First Edition 1930
Reprinted, with Corrections, 1931
Second Edition 1937
Reprinted 1940
Third Edition 1941
Reprinted, with Corrections, 1945
Reprinted 1948
Reprinted, with Corrections and
Revised Addenda, 1949, 1951
Reprinted, with Corrections, 1953
Reprinted, with Corrections and
Revised Addenda, 1955

The Little
OXFORD
DICTIONARY
OF
CURRENT ENGLISH

COMPILED BY

GEORGE OSTLER

THIRD EDITION
Revised and supplemented by
J. COULSON

OXFORD
AT THE CLARENDON PRESS
LONDON: GEOFFREY CUMBERLEGE

PUBLISHER'S NOTE

WHEN the demand arose for a dictionary which should be still smaller than the *Pocket Oxford Dictionary*, and yet cover the same or even a wider vocabulary, it soon became clear that the problem of compression required not merely lexicographical accuracy, but the technical skill of an experienced compositor. Mr. George Ostler, who served for forty-four years on the composing and reading staff of the Clarendon Press, and whose encyclopaedic knowledge had been of service to two generations of compositors and authors, was therefore entrusted with the task of packing all that could be packed into 640 of these pages. He had completed the Dictionary proper, revised all the proofs, and prepared the appendix of Abbreviations, when his death on 21 April 1929 prevented him from carrying through its last stages a work to which he had given his best energies. The publishers are grateful to Mrs. J. Coulson, of the staff of the Oxford Dictionary, for reading the early proofs with the editor, for preparing the appendix of Difficult Proper Names, and for finishing the work after Mr. Ostler's death. It is not possible to make more than a general acknowledgement of the helpful suggestions received from many quarters; but particular thanks are due to Sir William Craigie, the organizing editor of the forthcoming great *Dictionary of American English*, and to his assistant, Mr. M. M. Mathews, for their help in selecting and distinguishing words and meanings that have their origin or principal use in the United States.

In the second edition of 1937 the Dictionary was revised throughout by Mrs. J. Coulson with the aid of the Supplement to the *Oxford English Dictionary*.

NOTE TO THE THIRD EDITION, 1941

FOR this third edition, Mrs. Coulson has revised the Dictionary in points of detail. Words that have recently made good their claim to inclusion will be found in the *Addenda*.
The list of Abbreviations has also been revised to include many that war has brought into general use.

Printed in Great Britain

PREFACE

THIS work is based on the *Pocket Oxford Dictionary* edited by F. G. Fowler and H. W. Fowler; and, like it, rests ultimately upon the authority of the great Oxford Dictionary edited by Drs. Murray, Bradley, Craigie, and Onions [1884–1928]. The choice of words is in the main that of the *Pocket Oxford Dictionary*, but new words and phrases, whose place and dignity in the language is not yet assured, have been admitted rather more freely. It has been thought advisable to give more space to the usage of the United States of America than is commonly done in smaller English dictionaries, because the interaction of the two great branches of the English language is steadily increasing. We think at once of the wider spread of American books and journals; of cinema captions and of the new power of wireless; but these are only striking examples of the growing rapidity and frequency of all means of communication; and free communication is the great leveller of differences in language. As the distinction of American usages is of considerable importance, they are marked by an asterisk * prefixed to a word, phrase, or meaning; and the sign must be understood as a mark of territorial origin or use, not as an indication of inferiority. Attention has also been given to words and meanings common in the British Empire overseas; and if, in this or other respects, a user of the dictionary finds it incomplete, he is asked to remember that it is a *Little* Dictionary, in which rigorous selection has been necessary.

COMPOUNDS AND DERIVATIVES. Generally words are given in their alphabetical order; but for brevity compounds and some derivatives are grouped under the main word.

FOREIGN WORDS AND PHRASES are entered among English words in their alphabetical order, and are printed in the same black type as the English words; but a parallel sign ‖ prefixed marks those foreign words and phrases that are not yet naturalized in English and are therefore commonly found printed in italic type.

P. at the end of a definition indicates that the word defined is or appears to be a proprietary term, trade mark, or the like; but competence to settle the question whether a word is or is not proprietary is disclaimed.

In order to save space, definitions have been omitted from derivatives where the meaning is sufficiently clear from the meanings given for the main word. For the same reason many words have been shortened by the use of the tilde ∼; e.g. under **fulfil**, ∼ment = fulfilment; **fusible**, ∼bility = fusibility; **emerge**, ∼nce = emergence.

Where more than one spelling is given the first is to be preferred.

3495   A 2

PRONUNCIATION

1. Accent. The accentuation mark ′ is usually placed at the end of the stressed syllable.

2. Phonetic System. Where the pronunciation of a word or part of a word cannot be shown by the ordinary spelling and markings, a phonetic spelling is given in round brackets immediately after the black-type word. The phonetic scheme is as follows:

CONSONANTS: b; ch (chin); d; dh (dhe =the); g (go); h; j; k; l; m; n; ng (sing); ngg (finger); p; r; s (sip); sh (ship); t; th (thin); v; w; y; z; zh (vizhn =vision).

VOWELS: ā ē ī ō ū ōō (mate mete mite mote moot)
ă ĕ ĭ ŏ ŭ ŏŏ (rack reck rick rock ruck rook)
ār ēr īr ōr ūr (mare mere mire more mure)
är ẽr ôr (part pert port)
ah aw oi oor ow owr (bah bawl boil boor brow bower)

Vowels printed in italic within the brackets indicate vague sounds.

3. Pronunciation without Respelling. As far as possible pronunciation is shown without respelling by placing symbols over the words (e.g. ā, ĕ, ār, ẽr, ōō, &c.) in the black type.

(a) The ordinary spelling often coincides with the phonetic system described in par. 2.

(b) The following additional symbols are used in the black type:

ė =ĭ (nā′kėd, rėlȳ′, cŏll′ėge, prĭv′ėt)
ĩr, ũr =ẽr (bĩrth, bũrn)
ȳ, y̆ =ī, ĭ (implȳ′, sŭnn′y̆)

(c) final e when unmarked is mute, i. e. not to be pronounced. Thus ape is to be pronounced āp. Where final e is pronounced, it is marked as in rĕ′cĭpė.

(d) Unless another pronunciation is indicated, the following letters and combinations have the usual values in English spelling which are shown alongside them:

Vowels.

ae = ē (aegis)
ai = ā (pain)
air = ār (fair)
au = aw (maul)
ay = ā (say)
ea, ee = ē (mean, meet)

ear, eer = ēr (fear, beer)
eu, ew = ū (feud, few)
ie = ē (thief)
ier = ēr (pier)
oa = ō (boat)
ou = ow (bound)
oy = oi (boy)

Consonants.

c is 'hard' and = k (cob, cry, talc) *but*
c before e, i, y, is 'soft' and =s (ice, icy, city)
dg = j (judgement)

g before e, i, y, is 'soft' and =j (age, gin, orgy)
n before k, 'hard' c, q, x =ng (zinc, uncle, tank, banquet, minx)

ṅ indicates French nasaliza-
   tion of preceding vowel
ph = f (photo)

qu = kw (quit)
tch = ch (batch)
x = ks (fox)

Thus in **gĕm** the pronunciation of *g* is not marked
because it comes under the rule above: 'g before **e, i,
y**, is soft and = **j**'; but **gĕt** is followed by [g-] to show
that here exceptionally g before **e** is 'hard' as in go.

  (*e*) The following terminations have the values shown:

-age = -ĭj (garbage)
-ate = -ĭt or -*at* (mandate)
-ey = -ĭ (donkey)
-ous = -*us* (furious)

-sm = -zm (atheism, spasm)
-tion = -shon (salvation)
-ture = -ch*er* as well as -tū̇r,
  esp. in common words.

☞The principal symbols used to show the pronunciation
are given at the foot of the pages, the series running across
four consecutive pages.

SPECIAL SIGNS

* = originating in or used chiefly in the United States.
‖ = foreign word or phrase not thoroughly at home in English and commonly printed in italic.
P = proprietary term (see above).

ABBREVIATIONS

a., aa., adjective(s)	Bibl., biblical	esp., especially
abbr., abbreviation	Biol., biology	Eth., ethics
abs., absolute	Bot., botany	Etym., etymology
acc., according		euphem., euphemism
act., active	c., cc., century, -ries	Eur., European
adj., adjective, -val	Chem., chemistry	ex., exx., example(s)
adv., advv., adverb(s)	collect., collective(ly)	exc., except
advl., adverbial	colloq., colloquial(ly)	excl., exclamation
Alg., algebra	comb., combination	expr., expressing
Amer.-Ind., Ameri-	commerc., commercial	
can-Indian	comp., comparative	facet., facetiously
Anat., anatomy	*conj., conjj.,* conjunc-	fem., feminine
Anglo-Ind., Anglo-	tion(s)	fig., figurative(ly)
Indian	contempt., contemp-	Footb., football
Ant., antiquities	tuous(ly)	ft., foot, feet
arch., archaic	Crick., cricket	fut., future
Archaeol., archaeo-		
logy	dial., dialect	gal., gals., gallon(s)
Archit., architecture	Dynam., dynamics	G.B., Great Britain
Arith., arithmetic		gen., general(ly)
Astrol., astrology	eccl., ecclesiastical	Geog., geography
Astron., astronomy	E.-Ind., East-Indian	Geol., geology
attrib., attributive(ly)	Electr., electricity	Geom., geometry
Austral., Australasian	Entom., entomology	Gk., Greek
	erron., erroneously	

Herald., heraldry
hist., historical
hr., hrs., hour(s)

imit., imitative
imperat., imperative
in., inch(es)
ind., indicative
inf., infinitive
int., interj.. interjection
interrog., interrogative(ly)
intr., intransitive
Ir., Irish
irreg., irregular(ly)
i. & t., intr. & trans.

joc., jocose, jocular

leg., legal
lit., literal(ly)
Log., logic

Magn., magnetism
Math., mathematics
Mech., mechanics
Med., medicine
metaph., metaphorical
Metaphys., metaphysics
Meteor., meteorology
Mil., military
Min., mineralogy
mod., modern
Mus., music
Mythol., mythology

n., nn., noun(s)
N.-Amer.. North-American
Nat. Hist.. natural history
Naut., nautical
Nav., naval
neg., negatively
nom., nominative
N.T., New Testament

obj., object(ive case)
obs., obsolete
opp., (as) opposed (to)
Opt., optics

orig., origin(al)(ly)
Ornith.. ornithology
O.T., Old Testament

P.. proprietary
Parl., Parliament(ary)
part., participle
pass., passive(ly)
Path., pathology
pedant., pedantic(ally)
perf., perfect tense
perh., perhaps
pers., person
Philol., philology
Philos., philosophy
Photog., photography
phr., phrr., phrase(s)
Phys., physics
Physiol., physiology
pl., plural
poet., poetical
Pol., politics
Pol. Econ., political economy
pop., popular
p.p., past or passive participle
pr., pronounce(d)
pred. a., predicative adjective
pref., (as) prefix
prep., prepp., preposition(s)
pres., present tense
Print., printing
prob., probable, -ably
pron., pronoun
pronunc., pronunciation
prop., proper(ly)
Pros., prosody
prov., proverb
prov., provincial
pt., pint

R.C., Roman Catholic
ref., reference
refl., reflexive(ly)
rel., relative
repr., representing
rhet., rhetoric(al)
Rom., Roman

Rom. Ant., Roman antiquities

s., singular
S.-Afr., South-African
S.-Amer., South-American
Sc., Scotch
sch. sl., schoolboy slang
Sci., science
Sculp., sculpture
sent., sentence
sing., singular number
sl., slang
St. Exch., Stock Exchange
subj., subject(ive case)
subj., subjunctive
suf., suffix
sup., superlative
Surg., surgery

tech., technical(ly)
telegr., telegraphic
theatr., theatrical
Theol., theology
trans., transitive(ly)
trans., by transference
transl., translation
Typ., typography
t. & i., trans. & intr.

U.K., United Kingdom
U.S., United States
usu., usually

v., vv., verb(s)
var., variant
v. aux., verb auxiliary
vb., vbl., verb(al)
v.i., verb intransitive
v. impers., verb impersonal
voc., vocative(ly)
v. refl., verb reflexive
v.t., verb transitive
vulg., vulgar

W.-Afr., West-African

yd., yds., yard(s)

Zool., zoology

LITTLE OXFORD DICTIONARY

A, ā¹, (Mus.) 6th note in scale of C major.

a², **an**¹ (a, an : emphat. ā, ăn), *a.* one but no matter which.

a³, *prep.* on, to, in (now chiefly pref. in *abed*, *afoot*, &c.).

aard-vàrk (ärd-), *n.* S.-Afr. quadruped between armadillos and ant-eaters. **aard-wolf** (ärd-wŏŏ-), *n.* S.-Afr. carnivore between hyenas and civets.

Aar'on (ăr-), *n.* ~'s beard, ~'s rod, kinds of plant.

abăck', *adv.* backwards, behind. **taken** ~, disconcerted, surprised.

ăb'acus (pl. *-ci*), *n.* frame used for calculating ; (Archit.) upper member of capital, slab supporting architrave.

abaft' (-ah-), *adv.* in stern of ship. *prep.* towards stern.

abăn'don, *v.t.* give up, surrender. *n.* easy manner. ~ed, *a.* profligate. ~ment, *n.*

abăndonee', *n.* underwriter to whom salvage of wreck is abandoned.

abāse', *v.t.* (-*sable*), humiliate, lower, degrade. ~ment, *n.*

abăsh', *v.t.* put out of countenance. ~ed, *a.* ; ~ment, *n.*

abāte', *v.t. & i.* (-*table*), diminish, make or become less ; deduct ; (Law) put an end to ; make null and void. ~ment, *n.*

ăb'atis, *n.* defence made of felled trees.

abattoir (abăt'wahr), *n.* public slaughter-house.

Abb'a (à-), *n.* Father.

ăbb'acy̆, *n.* office of an abbot.

abbé (ăb'ā), *n.* French ecclesiastic.

ăbb'ess, *n.* head of a nunnery.

ăbb'ey̆, *n.* (pl. *-eys*), body of monks or nuns ; monastic buildings ; church of an abbey.

ăbb'ot, *n.* head of an abbey.

abbrē'viāte, *v.t.* shorten. ~tion, ~tor, *nn.*

ā b c, *n.* alphabet ; rudiments.

ăb'dicāte, *v.t. & i.* renounce for mally or by default. ~tion, ~tor, *nn.*

ăb'dō'mĕn, *n.* belly : hinder part of an insect, &c. **ăbdŏm'inăl.** *a.*

abdŭct', *v.t.* carry off illegally ; (of muscle, &c.) draw from normal position. ~ion, ~or, *nn.*

abeam', *adv.* on a line running from a ship at right angles to her length.

abēle', *n.* the white poplar.

ăberdevíne', *n.* bird allied to goldfinch, siskin.

ăberrā'tion, *n.* mental or moral slip or error ; deviation from type ; displacement of heavenly body's true position to observer. **abĕ'rrant**, *a.* ; ~rance, *n.*

abĕt', *v.t.* (-*tt*-), countenance or assist. ~ment, ~tor, *nn.*

abey'ance (-bā-), *n.* suspension, temporary disuse.

‖**ăb ĕx'trā**, from outside.

abhŏr', *v.t.* (-*rr*-), regard with disgust and hatred, detest. ~rence, *n.* ; ~rent, *a.*

abīde', *v.t. & i.* (*abōde*, also *abided* ; *-dable*), dwell ; remain, continue ; submit to. **abī'dance**, *n.* (esp., *by* terms, &c.) ; ~ding, *a.*

ăb'igail, *n.* lady's-maid.

abil'ity̆, *n.* power to do a thing ; cleverness, mental faculty.

‖**ăb init'ĭō**, from the beginning.

ăbiogĕn'esis, *n.* spontaneous generation.

ăb'jĕct, *a.* craven, degraded. **abject** person. ~tion, *n.*

abjūre' (-joor), *v.t.* (-*rable*), renounce on oath. ~ation, *n.*

ăb'lative, *a. & n.* case in Latin nouns, expressing agent, &c.

ăb'laut (owt), *n.* vowel-change in related words.

ablāze', *adv. & pred. a.* on fire ; excited ; glittering.

ā'ble, *a.* (*abler*, *ablest*), having the power ; talented. ~bodied, *a.* robust, skilled. **ā'bly̆**, *adv.*

ablu'tion (-lōō-), *n.* ceremonial or ordinary personal washing.

ăb′nĕgāte, *v.t.* (*-gable*), deny oneself; renounce. ~**tion**, ~**tor**, *nn.*

abnŏrm′al, *a.* (*-lly*), exceptional, deviating from type. ~**ity**, *n.*

aboard′ (-ōrd), *adv.* & *prep.* on board; *on a train; alongside.

abŏde′, *n.* dwelling-place.

abode, *p.t.* & *p.p.* of abide.

abŏl′ish, *v.t.* do away with. ~**ment**, ~**ition**, *nn.*

aboli′tionist (-shon-), *n.* supporter of movement against negro slavery.

abŏm′inable, *a.* detestable, revolting.

abŏm′ināte, *v.t.* loathe, detest. ~**tion**, ~**tor**, *nn.*

abŏri′ginal, *a.* (*-lly*), indigenous, existing at dawn of history. *n,* aboriginal inhabitant, plant, &c.

abŏri′ginēs (-z), *n., pl.* aboriginal inhabitants.

abŏrt′, *v.i.* miscarry; become sterile.

abŏr′tion, *n.* miscarriage; dwarfed or misshapen creature. ~**ist**, *n.* one who procures abortion.

abŏrt′ive, *a.* premature; fruitless.

abound′, *v.i.* be plentiful; be rich in; be infested with.

about′, *adv.* around from outside or centre; astir; approximately. *prep.* around; near; at a time near to.

above′ (-ŭv), *adv.* higher up, overhead, up stream; in addition to. *prep.* over, higher than; of higher rank, &c. than. ~**board**, without concealment.

ăbracadăb′ra, *n.* cabalistic word used as spell; gibberish.

abrāde′, *v.t.* (*-dable*), scrape off, injure by rubbing.

abrā′sion (-zhn), *n.* rubbing off; wound made by scraping. abrā′sive, *a.* grazing; grinding down.

abreast′ (-rĕst), *on* a level and facing the same way; not behind.

abridge′, *v.t.* (*-geable*), condense, shorten; curtail. ~**ment**, *n.*

abroach′, *adv.* pierced to let liquor run from cask.

abroad′ (-rawd), *adv.* widely, in different directions; away from one's country.

ăb′rogāte, *v.t.* (*-gable*), repeal, cancel. ~**tion**, ~**tor**, *nn.*

abrŭpt′, *a.* sudden, hasty, disconnected; steep.

ăb′scess (-sĕs), *n.* collection of pus in cavity of the body.

abscŏnd′, *v.i.* go away secretly, fly from the law. ~**ence**, *n.*

ăb′sence, *n.* being away; non-existence; abstracted state.

ăb′sent[1], *a.* not present; not existing. ~**minded**, *a.* abstracted. ~**ly**, *adv.* in absent-minded way.

absĕnt′[2], *v. refl.* to keep away purposely.

absĕntee′, *n.* person not present; landlord living away from home. ~**ism**, *n.* this practice among landlords.

ăb′sinth, *n.* wormwood; liqueur made from this.

‖ **ăb′sit ō′men!** may a suggested foreboding not be realized.

ăb′solute (-ōot), *a.* complete, entire, perfect; unqualified. ~**ly**, *adv.* in an absolute manner or sense; (colloq.) quite so, yes.

absolu′tion (-ōo-), *n.* forgiveness, esp. eccl. declaration of pardon.

ăb′solutism (-ōot-), *n.* principle of despotic government. ~**tist**, *n.*

absŏlve′, *v.t.* set or pronounce free; acquit.

absŏrb′, *v.t.* swallow up; assimilate; suck up; engross the attention of. ~**ability**, *n.*

absŏrb′ent, *a.* tending to absorb. *n.* such substance, organ, &c.

absŏrp′tion, *n.* the act of absorbing. ~**tive**, *a.* ~**tivity**, *n.*

abstain′, *v.i.* keep oneself away, refrain; drink no alcohol. ~**er**, *n.* one who abstains from all alcoholic liquors.

abstē′mious, *a.* sparing or moderate in food, drink, &c.

abstĕn′tion, *n.* the act of refraining or holding back.

abstĕr′gent, *a.* cleansing, *n.* cleansing substance. abstĕr′sion, *n.;* ~**sive**, *a.*

ăb′stinence, *n.* refraining from food, pleasure, &c. total ~, abstaining from alcohol. ~**ment**, *n.*

ăb′stră̆ct[1], *a.* not concrete; ideal,

---

māte, mēte, mīte, mōte, mūte, mōōt; răck, rĕck, rick, rŏck, rŭck, rōōk;

theoretical ; abstruse. *n.* essence, summary.

abstract'², *v.t.* deduct, take away ; steal ; summarize. **~ed,** *a.* absent-minded.

abstrāc'tion, *n.* withdrawal ; stealing ; absent-mindedness.

abstruse' (-ōōs), *a.* hard to understand, profound.

absŭrd', *a.* unreasonable, ridiculous. **~ity,** *n.*

abŭn'dance, *n.* plenty, more than enough ; affluence, wealth.

abŭn'dant, *a.* plentiful, rich.

|| **ăb ŭrb'é cŏn'dită,** from Rome's foundation (A.U.C.).

abūse' (-z), *v.t.* (**-sable**), make bad use of ; revile. (**-s**), *n.* misuse ; corrupt practice ; reviling.

abū'sive, *a.* insulting, vituperative. **~ness,** *n.*

abŭt', *v.t.* & *i.* (**-tt-**), border upon ; touch upon, lean against. **~ter,** *n.* owner of adjoining property.

abŭt'ment, *n.* lateral support, masonry supporting end of arch, &c.

abў(e)', *v.t.* pay the penalty of.

abўss', **abўsm',** *nn.* the bowels of the earth ; bottomless or deep chasm. **abўs'mal** (-z-), *a.* bottomless. **abўss'al,** *a.* more than 300 fathoms below sea-surface.

acā'cia (-sha), *n.* genus of tree, some species of which yield gum arabic.

ăcadĕm'ic, *a.* of an academy ; scholarly ; abstract, unpractical. *n.* member of university ; (*pl.*) academic arguments. **~ally,** *adv.*

ăcadĕm'ical, *a.* of college or university. *n.pl.* college costume.

acadēmi'cian, *n.* member of an academy, esp. the Royal Academy of Arts.

acăd'emў, *n.* place of study, university, college, or school ; place of special training ; society for cultivating art, learning, &c.

acăn'thus, *n.* kinds of plant, esp. bear's-breech.

Accā'dian, *a.* of Accad. *n.* a language found in cuneiform inscriptions.

accēde' (aks-), *v.i.* consent ; agree ; enter an office ; join a party.

|| **accĕlerăn'dō** (-ks-), *adv.* with gradually increasing pace. *a.* so performed. *n.* passage so performed.

accĕl'erāte (aks-), *v.t.* & *i.* (**-rable**), make quicker ; cause to happen earlier. **~tion,** *n.* **~tor,** *n.* person or thing that increases anything's speed, esp. an attachment in motor-cars for this purpose.

ac'cent¹ (aks-), *n.* prominence given to a syllable by stress or higher musical pitch ; national or other peculiar mode of pronunciation ; (*pl.*) speech ; rhythmical stress. **accĕnt'²** (aks-), *v.t.* pronounce with accent ; emphasize, dwell upon. **~ual,** *a.* ; **~uate,** *v.t.* ; **~uation,** *n.*

accĕpt' (aks-), *v.t.* & *i.* to receive (gift, &c.) ; answer affirmatively (offer, &c.) ; receive as true ; agree to meet (bill). **~able,** *a.* worth accepting, welcome ; **~ability,** *n.* **~ance,** *n.* a consent to receive ; accepted bill. **~ation,** *n.* sense in which a word is used. **accĕp'tor,** *n.* one who accepts bill ; (Wireless) a tuned oscillatory circuit, consisting of inductance and capacity in series, offering low resistance to currents of the frequency to which it is tuned.

ăc'cĕss (-ks-), *n.* approach ; addition ; attack (of illness). **~ible,** *a.* able to be reached. **~ibility,** *n.*

accĕssary' (aksĕs'-, ăk'sĭs-), *n.* helper in, or privy to, an act.

accĕssion (aksĕ'shn), *n.* coming to the throne ; acceding to office ; attaining to manhood ; addition.

accĕssorў (aksĕs'-, ăk'sĭs-), *a.* additional, adventitious. *n.* such thing, accompaniment.

ac'cidence (ăks-), *n.* part of grammar dealing with inflexions.

ac'cident (ăks-), *n.* event without apparent cause ; unexpected event ; unintentional act ; mishap. **~al,** *a.* ; **~ally,** *adv.*

acclaim', *v.t.* welcome loudly ; hail. *n.* shout of applause.

ăcclamā'tion, *n.* loud and eager assent ; (*pl.*) shoutings.

---

accli'matize, accli'mate, *vv.t.* (*-zable*), habituate to new climate. ~tization, àcc'limātion, *nn.*

accliv'ity, *n.* an upward slope.

àccolāde' (*or -ahd*), *n.* ceremony of conferring knighthood; (Mus.) vertical line or brace coupling staves.

accŏm'odāte (*-dable*), adapt, harmonize; reconcile; find lodging for. ~ting, *a.* obliging. ~tion, *n.* adaptation, adjustment; settlement; lodging; loan. ~tor, *n.*

accom'paný (*-ŭm-*), *v.t.* (*-iable*) go with, escort, attend; (Mus.) perform a subsidiary part. ~niment, *n.* accompanying thing; (Mus.) subsidiary part. ~nist, *n.*

accŏm'plice, *n.* partner in crime or guilt.

accŏm'plish, *v.t.* perform, carry out, succeed in doing. ~ment, *n.* achievement, fulfilment; (pl.) attainments.

accŏrd', *v.i. & t.* to agree, be consistent with; grant, give. ~ consent; treaty of peace; harmony, agreement. ~ance, *n.* ~ant, *a.*

accŏrd'ing, *adv.* In comb.: ~ as, in proportion as; ~ to, in a manner consistent with; on the authority of.

accŏrd'ingly, *adv.* consequently.

accŏrd'ion, *n.* portable musical instrument with bellows, keys, and metal reeds. ~ist, *n.*

accŏst', *v.t.* make up to and address; solicit.

accouchement (ăkoo'shmahn), *n.* lying-in, delivery.

accoucheur (ăkoo'sher), *n.* man midwife; (fem.) ~euse, midwife.

account', *v.t. & i.* reckon; regard; give reckoning for; answer, explain. *n.* counting, reckoning; statement of money received and expended; explanation; ground, reason; narration. accoun'tancy, *n.*

accoun'table, *a.* responsible, liable; explicable. ~ability, *n.*

accoun'tant, *n.* keeper or inspector of accounts.

account'rements (*-oot-*), *n.pl.* equip-

ment, trappings. accou'tred (*-ooterd*), *a.* equipped, attired.

accrĕd'it, *v.t.* gain credit for, dispose one to believe; send out with credentials; attribute to. ~ed, *a.*

accrē'tion, *n.* growth by organic enlargement; increase by external additions.

accrue' (*-oo-*), *v.i.* to come to; increase; be added.

accū'mulāte, *v.t. & i.* (*-lable*), heap up, get together; produce or acquire; grow numerous. ~tion, *n.*; ~tive, *a.*

accū'mulātor, *n.* apparatus for storing electricity.

ăcc'urate, *a.* precise, exact, correct. ~acy, *n.*

accurs'ed, *a.* detestable, annoying; (also *accurst*) lying under a curse.

accū'sative (*-z-*), *a. & n.*, ~ *case* or *accusative*, that used in Greek and Latin for goal of motion or object of action.

accuse' (*-z*), *v.t.* (*-sable*), indict, charge; lay the blame on. ~sation, *n.*; ~satorial, ~satory, *aa.*

accūs'tom, *v.t.* habituate. ~ed, *a.*

āce, *n.* the one on dice, cards, &c.; one point at racquets, &c.; (Tennis) service that beats opponent; (Mil.) French airman who has destroyed ten or more hostile aircraft.

Acĕl'dama (*ak-*), *n.* scene of bloodshed or butchery.

acĕrb'ity, *n.* bitterness of speech, temper, &c.; sourness, harsh taste.

acē'tic (*or -ĕt-*), *a.* of vinegar, sour. ~ acid, acid which gives sourness to vinegar. ā'cĕtāted, *a.* treated with acetic acid.

acĕt'ify, *v.t. & i.* (*-fiable*), turn into vinegar, make or become sour. ~fication, *n.*

ă'cĕtone, *n.* colourless liquid used as solvent.

ă'cĕtous, *a.* of vinegar, sour.

acĕt'ylene, *n.* colourless gas burning with bright flame.

Achātes (akā'tēz), *n.* faithful friend.

ache (āk), *v.i.* suffer continuous or prolonged pain. *n.* such pain.

achieve, *v.t.* (*-vable*), accomplish, perform; attain, acquire, reach. ~**ment**, *n.* feat achieved; escutcheon, hatchment.

achromat'ic (ăk-), *a.* free from colour; transmitting light without decomposing it. **achrōmat'ically**, *adv.* **achrō'maticity**, **achrō'matism**, *nn.* achromatic quality. ~**tize**, *v.t.* make achromatic.

a'cid, *a.* sour, sharp. *n.* sour substance; (Chem.) any of a class of compounds of other elements with hydrogen, most of which are sour. ~**test**, one in which acid is applied to test composition, &c.; often used fig. **acid'ify**, *v.t. & i.* ; ~**ification**, ~**ity**, *nn.*

acidim'eter, *n.* instrument measuring strength of acids.

acid'ulous, *a.* somewhat acid. ~**lated**, *a.* made acidulous.

ăck emm'a, *adv. & n.* (sl.), *ante meridiem*; air-mechanic.

acknowledge (aknŏl'ij), *v.t.* (*-geable*), admit the truth of, admit, own; announce receipt of letter, &c.; express appreciation of services, &c. **acknowledg(e)ment**, *n.* thing given or done in return for a service, &c.

aclin'ic, *a.* ~ **line**, magnetic equator, on which magnetic needle has no dip.

ăc'mē, *n.* highest point.

ăc'nē, *n.* pimply disease.

ăc'olyte, *n.* inferior officer in church attending priest.

ăc'onite, *n.* the plant monk's-hood; the poison found in it.

ā'côrn, *n.* fruit of the oak. ~**shell**, cirriped allied to barnacles.

acŏtylē'don, *n.* plant with no distinct seed-lobes. ~**ous**, *a.*

acous'tic, *a.* of the sense of hearing. ~**al**, *a.*; **acousti'cian** (-shn), *n.*

acous'tics, *n.* the science treating of the laws of sound.

acquaint', *v.t.* make aware or familiar; inform.

acquain'tance, *n.* being acquainted with (person, fact, &c.); person one knows. ~**ship**, *n.*

ăcquiĕsce', *v.i.* agree, esp. tacitly; not object. **ăcquiĕs'cence**, *n.* ~**ent**, *a.*

acquire', *v.t.* (*-rable*), gain, get, come to have. ~**ment**, *n.* (pl.) mental attainments.

acquisi'tion (-z-), *n.* the thing acquired; useful addition. ~**ive**, *a.* desirous of acquiring.

acquit', *v.t.* (*-tt-*), declare not guilty, free of blame, &c.; *refl.* perform one's part. ~**tal**, *n.* deliverance from a charge by verdict, &c. ~**tance**, *n.* payment of or release from debt; receipt in full.

ā'cre (-ker), *n.* measure of land, 4,840 sq. yds.; (pl.) lands, fields. ~**age**, number of acres, extent of land.

ăc'rid, *a.* bitterly pungent; of bitter temper, &c. **acrid'ity**, *n.*

ăc'rimony, *n.* bitterness of temper. **ăcrimō'nious**, *a.*

ăc'robat, *n.* rope-dancer, tumbler. **acrobăt'ic**, *a.* ~**ism**, *n.*

acrŏp'olis, *n.* citadel or elevated part of a Greek city, esp. Athens.

across' (-aws), *prep. and adv.* from side to side, to or on the other side; across one another.

acros'tic, *n.* poem, &c. in which first or first and last letters of lines form word(s).

ăct, *n.* thing done, deed; decree of legislative body; main division of a play. *v.t. & i.* perform, play one's part; personate character; carry out.

ăct'inism, *n.* property of sun's rays that produces chemical changes, as in photography.

actin'ium, *n.* radio-active substance found in pitchblende.

ăc'tion, *n.* doing, working, exertion of energy; thing done; mode or style of movement of horse, machine, batsman, &c.; mechanism of instrument; legal process; battle. *v.t.* bring an action against. ~**able**, *a.* affording grounds for an action.

ăc'tive, *a.* working, acting, operative; consisting in or marked by action; energetic, diligent;

(Gram.) attributing the verbal action to the person or thing whence it proceeds. **~ voice,** active of transitive and all forms of intransitive verbs.

ăc'tĭvāte, v.t. make (radio-)active.

actĭv'ĭtý, n. exertion of energy; (pl.) spheres of action.

ăc'tor, n. dramatic performer; a doer. **ăc'trĕss,** n.

ăc'tŭal, a. existing, real; present, current.

actŭăl'ĭtý, n. reality; realism.

ăc'tŭālize, v.t. realize in action; treat realistically. **~zation,** n.

ăc'tŭally, adv. in actual fact; for the time being.

ăc'tŭarў, n. expert authority on rates of mortality and insurance statistics. **ăctŭăr'ial,** a.

ăc'tŭāte, v.t. (-uable), serve as motive to; communicate motion to. **~ation,** n.

acū'ĭtý, n. sharpness, acuteness.

acū'mĕn, n. keen perception, penetration.

acūte', a. sharp, keen, penetrating; clever; (of disease) coming sharply to a crisis, not chronic; (of letter) bearing acute accent. **~ accent,** stress mark (').

ăd, n. advertisement (colloq.).

|| **adā'gĭo** (adahj'ŷō), adv. (in music) slowly. n. slow movement.

Ad'ăm (ă-), n. the first man. **~'s ale** or **wine,** water. **~'s apple,** a cartilaginous projection of the throat.

ăd'amănt, n. impenetrably hard substance. **~ine,** a.

adăpt', v.t. suit, fit; modify, alter. **~ability,** **~ation,** nn. **~ive,** a.

|| **ăd căptăn'dum (vulgus),** to take the fancy of the mob).

ădd, v.t. & i. join by way of increase or supplement. **~ up** or **together,** find the sum of.

addĕn'dum, n. (pl. -da), something added, additional remark.

ădd'er, n. small venomous snake. **~'s tongue,** a fern.

addĭct', v.t. devote or habituate oneself to. (-'ĭct) n. one addicted to specified drug, &c. **~ion,** n.

addĭ'tion, n. adding; thing added.

addĭ'tional (-shon-), a. (-ŭly), added, extra.

ăd'dle, a. (of egg) rotten, producing no chicken; muddled, crazy. v.t. make or grow addled. **~-headed** or **-brained,** a. confused in mind.

addrĕss', v.t. to direct in speech or writing; write directions for delivery on cover of letter, &c.; apply oneself. n. speech delivered to audience; manner, bearing; superscription of letter; place of residence; (pl.) courtship. **~ee,** n. person to whom letter, &c. is addressed.

addūce', v.t. (-cible), cite as proof or instance.

addūct', v.t. (of muscles) draw to a common centre. **~ion,** n.

ăd'ĕnoids (-z), n.pl. spongy tissue at back of nose, often hindering breathing.

adĕpt', a. thoroughly proficient. n. skilled person.

ăd'ĕquate, a. sufficient, such as meets the case. **~acy,** n.

|| **à deux** (ah dẽr'), for two.

|| **ad ĕūn'dem,** adv. Admitted **~.** to the same degree (at another university).

adhēre' (-h-), v.i. stick fast to. **adhēr'ence,** (-h-), n. **adhēr'ent** (-h-), n. a supporter. **~ sticking;** due or incident to.

adhē'sion (-hēzhn), n. the act of adhering or sticking. **~ive,** a. sticking, sticky.

|| **ăd hŏc,** for this purpose.

ădiăn'tum, n. kinds of fern, esp. the black maiden-hair.

adieu (adū'), int. & n. good-bye.

|| **ăd infīnī'tum,** for ever.

|| **ăd in'terim,** for the meantime.

ăd'ipōse, a. of fat, fatty. **ădĭpŏs'ĭtý,** n.

ăd'it, n. horizontal entrance to, or passage in, a mine.

adjā'cent, a. lying near to, contiguous. **~ncy,** n.

ădj'ĕctive, n. name of an attribute added to a thing to describe it more fully. a. additional, not standing by itself. **~i'val,** a.

---

māte, mēte, mīte, mōte, mūte, mōōt; răck, rĕck, rĭck, rŏck, rŭck, rōōk;

adjoin', *v.t.* be adjacent to.

adjourn (ajĕrn'),*v.t.* & *i.* put off till another time; defer. **~ment**, *n.*

adjudge', *v.t.* (*-geable*), pronounce judgement on; condemn; award (prize, &c.). **~ment**, *n.*

adjud'icate (ajōō-), *v.t.* & *i.* to pronounce judicially upon. **~tion**, **~tor**, *nn.*; **~tive**, *a.*

adj'unct, *n.* subordinate or incidental thing, accompaniment; (Gram.) amplification of predicate, subject, &c.

adjure (ajoor'), *v.t.* (*-rable*), charge or request solemnly or earnestly. **~ration**, *n.*

adjust', *v.t.* arrange, put in order; harmonize; adapt. **~ment**, *n.*

adj'utant[1] (-ōō-), *n.* army officer assisting superior by communicating orders, conducting correspondence, &c. **~general**, assisting general thus. **~ncy**, *n.*

adj'utant[2] (-ōō-), *n.* large Indian stork.

|| **ăd lib'itum**, at pleasure.

admin'ister, *v.t.* & *i.* (*-trable*), manage (affairs, estate, &c.); dispense, supply, furnish, give. **~tration**, *n.* act of administering; the ministry, Government. **~trative**, *a.*; **~trator**, *n.*; **~tratrix**, *n.* (pl. *-trices*).

ăd'mirable, *a.* worthy of admiration; excellent.

ăd'miral, *n.* (hist., in full *Lord High Admiral*) commander-in-chief of the navy; naval officer, commander of fleet or squadron; ship carrying the admiral; commander of fishing or merchant fleet. **~ ship**, *n.* Red, White~, kinds of butterfly.

ăd'miralty, *n.* office of admiral; the (Lords Commissioners of) *A.*, branch of executive managing the navy; (Rhet.) command of the seas.

admire', *v.t.* approve warmly of; look with wonder and pleasure at; (colloq.) compliment person on. **ădmiration**, *n.* **admir'er**, *n.* one who admires; a lover.

admiss'ible, *a.* capable of being admitted or allowed. **~bility**, *n.*

admi'ssion (-shn), *n.* act of admitting; fee for admitting; acknowledgement of error, &c.

admit', *v.t.* & *i.* (*-tt-*), let in, allow entrance of; accept as valid; acknowledge. **~tance**, *n.* **~tedly**, *adv.* confessedly.

admix', *v.t.* add as ingredient, mix with. **~ture**, *n.*

admon'ish, *v.t.* exhort, warn, remind; reprove. **~ment**, *n.*

ădmoni'tion, *n.* warning; reproof. **admon'itory**, *a.*

|| **ăd naus'eăm**, to a disgusting extent.

ado (adōō'), *n.* fuss; difficulty.

ado'be, *n.* unburnt brick dried in the sun.

ădoles'cent, *a.* between childhood and manhood or womanhood. *n.* an adolescent person. **~nce**, **~ncy**, *nn.*

Ado'nis, *n.* a beautiful youth loved by Venus; beau, dandy.

ăd'onīze, *v.t.* & *i.* adorn; adorn oneself.

adopt', *v.t.* take into a relationship; take as one's child; take another's idea; choose (profession, &c.). **~ion**, *n.*; **~ive**, *a.*

ador'able, *a.* worthy of love; (colloq.) charming, delightful.

ădora'tion, *n.* homage; worship.

adore', *v.t.* regard with deep respect and affection; worship; pay divine honours to.

ador'er, *n.* an admirer, lover.

adorn', *v.t.* deck with ornaments; add beauty to, be an ornament to. **~ment**, *n.*

|| **ăd rĕm**, to the purpose.

adre'nal, *a.* near the kidney. *n.* the suprarenal capsule. **adre'nalin**, *n.* a secretion of the adrenal ductless glands; this extracted from animals for medicinal use.

adrift', *adv.* in a drifting state; (fig.) at the mercy of circumstances.

adroit', *a.* dexterous, skilful.

ădsciti'tious (-sĭti'shus), *a.* added from without; supplemental.

adscrip'tus glē'bae, *a.* (of serf) attached to the soil.

|| **ăd'sŭm**, I am here.

---

māre, mēre, mīre, mōre, mūre; pärt, pĕrt, pört; *italics*, vague sounds.

ăd'ŭlāte, *v.t.* (-*lable*). flatter basely. ~tion, ~tor, *nn.* ; ~tory, *a.*

adŭlt', *a.* grown up ; mature. *n.* a grown-up person.

adŭl'terāte[1], *v.t.* (-*rable*), falsify by mixing with baser ingredients. ~tion, ~tor, *nn.*

adŭl'terāte[2], *a.* spurious, counterfeit ; stained by, born of, adultery. ~ant, *a.* used in adulterating. *n.* such substance.

adŭl'tery, *n.* sexual intercourse of man with woman not his wife, either or both being married. adŭl'terer, ~ess, *nn.* adŭl'terine (*or* -īn), *a.* of adultery ; adulterated, spurious. ~rous, *a.* guilty of adultery.

ăd'ŭmbrate (*or* adŭm'-), *v.t.* (-*table*), sketch in outline ; indicate faintly ; foreshadow ; overshadow. ~tion, *n.* ; ~tive, *a.*

|| ăd ŭng'uěm (făc'tus) (-nggw-), highly finished.

adŭst', *a.* parched ; sunburnt.

|| ăd valōr'ěm, in proportion to estimated value of goods.

advance' (-vah-), *v.t. & i.* (-*ceable*), move or put forward ; help on ; make claim, &c. ; hasten event ; lend money ; raise price. *n.* going forward ; progress ; overture ; rise in price ; loan. ~ment, *n.*

advanced' (-vah-), *a.* in the front rank. ~ student. ~ studies, not elementary. ~ ideas, ~ thinkers, ahead of the times.

advan'tage (-vah-), *n.* stronger position, superiority, gain ; favourable circumstance, &c. (Tennis) next point won after deuce. *v.t.* be an advantage to ; help, profit. ădvantā'geous (-jus), *a.* giving advantage ; beneficial to.

ăd'vent, *n.* season before the Nativity ; the Incarnation ; coming of important person or event.

ădventī'tious (-shus), *a.* accidental, casual.

advĕn'ture, *n.* unexpected or exciting experience ; daring enterprise. *v.t. & i.* to risk, venture. advĕn'turer (-cher-), *n.* one who seeks adventures ; speculator ; one who lives by his wits. ~ess, *n.*

advĕn'turous (-cher-), *a.* venturesome, enterprising.

ăd'vĕrb, *n.* word qualifying an adjective, verb, or adverb. ~ial, *a.*

|| ăd vĕrb'um, word for word.

ăd'versary, *n.* antagonist, enemy.

ăd'vĕrse, *a.* opposed, hostile ; placed opposite. ~sative, *a.* (of word) expressing opposition.

advĕrs'ity, *n.* trouble ; misfortune.

advĕrt', *v.i.* refer or allude to.

ăd'vertise (-z), *v.t. & i.* (-*sable*), give public notice of by placards ; announce for sale, or make one's wants known, in newspapers, &c. ; notify. advĕr'tisement, *n.*

advīce', *n.* opinion given as to future action ; information ; (pl.) notice of dispatch of goods ; communications from a distance.

advī'sable (-z-), *a.* expedient, judicious. ~bility, *n.*

advīse' (-z), *v.t. & i.* give advice to ; take counsel with ; announce consignment ; notify. advī'ser, *n.* counsellor, esp. person habitually consulted.

advīsed' (-zd), *a.* deliberate ; judicious. advī'sĕdly, *adv.*

advī'sory (-z-), *a.* giving advice.

|| ăd vī'ǐam aut cŭl'păm, during good behaviour.

ăd'vocate[1], *n.* one who pleads for another ; professional pleader ; one who supports or speaks in favour of a policy, &c. ăd'vocāte[2], *v.t.* (-*cable*), to plead for or support a policy, &c. ăd'vocacy, *n.* support, recommendation, of policy, &c.

advowson (-z-), *n.* right of presentation to a benefice.

ăd'ytum, *n.* (pl. -*ta*), innermost part of temple ; sanctum.

ădze, *n.* kind of axe with arched blade.

ae'dīle, *n.* Roman magistrate superintending public works, &c.

ae'ger, *n.* note certifying that student is ill.

ae'gis, *n.* shield of Zeus or Athena ; impregnable defence.

aegrō'tăt, *n.* certificate that student is too ill to attend examination, &c.

Aeo′lian, a. of Aeolis; of Aeolus, god of winds. ~ harp, instrument giving musical sounds on exposure to wind.

ae′on, ē′on, n. immense period.

ā′erāte, v.t. (-table), expose to action of air; charge with carbon dioxide. ~tion, n.

āēr′ial (or ār-), a. of air, gaseous; ethereal; existing in the air. n. (Wireless) collecting-wire.

aerie, aery (ā′eri, ī′ī), n. nest of bird that builds high up; dwelling perched high up.

ā′eriform, a. of the form of air, gaseous; unsubstantial.

āero- (or ār-), in comb. air- of aircraft. āerobāt′ics, n.pl. feats of expert aviation. ā′erobus, n. (sl.) aeroplane. ~drōme, n. aviation ground. ~foil, aeroplane wing or plane. ~grām, n. wireless message. ~hȳ′droplāne, n. flying-boat.

ā′erolite, ~lith, n. meteorite.

āerodȳnăm′ics, n.pl. the physics of gases in motion.

ā′eronaut (or ār-), n. aerial navigator. ~ic, ~ical, aa.

ā′eroplāne (or ār-), n. a flying-machine heavier than air using planes.

ā′erostāt, n. balloonist. ~ic, a.

āerostāt′ics, n.pl. physics of gases in equilibrium; science of air navigation.

Aescula′pius, n. god of medicine; a physician.

aesthet′ic, a. concerned with appreciation of the beautiful. ~al, a.; ~ism, ~s, nn. aes′thēte, n. appreciator of beauty.

‖ aetā′tis, ae′tāt., aet., pred. a. aged, of or at the age of.

aetiōl′ogy, n. assignment of a cause. ~gical, a.

afar′, adv. at a distance.

ăff′able, a. easy of address, courteous. ~bility, n.

affair′, n. business, concern.

affect′, v.t. produce an effect on; pose, pretend; move, touch the feelings.

ăffectā′tion, n. artificial manner; pretentious display.

affec′ted, a. disposed; full of affectation.

affec′tion, n. goodwill, love; malady, disease. ~āte, a. loving.

affi′ance, v.t. (-ceable), promise in marriage. n. trust; betrothal.

ăffidā′vit, n. written statement on oath.

affil′iāte, v.t. (-liable), adopt, attach to; fix paternity and maintenance of illegitimate child on. ~tion, ~tor, nn.

affin′itȳ, n. relationship; resemblance; attraction; (Chem.) tendency of elements to unite.

affirm′, v.t. & i. state as a fact; make affirmation. affirmā′tion, n. (esp.) declaration by one who conscientiously declines oath. ~ative, a. affirming; n. in phr. the answer is in the affirmative. ~atory, a.

affix′¹, v.t. fasten, append, attach. ăff′ix², n. thing affixed, addition; prefix or suffix.

afflā′tus, n. inspiration.

afflict′, v.t. distress, trouble; (pass.) be troubled. ~ion, n. distress, pain.

ăff′luence (-loo-), n. wealth, abundance.

ăff′luent (-loo-), a. rich, abundant. n. tributary stream.

ăff′lux, n. a flow to a point.

afford′, v.t. spare time or money for; supply, furnish.

affō′rest, v.t. convert into a forest. ~ation, n.

affray′, n. breach of the peace by fighting or riot.

affright′ (-īt), v.t. frighten. n. alarm, terror.

affront′ (-ŭnt), v.t. insult openly; face defiantly. n. open insult.

affū′sion (-zhn), n. pouring on, esp. of water in baptism.

afield′, adv. on, in, or to the field; away, at a distance.

aflāme′, adv. in flames, in a glow.

afloat′, adv. in a floating condition; at sea; out of debt.

‖ a fond (ah fawn′), thoroughly.

afoot′, adv. on foot, in progress.

afore′, adv. in front. prep. in

front of. ~named, ~said, previously named, &c. ~thought, premeditated. ~time, previously.

‖ ā fŏrtiŏr ī, with stronger reason.

afraid', a. in fear, feeling fear or dread; timid.

afresh', adv. with a fresh start.

Af'rikaans (ā-; -ahns), n. one of the official languages of S. Africa.

Afrikăn'der (ā-), n. native of S. Africa born of European (esp. Dutch) settlers. ~ Bond, organization for furtherance of Afrikander interests.

aft (ahft), adv. in, near, to, or towards stern of ship.

af'ter (ah-), adv. behind; later. prep. behind; *past (an hour); in pursuit or quest of; about, concerning; later than; according to. conj. after the time at which. a. later, hinder.

af'terbirth, n. membrane enveloping foetus in womb.

af'ter-crŏp, n. a second crop.

af'terdămp, n. gas left in mine after fire-damp explosion.

af'terglow (-ō), n. glow in the west after sunset.

af'termăth, n. grass growing after first crop is mown; results.

af'termŏst (ah-), adv. most aft.

afternoōn', n. time between noon and evening.

af'terthought (-awt), n. idea, &c. that occurs to one later.

af'terwards (ah-, -z), adv. later, subsequently.

aga (ä'gä, ä'gă), n. chief officer in Ottoman empire.

again', adv. another time, once more; further, besides.

against', prep. in opposition to; in contrast to; in anticipation of. conj. by the time that.

agāpe', adv. open-mouthed.

ăg'ate, n. kinds of chalcedony.

agä'vě, n. kinds of plant, including the American aloe.

āge, n. length of life or existence; historical or other period; (colloq.) a long time. v.i. & t. (-geable), grow old; show signs of age; cause to grow old. ~less, a. never growing old.

aged, a., (ājd) of the age of; (ā'jĭd) old; (of horses) over six years old.

ā'gencў, n. active operation, action; instrumentality; office of agent; business establishment.

agĕn'da, n.pl. items of business to be considered at meeting.

ā'gent, n. person or thing producing an effect; one who represents a person or firm in business.

‖ agent provocateur (ah'zhahn prŏvŏkahtĕr'), person employed to detect suspected offenders by tempting them to overt action.

agglŏm'erāte, v.t. & i. (-rable), collect into a mass. ~tion, n. ~mass. ~tive, a.

agglut'ĭnāte (-lŏo-), v.t. & i. (-rable), unite as with glue; turn into glue; form (words) into compounds. ~tion, n.; ~tive, a.

ăg'randize, v.t. (-zable), increase power, rank, or wealth of (State, person). ~ment, n.

ăg'ravāte, v.t. (-vable), increase the gravity of; (colloq.) annoy. ~tion, ~tor, nm.

ăg'regate, a. collected, total. n. whole collection, sum total; broken stone for concrete. v.t. & i. (-gable), collect together, unite. ~tion n.; ~tive, a.

aggrĕ'ssion (-shn), n. unprovoked attack. ~sive, a.; ~sor, n.

aggriev'ed (-vd), a. injured, having a grievance.

aghast' (-gahst), a. terrified, amazed.

ā'gile, a. quick-moving; nimble, active. agil'itў, n.

ā'giŏ (or ă-), n. (pl. -os), charge for changing paper-money into cash or one currency into another. ~tage, n. exchange business.

ā'gitāte, v.t. & i. (-itable), shake about; disturb, excite; discuss. ~tion, n. disturbed state of mind; keeping of a matter before the public. ~tor, n.

ăg'lĕt, ăig'lĕt, n. metal tag of a lace; tag or spangle as ornament of a dress; catkin.

ăg'nail, n. torn skin at root of finger-nail; resulting soreness.

---

māte, mēte, mīte, mōte, mūte, mōŏt; răck, rĕck, rĭck, rŏck, rŭck, rōōk;

ăg′nāte, *a.* descended from same male ancestor; of same clan or nation. *n.* such person.

ăgnō′měn, *n.* additional name.

agnŏs′tic, *n.* one who holds that nothing is to be known of a God or of anything but material phenomena. *a.* of or holding this theory. **~ism**, *n.*

Ag′nus Dē′ī (ä-), part of Mass.

agō′, *adv.* (of past event) from now.

agŏg′, *adv.* eager, on the look-out.

ăg′onīze, *v.t. & i.* cause agony to, torture; make desperate efforts.

ăg′ony, *n.* intense bodily or mental suffering; a severe struggle.

ăgorophō′bia, *n.* morbid dread of public places.

agrā′rian, *a.* relating to landed property; of cultivated land. *n.* advocate of redistribution of landed property. **~ism**, *n.*

agree′, *v.i.* consent; concur; become or be in agreement with.

agree′able (-ria-), *a.* pleasing; well-disposed; conformable.

agree′ment, *n.* mutual understanding; legal contract.

agrĕs′tic, *a.* rural, rustic.

ăg′riculture, *n.* cultivation of soil. **~ral**, *a.*; **~ralist, ~rist**, *nn.*

aground′, *adv.* upon the bottom of shallow water.

ā′gūe, *n.* malarial fever with cold, hot, and sweating stages; fit of shivering. **ā′gūed**, *a.* having ague. **ā′gūish**, *a.* of or like ague; subject to, suffering from ague.

ahead′ (ahĕd′), *adv.* in advance, in front; forward.

ahoy′ (a-h-), *int.* (naut.) used in hailing.

aid, *v.t.* help, assist, promote. *n.* help, helper; helpful thing.

aide-de-camp (ā *de* kahn), *n.* (pl. *aides-de-camp*, pr. ā′ *de* kahnz), officer assisting general by carrying orders, &c.

ai′grĕtte, *n.* tuft of feathers or hair; spray of gems, &c.

ai′guille (-gw-), *n.* sharp peak.

ail, *v.t. & i.* trouble, afflict, in body or mind; be ill. **~ment**, *n.*

aim, *v.t. & i.* direct at; point at; direct one's ambition. *n.* aim-

ing; object aimed at; purpose. **~less**, *a.* purposeless.

air, *n.* gaseous mixture of oxygen and nitrogen enveloping earth; atmosphere; open space; confident bearing; melody; (pl.) affected manners. *v.t.* expose to air, ventilate; make known, show off. Compounds denoting things containing air. **~ball, ~bladder, ~cushion, ~jacket.**

air′craft (-ahft), *n.* aeroplanes, airships, and balloons. **~ carrier**, ship that carries and serves as base for aeroplanes.

air′-gun, *n.* gun using compressed air as propelling force.

air′less, *a.* stuffy; still, calm.

air′-line, *n.* *direct line; line of passenger aircraft. **air′-liner**, *n.* large passenger aircraft.

air′-mail, *n.* mail carried by aircraft.

air′man, *n.* aviator.

air′plāne, *n.* aeroplane.

air′-port, *n.* aerodrome for passenger aircraft.

air′pump, *n.* instrument for pumping out air.

air′-raid, *n.* attack by aircraft.

air′ship, *n.* flying-machine lighter than air, Zeppelin, &c.

air′-tight, *a.* impermeable to air.

air′way, *n.* ventilating passage in mine; route regularly followed by aircraft.

air′y, *a.* (-ier, -iest, -ily, -iness), breezy; light, thin; sprightly.

aisle (īl), *n.* division of church; passage between rows of pews; *passage-way in building or train.

aitch′-bone, *n.* rump-bone; cut of beef lying over this.

ajār′, *adv.* (of door) slightly open.

a-kim′bŏ, *adv.* with hands on hips and elbows turned out.

akin′, *pred. a.* in relationship, related.

‖ à la (ah lah), in the manner known as.

ăl′abaster (-bah-), *n.* kinds of carbonate or sulphate of lime used for vases, &c. *a.* of alabaster.

‖ à la carte (ah lah kärt′), by the bill of fare.

---

māre, mĕre, mīre, mōre, mūre; pärt, pĕrt, pŏrt; *italics*, vague sounds;

aláck', *int.* expressing sorrow.

alác'ritŷ, *n.* briskness, readiness.

‖ à la mode (ah lah mŏd'), in the fashion.

alárm', *n.* call to arms, warning sound ; warning or excited anticipation, of danger. *v.t.* give the alarm to ; disturb, frighten. ~ism, *n.* panic-mongering. ~ist, *n.* a panic-monger.

alá'rum, *n.* signal of alarm ; an alarm-clock.

alas' (-ahs), *int.* expressing grief.

álb, *n.* white vestment reaching to feet, worn by priests, &c.

ál'bacŏre, *n.* large sea-fish of the tunny kind.

ál'batrŏs, *n.* type of Austrian aeroplane.

ál'batrŏss, *n.* kinds of bird allied to petrel ; largest sea-fowl.

albē'it (awl-), *conj.* although.

ál'bert, *n.* kind of watch-chain.

albēs'cent, *a.* growing white.

albī'nō (-bē-), *n.* (pl. -os), person (or animal) with white hair and skin, and eyes of a pink colour. ~něss (-bē-), ál'binism, *nn.*

ál'bum, *n.* book for autographs, photographs, &c.

ál'būmĕn, *n.* white of egg ; a constituent of animal solids and fluids and of seeds, found in white of egg.

ál'būminoid, *a.* like albumen. *n.* any of a class of organic compounds forming chief parts of organs and tissues of animals and plants. ~nous, *a.*

ál'būrnum, *n.* sap-wood.

Alcā'ic (ă-), *a.* of, or in, the metre invented by Alcaeus. *n.pl.* Alcaic strophes.

ál'chemŷ (-k-), *n.* transmutation of baser metals into gold. ~mist, *n.* ~mize, *v.t.* change as by alchemy.

ál'cohŏl, *n.* pure spirit of wine ; any liquor containing alcohol. ~ic, *a.* ~ism, *n.* effect of alcohol on the system. ~ize, *v.t.* saturate, treat, with alcohol.

Alcoran (ăl'korahn), *n.* Koran, sacred Mohammedan book.

ál'cŏve, *n.* recess in room, garden.

al'der (awl-), *n.* tree related to birch.

al'derman (awl-), civic dignitary next below mayor. aldermánic, *a.* ; ~rŷ, ~ship, *nn.*

Al'derney (awl-), *n.* cow, &c., from Alderney.

Al'dine (awl-), *n.* of or by Aldus Manutius, Venetian printer.

āle, *n.* malt liquor, beer. ~ house, place where ale is retailed.

alĕm'bĭc, *n.* apparatus formerly used in distilling.

alĕrt', *a.* watchful, vigilant ; nimble. ~ness, *n.*

Aléxán'drine (ă-), *a.* consisting of six iambic feet. *n.* A. verse.

ălfál'fa, *n.* lucerne.

ălfrĕs'cō, *adv.* & *a.* in the open air.

ál'ga, *n.* (pl. -gae, pr. -jē), seaweed.

ál'gŏl'ogist, ~gŷ, *nn.*

ál'gĕbra, *n.* investigation of the properties of numbers by means of general symbols. ălgébrá'ic(al), *aa.* ; ăl'gĕbr(ă)ist, *nn.*

ā'lias, *adv.* on other occasions. *n.* (pl. -ases) assumed name.

ăl'ĭbī, *n.* (pl. -bis), plea of being elsewhere ; *excuse.

ā'lien, *a.* not one's own ; foreign ; out of harmony. *n.* stranger, foreigner.

ā'lienāte, *v.t.* (-nable), estrange ; transfer ; divert. ~ability, ~tor, *nn.* ~tion, *n.* estrangement ; insanity.

ā'lienism, *n.* study and treatment of mental diseases. ~ist, *n.* specialist in such diseases.

alĭght'¹ (-īt), *v.i.* dismount, descend ; (of birds) come down.

alĭght'² (-īt), *a.* on fire.

alĭgn' (-īn), aline, *v.t.* & *i.* place or form in line. ~ment, *n.*

alīke', *a.* similar, like. *adv.* similarly, in like manner.

ăl'ĭment, *n.* food. ălĭmĕn'tal, *a.* supplying food. ~ary, *a.* nourishing ; concerned with nutrition. ~ation, *n.* nourishment.

ăl'imonŷ, *n.* allowance due to a wife for support.

ă'lĭquŏt, *a.* (of part) contained an exact number of times in a whole. *n.* aliquot part.

alive′, *a.* living; brisk, active; fully susceptible to.

ăl′kalĭ, *n.* (pl. -*lis*), any of a series of compounds called bases that neutralize strong acids. ălkalēs′cent, *a.* slightly alkaline. ălkalēs′cence, *n.*; ălkăl′ĭfў, *v.t.* ăl′kaline, *a.* of alkalis.

ăl′kaloĭd, *n.* nitrogenous basic substance. ~al, *a.*

all (awl), *a.* the whole amount, extent, or number. *pron.* the whole number; every one. *n.* the whole world; everything. *adv.* entirely, quite. *~ in,* quite exhausted.

Allah (ăl′a), *n.* Mohammedan name of God.

*all′-around, *a.* all-round.

allay′, *v.t.* repress; assuage.

allēge′, *v.t.* (-*geable*), state or advance as a fact. ăllēgā′tion, *n.*

allē′giance (-*jans*), *n.* duty of subject to sovereign or government; loyalty.

ăll′egorў, *n.* narrative describing one subject under the guise of another. ~ric(al), *aa.*; ~rist, *n.*; ~rize, *v.t.*

ăllegrĕt′to, *adv. & a.* (Mus.) in somewhat lively time. ălle′gro (-lā-) *adv. & a.* in quick, lively time.

ăllēlu′ia (-lōōya), *n.* song of praise.

allē′viāte, *v.t.* (-*iable*), mitigate, lessen (pain, evil). ~tion, *n.*, ~tor, *nn.*; ~tory, *a.*

ăll′ey, *n.* (pl. -*eys*), narrow street, passage; *back-lane; enclosure for skittles.

All Fools′ Day, 1st April.

all-fours, *n.* one's hands & knees.

All Hăll′ows, All Saints′ Day.

ălli′ance, *n.* relation of allies, confederation; union by marriage.

ăll′igātor, *n.* American crocodile. ~ apple, ~ pear, fruit of W.-Ind. trees.

ăllĭterā′tion, *n.* commencement of several words in same sentence with same letter. ~ate, *v.i.*; ~ative, *a.*

ăll′ocāte, *v.t.* (-*cable*), assign to. ~tion, ~tor, *nn.*

ăllocū′tion, *n.* formal hortatory address, esp. by Pope.

ăllŏp′athў, *n.* treatment of disease by inducing a different tendency. ăllopă′thic, *a.*; ~pathist, *n.*

allŏt′, *v.t.* (-*tt*-), assign; distribute by lot. ~ment, *n.* assignment; small plot of land let for cultivation. ~tee, *n.* one to whom allotment is made; a plot-holder.

ăllŏt′ropў, *n.* variation of physical properties without change of substance. ăllotrŏp′ic(al), *aa.*

allow′, *v.t. & i.* admit; permit; give periodically; add, deduct, in estimating. ~able, *a.* ~ance, *n.* fixed sum allowed; deduction from account, &c. ~ĕdly, *adv.* admittedly.

alloy′, *v.t.* mix with baser metal; debase. *n.* baser metal mixed with gold; any base mixture.

all right, *adv.* in good state.

all′-round′, *a.* good 'all round', or with ability in all departments. ~ man, all-roun′der, *nn.* one who is able 'all round'.

All Saints′ Day, 1st Nov.

All Souls′ Day, 2nd Nov.

all′spice, *n.* Jamaica pepper.

allude′ (-lōō-), *v.i.* refer covertly or indirectly to, hint at.

allure′, *v.t.* (-*rable*), entice, tempt; charm. ~ment, *n.*

allu′sion (-lōōzhn), *n.* indirect reference; hint. ~ive, *a.*

alluv′ion (-lōō-), *n.* wash of sea or river against shore; matter deposited by flood. ~ium, *n.* (pl. -*ia*, -*iums*), deposit of flood. ~ial, *a.*

allў′ⁿ, *v.t.* (-*iable*), join in confederation or marriage for special object. *n.* (also ăl′ī) allied State or person.

ăll′ў², *n.* choice playing-marble.

Al′ma Mā′ter (ă-), *n.* one's university or school.

al′manăc (awl-), *n.* yearly calendar of months and days.

almighty (awlmī′tĭ), *a.* infinitely powerful; (colloq.) very great. A. God, the Deity.

|| almīr′a, *n.* (Anglo-Ind.) cupboard, press, chest of drawers, &c.

alm′ond (ahm-), *n.* kernel of a fruit allied to plum. ~ cake, *n.*; ~ eyes, *n.pl.* (almond-shaped).

al'moner (*also* ahm'ner), *n.* official distributor of alms.

al'most (awl-), *adv.* very nearly, all but.

alms (ahmz), *n.* charitable relief or donation. ~**house**, ~**man**, *nn.*

al'öe, *n.* plant with erect spikes of flowers and bitter juice; (pl.) purgative drug from aloe juice.

aloft' (-awft), *adv.* high up, over-head.

alöne', *a.* solitary, by or to one-self. *adv.* only, singly.

alöng', *prep.* through the length or any part of the length of. *adv.* within the limits of a thing's length; in company, with one; onward, in progress. ~**side**, *adv.* close to side of ship, &c.

aloof', *adv.* away, apart. ~**ness**, *n.* unconcern, lack of sympathy.

aloud', *adv.* in the normal voice, not in a whisper; loudly.

älp, *n.* mountain-peak.

älpăc'a, *n.* llama with long wool; its wool; fabric thence made.

äl'penstöck, *n.* iron-shod staff used in climbing.

äl'pha, *n.* first letter in Greek alphabet. ~**particles, rays,** kinds emitted by radium.

äl'phabét, *n.* letters used in a language. **älphabét'ic**(al), *aa.*

Al'pine (ă-), *a.* of the Alps; lofty. ~**nist**, *n.* Alpine climber.

already (awlrĕd'ĭ), *adv.* before-hand; by this time, thus early.

Alsatian (ălsā'shn) (**wolf-hound**), *n.* a breed of dog.

al'sö (awl-), *adv.* besides, too.

ält, *n.* (Mus.) high tone.

al'tar (awl-), *n.* flat-topped block for offerings to a deity; Communion table. ~**piece**, *n.* painting or sculpture behind altar.

al'ter (awl-), *v.t. & i.* change in character, position, &c.; modify. ~**ation**, *n.*

al'terative (awl-), *a.* tending to alteration. *n.* medicine or treatment that alters the processes of nutrition.

al'tercāte (awl-), *v.i.* dispute, wrangle. ~**tion**, *n.*

|| **äl'ter ĕg'ō**, *n.* one's other self, intimate friend.

alternate, *a.* (awltĕrn'at), (of things of two kinds) occurring each after one of the other kind; (of a series or whole) composed of alternate things. *v.t. & i.* (awl'ternāt), arrange, occur, in alternate order. ~**tion**, *n.* alternating current, (Electr.) current which flows in alternate directions in a circuit.

altern'ative (awl-), *a.* offering a choice between two things. *n.* choice between two (or more) things.

al'ternātor (awl-), *n.* dynamo for producing alternating currents.

although (awldhō'), *conj.* though.

ältim'éter, *n.* aeronautical instrument showing height above sea level.

al'titūde, *n.* vertical height; height above sea level; (usu. pl.) high place.

äl'tö, *a.* high. *n.* (pl. -ōs), highest male voice.

altogĕther (awltogĕdh'er), *adv.* entirely; on the whole.

äl'tō-relievv'ō (-lĕ-), *n.* (pl. -ōs), (Sculpt.) high relief.

äl'truism (-rōō-), *n.* regard for others as a principle of action. ~**ist**, *n.*; ~**istic**, *a.*

äl'um, *n.* a mineral salt.

alum'ina (-lōō-), *n.* oxide of aluminium. **älūmin'ium**, *n.* a white metal. ~**nous**, *a.* of alum or alumina.

älū'minum, *n.* aluminium.

alūm'na, *n.* (pl. -nae), fem. of *alumnus.*

alūm'nus, *n.* (pl. -nī), (former) pupil of school or university.

always (awl'wiz), *adv.* at all times, on all occasions.

am, 1st pers. sing. of verb *to be.*

ämadavat', **äva-**, *n.* an Indian song-bird.

|| **a'mah** (ah-), *n.* (Anglo-Ind.) a child's nurse.

amain', *adv.* with force; in haste.

amăl'gam, *n.* mixture of a metal with mercury; plastic mixture.

amăl'gamāte. *v.t. & i.* (*-mable*). mix; unite, combine. ~tion, ~tor, *nn.*; ~tive, *a.*

amănŭĕn'sis, *n.* (pl. *-nsēs*), clerk who writes from dictation.

ăm'aranth, *n.* kinds of plant with coloured foliage; imaginary unfading flower. āmarăn'thine, *a.*

ămaryl'lis, *n.* kinds of flowering plant.

amăss', *v.t.* heap together, accumulate.

ăm'ateur (-ūr), *n.* one who cultivates a thing as a pastime. ~ish, *a.* suggesting the amateur.

ăm'ative, *a.* disposed to love. ~ness, *n.* ~tory, *a.* of lovers.

ăm'atōl, *n.* a high explosive.

amāze, *v.t.* overwhelm with wonder. ~zing, *a.* astonishing. ~ment, *n.*

Am'azon (ă-), *n.* female warrior; masculine woman. ~ō'nian, *a.*

ămbăss'ador, *n.* minister sent to foreign court as permanent representative or on a mission. ămbăssadōr'ial, *a.*; ~dress, *n.*

ăm'ber, *n.* a yellow translucent fossil resin.

ăm'bergris (-ēs), *n.* wax-like substance from the sperm-whale.

ămbidex'ter, *a.* able to use both hands alike; double-dealing. dĕxtĕr'ity, *n.*; ~t(e)rous, *a.*

ăm'bient, *a.* surrounding.

ambĭg'ūous, *a.* of doubtful meaning; uncertain. ămbĭgū'ĭty, *n.*

ăm'bĭt, *n.* confines, scope.

ambĭ'tion, *n.* desire for distinction; aspiration; object of this. ambĭ'tious (-shus), *a.* ardently desirous; full of ambition.

ăm'ble, *v.i.* (of horse, &c.) move at easy pace. *n.* easy pace.

ămbrō'sia (-zia, -zhya), *n.* food of the gods; thing delightful to taste or smell. ~ial, *a.*

ăm'bŭlance, *n.* moving hospital following army; conveyance for sick or wounded persons.

ăm'bŭlatory, *a.* (-lă-) of or for walking. *n.* (-la-) place for walking; cloister.

ămbuscāde', *n.* an ambush.

ăm'bush (-ŏŏsh), *n.* troops con-

cealed in wood, &c.; such concealment. *v.t.* lie in wait for.

‖ âme damnée (ahm dahn'ā), tool, devoted adherent.

ameer', amir' (-ēr), *n.* title of various Mohammedan rulers.

amē'liorāte, *v.t. & i.* (*-rable*). make or become better. ~tion, ~tor, *nn.*; ~tive, *a.*

amĕn' (ah-, ā-), so be it.

amē'nable, *a.* responsible, accountable; tractable. ~bility, *n.*

amĕnd', *v.t. & i.* correct, improve; make improvements. ~ment, *n.*

‖ amende honorable (âmahnd' ŏnŏrah'bl), public apology.

amĕnds' (-z), *n.* compensation.

amē'nĭty, *n.* pleasantness; ~s (pl.) agreeable manners.

amĕrce', *v.t.* fine; punish. ~able, *a.*; ~ment, *n.*

Amĕ'rĭcan, *a.* of America or United States. *n.* citizen of the U.S. ~ism, *n.* word or phrase borrowed from the U.S.; adherence to American principles, &c. ~ize, *v.t. & i.* make or become American.

ăm'ĕthyst, *n.* a precious stone of purple or violet colour. ~ine, *a.*

ā'miable, *a.* lovable, inspiring friendliness. ~bility, *a.*

ămĭăn'tus, ~thus, *n.* kind of asbestos.

ăm'ĭcable, *a.* friendly. ~bility, *n.*

ăm'ĭce, *n.* (1) square of white linen on shoulders of celebrant priest (R.C.); (2) cap, hood, badge, of religious orders.

‖ amī'cus cūr'iae, *n.* friend of the court, disinterested adviser.

amĭd', ~st, *prep.* in the middle of, among. ~ships, in middle of ship.

amĭss', *adv.* out of order; badly.

ăm'ĭty, *n.* friendly relations.

ăm'mēter, *n.* instrument for measuring electric currents.

ammō'nia, *n.* a colourless pungent gas with strong alkaline reaction. ~ăc, ~i'acal, ~āted, *aa.*

ammō'nium, *n.* hypothetical radical of ammonia salts.

ămm'onite, *n.* coil-shaped fossil shell.

ămmūni'tion, *n.* military stores (now only of powder, shot, &c.).

ăm'nĕsty, *n.* act of oblivion; general pardon.

amœ'ba (-mē-), *n.* (pl. *-bae, -bas*), microscopic animalcule perpetually changing shape.

among', **~st** (-mŭ-), *prep.* in the midst of, in the number of.

amō'ral, *a.* non-moral.

ăm'orous, *a.* in love; loving.

amŏr'phous, *a.* shapeless; anomalous.

amŏrt'īze, *v.t.* (*-zable*), extinguish debt, esp. by means of a sinking fund. **~zā'tion**, *n.*

amount', *v.i.* be equivalent to, reach the total of. *n.* total; quantity.

amour' (-oor), *n.* love affair, intrigue.

‖ amour-propre (ăm'oor-prŏp'r), self-esteem.

ămpelŏp'sis, *n.* vine-creeper.

ampere (ăm'pĕr), *n.* unit of electric current.

ămpersănd', *n.* the sign & (and).

amphĭb'ian, *a.* & *n.* (animal) living both on land and in water; (aeroplane) designed to rise from and alight on either land or water.

amphĭb'ious, *a.* living both on land and in water.

ăm'phitheatre (-later), *n.* round building with tiers of seats surrounding central space; semicircular gallery in theatre.

ăm'phora, *n.* (pl. *-ae, -as*), Gk. or Rom. two-handled vessel.

ăm'ple, *a.* spacious, extensive; abundant; quite enough.

ăm'plĭfy, *v.t.* & *i.* (*-iable*), enlarge, add details. **~fĭcā'tion**, *n.* (esp. Electr.) process of increasing the strength of varying or alternating currents.

ăm'plĭfier, *n.* (esp.) appliance increasing force of electric signals in wireless reception.

ăm'plĭtūde, *n.* spaciousness.

ămpŭll'a, *n.* (pl. *-ae*), Roman globular two-handled flask. **ămpŭllā'ceous**, *a.* bottle-shaped.

ăm'pūtāte, *v.t.* (*-utable*), cut off (limb, &c.). **~tion**, **~tor**, *nn.*

amŭck', *adv.* In phr. *run ~*, run about in frenzied state.

ăm'ūlĕt, *n.* thing worn as a charm against evil.

amūse' (-z), *v.t.* (*-sable*), excite the risible faculty; find diversion or light occupation for; entertain. **~ment**, *n.*

ăm'yl, *n.* (Chem.) the radical of various alcohols some of which are constituents of fusel oil. **amȳl'ic**, *a.*

ămylā'ceous (-shus), *a.* starchy.

ăm'yloid, *a.* starchy. *n.* starchy food.

an¹: see **a¹**. **ăn²**, *conj.* (arch.) if.

ā'na, *n.* (pl. *anas*), collection of sayings; (pl.) anecdotes of a person.

ănabăp'tist, *n.* one who baptizes over again. **~ism**, *n.* re-baptism; doctrine of anabaptists.

anăc'hronism (-k-), *n.* chronological error; thing out of harmony with the period. **~is'tic**, *a.*

ănacŏn'da, *n.* large snake of Ceylon; large S.-Amer. boa.

anae'mia, *n.* lack of blood; unhealthy pallor. **~ic**, *a.*

ănaesthē'sia, *n.* insensible condition. **~thĕt'ic**, *a.* producing anaesthesia; *n.* drug, &c. producing a. **~thetist**, *n.* one who administers anaesthetics. **~thetize**, *v.t.*; **~thetizā'tion**, *n.*

ăn'agrăm, *n.* word or phrase formed from letters of another. **~mă'tic(al)**, *aa.*; **~matist**, *n.*

ā'nal, *a.* of the anus.

ăn'alĕcts, *n.pl.* literary gleanings.

ănălgē'sia, *n.* absence of pain. **~ĕt'ic**, **~esic**, *aa.* giving analgesia; *nn.* such drug.

anăl'ogous, *a.* similar, parallel. **anăl'ogue**, *n.* analogous thing.

anăl'ogy, *n.* parallelism, similarity; reasoning from parallel cases. **analŏg'ical**, *a.*; **~gize**, *v.t.* & *i.*; **~gist**, *n.*

ăn'alyse (-z), *v.t.* (*-sable*), ascertain the elements of, examine minutely the constitution of.

anăl'ysis, *n.* (pl. *-es*), resolution into simple elements.

ăn'alyst, *n.* one who analyses.

ănalўt′ic, ~al, aa. of or employing analysis.

ană′nas (or -ahn-), n. pine-apple.

ăn′apaest, n. a metrical foot of three syllables (‿‿–). **~ic,** a.

an′archў (-k-), n. absence of government; disorder. **anăr′chic(al),** aa. lawless. **~chism,** n. **~chist,** n. advocate of anarchy.

anastig′măt, n. anastigmatic lens. **~ic,** a. (of lens) with astigmatism corrected.

anăth′ema, n. solemn curse; accursed thing. **~tize,** v.t.

anăt′omў, n. science of bodily structure; dissection; a mere skeleton. **ănatŏm′ical,** a. **~mize,** v.t. & i. practise anatomy, dissect. **~mist,** n.

ăn′burў, n. soft tumour on horses, &c.; disease of turnips.

ăn′cestor, n. any of those from whom one's father or mother is descended; forefather. **ances′tral,** a. inherited from ancestors. **~tress,** n. **~trў,** n. ancient descent.

ănc′hor (-k-), n. heavy iron instrument, with hooks, for mooring ship to bottom of water. v.t. & i. secure ship with anchor; fig. fix one's hope on. **~age,** n. place for ship lying at anchor.

ănc′horět, ~rīte (-k-), n. hermit, recluse. **~ess, ăn′crĕss,** nn. fem.

ănchō′vў (or ăn′cho-), n. small fish of the herring family. **~ paste, sauce,** &c.

anchylō′sis (ăngkĭ-), n. stiffening of a joint by uniting of the bones.

|| ancien régime (ahn′syăn rā′zhĕm′), n. time before French Revolution.

ăn′cient[1] (-shent), a. of times long past; old. **A. of Days,** God.

ăn′cient[2] (-shent), n. an ensign.

ăn′cillarў, a. subservient.

and (and; emphat. ănd), conj. connecting words, clauses, and sentences.

ăndăn′tè, a. moderately slow.

ăn′diron (-īrn), n. firedog.

ăn′ecdōte, n. narrative of detached incident. **~tage,** n. telling of anecdotes, esp. in old age. **~tal,** a.; **~tist,** n.

ănēle′, v.t. anoint; give extreme unction to.

anĕmŏm′ēter, n. instrument for measuring force of wind. **ănĕmŏmĕt′ric,** a.; **ănĕmŏm′ĕtrў,** n.

anĕm′onè, n. a woodland flower. also called wind-flower. **sea~,** kinds of zoophyte.

anĕnt′, prep. concerning.

ăn′eroid, a. not employing fluid. **~ barometer,** n. one that measures air-pressure by its action on lid of box exhausted of air.

ăn′eurўsm, ~ism (-nūr-), n. morbid dilatation of artery.

anew′, adv. again, once more.

ăn′garў, n. (Law) belligerent's right of seizing or destroying neutral property.

ā′ngel (-j-), n. divine messenger; attendant spirit; obliging person; old English gold coin. **ăngĕl′ic,** a. **~fish,** kind of shark. **ăngĕl′ica** (-j-), n. aromatic plant. **ăn′gelus** (-j-), n. devotional exercise said at morning, noon, and sunset, at sound of bell. **~ bell,** such bell.

ăng′er (-ngg-), n. hot displeasure. v.t. excite anger in.

ăngī′na (-j-), n. quinsy. **~ pectoris** (pĕk′toris), spasm of chest due to over-exertion when heart is diseased.

angle[1] (ăng′gl), n. space between two meeting lines, inclination of two lines to each other; a corner.

angle[2] (ăng′gl), n. fish-hook. v.i. fish with rod, hook, and bait. **ăng′ler** (-ngg-), n. a fisher.

Ang′lican (ăngg

-), a. of the reformed Church of England, esp. of High Church principles. n. such person. **~ism,** n.

|| Anglice (ăng′glĭsē), adv. in English.

Ang′licism (ăngg-), n. English idiom. **~cize,** v.t. make English.

Anglo- (ăngg

-), in comb. English. **~Căth′olic,** a. & n. (member) of the party that insists on the catholicity of the Church of England and repudiates the epithet protestant. **~In′dian,** a. & n. (person) of British birth but living

or having lived long in India.
~mā'nia, *n.* strong desire to imitate things English; ~mā'niăc, *n.*
~phōbe, *n.* one with an excessive dread of the English; ~phō'bia, *n.* ~-Săx'on, *a.* of the English before the Norman Conquest; *n.* such person; Old English language before 1100.

ăngō'la (-ngg-), *n.* fabric made from wool of Angora goat.

ăngōr'a, *n.* (usu.) angola. ~ goat, goat with long silky hair from Angora in Asia Minor. ~ cat, ~ rabbit, long-haired varieties of cat and rabbit.

ăng'rў (-ngg-), *a.* feeling or showing anger; (of sore, &c.) inflamed, painful.

ăng'uish (-nggw-), *n.* severe mental or bodily pain.

ăng'ūlar (-ngg-), *a.* having angles; sharp-cornered. ~ă'rity, *n.*

ăn'iline, *n.* a product of coal-tar, the source of many dyes.

ănimadvert', *v.i.* pass criticism or censure upon. ~version, *n.*

ăn'imal, *n.* a being endowed with life, sensation, and voluntary motion; (pop.) a creature other than man. *a.* of animals, of the nature of animals; carnal; sensual. ~ism, *n.* exercise of animal faculties. ~ity, *n.* animal nature. ~ize, *v.t.* convert into animal substance; sensualize. ~ization, *n.*

ănimăl'cūle, *n.* microscopic animal.

ăn'imāte, *v.t.* breathe life into; encourage, inspirit. *a.* (-at) living, not inanimate. ~tion, *n.* ardour, life, vivacity. ~tor, *n.*

ăn'imism, *n.* attribution of a soul to inanimate objects and natural phenomena. ~ist, *n.*; ~istic, *a.*

ănimŏs'itў, *n.* hostility, enmity.

ăn'imus, *n.* bitter feeling against.

ăn'ise, *n.* plant with aromatic seeds. ăn'iseed, *n.* seed of anise.

ankle (ăng'kl), *n.* joint connecting foot with leg. ănk'lĕt, *n.* support or ornament for the ankle.

ănn'a, *n.* sixteenth part of rupee; *half*~, *quarter*~, E. Indian coins.

ănn'als (-z), *n.pl.* narrative of events year by year; records. ănn'alist, *n.* writer of annals.

anneal', *v.t.* temper by gradually diminishing heat; temper.

ănn'elid, *n.* red-blooded worm, e. g. earth-worm, leech. ~an, *a.*

annex', *v.t.* add, append, attach; take possession of. *n.* (also ann'exe), supplementary building, addition to document, &c. ~ation, *n.*

annihilāte (-nī-), *v.t.* (-lable), destroy utterly. ~tion, ~tor, *nn.*

ănnivèrs'arў, *n.* yearly return of a date; celebration of this.

ănn'ō aetā'tis sū'ae, *adv.* in the — year of his age.

Ănn'ō Dŏm'ini (ā-), *adv.* (usu. abbr. A. D.), in the year of our Lord. *n.* (slang) advancing age.

ănn'otāte, *v.t.* & *i.* (-tatable), add notes to book, &c.; make notes on. ~tion, ~tor, *nn.*

announce', *v.t.* (-ceable), proclaim, give notice of. ~ment, *n.*

announ'cer, *n.* (esp.) official at broadcasting station who announces each item of the programme.

annoy', *v.t.* irritate, molest. ~ance, *n.* molestation, vexation.

ănn'ūal, *a.* reckoned by the year; recurring yearly. *n.* plant living only a year; yearly periodical.

annū'itў, *n.* yearly grant or sum; investment entitling one to a fixed annual sum. ~tant, *n.*

annŭl', *v.t.* (-ll-), abolish, cancel; declare invalid. ~ment, *n.*

ănn'ūlar, *a.* ring-shaped. ~late, ~lated, *aa.* marked with rings.

annŭn'ciāte (-shi-), *v.t.* (-ciable), proclaim. ~tion, *n.* announcement, esp. of the Incarnation. ~tor, *n.*

ăn'ōde, *n.* the path by which electric current leaves the positive pole; the positive pole.

ăn'odyne, *a.* pain-killing, soothing. *n.* drug to allay pain.

anoint', *v.t.* apply ointment or oil to; smear, rub, &c.

anŏm'alous, *a.* irregular, abnormal. anŏm'alў, *n.* irregularity.

anŏn', *adv.* soon, presently.

anŏn´ymous, a. of unknown name; of unknown authorship. anŏn´ymity, n.

anŏph´elēs, n. kinds of (esp. malarial) mosquito.

anoth´er (-ŭdh-), a. an additional; a different. pron. another one.

an´serine, a. of geese; silly.

answer´ (ahn´ser), v.t. & i. make a reply to; be responsible for; correspond to. n. thing said, written, or done in reply to. ~able, a. responsible.

ant, n. a small insect. ~-eater, animal living on ants. ~-hill, a mound over ants' nest.

antăg´onism, n. active opposition. ~ist, n. opponent. ~istic, a. ~ize, v.t. oppose actively; counteract.

antărc´tic, a. of south polar regions.

ante-, pref. before.

antecē´dent, a. previous to. n. preceding event or circumstance; (pl.) a person's past history. ~nce, n.

an´techamber, n. room leading to chief apartment.

an´techăpel, n. outer part at west end of chapel.

antedāte´, v.t. (-table), affix or assign an earlier than the true date to; precede; anticipate.

antedilū´vian (-lōō-), a. before the flood; antiquated.

an´telope, n. deer-like ruminant.

an´tē mĕrid´iĕm, adv. (abbrev. a.m.), before noon.

antenā´tal, a. before birth.

antĕnn´a, n. (pl. -ae), feelers or horns found on heads of insects and crustacea; (Wireless) a conductor which sends out or receives electric waves, an aerial. antĕnn´al, ~ary, aa.

antepĕnŭlt´, ~imate, aa. last but two. nn. antepenult syllable.

antēr´ior, a. prior to; more to the front. antēriŏr´ity, n.

an´tē-rŏŏm, n. antechamber.

an´them, n. composition set to sacred music; song of praise.

an´ther, n. part of stamen containing pollen. ~al, a.

anthŏl´ogy, n. collection of small choice poems, &c. ~gist, n.

an´thracite, n. non-bituminous kind of coal. ~it´ic, ~tous, aa.

an´thrax, n. malignant boil; a disease of sheep and cattle.

an´thropoid, a. man-like. n. anthropoid ape.

anthropŏl´ogy, n. whole science of man; study of man as an animal. ~olŏg´ical, a.; ~gist, n.

anthrŏpomŏr´phize, v.t. (-zable), attribute human form or personality to God, &c. ~phic, a.; ~phism, ~phist, nn.

anthropŏph´agi, n.pl. cannibals. ~gous, a. man-eating. ~gy, n.

anti-, pref. opposite, against.

anti-air´craft, a. ~ gun, &c., for shooting down hostile aircraft.

an´ti-bŏdy, n. kinds of substance in the blood tending to neutralize others that are harmful.

an´tic, n. grotesque posture or trick. a. grotesque; fantastic.

An´tichrist (ä-, -k-), n. the Great Enemy of Christ.

antichris´tian (-k-), a. opposed to Christianity. ~ism, n.

antic´ipate, v.t. (-pable), look forward to, expect; forestall; use in advance. ~tion, ~tor, nn.; ~tive, ~tory, aa.

anticli´max, n. lame conclusion to anything promising a climax.

anticy´clone, n. rotatory outward flow of air from atmospheric area of high pressure.

an´tidote, n. medicine used to counteract disease or poison.

an´tigĕn, n. substance introduced into the blood to stimulate production of anti-bodies.

antimacăss´ar, n. protective covering for chair-back.

an´timony, n. a brittle metallic element used in medicine, &c.

Antinō´mian (ä-), n. one who holds that the moral law is not binding on Christians.

antin´omy, n. contradiction in a law, authorities, or conclusions.

antip´athy, n. constitutional or settled aversion to. ~thĕt´ic, a.

an´tiphon, n. verse or sentence

sung by one choir in answer to another. **ăntiph'onal**, *a.* sung alternately. **~ary**, *n.* book of antiphons. **~y**, *n.* antiphonal singing.

ăntip'odēs (-z), *n.pl.* region of the earth diametrically opposite, esp. to our own. **~dal**, **~dē'an**, *aa.*

ăn'tipōpe, *n.* opposition pope.

ăntipyrēt'ic, *a. & n.* (drug) allaying or preventing fever. **ăntipy'rin**, *n.* a particular antipyretic. P.

ăn'tiquary, *n.* student or collector of antiquities. **ăr'ian**, *a. & n.* **~rianism**, *n.*

ăn'tiquated, *a.* out of date.

ăntique' (-ēk), *a.* of or dating from old times; old-fashioned. *n.* antique relic, esp. work of art.

ăntiq'uity, *n.* old times, esp. before the middle ages; (pl.) customs, &c. of the ancients; ancient relics.

ăntirrhī'num (-rī-), *n.* snapdragon.

ăntiscorbū'tic, *a.* of use against scurvy. *n.* a medicine, &c.

ănti-Sĕmīt'ic, *a.* opposed to or hostile to Jews. **~Sĕ'mite**, **~Sĕ'mitism**, *nn.*

ăntisĕp'tic, *a.* preventing putrefaction. *n.* a drug, treatment, &c.

ăntis'trophē, *n.* lines recited during returning movement from left to right in Greek chorus. **~ŏph'ic**, *a.*

ăntith'esis, *n.* (pl. *-theses*), contrast of ideas marked by parallelism of contrasted words; direct opposite. **~thĕt'ic(al)**, *aa.*

ăntitŏx'ic, *a.* serving to neutralize a toxin. **ăntitŏx'in**, *n.* a serum.

ăn'ti-trāde, *n.* wind blowing in opposite direction to trade wind.

ăn'titype, *n.* that which a type represents.

ănt'ler, *n.* branched horn of deer.

ăn'tonym, *n.* a word of contrary meaning to another.

ăn'vil, *n.* block on which smith works metal.

anxi'ety (ăngz-), *n.* troubled state of mind; uneasiness.

anxious (ăngk'shus), *a.* troubled; uneasy in mind; desirous to do.

any (ĕn'ĭ), *a.* one, some, every,

pron. one, some. *adv.* at all, in any degree. **~body**, *n.* any person; a person of consequence. **~how**, *adv.* in any way; in any case; at random. **~one**, *n.* anybody. **~thing**, *n.* any thing, any whit. **~way**, *adv.* at any rate. **~ways**, **~wise**, *advv.* in any way. **~where**, *adv.* in any place.

An'zăc (ă-), *n.* (pl.) the Australian and New Zealand Army Corps in the great war.

ā'orist, *n.* Greek tense denoting occurrence simply.

aŏrt'a, *n.* great artery issuing from left ventricle of heart. **~tic**, *a.*

à outrance (ah ōō'trahns), to the death.

apāce', *adv.* swiftly; fast.

apache' (-ahsh), *n.* street ruffian.

ăp'anage, **ăpp-**, *n.* provision for younger children; dependency; perquisite.

apárt', *adv.* aside, separately.

apárt'ment, *n.* single room; *set of rooms; (pl.) set of rooms.

ăp'atny, *n.* insensibility, indifference; mental indolence. **ăpa-thĕt'ic**, *a.*

āpe, *n.* tailless monkey; imitator. *v.t.* imitate. **ā'pery**, *n.* mimicry.

apercu (ahp'ārsōō), *n.* summary exposition of subject.

apē'rient (or -ēr-), *a.* laxative. *n.* medicine to open the bowels.

ăp'erture, *n.* opening, gap.

ā'pĕx, *n.* (pl. *-icĕs*, *-exes*), tip, topmost point, pointed end.

aphā'sia (-zyǎ), *n.* loss of speech.

aphē'lion, *n.* (pl. *-ïă*), point of orbit farthest from sun.

ăph'is, *n.* (pl. *aphidēs*), small insect, plant-louse, ant-cow, &c.

ăph'orism, *n.* short pithy maxim; definition. **~ist'ic**, *a.*

ā'piary, *n.* place where bees are kept. **āpiār'ian**, *a.* ; **~rist**, *n.*

ā'pical (or ă-), *a.* of or at the apex.

ā'piculture, *n.* bee-keeping.

apiece', *adv.* severally, each.

ā'pish, *a.* of or like an ape.

aplomb (ahplawn'), *n.* self-possession.

apŏc'alypse, *n.* revelation, esp. that of St. John. **~lyp'tic(al)**, *a.*

---

ah, awl, oil, boor, cow, dowry; chin, go, bang, so, ship, thin; dh, as th(e):

apŏc'opĕ, *n.* cutting off of end of word.

apŏc'rypha, *n.* O.T. books not counted genuine. **~phal**, *a.* doubtful.

apŏd'osis, *n.* (pl. *-doses*), consequent clause in conditional sentence.

ăp'ogee, *n.* point in an orbit farthest from the earth; climax.

Apŏll'o, *n.* Greek sun-god; the sun; man of great beauty.

Apŏll'yon, *n.* the Devil.

apŏlogĕt'ic, *a.* regretfully acknowledging fault; of the nature of an apology. **~s**, *n.pl.* reasoned defence, esp. of Christianity.

ăp'ologue (-ŏg), *n.* moral fable.

apŏl'ogy, *n.* regretful acknowledgement of offence; explanation, vindication. **~gist**, *n.* one who defends by argument. **~gize**, *v.i.* make an apology.

ăp'ophthegm (*-ŏfthĕm*, *-ŏthĕm*), *n.* terse or pithy saying. **~atic**, *a.*

ăp'oplexy, *n.* a malady suddenly arresting powers of sense and motion. **~plec'tic**, *a.* of apoplexy.

ăposiopē'sis, *n.* (pl. *-peses*), sudden stop in speech for effect.

apŏs'tasy, *n.* abandonment of one's religion, party, &c. **~tate**, *n.* one guilty of apostasy. **~tatize**, *v.i.*

|| ā pŏstĕriŏr'ī, *adv.* from effect to cause.

apŏs'tle, *n.* any of the twelve sent forth by Christ; missionary; leader of reform. **~tolate**, *n.* apostleship. **~tŏl'ic**, *a.* of the Apostles; of the Pope.

apŏs'trophe, *n.* exclamatory address; sign of omitted letter (*can't*); sign of possessive case (*boy's*, *boys'*).

apŏth'ecary, *n.* druggist, chemist.

apŏthēō'sis, *n.* (pl. *-osēs*), deification; transformation; deified ideal. **apŏth'eosize**, *v.t.*

appal' (*-awl*), *v.t.* dismay, terrify.

ăpparā'tus (pl. *-tuses*), *n.* appliances for scientific or other work.

appă'rel (*-ll-*), *v.t.* dress, attire. *n.* dress, clothing.

appă'rent (*or -ār-*), *a.* manifest.

ăppari'tion, *n.* appearance, esp. of startling kind; a ghost.

appā'ritor, *n.* herald; usher.

appeal' (*-ēl*), *v.i. & t.* apply to higher court; call upon for corroboration; make a request. *n.* act or right of appealing.

appear', *v.i.* become visible; present oneself; be published; seem.

appear'ance, *n.* appearing; seeming; look, aspect; (pl.) outward show of prosperity, friendly relations, &c.

appease' (*-z*), *v.t.* (*-sable*), pacify, soothe; satisfy. **~ment**, *n.*

appell'ant, *a.* concerned with appeals. *n.* one who appeals to higher court.

appell'ate, *a.* (of court) hearing appeals.

appellā'tion, *n.* name, title.

appell'ative, *a.* (of nouns) common, not proper. *n.* such noun.

append', *v.t.* attach as an accessory; add to. **~age**, *n.* accompaniment.

appendici'tis, *n.* inflammation of vermiform appendix of intestine.

appen'dix, *n.* (pl. *-ixes* or *-icēs*) subsidiary addition (to book, &c.).

ăppertain', *v.i.* belong to, relate to.

ăpp'etite, *n.* desire or craving for food, pleasure, &c.; relish for food. **ăpp'etizer**, *n.* thing that gives appetite. **~izing**, *a.* inviting.

applaud', *v.t. & i.* express approval, esp. by clapping; commend.

applause' (*-z*), *n.* loud approbation.

ăp'ple, *n.* fruit of the apple-tree. **~cart**, *n.* in phr. *upset one's apple-cart*, upset one's plans. **~dumpling**, *n.* apple cooked in paste. ***-jack**, spirit distilled from cider. **~ of the eye**, the pupil; a cherished object. **~pie bed**, with sheets so folded that one cannot get one's legs down. **~pie order**, perfect order. ***-sauce**, *n.* flattery; *int.* nonsense!

appli'ance, *n.* thing applied as a means; instrument, device.

app'licable, *a.* that applies or may be applied. **~bility**, *n.*

app'licant, *n.* one who applies.

applica'tion, *n.* applying; request; diligence; bringing to bear.

appliqué (-e'kā), *n.* cut-out material applied to a surface.

apply', *v.t. & i.* put close, put in contact; administer (remedy); request; attend closely to.

appoint', *v.t.* fix (time, &c.); prescribe, ordain; assign post to.

appoint'ment, *n.* engagement, assignation; (pl.) outfit.

app'ort, *n.* material thing produced at spiritualist séance.

appor'tion, *v.t.* assign as share, portion out. **~ment**, *n.*

app'osite (or -I-; -z-), *a.* well put, to the point. **~ness**, *n.* juxtaposition.

appraise' (-z), *v.t.* (*-sable*), fix price of; estimate. **~sal**, **~ment**, *nn.*

appre'ciable (-sha-), *a.* perceptible.

appre'ciate (-shi-), *v.t. & i.* set high value on; estimate rightly; rise in value. **~tion**, **~tor**, *nn.*; **~tive, ~tory**, *aa.*

apprehend', *v.t.* seize, arrest; understand; anticipate with fear.

apprehen'sible, *a.* perceptible to senses. **~bility**, *n.* **~sion**, *n.* arrest; understanding; dread. **~sive**, *a.* afraid, fearful.

appren'tice, *n.* learner bound to employer for specified term. *v.t.* (*-ceable*), bind as apprentice. **~ship**, *n.*

apprise' (-z), *v.t.* give notice of, inform.

apprize' (-z), *v.t.* set a value on.

approach', *v.t. & i.* come near to; make overtures to; play a shot. *n.* access, way towards; (golf) shot that should reach green. **~ability**, *n.*

*app'robate, *v.t.* approve.

approba'tion, *n.* sanction, approval. **app'robatory**, *a.*

appro'priate¹, *a.* suitable, proper.

appro'priate², *v.t.* (*-iable*), take possession of; devote to. **~tion**, **~tor**, *nn.*; **~tive**, *a.*

approve' (-ōov), *v.t. & i.* (*-vable*), pronounce good; have favour-

able opinion of; (p.p.) pronounced satisfactory, accepted. **~val**, *n.* favourable opinion.

approv'er (-ōo-), *n.* one who turns king's evidence.

approx'imate¹, *a.* fairly correct, near to. **approx'imate²**, *v.i. & t.* be or make near to. **~ation**, *n.* close approach.

appur'tenance, *n.* appendage; belonging (usu. pl.).

a'pricot (ā-), *n.* fruit allied to plum.

A'pril (ā-), *n.* month noted for frequent showers. **~ fool**, person hoaxed on Apr. 1.

ā prio'ri, from cause to effect.

‖ **ā prio'ri**, from cause to effect.

a'pron, *n.* garment worn in front of body; (Theatr.) advanced strip of stage for playing scenes before curtain. **~ful**, *n.* (pl. **-ls**).

à propos (-pō), *adv.* to the point or purpose. **~ of**, in connexion with.

apse, *n.* (pl. **-es**), arched or domed recess at end of church.

ap'sidal, *a.* of the form of an apse; of the apsides.

ap'sis, *n.* (pl. **ap'sīdēs** or **apsi'dēs**), aphelion or perihelion of planet, apogee or perigee of moon.

apt, *a.* suitable, appropriate; quick, ready; inclined. **~ly**, *adv.*; **~ness**, *n.*

ap'teryx, *n.* New Zealand bird with rudimentary wings and no tail.

ap'titude, *n.* fitness, talent.

à'qua-fort'is, *n.* nitric acid.

aquamarine' (-ēn), *n.* bluish-green beryl; colour of this.

aquarelle', *n.* painting with Indian ink and thin water-colours.

aquar'ium, *n.* tank for aquatic plants or animals; place with such tanks.

aquat'ic, *a.* living in or near water. *n.pl.* water sports.

à'quatint, *n.* engraving on copper.

àqua-vitae, *n.* ardent spirits.

à'queduct, *n.* artificial channel for water; conduit.

à'queous, *a.* of water, watery.

Aquiline, *a.* like an eagle.

A'rab (ā-), *n.* native of Arabia; A. horse. **street~**, homeless child.

---

māte, mēte, mīte, mōte, mūte, mōōt ; răck, rĕck, rick, rŏck, rŭck, rōōk ;

Arā′bian, a. of Arabia. n. Arab. ~ bird, phoenix.

árabésque′ (-k), n. style of decoration with intertwined leaves; scroll-work. a. in this style.

A′rabic (ă-), a. of Arabia (~ numerals; gum arabic). n. language of Arabians.

ā′rable, a. fit for tillage.

arāc′hnid (-k-), n. any of a class comprising spiders, &c.

árb′alèst, n. machine crossbow.

árb′iter, n. judge; arbitrator.

árb′itrament, n. decision.

árb′itrary, a. capricious; despotic.

árb′itrāte, v.t. & i. (-rable), determine, settle dispute. ~tor, ~tress, nn. one appointed to settle dispute. ~tion, n.

ár′bor, n. main support of machine; axle or spindle of wheel.

árborā′ceous (-shus), a. tree-like.

árbōr′eal, a. pertaining to trees.

árbōr′éous, a. abounding in trees.

árborès′cent, a. tree-like in growth or form. ~nce, n.

árborē′tum, n. (pl. -ta), a botanical tree-garden.

árb′oricúlture, n. cultivation of trees or shrubs. ~ral, a.; ~rist, n.

árb′our (-er), n. shady nook.

árb′ūtus, n. kinds of evergreen.

arc, n. part of circumference of circle; luminous discharge between two separate carbons, &c. ~lamp, electric lamp with luminous arc.

árcāde′, n. covered walk lined with shops; row of arches. ~d, a.

Arcā′dian (ár-), a. ideally rustic.

arcā′num, n. (pl. -na), mystery.

árch[1], n. curved structure supporting bridge, &c.; curve. ~way, arched entrance. ~wise, adv.

árch[2], a. roguish, saucy.

árchaeōl′ogy (-kĭ-), n. study of antiquities or of prehistoric remains. ~ōg′ical, a.; ~gist, n.

árchā′ic (-kĭ-), a. primitive, antiquated. ~ism, n. use of the archaic. ~istic, a.; ~ize, v.t. & i.

árc′hängel (-k-), n. angel of highest rank. árchängel′ic, a.

árchbish′op, n. chief bishop, metropolitan. ~ric, n. office of a.

árchdeac′on, n. Church dignitary next below bishop. ~ry, n. jurisdiction of archdeacon.

árchdī′ocèse, n. archbishop's see.

árch′dūke, n. son of Emperor of Austria. ~dū′cal, a.; ~dúch′ess, ~dúchy, nn.

árch′er, n. one who shoots with bow and arrows. árch′ery, n. use of bow and arrows.

árc′hétype (-k-), n. original model.

árch′-fiend′, n. Satan.

ār′chibald, ār′chie, n. anti-aircraft gun.

árchidīāc′onal (-k-), a. of an archdeacon. árchiépis′copa[1] (-kĭ-), a. of an archbishop.

árchimán′drīte (-k-), n. superior of Greek-Church monastery.

árchipél′agō (-k-), n. (pl. -os), sea with many islands; group of islands.

árc′hitèct (-k-), n. one who prepares plans for building.

árc′hitèc′ture (-k-), n. science of building. ~ral, a. ~tōn′ic, a. of architecture; of the systematization of knowledge.

árc′hitrāve (-k-), n. beam resting on abacus of column; various parts round doorway or window.

árc′hives (-kīvz), n.pl. public records; place for these. ~vist, n.

árc′tic, a. of the north pole.

árd′ent, a. eager, zealous, fervent; burning. ~ncy, n.

árd′our (-der), n. zeal; warmth.

árd′uous, a. hard; strenuous.

ār′ea, n. extent of surface; region; scope, range; sunk court in front of basement of house.

á′reca, n. kinds of palm. ~nut, astringent seed of areca.

arē′na, n. centre of amphitheatre; scene of conflict.

arénā′ceous (-shus), a. sandy.

ár′gali, n. Asiatic wild sheep.

árg′and. In comb. ~burner, ~lamp, kinds with circular flame.

ár′gent, n. & a. silver, or like silver. ~i′ferous, a. yielding silver.

ár′gil, n. potter's clay. ~lā′ceous, a. of the nature of clay.

árg′on, n. a gas, an inert constituent of the atmosphere.

ăr'gŏsy, n. richly laden ship.

ăr'ot (-ŏ), n. slang, esp. thieves'.

ăr'ūe, v.t. & i. (-ġuable), maintain by reasoning; prove; reason.

ăr'ūfy, v.i. argue for the sake of controversy.

ăr'ūment, n. reason advanced; debate; summary of book. ~ation, n. ărgūmĕn'tative, a. fond of arguing.

Arg'us (ăr-), n. fabulous person with hundred eyes. ~eyed, a. vigilant.

ăr'gyrodīte (-jī-), n. a rare mineral containing silver.

‖ ăr'ia, n. air, melody.

Ar'ian (ăr-), a. of the doctrine of Arius, who denied Christ's divinity. n. holder of this doctrine. ~ism, n.

ă'rid, a. dry, parched. ~ity, n.

aright' (-īt), adv. rightly.

arise' (-z), v.i. (arōse, arisen), appear, spring up, occur.

arīstŏc'racy, n. the nobility; government by the best citizens. ă'rīstocrat, n. member of aristocracy. ~crăt'ic, a. of the aristocracy; grand.

Aristŏtē'lian (ă-), a. of Aristotle.

arith'mĕtic, n. science of numbers; computation, use of figures. ărithmĕt'ical, a.; ~ian, n.

ark, n. covered floating vessel; wooden coffer containing tables of Jewish law; a chest. Noah's ~, toy ark with animals.

arm[1], n. upper limb of human body; sleeve; branch; armlike thing. ~chair, chair with arms. ~ful (pl. -ls). ~pit, hollow under shoulder.

arm[2], n. particular kind of weapon; (pl.) weapons; heraldic devices. v.t. & i. furnish with arms; take up arms; provide, furnish.

armā'da, n. fleet of war-ships.

armadill'o, n. (pl. -os), animal with body cased in bony armour; small terrestrial crustacean.

Armagĕdd'on (ăr-, -g-), n. supreme conflict of the nations.

ărm'ament, n. force equipped for war; military equipments.

ărm'ature, n. arms, armour; piece of soft iron placed in contact with poles of magnet; essential part of a dynamo.

Armĭn'ian (ăr-), a. of the doctrine of Arminius. n. adherent of this doctrine.

ărm'istice, n. cessation from arms; short truce. A. Day, 11th Nov., kept as anniversary of the armistice (1918) that ended hostilities in the great war.

ărm'lĕt, n. band worn round arm.

ărmō'rial, a. of heraldic arms.

ărm'ory, n. heraldry.

ărm'our (-mer-), n. defensive covering worn in fighting; protective covering of war-ship. v.t. furnish with armour.

ărm'ourer (-mer-), n. maker of arms; official in charge of arms.

ărm'oury (-mer-), n. place where arms are kept; arsenal; *armourer's workshop.

ărm'y, n. land forces of a State; vast number; organized body. ~list, n. of commissioned officers.

ărn'ica, n. kinds of plant, including mountain tobacco; medicine, esp. tincture, made from this.

arō'ma, n. fragrance, sweet smell; a subtle quality. arose, p.t. of arise.

arōmăt'ic, a.

around', adv. on every side, all round; about (fool~). prep. on every side of.

arouse' (-z), v.t. (-sable), rouse.

ărpĕ'ggio (-ĕjŏ), n. (pl. -os), striking of notes of chord in rapid succession; chord so struck.

arquebus. See harquebus.

‖ ă'rrack (or ărăk'), n. any Eastern spirituous liquor, esp. one made from coco-palm.

arraign' (-ān), v.t. indict, accuse; find fault with. ~ment, n.

arrange', v.t. & i. (-ġeable), put in order; settle; form plans; (Mus.) adapt (composition).

arrange'ment (-jm-), n. thing arranged; settlement; (pl.) plans.

ă'rrant, a. downright, notorious.

ă'rras, n. tapestry; hangings of this.

array', v.t. dress, esp. with display; marshal (forces). n. dress; imposing series; martial order.

arrear′, n. that which is behind ; (pl.) outstanding debts ; work, &c. in which one is behindhand. ~age, n. being in arrears ; debt.

arrest′, v.t. stop, seize by authority ; apprehend ; catch the attention of. n. legal apprehension ; stoppage. ~ment, n.

‖arrière-pensée (ă´riĕr pahǹ′sā), n. ulterior motive ; mental reservation.

arrive′, v i. come to destination or end of journey ; attain an object ; establish one's position. ~val, n. appearance on scene.

a′rrogant, a. overbearing ; presumptuous. ~rrogance, n.

a′rrogate, v.t. (-gable), claim unduly. ~tion, n.

‖arrondissement (ărŏndĕ′smahǹ), n. administrative subdivision of French department.

a′rrow (-ō), n. pointed missile shot from bow ; indication mark.

a′rrowroot, n. plant from which a nutritious starch is prepared.

a′rsenal, n. place for storage or manufacture of war material.

a′rsenic, n. a semi-metallic element ; trioxide of this, a violent poison. ~al, arsē′nious, aa.

a′rsis, n. (pl. arsēs), accented syllable in English scansion.

a′rson, n. wilful setting on fire of houses or other property.

art¹. See be.

art², n. skill, esp. applied to design ; cunning ; (pl.) certain branches of learning ; fine arts, music, painting, &c. ~ful, a. sly.

arter′ial, a. of the nature of an artery. ~ road, main highway.

arter′ialize, v.t. convert into arterial blood. ~zation, n.

arteriosclero′sis, n. hardening of walls of arteries.

art′ery, n. any of the tubes by which blood is conveyed for this.

arte′sian (-zhn) well, n. deep well in which water rises to surface when hole is bored through strata.

arthri′tis, n. inflammation of joint ; gout. arthrit′ic, a.

art′ichoke, n. an edible vegetable.

art′icle, n. clause of agreement, treaty, &c. ; short literary composition ; any particular thing. v.t. bind by articles of apprenticeship ; set forth in articles.

artic′ulate¹, a. having joints ; divided into words or syllables.

artic′ulate², v.t. & i. (-lable). speak distinctly ; connect by joints. ~lar, a. of the joints. ~tion, n. articulate speech ; jointing. ~tor, n. ; ~tory, a.

art′ifice, n. device ; cunning ; skill.

art′ificer, n. craftsman.

artifi′cial (-shl), a. produced by art ; feigned ; affected. ~iăl′ity, n. ; ~ize, v.t. ~ silk, lustrous fabric made from cellulose, &c., used as substitute for silk.

artill′ery, n. cannon ; ordnance branch of army. ~rist, n. ~ man, man in the Artillery. ~train, number of guns mounted and ready for marching.

artisăn′ (-z-), n. mechanic, craftsman.

art′ist, n. one who practises one of the fine arts ; one who makes his craft a fine art. ~ic, a. ; ~ry, n.

artiste′ (-tē-), n. professional singer, dancer, &c.

art′less, a. guileless, simple ; lacking art, crude. ~ness, n.

ar′um, n. kinds of plant including wake-robin. ~ lily, white arum.

Ar′yan (ār′-), a. Indo-European. n. Aryan language ; speaker of this.

as¹ (az, ăz), adv. & conj. in the same degree ; similarly ; while, when ; since, seeing that. rel. pron. that, who, which.

as², n. Roman copper coin.

ăsafoet′ida (-fĕt-), n. resinous gum with smell of garlic.

asbes′tos (ăz-), n. a fibrous mineral ; incombustible fabric woven from this. ~tine, a. of asbestos ; incombustible.

ascend′, v.t. & i. go or come up ; rise, mount, climb.

ascen′dancy, -ency, n. sway, powerful influence.

ascen′dant, -ent, a. rising ; predominant. n. ascendant point of ecliptic or degree of zodiac; horoscope.

ascĕn′sion (-shn), n. ascent, esp. of Christ to heaven; rising of celestial body. **A.** Day, Holy Thursday.

ascĕnt′, n. ascending; rising; upward path or slope.

ăscertain′, v.t. find out. ~able, a.; ~ment, n.

ascĕt′ic, a. severely abstinent, severe in self-discipline. n. ascetic person. ~ism, n.

ăscribe′, v.t. (-bable), attribute, impute; assign.

ăscrip′tion, n. act of ascribing.

asĕp′sis, n. absence of putrefactive matter or harmful bacteria; the aseptic method in surgery.

asĕp′tic, a. preventing putrefaction by securing absence of bacteria; surgically sterile, sterilized. n. aseptic substance.

asĕx′ŭal, a. non-sexual.

ăsh′, n. a forest tree. ~en, a. of ash. ~key, seed of ash.

ăsh², n. powdery residue left after combustion of a substance; (pl.) remains of human body after cremation. **A.** Wednesday, first day of Lent. ăsh′en, a. of ash; like ashes, pale; grey.

ashāmed′ (-md), a. abashed, conscious of shame.

ăsh′lar, n. square hewn stone; masonry of this. ~ing, n. short upright wall in garret cutting off angle of rafters.

ashôre′, adv. to or on shore.

ăsh′ў, a. of or like ashes; pale.

Asiăt′ic (āshi-), a. of Asia. n. native of Asia.

aside′, adv. to or on one side, away, apart. n. words spoken aside, esp. by actors.

ăs′inīne, a. of asses; stupid.

ask (ah-), v.t. & i. inquire, put a question; make a request.

askănce′, ~nt′, adv. sideways.

askew′, adv. obliquely, awry.

aslant′ (-ahnt), adv. obliquely. prep. slantingly across.

asleep′, adv. or pred. a. in a state of sleep; (of limbs) benumbed; (of a top) spinning without apparent motion.

aslōpe′, adv. on a slope, crosswise.

ăsp, n. small venomous serpent.

aspă′ragus, n. plant whose vernal shoots are a table delicacy.

ăs′pĕct, n. way a thing presents itself to eye or mind; direction in which a thing fronts.

ăs′pĕn, n. kind of poplar with tremulous leaves.

ăspĕ′rity, n. harshness; roughness.

aspĕrse′, v.t. (-sable), attack the reputation of, calumniate. ~sion, n.

ăs′phalt, n. a bituminous substance; pitch used for paving, &c.

ăs′phodĕl, n. kinds of lily.

asphyx′ia, —xў, nn. suffocation. ~ial, a. ~iate, v.t. suffocate. ~tion, ~tor, nn.

ăs′pic, n. savoury jelly with cold game, eggs, &c. in it.

ăspidĭs′tra, n. foliage plant with broad taper leaves.

ăs′pirate¹, n. sound of h, consonant blended with this. a. so blended.

ăs′pirate², v.t. (-rable), pronounce with h; draw out (gas) from vessel. ~tor, n. apparatus for aspirating gas, &c.; winnowing-machine.

aspīre′, v.i. feel earnest desire or ambition; reach high. ~rant, n. one who aspires. ~rā′tion, n.

ăs′pirin, n. an analgetic and febrifuge. P.

asquint′, adv. with a squint.

ăss (or ahs), n. long-eared quadruped; stupid fellow.

ăss′agai, -ēgai (-gī), n. throwing spear of S.-Afr. tribes; also applied to a large S.-Afr. tree (~ tree, ~ wood).

assail′, v.t. attack, assault. ~able, a. open to attack. ~ant, n.

assăss′in, n. one hired to kill another treacherously; a murderer. ~ate, v.t. kill by treacherous violence. ~ation, ~ator, nn.

assault′, n. attack on fortress, &c. by sudden rush; unlawful personal attack. v.t. make attack upon. ~ of or at arms, display of fencing, &c.

assay′, n. trial of metal, test. v.t. make trial; attempt task.

---

mäte, mēte, mīte, mŏte, mūte, mōōt; răck, rĕck, rick, rŏck, rŭck, rōōk;

assem'blage, *n.* collection, concourse.

assem'ble, *v.t. & i.* bring or come together; collect; fit together the parts of (machine, &c.).

assem'bly, *n.* gathering of persons, esp. of deliberative body.

assent', *v.i.* agree to; defer or accede to. *n.* concurrence; sanction. **~tient** (-shi-), *a.* ; **~or,** *n.*

assert', *v.t.* maintain one's claim to; declare, state. **~ion,** *n.* thing asserted. **~ive,** *a.* positive, dogmatic. **~or,** *n.*

assess', *v.t.* fix amount of rate, tax, &c.; value for taxation. **~ment,** *n.* **~or,** *n.* one who assesses taxes; adviser to judge or magistrate.

ass'ets, *n.pl.* all the available property of person or company; (sing.) item of this; any possession, useful quality, &c.

assev'erate, *v.t.* (-rable), declare solemnly. **~tion,** **~tor,** *nn.*

assidu'ity, *n.* constant attention.

assid'uous, *a.* diligent, unremitting.

assign' (-in), *v.t.* make over formally; allot; appoint; ascribe. **~able,** *a.* **~ee,** *n.* one appointed to act for another. **~ment,** *n.* **~or,** *n.* one who assigns property.

ass'ignat, *n.* piece of paper money secured on state lands, esp. in the French Revolution.

assigna'tion, *n.* appointment of time and place for interview.

assim'ilate, *v.t. & i.* (-lable), make or become like; absorb, be absorbed, digest. **~tion,** **~tor,** *nn.* ; **~tive,** **~tory,** *aa.*

assist', *v.t. & i.* help, aid; be present at. **~ance,** *n.*

assis'tant, *a.* helping. *n.* helper, subordinate worker.

assize', *n.* (usu. pl.) periodical county sessions held by judges on circuit for administration of civil and criminal justice; (sing.) statutory price of bread and ale.

asso'ciate¹ (-shi-), *v.t. & i.* join, unite together; have intercourse with; connect in idea.

asso'ciate² (-shi-), *n.* partner, companion; subordinate member of an association. *a.* allied.

associa'tion, *n.* organized body of persons; connexion of ideas; intercourse. **A.** football, game played with round ball which must not be carried.

ass'onance, *n.* resemblance of sound between two syllables; rhyme depending on identity of vowel-sounds only. **~ant,** *a.*

assort', *v.t. & i.* arrange in sorts; suit, harmonize. **~ed,** *a.* selected, classified. **~ment,** *n.*

assuage' (-sw-), *v.t.* soothe, allay. **~ment,** *n.* mitigation.

assume', *v.t.* (-mable), take upon oneself; simulate; usurp authority; take for granted.

assump'tion, *n.* assuming; arrogance. **~tive,** *a.* taken for granted.

assure (ashoor'), *v.t.* (-rable), make positive or confident assertions; satisfy, convince; insure (life). **~rance,** *n.* positive assertion; self-confidence; impudence; insurance (of life). **~redly,** *adv.* certainly.

as'ter, *n.* kinds of plant with showy radiated flowers; *Mi-chaelmas daisy.

as'terisk, *n.* mark of reference (*).

astern', *adv.* in the stern; behind.

as'teroid, *n.* any of the small planets revolving round sun between orbits of Mars and Jupiter. *a.* star-shaped. **~al,** *a.*

asth'ma (-sm-), *n.* a disease marked by difficulty in breathing.

asthmat'ic, *a.* caused by asthma. *n.* person suffering from asthma.

astig'matism, *n.* defect in eye or lens preventing rays from being brought to proper focus. **~tic,** *a.*

astir', *adv.* in motion; out of bed.

aston'ish, *v.t.* amaze, surprise. **~ing,** *a.* surprising. **~ment,** *n.*

astound', *v.t.* amaze, astonish.

astrakhan' (-kän), *n.* skin of Astrakhan lamb, with woolly fur.

as'tral, *a.* of stars; spiritual.

astray', *adv.* out of the right way.

astride', *adv.* with legs wide apart or one on each side of.

---

astrin'gent (-nj-), *a.* causing contraction or compression. *n.* such medicine. **~ncy,** *n.*

as'trolābe, *n.* instrument formerly used in taking altitudes, &c.

astrol'ogy, *n.* study of occult influence of stars on human affairs; (formerly) astronomy. **~ger,** *n.* student of astrology. **~gical,** *a.*

astron'omy, *n.* science of the heavenly bodies. **~mer,** *n.* student of astronomy. **~mic(al),** *aa.*

astūte', *a.* shrewd; crafty.

asun'der, *adv.* apart, in pieces.

asy'lum, *n.* institution for afflicted persons; refuge; sanctuary.

asymm'etry, *n.* want of symmetry or proportion.

at (*usu. at; ăt when emphatic*), *prep.* in, by, toward, on.

at'avism, *n.* resemblance to remote ancestors rather than parents; recurrence of disease after some generations. **~istic,** *a.*

atax'y, *n.* irregularity of animal functions. **atax'ic,** *a.*

|| **atelier** (ăt'elyā), *n.* studio.

ā'theism, *n.* disbelief in the existence of God. **~ist,** *n.*; **~istic,** *a.*

āthenae'um, *n.* literary or scientific club; library.

athirst', *a.* thirsty; eager for.

ăth'lēte, *n.* one who competes at or excels in physical exercises.

athlet'ic, *a.* physically powerful; of athletes. *n.* (pl.) physical exercises; athletic sports. **athlēt'icism,** *n.*

athwart' (-ôrt), *adv.* across, esp. obliquely. *prep.* across.

ăt'las, *n.* volume of maps.

ăt'mosphēre, *n.* spheroidal gaseous envelope, esp. that surrounding earth; mental or moral environment; air. **~ĕr'ic(al),** *aa.* **ătmosphē'rics,** *n.pl.* electric disturbances in the air interfering with the reception of wireless or other telephone messages.

atŏll' (*or* ăt'ŏl), *n.* round coral reef enclosing lagoon.

ăt'om, *n.* body too small to be divided; minute portion or thing. **~ic,** *a.* of atoms. **~ism,** *n.* atomic philosophy or theory.

~ist, *n.*; **~istic,** *a.* **~ize,** *v.t.* reduce to atoms. **~ization,** *n.*

atomic'ity, *n.* the number of atoms in the molecule of an element.

at'omizer, *n.* instrument for spraying liquids.

at'omy, *n.* atom, tiny being; emaciated body.

atōne', *v.i.* expiate, make up for. **~ment,** *n.* act of atoning.

atŏn'ic, *a.* unaccented.

ātrabil'ious (*also* ă; -lyus), *a.* melancholy, gloomy; splenetic.

atrō'cious (-shus), *a.* heinous, gross. **atrŏc'ity,** *n.* wicked deed.

at'rophy, *n.* wasting away for lack of nourishment. *v.t. & i.* cause atrophy in; suffer atrophy.

ăt'ropine, *n.* poison of Deadly Nightshade.

attach', *v.t. & i.* fasten, join; attribute to; adhere, be incident to; bind in friendship; seize by legal authority. **~ment,** *n.* a fastening; esp. affection for.

attaché (atăsh'ā), *n.* one attached to ambassador's suite. **~ case,** *n.* small rectangular valise.

attack', *v.t.* fall upon, assault, assail. *n.* assault, onset.

attain', *v.t. & i.* reach, gain, accomplish. **~ability,** *n.*; **~able,** *a.* **~ment,** *n.*; (pl.) degree of education or kinds of skill attained.

attain'der, *n.* consequences of sentence of death or outlawry.

attaint', *v.t.* subject to attainder; infect; sully.

ătt'ar, *n.* fragrant oil from rosepetals.

attem'per, *v.t.* qualify by admixture; modify; temper.

attempt', *v.t.* try; try to overpower (person, fortress, &c.). *n.* attempting; endeavour.

attend', *v.t. & i.* apply one's mind to; be present; accompany.

atten'dance, *n.* attending (lectures, &c.); the persons present.

atten'dant, *a.* waiting on; accompanying. *n.* servant.

atten'tion, *n.* act of applying one's mind, attending; (pl.) ceremonious politeness, courtship, addresses. *int.* calling to attention. ~ive, *a.* heedful, observant ; polite.

attĕn'ūāte¹, *v.t.* (-*uable*), make slender or thin ; reduce in force or value. attĕn'ūāte², *a.* slender ; rarefied. ~tion, *n.*

attĕst', *v.t.* bear witness to, certify ; put on oath or solemn declaration. ~ation, *n.* ; (esp.) formal confirmation by signature, oath, &c. ~or, *n.*

ăt'tic, *n.* room in top story of house ; a garret.

Att'ic (ă-), *n.* Attic dialect. *a.* of Athens or Attica. ~ order, square column of any of the five orders.

attīre', *v.t.* (-*rable*), dress, array. *n.* dress, apparel.

ăt'titūde, *n.* posture of body ; settled behaviour as showing opinion. ăttitū'dinīze, *v.i.* assume attitudes ; show affectation.

attorn'ey (-tẽr-), *n.* (*pl.* -*eys*), one's business or legal representative ; solicitor. A. General, chief legal officer appointed to act in cases in which the State is a party.

attrăct', *v.t.* draw to oneself ; allure, entice. ~ion, *n.* act of attracting ; thing that attracts ; charm, inducement. ~ive, *a.* inviting, pleasing. ~or, *n.*

attrĭb'ūte¹, *v.t.* (-*table*), ascribe as belonging or appropriate to ; refer. ăt'trĭbūte², *n.* quality ascribed to a person or thing ; characteristic quality. ~tion, *n.* ascription. ~tive, *a.* expressing an attribute ; qualifying.

attri'tion, *n.* friction ; abrasion ; wearing out.

attūne', *v.t.* (-*nable*), bring into musical accord ; adapt ; tune.

aub'urn (-ẽrn), *a.* golden-brown.

auc'tion, *n.* sale in which articles are sold to highest bidder ; (cards) form of bridge. ~ , *v.t.* sell by a. ~eer', *n.* holder of a.

audā'cious (-shus), *a.* daring, bold ; impudent. audā'cĭtÿ, *n.*

aud'ible, *a.* that can be heard. audĭbĭl'ĭtÿ, *n.*

aud'ience, *n.* a hearer's attention ; assembly of listeners.

aud'it, *n.* official examination of accounts. *v.t.* examine accounts officially. ~or, *n.* one who audits ; a hearer. ~ōr'ial, *a.*

audĭ'tion, *n.* faculty of hearing ; trial hearing of applicant.

audĭtōr'ium, *n.* part of building occupied by audience.

aud'itorÿ, *a.* of hearing. *n.* hearers, audience.

‖ au fait (ō fā'), at home in ; conversant, instructed.

‖ au fond (ō fawn'), at bottom.

Augē'an, *a.* filthy, like the stables of Augeas.

aug'er (-g-), *n.* a boring-tool.

aught (awt), *n.* anything.

augmĕnt'¹, *v.t.* & *i.* increase ; prefix the augment to. aug'mĕnt², *n.* increase ; vowel prefixed to past tenses in Greek and Sanskrit. ~ation, *n.* enlargement, increase. ~ative, *a.* increasing in force the idea of the original word.

‖ au grand sérieux (ō grahn sārēēr'), quite seriously.

aug'ur (-er), *n.* soothsayer, prophet. *v.t.* & *i.* foresee, prognosticate ; betoken, promise. aug'urÿ, *n.* divination ; omen ; prophecy.

augŭst'¹, *a.* venerable, imposing.

Aug'ust², *n.* eighth month of the year, associated with summer heat and holiday season.

auk, *n.* northern sea-bird with short wings used as paddles.

‖ au naturel (ō nătürĕl'), (cooked) in the simplest way.

aunt (ahnt), *n.* parent's sister or sister-in-law. A. Sally, game of throwing sticks at wooden head.

aur'a, *n.* subtle emanation from anything ; atmosphere diffused by or attending a person, &c.

aur'al, *a.* of the ear.

aurē'ola, *n.* a celestial crown. aur'ēōle, *n.* gold disk or circle of light depicted round head ; halo, esp. that seen in eclipses.

‖ au revoir (ōrevwahr'), (goodbye) till we meet again.

aur'icle, *n.* external ear ; either upper cavity of the heart.

auric'üla, *n.* kinds of primula.

auric'ŭlar, a. of the ear or hearing. ~ confession, told privately in the ear (of priest).

aurif'erous, a. yielding gold.

aur'ŏchs (-ks), n. extinct wild ox; European bison.

auror'a (ar-), n. (A-) goddess of dawn; a luminous electrical radiation from northern (~ bŏrēā'lis) or southern (~austrā'lis) magnetic pole.

auscultā'tion, n. listening to movement of heart, &c. ~tory, a.

aus'pice, n. omen, prognostic; (pl.) patronage. auspi'cious (-shus), a. of good omen, promising.

austēre', a. morally strict; severely simple; stern. ~ē'rity, n.

aus'tral, a. southern.

Australā'sian (-shn), a. of Australasia. n. A. native.

Austrā'lian, n. native of, colonist or resident in, Australia. a. of Australia.

authěn'tic, a. trustworthy, entitled to acceptance; genuine, not forged.

authěn'ticāte, v.t. (-cable), establish the truth, authorship or validity of. ~tion, ~tor, authěnti'city, nn.

auth'or, n. writer of book, &c.; originator. ~ess, n.; author'ial, a.; ~ship, n.

authŏr'ity, n. power or right to enforce obedience; personal influence; person, book, &c. cited as authority. ~tative, a. possessing or claiming authority.

auth'orize, v.t. (-zable), sanction; give authority to. ~zation, n.

autobiŏg'raphy, n. one's life written by oneself. ~pher, n. writer of such life. ~phic(al), aa.

aut'ocăr, n. motor-vehicle.

autŏch'thon (-k-), n. (usu. pl.) aboriginal inhabitants. ~ous, a.

aut'ocrăt, n. absolute ruler. ~acy, n. absolute rule. ~ic, a.

‖ auto-da-fé (awt'odahfā'), n. (pl. autos-da-fé), sentence of the Inquisition; execution of this.

autogƫr'ō ~gyr'ō, n. form of aeroplane that can descend vertically by means of a windmill revolving freely on its own shaft.

aut'ograph (-ahf), n. own handwriting, esp. signature. ~ic, a.

autŏm'aton, n. (pl. -ta, -tons), piece of mechanism with concealed motive-power; person acting like a. automǎt'ic, a. mechanical, unconscious; self-acting; n. a pistol. autŏm'atism, n. mechanical routine; involuntary action.

automobile' (-ēl), n. motor-car. *v.i. ride in motor-car.

autŏn'omў, n. right of self-government. ~mous, a.

autŏp'sў (or awt'-), n. personal inspection; post-mortem. ~ptic, a.

auto-suggestion (-sujěs'chon), n. hypnotic suggestion proceeding from the subject himself.

aut'otype, n. photographic process for reproducing in monochrome; facsimile so produced. v.t. reproduce thus.

aut'umn (-m), n. third season of the year; (fig.) season of incipient decay. autumnal, a.

auxil'iary (-lya-), a. helpful, subsidiary; (of verbs) serving to form tenses, &c. of other verbs. n. helper; (pl.) foreign or allied troops in a nation's service.

avail', v.t. & i. be of use or assistance; help, benefit. n. use, profit. ~able, a. capable of being used, at one's disposal. ~ability, n.

av'alanche (-ahnsh), n. falling mass of snow, earth, and ice.

av'arice, n. greed of gain, cupidity. ~i'cious (-shus), a. greedy.

avast' (-ahst), int. stop, cease.

av'atār, n. descent of deity to earth in incarnate form; incarnation.

avaunt', int. begone.

ā'vē, int. hail; farewell. n. the cry ave. A. Maria, devotional recitation and prayer to the Virgin.

avěnge' (-j), v.t. (-geable), inflict retribution on behalf of; exact retribution for.

av'ěnue, n. roadway, approach to house bordered by trees; way of approach (also used fig.).

---

mǎte, mēte, mite, mōte, mūte, mōōt : rǎck, rěck, rick, rŏck, rŭck, rōōk :

avĕr', *v.t.* (*-rr-*), assert, affirm. **~ment**, *n.* positive assertion.

ăv'erage, *n.* arithmetical mean; ordinary standard. *a.* estimated by average, of the usual standard. *v.t.* (*-geable*), estimate or reach the average of.

avĕrse', *a.* opposed, disinclined, unwilling. **~sion**, *n.* dislike or antipathy; thing or person one dislikes.

avĕrt', *v.t.* (*-tible, -table*), ward off; turn away from.

ā'viarÿ, *n.* large cage or building for keeping birds.

ā'viāte, *v.i.* manage or travel in aircraft. **~tion**, **~tor**, *nn.*

ăvid, *a.* eager, greedy. **~itÿ**, *n.*

ăv'ifauna, *n.* birds of district, &c.

ăvocā'dō (*-kah*), *n.* alligator pear.

ăvocā'tion, *n.* vocation; calling.

avoid', *v.t.* shun, keep away from; (Law) annul. **~ance**, *n.*

avoirdupois (ăverdŭpoiz'), *n.* system of weights used for ordinary goods; *weight, heaviness.

avŏuch', *v.t.* guarantee the truth or existence of; affirm. **~ment**, *n.*

avŏw', *v.t.* admit, confess. **~al**, *n.* an open admission. **~ĕdlÿ**, *adv.*

avŭnc'ŭlar, *a.* of an uncle.

await' (*a-*), *v.t.* wait for.

awāke' (*a-*), *v.i. & t.* (past *awŏke*, p.p. *awaked* or *awoke*), cease to sleep; become active; rouse from sleep. *pred.a.* not asleep; vigilant.

awā'ken (*a-*), *v.t. & i.* awake, arouse the consciousness of.

award (awŏrd'), *v.t.* adjudge to. *n.* judicial sentence; thing awarded.

awāre' (*a-*), *a.* conscious, not ignorant of. **~ness**, *n.*

awash' (*-wŏ-*), *pred. a.* flush with or washed by the waves.

awāy' (*a-*), *adv.* to or at a distance from place, person, &c.

awe, *n.* reverential fear. *v.t.* inspire with awe. **~some**, *a.* dread, terrible. **~struck**, *a.*

aw'ful, *a.* inspiring awe; (colloq.) notable in its kind. **~lÿ**, *adv.* (colloq.) very.

awhile (awīl'), *adv.* for a time.

aw'kward, *a.* ill-adapted for use; hard to deal with; clumsy.

awl, *n.* small pricking-tool.

awn, *n.* beard of grain, &c.

awn'ing, *n.* canvas roof; shelter.

awrÿ (arī), *adv.* crookedly; amiss.

āxe, *n.* tool for chopping.

ăx'ial, *a.* pertaining to an axis.

ăx'iom, *n.* self-evident truth; established principle, maxim. **ăxiomăt'ic**, *a.*

ăx'is, *n.* (pl. *axēs*), imaginary line round which a body rotates; straight line between poles or ends.

ă'xle, *n.* spindle on or with which wheel revolves; axle-tree or either end of this. **~tree**, bar connecting pair of carriage-wheels.

Ax'minster, *a.* *A. carpet*, kind formerly handwoven at Axminster.

ay (ī), *int.* yes. *n.* (pl. *ayes*), affirmative answer or vote.

ayah (ī'a), *n.* native Indian nurse or lady's maid.

aye (ā), *adv.* always.

azā'lėa, *n.* kinds of flowering shrubby plant.

ăz'imuth, *n.* vertical arc of sky from zenith to horizon; angular distance of this from a meridian.

ā'zure (*-zher, -zhyer*), *n.* blue unclouded sky; (Herald.) blue colour; bright blue pigment. *a.* sky-blue.

B

B, b (bē), (Mus.) 7th note in scale of C major.

baa (bah), *n.* bleat of a sheep. *v.i.* (*baaing*; past *baa'd*), bleat.

baas (bahs), *n.* (S.-Afr.) native mode of addressing white man.

băb'ble, *v.i. & t.* talk half articulately or excessively; divulge foolishly. *n.* idle talk. **~r**, *n.*

bābe, *n.* baby.

bā'bel, *n.* confused noise of talk; confused scene.

babīrous'sa (*-rōō-*), *n.* E.-Asiatic wild hog.

ba'bōō (bah-), *n.* Hindu gentleman (as title=Mr.); Indian English-writing clerk; (contempt.) half-anglicized Hindu.

baboon', *n.* large monkey.

ba'by, *n.* very young child; childish person. ~car. very small car. ~ grand, small grand piano. ~ish, *a.*

baccalaur'eate, *n.* degree of Bachelor.

bacc'arat (-ra), *n.* a card game.

bacc'hanal (-ka), *a.* of Bacchus or his rites. *n.* Bacchant; reveller. ~a'lia, *n. pl.* festival of Bacchus, drunken revelry. ~ian, *a.*

Bacc'hant (-ka), *n.* priest, priest-ess, votary of Bacchus. Bacc-hante (bak'ant, bakan'ti), *n.* (pl. -tes), female Bacchant.

Bacc'hus (-kus), *n.* Greek god of wine. ~hic, *a.* bacchanal.

*bach, *v.i.* (colloq.) to keep house as a bachelor.

bach'elor, *n.* unmarried man; university degree below Master. ~hood, *n.* unmarried life.

bacill'us, *n.* (pl. -li), microscopic rod-like vegetable organism, esp. as found in diseased tissues in phthisis, &c. bacill'ary, *a.*

back, *n.* hinder surface of human body; upper surface of animal's body; hind part of things; the rear; football player stationed behind (full, three-quarter, half, back). *a.* situated behind; covering past period. *adv.* to the rear; into an earlier position; to a re-tired or remote position; *back of, behind. *v.t. & i.* put or be a back or background to; support with money, argument, &c.; bet on; endorse (cheque, &c.); *ad-dress (letter); ride (horse); cause to move back; go backwards; *carry on the back. ~blocks, (Austral.) furthermost fringe of settlement. ~ number, (sl.) out-of-date method, person, &c. ~ out of, withdraw from. ~ seat, (take a back ~), efface or humble oneself. ~ talk, (sl.) impudent answer. ~ up, support.

back'bite, *v.i.* slander. ~biter, *n.*

back'bone, *n.* spine, main sup-port; firmness of character.

backdoor' (-or), *n.* door at back of house.

back'er, *n.* one who bets.

backgamm'on, *n.* game on double board with draughts and dice.

back'ground, *n.* back part of scene; obscurity, retirement.

back'hand, -hån'ded, *aa.* delivered with back of hand; indirect. ~r, *n.* such blow, indirect attack.

back'slide, *v.i.* relapse into sin or disbelief. ~r, *n.*

back'stairs, *n.pl.* back or second-ary stairs. *a.* secret, under-hand.

back'stitch, *v.t.* sew with over-lapping stitches. *n.* such stitch.

back'sword (-sōrd), *n.* one-edged sword; singlestick.

back'veld (-lt), *n.* (S.-Afr.), re-moter parts of the veld.

back'ward, *adv.* (also -wards), back foremost; back to starting-point; reverse way. *a.* slow in learning.

back'water (-waw-), *n.* still water beside stream and fed by its back flow.

back'woods, *n.pl.* remote un-cleared forest land. ~man, *n.* settler in this.

ba'con, *n.* cured back and sides of pig.

bactēr'ium, *n.* (pl. -ia), micro-scopic unicellular organism found almost everywhere, some causing disease. ~ial, *a.*; bactēriol'ogy, ~iologist, *nn.*

bad, *a.* (worse, worst), worthless, defective, inefficient, not valid; wicked, depraved; corrupt, de-cayed; injurious; painful; ill, injured, in pain.

bad, bade, *p.t.* of bid.

badge, *n.* thing worn as a mark of office, membership, &c.

bådg'er, *n.* quadruped between weasel and bear. *v.t.* worry, pester.

bad'inage (-ahzh), *n.* banter.

bad'ly, *adv.* defectively, unsuccess-fully; to a serious extent.

bad'minton, *n.* game with nets, rackets, and shuttle-cocks.

baf'fle, *v.t.* foil, frustrate, perplex. ~ling, *a.* bewildering.

baff'y, *n.* wooden golf club.

---

bäg, *n.* receptacle of flexible material with opening at top; sac in body for honey, poison, &c.; all a sportsman has shot; (pl., slang) trousers. *v.t. & i.* put in bag; secure (game); (colloq.) take possession of, steal; bulge; hang loosely. ~**ful**, *n.* (pl. -*ls*). ~**gy**, *a.* loose-hanging.

bägatélle', *n.* mere trifle; minor game of billiard kind.

bägg'age, *n.* portable equipment of army; luggage; (joc.) saucy girl.

bäg'man (-*an*), *n.* commercial traveller; packman.

bagnio (băn'yō), *n.* an Oriental prison; brothel.

bäg'pipe(s), *n.* musical wind instrument. ~**piper**, *n.*

Baha'dur (-ahd-), *n.* title of respect appended in India to a person's name (and other titles); (Anglo-Ind. sl.) consequential official.

¶ **bahar'**, *n.* measure of weight used in India and China, varying from 223 to 625 lb.

bail¹, *n.* security for prisoner's appearance; person who becomes surety. *v.t.* become bail for and secure liberation of; deliver goods in trust. ~**able**, *a.* admitting of bail. ~**ee**, *n.* one to whom goods are entrusted. ~**ment**, *n.* (of goods or prisoner). ~**or**, *n.* one who entrusts goods.

bail², *n.* bar separating horses in open stable; (Crick.) either of the crosspieces over the three stumps. ~**er**, *n.* ball so bowled as to hit the bails.

bail³, **bäle**, *v.t.* (-*lable*), throw water out of (boats, &c.) with bowls, &c. ~**or**, *n.* instrument for bailing.

bail'ie (-lĭ), *n.* Scotch municipal officer corresponding to alderman. **bail'iwick**, *n.* district of bailiff.

bail'iff, *n.* sheriff's officer; agent of lord of manor; steward.

bairn, *n.* (Sc.) child.

bait, *v.t. & i.* worry animals by setting dogs at them; worry persons by jeers; give (horse, &c.) food; (of horse) take food thus; stop at inn; put bait on or in (fishing-hook, trap, &c.). *n.* food to entice prey; allurement; halt for refreshment.

baize, *n.* coarse woollen stuff used for coverings.

bäke, *v.t. & i.* (-*kable*). cook by dry heat; harden by heat; be or become baked. ~**house**, *n.* place for baking bread, &c. **bā'ker**, *n.* professional breadmaker. ~**'s dozen**, thirteen. **bā'ker'y**, *n.* bakehouse. **baking-powder**, *n.* substitute for yeast.

bä'kelite, *n.* plastic material of phenol and formaldehyde. *P.*

bak'sheesh, *n.* gratuity, tip.

bak'ŭ, *n.* fine kind of straw woven in China.

bal'ance, *n.* weighing-apparatus; regulating-gear of clock, &c.; equilibrium; preponderating weight or amount; excess of assets over liabilities or *vice versa*; remainder. *v.t. & i.* (-*ceable*), weigh; equalize, match; bring or come into equilibrium. ~**sheet**, *n.* statement of assets and liabilities.

bäl'as, *n.* rose-red spinel ruby.

bäl'cony, *n.* outside balustraded platform with access from upperfloor window; in theatre, seats usu. between dress-circle and gallery.

bald (bawld), *a.* with scalp wholly or partly hairless; without feathers, &c.; bare; meagre, dull.

băl'dachin (-k-), ~**quin**, *n.* canopy over throne, &c.

bal'derdăsh (bawl-), *n.* jumble of words, nonsense.

bal'dric (bawl-), *n.* belt for sword, bugle, &c.

bäle¹, *n.* evil, destruction, woe.

bäle², *n.* package of merchandise.

baleen', *n.* whalebone.

bä'lefire (-lf-), *n.* great fire in the open, bonfire; beacon-fire.

bä'leful (-lf-), *a.* pernicious, destructive, malignant.

balk, baulk (bawk), *n.* roughly squared timber beam; stumbling-block ; sanctuary area on billiard table ; ridge left unploughed. *v.t. & i.* thwart, hinder ; discourage, startle ; jib, shy.

ball[1] (bawl), *n.* solid or hollow sphere, esp. one used in a game ; (Crick.) single delivery of ball by bowler ; missile for cannon, rifle, &c. *v.i.* (of snow, &c.) form lumps. *balled up, (of speaker) confused, and so unable to go on.

ball[2] (bawl), *n.* social assembly for dancing. ~room, *n.*

băll'ad, *n.* simple song ; narrative poem in short stanzas. ~ry, *n.* ballad poetry. ~monger, *n.* (contempt.) dealer in ballads.

ballade' (-ahd), *n.* poem of one or more triplets of 7- or 8-lined stanzas ending with refrain, and envoy.

băll'ast, *n.* heavy material placed in ship's hold for stability ; experience, &c. as steadying character. *v.t.* furnish with ballast.

băll'et (-lā), *n.* combined performance of professional dancers.

ballis'ta, *n.* (pl. -*ae*), ancient military engine for hurling stones, &c. **ballis'tic**, *a.* of projectiles. *n.pl.* science of these.

‖ **ballon d'essai** (băl'awǹ děsā'), experiment to see how a policy, &c. will be received ; a kite.

băll'onèt, *n.* one of the interior gasbags of an airship.

balloon', *n.* round or pear-shaped air-tight envelope inflated with gas so as to rise in air ; inflated thing. ~er, ~ist, *nn.*

băll'ot, *n.* secret voting ; ball, ticket, or paper used in ballot ; lot-drawing. *v.i.* vote by ballot ; draw lots.

băll'ȳ, *a. & adv.* (sl.) expressing speaker's impatience, disgust, &c.

băll'ȳrăg, *v.t. & i.* play practical jokes on ; indulge in horse-play.

balm (bahm), *n.* fragrant exudation ; ointment ; healing or soothing influence ; tree yielding balm.

bălmō'ral, *n.* kinds of boot, petticoat, and Scotch cap.

balmy (bahm'ĭ), *a.* of or like balm ; fragrant, mild, soothing ; silly.

bal'sam (bawl-), *n.* balm ; kinds of ointment ; tree yielding balm ; a flowering plant. **balsam'ic**, *a.*

băl'uster, *n.* short pear-shaped pillar ; post supporting handrail of staircase, (pl.) posts and handrail. **bălustrade'**, *n.* row of balusters with rail or coping as parapet to balcony, &c.

bămboo', *n.* (pl. *-oos*), tropical giant grass ; its stem as stick or material.

bămboo'zle, *v.t.* hoax, mystify.

băn, *v.t.* (-*nn-*), prohibit, interdict. *n.* a curse ; formal prohibition.

bă'nal (*or* -ā-), *a.* commonplace. **banăl'ity**, *n.* triviality.

bana'na (-nah-), *n.* tropical fruit-tree ; its finger-shaped fruit.

bănd, *n.* flat strip of thin material ; hoop of iron, rubber, &c. ; belt connecting wheels ; body of musicians ; group of persons. *v.t.* form into a league ; put a band on. ~box, box for millinery ~master, conductor of musical band. ~saw, endless saw running over wheels. ~smaṇ ~stand, member of platform for musical band.

bănd'age, *n.* strip of material for binding up wound, &c. *v.t.* tie up with bandage.

băndăn'a, *n.* yellow- or white-spotted coloured handkerchief.

băndeau' (-dō), *n.* (pl. *-x*, pr. *-z*) woman's hair-fillet ; fitting-band inside woman's hat.

băn'dicoot, *n.* large Indian rat (Austral.) insectivorous marsupial.

băn'dit, *n.* (pl. -*its*, -*itt'ĭ*) outlaw ; brigand.

‖ **băn'dobăst**, *n.* (Anglo-Ind.) organization, arrangement.

băn'dŏg, *n.* chained dog ; mastiff ; bloodhound.

băndoleer', -ier' (-ēr), *n.* shoulder belt with cartridge-loops.

băndōle'ro (-lā-), *n.* bandit robber

băn'dȳ,[1] *v.t.* throw or pass to and fro ; discuss ; exchange. *n* hockey ; curved stick used in the game. *a.* (of legs) wide apart a the knees.

bǎn'dỹ², n. Indian carriage, cart, or buggy. ~**ful**, a.

bāne, n. ruin; poison.

bǎng, v.t. & i. strike or shut noisily; make sound as of blow or explosion; thrash. n. sharp blow; loud noise. adv. with a bang, abruptly; (colloq.) quite, right.

bǎngle (bǎng'gl), n. ring bracelet or anklet.

bǎn'īan, **bǎn'yan**, n. Hindu trader; (Bengal) native broker to European house; Indian flannel jacket; Indian fig whose branches root themselves over large area.

bǎn'ish, v.t. condemn to exile; dismiss from one's presence or mind. ~**ment**, n.

bǎn'ister, n. = baluster.

bǎn'jō, n. (pl. -os), instrument like guitar with tambourine body. ~**ist**, n. banjo player.

bǎnk¹, n. raised shelf of ground; artificial slope; ground at edge of river; flat-topped mass of cloud. v.t. & i. contain, confine, as or with bank(s); (Aviation) travel with one side higher.

bǎnk², n. establishment for custody of money; the money before keeper of gaming-table. v.t. & i. keep a bank; deposit money at a bank; *~**on**, count or rely on. ~**bill**, bill drawn by one bank on another; *bank-note. ~**holiday**, day on which banks and most shops are closed. ~**note**, a banker's promissory note payable to bearer on demand.

bǎnk³, n. galley-rower's bench; tier in galley; row of organ keys.

bǎnk'er, n. proprietor, director, &c. of a bank; keeper of gaming bank; gambling card game.

bǎnket', n. auriferous conglomerate like pudding-stone found in S.-Africa.

bǎnk'rupt, n. insolvent person. a. insolvent; bereft of (quality, &c.). v.t. make bankrupt. ~**cy**, n. insolvency.

bǎnks'hall, n. (Anglo-Ind.) a warehouse; the office of a harbour-master or port authority.

bǎnk'sia (-sha), n. a flowering shrub.

bǎnn'er, n. flag of a king, country, army, friendly society, &c. *~**state** (&c.), leading or pre-eminent state (&c.).

bǎnn'erét, n. knight with vassals under his banner; one knighted on field for valour.

bǎnn'ock, n. Sc. home-made loaf, usu. unleavened and flat.

bǎnns (-z), n.pl. notice in church of intended marriage, thrice read.

bǎnq'uét, n. sumptuous feast; dinner with speeches. v.t. & i. regale (person); take part in banquet.

bǎnquette' (-kĕt), n. firing-step in trenches, &c.; bench behind driver in diligence.

bǎn'shee, n. spirit whose wail portends death in a house.

bǎnt, v.i. reduce weight by diet.

bǎn'tam, n. small kind of fowl, of which the cock is pugnacious; small but spirited person; a boxing-weight (8 st. 6 lb.).

bǎn'ter, n. humorous ridicule. v.t. & i. make fun of; jest.

bǎn'tling, n. brat, little child.

Bǎn'tu (-ōō), n. (pl. same) large group of Afr. negroid races; their languages.

banyan. See banian.

bā'obǎb, n. African tree with huge stem and edible fruit.

bǎp'tism, n. religious rite of immersing in or sprinkling with water in sign of purification and admission to the Church. **bǎptis'mal**, a. **Bǎp'tist**, n. one of a sect objecting to infant baptism and practising immersion. ~**ery**, n. part of building where baptism is administered. **bǎptize'**, v.t. (-zable), administer baptism to, christen; give a name to.

bǎr, n. long-shaped piece of rigid material; slip of silver below clasp of medal as extra distinction; (Mus.) vertical line dividing piece into equal time-parts; barrier; counter at which refreshments are served; barristers, their profession. *v.t.* fasten with bars, keep in (or out) thus; obstruct, prevent; exclude. ~maid, ~man, attendant at refreshment bar. ~ sinister, badge of bastardy.

barb¹, *n.* recurved point of arrow, fish-hook, &c. *v.t.* furnish with barb, barbed-wire, for fences, with wire prickles at intervals.

barb², *n.* Barbary horse or pigeon.

bārbā′rian, *a.* uncivilized, wild, uncultured. *n.* such person.

bārbā′ric, *a.* rude, uncultured.

bārb′arism, *n.* rude or uncultured state; uncultured expression.

bārbā′rity, *n.* savage cruelty.

bārb′arize, *v.t.* & *i.* make or become barbarous. ~**zation**, *n.*

bārb′arous, *a.* uncivilized.

bārb′ecūe, *n.* framework for smoking or broiling; hog, ox, &c. roasted whole; *social gathering where barbecue is served; floor for drying coffee-beans. *v.t.* roast whole.

bārb′el, *n.* a fresh-water fish with fleshy appendages at its mouth.

bārb′er, *n.* one who shaves beards and cuts hair, a hairdresger.

bārb′erry, *n.* a yellow-flowered shrub; its oblong red berry.

bārbétte′, *n.* platform in fort from which guns fire over parapet; raised gun platform in ship.

bārb′ican, *n.* outer defence to city or castle, esp. tower over gate.

bārc′arōle, *n.* gondolier's song.

bārd, *n.* Celtic minstrel or poet. ~**ic**, *a.* of Celtic bards. ~**ling**, *n.*

bāre, *a.* unclothed, uncovered; exposed; unadorned; scanty; mere. *v.t.* make bare, strip, expose. ~**backed**, *a.* on unsaddled horse. ~**faced**, *a.* shameless, impudent.

bāre′ly, *adv.* scarcely.

bārg′ain (-gin), *n.* agreement on terms of purchase, compact; thing acquired cheap or by bargaining. *v.i.* haggle, stipulate.

bārge, *n.* flat-bottomed freight-boat; house-boat. ~, *v.i.* bump heavily. **bārgee′**, *n.* bargeman.

bā′ritōne, *a.* between tenor and bass. *n.* baritone voice or singer.

bār′ium, *n.* a white metallic element.

bārk¹, *n.* outer sheath of tree trunk and branches; tan; quinine. *v.t.* strip tree of bark; abrade (shins, &c.).

bārk², **bārque** (-k), *n.* (usu. -*que*). vessel with fore and main masts square-rigged, mizen fore and aft rigged; (poet., usu. -*k*), ship, boat.

bārk³, *v.i.* & *t.* (of dog, fox, &c.) utter sharp explosive cry; speak petulantly; cough. *n.* sound of barking; report of gun; cough. ~**er**, *n.* pistol, gun; auction-tout, barking-deer, small species of deer with a short barking call. barking-iron, (sl.) pistol.

bārl′ey, *n.* (pl. -*eys*), cereal used as food and in malt liquors and spirits; its grain. ~**corn**, grain of barley. ~**meal**, flour ground from barley. ~**sugar**, a twisted sweetmeat. ~**water**, a soothing decoction for invalids.

bārm, *n.* froth on fermenting malt liquor, yeast. **bār′my**, *a.* frothy; (sl.) crazy.

Bārm′ecīde, *a.* (also—*dal*), illusory. *n.* giver of illusory gifts.

bārn, *n.* covered building for storing grain, &c. ~ **dance**, kind of schottische.

bārn′acle¹, *n.* (usu. pl.) pincers put on horse's nose to keep him still in shoeing, &c.

bārn′acle², *n.* Arctic goose visiting Britain in winter; crustacean clinging to ship's bottom.

barōm′eter, *n.* instrument measuring atmospheric pressure and used to forecast weather. **bāromĕt′ric(al)**, *aa.*

bā′ron, *n.* title of the lowest rank in the peerage. ~**ess**, *n.* baron's wife; female baron in her own right. ~**age**, *n.* the barons; book with list of barons. **barō′nial**, *a.* of barons or a baron. ~ **of beef**, double sirloin.

bā′ronet, *n.* one of lowest hereditary titled order. ~**age**, *n.* list of baronets. **~cy**, *n.* baronet's rank.

bā'rony, *n.* baron's rank or domain; (Ir.) division of county; (Sc.) large manor.

baróque' (-k), *a.* grotesque, whimsical. *n.* baroque style or ornamentation.

barouche' (-ōosh), *n.* four-wheeled carriage for four occupants.

barque. See **bark**. **bar'quentine** (-ēn), *n.* small barque.

bă'rrack, *n.* (usu. pl.) building for lodging soldiers; building of severely dull appearance. *v.t.* (sl.) jeer at, cheer ironically.

|| **bărracu'da**, **-cou'ta** (-ōo-), *n.* large W.-Ind. sea-fish.

bărr'age, *n.* dam built across a river; (bă'rahzh), concentrated gunfire.

bă'rrator, *n.* litigious person.

bă'rratry, *n.* vexatious litigation; fraud of master or crew to prejudice of ship's owners.

bă'rrel, *n.* cylindrical wooden vessel of hooped staves; contents of such vessel; metal tube of gun; a cylinder. *v.t.* put in barrels. **~organ**, *n.* musical instrument with pin-studded barrel acting on keys.

bă'rren, *a.* not bearing, incapable of bearing (children, fruit, &c.); unprofitable.

barrĕt'ter, *n.* instrument used in wireless receivers for controlling current supply to a valve filament.

bărricade', *n.* barrier. *v.t.* block or defend with a barricade.

bă'rrier, *n.* fence, rail, &c. barring advance or access; obstacle, circumstance, &c. that keeps apart.

bă'rrister, *n.* lawyer entitled to practise in the superior courts; *counsellor at law.

bă'rrow[1] (-ō), *n.* prehistoric gravemound, tumulus.

bă'rrow[2] (-ō), *n.* frame with short shafts used for carrying load, a hand-barrow; two-wheeled hand-cart.

bă'rrow[3] (-ō), *n.* infant's long sleeveless flannel coat.

bărt'er, *v.t.* & *i.* exchange (goods, rights, &c.). *n.* trade by exchange.

bărtizan', *n.* battlemented parapet.

bărt'on, *n.* farmyard.

basalt (băs'awlt, basawlt'), *n.* a dark green or brown igneous rock. **~ic**, **~iform**, *aa.*

băs'cule bridge, *n.* kind of bridge worked by counterpoise.

base[1], *a.* morally low, mean, ignoble; debased; of inferior value. **~born**, *a.* of low birth, illegitimate.

base[2], *n.* foundation, bottom, groundwork, principle, startingpoint; (Mil.) town or other area in rear of an army where drafts, stores, hospitals, &c. are concentrated; (Chem.) electro-positive compound body that combines with acid to form salt. *v.t.* found or rest on; establish. **bā'sal**, **bā'sic**, *aa.* of, at, forming, the base; fundamental; **~ic** (Chem.) (of salts) having the base atomically more than the acid. **basi'city**, *n.* acid's power of combining with bases.

base'ball, *n.* U.S. national game played with bat and ball, 9 players on each side; ball used in it.

base'less, *a.* groundless, unfounded.

base'ment, *n.* lowest part of structure; story below ground level.

băsh, *v.t.* strike so as to smash in.

bashaw', *n.* = **pasha**.

băsh'ful, *a.* shy; sheepish.

băshi-bazouk' (-ōōk), *n.* mercenary of Turkish irregulars.

basic, basicity. See **base**[2].

băs'il (-z-), *n.* an aromatic herb.

basil'ica, *n.* oblong hall with double colonnade and apse.

basil'icon, *n.* kinds of ointment.

băs'ilisk (-z-), *n.* fabulous reptile blasting by its breath or look; lizard with crest inflated at will.

bā'sin, *n.* round vessel for holding water, &c.; hollow depression, tract drained by river; a landlocked harbour.

bā'sis, *n.* (pl. *basēs*) foundation,

thing to work upon, main principle.

bask (bah-), *v.i.* lie or sit warming oneself in the sun.

bas′kĕt (bah-), *n.* wicker vessel of plaited osier, cane, &c. ~**ful**, *n.*

bäs-rélief′, *n.* shallow carving or sculpture on background.

băss¹, *n.* kinds of fish of perch family, including common perch.

băss², **băst**, *n.* inner bark of the lime-tree, other similar fibre. ~**broom**, coarse fibre broom.

bāss³, *a.* deep-sounding; of lowest part in music. *n.* bass voice or singer or part. ~ **viol, violoncello.**

bāss′ĕt, *n.* short-legged dog used for badgers, &c.

bässinĕt′, *n.* hooded wicker cradle or perambulator.

bassoon′, *n.* double-reed wood instrument, used as bass to oboe.

băst. See **bass²**.

bäs′tard, *a.* born out of wedlock; hybrid, counterfeit. *n.* illegitimate child, counterfeit thing. ~**ize**, *v.t.* declare bastard. ~**ization**, *n.* **bäs′tardy**, *n.* illegitimacy.

bäste¹, *v.t.* sew together with temporary stitches.

bäste², *v.t.* moisten (roasting meat) with fat; thrash, cudgel.

băstile (-ēl), *n.* fortress; prison.

băstinā′dō, *n.* (pl. *-oes*), caning on soles of feet. *v.t.* cane thus.

bäs′tion, *n.* pentagonal projection from a fortification. ~**ed**, *a.*

băt¹, *n.* nocturnal mouse-like winged quadruped.

băt², *n.* wooden implement for striking ball, esp. in cricket; batsman. *v.i.* & *t.* use bat, have innings. ~**sman**, ~**ting**, *nn.* performer, performance, with bat.

băt³, *n.* (sl.) pace; "spree, good time. ᵒ~ **round**, *v.i.* have a good time; go from place to place in quest of pleasure.

bătch, *n.* loaves baked at a time; group, collection of things.

bāte¹, *v.t.* & *i.* (*-table*), let down; fall off in force; restrain; deduct.

bāte², *n.* (sch. sl.) rage.

bateau′ (-tō; pl.*-eaux*, pr. -tōz), *n.* a light river-boat, esp. the long tapering boats with flat bottoms used by French Canadians.

bath (bahth), *n.* (pl. pr. -dhz), washing, immersion; vessel or place for bathing in; (pl.) bathing-place. *v.t.* (pr. -th) give a bath to. ~**room**, *n.*

Bath′-brick (bahth-), *n.* a preparation for cleaning metal. ~**chair**, invalid's wheeled chair. ~**stone**, building stone quarried at Bath.

bāthe (-dh), *v.t.* & *i.* immerse in water, &c.; moisten all over; take a bath; (of sunlight, &c.) envelop. *n.* the act of bathing.

bā′ther (-dh-), *n.* **bathing-machine**, wheeled dressing-box for sea-bathing.

bā′thŏs (or -ă-), *n.* fall from sublime to ridiculous.

băt-ĭk, *n.* (material patterned by) Javanese method of painting parts with wax and then dyeing.

bătiste′ (-eest), *n.* fine light cotton or linen fabric.

băt′man (-an), *n.* officer's or warrant-officer's servant.

băt′on, *n.* staff of office; conductor's wand for beating time.

batrā′chian (-k-), *n.* of frogs or other animals that discard gills and tail. *n.* such animal.

băt′ta, *n.* (Anglo-Ind.), extra pay during a campaign; addition to pay of officers serving in India.

battăl′ion (-yon), *n.* large body of men in battle array; body forming part of regiment.

băt′tels, *n.pl.* (Oxf. Univ.) college accounts, esp. for provisions.

băt′ten¹, *n.* board for flooring; strip of wood, esp. to secure hatchway tarpaulin. *v.t.* strengthen or fasten with battens.

băt′ten², *v.i.* feed; grow fat.

băt′ter, *v.t.* & *i.* strike repeatedly so as to bruise or break; criticize severely. *n.* mixture of ingredients beaten up with liquid for cooking. ~**ing-ram**, military engine for assailing walls.

băt′terў, *n.* (Law) infliction of

blows or menacing touch to clothes or person; (Mil.) emplacement for one or more guns, artillery unit of guns and men and vehicles or (more rarely) horses.

băt´tle, n. combat, esp. of organized forces. v.i. struggle with or against. ~axe, medieval weapon. ~cruiser, heavy-gunned ship of higher speed and lighter armour than battleship. ~plane, large fighting aeroplane. ~ship, war-ship of most heavily armed and armoured class.

băt´tledŏre (-teld-), n. wooden in-strument used in washing; bat for striking shuttlecock. ~ and shuttlecock, a game.

băt´tlement (-tel-), n. (usu. in pl.) indented parapet; this and roof.

battue (bătōō´), n. driving of game by beaters to sportsmen; battue shooting-party; whole-sale slaughter.

bau´ble, n. showy trinket.

bawb´ee, n. (Sc.) halfpenny.

bawd, n. procuress. ~y, a. obscene.

bawl, v.t. & i. speak noisily. *~ out, reprove loudly.

bay¹, n. kind of laurel with deep-green leaves; (pl.) conqueror's or poet's bay wreath. ~berry, a West-Indian tree; *wax-myrtle. ~ rum, perfume distilled from bayberry leaves.

bay², n. part of sea filling wide-mouthed opening of land; recess in mountains. ~ salt, salt got from sea-water by evaporation.

bay³, n. division of wall between buttresses, &c.; projecting win-dow-space. ~ window, window filling a bay.

bay⁴, n. bark of large dog, esp. chorus of pursuing hounds. v.i. & t. (of large dog) bark, bark at. at ~, said of hunted animals sur-rounded by dogs and unable to escape; often fig. of persons.

bay⁵, a. (of horse) reddish-brown. n. bay horse.

|bāyădēre´, n. Hindu dancing-girl.

bay´onet, n. stabbing blade at-tached to rifle. v.t. stab with bayonet.

*bayou (bī´ū), n. marshy offshoot of a river.

bazaar (-zăr´), n. Oriental market; fancy fair to raise funds.

be (bē, bǐ), v.i. (pres. ind. am, art, is, pl. are; past ind. 1 & 3 was, 2 wast, pl. were; pres. subj. be; past subj. were, exc. 2 sing. wert arch.; imperat. be; part. being; p.p. been), exist, occur; remain, continue; have a certain state or quality.

beach, n. sandy or pebbly shore of sea. v.t. run (boat, &c.) ashore, haul up. ~comber (-ŏmer), n. long rolling wave; white man in Pacific Islands, &c. who lives by collecting jetsam.

beac´on, n. signal-fire on hill or pole; signal; signal-station.

bead, n. small ball pierced for threading with others; small knob in front sight of gun; moulding like row of beads. v.t. furnish with beads; string to-gether. ~roll, list, bea´ding, n. bead moulding. bea´dў, a. small and bright.

bea´dle, n. parish officer; church or court officer; mace-bearer. ~dom, stupid officiousness.

beads´man (-zmạn), n. almsman.

bea´gle, n. small hound for hunt-ing hares; spy, bailiff, &c.

beak, n. bird's bill; hooked nose; prow of war-ship; spout; (sl.) a magistrate.

beak´er, n. large drinking-cup; lipped glass for experiments.

beam, n. long piece of squared timber supported at each end; bar of balance; horizontal cross-timbers of ship; ray of light or of electric radiation; bright look. v.t. & i. emit light; shine; look radiantly up. ~ends, side of ship. ~ system, wireless tele-graphy in which a short-wave beam is projected by reflection from a parabolic mirror.

bean, n. plant with kidney-shaped seed in long pods; such seed; seed of coffee and other plants; (sl.) coin; *(sl.) head. ~feast, work-men's annual outing. old bean.

(sl.) familiar term of address to a parent, &c. **bean′ŏ**, n. (sl.) any frolicsome enjoyment.

bear[1] (bār), n. heavy thick-furred quadruped ; rough surly person ; (Stock Exch.) speculator for a fall in price of stocks. ~-garden, scene of tumult. ~-leader, travelling tutor. ~'s-grease, pomade. ~skin, Guards' tall furry cap. ~ish, a. rough-mannered, surly.

bear[2] (bār), v.t. & i. (past *bore*, arch. *bare* ; p.p. *borne*), carry or support ; endure, tolerate ; give birth to ; produce, yield. ~able, a. endurable.

beard, n. hair of lower part of face ; chin tuft of goat, &c. ; awn of grass. v.t. oppose openly, defy. ~ed, a. ~less, a. youthful.

bear′er (bār-), n. bringer of letter, &c., presenter of cheque ; carrier of coffin ; (Anglo-Ind.) palanquin-carrier, domestic servant.

bear′ing (bār-), n. behaviour ; heraldic charge ; relation, aspect ; direction, relative position. ~rein, rein forcing horse to arch its neck.

beast, n. animal ; quadruped ; bovine animal ; brutal man ; person one dislikes. ~ly, a. dirty, disgusting ; (colloq.) annoying. ~liness, n. beastly conduct.

beat, v.t. & i. strike repeatedly ; flog or whip ; hammer metal ; (of sun, rain, &c.) strike persistently ; defeat, overcome ; perplex ; mark (time, &c.) with regular strokes ; rouse game ; *defraud, make (one's) way by fraud. n. stroke on drum ; movement of conductor's baton ; measured sequence of strokes, &c., e. g. in verse ; throbbing ; appointed round ; *election-district ; *something surpassing ; *newspaper success against rivals ; *a shiftless fellow. ~er, n. man employed to rouse game. *(sl.) ~ it, go, get out !

beatif′ic, a. making blessed. **beāt′ify**, v.t. make happy. ~fication, n. act of blessing. **beāt′itūde**, n. blessedness ; (pl.) the blessings in Matt. v. 3–11.

beau (bō), n. (pl. -x, pr. -z), fop ; lover.

‖ **beau geste** (bō zhěst′), n. a display of magnanimity.

beau idē′al (bō), n. one's highest type of excellence.

‖ **beau monde** (bō mawnd′), n. fashionable society.

Beaune (bon), n. a red Burgundy.

beaut′eous (bū-), a. endowed with beauty.

beaut′iful (bū-), a. having beauty ; capital, excellent.

beaut′ify (bū-), v.t. (-*fiable*), make beautiful. **beaut′ifier** (bū-), n. thing that beautifies.

beaut′y (bū-), n. combination of qualities that delights the sight or mind ; person or thing possessing this. ~-sleep, that before midnight. ~-spot, small patch stuck on woman's face as foil to complexion ; a beautiful scene.

beav′er[1], n. amphibious broadtailed soft-furred rodent ; its fur ; hat of this.

beav′er[2], n. lower face-guard of helmet.

bécall′ (-kawl), v.t. (arch. or vulg.) call (person) names.

bécalm′ (-ahm), v.t. make calm.

bécāme′, p.t. of become.

bécause′ (-kŏz, -kawz), adv. by reason, conj. for the reason that.

beck[1], v.t. & i. beckon. n. significant nod or gesture.

beck[2], n. brook, mountain stream.

beck′ĕt, n. (naut.) anything fixed as attachment for ropes, &c.

beck′on, v.i. & t. make mute signal ; summon thus.

bécloud′, v.t. cover with clouds.

bécome′ (-ŭm), v.i. & t. come to be, begin to be ; suit, befit, look well on. **bécom′ingly** (-kŭ-), adv. suitably, gracefully.

bĕd, n. couch to sleep on ; animal's resting-place, litter ; flat base on which thing rests ; garden plot for plants ; bottom of sea, river, &c. ; stratum. v.t. prepare bed for (horse, &c.) ; plant in a bed. ~-chamber, bedroom. ~-clothes, sheets, blankets, &c. ~-fellow, sharer of bed. ~-pan, chamber utensil for use in bed. ~plate, base of machine, &c. ~ridden, a. confined to bed by infirmity. ~rock, solid rock below superficial formations; (fig.) foundation, bottom. ~room, for sleeping in. ~spread, coverlet. ~stead, framework of bed. ~tick, large bag of feathers, &c. for bed.

bedab'ble, v.t. splash with liquid.

bedaub', v.t. smear with paint, &c.

bed'ding, n. mattress and bedclothes; litter for cattle, &c.

bedeck', v.t. adorn.

be'del, n. official with duties chiefly processional. See beadle.

bedev'il, v.t. (-ll-), treat diabolically; bewitch. ~ment, n. maddening trouble or confusion.

bedew', v.t. cover with drops.

bedim', v.t. (-mm-), make dim.

bedi'zen, v.t. dress out gaudily.

bed'lam, n. madhouse; scene of uproar. ~ite, n. lunatic.

bed'ouin (-ōō-), n. (pl. same) Arab of the desert; gipsy.

bedrag'gle, v.t. wet (dress, &c.) by trailing it.

bed'straw, n. kinds of plant.

bee, n. social insect producing wax and honey; busy worker; meeting for combined work, &c. ~hive, house for bees. ~line, straight line between two places. ~s'wax, wax secreted by bees.

beech, n. a smooth-barked glossy-leaved tree; its wood. ~mast, fruit of beech, beech-nuts. beech'en, a. of beech.

beef, n. flesh of ox, bull, or cow; (of men) muscle; ox or cow. ~eater, yeoman of guard. ~steak, slice of beef. ~tea, stewed beef juice. beef'y, a. solid, muscular.

been, p.p. of be.

beer, n. alcoholic liquor made from fermented malt, &c., flavoured with hops, &c. ~house, one licensed for beer but not for spirits. ~money, allowance in lieu of beer. beer'y, a. betraying influence of beer.

bees'tings (-z), n.pl. first milk of cow after parturition.

bees'wing (-z-), n. second crust in old port, old wine.

beet, n. kinds of plant with succulent root used for salad, &c. and sugar-making. ~root, root of beet plant.

bee'tle[1], n. heavy-headed tool for ramming, crushing, &c.

bee'tle[2], n. coleopterous insect. a. projecting, shaggy, scowling. v.i. overhang. ~browed, a. with overhanging brow. ~crusher, large boot or foot.

befall' (-awl), v.t. & i. happen, happen to.

befit', v.t. (-tt-), be suited to.

befog', v.t. (-gg-), envelop in fog.

befool', v.t. make a fool of.

before', adv. ahead; in front; previously, already. prep. in front of, ahead of; in the presence of; earlier than. conj. sooner than; rather than.

before'hand, adv. in anticipation, in readiness, before the time.

befoul', v.t. make foul.

befriend' (-rĕnd), v.t. act as a friend to, help at need.

beg, v.t. & i. (-gg-), ask for something by way of alms, live by begging; ask for favour, leave, &c.; make entreaty. ~ the question, assume by implication the very fact one is trying to prove.

began, p.t. of begin.

beget' (-g-), v.t. (past begot, arch. begat, p.p. begotten), procreate, give rise to. ~ter, n.

beg'gar, n. one who begs, esp. lives by begging; poor or penniless person; (colloq.) fellow. v.t. reduce to poverty. ~ly, a. poor, needy; mean. ~y, n. extreme poverty. ~my-neighbour, card game.

begin' (-g-), v.t. & i. (began, begun), set about, make a start with; originate; *get near (to being something). ~ner, n. one who starts anything; a learner. ~ning, n. time at which thing begins; source, origin.

begird' (-g-), v.t. (*begirt*), gird, encircle.

begone' (-awn), int. away with you!

bego'nia, n. plant with petal-less flowers and ornamental foliage.

begot, -ten, p.t. & p.p. of beget.

begrime', v.t. (*-mable*), make grimy.

begrudge', v.t. (*-geable*), grudge.

beguile' (-gil), v.t. (*-lable*), delude, cheat; charm, amuse; cause (time, &c.) to pass easily. ~ment, n.

be'gum, n. (In India) queen or lady of rank.

begun, p.p. of begin.

behalf' (-ahf), n. part, interest.

behave', v.i. & refl. conduct oneself, act in specified manner.

beha'viour (-yer), n. manners, conduct, way of behaving.

behead' (-hĕd), v.t. cut off the head of; execute thus.

beheld', p.t. & p.p. of behold.

behe'moth (or bē'i-), n. huge creature.

behest', n. command.

behind', adv. & prep. in or to the rear; in concealment; too late; in arrear. ~hand, a. & adv. in arrear, behind time, too late.

behold', v.t. see with the eyes; (imperat.) take notice, observe.

behol'den, a. under obligation to.

behoof', n. use, advantage.

behove', -hoove', v.t. be incumbent on; befit.

beige (bāzh), n. a dress-material of undyed unbleached wool; the colour of this. a. of this colour.

be'ing, n. existence; person or thing that exists; constitution.

bela'bour (-ber), v.t. thrash.

bela'ted, a. overtaken by darkness; coming too late.

belaud', v.t. heap praises on.

belay', v.t. (*-layed*), coil rope round cleat, &c. to secure it. ~ing-pin, n. fixed pin for belaying on.

belch, v.i. & t. emit wind noisily from stomach through mouth; (of volcano, gun, &c.) emit fire, smoke, &c. n. belching; eructation.

bel'cher, n. parti-coloured neckerchief.

bel'dam(e), n. hag; virago.

bèleag'uer (-ger), v.t. besiege.

bel'emnite, n. common fossil of pointed bullet shape.

bel'fry, n. bell tower; bell space in church tower.

belie', v.t. (*-lying*), fail to confirm or act up to; give false notion of.

belief', n. trust, confidence; acceptance of thing as true; what one believes.

believe', v.t. & i. (*-vable*), accept as true; have faith in.

believ'er, n. one who believes, (esp.) adherent of one's religion.

belike', adv. probably; perhaps.

belit'tle, v.t. disparage, dwarf.

bell, n. cup-shaped metal instrument emitting musical sound when struck; bell-shaped thing. *~boy, hotel page. ~founder, caster of bells. ~man, town-crier. *~hop, (sl.) hotel page. ~metal, alloy of copper and tin. ~pull, cord, &c., attached to bell wire. ~ringer, ~ringing, (person) ringing changes, &c. on church bells. ~tent, bell-shaped tent. ~wether, leading sheep of flock with bell on neck.

belladonn'a, a. deadly nightshade; drug got from this.

belle, n. handsome woman; reigning beauty.

belles-lettres (bĕl-lĕt'r), n. studies or writings of purely literary kind.

bell'icose, a. inclined to fight.

belli'gerent, a. waging regular war; engaged in conflict. n. belligerent nation, party, or person. ~ncy, n. status of a belligerent.

bell'ow (-ō), v.i. & t. roar like bull; roar or cry with pain. n. bellowing sound.

bell'ows (-ōz), n.pl. contrivance for driving air into fire, organ, &c.

bell'y, n. abdomen, stomach; cavity or bulging part of anything. v.t. & i. swell out. ~ful, a. as much as one wants.

belong', v.i. be the property of,

---

be attached to. **~ings,** *n.pl.* one's property or relatives.

belŏved, *a.* (-ŭv'ĭd) & *p.p.* (-ŭvd'), dearly loved. *n.* beloved person.

below' (-ō), *adv.* at or to a lower level; in a lower position or rank. *prep.* lower in position, amount, degree, rank, &c. than; unworthy of, beneath.

belt, *n.* strip of leather, &c. worn round waist; strap connecting wheels; a sash; zone or district. *v.t.* put belt round; thrash.

bĕl'vedēre, *n.* raised turret to view scenery from.

bemīre', *v.t.* besmirch.

bemoan', *v.t.* lament.

bemūse' (-z), *v.t.* stupefy.

bench, *n.* long seat of wood or stone; judge's or magistrate's seat; court of law; carpenter's or laboratory table; level stretch on mountain-side. **~er,** *n.* senior member of Inns of Court.

bend, *v.t.* & *i.* (bent), force into a curve or angle; receive such shape; incline from the vertical; submit, force to submit. *n.* bending, curve; bent part of thing. **~ sinister** (Herald.), parallel lines indicating bastardy.

bĕn'der, *n.* (sl.) sixpenny-bit.

beneath', *adv.* & *prep.* below, under.

Bĕnedī'cĭtē, *n.* canticle; grace at table. **~dĭc'tus.** *n.* canticle.

bĕn'edĭck, *n.* newly-married man.

benedic'tion, *n.* utterance of a blessing; a blessing. **~tory,** *a.*

benefăc'tion, *n.* doing good; charitable gift. **bĕn'efăctor,** *n.* patron, donor. **~tress,** *n.*

bĕn'efĭce, *n.* church living. **bĕn'eficed** (-st), *a.* holding a benefice.

benĕf'icent, *a.* doing good; actively kind. **benĕf'icence,** *n.*

benefi'cial (-shl), *a.* advantageous, serviceable.

benefi'ciary (-sha-), *a.* holding by feudal tenure. *n.* holder of living; receiver of benefits.

bĕn'efĭt, *n.* advantage, profit; allowance from Benefit Society, &c.; performance, game, &c., of which proceeds go to a particular player or person; (sl., iron.)

fine time or job. *v.t.* & *i.* do good to; receive benefit.

benĕv'olent, *a.* desirous of doing good; charitable. **~nce,** *n.*

Bengal' (-awl), *a.* ~ **light,** firework used for signals. **~ tiger,** the tiger proper.

Bengali (bĕnggawl'ĭ), *a.* of Bengal. *n.* native, language, of Bengal.

benight'ĕd (-nīt-), *a.* overtaken by night; involved in intellectual or moral darkness.

benign' (-īn), *a.* kindly, gentle; favourable, salutary. **bēnig'nant,** *a.* kindly, gracious. **~ncy,~nity,** *nn.* kindliness.

bĕn'īson (-zn), *n.* benediction.

bent', *n.* kinds of stiff-stemmed grass; stiff flower-stalk of grass; also called **bennet, bent-grass.**

bĕnt², *n.* inclination, bias.

bĕnt³, *p.t.* & *p.p.* of **bend.**

Bĕn'thamism (-ta-), *n.* doctrine of the greatest happiness of greatest number.

benŭmb' (-m), *v.t.* make numb or torpid; paralyse.

bĕn'zĕne, *n.* aromatic hydrocarbon got from coal-tar.

bĕn'zine, *n.* mixture of liquid hydrocarbons got from mineral oils and used for removing grease-stains.

bĕn'zŏin (or -oin), *n.* aromatic resin.

bĕn'zŏl, -ole, *n.* benzene.

bĕn'zoline, *n.* benzine.

bequeath' (-dh), *v.t.* leave by will; transmit to posterity. **bequest',** *n.* thing bequeathed.

***berāte',** *v.t.* scold.

bēre, *n.* kinds of barley.

bereave', *v.t.* (bereaved or bereft), rob, deprive; leave desolate. **~ment,** *n.* loss by death.

bē'ret'(-ĭ), *n.* kind of tam-o'-shanter cap.

bĕrg, *n.* iceberg; (S.-Afr.) mountain.

bĕrg'amŏt¹, *n.* tree of orange kind; perfume from its fruit.

bĕrg'amŏt², *n.* kind of pear.

bērhȳme', *v.t.* write verses about.

bĕ'rĭbĕrĭ, *n.* disease like dropsy.

---

mãre, mēre, mĭre, mōre, mūre; pãrt, pĕrt, pōrt; *italics,* vague sounds;

Berlin', *n.* four-wheeled covered carriage, with hood behind. ~wool, fine dyed knitting wool.

bĕ'rry, *n.* any small round juicy stoneless fruit. ~**ried**, *a.*

bĕrs'ĕrk(er), *n.* wild Norse warrior fighting with frenzy.

bĕrth, *n.* sea-room; ship's place at wharf; sleeping-place; situation. *v.t.* moor ship in berth; provide sleeping-berth for.

bĕ'ryl, *n.* kinds of (esp. green) precious stone; mineral species, including emerald.

bėseech', *v.t.* (-sought, pr. -sawt.) entreat; ask earnestly for.

bėseem', *v.t.* suit, be fitting for.

bėset', *v.t.* hem in, assail.

bėshrew' (-rōō) *v.t.* wish a curse to.

bėside', *prep.* at the side of, close to; compared with; wide of.

bėsides' (-dz) *prep.* in addition to; otherwise than. *adv.* also, as well; else.

bėsiege', *v.t.* lay siege to; crowd round; assail with request.

bėsläv'er, bėslŏbb'er, *vv.t.* cover with slaver; flatter fulsomely; (-slob-) kiss effusively.

bėsmear', *v.t.* smear.

bėsmirch', *v.t.* soil, discolour.

bĕ'som (or -ē-; -z-), *n.* long-handled broom made of twigs.

bėsot', *v.t.* stupefy mentally or morally. ~**ted**, *a.*

bėsought', *p.t.* & *p.p.* of beseech.

bėspangle (-ăng'gl), *v.t.* cover with spangles.

bėspatt'er, *v.t.* spatter all over; cover with abuse.

bėspeak', *v.t.* (past -spōke; p.p. -spŏken), engage beforehand; order (goods); be evidence of.

bėsprinkle (-ĭng'kl), *v.t.* sprinkle.

Bĕss'ėmer prŏ'cĕss, *n.* method of making steel by passing current of air through molten pig-iron.

bĕst, *a.* & *adv.* (superl. of *good*, *well*) of, in, the most excellent kind, way. *v.t.* (colloq.) get the better of.

bėstead' (-ĕd), *v.t.* & *i.* avail, help.

bĕs'tial, *a.* of beasts; brutish. ~**ăl'ity**, *n.*; ~**ize**, *v.t.* **bĕs'tiary**, *n.* medieval treatise on beasts.

bėstir', *v.refl.* exert, rouse oneself.

bėstow' (-ō), *v.t.* confer as gift; deposit, place. ~**al**, ~**ment**, *nn.*

bėstrew' (-rōō), *v.t.* (p.p. -*ewed*, -*ewn*), strew; lie scattered over.

bėstride', *v.t.* (past -ōde; p.p. -*idden*, -*id*, -ōde), sit astride on; stand astride over.

bĕt, *v.i.* & *t.* risk one's money, &c. against another's on result of event. *n.* a wager.

bėtake', *v.refl.* (-tōōk, -tāken), go to, have recourse to.

bĕ'tel, *n.* leaf of a plant, chewed by Indians with areca nut. ~**nut**, areca nut.

|| **bête noire** (bāt nwahr), *n.* one's abomination.

bĕth'el, *n.* hallowed spot; a place of worship.

bėthink', *v.refl.* (-thought, pr. -awt.) reflect, stop to think.

bėtide', *v.i.* & *t.* happen; happen to.

bėtimes' (-mz), *adv.* in good time.

bėtō'ken, *v.t.* be a sign of.

bĕt'ony, *n.* purple-flowered plant.

bėtook', *p.t.* of betake.

bėtray', *v.t.* give up or reveal treacherously; be disloyal to; reveal involuntarily. ~**al**, *n.*

bėtrŏth' (-dh), *v.t.* bind with promise to marry. ~**al**, *n.*

bĕtt'er, *a.* (compar. of *good*) having good qualities in a higher degree. *n.* one's *betters*, persons of higher rank; one's *better*, more skilful person. *adv.* (compar. of *well*) in a higher degree; in a better way. *v.t.* & *i.* improve; improve upon, surpass. ~**ment**, *n.* improvement.

bėtween', *prep.* in or into a space or interval; to and from; in shares among. *adv.* between two or more points; between two extremes. ~**maid**, servant helping two others. ~**whiles**, *prep.* in the intervals.

bėtwixt', *prep.* between.

bĕv'el, *n.* tool for setting off angles; sloping edge or surface. *v.t.* & *i.* reduce to a bevel; have other than right angle.

bĕv'erage, *n.* liquor for drinking.

bĕv'y, *n.* a company.

---

bewail', v.t. & i. mourn for.

beware', v.i. & t. take heed, be on one's guard.

bewil'der, v.t. perplex, confuse. ~ment, n. state of confusion.

bewitch', v.t. cast magic spell on; delight. ~ment, n.

bewray (bīrā'), v.t. reveal.

bey (bā), n. Turkish governor.

beyond', adv. at or to the farther side, further on; besides. prep. at or to the farther side of; more than; except. n. the ~, the future life, the unknown.

bez'el, n. sloped edge of chisel, &c.; groove for watch-glass, &c.

bezique' (-ēk), n. card-game.

bhang (bä-), n. Indian hemp used as narcotic and intoxicant.

biănn'ual, a. twice a year.

bi'as, n. (game of bowls) bowl's oblique course due to its lopsided or (orig.) lead loading; predisposition, prejudice; oblique direction. v.t. (-s- or -ss-), give a bias to; prejudice.

bib, v.i. & i. drink much or often; tipple. n. child's chin-cloth; apron-top. **bib'ber**, n. one who drinks frequently.

bib'-cock, n. cock or tap with turned-down nozzle.

Bi'ble, n. Old and New Testament. **bib'lical**, a. of the Bible.

bibliog'raphy, n. history of books, their editions, &c.; list of books of any author, subject, &c. ~pher, n. writer of bibliography. **bibliograph'ic(al)**, aa.

bibliol'ater, n. worshipper of books. ~try, n. such worship. ~trous, a.

bibliomā'nia, n. rage for collecting books. ~iac, n. great book-collector.

bib'liophile, n. book-lover.

bib'liopōle, n. seller of (esp. rare) books. **bibliop'oly**, n. selling of books.

bib'ulous, a. addicted to drink.

bicăm'eral, a. with two chambers.

bicărb'onate, n. carbonate containing a double amount of the acid.

bice, n. a dull blue or green pigment.

bicĕntē'nary, a. pertaining to 200 years. n. two hundredth anniversary or its celebration.

biceph'alous, a. two-headed.

bi'ceps, n. (pl. -pses), muscle with double head or attachment.

bick'er, v.i. quarrel, wrangle; (of stream, rain, &c.) brawl, patter. ~ing, n. wrangling.

bicus'pid, a. two-cusped.

bi'cycle, n. two-wheeled pedal-driven vehicle. v.i. ride on it.

bid, v.t. & i. (past băd, bāde, bid; p.p. bĭdden, bid), command; invite; offer price; proclaim (defiance, &c.). n. offer of prices; *(sl.) invitation. **bidd'able**, a. obedient. ~ding, n. command; offers at auction.

bide, v.t. & i. (bīded, bōde), abide.

bienn'ial, a. two-year long, two-yearly. n. plant lasting two years.

bier, n. stand on which coffin is taken to the grave.

biff (sl.), n. smart blow. v.t. strike (person).

biff'in, n. red cooking-apple.

bi'fid, a. cleft into two parts.

bifō'cal, a. (of spectacle-lenses) with two focal lengths, for distant and near vision.

bifō'liate, a. of two leaves.

bi'furcate (-fĕrkāt), v.t. & i. divide into two branches, fork. a. (-fĕrkat), forked. ~tion, n. fork of branch, &c.

big, a. large, of the largest kind; grown up; pregnant; important; boastful. *~ bug, n. important person. ~ end, crankpin end of engine connecting-rod. ~ noise, bigwig. ~ three, four, &c. (sl.) the predominant few in any affair. ~ wig, n. important person.

big'amy, n. having two wives or husbands at once. ~mist, n. such person. ~mous, a.

*big'-hôrn, n. Rocky Mountain sheep.

bight (bīt), n. loop of rope; recess of coast, small bay.

big'ot, n. violent and unreasonable adherent of a creed or view. ~ed, a.; ~ry, n.

---

zh, as (rou)ge; ē=ĭ; ñ, ûr, =êr; ў, y̆,=ĭ, ĭ; and see p. 4. * =U.S.

bijou (bē'zhōō), *n.* (pl. -*oux*, pr. -ōō), jewel, trinket. *a.* small and elegant. ~**terie,** *n.* jewelry.

bike. *n. & v.i.* (colloq.) bicycle.

bilā'bial, *a.* (of consonants) produced by the two lips.

bilăt'eral, *a.* of, on, or with two sides; between two parties.

bil-berry, *n.* a shrub and its deep-blue edible fruit, whortleberry.

bil'bō, *n.* (pl. -*os*), sword.

bil'boes (-ōz), *n.pl.* iron bar with sliding shackles for prisoner.

bile, *n.* bitter fluid secreted by liver to aid digestion; derangement of bile; peevishness.

bilge, *n.* the nearly horizontal part of ship's bottom; belly of barrel; rubbish, rot. *v.t. & i.* stave in the bilge of; spring leak in the bilge. ~**-water,** foul water in bilge.

bil'iary (-lya-), *a.* of the bile.

biling'ual (-nggw-), *a.* of, in, or speaking two languages.

bil-ious (-lyus), *a.* affected by derangement of the bile. ~**ness,** *n.*

bilk, *v.t.* evade payment; cheat.

bill¹, *n.* halberd; (also ~*hook*) concave-edged pruning-instrument.

bill², *n.* beak (of bird); narrow promontory; point of anchor-fluke. *v.i.* (of doves) stroke bill with bill; ~ *and coo,* exchange caresses.

bill³, *n.* draft of proposed Act of Parliament; (Law) written statement of case, bill of indictment; note of charges for goods, work done, &c.; promissory note; *bank-note; poster (to fill the bill).* *v.t.* announce on poster; plaster with bills. ~**-broker,** dealer in bills of exchange. ~**-head,** printed account form. ~**-sticker,** man who posts up bills.

bill'ét¹, *n.* order requiring person to board and lodge soldier; place where troops are lodged; appointment, job. *v.t.* quarter soldiers on town, &c.

bill'ét², *n.* thick piece of firewood; (Archit.) short roll at intervals in hollow moulding.

billet-doux (bīlĭdōō'), *n.* love-letter.

bill'iards (-lyardz), *n.* game with

cues and balls on cloth-covered table. **billiard-marker,** attendant marking score.

bill'ingsgate (-z-), *n.* violent abuse.

bill'ion (-yon), *n.* a million millions.

bill'ow (-ō), *n.* great wave. *v.i.* rise or move in billows. ~**y,** *a.*

bill'y, *n.* (Austral.) tin can serving as kettle, &c. in camping out.

bill'ycock, *n.* hard felt hat.

bill'y-goat, *n.* male goat.

bil'tong, *n.* (S.-Afr.) sun-dried meat in strips.

bĭmét'allism, *n.* use of both gold and silver as legal tender at fixed ratio to each other. **bĭmétăll'ic,** *a.*; ~**ist,** *n.*

bin, *n.* receptacle for corn, coal, wine, refuse, &c.; canvas receptacle used in hop-picking.

bī'nary, *a.* dual, of two.

bind, *v.t.* (*bound*), tie, fasten, attach together; wreathe (head, &c.) with material; be obligatory on, impose obligation on; ratify (bargain); fasten (sheets of book) into cover. *n.* (Mus.) curved line between two notes to be sounded continuously. ~**er,** *n.* book-binder; sheaf-binding machine; anything that binds. ~**ery,** *n.* bookbinder's workshop. ~**ing,** *a.* obligatory on; *n.* book-cover, bandage.

bĭ'ndweed, *n.* kinds of convolvulus, &c.

bīne, *n.* flexible shoot; stem of climbing plant, esp. hop.

bĭnn'acle, *n.* box of ship's compass.

bĭnŏc'ŭlar, *a.* for two eyes. *n.* a binocular field or opera glass.

bīnŏ'mial, *a. & n.* (Algebraic expression) consisting of two terms, joined by + or −. ~**ial,** ~**inal,** *aa.* (of scientific nomenclature) employing two names, esp. those of genus and species.

biogĕn'ésis, *n.* hypothesis that living matter arises only from living matter.

bīŏg'raphy, *n.* written life of a person. ~**pher,** *n.*; ~**phical,** *a.*

bīŏl'ŏgy, *n.* science of physical life of animals and plants. **bīŏlŏg'ical,** *a.*; ~**gist,** *n.*

bi'oplăsm (-zm), n. living proto-plasm. bi'oplăst, n. small separate portion of bioplasm.

bipărt'ite, a. consisting of two parts; in which two parties are concerned. bipărti'tion, n.

bi'pĕd, a. two-footed. n. such animal.

bi'plane, n. two-planed aeroplane.

biquadrăt'ic, a. of the fourth power. n. fourth power of a number.

bĭrch, n. a smooth-barked forest tree; bundle of birch twigs for flogging schoolboys. v.t. flog with birch-rod. ~en, a. of birch.

bĭrd, n. feathered vertebrate; *(sl.) first-rate person, animal, or thing. ~fancier, dealer in birds. ~lime, sticky stuff set to catch birds. ~seed, kinds of seed given to caged birds. ~ of passage, migratory. ~'s-eye view, of town, &c. as seen from above. ~'s-nesting, v.t. hunting for nests.

bĭrd's-eye (-ī), n. kinds of plant with small bright flowers; tobacco in which ribs are cut as well as fibre. ~maple, wood of the sugar maple.

birĕtt'a, n. square cap of R.C. and other clerics.

bĭrth, n. bringing forth of offspring; being born; origin, beginning; descent. ~day, anniversary of one's birth. ~mark, blemish on one's body from birth. ~place, where one was born. ~rate, births per thousand of population. ~right, rights to which one is born.

|| bis, adv. (in references) in two places; (Mus.) twice, repeat.

bis'cuit (-kit), n. kinds of unleavened bread, usu. dry and crisp; flat thin cake of this; *a small scone.

bisĕct', v.t. divide into two (usu. equal) parts. ~ion, n. ~or, n. bisecting line.

bisĕx'ual, a. of two sexes.

bish'op, n. governor of diocese; piece in chess; mulled and spiced wine. ~ric, n. office of bishop.

|| bismil'lah, int. in the name of Allah (Mohammedan exclamation).

bis'muth (-z-), n. a reddish-white metal used as alloy, &c.

bi'son, n. wild ox; buffalo.

bisque[1] (-k), n. right of scoring unearned point at tennis, or playing extra turn at croquet, &c.

bisque[2] (-k), n. unglazed white china for statuettes.

bissĕx'tile, a. & n. leap (-year).

bis'tort, n. herb with flesh-coloured flowers.

bis'tre (-er), n. brown pigment made from soot; this colour.

bit, n. small piece or amount; cutting part of tools, &c.; mouthpiece of bridle. v.t. put bit into mouth (of horse); restrain.

bĭtch, n. female dog, fox, or wolf; abusive term for a woman.

bīte, v.t. & i. (past bĭt; p.p. bĭtten, occas. bĭt; ~table), seize with the teeth; penetrate; grip; corrode. n. act of biting; wound so made.

bī'ting, a. cutting; severe.

bĭtt'er, a. tasting like wormwood; virulent; biting, harsh.

bĭtt'ern, n. a marsh bird allied to the heron.

bitū'mĕn (or -ī-), n. kinds of inflammable mineral substance (naphtha, asphalt, &c.). bitū'minous (or -ī-), a.

bi'valve, a. two-valved; (of shellfish) with double shell. ~vūlar, a.

biv'ouăc (-vŏŏ-), n. temporary encampment without tents, &c. v.i. (-ck-), resort to bivouac.

bizărre', a. of fantastic appearance or effect; whimsical.

*blaa (blah), blah, (sl.) blunder; foolish talk.

blăb, v.i. & t. be indiscreet in talk; tell secret.

blăck, a. darkest of all colours; dark-skinned; dusky, gloomy; wicked; sullen. n. black colour, paint, clothes, speck; negro. v.t. make black; polish with blacking. ~ art, magic. ~ belt, negro area of U.S. ~ cap, put on by judge in sentencing to death. ~ coffee, without milk. ~ draught, an aperient. ~jack, leather wine-bottle. ~letter, old type like German. ~out, obliterate. ~pudding, sausage of blood, suet, &c. ~Rod, chief usher of House of Lords. ~shirts, fascisti.

black'amoor, n. negro; black man.

black'ball (-bawl) n. reject candidate in club ballot by means of a black ball.

blackbee'tle, n. cockroach.

black'berry, n. fruit of bramble.

black'bïrd, n. European song-bird; *redwing, crow-blackbird, &c., negro.

black'board (-bôrd), n. for chalk writing in class-room, &c.

black'cap, n. kinds of bird.

black'cock, n. male of black grouse.

black'en, v.t. & i. make or grow black; speak evil of, defame.

blackguard (blăg'ärd), n. scoundrel, foul-mouthed fellow. v.t. abuse scurrilously. ~guardly (blăg'ärdl'), a.

black'ing, n. polish for boots.

black-lead' (-lĕd), v.t. polish with plumbago (black lead).

black'lĕg, n. swindler, esp. on turf; workman who works for employer whose men are on strike.

black'mail, n. extortion by threats. v.t. extort money from thus.

black'smith, n. smith working in iron. *~shop, smithy.

black'thörn, n. shrub bearing sloes.

black'wöod, n. name given to various species of trees and their timber in N.S. Wales, East Indies, and W. Australia.

bladd'er, n. membranous bag in human or other animal body; inflated thing.

blade, n. flat narrow leaf of grass and cereals; leaf-like part of bat, oar, spade, &c.; cutting-piece of knife, &c.; flat bone of shoulder; gay dashing fellow.

blae'berry (blā-), n. (north.) bilberry.

*blah. See blaa.

blain, n. inflamed sore.

blame, v.t. (-mable). find fault with. n. censure. ~ful, ~worthy, aa.

deserving blame. ~less, a. innocent.

blanch (-ah-), v.t. & i. make white; grow pale.

blancmange (blamahnzh'), n. white jelly of isinglass, &c. and milk.

bland, a. polite, suave, mild; balmy. blan'dishment, n. flattering attentions. ~ly, adv.

blank, a. not written or printed on; void of interest, result, &c. n. empty space in document, &c.; *printed form with blank spaces. *~book, book of clean paper. ~cartridge, n. without ball. ~cheque, n. one with amount left for payee to fill in. ~verse, n. unrhymed verse.

blank'ĕt, n. large woollen sheet as bed-covering, horse-cloth, &c. a. *covering, inclusive. v.t. cover with blanket; stifle, keep quiet (scandal, &c.); toss in blanket as punishment. *~Indian, wild or semi-civilized Indian.

blank'ly, adv. helplessly; flatly.

blare, v.i. & t. make sound of trumpet; trumpet forth. n. blaring sound.

blarn'ey, n. cajoling talk. v.t. & i. cajole, use blarney.

‖ **blasé** (blahz'ā), a. tired of pleasure.

blasphême', v.i. & t. (-mable). talk impiously; profane in words. blas'phemous, a. blas'phemy, n. impious speech, profanity.

blast (-ah-), n. strong gust; sound of wind-instrument; current in blast-furnace. v.t. blow up with explosive; blight, shrivel. ~furnace, one with draught of compressed hot air driven into it by engine.

blas'todĕrm, n. germinal skin round yolk in impregnated ovum.

blā'tant, a. loudly obtrusive.

blather. See blether.

blauw'bŏk (-ow-), n. (S.-Afr.) large antelope with bluish hair.

blaze¹, n. bright flame or fire; violent outburst of passion. v.i. flame; burn with excitement, &c.

blaze², n. white mark on face of horse or ox, or chipped in bark of tree to mark route. *v.t.* mark tree or path with blazes.

blaze³, *v.t.* (*-zable*), proclaim.

blā´zer, *n.* coloured jacket for boating, &c.

blā´zon, *n.* heraldic shield, coat of arms, or banner. *v.t.* describe or paint (arms) heraldically; proclaim. ~ment, *n.* ~ry, *n.* heraldic devices, art of blazoning.

bleach, *v.t.* & *i.* whiten in sunlight or by chemical process.

***bleach´ers**, *n.* unroofed seats at baseball field, &c.

bleak¹, *n.* kinds of small fish.

bleak², *a.* dreary; bare; chilly.

blear, *a.* dim-sighted, filmy. ~-eyed, *a.* with blear eyes.

bleat, *v.i.* & *t.* utter cry of sheep, goat, or calf; speak foolishly. *n.* cry of sheep, goat, or calf.

bleed, *v.t.* & *i.* (*bled*), emit blood; draw blood surgically from; extort money from; feel pity.

blem´ish, *v.t.* spoil the beauty of, mar. *n.* flaw, defect, stain.

blench, *v.i.* flinch, quail.

blend, *v.t.* & *i.* (*blended*; also *blent*), mix; mingle intimately; become one. *n.* mixture.

blende, *n.* sulphide of zinc.

Blen´heim (*-nim*), *n.* kind of spaniel. ~ orange, kind of apple.

blent. See blend.

bless, *v.t.* (past & p.p. *blessed*, pr. usu. *-st*; also *blest*), consecrate; praise; invoke God's favour on; make happy; thank. **bless´ed**, **blest**, *aa.* consecrated; revered; in paradise. ~edness, *n.* ~ing, *n.* declaration, invocation, or bestowal of divine favour; grace at meals; thing one is thankful for.

bleth´er, **blath´er** (*-dh-*), *v.i.* talk nonsense. *n.* such talk.

blew, *p.t.* of blow¹.

blew´it (*-ōō-*), *n.* a mushroom.

blight (*-īt*), *n.* kinds of plant disease; species of aphis; hazy atmosphere. *v.t.* exert baleful influence on; wither. **blight´er** (*-īt-*), *n.* (sl.) annoying person.

Blight´y (*-īt-*), *n.* (Army sl.) home after foreign service.

bli´mey, *int.* (sl.) expr. surprise.

blind, *a.* without sight; without moral or mental discernment; reckless. *v.t.* deprive of sight, make mentally blind. *n.* obstruction to sight; *screen in hunting; screen on window; *horse's blinker. ~ alley, one closed at one end (often fig.). *~ pig, ~ tiger (sl.) illicit liquorshop. ~ness, *n.*

blind´fold, *a.* & *adv.* with eyes bandaged, without circumspection. *v.t.* deprive of sight with bandage.

blind´ly, *adv.* without seeing, recklessly.

blind´-man's-buff´, *n.* indoor game.

blind´-worm (*-ẽrm*), *n.* slow-worm.

blink, *v.i.* & *t.* move the eyelids; look with eyes opening and shutting; ignore or shirk (facts). *n.* blinking movement.

blink´ers, *n.pl.* horse's eye-screens.

bliss, *n.* gladness, joy. ~ful, *a.*

blis´ter, *n.* vesicle on skin filled with serum; plaster applied to raise blister. *v.t.* & *i.* raise blister on; become covered with blisters; (sl.) bore, weary.

blithe (*-dh*), *a.* gay, joyous. ~some, *n.* somewhat blithe.

blizz´ard, *n.* blinding snowstorm.

bloat, *v.t.* & *i.* cure (herring) by salting and smoking slightly; inflate, become inflated. **bloat´er**, *n.* bloated herring.

blob, *n.* drop of liquid; small round mass or spot; (Crick.) duck's egg.

block, *n.* log, tree-stump; large piece of wood or stone; mould for shaping hats on; piece of wood engraved for printing; obstruction; spot on which batsman rests bat before play; square of buildings in town. *v.t.* obstruct; stop (ball) with bat; shape (hat).

blockáde´, *n.* shutting-up of a place by hostile forces. *v.t.* subject to blockade.

block´head (*-hĕd*), *n.* dolt.

block´house, *n.* detached fort; timber building with loopholes.

blond, **blonde**, *a.* light auburn,

of fair complexion. *n.* blond person.

blood (blŭd), *n.* red liquid circulating in veins of higher and lower animals; murder, bloodshed; race, descent; relationship; man of fashion. *v.t.* give first taste of blood to hound; (Med.) bleed.

*blood'ed (-ŭ-), *a.* of good stock.

blood'hound (-ŭ-), *n.* large dog formerly used for tracking cattle, slaves, &c.; (fig.) detective.

blood'less (-ŭ-), *a.* without blood or bloodshed; unfeeling.

blood'shed (-ŭ-), *n.* spilling of blood, slaughter.

blood'shot (-ŭ-), *a.* (of eye) suffused with blood.

blood'-stained (-ŭ-), *a.* stained with blood.

blood'sucker (-ŭ-), *n.* leech; extortioner, sponger.

blood'thirst'y (-ŭ-), *a.* eager for bloodshed.

blood'-vessel (-ŭ-), *n.* vein or artery conveying blood.

bloody (blŭd'ĭ), *a.* pertaining to blood; involving bloodshed; cruel; (in foul language) damned.

bloom¹, *n.* flower; florescence; prime; freshness. *v.i.* bear blooms; be in flower; flourish.

bloom², *n.* mass of puddled iron hammered into thick bar. ~ery, ~ary, *nn.* place where blooms are made.

bloom'er, *n.* (sl.) blunder.

bloom'ers (-z), *n.pl.* woman's knickerbockers.

bloss'om, *n.* flower; mass of flowers on tree. *v.i.* open into flower.

blot¹, *n.* spot of ink, &c.; blemish; disgraceful act. *v.t.* make blot on; stain (character); dry with blotting-paper; obliterate.

blot², *n.* exposed piece in backgammon.

blotch, *n.* inflamed patch, &c. on the skin; dab of ink, &c.; (sl.) blotting-paper. ~ed, ~y, *aa.*

blott'er, *n.* pad of blotting-paper.

blott'ing-päper, *n.* absorbent paper for drying inkmarks.

blouse (-owz), *n.* workman's loose

upper garment; woman's loose dress-body visible to waist; *(U.S. army) undress uniform jacket.

blow¹ (-ō), *v.i. & t.* (*blew*, pr. blōō blown), move as wind does; puff, pant; make or shape (bubble, glass) by blowing; sound by blowing; (of fly) deposit eggs on; (of electric fuse) melt when overloaded. *n.* blowing, puff of fresh air; fly-blow. (sl.) ~ in, spend; drop in. ~out, (sl.) large meal; burst in pneumatic tyre.

blow² (-ō), *v.i.* (*blew*, pr. -ōō; blown), come into, be in, flower. *n.* flowering condition.

blow³ (-ō), *n.* hard stroke with fist, hammer, &c.; disaster, shock.

blow'er (-ŏer), *n.* sheet of iron increasing draught of fire.

blow'fly (-ō-), *n.* meat fly.

blow'-pipe (-ō-), *n.* tube for heating flame by blowing air into it.

blow'y (-ōĭ), *a.* windy.

blowzed (-zd), *a.* red-faced, coarse-looking; dishevelled. ~zy, *a.*

blub (sl.) (school sl.) shed tears.

blubb'er, *n.* whale fat; weeping. *a.* (of lips) swollen, protruding. *v.t. & i.* sob out (words), sob.

bluchers (blōōk'erz), *n.pl.* low-cut laced boots.

bludg'eon (-ŭjn), *n.* heavy stick.

blue (blōō), *a.* coloured like sky or deep sea, *n.* blue colour; *blue uniform; laundress's blue powder; sky, sea; colour, member, of party; (badge of) athlete representing university; (pl.) dumps; Royal Horse Guards. *v.t.* make blue; (sl.) spend extravagantly. ~bell, *n.* wild hyacinth, (north.) harebell. ~book, Parliamentary or Privy-Council report; *directory of prominent persons. ~bottle, blowfly, blue cornflower. ~coat boy, scholar in Christ's Hospital and certain charity schools. *~ grass, a field-grass of Kentucky and Virginia; region of this. ~gum, kind of eucalyptus. ~jacket, seaman in Navy. *~ laws, severe Puritanical laws. **~** Peter, blue flag with white square, hoisted before sailing. **~** ribbon, ribbon of the Garter; badge of teetotalism. **~** rock, kind of pigeon. **~** stocking, woman having or affecting literary tastes and learning.

bluff, *a.* with perpendicular broad front; blunt, frank, hearty. *n.* bluff cliff, headland; bluffing demeanour, threat, &c. *v.t. & i.* impose upon; hoodwink.

blun'der, *v.i. & t.* move blindly; make gross mistake; mismanage. *n.* stupid or careless mistake.

blun'derbuss, *n.* short gun with large bore firing many balls.

blunt, *a.* dull, not sensitive; without edge or point; plain-spoken. *n.* (sl.) ready money; (pl.) grade of short thick needle. *v.t.* make blunt.

blur, *n.* smear; dimness. *v.t.* smear with ink; make indistinct.

*blurb, *n.* (sl.) publisher's commendatory advertisement of book; summary, &c. preceding magazine stories and articles.

blurt, *v.t.* utter abruptly or tactlessly (usu. *blurt out*).

blush, *v.i.* become red in the face; be ashamed. *n.* glance, glimpse; blushing.

blus'ter, *v.i. & t.* (of wind, waves, person) storm boisterously; bully. *n.* blustering; self-assertive talk.

bo'a, *n.* large non-poisonous snake; woman's throat-wrap. **~** constrictor, boa or python.

Boaner'ges (-z), *n.* loud-voiced preacher or orator.

boar (bōr), *n.* uncastrated pig.

board (bōrd), *n.* thin plank; slab of board or boards; cardboard used in bookbinding; (pl.) the stage; table; daily meals; counciltable, councillors, committee; *on board*, on ship, train, &c. *v.t. & i.* cover with boards; provide, be provided, with meals at fixed rate; come alongside (ship), embark on. **~** fence, close fence of boards. **~** wages, servant's pay in lieu of food. **~** walk, footway of boards.

board'er (bōr-), *n.* one who is lodged and fed at a certain price; boy at boarding-school; one who boards ship.

board'ing (bōr-), *n.* erection of boards. **~** house, **~** school, where persons or boys and girls board.

boast, *n.* vainglorious statement; thing one is proud of. *v.i. & t.* brag; magnify one's actions. **~** ful, *a.* apt to boast.

boat, *n.* small open oared or sailing vessel; steamer; boat-shaped receptacle. *v.i.* sail or row or go in a boat, esp. for amusement. **~** hook, long pole with hook. **~** house, shed for boats. **~** man, one who lets out boats; a waterman. **~** race, rowing contest. **boat'er**, *n.* hard straw hat.

boatswain (bō'sn), *n.* ship's officer in charge of sails, &c.

bob[1], *n.* weight on pendulum, &c.; bobbed hair; knot of hair, curl; horse's docked tail; jerk, curtsy; kinds of change in bell-ringing. *v.i. & t.* move up and down; rap, jerk; cut (hair) to hang short of shoulders. **~** sled, **~** sleigh, two short sleighs coupled for drawing logs or for tobogganing. **~** tail, docked tail, horse or dog with this; *a.* bobtailed. **~** wig, shortcurled, not full-bottomed.

bob[2], *dry* **~**, *wet* **~**, *nn.* cricketing or boating Etonian.

bob[3], *n.* (sl.; pl. same) shilling.

bob'bery, *n.* (Anglo-Ind., sl.), noisy disturbance, row.

bob'bin, *n.* cylinder for holding thread, &c., reel, spool; small bar and string for raising doorlatch.

bob'inet, *n.* machine-made cotton net imitating lace.

bob'bish, *a.* (sl.) brisk, well.

bob'by, *n.* (sl.) policeman.

bob'olink, *n.* N.-Amer. song-bird.

bob'stay, *n.* rope holding bowsprit down.

Boche (-sh), *n. & a.* (sl.) German.

bode, *v.t. & i.* foresee, foretell; portend. **~** ful, *a.* ominous.

bod'ice, *n.* close-fitting part of

woman's dress down to waist; inner vest over stays.

bod′iless, bodily. See body.

bod′kin, n. blunt thick needle for drawing tape, &c. through hem; pin for fastening hair.

bod′y, n. man or animal dead or alive; trunk apart from head and limbs; bodice; person; aggregate of persons or things; solidity, substance. v.t. give shape to. ~guard, retinue, escort. ~servant, valet. **bod′iless,** a. incorporeal, separated from the body. **bod′ily,** a. of or affecting the body; adv. in person, as a whole.

Bo′er (boor, bōr), n. Dutch-descended S.-African, a. of the Boers.

bog, n. wet spongy ground, morass. v.t. submerge in bog. ~trotter, Irishman.

bog′gle, v.i. start with fright; demur; equivocate; fumble.

bogg′y (-g-), a. spongy.

bo′gie (-gi), n. under-carriage pivoted below end of locomotive, &c.

bo′gle, n. goblin; scarecrow.

bo′gus, a. sham.

bo′gy, -gey (-gi), n. (pl. -ies, -eys), the devil; goblin; bugbear; (-gey) also Colonel Bogey) score that good golfer should do hole or course in.

bōhea′ (-hē), n. black tea of lowest quality.

Bōhē′mian, a. socially unconventional; of free-and-easy habits. n. such person, esp. artist. ~ism n.; ~ize, v.i.

boil¹, n. hard inflamed suppurating tumour.

boil², v.i. & t. bubble up with heat; be agitated like boiling water; cook by boiling. n. boiling-heat. *boiled, a. (sl.) intoxicated. ~ shirt, (sl.) cotton or linen shirt with starched front.

boil′er, n. vessel for boiling, esp. for making steam in engine; water-heating tank of kitchen-range. *~ deck, lower deck of steamer.

boil′ing, n. food prepared by boil-

ing. ~hot (colloq.), very hot. ~point, temperature at which water boils.

bois′terous, a. violent, rough; noisily cheerful.

bold, a. courageous, enterprising, confident; impudent, immodest; vigorous, well-marked, clear.

bole, n. stem, trunk.

bolēr′ō (-ār-), n. (pl. -os), Spanish dance; woman's short loose jacket with or without sleeves.

boll, n. round seed-vessel of flax, cotton, &c. *~weevil, *~worm, (attacking cotton bolls).

boll′ard, n. post on ship or quay for securing rope.

Bol′shevik, n. advocate of proletarian dictatorship in Russia by soviets; (pop.) any revolutionary. ~vism, ~vist, n. & a.

bō′lster, n. long stuffed pillow. v.t. & i. support with bolster, prop up; fight with bolsters.

bŏlt¹, n. short heavy arrow of crossbow; discharge of lightning; door-fastening; headed metal pin secured with rivet or nut; running away v.i. & t. dart off, run away, (of horse) break from control; *desert political party, 'rat'; *run away from, avoid; gulp down unchewed; fasten with bolt. adv. quite (upright).

bŏlt², boult (bōlt), v.t. sift.

*bō′lter¹, n. political deserter.

bŏl′ter², boul′ter (bōl-), n. sieve, sifting-machine.

bō′lus, n. big pill.

bomb (-ŏm), n. case of explosive fired from gun or thrown by hand. v.t. & i. assail with or throw bombs. ~proof, a. safe from bombs.

bŏm′ber (-mer), n. soldier, aeroplane, using bombs.

bŏmbard′, v.t. batter with shot and shell; assail with abuse, &c. ~ment, n.

bombardier′ (bŭmb-), n. artillery N.C.O. below sergeant.

bŏm′basine (-zēn; also bŭ-), n. twilled dress-material of worsted with silk or cotton, or alone.

---

ah, awl, oil, boor, cow, dowry; chin, go, bang, so, ship, thin; dh, as th(e):

bŏm′bast, n. inflated talk. ~**ic,** a.

‖ **bŏ′na fī′dē,** a. genuine, sincere. adv. genuinely. ~ **fī′dēs** (-z), n. honest intention, sincerity.

***bŏnán′za,** n. rich mine; source of great wealth.

bŏn′bŏn, n. sweetmeat; Christmas cracker.

bŏnd[1], n. that which binds or unites; covenant or binding agreement; (pl.) fetters, chains. v.t. place goods in bond; guarantee payment by issue of bonds. ~**holder,** person holding a bond. **bonded warehouse,** place in which importer's dutiable goods are stored to await Customs duty.

bŏnd[2], a. (obs. exc. in comb.) in slavery, not free. ~**man,** ~**maid,** ~**servant,** ~**slave,** ~**woman,** serf or slave. ~**service,** serfdom.

bŏn′dage, n. serfdom or slavery; confinement, constraint.

bone, n. any of the separate parts of a vertebrate skeleton; thing made of bone or ivory; *dollar. v.t. rid of bones; (sl.) steal. ~**dry,** a. dry as a bone. *~**head,** stupid person. ~**setter,** person who treats fractures, &c. without being a qualified surgeon. ~**shaker,** (colloq.) bicycle without rubber tires.

bŏn′fīre, n. large open-air fire.

bŏn′gō, n. large striped African antelope.

bŏn′homie (-nŏmē), n. geniality.

Bŏn′ifàce, n. innkeeper.

‖ **bon mot** (bawn mō) (pl. *bons mots,* bawn mō), witty saying.

‖ **bŏnne,** n. nursemaid or servant-maid. ~ **bouche** (boōsh), titbit.

bŏnn′ét, n. woman's brimless outdoor headdress; Scotch cap; bonnet-like structure; hinged cover over motor of car; accomplice or decoy. v.t. provide with bonnet; crush down hat over eyes of a person.

bŏnn′y, a. comely, healthy-looking.

bŏn′tébŏk, n. S.-Afr. antelope, also called Pied Antelope.

‖ **bon ton** (bawn tawn), good breeding, the fashionable world.

addition to dividends or wages.

‖ **bon vivant** (bawn vē′vahn), gourmand.

bō′nÿ, a. having much bone.

bonze, n. Buddhist priest.

boō, int. expressing contempt. n. (pl. -s), the sound boo. v.i. & t. emit boos, hoot (speaker, &c.).

*boōb, n. (sl.) booby.

boōb′ÿ, n. silly or awkward fellow; kinds of gannet. ~ **prize,** for last or lowest competitor. ~**trap,** things balanced on door ajar to fall on head of first comer

boō′dle, n. *money for political bribery, &c.; a card-game.

book, n. a number of leaves of paper, either written or printed on, fastened together and bound in cover; a literary composition made available for reading in such manner; main division of treatise, &c. or of the Bible; libretto; (pl.) merchant's accounts, list of members, &c.; (Turf) person's bets on a race. v.t. enter in book or list; secure (seat, &c.) in advance. ~**binder,** one who binds books. ~**binding,** n. ~**case,** case with shelves for books. *~**concern,** publishing house. ~**keeper,** one who keeps business accounts. ~**keeping,** n. ~**maker,** one who compiles books for profit; a professional betting man. ~**muslin,** fine kind of muslin folded like a book. ~**plate,** label with owner's name, crest, &c. for pasting in books. ~**seller,** one who sells books. ~**selling,** n. ~**shop,** ~**stall,** *~**store,** for sale of books. ~**work,** study of rule, &c. as opposed to practice. ~**worm,** book-ᵈestroying maggot; great reader. ᵇooking-clerk, clerk who issues tickets. ~**hall,** ~**office,** esp. for sale of tickets.

book′ie, n. (sl.) betting bookmaker.

book′ish, a. given to book-lore.

boom[1], n. spar stretching sail-foot and attached at one end to mast;

floating timber barrier across harbour, &c.

boom², *n.* deep resonant sound; sensational activity in commerce, &c. *v.i. & t.* emit boom; (of commodity, &c.) be in great demand; create boom by advertising, &c.

boo'merang, *n.* Australian missile of curved wood that can be so thrown as to return to thrower.

boon¹, *n.* a request; favour, gift.

boon², *a.* bounteous; convivial.

boor, *n.* ill-mannered man. ~ish, *a.* unmannerly.

boost, *n.* *a hoist, lift-up; puff. *v.t.* *help with a push, boom; (Electr.) supplement voltage of battery. *boo'ster**, *n.* indefatigable promoter.

boot¹, *n.* advantage (now only in phr. *to boot* as well, into the bargain). *v.i. impers.* be of avail. ~less, *a.* unavailing.

boot², *n.* foot-covering of leather, &c. coming above the ankle; (hist.) instrument of torture, luggage-receptacle in coach. ~jack, appliance for pulling boots off. ~lace, ~maker, *nn.* ~trees, *n.pl.* moulds for keeping boots in shape. **boo'ted**, *a.* having boots on. ~less, *a.* without boots. **bootee'**, *n.* kinds of lady's and infant's boot.

booth (-dh), *n.* structure of canvas or wood erected at fairs, &c.

*boo'tlegger** (-g-), *n.* one who smuggles or sells by retail prohibited liquor. ~ging, *n.*

boots, *n.* servant at an inn.

boo'ty, *n.* plunder or profit acquired in common; a prize.

booze, *v.i.* fuddle oneself with drink. *n.* drinking-bout; drink. ~hoisting, (sl.) drinking liquor.

boo'zy, *a.* drunk, given to drink.

bora'cic, *a.* of borax.

bo'rage (bū-), *n.* blue-flowered plant used to flavour claret-cup, &c.

bor'ax, *n.* a salt used as antiseptic and in soldering.

bord'er, *n.* side, edge, boundary or part near it; distinct edging

round anything. *v.i. & t.* be a border to; finish thing off with a border. **bord'erer**, *n.* dweller on the English and Scottish frontier.

bore¹, *p.t.* of *bear.*

bore², *v.t. & i.* (-rable), make hole, esp. with revolving tool; (Racing) push another, push aside; weary by tediousness. *n.* hollow of gun-barrel, its diameter, calibre; tiresome person, twaddler.

bore³, *n.* tide-wave of exceptional height rushing up estuary.

Bor'eas, *n.* the north wind. **bor'eal**, *a.* of Boreas, of the north.

bore'dom (-ōrd-), *n.* bored state.

bo'ric, *a.* of boron.

born, *p.p.* of *bear. a.* destined from birth (*to be a poet,* &c.).

bor'on, *n.* non-metallic element.

borough (bū'ra), *n.* town with a municipal corporation.

bo'rrow (-ō), *v.t. & i.* get temporary use of, with promise of returning; borrow money; plagiarize; (Golf) allow for wind or slope.

Bor'stal, *n.* ~system, of imprisonment for young criminals.

bor'zoi, *n.* Russian wolf-hound.

bos (sl.), *n.* bad shot or guess. *v.i. & t.* make bos, miss, bungle.

bos'cage, -k-, *n.* shrubs or trees.

bosch (bŏsh), (S.-Afr.) *n.* a wood, bush. ~bok, antelope, bushbuck. ~man, Bushman. ~vark, species of wild pig. ~veld(t), bush country.

bosh (colloq.), *n.* foolish talk, nonsense. *int.* ridiculing thing said.

bos'ky, *a.* with shrubs or trees.

bo'som (booz-), *n.* the breast, that part which is about the breast; an expanse or enfolding space. ~ friend, *n.* confidential friend.

boss¹, *n.* master, manager, or overseer. *v.t.* be boss of, control.

boss², *n.* protuberance, round knob or stud. ~ed, *a.* having bosses.

bot, *n.* a parasitic worm; (pl.) horse-disease caused by it.

botan'ic, ~al, *a.* of botany.

bot'anist, *n.* student of botany.

bot'anize, *v.i.* study plants.

bot'any, *n.* science of plants.

mäte, mēte, mīte, mōte, mūte, mŏŏt; răck, rĕck, rick, rŏck, rŭck, rŏŏk;

bŏtch, *v.t.* patch, mend clumsily. *n.* clumsy patch. ~**er**, *n.*

bŏth, *a.* the pair of. *pron.* both persons or things.

bŏth'er (-dh), *v.t. & i.* give trouble to, perplex; take trouble. *n.* worried state, fuss. *int.* of impatience. ~**ation**, *n. & int.* bother. ~**some**, *a.* bothering.

bŏth'ў, -ie, *n.* (Sc.) hut, cottage; one-roomed building.

bō'-tree, *n.* name given in Ceylon to the Pipal tree, allied to the Banian.

bŏt'tle[1], *n.* narrow-necked vessel, with cork or stopper. *v.t.* store in bottles; (sl.) nab, catch. ~**-holder**, pugilist's attendant at fight. ~**washer**, underling.

bŏt'tle[2], *n.* bundle of hay or straw.

bŏtt'om, *n.* lowest part of anything, the base; what is below the surface; bottom of ship's hull; **=*bottom-land. *v.t.* touch bottom of (sea, &c.); find truth of. **~-land*, low land along river. ~**less**, *a.* unfathomable. ~**most**, *a.* lowest down. ~**ry**, *n.* borrowing of money by owner on security of ship.

bŏt'ūlism, *n.* sausage-poisoning.

boudoir (bōō'dwàr), *n.* lady's private room.

bough (-ow), *n.* branch of tree.

bought, *p.t. & p.p.* of buy.

bougie (bōō'zhē), *n.* surgical instrument for exploring passages of the body.

bouillon (bōōl'yawn), *n.* broth.

boul'der (bōl-), *n.* detached rock; large water-worn stone.

boulevard (bōōl'vàrd), *n.* broad tree-lined street.

bounce, *v.i. & t.* (of ball, &c.) spring up after striking ground; (of person) jump up, esp. in anger; boast; hustle or bluff; **eject* summarily. *n.* a rebound from ground; boastfulness, assurance. *adv.* startlingly. **boun'cer**, *n.* (esp. sl.) big specimen, great lie; **chuckerout.* ~**cing**, *a.* big and hearty.

bound[1], *n.* (usu. in pl.) encircling

boundary, limit. *v.t.* be the boundary of. ~**less**, *a.*

bound[2], *v.i.* (of ball, &c.) recoil from wall or ground; spring, leap. *n.* recoil of ball, &c.; a springy upward or forward movement.

bound[3], *a.* ready to start or on the way for.

bound[4], **bounden**, *p.t. & p.p.* of bind.

boun'dary, *n.* limiting line; (cricket) hit to limit of field scoring 4 or 6 runs.

boun'der, *n.* (colloq.) cheerfully or noisily ill-bred person.

boun'tèous, ~**tiful**, *aa.* showing bounty, generous, profuse.

boun'tў, *n.* profuse giving, charitable gifts; State payment to manufacturers of a commodity to encourage its production.

bouquet (bōōkā'), *n.* cut flowers arranged for carrying in the hand; perfume of wine.

bouquetin (bōō'ketin), *n.* the Alpine ibex.

*bourb'on (boor-), *n.* (polit.) stubborn conservative; Kentucky whisky.

bourgeois[1] (boorzh'wah), *a.* of the class between the gentry and the labourers. *n.* bourgeois person.

bourgeois[2] (berjois'), *n.* a size of printing-type (9-point).

bourgeoisie (boorzhwahzē'), *n.* the bourgeois class.

bourn[1] (-oor-), *n.* a stream.

bourn[2], **bourne** (-oor-), *n.* goal or destination.

bourse (-oor-), *n.* foreign money-market.

bout, *n.* spell or turn; trial of strength.

‖ **bouts rimés** (bōō rēmā'), *n.* (versifying to) set rhymes.

bō'vine, *a.* of oxen; dull, inert.

bŏv'rîl, *n.* kind of beef-tea. **P.**

bow[1] (bō), *n.* weapon for shooting arrows; implement used in playing fiddle, &c.; slip-knot with one loop or two; ribbon, &c. so tied. ~**-head**, Greenland whale. ~**-legged**, *a.* bandy. ~**-man**, archer. ~**-window**, curved bay window.

bow², *v.i. & t.* bend or kneel in sign of submission or reverence, signify submission to authority; incline one's head in salutation. *n.* bowing of head or body.

bow³, *n.* fore-end of boat or ship; rower nearest bow.

bowd'lerize, *v.t.* expurgate book. ~**ism**, ~**ization**, *nn.*

bow'el, *n.* (pl.) entrails, one's inside, feelings of compassion.

bow'er¹, *n.* anchor at ship's bow.

bow'er², *n.* dwelling, lady's room; arbour; leafy nook.

•**bowie** (bō'i), ~**knife**, *nn.* long hunting-knife used in U.S.

bowl¹ (bōl), *n.* basin, esp. for drink or food; hollow of tobacco-pipe, spoon, &c. ~**ful**, *a.*

bowl² (bōl), *n.* (pl.) game played on green with biased wooden balls, (sing.) such ball; ball used in skittles. *v.i. & t.* play bowls or skittles; roll; go along at smart even pace; (Crick.) deliver ball, put batsman out by bowling.

•**bowl'ing** (bōl-), *n.* game of skittles. ~**alley**, enclosure for skittles. ~**crease**, line from behind which bowler in cricket delivers ball. ~**green**, ground for bowls.

bowl'er¹ (bō-), *n.* person bowling at cricket; player at bowls.

bowl'er² (bō-), *n.* hard felt hat.

bow'line (bō-), *n.* knot used in making fixed end loop.

bow'sprit (bō-), *n.* spar running forward from ship's bow.

bow'yer (bō-), *n.* maker or seller of bows.

box, *n.* kinds of evergreen shrub; wood of these; receptacle of rigid material; driver's seat in front of carriage; small compartment in a theatre. *v.t. & i.* put in box; fight with boxing-gloves or (rarely) bare fists. •~**car**, enclosed freight-car. ~**cloth**, close-woven stuff like buff. ~**office**, place for booking seats. ~**seat**, seat beside the driver on box. ~ **the compass**, (Naut.) rehearse points of compass correctly, (transf.) make complete

revolution (in opinion, &c.) and end where one began. ~**tree**, *n.* ~**wood**, wood of the box-tree.

box'er¹, *n.* glove-fighter, pugilist.

Box'er², *n.* member of Chinese anti-foreign secret society.

box'ing, *n.* act of fighting with fists, usu. gloved. ~**day**, first week-day after Christmas when Christmas-boxes are given. ~**gloves**, padded gloves used in boxing. ~**weights**, am. Heavy (over 12st. 10 lb.), Light Heavy (12st. 10 lb.), Middle (11st. 11 lb.), Light Middle (11st. 2 lb.), Welter (10 st. 8 lb.), Light Welter (10st.), Light (9 st. 7 lb.), Feather (9 st.), Bantam (8 st. 7 lb.), Fly (8 st.).

boy, *n.* male child or youth, son; used familiarly instead of 'man', often with *my*, *old*; native male servant. ~ **scouts**, ~**s' brigade**, movements for developing character and physique of boys.

boy'cott, *v.t.* refuse to hold relations with. *n.* such refusal.

boy'hood, *n.* boyish age, boys.

boy'ish, *a.* of boys, lively or high-spirited.

brace, *v.t.* (-*ceable*) strengthen or tighten, make taut. *n.* thing that braces or connects; (pl.) trouser-suspenders; pair or couple. •**brā'cer**¹, *n.* (sl.) pick-me-up.

brace'let (-sl-), *n.* ornament for arm or wrist. ~**ed**, *a.*

brā'cer², *n.* wrist-guard in archery and fencing.

brāck'en, *n.* fern abundant on heaths; mass of this.

brāck'et, *n.* projection from wall serving as a support, corbel; angular support for something fastened to a wall; marks used in pairs for enclosing words or figures, viz. ( ), [ ], { }. *v.t.* support with bracket; enclose in brackets; couple names, &c. together.

brāck'ish, *a.* saltish (of water).

bract, *n.* (Bot.) small leaf or scale below calyx. **brăc'teate**, *a.* having bracts.

brăd, *n.* thin small nail.

brăd'awl, *n.* small boring tool.

brăd´burў, n. (sl.) currency note.

brăe, n. (Sc.) hill-side.

brăg, v.i. & t. talk boastfully, boast of. n. boastful statement or talk ; a card-game.

brăggădo´ciŏ (-shǐ-), n. bragging talk ; boaster. brăgg´art, n. boaster ; (attrib.) bragging.

Brahm´a, n. supreme Hindu deity.

brahmapoō´tra, usu. shortened to brahma, n. breed of fowl.

brahm´in, n. member of Hindu priestly caste. ~ee´, n. female brahmin. ~ism, n.

brahm´inee, a. belonging to brahmin caste, &c. ~ duck, the ruddy sheldrake.

braid, n. plaited tress of hair; silk or thread or wire woven into a band ; v.t. form into braid ; trim with braid ; interweave.

brail, n. (pl.) trussing-cords along sail-edge. v.t. truss (sail).

braille, n. printing for the blind with embossed letters.

brain, n. nervous organ in interior of skull; (pl.) substance of the brain, intellectual ability. v.t. dash out brains of. ~fag, nervous exhaustion. ~fever, inflammation of brain. ~pan, cranium. ~wave, bright idea. brain´ў, a. mentally smart, inventive.

braise (-z), v.t. stew tender with bacon, herbs, &c.

brāke[1], n. bracken.

brāke[2], n. thicket, brushwood.

brāke[3], v.t. crush (hemp, flax) by beating. n. toothed braking-instrument ; heavy harrow.

brāke[4], n. apparatus for checking motion of wheel, vehicle, or train ; a large wagonette. v.t. & i. apply brake, check with brake. ~van, guard's compartment in which train-brake is worked. brakes´man (-an), n. man in charge of brake.

brăm´ah, n. kind of lock ; its key.

brăm´ble, n. blackberry bush ; any wild prickly shrub ; (Sc.) blackberry. brăm´blў, a.

brăm´bling, n. the mountain finch.

brăn, n. husks separated from flour. ~pie, n. tub of bran into which children dip for toys.

branch (-ah-), n. shoot of a tree, small bough, twig ; offshoot or subdivision of something. v.i. send branches forth ; divide into distinct parts. ~ed, ~ў, aa.

brănd, n. piece of burning or smouldering wood, torch ; sword (poet.) ; iron stamp used red-hot, mark left by it ; stigma ; particular kind of goods. v.t. stamp with brand, impress indelibly ; stigmatize. brănd´-new´, a. conspicuously new.

brăn´dish, v.t. wave or flourish.

brant, n. = brent.

brăn´dў, n. strong spirit distilled from wine or grapes. ~pawnee, (Anglo-Ind.) brandy and water.

brăsh[1], n. loose broken rock or ice ; hedge refuse, &c.

*brăsh[2], a. (sl.) brittle ; hasty, saucy.

brass (-ahs), n. yellow alloy of copper with zinc ; sepulchral table of brass ; (fig.) effrontery ; (sl.) money. ~hat, (Army sl.) officer of high rank. ~tacks, (sl.) actual details.

brassărd´, n. badge on arm.

brass´ў (-ah-), a. like brass in colour or sound or taste. n. brass-soled golf-club.

brăt, n. child (contempt.).

brava´dŏ (-ah-), n. (pl. -os), ostentatious or simulated boldness.

brāve, a. ready to confront and steady in enduring danger or pain ; finely dressed, showy, excellent. n. Red-Indian warrior. v.t. defy, dare, challenge.

brā´verў, a. brave conduct or temper ; bright colours, fine clothes.

bra´vŏ (-ah-), n. (pl. -os), hired assassin or bully ; cry of bravo! int. excellent! well done!

bravur´a (-oor-), n. (Mus.) brilliant execution, passage requiring this.

brawl, n. noisy quarrel. v.i. engage in brawl ; (of stream) be noisy.

brawn, n. muscle, lean flesh ; meat of pig's head. ~ў, a. muscular.

zh, as (rou)ge ; è = Ī ; ŭ, ŭr, = êr ; ў, ў, = ī, ĭ ; and see p. 4. * = U.S.

3495 Q

brā'xӯ, (Sc.) *n.* splenic apoplexy in sheep; mutton of sheep dying from this. *a.* suffering from braxy.

bray[1], *n.* ass's cry; blare of trumpet, &c.; loud asinine utterance. *v.i. & t.* emit bray, utter in braying tone.

bray[2], *v.t.* pound in mortar.

brāze, *v.t.* solder with alloy of brass and zinc, colour like brass.

brā'zen, *a.* of or like brass; shameless. *v.t.* carry off shamelessly.

brā'zier[1] (-zher), *n.* brass-worker.

brā'zier[2] (-zher), *n.* pan or iron basket with lighted charcoal or coke as portable heater.

brazil', *n.* red wood of an East-Indian tree; similar wood of a S.-Amer. species; now usu. called ∼*wood.*

brazil'-nŭt, *n.* three-cornered nut.

breach, *n.* infringement or breaking of rule, duty, promise, &c.; breaking off of relations, a quarrel; fissure; gap made in fortifications by artillery, &c. *v.t.* make breach (in wall, &c.).

bread (-ĕd), *n.* flour kneaded into dough, made into loaves, and baked; this as staple food.

breadth (-ĕd-), *n.* broadness, distance from side to side; freedom from mental limitations or prejudices. ∼**ways,** ∼**wise,** *adv.*

break (-āk), *v.t. & i.* (*broke, broken*), divide or separate by force; tame, subdue, crush; make or become bankrupt; discard; lay open; fall to pieces, burst, issue forth; become feeble; grow weaker; fall out; (of cricket-ball) deviate from direction on pitching. *n.* breaking, breach, gap, broken place; pause in work, &c.; deviation of cricket-ball on pitching; player's scoring sequence in billiards.

break'able (-āk-), *a.* capable of being broken. *n.* (pl.) breakable things.

break'age (-āk-), *n.* breaking.

break'down (-āk-), *n.* a collapse, failure of health; negro dance.

break'er (-āk-), *n.* heavy wave breaking on coast or over reef.

breakfast (brĕk'fast), *n.* first meal of day. *v.i.* take breakfast.

break'nĕck (-āk-), *a.* (of pace, hill, &c.) dangerous.

break'water (-āk : waw-), *n.* mole built to break force of waves.

bream, *n.* a fresh-water fish.

breast (-ĕst), *n.* either milk-secreting organ in woman; (fig.) source of nourishment; the chest; seat of affections. *v.t.* oppose the breast to, struggle with (waves, &c.). ∼**bone,** that connecting ribs in front. ∼**plate,** piece of armour for breast.

breath (-ĕth), *n.* air as used by the lungs; breathing, one respiration; slight movement of air; a mere word.

breathe (-dh), *v.i. & t.* (*-thable*), use the lungs, live; take breath or rest; inhale or exhale or instil; speak or utter softly.

breath'er (-dh-), *n.* spell of hard exercise or of rest.

breath'ing (-dh-), *n.* respiration; (Gk. gram.) signs (*rough '*, *smooth '*) indicating that the initial vowel is or is not aspirated.

breath'lĕss (-ĕth-), *a.* panting; unstirred by wind; holding breath.

brĕd, *p.t. & p.p.* of breed.

breech, *n.* the buttocks; back end of gun or gun-barrel. ∼**loader,** *n.* gun loaded at breech, not muzzle.

breeches (-ĭch'ĭz), *n.* man's garment fastened below the knees; (colloq.) trousers. ∼ buoy, life-buoy with canvas b. for legs.

breech'ing (-ĭch-), *n.* strap round horse's breech for backing; rope securing gun to ship's side.

breed, *v.t. & i.* (*brĕd*), produce offspring, propagate, give birth to; raise (cattle, &c.); educate, train the faculties or manners. *n.* race, strain, family, with hereditary qualities.

breed'ing, *n.* nurture, good manners.

breeze[1], *n.* a gadfly.

breeze[2], *n.* gentle wind; (sl.) quarrel. **breez′ȳ**, *a.* pleasantly windy ; lively, irresponsible.

brent, or **~-goose**, *n.* smallest kind of wild goose.

breth′ren, pl. of brother.

***brer**, *n.* (negro dial.) brother.

brēve, *n.* (Mus.) a note equal to two semibreves.

brēv′et, *n.* document conferring nominal rank on army officer.

brē′viarȳ, *n.* book containing Divine Office of R.C. Church.

brēvier′, *n.* a size of type (8-pt.).

brēv′itȳ, *n.* conciseness, shortness.

brew (-ōō-), *v.t. & i.* make beer by fermenting malt ; make punch, tea, &c. *n.* amount brewed at once ; liquor brewed. **~house**, building in which beer is brewed. **~er**, *n.* one who brews beer or malt liquors. **~ery**, *n.* commercial brew-house.

brews′ter, *n.* (arch.) brewer. **B. Sessions**, court for issue of licences to trade in alcoholic liquors.

briar. See brier.

bribe, *n.* inducement offered to persuade some one to do the briber a dishonest or illegal service. *v.t. & i.* give bribe to. **brī′berȳ**, *n.* act of giving or receiving bribes.

bric′-a-brāc, *n.* antiquarian or artistic odds and ends.

brick, *n.* building-material of baked clay made in oblong blocks ; (sl.) warmly approved person. *v.t.* face, block *up*, close *in*, &c. with brick. **~bat**, piece of brick, esp. as missile. **~dust**, powdered brick. **~field**, **~kiln**, places for making and baking bricks. **~layer**, workman building in brick.

brī′dal, *n.* wedding feast or ceremony. *a.* of bride or wedding.

bride, *n.* woman on wedding day and through the honeymoon. **~groom**, man on wedding day, &c. **brīdes′maid** (-z-), unmarried woman or girl of bride's train.

bride′well (-dw-), *n.* (arch.) gaol, House of Correction.

bridge[1], *n.* structure carrying road or path across stream, ravine,

&c. ; (Naut.) platform amidships for officer in charge ; upper bony part of nose ; prop under violin-strings. *v.t.* make bridge over, span as with a bridge. **~head**, *n.* position held on enemy's side of water-barrier as starting-point for future attack.

bridge[2], *n.* card-game developed from whist.

brī′dle, *n.* controlling head-gear for horse, &c. *v.t. & i.* put bridle on ; control, curb ; draw one's head up in offence. **~path**, **~road**, fit or meant for riders but not vehicles. ***~wise**, trained to obey reins.

brief, *a.* of short duration ; concise. *n.* solicitor's summary for guidance of barrister ; size of writing-paper. *v.t.* instruct by brief, employ (barrister). **~less**, *a.* without clients.

brī′er[1], **-ar**,[1] *n.* wild rose bush.

brī′er[2], **-ar**,[2] *n.* heath with root used for pipe-bowls : brier pipe.

brig[1], *n.* (Sc.) bridge.

brig[2], *n.* two-masted vessel ; ***(U.S. Navy sl.) guardhouse.

brigāde′, *n.* military unit composed of 2-4 battalions or regiments or batteries ; kinds of organization on military model.

brigadier′, *n.* brigade-commander.

brig′and, *n.* member of a robber gang. **~age**, *n.* pillage, blackmail.

brig′antine (-ēn), *n.* two-masted vessel.

bright (-īt), *a.* shining, brilliant ; cheerful ; vivacious, quick-witted. **bright′en** (-īt-), *v.t.* make bright. **Bright's disease** (-īts, -zēz), *n.* a kidney disease.

brill, *n.* a flat-fish.

brill′iant (-lya-), *a.* bright, sparkling, distinguished. *n.* diamond of finest quality ; size of type (3½ pt.). **~nce**, *n.* **brill′iantine** (-ēn), *n.* cosmetic for hair.

brim, *n.* edge of cup, hollow, channel, &c. ; projecting rim of hat. *v.i. & t.* fill or be full to the brim. **~ful**, *a.*

brimm′er, *n.* a full cup ; a hat.

māre, mēre, mīre, mōre, mūre ; pärt, pĕrt, pört ; *italics*, vague sounds ;

C 2

brim'stone, n. sulphur.

brin'dled (-dld), a. brown with streaks of other colour.

brine, n. salt and water for pickling; salt water, the sea; tears. *v.t.* treat with brine.

bring, *v.t.* (brought, pr. -awt), fetch, cause to come along with one; convey in one's hand; conduct; prevail upon; prefer (charge). ~ about, cause. ~ off, succeed in. ~ round, restore to consciousness. ~ up, raise; rear; sue in court.

|| brin'jal, -jaul (-awl), n. (Anglo-Ind.) fruit of the egg-plant.

brink, n. edge of precipice, &c.

bri'ny, a. of brine or sea, salt. n. (joc.) the sea.

briquette' (-kĕt), n. block of compressed coal-dust.

brisk, a. active, lively, quick.

brisk'ět, n. animal's breast next ribs, esp. as joint of meat.

bri'stle (-sl), n. a short stiff hair. *v.i. & t.* (of hair, &c.) stand up, make bristle; show temper; be thickly set (with obstacles, &c.).

bris'(t)ling, n. sardine-like fish.

Bris'tol, n. (attrib.) ~ board, kind of cardboard for drawing on. ~ fighter, type of aeroplane.

Britann'ia (-ya), n. Britain personified. ~ metal, a silvery alloy.

Britann'ic, a. of Britain.

Brit'ish, a. of the ancient Britons or of Great Britain. ~warm, kind of short military overcoat for officers. *Brit'isher, n. native of G.B. ~ism, n. idiom of G.B.

Brit'on, n. one of the race found by the Romans in S. Britain; (poet., rhet.) modern British person.

brit'tle, a. apt to break, fragile.

broach, n. roasting-spit; kinds of boring-bit. *v.t.* bore or begin drawing from (cask), start using; bring up for discussion.

broad (-awd), a. large across, extensive; comprehensive, tolerant; of specified breadth; manifest, unmistakable. n. expanse of water formed by widening of stream; broad part of the back. *adv.* broadly. ~~arrow, mark

cut or stamped on Government stores. B. Church, section favouring comprehension.

broad'cast (-awd-), a. (of seed) scattered or thrown about by the hand without drills or rows. *adv.* in this manner. *v.i. & t.* (past broadcasted, p.p. -cast), to sow thus; (of news, &c.) disseminate widely; (Wireless) transmit speeches, music, &c. by wireless telephony to owners of receiving-sets; speak, sing, &c. for such transmission. n. (esp. attrib.) the practice, &c. of broadcasting (broadcast licences, programmes, &c.).

broad'cloth (-aw-), n. fine black kind of cloth.

broad'en (-aw-), *v.t. & i.* make broader.

broad'sheet (-aw-), n. large sheet of paper printed on one side.

broad'side (-aw-), n. ship's side; all guns on one side; simultaneous firing of these; a broadsheet.

broad'sword (-aw-; -sôrd), n. sword with broad straight blade.

brocade', n. fabric with raised pattern. ~ed, a. so woven.

broc'coli, n. species of cauliflower.

bro'chure (-shoor), n. stitched booklet, pamphlet.

brock, n. badger.

brogue (-g), n. rude form of shoe; marked Irish or other accent.

broil, n. quarrel, tumult.

broil, *v.t. & i.* cook on fire or gridiron; make or be very hot.

broke, *p.t.* of break.

bro'ken, n. in pieces, shattered; ruined, infirm, incomplete. ~-hearted, a. crushed by grief. ~ meat, n. scraps. ~-winded, a. disabled by ruptured air-cells.

bro'kenly, adv. spasmodically.

bro'ker, n. middleman, agent; dealer in second-hand furniture; appraiser and seller of distrained goods. ~age, n. broker's fees or commission. bro'king, n. broker's trade.

broll'y, n. (sl.) umbrella.

bro'mate, bro'mide, nn. kinds of compound of bromine.

---

ah, awl, oil, boor, cow, dowry; chin, go, bang, so, ship, thin; dh, as th(e);

brŏ′mic, *a.* containing bromine.

brŏ′mine, *n.* (Chem.) a liquid element with rank smell.

brŏ′mism, *n.* morbid state due to use of bromine.

brŏnc′hial (-ngk-), *a.* of the ramifications of the windpipe.

brŏnchī′tis (-ngk-), *n.* inflammation of bronchial mucous membrane.

brŏn′co, *n.* wild or half-tamed horse of California, &c.

brŏnze, *n.* brown alloy of copper and tin; its colour; work of art in it; (attrib.) made of or coloured like bronze. *v.t. & i.* give bronze surface to, make or grow brown, tan.

brooch (-ō-), *n.* ornamental safety-pin worn as fastening of dress.

brood, *n.* birds or other animals produced at a hatch or birth; (contempt.) children of a family, a gang or crew. *v.i.* sit on eggs; meditate deeply, fret over. brood′y, *a.* (of hen) wishing to sit.

brook¹, *v.t.* tolerate, put up with; admit of (delay, &c.).

brook², *n.* small stream. ∼let, *n.*

broom, *n.* yellow-flowered shrub; long-handled sweeping-brush. ∼stick, *n.* broom-handle.

broth (-aw-), *n.* thin meat soup.

broth′el, *n.* house of prostitution.

broth′er (-ŭdh-), *n.* son of the same parents; companion, equal; member of religious order; (pl. *brethren*) fellow member of Church, guild, order, &c. ∼in-law, *n.* one's wife's or husband's brother, one's sister's husband.

broth′erhood (-ŭdh-), *n.* set of brothers or comrades; brotherliness.

broth′erly (-ŭdh-), *a.* like a brother. ∼liness, *n.*

brough′am (-ōŏam), *n.* short closed 4-wheel horse or electric carriage or car.

brought, *p.t. & p.p.* of *bring.*

brow, *n.* arch of hair over eye (usu. in pl.); forehead; edge of cliff, hill, &c.; summit of pass. ∼beat, *v.t.* bear down with looks and words.

brown, *a.* toast-coloured, dark-skinned. *n.* brown colour or pigment. *v.t. & i.* make or grow brown. ∼ bread, bread made of unbolted flour. ∼ paper, kind used for packing, &c. ∼ study, reverie.

brown′ie, *n.* benevolent sprite haunting house and doing household work; junior member (ages 8–11) of Girl Guides.

Brown′ing, *n.* automatic pistol. P.

browse (-z), *v.i. & t.* feed on leaves and young shoots; (fig.) read for enjoyment. *n.* browsing or material for it.

Bru′in (-ōō-), *n.* name for a bear.

bruise (-ōōz), *n.* injury caused by blow or pressure; dint in wood, &c. *v.t. & i.* pound, grind small, batter; inflict bruise on, be susceptible to bruises.

bruis′er (-ōōz-), *n.* a prize-fighter.

bruit (-ōō-), *v.t.* spread about.

Brumm′agem, *a.* counterfeit, cheap and showy.

brunette′ (-ōō-), *n.* woman of dark complexion; also used attrib.

brunt, *n.* stress of shock or attack.

brush, *n.* cleaning or hair-dressing or painting implement; fox's tail; skirmish; *brushwood. v.t. & i.* touch lightly, graze in passing; use brush on. ∼wood, undergrowth, bushes and saplings. ∼work, painter's manipulation.

brusque (-ōōsk), *a.* blunt, offhand.

Brüss′els (-z). In comb. ∼ carpet, ∼ lace, kinds made at Brussels. ∼ sprouts, kind of cabbage with buds.

bru′tal (-ōō-), *a.* as of the brutes; coarsely sensual or callously cruel. brutāl′ity (-ōō-), *n.*

bru′talize (-ōō-), *v.t.* destroy the human qualities in.

brute (-ōōt), *a.* not gifted with reason. *n.* animal other than man, large or formidable beast; human being of low type; (colloq.) person one dislikes.

‖ bru′tum fŭl′men (-ōō-), *n.* empty threat.

bry′ony, *n.* climbing hedge plant.

*bub, *n.* brother (child's use).

bŭb'ble, n. globe or half-globe of liquid enclosing air or gas; a visionary project. v.i. send up or rise in bubbles; (fig.) boil over (with joy, anger, &c.).

bŭbb'ly, a. full of bubbles, gurgling. ~jock, (Sc.) turkey-cock.

bū'bō, n. (pl. -oes), inflamed swelling in groin or armpit. būbŏn'ic, a. accompanied by buboes.

bŭccaneer', n. sea-rover. ~ing, a. piratical; ~ing, n. piratical roving.

bŭck,[1] n. male of fallow-deer, reindeer, chamois, antelope, hare, or rabbit; *male sheep, ram; *male negro or Indian; dandy; act of buckjumping; *buck-shot; *(sl.) dollar; *(sl.) object to mark position of the deal in card-games (to pass the buck). v.i. (of horse) = buck-jump. ~horn, horn of deer. ~hound, small variety of deer-hound. ~jump, (of horse) jump vertically with back arched. ~shot, large coarse shot. ~skin, soft leather made from skin of deer, goat, &c. ~tooth, a projecting tooth. ~up, (sl.) make haste, cheer up. buck'er, n. bucking horse. bŭck'ish, a. dandified.

bŭck,[2] v.i. butt (against, at, or in).

bŭck'et, n. a vessel for carrying or holding water, &c.; socket for whip, carbine, &c. v.t. & i. ride (horse) hard, go at utmost speed, row hurried stroke. ~ful, n. (pl. -ls). ~shop, office for speculative dealings in stocks, &c.

bŭc'kle, n. clasp with hinged tongue used for straps, &c. v.t. & i. fasten with buckle; put on; bend one's energies to work; crumple up under pressure.

bŭck'ler, n. small round shield; (fig.) protector or protection.

bŭck'ram, n. coarse linen or cloth stiffened with paste, &c.

bŭck'shee, a. & adv. (sl.), free.

bŭck'wheat (-wēt), n. cereal with seeds shaped like beech-mast.

bŭcŏl'ic, a. farming, rustic, pastoral. n. pastoral poem.

bŭd,[1] n. projection from which branch or leaf-cluster or flower

develops; flower or leaf not fully open; *débutante. v.i. & t. put forth buds, sprout as buds; begin to grow or develop; graft.

*bŭd[2], n. brother (familiar form of address).

Budd'hism (-ōŏdi-), n. Asiatic religion founded by Gautama Buddha. ~ist, n.

bŭddlei'a (-lēa), n. shrub with lilac or yellow flowers.

*bŭdd'y, n. (sl.) chum.

bŭdge, v.i. & t. (-geable), move in the least degree.

bŭd'gĕrigăr', n. Australian love-bird.

bŭd'ĝet, n. contents of bag, bundle of letters, &c.; Chancellor of Exchequer's annual estimate of revenue and expenditure, similar estimate of body or person. v.i. ~ for, allow or arrange for in budget.

bŭff, n. stout velvety dull-yellow leather; colour of this. a. of this colour. v.t. polish with buff.

bŭff'alō, n. (pl. -oes), kind of ox. v.t. to overpower, overawe.

bŭff'er, n. apparatus for deadening or sustaining concussions, esp. on railways; (sl.) man, fellow.

bŭff'ĕt, n. blow with the hand; blow dealt by wave, &c. or by fortune; side-board or recessed cupboard; (pron. bōŏf'ā) refreshment bar. v.t. & i. deal blows to, struggle with.

buffōŏn', n. person who makes himself ridiculous to raise laughter, coarse jester. v.i. play the buffoon. ~ery, n.

bŭg, n. small blood-sucking insect infesting beds; *any insect. ~hunter, n. (colloq.) entomologist.

bŭg'abŏŏ, n. object of baseless terror.

bŭg'bear (-bār), n. object of terror; dreaded event, &c.

bŭg'ġy, n. light horse-drawn vehicle for one or two persons (formerly used esp. in U.S., India).

*bŭg'house, a. crazy.

bū'gle[1], n. kinds of plant.

---

māte. mēte. mīte. mōte. mūte. mōŏt : rӑck. rĕck. rĭck. rŏck. rŭck. rōŏk ;

bū′gle², *n.* (pl.) long glass beads sewn on dresses as ornament.

bū′gle², *n.* brass instrument like small trumpet. *v.i. & t.* sound bugle, sound call on bugle.

bū′gler, *n.* bugle-signaller.

bū′gle, *n.* bicyclist's small bugle.

bū′gloss, *n.* rough-leaved plant.

buhl (-ool), *n.* inlaid work of brass and tortoise-shell.

build (bĭ-), *v.t. & i.* (built), construct or erect by successive additions; (fig.) base hopes on. *n.* make or proportions of ship, carriage, or of person's or animal's body.

buil′der (bĭ-), *n.* (esp.) a contractor for building houses.

buil′ding (bĭ-), *n.* house or other structure with roof and walls.

*built (bĭ-), *p.p.* constituted by nature.

bŭlb, *n.* globular stem of some plants; roundish swelling in cylindrical organ or tube.

bŭl′bous, *a.* bulb-shaped, having bulb or bulbs; swollen.

bulbul (bool′bool), *n.* Eastern song-thrush.

bŭlge, *n.* irregular swelling-out of a surface or line; *advantage, upper hand. *v.i.* form or show bulge.

bŭl′ger, *n.* wooden golf-club with bulging face.

bŭlk, *n.* contents of ship's hold, cargo; the mass or greater part; size, magnitude, volume. *v.i.* seem of specified bulk or importance. ~head, upright partition in ship's hull between cabins or watertight compartments.

bŭl′ky, *a.* large, unwieldy.

bull¹ (-ool), *n.* Papal edict.

bull² (-ool), *n.* statement so made as to imply an absurdity.

bull³ (-ool), *n.* male of ox, elephant, whale, and other large animals; bull's-eye in shooting; (Stock Exch.) person interested in sending prices up. ~calf, young bull. *~doze, (sl.) compel by show of force; bully. ~fight, baiting of bulls with horsemen, &c. ~puncher, (Austral.) bul-

lock-driver. ~terrier, cross between bulldog and terrier.

bullace (bool′is), *n.* small wild plum.

bull′dog (-ool-), *n.* breed of dog noted for tenacity; tenacious person; (sl.) University proctor's attendant.

bull′et (-ool-), *n.* missile for rifle, pistol, or machine-gun.

bull′etin (-ool-), *n.* short official statement of invalid's condition, &c.

bull′finch (-ool-), *n.* fine-plumaged song-bird; quickset hedge with ditch.

bullion (bool′yon), *n.* gold or silver in the lump or by weight. ~ist, *n.* advocate of metallic currency.

bull′ock (-ool-), *n.* gelded bull.

bull's-eye (-oolz-ī), *n.* hemispherical lens, lantern having it; centre of target; kind of sweetmeat.

bull′y (-ool-), *n.* hired ruffian; blusterer, browbeater; schoolboy tyrant; tinned beef; (Footb.) scrummage in the Eton game. *v.i. & t.* play the bully, browbeat, overawe by threats. *a.* (sl.) first-rate, slap-up. ~ off, start play in hockey with crossed sticks. *~rag, (sl.) maltreat, ballyrag.

bul′rush (-ool-), *n.* tall rush, reed-mace; papyrus.

bul′wark (-ool-), *n.* earthwork or other material defence; person or principle that protects; ship's side above deck.

*bum (sl.) *a.* worthless, good-for-nothing. *n.* loafer, ne'er-do-well. *v.i. & t.* drink to excess; tramp, live life of a vagabond.

bŭm-bail′iff, *n.* sheriff's officer for arrests, &c.

bŭm′-boat, *n.* boat plying with fresh provisions for ship.

bŭm′ble-bee, *n.* loud-humming bee.

bŭm′bledom (-ld-), *n.* consequential minor officials and their ways.

bŭm′ble-pŭppy, *n.* unskilled whist, tennis, &c.; game with tennis-ball slung to post.

bŭm′malo, *n.* small fish found off

southern Asia, used, when dried, as a relish.

*bŭm'mer, n. worthless loafer.

bŭmp, n. collision of two surfaces, swelling caused by it; a protuberance. adv. with a bump. v.t. & i. inflict bump or bumps on; strike or come bump against; jolt; (of cricket-ball) rise abruptly. bŭm'pў, a.

bŭm'per, n. brimming glass; great harvest, record score, &c.; (Motoring) spring fender for mitigating collisions.

bŭmp'kin, n. awkward country lout.

bŭmp'tious (-shus), a. self-assertive.

bŭn, n. small soft currant cake; hair dressed in bun-shape; *(sl.) have bun on, be intoxicated.

bŭnch, n. set of things growing or fastened together; group of people; *herd of cattle. v.t. & i. arrange in bunch or bunches; gather in bunch; come or cling together. *~grass, various grasses of western U.S. bŭn'chў, a. forming a bunch.

*bŭn'cō, v.t. (sl.) swindle (~ game, man, steerer).

bŭnd, n. (Anglo-Ind.) embankment, causeway, quay.

bŭn'der, n. (Anglo-Ind.) landing-place or quay; seaport; harbour. ~boat, boat used for communicating with ships in harbour, &c.

bŭn'dle, n. odds and ends tied up in cloth, &c.; sticks, &c. bound up together. v.t. & i. tie in a bundle; throw confusedly into a receptacle; go or send unceremoniously away.

bŭng, n. stopper of cork or other material for bung-hole; (sl.) lie. v.t. stop up. ~hole, hole by which cask is filled. bunged up, (of eye, nose, pipe, &c.) stopped up.

bŭng'alow (-nggalō), n. one-storied house, orig. lightly built.

bungle (bŭng'gl), v.i. & t. go awkwardly to work, mismanage, fail. n. piece of bungling.

bŭn'ion (-yon), n. inflamed swelling on foot.

bŭnk¹, n. sleeping-birth. *~v.i. to have a, go to, bed. *~house, h. with berths for lumberers, &c.

bŭnk², v.i. & n. (sl.) Bunk, do a ~, abscond, vanish.

*bŭnk³, n. big talk, bunkum.

bŭnk'er, n. ship's coal-bin; a receptacle; military dug-out; pit or hollow impeding golfer, (fig.) obstacle. bŭnk'ered (-erd), p.p. entangled in bunker.

bŭnk'um, ~combe (-m), n. insincere talk, claptrap.

bŭnn'ў, n. pet name for rabbit. ~hug, an American dance.

Bun'sen bŭrn'er (-ōŏn-), n. an invention for burning mixed air and gas, giving great heat.

bŭnt, n. (Naut.) baggy middle of sail; *baseball batted to point within the infield. ~line, n. rope used in furling.

bŭn'ting, n. kinds of small bird; flags or their material.

buoy (boi), n. anchored float as navigation mark, &c. v.t. bring to surface of water, keep afloat; sustain; mark with buoys.

buoy'ant (boi-), a. apt to float, light; cheerful. ~ncy, n.

bŭr, n. clinging seed-vessel or other part of plant, plant producing burs; person hard to shake off.

bŭrb'errў, n. a waterproof material; garment made of it. P.

bŭrb'ot, n. eel-like freshwater fish.

bŭrd'en, n. load, task, weight of grief, obligatory expense; (often -then) ship's tonnage; refrain of song, theme. v.t. load, encumber, lie heavy on. ~some, a. imposing a burden.

bŭr'dock, n. plant with prickly flowers and dock-like leaves.

bureau' (-rō), n. (pl. -eaux, pr. -ōz), escritoire; chest of drawers; office, esp. of a Government department.

bureau'cracў (-rō-), n. government by bureaus, centralization, officialism. ~crat, n. ~cratic, a.

*burg, n. (sl.) town.

bŭrgee', n. small swallow-tailed pennant of yacht, &c.

bur'geon (-jn), n. & v.i. bud, shoot.

bur'gess, n. freeman of borough, citizen; M.P. for borough or corporate town or university.

burgh (bŭ'ru), n. Scotch borough.

burg'her (-ger), n. citizen or member of a burgh.

burg'lar, n. person attempting burglary.

burg'lary, n. breaking into house by night with felonious intent. **burglar'ious**, a. **bŭr'gle** (colloq.), v.t. & i. commit burglary.

burg'omaster (-ah-), n. Dutch or Flemish mayor.

burg'undy, n. kinds of wine.

bu'rial (bě-), n. burying, esp. of dead body; funeral. **~-case, coffin.**

bur'in, n. engraver's tool.

burke, v.t. murder, esp. by stifling; (fig.) stifle inquiry, &c.

burlesque' (-k), a. of derisively imitative kind. n. dramatic or literary parody; this branch of art. v.t. make or give burlesque of.

burl'y, a. of stout sturdy build.

burn[1], n. (Sc.) brook, stream.

burn[2], v.i.s. & t. (burnt, sometimes -ed), consume or be consumed by fire, blaze or smoulder; feel intense heat or emotion; injure by burning; brand; (of seeker in hiding-game) draw near object of search. n. sore or mark made by burning; *burnt area in forest, &c.

burn'er, n. part of lamp, &c. that shapes the flame.

burn'et, n. brown-flowered plant.

burn'ish, v.t. & i. polish by friction, take such polish.

burnt, p.t. of burn.

burr, n. whirring sound; sound of a strongly pronounced r.

*burrō, n. donkey.

bŭ'rrow (-ō), n. hole excavated by animals as dwelling. v.i. & t. make or live in burrow; excavate.

bŭrs'ar, n. treasurer of college, &c.; holder of bursary. **bŭrsār'ial**, a. **bŭrs'ary**, n. bursar's office; allowance to poor scholar.

burst, v.i. & t. fly violently asunder or give way suddenly, explode, rush forth; (part.) full to overflowing. n. bursting, explosion, outbreak; spurt, continuous gallop.

bu'ry (bě-), v.t. commit (corpse) to earth or tomb or sea, celebrate burial rites over; inter, hide in earth; consign to oblivion.

bus, n. (pl. buses), omnibus; (Air Force sl.) aeroplane; motor-car. v.i. go by bus.

bus'by (-z-), n. tall fur cap with cloth bag on right side worn by hussars and others.

bush[1] (-ōō-), n. shrub, clump of shrubs; (Austral., S.-Afr.), woodland, forest. **~-bean, kidney-bean. ~buck, small African antelope. ~hog, wild pig of S. Africa. *~-hook, bill-hook. ~lawyer, New Zealand bramble. ~man, earliest known S. Afr. native race; dweller or traveller in Australian bush. ~ranger, Australian brigand living in bush. *~-whacker, person who cuts down bush; backwoodsman; implement for cutting brushwood.** **bushed** (bōōsht), (Austral.) lost in bush.

bush[2], n. perforated plug; metal lining of orifice.

bush'el (-ōō-), n. measure of capacity (8 gal.) for corn, fruit, &c.

bush'y (-ōō-), a. like a bush.

business (biz'nis), n. one's occupation or affairs; one's province or duty; work, employment; (Theatr.) dumb-show; a commercial firm or its interests.

busk, n. stiff rib in stays.

busk'er, n. (sl.) wandering actor, &c.

bus'kin, n. high boot; ancient tragic actor's boot; the tragic drama.

buss, n. & v.t. kiss.

bust[1], n. sculptured head, shoulders, and chest; contour of breast and neck.

bust[2], n. (sl. or vulgar) burst. v.i. burst, go bankrupt.

bus'tard, n. large running bird.

bŭ'stle (-sl), v.i. & t. make show of activity, hurry about. n. excited activity; padding inside top of woman's skirt behind.

busy (bĭz'ĭ), *a.* working with concentrated attention, fully employed; fussy, meddlesome. *v.t.* engage, occupy, keep busy.

but, *adv.* only. *prep.* except, without, outside of or apart from. *conj.* unless, if not, yet, still.

butch′er (-ŏŏ-), *n.* slaughterer of animals for food, meat-dealer; one who delights in bloodshed. *v.t.* slaughter (people) mercilessly or wantonly. **butch′ery** (-ŏŏ-), *n.* wanton slaughter, massacre; slaughtering department in camps, &c.

but′ler, *n.* man-servant in charge of wine, plate, &c.

butt¹, *n.* large cask (108–140 gal.).

butt², *n.* mound behind target; (pl.) shooting-range; object of ridicule, person habitually teased.

butt³, *n.* thicker end of an object.

butt⁴, *v.i. & t.* push or run one's head into; go headlong into (affair, &c.).

*butte (būt), *n.* isolated hill or peak rising abruptly.

butt′er, *n.* yellow fatty food-substance made from cream. *v.t.* spread butter on bread, &c.; (colloq.) flatter. **~boat,** sauce-boat. **~fingered,** *a.* given to letting things slip. **~fingers,** butter-fingered person. **~milk,** liquid left after butter-making. **~sauce,** made of melted butter, flour, &c.

butt′ercup, *n.* kinds of yellow-flowered ranunculus.

butt′erfly, *n.* diurnal insect with large wings, often of brilliant colours; showy person, trifler.

*butt′ernut, *n.* large oily nut of the white walnut-tree of N. America; also, the tree itself.

butt′erwort (-wĕr-), *n.* violet-flowered bog-plant.

butt′ery, *n.* place in colleges, &c. where provisions are kept.

butt′ock, *n.* either protuberance of seat of body, hind part of beasts; (pl.) seat, hind-quarters.

butt′on, *n.* disk sewn to garment, &c. to fasten part of the dress; (pl. as sing.) page with many-buttoned coat; small knob or projection; unopened flower-bud. *v.t. & i.* fasten with button(s); enclose in buttoned garment, &c. (usu. with *up, in, into*). **~hole,** *n.* hole into which button fits; flower(s) to be worn in button-hole; *v.t.* seize person to secure his attention. **~hook,** hook for fastening buttons.

butt′ress, *n.* support built against a wall, &c.; a prop; person, &c. that strengthens a cause, &c. *v.t.* support or strengthen.

bux′om, *a.* plump, comely.

buy (bī), *v.t.* (bought, pr. -awt), obtain in exchange for money or other consideration; obtain by bribery. **n.* bargain.

buy′er (bī-), *n.* one who buys.

buzz, *n.* humming like bees, confused sound. *v.i. & t.* make a buzz; spread secretly. **~saw,** circular saw.

buzz′ard, *n.* kinds of falcon; **kind of vulture.*

buzz′er, *n.* steam-whistle; electric buzzing-machine for sending signals; (Army sl.) signaller.

by (bī), *adv.* near, at hand; aside, in reserve; past. *prep.* near to, beside, within reach of; along, viâ, past; surrounded with; through the action, agency, means, or instrumentality of; as soon as, not later than; in accordance with. **~ and by,** before long; *n.* the future. **~blow,** a side-blow; bastard child. **~-election,** election caused by death or resignation. **~lane,** side lane. **~name,** nickname. **~pass,** secondary gas-jet always alight from which main jet is lit when wanted; piece of new road relieving traffic by connecting two points of the old. **~path,** unfrequented path. **~play,** dumb show of minor characters on stage. **~product,** substance, &c. produced incidentally in the making of something else. **~road,** side road. **~street,**

side street. **~ the by**, incidentally, parenthetically. **~-way**, secluded road, &c.; less known department of subject.

bỹe, n. run made at cricket without ball being struck by the batsman; a goal at lacrosse; (in sports where competitors are paired) position of an individual or crew or team left over after heats are drawn.

by'gone (bīgawn), a. no longer existent. n.pl. the past.

by'-law, bye-, (bī-), n. regulation made by local authority, &c.

bỹre, n. cow-house.

bỹ'stănder, n. spectator.

by'word (bī'wẽrd), n. familiar saying; object of derision.

bỹ'wõner, n. (S.-Afr.) sub-occupier of farm land, paying rent in kind or service.

Bӯzăn'tine (or -ỹ-), a. of Byzantium or Constantinople; of the architectural style of the Eastern Roman Empire.

C

C, c (sē), as roman numeral, 100; (Mus.) first note of natural major scale.

căb, n. hackney carriage, esp. of brougham or hansom shape or taxi; shelter on engine for crew. v.i. go by cab. **~man**, driver of cab. **~stand**, place where cabs stand for hire.

cabăl', n. secret intrigue; political clique. v.i. join in or act as cabal.

‖ **căb'aret** (-ā), n. French tavern; entertainment in restaurant, &c. while guests are at table.

căbb'age[1], n. kinds of green vegetable with round heart. v.i. form a head like a cabbage.

căbb'age[2], n. shreds (or large pieces) of cloth appropriated by tailors in cutting out clothes. v.t. appropriate (cloth, &c.) surreptitiously.

căb(b)'ala, n. Jewish oral tradition; occult lore. **căb(b)'alism**, **~ist**, nn.; **căbbalis'tic**, a.

căbb'ỹ, n. (colloq.) cabman.

că'ber, n. pine-trunk used in Sc. sport of tossing the caber.

căb'in, n. small dwelling, esp. of wood; hut; private or public room on ship. **~boy**, ship's waiter. **căb'ined** (-nd), a. cramped in small space.

căb'inět, n. closet, private room; body of Ministers attending councils with Prime Minister; case with drawers or shelves or compartments. **~-maker**, skilled joiner.

că'ble, n. anchor rope or chain, (as measure) 100 fathoms; thick rope of wire or hemp; (Teleg.) submarine line containing insulated wires, message sent by this. v.i. & t. use telegraphic cable, wire message thus. **~-car**, tram-car worked by underground cable. **~-gram**, message sent by cable.

căbôbs', n.pl. meat cooked in small pieces on skewers.

*cabōō'dle, n. (sl.) group, lot, set.

caboose', n. cook-room on ship's deck; *car for use of conductor, brakemen, &c. on a freight-train.

căbriolet' (-lā), n. kind of chaise.

cacā'o, n. tree, or its seed, yielding cocoa and chocolate.

căch'alŏt (-sh-), n. kinds of whale.

căche (-sh), n. hidden store of provisions, &c. v.t. store in cache.

cachet (kăsh'ā), n. marks of authenticity; any distinctive stamp; capsule for medicine.

că'chinnāte (-k-), v.i. laugh loudly. **~tion**, n.; **~tory**, a.

cachou (kăsh'ōō), n. pill for sweetening the breath.

cacique' (-ēk), n. Amer.-Ind. chief.

că'ckle, n. clucking of hen, calling of geese; glib inconsequent talk. v.i. & t. emit cackle; utter or express with cackle.

cacōde'mon, n. an evil spirit.

cacōē'thes (-z), n. itch for doing something foolish.

cacŏph'ŏnỹ, n. ugly sound, esp. of words or music. **~nous**, a.

că'ctus, n. succulent shiny plant. **căctā'ceous** (-shus), a.

căd, n. low ill-bred fellow. **~dish**, a. dishonourable, ill-bred.

---

mãre, mēre, mĩre, mõre, mūre; pãrt, pẽrt, põrt; *italics*, vague sounds;

cadav′erous, a. of corpse-like pallor.

cădd′ie, n. golfer's attendant.

cădd′is, -ice, n. water-larva in cylindrical case of stems, &c.

cădd′ŷ, n. small box for tea.

ca′dence, n. measured movement of sound; intonation.

cadet′, n. younger son; student in naval or military college. ~ corps, of schoolboys, &c., receiving military training.

cădge, v.i. & t. (-geable), get by begging or sponging. cădg′er, n. pedlar, hawker; sponger.

cadi, k- (kahd′ĭ), n. (pl. -ĭs), Mohammedan judge.

căd′mium, n. a tin-like metal.

cadre (kahd′er), n. permanent expandable regimental establishment.

cadū′ceŭs, n. (pl. -eī), ancient herald's wand, esp. as symbol of Mercury.

cadū′cous, a. fleeting, unenduring; (Bot., Zool., of parts) falling off when work is done.

caec′um (s-), n. (pl. -ca), blind gut or first part of large intestine.

Caes′arism, ~ist (sēz-), nn. belief, believer, in autocracy.

caesūr′a (siz-), n. point of natural pause in a metrical line. cae-sūr′al (siz-), a.

café (kăf′ā), n. coffee-house or restaurant; *bar-room.

*căfetēr′ia, n. restaurant where the patrons serve themselves with food.

căff′eine, n. alkaloid in coffee and tea plants.

căge, n. prison of wire or with bars, esp. for animals; open framework, mineshaft car, &c. v.t. confine in cage.

*cahoot′, n. (colloq.) in cahoot(s), in league or partnership.

caique (ka-ēk′), n. Turkish boat.

cairn, n. pyramid of stones.

cairngŏrm′, n. yellow or wine-coloured gem-stone.

caiss′on (or kasōn′), n. water-tight case used in laying foundations under water; ammunition chest or wagon.

cait′iff, n. coward or rascal.

cajōle′, v.t. (-lable), persuade or soothe by flattery or deceit. ~ment, cajolery (-ĕrĭ), nn.

cāke, n. small flat loaf; a compound of bread sweetened with sugar, currants, and other ingredients; flattish compact mass. v.t. & i. form into cohesive mass, harden. ~walk, dance developed from negro contest in graceful walking with cake for prize. cā′kў, a. lumpy, cohesive.

căl′abash, n. kinds of gourd and fruit-tree; a shell from these as drinking or cooking vessel.

*călabōose′, n. (colloq.) prison.

călaman′der, n. a hard cabinet wood of Ceylon and India.

călăm′itў, n. grave disaster; distressed state. ~tous, a. causing or marked by calamity.

călash′, n. hooded carriage; (Canada) two-wheeled one-seated vehicle with driver's seat on splash-board; carriage-hood; hood protecting bonnet, &c.

călcā′reous, a. containing carbonate of lime; of limestone.

călcēolā′ria, n. plant with slipper-shaped flower.

căl′cifў, v.t. & i. (-iable), convert into lime; suffer such change. ~fication, n.

căl′cine, v.t. & i. (-nable), reduce to quicklime or powder by burning or roasting; suffer this. ~nation, n.

căl′cium, n. a metal, the base of lime.

căl′culate, v.t. & i. (-lable), compute by figures, ascertain by exact reckoning; *suppose, believe; (p.p.) intentional, pre-arranged. ~tion, ~tor, nn.

căl′culus, n. (pl. -li), (Med.) concretion in some part of body; (Math.) particular method of calculation.

caldron. See cauldron.

Cālēdō′nian, a. pertaining to Scotland. n. a Scot.

căl′endar, n. system fixing civil year's beginning, &c.; almanac or table exhibiting year's arrangement; register or list. *v.t.* enter in list; arrange, analyse, and index (documents).

căl'énder, *n.* roller-machine for cloth, &c.; steam mangle. *v.t.* press in calender.

căl'ends, k-, *n.pl.* first of month in ancient-Roman calendar.

căl'enture, *n.* sailor's delirium in tropics showing sea as fields.

calf[1] (kahf), *n.* (*pl. -ves*) young of cow or of elephant, whale, deer, seal, &c.; stupid fellow.

calf[2] (kahf), *n.* (*pl. -ves*) fleshy hinder part of leg below knee.

căl'ibrate, *v.t.* find calibre of, correct irregularities before graduating. **~tion**, *n.*

căl'ibre (-er), *n.* internal diameter of gun or tube; moral weight, degree of importance.

căl'icō, *n.* (*pl. -oes*) cotton cloth, esp. plain white kinds; *printed cotton cloth. *a.* variegated.

căl'iph, -if, *n.* successor of Muhammed, official head of Islam, **căl'iphate**, *n.* caliph's office.

căl'ix, *n.* (*pl. -ices*), (*Anat.*) cuplike cavity or organ.

calk (kawk), *n.* sharp iron set in horse-shoe or boot to save slipping. *v.t.* provide with a calk.

calkin (kawk'ĭn), *n.* turned-down edge of horse-shoe.

call (kawl), *v.i. & t.* speak in loud tone; utter a summons; pay brief visit; convoke; name, describe. ***~ down**, reprove, abuse. *n.* shout, bird's cry; signal on bugle, &c.; a summons; short visit; (*Bridge*) turn to bid.

call'er[1] (kaw-), *n.* visitor.

call'er[2], *a.* (*Sc.*) fresh (fish, air, &c.).

callig'raphý, *n.* handwriting.

call'ing (kaw-), *n.* profession.

căll'iper, *n.* (*pl.*) compasses for measuring diameter of bullets, tubes, &c. *v.t.* measure with callipers.

căllisthěn'ics, *n.pl.* exercises to develop strength and grace.

callōs'itý, *n.* hardness of skin, hardened part, insensible lump.

căll'ous, *a.* hardened, horny; unfeeling, unsympathetic.

căll'ow (-ō), *a.* unfledged; raw, inexperienced.

calm (kahm), *a.* tranquil, windless, unagitated; (*colloq.*) impudent. *v.t. & i.* make or become calm, pacify. *n.* calm state.

căl'omel, *n.* a purgative medicine.

calō'ric, *n.* heat, bodily warmth.

căl'orie, *n.* unit of heat.

calōrif'ic, *a.* heat-producing.

călōrim'éter, *n.* heat-measuring instrument.

căl'trop, *n.* four-spiked iron ball thrown down to maim cavalry horses; kinds of plant.

căl'umět, *n.* Amer.-Ind. tobacco-pipe, esp. as symbol of peace.

calŭm'niate, *v.t.* (*-iable*), slander, utter calumny about. **~tor**, *n.*; **~nious**, *a.*

căl'umný, *n.* defamation, slander.

căl'varý, *n.* representation of the Crucifixion.

calve (kahv), *v.i.* produce a calf.

Căl'vinism, *n.* Calvin's theology, esp. his doctrine of predestination; adherence to this. **~ist**, *n.*

călx, *n.* (*pl. calcēs*) ashes left after smelting.

cā'lyx (*or -ă-*), *n.* (*pl. -cēs, -xes*) whorl of leaves called sepals forming outer case of bud.

căm, *n.* (in a wheel, &c.) part so shaped as to convert rotary into reciprocal motion.

‖ **camaraderie** (kămˈrahˈdereˊ), *n.* fraternizing disposition or conduct of comrades.

‖ **cămarill'a**, *n.* cabal or junto.

căm'ber, *n.* convex form of deck, road, &c. *v.t.* construct with camber.

Căm'brian, *a.* of Wales. *n.* Welshman.

căm'bric, *n.* fine linen.

came, *p.t.* of come.

căm'el, *n.* large quadruped with one hump (*Arabian ~*) or two (*Bactrian ~*); type of aeroplane.

camē'llia (*or -ē-*), *n.* a flowering evergreen.

camĕl'opărd, *n.* (rare) giraffe.

Căm'embert (-âr), *n.* small cheese.

căm'ĕō, *n.* (*pl. -os*) onyx or similar stone carved in relief.

căm'era, *n.* photographing apparatus. ∼ **obscūra,** *n.* apparatus projecting on paper image of distant object.

cămi-knick'ers, *n.pl.* woman's undergarment of camisole and knickers combined.

căm'ion, *n.* low flat four-wheeled horse or motor truck.

căm'isōle, *n.* under-bodice.

căm'lĕt, *n.* a light cloth.

căm'omīle, *n.* aromatic herb. ∼ **tea,** infusion of the flowers.

căm'ouflage (-ōoflahzh), *n.* disguise of guns, ships, &c. by obscuring outline with splashes of various colours; (transf.) means of throwing people off the scent. *v.t.* hide by camouflage.

cămp, *n.* place where troops, &c. are lodged in tents, &c. *v.i.* & *t.* encamp, be in camp. ∼**bed,** ∼**chair,** ∼**stool,** folding-up bed, &c. ∼**follower,** non-military hanger-on of camp. *∼**meeting,** religious open-air meeting.

cămpaign' (-ān), *n.* series of military operations; military service in the field; organized course of action (e.g. in politics). *v.i.* serve on campaign.

cămpanil'ē (-nē-), *n.* detached bell-tower. ∼**nology,** *n.* bell-lore.

cămpăn'ūla, *n.* kinds of plant with bell-shaped flowers.

căm'phor, *n.* crystalline aromatic bitter substance. ∼**ate,** *v.t.* impregnate with camphor.

căm'pion, *n.* wild flowering-plant.

‖ **căm'pōo,** *n.* (Anglo-Ind.) camp.

cămp'us, *n.* (Antiq.) open space for martial exercises; *grounds of a school or college.

căn¹, *n.* metal vessel for liquid. *v.t.* pack (food) in cans for preserving; (sl.) discharge, suppress.

căn², *v. aux.* (2 s. canst, 3 can; neg. cannot, can't pr. kahnt; past & cond. could pr. kŏŏd, couldst or couldest), be able to; have the right to (do); be permitted to; feel inclined to.

Canā'dĭan, *a.* of Canada. *n.* Canadian person. ∼ **canoe,**

---

open canoe with single-bladed paddle.

‖ **canaille** (kanah'y), *n.* the rabble.

canàl', *n.* artificial watercourse. ∼**ize,** *v.t.* make into canal; direct into channel.

canàrd', *n.* an unfounded rumour.

canàr'ў, *n.* cage songbird of yellow plumage; wine from the Canary Islands. *a.* bright-yellow.

canàs'ter, *n.* tobacco-leaf dried and broken up.

‖ **cancan** (kahn'kahn), *n.* high-kicking dance.

căn'cel, *v.t.* & *i.* cross out, annul, countermand, neutralize; (Arith.) strike out factor. ∼**lation,** *n.*

căn'cer, *n.* the Crab in the zodiac; malignant tumour; (fig.) corruption. tropic of C. northern tropic. ∼**ed,** ∼**ous,** ∼**croid,** *aa.*

cāndělā'brum, *n.* (pl. -a), large, usu. branched, candlestick.

căn'did, *a.* unprejudiced; free from dissimulation; outspoken.

căn'didāte, *n.* one who seeks some office or honour. ∼**acy,** ∼**ature,** *n.* being candidate.

candied. See candy.

căn'dle, *n.* cylinder of wax or tallow enclosing wick for giving light. ∼**light,** artificial light. ∼**power,** unit of light-measure. ∼**stick,** stand for holding candle.

Căn'dlemas, *n.* feast of Purification of the Virgin, 2nd Feb.

căn'dour (-der), *n.* candidness.

căn'dў, *n.* crystallized sugar *a sweetmeat; sweets *v.t.* & *i.* preserve, fruit, &c. by coating with candy. **căn'died** (-ĭd), *a.* coated with sugar; (fig.) sugared, honeyed.

căn'dўtŭft, *n.* plant with white, pink, or purple flowers.

cāne, *n.* (collect.) stems of giant reeds and grasses or slender palms; stem of raspberry, &c.; walking-stick, rod for punishment. *v.t.* beat with cane; weave cane into (chair, &c.).

canē'phorus, *n.* (pl. -rī), sculptured youth or maid with basket on head.

---

mäte, mēte, mīte, mōte, mūte, mŏŏt; răck, rĕck, rĭck, rŏck, rŭck, rōŏk;

că′nīne, a. of the dog. ~ **tooth**, between incisors and molars.

căn′ister, n. small box for tea, &c. ~**shot**, case-shot.

cănk′er, n. kinds of disease (of human mouth, horse's hoof, fruit-trees); (fig.) corrupting influence; destructive caterpillar or larva. v.t. consume with canker, corrupt; (p.p.) soured, malignant.

cănn′a, n. bright-flowered ornamental-leaved plant.

cănn′el, n. hard bright-flamed coal rich in oil and gas.

cănn′ibal, n. man or animal that feeds on his own species; (attrib.) having this habit. ~**ism**, n.; ~**istic**, a.

cănn′ikin, n. small can.

cănn′on¹, n. (billiards) hitting of two balls successively by player's ball. v.i. make cannon; (of person or thing) come into collision without stopping.

cănn′on², n. mounted gun throwing projectile larger than bullet. ~**ball**, round shot. **cănnonāde′**, n. continuous gunfire; v.i. & t. fire continuously, bombard.

cannot. See can².

cănn′y, a. shrewd, quiet, circumspect. ca′ ~, v.i. go gently; n. practice or policy of limiting output of labour.

canoe′ (-nōō), n. light boat propelled with paddles. v.i. (-oeing), go in canoe. ~**ist**, n.

căn′on, n. Church decree; criterion; list of Bible books accepted by the Church; member of cathedral chapter.

cañon. See canyon.

canŏn′ical, a. appointed by canon law; authoritative or accepted. n.pl. clergy's appointed costume.

căn′onīze, v.t. admit to calendar of saints. ~**zation**, n.

căn′onry, n. office of canon.

căn′opy, n. covering hung or held up over throne, bed, person, &c.; a roof-like projection; (fig.) sky or overhanging shelter. v.t. supply or be a canopy to.

canō′rous, a. melodious.

cănt¹, n. bevel, slanting surface; tilted position; oblique push or jerk. v.t. & i. push or jerk or hold out of level; be in tilted position.

cănt², n. temporary catchwords; insincere pious or moral talk. v.i. use cant.

can′t. See can².

căn′taloup (-ōōp), n. small melon.

căntănk′erous, a. cross-grained, quarrelsome.

cănta′ta (-ah-), n. choral work like oratorio but usu. shorter.

canteen′, n. camp or barrack shop for liquor, provisions, &c.; refreshment-room in works, &c.; soldier's mess-tin or water-bottle; chest fitted with cooking or table utensils.

căn′ter, n. easy gallop. v.i. & t. go, make go, at a canter.

căn′terbury, n. stand for portfolios, music, &c.

Căn′terbury běll, n. kinds of campanula.

cănthă′ridēs (-z), n.pl. (Med.) dried Spanish Fly.

căn′ticle, n. a divine song.

căn′tilever, n. bracket projecting from wall to support balcony, &c. ~ **bridge**, bridge in which great cantilevers run out from the piers.

căn′tle, n. slice cut off; hind bow of saddle.

căn′tō, n. (pl. -os), division of poem.

canton, n. (kăn′ton or kăntŏn′) any state of the Swiss Confederation. v.t. (kăntōōn′) put (troops) in quarters. **canton′ment** (ōōn-), n. lodgings of troops; (in India) permanent military station.

cantō′rial, a. of the precentor's or north side of the choir.

Canŭck′, n. (sl.) French-Canadian; *Canadian (horse).

căn′vas, n. coarse cloth of hemp or flax; a picture. *~**back**, species of wild duck.

căn′vass, v.t. & i. discuss, ask votes of. n. canvassing for votes.

canyon, cañon (kăn′yon), n. deep gorge.

caoutchouc (kowch'ōŏk), *n.* unvulcanized rubber.

cap, *n.* soft brimless outdoor headdress: indoor head-dress; caplike covering. *v.t.* confer degree on; (Sport) select for representative team; crown; take off or touch one's cap to.

cā'pable, *a.* able, competent; susceptible of. **~bility**, *n.*

capā'cious (-shus), *a.* roomy, of large content.

capā'citāte, *v.t.* make capable.

capā'city, *n.* cubic content; mental power; function or character.

cap-a-pie' (-pē), *a.* from head to foot.

capā'rison, *n.* harness, trappings. *v.t.* put caparison upon.

cāpe[1], *n.* short sleeveless cloak.

cāpe[2], *n.* headland, promontory. the C~, Cape of Good Hope, also =Cape Province. Cape boy, ~coloured people, S. African(s) of mixed black and white descent. Cape cart (S.-Afr.), hooded cart usu. drawn by oxen.

cā'per[1], *n.* a shrub; (pl.) its buds pickled. **~sauce**, *n.*

cā'per[2], *n.* frisky jump; lark, spree. *v.i.* cut capers.

căpercail'yé, **~lzie**, *n.* largest bird of grouse kind.

cap'ful (-ōŏl), *n.* (pl. -ls), enough to fill a cap.

căpillā'rity, *n.* degree of capillary attraction or repulsion.

capill'ary, *a.* of the hair; of hairlike fineness. *n.* capillary tube, minute blood-vessel.

cap'ital, *a.* of chief importance, principal, leading, first-class, excellent; fatal, vital; punishable with death. *n.* capital city; capital letter; head or cornice of a pillar; stock with which company, &c. starts; accumulated wealth. ~levy, confiscation of a proportion of all capital.

cap'italism, *n.* organization of production by capitalists. **~istic**, *a.*

cap'italist, *n.* person who uses or possesses capital; a rich man.

cap'italize, *v.t.* use as capital;

compute or realize present value of; print in capitals. **~zation.** *n.*

capitā'tion, *n.* reckoning by the head (usu. used attrib).

Cap'itol, *n.* temple of Jupiter in Rome; *Congress house; *State house.

capit'ular, *a.* of a cathedral chapter.

capit'ulāte, *v.i.* surrender on terms.

capitulā'tion, *n.* summary of headings; terms of agreement; surrender on terms; *the Capitulations*, agreements securing privileged legal status to foreigners in Turkey, &c.

cā'pon, *n.* castrated cock.

căp'oral (-ahl), *n.* a French tobacco.

capôt', *n.* taking of all tricks in piquet. *v.t.* beat by capot.

caprice' (-ēs), *n.* unaccountable change of mind or conduct; freakish fancy. **capri'cious** (-shus), *a.* liable to caprice.

Cap'ricŏrn, *n.* the goat in the zodiac. tropic of ~, southern tropic.

cap'riole, *n.* trained horse's high leap and kick. *v.i.* do this.

cap'sicum, *n.* kinds of plant with hot capsules; the red pepper made from them.

capsize', *v.t. & i.* overturn (of boat).

cap'stan, *n.* a revolving barrel for winding cable in, &c.

cap'sūle, *n.* enclosing membrane; plant's seed-case; gelatine case for taking physic in.

cap'tain (-tin), *n.* chief, leader; naval or military officer; master of merchant ship; leader of side in games.

cap'taincy (-tin-), *n.* position of captain.

cap'tion, *n.* a heading, headline.

cap'tious (-shus), *a.* given to carping, quibbling.

cap'tivāte, *v.t.* (-vable), fascinate by one's beauty or other attraction. **~tion**, *n.*

cap'tive, *a.* taken prisoner; in confinement; unable to escape. *n.* captive person or animal. **captiv'ity**, *n.*

căp'tor, ~trĕss, nn. taker, female taker, of captive.

căp'ture, n. seizing of person, &c. as captive; taking of fortress, &c. v.t. make capture of.

Căp'ŭchin, n. Member of order of Franciscan friars (after 1528).

căr, n. chariot or other wheeled vehicle; motor-car, tram-car; *railway carriage; pendant of air-ship or balloon.

cărabineer', n. horse-soldier armed with a carbine.

că'racōle, n. trained horse's half turn to right or left. v.i. perform caracole.

că'racul (-ōol), n. kind of astrakhan.

carafe' (-ahf), n. table water-bottle.

că'ramĕl, n. burnt sugar for colouring spirit, &c.; a sweetmeat.

că-rapāce, n. tortoise's and crustaceans' upper shell.

că'rat, n. unit of weight for gems and of fineness for gold.

căravăn', n. company travelling together for safety in the East, &c.; house on wheels.

căravăn'serai (- rī), n. Eastern inn with inner court for caravans.

că'ravel, cărv'el, n. kinds of light ship.

că'raway (-a-w-), n. plant with small fruit (~-seeds) used in cakes.

cärb'ide, n. compound of carbon with an element.

cärb'ine, n. short rifle.

cärbohy'drate, n. kinds of compound of carbon with hydrogen and oxygen.

cärbŏl'ic ā'cid, n. a disinfectant and antiseptic. **cärb'olīze,** v.t. treat with this.

cärb'on, n. a non-metallic element found as diamond, graphite, and charcoal, and in compounds; charcoal pencil used in electric lighting. **~-paper,** thin paper laid with carbon for taking copies of letters, &c. **cärbonā'ceous (-shŭs),** a. containing carbon.

cärbonā'ri (-rē), n.pl. members of Italian secret republican society.

cärb'onate, n. salt of carbonic acid.

cärbŏn'ic, a. of carbon. **~ acid,** n. gas formed in combustion of carbon.

cärbonif'erous, a. coal-producing.

cärb'onīze, v.t. (-zable), convert into carbon. **~zation,** n.

cärbor'un'dum, n. compound of carbon and silicon used in polishing. **P.**

cärb'oy, n. bottle of strong glass protected by wicker.

cärb'uncle, n. garnet cut in boss shape; inflamed skin-tumour. **cärbŭn'cular,** ~cled, aa.

cärb'ürĕt, v.t. combine (element) with carbon; charge with carbon. **cärbürĕt'tor,** ~ter, n. apparatus mixing air with petrol vapour for combustion in motor engines, &c.

cär'cass, n. dead body of beast or (contempt.) person; framework or skeleton or worthless remains.

cärd¹, n. toothed instrument or wire brush. v.t. treat with card. comb.

cärd², n. thick paper or pasteboard; ticket of admission, invitation, label, &c.; one of the 52 pieces making up a pack; (pl.) card-playing; (sl.) a queer character. **~board,** pasteboard for making boxes, &c. **~-case,** receptacle for one's visiting cards. **~ index,** index with each item on separate card. **~-sharper,** swindler at card-games.

cärd'amom, n. an E.-Ind. spice.

cärd'iac, a. of the heart. n. heart-stimulant.

cärd'igan, n. warm sleeved overwaistcoat.

cärd'inal, a. fundamental, central; of deep scarlet. n. a prince of R.C. Church; cardinal colour or number; *scarlet grosbeak. **~ numbers,** one, two, &c.

căre, n. anxiety, concern; task, thing to be seen to; serious attention. v.i. & t. feel concern or interest.

careen', v.t. & i. turn (ship) on one side for repair; heel over.

career', n. spell of rapid progression; course through life. v.i. go swiftly or wildly.

care′ful (-ārf-), a. painstaking, watchful, cautious, solicitous.

care′less (-ārl-), a. unconcerned, thoughtless, negligent, inaccurate.

caress′, n. fondling touch, kiss. v.t. bestow caress on.

că′ret, n. omission-mark (∧).

căre′-tā′ker, n. person left in charge of house, &c.

căre′wŏrn, a. showing effects of anxiety.

cărg′ō, n. (pl. -oes), ship's freight.

Că′rĭb, n. aboriginal native of some W.-Ind. islands; their language.

caribou′ (-boō), n. N.-Amer. reindeer.

căricature′, n. grotesque representation of person, &c. v.t. make or give caricature of. ~rist, n.

căr′ĭes (-z), n. decay of tooth or bone.

că′rillon (-lyon), n. chime of bells; air played on bells.

căr′ious, a. affected with caries.

cărk′ĭng, a. burdensome.

căr′man (-an), n. van-driver.

Cărm′elite, n. a white friar.

cărm′ine, n. vivid crimson pigment and colour.

cărn′age, n. great slaughter.

căr′nal, a. fleshly, sexual, worldly. ~ism, ~ăl′ity, nn.; ~ize, v.t.

cărnā′tion, n. rosy-pink colour; clove-pink, a. of rosy pink.

cărn′ĭval, n. festive days preceding Lent; riotous revelry.

carnĭv′ora, n.pl. the carnivorous order of mammals.

cărn′ĭvŏre, n. one of the carnivora.

carnĭv′orous, a. flesh-eating.

că′rŏl, n. joyous song, warbling, Christmas hymn. v.i. utter carol.

*căr′om, n. cannon at billiards.

carŏt′ĭd, n. & a. either of two main arteries serving the head.

carouse′ (-z), n. drinking-bout, drunken revelry. v.i. hold carouse.

cărp[1], n. a pond fish.

cărp[2], v.i. take exceptions, indulge in fault-finding.

cărp′al, a. of the carpus.

cărp′el, n. pistil or pistil-cell.

cărp′enter, n. artificer in woodwork. v.i. & t. do carpenter's work. ~try, n. such work.

cărp′et, n. textile fabric for covering floor; expanse of grass, &c. v.t. cover with carpet. ~bag, travelling bag. ~bagger, adventurer, itinerant politician.

cărp′us, n. (pl. -pī), the small bones connecting hand and forearm, wrist, horse's knee, &c.

că′rriage (-rĭj), n. conveying of goods, &c., cost of this; manner of carrying oneself; wheeled vehicle.

că′rrier, n. person conveying parcels for hire; part of bicycle, &c. for carrying luggage, &c.; person or animal conveying germs of disease. ~ wave, tone-modulated high-frequency oscillations from a wireless transmitter.

că′rriole, n. small open carriage.

că′rrion, n. dead flesh; garbage.

cărronāde′, n. kind of ship's gun.

că′rrot, n. an edible root; (pl., sl.) red hair, red-haired person. că′rroty, a. (sl.) red-haired; red.

că′rry, v.t. & i. (-iable), convey, transport, bear, support; have about the person ready for use. ~on, go on; flirt. n. (Mil.) the position of carrying sword; (Golf) ball's flight before pitching; portage between rivers, &c.

cărt, n. strong two-wheeled vehicle for heavy work. v.t. & i. carry in cart, use cart. ~horse, horse of heavy build. ~wright, maker of carts. cărt′age, n. carting or its cost. cărt′er, n. driver of cart. cărt′ful (-ŏŏl), n. (pl. -ls).

cărte, n. a bill of fare.

‖ carte blanche (kărt blahńsh), authorization to do what one will. ‖ carte-de-visite (vĭzēt′), photograph 3¼ in. by 2¼.

cărtel, k-, n. written challenge to duel; agreement for exchange of prisoners; manufacturers' union.

Cărthu′sian (-zhn), n. (pl.) order of monks; (sing.) member of it or of the Charterhouse or of Charterhouse School.

cărt′ilage, n. firm elastic structure

<hr />

māte, mēte, mīte, mōte, mūte, moōt ; răck, rĕck, rĭck, rŏck, rŭck, rōōk ;

in vertebrates. **cartila'ginous,** *a.* of or like cartilage, gristly.

cartog'raphy, *n.* map-drawing. **~pher,** *n.* worker in cartography.

cart'omancy, *n.* divination by playing-cards.

cart'on, *n.* inner bull's-eye on targets; cardboard box, cardboard.

cartoon', *n.* design-sketch on stout paper; humorous topical illustration. *v.t.* draw cartoon of. **~ist,** *n.*

cartouche' (-ōōsh), *n.* scroll ornament; oval ring enclosing name and title of Egyptian king.

cart'ridge, *n.* charge of explosive made up in case. **~paper,** thick and rough paper for drawing and large envelopes.

ca'runcle, *n.* fleshy lump.

carve, *v.t. & i.* cut up (meat) at or for the table; cut figures or patterns in wood, &c.

carvel. See caravel.

carv'er, *n.* one who carves; (pl.) carving knife and fork.

carv'ing, *n.* carved wood, &c. **~fork,** **~knife,** implements for meat-carving.

caryat'id, *n.* female figure as pillar.

cascade', *n.* small or artificial waterfall; wavy fall of lace, &c.

case[1], *n.* instance of thing's occurring; hypothetical or actual situation; plight or condition; (Law) suit or cause; (relation expressed by) inflexion of nouns.

case[2], *n.* box, cabinet, crate, bag, or sheath designed to hold something. *v.t.* (-sable), enclose in case. **~bottle,** square bottle to fit in case with others. **~harden,** *v.t.* harden surface of; (fig.) render callous. **~knife,** large knife kept in sheath. **~shot,** bullets in tin box fired from gun.

ca'sein, *n.* protein in cheese.

case'mate (-sm-), *n.* embrasured room in wall of fortress.

case'ment (-zm-, -sm-), *n.* hinged window or part of window.

cash[1], *n.* money in the form of coin or bank-notes. *v.t.* give or obtain cash for (cheque, &c.). **~ in,** settle accounts; die.

cash[2], *n.* (pl. same), one of various

coins of low value in the East Indies and China.

cash'ew (-ōō), *n.* W.-Ind. tree bearing cashew-nut.

cashier'[1], *n.* person in charge of cash in bank or office.

cashier'[2], *v.t.* dismiss from service.

cash'mere, *n.* soft fabric of Cashmere goat's wool.

ca'sing, *n.* enclosing material.

casi'no (-ē-), *n.* (pl. -os), public hall for gambling, dancing, &c.

cask (-ah-), *n.* vessel for holding liquor, a barrel.

cas'ket (-ah-), *n.* small box for holding valuables.

casque (-k), *n.* (arch.) helmet.

cassa'tion, *n.* act of annulling.

cassa'va (-sah-), *n.* W.-Ind. plant; its starch or flour.

cass'erole, *n.* vessel in which food is both cooked and served.

cā'ssia (-sha), *n.* kind of cinnamon.

cass'ock, *n.* long close tunic worn by some clergymen.

cass'owary (-o-w-), *n.* kinds of large bird related to ostrich.

cast[1] (-ah-), *v.t. & i.* throw, fling, drop; give or get decision against; (of animals) slough or shed or lose; (of dam) drop prematurely; give vote; add up; shape in mould; assign part to.

cast[2] (-ah-), *n.* throw of missile, dice, net, lead, fishing-line, &c.; mould for casting, thing cast in it; forme or type; slight squint.

cas'tanet, *n.* dancer's chinking-instrument.

cast'away (-ah-), *n.* shipwrecked person; reprobate.

caste (-ah-), *n.* any of the E.-Ind. hereditary classes with members shunning intercourse with other castes; exclusive class elsewhere.

cas'tellan, *n.* castle-warden.

cas'tellated, *a.* built like castle, with battlements, &c.

cas'tigate, *v.t.* (-gable), punish, chastise. **~tion,** **~tor,** *nn.*

Castile (-ēl) **soap,** *n.* hard, usu. mottled kind.

cast'ing-vote (-ah-), *n.* vote to decide an equal division.

cast iron (cahst īrn), *n.* iron shaped

by casting. **cast′-iron′**, *a.* of cast iron ; of extreme rigidity.

castle (kah′sl), *n.* building designed to serve both as residence and fortress ; (Chess) piece with battlemented top, rook.

cas′tor¹ (-ah-), *n.* substance from beaver used in medicine and perfumery ; (sl.) hat.

cas′tor² (-ah-), *n.* condiment-holder, (pl.) cruet-stand ; small swivelled wheel of table-leg, &c.

cas′tor oil (-ah-), *n.* purgative and lubricant vegetable oil.

cās′trāte′, *v.t.* (-*table*), remove testicles of, geld. **~tion,** *n.*

cā′sual (-zhōō-, -zū-), *a.* due to chance ; not permanent. *n.* casual labourer ; one in receipt of occasional poor-relief.

cā′sualty (-zhōo-, -zū-), *n.* mishap ; (pl.) losses in battle, &c.

cā′suist (-zhōō-, -zū-), *n.* person who examines special cases as affected by conflicting moral rules ; sophist, quibbler. **~ic(al),** *aa.* ; **~ry,** *n.*

‖ **cā′sus běll′ī,** *n.* act justifying war.

cǎt, *n.* small feline quadruped ; any feline animal ; spiteful woman, scratching child ; cat-o′-nine-tails ; tapered wood used in tip-cat. **~call,** shrill whistle. **~fish,** kinds of fish. **~ice,** unsound, bubbly ice. **~o′-nine-tails,** 9-lashed rope whip for flogging. **cat′s-cradle,** child′s game. **~′s-eye,** a precious stone. **~′s-meat,** horseflesh prepared for cats. **~′s-paw,** person used as tool by another ; slight breeze rippling the water.

cǎtachrē′sis (-k-), *n.* misapplication of words.

cǎt′aclysm, *n.* deluge, political or social upheaval. **~clȳs′mic,** *a.*

cǎt′acōmb (-m), *n.* subterranean gallery with recesses for tombs.

cǎt′afǎlque (-k), *n.* stage for display of coffin at funeral.

cǎtalěc′tic, *a.* a syllable short.

cǎt′alĕpsy, *n.* disease with recurrent trances. **cǎtalěp′tic,** *a.* & *n.* (person) having catalepsy.

cǎt′alŏgue (-g), *n.* complete list, usu. in alphabetical or other systematic order. *v.t.* make catalogue of. ‖ **~raisonné** (-zonä′), descriptive catalogue arranged in subjects, &c.

catǎl′ysis, *n.* effect of substance that produces chemical change without itself changing. **~ȳst,** *n.* **~ȳt′ic,** *a.*

cǎtamarǎn′, *n.* raft of yoked logs or boats ; cross-grained woman.

cǎt′apǔlt, *n.* ancient engine for hurling stones or darts ; boy′s shooting contrivance.

cǎt′aract, *n.* waterfall ; downpour ; opacity of crystal lens of eye producing partial blindness.

catǎrrh′ (-ār), *n.* inflammation of a mucous membrane ; cold in the head ; catǎr′rhal (-ral), *a.*

catǎs′trophe, *n.* dénouement of drama ; subversive event ; great disaster. **catǎstrŏph′ic,** *a.*

cǎtch, *v.t.* & *i.* (*caught,* pr. kawt), capture, lay hold of, seize ; hold ; overtake ; receive infection ; become entangled ; apprehend. *n.* act of catching ; thing or person caught or worth catching ; question designed to trick ; (Crick.) chance or act of catching ; musical round. **~ing,** *a.* highly infectious ; (of melody, &c.) attractive. **~ment,** *n.* basin from which rainfall flows into river. **~penny,** *a.* intended merely to sell, claptrap. **~pōle,** *n.* sheriff′s officer. **~word,** *n.* influential temporary phrase in politics, &c. **~y,** *a.* (of tune) easily caught up.

cāte, *n.* (arch.) a dainty.

cǎtéchĕt′ical (-k-), *a.* teaching orally ; proceeding by question and answer ; of the Catechism.

cǎt′echism (-k-), *n.* piece of catechizing ; form of instruction drawn up by way of question and answer. **cǎt′echist** (-k-), *n.* one who catechizes.

cǎt′echize (-k-), *v.t.* (-*zable*), instruct by question and answer ; put questions to.

cǎt′echu (-tshōō), *n.* astringent

substances with much tannin from bark, wood, or fruits, of Eastern plants.

căt′échu′mĕn (-k-), *n.* convert under instruction before baptism.

cătégŏ′rĭcal, *a.* (of statements) unconditional, absolute, explicit.

căt′egorў, *n.* a class, rank, or order of ideas or things.

caté′na, *n.* connected series.

caté′narў, *n.* curve formed by a hanging chain.

ca′ter, *v.i.* purvey food; provide amusement &c. for.

căt′eran, *n.* (Highland) marauder, fighting-man.

căt′erpĭllar, *n.* larva of butterfly or moth.

căt′erwaul, *v.i.* scream like cats.

căt′gŭt, *n.* twisted intestines of beasts used for fiddle-strings, &c.

cathăr′sĭs, *n.* (pl. *-ēs*) purgation; outlet to emotion afforded by drama.

cathăr′tĭc, *a.* purgative. *n.* such drug.

cathé′dral, *n.* principal church of diocese with bishop's throne.

Căth′erine-wheel, *n.* rotating firework; somersault turned sideways.

căth′eter, *n.* tube for passing into the bladder.

căth′olic, *a.* universal, all embracing, broad-minded; including all Christians, or all of the Roman Church. *n.* member of the Catholic Church, more esp. of the R.C. Church. **cathŏl′ĭcism**, *n.* adherence to the Catholic Church.

căthŏl′ĭcitў, *n.* comprehensiveness; accordance with Catholic Church doctrine. **cathŏl′ĭcīze**, *v.t.*

căt′kin, *n.* hanging flower of willow, hazel, &c.

căt′mĭnt, ***căt′nĭp**, *n.* aromatic plant.

catŏp′trĭc, *a.* of reflexion of light. **catŏp′trĭcs**, *n.*

catsup. See ketchup.

căt′tle, *n.* livestock, esp. oxen; (sl.) horses; contemptible people. **~plague**, rinderpest.

cauc′us, *n.* local committee for political party organization.

caud′al, *a.* of the tail.

caud′āte, *a.* tailed.

caud′le, *n.* warm spiced gruel.

caught, *p.t.* & *p.p.* of catch.

caul, *n.* membrane sometimes enclosing child's head at birth.

caul′dron, *n.* large boiling vessel.

caul′iflower (kŏl-), *n.* cabbage with large edible flower-head.

caulk (-awk), *v.t.* stop up seams of ship with oakum and pitch.

caus′al (-z-), *a.* of the nature of cause and effect.

causăl′itў (-z-), *n.* universal operation of cause and effect as a belief. **causā′tion** (-z-), *n.* causing, causality.

cause, *n.* what produces an effect; ground or reason or motive for action; justification; case of party to law-suit; side in a struggle, &c. *v.t.* (-*sable*), effect; occasion to do something. ‖ **cause** célèbre (kŏz sĕlĕ′br; pl. *-s -s*, pr. as sing.), law-suit that excites much interest.

cause′lĕss (-zl-), *a.* groundless, without justification.

causerie (kōzerē′), *n.* (pl. *-s*, pr. as sing.), newspaper or magazine article of informal kind.

cause′way (-zw-), **caus′ey** (-z-), *nn.* raised road across low or wet ground, raised footway.

caus′tic, *a.* that burns or corrodes; sarcastic, biting. *n.* a caustic substance. **causti′citў**, *n.*

caut′erīze, *v.t.* sear with caustic or cautery. **~zation**, *n.*

caut′erў, *n.* hot iron for surgical searing; such searing.

cau′tion, *n.* avoidance of rashness, attention to safety; warning; (sl.) strange person, staggering event. *v.t.* warn, admonish.

cau′tionarў (-sho-), *a.* of a warning kind.

cau′tious (-shus), *a.* disposed to or exhibiting caution.

căvalcāde′, *n.* company of riders.

căvalier′, *n.* horseman; gallant; lady's protector or escort; 17th c. royalist. *a.* brusque, discourteous.

căv'alrў, n. horse-soldiers.

|| **căvati'na** (-tē-), n. short simple song; smooth melodious air.

cāve[1], n. underground hollow, usu. with horizontal entrance. **~-dwellers**, prehistoric men living in caves. **~-man**, cavedweller. v.t. & i. hollow out. **~ in**, subside or give inwards; yield to pressure, submit.

cā'vē[2], int. (sch. sl.) look out! (as warning of approach of master, &c.).

cā'vĕat, n. (Leg.) process to suspend proceedings.

căv'endish, n. kinds of strong cake tobacco.

căv'ĕrn, n. cave. **~ed**, a.

căv'ĕrnŏus, a. full of caverns; huge or deep as a cavern.

căviăr(e)', n. pickled sturgeon-roe. **~ to the general**, good thing unappreciated by the ignorant.

căv'il, v.i. take exception at, find fault. n. frivolous objection.

căv'itў, n. a hollow place.

*"**cavŏrt'**, v.i. prance.

caw, n. cry of crows. v.i. utter caw.

cayenne (kăĕn'), n. red capsicum pepper.

caym'an, cai-. n. S.-Amer. reptile allied to crocodile.

cēanō'thus, n. a flowering shrub.

cease, v.i. & i. desist from; stop doing; come to an end.

cease'less (-sl-), a. incessant.

cēc'ils (-z), n.pl. kind of fried forcemeat balls.

cē'dar, n. tree with fragrant finegrained wood; its wood.

cēde, v.t. (-dable), transfer territory to; give up, yield.

cĕdill'a, n. mark written under c (ç) to show sibilance.

ceil'ing (sēl-), n. lining of plasterwork at top of a room.

cĕl'andine, n. kinds of yellow spring flower.

cĕlanēse', n. kind of artificial silk. P.

cĕl'ĕbrant, n. priest celebrating Mass or Eucharist.

cĕl'ĕbrāte, v.t. & i. (-brable), duly perform (rite, &c.); keep festival or commemorate event; publish abroad, extol; (p.p.) famous. **~tion**, **~tor**, nn.

cĕlĕb'ritў, n. fame; widely known person.

cĕl'ĕriăc, n. turnip-rooted celery.

cĕlĕr'itў, n. dispatch, swiftness in acting.

cĕl'erў, n. a salad vegetable.

cĕlĕs'tial, a. of the sky; of Heaven, divinely good or beautiful; Chinese. n. inhabitant of China.

cĕl'ibacў, n. unmarried state; **cĕl'ibate**, a. practising celibacy; n. such person.

cĕll, n. anchoret's one-roomed dwelling; small room; unit of voltaic battery; sac or cavity or interstice in natural structure.

cĕll'ar, n. underground room for storing wine, coal, &c. **~age**, n. cellar accommodation. **~er**, n. keeper of monastery's wine and food. **~ĕt'**, n. case, &c., for winebottles in dining-room.

*"**cĕllō** (ch-). See **violoncello**.

cĕll'ular, a. consisting of cells.

cĕll'ūle, n. cavity-cell or ceil of protoplasm; small cell.

cĕll'ūloid, n. hard elastic substance made chiefly of cellulose.

cĕll'ūlōse, n. substance forming framework of plants.

cĕlt[1], n. chisel-edged prehistoric tool.

Cĕlt[2], K-, (pl.) peoples speaking or having spoken languages akin to that of the Gauls; (sing.) member of such people. **~ic**, a. of the Celts; n. the Celtic language.

cĕmĕnt', n. substance of lime and clay, setting like stone; substitute for glue; binding agency. v.t. apply cement to; unite firmly.

cĕm'ĕterў, n. burial-ground other than churchyard.

cĕn'otaph (-ahf), n. monument to one whose remains are elsewhere.

cĕnse, v.t. adore or perfume with incense. **cĕn'ser**, n. incenseburning vessel.

cĕn'sor, n. official who examines plays, books, news, &c. to suppress what is immoral or seditious or inopportune; person assuming the right of judging others. v.t.

---

examine plays, &c. as censor. ~ship, n.

cen′sor′ial, ~ious, aa. given to judging others.

cen′sure (-sher), n. expression of disapproval or blame. v.t. (-rable), issue or utter censure.

cen′sus, n. official numbering of the population.

cent, n. a hundred as standard number; hundredth of a dollar.

cen′tal, n. 100 lb.

cen′taur (-tor), n. man-horse of mythology; a perfect horseman.

cen′taury, n. kinds of plant.

centenār′ian, n. one aged 100 or more.

centē′nary, a. centennial. n. hundredth anniversary.

centēnn′ial, a. of or having lasted 100 years. n. centenary.

centēs′imal, a. reckoning or reckoned by hundredths.

cen′tigrāde, a. having 100 degrees.

cen′tigramme, cen′tilitre (-ēter), ~mètre (-ter), nn. the hundredth part of a gramme, litre, metre.

|| **centime** (sahntēm′), n. French coin, 1/100 franc.

cen′tipēde, n. many-footed crawling wingless animal.

cen′tō, n. (pl. -os), work composed of quoted scraps.

cen′tral, a. relating to the centre; leading, principal. ~ăl′ity, n.

cen′tralism, ~ist, nn. belief, believer, in centralization.

cen′tralize, v.t. & i. (-izable), concentrate (administration) under one control, subject (State, &c.) to this system. ~zation, n.

cen′tre (-ter), n. middle point of anything; (Footb.) centre forward. a. at or of the centre. v.i. & t. (-tring, -trable), be concentrated; place in centre; find centre of. ~ forward, player in Association football.

cen′trebit, n. kind of boring-tool.

cen′treboard, n. (boat with) board that can be lowered to deepen keel.

cen′tric(al), aa. at or near the centre; from a centre.

centri′cĭty, n. relation to centre.

centrif′ūgal, a. flying or tending from a centre.

centrip′ĕtal, a. tending to a centre.

cen′tūple, a. hundredfold. **cĕntū′plicate,** v.t. make a hundredfold.

centūr′ion, n. captain of a century in Roman army.

cen′tūry, n. (Rom. hist.) company in army; 100 years; any set of 100. ~plant, American aloe.

cĕphăl′ic, a. of, in the head. ~index, ratio of width to length of skull.

cĕrăm′ic, a. of the art of pottery. ~s, cĕ′ramist, nn.

cĕrăs′tium, n. hoary-leaved herb.

Cĕrb′erus, n. three-headed dog guarding Hades.

cēre, n. naked waxlike membrane at base of some birds' beaks. ~cloth, waxed or other winding-sheet.

cōr′ĕal, a. of edible grain. n. (usu. pl.) kinds of edible grain; *breakfast dish of some cereal.

cĕrēbĕll′um, n. little or hinder brain.

cĕ′rēbral, a. of the brain.

cĕrēbrā′tion, n. working of the brain. **cĕrēbro-spī′nal,** a. of brain and spine.

cĕ′rēbrum, n. the brain proper.

cere′ment (sērm-), n. (usu. pl.) grave-clothes.

cĕrēmō′nial, a. with or of ceremony, formal. n. system of rites or ceremonies. ~ism, ~ist, nn.

cĕrēmō′nious, a. addicted to or showing addiction to ceremony.

cĕ′rēmony, n. religious rite, piece of formal procedure, polite observance; punctilious behaviour. ceriph. See serif.

ceri′se (-ēs), n. & a. light clear red.

cĕrt′ain (-tn), a. settled, unfailing; unerring; reliable; indisputable; some. ~ly, adv. I admit it, no doubt, yes. ~ty, n. undoubted fact, absolute conviction.

cĕrt′ĕs (-z), adv. assuredly.

certif′ĭcate, n. (-it), document formally attesting a fact. v.t. (-āt), furnish with certificate.

cĕrt′ĭfy, v.t. (-fiable), give certain information of, testify.

cĕrt′ĭtŭde, *n.* feeling certain.

cerul′ĕan (-ōō-), *a.* sky-blue.

ceruse′ (-ōōs), *n.* white lead.

cérvĭ′cal (*or* sĕrv′ĭ-), *a.* of the neck.

cĕss, *n.* a rate or tax.

cessā′tion, *n.* ceasing.

cĕ′ssion (-shn), *n.* ceding.

cĕss′pōol, *n.* well sunk to receive house-drainage.

cētā′cean (-shn), *a.* of the *Cetacea* or marine mammals. *n.* such animal. cētā′ceous (-shus), *a.*

cĕt′erăch (-k), *n.* kinds of fern.

cha (-aw, -ah), *n.* (Army sl.) Chinese name (*ch′a*) for tea.

Chablis (shăb′lē), *n.* a white wine.

chāfe, *v.t.* & *i.* (-fable), rub (skin, &c.) to restore warmth ; make or become sore by rubbing ; irritate or show irritation ; fret. *n.* sore ; heated state.

chā′fer, *n.* kinds of beetle.

chaff (-ahf), *n.* separated grain-husks ; chopped hay and straw, worthless stuff ; light irony or banter. *v.t.* banter, tease with irony.

chăff′er, *v.i.* bargain, haggle. *n.* chaffering. ~er, *n.*

chăff′inch, *n.* commonest finch.

chagrin (shagrēn′), *n.* acute disappointment. *v.t.* mortify, vex.

chain, *n.* series of links ; set of facts linked together ; (pl. or sing.) fetters, binding influence ; measuring-line, its length (66 ft.). *v.t.* secure with a chain. ~-armour, armour of interlaced rings. ~ bridge, suspension bridge. ~-gang, convicts chained together at work, &c. ~-mail, chain-armour. ~-smoker, one who lights cigarette, &c. from stump of last one smoked. ~-stores, shops belonging to one firm.

chair, *n.* seat for one, usu. movable ; seat of authority, professorship, mayoralty ; chairman ; a sedan. *v.t.* install in chair ; carry aloft in chair. ~man, person who presides over meeting, Board, or Committee. ~woman, woman chairman.

chaise (shāz), *n.* pleasure or travelling carriage.

chălcĕd′onŷ (k-), *n.* precious stones of quartz kind.

chald′ron (-awl-), *n.* coal measure, 36 bushels.

chalet (shăl′ā), *n.* Swiss wooden cottage ; street lavatory.

chăl′ice, *n.* goblet (poet.) ; Eucharist-cup.

chalk (-awk), *n.* white soft limestone ; coloured substance used in crayons. *v.t.* rub, draw, or write with chalk. chalk′ŷ (-awk-), *a.*

chăll′enge (-j), *n.* calling to account ; invitation to a contest. *v.t.* (-geable), call to account ; take exception to ; dispute statement ; claim attention ; invite to a contest.

chalŷb′eate (ka-), *a.* impregnated with iron (of water).

chā′mber, *n.* bedroom or other room ; (pl.) set of rooms ; deliberative body ; house of parliament or its debating-room ; cavity in machinery, revolver, &c.

chā′mberlain (-lin), *n.* officer managing royal or princely household, treasurer of corporation, &c.

chā′mbermaid, *n.* inn housemaid.

chamē′léon (ka-), *n.* lizard noted for changing colour.

chăm′fer, *n.* groove cut in a surface ; bevel on an edge. *v.t.* make chamfer(s) on.

chamois, *n.* 1 (shăm′wah). small European mountain antelope. 2 (shăm′), soft leather from sheep, goats, &c.

chămp, *v.t.* & *i.* munch (fodder) or mouth (bit) noisily. *n.* sound of champing.

champagne (shămpān′), *n.* kinds of sparkling wine.

chăm′paign (-ān), *n.* open country.

chăm′pertŷ, *n.* offence of assisting in a suit with a view to sharing the proceeds. ~tous, *a.*

chăm′pion, *n.* person who fights for others ; athlete, beast, &c. that has defeated all competitors. *a.* (vulg.) first-class, prime. *v.t.* maintain the cause of. ~ship, *n.* position of having defeated all rivals in some sport.

champlevé (shămp'levā), or ~**enamel**, *n.* enamel in which the colours are filled into hollows made in the surface.

chance (-ahns), *n.* way things fall out, probability or prospect of any occurrence; a possible catch at cricket; *(dial.) number, quantity. a. fortuitous. v.i. & t. befall, happen; risk, leave to fate.

chan'cel (-ah-), *n.* railed-off eastern part of church.

chan'cellery (-ah-), *n.* chancellor's department or staff or offices; office attached to an embassy.

chan'cellor (-ah-), *n.* kinds of State or law official; titular head of a university.

Chan'cery (-ah-), *n.* division of the High Court of Justice.

chan'cy (-ah-), *a.* risky.

chändelier' (sh-), *n.* branched hanging support for lights.

chand'ler (-ah-), *n.* dealer in candles, oil, &c. ~**y**, *n.*

change (-j), *n.* variation, alteration; substitution of one for another; money in small coins; (pl.) different orders in which peal of bells can be rung. v.i. & t. make or become different, alter; interchange or exchange; give or get money change. **change'able** (-ja-), a. inconstant, given to change. ~**ability**, ~**ful**, ~**less**, *aa.*

change'ling (-jl-), *n.* elf-child; child substituted for another.

‖ **chänk**, *n.* a large kind of shell used by the Hindus for offering libations, &c.

chänn'el, *n.* bed in which water runs; passage for liquid; groove or flute; medium or agency; narrow piece of water connecting two seas. *v.t.* form channel(s) in; groove.

chant (-ah-), *n.* song; melody for psalms; droning music, singsong talk. *v.i. & t.* sing; intone, sing to a chant.

chan'ter (-ah-), *n.* melody-pipe of bagpipe.

chan'ticleer (-ah-), *n.* domestic cock.

chan'tress (-ah-), *n.* female singer.

chan'try (-ah-), *n.* endowment for singing of masses; its chapel or priests.

chan'ty (-ah-), **shăn'ty**, *n.* sailors' heaving-chorus.

chä'os (k-), *n.* formless welter of matter conceived as preceding creation; utter confusion. **chäŏt'ic**, *a.* utterly without order.

chăp[1], *n.* (sl.) fellow; boy.

chăp[2], *n.* (pl., also **chops**) jaws, cheeks; (usu. pl.) crack(s) in skin, &c. *v.i. & t.* develop chaps; cause to chap. ~**fallen**, or **chop-fallen**, *a.* dejected.

chăpp'y, *a.* chapped.

chaparajos (chapparah'hōs), **chăps** (or sh-), *n.* cowboy's leather or sheepskin leggings.

chăparrăl', n. (thicket of) dwarf evergreen oak.

chăp'-book, *n.* cheap book of tales, ballads, tracts, &c.

chăp'el, *n.* place of worship attached to institution or private house; oratory with altar in church; Nonconformist place of worship.

chăp'erŏn (sh-), *n.* lady in charge of girl on social occasions. *v.t.* act as chaperon to. ~**age**, *n.*

chăp'lain (-lĭn), *n.* clergyman of institution, private chapel, ship, regiment, &c. ~**cy**, *n.*

chăp'lêt, *n.* wreath or circlet for head; string of beads; rosary.

chăp'man, *n.* hawker, pedlar.

chăp'ter, *n.* division of a book; canons of cathedral or collegiate church, or members of monastic or knightly order; meeting of these. ~**house**, room in which chapter meets.

chär[1], *v.i.*, see **chare**. **char'woman**, *n.* woman hired by the day or hour for house-work.

chär[2], *n.* fish of trout kind.

chär[3], *v.t. & i.* burn to charcoal; scorch or blacken with fire.

char-à-banc (shă'rabăng) (pl. *chars-à-bancs*) or **charabanc** (pl. *charabancs*), *n.* long vehicle with seats looking forward.

cha'racter (kărĭk-), *n.* distinctive mark; a letter, sign; mental or moral nature, reputation; testimonial of qualities; actor's part; person in novel, play, &c.

characteris'tic (k-), *a.* distinguishing, in character. *n.* such trait or mark or quality.

chă'racterize (k-), *v.t.* (-*zable*), describe character of; impart character to. ~**zation**, *n.*

charade (sharahd'), *n.* game of guessing word from acted clue.

char'coal, *n.* residue of burnt wood, &c.; form of carbon.

chāre, chăr, *n.* (usu. in pl.) odd job(s) of house-work. *v.i.* (-*ared, -aring*) **work by the day at house-cleaning.**

charge, *n.* filling of explosive or electricity or the like; (Herald.) device, bearing; expense, price demanded; task, duty, or commission; exhortation; trust, custody; thing or person entrusted; accusation; impetuous attack. *v.t. & i.* supply with charge of explosive, &c.; entrust with task; solemnly urge; accuse; demand as price of, enter cost to; attack at a gallop or run. ***~account**, running account at shop, &c.

charge'able (-ja-), *a.* subject to charge or expense; accusable.

‖ **chargé d'affaires** (shärzh'ā dafār'), *n.* (pl. -*gés*, pr. as sing.), deputy ambassador, ambassador at minor court.

chăr'ger, *n.* military officer's horse; a large flat dish.

chă'riot, *n.* stately vehicle; car used in ancient fighting.

chărioteer', *n.* chariot-driver.

chă'ritable, *a.* kind in giving alms; lenient in judging others.

chă'rity, *n.* Christian good feeling; kindness; lenience in judging others; almsgiving; institution for helping the helpless (often used attrib.).

chăr'ivari (sh-), *n.* hurly-burly.

chăr'latan (sh-), *n.* impostor pretending to knowledge or skill. ~**ism**, ~**ry**, *nn.*

Chăr'leston, *n.* and *v.i.* dance with side-kicks from the knee.

chăr'lock, *n.* field mustard.

chăr'lotte (sh-), *n.* pudding of cooked fruit under bread-crumbs.

charm, *n.* word(s) or act(s) or object having occult power; attractiveness or power of giving delight; trinket resembling amulet. *v.t.* subject to a spell, bewitch, protect by magic; captivate, delight. ~**er**, *n.* (esp., joc.) beautiful woman.

charm'euse (sh-, -ĕrz), *n.* soft smooth silk fabric.

chăr'nel-house, *n.* place containing corpses or bones.

‖ **chăr'poy**, *n.* (Anglo-Ind.) light Indian bedstead.

chart, *n.* navigator's sea map; sheet of tabulated or diagrammatic information. *v.t.* make chart of.

chart'er, *n.* written grant of rights by sovereign or legislature; privilege or admitted right. *v.t.* grant charter to; hire ship by charter-party; hire vehicle, &c. ~**party**, indenture between ship-owner and merchant.

chart'ered (-ĕrd), *a.* granted or protected by charter; privileged.

chart'ism, ~**ist**, *nn.* principles, adherent, of the People's Charter movement of 1837–48.

chartreuse (shärtrĕrz'), *n.* kinds of liqueur.

chă'ry, *a.* cautious; sparing of praise, &c.

chāse¹, *v.t.* (-*sable*), emboss or engrave metal.

chāse², *v.t.* (-*sable*), try to overtake, pursue; *~ *oneself*, (sl.) go away. *n.* hunting; the attempt to catch anything by pursuit; unenclosed park-land. **chā'ser**, *n.* pursuer; gun in bow or stern for use during chase; (sl.) water or beer drunk after spirit; horse for steeple-chasing.

chāse³, *n.* frame for pages of type.

chasm (kă'zm), *n.* deep cleft, gulf, fissure; wide difference.

chassis (shăs'ē), *n.* (pl. same), base-frame of carriage, motor-car, &c.

chāste, *a.* pure, virtuous, modest; pure in taste or style, unadorned, ~ness, *n.* purity, chastity.

chā'sten (-sn), *v.t.* discipline by pain, punish; refine, temper.

chāstīse' (-z), *v.t.* punish, beat. ~ment, *n.* punishment.

chās'tĭty, *n.* chasteness.

chās'ūblė (-z-), *n.* sleeveless mantle as celebrant's vestment.

chăt, *v.i.* exchange views and news. *n.* such talk; stone-chat or whin-chat or warbler.

château (shăt'ō), *n.* (pl. -x, pr. -z), French country-house.

chăt'elaine (sh-), *n.* appendage to woman's belt for carrying keys, &c.; mistress of household.

chăt'tel, *n.* (usu. in pl.), movable possessions.

chăt'ter, *v.i. & t.* talk fast, incessantly, trivially, or indiscreetly; (of teeth) rattle together. *n.* chattering. ~box, *n.* child given to chatter. **chătt'ÿ¹**, *a.* talkative, fond of chat.

|| **chăt'tÿ²**, *n.* (Anglo-Ind.) an E.-Ind. pot for water.

chauffeur (shō'fer), *n.* motor-car driver.

chaulmoo'gra oil, *n.* vegetable fat used in treatment of leprosy.

chauv'ĭnĭsm (shŏv-), *n.* bellicose patriotism. ~ist, *n.*; ~istic, *a.*

chaw, *v.t.* chew (vulg.); *~ up*, utterly defeat. ~~bacon, (sl.) bumpkin.

cheap, *a.* inexpensive; easily got; of little account. *~ Jack*, travelling hawker.

cheap'en, *v.t. & i.* haggle, beat down the price of.

cheat, *v.t. & i.* trick, defraud; get by fraud. *n.* a deception; swindler; unfair player.

chĕck, *int.* announcing check at chess. *n.* exposure of king at chess involving loss of game unless he can be extricated; sudden arrest of motion, stoppage; rebuff; slight military reverse; restraint; means of checking accuracy; *receipt or registration ticket; *cheque; crosslined pattern. *v.t. & i.* (Chess) subject

(opponent or his king) to check; arrest motion of, restrain; test accuracy of; find fault with, rebuke; *give in return for receipt; *dispatch as registered or booked.

chĕcked (-kt), *a.* of check pattern.

*chĕck'ers, *n.* game of draughts.

chĕck'māte, *n.* inextricable check at chess; final defeat in any enterprise. *v.t.* defeat at chess; discomfit or frustrate.

chĕdd'ar, *n.* kind of cheese.

cheek, *n.* side of face below the eye; (colloq.) saucy speech, effrontery; (pl.) jaws of vice, twin pieces in machines. **cheek'ÿ**, *a.* (colloq.) impudent.

cheep, *v.i. & n.* (make) chick's shrill note. ~er, *n.* young bird.

cheer, *n.* frame of mind; food, fare; shout of applause. *v.t. & i.* comfort, gladden; urge on; applaud. ~ful, *a.* in good spirits. ~less, *a.* gloomy, dreary. ~ly, *adv.* with a will. ~y, *a.* lively and genial. **cheerĭō**, (sl.) *int.* of encouragement.

cheese (-z), *n.* food made by pressing curds, cake or ball of this within rind. ~cake, tartlet filled with compound of curds, &c. ~monger, *n.* dealer in cheese, butter, &c. **chees'ÿ** (-z), *a.* like cheese; (sl.) stylish.

cheet'ah, *n.* kind of leopard, used for hunting deer in India.

chĕf (sh-), *n.* male head-cook.

|| **chef-d'œuvre** (shĕdĕr'vr), *n.* (pl. -fs-, pr. as sing.), a masterpiece.

Chĕllē'an (sh-), *a.* (Archæol.) of the palæolithic epoch represented by remains found at Chelles in France.

chem'ĭcal (kĕ-), *a.* of or made by chemistry. *n.* substance obtained by or used in chemical process.

chemise (shĭmēz'), *n.* woman's body under-garment. **chémisétte'** (sh-, -z-), *n.* bodice filling neck-opening of dress.

chem'ĭst (kĕ-), *n.* expert in chemistry; dealer in drugs.

chem'ĭstrÿ (kĕ-), *n.* science of the

elements and their laws of combination and behaviour.

chenille (shĭnēl'), *n.* velvety cord for trimming dresses and furniture.

chĕque (-k), *check, n.* written order to banker to pay sum of money.

chĕq'uer (-ker), **chĕck'er,** *n.* (often pl.) pattern consisting of squares often alternately coloured. *v.t.* mark with chequers, variegate, break uniformity of.

chĕr'ish, *v.t.* tend lovingly; keep in one's heart, cling to.

cheroot' (sh-), *n.* cigar with both ends open.

chĕr'ry, *n.* small stone-fruit, tree bearing it, wood of this. *a.* cherry-coloured, of bright red. ~ **pie,** *n.* heliotrope.

chĕr'ub, *n.* (pl. -s, -ĭm), angelic being; beautiful child. ~**ic,** *a.*

chĕr'vil, *n.* a salad herb.

chess, *n.* game for two players with 32 ~**men** on chequered ~**board** of 64 squares.

chĕst, *n.* large box of wood or other material; coffer; part of the body enclosed by ribs.

chĕs'terfield, *n.* kinds of overcoat, and couch.

chĕst'nŭt (-sn-), *n.* glossy brown seed or nut of edible and non-edible kinds, tree bearing either; bright brown, horse so coloured; stale anecdote. *a.* chestnut-coloured.

chĕvál'-glass (sh-, -ahs), *n.* tall mirror swung on uprights.

chĕvalier' (sh-), *n.* member of certain orders of knighthood.

chevaux-de-frise (shevōdefrēz'), *n.* line of iron spikes set in timber, &c. to stop cavalry.

chĕv'iot, *n.* cloth of Cheviot sheep's wool.

chĕv'ron (sh-), *n.* V-shaped bar in heraldry and architecture; on sleeve of Services, sign of N.C.O. rank or (inverted) long service.

chĕv'y (-ĭ-), **chiv'y,** *n.* chase; game of prisoner's base. *v.t. & i.* chase; scamper.

chew (-ōō), *v.t. & i.* work about

between teeth, crush or indent thus; meditate on, ruminate over. *n.* spell of chewing; quid of tobacco.

chiaroscuro (kyȧroskoor'ō), *n.* treatment of light and shade in painting; use of contrast and relief in literature.

chias'mus (kĭȧz-), *n.* cross-correspondence in order of two phrases.

chibouk', **-que** (-ōōk), *n.* long Turkish tobacco-pipe.

chic (sh-), *a.* stylish, in the fashion.

chicāne' (sh-), *v.i. & t.* use chicanery, cheat. *n.* chicanery; (Bridge) hand with no trumps, holding of it.

chicā'nery (sh-), *n.* legal trickery, underhand dealing, sophistry.

chick,[1] *n.* young bird or child. *~-wire, *~-yard,* for enclosing domestic fowl. **chickabiddy,** *n.* term of endearment to child, &c. ‖ **chick**[2]**,** **cheek,** *n.* (Anglo-Ind.) screen-blind made of finely-split bamboo laced with twine.

chick'en, *n.* young of domestic fowl; *fowl of any age; its flesh as food; youthful person. ~-hearted,* *a.* cowardly, fearful. ~**pox,** mild eruptive disease.

chick'ling, *n.* common cultivated vetch.

chick'-pea, *n.* dwarf pea.

chick'weed, *n.* small plant.

chic'ory, *n.* root ground and used with or instead of coffee.

chide, *v.t. & i.* (chid, p.p. chidden or chid; -dable), rebuke, scold.

chief, *n.* leader or ruler; head of tribe or clan; (colloq.) head of department, &c. *a.* first in importance or influence; prominent, leading. ~**dom,** ~**ship,** *nn.*

chief'ly, *adv.* above the rest; mainly but not exclusively.

chief'tain (-tĭn), *n.* military leader; chief of clan or tribe or robber-band. ~**cy,** ~**ship,** *nn.* chieftain's position.

chiff-chaff, *n.* bird of warbler kind.

chiffon (shĭf'ŏn), *n.* thin gauze; (pl.) dress-trimmings, frills, &c.

chiffonier' (sh-), *n.* low movable cupboard or sideboard.

chignon (shĭnŏn'), n. mass of hair over pad at back of head.

chig'oe, n. W.-Ind. flea.

chil'blain, n. itching blain on hand, foot, ear, or nose.

child, n. (pl. *children*), young human being; descendant or follower or product of. ~bed, ~birth, parturition; ~hood, period of being a child. ~ish, a. of or like a child. ~like, a. innocent or frank or simple.

Chil'dermas, n. festival of Holy Innocents (28 Dec.).

chill, n. unpleasant coldness of air, &c. a. lacking warmth. v.t. & i. make or become cold; depress, dispirit.

chill'i, n. dried capsicum pod.

|| chill'um, n. (Anglo-Ind.) the part of the hookah containing the tobacco, &c.; loosely, the hookah, act of smoking.

|| chill'umchee, n. (Anglo-Ind.) wash-hand basin of brass or tinned copper.

chill'y, a. rather cold, sensitive to cold; cold-mannered.

chime, n. set of attuned bells; succession of notes given by them. v.i. & t. (-mable), ring chimes on bells; show hour by chiming; agree, fall in with.

chimēr'a (kī- or kĭ-), n. a bogy; wild impossible scheme or fancy. chimē'rical, a. imaginary.

chim'ney (pl. -eys), n. structure by which smoke or steam is carried off; glass tube protecting lamp-flame. ~piece, mantel. ~pot, pipe at top of chimney. ~pot hat, man's silk hat. ~sweep, man or boy who cleans chimneys of soot.

chimpänzee', n. manlike ape.

chin, n. front of lower jaw.

chi'na, n. ware made of china-clay or kaolin, porcelain. a. made of china.

*chinch, n. bed-bug. ~bug, insect destructive to wheat, &c.

chinchill'a, n. a grey fur.

chin'-chin, int. of greeting and farewell (sl.; also as n. & v.i.).

chine¹, n. deep narrow ravine.

chine², n. backbone; joint of meat from backbone; hill-ridge.

Chinēse' (-z), a. of China. n. Chinese language or native (pl. same). ~ lantern, collapsible lantern of coloured paper. Chinee', n. (sl.) Chinaman.

chink¹, n. clinking sound; narrow slit, peep-hole; (sl.) coin. v.i. & t. emit chink, shake coins together with chink.

Chink², n. (sl.) Chinaman.

chink'apin, chinqu'apin (-ingka-), n. N.-Amer. dwarf chestnut.

chintz, n. colour-printed glazed cotton cloth.

chip, v.t. & i. break edge of, cut into small pieces; suffer chipping. n. piece cut off, chipped place; (pl., colloq.) potatoes cut small and fried; counter in games of chance.

chip'muck, -munk, n. N.-Amer. squirrel.

Chipp'endäle, n. a light and solid style of drawing-room furniture.

chipp'y, a. dry, uninteresting; (sl.) parched, irritable.

chi'rōmancy (kī-), n. foretelling by inspecting the hands.

chirop'ody (kīr-), n. treatment of hands, feet, &c. ~dist, n.

chirp, n. short sharp note as of sparrow. v.i. & t. emit chirp(s); express thus; talk merrily. chirp'y, a. cheerful. chir'rup, n. chirping sound. v.i. make chirrup.

chis'el (-zl), n. edged tool for cutting. v.t. cut with chisel; (sl.) defraud, treat unfairly.

chit¹, chitt'y, nn. (Anglo-Ind.) report, certificate of character, or other document.

chit², n. young child, little woman. chit-chät, n. small-talk, gossip.

chitt'erlings, n.pl. smaller intestines of pig, &c. as food.

chiv'alry, n. medieval knightly system; inclination to defend weaker party; knights or gallant gentlemen. ~ric, ~rous, aa.

chive, n. herb of leek kind.

chivy. See chevy.

chlor'al (kl-), n. a hypnotic and anaesthetic.

---

chlor′ide (klī-), n. compound of chlorine; bleaching agent.

chlor′ine (kl-, -ēn), n. non-metallic element; a yellow-green gas.

chlor′odyne (kl-), n. a patent anodyne. P.

chlor′ofŏrm (kl-), n. thin liquid whose inhaled vapour produces insensibility. v.t. render insensible with this. ~ist, n. surgeon's assistant giving chloroform.

chlor′ophŷll (kl-), n. colouring matter of green parts of plants.

chlōrō′sĭs (kl-), n. anaemic disease in young women, green-sickness.

chŏck, n. block of wood, a wedge. v.t. make fast with chocks.

chŏck-full, adv. stuffed.

chŏc′olate, n. paste or cake of ground cacao seed; drink made of this; (pl.) sweets made with it; dark brown colour. a. chocolate coloured.

choice, n. act of choosing; preference; variety to choose from; thing chosen. a. of picked quality; exquisite.

choir (kwīr), quïre (arch.), n. organized band of singers; chancel of a church; birds singing. v.t. & i. (poet.) sing in chorus.

chōke, v.t. & i. (-kable), stop breath of, suffocate, block up passage; have coughing-fit. n. fit of choking; (Electr.) low-resistance coil cutting down current or changing its phase. *~ cherry, astringent wild cherry. ~damp, carbonic acid gas in mines, &c.

chō′ker, n. (sl.) white tie; high stand-up collar.

‖ **chō′kidār**, n. (Anglo-Ind.) a watchman.

chō′kŷ, n. (Anglo-Ind.) custom or toll station; a lock-up.

chŏl′er (kŏ-), n. bile; anger, irascibility. **chŏl′eric** (kŏ-), a. irascible.

chŏl′era (kŏ-), n. (English~) bilious disorder with diarrhoea and vomiting; (Asiatic~) non-bilious often fatal endemic disease.

chōose (-z), v.t. & i. (chōse, chōsen; -sable), decide as between greater number; decide as between alternatives.

chŏp¹, v.t. & i. cut with axe or heavy edge-tool; mince; cut words short; (of waves, &c.) swing this way and that. n. chopping stroke; small cut-off portion of mutton, pork, &c.

chŏp′per, n. large-bladed short axe; cleaver. **chŏp′pŷ**, a. (of wind, sea) jerky, rough.

chŏp², v.i. (India, China) seal; official impress or stamp; licence; trade-mark, brand of goods.

chŏp³. See **chap³**.

chŏp′stick, n. (pl.) pair of ivory, &c. slips used as fork in China.

***chŏp suey** (sōō′ĭ), n. kind of Chinese stew.

chŏr′al¹ (k-), a. of, for, or sung by choir; or with chorus.

chorale, chorāl² (korahl′), n. simple tune or hymn.

chŏr′alist, n. choral singer.

chŏrd¹ (k-), n. string of harp, &c.; also fig., of the emotions; straight line joining ends of arc.

chŏrd² (k-), n. harmonious combination of simultaneous notes.

***chŏre**, n. odd job; (usu. pl.) daily light work of house, farm, &c. v.i. do odd jobs; chare.

chŏr′eograph, ~er (k-), nn. designer of ballet. **~ŷ**, n.

chŏr′ic (k-), a. of, for, or like a Greek chorus.

chŏr′ister (k-), n. member of choir; choir-boy; *leader of choir.

chŏr′tle (sl.), v.i. chuckle loudly. n. such sound.

chŏr′us (k-), n. band of singers; choir; thing sung or said by many at once; refrain of a song. v.t. (-used), say or sing in chorus.

chose jugée (shōz zhōō′zhā), n. thing it is idle to discuss.

chose(n). See **choose**.

chō′ta ha′zri (hah-), n. (Anglo-Ind.) light early breakfast.

chou (shōō), n. large ornamental knot or rosette of ribbon, &c.

chough (chŭf), n. red-legged crow.

chouse (k-), v.t. & n. (colloq.) swindle.

chow¹, n. *(Army sl.) food.

Chow², n. Chinese breed of dog.

---

māte, mēte, mīte, mōte, mūte, mōōt; răck, rĕck, rĭck, rŏck, rŭck, rōŏk;

*chow′der, n. stew of fresh fish or clams, with pork, onions, biscuit, &c.

|| chow′ry, n. (Anglo-Ind.) a whisk or fly-flapper.

chri′sm (k-), n. consecrated oil.

christen (kri′sn), v.t. baptize and give name to child. ~ing, n. ceremony of baptism.

Christendom (kri′sn-), n. Christian countries as a whole.

Christian (kris′tyan), a. of Christ or his teaching; professing the Christian religion; (sl.) civilized or decent. n. a professor of the religion of Christ; (colloq.) civilized being; decent person. ~era, the era counted from supposed year of Christ's birth. ~name, the name given at christening. ~Science, system by which Christian faith is alleged to overcome disease, &c. without medical treatment. ~Scientist, adherent of this.

Christian′ity (k-), n. Christian faith, quality or character.

Chris′tianize (krischa-), v.t. make Christian.

Christ′like (k-), a. partaking of the nature and attributes of Christ.

Christmas (kris′m-) n. Christmas-day or Christmas-tide. ~box, small present given at C. ~card, greeting of good will. ~Day, festival of Christ's birth, 25 Dec. ~rose, white-flowered winter-blossoming hellebore. ~tide, holiday season, 24 Dec. to 1 Jan. ~tree, small fir hung with candles and presents. Christ′masy (krism-), a. of festive appearance, &c.

chromat′ic (k-), a. of colour, in colours; of or having notes not included in diatonic scale.

chromat′ics (k-), n. science of colour.

chrōme (k-), n. pigment got from compounds of chromium.

chrō′mium (k-), n. a metal.

chrōmolith′ograph (-ahf), chrō′mō (pl. -os), (k-), n. picture lithographed in colours.

chron′ic (k-), a. constantly present or recurring; confirmed, permanent; (vulg.) bad, intense.

chron′icle (k-), n. register of events in order of time. v.t. enter in chronicle or diary, record in newspaper. chron′icler (k-), n.

chronolō′gical (k-), a. according to sequence of time.

chronŏl′ogy (k-), n. science of computing dates; arrangement or table of events with dates.

chronŏm′eter (k-), n. time-measuring instrument.

chrys′alis (k-), n. form taken by insect in stage between larva and imago; case enclosing it.

chrysăn′themum (k-), n. garden plant flowering in autumn.

chrysŏbĕ′ryl, chrys′olite, chrys′oprāse (-z), (k-), nn. yellowish-green, olive-green, apple-green, precious stones.

chŭb, n. thick river fish.

chŭbb′y, a. plump, round-faced.

chŭck[1], n. part of lathe holding work. v.t. fix in chuck.

chŭck[2] (colloq.), v.t. fling, throw carelessly; jerk (under the chin); (with out) expel (intruder, &c.); (sl.; with it) cease, give up. n. act of chucking. ~farthing, quoit-game with coins. chŭcker-out, n. (sl.) one who expels (troublesome person) from meeting, &c.

chŭck[3], n. (usu. voc.) darling.

*chŭck[4], n. (sl.) food, 'grub'.

chŭck[5], int. calling noises of urging horse. v.i. utter this.

chŭc′kle, n. quiet laugh; hen's call. v.i. make chuckle.

chŭc′kle-head (-hĕd), n. dolt. ~headed, a. stupid.

|| chŭd′dar, n. (Anglo-Ind.) large sheet worn as a shawl by women.

chŭkk′er, n. each period of play in game of polo.

chŭm (colloq.), n. familiar friend. v.i. be intimate with, occupy same rooms together.

chŭm′my, n. type of car-body.

chŭmp, n. (colloq.) lump of wood; thick end of loin of mutton; (sl.) head; blockhead.

māte, mēte, mīte, mōte, mūte; pārt, pĕrt, pōrt: italics, vague sounds;

chŭnk, n. (colloq.) lump cut or broken off.

‖ chupatty (chōopaht´y), n. (Anglo-Ind.) a small cake of unleavened bread.

chuprassi (chōoprahs´ī), n. (Anglo-Ind.) uniformed servant of high Government official or of Government office; attendant, messenger.

church, n. building for Christian worship; collective body of Christians; body adhering to one particular form of worship; the clerical profession. v.t. hold church service over woman after childbirth. ~man, ~woman, member of established Church. ~ward´en, elected lay representative of parish; a long clay pipe. ~yard, enclosed ground round church.

churl, n. ill-bred or cross-grained fellow; a niggard; (arch.) peasant, low-born person. ~ish, a.

churn, n. butter-making machine; large milk-can. v.i. & t. make butter by agitating in churn; stir to and fro.

‖ chŭrr´us, n. resinous exudation of the hemp-plant, used in India as an intoxicant.

chute (shōot), n. slide for conveying things to lower level; rapid smooth fall of water over slope.

chŭt´ney, n. (pl. -eys), hot relish of fruits, chillies, &c.

chyle (kīl), n. milky fluid into which chyme is converted.

chyme (kīm), n. pulp into which gastric secretion converts food.

cicā´da, n. winged chirping insect.

cic´atrice, n. scar of healed wound. cic´atrize, v.i. & t. skin over, heal. ~zation, n.

ci´cely, n. kinds of flowering plant allied to parsley and chervil.

ciceró´nē (chiche-), n. (pl. -ni, pr. -nē), guide who explains things.

Ciceró´nian, a. pure as Cicero's Latin. n. expert in Cicero.

ci´der, n. fermented apple-juice as drink.

‖ ci-devant (sē devahń´), a. former, late.

cigar´, n. tobacco-leaf rolled into cylinder. cigarĕtte´, n. cut tobacco rolled in paper.

cil´ia, n.pl. eye-lashes; similar fringe on leaf or insect's wing. cil´iarў (-lya-), a.

Cimmē´rian, a. extremely dark.

*cinch (sinch), n. saddle-girth; (sl.) sure hold, advantage, easy job, foregone conclusion. v.t. girth tightly up; (sl.) get a sure hold on a thing.

cinchō´na (-k-), n. kinds of tree yielding Peruvian bark.

cinc´ture, n. girdle, belt, fillet.

cin´der, n. slag; piece of coal that has ceased to burn. ~path, running track. cin´derў, a.

Cinderĕll´a dance (dah-), n. dance ending at midnight.

cin´é-cãm´era, n. motion-picture camera.

cin´ema, n.cinematograph theatre; the ~, cinematography, moving pictures.

cinĕmat´ograph (-ahf), n. apparatus producing pictures of motion by the rapid projection on a screen of a great number of photographs taken successively on a long film. cinĕmatograph´ic, a. cinĕmatog´raphў, n.

ciné-project´or, n. projector for cinematograph pictures.

cinerā´ria, n. kinds of flowering plant with ashy down on leaves.

cin´erarў, a. of ashes (esp. of urn holding cremated ashes).

Cingalese´ (-nggalēz), obsolete form of Sinhalese.

cinn´abãr, n. red mercuric sulphide; vermilion.

cinn´amon, n. an E.-Ind. tree, its aromatic yellowish-brown inner bark as spice; colour of the bark. a. cinnamon-coloured.

cinque´foil (-kf-), n. plant with five-lobed leaves.

Cinque Pŏrts (-nk), n.pl. certain ports (orig. five) on SE. coast with ancient privileges.

cī´pher, n. arithmetical symbol 0; any single arabic figure; secret writing; a monogram. v.i. & t.

ah, awl, oil, boor, cow, dowry; chin, go, bang, so, ship, thin; dh, as th(e);

do sums, work (sum) out; put into cipher writing.

|| **cîr′ca**, *prep.* (abbr. *c.*, *circ.*) about.

Cîr′cè, *n.* enchantress, temptress. **Cîrcē′an**, *a.* pertaining to Circe, bewitching, tempting.

cîrcle, *n.* perfectly round plane figure, line enclosing it; roundish enclosure, ring; set or coterie or class; period or cycle. *v.i.* & *t.* move in a circle, revolve; surround.

cîr′clet, *n.* small circle; circular band as ornament for head.

cîr′cuit (-kit), *n.* circular or circuitous course; judge's progress through district to hold courts, such district; (Electr.) path of current. **circū′itous**, *a.* roundabout, indirect.

cîr′cular, *a.* having the shape of a circle; moving in a circle, *n.* notice sent round to customers and others. **∼ize**, *v.t.* send circular to.

cîr′cūlāte, *v.i.* & *t.* (-*lable*), be or put in circulation.

cîr′cūlā′tion, *n.* movement from and back to a starting-point; passing from place to place or hand to hand; current coins; extent of sale of newspapers, &c. **∼tor**, *n.*; **∼tory**, *a.*

cîrcumâm′bient, *a.* (of fluids) surrounding.

cîr′cumcise (-z), *v.t.* (-*sable*), cut off the foreskin; (fig.) purify.

cîrcumci′sion (-zhn), *n.* action of circumcising; practised as religious rite by Jews and Mohammedans; surgical operation.

circûm′ference, *n.* line enclosing circle; distance round thing.

cîr′cumflêx, *a.* & *n.* mark (^) over vowel to indicate length, &c.

circûm′fluent (-lōō-), *a.* flowing round anything.

cîrcumfūse′ (-z), *v.t.* (-*sable*), pour round; bathe or surround.

cîrcumgŷrā′tion, *n.* rotation, turning this way and that.

cîrcumjā′cent, *a.* situated around.

cîrcumlocū′tion, *n.* roundabout expression; evasive talk. **∼tory**, *a.*

cîrcumnāv′igāte, *v.t.* (-*gable*), sail round. **∼tion**, **∼tor**, *nn.*

cîrcumpō′lar, *a.* about or near one of the earth's poles.

cîr′cumscrîbe, *v.t.* (-*bable*), (of line, &c.) enclose or outline; mark or lay down limits of; confine.

cîrcumscrip′tion, *n.* limitation; inscription round coin, &c.

cîrcumsō′lar, *a.* moving round sun.

cîr′cumspêct, *a.* wary, taking everything into account. **∼ion**, *n.* exercise of caution.

cîr′cumstance, *n.* (pl.) all the surroundings of an act, a person's material welfare or situation; an occurrence or detail; *(colloq.)* comparable thing. **cîr′cumstanced** (-st), *a.* in such and such circumstances.

cîrcumstân′tial (-shl), *a.* with many details; accidental, not essential; particular, minute. **cîrcumstân′tiâl′ity** (-shi-), *n.*

cîrcumvallā′tion, *n.* rampart or entrenchment made round place.

cîrcumvênt′, *v.t.* overreach, outwit.

cîr′cus, *n.* arena for equestrian and other exhibitions; open circle with streets converging on it; show of trained horses, &c.

cîrque (-k), *n.* natural amphitheatre.

cî′rrīped, *n.* kinds of crustacean.

cî′rrus, *n.* (pl. **-rī**), form of cloud with diverging woolly filaments.

cis′tern, *n.* reservoir for water.

cis′tus, *n.* kinds of flowering shrub, rock-rose.

cit′adel, *n.* fortress protecting or dominating a city.

cite, *v.t.* (-*table*), summon at law; adduce as instance, quote in support. **citā′tion**, *n.* summons; reference; *(Mil.)* official commendation of conduct of soldier or unit.

cit′ern, **citt′ern**, *n.* lute, guitar.

cit′izen, *n.* burgess or freeman of city; townsman, civilian (inhabitant of State). **∼ship**, *n.*

cit′rāte, *n.* salt of citric acid.

cit′ric ā′cid, *n.* an acid existing in the juice of the citron.

---

zh, as (*rou*)*ge*: è = **ī**; **ĭr**, **ūr**, = **ĕr**; **ȳ**, **ў**, = **ī**, **ĭ**; and see p. 4. *° = U.S.*

cit'ron, n. fruit of lemon kind but larger; tree bearing it.

cit'y, n. important town created city by charter; cathedral town.

civ'et, n. strong musky perfume got from the civet-cat.

civ'ic, a. of city or citizenship.

civ'ics, n. principles of civic duty.

civ'il, a. of a citizen community; non-military; polite, obliging. ~ list, Parliamentary allowance for Sovereign's household and royal pensions. ~ Service, all non-warlike branches of State administration. ~ war, war between sections of one State.

civil'ian (-yan), a. not in or of armed forces. n. such person.

civil'ity, n. readiness to oblige; (pl.) acts of courtesy.

civiliza'tion, n. advanced stage of social development.

civ'ilize, v.t. (-zable), bring out of barbarism; enlighten, refine.

clack, n. sharp sound; clatter of tongues. v.i. make clack.

clad, p.t. & p.p. of clothe.

claim, v.t. demand as one's due; proclaim; have a right to; assert claim; assert. n. a demand; right or title to; (Mining, &c.) piece of ground marked out or allotted. *~-jumper,* appropriator of another's claim.

claim'ant, n. claiming party, esp. in law-suit.

clairvoy'ance, n. abnormal faculty of seeing what is out of sight; deep insight. ~ant, n. & a.

clam, n. edible shell-fish.

cla'mant, a. noisy, insistent.

clam'ber, v.i. climb with help of hands, or with difficulty.

clamm'y, a. stickily moist.

clam'our (-mer), n. shouting, confused noise; loud protest or demand. v.i. vociferate, make clamour. **clam'orous,** a.

clamp, n. brace or band of iron; gripping appliance tightened by screw. v.t. strengthen or fasten with a clamp.

clan, n. Scottish highlanders with common ancestor; family holding much together; party or coterie. **clann'ish,** a.

clandes'tine, a. done secretly.

clang, n. loud resonant metallic sound. v.i. make clang. *~our* (-ngg-), n. continued clanging.

clank, n. sound as of chain shaken. v.i. & t. make, cause (chain, &c.) to make, clank.

clan'ship, n. prevalence of clannish feeling.

clap, v.t. & i. strike palms loudly together; strike with a quick motion; flap (wings) audibly; add one thing to another. n. explosive noise, esp. peal of thunder; spell of hand-clapping. *~-board,* narrow board for weather-boarding frame buildings.

clap'net, n. fowler's, &c. net, closed by pulling string.

clapp'er, n. tongue or striker of bell; bird-scaring rattle.

clapp'erclaw, v.t. scratch and hit.

clap'trap, n. language or doings meant to catch applause. a. showy, playing to the gallery.

claque (-ahk), n. hired body of applauders in theatre, &c.

Clarencieux' (-sū), n. one of the kings-of-arms in England.

cla'rendon, n. thick-faced type.

cla'ret, n. kinds of red wine imported from Bordeaux.

cla'rify, v.t. & i. (-fiable), free (mind, &c.) from obscurity; free (liquid, &c.) from impurities; become transparent.

cla'rinet, n. reed instrument with holes and keys; organ-stop of like quality. ~tist, n.

cla'rion, n. shrill trumpet; organ-stop of like quality; rousing call to action.

clarionet', n. clarinet.

cla'rity, n. clearness.

clark'ia, n. a garden flower.

clash, n. loud broken sound as of cymbals; collision, conflict, discord of colours, &c. v.t. & i. make clash; be at variance with; bring together with clash.

clash'y, -ee, n. (Anglo-Ind.) tent-pitcher; native sailor.

clasp (-ah-). *n.* contrivance for fastening; buckle, &c.; grip of arms or hand, embrace, handshake; silver bar on medal-ribbon. *v.t. & i.* fasten up, fasten clasp of (belt, &c.); encircle, embrace, grasp. **~knife,** large folding knife.

class (-ah-). *n.* rank or order of society; set of students taught or *graduating together; any set of persons or things differentiated by quality from others. *v.t.* assign to a class. **~book,** designed for use by student-classes. *~day, day of display by graduating class.

clǎss'ic, *a.* allowed excellence, standard; of the first order or rank. *n.* classic writer or artist; ancient Greek or Latin writer; any great literary work; (pl.) study of ancient Greek and Latin.

clǎss'ical, *a.* of the standard Greek and Latin authors; (of education) based on these.

clǎss'icism, *n.* following of or belief in the classics; a Greek or Latin idiom. **~cist,** *n.*

clǎss'ify, *v.t.* (*-fiable*), arrange in classes, class. **~fication,** *n.*; **~ficatory,** *a.*

class'y (-ah-). *a.* (sl.) superior.

clǎtt'er, *n.* rattling sound; noisy talk. *v.i.* make clatter, fall with a clatter.

clause (-z). *n.* single proviso in treaty, law, or contract; a sentence or part of a sentence.

claus'tral, *a.* relating to a cloister.

claustrophō'bia, *n.* morbid dread of closed places.

clave, *p.t.* of cleave[1].

clǎv'ichŏrd (-k-). *n.* key-board instrument, predecessor of piano.

clǎv'icle, *n.* collarbone; merry-thought of birds. **clavic'ular,** *a.*

claw, *n.* pointed horny nail of beast's or bird's foot; ugly hand; grappling-iron. *v.t. & i.* scratch or maul with claws or fingernails; clutch hold of. *~hammer (coat), evening dress-coat.

clay, *n.* stiff tenacious earth; substance of the body. **clay'ey,** *a.*

clay'mŏre, *n.* ancient Scottish two-edged broadsword.

clean, *a.* free from dirt (lit. & fig.); unsoiled; free of defilement or disease; complete, decisive. *adv.* completely, altogether. *v.t.* make clean (of dirt, &c.). *n.* process of cleaning.

clean'lȳ[1], *adv.* in clean manner.

clean'lȳ[2] (-ĕn-). *a.* habitually clean; attentive to cleanness.

cleanse (-ĕnz), *v.t.* (*-sable*), purify from sin; make clean.

clear, *a.* transparent; not clouded; distinct, intelligible, manifest; not dim; well-defined, unobstructed, open; unhampered. *v.t. & i.* make or become clear; show or declare innocent; remove any encumbrance; make sum as net gain. ~ out, go away, decamp.

clear'ance, *n.* removal of obstructions; space allowed for the passing of two parts in machinery, &c.

clear'ing, *n.* piece of land cleared for cultivation.

clear'lȳ, *adv.* (in answers), yes, no doubt, evidently.

clear'-sight'ed (-sīt-), *a.* discerning.

cleat, *n.* tightening-wedge; slip of wood, &c. fastened on to form projection or attachment.

cleav'age, *n.* way in which thing tends to split.

cleave[1], *v.i.* (cleaved or clāve; p.p. cleaved), be faithful to, hold together; stick, adhere.

cleave[2], *v.t. & i.* (clōve or clĕft; p.p. clōven or clĕft; *-vable*), split, divide; chop asunder; make way through.

cleav'er, *n.* butcher's chopper.

cleav'ers (-z), *n.* goose-grass.

cleek, *n.* iron-headed golf-club.

clĕf, *n.* (Mus.) symbol showing pitch of stave.

cleft[1], *p.t. & p.p.* of cleave[2].

clĕft[2], *n.* split; fissure in earth.

clĕg, *n.* large grey fly, gadfly.

clĕm, *v.t. & i.* (dial.) starve.

clĕm'atis, *n.* flowering climber.

clĕm'ency, *n.* merciful treatment or feeling.

clĕm'ent, *a.* (rare) merciful.

---

clench, clinch, *v.t. & i.* secure nail by hammering point sideways; (of fingers, teeth, hand) close tight; make conclusive, confirm; (of boxers) come to close quarters. *n.* clenching or clenched state. clin′cher, clěn′-cher, *n.* argument, &c. that settles a question.

clere′stŏry (-ērs-), *n.* windowed part of wall of cathedral, &c. above aisle roof.

clēr′gў, *n.* all persons in holy orders. ~man, *n.*

clēr′ic, *n.* clergyman. *a.* clerical. clě′rical, *a.* of clergy(man), of clerk(s). *n.* member of clergy party in a parliament, &c. ~ism, ~ist, *nn.* ; ~ize, *v.t.*

clerk (-ärk, *·-ērk), *n.* person employed to keep accounts, &c. ; lay officer of parish church; man of business and keeper of records in municipal and other public offices; clergyman; scholar or penman. *v.i.* act as clerk. ~ess, *n.* ~ly, *a.* good in penmanship. ~ship, *n.*

clěv′er, *a.* quick and neat in movement; skilful, ingenious.

clew, *n.* ball of thread or yarn; sail-corner to which tacks and sheets are fastened. *v.t.* draw up or let down clews in furling and unfurling sails.

cliché (klēsh′ā), *n.* hackneyed literary phrase.

click, *n.* sharp sound; (S.-Afr. languages) sharp non-vocal sucking sound as articulation; catch in machinery.*v.i.* make click; (sl.) have luck, secure one's object; (sl.) get on friendly terms *with*.

cli′ent, *n.* person using the services of a lawyer or other professional man; customer.

cli′entèle, *n.* clients; customers, frequenters of theatre, &c.

cliff, *n.* a steep rock-face.

climactě′ric, *a.* constituting a turning-point, critical. *n.* critical point in physical development.

cli′mate, *n.* place's weather characteristics; region of certain climate. ~ăt′ic, *a.* ; ~tŏ′logy, *n.*

cli′măx, *n.* ascending scale; series arranged in climax; culmination.

climb (-m), *v.t. & i.* make way up hill, tree, ladder, &c. ; (of sun, aeroplane, &c.) mount slowly; (of plant) go up wall or other support by clinging; rise in social scale. *n.* piece of climbing; place to be climbed.

cli′mber (-mer), *n.* one who climbs; climbing-plant.

clime, *n.* region, tract.

cling, *v.i.* (clŭng), maintain grasp, keep hold, adhere closely.

cling′stŏne, *n.* peach, nectarine, with pulp adhering to stone.

clin′ic, *n.* clinical method of teaching; class so taught.

clin′ical, *a.* of or at the sickbed.

clink[1], *n.* sharp ringing sound. *v.i. & t.* emit clink; touch glasses together in toasts, &c.

clink[2], *n.* (sl.) prison.

clink′er[1], *n.* brick vitrified on surface; mass of slag or fused brick.

clink′er[2], *n.* (sl.) first-class specimen; good shot or stroke.

clink′er-built′ (-bi-), *a.* (of boat) with planks overlapping; secured with clinched nails.

clip[1], *v.t.* grip tightly. *n.* appliance for holding things together.

clip[2].*v.t.* cut short with shears; pare edge of coin; curtail. *n.* shearing or haircutting; yield of wool.

clipp′er, *n.* instrument for clipping (usu. pl.); swift mover; ship of raking build; (sl.) thing excellent of its kind.

clipp′ing, *n.* piece clipped off. *a.* (sl.) firstrate.

clique (-ēk), *n.* exclusive set of associates. cli′quy (-ēki), *a.*

cloak, *n.* loose sleeveless outdoor garment; pretext. *v.i. & t.* put on one's cloak; cover, hide. ~-room, room for temporary deposit of luggage.

clock[1], *n.* machine measuring time and indicating on a dial. ~work, *n.* mechanism on clock principle; (attrib.) mechanical, precise, regular.

clŏck², n. ornamental pattern on sides of stocking or sock.

clŏd, n. lump of earth or clay; a lout. ~dish, a. stupid, phlegmatic. ~hopper, bumpkin, lout. ~pole, stupid rustic.

clŏg, n. log fastened to leg as impediment; wooden-soled shoe. v.t. & i. confine with clog; be an encumbrance to, impede; choke up; adhere. clŏgg'ỹ, a. apt to clog, sticky.

clois'ter, n. convent, monastic house; covered walk, esp. of convent, college, or cathedral buildings. v.t. shut up in convent, immure. clois'tral, n. clois'tered (-erd), a. having cloister-walls; secluded; monastic.

clōse¹, a. shut; tight; stifling, secret; niggardly; near together; compact, dense; nearly equal. adv. closely. n. enclosed place; a passage or entry; small enclosed field. ~stool, chamber-pot mounted in stool with cover.

clōse² (-z), v.t. & i. (-sable), shut; be declared shut; finish; draw near to; come to terms with. n. conclusion, end; a grapple. clō'sing-time, n. shutting-up time.

clŏs'ĕt (-z-), n. private or small room; cupboard; water-closet. ~ĕd, a. in private consultation.

clō'sure (-zher), n. closing, closed state; closing of debate. v.t. apply closure to.

clŏt, n. lump of adhesive matter; coagulated mass. v.i. & t. form into clots; curdle.

cloth (-aw-; pl. -dhz), n. woven or felted stuff; table-cover; woollen material for clothes.

clōthe (-dh), v.t. (clothed or clăd), provide with clothes, put clothes upon, be as clothes to.

clōthes (-ōz, -ōdhz), n.pl. wearing-apparel, garments.

clō'thier (-dh-), n. cloth-maker; dealer in cloth or clothes.

clō'thing (-dh-), n. clothes.

cloud, n. visible condensed watery vapour floating in the air; mass of smoke or dust; great number moving together; louring look.

v.t. & i. overspread or darken with clouds, gloom, trouble, or imbecility; become overcast. ~berry, n. mountain raspberry. ~less, a. ~scape, picture of clouds. ~ỹ, a. obscured with clouds; lacking clearness.

clough (klŭf), n. ravine.

clout, v.t. patch (shoe, garment); hit or rap. n. a cloth; piece of clothing; rap or blow; iron plate on boot &c. to save wear.

clōve¹, n. dried bud of tropical tree, spice; the tree. ~ gilly-flower, n. clove-scented Pink.

clōve², n. one sector of a bulb of garlic, &c.

clōve³(n). See cleave².

clōve hitch, n. hitch securing rope round spar, &c., at right angles.

clō'ver, n. kinds of trefoil used as fodder. in ~, in luxury.

clown, n. rustic, lout; jester in pantomime or circus. ~ish, a.

cloy, v.t. sate, surfeit.

club, n. heavy stick used as weapon; kinds of stick used in golf, &c.; body of persons associated for social or other purposes. v.t. & i. strike with club; bring or come together; contribute to a common expense. clŭbb'able, a. sociable.

club'foot, n. a malformation of the foot. ~ed, a.

cluck, n. hen's cry. v.i. make cluck.

clue (-ōō), n. guiding or suggestive fact; thread of story; train of thought.

clŭm'ber, n. breed of spaniel.

clŭmp, n. cluster of trees; a lump. v.i. & t. tread heavily; plant in clump.

clŭm'sỹ (-z-), a. awkward in movement or shape; ill-contrived, ill-conceived; tactless.

clung, p.t. & p.p. of cling.

clŭs'ter, n. bunch of flowers or fruits; group of things. v.i. & t. form a cluster; arrange in a cluster.

clŭtch¹, v.t. & i. seize eagerly, grasp tightly. n. tight grasp; coupling device in machine.

clŭtch², n. brood of chickens.

clutt'er, *n.* untidy state; turmoil. *v.i. & t.* bustle about; litter.

coach, *n.* state carriage; four-wheeled vehicle; railway carriage; tutor or trainer. *v.i. & t.* travel by coach; prime with facts. ~**man**, *n.* driver of any horse carriage.

cŏädj'utor (-ōō-), *n.* assistant.

cŏăg'ŭlant, *n.* coagulating agent.

cŏăg'ŭlāte, *v.i. & t.* (-*lable*), change from fluid to solid state; clot, curdle, set. ~**tion**, *n.*

coal, *n.* black mineral used as fuel &c. *v.t. & i.* put coal into (ship &c.); take in coal. ~**box**, coal-scuttle. ~**cellar**, underground room for keeping coal. ~**field**, district in which coal is found. ~**gas**, gases extracted from coal. ~**heaver**, one who carries and loads coal. ~**hole**, a small place for keeping coal. ~**master**, ~**owner**, owner or lessee of colliery. ~**measures**, seams of coal with intervening strata. ~**mine**, ~**pit**, mine or pit from which coal is dug. ~**scuttle**, portable vessel for coal.

cŏălēsce', *v.i.* come together and form one; combine in a coalition. **cŏălēs'cence**, *n.* ; ~**nt**, *a.*

cŏăli'tion, *n.* fusion into one whole; temporary combination between parties. ~**ist**, *n.*

coal'mouse, ~**tit**, *nn.* dark species of titmouse.

coarse (kōrs), *a.* common, inferior; rough; lacking delicacy, unrefined; vulgar; (of language) obscene. ~**ness**, *n.*

coars'en (kōr-), *v.t. & i.* make or become coarse.

coast, *n.* sea boundary, line of shore. *v.i.* sail along coast; travel downhill on toboggan or without work on bicycle. ~**guard**, *n.* coast police. ~**line**, shape of coast. ~**wise**, *a. & adv.* along coast.

coat, *n.* sleeved outer body garment; covering of any animal; covering of paint, &c. *v.t.* cover with paint, dust, &c. ~**armour**, heraldicarms. ~**ofarms**, herald's tabard; heraldic bearings.

coatee', *n.* short-tailed coat.

coat'ing, *n.* coat of paint, &c.; cloth for coats.

coax, *v.t.* use blandishments on, persuade; force gently.

cŏäx'ial, *a.* with common axis.

cŏb, *n.* stout short-legged riding-horse; male swan; cob-nut; *stalk of maize-ear; (pl.) coal in roundish lumps; round-headed loaf; wall-material of clay, &c.

cŏ'balt (-awlt), *n.* a metal; deep blue pigment made from it.

cŏb'ble, *n.* (pl.) paving pebbles; coals of cobble size. *v.t.* mend, patch coarsely.

cŏbb'ler, *n.* mender of shoes; clumsy workman; iced drink.

cŏb'le, *n.* kind of fishing-boat.

cŏb'nut, *n.* kind of hazel nut.

cŏ'bra, *n.* venomous hooded snake.

cŏb swan (-ŏn), *n.* male swan.

cŏb'wĕb, *n.* spider's network or thread; entanglement.

cō'ca, *n.* Bolivian shrub.

cocaine', *n.* drug from coca producing numbness. ~**nism**, *n.* morbid state resulting from excess of cocaine.

cocain'ize, *v.t.* treat with cocaine.

cŏc'cyx (-ks-), *n.* bone ending spinal column.

cŏch'in-chi'na, *n.* breed of fowl.

cŏch'ineal, *n.* dried insects yielding scarlet dye and carmine.

cŏck¹, *n.* male of domestic fowl; any male bird; hammer of gunlock, cocked position of hammer. *v.t. & i.* set in upright or slanting position; glance knowingly. ~**a-hoop**, *a.* exultant. ~**eyed**, *a.* (sl.) squinting; set aslant, one-sided. ~**of the walk**, dominant person in any company. ~**shot**, ~**shy**, object set up to be thrown at; throw at this.

cŏck², *n.* small conical heap of hay, &c. *v.t.* put (hay) in cocks.

cŏckāde', *n.* badge in hat.

cŏck-a-lee'kie, *n.* Scotch dish of broth with leeks.

cŏckātoo', *n.* crested parrot.

cŏck'atrice (*or* -ĭ-), *n.* basilisk.

cŏck'boat, *n.* small ship's boat.

cŏck′chāfer, *n.* chestnut-coloured loud-humming beetle.

cŏcked hat, *n.* brimless hat with points before, behind, and above.

cŏck′er¹, *v.t.* pamper, coddle.

Cŏck′er², *n. According to* ~, correct, regular.

cŏck′er³, *n.* breed of spaniel.

cŏck′erel, *n.* young cock.

cŏc′kle¹, *n.* plant growing in corn. ~bur, kind of weed.

cŏc′kle², *n.* edible bivalve; cockleshell; bulge or wrinkle. *v.i. & t.* wrinkle, pucker.

cŏck′ney, *n.* (pl. *-eys*), native of London; London English. *a. of* cockneys. ~ism, *n.* cockney idiom or pronunciation.

cŏck′pit, *n.* cock-fighting arena; place of many battles; place on orlop deck on man-of-war, used as hospital in action (Aeronaut.) space for pilot, &c. in fuselage of aeroplane.

cŏck′roach, *n.* the black-beetle.

cŏcks′cŏmb (-m), *n.* cock's crest; kinds of plant.

cŏcksure′ (-shoor), *a.* quite convinced; dogmatic, confident.

cŏck′tail, *n.* horse of racing stamp but not thoroughbred; social upstart; drink of spirit with bitters and sugar.

cŏck′y, **cŏck′sy**, **cŏx′y**, *aa.* conceited, pert; (pred.) cock-a-hoop.

cō′cō, *n.* (pl. *-os*), tropical palm bearing coco-nut. ~nut, seed of coco with edible white lining enclosing liquid called *coco-nut milk*.

cō′coa (-kō), *n.* powder of crushed cacao seeds, often with other substances; drink made from this or the seeds.

cocoon′, *n.* silky case spun by larva (esp. of silkworm) to protect it as chrysalis.

cŏd¹, *n.* large sea fish. ~-liver oil, a medicinal oil.

cŏd², *v.t. & i.* (sl.) hoax, fool.

cŏd′dle, *v.t. & i.* treat, treat oneself, as invalid; pamper. ~ per-son who coddles.

cōde, *n.* a systematized body of laws; set of rules; system of

signals; arbitrary symbols used for brevity or secrecy. *v.t.* put into code symbols.

cō′dex, *n.* (pl. *-dicēs*), ancient manuscript volume.

cŏdg′er, *n.* (sl.) queer fellow.

cŏd′icil, *n.* supplement modifying or revoking a will.

cŏd′ify, *v.t.* (-*fiable*), frame laws into code. ~fication, *n.*

cŏd′ling, *n.* variety of apple.

***cō′-ĕd**, *n.* (sl.) girl student at co-educational institution.

cō-ĕdūcā′tion, *n.* training boys and girls in same school &c.

cŏĕffi′cient (-shnt), thing or person that contributes to an effect; (Alg.) expression of quantity standing before another as multiplying it.

cōĕ′qual, *a. & n.* equal.

cōĕrce′, *v.t.* (-*ceable*), constrain into obedience. ~cive, *a.* cōĕr′cion (-shn), *n.* forcible compulsion, government by force. ~ist, *n.*

cōĕssĕn′tial (-shl), *a.* of the same substance.

cōĕtĕr′nal, *a.* alike eternal.

cōē′val, *a.* of same age, duration, or epoch. *n.* same-aged person.

cōĕxĕc′ūtor, ~trix (-gz-), *nn.* joint executor.

cōĕxist′ (-gz-), *v.i.* exist at the same time. ~ent, *a.*; ~ence, *n.*

cōĕxtĕn′sive, *a.* extending over same space or time.

cŏff′ee (-fi), *n.* a shrub; its seeds or a powder made from them; infusion of this as hot drink. ~house, refreshment place. ~room, dining-room of inn.

cŏff′er, *n.* box for valuables; (pl.) funds or treasury.

cŏff′in, *n.* burial-chest.

cŏg, *n.* the tooth of a wheel.

cō′gency, *n.* force, strength.

cō′gent, *a.* (of reasoning, &c.) compelling assent, convincing.

cō′gitable, *a.* that can be conceived by thought.

cō′gitāte, *v.i. & t.* think deeply. ~tion, ~tor, *nn.*; ~tive, *a.*

cognac (kŏn′yäk), *n.* French brandy.

cŏg′nāte, *a.* descended from same

---

ancestor; kindred; related to. *n.* relative; cognate word.

cogni'tion, *n.* knowing or perceiving or conceiving; knowledge, notion. ~al, *a.*

cŏg'nitive, *a.* having the power of knowing.

cogn'izable (kŏgn-), *a.* within the cognizance of a court; knowable.

cogn'izance (kŏgn-), *n.* being aware; judicial notice; crest or other badge.

cogn'izant (kŏgn-), *a.* having cognizance of; having cognition.

cŏgnō'mĕn, *n.* nickname, surname.

cŏgnō'vit, *n.* defendant's acknowledgement that plaintiff's cause is just.

cohăb'it, *v.i.* live together as husband and wife. ~ation, *n.*

coheir', **coheir'ess** (kōăr-), *nn.* male, female, joint heir.

cohēre', *v.i.* stick together, remain united; be well knit or consistent; cohēr'ence, *n.* ~ent, *a.* holding together; not inconsequent or rambling.

cohē'sion (-zhn), *n.* force with which parts cohere; union; dependence. cohē'sive, *a.*

cō'hŏrt, *n.* tenth part of Roman legion; (pl.) troops; band.

coif, *n.* kind of close cap.

‖ **coiffeur** (kwah'fĕr), *n.* hairdresser. ‖ **coiffure** (kwah'fūr), *n.* way hair is dressed.

coign (koin), *n.* corner or external angle; wedge.

coil, *v.t. & i.* dispose in concentric rings; take or twist into spiral or circular shape. *n.* coiled length of rope, wire, &c.

coin, *n.* piece of stamped metal money; (collectively) money. *v.t. & i.* make money by stamping metal; turn into money.

coin'age, *n.* coining; coins; system of coins in use.

coïncide', *v.i.* occur simultaneously; agree or be identical with. **coïn'cidence**, *n.* notable concurrence of events. ~nt, ~en'tal, *aa.*

coin'er, *n.* maker of false coin.

coir (koi'er), *n.* coco-nut fibre.

cōi'tion, *n.* sexual copulation.

cōke, *n.* residue of coal after distillation of volatile parts.

cŏl, *n.* depression in mountain-chain.

cō'la, **k-**, *n.* W.-Afr. tree; its seed. ~nut, ~seed.

col'ander (kŭ-), *n.* perforated vessel, cook's strainer.

cŏl'chicum (-kï-), *n.* meadow-saffron; drug from it.

cōld, *a.* of low temperature; feeling cold; lacking ardour; undemonstrative, apathetic. *n.* prevalence of low temperature; catarrh of nose or throat. ~ cream, a cosmetic.

cōle, *n.* kinds of cabbage. ~seed, plant yielding colza oil.

cŏlĕŏp'terous, *a.* of the order *Coleoptera* or beetles.

**cōle'slaw, cōld-, *n.* salad of cabbage sliced or chopped.

cŏl'ic, *n.* griping belly-pain.

colitis. See colon.

collăb'orāte, *v.i.* work in combination with another. ~tion, ~tor, *nn.*

collăp'sable, **-ible**, *a.* folding.

collapse', *n.* tumbling down or falling to ruin; physical or mental break-down. *v.i.* suffer collapse; fall to ruin; break down.

cŏll'ar, *n.* neckband of shirt or dress; chain or band round animal's neck; chain worn as ornament by knights of several orders. *v.t.* seize by the collar, lay hold of; (Rugby Footb.) stop opponent by clasping hold of him; (sl.) appropriate.

cŏll'arbone, *n.* the bone joining breastbone and shoulder-blade.

cŏllarětte', *n.* woman's collar of lace, fur, &c.

collāte', *v.t.* <table>, compare in detail; gather and place in order; appoint to benefice.

collăt'eral, *a.* side by side; subordinate but from same source; connected but aside from main line. *n.* collateral kinsman.

collā'tion, *n.* collating; bestowing; a light repast.

cŏll'eague (-g), *n.* an associate in office; a coadjutor.

cŏll'ect[1], *n.* a short prayer.

collect'², *v.t.* & *i.* assemble, accumulate, bring or come together; gather contributions, rates, &c.; concentrate one's thoughts.

collectá'néa, *n.pl.* miscellany of passages, &c.

collec'tion, *n.* collecting; collecting of money at church service &c.; sum so collected; set of collected specimens.

collec'tive, *a.* representing or including many; combined, aggregate, common. *n.* (Gram.) collective noun. ~ **noun**, used in sing. to express many individuals. ~ **ownership**, by all for common benefit.

collec'tivism, *n.* (theory of) collective ownership of land and means of production. ~**ist**, *n.* & *a.*

collec'tor, *n.* one who collects specimens, curiosities, money due, &c.; in India, the chief administrative official of a district, whose special duty is the collection of revenue. ~**ship**, *n.*

coll'een, *n.* (Anglo-Ir.) girl.

coll'ege, *n.* body of colleagues; corporation of scholars forming part of a university; school for boys with similar foundation; (Sc., U.S., &c.) incorporated and endowed institution of highest grade; (name assumed by) other educational institutions; buildings of any college.

colle'gian, *n.* member of a college; (vulg.) university man.

colle'giate, *a.* constituted as a college.

collide', *v.i.* come into collision.

coll'ie, *n.* Scotch sheep-dog.

coll'ier (-yer), *n.* coal-miner; coal-ship, member of its crew.

coll'iery (-yer-), *n.* coal-mine.

colli'sion (-zhn), *n.* violent encounter of moving bodies; clash of opposed interests, &c.

collocā'tion, *n.* relative situation.

coll'ocūtor, *n.* one's partner in colloquy.

collō'dion, *n.* solution of gun-cotton in ether.

collōgue' (-g), *v.i.* (colloq.) talk confidentially.

coll'oid, *a.* gluey; (Chem., of substances) in non-crystalline solid state. *n.* colloid substance.

coll'op, *n.* slice of meat.

collō'quial, *a.* proper or peculiar to everyday talk; not literary, &c. ~**ism**, *n.* colloquial word or idiom; use of these.

coll'oquy, *n.* talk, dialogue.

coll'otype, *n.* gelatine photographic plate that can be printed from in ink.

collu'sion (-ōozhn), *n.* fraudulent secret understanding between ostensible opponents. ~**ive**, *a.*

colly'rium, *n.* (pl. -*ia*), eye-salve; suppository.

col'ocynth, *n.* bitter-apple; purgative of colocynth.

cō'lon¹, *n.* greater part of the large intestine. **coli'tis, colōni'tis**, *nn.* inflammation of the colon.

cō'lon², *n.* punctuation-mark or stop (:).

colonel (kĕrn'el), *n.* army officer next in rank to a brigadier. **lieutenant-** ~, commander of a military unit (*colonel* used as courtesy title). ~**cy**, *n.* colonel's status.

colō'nial, *a.* of a colony. *n.* inhabitant of a colony.

col'onist, *n.* settler in or part-founder of a colony. **col'onize**, *v.t.* & *i.* (-*zable*), establish or join colony. ~**zation**, *n.*

colonnāde', *n.* series of columns with entablature.

col'ony, *n.* settlement of emigrants in a new country; persons of foreign nation or of one trade living in a town; birds, &c. similarly congregated.

col'ophon, *n.* tail-piece at end of old books.

coloph'ony, *n.* kind of dark resin.

Colora'dō bee'tle (-rah-), *n.* a potato pest.

colorā'tion (kŏ-, kŭ-), *n.* disposition of colours.

‖ **coloratur'a** (-oora), *n.* florid passages in vocal music.

colorif'ic (kŏ-, kŭ-), *a.* colour-producing.

---

colŏss'al, a. like a colossus, huge; (colloq.) splendid, glorious.

colŏss'us, n. (pl. ĭ-, -uses), statue of gigantic size; gigantic person or personified power.

colŏt'omy, n. incision in colon to provide artificial anus in stricture, &c.

colour (kŭl'er), n. sensation produced in eye by rays of decomposed light; any particular hue; pigment; (pl.) flag of regiment or ship; show of reason; pretext. v.t. & i. give colour to; paint or stain or dye; blush; make plausible. ~able, a. specious, plausible, counterfeit. ~blind, a. unable to distinguish some colours. *~ed, a. negro, of negro origin. ~ful, a. ~ing, n. coloration; artist's use of colour. ~ist, n. artist. ~less, a. wanting in character or vividness.

colpŏrteur' (-tẽr), n. book-hawker, esp. one employed to distribute Bibles and religious literature.

cŏlt¹, n. young horse; tiro, esp. cricket professional in first season; (Naut.) rope-end used in thrashing. v.t. thrash with colt.

Cŏlt², n. Colt revolver or pistol. P.

cō'ltsfŏŏt, n. large-leaved yellow flowered weed.

Colŭm'bia, n. America; the United States personified.

cŏl'umbine, n. garden plant; (C-) female character in pantomime.

cŏl'umn (-m), n. a round pillar, esp. one with base and capital; column-shaped thing; narrow-fronted deep arrangement of troops in successive lines.

cŏl'za, n. cole-seed. ~ oil, n. oil used in lamps.

cō'ma, n. unnatural heavy sleep or stupor. cō'matōse, a. in or like coma.

cŏmb (-m), n. toothed strip of rigid material for the hair; part of machine having similar shape; red fleshy crest of cock, &c.; honey-comb. v.t. & i. draw comb through hair; curry horse; dress wool with comb; to search.

cŏm'bat (kŭ-, kŏ-), n. fight. v.t. & i. do battle; engage in contest; oppose or strive against.

cŏm'batant (kŭ-, kŏ-), a. having actual fighting as function. n. combatant soldier, &c.

cŏm'bative (kŭ-, kŏ-), a. pugnacious or disputatious.

combinā'tion, n. set of things or persons combined; united action; chemical union; (pl.) under-garment for body and legs.

combīne', v.t. & i. (-nable), bring into union; possess in combination; co-operate. n. combination of persons, esp. to influence prices or course of trade.

combŭs'tible, a. capable of burning, easily set alight. n.pl. combustible things. ~bility, a.

combŭs'tion (-schn), n. destruction by fire; oxidation.

come (kŭm), v.i. (cāme, p.p. come), draw near, advance towards; arrive at; happen; become; prove, turn out. *~ across, (sl.) pay what one owes. ~down, n. downfall.

come-ăt-able (kŭ-), a. accessible.

comē'dian, n. actor; player of comic parts.

comēdiĕnne', n. comedy actress.

comēdiĕtt'a, n. short comedy.

cŏm'edy, n. amusing play satirizing everyday life; branch of drama concerned with comedies.

comely (kŭm'li), a. pleasant to look at; proper, decent.

comĕs'tibles, n.pl. things to eat.

cŏm'et, n. heavenly body with starlike nucleus and tail of light. cŏm'etarў, a.

cŏm'fit (kŭ-), n. sweetmeat.

cŏm'fort (kŭ-), n. relief in trouble, consolation; (pl.) things that make life easy. v.t. soothe, console; make easy.

cŏm'fortable (kŭ-), a. at ease in body or mind; promoting comfort. *n. stuffed or quilted coverlet for bed.

cŏm'forter (kŭ-), n. one who comforts, esp. the Holy Ghost; woollen scarf; baby's dummy teat.

cŏm'fortless (kŭ-), a. without provision for comfort.

com'frey (kŭ-), n. (pl. -eys), tall bell-flowered ditch-plant.

com'ic, a. of or like comedy; facetious, burlesque, funny. n. music-hall comedian. *~ strip, c. drawings in newspaper &c.

com'ical, a. comical'ity, queer, odd. comical'ity, n.

com'ity, n. courtesy; civility.

comm'a, n. punctuation-mark (,).

command' (-ah-), v.t. & i. order; issue orders; be in command; restrain or hold in check; have at disposal; look down over, dominate. n. order given; exercise or tenure of authority; troops or district under commander.

commandant', n. military governor of fortress, &c.

commandeer', v.t. impress or seize for military purposes.

comman'der (-ah-), n. a leader; naval officer ranking next to captain. ~-in-chief, n. commander of all land-forces of a State, or of all ships on a station.

comman'ding (-ah-), a. in command; exalted or impressive; dominant.

command'ment (-ah-), n. divine command; mandate, order.

comman'dō (-ah-), n. (pl. -os), (S.-Afr.) body of troops under one command.

commem'orāte, v.t. (-rable), celebrate in speech or writing or by some ceremony; be a memorial of. ~tion, n. a public celebration. ~tive, a.; ~tor, n.

commence', v.t. & i. (-ceable), begin. ~ment, n. beginning, start.

commend', v.t. entrust for safe keeping; praise. ~able, a. praiseworthy. ~ation, n. praise. ~atory, a. commending.

commen'surable (-sher-), a. measurable by same standard; proportionate to. ~bility, n. ~rate, a. coextensive, proportionate.

comm'ent, n. explanatory remark; criticism; observation; annotation. v.i. annotate, expound; make remarks upon.

comm'entary, n. running com-

ments on a book or remarks on a speech or performance. comm'entātor, n. writer or speaker of commentary.

comm'erce, n. exchange of merchandise; intercourse or dealings; a card game.

commer'cial (-shl), a. pertaining to commerce. n. (vulg.) commercial traveller. ~ traveller, agent sent out to solicit custom for firm.

commina'tion, n. cursings, denunciation. comm'inātory, a. threatening vengeance.

commingle (koming'gl), v.t. & i. mix, unite.

comm'inūte, v.t. reduce to minute particles. ~tion, n. pulverization.

commis'erāte (-z-), v.t. & i. (-rable), pity, have commiseration for.

commisera'tion (-z-), n. compassion, pity. commis'erātive, a.

commissar', n. head of a Government department of the U.S.S.R.

commissar'iat, n. food and store department of army; family's or person's food supply.

comm'issary, n. person deputed by superior power; head of commissariat. commissar'ial, a.

commi'ssion (-shn), n. act of committing; task committed to person; body or board of persons constituted to discharge a task; (Mil., Nav.) warrant appointing a commissioned officer; brokerage; percentage on sales, &c. v.t. empower or appoint by commission; empower a person to do some service.

commissionaire' (-sho-), n. pensioned soldier employed as porter, &c.

commi'ssioner (-sho-), n. member of a permanent Government board or other commission; representative of supreme authority in a district or Government department.

comm'issure (-shoor), n. (Anat.) a band, seam, suture.

commit', v.t. entrust; consign, imprison; perpetrate; pledge, involve, compromise. ~ment, n. engagement that restricts freedom of action. ~tal, n. committing to prison ; committing of oneself.

commit'ee (-tǐ), n. body to which the considering or ordering of any matter is referred.

commix', v.t. & i. mix, mingle. ~ture, n. blending.

commode', n. chest of drawers ; close-stool.

commo'dious, a. roomy.

commod'ity, n. article that meets needs or can be traded in.

commodore', n. commander of squadron of ships ; senior captain of ships sailing together or of ships of one shipping line ; captain of pilots. Air C~, officer of Royal Air Force.

comm'on, a. shared by all ; of ordinary kind ; occurring often ; of inferior quality ; vulgar ; (of gender or a noun) indifferently masculine and feminine. n. lands belonging to a community ; piece of unenclosed waste land. ~ law, unwritten law of England derived from ancient usage. ~ sense, good practical sense in everyday matters.

comm'onage, n. right of common ; land held in common.

comm'onalty, n. the common people.

comm'oner, n. person below rank of peer ; person with right of common.

comm'only, adv. usually, frequently.

comm'onplace, n. trite quotation or everyday saying ; platitude. a. lacking originality or individuality.

comm'ons (-z), n.pl. the common people ; the lower house of Parliament ; food, diet.

comm'onwealth (-wĕl-), n. general body of the people ; a free community.

commo'tion, n. agitated stir.

comm'unal, a. of a commune ; on communalistic principles. ~ism, n. local autonomy as basis of State organization. ~istic, a.

comm'une, n. small territorial administrative district. v.i. (also

komūn') hold intimate converse with.

commū'nicant, n. receiver of Communion ; imparter of news.

commū'nicate, v.t. & i. (-cable), impart to others, have communication with ; receive Communion.

communica'tion, n. imparting or exchange of information ; connexion between places.

commū'nicative, a. given to talking openly ; not reserved.

commū'nion (-yon), n. intercourse ; fellowship ; celebration of the Lord's Supper or participation in it.

||communiqué (komū'nĭkā), n. official intimation.

comm'unism, n. community of goods as a social system. ~ist, n. ; ~istic, a.

commū'nity, n. joint ownership ; body of persons, &c. having community of life (e.g. members of a State, town, convent, &c.). ~ singing, in which all present join.

commū'tator, n. device for altering direction of current.

commute', v.t. & i. (-table), buy off by exchange ; diminish ; change ; *buy and use commutation ticket. ~tation, n. *commutation ticket, season-ticket issued by railroad for trips between specified places. *commū'ter, n. holder of season-ticket.

com'pact[1], n. binding agreement or understanding.

compact'[2], a. close, dense ; well-knit ; terse. v.t. make compact.

compan'ion (-yon), n. comrade, mate ; an associate ; thing that matches with another ; member of lowest grade of knightly Order. v.t. & i. act as companion to ; associate with. ~able, a. sociable. ~ship, n. fellowship.

com'pany (kŭ-), n. being with another or others ; persons assembled together ; guests ; body of persons combined for commercial or other end ; (Mil.) part of battalion.

com'parable, a. susceptible of

comparison (*with*) ; fit to be compared (*to*).

compa´rative, *a.* working or perceiving by comparison ; not absolute. ~ly, *adv.*

compare´, *v.t. & i.* liken to ; estimate similarity of ; put side by side for comparison ; bear comparison with. *n.* comparison.

compa´rison, *n.* comparing ; a simile or illustration.

compart´ment, *n.* a division, space partitioned off.

com´pass (kŭ-), *n.* circuit, extent, area, range ; instrument with magnetic needle indicating points of the compass ; instrument for describing circles on paper. *v.t.* go round, surround, hem in ; attain or bring about.

compa´ssion (-shn), *n.* pity. compa´ssionate[1] (-sho-), *a.* feeling or showing compassion. compa´ssionate[2] (-sho-), *v.t.* regard or treat with compassion.

compat´ible, *a.* consistent ; agreeable with. ~bility, *n.*

compat´riot, *n.* fellow-countryman.

compeer´, *n.* an equal.

compel´, *v.t.* force or constrain ; bring about irresistibly.

compen´dious, *a.* abridged ; brief.

compen´dium, *n.* (pl. *-s*, *-dia*), an abridgement or summary.

com´pensate, *v.t. & i.* (*-sable*), counterbalance ; recompense.

compensa´tion, *n.* that which compensates. ~tor, *n.* ; ~tory, *a.*

compete´, *v.i.* strive against others ; contend for a prize.

com´petence, *n.* competent ability ; a sufficiency. ~cy, *n.*

com´petent, *a.* having the qualifications required by law or by the work in hand ; open or permissible.

competi´tion, *n.* competing ; contest. compet´itive, *a.* ; ~tor, *n.*

compila´tion, *n.* that which is compiled ; compiled book.

compile´, *v.t.* (*-lable*), collect together (facts, quotations, &c.).

compla´cency, *n.* pleasure ; self-satisfaction ; gratification.

compla´cent, *a.* self-satisfied ; in pleasant mood.

complain´, *v.i.* bewail ; make complaint ; inform against. ~ant, *n.* plaintiff in certain suits.

complaint´, *n.* statement that one is aggrieved or dissatisfied ; formal protest ; bodily ailment.

complais´ance (-z-), *n.* civility ; desire of pleasing.

complais´ant (-z-), *a.* disposed to please ; obliging.

com´plement[1], *n.* what completes or coexists with ; complete set or provision ; full number.

com´plement[2], *v.t.* act as complement to. ~ary, *a.*

complete´, *a.* having all its parts ; finished. *v.t.* (*-table*), bring to entirety ; finish.

comple´tion, *n.* completing.

com´plex, *a.* consisting of parts ; complicated, involved. *n.* a complex whole ; (Psychol.) kind of mental abnormality. ~ity, *n.* state of being complex.

comple´xion (-kshn), *n.* colouring and skin-texture of the face.

compli´ance, *n.* acquiescence.

compli´ant, *a.* yielding.

com´plicate, *v.t.* (*-cable*), make complicated, entangle. ~d, *a.* intricate, involved, hard to unravel. ~tion, *n.* complicated state ; complicating circumstances.

complic´ity, *n.* accompliceship.

com´pliment[1], *n.* polite expression or implication of praise.

com´pliment[2], *v.t.* pay compliments to ; flatter. ~ary, *a.* laudatory ; by way of compliment.

com´plin(e), *n.* (in Catholic ritual) last daily service.

comply´, *v.i.* act according to request or command or rules.

compo´nent, *a.* going to the making of a whole ; constituent. *n.* component part.

comport´, *v.t. & i.* behave or conduct oneself ; be compatible or in harmony with.

compose´ (-z), *v.t. & i.* (*-sable*), (of elements, &c.) form or constitute ; construct in one's mind ;

become tranquil; make up or reconcile; set up type. ~ed, a. quiet, calm. ~edly, adv. calmly.

compo'ser (-z-), n. one who composes, esp. music.

com'posite (or -īt; -z-), a. consisting of different parts or materials. n. whole made of different elements.

compoṣi'tion, n. composing; thing composed; a mixture; agreement or compromise.

compoṣ'itor (-z-), n. type-setter.

com'post, n. compound manure.

compo'ṣure (-zher), n. calmness.

com'pōte, n. fruit in syrup.

compound¹, v.t. & i. mix or combine into a whole; settle by mutual concession; commute.

com'pound², a. composite, compounded; not simple. n. a mixture; compound word.

com'pound³, n. (India, China, &c.) enclosure round buildings.

comprᵉhend', v.t. grasp mentally; be inclusive of; comprise.

comprehen'sible, a. intelligible.

comprehen'sion (-shn), n. understanding; inclusion; grasp.

comprehen'sive, a. embracing much; of wide scope.

compreṣṣ'¹, v.t. (-ible), squeeze together; bring into smaller compass. ~ibility, ~ion, nn.

com'preṣṣ², n. pad for compressing artery, &c.

compriṣe' (-z), v.t. (-sable), contain; include.

com'promiṣe (-z), n. agreement attained by mutual concession. v.t. (-sable), adjust by mutual concessions; bring oneself (or another) under suspicion.

comprovin'cial (-shl), a. & n. (person, esp. bishop) of the same (esp. archiepiscopal) province.

comptrō'ller, n. controller.

compul'sion (-shn), n. compelling.

compul'sory, a. done or acting under compulsion.

compunc'tion, n. pricking of conscience.

compute', v.t. calculate, reckon, count. ~table, a.; ~tation, n.

comrade (kŭm'rĭd, kō-), n. mate

or fellow; companion or associate. ~ship, n.

Com'tism, n. positivism.

con¹, v.t. study or learn.

con², v.t. direct steering of ship.

|| con amōr'ē, adv. with enthusiasm.

conā'tion, n. the exertion of willing that desire or aversion shall issue in action.

concaténā'tion, n. connexion as of chain-links; string or series of ideas, events, &c.

con'căve, a. of interior curvature; opp. to convex. concăv'ity, n.

conceal', v.t. hide or keep secret. ~ment, n.

concēde', v.t. (-dable), grant; admit as true; allow.

conceit' (-sēt), n. one's notion of oneself; vanity; far-fetched comparison. ~ed, a.

conceive' (-sēv), v.t. & i. (-vable), become pregnant; form in the mind; formulate in words.

con'centrāte, v.t. & i. (-trable), bring to bear on one point; collect one's thoughts or efforts. ~tion, n. collection to one point; mental faculty of exclusive attention. ~tive, a.; ~tor, n.

concen'tric, a. having common centre. concentri'city, n.

con'cept, n. idea of a class of objects; general notion.

concep'tion, n. conceiving; pregnancy; an idea. ~al, a. ~tive, a. capable of conceiving. ~tual, a. of mental conceptions.

concern', v.t. relate to; affect; be relevant to; mix oneself up in; feel anxiety about. n. thing that concerns one; (pl.) one's affairs; solicitude; firm or enterprise. ~ing, prep. about. ~ment, n.

con'cert¹, n. combined state; a musical entertainment.

concert'², v.t. plan, contrive; prearrange; (p.p., Mus.) arranged in parts.

concerti'na (-tē-), n. wind-instrument pumped by the hands.

concert'o (-cher-), n. (pl. -os), musical piece for solo instrument with orchestral accompaniment.

conceṣ'sion (-shn), n. conceding or

thing conceded; monopoly or similar privilege. **~aire'**, n. holder of concession. **~ive**, a.

conch (-ngk), n. shellfish or its shell. **~ol'ogy**, n. study of shells.

concil'iate, v.t. (-iable), propitiate; win over from hostility; reconcile. **~tion**, n. bringing of opponents into harmony. **~tor**, n.; **~tory**, a.

concise', a. brief, condensed.

con'clave, n. cardinals' meeting-place for papal election; any meeting for secret consultation.

conclude (kon-klood'), v.t. & i. (-dable), bring or come to an end; finish, settle; infer.

conclusion (kon-kloo'zhn), n. ending, close; inference; final opinion. **conclu'sive**, a. convincing.

concoct', v.t. compound; fabricate; make in concert. **~ion**, n. concocting, concocted thing.

concom'itance, n. co-existence.

concom'itant (-n-k-), a. attendant, accompanying. n. (usu. in pl.) concomitant circumstances.

conc'ord, n. harmonious relations; (Gram.) agreement in gender, person, &c. between words. **~ant**, a. agreeing; in harmony.

concord'ance (-n-k-), n. agreement; index of words used by author or in book, esp. Bible.

concord'at (-n-k-), n. compact between church and state.

conc'ourse (-ors), n. a flocking together; a crowd, throng.

conc'rete, a. having objective reality; not abstract. n. a concrete thing or word; composition of gravel, cement, &c. **concrete'**, v.t. solidify; form into a mass.

concre'tion (-n-k-), n. mass of coalesced particles; morbid formation in the body. **~ary**, a.

conc'ubine, n. woman who cohabits with a man without marriage. **concu'binage**, n. such cohabitation.

concu'piscence (-n-k-), n. sexual lust. **concu'piscent**, a. lustful.

concur' (-n-k-), v.i. occur together, coincide; agree. **concu'rrence**, n. **~rent**, a. concurring.

concu'ssion (kon-kŭshn), n. violent shaking or shock; head injury due to heavy blow.

condemn' (-m), v.t. censure, blame; give judicial decision against; pronounce unfit for use. **condemnā'tion**, n.; **condem'natory**, a.

condense', v.t. & i. (-sable), make denser or briefer; compress; consolidate. **~sability**, **condensā'tion**, nn.

conden'ser, n. apparatus for converting steam to water.

condescend', v.i. deign to do; stoop; (part.) patronizing.

condescen'sion (-shn), n. condescending manner or act.

condign' (-in), a. adequate.

con'diment, n. relish or seasoning for use with food.

condi'tion, n. quality; state; attribute; (pl.) circumstances; stipulation; social rank. v.t. be a condition of; make terms; stipulate. **~al**, a. not absolute.

condole', v.i. express sympathy in sorrow with. **condo'lence**, n.

condomin'ium, n. joint control of a State by other States.

condone', v.t. (-nable), treat as non-existent. **condonā'tion**, n.

con'dor, n. large S.-Amer. vulture.

condottier'e (-tyāri), n. (pl. -ri, pr. -rē), captain of mercenaries.

conduce', v.i. tend to produce or effect. **~cive**, a.

con'duct[1], n. one's actions; management; convoy, escort. **conduct'[2]**, v.t. lead, escort; control; manage; behave oneself; transmit (heat, &c.). **~ion**, n. (Phys.) conducting of heat, electricity, &c. **~ive**, a.; **~ivity**, n. (Phys.)

conduc'tor, n. director of orchestra; official in charge of passengers; conductive substance or object. **~tress**, n.

con'duit (kŭn'dit), n. channel or pipe, aqueduct.

cone, n. tapering figure with circular base; pine-cone, fir-cone.

confab'ulate, v.i. talk together. **~tion**, **~tor**, nn.

confec'tion, n. sweetstuff; light

---

and elegant article of female attire. ~er, n. dealer in pastry, sweets, &c. ~ery, n.

confed'eracy, n. league, conspiracy ; league of confederate States.

confed'erate, a. leagued together. n. partner in a design; accomplice. v.t. & i. (-at; -rable), make league with ; make a confederation. ~a'tion, n. permanent union of sovereign States for common external action.

con'fer¹, cf., v. imperat. compare.

confer'², v.t. & i. bestow ; take counsel ; meet for discussion.

con'ference, n. meeting for discussion ; exchange of views.

confer'ment, n. conferring of honours, &c.

confess', v.t. & i. acknowledge ; plead guilty to ; disclose one's sin to confessor ; (of priest) hear confession of.

confess'edly, adv. avowedly.

confes'sion (-shn), n. acknowledgement of guilt, &c. ; confession to priest ; statement of one's principles. ~al, a. of confession. n. confessor's stall.

confess'or, n. one who avows his religious faith ; priest who hears confessions and gives absolution.

confett'i, n.pl. sweets or disks of coloured paper used as missiles in carnival, at weddings, &c.

confidant', n. (fem. -ante), person to whom one confides one's private affairs.

confide', v.i. & t. repose confidence in ; impart ; (part.) unsuspicious.

con'fidence, n. firm trust ; confidence in oneself ; assurance. ~ trick, method of swindling.

con'fident, a. feeling or showing assurance ; positive.

confiden'tial (-shl), a. imparted in confidence ; enjoying confidence.

configura'tion, n. aspect as produced by relative position of parts.

confine'¹, v.t. (-nable), keep within limits ; confine to limits ; imprison, hold in custody ; (pass.) be brought to bed of a child.

con'fine², n. a boundary ; (pl.) the border or edge of.

confine'ment, n. being confined ; imprisonment ; child-birth.

confirm', v.t. make stronger ; ratify ; corroborate ; administer confirmation to. ~and, n. candidate for confirmation. ~ation, n. corroborating circumstance or statement ; rite in which persons confirm the vows made for them at baptism. ~ative, ~atory, aa. corroborating.

con'fiscate, v.t. (-cable), seize private property for the public treasury ; seize as by authority. ~tion, ~tor, nn. ; ~tory, a.

conflagra'tion, n. a widespread fire ; great outbreak of war, &c.

con'flict¹, n. trial of strength ; strife ; conflicting state.

conflict'², v.i. be at odds or inconsistent with ; contest with.

con'fluent (-ooent), a. merging into one. n. one of confluent streams, &c. con'fluence (-ooens), con'flux, nn. meeting of confluents ; concourse.

conform', v.t. & i. adapt ; make like ; comply with rules or general custom. ~able, a. adapted or corresponding to. ~ation, n. thing's structure. ~ist, n. conformer to Anglican usages. ~ity, n. correspondence to or harmony with.

confound', v.t. mix up, confuse ; astound ; baffle ; ~ it, you, a mild imprecation ; (p.p.) accursed, disagreeable.

confrater'nity, n. a brotherhood.

|| confrère (kòn fràr), n. fellowmember of profession, &c.

confront' (-ŭnt), v.t. bring face to face ; face or be confronted with. ~ation, n.

confuse' (-z), v.t. (-sable), throw into disorder ; obscure, mix up.

confu'sion (-zhn), n. confused state ; tumult ; discomfiture.

confute', v.t. (-table), prove erroneous. confuta'tion, n.

|| congé (kawn'zhā), n. dismissal.

congeal' (-j-), v.t. & i. solidify by freezing or otherwise.

|| congee. See conjee.

congela'tion (-j-), n. congealing.

côn′gener (-j-), *n.* thing or person of the same kind.

conge′nial (-j-), *a.* of kindred temper; suiting one's disposition; pleasurable to. ~**al′ity,** *n.*

congĕn′ital (-j-), *a.* born with one; dating from birth.

cŏng′er (-ngg-), *n.* large sea eel.

conge′ries (-jĕrĭēz), *n.* mass of small bodies heaped together.

conges′tĕd (-j-), *a.* suffering congestion.

conges′tion (-jĕschon), *n.* abnormal accumulation of blood in an organ, population in a district, &c.

conglŏm′erate (-n-g-), *n.* mass of pebbles cemented into a kind of stone; mixture of things. ~**ed,** *a.* stuck together in a mass. **conglŏmerā′tion,** *n.*

cŏng′ou (-nggōō), *n.* a black China tea.

congrăt′ūlāte (-n-g-), *v.t.* (-*lable*), offer congratulations to; felicitate.

congrătūlā′tion (-n-g-), *n.* expression of pleasure in another's good fortune (usu. in pl.). ~**tory,** *a.*

cŏng′regāte (-ngg-), *v.t. & i.* (-*gable*), flock together, assemble.

congregā′tion, *n.* assembly of people, esp. for religious worship. ~**al,** *a.* public; of Congregationalism. **Cŏngregā′tionalism,** *n.* system by which individual churches are self-governing. ~**alist,** *n.* adherent of such church.

cŏng′ress (-ngg-), *n.* formal meeting of delegates for discussion; Senate and House of Representatives of the U.S. ~**man,** *n.* member of U.S. Congress, esp. of House of Representatives. **congre′ssional** (-nggrĕssho-), *a.*

cŏng′ruence (-nggrōō-), **congru′ity** (-nggrōō-), *nn.* accordance; harmonious relation; correspondence. **cŏng′ruent, cŏng′ruous,** *aa.*

cŏn′ic, *a.* of the form of a cone. ~**sections,** curves made by intersection of right circular cone with plane. ~**al,** *a.* cone-shaped. **cŏn′ics,** *n.* study of conic sections.

‖ **cŏnĭcŏp′olў,** *n.* (Anglo-Ind.) a native clerk or writer in the Madras Presidency.

cŏn′ifer, *n.* coniferous tree.

conif′erous, *a.* bearing fruit-cones.

conjec′ture, *n.* guessing, guesswork. *v.t. & i.* (-*rable*), make conjecture, guess. ~**ral,** *a.* depending on conjecture.

‖ **cŏn′jee,** -**gee** (-j-), *n.* (Anglo-Ind.) water in which rice has been boiled.

conjoin′, *v.t. & i.* make into or become a single whole. **conjoint′,** *a.* conjoined, combined.

cŏn′jugal (-ōō-), *a.* of marriage; between married persons.

cŏn′jugate (-ōō-), *v.t. & i.* (-*āt* -*gable*), inflect (verb); enter into conjugation. *a.* (-it) conjoint; growing in pairs.

cŏnjugā′tion (-ōō-), *n.* conjoining; reproductive fusion of cells; inflexion scheme of verbs.

conjunct′, *a.* associated with or assisting another.

conjunc′tion, *n.* conjoining; simultaneous occurrence; word used to connect sentences together. ~**al,** *a.* ~**tive,** *a.* serving to join.

cŏnjuncti′va, *n.* mucous membrane connecting eyelid and eyeball. **conjuncti′tis,** *n.* inflammation of this.

conjunc′ture, *n.* position of affairs at particular moment.

cŏnjurā′tion (-ōō-), *n.* solemn entreaty; incantation.

conjure[1] (-oor), *v.t.* entreat solemnly to do something.

conjure[2] (kŭn′jer), *v.i. & i.* produce magical effects; do sleight-of-hand tricks; call up spirits.

conjurer, ~**or** (kŭn′jerer), *n.* adept at sleight-of-hand.

cŏnk, *n.* nose. ~**y,** *a.* big-nosed.

cŏnk, *v.i.* (sl.) break down, give *out* (esp. of mechanism).

connâte′, *a.* congenital; (of leaves) united at base.

connâ′tural (-cher-), *a.* congenital of the same nature.

connect′, *v.t. & i.* join, link, unite; (*p.p.,* of narrative, &c.) having internal connexion; coherent. ~**ive,** *a.* serving as connexion. = U.S.

conne'xion (-kshon), ~nec'tion, n. being linked together or in communication or intercourse ; that which connects ; set of persons linked by some bond ; relationship.

con'ning'-tow'er, n. warship's shot-proof pilot-house.

*connip'tion, n. (sl.) attack of hysteria ; fit of rage.

conni'vance, n. pretence of being unaware ; winking at offence.

connive', v.i. look on in connivance at misdoing.

connoisseur' (-naser), n. a critical judge, esp. of the fine arts.

connote', v.t. (-table), imply, betoken ; mean ; include in its meaning. ~tation, n. ; ~tative, a.

connu'bial, a. connected with marriage.

co'noid, a. more or less conical. n. conoid object.

conq'uer (-ngker), v.t. & i. overcome ; acquire by conquest ; master one's difficulties or passions.

conq'ueror (-ngke-), n. person who conquers ; deciding game ; horse-chestnut that has broken others in boys' game of conquerors.

conq'uest, n. conquering, what is won by it ; winning of person to affection, person so won.

consanguin'eous (-nggw-), a. related by birth ; near of kin.

consanguin'ity (-nggw-), n. kinship.

con'science (-shens), n. faculty distinguishing between right and wrong ; consciousness that one's actions are right or wrong.

conscien'tious (-shus), a. obedient to dictates of conscience. ~ objector, person who pleads conscience as a reason for refusing to obey some law or command.

con'scious (-shus), a. having knowledge of one's thoughts and feelings ; awake to one's surroundings ; aware of. ~ness, n. person's thoughts and feelings as a whole.

conscribe', (-bable), enrol by conscription. conscript', vv.t.

con'script, n. conscribed man.

conscrip'tion, n. compulsory enlistment for national service.

con'secrate, v.t. (-rable), make sacred ; devote to sacred purpose ; sanctify. ~tor, n. ; ~tory, a.

consecra'tion, n. setting apart for sacred purposes ; dedication.

consec'utive, a. following, consequential ; orderly and unbroken.

consen'sus, n. agreement of opinion on the part of all concerned.

consent', v.i. agree to ; acquiesce in. n. agreement ; consenting or words expressing it.

consenta'neous, a. in accord ; done by common consent.

consen'tient (-shnt), a. agreeing.

con'sequence, n. that which comes from any cause or principle ; importance ; moment ; influential position.

con'sequent, a. that results ; following as a consequence.

consequen'tial (-shl), a. of the nature of a corollary ; self-important. ~tial'ity (-shi'-), n.

con'sequently, adv. & conj. as a result ; accordingly ; therefore.

conserv'ancy, n. board controlling river or port.

conserva'tion, n. preserving ; continuance ; conserved state.

conserv'ative, a. of conserving tendency, opposed to change ; (of estimate) moderate. n. member of Conservative party ; person of conservative disposition. ~tism, n.

conservatoire' (-twahr), n. public school of music and declamation (on Continent).

con'servator, n. member of conservancy ; custodian of museum, &c. ; person who secures the conserving of.

conserv'atory, n. greenhouse for tender plants.

conserve', v.t. (-vable), preserve ; keep from decay or change. n. preserved fruit, &c.

consid'er, v.t. & i. contemplate ; deliberate thoughtfully ; reckon with, take into account ; show consideration for.

consid'erable, *a.* of some importance ; worthy of regard.

consid'erate, *a.* thoughtful for the feelings or rights of others.

considera'tion, *n.* considering ; thing worth considering ; thing given or done as inducement ; considerateness. consid'ering *prep.* in view of.

consign' (-ĭn), *v.t.* commit or hand over ; send goods for delivery. ∼ee, ∼or, *nn.* person to whom, by whom, goods are consigned. ∼ment, *n.* consigning ; goods consigned.

consist', *v.i.* be composed of ; be compatible with. ∼ence, *n.* degree of density in liquids, &c. ∼ency, *n.* being consistent. ∼ent, *a.* compatible, not contradictory ; constant to same principles.

con'sistory, *n.* kinds of ecclesiastical council or court.

consola'tion, *n.* alleviation of grief or disappointment. consol'atory, *a.* giving comfort.

console'[1], *v.t.* (-lable), bring consolation to.

con'sole[2], *n.* bracket serving as ledge to support something.

consol'idate, *v.t.* & *i.* (-dable), solidify ; strengthen ; combine (statutes, debts, &c.) into one. ∼tion, ∼tor, *nn.* ∼tory, *a.*

consols' (-z), *n.pl.* Government consolidated stock.

con'sonance, *n.* agreement in sound, musical concord ; agreement in meaning, taste, &c.

con'sonant, *a.* agreeable, consistent. *n.* non-vowel letter ; sound that forms a syllable only in combination with a vowel. ∼al, *a.*

con'sort[1], *n.* spouse ; partner ; ship sailing with another.

consort'[2], *v.i.* associate or keep company ; be in harmony.

conspec'tus, *n.* general view ; synopsis.

conspic'uous, *a.* striking to the eye, readily seen ; eminent.

conspi'racy, *n.* plot or plotting for evil-doing. ∼ator, *n.*

conspire', *v.i.* take part in conspiracy ; agree together.

con'stable (kŭ-), *n.* great officer of royal household ; policeman below sergeant's rank. Chief ∼, head of police force of county, &c. constab'ulary, *a.* & *n.* (organized body) of police.

con'stancy, *n.* faithfulness ; tenacious adherence ; steadiness.

con'stant, *a.* not subject to variation ; continual ; firm. *n.* quantity that does not vary. ∼ly, *adv.* always ; often.

constella'tion, *n.* fixed stars forming a group to the eye.

consterna'tion, *n.* paralysing sense of calamity.

con'stipate, *v.t.* affect with constipation. ∼tion, *n.* difficulty in evacuating the bowels.

constit'uency, *n.* body electing representative ; place represented.

constit'uent, *a.* making part of a whole ; appointing, electing. *n.* constituent part ; member of elective body ; voter.

con'stitute, *v.t.* (-uable), appoint, make into ; establish ; be the essence or components of.

constitu'tion, *n.* constituent parts, essential nature ; bodily predisposition ; form in which a State is organized ; system of laws and customs.

constitu'tional (-sho-), *a.* of or due to one's constitution ; in harmony with the constitution of the State. *n.* walk taken as healthy exercise. ∼ism, ∼ist, *nn.*

con'stitutive, *a.* having power to constitute ; constituent.

constrain', *v.t.* compel ; hinder by force ; hold in constraint.

constraint', *n.* compulsion ; repression of feeling ; embarrassment.

constrict', *v.t.* compress ; encircle and squeeze. ∼ion, *n.* ∼ive, *a.* ∼or, *n.* constrictive muscle.

construct', *v.t.* fit together, frame, build. ∼or, *n.*

construc'tion, *n.* thing constructed ; syntactical connexion ; interpretation. ∼al, *a.*

construc'tive, *a.* tending to construction ; of a positive kind.

māre, mēre, mīre, mōre, mūre ; part, pert, port ; *italics*. vague sounds ;

cŏn'strue (-ōō), *v.t.* combine grammatically *with*; interpret; translate word for word.

cŏnsŭbstăn'tial (-shl), *a.* of one substance. **cŏnsŭbstăntiā'tion** (-si-), *n.* presence of body and blood of Christ in the Eucharist.

cŏn'sul, *n.* a Roman official; State agent in foreign town.

cŏn'sular, *a.* relating to a consul.

cŏn'sulate, *n.* office of consul; consul's official residence.

cŏnsŭlt', *v.t.& i.* take counsel with; seek information or advice from. **~ation**, *n.* **~ative**, *a.* deliberative; advisory.

cŏnsūme', *v.t. & i.* (-mable), destroy, use up, eat or drink; waste away; be exhausted.

cŏnsū'mědly, *adv.* excessively.

cŏnsū'mer, *n.* user of product.

cŏnsŭmm'ate², *a.* of the highest perfection or completeness.

cŏn'summate², *v.t.* (-table), bring to completion; be the crown of. **~tion**, **~tor**, *nn.*

cŏnsŭmp'tion, *n.* consuming; wasting disease, esp. tuberculosis.

cŏnsŭmp'tive, *a.* tending to or affected with tuberculosis, &c. *n.* consumptive person.

cŏn'tact, *n.* touch; connexion.

contā'gion (-jn), *n.* communication of disease by contact; corrupting influence. **~gious**, *a.*

contāin', *v.t.* have within, include; comprise; restrain.

contăm'ināte, *v.t.* (-nable), pollute, infect. **~tion**, **~tor**, *nn.*

contăng'ō (-ngg-), *n.* (pl. -os), percentage paid by buyer of stock for postponement of transfer.

contĕmn' (-m), *v.t.* feel contempt for; scornfully regard.

cŏn'template *v.t.* (-lable), survey steadily with eyes or mind; have in view. **~tion**, *n.* meditative state. **~tor**, *n.*

contĕm'plative, *a.* thoughtful.

contĕmporā'neous, *a.* belonging to, existing at, the same time.

contĕm'porary, *a.* of these times; contemporaneous. *n.* contemporary person or newspaper.

contĕmpt', *n.* feeling of scorn;

disrespect; disobedience to lawful authority.

contĕmp'tible, *a.* deserving contempt.

contĕmp'tuous, *a.* feeling or showing contempt; apt to despise.

contĕnd', *v.i. & t.* strive for; act in emulation; dispute, contest.

contĕnt', *a.* satisfied with; ready to accept. *v.t.* make content; meet demands of. *n.* contentment; (*also* kŏn'tĕnt) amount that vessel can contain; (pl.) what is contained; table of contents of book. **~ed**, *a.* enjoying contentment. **~ment**, *n.* satisfaction; happiness.

contĕn'tion, *n.* strife; what a disputant contends.

contĕn'tious (-shus), *a.* given to or involving contention.

contĕr'minous, *a.* having a common boundary or end.

contĕst'¹, *v.t.* impugn, controvert; contend or compete for. **~ant**, *n.*

cŏn'tĕst², *n.* contending; a competition.

cŏn'text, *n.* what precedes and follows word or passage of a discourse. **contĕx'tual**, *a.*

contĕx'ture, *n.* inter-relation of components; style of composition.

contigū'ity, *n.* contact; nearness.

contig'ūous, *a.* adjoining, next to; neighbouring.

cŏn'tinence, *n.* restraint; chastity.

cŏn'tinent¹, *a.* self-restraining.

cŏn'tinent², *n.* the mainland of Europe; any of the main divisions of the earth. **~al**, *a.* characteristic of the Continent (Europe).

contin'gency, *n.* being contingent; contingent event.

contin'gent (-j-), *a.* that may happen; conditional. *n.* quota or draft of troops.

contin'ual, *a.* occurring on every occasion; seeming incessant.

contin'ūance, *n.* continuing in existence or operation; duration.

continūā'tion, *n.* going on with or resuming something; thing that continues something else; (pl., sl.) trousers. **contin'ūative**,

contin′ue, *v.t. & i.* (-*uable*), go on with; remain in existence; take up again. **continū′ity**, *n.* uninterrupted connexion.

contin′uous, *a.* connected without break; uninterrupted.

contort′, *v.t.* twist or force out of normal shape. **contor′tion**, *n.* ~**ionist**, *n.* acrobat.

con′tour (-oor), *n.* outline of a figure, object, coast, &c.

con′traband, *n.* prohibited traffic; smuggled goods. ~**ist**, *n.* smuggler.

contracep′tive, *a. & n.* preventive of conception. **contracep′tion**, *n.* use of contraceptives.

con′tract[1], *n.* business agreement, bargain; compact.

contract′[2], *v.t. & i.* make a contract; catch (cold, &c.); draw together; make or become smaller; shorten.

contrac′tile (*or* -ī-), *a.* capable of or producing contraction.

contrac′tion, *n.* shrinking; diminution; word-shortening or contracted word.

contrac′tor, *n.* maker of a contract; a builder; contracting muscle.

contrac′tual, *a.* of a contract.

contradict′, *v.t. & i.* deny; oppose verbally; be at variance with.

contradic′tion, *n.* verbal denial; direct opposition; inconsistency.

contradic′tory, *a.* given to contradiction; conflicting.

contradistinc′tion, *n.* distinction by opposite qualities.

contradistin′guish (-nggw-), *v.t.* distinguish by opposite qualities; set in sharp contrast.

contral′to, *n.* (pl. -*os*), lowest of the female voices; contralto singer.

contrap′tion, *n.* (sl.) queer machine or appliance.

contrapun′tal, *a.* of counterpoint. ~**tist**, *n.* contrapuntal expert.

contrari′ety, *n.* contrariness.

con′trariwise (-z), *adv.* on the other hand; in the opposite way.

con′trary, *a.* opposed in nature or tendency or direction; (kontrār′ĭ) perverse, vexatious. *n.* thing's opposite. *adv.* contrarily.

con′trast[1] (-ah-), *n.* difference between things as shown by placing them against each other; thing in marked contrast to another.

contrast′[2] (-ah-), *v.t. & i.* put in or subject to or be in contrast.

contravēne′, *v.t.* (-*nable*), infringe, conflict with. ~**vēn′tion**, *n.* opposition; infringement.

contretemps (kawn′trĕtahn), *n.* unexpected hitch.

contrib′ute, *v.t. & i.* (-*table*), give to a common stock; bear a part.

contribū′tion, *n.* payment made in aid of a common fund or collection; something contributed.

contrib′utor, *n.* one that bears a part; a subscriber; writer in a newspaper, &c.

contrib′utory, *a.* that contributes; contributing to some purpose or fund.

con′trite, *a.* sorrowing for sin.

contri′tion, *n.* sorrow for sin.

contri′vance, *n.* contriving; contrived article or appliance.

contrive′, *v.t. & i.* (-*vable*), devise, think out; plan, manage.

control′, *n.* restraint; means of checking the results of bookkeeping or experiment; safeguarding; supervision; (Spiritualism) personality actuating a medium; station at which aeroplanes, motors, &c., in races are allowed time to stop for overhauling, &c.; (pl.) devices giving stability to aeroplane in turning, &c.; gear-lever, &c. of motor-car, &c. *v.t.* have control of; govern; restrain.

control′ler, *n.* officer controlling expenditure; one that governs.

controver′sial (-shl), *a.* of controversy; disputable. ~**ist**, *n.*

con′troversy, *n.* disputation, esp. argument conducted in the press.

controvert′, *v.t.* call in question; dispute the truth of.

contumā′cious, *n.* stubborn disobedience. **con′tumācious**, *a.*

con′tumely, *n.* insulting language or treatment. ~**ē′lious**, *a.*

contūse′ (-z), *v.t.* (-*sable*), bruise.

---

contū'sion (-zhn), n. bruise.

conŭn'drum, n. riddle.

cŏnvălěs'ce', v.i. be convalescent.

cŏnvălěs'cence, n. convalescent state.

cŏnvălěs'cent, a. recovering from sickness. n. convalescent person.

‖ convenances (kawn'venăhs), n.pl. conventional propriety.

convēne', v.t. & i. (-nable), summon; hold meeting.

convē'nience, n. what suits one; useful appliance; water-closet; (pl.) comforts.

convē'nient, a. fit, suitable; well-adapted; opportune.

cŏn'vent, n. religious community, esp. of women; its house.

convěn'ticle, n. meeting or meeting-house, esp. of dissenters.

convěn'tion, n. convening; assembly for transaction of business; an agreement; custom.

convěn'tional (-sho-), a. depending on custom. ~ity, a.; ~ize, v.t.

convěn'tūal, a. of conventuals.

convērge', v.i. (-geable), move with or show gradual approximation. ~ent, a.; ~ence, n.

convērs'able, a. fond of or pleasant in conversation.

cŏn'versant, a. well acquainted with subject; familiar.

conversā'tion, n. familiar discourse; intercourse; ~al, a. of or in conversation; colloquial. ~alist, n. practised talker.

cŏnversaziō'ně (-ăts-), n. social meeting of scientific or artistic kind.

converse', v.i. hold converse; commune. con'verse², n. familiar talk; communings.

cŏn'verse³, a. turned round or upside down; put the other way. n. converse statement or position.

conver'sion (-shn), n. change from one state into another.

convert'¹, v.t. change into another substance; bring over to another opinion; turn to godliness. ~ible, a. capable of conversion.

cŏn'vert², n. person converted.

cŏn'věx, a. of exterior curvature. convěx'ity, n. convex surface.

convey' (-vā), v.t. transport; transmit; transfer; make known; seem to mean.

convey'ance (-āa-), n. a carriage; deed conveying property. ~cer, ~cing, nn. lawyer preparing conveyances; his work.

convict'¹, v.t. prove guilty.

cŏn'vict², n. sentenced criminal.

convic'tion, n. convicting; verdict of guilty; firm belief.

convince', v.t. (-cible), bring to a belief; produce conviction.

conviv'ial, a. of or for a feast; festive. convivial'ity, n. convivial temper.

cŏnvocā'tion, n. convoking; provincial synod of clergy.

convōke', v.t.(-cable), call together; summon to an assembly.

cŏn'volute(d) (-ōōt, -ōōtid), aa. coiled or spiral.

cŏnvolu'tion (-ōō-), n. coiled state; one turn of a coil or spiral.

convŏl'vūlus, n. kinds of twining plant, esp. bindweed.

cŏn'voy¹, v.t. escort (ship, &c.) for defence; (joc.) conduct or escort.

cŏn'voy², n. an escort; convoyed party.

convŭlse', v.t. (-sable), affect with convulsion or convulsions.

convŭl'sion (-shn), n. bodily seizure with muscular spasms (usu. pl., and esp. as a disorder of children); any irregular or violent motion; (pl.) uncontrollable laughter.

convŭl'sive, a. as in convulsions.

cō'ny, ~ey, n. (pl. -ies, -eys), rabbit; (Bibl.) rock-badger.

cōō, n. soft murmuring sound. v.i. & t. talk amorously or softly.

cōō'ee, int. used as long-distance signal by Australians.

cook, v.t. & i. prepare food by heat; cook food; undergo cooking; (colloq.) falsify (accounts, &c.); (sl.) exhaust. n. one who does cooking. *~-book, cookery-book. ~-house, (Naut.) ship's galley. ~-maid, maid who assists the cook. ~-room, kitchen (in Anglo-Ind. establishments always detached from house).

---

cook'er, *n.* cooking apparatus; apple, &c. suited for cooking.

cook'ery, *n.* art of cooking.

cook'ie, -ky, *n.* (Sc.) plain bun; *small flat cake.

cool, *a.* cold to a slight degree; unperturbed, self-possessed; lacking zeal or cordiality. *v.t. & i.* make or become cool.

cool'er, *n.* vessel for cooling.

cool'ie, *n.* East Indian or Chinese hired labourer.

coomb, combe (kōōm), *n.* hollow on flank of hill; steep valley.

coon, *n.* racoon; *negro; *fellow, child.

coop, *n.* cage or pen for confining fowls. *v.t.* put in coop; shut up in narrow compass.

coop'er, *n.* maker or repairer of casks, pails, &c. *v.t.* repair (casks, &c.). **~age**, *n.* cooper's work (-shop) or charges.

co-op'erate, *v.i.* make joint efforts. **~tion**, *n.* production or distribution by co-operators who share the profits. **~tive**, *a.* on basis of co-operation. **~tor**, *n.*

co-opt', *v.t.* elect as colleague or member. **~ation**, *n.* **~ative**, *a.* of or by co-optation.

co-ord'inate, *a.* equal in status. *n.* (pl.) set of distances from known points or lines or planes sufficing in combination to fix thing's position. *v.t.* put in co-ordinate relation. **~tion**, *n.* **~tor**, *nn.*; **~tive**, *a.*

coot, *n.* kinds of water-bird.

cop, *v.t.* (sl.) catch. **~ it**, catch it, receive punishment.

copaiba (-pīb-), *n.* a balsam.

co'pal, *n.* kinds of resin used for varnish.

copart'ner, *n.* a joint partner. **~ship**, *n.* association with others in something. **~y**, *n.*

cope[1], *n.* vestment like long cloak; (fig.) vault (of heaven); coping of wall, &c. *v.t.* provide with coping.

cope[2], *v.i.* contend with; oppose; keep level with (task, &c.).

co'peck, *n.* Russian coin (½d.).

Copern'ican, *n.* according to the theory of Copernicus.

co'ping, *n.* top course of masonry. **~-stone**, stone used in coping; (fig.) consummation.

co'pious, *a.* plentiful; abounding in words; exuberant.

copp'er[1], *n.* (sl.) policeman.

copp'er[2], *n.* metal of brownish-pink colour; bronze coin; washing cauldron; (attrib.) made of copper. *v.t.* cover with copper. **~-head**, venomous species of serpent. **~plate**, *n.* copper plate for engraving or etching; print taken from it. **~smith**, artificer in copper; (India) the crimson-breasted barbet.

copp'eras, *n.* ferrous sulphate.

copp'ice, copse, *n.* wood of small trees grown for periodical cutting.

cop'ra, *n.* dried coco-nut kernels.

cop'rolite, *n.* fossil dung.

coproph'agous, *a.* feeding on dung.

Copt, *n.* native Egyptian Christian. **~ic**, *n.* language of the Copts.

cop'ula, *n.* part of verb *be* connecting subject with predicate. **~late**, *v.i.* unite sexually. **~tion**, *n.* **cop'ulative**, *a.* serving as copula, connecting predicate with subject; of sexual union.

cop'y, *n.* reproduction of something; pattern of handwriting; matter to be set up in type; school exercise for translation. *v.t. & i.* (-iable), make copy of; imitate; crib from neighbour in examination. **~book**, book of handwriting exercises.

cop'yhold, *n.* land tenure resting on custom of a manor. *a.* held by this tenure. **~er**, *n.*

cop'yist, *n.* imitator, transcriber.

cop'yright (-rīt), *n.* exclusive right to sell copies of a work. *a.* protected by copyright. *v.t.* secure copyrights of.

coquet' (-kĕt), *v.i.* play the coquette, flirt; dally or trifle.

co'quetry (-kit-), *n.* coquetting, coquettish appearance.

coquette' (-kĕt), *n.* woman who plays with men's affections.

---

mäte, mēte, mīte, mōte, mūte; pärt, pĕrt, pört; *italics*, vague sounds;

coquett′ish (-kĕt-), a. artfully enticing or consciously pretty.

cŏ′racle, n. boat of skin-covered wicker.

cŏ′ral, n. hard substance secreted by kinds of sea polyp; toy of polished coral for children cutting teeth; (attrib.) red as coral. ~island, one formed by growth of coral.

cŏ′ralline, a. of or like coral.

corb′el, n. stone or timber projection from a wall.

corb′ie, n. raven, carrion crow.

cord, n. rope of small diameter or thick string; measure for wood; (pl.) corduroy breeches. v.t. securewith cord; make (wood) into cords. ~age, n. cords or ropes.

cord′āte, a. heart-shaped.

cordélier′, n. Franciscan friar with knotted cord round waist.

cord′ial, a. stimulating; heartfelt, sincere, heartily, warm. n. cordial drink; liqueur; heartening influence. cordiăl′ity, n.

cord′ite, n. a smokeless explosive.

cord′on, n. string-course; chain of military posts; line or ring of police, &c.; ornamental cord or braid.

cord′ovan, a. & n. (leather) of Cordova.

corduroy′, n. coarse thick ribbed cotton stuff for working-clothes. *~road, road made of tree-trunks laid across swamp, &c.

cord′wainer, n. shoemaker.

core, n. the heart or innermost part of anything; horny capsule containing seeds of apple, &c.; hard centre of boils or corns.

cŏ-rěli′gionist (-jo-), n. person of same religion.

cŏrěŏp′sis, n. plant with rayed, usu. yellow, flowers.

cŏ-respŏn′dent, n. person proceeded against together with respondent in divorce suit.

cŏriǎ′ceous (-shus), a. leathery.

cŏriăn′der, n. plant with fruit used as flavouring.

Corin′thian, a. of Corinth; of the C. order. ~ order, one of the five orders of architecture.

cork, n. bark of the cork-tree: piece of cork as float or as bottle-stopper. v.t. close up with cork; bottle up one's feelings. ~ jacket, lifebelt of cork. ~screw, implement for extracting corks. cork′y, a. buoyant, lively.

cork′er, n. (sl.) thing that is meant to close a matter (e.g. final blow, retort, notable lie).

corm′orant, n. voracious sea-bird; rapacious person.

corn[1], n. a grain or seed of a cereal plant; (collect.) cereals in growth or their seed after threshing; *maize. v.t. preserve (meat) by sprinkling with salt. *~bread, of maize. ~chandler, retail dealer in corn. *~-cob, centre of ear of maize, used for tobacco-pipe bowls, &c. ~crake, the landrail. *-dodger, fried cake of cornflour. ~-exchange, corn mart. ~factor, corn merchant. ~flour, fine-ground maize flour. ~flower, blue-flowered plant growing among corn. *~-juice, (sl.) whisky. *~-meal, Indian meal. *~-pone, corn-bread. ~stalk, (colloq.) tall slight person (applied as nickname to Australians). *~-starch, starch made from corn, esp. a fine flour used for puddings, &c.

corn[2], n. tender place on foot with hard centre.

corn′ea, n. horny transparent structure in front of eyeball.

corn′el, n. kinds of tree, esp. Cornelian Cherry; fruit of this.

cornē′lian (also car-), n. dull-red chalcedony.

corn′er, n. angle of a room, box, &c.; remote place; humble niche; monopolistic buying up of the whole of a commodity. v.t. drive into a corner; establish corner in commodity. ~boy, -man[1], street loafer. ~man[2], man at either end of a row of minstrels. ~stone, (fig.) indispensable part or basis.

corn′ĕt, n. instrument of trumpet class (also ~à-piston, cornō′péan); kinds of organ-stop;

(hist.) junior officer of cavalry troop; conical ice-cream wafer.

cŏrn´ice, n. moulding of room-wall just below ceiling; projection under which curtains hang.

cornopean. See cornet.

cŏrnū´cō´pia, n. horn of plenty.

cŏrŏll´a, n. flower's inner envelope consisting of petals.

cŏrŏll´ary, n. proposition that follows without need of separate proof from one proved.

cŏ´ronăch (-k), n. Highland dirge.

cŏ´ronal, n. circlet for the head. a. of the crown of the head.

cŏronā´tion, n. ceremony of crowning a sovereign.

cŏ´roner, n. officer holding inquest on corpse to ascertain cause of death. ~ship, n.

cŏ´ronĕt, n. peer's or peeress's small crown. ~ed, a.

coro´zō, n. (pl. -os), S.-Amer. tree yielding corozo-nuts.

cŏrp´oral¹, n. non-commissioned officer below sergeant.

cŏrp´oral², a. of the body. ~ punishment, flogging. cŏrporăl´ĭty, n. being or having a body.

cŏrp´orate, a. of, forming, or having a corporation.

cŏrporā´tion, n. body of persons authorized to act as an individual; (colloq) large belly. municipal ~, the ~, mayor, aldermen, and councillors.

cŏrpŏr´eal, a. having body; material, tangible. ~ăl´ity, n.

cŏrp´osant (-z-), n. ball of light seen on ship in storm.

corps (kōr, pl. kōrz), n. a military force; organized body.

cŏrpse, n. dead body of person.

cŏrp´ulence, n. bulkiness of body.

cŏrp´ulent, a. fleshy, bulky.

cŏrp´us, n. body of writings of a particular kind; collection.

cŏrp´uscle (-sl), n. microscopic or minute body; atom, particle.

cŏrpŭs´cular, a. of corpuscles.

cŏrral´, n. *pen or enclosure for cattle, &c.; (Ceylon) enclosure for capture of wild elephants; laager. *v.t. put or keep in corral; surround, encircle.

cŏrrĕct´, a. in accordance with the facts; true, accurate, proper. v.t. set right; admonish for fault; counteract or neutralize. ~ion, n. correcting. ~itude, n. correct behaviour. ~ive, a. serving to correct; n. corrective measure or drug. ~or, n.

cŏ´rrĕlate, n. either of two things or words necessarily implying each other. v.i. & t. (-table), be in or have correlation; bring into correlation.

cŏrrĕlā´tion, n. mutual relations; the relation of correlates.

cŏrrĕl´ative, a. having reciprocal relation. n. a correlate.

cŏrrĕspŏnd´, v.i. have points of agreement with; be analogous; exchange letters with.

cŏrrĕspŏn´dence, n. relation between things that answer to each other in some respect; analogy; exchange of letters; letters.

cŏrrĕspŏn´dent, a. corresponding. n. one who writes a letter to another or for a newspaper; an agent.

cŏ´rridor, n. passage or gallery with doors leading into many rooms.

cŏrrigĕn´dum, n. (pl. -da), thing to be corrected, esp. in book.

cŏ´rrigible, a. that can be corrected.

cŏrrŏb´orant, a. & n. tonic.

cŏrrŏb´orate, v.t. (-rable), give support to; confirm. ~tion, ~tor, nn.; ~tive, ~tory, aa.

cŏrrŏb´oree, n. Australian native dance.

cŏrrōde´, v.t. & i. (-dable), affect with or suffer corrosion; eat into.

cŏrrō´sion (-zhn), n. wearing away from the surface inwards.

cŏrrō´sive, a. producing corrosion. n. corrosive agent.

cŏ´rrugate (-ōō-), v.t. & i. (-gable), contract into wrinkles; bend (iron) into wavy ridges. ~tion, n. ~tor, n. brow-contracting muscle.

cŏrrupt´, a. rotten; depraved; venal. v.t. & i. (-ible), make corrupt, deprave, bribe; rot, decompose. ~ibility, n.

corrŭp'tion, n. corrupting; corrupt state; depravity.

cŏrs'age (-ahzh), n. what a woman is wearing about the bust.

cŏrs'air, n. Mohammedan or (loosely) other privateer.

cŏrse, n. (poet.) corpse.

cŏrs'ĕt, n. pair of stays.

cŏrs'lĕt, ~sĕlĕt (-sl-), n. piece of armour covering trunk; woman's tight-fitting garment.

|| cortège (kŏrtāzh), n. procession.

Cŏr'tĕs, n. Spanish or Portuguese parliament.

cŏrt'ĕx, n. outer covering of some organs, esp. outer grey matter of brain; bark.

cŏrt'ical, a. of the nature of a cortex or of rind or bark. cŏrt'i-cātĕd, a. having cortical covering.

corŭn'dum, n. crystallined mineral allied to sapphire and ruby.

cŏ'ruscāte, v.i. sparkle. ~tion, n. flash; quick vibration of light.

corvée (kŏrvā'), n. system of exacting unpaid labour.

corvette', n. flush-decked warship with one tier of guns.

cŏrv'ine, a. of raven or crow.

Cŏ'rўbănt, n. priest of Cybele performing rites with frenzied dances and cries. cŏrўbăn'tic, a.

cŏ'rўmb, n. raceme with flat or flattish top. cŏ'rўmbōse, a.

cŏrўphæ'us, n. leader of a chorus; spokesman, &c. of party.

cŏs, n. crisp long-leaved lettuce.

cō-sig'natŏrў, n. person or State signing document with others.

cō'sine, n. (Trigonometry) sine of complement of given angle (abbrev. cos).

cŏsmĕt'ic (-z-), a. beautifying. n. preparation for hair or skin.

cŏs'mic, a. of the universe.

cŏsmŏg'onў (-z-), n. genesis of the universe; theory of this.

cŏsmŏg'raphў (-z-), n. description or mapping of universe or earth. ~pher, n.; ~ăph'ic(al), aa.

cŏsmŏl'ogў (-z-), n. study of the universe in all its parts. cŏsmo-lŏg'ical, a.; ~gist, n.

cŏsmopŏl'itan (-z-), a. of all parts

of the world; free from national prejudices. n. cosmopolitan person. ~ism, n.

cŏsmŏp'olite (-z-), n. citizen of the world. ~tism, n.

cŏs'mŏs¹ (-z-), n. the ordered universe; ordered system of ideas, &c.

cŏs'mŏs² (-z-), n. plant with single dahlia-like flower.

Cŏss'ăck, n. & n. one of a south Russian people skilled in horsemanship and famous as cavalry.

cŏss'ĕt, v.t. pamper, pet.

|| cŏss'id, n. (Anglo-Ind.) a courier.

cost (-aw-), v.t. involve the payment or sacrifice of; have as price. n. what thing costs; (pl.) legal expenses.

cŏs'tal, a. of the ribs.

cŏs'tard, n. large ribbed apple.

cŏs'ter(monger) (-ŭngg-), n. hawker of fruit, fish, &c.

cŏs'tive, a. constipated.

cost'lў (-aw-), a. costing much, expensive; sumptuous.

costūme', n. one's outer clothes; style of dress.

costū'mier, n. dealer in, maker of, costumes.

cō'sў (-z-), ~zў, a. snug, comfortable. n. quilted cover for teapot to retain warmth.

cŏt¹, n. cottage; small erection for shelter, cote.

cŏt², n. (Anglo-Ind.) light bedstead; swinging bed on board ship; child's bed.

cōte, n. shelter for animals.

cō'terie, n. set of persons with exclusive interests; select circle.

cothŭrn'us, n. (pl. -nī), buskin of Greek tragic actor.

cotill'ion, ~llon (-lyon), n. kinds of dance; music for these.

cŏtt'age (-ĭj), n. small house, esp. in the country; *residence at pleasure-resort. cŏtt'ager (-tĭ-), n. dweller in a cottage.

cŏtt'ar, n. Scottish peasant occupying cottage on farm.

cŏtt'er, n. kinds of wedge or pin.

cŏtt'on, n. a plant; the white downy fibrous covering of its seeds; thread spun or cloth woven from this. *v.i.* be compatible or congruous; take to person or custom. cŏtt'ony, *a.*

cŏtýle'don, *n.* primary or seed leaf in plant embryos.

couch[1], *n.* piece of furniture made for reclining on. *v.i. & t.* have one's bed or lair; lie ready to spring; set down or express in specified terms.

couch[2] (-ow-, -ōō-), *n.* usu. in comb. ~-grass, grass-weed with long creeping roots; quitch.

couch'ant, *a.* (Herald.) in couching attitude.

Couéism (kōō'āĭzm), *n.* systematic auto-suggestion of a sanguine kind.

coug'ar (kōō-), *n.* large feline beast.

cough (-awf), *n.* expulsion of air from the lungs; noise made by this; respiratory affection impelling to frequent coughs. *v.i. & t.* make cough. ~ up, (sl.) pay over money, &c.

could, *p.t.* of can[2].

*coulee, ‖ coulée (kōōl'ĭ, kōōl'ā), *n.* dry ravine; (Geol.) lava flow.

coulisse (kōōlēs'), *n.* groove for thing to slide in.

couloir (kōōl'wahr), *n.* steep gully in mountain-side.

coulomb' (kōōlom), *n.* quantity of electricity conveyed in one second by current of one ampere.

coul'ter (kōl-), *n.* vertical blade in front of share in plough.

coun'cil, *n.* any deliberative or administrative body.

coun'cillor, *n.* member of council.

coun'sel, *n.* deliberation or debate; advice; a barrister.

coun'sellor, *n.* adviser.

count[1], *v.i. & t.* reckon the number of by counting; include, or be included, in reckoning; have as numerical value. *n.* one's reckoning; a counting; item in an indictment.

count[2], *n.* title of foreign noble.

count'enance, *n.* expression of face; favouring look; moral sup-

port. *v.t.* (-ceable) give countenance to; look on with favour

coun'ter[1], *n.* small disk, &c. used in scoring at cards, &c.; token; piece at draughts, &c.; banker's or shopkeeper's table. ~-jumper, (contempt.) shop assistant.

coun'ter[2], *n.* part between horse's shoulders and below its neck; fencing-parry. *a.* opposite. *adv.* in the contrary direction. *v.t. & i.* meet or baffle (opponent, move) with answering move.

counteract', *v.t.* neutralize or hinder by contrary action.

coun'ter-attack', *n. & i., & n.* attack after close of enemy's attack.

counter-attrác'tion, *n.* attraction of contrary tendency; rival attraction.

coun'terbál'ance, *n.* weight balancing another. *v.t.* (-ceable) neutralize by contrary power or influence.

coun'terblast (-ah-), *n.* energetic declaration against something.

coun'ter-chárge, *n. & v.t.* charge in answer to another.

coun'tercheck, *n.* check that operates against another; retort.

coun'ter-claim, *n.* claim set up against another.

coun'terfeit, *a. & n.* (-fĭt) (thing) made in imitation; forged; not genuine. *v.t.* (-fēt) imitate; forge; simulate.

coun'terfoil, *n.* part of cheque, receipt, &c. retained as record.

counter-i'rritant, *n.* thing used to produce surface irritation and so relieve internal trouble.

coun'termand[1] (-ah-), *n.* order issued in revocation of previous one. countermand'[2], *v.t.* revoke order; recall by countermand.

coun'termárch, *n., & v.i. & t.* march in contrary direction to that previously followed.

coun'termark, *n.* additional mark on goods. *v.t.* put countermark upon.

coun'termine, *n.* mine made to blow up enemy mine before it is ready. v.t. & i. (-nable), make countermine; (fig.) counterplot.

coun'terpane (-in, -ān), n. coverlet or quilt of bed.

coun'terpart, n. thing resembling another; corresponding part.

coun'terplot, n. plot contrived to defeat another. v.i. make counterplot.

coun'terpoint, n. melody added as accompaniment to given melody.

coun'terpoise (-z), n. counterbalancing weight or force; equilibrium. v.t. counterbalance; compensate.

coun'ter-refŏrmā'tion, ~-revolu'tion (-ōō-), nn. movements undoing the original one wholly or in part.

coun'tersign (-īn), n. word to be given in answer to sentry's challenge; countermark. v.t. add confirming signature to. ~sig'nature, n.

countervail', v.t. & i. counterbalance; avail against.

coun'terwork (-ẽrk), v.t. try to frustrate.

coun'tess, n. wife or widow of count or earl.

coun'ting-house, n. building or room devoted to book-keeping.

count'less, a. too many to count.

coun'trified (kŭn-, -īd), a. rural in appearance or manners.

coun'try (kŭn-), n. region; territory of a nation; land of one's birth; rural districts. ~ dance, any native English dance. ~house, ~ seat, residence of country gentleman. ~man, rustic: member of rural-labourer class; man of one's own country or specified district. ~side, rural district or its inhabitants.

coun'ty, n. territorial division of U.K., a shire; *division of a State; people of a county, the county families. ~ borough, one ranking as administrative county. ~ council, elected governing body of administrative county. ~ court, court for civil actions. v.t. sue in county court for debt. *~ seat, county town.

coup (kōō), n. successful stroke or move. ‖ coup de grâce (de grahs), finishing stroke. ‖~ de main (de măn), sudden vigorous attack. ‖~ d'état (dětah'), violent or illegal change of government. ‖~ d'œil (-dū'ē), comprehensive glance; view as taken in by this. ‖~ de théâtre (de tẽah'tr), dramatically sudden or sensational act.

coupé (kōō'pā), n. close carriage for two; half-compartment at end of railway-carriage.

cou'ple (kŭ-), n. leash for two hounds; married or engaged pair; two, a brace. v.t. & i. link or fasten or associate together.

coup'let (kŭ-), n. pair of successive lines of rhyming verse.

coup'ling (kŭ-), n. link connecting railway-carriages or parts of a machine.

coup'on (kōō-), n. detachable ticket entitling holder to something.

cou'rage (kŭ-), n. bravery, boldness; fortitude. courā'geous, a.

cou'rier (kōō-), n. express messenger; servant employed to make travelling arrangements.

course (kōrs), n. going on in space or time; race or career; line of conduct or action; a series; ground on which race is run; distinct part of a meal; continuous layer of stone, &c. in building. v.t. & i. pursue (game); run about, run (esp. of liquids); chase; use hounds in coursing.

cours'er (kōr-), n. swift horse.

court (kōrt), n. space enclosed by wall or buildings; confined yard or area within walls or marked boundaries used in some games; sovereign's residence; his establishment and retinue; assembly of judges or other persons acting as tribunal; place in which justice is administered; qualified members of a corporation; meeting of these. v.t. pay court to; seek the favour or love of; invite. ~card, king, queen, knave. ~martial, n. judicial court of naval or military officers; v.t. try by this. **~yard**, space enclosed by buildings.

court'eous (kŏr-, kĕr-), *a.* polite or considerate in manners.

courtesan, **-zan** (kŏrtizăn'), *n.* refined or high-placed harlot.

court'esy (kŏr-, kĕr-), *n.* courteous behaviour or disposition.

court'ier (kŏr-), *n.* frequenter of royal Court.

court'ly (kōr-), *a.* in the manner of Courts; ceremonious; flattering.

court'ship (kōr-), *n.* courting, wooing, esp. of intended wife.

cous'in (kŭz-), *n.* child of one's uncle or aunt. **~hood**, **~ship**, *nn.*; **~ly**, *a.*

cove¹, *n.* small bay or inlet of coast; sheltered nook; (Archit.) concave arch, esp. of ceiling. *v.t.* provide (room, &c.) with cove; slope (fireplace) inwards.

cove², *n.* (sl.) fellow, chap.

co'venant (kŭ-), *n.* compact, bargain; sealed contract, clause of this. *v.t. & i.* make covenant with. **co'venanted** (kŭ-), *a.* bound by a covenant.

co'venanter, *n.* one who covenants, esp. (Sc. hist.) an adherent of the Covenants of 1638 and 1643.

Cov'entry, *n.* In phr. *send one to ~*, combine to cut him.

co'ver (kŭ-), *v.t.* be over the whole top of; overlie or lie above; conceal or shield; suffice to defray (expenses); report for newspaper. &c. *n.* thing that covers whole or part of something; shelter; screen or pretence, **~let**, bedcover lying over other bedclothes, **~point**, (Crick.) fielder behind point to stop balls first man misses; his place in the field.

co'vert¹ (kŭ-), *a.* secret, disguised; not open or explicit. **covert²** (kŭv'-er), *n.* wood or thicket affording cover for game.

co'verture (kŭ-), *n.* covering; wife's position under husband's care.

co'vet (kŭ-), *v.t.* long to possess; desire eagerly. **~ous**, *a.* avaricious, grasping.

co'vey (kŭ-), *n.* (pl. *-eys*), brood of partridges, young together.

cow¹, *n.* (pl. *-s*, arch. *kine*), female ox, esp. of domestic kind; female of elephant, rhinoceros, whale, seal, &c. **~boy**, boy in charge of cows; *man in charge of cattle on ranch. *~-catcher**, fender in front of locomotive. **~heel**, stewed foot of cow or ox. **~herd**, one who tends cows at pasture. **~-hide**, *n.* leather or whip of cow's hide; *v.t.* thrash with cowhide. **~-puncher**, (U.S. & (Austral.) cow-boy. **~-shot**, (Crick. sl.) violent pull made in crouching position. **~-spanker**, (Austral.) cow-boy.

cow², *v.t* intimidate.

cow'ard (kŭ-), *n.* faint-hearted, pusillanimous person; (attrib.) cowardly. **~ice**, *n.* cowardly conduct. **~ly**, *a.* of or like a coward.

cow'er, *v.i.* crouch or shrink with fear or with cold.

cowl, *n.* monk's hooded cloak; its hood; hood-shaped top of chimney or shaft. **~ed**, *a.*

cow'pox, *n.* disease on cows' teats, source of vaccine.

cow'rie, *n.* small sea-shell of Indian Ocean, used as money in parts of Asia, &c.

cow'slip, *n.* yellow-flowered plant growing in pastures.

cox, *n.* coxswain, esp. of racing boat. *v.t. & i.* act as cox.

cox'comb (-m), *n.* person given to showing off; (hist.) medieval jester's cap like cock's comb. **cöxcö'mbical**, *a.* **~ry**, *n.*

cŏx'swain (-ksn), *n.* boat's helmsman, esp. one in charge of ship's boat; steersman of racing boat. **~less**, *a.*

coy, *a.* modest, shy (usu. of girl).

coyo'te (ko-, ki'ōt), *n.* N.-Amer. prairie-wolf

co'zen (kŭ-), *v.t. & i.* cheat. **co'zenage** (kŭ-), *n.* cozening.

crăb, *n.* crustacean with ten legs, esp. edible species; crab-apple; kinds of winch and capstan. *v.t. & i.* cry down, depreciate; criticize with intent to frustrate.

~-apple, fruit of the crab-tree.
~-louse, parasite infesting human body. ~-tree, wild apple-tree with fruit of harsh sour flavour. catch a ~, in rowing, get oar jammed under water by faulty stroke.

crǎbb'ĕd, crǎbb'ў, aa. cross-grained, perverse, cantankerous.

crǎck, n. sudden sharp noise; sounding blow; fracture; piece of burglary; a talk. v.i. & t. suffer a crack or partial break; (of whip, &c.) make crack; (of voice) suffer change of tone; talk together; (p.p.) crazy. a. of great reputation. adv. sharply.

*crǎck'ajǎck, n. outstanding person.

crǎck'er, n. kind of firework; explosive bonbon; thin crisp biscuit; *unsweetened biscuit.

crǎc'kle, n. sound of repeated slight cracking. v.i. emit crackle.

crǎck'ling, n. cracking sound; crisp skin of roast pork.

crǎck'nel, n. crisp soft biscuit.

crǎcks'man, n. burglar.

crā'dle, n. infant's bed on rockers; place in which thing is first nurtured; frame for conveying something; gold-washing basket. v.t. be the cradle of; wash (ore).

crā'dling, n. wood or iron framework, used in building.

craft (-ah-), n. skill, cunning; art, trade; boat(s), vessel(s).

crafts'man (-ahf-), n. one who practises a craft. ~ship, n.

craf'tў (-ah-), a. cunning, artful.

crăg, n. steep rugged rock.

crăgs'man (-ăn), n. rock-climber.

crāke, n. bird of the rail kind.

crăm, v.t. & i. fill to repletion; fill mind with facts, &c required for examination; pack tightly; eat greedily. n. crowded or close-packed state; cramming for examination; (sl.) lie. ~mer, n. person who crams examinees; (sl.) lie.

crăm'bō, n. game in which one player gives word to which another finds a rhyme.

crămp, n. contraction of muscles from sudden chill, strain, &c.; kinds of clamp for holding masonry or timbers together. v.t. restrict; enclose too narrowly; (p.p.) affected with muscular cramp; (of space) too narrow; (of handwriting) too small or close.

crăm'pons (-z), n.pl. spiked appliances attached to boots for ice-climbing.

crăn, n. measure (37½ gal.) for fresh herrings

crā'nage, n. use of crane; dues paid for this.

crăn'berrў, n. a shrub or its acid red berry, used in tarts.

crāne, n. large wading bird; machine for moving heavy weights. v.t. & i. (-nable), stretch one's neck or head; move weights with crane. ~-fly, daddy-long-legs. ~'s-bill, kinds of wild geranium.

crā'nium, n. (pl. -ia), bones enclosing the brain, brain-pan; skull. crā'nial, a, crāniōl'ogical, a. crāniŏl'ogist, ~ogў, nn.

crănk, n. arm proceeding from an axis used to produce rotary motion; elbow-joint at angle of bell-wire; fanciful speech; eccentric notion, fad; faddist, v.t. set (motor engine) going by turning a crank. crănk'ў, a. shaky or crazy; capricious, crotchety, eccentric.

crăn'nŏg, n. ancient lake-dwelling in Scotland or Ireland.

crănn'ў, n. chink, crevice, crack. crănn'ied, a.

crāpe, n. gauzy wrinkled fabric. usu. of black silk.

*crăps, n.pl. simplified form of hazard.

crăp'ūlence, n. state following excessive drinking or eating. ~lent, ~lous, aa.

crăsh[1], n. violent fall or impact; sudden downfall or collapse. v.i. fall with a crash; make a loud crash.

crăsh[2], n. coarse linen cloth.

crăss, a. grossly stupid; without

sensibility; of thick coarse texture. ~itude, n.

crāte, n. open-work case of wooden bars or wicker for goods.

crā'ter, n. volcano-mouth; bowl-shaped cavity.

cravat', n. kind of neckcloth.

crāve, v.i. & t. have a vehement desire for; request, beg for.

crā'ven, a. cowardly, abject. n. cowardly person or animal.

craw, n. crop of birds or insects.

crawl, v.i. advance on hands or knees or on the belly; move with extreme slowness; creep, sneak about. n. crawling motion; slow walk; fast stroke in swimming. crawl'er, n. one that crawls; baby's overall; slow-moving cab; louse; *hellgramite.

cray'fish, craw'~, n. fresh-water lobsterlike crustacean.

cray'on, n. stick or pencil of coloured chalk; picture drawn with crayons.

crāze, v.t. drive crazy. n. general or individual mania.

crā'zy, a. unsound, shaky; mad; half-witted; madly eager for.

creak, n. harsh noise as of unoiled hinge. v.i. emit creak.

cream, n. oily part of milk convertible into butter; best part of anything, the pick; (attrib.) cream-coloured. v.i. & t. form cream or scum; skim off the cream. cream'ery, n. shop where milk, cream, &c. are sold. ~y, a.

crease, n. line made by folding; wrinkle; (Crick.) white line defining position of bowler (bowl-ing~) and limit of batsman's ground (popping~). v.t. & i. (-sable), make creases; develop creases.

creāte', v.t. (-table), bring into existence; invest with rank; originate; make a fuss. creā'tive, a.

creā'tion, n. creating (esp. the world); all created things; production of the human mind.

creā'tor, n. The C~, the Supreme Being; one who creates. ~tress.

crea'ture (krē'cher), n. human

being or animal; person's dependant or tool; contemptible person.

crèche (-āsh), n. public nursery for infants.

crē'dence, n. belief; credit.

crēden'tials (-shalz), n.pl. letters of recommendation.

cred'ible, a. believable; worthy of belief. ~bility, n.

cred'it, n. belief, trust; good reputation; allowing of deferred payment; sum at person's disposal in bank. v.i. believe; carry to credit side of account. ~able, a. praiseworthy.

cred'itor, n. person or body to whom one owes money.

crē'dō, n. (pl. -os), creed.

cred'ulous, a. too ready to believe. crēdū'lity, n.

creed, n. formal summary of Christian doctrine; set of opinions on any subject.

creek, n. inlet on sea-coast or arm of river; small stream.

creel, n. angler's fishing-basket.

creep, v.i. (crēpt), crawl along the ground; move stealthily or slowly; be servile; experience shivering sensation. n. (pl.) spell of creeping; shrinking horror. ~y, a.

creep'er, n. creeping or climbing plant.

crēmāte', v.t. (-table), consume by fire, as method of disposing of corpses. ~tion, n.

crēmā'tor, n. person, furnace, cremating corpses or rubbish.

crēmatōr'ium (pl. -s, -ia), n. establishment for cremation.

crēmō'na, n. violin made at C.

crēn'ellāted, a. having battlements or loopholes. ~tion, n.

crē'ole, n. person born in W. Indies, Mauritius, &c., but of European or negro race; *descendant of French or Spanish settlers in Louisiana.

crē'osŏte, n. oily antiseptic liquid distilled from wood-tar.

‖ crēpe (-āp), n. crapy fabric other than black mourning crape. ~ de Chine (deshēn), a strong glossy crêpe; ~ rubber, washed rubber.

crĕp'ĭtāte, v.i. make crackling noise. ~ation, n.

|| **crépon** (krĕp'ŏn), n. stuff like crape, but firmer.

crept, p.p. of creep.

crepŭs'cūlar, a. of twilight; (Zool.) active, &c. at twilight.

crescĕn'do (-sh-), adv., n., & a. (passage of music to be played) with gradually increasing volume.

crĕs'cent, n. figure of moon in first or last quarter; Mohammedan badge; row of houses of curved shape. a. crescent-shaped.

crĕss, n. kinds of plant with pungent edible leaves.

crĕss'et, n. fire-basket slung to give light.

crĕst, n. comb or tuft on animal's head; plume or central ridge of helmet; mane of horse, &c.; top of mountain; curl of foam on wave; heraldic device. v.t. & i. serve as crest to; crown; reach top of. ~fallen, a. mortified, dejected.

crētā'ceous (-shus), a. chalky.

crē'tĭn, n. deformed idiot.

crē'tĭnism, n. combination of idiocy and deformity. ~nous, a.

crĕt'onne, n. unglazed colour-printed cotton cloth.

crēvăsse', n. deep open split or chasm in glacier.

crĕv'ice, n. chink, fissure.

crew[1] (-ōō), n. ship's or boat's company; set; gang, mob.

crew[2]. See crow.

crew'el (-ōō-), n. thin worsted for tapestry and embroidery.

crib, n. barred rack for fodder; *bin for maize, salt, &c.; child's bed; (sl.) place of work; dealer's cards at cribbage, thrown out from other players' hands; plagiarism; translation for (esp. illegitimate) use of students. v.t. & i. confine in small space; plagiarize or copy or use cribs.

cribb'age, n. card-game for two, three, or four persons. ~board, board with holes for scoring.

crick, n. spasmodic affection of muscles. v.t. produce crick in.

crick'et[1], n. chirping insect.

crick'et[2], n. open-air game with ball, bats, and wickets. ~er, ~ing, nn. not ~, (colloq.) infringing the code of fair play.

cried, p.t. of cry.

cri'er, n. officer who makes public announcements.

cri'key, int. (sl.) expressing astonishment.

crime, n. act punishable by law; wicked act; sin. v.t. (Mil.) charge with or convict of military offence.

crim'inal, a. of the nature of crime. n. person guilty of crime. ~ity, n. state of being criminal.

crim'ĭnāte, v.t. & i. (-nable), impute crime to; prove guilty of crime; censure. ~tion, n.; ~tive, ~tory, aa.

crimĭnŏl'ogÿ, n. study of crime.

crim'inÿ, int. (arch.) expressing surprise.

crimp[1], n. agent who entraps men for seamen or soldiers. v.t. impress.

crimp[2], v.t. press into small folds; frill, corrugate.

crim'son (-z-), a. & n. rich deep red (colour). v.t. & i. turn crimson; dye crimson.

cringe (-j), v.i. cower; behave obsequiously. n. act of cringing.

crinkle (kring'kl), n. wrinkle; short bend or turn. v.i. & t. form crinkles (in). **crink'lÿ**, adv.

crin'oline, n. hooped petticoat used to expand skirt; structure to ward off torpedoes.

crip'ple, n. lame person. v.t. lame, disable; (fig.) impair.

cri'sis, n. (pl. -ēs), turning-point; time of acute danger.

crisp, a. brittle; bracing; brisk, decisive; curly. n. (sl.) bank-notes. v.t. & i. press into short folds; make or become crisp.

criss'-cross (-aws), n. ~row, the alphabet; crossing of lines, currents, &c. a. crossing; in criss-cross lines. adv. in criss-cross manner. v.i. & o. make criss-cross.

cris'tāte, a. (Nat. Hist.) crested.

crĭtēr'ion, n. (pl. -ia), principle taken as standard in judging.

---

ah, awl, oil, boor, cow, dowry; chin, go, bang, so, ship, thin; dh, as th(e).

crit'ic, n. person who attempts or is skilled in criticism.

crit'ical, a. censorious, fault-finding; skilled in criticism; of the nature of a crisis.

crit'icaster, n. feeble critic.

crit'icism, n. judging of merit; animadversion; critical observation.

crit'icize, v.t. & i. (-zable). discuss critically; find fault with.

critique' (-ēk), n. critical essay.

croak, n. deep hoarse note of a frog or raven. v.i. & t. utter croak, be hoarse; talk gloomily. ~er, n. prophet of ill. ~y, a.

cro'chet (-shī), n. kind of knitting with hooked needle. v.i. & t. (-cheted, pr. -shid), do crochet, make by crochet.

crock, n. earthenware jar; broken-down horse; worn-out or disabled person. v.t. make (person) into a crock. **crock'ery,** n. earthenware vessels, plates, &c.

crock'et, n. ornament on inclined sides of a pinnacle, &c.

croc'odile, n. large amphibious reptile; hypocritical enemy; (joc.) school walking two-and-two.

cro'cus, n. dwarf bulbous plant with yellow or purple flowers.

Croes'us (krēs-), n. wealthy man.

croft (-aw-), n. small piece of arable land close to house; crofter's holding. **crof'ter** (-aw-), n. joint tenant of Scotch divided farm.

Cro-Magnon (-mănyoń'), a. applied to a European race of the Stone Age, so called from the discovery of remains in the cave of Cro-Magnon in Dordogne.

crŏm'lĕch (-k), n. stone circle (esp. in France); (formerly) tomb of huge stones.

crône, n. withered old woman.

cro'nў, n. intimate friend.

crook, n. hooked staff, esp. of shepherd or bishop; bend, curve; wry turn; (sl.) swindler, criminal. v.t. & i. bend into a crook.

crooked¹ (-kt), a. crutched.

crook'ĕd², a. not straight, bent, twisted; not straightforward.

croon, n. low monotonous singing. v.i. & t. utter croon; hum softly.

crop, n. pouch in bird's gullet; thick end of whip, whip-handle; produce of cultivated lands; cropping of hair. v.t. & i. poll or clip; bite off or eat down grass, &c.; sow, plant, raise crop; reap; yield harvest.

cropp'er, n. person or thing that crops; (sl.) heavy fall.

cro'quet (-kī), n. lawn game with hoops, wooden balls, and mallets; croqueting. v.t. & i. (-quet'ing, -ted, pr. -kīng, -kĭd), drive away (player's ball) by striking one's own ball placed in contact with the other; do this.

croquette' (-kĕt), n. rissole.

crôre, n. one hundred lacs.

cro'sier, ~zier (-zhyer), n. pastoral staff of bishop or abbot.

cross (-aws), n. stake used by the ancients for crucifixion, usu. with transverse bar; model of this as emblem of the Christian religion; cross-shaped thing; decoration in some Orders of knighthood; sign of cross as religious act; line that intersects another; affliction; trial or annoyance; intermixture of breeds; a hybrid. a. transverse; reaching from side to side; intersecting; (colloq.) peevish, out of humour. v.t. & i. place crosswise; make sign of cross; draw line across; go across (road, sea, &c.); meet and pass (each other); thwart, interpose obstacles; (of animals or plants) interbreed, cross-fertilize; (of persons) cause (animals, plants, &c.) to cross.

cross'-bearer (-aws-; -âr-), n. person carrying processional cross.

cross'bĕlt (-aws-), n. belt for cartridges, &c. from shoulder to opposite hip.

cross'bill (-aws-), n. bird whose mandibles cross when bill is closed.

zh, as (rou)ge; ö=1; ȣ, ür, =ȝr; ў, ў, =ĭ, ĭ; and see p. 4. *=U.S.

3495 E

cross′bones (-aws-), *n.pl.* two arm or thigh bones crossed.

cross′bow (-aws-; -ō), *n.* weapon formed of a bow fixed across a wooden stock.

cross′-breed (-aws-), **n.** hybrid animal.

cross-bŭtt′ock (-aws-), *n.* wrestling-throw over the hip.

cross-coun′try (-aws-kŭn-), *a.* across fields, not following roads.

crŏsse, *n.* netted crook used in lacrosse.

cross-exămĭna′tion (-aws-ĕgz-), *n.* examination of witness with a view to shaking his evidence. ~-exăm′ine, *v.t.* subject to cross-examination.

cross′-grained (-aws-), *a.* (of wood) with grain running irregularly; (fig.) perverse, intractable.

cross-hătch′ (-aws-), *v.t.* engrave with intersecting parallel lines.

cross′ing (-aws-), *n.* an intersection; place where street is crossed.

cross′pătch (-aws-), *n.* ill-tempered child or woman.

cross′-pŭr′pose (-aws-), *n.* contrary purpose; (pl.) a game.

cross-quĕs′tion (-aws-, -chn), *n.* question put in cross-examination, *v.t.* cross-examine.

cross′-road (-aws-), *n.* one that crosses another or joins two.

*cross′tie, *n.* transverse piece of timber, &c.

cross′wise (-awswiz), *adv.* in the manner of a cross.

cross′-word (-aws-wĕrd), *n.* ~ puzzle, puzzle in which words to be written horizontally and others crossing them vertically on chequered paper are indicated by means of clues.

crŏtch′ĕt, *n.* (Mus.) black-headed note with stem; whim or fad. ~-eer′, *n.* faddist. ~-y, *a.*

crō′ton, *n.* kind of plant. ~ oil, drastic purgative.

crouch, *v.i.* stoop, bend, esp. timidly or servilely. *n.* crouching.

croup¹ (-ōō-), *n.* throat-disease of children, with sharp cough.

croup(e)² (-ōō-), *n.* rump, hind-quarters, esp. of horse.

croup′ier (-ōō-), *n.* raker-in of money at gaming-table.

crow (-ō), *v.i.* (past crowed, arch. crew, -ōō), utter cock's cry; (of infants) utter joyful sounds; exult. *n.* cock's cry; infant crowing; kinds of bird of black or black and grey plumage. *~-blackbird, the purple grackle and allied species. ~-pheasant, (Anglo-Ind.) popular name of a bird held in India to give omens.

crow′bar (-ō-), *n.* bar of iron used as a lever.

crow′berry (-ō-), *n.* black-berried heath shrub; *large cranberry.

crowd, *n.* throng, dense multitude; (colloq.) set, lot. *v.i. & t.* form a crowd, come in crowds; fill, occupy; force into; thrust out.

crow′-fōōt (-ō-), *n.* kinds of buttercup.

crown, *n.* wreath for the head; monarch's head-covering or circlet; supreme governing power in a monarchy; British coin of 5s.; top of the head or of a hat; completion. *v.t.* put crown on; make king or queen; be the consummation or reward of; put finishing touch to.

crow's′-fōōt (-ō-), *n.* small compound wrinkle about the eye.

crow's-nĕst′ (-ō-), *n.* barrel at mast-head for look-out man.

cru′cial (-ōōshl), *a.* decisive, critical; (Anat.) transverse.

cru′cible (-ōō-), *n.* vessel in which metals can be fused.

crucif′erous (-ōō-), *a.* with four equal petals arranged crosswise.

cru′cifix (-ōō-), *n.* image of Christ on the cross. crucifi′xion (-kshon), *n.* crucifying, esp. that of Christ. cru′ciform (-ōō-), *a.* cross-shaped. cru′cify (-ōō-), *v.t.* put to death on a cross; mortify or chasten.

crude (-ōō-), *a.* in the natural or raw state; not digested; unripe; (fig.) ill-digested, unpolished, lacking finish. crud′ity (-ōō-), *n.* crudeness.

cru′él (-ŏŏ-), a. callous to others' pain; painful, distressing.

cru′élty (-ŏŏ-), n. cruel temper or conduct.

cru′et (-ŏŏ-), n. small stoppered bottle for use at table; cruet-stand. ~**stand**, one holding cruets, mustard-pot, &c.

cruise (-ŏŏz), v.i. sail about without precise destination. n. cruising voyage. **cruis′er** (-ŏŏz-), n. high-speed warship of intermediate armament.

crumb (-m), n. small fragment, esp. soft bread; soft inner part of bread. v.t. cover, thicken, with crumbs; break into crumbs. **crumb′y** (-mĭ), a.

crum′ble, v.t. & i. break, fall, into crumbs or fragments.

crum′blÿ, a. apt to crumble.

crum′mÿ, a. (sl.) (of women) plump, comely, jolly; rich.

crump (colloq.), v.t. hit (esp. cricket-ball) hard. n. hard hit; heavy fall; exploding shell.

crum′pét, n. flat soft cake eaten hot with butter; (sl.) head.

crum′ple, v.t. & i. crush together into creases; become creased.

crunch, n. sound made by chewing crisp food or treading on gravel. v.t. & i. chew food; make or emit this sound.

crupp′er, n. strap passing round horse's tail; horse's croup.

crusade′ (-ŏŏ-), n. medieval military expedition to recover Palestine; campaign or movement against recognized evil. v.i. take part in crusade.

cruse (-ŏŏz), n. earthenware jar.

crush, v.t. compress with violence so as to break, bruise, or crumple; overwhelm. n. crowded mass of persons, &c.; (colloq.) crowded social gathering.

crust, n. hard outer part of bread; pastry covering pie; surface of earth, &c.; deposit of port. v.t. & i. cover with, form into, crust; become covered with crust.

crustā′cean (-shn), n. crustaceous animal.

crustā′ceous (-shus), a. crust-like

or crusted; of the *Crustacea* or hard-shelled animals.

crus′tÿ, a. with much or hard crust; irritable, surly.

crutch, n. staff for lame persons; support, prop.

crutched (-cht), a. supported on crutch; having cross-piece.

crux, n. knotty point, puzzle.

cry, n. & t. (*cried*; -*iable*), utter a shrill call; weep or wail. n. (pl. -*ies*), loud inarticulate utterance of grief, pain, fear, joy, &c.; urgent appeal; phrase, &c. that serves to rally partisans; spell of weeping. ~**ing**, a. (of evils) flagrant, demanding redress.

crypt, n. vault, esp. one below church used as burial-place.

cryp′tic, a. of mysterious import; veiled in obscurity.

cryp′togam, n. plant without stamens or pistil; non-flowering plant. ~**ic**, **cryptŏg′amous**, aa. **cryp′togram**, n. piece of cipher-writing. ~**graph′ic**, a.

crys′tal, n. a transparent mineral like ice or glass; glass of especial transparency; cut-glass vessels; (Nat. Sci.) aggregation of molecules. a. made of, like, as clear as, crystal. ~ **receiver**, ~**set**, simple form of wireless receiving apparatus.

crys′talline, a. of or like or clear as crystal.

crys′tallize, v.t. & i. (-*zable*), form into crystals or (fig.) into definite permanent shape. ~**zā′tion**, n.

crys′talloid, a. & n. crystal-like; (body) of crystalline structure.

cub, n. young fox or other wild beast; ill-mannered child or youth. **cubb′ing**, n. cub-hunting. **cubb′ish**, a. ill-mannered.

cubb′y-hōle, n. snug place.

cube, n. solid figure contained by six equal squares; product of a number multiplied by its square. v.t. find cube of (number).

cū′bic, a. of three dimensions; involving the cubes of numbers. **cū′bical**, a. cube-shaped.

cū′bicle, n. small separate sleeping compartment in dormitory.

---

māre, mēre, mīre, mōre, mūre; pàrt, pért, pórt; *italics*, vague sounds;

E 2

cŭ′biform, *a.* cube-shaped.

cŭ′bism, *n.* recent style in art of so presenting objects as to give the effect of an assemblage of geometrical figures. **cŭ′bist**, *n.*

cŭ′bit, *n.* measure about 18 in.

cŭck′old, *n.* husband of adulterous wife. *v.t.* make a cuckold of.

cŭc′koo (kŏŏ-), *n.* migratory bird appearing in spring; its call.

cŭ′cŭmber, *n.* long fleshy fruit of a creeping plant; the plant.

cŭd, *n.* ruminant's half-digested food.

cŭd′bear (-bār), *n.* a dye-stuff; the lichen it is made from.

cŭd′dle, *v.t. & i.* fondle; nestle together. *n.* close embrace.

cŭdd′y, *n.* cabin of half-decked ship; (Sc.) donkey.

cŭd′gel, *n.* thick stick as weapon. *v.t.* beat with cudgel.

cŭe, *n.* actor's words serving as signal for another to speak, &c.; hint, intimation; billiard-player's rod.

cŭff, *v.t.* strike with the hand. *n.* a blow; end of coat or shirt sleeve; linen wrist-band.

‖ **cui bŏ′nŏ?** (kī), who profited by it? (pop.) to what purpose?

cuirăss′ (kw-), *n.* breast and back plate forming body armour. **cuirassier′** (kūr-), *n.* cavalryman with cuirass.

cuisine (kwizēn′), *n.* cooking methods; the feeding at hotel, &c.

cul-de-sac (kŏŏl′ de săk), *n.* blind alley.

cŭ′linary, *a.* of or for cooking.

cŭll, *v.t.* pick (flowers); select.

cŭl′minate, *v.i.* reach highest point of development; (Astron.) reach meridian. ~**tion**, *n.*

cŭl′pable, *a.* blameworthy, criminal. ~**bility**, *n.*

cŭl′prit, *n.* prisoner at the bar; an offender.

cŭlt, *n.* system of religious worship; devotion to person or thing.

cŭl′tivate, *v.t.* (-*vable*), till, raise crops from land; (fig.) improve, develop; pay attention to, cherish. ~**tion**, ~**tor**, *nn.*

cŭl′ture, *n.* tillage; refinement; artificial rearing of bees, fish, bacteria, &c. **cŭl′tural** (-cher-), *a.*

cŭl′tured (-cherd), *a.* exhibiting culture.

cŭl′verin, *n.* obsolete cannon.

cŭl′vert, *n.* tunnel-drain for water crossing road, canal, &c.

cŭm′ber, *v.t.* hamper, hinder; burden. *n.* embarrassments. ~**some**, ~**brous**, *aa.* hampering; inconveniently large or heavy.

‖ **cŭm(m)′in**, *n.* plant with aromatic seed.

cŭmm′erbŭnd, *n.* waist-sash.

‖ **cŭm′shaw**, *n.* (in Chinese ports) a gratuity; baksheesh.

cŭ′mŭlative, *a.* representing the sum of many items.

cŭ′mŭlus, *n.* (pl. -*li*), heaped-up mass of cloud.

cŭ′nĕiform, *a.* wedge-shaped; of inscriptions, composed of cuneiform marks. *n.* cuneiform characters.

cŭnn′ing, *n.* skill, dexterity; skill in deceit or evasion. *a.* possessed of cunning.

cŭp, *n.* drinking-vessel of any material or form; (fig.) draught of sorrow or joy; gold or silver or plated trophy in wine-cup shape as prize; rounded cavity, socket, &c. *v.t.* bleed by means of a *cupping-glass*. **cŭp′ful** (-ŏŏl), *n.*

cŭpboard (kŭb′erd), *n.* shelved closet or cabinet.

cŭpid′ity, *n.* greed of gain.

cŭ′pola, *n.* rounded dome forming roof; kind of furnace; ship's or fort's revolving gun-turret.

cŭ′prous, *a.* of copper, coppery.

cŭr, *n.* worthless or snappish dog; ill-bred or cowardly fellow.

cŭr′açao (-sō), *n.* orange-peel liqueur.

cŭr′acy, *n.* curate's office.

cŭrā′rĕ, *n.* vegetable poison paralysing motor nerves.

cŭr′assow (-ō), *n.* S.-Amer. bird like turkey.

cŭr′ate, *n.* parish priest's salaried clerical assistant.

---

a̤h, awl, oil, boor, cow, dowry; **ch**in, go, ba**ng**, **s**o, **sh**ip, **th**in; dh, as th(**e**)

cūr′ative, *a.* tending to cure. *n.* curative drug or measure.

cūrā′tor, *n.* person in charge of something, esp. of museum or library; member of a board. **~ship**, *n.*

curb, *n.* part of a bridle; (fig.) constraint, check; a kerb. *v.t.* apply curb to; restrain.

curd, *n.* coagulated substance formed by action of acids on milk; (pl.) broken-up curd as food. **curd′y**, *a.*

cur′dle, *v.t. & i.* coagulate, form into curd.

cure¹, *n.* remedy; course of treatment; spiritual charge. *v.t.* (-rable), restore to health, heal, remedy; preserve (meat, &c.). **cure′less**, *a.* incurable.

cure², *n.* (sl.) eccentric person.

‖ **curé**, *n.* (kū′rā), French parish priest.

curette′, *n.* surgeon's scraping instrument. *v.t.* scrape with this.

cur′few, *n.* ringing of bell at fixed evening hour.

cur′io, *n.* (pl. -os). curious object of art.

cūriŏs′ity, *n.* desire to know; inquisitiveness; strange or rare thing.

cūr′ious, *a.* eager to learn; inquisitive; strange, surprising.

curl, *v.t. & i.* bend; coil into spiral shape; proceed in a curve; play at curling. *n.* spiral lock of hair; spiral or incurved form.

curl′ew, *n.* long-billed wading bird with musical cry.

curl′ing, *n.* game played on ice with large flattish stones.

curl′y, *a.* having curls.

cur̄mŭdg′eon (-jn), *n.* churlish or miserly fellow.

cŭr′rant, *n.* a dried fruit; fruit of kinds of Ribes.

cŭr′rency, *n.* time during which a thing is current; money current in a country. **~ note**, inconvertible legal-tender note for £1 or 10s.

cŭr′rent, *a.* in circulation or general use; not yet superseded.

n. moving body of water, air, or electricity; general tendency or course.

cŭr′ricle, *n.* light two-wheeled two-horse carriage.

curric′ulum, *n.* (pl. -la), appointed course of study.

cŭr′rier, *n.* leather-dresser.

cŭr′ry¹, *n.* (Anglo-Ind.) dish of rice, dressed with spiced mincemeat, fish, &c.; (Eng.) dish of meat, &c. cooked with curry-powder, a preparation of turmeric.

cŭr′ry², *v.t.* rub down or dress (horse); dress (leather). **~comb**, metal comb for horses, &c.

cûrse, *n.* invocation of destruction or punishment; thing whose effects are disastrous. *v.t. & i.* (-sable), utter curse against; be a curse to. **cûrs′ed**, *a.* under a curse; damned.

cûrs′ive, *n.* running script. *a.* in cursive.

cûrsō′rial, *a.* (Zool.) having limbs adapted for running.

cûrs′ory, *a.* without attention to details; rapid, desultory.

cûrt, *a.* noticeably or rudely brief; over-concise.

curtail′, *v.t.* cut down, shorten, reduce. **~ment**, *n.*

cûr′tain (-tn), *n.* cloth, &c. suspended as screen. *v.t.* provide, shut off, with curtains. **~fire**, barrage.

cûr′tilage, *n.* area attached to dwelling-house.

cûrt′sy, *n.* woman's act of deference. *v.t.* drop curtsy.

cûrve, *n.* line of which no part is straight. *v.i. & t.* (-vable), bend so as to form a curve. **cûrv′ature**, *n.* curving, curved shape.

cûrvĕt′, *n.* horse's frisky leap. *v.i.* perform this.

cûrvilin′ear, *a.* of curved lines.

cŭsh′at, *n.* wood-pigeon.

cushion (koŏ′shn), *n.* bag of silk, cloth, &c. filled with soft material; elastic lining of billiard-table's sides. *v.t.* furnish with cushions; place or leave (billiard-ball) close to cushion.

cush'y (kŏŏ-), *a.* (sl.) (of job, &c.) easy and well paid.

cŭsp, *n.* point of meeting of two curves. **cŭsped** (-pt), ~**idal,** *aa.*

*****cŭss,** (sl.) *n.* creature, chap. *v.t.* & *i.* curse.

cŭss'ĕdnĕss, *n.* (sl.) perversity.

cŭs'tard, *n.* flavoured mixture of eggs and milk.

cŭstō'dian, *n.* curator, caretaker.

cŭs'tody, *n.* keeping; imprisonment.

cŭs'tom, *n.* usual practice; established usage; business patronage or support; (pl.) duties levied on imports. ~**house,** office at which customs duties are collected.

cŭs'tomary, *a.* usual; based on custom rather than law.

cŭs'tomer, *n.* a purchaser; person dealing with a business establishment.

cŭt, *v.t.* & *i.* divide or wound with edged instrument; detach by cutting; cross, intersect; reduce by cutting (hair, &c.); shape by cutting; (of batsman) hit (off ball) at wide angle to off with horizontal bat; decline to recognize person; reduce expenses; (sl.) go quickly; (sl.) *cuts no ice,* effects little or nothing. *n.* act of cutting, wound made by it; stroke with sword, whip, or cane; cutting of cricket-ball; cutting of an acquaintance; excision; joint or piece of meat; way thing is cut. ~**in,** drive vehicle between two passing each other.

cŭtā'nĕous, *a.* of the skin.

‖ **cŭt'cha,** k-, *a.* (Anglo-Ind.) slight, makeshift.

‖ **cutchě'rry,** **cŭt'cherý,** *n.* (Anglo-Ind.) court-house; business office.

cūte, *a.* (colloq.) clever, ingenious; *****attractive (esp. of child).

cū'ticle, *n.* outer skin, epidermis.

cŭt'lass, *n.* sailor's short broad-bladed sword.

cŭt'ler, *n.* knife maker or dealer.

cŭt'lerý, *n.* knives, scissors, &c.

cŭt'lĕt, *n.* neck-chop of mutton; small piece of veal, minced fish, &c.

cŭt'ter, *n.* person or thing that cuts; tailor's cutting-out hand; war-ship's rowing and sailing boat; small sloop-rigged vessel.

cŭt'ting, *n.* excavation of high ground for railway, &c.; piece cut from newspaper, &c.

cŭt'tle, *n.* sea mollusc ejecting black fluid when pursued.

cŭt'ty, *n.* short clay pipe.

cŭt'water, *n.* edge of ship's stem.

cȳăn'ic, *a.* of or containing cyanogen. **cȳ'anide,** *n.* compound of cyanogen. **cȳăn'ogen,** *n.* a colourless poisonous gas.

cȳc'lamĕn, *n.* bulbous plant with purple or white flowers.

cȳ'cle, *n.* recurrent period; complete set or series; bicycle, tricycle, or similar machine. *v.i.* move in cycles; use bicycle, &c. ~**car,** light motor vehicle.

cȳc'lĭc(al), *aa.* recurring in cycles; belonging to a period.

cȳ'clist, *n.* user of wheeled cycle.

cȳ'cloid, *n.* curve traced by a point on the circumference of a circle as the circle rolls along a straight line. **cȳcloid'al,** *a.*

cȳc'lomĕ'ter, *n.* instrument for measuring circular arcs; instrument recording distances travelled by cycle, &c.

cȳ'clone, *n.* hurricane of limited diameter, tornado. **cȳclŏn'ic,** *a.*

cȳclopaed'ia, *n.* encyclopaedia.

cȳ'clostȳle, *n.* apparatus printing copies of writing from stencil-plate cut by pen with small toothed wheel.

cȳg'nĕt, *n.* young swan.

cȳl'inder, *n.* solid or hollow roller-shaped body. **cȳlin'drical,** *a.*

cȳm'bal, *n.* (Mus.) one of two brass plates clashed together.

cȳme, *n.* an inflorescence in which each flower-stem ends in a flower. **cȳ'mōse,** *a.*

Cȳm'ric (k-), *a.* Welsh.

cȳn'ic, *n.* member of Greek sect of philosophers; sneering fault-finder. ~**al,** *a.* churlish; captious; incredulous of human goodness; sneering. ~**ism,** *n.*

cȳn′osure (-shoor). *n.* guiding star; centre of attraction or interest.

cȳ′press, *n.* coniferous tree with dark foliage; twigs of it as symbol of mourning.

cȳst, *n.* bladder or sac containing liquid secretion, morbid matter, or embryos. ~ic, *a.*

cȳs′toscōpe, *n.* instrument for cystic examination. ~scŏp′ic, *a.*

Czar, Tsar, Tzar (tsär), *n.* emperor or king. Czarit′sa, Ts~, Tz~, *n.* Russian Czar′s wife.

D

D, d (dē), *n.* as roman numeral, 500; (Mus.) second note in scale of C major.

dăb, *v.t. & i.* apply a wet surface to; strike lightly, aim feeble blow at. *n.* dabbing, light blow; kind of flatfish; (sl.) adept *at.*

dăb′ble, *v.i. & t.* move the feet or hands about in water; do anything in a slight manner.

dăb′chick, *n.* kind of water-bird.

‖ da ca′pō (dahkah-), (Mus.) repeat from the beginning.

dāce, *n.* small fresh-water fish.

dachs′hund (dahks-hoō-), *n.* kind of short-legged dog.

dacoit′, *n.* Indian or Burmese bandit.

dacoit′y, *n.* piece of dacoit′s work.

dăc′tyl, *n.* metrical foot (— ∪∪).

dăd, da (dah), dăd′a, dădd′ȳ, *nn.* (colloq.) father.

dădd′ȳ-lŏng′-lĕgs, *n.* crane-fly.

dā′dŏ, *n.* (pl. -os), the plane-faced body of a pedestal; lower part of room wall when distinguished by wainscot or colour. dā′dŏed, *a.* having dado.

daed′al, *a.* of mysterious complexity or skill.

dăff′odil, *n.* kinds of pale yellow narcissus.

daft (-ahft), *a.* foolish, wild, crazy.

dăgg′er (-g-), *n.* short edged stabbing weapon; obelus (†).

*dā′gŏ, *n.* (sl.) Spaniard, Portuguese, or Italian.

dague′rreotȳpe (-gĕrot-), *n.* early kind of photograph.

‖ dahabee′yah (dah-h-), *n.* a Nile sailing-boat.

dahl′ia (dāl-), *n.* a garden plant.

Dail Eireann (doilyē′ran), *n.* parliament of the Republic of Ireland.

dail′ȳ, *adv.* every day, constantly. *a.* done, occurring, published, &c. daily. *n.* daily newspaper.

dain′tȳ, *n.* choice morsel, a delicacy. *a.* choice; prettily neat; hard to please.

dair′ȳ, *n.* place for dealing with milk, &c. ~maid, woman employed in dairy. ~man, dealer in milk, &c. ~ing, dairy-keeping.

dais, *n.* low platform, usu. at upper end of room or hall.

dais′ȳ (-z-), *n.* small field and garden flower; (sl.) first-rate specimen of anything, often used contemptuously of persons. ~ -chain, string of daisies fastened together. ~cutter, horse lifting feet very little; ball running along ground in cricket.

dāle, *n.* valley. dāles′man (-ǎn), *n.* dweller in dales of N. England.

dăll′ȳ, *v.i.* spend time in idleness or vacillation. dăll′iance, *n.* love-making; delay.

Dălmā′tian (-shn), *n.* kind of spotted dog.

dăl′mat′ic, *n.* an ecclesiastical and royal vestment.

‖ dăl segno (sā′nyō), (Mus.) repeat from point indicated.

dăm[1], *n.* barrier checking the downward flow of water. *v.t.* confine with dam.

dăm[2], *n.* mother (usu. of beast).

dăm′age, *n.* harm; injury; loss; (pl.) sum claimed or adjudged for damage; (sl.) cost. *v.t.* (-geable), do harm to; injure.

dămascēne′, *n.* damson.

dăm′ask, *n.* kinds of woven material of silk or linen; colour of the damask rose, velvety red. *a.* made of damask; coloured like damask. ~ rose, kinds of red rose.

dămaskeen′, -scēne′, *v.t.* ornament (steel, &c.) by inlaying.

dâme, n. lady. esp. (arch.) as prefix to name of knight's or baronet's wife; lady member of O.B.E.; a matron.

dăm'măr, n. various resins.

dămn (-m), v.t. & i. doom to eternal torment; condemn with curses; give hostile reception to (play); censure or condemn, curse. dăm'nable, a. deserving damnation, hateful. dămnâ'tion, n. eternal punishment in hell. dăm'natory, a. conveying censure. dămned (-md), a. & adv. damnable, damnably.

dăm'nify, v.t. (legal), cause injury to. ~fication, n.

|| dămnō'sa hērēd'ĭtās, n. inheritance that brings more burden than profit.

dămp, n. diffused moisture. a. not in the normal dry state: affected with moisture. v.t. make damp; deaden, make spiritless. ~ course, layer of slate, &c., in wall to keep d. from rising.

dăm'per, n. person or thing that depresses metal plate in flue controlling combustion; (Austral.) unleavened cake baked in wood ashes.

dăm'sel (-z-), n. (arch.) girl.

dăm'son (-z-), n. small dark-purple plum; tree bearing it. ~ cheese, solid conserve of damsons.

dance (dah-), v.i. & t. (-ceable), move with rhythmic steps, glides, &c., usu. to music; jump about, move in lively way. n. piece of dancing; dancing-party. dan'cer (dah-), n. one who engages in dancing, esp. one who dances in public for pay. dan'cing-girl, n. a female professional dancer, esp. in India, a nautch-girl.

dăn'dēlion, n a yellow-flowered wild plant.

dăn'der, n. (sl.) fighting spirit.

Dăn'die Din'mont, n. breed of terrier.

dăn'dle, v.t. dance or nurse (child) in the arms.

dăn'druff, -riff, n. dead skin in small scales among the hair.

dăn'dy, n. man paying excessive attention to smartness in dress, &c.; *(attrib., colloq.) excellent. ~ism, n.

Dāne, n. native of Denmark. (hist.) Northman invader of England. great~, large breed of dog.

dă'nger (-j-), n. liability or exposure to harm. ~ous, a.

dangle (dăng'gl), v.i. & t. be loosely suspended; hold in suspense; linger as lover. dăng'ler, n.

dănk, a. oozy; damp.

dăph'nē, n. a flowering shrub.

dăp'per, a. neat, precise.

dăp'ple, v.t. variegate with rounded spots. ~grey, a. of grey dappled with darker spots. n. dapple-grey horse.

dar'bies (-biz), n.pl. handcuffs.

Dar'by & Joan, n. devoted old married couple.

dāre, v.t. venture; have courage or impudence for any purpose; defy, challenge. ~devil, a. reckless. n. reckless person.

dâr'ing, n. adventurous courage. a. bold, fearless.

dârk, a. with little or no light; gloomy; obscure, secret; brown-complexioned. n. absence of light; want of knowledge; dark colour. ~ ages, the middle ages. ~ continent, Africa. ~ horse, one of whose racing form little is known (often fig. of persons).

dârk'en, v.t. & i. make or become dark; perplex.

dârk'ling, adv. & a. in the dark.

dârk'ness, n. absence of light; wickedness.

dârk'some, a. gloomy; obscure.

dârk'y, n. (colloq.) negro.

dâr'ling, n. beloved person or animal. a. beloved or prized.

dârn¹, v.t. mend hole with needle and yarn or thread. n. place darned. *darning-needle, dragonfly.

dârn², v.t. (sl.) damn (in cursing).

darnâ'tion, n. (sl.) used as exclamation of chagrin, &c.

dâr'nel, n. a weed growing in corn.

dârt, n. light javelin or pointed missile; darting motion; (pl.) in-

door game. *v.t.* & *t.* throw missile; emit suddenly; go rapidly.

Dar′win·ian, *a.* of or according to Darwin or his doctrines, esp. on evolution of species. **n.** follower of Darwin. **~ism,** **~ist,** *nn.*

dash, *v.t.* & *i.* shatter; send violently; go with haste; flavour *with.* **n.** rush or sudden advance; showy smartness; a stroke (—); slight infusion of. **~board,** mudshield in front of vehicle.

dash′ing, *a.* spirited; showy.

das′tard, *n.* brutal coward. **~ly,** *a.*

date¹, *n.* an oblong stone-fruit; tree bearing this.

date², *n.* day or time of thing's occurrence; period to which a work belongs; *(colloq.)* appointment for a specified time. *v.t.* & *i.* (*-table*), mark with date; count time, reckon; (of art, style, &c.) become recognizable as of a particular period. **~less,** *a.* undated; endless.

da′tive, *a.* & *n.* (the case in nouns, &c.) proper to the remoter object or recipient. dati′val, *a.*

da′tum, *n.* (pl. *-ta*), thing known or assumed as basis for inference; fixed starting-point of scale, &c.

|| **datūr′a,** *n.* (Anglo-Ind.) kinds of narcotic plant.

daub, *v.t.* & *i.* coat (wall, &c.) with clay, &c.; smear; paint roughly or unskilfully. **n.** stuff daubed on; rough picture. **~er,** **~ster,** *nn.* bad painter.

daught′er (dawt-), *n.* one's female child; female member of family, race, &c. **~in-law,** son's wife.

daunt, *v.t.* frighten into giving up a purpose. **~less,** *a.* not to be daunted.

dauph′in, *n.* king of France's eldest son. **~ess,** dauphin's wife.

dav′enport, *n.* kind of escritoire; *kind of settee.

dav′it, *n.* crane at ship's side.

Da′vy¹ (lămp), *n.* miner's safety lamp.

da′vy², *n.* (sl.) *take one's* **~,** swear that, swear to fact.

Da′vy Jones's lŏck′er (jōnzĭz), *n.* the sea regarded as a grave.

daw, *n.* kind of small crow.

daw′dle, *v.i.* idle, waste time.

|| **dawk,** dăk (dawk), *n.* (Anglo-Ind.) post or transport by relays of men or horses; relay. **~ bungalow,** house for travellers at dawk station.

dawn, *v.i.* begin to grow light; appear faintly. **n.** first light; daybreak; incipient gleam.

day, *n.* time during which sun is above the horizon; daylight; dawn; a distinctive period. **~book,** one in which sales, &c. are noted for later transfer to ledger. **~boy,** schoolboy living at home. **~-letter,** telegram at a special rate. **~light,** light prevailing from sunrise to sunset, dawn; publicity. **~light-saving,** shifting of daily business to earlier hour in summer by use of fictitious time. **~-school,** one for day-pupils only. **~-spring,** dawn.

daze, *v.t.* stupefy, bewilder. **n.** bewilderment, stupefaction.

daz′zle, *v.t.* confuse the sight by overpowering brightness; tempt by brilliant prospects.

deac′on, *n.* minister of third order in Episcopal Church; secular officer of non-episcopal churches. **~ess,** churchwoman appointed to perform charitable functions; a female deacon in non-episcopal churches.

dead (dĕd), *a.* no longer alive; without spiritual life; obsolete; inanimate; dull, devoid of force. *adv.* profoundly, absolutely, completely. **~alive,** dull, spiritless. **~ball,** out of play. **~beat,** utterly exhausted. **~head,** nonpaying member or passenger. **~ heat,** race in which horses finish exactly even. **~ letter,** law no longer observed; unclaimed letter at post office. **~light,** shutter blacking out cabin-window or port-hole. **~lock,** state of affairs in which it is impossible to advance or recede. **~ march,** funeral music. **~nettle,** nonstinging nettle-like weed. **~ shot,** one who never misses.

dead'en (dĕd-), *v.t. & i.* deprive of or lose vitality, force, &c.; make insensible to.

dead'ly (dĕd-), *a.* causing fatal injury or death; intense.

deaf (dĕf), *a.* wholly or partly without hearing; inattentive.

deaf'en (dĕf-), *v.t.* deprive of hearing, esp. temporarily.

deal[1], *n.* fir or pine wood; a 9 in. deal board.

deal[2], *v.t. & i.* (dealt, pr. dĕlt), distribute to a number of people; assign as share; deliver blow; bargain or do business with. *n.* a part, quantity, amount; dealing at cards; piece of bargaining. **~er**, *n.* person dealing at cards; trader; trafficker.

deal'ings, *n.pl.* person's conduct or transactions; intercourse.

dean, *n.* head of the chapter of a cathedral; fellow of a college with disciplinary functions. **dean'ery**, *n.* dean's house or office; rural dean's division of archdeaconry.

dear, *a.* beloved; precious to; costly; not cheap. *n.* beloved one; charming person or thing. *adv.* at high price. *int.* expressing surprise, distress, &c.

dear'est, *n.* most beloved one.

dearth (dĕr-), *n.* scarcity and dearness of food; a deficiency.

dear'y, *n.* (colloq.), dear one.

death (dĕth), *n.* dying, end of life; being dead; want of spiritual life. **~adder**, kinds of venomous snake. **~duties**, tax levied before property passes to heir. **~mask**, cast taken of dead person's face. **~rate**, yearly number of deaths to 1,000 of population. **~'s-head**, skull as emblem of mortality. **~trap**, unwholesome or dangerous place. **~warrant**, order for criminal's execution (also fig.). **~watch**, kinds of wood-boring insect whose ticking portends a death.

death'less (dĕth-), *a.* immortal; never dying.

death'ly (dĕth-), *a. & adv.* resembling death; still; pale.

‖ **débâcle** (dībah'kl), *n.* utter collapse or disorganization or rout.

débar', *v.t.* exclude; preclude.

débarka'tion, *n.* disembarkation.

débase', *v.t.* (-sable), lower in character, quality, or value; adulterate metal (of coinage). **~ment**, *n.*

débate', *v.t. & i.* contest, fight for; discuss; consider or deliberate in one's mind. *n.* controversy; discussion. **déba'table**, *a.* subject to dispute. **déba'ter**, *n.* person skilled in argument. debating-society, *n.* one in which political and other questions are debated.

débauch', *v.t.* pervert from virtue; vitiate (taste); seduce. *n.* bout of sensual indulgence. **débauchee'** (-bosh-), *n.* viciously sensual person. **débauch'ery**, *n.* indulgence in or prevalence of sensual habits.

dében'ture, *n.* sealed bond of corporation acknowledging sum on which fixed interest is due till principal is repaid.

débil'itate, *v.t.* cause debility in.

débil'ity, *n.* feebleness; weakness.

deb'it, *n.* entry in account of sum owing. *v.t.* charge with sum, enter against.

débonair', *a.* genial, unembarrassed.

débouch' (-ōōsh), *v.i.* issue from ravine, woods, &c. into open ground (of troops, rivers, &c.). **~ment**, *n.*

déb'ris (-rē), *n.* strewn fragments, drifted accumulation.

debt (dĕt), *n.* what is owed; state of owing something.

debt'or (dĕt-), *n.* person in debt.

débus', *v.t. & i.* (Mil.) unload (men, stores) or alight from motor vehicles.

début (dā'bōō), *n.* one's first appearance in society or as a performer. **débutant** (dā'bōōtahn), **-e** (dā'bōōtahńt), *nn.* male, female, making début.

déc'ade (-ad), déc'ad, *n.* ten-year period; set of ten, &c.

déc'adence, *n.* deterioration; decline of a nation, art, &c.

déc'adent, *a.* declining, showing

---

māte, mēte, mīte, mōte, mūte, mŏŏt ; răck, rĕck, rick, rŏck, rŭck, rŏŏk ;

decadence. *n.* decadent person, esp. a writer or artist affecting a turgid or obscure style.

dĕc'agon, *n.* plane figure with ten sides and angles. dĕcăg'onal, *a.*

dĕc'agram(me), *n.* ten grammes; ·353 oz. avoirdupois.

dĕcahēd'ron, *n.* solid figure or body with ten sides. ~dral, *a.*

dĕc'alitre (-tēr), *n.* ten litres; about 2 1/5 gall.

dĕc'alogue (-ŏg), *n.* the ten commandments.

dĕc'amĕtre (-tēr), *n.* ten metres.

dĕcămp', *v.i.* break up or leave camp; abscond. ~ment, *n.*

dĕcā'nal, *a.* of a dean; of the dean's or south side of the choir. ‖ dĕcā'nĭ, (mus. direction) to be sung by dean's side.

dĕcănt', *v.t.* pour off (wine, &c.) leaving sediment behind.

dĕcăn'ter, *n.* stoppered bottle in which wine is brought to table.

dĕcăp'ĭtāte, *v.t.* (-*itable*), behead. ~tion, ~tor, *nn.*

dĕc'apŏd, *n.* ten-footed crustacean, e.g. crab.

dĕcasyll'able, *n.* line of ten syllables. dĕcasyllăb'ic, *a.*

dĕcay', *v.i. & t.* rot, decompose; decline in power, wealth, energy, &c. *n.* decline, falling off; break-up of health; decomposition.

dĕcease', *n.* death, departure from life. *v.i.* die (usu. in *p.p.*).

dĕceit' (-sēt), *n.* piece of deception; deceitfulness. ~ful, *a.* given to or marked by deceit.

dĕceive (-sēv), *v.t.* (-*vable*), persuade of what is false; mislead, take in; disappoint.

Dĕcĕm'ber, *n.* twelfth month.

dē'cency, *n.* decentness; the recognized code of propriety.

dĕcĕnn'ial, *a.* recurring in ten years.

dē'cent, *a.* seemly; not immodest or obscene; respectable; passable; good enough; (school sl.) kindly; not severe.

dĕcĕp'tion, *n.* deceiving or being deceived; thing that deceives. ~ive, *a.* apt to mislead; of a misleading kind.

dĕcīde', *v.t. & i.* (-*dable*), settle by giving victory to one side; give judgement; resolve.

dĕcī'dĕd, *a.* definite or unquestionable; not vacillating. ~ly, *adv.* undeniably, undoubtedly.

dĕcĭd'ūous, *a.* subject to periodical or normal shedding.

dĕ'cigram(me), *n.* (metric system) one-tenth of a gramme. dĕ'cilitre (-lētēr), *n.* one-tenth of a litre.

dĕcill'ion (-yon), *n.* tenth power of a million.

dē'cĭmal, *a.* of tenths; proceeding by tens. *n.* a decimal fraction. ~ coinage, one in which the value of each denomination is 10 times that of the one next below it. ~ fraction, a fraction with a power of 10 as denominator. ~ system, a system of weights and measures with denominations rising as in decimal coinage. dē'cĭmalize, *v.t.*; ~zation, *n.*

dē'cĭmāte, *v.t.* (-*table*), kill a tenth or a large proportion of. ~tion, ~tor, *nn.*

dē'cĭmĕtre (-tēr), *n.* one-tenth of a metre, or 3·937 in.

dĕcī'pher, *v.t.* make out (cipher, bad writing, hieroglyphics, &c.). ~ment, *n.*

dĕcī'sion (-zhn), *n.* act of deciding; settlement of an issue; conclusion come to; firmness.

dĕcī'sive, *a.* that decides an issue or contributes to a decision.

dĕck, *n.* platform in ship. *v.t.* array, decorate; (*p.p.*) having a deck. ~chair, camp-stool; long-armed reclining chair. ~hand, man employed about ship's deck.

dĕclaim', *v.i. & t.* speak oratorically; inveigh passionately. dĕclamā'tion, *n.* declaiming; impassioned speech. dĕclăm'atory, *a.*

dĕclarā'tion, *n.* declaring; an emphatic or deliberate or formal statement. dĕclă'ratory, *a.*

dĕclāre', *v.t. & i.* (-*rable*), assert emphatically; affirm; publish; proclaim; (bridge) name (trumps).

dĕclĕn'sion (-shn), *n.* a falling-off

from a standard; (Gram.) manner of declining nouns.

declina′tion, n. downward bend; angular distance of star, &c. N. or S. of celestial equator; deflexion of compass-needle from true N. and S. ~al, a.

decline′, v.i. & t. (-nable), show a downward tendency; decrease, deteriorate; refuse; rehearse or make the case-forms of (nouns, &c.). n. gradual decrease or deterioration; decay; wasting disease.

decliv′ity, n. downward slope.

declutch′, v.i. disengage clutch.

decoc′tion, n. extraction of essence by boiling.

decode′, v.t. (-dable), decipher.

∥ **décolleté** (dicŏl′tā), a. (fem. -ée), low-necked; in low-necked dress.

decompōse′ (-z), v.t. & i. separate (substance) into its elements; rot. **decomposi′tion**, n.

decontrol′, v.t. release (trade, &c.) from Government control.

dec′orāte, v.t. (-rable), adorn, beautify; invest with badge of honour. ~tive, a.

decora′tion, n. decorating; badge, medal, &c.; (pl.) flags, &c. put up on festive occasion. *D~ Day, Memorial Day.

dec′orātor, n. tradesman who paints and papers houses.

decō′rous, a. not offending against decency or seemliness.

decō′rum, n. seemliness, propriety, etiquette.

decoy′, n. netted pond into which wild duck may be enticed; bird, or person, used to entice others; an enticement. v.t. entice by a decoy.

decrease′, v.t. & i. (dikrēs′) diminish. n. (dē′krēs) diminution.

decrēe′, n. authoritative order; judicial decision. v.t. ordain by decree. ~ nis′ī, (esp.) order for divorce after fixed period.

dec′rement, n. decrease.

decrep′it, a. enfeebled with age; infirm. ~ūde, n.

decrē′tal, n. Papal decree.

decry′, v.t. disparage, cry down.

dec′uple, a. tenfold amount. v.t. & i. multiply by 10.

ded′icāte, v.t. (-cable), devote to the service of God; give up to some special purpose; inscribe (book, &c.). ~tion, n. dedicating; words in which book is dedicated. ~tor, n. ~tory, a.

dedūce′, v.t. (-cible), infer; draw as conclusion from facts.

dedūct′, v.t. subtract; take away or withhold. ~ion, n. deducting, amount deducted; inference. ~ive, a. deducing.

deed, n. thing consciously done; fact, reality; legal document. *v.t. convey or transfer by deed.

deem, v.t. believe, consider, judge. ~ster, n. Manx judge.

deep, a. going far down or far in; immersed in; profound; heartfelt; hard to fathom. n. abyss, pit; the sea. adv. far down or in. **deep′en**, v.t. & i.

deer, n. kinds of ruminant quadruped. ~forest, wild land reserved for deer-stalking. ~hound, large rough-haired greyhound. ~stalker, sportsman stalking deer; pattern of cloth hat.

deface′, v.t. (-ceable), disfigure; make illegible. ~ment, n.

∥ **dē fāc′to**, in fact, whether by right or not.

dē′falcāte, v.i. be guilty of defalcation. ~tor, n.

dēfalcā′tion, n. misappropriation of funds; breach of trust concerning money.

dēfāme′, v.t. (-mable), attack the good fame of. **dēfamā′tion**, n.; **dēfām′atory**, a.

default′, n. failure to act or appear or pay. v.i. fail to meet obligations.

dēfeat′, v.t. worst in battle or other contest; frustrate, baffle. n. lost battle or contest; frustration. ~ism, n. conduct tending to bring about acceptance of defeat. ~ist, n. & a.

def′ecāte, v.t. & i. (-cable), clear of impurities, refine; void excrement. ~tion, n.; ~tor, n.

deféct', n. lack of something; shortcoming, blemish.

deféc'tion, n. abandonment of one's leader or cause.

deféc'tive, a. incomplete, faulty; wanting, deficient.

defénce', n. defending from, resistance of, attack; (Mil., pl.) fortifications; defendant's case in law-suit. ~less, a.

defénd', v.t. & i. ward off attack from; keep safe, protect; conduct the defence in law-suit.

defén'dant, n. person accused or sued in court of law.

defén'der, n. one who defends.

defén'sible, a. easily defended; justifiable. ~bility, n.

defén'sive, a. serving for defence. n. state or posture of defence.

defér'¹, v.t. put off, postpone. ~ment, n. defér'²², v.i. change one's course in deference to another's advice.

déf'erence, n. compliance with advice, &c. of another; respectful conduct. deferén'tial (-shl), a. showing deference.

defí'ance, n. challenge to fight; open refusal to obey.

defí'ant, a. expressing defiance.

defí'ciency (-shn-), n. lack or shortage; thing wanting, deficit.

defí'cient (-shnt), a. insufficient in quantity, force, &c.

dé'ficit (or déf'-), n. deficiency in a sum of money, &c.; excess of liabilities over assets.

defile¹, v.i. (diffil') march in file. n. (dé'fil) gorge or pass.

defile², v.t. (-lable), make dirty, pollute; profane. ~ment, n.

define', v.t. (-nable), mark out (limits, boundary); fix or show clearly; state meaning precisely.

déf'inite, a. with exact limits; determinate, distinct, precise.

defini'tion, n. statement of the precise meaning of a term.

defin'itive, a. to be regarded as final; not subject to revision.

defla'te, v.t. (-lable), empty (balloon, &c.) of its gas or air; reduce inflation of (currency). ~tion, n.

defléct', v.t. & i. turn aside from the straight course. defléx'ion (-kshn), ~éc'tion, n.

deflow'er, v.t. deprive of virginity; ravage; strip of flowers.

defórm', v.t. spoil the aspect or shape of; disfigure; (p.p.) misshapen. defórma'tion, n. perverted or changed form. ~ity, n. deformed state; abnormality.

defráud', v.t. fraudulently deprive, cheat.

defráy', v.t. provide money for.

déft, a. dextrous, adroit.

defúnct', a. dead; obsolete.

defý', v.t. challenge to do or prove something; resist openly; present insuperable obstacles to.

degén'eracy, n. degenerate state.

degén'erate, a. (-it) having lost qualities proper to the kind. n. (-it) degenerate person. v.i. (-āt) become degenerate. ~ā'tion, n.

deglutí'tion (-lōo-), n. swallowing.

degrada'tion, n. degrading; disgrace; thing that degrades.

degrá'de, v.t. (-dable), reduce to lower rank; debase. ~ding, a.

degree', n. stage in ascending or descending scale; unit of angular or of thermometric measurement; university rank.

dehis'cent, a. (of seed-vessels) gaping, bursting open.

dé'ify, v.t. (-lable), make a god of; worship. ~fica'tion, n.

deign (dān), v.t. & i. condescend to do; vouchsafe, grant. ‖ dé'i grā'tiā (shi-), adv. by God's grace.

dé'ism, n. belief in the existence of God without accepting revelation. dé'ist, n.; déist'ic, a.

dé'ity, n. divine status or nature; a god. The D—, God.

dejéct', v.t. dispirit, cast down. ~ion, n. downcast mood. ‖ déjeuner (dé'zhonǎ), n. ceremonial luncheon.

‖ dé jure' (joor-), rightful, by right.

délaine', n. a light dress-fabric.

déla'tion, n. act of informing against a person.

delay', v.t. & i. put off; hinder,

frustrate; be tardy. n. lack of dispatch; hindrance.

delec'table, a. delightful.

delecta'tion, n. enjoyment.

del'egacy, n. body of delegates.

del'egate, v.t. (-āt) send as representative(s) to a council or conference; commit (authority) to representative(s). n. (-ĭt) such representative.

delega'tion, n. delegating; delegacy; *representatives of a single State in Congress.

delete', v.t. (-table), strike out (word, passage, &c.). ~tion, n.

deleter'ious, a. harmful.

delf, n. kind of earthenware.

delib'erate, v.i. & t. (-āt), take counsel, hold debate; weigh, consider. a. (-ĭt), intentional, fully considered. ~a'tion, n. deliberating; being deliberate.

delib'erative, a.

del'icacy, n. delicateness; refined feeling; a dainty.

del'icate, a. dainty, luxurious; tender or easily harmed; fastidious; slender, fine, exquisite; sensitive.

*delicatess'en, n. (shop selling) delicacies for table.

deli'cious (-shus), a. highly delightful, esp. to taste or smell.

delight' (-īt), v.t. & i. please highly; take great pleasure in. n. high pleasure; thing that gives it. ~ful, ~some, aa.

delimita'tion, n. assigning of boundaries.

delin'eate, v.t. (-neable), portray by drawing or description. ~tion, ~tor, nn.

delin'quency, n. neglect of duty; guilt; misdeed.

delin'quent, n. person who fails in his duty or commits an offence.

deliquesce', v.i. undergo change to liquid form; (fig.) melt away. ~ence, n. ; ~ent, a.

deli'rious, a. affected with delirium; raving; wildly excited.

deli'rium, n. disordered state of mind; wildly excited mood. ~ tre'mens (-z), disorder due to heavy drinking.

deliv'er, v.t. rescue, save, set free; transfer or hand over to another; convey (letters, goods) to addressee or purchaser; aim (blow, cricket-ball, attack); (be ~ed of) give birth to; utter (speech).

deliv'erance, n. setting free; a consequential utterance.

deliv'ery, n. delivering or being delivered; periodical distribution of letters or goods; person's manner of delivering a speech or a ball, &c.

dell, n. little wooded hollow.

Del'phian, -phic, aa. oracular, ambiguous.

del'ta, n. Greek letter written Δ; triangular alluvial tract at some rivers' mouths.

del'toid, a. Δ-shaped. n. deltoid muscle in shoulder.

delude' (-ōō-), v.t. fool, deceive.

del'uge, n. & v.t. flood.

delu'sion (-ōōzhn), n. a false belief; source of vain hope.

delu'sive (-ōō-), a. raising vain hopes; deceptive.

|| **de luxe'**, of unusual sumptuousness.

delve, v.t. & i. (arch.) dig.

dem'agogue (-g), n. democratic orator or agitator. ~gŏg'ic(-g-),a.

demand' (-ah-), n. request made as of right; call for a commodity, &c. v.t. claim; ask for peremptorily.

demarca'tion, n. division between adjacent areas.

demean', v.t. lower the dignity of.

demean', v.refl. ~ oneself, behave, conduct oneself. demean'our (-ner), n. one's bearing.

dement'ed, a. beside oneself.

|| **dementi** (dāmahn'tē), n. official denial of rumour.

demer'it, n. fault, defect.

demesne' (-ēn), n. possession of land with unrestricted rights; territory; a landed estate.

dem'igŏd, n. being half divine and half human or bestial.

dem'ijohn (-ŏn), n. large wicker-cased bottle.

---

māte, mēte, mīte, mōte, mūte, mōōt ; răck, rĕck, rick, rŏck, rŭck, rŏŏk ;

dĕm'ĭ-mŏnde, *n.* class of women of doubtful reputation.

dĕm'ĭ-rĕp, *n.* woman of suspected chastity.

dĕmīse' (-z), *v.t.* (*-sable*), convey to another by will or lease; transmit by death or abdication. *n.* demising; death.

dĕm'ĭsĕm'ĭquāver, *n.* note equal to half a semiquaver.

dĕmŏc'racў, *n.* government by the people; State having this.

dĕm'ŏcrăt, *n.* advocate of democracy; member of U.-S. democratic party. ~ic, *a.* ~ *party,* one of the two chief political parties, opp. *republican.* **dĕmŏc'ratize,** *v.t.* ~ization, *n.*

dĕmŏl'ĭsh, *v.t.* overthrow; batter or crush to pieces; (colloq.) eat up. **dĕmŏlĭ'tion,** *n.* demolishing.

dē'mon, *n.* devil or evil spirit. **dēmō'nĭac,** *n.* person possessed with a devil. **dēmŏnī'acal,** *a.* devilish; cruel or malignant.

dēmŏn'ĭc, *a.* demoniac; abnormal.

dēmŏnŏl'atrў, dēmŏnŏl'ogў, *nn.* worship, study, of demons.

dĕm'onstrāte, *v.t. & i.* (*-rable*), give or be a proof of; establish the truth of; make or take part in a demonstration. ~tion, *n.* proving or proof; setting forth of a case; show of feeling; display of armed force or organized expression of opinion. **dĕmŏn'strative,** *a.* conclusive; unreserved; (of pron. or adj.) serving to point out or identify; *n.* demonstrative word. ~tor, *n.* professor's assistant.

dĕmŏr'alize, *v.t.* (*-zable*), ruin the morals or morale of. ~zation, *n.*

Dē'mŏs, *n.* democracy personified. *dēmōte', v.t.* (colloq.) reduce (soldier, student, &c.) to lower grade.

dēmur', v.i. raise objections; take exception to. *n.* raising of objections.

dēmure', *a.* quiet or undemonstrative; affectedly coy.

dēmur'rage, *n.* amount payable for delay in loading or discharging ships or railway trucks.

dēmur'rer, *n.* (legal) exception taken to opponent's point.

dēmў', *n.* a size of paper.

dĕn, *n.* wild beasts' lair; person's private room. *v.i.* live in den.

dēnā'rĭus, *n.* (pl. *-iī*), ancient-Roman silver coin.

dē'narў, *a.* of ten; decimal.

dēnā'ture, *v.t.* charge essential qualities of; make (alcohol) undrinkable.

dēnăt'uralize (-chōo-), *v.t.* change nature of; divest of citizenship. ~zation, *n.*

dēne, *n.* deep wooded valley.

dĕng'ue (-nggā), *n.* infectious eruptive fever with acute pain in joints.

dēnī'al, *n.* act of denying or refusing; contradiction.

dĕn'im, *n.* twilled cotton fabric.

dĕn'izen, *n.* inhabitant; species permanently established but not native of a place.

dēnŏm'ĭnāte, *v.t.* (*-nable*), give specified name to; designate. **dēnŏmĭnā'tion,** *n.* name, title; class of units in money, &c.; a distinctively named Church or sect. ~al, *a.* of religious denominations. ~alize, *v.t.* ~tor, *n.* number below the line in a vulgar fraction; divisor.

dēnotā'tion, *n.* denoting; term's primary meaning; designation. **dēnō'tative,** *a.* indicative of. **dēnōte',** *v.t.* (*-table*), stand for; be the sign of; indicate.

‖ **dénouement** (dānōō'mahn), *n.* the issue of a tale.

dēnounce', *v.t.* (*-ceable*), inform or inveigh against; give notice of intention to withdraw from.

‖ **de nouveau** (nōōvō'), dē nō'vō', afresh; once more.

dense, *a.* closely compacted; crowded together; stupid.

dĕn'sitў, *n.* closeness of substance; crowded state; stupidity.

dĕnt, *n.* depression left by a blow. *v.t.* mark with dent.

dĕn'tal, *a.* of tooth, teeth, or dentistry; (of sound) made with tongue-tip against front teeth. *n.* dental sound or letter.

---

mãre, mēte, mĩre, mõre, mũre ; pãrt, pĕrt, põrt ; *italics*, vague sounds :

dĕn'tāte, *a.* toothed; notched.

dĕn'tifrice, *n.* powder, paste, or wash for tooth-cleaning.

dĕn'tine, *n.* substance of which the teeth are mainly composed.

dĕn'tist, **dĕn'tistry**, *nn.* dental surgeon, his art.

dĕnti'tion, *n.* teething; characteristic arrangement of teeth.

dĕn'ture, *n.* set of teeth.

dĕnūdā'tion, *n.* stripping; (Geol.) disappearance of forests or surface soil.

dĕnūde', *v.t.* (-dable), make naked or bare; strip.

dĕnŭncīā'tion, *n.* denouncing, invective. **dĕnŭn'ciatorў,** *a.*

dĕnŷ', *v.t.* (-iable), declare untrue; disavow; refuse.

dē'ŏdār, *n.* Himalayan cedar; also applied in India to other trees.

dēŏd'orize, *v.t.* (-zable), rid of smell, disinfect. **~zā'tion,** *n.* **~zer,** *n.* disinfecting substance.

|| Dē'ō vŏlĕn'tĕ, *adv.* (abbr. D.V.) if God wills, if nothing prevents.

dĕpärt', *v.i.* & *t.* go away (from); die; diverge or deviate from. **~ure,** *n.* departing.

dĕpärt'ment, *n.* separate part of complex whole; branch of a business or of municipal or State administration. **'~ store,** store keeping a variety of goods. **dĕpärtmĕn'tal,** *a.*

dĕpĕnd', *v.i.* be suspended from; be contingent; rely upon.

dĕpĕn'dable, *a.* reliable.

dĕpĕn'dant, *n.* one who depends on another; a retainer.

dĕpĕn'dence, *n.* depending; reliance; thing relied on.

dĕpĕn'dencў, *n.* something subordinate; a dependent State.

dĕpĕn'dent, *a.* depending on; contingent, subordinate; subject.

dĕpict', *v.t.* give a picture or description of. **~or,** *n.*

dĕpilā'tion, *n.* extirpation of hair from the face, &c. **dĕpil'atorў,** *a.* used in depilation.

dĕplēte', *v.t.* (-table), exhaust or nearly exhaust (stock). **~tion,** *n.*

dĕplōr'able, *a.* lamentable; much to be regretted; blameworthy.

dĕplōre', *v.t.* bewail; grieve over.

dĕploy', *v.t.* & *i.* spread out from column into line. **~ment,** *n.*

dēpō'nent, *n.* maker of a legal deposition; a deponent verb. *a.* (of verbs) of passive form but active meaning.

dēpŏp'ŭlāte, *v.t.* (-lable), reduce population of. **~tion,** **~tor,** *nn.*

dēpört', *v.t.* carry into exile, banish; (refl.) behave or conduct oneself. **dēpörtā'tion,** *n.* conveyance into exile. **~ment,** *n.* behaviour, bearing.

dēpōse' (-z), *v.t.* & *i.* (-zable), remove from office, dethrone; state that, testify.

dēpŏs'it (-z-), *n.* thing stored for safe keeping; sum placed in a bank; earnest money; layer of accumulated matter. *v.t.* lay down in a place; leave as a deposit; entrust for keeping.

dēpŏs'itarў (-z-), *n.* person with whom thing is deposited.

dĕposi'tion (-z-), *n.* deposing; removing; piece of sworn evidence.

dēpŏs'itor (-z-), *n.* person who deposits money, property, &c.

dēpŏs'itorў (-z-), *n.* storehouse.

dĕp'ot (-ō), *n.* storehouse; (Mil.) place for stores, head-quarters.

dĕprāve', *v.t.* (-vable), corrupt morally. **~d,** *a.* wicked, dissolute.

dĕprăv'itў, *n.* wickedness, moral corruption.

dĕp'rĕcāte, *v.t.* (-cable), advise the avoidance of; plead against. **~tion,** **~tor,** *nn.* **~torў,** *a.*

dēprē'cīāte (-shi-), *v.t.* & *i.* (-iable), disparage; lower in value. **~tion,** *n.* depreciating; fall in value. **~tor,** *n.* **~torў,** *a.* disparaging.

dĕprēdā'tion, *n.* spoliation; (pl.) ravages. **~tor,** *n.* spoiler.

dĕprĕss', *v.t.* lower or reduce; affect with low spirits. **~ible,** *a.*

dĕprĕ'ssion (-shn), *n.* part of surface below the general level; low spirits; a lowering of barometric pressure, trade, &c.

dĕprīve', *v.t.* dispossess or strip of.

dĕprīvā'tion (*or* dĕpri-), *n.* (esp.) felt loss.

dĕpth, *n.* deepness; deep place; abyss; deep thought, feeling, &c. **~chärge,** bomb for dropping on submerged submarine.

dĕpŭtā'tion, *n.* body of persons sent to represent others.

dĕpūte', *v.t.* (*-table*), commit (task, authority) to another.

dĕp'ūtize, *v.i.* act as deputy for.

dĕp'ŭty, *n.* person acting as substitute; parliamentary representative (in foreign countries).

dėrail', *v.t.* make (train) leave the rails. **~ment,** *n.*

dėrānge' (-j), *v.t.* (*-geable*), throw into confusion, disorganize; (*p.p.*) of deranged mind, mad. **~ment,** *n.*

dėrāte', *v.t.* relieve of rates; diminish burden of rates. **~ting,** *n.*

Derby (där-), *n.* Epsom horse-race, counted chief flat-racing event of the year. ***Dĕr'by** (hat), bowler.

dė'rĕlict, *a.* left ownerless (esp. of ship at sea); *neglectful of duty. *n.* a derelict ship or article.

dĕrėlic'tion, *n.* neglect (of duty); sin of omission.

dėrīde', *v.t.* (*-dable*), scoff at.

‖ **de rigueur** (rēgẽr'), required by etiquette.

dėri'sion (-zhn), *n.* ridicule, scoffing; a laughing-stock.

dėri'sive, *a.* mocking, scoffing.

dėri'sory, *a.* mocking, ridiculing.

dėrivā'tion, *n.* source to which thing is traced; descent.

dėriv'ative, *a.* of a derived kind. *n.* derivative word or substance; an offshoot.

dėrive', *v.t. & i.* (*-vable*), obtain or have from a source; be descended from.

dĕrmatŏl'ogy, *n.* study of the skin.

dė'rogate, *v.i.* detract; lessen in value. **~tion,** *n.*, derogating; impairment of a right. **dėrŏg'atory,** *a.* involving impairment or disparagement.

dĕ'rrick, *n.* kinds of hoisting-machine.

dĕ'rringer (-j-), *n.* small pistol.

dĕr'vish, *n.* Mohammedan friar.

dėscänt'[1], *v.i.* talk at large, dwell upon. **dĕs'cant**[2], *n.* song, melody.

dėscĕnd', *v.i. & t.* come or go down; slope downwards; stoop (to meanness); succeed in passing; have as ancestor. **~ant,** *n.* person descended from another.

dėscĕnt', *n.* descending; slope; way down; sinking in scale; sudden attack; lineage.

dėscrībe', *v.t.* (*-bable*), give description of; delineate.

dėscrĭp'tion, *n.* verbal portraiture; sort, kind, or class (of thing). **~tive,** *a.* full of description; graphic.

dėscrȳ', *v.t.* (*-iable*), make out dimly; succeed in discerning.

dĕs'ėcrāte, *v.t.* (*-crable*), violate the sanctity of. **~tion,** *~tor,* *nn.*

dĕsẽrt'[1] (-z-), *n.* (pl. or, rarely, sing.) conduct or qualities deserving reward or punishment; merit.

dĕsẽrt'[2], *v.t. & i.* (dĭzẽrt') abandon; cease to frequent; withdraw from. *a.* (dĕz'ẽrt) uninhabited and barren. *n.* (dĕz'ẽrt) a desert tract; depopulated place.

dėsẽrt'er (-z-), *n.* one who forsakes a cause or a duty.

dėsẽr'tion (-z-), *n.* deserting or being deserted.

dėsẽrve' (-z-), *v.t. & i.* show oneself worthy of either good or ill; (of things) be worth mention. **dėsẽr'vėdly** (-z-), *adv.* as he, &c. fully deserved. **dėsẽr'ving** (-z-), *a.* meritorious; worthy of.

‖ **déshabillé** (dāzahēb'yā), *n.* dishabille.

dĕs'iccāte, *v.t.* (*-cable*), exhaust of moisture; dry up. **~tion,** *n.*; **~tive,** *a.* **~tor,** *n.* desiccating apparatus.

dėsĭd'ėrāte, *v.t.* feel to be missing. **~tive,** *a.* expressing desire; *n.* such verb or form. **~tum,** *n.* (pl. *-ta*), thing missing; felt want.

dėsīgn' (-zīn), *v.t.* purpose or intend; formulate plan. *n.* purpose; plan; outline or sketch.

dĕs'ignāte[1] (-z-), *v.t.* (*-nable*), style or describe as; specify; appoint to office. **dĕs'ignāte**[2] (-z-, -ĭt), *a.* (placed after noun) appointed to but not yet installed in office.

designa'tion (-z-), *n.* designing; name or title; description.

design'édly (-zin-), *adv.* purposely.

design'er (-zīn-), *n.* contriver; plotter; one who draws designs.

design'ing (-zin-), *a.* crafty, artful, scheming.

desir'able (-z-), *a.* worth wishing for; pleasing. ~bility, *n.*

desire' (-z-), *n.* eagerness to obtain; expressed wish or request. *v.t.* wish, long for; request. desīr'ous, *a.* wishful, desiring.

desist', *v.i.* abandon course, cease.

desk, *n.* table with sloping top for reading or writing.

des'olate, *a.* (-it) left alone; uninhabited; ruinous; disconsolate. *v.t.* (-āt) depopulate; devastate. ~tion, ~tor, *nn.*

despair', *v.i.* lose all hope; despond. *n.* hopelessness.

despatch. See dispatch.

despera'dō, *n.* (pl. -*oes*), person who will stick at nothing.

des'perate, *a.* hopelessly bad; difficult or dangerous; reckless. despera'tion, *n.* reckless state of mind; hopelessness.

des'picable, *a.* contemptible; vile.

despise' (-z-), *v.t.* regard with contempt; look down upon.

despīte', *n.* malice; anger; offended pride. ~ful, *a.* malicious, cruel.

despoil', *v.t.* plunder or strip. ~ment, despoliá'tion, *nn.*

despond', *v.i.* lose heart or hope; be dejected. ~ency, *n.*; ~ent, *a.*

des'pot, *n.* tyrant, oppressor; absolute ruler. despot'ic, *a.* subject to no constitutional checks; tyrannous. ~ism, *n.* tyrannical conduct; autocratic government.

dés'quamāte, *v.i. & t.* throw off or make throw off scales. ~tion, *n.*

dessert' (-z-), *n.* course of fruit, sweetmeats, &c., ending dinner; *"pastry, pudding, &c., ending dinner. ~spoon,* spoon used in eating dessert.

destinā'tion, *n.* place to which person or thing is bound.

des'tine, *v.t.* (-*nable*), foreordain or mark out beforehand.

des'tiny, *n.* the power that foreordains; predetermined events.

des'titūte, *a.* in want of necessaries; resourceless. ~tion, *n.*

destroy', *v.t.* make away with; demolish; kill.

destroy'er, *n.* one that destroys; warship designed to attack by torpedo and guard own fleet against torpedo attack.

destruc'tible, *a.* destroyable.

destruc'tion, *n.* destroying.

destruc'tive, *a.* causing destruction; pulling to pieces.

destruc'tor, *n.* furnace for refuse.

désuetūde (-swi-), *n.* state of disuse.

des'ultory, *a.* changing from one thing to another; unmethodical.

détach', *v.t.* unfasten and remove; separate. ~ed, *a.* standing apart; isolated. ~ment, *n.* detached party of soldiers, &c.; detached state.

detail, *n.* (dē'tāl) treatment of things item by item; (pl.) parts of a composite whole; (sing.) an item or particular. *v.t.* (ditāl') relate circumstantially. dē'tailed, *a.* going into detail.

detain', *v.t.* keep in custody; withhold; keep waiting.

detéct', *v.t.* discover; find out. ~ion, *n.*

detéc'tive, *a.* engaged in detection. *n.* policeman, &c. so employed.

detéc'tor, *n.* (esp.) device by which high-frequency oscillations are rectified in a wireless receiver.

deten'tion, *n.* detaining, being detained; confinement.

detér', *v.t.* discourage, hinder.

detér'gent, *a.* surface-cleaning. *n.* a detergent substance.

detér'iorāte, *v.i. & t.* (-*rable*), make or grow worse. ~tion, *n.*

detér'minant, *n.* decisive factor.

detér'minate, *a.* limited; of a definite scope or nature.

detérminā'tion, *n.* termination; resolve; resolute conduct.

detér'minative, *a.* tending to decide something.

detér'mine, *v.t. & i.* (-*nable*), ascertain or fix with precision; resolve; bring to a decision. ~d, *a.* resolute.

---

detěrm'inism, n. theory that action is determined by forces regarded as independent of the will. ~ist, n.; ~istic, a.

detě'rrent, a. serving to deter.

detest', v.t. hate, loathe.

detes'table, a. abominable.

detestā'tion (or -ē-), n. abhorrence.

dethrōne', v.t. (-nable), depose (sovereign). ~ment, n.

det'onāte (or -ē-), v.i. & t. explode with report. ~tion, n. ~tor, n. detonating apparatus.

detour' (-oor), n. course that leaves and rejoins direct route.

detract', v.t. reduce the credit due to; depreciate. ~ion, n. disparagement. ~or, n.

detrain', v.i. & t. alight, make (troops) alight, from train.

det'riment, n. harm, damage.

detrimen'tal, a. harmful, causing loss. n. (sl.) undesirable suitor.

detrī'tus, n. worn-down matter such as gravel or rock-debris.

‖ **de trop** (trō), not wanted, in the way; unwelcome.

deuce[1], n. the two at dice and cards; (Tennis) state of score (40 all, games all) at which only two successive wins by one side can decide game or set.

deuce[2], n. plague, mischief; the devil. **deu'ced**, a. & adv. confounded(ly), surprising(ly).

‖ **dē'us ex māch'inā** (-k-), n. divine interposition or other artificial solution of difficulties.

‖ **deux-temps** (dẽr tahṅ), n. quicktime waltz.

Dē'va, n. a god; one of the good spirits of Hindu mythology.

dē'vastāte, v.t. (-atable), lay waste. ~tion, ~tor, nn.

devěl'op, v.t. & i. unfold, reveal; grow bigger; bring or come to maturity; become fuller; make progress; (Photog.) treat (plate, film) so as to make picture visible. ~ment, n.

dē'viāte, v.i. leave the beaten track; digress; lapse. ~tion, n. act of deviating. ~tor, n.

device', n. a devised method or design; stratagem; emblem.

děv'il, n. the personified spirit of evil; any cruel or malignant being; person of notable energy; person who devils for author or barrister. v.t. do work for author or barrister; grill with hot condiments. ~may-care, happy-go-lucky; irrepressible. ~'s advocate, person who sees objections and weaknesses only. **děv'ilish**, a. monstrously cruel or wicked; adv. (colloq.) very. **děv'ilment**, n. mischief; wild spirits; wizardry. **děv'ilry**, n. black magic; iniquity; reckless daring.

dē'vious, a. winding, circuitous; erratic.

devīse' (-z), v.t. (-sable), leave by will; think out; contrive.

devīsee', **devī'sor** (-z-), nn. person to whom, by whom, property is devised.

devoid', a. destitute; empty of.

dēv'oir (-vwar), n. duty; one's best; (pl.) courteous attentions.

dēvolū'tion (-lōo-), n. descent through a series of changes; transfer of business from Parliament to subsidiary bodies.

devōlve', v.t. & i. (-vable), throw (task, duty), or be thrown, upon another; descend or pass (to, upon).

devōte', v.t. (-table), consecrate, dedicate; give up exclusively to. ~d, a. zealously loyal or loving.

devotee', n. votary of a pursuit or person; one who devotes himself to religion.

devō'tion, n. devotedness; devoutness; self-surrender; (pl.) one's religious exercises. ~al, a. of or assisting the devotions.

devour' (-owr), v.t. eat up; eat greedily or fast; destroy or consume; take in greedily with eyes or ears.

devout', a. earnestly religious, reverent, prayerful.

dew, n. atmospheric vapour; beaded moisture resembling it. v.i. & t. form or fall as dew; bedew; moisten. ~berry, kind of blackberry. ~claw, rudimen-

tary inner claw of some dogs.
~pond, shallow pond, usu. on
downs, fed by atmospheric condensation.

‖ dêwan' (-ah-), *n.* (in India) prime
minister of a native state; the
chief native officer of certain
Government establishments.
dêwan'ī, *n.* the office of dewan.

dew'lâp, *n.* fold of loose skin hanging from throat, esp. in cattle.

dew'y̆, *a.* wet with dew.

dêx'ter, *a.* on the right-hand side
(Herald., to spectator's left).

dêxtĕ'rĭtў, *n.* dextrousness.

dêx'tĕ(e)rous, *a.* neat-handed,
adroit; clever.

‖ dhak (-ah-), dhawk, *n.* E.-Ind.
tree noted for its brilliant flowers.

‖ dhal (-ah-), *n.* (Anglo-Ind.) kind
of pulse used as a porridge.

‖ dhō'bĭ, *n.* (Anglo-Ind.) native
washerman.

‖ dhō'ney, dō'ney, *n.* small native
sailing vessel of Southern India.

‖ dhō'tī, dhōō'tī, *n.* the loin-cloth
worn by Hindus.

dhow (dow), *n.* Arabian-Sea ship of
kind used in slave-trade.

‖ dhŭr'rie (d-), dŭr'rie, *n.* Indian
rectangular fringed cotton carpet
used for sofa-covers, &c.

dīabē'tēs (-z), *n.* disease with excessive glucose-charged urine.
dīabĕt'ĭc, *a.* of or having diabetes.
n. diabetic patient.

dīa'blerīe (-ahblĕrē), *n.* sorcery;
devil-lore; uncanny proceedings.

dīabŏl'ĭc(al), *a.* of the Devil;
monstrously cruel or wicked.
dīăb'olĭsm, *n.* sorcery; diabolical
conduct; devil-worship.

dīăb'olō, *n.* air-top sent up from
a string attached to two sticks.

dīăc'hȳlon (-k-), *n.* kind of sticking plaster.

dīăc'onal, *a.* of a deacon.
dīăc'onate, *n.* deacon's office; body
of deacons.

dīacrĭt'ical, *a.* distinguishing, distinctive.

dī'adĕm, *n.* crown or fillet.

dīaer'esis, *n.* (pl. -esēs) mark (¨)
placed over a vowel to show that
it is sounded separately.

diagnōse' (-z), *v.t.* determine from
symptoms the nature of a disease.

diagnō'sĭs, *n.* (pl. -osēs), identification of disease by means of
patient's symptoms, &c.

diagnŏs'tĭc, *a.* of or assisting diagnosis. *n.* symptom.

dīăg'onal, *a.* traversing obliquely
from angle to angle. *n.* a line so
drawn; any oblique line.

dī'agrăm, *n.* drawing made to
illustrate a statement, &c.

dī'al, *n.* face of clock or watch;
sun-dial. *v.t.* indicate on dial.

dī'alĕct, *n.* form of speech peculiar
to a district or class. ~al, *a.*

dīalĕc'tĭc, *n.* (often pl.) the art of
arguing; logical dexterity. dialĕc'tĭc(al), *aa.* concerned with
dialectics. dīalĕctĭ'cian (-shn), *n.*
expert in dialectics.

dī'alŏgue (-g), *n.* a conversation
between two or more persons.

dīăm'ĕter, *n.* straight line passing
from side to side of any body or
figure through its centre; transverse measurement. diăm'ĕtral,
a. of or along a diameter.

dīamĕt'rical, *a.* of or along a diameter; directly opposite.

dī'amond, *n.* a transparent precious stone; a rhomb.

dīapā'son (-zn), *n.* grand swelling
burst of harmony; organ-stop.

dī'aper, *n.* fine linen towelling;
small towel, napkin; reticulated
decorative work. ~ed, *a.* with
diaper decoration.

dīaph'anous, *a.* transpareat.

dīaphorĕt'ĭc, *a.* inducing perspiration. *n.* a diaphoretic drug, &c.

dī'aphragm (-ăm), *n.* partition
between thorax and abdomen in
mammals; partition in various
instruments, esp. in optics, telephony, and wireless, vibrating
disk pierced with circular hole.
dīaphrăgmăt'ĭc, *a.*

dī'archy (-kĭ), *n.* government by
two independent authorities.

dī'arist, *n.* keeper of diary.

dīarrhoe'a (-rēa), *n.* excessive
looseness of bowels.

dī'arў, *n.* daily record of events;
book designed for such purpose.

---

di'astāse, n. (Chem.) a ferment converting starch to glucose.

diás'tolē, n. dilatation alternating with systole in pulsation.

diàth'esis, n. (pl. -esēs), constitutional predisposition.

di'atŏm, n. kinds of minute one-cell water-plant. ~ē'ceous, a.

diatŏm'ic, a. of two atoms.

diatŏn'ic, a. (Mus.) (of scale) proceeding by notes proper to the key without chromatic alteration.

di'atrìbe, n. bitter criticism; denunciatory harangue.

dib'ber, n. a dibble.

dib'ble, n. gardener's implement for planting. v.t. use a dibble.

dibs (-z), n.pl. (sl.) money.

dice, n.: see die[1]. v.i. gamble with dice. ~box, n. box from which dice are thrown. di'cer, n. person addicted to dicing.

dichŏt'omy (-k-), n. division into two, esp. in classification.

dichrŏmat'ic (-k-), a. of two colours.

dick, n. (sl.) Take one's ~, swear, affirm. Up to ~, knowing.

dick'ens (-z), n. deuce, the Devil.

*dick'er, v.i. trade by barter.

dick'ȳ, n. donkey (sl.); dicky-bird; false shirt-front; seat at back of carriage or car. a. (sl.) shaky, rickety. ~bird (child's talk), small bird.

dicŏtȳlē'don, n. flowering plant with two cotyledons. ~ous, a.

dic'taphŏne, n. machine recording, for subsequent reproduction in type, what is spoken into it.

dictate, v.t. & i. (dĭktāt'), say aloud matter to be written down; give peremptory orders to. n. (dĭk'tāt) (usu. in pl.), the bidding of conscience, self-interest, or the like. dicta'tion, n.

dicta'tor, n. absolute ruler; person in a position of supreme authority. ~ship, n.

dictatŏr'ial, a. absolute or free of checks; despotic or overbearing.

dic'tion. n. choice and use of words in speech or writing.

dic'tionarȳ (-sho-), n. book con-taining the words of a language with their meaning; word-book, lexicon; book arranged alphabetically, containing homogeneous articles on some particular branch of knowledge.

dic'tograph (-ahf), n. a loud-speaking internal telephone.

dic'tum, n. (pl. -ta), pronouncement; maxim, current saying.

did, didst, p.t. of do.

didăc'tic (or di-), a. meant or meaning to instruct. ~ism, n.

di'dăpper, n. a diving bird.

did'dle, v.t. (sl.) cheat, take in.

*di'dō, n. (pl. -oes), (sl.) prank, caper.

die[1], n. 1 (pl. dice), one of the cubes used in games of chance; (pl.) dice-play. 2 (pl. dies), coining or embossing stamp.

die[2], v.i. (dying), cease to live; suffer spiritual death; fade away; wither. ~hard, person who resists to the end.

diélec'tric, a. & n. insulating (medium or substance); non-conductive, non-conductor.

|| Di'es irae (ī'rē), n. the Day of Judgement; Latin hymn.

di'et[1], n. a congress, esp. as Eng. name for foreign parliaments, &c.

di'et[2], n. kind of food on which a person, &c. lives; a food-regimen. v.t. keep person, oneself, &c. to a particular diet.

di'etarȳ, a. dietetic. n. allowance or character of food provided.

dietět'ic, a. of or in the matter of diet. ~s, n.pl. science of diet.

diff'er, v.i. be unlike; be distinguishable; diverge in opinion.

diff'erence, n. unlikeness; degree or amount of unlikeness; disagreement.

diff'erent, a. dissimilar; not the same; of diverse qualities.

differěn'tia (-shia), n. (pl. -ae), distinguishing mark, esp. of species.

differěn'tial (-shl), a. varying with circumstances; distinctive. n. mechanism enabling motor-car's hind wheels to revolve at different speeds in rounding a corner.

differen'tiate (-shǐ-), *v.t.* & *i.* (*-iable*), constitute the difference between, or in; develop into unlikeness; discriminate. ~**tion.** *n.*

diff'icult, *a.* hard to do, deal with, or understand; troublesome.

diff'iculty, *n.* difficultness; difficult point or situation; obstacle.

diff'idence, *n.* self-distrust; shyness.

diff'ident, *a.* wanting in self-confidence.

diffract', *v.t.* break up (beam of light) into series of dark and light bands. ~**ion,** *n.*; ~**ive,** *a.*

diffuse', *v.t.* (-z), shed or spread around; cause to intermingle. *a.* (-s), not terse or brief; verbose. ~**sible,** *a.*; ~**sion,** *n.*

diffu'sive, *a.* spreading readily; radiating; genial.

dig, *v.i.* & *t.* (*dǔg*), turn up soil with spade; thrust one's nails into; make research; *(sl.)* study hard. *n.* piece of digging; thrust or poke.

digamm'a, *n.* letter (F) of early Greek alphabet, later disused.

digest, *v.t.* & *i.* (dǐjěst'), reduce into systematic or assimilable form; summarize; absorb and assimilate; (of food) undergo digestion. *n.* (dī'jěst), a compendium, esp. of laws. **diges'tible,** *a.*; ~**ibility,** *n.* (esp. of food).

diges'tion (-schon), *n.* digesting; power of digesting food.

diges'tive, *a.* assisting digestion.

digg'er (-g-), *n.* one who digs with spade; man who digs for gold; *root-digging Indian; (sl.)* Australian.

digg'ing, *n.* act of digging; (usu. pl.) gold-field; (pl. colloq., also *digs*) lodgings; *(pl., colloq.)* place.

dight (dīt), *a.* clad, adorned.

di'git, *n.* any of the figures 0-9; finger or toe; finger's breadth.

digitā'lis, *n.* drug made from foxglove.

di'gitigrade, *a.* walking on the toes only. *n.* such animal.

dig'nify, *v.t.* (*-iable*), give dignity to; (*p.p.*) stately.

dig'nitary, *n.* holder of high office, esp. in the Church.

dig'nity, *n.* claims to respect; office or title; dignified behaviour.

di'graph, *n.* two letters composing a single sound.

digress' (*or* dī-), *v.i.* diverge temporarily from the main track, esp. in discourse. ~**ion,** *n.*; ~**ive,** *a.*

dīke, dȳke, *n.* long ridge of earth, embankment; channel or ditch. *v.t.* protect with dike.

dilapidā'tion, *n.* state of bad repair; falling into decay. **dilap'idāted,** *a.* in decay.

dilāte', *v.t.* & *i.* (*-table*), widen or expand; expatiate or enlarge. **dilatā'tion** (also **dīlā'tion,** incorrect but usual), **dilātabil'ity,** *nn.*

dil'atory, *a.* tending to or designed to cause delay; tardy.

dilemm'a, *n.* position leaving only a choice between equal evils.

dilettän'tē, *n.* (pl. *-ti,* pr. *-tē*), person with taste for the fine arts; amateur, smatterer. *a.* amateur; desultory. ~**tism,** *n.*

dil'igence, *n.* unremitting application to work. **dil'igent,** *a.*

dill, *n.* herb with scented seeds.

dill'y-dally, *v.i.* (colloq.) procrastinate or vacillate.

dilute (dīlōōt'), *v.t.* reduce in strength by addition of water. *a.* diluted. ~**tion,** *n.*

dilu'vial (*or* dī-; *-ōō-*), *a.* of a flood, esp. the Flood in Genesis.

dim, *a.* deficient in brightness or clearness; obscure; indistinct. *v.t.* & *i.* make or grow dim.

***dime,** *n.* tenth of dollar.

dimen'sion (-shn), *n.* any of the three linear measurements, length, breadth, and depth; (pl.) size or extent. ~**al,** *a.*

dimin'ish, *v.t.* & *i.* make or become less; impair.

diminuěn'dō, *adv.* (Mus.) with decreasing volume of sound.

diminū'tion, *n.* lessening.

dimin'ūtive, *a.* (of words, suffixes, &c.) implying smallness; (transf.)

---

māte, mēte, mīte, mōte, mūte, mōōt; răck, rĕck, rick, rŏck, rŭck, rōōk;

tiny, undersized. *n.* a diminutive word.

dim'ity, *n.* cotton fabric for bedroom hangings, &c.

dim'ple, *n.* small hollow, esp. in cheek or chin; ripple in water. *v.t.* & *i.* produce dimples in, show dimples. dim'ply, *a.*

din, *n.* continuous roar of confused noises. *v.t.* stun with noise; ram (fact, advice) into person or his ears.

dine, *v.t.* & *i.* take dinner; entertain at dinner. di'ner, *n.* one who dines; *dining-car. dining-room, used for meals.

ding¹, *v.t.* throw, dash, hurl.

ding², *v.i.* & *t.* ring, keep sounding; reiterate in a wearisome way; *nag. ding-dong, *n.* sound of two bells rung alternately. *adv.* with persistent alternation.

dinghy, ~gey (ding'gi), *n.* kinds of small boat.

dingle (ding'gl), *n.* deep dell.

ding'ō (-ngg-), *n.* (pl. -oes), Australian wild dog.

din'gy (-ji), *a.* dull-coloured; grimy; dirty-looking.

din'ky, *a.* (colloq.) pretty, neat; of engaging appearance.

dinn'er, *n.* chief meal of the day; banquet. ~wagon, movable sideboard.

di'nosaur (-ôr), *n.* large extinct reptile. ~ian, *a.*

di'nothēre, *n.* huge extinct quadruped with trunk and tusks.

dint, *n.* blow or stroke; dent. *v.t.* dent.

diō'cĕsan (-zn), *a.* of a diocese. *n.* bishop in relation to diocese.

di'ocēse, *n.* bishop's district.

diora'ma (-rah-), *n.* spectacular panoramic painting. ~âm'ic, *a.*

diōx'ide, *n.* oxide with two atoms of oxygen to one of the metal.

dip, *v.t.* & *i.* put or let down into liquid, immerse; go under water and emerge quickly; read or study cursorily. *n.* act of dipping; downward slope; short bathe; tallow candle.

diphthĕr'ia, *n.* infectious disease with membranous growth in throat, &c. diphtherit'ic, *a.*

diph'thong, *n.* union of two vowels in one sound; digraph; ligature. diphthŏng'al (-ngg-), *a.*

diplō'ma, *n.* voucher of person's title to some degree or status.

diplō'macy, *n.* management of international relations; tact.

dip'lomat, *n.* diplomatist.

diplomat'ic, *a.* of diplomacy; engaged or skilled in diplomacy; (of statements) uncandid.

diplō'matist, *n.* member of diplomatic service; adroit negotiator.

dipp'er, *n.* one who dips in the water; kinds of bird. *the D~, Great Bear constellation.

dipsomā'nia, *n.* inability to keep from alcohol. dipsomā'niac, *n.*

dip'tych (-k), *n.* pair of pictures or carvings on two folding tablets.

dīre, *a.* dread, terrible.

dĭrĕct', *a.* straight, not crooked or round about; frank. *adv.* by the direct route; without intermediaries. *v.t.* put in the direct way by instructions; tell the way to (place, &c.); address (letter, &c.) to; command, order. ~ action, exertion of pressure on the community by strikes to force political measures on the Government.

dĭrĕc'tion, *n.* directing; orders or instructions; address of letter, &c.; course; aim. ~ finder, wireless apparatus for determining the geographical bearings of transmitting stations.

dĭrĕc'tive, *a.* giving guidance.

dĭrĕct'ly, *adv.* in direct manner; at once, without delay.

dĭrĕc'tor, *n.* superintendent, manager, esp. member of board directing affairs of company, &c. ~ate, *n.* such board. ~ship, *n.* ~ress, *n.*

dĭrĕc'tory, *n.* book of rules; list of inhabitants of town, &c., with addresses and other details.

dire'ful (-rf-), dire, dreadful.

dirge, *n.* song of mourning.

di'rigible, *a.* that can be directed or steered (esp. of balloons). *n.* dirigible balloon or airship.

---

māre, mēre, mīre, mōre, mūre; pärt, pĕrt, pôrt; *italics*, vague sounds:

dirk, *n.* kind of dagger.

dirt, *n.* mud, filth, mire; earth, soil; worthless things or people; foul talk. *v.t.* make foul.

dirt'y, *a.* soiled; foul; unclean; obscene, filthy; mean, despicable; wet and windy; muddy-looking. *v.t.* foul, soil.

disabil'ity, *n.* thing that incapacitates or disqualifies.

disa'ble, *v.t.* make unable to act or move. ~ment, *n.*

disabuse' (-z), *v.t.* undeceive; relieve of illusion.

disaccord', *v.i.* be at variance.

disadvan'tage (-vah-), *n.* unfavourable condition. ~ous, *a.*

disaffec'ted, *a.* discontented; ill-disposed; disloyal. ~tion, *n.*

disagree', *v.i.* differ; fail to agree with; quarrel. ~ment, *n.*

disagree'able (-rī-), *a.* unpleasant; ill-tempered.

disallow', *v.t.* reject; prohibit.

disappear', *v.i.* pass from sight; vanish. ~ance, *n.*

disappoint', *v.t.* fail to fulfil; defeat the hopes of; break appointment with. ~ment, *n.*

disapproba'tion, *n.* disapproval.

disapprove' (-ōōv), *v.t. & i.* have or express an unfavourable opinion of. ~val, *n.*

disarm', *v.t.* deprive of weapons; pacify hostility or suspicions of. ~ament, *n.* abandonment or reduction of warlike establishment.

disarrange', *v.t.* put into disorder; disorganize. ~ment, *n.*

disarray', *n.* disorder, confusion. *v.t.* throw into disorder.

disas'ter (-zah-), *n.* sudden or great misfortune. ~trous, *a.*

disavow', *v.t.* disown; deny knowledge of; repudiate. ~al, *n.*

disband', *v.t. & i.* disembody (troops); be broken up; disperse. ~ment, *n.*

disbar', *v.t.* deprive (barrister) of right to plead. ~ment, *n.*

disbelieve', *v.t. & i.* refuse credence to; be a sceptic. ~belief, *n.*

disbur'den, *v.t.* relieve of a burden; unload; ease the mind.

disburse', *v.t. & i.* (-sable), pay out; make outlay. ~ment, *n.*

disc. See disk.

discard', *v.t. & i.* throw out or reject; give up; dismiss.

discarn'ate, *a.* parted from the flesh; disembodied.

discern', *v.t.* make out or descry; distinguish; (*part.*) having insight. ~ible, *a.* ~ment, *n.* insight; critical sagacity.

discharge', *v.t. & i.* (-geable), unburden; unload; disembark; dismiss, cashier; release; let flow; send as missile; fire; acquit oneself of (duty, debt). *n.* discharging or being discharged; matter discharged from tumour, &c.

disci'ple, *n.* one who takes another as his teacher or leader.

disciplinar'ian, *n.* maintainer of strict discipline.

dis'ciplinary, *a.* of or promoting discipline.

dis'cipline, *n.* training, esp. of the kind that produces self-control, orderliness, and obedience. *v.t.* train with discipline.

disclaim', *v.t.* disown, disavow. ~er, *n.* disavowal.

disclose' (-z), *v.t.* (-sable), expose to view, reveal. **disclo'sure** (-zher), *n.* disclosing; thing disclosed.

discol'our (-ŭler), *v.t. & i.* impair the colour of; suffer such impairment. ~colo(u)ra'tion, ~col'ourment (-ŭler-), *nn.*

discomfit (-ŭm-), *v.t.* defeat; baffle; disconcert. ~ure, *n.*

discom'fort (-ŭm-), *n.* uneasiness of body or mind. *v.t.* make uneasy.

discom'mon, *v.t.* enclose (common land).

discompose' (-z), *v.t.* disturb composure of. ~pō'sure (-zher), *n.*

disconcert', *v.t.* derange or upset; embarrass. ~ment, *n.*

disconnect', *v.t.* sever the connexion of. ~ed, *a.* incoherent, badly connected. ~nexion, *n.*

discon'solate, *a.* inconsolable; downcast for loss of something.

discontent', *n.* unsatisfied state of mind. ~ed, *a.* feeling discontent.

---

discontin′ūe, v.t. leave off; not go on with. **~uance**, n. discontinuing. **~uous**, a.; discontinu′ity, n.

discord (dis′kŏrd), n. disagreement, strife; harsh noise; want of harmony. **discord′ant**, a. showing discord. **~ance**, n.

discount, n. (dis′kownt), deduction from amount of a bill; (fig.) allowance made for exaggeration. v.t. (diskownt′), lessen, detract from; allow for exaggeration.

discount′enance, v.t. refuse to countenance; discourage.

discou′rage (-kŭ-), v.t. (-geable), reduce the confidence or spirits of; deter. **~ment**, n.

discourse, n. (dis′kŏrs), a lecture, sermon, or other exposition; talk or conversation. v.i. (diskŏrs′), utter a discourse; converse, talk.

discourt′eous (-kŏr-, -kĕr-), a. rude, uncivil. **~esy**, n. incivility.

disco′ver (-kŭ-), v.t. find out, detect; make known. **~er**, n. **~y**, n. discovering; thing discovered.

discred′it, v.t. refuse belief to; bring disrepute on. n. discredited state; disrepute. **~able**, a.

discreet′, a. prudent; cautious in speech or action.

discrep′ancy, n. difference; failure to tally. **~ant**, a.

dis′crēte, a. separate; distinct.

discre′tion, n. discreetness; liberty of action. **~ary**, a.

discrim′inate, v.t. & i. (-nable), draw or make distinctions between. **~tion**, **~tor**, ns.; **~tive**, a.

discrown′, v.t. take crown from.

discur′sive, a. rambling, not sticking to the main subject.

discuss′, v.t. examine by argument; debate; (joc.) eat or drink. **~ible**, a.; **~ion**, n.

disdain′, v.t. scorn; treat as unworthy of notice or of oneself. n. contemptuous neglect or dislike. **~ful**, a. showing disdain.

disease′ (-zēz), n. serious derangement of health; bodily disorder. **diseased′** (-zēzd), a. affected with disease; morbid; depraved.

disembark′, v.t. & i. put or go ashore. **disembarka′tion**, n.

disembar′rass, v.t. free from embarrassment; disentangle; rid or relieve of. **~ment**, n.

disembod′iment, n. act of disembodying, disembodied state.

disembod′y, v.t. divest of the body; (of troops) disband.

disembogue′ (-g), v.i. (of river, &c.) issue.

disembow′el, v.t. remove entrails of; rip up.

disembroil′, v.t. extricate from confusion or entanglement.

disenchant′ (-ah-), v.t. free from enchantment or fascination; disillusion. **~ment**, n.

disencum′ber, v.t. disburden; free from encumbrance.

disendow′, v.t. strip of endowments. **~ment**, n.

disengāge′, v.t. (-geable), detach; liberate; loosen. **~ment**, n.

disengāged′ (-jd), a. at leisure; vacant; not occupied.

disentail′, v.t. free from entail.

disentan′gle (-nggl), v.t. extricate; unravel; untwist. **~ment**, n.

disenthral′ (-awl), v.t. free from bondage. **~ment**, n.

disentomb′ (-ōōm), v.t. take out of tomb; find out by research.

disestab′lish, v.t. undo establishment of; sever Church from connexion with State. **~ment**, n.

disfā′vour (-ver), n. dislike; disapproval. v.t. discountenance.

disfig′ure (-ger), v.t. mar the appearance of; sully. **~ment**, n.

disfran′chise (-z), v.t. (-sable), deprive of right of electing or voting. **~isement** (-zm-), n.

disfrock′, v.t. deprive of clerical status.

disgorge′, v.t. (-geable), eject; give up; (of river) discharge.

disgrāce′, n. loss of favour; downfall; ignominy. v.t. (-ceable), dismiss from favour; be a disgrace to. **~ful**, a. shameful.

disgrun′tled (-ld), a. discontented.

disguise′ (-gīz), v.t. (-sable), make unrecognizable; pass off as something else; cloak or hide.

n. disguised state; device or garb used to disguise.

disgŭst', *n.* a violent distaste; keen disappointment. *v.t.* affect with disgust. **~ful**, *a.*

dish, *n.* shallow vessel for holding food; a particular kind of food. *v.t.* put in dish(es) for serving; (sl.) baffle by superior strategy.

dishabille' (-sabēl), *n.* negligently or partly dressed state; undress.

disheart'en (-hār-), *v.t.* discourage; deject. **~ment**, *n.*

dishěv'elled (-ld), *a.* with disordered hair; unkempt, untidy.

dishŏn'ĕst (-s-ŏn-), *a.* fraudulent; knavish; insincere. **~y**, *n.*

dishŏn'our (-s-ŏnér), *v.t.* treat with contumely; bring dishonour upon. *n.* dishonoured state; loss of repute. **~able**, *a.* shameful; unprincipled.

disillū'sion, **~ize** (-ōōzho-), *v.t.* open the eyes of; wake to (disappointing) realities. **~ment**, *n.*

disinclinā'tion, *n.* slight dislike or unwillingness.

disincline', *v.t.* inspire with disinclination; make disaffected.

disinfĕct', *v.t.* purge of infection. **~ant**, *a.* having disinfecting qualities. *n.* disinfectant substance. **~ion**, *n.*

disingĕn'ūous, *a.* insincere; not candid.

disinhĕr'it, *v.t.* deprive of right of inheriting. **~ance**, *n.*

disin'tĕgrāte, *v.t.* & *i.* (-rable) separate into component parts; lose cohesion. **~tor**, **~tion**, *nn.*

disintĕr', *v.t.* unbury, exhume; unearth. **~ment**, *n.*

disin'terĕsted, *a.* not influenced by self-interest or partiality.

‖ **disjĕc'ta mĕm'bra**, *n.pl.* fragments, scattered remains.

disjoin', *v.t.* separate, disunite.

disjoint', *v.t.* take in pieces at the joints; dislocate ; (*p.p.*, of talk or style) incoherent.

disjŭnc'tion, *n.* disjoining, separation. **~ive**, *a.* disjoining.

disk, **disc**, *n.* thin flat circular object or semblance of this.

dislīke', *v.t.* (-kable), feel aversion to. *n.* such feeling.

dis'locāte, *v.t.* (-table), put limb out of joint; force out of gear. **~tion**, *n.*

dislŏdge', *v.t.* (-geable), force out of position occupied. **~ment**, *n.*

disloy'al, *a.* unfaithful; untrue to allegiance; disaffected. **~ty**, *n.*

dis'mal (-z-), *a.* cheerless, dreary.

disman'tle, *v.t.* deprive of defences, equipment, or furniture.

dismast' (-ah-), *v.t.* deprive (ship) of mast(s).

dismay', *n.* loss of courage; horrified amazement. *v.t.* affect with dismay; reduce to despair.

dismĕm'ber, *v.t.* tear or cut limb from limb; partition (country). **~ment**, *n.*

dismiss', *v.t.* send away, disband; discharge, cashier; put out of one's thoughts; (Crick., of fielding side) put (batsman, side) out (usu. for so many runs). **~al**, *n.*

dismount', *v.i.* & *t.* alight or cause to alight from horseback; take (gun, &c.) from its mount.

disobē'dience, *n.* disobeying; rebelliousness. **~nt**, *a.*

disobey' (-bā), *v.i.* & *t.* disregard orders; break rules.

disoblige', *v.t.* (-geable), refuse to consult the convenience or wishes of. **~oblī'ging**, *a.*

disord'er, *n.* confusion; bodily or mental ailment; infractions of discipline. *v.t.* disturb the healthy working of. **~ly**, *a.* untidy; riotous or ill-disciplined.

disŏr'ganize, *v.t.* destroy system, &c. of; throw into disorder. **~zation**, *n.*

disown' (-ōn), *v.t.* refuse to own; repudiate, disclaim; renounce.

dispä'rage, *v.t.* (-geable), speak slightingly of; depreciate. **~ment**, *n.*

dis'parate, *a.* essentially different.

dispăr'ity, *n.* unequal state or degrees.

dispark', *v.t.* convert park-land to other uses.

dispart', *v.t.* & *i.* separate.

dispa'ssionate (-sho-), a. devoid of emotion; impartial.

dispatch', dĕs-, v.t. send to destination; kill; get business done promptly. n. dispatching; rapidity; official message.

dispel', v.t. dissipate; disperse.

dispen'sable, a. that can be dispensed with or dispensed.

dispen'sary, n. place where medicine is dispensed.

dispensa'tion, n. distributing, dealing out; an exemption; order of things regarded as established by Providence.

dispense', v.t. & i. deal out (justice, &c.); make up and issue medicines; exempt; ~ with, do without, discharge.

dispen'ser, n. one who dispenses, esp. maker-up of medicines.

dispeo'ple (-pēpl), v.t. depopulate.

dispers'al, n. act of dispersing.

disperse', v.t. & i. (-sable), break up from assembled state; go or make go various ways. ~sion, n. dispersed state; dispersal.

dispi'rit, v.t. make despondent.

displace', v.t. (-ceable), shift from proper position; oust, remove from office. ~ment, n. displacing; weight of liquid displaced by an object floating or immersed in it.

display', v.t. spread out to view; exhibit. n. displaying; exhibition; ostentation.

displease' (-z), v.t. (-sable), offend; make angry; excite disapprobation of.

displea'sure (-lezher), n. resentment; annoyance; vexation.

displume' (-ōō-), v.t. strip of feathers.

disport', v.refl. move about for enjoyment. n. (arch.) pastime.

dispo'sable (-za-), a. that can be disposed of or disposed.

dispo'sal (-zl), n. disposing of; bestowal; sale; management.

dispose' (-z), v.t. & i. place in order; adjust; incline mind to do; bestow. ~ of, get rid of.

disposi'tion (-zi-), n. disposing or arrangement; temperament.

dispossess' (-og-), v.t. oust or dislodge. ~ion, ~or, nn.

dispraise' (-z), v.t. disparage; censure. n. disparagement; blame.

disproof', n. refutation.

dispropor'tion, n. want of symmetry; being out of proportion. ~ed, a. ~ate, a. unsymmetrical.

disprove' (-ōōv), v.t. prove false; show fallacy of; refute.

dis'putable, a. open to question.

dis'putant, n. controversialist.

disputa'tion, n. argumentative debate, discourse, or treatise.

disputa'tious (-shus), a. fond of argument or controversy.

dispute', v.i. & t. hold debate; quarrel, controvert; contend; resist. n. controversy, debate; quarrel; difference of opinion.

disqualifica'tion (-ŏl-), n. that which disqualifies.

disqual'ify (-ŏl-), v.t. (-iable), make unfit or ineligible.

disqui'et, n. uneasiness, perturbation, anxiety. v.t. perturb. ~ness, disquietude, nn.

disquisi'tion (-zi-), n. an elaborate exposition or disputation.

disregard', v.t. ignore, be uninfluenced by. n. neglect.

disrel'ish, n. want of liking for. v.t. regard with distaste.

disrepair', n. bad state for want of repairing.

disrep'utable, a. bearing a bad character; not respectable.

disrepute', n. ill repute; discredit.

disrespect', n. lack of deference. ~ful, a. showing disrespect.

disrobe', v.t. & i. undress; uncover.

disrupt', v.t. shatter; separate. ~ion, n. violent severance; split, schism. ~ive, a.

dissatisfac'tion, n. discontent.

dissat'isfy, v.t. fail to satisfy; make discontented.

dissect', v.t. cut in pieces; anatomize; examine or criticize. ~ion, ~or, nn.

dissem'ble, v.t. & i. conceal or disguise; be hypocritical.

dissem'inate, v.t. (-nable), spread abroad. ~tion, ~tor, nn.

dissen'sion (-shn), n. disunion.

---

dissent', v.i. differ in opinion. n. disagreement; difference of opinion; refusal to accept doctrines of established church. ~er, n. one who dissents, esp. from an established church.

dissen'tient (-shnt), a. not agreeing, dissenting. n. dissentient person.

disserta'tion, n. formal discourse.

disser'vice, n. an ill turn done to a person or cause.

dissev'er, v.t. & i. sever, divide.

diss'idence, n. disagreement.

diss'ident, a. not in agreement; conflicting. n. dissentient.

dissim'ilar, a. unlike. ~a'rity, n.

dissim'ulate, v.t. & i. (-lable), practise deceit. ~tion, ~tor, nn.

diss'ipate, v.t. & i. (-pable), dispel; squander or fritter away. ~d, a. given to dissipation. ~tion, n. dispersion; dissolute living.

disso'ciate (-shi-), v.t. (-ciable), separate, disunite, part; (Chem.) decompose. ~tion, n.; ~tive, a.

dissolubil'ity (-lŏŏ-), n. capacity of being dissolved.

diss'oluble, a. dissolvable.

diss'olute (-ŏŏt), a. licentious.

dissolu'tion (-lŏŏ-), n. dissolving; death; annulment of marriage or other bond.

dissolve' (-z-), v.t. & i. (-vable), decompose; make or become liquid; put an end to.

diss'olvent, n. substance having the power of dissolving another.

diss'onant, a. jarring, clashing, discordant. diss'onance, n.

dissuade' (-wā-), v.t. advise to refrain; deprecate; hinder. dissua'sion (-wāzhn), n.; ~ive, a.

dis'taff (-ahf), n. cleft stick holding wool, &c. used in spinning.

dis'tance, n. length from one point to another; remoteness; distant behaviour. v.t. (-ceable), leave far behind.

dis'tant, a. at a considerable or specified distance; reserved.

distaste', n. dislike; aversion. ~ful, a. exciting distaste.

distem'per, n. a disordered condition; a dog-disease; pigment used in painting on plaster. v.t. paint in distemper; (usu. in p.p.) derange (mind, &c.).

distend', v.t. swell out or be dilated by pressure from within. disten'sible, a.; ~sion, n.

dis'tich (-k), n. (prosod.) couplet.

distil', v.i. & t. trickle, come or give forth in drops; make (spirit, essence) by distillation. ~lation, n. distilling. ~ler, n. maker of alcoholic spirit. ~lery, n. spirit-distilling establishment.

distinct', a. easily discernible; separate or differing in identity.

distinc'tion, n. difference; thing that differentiates; mark of honour; excellence; individuality. ~ive, a. distinguishing; characteristic.

distingué (distăng'gā), a. of distinguished air, manners, &c.

disting'uish (-nggw-), v.t. & i. draw or make distinctions between; characterize; recognize; make oneself prominent. ~ed, a. eminent, having distinction.

distort', v.t. pull or twist out of shape; misrepresent. ~ion, n.

distract', v.t. divert; draw away or in different directions; bewilder; (chiefly p.p.) drive mad or infuriate. ~ion, n. diversion; anger, perplexity; confusion, dissension.

distrain', v.i. resort to distraint.

distraint', n. legal seizure of goods as payment for debt.

distrait' (-rā), a. with thoughts engaged on something else.

distraught' (-awt), a. crazed with grief, &c.; distracted.

distress', n. mental pain; pressure of want, danger, or fatigue; (Law) distraint. v.t. pain mentally; exhaust. ~ful, a. giving or suffering distress.

distrib'ute, v.t. (-table), deal out, give each a share of; classify. ~tion, ~tor, nn.

distrib'utive, a. effecting or concerned in distribution.

dis'trict, n. a region; province; territory.

distrust', n. want of trust; doubt,

ah, awl, oil, boor, cow, dowry; chin, go, bang, zo, ship, thin; dh, as th(e);

suspicion. *v.t.* have no confidence in. ~ful, *a.*

disturb', *v.t.* break the rest or quiet of; worry; disorganize.

disturb'ance, *n.* disturbing; disturbed state; tumult.

disu'nion (-yon), *n.* separation; want of union; dissension.

disunite', *v.t. & i.* separate or become separate; divide.

disuse', *v.t.* (-z), cease to use. *n.* (-s), disused state; desuetude.

disyll'able, *n.* word or metrical foot of two syllables. ~ab'ic, *a.*

ditch, *n.* excavation serving to drain land, &c. *v.i. & t.* make or repair ditches; *throw (railway train, &c.) off track; (fig.) ruin.

dith'er (-dh-), *v.i.* tremble, quiver.

dith'yramb (-m), *n.* (usu. in pl.) outpouring of ecstatic kind; wild eulogy or invective. ~ic, *a.*

ditt'o, substitute for repetition of word or phrase.

ditt'y, *n.* a short simple song.

diuret'ic, *a.* promoting urination. *n.* a diuretic agent.

diur'nal, *a.* in or of the day; (Astron.) occupying a day.

di'vagate, *v.i.* digress. ~tion, *n.*

divan', *n.* oriental council or council-room; low seat running along room-side.

dive, *v.i.* plunge, esp. head foremost, into water, &c.; seek for by diving; make deep inquiry into. *n.* act of diving; *(sl.) cheap restaurant; *low resort. di'ver, *n.* one who descends into deep water; kinds of diving-bird.

di'ving-bell, ~dress, ~helmet, kinds of apparatus for use of divers.

diverge' (or dī-), *v.i.* take a different direction; go off sideways; digress. ~nce, *n.*; ~nt, *a.*

di'vers (-z), *a.* sundry, several.

diverse' (or dī-), *a.* of differing kinds; differing from.

diver'sify (or dī-), *v.t.* (-fiable), introduce variety into; vary.

diver'sion (or dī-), *n.* diverting, deviation; amusement.

diver'sity (or dī-), *n.* diverseness.

divert' (or dī-), *v.t.* turn in another direction; get rid of; draw off attention of; entertain, amuse. diver'ting, *a.* amusing.

divest' (or dī-), *v.t.* unclothe, strip, lay bare. ~ment, *n.*

divide', *v.t. & i.* (-dable), separate into parts; sunder, cut off; set at variance; distribute; share with others; ascertain how many times one number contains another. *n.* water-shed.

div'idend, *n.* number to be divided by divisor; sum payable as interest or profit or share.

divi'der, *n.* that which divides; (pl.) pair of measuring-compasses.

divina'tion, *n.* divining, esp. by aid of magic.

divine', *a.* of, from, or like God or a god; sacred; superhumanly beautiful or excellent. *n.* theologian. *v.t. & i.* (-nable), make out by intuition, magic, or inspiration; foresee, predict, conjecture; practise divination.

divi'ner, *n.* expert in divination.

divi'ning-rod, *n.* switch used by dowser to detect underground water or minerals.

divin'ity, *n.* divineness; a god; the divine Being; theology.

divis'ible (-z-), *a.* that can be divided. ~bility, *n.*

divi'sion (-zhn), *n.* dividing or being divided; one of the parts into which something is divided; (Mil.) unit of two or more brigades. ~al, *a.*

divi'sor (-z-), *n.* the number by which dividend is to be divided.

divorce', *n.* dissolution of marriage; separation between things that should go together. *v.t.* (-ceable), separate by divorce; sunder. divorcée' (or dī-), *n.* divorced person.

div'ot, *n.* a turf, sod; (Golf) piece of turf cut out by bad stroke.

divulge', *v.t.* (-geable), let out (secret); make public.

diwan, = dewan, divan.

*Dix'ie, *n.* Southern States of U.S.; a song.

dix′y̆, n. large iron pot in which stew, tea, &c. are made.

diz′en (or dī-), v.t. bedizen.

dizz′y̆, a. giddy, dazed, unsteady; causing dizziness.

dō′, n. (Mus.) first note of scale.

do² (dōō), n. (colloq.) an impostor, hoax, swindle.

do³ (dōō, doo, do), v.t. & i. (dĭd, done pr. dŭn; 2 sing. pres. dost pr. dŭ-, & doest pr. dōō′ĭst; 3 sing. pres., does pr. dŭz, & arch. doth pr. dŭ-; 2 sing. past, dĭdst) v.t. perform, effect, execute; deal with, set in order, solve; (colloq.) outwit, cheat; exhaust; (sl.) cater for (well, &c.). v.i. act or proceed, succeed, make an end; fare, be suitable, suffice.

Dŏbb′in, n. carthorse.

dō′cile, a. easy to teach and willing to obey. docĭl′ĭty̆, n.

dŏck¹, n. tall coarse weed.

dŏck², v.t. cut short (tail, hair, food, money, or supplies).

dŏck³, n. basin for loading and repairing of ships; enclosure in court for prisoner. ~, put in dock for repair. ~-yard, enclosure for building and repairing ships.

dŏck′er, n. dock-labourer.

dŏck′ĕt, n. endorsement on document showing its subject or contents; *calendar of matters for action. v.t. endorse with docket.

dŏc′tor, n. holder of highest university degree in any faculty; qualified medical practitioner. v.t. treat medically; patch up; garble. ~al, a. of the degree of doctor. ~ate, n. doctor's degree.

dŏctrinaire′, n. person who applies principles pedantically with no allowance for circumstances.

dŏctrī′nal (or dŏk′trĭ-), a. containing doctrine.

dŏc′trine, n. what is taught; a particular dogma (of Church, &c.).

dŏc′ŭment, n. something that furnishes evidence, esp. a legal deed or other piece of writing. v.t. furnish with documents. dŏcŭmĕnt′ary̆, a.; ~ation, n.

dŏdd′er¹, n. parasitic plant resembling tangled red twine.

dŏdd′er², v.i. shake with palsy; totter or potter with senility.

dōdĕc′agon, n. plane figure of twelve sides. dōdĕcahē′dron, n. solid figure of twelve faces. dōdĕcasyll′able, n. verse of twelve syllables.

dŏdge, n. swerving or zigzag movement; piece of duplicity; wrinkle or ingenious method. v.t. & i. (-geable) elude; make a dodge into hiding; treat evasively. dŏdg′er, n. shifty person; *small handbill.

dō′dō, n. (pl. -os), an extinct bird.

dōe, n. female of fallow deer, hare, or rabbit.

does, 3 pers. sing. pres. of do.

dŏff, v.t. take off (hat, &c.).

dŏg, n. quadruped of various breeds, wild and domesticated; worthless man or boy; lucky or sly fellow; *(sl.) style, side; (pl.) metal supports for grate or fire-irons. v.t. follow closely; pursue, track. ~-box, railway van for dogs. ~-cart, two-wheeled driving-cart. ~-days, hot season variously dated with reference to the dog-star. ~-fish, kinds of shark and other fish. ~-rose, wild hedge rose. ~'s-ear, n. corner of page curled with use; v.t. make dog's-ear in book. ~-star, Sirius, chief star of Canis Major. ~-tired, a. tired out. ~-tooth, sharp-pointed human tooth growing next the grinders. ~-watch, (Naut.) short half-watch of two hours.

dōge, n. (hist.) Venetian or Genoan chief magistrate. dō′gate, n. office of doge.

dŏgg′ĕd (-g-), a. tenacious.

dŏgg′erel (-ge-), n. slipshod or unpoetic verses (often attrib.).

dŏgg′y̆ (-g-), a. devoted to dogs.

dŏg′ma, n. (pl. -s, rarely -ata), principle, tenet; doctrinal system. ~ăt′ic, a. of the nature of dogma; given to dogmatizing. ~tism, n. dogmatizing temper or habit. ~tize, v.i. assert positively.

---

māte, mēte, mīte, mōte, mūte, mōōt ; răck, rĕck, rĭck, rŏck, rŭck, rōōk ;

doil′y, n. small napkin placed below finger-glass, &c.

do′ings (dōō-; -z), n.pl. things done; events; behaviour.

doit, n. very small sum.

doit′ed, a. (Sc.) crazed, mad.

dol′drums (-z), n.pl. depressed state, dumps; equatorial ocean region of calms and light variable winds.

dōle[1], n. charitable gift, esp. of measured amount; payment of unemployment insurance. v.t. (-lable), deal out; distribute.

dōle[2], n. woe. ~ful, a. dreary, dismal, melancholy.

dōlichŏcĕphāl′ic (-ĭk-), a. long-headed.

dŏll, n. child's toy representing a baby; pretty silly woman or child. v.t. & i. (sl.) dress (oneself) up smartly. **dŏll′y,** n. doll.

dŏll′ar, n. unit of currency in U.S., Canada, and elsewhere = 100 cents.

dŏll′op, n. (colloq.) lump of food or some soft substance.

dŏl′man, n. kinds of cloak.

dŏl′men, n. cromlech.

dŏl′omite, n. magnesian limestone.

dŏl′orous, a. painful, sad, dismal. **dŏl′our** (-ler). n. sorrow, distress.

dŏl′phin, n. porpoise-like sea mammal; a fish noted for its changes of colour in dying.

dōlt, n. stupid fellow. ~ish, a.

Dŏm, n. title prefixed to names of some R.C. dignitaries and some Portuguese and Brazilian nobles and ecclesiastics.

domain′, n. lands as held or ruled over; an estate or realm; (rhet.) sphere or scope.

dōme, n. rounded vault as roof; stately building; (fig.) the sky; *(sl.) head. dōmed (-md), a.

Domesday (Bŏŏk) (dōōmz-). n. land record made in 1086.

domĕs′tic, a. of the home, household, or family affairs; of one's own country; home-keeping. n. household servant.

domĕs′ticāte, v.t. (-cable), naturalize (plant, &c.); tame (animal);

(p.p.) devoted to home life. ~tion, ~tor, nn.

dŏmĕsti′city (or dō-), n. home life or privacy; homeliness.

dŏm′icile (or -il), n. person's regular place of abode. ~ciled (or -ild), a. having domicile at or in. ~cil′iary (-lya-), a. of a dwelling-place.

dŏm′inant, a. dominating, prevailing, established in power. ~nce, n.

dŏm′ināte, v.t. & i. (-nable), have commanding influence over; overlook. ~tion, n. ascendancy.

dŏmineer′, v.i. behave overbearingly; tyrannize over.

domin′ical, a. of Sunday.

Domin′ican, a. of St. Dominic or his order of friars. n. D. friar.

domin′ie, n. (Sc.) schoolmaster.

domin′ion (-yon), n. sovereignty or lordship; domination; territory of sovereign or government.

dŏm′inō, n. (pl. -oes), cloak worn with half-mask to conceal identity; (pl.) game played with 28 pieces marked with pips; one of these pieces.

dŏn[1], v.t. put on (garment).

dŏn[2], n. member of college or university staff; Spanish gentleman.

dō′na(h), n. (sl.) woman, sweetheart.

donā′tion, n. gift to a fund or institution; benefaction. **donāte′,** v.t. make a donation. *(pop.) give. ~tive, n. a largess or gratuity.

done, p.p. of **do.**

|| **doney.** See **dhoney.**

dŏn′ga (-ngga), n. (S.-Afr.) gully, ravine.

dŏn′jon, n. keep of castle.

dŏnk′ey, n. (pl. -eys), the ass; a stupid fellow.

dŏnn′a, n. Italian or Spanish or Portuguese lady.

dō′nor, n. giver, bestower.

do-nothing (dōō-nŭ-), a. & n. idle, idler.

dŏn′t, abbr. of do not.

|| **dŏŏb,** n. the dog's-tooth grass, used for fodder in India.

|| **dōŏ′lie** (-l), **dōŏ′ly,** n. a rudimentary litter or palanquin used by

the lower classes in India, and as an army ambulance.

dōom, *n.* fate, destiny; judicial sentence; the Last Judgement. *v.t.* condemn, sentence (esp. in *p.p.*). **dooms'day**, *n.* the Last Judgement.

door (dōr), *n.* barrier at the entrance to a building, room, safe, &c.; (fig.) means of approach. **~-keeper**, porter. **~-mat**, for rubbing boots on before entering. **~-way**, entrance to a building.

dōpe, *n.* thick liquid; kinds of varnish; (sl.) drug, esp. narcotic; *(sl.) information secured before race, &c. about past performance of athlete, &c. *v.t. & i.* (-*pable*). treat with dope; take narcotics. *(sl.) predict result of race, &c.

dōr, *n.* kinds of beetle.

Dōr'a, *n.* nickname (initials) of the Defence of the Realm Act.

Dōr'cas, *n.* In comb. Dorcas meeting, meeting of a society of ladies to make clothes, &c. for the poor. **~ society**, such body.

|| **dōr'ia**, **dōr'ea**, *n.* a kind of striped Indian muslin.

Dō'ric, *a.* of the Dorian race in ancient Greece; (of dialect) broad, rustic. *n.* dialect of ancient Greece. **~ order**, one of the five orders of architecture.

Dork'ing, *n.* breed of fowl.

dōrm'ant, *a.* lying inactive as in sleep; concealed. **~ncy**, *n.*

dōrm'er, **~-window**, *n.* upright window set in sloping roof.

dōrm'itory, *n.* sleeping-room with a number of beds; suburban or country district of city people's residences.

dōrm'ouse, *n.* (pl. -*mice*), small hibernating rodent.

dōrm'y, *a.* (Golf) as many holes ahead as holes to play.

dō'rothy bag, *n.* lady's open-topped handbag hung at wrist.

dōrp, *n.* (S.-Afr.) small town.

dōrs'al, *a.* of or on the back.

dōr'ter, **~-tour**, *n.* (hist.) bedroom, dormitory.

dōr'y, *n.* edible sea-fish.

dōse, *n.* amount of medicine, &c.

administered at one time. *v.t.* (-*sable*), give medicine to; blend or adulterate with.

dōss, *v.i.* (sl.) sleep in dosshouse. **~-house**, *n.* common lodging-house.

dōss'ier, *n.* set of documents bearing on person's antecedents.

dost, 2 pers. sing. pres. of do.

dōt[1], *n.* small spot, a point; small child, tiny object. *v.t.* mark with dot(s); place here and there.

dōt[2], *n.* woman's marriage-portion.

dō'tage, *n.* feeble-minded senility.

dō'tard, *n.* man in his dotage; old fool.

dōte, *v.i.* be feeble-minded or silly; be passionately fond of.

doth, 3 pers. sing. pres. of do.

dōtt'(e)rel, *n.* kind of plover.

dōt'tle, *n.* remnant of tobacco in smoked pipe.

dōtt'y, *a.* dotted; (sl.) limping or shaky; rather mad.

dou'ble (dŭ-), *a.* twofold; consisting of two parts; of twice the amount or intensity; of two kinds; deceitful. *adv.* twice the amount; two together. *n.* person or thing mistakable for another; game between two pairs of players; twice the amount; (Mil.) double time. *v.t. & i.* make or become double; increase twofold; clench (fist); (Mil.) go at the double; make sudden turn; play two parts in same piece. **double-barrelled**, (of gun) with two barrels. **~-bass**, deepest-toned instrument of violin kind. *~-cross, betray, sell to both sides. **~-dealer**, insincere person. **~-dyed**, (of scoundrel, &c.) confirmed, utter. **~-edged**, (of argument, &c.) damaging to user as well as opponent. || **double entendre** (dōōbl ahntahn'dr), phrase capable of two meanings; use of such phrases. **~-faced**, hypocritical. *~-header. (Baseball) two games between the same teams in immediate succession on the same day.

doub'let (dŭ-). *n.* man's close

body-garment in 14th–18th centuries; word that is etymologically the same as another.

doubloon' (du-), n. Spanish gold coin slightly over £1.

doubt (dowt), n. feeling of uncertainty; state not allowing of certainty; suspicion. v.t. & i. feel doubt; disbelieve in; feel distrust of; be apprehensive.

doubt'ful (-owt-), a. feeling or giving rise to doubt; uncertain.

doubt'less (-owt-), adv. certainly.

douce (dōōs), a. (Sc.) sedate; quiet-mannered.

|| douceur (dōō'sĕr), n. gratuity, bribe.

douche (dōōsh), n. jet of water applied externally or internally. v.t. & i. (-chable), administer douche to; douche oneself.

dough (dō), n. flour moistened and kneaded; *(sl.) money. ~boy, boiled dumpling; *(sl.) infantryman in U.S. army. doughy (dō'ĭ), a. like dough.

dought'y (dowt-), a. valiant.

dour (-oor), a. (Sc.) grim, stubborn.

dove (dŭv), n. pigeon; a type of gentleness or innocence. ~côt(e), pigeon-house.

dove'tail (-ŭv-), n. joint made with tenon shaped like dove's tail. v.t. & i. fit together thus.

dow'ager, n. woman with title or property derived from her late husband.

dowd'y, a. lacking smartness, illdressed. n. dowdy woman.

dow'er, n. widow's share for life of husband's estate; natural gift or talent. v.t. give dowry to; endow with talent, &c.

dowl'as, n. kind of strong calico.

down¹, n. open high land.

down², n. fine soft short hair or feathers or fluff.

down³, adv. towards or in a lower place or state; from earlier to later time; on the ground. prep. downwards along, through, or into; at a lower part. a. directed downwards. v.t. (colloq.) put, throw, knock, or bring down.

down'cast (-ah-), a. (of eyes) looking down; (of person) dejected.

*down-eas'ter, n. New-Englander, esp. inhabitant of Maine.

down'fall (-awl), n. fall from prosperity or power; downpour.

down'-heart'ed (-hār-), a. despondent.

down'hill, n. downward slope. a. descending; declining.

down'pour (-pōr), n. heavy fall of rain, &c.

down'right (-rīt), a. plain, straightforward, blunt. adv. thoroughly, quite.

downstairs', adv., n., & a. (to, in of) lower part of a house.

down'ward (a. & adv. ~wards (-z), adv. from a higher to a lower place.

down'y, a. of or like down; (sl.) knowing, sly.

dow'ry, n. property brought by a wife at marriage; a talent.

dowse, douse, v.t. & i. (-sable), throw water over, drench; extinguish (light); (pr. -z) use dowsing-rod. dows'er (-z-), n. user of dowsing-rod. dowsing-rod (-z-), n. divining rod.

doxol'ogy, n. formula of praise.

doyen (doi'yen), n. senior member of a body of colleagues.

dōze, v.i. yield to sleep, be half asleep. n. light sleep.

do'zen (dŭ-), n. set of twelve.

dráb¹, a. of dull light brown; dull, monotonous. n. drab colour.

dráb², n. slut, prostitute.

drachm (-ăm), n. unit of weight, 1/16 oz. avoird., 1/8 oz. apoth.; ancient drachma.

drách'ma (-k-), n. (pl. -ae, -as), ancient and modern Greek coin (franc).

Draco'nian, ~ŏn'ic, aa. rigorous as the laws of Draco.

draff (-ahf), n. dregs, refuse.

draft (-ah-), n. body of men drawn from depot, &c.; order for drawing money, bill or cheque drawn; sketch of work to be done, rough copy of document. v.t. dispatch (men) as draft; make draft of

gh. as (rou)ge: ě =ĭ; ĭf, ŭf, =ĕf; ӯ, ỹ, =ĭ, ĭ; and see p. 4. *=U.S.

3495 F

(document). ~s'man, drafter of documents.

dråg, v.t. & i. draw along with force; trail or go heavily; use grapnel; harrow; check with drag. n. check on progress, retarded motion; iron shoe to retard wheel and vehicle; coachlike 4-horse vehicle; hunt using lure drawn before hounds; kinds of harrow, sledge, rake, net, and grapnel.

dråg'gle, v.t. & i. make dirty and wet by trailing; hang trailing. ~tail(ed), n. & a. (woman) with draggled skirts.

dråg'oman, n. (pl. -ans, -en), interpreter in Near East.

dråg'on, n. fire-breathing monster like winged crocodile or snake; vigilant person, duenna.

dråg'onfly, n. long-bodied gauze-winged insect.

dragoon', n. cavalryman of certain regiments (hist.) mounted-infantry man. v.t. subject to oppression; force into submission.

drain, v.t. & i. draw off (liquid) by ditches, pipes, &c.; drink to the dregs; exhaust; run dry. n. channel or pipe carrying off water, sewage, &c.; (colloq.) drop of liquor. drain'age, n. draining; what is drained off.

dråke¹, n. fly used in fishing.

dråke², n. male duck.

dråm, n. a drachm; small draught of strong drink.

dra'ma (-ah-), n. a stage play; dramatic art; play-like series of events.

dramåt'ic, a. of drama; forcible, theatrical; striking.

|| dråm'atis pěrső'nae, n.pl. characters of drama.

dråm'atist, n. playwright.

dråm'atize, v.t. (-zable), turn into drama. ~zation, n.

drank, p.t. of drink.

dråpe, v.t. (-pable), cover, hang, adorn, with cloth, &c.; arrange in graceful folds. drå'per, n. dealer in cloth, linen, &c. drå'pery, n. draper's wares or trade; clothing or hangings disposed in folds.

drås'tic, a. strongly operative; vigorous; violent.

dråt, v.t. curse, bother (person, thing). drått'ěd, a. cursed.

draught (-ahft), n. traction; one drawing of net; one continuous act of drinking; dose of medicine; depth of water ship draws; current of air; (pl.) game on chessboard with 12 uniform pieces (draughtsmen) on each side; artist's sketch for picture.~y, a. abounding in currents of air.

draughts'man (fem. -woman), person who makes drawings; piece in draughts. ~ship, n.

draw¹, n. act of drawing; thing that draws custom or attention drawing of lots; drawn game.

draw², v.t. & i. (drew, pr. -ōō, drawn) pull, drag, haul; attract; derive, deduce, infer; inhale; extract; entice; extort, force; elicit; take from or out; pull into or out of position; protract; make picture by tracing lines; describe in words; write out (bill, cheque, &c.); bring (game, &c.) to undecided conclusion; obtain by lot.

draw'back, n. thing that qualifies satisfaction; amount of excise or import duty remitted or repaid on exports.

draw'bridge, n. bridge hinged for drawing up or drawing aside.

draw'er, n. one who draws; sliding receptacle in table, chest, &c.; (pl.) two-legged undergarment.

draw'ing, n. act of pulling, dragging, or hauling; delineation with pencil; a sketch.

draw'ing-room, n. reception-room; levee or court reception.

drawl, n. indolent or affected slowness of speech. v.i. & t. speak or utter with drawl.

draw'-well, n. well with rope and bucket for drawing water.

dray, n. low cart for carrying heavy loads, esp. beer-barrels. ~horse, ~man, nn.

dread (-ĕd), v.t. & i. anticipate with terror; be in great fear of. n. great fear; awe. a. dreaded.

māte, mēte, mīte, mōte, mūte, mōōt; răck, rěck, rǐck, rŏck, rŭck, rŏŏk;

dread'ful (-ĕd-), *a.* terrible; troublesome or horrid.

dread'nought (drĕdnawt), *n.* kind of heavy coat and cloth; powerful modern battleship type.

dream, *n.* a sleeping vision; indulgence in fancy; a day dream, reverie. *v.i. & t.* (*-eamt* pr. *-ĕmt,* or *-ed*) experience a dream; allow oneself to believe or think that; fall into reverie. ~**land,** *n.* region outside the laws of nature. ~**y,** *a.* given to reverie; vague.

drear'y (poet.) **drear,** *aa.* dismal, gloomy, dull.

dredge¹, *n.* apparatus for clearing mud, &c.; oyster-dredge. *v.i. & t.* (*-geable*), use dredge; clean or fetch up with dredge. **dredg'er¹,** *n.* one who fishes with a dredge; a dredge.

dredge², *v.t.* (*-geable*), sprinkle with flour, &c. **dredg'er²,** *n.* box for sprinkling flour, &c.

dreg, *n.* (pl.) sediment, grounds, refuse; (sing.) small remnant.

drench, *v.t.* wet all over; force (beast) to take dose. *n.* dose for beast. **dren'cher,** *n.* heavy rainstorm. ~**ing,** *n.* a soaking.

Dres'den (-z-), *n.* ~**china,** ~**porcelain,** kind produced in Saxony, esp. in 18th c.

dress, *v.t. & i.* (Mil.) take up exact alignment; clothe, clothe oneself; put dressing on (wound, &c.); prepare food; trim. *n.* clothing, esp. external. ~**circle,** first gallery in theatres. ~**coat,** swallow-tailed for evening dress. ~**maker,** woman making women's dresses. ~**rehearsal,** final one in costume.

dress'er, *n.* one who dresses; kitchen sideboard with shelves.

dress'ing, *n.* ointment, &c. applied to a wound; manure; sauce or stuffing; a scolding or thrashing. ~**case,** case with toilet requisites. ~**gown,** loose girdled gown.

dress'y, *a.* given to smart dress.

drew, *p.t.* of draw.

drib'ble, *v.t. & i.* flow or let flow in drops; (Footb.) work ball forward with repeated touches of feet. *n.* dribbling flow; piece of dribbling.

drib'let, *n.* small instalment.

dried, *p.t.* of dry.

drift, *n.* being driven by current; inaction; bearing of speaker's words; matter heaped by wind or collected by water; (S.Afr.) ford. *v.i. & t.* be carried by current; heap or be heaped into drifts; go aimlessly. ~**net,** net employed in fishing for herring, mackerel, &c.

drif'ter, *n.* boat with drift-net.

drill¹, *n.* boring tool or machine; exercising of soldiers; drill; seed-sowing machine; small furrow. *v.t. & i.* bore (hole, &c.); subject to or undergo drill; sow in rows.

drill², *n.* coarse twilled fabric.

drill³, *n.* kind of baboon.

drink, *v.i. & t.* (*drank; drunk & drunken*) swallow liquid; absorb moisture. *n.* liquid for drinking; act of drinking. ~**ables,** *n.pl.* things to drink.

drip, *v.i. & t.* fall or let fall in drops. *n.* process of dripping.

drip'ping, *n.* grease that has dripped from roasted meat.

drive, *v.t. & i.* (*drove, driven; -vable*), urge onwards by force; chase (game, &c.) from large area into small; convey or be conveyed in vehicle; impel, propel, carry along. *n.* excursion in carriage; carriage road; driving of game, cattle, or enemy; strokes in cricket, golf, tennis.

driv'el, *v.i.* slaver; talk silly stuff. *n.* silly nonsense. ~**ler,** *n.*

dri'ver, *n.* one who or that which drives; coachman; golf-club.

driz'zle, *v.i.* fall in fine dense rain. *n.* such rain.

droll, *a.* amusing, odd, queer.

droll'ery, *n.* quaint humour.

drom'edary (or *-ŭm-*), *n.* camel bred for riding.

drone, *n.* male or non-worker bee; idler; deep monotonous hum. *v.i. & t.* buzz; talk or utter with drone.

drool, *v.i.* drivel.

droop, *v.i. & t.* incline or hang

---

down; languish, lose heart. *n.* drooping state.

drŏp, *n.* portion of liquid; draught of strong drink; sweetmeat; dropping or fall; drop-kick. *v.i.* & *t.* fall or shed in drops; let fall; lose money; leave hold of; sink to lower level; lower (eyes, &c.); sink to ground; (Footb.) make goal by drop-kick, take drop-kick. ~ curtain, curtain let down between the acts in theatre. ~kick, kicking of football as it bounds after being dropped from hands. *~letter*, letter delivered from office where it is posted.

drŏp´lĕt, *n.* a little drop.

drŏpp´ings (-z), *n.pl.* what has dropped; dung of beasts, &c.

drŏp´sў, *n.* disease with watery fluid collecting in body. **drŏp´sical,** *a.*

drŏs(h)´kў, *n.* Russian carriage; cab in German towns.

drŏss, *n.* scum of molten metal; impurities; refuse. **drŏss´ў,** *a.*

drought (-owt), (poet.) **drouth,** *nn.* thirst; continuous dry weather, wanting rain. **drought´ў,** *a.*

drŏve¹, *n.* moving herd or flock; crowd in motion. **drō´ver,** *n.* driver of or dealer in cattle.

drŏve², *p.t.* of drive.

drown, *v.i.* & *t.* be suffocated or suffocate by immersion; drench or flood; (of sound, &c.) overpower; deaden (grief) with drink.

drowse (-z), *v.i.* be half asleep.

drow´sў (-z-), *a.* half asleep.

drŭb, *v.t.* thrash, whack; beat into or out of. *~bing, n.*

drŭdge, *v.i.* work hard at distasteful tasks. *n.* person who drudges. **drŭdg´erў,** *n.*

drŭg, *n.* simple substance used in medicine; unsalable commodity. *v.t.* & *i.* adulterate or stupefy with drugs; administer or take drugs. *~store,* druggist's shop.

drŭgg´ĕt (-g-), *n.* coarse woollen stuff; over-carpet.

drŭgg´ist (-g-), *n.* dealer in drugs.

Dru´id (-ōō-), *n.* ancient Gallic or

British priest; Eisteddfod official; member of a modern Order of Druids. *~ess, ~ism, nn.*

drŭm, *n.* musical instrument of various kinds; cylindrical structure or object; tympanum of the ear; (arch.) large evening part. *v.i.* & *t.* play drum; tap or thump continuously; *~fire*, heavy continuous rapid artillery fire. *~head,* skin of drum. *~major,* regimental band-leader. *~stick,* stick for beating drum; lower joint of cooked fowl's leg; *the stilt-sandpiper.

drŭmm´er, *n.* player of drum; *commercial traveller.

drŭnk, *p.p.* of drink. *pred. a.* intoxicated; overcome by strong drink. *n.* (sl.) drinking-bout; case of drunkenness. **drŭnk´ard,** *n.* person often drunk. *~en, a.* given to drunkenness.

drupe (-ōō-), *n.* stone-fruit.

drў, *a.* without or deficient in moisture; without rain; thirsty; hard; teetotal, free from sale of intoxicants; uninteresting. *v.t.* & *i.* make or become dry. *~ goods,* non-liquid goods; *drapery,* mercery. *~nurse,* woman tending but not suckling child. *~ rot,* decay in wood not exposed to air; moral or social decay.

drў´ad, *n.* wood-nymph.

Drў´asdŭst, *n.* dull antiquary or historian. *a.* dry, uninteresting.

drў´salter (-awl-), *n.* dealer in tinned foods, drugs, oils, &c.

drў´shŏd, *a.* with feet dry.

dū´al, *a.* of double nature; forming a pair; twofold. *n.* (Gram.) dual number or form. *~ism, n.* duality; recognition of two independent principles or powers. *~ist, n.; ~istic, a.; dūăl´itў, n.; ~ize, v.t.*

dŭb¹, *v.t.* confer knighthood on; give person a title or nickname.

dŭb², *n.* (sl.) fool.

dŭb³, *n.* (Anglo-Ind.) a small copper coin; money in general. 'cash.'

dŭb´ber, *n.* (Anglo-Ind.) a large

oval leathern vessel, used for holding and transporting ghee or oil.

dubb'ing, *n.* grease for suppling leather.

dubi'ety, *n.* feeling of doubt.

du'bious, *a.* occasioning doubt; not clear or decided; uncertain.

dubita'tion, *n.* hesitation.

du'bitative, *a.* expressing doubt.

du'cal, *a.* pertaining to a duke.

duc'at, *n.* gold coin about 9*s.*, formerly current in Italy, &c.

Duce (dōō'chā), *n.* (It.) chief.

duch'ess, *n.* duke's wife or widow; (sl.) coster's wife (abbr. *dutch*).

duch'y, *n.* reigning duke's territory.

duck¹, *n.* kinds of swimming bird; darling; bob of head; (Crick.) duck's-egg. ~**bill**, ornithorhyncus. ~**'s-egg**, batsman's score of 0. ~**-hawk**, peregrine falcon. ~**weed**, a water-plant.

duck², *v.i.* & *t.* dip head under water and emerge; push head of (person) under water; bob down to avoid blow, &c.; drop curtsy. ~**out**, leave.

duck³, *n.* strong linen or cotton material; (pl.) trousers of it.

duck'ling, *n.* young duck.

duck'y, *n.* (nursery) darling.

duct, *n.* conduit; (Anat.) tube conveying chyle or other liquid.

duc'tile (*or* -īl), *a.* capable of being drawn into wire; plastic; docile.

ductil'ity, *n.*

dud, *n.* (sl.), (pl.) clothes, rags; shell, &c. that fails to go off; futile plan or person.

dude, *n.* foppish person.

dudg'eon (-jn), *n.* resentment; state of wrath or indignation.

dud(h)een' (dŏŏ-), *n.* (Ir.) short clay pipe.

due, *a.* that ought to be given to a person; proper, adequate; owing, payable as a debt or an obligation. *adv.* exactly; duly. *n.* person's fair share; (usu. pl.) fixed toll(s) or fee(s). ~**bill**, written acknowledgement of debt.

du'el, *n.* fight with weapons between two persons; two-sided

contest. *v.i.* fight duel(s). **du'ellist**, *n.* duel-fighter.

duén'na, *n.* governess, female guardian, chaperon.

duèt', *n.* musical composition for two voices or instruments.

duff, *n.* (sl.) dough; plum-pudding.

duff'el, *n.* coarse woollen cloth.

duff'er, *n.* (colloq.) inefficient or stupid person.

dug¹, *n.* udder, beast's teat.

dug², *p.t.* & *p.p.* of dig.

du'gong (-ōō-), *n.* herbivorous sea mammal of Indian seas.

dug'-out, *n.* underground shelter for use of troops in trenches; hollowed tree as canoe; retired officer, &c. recalled to service.

dui'ker (dī-), *n.* small S.-Afr. antelope.

duke, *n.* sovereign of a duchy; British peer of highest rank. ~**dom**, duchy; duke's dignity.

dul'cet, *a.* sweet, soothing.

dul'cimer, *n.* musical instrument from which piano descends.

dull, *a.* lacking intelligence; not bright; wanting liveliness. *v.t.* & *i.* make or grow dull; lose keenness. **dull'ard**, *n.* slow-witted person.

du'ly, *adv.* properly, fitly, rightly; sufficiently; punctually.

du'ma (dŏŏ-), *n.* Russian pre-revolutionary parliament.

dumb (-m), *a.* unable to speak; silent, taciturn; *(colloq.) dull, stupid. ~**bell**, short bar used in pairs to exercise muscles; *(sl.) stupid tongue-tied person. ~**found**, confound to dumbness.

dum'dum (bullet), *n.* soft-nosed expanding bullet.

dumm'y, *n.* sham article; mere tool; lay figure. *a.* sham.

dump, *v.t.* shoot or deposit rubbish; throw down; send surplus goods to foreign market at low price. *n.* rubbish-heap; (Mil.) temporary depot of munitions at front; (pl.) depression, melancholy.

dump'ling, *n.* ball of dough boiled in stew, &c.

dum'py, *a.* short and stout.

dŭn[1], *a.* of dull greyish brown. *n.* dun colour; dun horse, &c.

dŭn[2], *n.* importunate creditor. *v.t.* importune for payment.

dŭnce, *n.* bad learner; dullard.

dŭn′derhead (-ĕd), *n.* blockhead. ~-headed, *a.* grossly stupid.

dŭne, *n.* mound of dry shifting sand on coast.

dŭng, *n.* excrement of animals; manure. *v.t.* manure (land). ~hill, manure-heap. dŭng′ȳ, *a.*

dŭng′aree (-ngg-), *n.* coarse Indian calico; (pl.) overalls.

dŭn′geon (-jn), *n.* subterranean cell for prisoners.

dŭn′lin, *n.* red-backed sandpiper.

dŭodĕ′cimal, *a.* of twelve; proceeding by twelves.

dŭodĕ′cimo (or 12mo). *n.* booksize, 12 leaves to the sheet.

dŭodĕ′num, *n.* part of small intestine next stomach.

dū′ologue (-g), *n.* dialogue of two speakers.

dūpe, *v.t.* (-*pable*), deceive and make use of. *n.* duped person.

dū′ple, *a.* (of ratio) double; (mus.) of two beats to the bar.

dū′plex, *a.* of two parts; twofold. ~ telegraphy, by which one wire transmits messages both ways at once.

dū′plicate, *a.* (-kit), double; exactly like or reproducing another example. *n.* (-kit), such example. *v.t.* (-āt), make copies of. ~tion, *n.* doubling; making of copies. ~tor, *n.* apparatus for making copies.

dŭpli′city, *n.* deceitfulness.

dūr′able, *a.* capable of lasting; resisting wear. dūrabil′itȳ, *n.*

‖ **dūr′a māter**, *n.* outer membrane of the brain.

dūr′ance, *n.* imprisonment.

dūrā′tion, *n.* time thing lasts.

dŭrb′ar, *n.* levee of Indian sovereign or Anglo-Ind. governor.

dūr′ess(e) (also dūrĕs′), *n.* forcible restraint; threats or other illegal compulsion.

dūr′ing, *prep.* throughout or at a point in the duration of.

‖ **dŭr′ra**, dh- (doo-), Indian millet.

dŭrst, *p.t.* of dare.

dŭsk, *n.* partial darkness; obscurity. dŭs′kȳ, *a.* in scanty light; dark-coloured.

‖ **Dŭss′erah**, *n.* annual Hindu festival extending over nine nights (or ten days).

dŭst, *n.* powder of earth or fine particles of matter. *v.t.* sprinkle with powder; clear of dust. ~bin, receptacle for rubbish. ~man, scavenger.

dŭs′ter, *n.* cloth for dusting furniture; person who does this.

dŭs′ting, *n.* clearing of dust; (sl.) thrashing; tossing at sea.

‖ **dŭstoor′**, -ȳ, *n.* (Anglo-Ind.) custom, usage, fashion; customary commission.

‖ **dŭs′tŭck**, dŭs′tŭk, *n.* (Anglo-Ind.) passport.

dŭs′tȳ, *a.* powdery, dust-covered.

Dŭtch[1], *a.* of Holland or its people or in their language. *n.* the Dutch language. ~ auction, sale in which price is reduced till purchaser is found. ~man, native of Holland; *(colloq.)* a German. ~ oven, metal box with open side attachable to grate. *~* treat, (colloq.) one in which each pays his own way.

dŭtch[2], *n.* (coster sl.) wife.

dū′teous, *a.* dutiful.

dū′tiable, *a.* liable to customs duties, &c.

dū′tiful, *a.* regular and willing in the discharge of duty.

dū′tȳ, *n.* moral or legal obligation; office or function; tax levied on article or transaction.

dūŭm′vir (-er), *n.* (pl. -*rs*, -*rī*), member of board of two equal officials. ~ate, *n.* such board.

dwāle, *n.* Deadly Nightshade.

dwarf (-awf), *n.* much undersized person; (attrib.) stunted or undersized. *v.t.* stunt in growth; make look small. ~ish, *a.*

dwĕll, *v.i.* (*dwĕlt*), keep one's attention fixed; write or speak at length on; inhabit; reside.

dwĕll′ing, *n.* house, residence.

dwin′dle, *v.i.* waste away; diminish; lose importance.

---

māte, mēte, mīte, mōte, mūte, mōōt; răck, rĕck, rĭck, rŏck, rŭck, rōōk;

dȳ'ad, n. two; set of two.

dȳe, v.t. (dyed, dyeing), colour, tinge; make of specified colour. n. colour produced by dyeing; hue; matter used to dye with. dȳ'er, n.

dẏnăm'ic, a. of motive force or force in operation; of dynamics. n. energizing or motive force. ~al, a. of or in dynamics.

dẏnăm'ics, n.pl. (usu. with sing. vb. &c.), branch of physics treating of the action of force; physical or moral forces in any sphere.

dȳ'namist, n. expert in dynamics.

dȳ'namite, n. high explosive of nitro-glycerine and absorbent. v.t. shatter with this. dȳ'namiter, ~tard, nn. user of explosives, esp. for revolutionary purposes.

dȳ'namō, n. (pl. -os), machine converting mech. into electr. energy. ~electric. a. of current electr.

dẏnamom'eter, n. instrument measuring energy expended.

dȳn'ast (or dȳ-), n. member of dynasty.

dȳn'astẏ, n. line of hereditary rulers. dẏnăs'tic (or dȳ-), a.

dȳne, n. (Phys.) unit of force.

dȳs'enterẏ, n. a disease of the bowels. dẏsentĕ'ric, a.

dẏspĕp'sia, n. indigestion.

dẏspĕp'tic, a. having or subject to dyspepsia. n. dyspeptic person.

E

E, e (ē), n. (Mus.) third note in scale of C major.

each, a. & pron. (of two or more) every one taken separately.

eag'er (-g-), a. full of keen desire; ardent; impatient.

ea'gle, n. large bird of prey; figure of eagle as ensign, or lectern in church; U.S. gold coin worth 10 dollars. eag'let, n. young eagle.

eagre (ā'ger, ē-), n. large tidal wave in a river.

ear[1], n. organ of hearing; ear-shaped thing. ~ache, pain in

drum of ear. ~mark, n. owner's mark on ear of sheep, &c. v.t. mark sheep, &c. thus; assign (fund, &c.) to some definite purpose. ~phone, head-phone. ~ring, ornament worn in lobe of ear. ~trumpet, tube used by partly deaf person.

ear[2], n. spike or head of corn containing the flowers or seeds.

earl (ĕrl), n. nobleman ranking next to marquis. ~dom, n.

earl'ẏ (ĕr-), a. & adv. soon; betimes; in advance of others.

earn (ĕrn), v.t. obtain as reward of work or merit. earn'ings (ĕrn-), n.pl. money earned.

earn'ĕst[1] (ĕr-), a. serious, not trifling; ardent, zealous. n. seriousness. earn'ĕst[2] (ĕr-), n. money paid as instalment to confirm contract; foretaste.

earth (ĕrth), n. the world we live on; dry land; soil, mould; the ground. v.t. & i. cover roots with earth; (of fox) run to earth. ~born, mortal. ~closet, substitute for water-closet. ~nut, kinds of tuber, esp. pignut. ~work, bank of earth in fortification. ~worm, worm living in earth.

earth'en (ĕr-), a. made of earth or of baked clay. ~ware, n. baked clay; vessels made of this.

earth'lẏ (ĕr-), a. of the earth; terrestrial. ~liness, n. worldliness.

earth'quake (ĕr-), n. volcanic convulsion of earth's surface.

earth'ẏ (ĕr-), a. of or like earth or soil; grossly material.

ear'wig, n. insect formerly thought to enter head by ear; *(colloq.) small centipede.

ease (ēz), n. freedom from pain, trouble, or constraint; quiet, rest; facility. v.t. & i. relieve from pain, &c.; relax, slacken. ~ful, a. at rest.

eas'el (-z-), n. frame to support picture, blackboard, &c.

ease'ment (-zm-), n. right of way; supplementary building; relief from pain, &c.

māre, mēre, mīre, mōre, mūre; părt, pĕrt, pŏrt; *italics*, vague sounds;

east, *n.* part of horizon where the sun rises; eastern parts, orient. *a.* from or towards the east.

Eas´ter, *n.* festival of Christ's resurrection. ~**dues** or **offerings,** voluntary gifts collected for the parson of a parish at Easter. ~**egg,** painted or imitation egg as Easter gift.

eas´terly, *a.* from or to the east.

eas´tern, *a.* of or in the east. *n.* inhabitant of the east.

east´ward(**s**), *adv.* towards the east.

eas´ỹ (-z-), *a.* free from bodily or mental pain, worry, &c.; not difficult; easily gained (money); not ceremonious; compliant; tranquil. *adv.* in comfortable fashion. *n.* short stop in rowing. ~**chair,** arm-chair designed for comfort. ~**going,** not fussy; content with things as they are. **~mark,** one who is easily fooled.

eat, *v.t. & i.* (past *ate* or *eat,* pr. ĕt; p.p. *eaten,* pr. ētn), masticate and swallow (food); destroy, consume. ~**able,** *n.* (usu. pl.) solid food. **eat´ing,** *n.* act of consuming food. ~**house,** restaurant. ***eats,** (sl.) food.

‖ **Eau-de-Cologne** (ō´dekolōn´), *n.* perfume made at Cologne. ‖ **eau-de-vie** (ōdevē´), *n.* brandy.

eaves (ēvz), *n.pl.* projecting lower edge of roof. ~**dropper,** *n.* one who stands under eaves, &c., to overhear secrets. ~**dropping,** *n.*

ebb, *n.* reflux of tide; decline, decay. *v.i.* flow back; decline.

eb´on, *a.* (poet.) of ebony.

eb´onite, *n.* vulcanized rubber.

eb´onỹ, *n.* kinds of hard black wood. *a.* made of, black as, ebony.

ebull´ient, *a.* boiling; exuberant. ~**nce,** ~**ncy,** *nn.*

ebulli´tion, *n.* boiling; outburst.

écarté (ĕkärt´ā), *n.* a card-game for two.

eccen´tric (-ks-), *a.* not concentric; not placed centrally; not circular; irregular; odd, whimsical. *n.* eccentric person.

eccentri´citỹ, *n.* deviation from a centre; singularity of conduct.

ecclēsiás´tic (-zi-), *n.* clergyman. ~**al,** *a.* of the church or clergy.

ecclēsiol´ogỹ (-zi-), *n.* science of church building and decoration. **ecclēsiolō´gical,** *a.* ~**gist,** *n.*

e´chelon (-sh-), *n.* formation of troops in parallel divisions, each with its front clear of that in advance.

echi´nus (-k-), *n.* animal inhabiting spheroidal prickly shell; sea-urchin.

ec´hō (-k-), *n.* (pl. -*oes*), repetition of sound by reflexion of sound-waves; close imitation. *v.i. & t.* resound with echo; be repeated; repeat (person's words).

éclair (ĕk´lār), *n.* finger-shaped cake filled with cream and iced.

‖ **éclaircissement** (ĕklārsē´smahn), *n.* explanation of conduct or situation.

‖ **éclat** (ĕklah´), *n.* brilliant success; prestige.

eclec´tic, *a.* drawing one's philosophy from various schools; catholic. *n.* eclectic person.

eclipse´, *n.* interception of light of sun, moon, &c. by another body; loss of brilliance or splendour. *v.t.* intercept light; outshine, surpass.

eclip´tic, *a.* of eclipse. *n.* the sun's apparent orbit.

ec´logue, *n.* a pastoral poem.

econom´ic, *a.* pertaining to economy; on business lines; paying costs. *n.pl.* political economy. ~**al,** *a.* saving, frugal; of economics.

econ´omist, *n.* manager, user (of money, &c); thrifty person; writer on political economy.

econ´omize, *v.t. & i.* (-*zable*), use sparingly; practise economy; avoid expense. ~**zation,** *n.*

econ´omỹ, *n.* management of concerns and resources of a state, a business, or a household; frugality, frugal use.

ec´stasỹ, *n.* exalted state of feeling; trance; poetic frenzy.

ecstăt´ic, of or in ecstasies;

---

ah, awl, oil, boor, cow, dowry; chin, go, bang, so, ship, thin; dh, as *th(e)*

ĕc′zema, *n.* a skin disease.

ĕdā′cious (-shŭs), *a.* fond of eating; greedy. **ĕdā′cĭtў**, *n.*

Edd′a (ĕ-), *n.* collection of ancient Icelandic poems.

ĕdd′ў, *n.* small whirlpool; smoke, &c. moving like this. *v.t. & i.* move in eddies.

edelweiss (ā′dĕlvīs), *n.* Alpine white-flowered plant.

E′den (ē-), *n.* abode of Adam and Eve; delightful place or state.

ĕdĕn′tāte, *a.* toothless.

ĕdge, *n.* cutting side of blade; edge-shaped thing; boundary-line. *v.t. & i.* sharpen; give or form a border to; advance obliquely. ~bone, the stitch-bone. ~tool, cutting-tool (in fig. sense *edged tool*). ~ways (-jwāz), ~wise (-jwīz), *advv.* with edge foremost; edge to edge.

ĕdg′ing, *n.* border; fringe.

ĕd′ĭble, *a.* fit to eat. *n.* (usu. in pl.) edible thing. **ĕdĭbĭl′ĭtў**, *n.*

ē′dĭct, *n.* order proclaimed by authority.

ĕd′ĭfĭce, *n.* building; fabric.

ĕd′ĭfў, *v.t.* instruct; improve morally. ~fĭcation, *n.*

ĕd′ĭt, *v.t.* prepare for publication (book, newspaper, &c.). **edĭ′tion**, *n.* copies of book, news-paper, &c. printed at one time. ‖ **édition de luxe** (edish′on de looks), *n.* handsome edition. **ĕd′ĭtor**, ~tress, *nn.* one who con-ducts a newspaper or periodical or prepares a work for publica-tion. **ĕdĭtō′rĭal**, *a.* of an editor. *n.* article written or sanctioned by an editor; newspaper leader.

ĕd′ūcāte, *v.t.* (-cable), bring up (child); train mentally and morally; instruct. ~ā′tion, *n.*; ~tĭonal, *a.* tĭon(al)ist, *nn.* advo-cate of, person concerned with, education. ~tĭve, *a.*; ~tor, *n.*

ĕdūce′, *v.t.* bring out, develop; infer; extract. **ĕdū′cĭble**, *a.*; **ĕdūc′tĭon**, *n.*

eel, *n.* a snake-like fish (often as type of evasiveness).

e′en, *adv.* poet. for even, ever.

eer′ĭe, ~rў, *a.* strange; weird.

ĕfface′, *v.t.* (-ceable), rub or wipe out; eclipse. ~ment, *n.*

ĕffect′, *n.* result, consequence; impression; (pl.) property. *v.t.* bring about; accomplish.

ĕffĕc′tĭve, *a.* operative; striking; fit for service; existing.

ĕffĕc′tūal, *a.* answering its pur-pose. ~ly, *adv.* efficaciously.

ĕffĕc′tūāte, *v.t.* bring about, fulfil. ~tĭon, *n.*

ĕffĕm′ĭnate, *a.* womanly; woman-ish; voluptuous. ~acy, *n.*

ĕffĕn′di, *n.* Turkish title of government officials and mem-bers of learned professions.

ĕffervĕsce′, *v.i.* give off bubbles of gas. ~ent, *a.*; ~ence, ~ency, *nn.*

ĕffēte′, *a.* worn out; feeble.

ĕffĭcā′cious (-shŭs), *a.* producing desired effect. **ĕff′ĭcacў**, *n.*

ĕffĭ′cient (-shĕnt), *a.* competent, capable. **ĕffĭ′ciencў**, *n.*

ĕff′ĭgў, *n.* portrait, image.

ĕfflorĕsce′, *v.i.* burst into flower; (Chem.) turn to powder on ex-posure to air. ~nt, *a.*; ~nce, *n.*

ĕff′luence (-loō-), *n.* flowing out (of liquid, &c.); what flows out.

ĕff′luent (-loō-), *a.* flowing out. *n.* stream from larger stream, sewage tank, &c.

ĕ′fflū′vĭum (-loō-), *n.* (pl. -ia), ex-halation affecting sense of smell.

ĕff′lux, efflux′ĭon (-kshon), *nn.* effluence.

ĕff′ort, *n.* exertion; endeavour.

ĕffron′terў (-ŭn-), *n.* impudence.

ĕfful′gence, *n.* lustre, brightness. **ĕfful′gent**, *a.* bright, radiant.

ĕffūse′ (-z), *v.t.* pour forth. ~sĭon, *n.* outpouring, poem, &c. ~sĭve, *a.* demonstrative, gushing.

ĕft, *n.* newt.

ĕgg¹, *n.* spheroidal body produced by female of birds, &c., contain-ing germ of new individual.

ĕgg², *v.t.* incite, urge on.

ĕg′lantĭne (or -ĭn), *n.* sweet briar.

ĕg′ō, *n.* I; one's self.

ĕg′ōism, *n.* systematic selfishness; self-opinionatedness. ~ist, *n.*; ~ĭstĭc(al), *aa.*

ĕg′ōtism, *n.* practice of talking

about oneself; self-conceit. ~ist, *n.*; ~istic(al), *aa.*

ègrē'gious (-jus), *a.* notable, distinguished (now depreciatory).

ē'grèss, *n.* going out; way out.

è'grét (*or* ēg-), *n.* Lesser White Heron; down on thistle, &c.

Egyptian (ijǐp'shn), *a.* of Egypt. *n.* Egyptian native; gipsy.

Egyptól'ogў (ē-), *n.* study of Egyptian antiquities. ~gist, *n.*

eid'er (ī-), *n.* an Arctic duck. ~down, breast-feathers of eider; quilt stuffed with eiderdown.

eight (āt), *n.* one more than seven (8, VIII); crew of eight in rowing-boat. ~fold, *a.* eight times the number. eighth (ātth), *a.* & *n.*; eighth'ly, *adv.*

eight·een' (āt-), *n.* one more than seventeen (18, XVIII). ~th, *a.* & *n.*

eight'ў (āt-), *n.* eight times ten (80, LXXX). ~tieth, *a.* & *n.*

eirē'nĭcŏn (ĭr-), *n.* step tending to peace.

eisteddfod (āstĕdh'vŏd), *n.* congress of Welsh bards.

eith'er (īdh-, ē-), *a.* one or other of two. *pron.* each one.

èjăc'ūlāte, *v.t.* & *i.* (*-table*), utter suddenly, cry out. ~tion, ~tor, *nn.*; ~tory, *a.*

èjĕct', *v.t.* throw out, expel, emit. ~ion, ~ment, ~or, *nn.*

ĕk dŭm, *adv.* (Anglo-Ind.) at once, quickly.

ēke[1], *v.t.* (with *out*) supply the deficiencies of; prolong.

ēke[2], *adv.* (arch.) also.

èlăb'orate, *a.* (*-at*), minutely worked out; highly finished. *v.t.* work out in detail. ~tion, ~tor, *nn.*; ~tive, *a.*

‖ élan (ā'lahń), *n.* vivacity, dash.

ē'land, *n.* a S.-Afr. antelope.

èlápse', *v.i.* (of time) pass away.

èlăs'tíc (*or* -lah-), *a.* having power to resume normal shape; springy; buoyant; not inflexible. *n.* elastic cord or string; *elastic band worn as garter, &c. èlăstí'cítў (*or* ěl-), *n.*

èlāte', *a.* in high spirits; exultant;

proud. *v.t.* (*-table*), make elate. èlā'tion, *n.*

ěl'bow (-ō), *n.* bend of the arm; elbow-shaped bend, &c. *v.t.* thrust, jostle. ~grease, vigorous polishing, hard work.

ěld, *n.* old age; olden time.

ěl'der[1], *n.* a white-flowered tree. ~wine, from elder berries.

ěl'der[2], *a.* of greater age; senior. *n.* person of greater age; official in certain religious bodies.

ěl'derlў, *a.* growing old.

ěl'dest, *a.* first-born or oldest surviving (son, daughter, &c.).

El Dorado (ěldorahd'ō), *n.* (pl. *-os*), fictitious region rich in gold.

ěl'dritch, *a.* weird, hideous.

èlècămpāne', *n.* plant with bitter leaves and root; a sweetmeat.

èlěct', *v.t.* choose, pick out; choose by vote; choose for salvation. *a.* chosen; select.

èlěc'tion, *n.* choosing, esp. by vote.

èlèctioneer' (-shon-), *v.i.* busy oneself in political elections.

èlěc'tive, *a.* appointed by election; entitled to elect; *(of course of study) optional, chosen voluntarily.

èlěc'tor, *n.* one entitled to elect. ~al, *a.* ~ate, *n.* body of electors.

èlěc'trèss, *n.* female elector.

èlěc'tric, *a.* of, charged with, or capable of developing electricity. ~al, *a.* concerned with electricity. èlèctri'cian (-shn), *n.* one skilled in electricity.

èlèctri'cítў (*or* ěl-), *n.* condition of molecules or ether produced by chemical action, heat, or magnetism; study of this.

èlěc'trifў, èlěc'trize, *vv.t.* charge with electricity; convert (railways, transport, &c.) to electric working; startle, excite. ~fication, ~zation, *nn.*

èlěc'trō, *n.* & *v.t.* (colloq.) electroplate, electrotype.

èlěc'trō-, in comb. = of, by, or caused by electricity. ~cūte, *v.t.* execute (criminal) by electricity; ~cū'tion, *n.* èlěc'trŏde, *n.* either pole of galvanic battery. èlěctrodÿnăm'ícs, ~kĭnět'ícs, *nn.*

dynamics, kinetics, of electricity. ~lȳse (-z), v.t. decompose by galvanic action; ĕlĕctról'ўsis, n. this process. ~măg'nĕt, piece of soft iron surrounded by wire coil through which electricity has passed. ~măg'nĕtism, production of magnetism by electric current. ĕlĕctrŏp'athў, n. electrical treatment of disease. ~plāte, v.t. coat with silver by electrolysis; n. ware so coated. ~pŏs'itive (-z-), a. of positive electricity. ~scōpe, n. instrument indicating presence or quantity of electricity. ~stăt'ics, n. statics of electricity. ~tȳpe, n. copy in metal formed by deposition of copper on a mould by galvanic action; v.t. make copy thus.

ĕlĕc'trŏn, n. (Phys., Chem.) indivisible unit of the charge of negative electricity of an atom, rotating (in numbers constant for each element) about the positive nucleus of every atom. ~ic, a.

ĕlĕc'trum, n. alloy of silver and gold used by the ancients; (Mineral.) native argentiferous gold.

ĕlĕc'tuarў, n. medicinal powder, &c. mixed with honey.

ĕlĕēmŏs'ўnarў (or -z-), a. of or dependent on alms; charitable.

ĕl'ĕgance, n. grace, refinement.

ĕl'ĕgant, a. graceful, tasteful; of refined luxury. n. person with pretensions to taste and fashion.

ĕlēgī'ăc, a. suited to elegies, mournful. n. (pl.) elegiac verses.

ĕl'ĕgў, n. song of lamentation, esp. for the dead; poem in elegiac metre.

ĕl'ĕment, n. component part; unanalysable substance; any of the four elements—earth, water, air, fire; congenial surroundings; (pl.) rudiments of learning or of an art.

ĕlĕmĕn'tal, a. of or like the powers of nature; essential.

ĕlĕmĕn'tarў, a. rudimentary; unanalysable.

ĕl'ĕphant, n. quadruped with proboscis and ivory tusks. ĕlĕphăni'īne, a. clumsy, unwieldy.

ĕlĕphăn̄ti'asis, n. disease of skin causing it to resemble elephant's hide.

ĕl'ĕvāte, v.t. lift up, raise.

ĕlĕvā'tion, n. raising aloft; exaltation, dignity; height above given level.

ĕl'ĕvātor, n. that which elevates; lift; hoisting-machine; *warehouse for storing grain.

ĕlĕv'en, n. one more than ten (11, XI); side of eleven persons at cricket, &c. ĕlĕv'enth, a.

ĕlf, n. (pl. elves), a supernatural being; small or mischievous creature. ~ish, a. ~lock(s), tangled mass of hair.

ĕl'fin, n. of elves, elf-like. n. dwarf, child.

ĕli'cit, v.t. draw out.

ĕlīde', v.t. omit in pronunciation.

ĕl'igible, a. desirable, suitable. ĕligibil'itў, n.

ĕlim'ināte, v.t. remove, expel; set aside. ~tion, ~tor, nn.

ĕli'sion (-zhn), n. suppression of vowel or syllable in pronouncing, of passage in book, &c.

|| élite (ĕlēt'), n. the pick of.

ĕlix'ir (-er), n. alchemist's preparation designed to change metal into gold; sovereign remedy.

ĕlk, n. animal of the deer kind; kinds of deer and antelope.

ĕll, n. a measure of 45 inches.

ĕllipse', n. an oval figure.

ĕllip'sis, n. (pl. -pses, pr. -psēz), n. omission of words needed to complete sense. ĕllip'tic(al), aa.

ĕllip'soid, n. solid of which all plane sections through one axis are ellipses and through the other ellipses or circles.

ĕlm, n. tree with rough doubly-serrated leaves.

ĕlocū'tion (or ĕl-), n. mode or art of oral delivery. ~arў, a.; ~ist, n.

|| ĕloge (ĕlōzh'), n. discourse in honour of a deceased person.

ĕlō'gium, ĕl'ogў, nn. panegyric or eulogy; éloge.

ĕ'lŏngāte (-ngg-), v.t. lengthen, extend, draw out. ~tion, n.

élōpe', *v.i.* run away clandestinely ; abscond. ~ment, *n.*

el'oquence, *n.* fluent and powerful speech. él'oquent, *a.*

else, *adv.* besides ; instead ; otherwise ; if not. ~where, *adv.* in or to some other place.

élu'cidāte (-loo-), *v.t.* throw light on, explain. ~tion, ~tor, *nn.* ; ~tive, ~sory, *aa.*

élude' (-loo-), *v.t.* escape adroitly from ; avoid ; baffle.

élu'sion (-loozhn), *n.* an escape ; artifice. ~sive, ~sory, *aa.*

Elys'ium (lliz-), *n.* (Gk. Myth.) abode of the blessed after death ; (place of) ideal happiness. Elys'ian, *a.*

émā'ciāte (*or* -ā- ; -shī-), *v.t.* make lean, waste. ~tion, *n.*

em'anāte, *v.i.* issue, originate, proceed. ēmanā'tion, *n.* that which proceeds from a source. ~tive, *a.*

émān'cipāte, *v.t.* free from legal, social, or other restraint. ~tion, *n.* liberation from slavery, &c. ~tor, *n.* ; ~tory, *a.*

émas'culāte, *v.t.* (-āt), castrate ; enfeeble ; weaken by excisions. *a.* (-at), castrated ; effeminate. ~tion, *n.* ; ~tive, ~tory, *aa.*

émbalm' (-ahm), *v.t.* preserve (body) with spices ; preserve from oblivion ; make fragrant. ~ment, *n.*

émbānk', *v.t.* shut in by banks, stone structure, &c. ~ment, *n.*

émbárg'ō, *n.* (pl. -oes), order for bidding ships to enter or leave a port ; suspension of commerce.

émbárk', *v.t. & i.* put or go on board ship ; engage in enterprise. émbárkā'tion, *n.* embarking on ship.

émbā'rrass, *v.t.* encumber, esp. with debt ; perplex. ~ment, *n.*

ém'bassy, *n.* ambassador's function, office, or residence ; deputation.

émbat'tle, *v.t.* set in battle array ; furnish with battlements.

émbay', *v.t.* bring (vessel) into bay ; enclose as in bay. ~ment, *n.*

ómbéd', im~, *v.t.* fix in surrounding mass.

émbéll'ish, *v.t.* beautify, adorn ; enrich. ~ment, *n.*

ém'ber[1], *n.* (usu. pl.) small piece of fuel in dying fire.

ém'ber[2], *a.* E. days, days of fasting and prayer.

ém'ber[3], *n.* usu. ~-goose, ~-diver, an Orkney sea-fowl.

émbéz'zle, *v.t.* appropriate fraudulently. ~ment, *n.*

émbitt'er, *v.t.* make bitter ; aggravate ; exasperate. ~ment, *n.*

émblā'zon, *v.t.* adorn with figures of heraldry ; celebrate, extol.

ém'blēm, *n.* symbol, type ; device. ~ātic, ~ātical. ~ātic(al), *aa.*

émbŏd'y̆, *v.t.* (-iable), clothe (spirit) with body ; form into unit ; include. ~diment, *n.*

émbō'lden, *v.t.* encourage.

ém'bolism (-zm), *n.* obstruction of artery, &c. by clot of blood, &c., esp. as cause of paralysis.

‖ embonpoint (ahnbawnpwăn'), *n.* plumpness, usu. of women.

émbos'om (-ooz-), *v.t.* embrace.

émbŏss', *v.t.* carve or mould in relief. ~ment, *n.*

émbow'el, *v.t.* disembowel.

émbow'er, *v.t.* enclose in bower.

émbrāce', *v.t.* fold in the arms, clasp, enclose ; accept, adopt ; include. *n.* folding in the arms.

émbrā'sure (-zher, *also* émbrazhoor'), *n.* bevelling of wall at sides of window, &c. ; opening in parapet for gun.

ém'brocāte, *v.t.* bathe, foment. ~tion, *n.* liquid for rubbing limb, &c.

émbroid'er, *v.t.* ornament with needlework ; embellish.

émbroid'ery̆, *n.* embroidered work ; adventitious ornament.

émbroil', *v.t.* confuse, distract ; involve in hostility. ~ment, *n.*

ém'bryō, *n.* (pl. -os), unborn offspring ; thing in embryo. ~ŏl'ogy̆ ~logist, *nn.* ; ~ŏn'ic, *a.*

émênd', *v.t.* remove errors ; correct. ~ation, ~ator, *nn.* ; ~atory, *a.*

ém'erald, *n.* bright-green precious stone ; colour of emerald.

émérge', *v.i.* come up or out into

view; issue; appear; crop up. ~nce, n. emerging. ~nt, a.

émèr'gency, n. sudden juncture needing prompt action.

émé'ritus, a. E. professor, retired from service.

émèr'sion (-shn), n. emerging; re-appearance after an eclipse.

ém'erẏ, n. coarse corundum for polishing metal, &c.

émèt'ic, a. that causes vomiting. n. emetic medicine.

ém'ïgrant, a. emigrating. n. one who emigrates.

ém'ïgrate, v.i. & t. (-rable), go to settle in another country; assist to emigrate. ~tion, n.

ém'inence, n. recognized superiority; rising ground.

ém'inent, a. distinguished, notable. ~ly, adv. notably, decidedly.

émïr' (-ēr), n. Arab prince or governor. ~ate, n. district under an emir.

ém'issarẏ, n. one sent on (esp. odious or underhand) mission.

émï'ssion (-shn), n. act of giving out; thing given out. ~ive, a.

émït', v.t. give out, put forth.

émm'èt, n. (dial.) ant.

émöll'ient (-lye-), a. softening; suppling. n. emollient application.

émöl'ūment, n. (usu. in pl.) profit from employment; salary.

émō'tion, n. mental agitation or feeling; excited mental state.

émō'tional (-shon-), a. of the emotions, given to emotion.

émpán'el, v.t. enter on panel.

ém'peror, n. ruler of an empire.

ém'phasis, n. significant stress on word(s); vigour of expression.

ém'phasize, v.t. lay stress on.

émphàt'ic, a. forcible, strong; (of words) bearing the emphasis.

ém'pïre, n. supreme and wide dominion; territory of an emperor. ~ Day, May 24th.

émpïr'ic, n. relying on experiment, not on theory. n. empiric scientist, physician, &c.; quack. ~al, a.; ~ism, ~ist, nn.

émplàce'ment (-sm-), n. putting in position; platform for gun(s).

émplāne', v.i. & t. go or put on board aeroplane.

émploy', v.t. use (thing, time, energies, &c.); use services of; keep at work. n. service.

émployé, fem. ~ée (émploi'ē), émployee', nn. person employed for wages.

émploy'er, n. one who uses another's services.

émploy'ment, n. work; one's trade; business entrusted to one.

émpor'ium, n. centre of commerce; (vulg.) shop.

émpow'er, v.t. authorize; enable.

ém'press, n. wife of an emperor; female ruler of an empire.

émprïse' (-z), n. an enterprise.

émp'tẏ (-mt-), a. containing nothing; (colloq.) hungry; meaningless. n. empty truck, box, &c. v.t. & i. remove contents of; transfer; become empty; (of river) discharge itself.

émpur'ple, v.t. make purple.

émpȳrē'an, a. & n. (of the) highest heaven as sphere of fire or abode of God; (of) the sky. ~real, a.

ē'mū, n. Australian bird allied to the cassowary.

ém'ūlate, v.t. try to equal or excel; imitate. ~tion, ~tor, nn. ~tive, a. ém'ūlous, a. desirous of fame, &c.; zealously imitative of.

émul'sion (-shn), n. milky liquid with oily particles suspended in it. émul'sifẏ, v.t. make an emulsion of. ~sive, a.

énā'ble, v.t. empower; supply with means (to do).

énàct', v.t. ordain, decree; play (part). ~ment, n. law enacted.

énàm'el, n. glass-like coating on metal; any hard smooth coating; kinds of complexion-veneer; painting done on enamel. v.t. coat with enamel.

énàm'our (-mer), v.t. inspire with love; make fond of.

‖ en blóc (ahñ), in a lump.

éncaen'ia (-sēn-), n. dedication festival.

éncāge', v.t. put in a cage.

éncàmp', v.t. & i. settle in camp; lodge in tents. ~ment, n.

encāse′, *v.t.* surround as with a case. **~ment**, *n.*

encaus′tic, *a.* burnt in. *n.* encaustic painting.

enceinte (ahṅsäṅt′), *a.* pregnant. *n.* (fortif.) enclosure.

enchāin′, *v.t.* chain up; fetter.

enchant′ (-ah-), *v.t.* bewitch; delight. **~ment**, **~ress**, *nn.*

encir′cle, *v.t.* surround.

enclasp′ (-ah-), *v.t.* clasp.

enclāve′, *n.* territory surrounded by foreign dominion.

enclōse′ (-z), *v.t.* (*-sable*), surround, fence in; shut up; hem in.

enclō′sure (-zher), *n.* enclosing; enclosed land; thing enclosed.

encō′miast, *n.* panegyrist; composer of encomiums. **~ic**, *a.*

encō′mium, *n.* eulogy; formal or high-flown praise.

encom′pass (-ŭm-), *v.t.* shut in, surround, encircle.

encore (ŏngkōr′), *int.* again! once more! in the cry *encore*. *v.t. & i.* call for repetition.

encoun′ter, *v.i.* meet hostilely; meet with (person, obstacle, &c.). *n.* hostile or casual meeting.

encou′rage (-kŭ-), *v.t.* (*-geable*) make bold; urge; further, promote. **~ment**, *n.*

encroach′, *v.i.* intrude on others' territory, &c. **~ment**, *n.*

encrŭst′, *v.t. & i.* cover with or form a crust.

encŭm′ber, *v.t.* hamper, impede; burden with debt. **~brance**, *n.* burden, impediment; mortgage, &c. on property.

encyˊ′clic(al), *aa.* for wide circulation. *n.* Pope's e. letter.

encyˊclop(a)ed′ia (-pē-), *n.* (pl. *-as*), book of information on all branches of knowledge. **~ic**, *a.*; **~ist**, *n.*

end, *n.* limit; extreme point or part; conclusion; destruction; death; result; object. *v.t. & i.* bring or come to an end.

endā′nger (-j-), *v.t.* bring into danger.

endear′, *v.t.* make dear. **~ment**, *n.* act, &c. showing affection.

endeav′our (-dĕver), *v.i. & t.* try, strive. *n.* attempt, effort.

endēm′ic, *a.* regularly found among a people. *n.* e. disease.

end′ing, *n.* result, conclusion; end of word, verse, or story.

en′dive, *n.* curly-leaved chicory, used as salad.

end′less, *a.* unending, continual.

endō-, *pref.* within. **~car′diac**, *a.* pertaining to the endocardium. **~cardi′tis**, inflammation of the endocardium. **~car′dium**, lining membrane of the heart. **~carp**, inner layer of pericarp. **~crāne**, inner surface of skull. **~crīne**, secreting internally, ductless. **~derm**, inner layer of blastoderm. **~gen**, plant that develops wood in interior of stem. **endŏg′enous**, growing fruit from within. **~plasm**, **~sarc**, inner soft layer of protoplasm. **~scōpe**, instrument for viewing internal parts of body. **~sperm**, albumen enclosed with embryo in seeds. **~spore**, inner coat of spore; spore formed in a case.

endŏg′amy, *n.* custom of marrying only within the tribe. **~mous**, *a.*

endorse′, *v.t.* write on back of document, cheque, &c.; confirm. **~ment**, *n.*

endow′, *v.t.* give permanent income to; invest with powers, qualities, &c. **~ment**, *n.*

endūe′, *v.t.* (*-uable*), clothe; put on; endow with qualities, &c.

endūr′ance, *n.* power of enduring.

endūre′, *v.t. & i.* undergo; bear; last.

en′ema (pop. inē′-), *n.* injection of liquid, &c. into the rectum; the syringe used.

en′emy, *n.* hostile person, opponent; hostile force or ship. *a.* of or belonging to the enemy.

energet′ic, *a.* forcible; operative; vigorous; full of energy.

en′ergize, *v.t.* infuse energy into.

en′ergy, *n.* force, vigour, activity; capacity for work.

ener′vāte, *v.t.* deprive of vigour. **~tion**, *n.*

|| **enfant terrible** (ahṅ′fahṅ tērēbl′),

---

n. child who asks awkward questions, repeats talk, &c.

enfee'ble, *v.t.* make feeble. ~ment, *n.* weakness.

enfeoff' (-fĕf), *v.t.* invest with fief; convey. ~ment, *n.*

‖ **en fête** (ahn fāt), engaged in holiday-making.

enfilade', *n.* artillery fire sweeping a line from end to end. *v.t.* subject (troops, &c.) to enfilade.

enfold', *v.t.* wrap; embrace.

enforce', *v.t.* press, urge; compel observance of. ~ment, *n.*

enfran'chise (-z), *v.t.* (-sable). set free; give electoral franchise to. ~isement (-zm-), *n.*

engage' (-n-g-), *v.t.* (-geable). bind by contract or promise; pledge oneself; employ, occupy; bring or come into conflict. ~ment, *n.*

engen'der (-j-), *v.t.* give rise to.

en'gine (-j-), *n.* complex mechanical contrivance; locomotive; means, instrument. ~-driver, driver of locomotive.

engineer' (-j-), *n.* one who designs and constructs military works or works of public utility; one skilled in mechanical engineering work. *v.i. & t.* construct, manage, act, as engineer; (colloq.) contrive.

engir'd(le) (-n-g-), *vv.t.* surround as with a girdle.

Eng'lish (ĭngg-), *a.* of England. *n.* the English language.

engraft' (-ah-), *v.t.* insert; implant; incorporate; add.

engrain', *v.t.* make (dye) sink deeply in; also used fig.

engrave', *v.t.* (-vable). cut in lines on metal plate for printing; carve; impress deeply (on memory). engra'ving, *n.* copy of picture from engraved plate.

engross', *v.t.* write out in large letters or in legal form; monopolize; absorb. ~ment, *n.*

engulf', *v.t.* swallow up (usu. in pass.). ~ment, *n.*

enhance', *v.t.* (-ceable). heighten, intensify; exaggerate. ~ment, *n.*

enig'ma, *n.* riddle; puzzling person or thing. enigmat'ic(al), *aa.*

enjoin', *v.t.* prescribe; command.

enjoy', *v.t.* take delight in; have use of. ~able, *a.*; ~ment, *n.*

enkin'dle, *v.t.* set on fire.

enlace', *v.t.* encircle; enfold.

enlarge', *v.t. & i.* expand; grow larger; expatiate; reproduce on larger scale. ~ment, *n.*

enlight'en (-īt-), *v.t.* instruct; inform; shed light on. ~ment, *n.*

enlist', *v.t. & i.* engage, be engaged, for military service; get the support of. ~ment, *n.*

enli'ven, *v.t.* animate, inspirit, brighten. ~ment, *n.*

‖ **en masse** (ahn), all together.

enmesh', *v.t.* entangle as in a net.

en'mity, *n.* hatred, hostility.

enno'ble, *v.t.* make (person) a noble; make noble. ~ment, *n.*

ennui (ŏn'wē), *n.* feeling of boredom.

enor'mity, *n.* great wickedness; crime; deviation from right.

enor'mous, *a.* very large.

enough (-nŭf'), *a.* sufficient. *n.* as much or many as necessary. *adv.* to the necessary degree.

enounce', *v.t.* (-ceable). enunciate.

‖ **en passant** (ahn păs'ahn), *adv.* by the way.

enquire. See inquire.

‖ **en rapport** (ahn rapŏrr'), *adv.* in touch with.

enrage', *v.t.* make furious.

‖ **en rapport** (ahn rapŏrr'), *adv.* in touch with.

enrap'ture, *v.t.* delight intensely.

‖ **en règle** (ahn'rāgl), *adv.* in due form.

enrich', *v.t.* make rich. ~ment, *n.*

enrobe', *v.t.* put robe on.

enrol', *v.t.* (-ll-). insert name in list; incorporate as member; register deed; record. ~ment, *n.*

‖ **en route** (ahn rōōt), *adv.* on the way.

ensconce', *v.t.* establish safely.

‖ **ensemble** (ahnsahnbl'), *n.* thing viewed as a whole.

enshrine', *v.t.* (-nable). enclose as in shrine; cherish.

enshroud', *v.t.* cover completely.

en'sign (-īn), *n.* badge, emblem; banner, flag; (hist.) lowest commissioned officer in infantry; *(U.S. navy, ĕn'sīn) lowest commissioned officer.

ĕn'silage, n. storage in silo; fodder so stored.

ensile', v.t. put into silo.

ĕnslāve', v.t. (-vable), make a slave (often to habit). ~ment, n.

ĕnsnāre', v.t. (-rable), entrap.

ĕnsphēre', v.t. enclose (poet.).

ĕnsūe', v.i. & t. happen later; result from; (Bibl.) seek after.

ĕnsure' (-shoor'), v.t. (-rable), make sure or certain; secure.

ĕntăb'lature, n. the architrave, frieze, and cornice of a column.

ĕntail', v.t. settle landed estate on persons successively so that it cannot be bequeathed at pleasure; impose on; necessitate. n. such settlement; estate so secured.

ĕntăng'le (-nggl), v.t. catch in snare, &c.; involve in difficulties; make (thing) tangled; complicate. ~ment, n.

‖ entente (cordiale) (öntŏ'nt kŏr'diahl'), n. friendly understanding between States.

ĕn'ter, v.i. & t. go or come in; engage in; insert in book, &c.; give in name as competitor for, or for admission.

ĕntĕ'ric, a. of the intestines. n. enteric fever. ~ fever, typhoid.

ĕnteri'tis, n. bowel inflammation.

ĕn'terprise (-z), n. bold undertaking; readiness to engage in one.

ĕn'terprising, a. full of enterprise.

ĕntertain', v.t. receive as guest; amuse; harbour; keep in mind. ~ment, n. hospitality; amusement; public performance.

ĕnthral' (-awl), v.t. enslave; captivate. ~ment, n.

ĕnthrōne', v.t. place (king, bishop, &c.) on throne. ~ment, n.

ĕnthū'siăsm (-zĭ-), n. ardent zeal.

ĕnthūse', v.i. (colloq.) show enthusiasm.

ĕnthū'siăst (-zĭ-), n. person full of enthusiasm; visionary. ~ic, a.

ĕntīce', v.t. allure. ~ment, n.

ĕntīre', a. complete; not broken; not castrated; of one piece.

ĕntīre'ly (-īrlĭ), adv. wholly.

ĕntīre'ty (-īrtĭ), n. sum total.

ĕnti'tle, v.t. give book, &c. the title of; give a claim to.

ĕn'tĭty, n. thing with real existence.

ĕntomb' (-ōōm), v.t. place in tomb; serve as tomb for. ~ment, n.

ĕntomŏl'ogy, n. study of insects. ~gical, a.; ~gist, n.; ~gize, v.t.

‖ entourage (öntōōrahzh'), n. surroundings; attendant persons.

‖ entr'acte (ö'nträkt), n. interval between acts of a play.

ĕn'trails (-z), n.pl. inner parts.

ĕntrain', v.t. & i. put (troops, &c.) or get into a train.

ĕntrance'[1] (-ah-), v.t. throw into trance; overwhelm with joy, &c.

ĕn'trance[2], n. coming or going in; right of admission; door or passage for entrance.

ĕn'trant, n. one who enters room, profession, &c., or for race.

ĕntrăp', v.t. catch as in trap.

ĕntreat', v.t. ask earnestly; beg.

ĕntreat'y, n. earnest request.

entrée (ŏn'trā), n. right or privilege of admission; made dish.

ĕntrĕnch', v.t. surround with trench; also fig. ~ment, n.

‖ entrepôt (ö'ntrepō), n. mart.

‖ entre nous (öntre nōō), adv. between you and me.

‖ entresol (ö'ntresöl), n. low story between first and ground floor.

ĕntrŭst', v.t. charge with (duty, &c.); confide to (thing, secret, &c.).

ĕn'try, n. coming or going in; entrance; alley; entering; item entered.

ĕntwīne', v.t. interweave.

ĕnū'merāte, v.t. count; specify. ~tion, ~tor, nn.; ~tive, a.

ĕnūn'cĭāte (-shĭ-), v.t. state definitely; proclaim; pronounce. ~tion, ~tor, nn.; ~tive, a.

ĕnvĕl'op, v.t. wrap up, cover; surround (enemy). ~ment, n.

ĕn'velōpe (also ŏn-), n. cover of letter; wrapper, covering.

ĕnvĕn'om, v.t. put poison on or into; infuse venom into.

ĕn'viable, a. calculated to excite envy. ĕn'vious, a. full of envy.

ĕnvī'ron, v.t. form a ring round.

surround. ~ment, n. surrounding; surrounding objects or circumstances. énvir′ons (-z; or én′vironz), n.pl. district round town, &c.

énvi′sage (-z-), v.t. look in the face; view; contemplate.

én′voy, n. messenger; minister plenipotentiary; (also -oi) short final stanza of some poems.

én′vy, n. bitter contemplation of another's success; object of this. v.t. feel envy of.

énwráp′, v.t. wrap, enfold.

énzóöt′ic, a. & n. (disease) regularly affecting cattle, &c. in a particular district or at a particular season.

én′zyme, n. (Chem.) a chemical or unorganized ferment as distinguished from yeast and other living ferments.

éo′céne, a. (Geol.) of the lowest division of Tertiary strata.

éolith′ic, a. of the period preceding the palaeolithic age.

éozó′ic, a. (of strata) showing the earliest indications of animal life.

é′pact (or ép′-), n. number indicating excess of solar over lunar year.

ép′aulét(te) (-pol-), n. shoulderpiece of officer's uniform.

epergne (épérn′), n. centre ornament for dinner-table.

éphém′era (pl. -ras), ~ron (pl. -rons, -ra), n. insect living only a day; short-lived thing.

éphém′eral, a. short-lived, transitory. éphémerál′ity, n.

éph′od, n. Jewish priestly vestment.

éph′or, n. a Spartan magistrate.

ép′ic, a. narrating heroic deeds or embodying a nation's history; of heroic type or scale. n. epic poem. ~al, a.

ép′icéne, a. for or having the characteristics of both sexes.

ép′icüre, n. one who is dainty in eating or drinking. ép′icürism, n. such daintiness.

épicürē′an, a. devoted to refined sensuous enjoyment. n. such person. ~ism, n.

ép′icycle, n. circle with centre on circumference of a greater.

épidém′ic, a. (of disease, craze, &c.) prevalent for the time among community. n. such disease.

épidérm′is, n. outer layer of animal's skin, cuticle; plant's true skin below cuticle.

épigas′trium, n. part of abdomen above stomach. ~tric, a.

épiglott′is, n. cartilage at root of tongue, depressed in swallowing. ~tic, a.

ép′igram, n. short poem with witty ending; pointed saying. ~mát′ic, a.; ~matist, n.

ép′igraph (-ahf), n. inscription. ~y, n. study of epigraphs.

ép′ilepsy, n. disease in which person falls down unconscious, with spasms and foaming.

épilép′tic, a. of or subject to epilepsy. n. such person.

ép′ilogue (-g), n. concluding part of book, &c.; speech or short poem delivered at end of a play.

épiph′any, n. manifestation of Christ to the Magi.

ép′iphyte, n. plant growing on another; vegetable parasite on animal.

épis′copacy, n. government of church by bishops; the bishops.

épis′copal, a. of or governed by bishop(s). épiscopā′lian, a. of e. government or church; n. adherent of e. church. épis′copate, n. e. office, see; the bishops.

ép′isóde, n. incidental narrative or digression. épisód′ic(al), aa.

épis′tle (-sl), n. a letter; poem, &c. in form of letter.

épis′tolary, a. of or carried on by letters.

épis′toler (-stol-), n. (Eccl.) reader of the Epistle.

ép′itaph (-ahf), n. words inscribed on tomb.

épithalā′mium, n. (pl. -ums, -a), nuptial song or poem.

ép′ithet, n. adjective expressing quality or attribute; appellation.

épit′ome, n. summary, abstract. épit′omize, v.t.

ĕpĭzŏŏt′ĭc, a. & n. (disease) temporarily prevalent among animals.

ĕ′pŏch (or ĕ-; -k), n. beginning of an era; period marked by notable events.

ĕp′ōde, n. third division in lyric ode.

ĕpŏn′ȳmous, a. commemorated by adoption of the name.

ĕp′opee, n. epic poem.

ĕp′ŏs, n. early unwritten epic poetry; epic poem.

ē′quable, a. uniform, even; not easily disturbed. ~bility, n.

ē′qual, a. the same in number, size, merit, &c.; adequate; evenly matched. n. person, &c. equal to another. v.t. be equal to.

ēqual′itȳ (-ŏl-), n. being equal.

ē′qualize, v.t. make equal. v.i. (in games) reach opponent's score. ~zation, n.

ēquanĭm′itȳ, n. composure, calm.

ēquāte′, v.t. state equality of; treat as equivalent.

ēquā′tion, n. making equal, balancing; (Math.) statement of equality. ~al, a.

ēquā′tor, n. a great circle of the earth, equidistant from poles. ēquātŏr′ial, a. of or near the e.

ĕq′uerrȳ, n. officer of prince, &c. in charge of horses; an officer of British royal household.

ēqŭes′trian, a. of horseriding. n. (fem. -iĕnne′), rider or performer on horse.

ēquĭang′ular (-ngg-), a. having equal angles.

ēquĭdis′tant, a. at equal distances.

ēquĭlăt′eral, a. having all sides equal.

ĕq′uilĭbrāte, v.t. & i. balance; counterpoise. ~tion, n.

ēquĭlĭb′rium, n. state of balance; mental balance.

ēquĭmŭl′tĭple, n. number having common factor with another.

ē′quine, a. of or like a horse.

ēquĭnŏc′tial (or ĕ-; -shal), a. of, or happening at or near, the equinox. n. equinoctial line; (pl.) equinoctial gales.

ē′quĭnŏx, n. time at which sun crosses equator and day and night are equal.

ēquĭp′, v.t. supply with requisites; dress for journey. ēq′uipage, n. carriage, horses, and attendants; requisites, outfit. ~ment, n. equipage; soldier's accoutrements.

ē′quipoise (-z), n. equilibrium; counterbalancing weight. v.t. counterbalance; hold in suspense.

ēquĭpŏll′ent, a. equal in power, force, &c. ~nce, n.

ēq′uitable, a. fair, just.

ēquĭtā′tion, n. riding.

ĕq′uitȳ, n. fairness; principles of justice supplementing law.

ēquĭv′alent, a. equal in value; corresponding. n. equivalent amount, &c. ~nce, ~ncȳ, nn.

ēquĭv′ocal, a. of double or doubtful meaning; dubious. ēquĭvocāl′itȳ, n. ~ate, v.i. use words ambiguously. ~ation, ~ator, nn.

ē′quivŏque (or ĕ-; -k), ~ōke, n. a pun; ambiguity.

ēr′a, n. system of chronology starting from particular period.

ĕrăd′ĭcāte, v.t. root out, extirpate.

ērāse′ (-z), v.t. rub out, obliterate.

Ērăs′tian (ĭ-), a. & n. (adherent) of the doctrine of subordinating ecclesiastical to secular power. ~ism, n.

ērā′sure (-zher), n. rubbing out.

ere (âr), prep. & conj. before; sooner than. ~while, adv. of old.

ērĕct′, a. upright, vertical. v.t. make erect; build, form. ērĕc′tile (or -ĭl), a. that can be erected. ~ion, ~tor, nn.

ē′rēmite, n. hermit. ~it′ic, a.

|| ĕrg′ō, adv. (usu. joc.) therefore.

ĕrg′ot, n. a disease of rye, &c. ~ism, n. disease caused by bread of flour so affected.

E′rin (ē-), n. (poet.) Ireland.

ĕris′tic, a. controversial; aiming at victory rather than truth.

ĕrm′ine, n. animal of weasel kind; its fur.

ĕrn, n. the golden eagle.

ērōde′, v.t. gnaw away; wear out.

ērō′sion (-zhn), n. ~ive, a.

ērŏt′ĭc, a. of love; amatory.

mãte, mēte, mīte, mōte, mūte, mōōt; răck, rĕck, rick, rŏck, rŭck, rōōk.

ĕrr, *v.i.* make mistakes ; be incorrect ; sin.

ĕ'rrand, *n.* short journey with a message, commission, &c. **~boy**, one employed on errands.

ĕ'rrancy̆, *n.* erring state or conduct.

ĕ'rrant, *a.* roaming in quest of adventure ; itinerant ; erring. **~ry̆**, *n.* condition, conduct, &c. of knight errant.

ĕrrăt'ic, *a.* uncertain in movement, conduct, opinion, &c.

ĕrrā'tum, *n.* (pl. *-ta*), error in printing, &c.

ĕrrō'neŏus, *a.* incorrect.

ĕ'rror, *n.* mistake ; wrong opinion ; transgression.

Erse (ĕrs), *a.* & *n.* Irish form of Celtic.

ĕrst(while), *adv.* formerly.

ĕrubĕs'cent (-rōō-), *a.* reddening.

ĕrŭctā'tion, *n.* belching.

ĕ'rudite (-rōō-), *a.* learned.

ĕrudi'tion (-rōō-), *n.* learning.

ĕrŭpt', *v.i.* break out. **~ion**, *n.* outbreak (of volcano, anger, &c.) ; rash, pimples. **~ive**, *a.* bursting forth.

ĕry̆sip'elas, *n.* a disease producing red colour on skin.

ĕscalāde', *n.* scaling of walls with ladders.

ĕs'calātor, *n.* moving staircase.

ĕscapāde', *n.* flighty piece of conduct.

ĕscāpe', *v.i.* & *t.* get free ; find a way out ; elude, avoid. *n.* escaping ; leakage.

ĕscāpe'ment (-pm-), *n.* mechanism regulating motion of watch, &c.

ĕscarp', *n.* steep bank under rampart. **~ment**, *n.*

ĕschatŏl'ŏgy̆ (-k-), *n.* doctrine of death and judgement.

ĕscheat', *n.* lapse of property to crown, &c. ; property so lapsing. *v.t.* & *i.* confiscate ; revert by e.

ĕschew' (-ŏŏ), *v.t.* abstain from.

ĕscort', *n.* (ĕs'kŏrt), *n.* body of armed men as guard ; person accompanying another as protection. *v.t.* (ĭskŏrt'), act as escort.

ĕs'critoire (-twahr), *n.* writing-desk with drawers, &c.

ĕs'cŭlent, *a.* fit for food. *n.* esculent thing.

ĕscŭtch'eon (-chon), *n.* shield with armorial bearings ; pivoted key-hole cover.

Eskimo (ĕskĭmō'), *n.* (pl. *-os*, pr. -ōz), one of a race in north polar regions.

ĕsŏtĕ'ric, *a.* meant for the initiated ; private, confidential.

ĕspăl'ier, *n.* lattice-work for tree, &c. ; tree trained on espalier.

ĕspărt'ō, *n.* kind of grass.

ĕspē'cial (-shal), *a.* chief ; more than ordinary ; particular.

ĕspē'cially̆ (-sha-), *adv.* chiefly ; more than in other cases.

Esperăn'tō (ĕ-), *n.* an artificial universal language.

ĕspī'al, *n.* espying ; spying.

ĕs'pionage (-nahzh), *n.* use of spies.

ĕsplanāde', *n.* level space, esp. one used as promenade.

ĕspous'al (-zl), *n.* espousing ; (usu. pl.) marriage, betrothal.

ĕspouse' (-z), *v.t.* (*-sable*), marry ; support (cause).

‖ **ĕsprit'** (-rē), *n.* sprightliness, wit. **~ de corps** (de kōr), regard for a body one belongs to.

ĕspy̆', *v.t.* catch sight of.

ĕsquire', *n.* (abbr. *Esq.*), title of courtesy ; (arch.) squire.

essay, *n.* (ĕs'ā), literary composition ; attempt. *v.t.* (ĕsā'), attempt ; test. **ĕss'ay̆ist**, *n.* essay-writer.

ĕss'ence, *n.* an existence or entity ; indispensable quality or element ; perfume.

ĕssĕn'tial (-shl), *a.* of or constituting a thing's essence. *n.* indispensable element. **~ity̆**, *n.*

ĕstăb'lish, *v.t.* set up ; settle ; place beyond dispute.

ĕstăb'lishment, *n.* establishing ; established church ; staff ; household ; house of business.

ĕstāte', *n.* landed property or movables ; one's assets and liabilities.

ĕstēem', *v.t.* think highly of ; consider. *n.* favourable opinion.

ĕs'timable, *a.* worthy of esteem.

ĕs'timate, *n.* (-ĭt), approximate

---

judgement of value, &c.; price quoted for specified work. *v.t.* (-āt), form an estimate of. ~tion, *n.* judgement; opinion; esteem. ~tor, *n.*

estŏp', *v.t.* (Law) bar, preclude. **estŏpp'age**, *n.* **estŏpp'el**, *n.* the being precluded from a course by previous action of one's own.

estrade' (-ahd), *n.* low platform.

estrānge' (-j), *v.t.* alienate person from another. ~ment, *n.*

estreat', *v.t.* take out record of (fine, &c.) and return it to Court of Exchequer to be prosecuted. *n.* copy of such record.

ĕs'tūarÿ, *n.* tidal mouth of river.

ĕsūr'ient, *a.* hungry; starveling.

ĕt cĕt'era (abbr. *etc.*, *&c.*), *phr.* and the rest; and so on.

ĕtch, *v.t. & i.* reproduce (picture, &c.) by engraving metal plate, &c. with acid, &c.; practise this art. **ĕtch'ing**, *n.* art of engraving thus; copy from plate.

ĕtĕrn'al, *a.* that always (has existed and) will exist; constant. **ĕtĕrn'(al)ize**, *vt.*

ĕtĕrn'itÿ, *n.* being eternal; infinite time; future life.

Etēsian (tēzh'an), *a.* ~ winds, NW. wind in Mediterranean for about 40 days in summer.

ē'ther, *n.* clear sky; upper air; a medium assumed to permeate space; volatile liquid used as anaesthetic.

ēthēr'ēal, ~ial, *a.* light, airy; heavenly. ~ăl'ity, *n.*; ~ization, *n.*; ~ize, *v.t.*

ē'therīze, *v.t.* put (patient) under ether. ~ization, *n.*

ĕth'ic, **ĕth'ical**, *aa.* of ethics.

ĕth'ics, *n.pl.* (rarely, sing.) science of morals; moral principles.

ĕth'nic(al), *aa.* of race; heathen.

ĕthnŏg'raphÿ, *n.* description of races of men. **ĕthnŏgráph'ic(al)**, *aa.*

ĕthnŏl'ogÿ, *n.* science of races. **ĕthnŏlō'gic(al)**, *aa.*

ē'thŏs, *n.* characteristic spirit of community, people, or system.

ē'tiolāte, *v.t.* (*-table*), make pale by

excluding light; give sickly hue to. ~tion, *n.*

ĕtiquette' (-kĕt), *n.* conventional rules of manners; unwritten code of professional conduct.

ĕt'na, *n.* small spirit-lamp and boiler in one piece.

ĕtui' (-wē), **ĕtwee'**, *n.* case for needles, &c.

ĕtÿmŏl'ogize, *v.t. & i.* trace the etymology of; study etymology. ~ist, *n.*

ĕtÿmŏl'ogÿ, *n.* (account of) word's formation and sense-development. **ĕtÿmŏlō'gical**, *a.*

ĕt'ÿmŏn, *n.* primary word whence another is derived.

eucalýp'tus, *n.* (pl. *-tuses*), kinds of plant, esp. Australian gum tree. ~ oil, a disinfectant.

euc'harist (-k-), *n.* the sacrament of the Lord's Supper. ~ic, *a.*

eu'chre (-ker), *n.* a card-game. *v.t.* gain advantage over.

Eu'clid, *n.* (pop.) geometry as a science or subject; (mod.) the geometry of ordinary experience, accepting Euclid's axioms as indisputable.

eugĕn'ic, *a.* of the production of fine offspring. *n.pl.* science of this. **eu'genist**, *n.*

eul'ogize, *v.t.* extol, praise highly. **eul'ogist**, *n.*; eulogist'ic, *a.*

eul'ogÿ, *n.* speech or writing in praise of person; praise.

eun'uch (-k), *n.* castrated person.

eupĕp'tic, *a.* having good digestion.

euph'ĕmism, *n.* substitution of mild for blunt expression; such substitute. ~ist'ic, *a.*

euphō'nium, *n.* bass saxhorn.

euph'onÿ, *n.* pleasantness or smoothness of sounds, esp. in words. **euphŏn'ic**, **euphō'nious**, *aa.*; euph'onize, *v.t.*

euph'rasÿ, *n.* the plant eyebright.

euph'üism, *n.* high-flown style of writing. ~ist, *n.*

Eurāsian (ūrāsh'an), *a.* of mixed European and Asiatic (esp. Indian) parentage; of or pertaining to Europe and Asia considered as one continent. *n.* Eurasian person.

---

eurē'ka (ūr-), *int.* I have found it.

eurhȳth'mic, *a.* in or of harmonious proportion (esp. in architecture). eurhȳth'mics, *n.pl.* harmony of bodily movement, esp. as developed with the aid of music into a system used in education.

eu'sŏl, *n.* a solution of hypochlorous acid, an antiseptic.

euthanā'sia (-z-, -s-), *n.* gentle and easy death.

evăc'ūāte, *v.t.* (-*uable*), make empty, clear; withdraw from. ~tion, *n.*

evāde', *v.t.* (-*dable*), escape from, avoid; elude, baffle.

evă'lūāte, *v.t.* find, state, the number or amount of. ~tion, *n.*

evanĕsce', *v.i.* fade from sight; disappear. evanĕs'cence, *n.* ~cent, *a.* quickly fading.

evăn'gel (-j-), *n.* the Gospel; political or other creed.

evăngĕl'ic(al) (-j-), *aa.* of or according to the Gospel teaching; (usu. -*ical*) of the Protestant or Low Church school. *n.* member of evangelical school. ~alism, *n.* doctrine of evangelical school.

evăn'gelist (-j-), *n.* writer of any of the four Gospels; preacher of the Gospel; mission-worker; revivalist. ~ism, *n.* preaching of the Gospel; evangelicalism. ~istic, *a.*

evăn'gelīze (-j-), *v.t.* preach the Gospel to. ~zation, *n.*

evăp'orāte, *v.t. & i.* turn into vapour; exhale moisture. ~tive, *a.*; ~tion, ~tor, *nn.*

evā'sion (-zhon), *n.* act or means of evading; shuffling excuse. evā'sive, *a.* elusive.

eve, *n.* evening or day before a festival, &c.; time just before event; evening.

ē'ven¹, *n.* evening. ~song, Evening Prayer. ~tide, evening.

ē'ven², *a.* level, smooth; uniform; equal; equable, calm; divisible by 2. *v.t.* make equal; treat as equal. *adv.* neither more nor less than; simply; notwithstanding.

ēve'ning (-vn-), *n.* close of day, esp. sunset to bedtime.

evĕnt', *n.* occurrence of a thing;

item of programme, esp. in sports; result; happening.

evĕnt'ful, *a.* full of incidents.

even'tūal, *a.* happening under certain conditions; final.

evĕntūal'itў, *n.* possible event.

even'tūāte, *v.i.* turn out; end; *happen, come to pass.

ev'er, *adv.* at all times; always; at any time; *ever so* (colloq.) very.

ev'ergreen, *a.* always green or fresh. *n.* such tree or shrub.

everlas'ting (-ah-), *a.* lasting for ever; perpetual. *n.* eternity; flower retaining colour when dried.

evermôre', *adv.* for ever, always.

ev'erў (-vr-), *a.* each one of all. ~body, *pron.* every person. ~day, *a.* occurring every day; ordinary. ~one, *pron.* everybody. ~thing, *pron.* all things. ~where, *adv.* in every place.

evict', *v.t.* expel by legal process. ~ion, *n.* dispossession. ~or, *n.*

ev'idence, *n.* indication, sign; facts available as proof. *v.t.* be evidence of; indicate.

ev'ident, *a.* obvious, manifest.

ēvidĕn'tial (-shal), -iarў, *aa.* relating to or furnishing evidence.

ē'vil (-vl, -vīl), *a.* bad, harmful. *n.* evil thing; sin; harm. *adv.* in evil manner. ~doer, *n.* sinner.

evince', *v.t.* show, indicate.

evis'cerāte, *v.t.* disembowel.

evocā'tion (or ĕ-), *n.* act of calling out. evŏc'atorў, *a.*

evōke', *v.t.* call up (feelings, &c.).

evolū'tion (or ĕ-; -lōō-), *n.* evolving; origination of species by development from earlier forms; change in disposition of troops or ships. ~al, ~arў, *aa.*; ~ism, ~ist, *nn.*

evŏlve', *v.t. & i.* (-*vable*), unfold, open out; set forth in order; develop by natural process.

evŭl'sion, *n.* forcible extraction.

ewe (ū), *n.* female sheep.

ew'er, *n.* pitcher; water-jug.

exă'cerbāte, *v.t.* aggravate; irritate. ~tion, *n.*

exăct' (-gz-), *a.* precise, accurate, strictly correct. *v.t.* enforce payment of (fees, obedience, &c.).

exăc'tion (-gz-). *n.* exacting ; illegal or exorbitant demand.

exăc'titūde (-gz-). *n.* exactness.

exăct'ly (-gz-), *adv.* quite so.

exa'ggeràte (ĭgzăj-), *v.t.* carry beyond truth ; overstate. ~**tion,** ~**tor,** *nn.* ~**tive,** *a.*

exalt' (ĭgzawlt'), *v.t.* raise in rank, power, &c. ; praise, extol.

exalta'tion (-awl-). *n.* elevation, raising on high ; elation.

exămĭna'tion (-gz-). *n.* minute inspection ; testing of knowledge or ability by questions.

exăm'ine (-gz-), *v.t. & i.* (-nable), investigate or inquire into ; test proficiency of (pupils, &c.) by questions. **exăminee', exăm'iner** (-gz-), *nn.*

exăm'ple (ĭgzah-). *n.* thing illustrating general rule ; model, pattern ; specimen ; precedent.

ĕx'ärch (-k), *n.* (Byzantine empire) governor of distant province ; (Eastern Ch.) patriarch, bishop. ~**ate,** *n.* office, province, of exarch.

exăs'peràte (-gz-), *v.t.* (-rable), irritate (person) ; (*p.p.*) angry at or irritated by ; aggravate (pain, &c.). ~**tion,** ~**tor,** *nn.*

‖ **ĕx cathĕd'rā,** *adv. & a.* authoritatively (lit. from the chair).

ĕx'cavàte, *v.t.* (-vable), hollow out ; remove soil by digging. ~**tion,** ~**tor,** *nn.*

exceed', *v.t. & i.* be greater than, go beyond ; be pre-eminent.

exceed'ingly, *adv.* very.

excĕl', *v.t. & i.* surpass ; be preeminent.

ĕx'cellence, *n.* great merit.

ĕx'cellency, *n.* title of ambassadors, governors, &c.

ĕx'cellent, *a.* very good.

excĕl'sior, *int.* higher ! *n.* soft shavings of wood for stuffing, &c.

excĕpt', *v.t. & i.* exclude from general statement, &c. ; make objection against. *prep.* (*excepting* is also used) not including ; but. *conj.* unless.

excĕp'tion, *n.* excepting ; thing or case excepted ; objection.

excĕp'tionable (-shon-), *a.* open to exception.

excĕp'tional (-shon-), *a.* forming an exception ; unusual.

excĕrpt', *v.t.* extract, quote (passage from book, &c.). *n.* (also ĕk's-), such passage. ~**ion,** *n.*

excĕss', *n.* fact of exceeding ; amount by which thing exceeds ; unreasonable indulgence. ~**ive,**a.

exchānge', *n.* giving one thing and receiving another in its place ; mode of settling debts without use of money ; building where merchants assemble for trade. *v.t. & i.* give in exchange ; take back in exchange ; interchange.

exchā'ngeable (-jabl), *a.* that may be exchanged. ~**bility,** *n.*

exchĕq'uer (-ker), *n.* national treasury ; money of private persons. ~**bill,** bill of credit issued by authority of parliament.

excīse'¹ (-z), *n.* duty charged on certain home goods ; tax on licences to pursue certain trades. &c. *v.t.* make person pay excise. ~**man,** officer collecting excise and enforcing excise laws.

excī'sable, *a.* liable to excise.

excīse'² (-z), *v.t.* cut out or away. **excī'sion** (-zhon), *n.*

excī'table, *a.* capable of being excited. ~**bility,** *n.*

ĕx'citant, *a. & n.* stimulant.

excĭta'tion, *n.* exciting, rousing ; stimulation. ~**tive,** ~**tory,** *aa.*

excīte', *v.t.* set in motion ; stir up ; stimulate to activity ; move to strong emotion.

excīte'ment (-tm-), *n.* agitation ; excited state of mind.

exclaim', *v.i. & t.* cry out, esp. in anger, surprise, &c.

exclama'tion, *n.* vehement outcry ; clamour. **exclăm'atory,** *a.*

exclūde' (-lŏŏd), *v.t.* shut out ; make impossible, preclude.

exclū'sion (-lŏŏzhn), *n.* act of shutting out or rejecting.

exclū'sive (-lŏŏ-), *a.* excluding ; not inclusive ; (of society, &c.) disposed to exclude outsiders.

ĕxcō'gĭtàte, *v.t.* think out, devise. ~**tion,** ~**tor,** *nn.*

excommŭ'nĭcāte, v.t. cut off from sacraments or communication with the Church. ~tion, ~tor, nn.; ~tive, ~tory, aa.

excō'rĭāte, v.t. strip, peel off (skin). ~tion, n.

ex'crément, n. waste matter discharged from bowels; dung.

excres'cence, n. abnormal or morbid outgrowth.

excres'cent, a. redundant.

excrēte', v.t. separate and expel from system. ~tion, n.; ~tive, ~tory, aa.

excru'ciāte (-krōōshĭ-), v.t. pain acutely; torture. ~tion, n.

ex'culpāte, v.t. (-table), clear from imputation. ~tion, n.; ~tory, a.

excŭr'sion (-shon), n. short journey or trip, taken for pleasure. ~ist, n. member of excursion party.

excŭr'sive, a. digressive.

excŭr'sus, n. (pl. -uses) discussion of special point in book.

excūse', v.t. (-z), (-sable), lessen blame; forgive; grant exemption to. n. (-s), apology; exculpation. excū'satory, a.

ex'eāt, n. leave of absence.

ex'ecrable, a. abominable.

ex'ecrāte, v.t. & i. express or feel abhorrence for; utter curses. ~tion, n.; ~tory, a. & n.

exĕc'ūtant (-gz-), n. performer, esp. of music.

ex'ecūte, v.t. (-table), carry out, perform; put to death.

execū'tion, n. executing; skill in performing music; destructive work; seizure of goods for debt; capital punishment. ~er, n. one who executes criminals.

exĕc'ūtive (-gz-), a. concerned with execution esp. of laws and sentences. n. executive branch of government of a society. **the E~**, Governor of a State, President of U.S.

exĕc'ūtor (-gz-), n. person appointed by testator to execute his will. ~trix (pl. -trīcēs), female executor. exĕcūtŏr'ial, a.

exēgē'sis, n. exposition, esp. of Scripture. exēgĕt'ĭc(al), aa.

exēm'plar (-gz-), n. model; type.

exēm'plarẏ (-gz-), a. fit to be imitated; serving as an example.

exēm'plify (-gz-), v.t. (-fiable), give or be an example of. ~fĭcation, n.

exēmpt' (-gz-), a. free (from taxation, disease, &c.). v.t. make exempt.

exēmp'tion, n. being exempt.

ex'ĕquies (-kwiz), n.pl. funeral rites.

ex'ercīse (-z), n. employment of faculties, &c.; practice; use of limbs in walking, &c.; task set for bodily or mental training; *formal programme of events. v.t. & i. use; give exercise to; take exercise; perplex, worry.

exĕrt' (-gz-), v.t. exercise; bring to bear; put forth. ~ion, n.

exfō'lĭāte, v.i. come off in scales or layers. ~tion, n.

exhalā'tion (ĕksa-), n. evaporation; puff of breath; effluvium.

exhāle', v.t. & i. give off, be given off, in vapour; breathe out.

exhaust' (igzawst-), v.t. draw off; consume, use up; empty of contents; tire out. n. passage for exit of used steam or motive fluid from engine cylinder; process of exhausting air in vessel. ~ible, a.; ~ibility, ~ion, nn.

exhaus'tive (igzaw-), a. tending to exhaust; comprehensive.

exhib'it (igzĭ-), v.t. display; manifest; show publicly. n. thing exhibited.

exhibĭ'tion (ĕksĭ-), n. display; public show; allowance to students. ~er, n. student holding an exhibition. exhib'itor (igzĭ-), n. one who exhibits in show, &c.

exhil'arāte (igzĭ-), v.t. (-rable), enliven, make cheerful. ~tion, n.

exhort' (igzŏrt'), v.t. admonish earnestly; urge to action. exhortā'tion (ĕksŏr-), n.; exhort'ative, ~atory (igzŏr-), aa.

exhūme', v.t. (-mable), disinter. ~mation, n. disinterment.

ex'igence, ~encẏ (ŭ-), nn. urgent need; (pl. -cies) pressing needs.

ex'igent, a. urgent; exacting.

ex'igible, a. that may be exacted.

exig′uous, *a.* scanty. small,
slender. ˘xĭgŭ′ĭtŭ, *n.*

ex′ile, *n.* penal banishment; long
absence from one's country, &c.;
person in exile. *v.t.* banish.

exist′ (-gz-), *v.i.* be, have being;
live, sustain life. ~ent, *a.*

exis′tence (-ēns), *n.* fact, mode, of
living; all that exists.

ex′it², *n.* going out; way out; departure; death.

‖ ex′it², *v.i.* (pl. *exeunt,* pr. -lŭnt).
(stage direction) goes off stage.

‖ ex li′bris, *n.* book-plate.

ex′odus, *n.* a departure.

‖ ex offi′cio (-shĭō), *adv.* & *a.* in
virtue of one's office.

ex′ogamy, *n.* custom compelling
a man to marry outside his tribe.
&ebreve;x&obreve;g′amous, *a.*

exorb′itant (-gz-), *a.* grossly excessive; extravagant. ~nce, *n.*

ex′orcize, *v.t.* expel (evil spirit) by
invocation, &c.; clear of spirits
thus. ~ism, ~ist, *nn.*

exord′ium, *n.* (pl. *-iums, -ia*), introductory part of discourse or
treatise. exord′ial, *a.*

exote′ric, *a.* intelligible to outsiders; ordinary, popular.

exot′ic (-gz-), *a.* introduced from
abroad. *n.* exotic plant, &c.

expand′, *v.t.* & *i.* spread out; develop; increase; become genial.

expanse′, *n.* wide area or extent
of land, space, &c. ~sible, *a.*;
~sibility, ~sion, *nn.*

expan′sive, *a.* able or tending to
expand; extensive; genial.

‖ ex part′e, *adv.* & *a.* from or on
behalf of one side only.

expa′tiate (-shĭ-), *v.i.* speak or
write copiously. ~tion, *n.*

expat′riate (*or* -pā-), *v.t.* (-*iable*),
banish. ~tion, *n.*

expect′, *v.t.* reckon on; anticipate;
look for; suppose.

expec′tant, *a.* expecting; looking
for. *n.* one who expects office, &c.
~ncy, *n.*

expecta′tion, *n.* anticipation;
what one expects; probability;
(pl.) prospects of inheritance.

expec′torate, *v.t.* & *i.* cough or spit
out from chest or lungs. ~tion,
~tor, *nn.*

expe′dient, *a.* suitable, advisable;
more politic than just. *n.* contrivance, device. ~nce, ~ncy, *nn.*

ex′pedite, *v.t.* help on, facilitate,
the progress of; dispatch.

expedi′tion, *n.* promptness, dispatch; (men, fleet, sent on)
journey or voyage for some
definite purpose. ~ary, *a.* (to be)
employed on an expedition.

expedi′tious (-shŭs), *a.* done with
or marked by expedition.

expel′, *v.t.* throw out; eject.

expend′, *v.t.* spend (money, time,
care); use up, consume.

expen′diture, *n.* expending (of
money, &c.); amount expended.

expense′, *n.* cost, charge; (pl.) outlay in executing commission, &c.

expen′sive, *a.* costly.

expe′rience, *n.* knowledge based
on personal observation or contact; incident that affects one.
v.t. find by experience; suffer,
undergo.

expe′rienced (-st), *a.* having had
much experience; knowing.

expe′riment, *n.* (-ent) procedure
tried on the chance of success,
or as a test. *v.i.* (-&ebreve;nt) make an
experiment. ~ation, *n.*

experimen′tal, *a.* based on or done
by way of experiment. ~ist, *n.*;
~ize, *v.i.* try experiments.

expert′, *a.* (ĭkspert′), practised,
skilful. *n.* (ĕk′spert), person expert in subject.

ex′piate, *v.t.* pay the penalty of,
make amends for (sin). ~tion,
~tor, *nn.*; ~tory, *a.*

expire′, *v.i.* & *t.* breathe out; die;
die out; come to an end. expira′-
a′tion, *n.*; expir′atory, *a.*

expir′y, *n.* termination.

explain′, *v.t.* make known; make
intelligible; account for.

explana′tion, *n.* statement or circumstance that explains.

explan′atory, *a.* serving to explain.

ex′pletive (*or* ĭksplē′-), *a.* serving
to fill out sentence, &c. *n.* exple-
tive word, esp. oath.

---

ah, awl, oil, boor, cow, dowry; chin, go, bang, so, ship, thin; dh, as th(en).

ex′plicable, *a.* explainable.

ex′plicate, *v.t.* develop (idea, &c.). ~**tive**, ~**tory**, *aa.* explanatory.

expli′cit, *a.* expressly stated; definite; outspoken.

explōde′, *v.t. & i.* (-*dable*), discredit; (cause to) go off with loud noise.

exploit, *n.* (ĕks′ploit), brilliant feat. *v.t.* (ĭksploit′), work (mine, &c.); utilize for one's own ends. ~**ation**, *n.*

explōre′, *v.t.* (-*rable*), examine (country, &c.) by going through it; examine by touch; inquire into. ~**ration**, *n.*; ~**ative**, ~**atory**, *aa.*

explō′sion (-zhn), *n.* going off with loud noise; outbreak.

explō′sive, *a.* tending to explode. *n.* explosive agent or material.

expō′nent, *n.* person who explains or interprets; type, representative; algebraic symbol.

export, *v.t.* (ĭksport′), send goods to another country. *n.* (ĕks′-), exported article; (usu. pl.) amount exported. ~**ation**, *n.*

expōse′ (-z), *v.t.* (-*sable*), leave unprotected; subject to risk, criticism, &c.; exhibit for sale; disclose, unmask.

‖ **exposé** (ĕkspō′zā), *n.* statement of facts; showing up.

exposi′tion (-z-), *n.* description, explanation; exhibition of goods, &c. **expŏs′itor**, *n.*; ~**tory**, *a.*

‖ **ex post fac′tō**, *a.* retrospective.

expŏs′tūlāte, *v.i.* make (esp. friendly) remonstrance. ~**tion**, ~**tor**, *nn.*; ~**tory**, *a.*

expō′sure (-zher), *n.* exposing, being exposed; unmasking.

expound′, *v.t.* set forth in detail; explain, interpret.

express′, *v.t.* represent in words, make known; squeeze out; *not* send by express. *a.* definitely stated, explicit; meant, done, &c. for special purpose. *n.* express train, messenger; *express agent, company. adv.* with speed. ~**ible**, *a.*

expre′ssion (-shn), *n.* expressing; word, phrase; aspect of face; tone; style. ~**al**, *a.*

express′ive, *a.* serving to express; significant.

express′ly, *adv.* explicitly.

exprō′priate, *v.t.* dispossess; take away. ~**tion**, ~**tor**, *nn.*

expul′sion (-shon), *n.* expelling; banishment. ~**sive**, *a.*

expūnge′ (-j), *v.t.* remove, omit.

ex′purgate (-per-), *v.t.* (-*table*), purge, purify; remove objectionable parts (of book, &c.). ~**tion**, ~**tor**, *nn.*; **expurgātor′ial**, **ex′purgatŏry**, *aa.*

ex′quisite (-z-), *a.* of extreme beauty or delicacy; acute, keen. *n.* coxcomb.

ex-ser′vice, *a.* that has been but is no longer in one of the fighting services.

ex′tant (or ĭkstănt′), *a.* (of document, &c.) still existing.

extĕm′porĕ, *adv. & a.* without preparation; off-hand. ~**rā′neous**, ~**rary**, *aa.* extempore. ~**rize**, *v.t. & i.* speak extempore. ~**zation**, *n.*

extĕnd′, *v.t. & i.* stretch out; reach; accord to; prolong; enlarge; tax the powers of. ~**ible**, *a.* extĕn′sible, *a.*; ~**bility**, *n.*

extĕn′sile (or -ĭl), *a.* that can be protruded or enlarged.

extĕn′sion (-shn), *n.* extending; enlargement, additional part.

extĕn′sive, *a.* large, far-reaching.

extĕn′sor, *n.* muscle that straightens a joint.

extĕnt′, *n.* space covered; large space or tract; size.

extĕn′ūate, *v.t.* (-*uable*), lessen by partial excuse the gravity of; mitigate. ~**tion**, ~**tor**, *nn.*

extēr′ior, *a.* outer, outward. *n.* exterior aspect or part.

extĕrm′inate, *v.t.* root out, destroy utterly. ~**tion**, ~**tor**, *nn.*

extern′al, *a.* outside; outward. *n.pl.* non-essentials. ~**al′ity**, *n.* ~**ize**, *v.t.* give, attribute, external existence to. ~**ization**, *n.*

extērritōr′ial, *a.* free from jurisdiction of territory one resides in. **extērritōrial′ity**, *n.*

extĭnct′, *a.* no longer burning, quenched; that has died out.

extinc′tion, *n.* making or becoming extinct; destruction.

exting′uish (-nggw-), *v.t.* put out, quench; eclipse; annihilate; wipe out (debt).

exting′uisher (-nggw-), *n.* cap for extinguishing candle.

ex′tirpate, *v.t.* root out, destroy utterly. ~**tion,** ~**tor,** *nn.*

extol′, *v.t.* praise enthusiastically.

extort′, *v.t.* get by force, threats, importunity, &c.

extor′tion, *n.* extorting, esp. of money; illegal exaction. ~**ate,** *a.* exorbitant. ~**er,** *n.*

ex′tra, *a.* additional; larger, better. *n.* extra thing; thing charged extra; (Crick.) run not scored off bat.

extract, *v.t.* (ĭkstrăkt′), take out; draw forth; deduce, derive; copy out, quote. *n.* (ĕks′trăkt), essence; concentrated preparation; passage from book, &c. **extract′or,** *n.*

extrac′tion, *n.* extracting; descent, lineage. ~**ive,** *a.* of extraction.

extradi′table, *a.* liable to, (of crime) warranting, extradition.

ex′tradite, *v.t.* give up fugitive foreign criminal. **extradi′tion,** *n.* delivery of fugitive foreign criminal to proper authorities.

extrajudi′cial (-jōōdĭshal), *a.* not made in court; not legally authorized.

extramun′dāne, *a.* outside our world or the universe.

extramūr′al, *a.* outside the walls of town, &c.

extrā′neous, *a.* of external origin; not naturally belonging; foreign.

extra-offi′cial (-shl), *a.* not pertaining to an office.

extraord′nary (-rŏr-, -raŏr-), *a.* out of usual course, specially employed; exceptional, surprising.

extraparō′chial (-k-), *a.* outside the parish.

extraterritōr′ial, *a.* exterritorial.

extrāv′agance, *n.* extravagant expenditure; want of restraint.

extrāv′agant, *a.* wild, absurd; exorbitant; profuse, wasteful.

extrāvagan′za, *n.* fantastic composition, language, or behaviour.

extrāv′asāte, *v.t.* force out (blood, &c.) from its vessel; flow out. ~**tion,** *n.*

extrēme′, *a.* situated at the end; farthest from the centre; going to great lengths. *n.* thing at either end; extreme degree or measures. ~**ly,** *adv.* in an extreme degree; very.

extrē′mist, *n.* advocate of extreme measures.

extrem′ity, *n.* extreme point, end, esp. (pl.) hands and feet; extreme distress.

ex′tricate, *v.t.* disentangle, release. ~**tion,** ~**tor,** *nn.*

extrin′sic, *a.* not inherent or intrinsic; extraneous.

ex′trovert, *n.* (Psychol.) person not given to introspection.

extrude′ (-rōō-), *v.t.* thrust out.

extru′sion (-rōōzhn), *n.* expulsion.

exū′berant (-gz-), *a.* luxuriant, prolific; effusive. ~**nce,** *n.*

exūde′ (-gz-), *v.i.* & *t.* ooze out; give off (moisture). **exūdā′tion,** *n.*

exūlt′ (-gz-), *v.i.* rejoice; triumph (at, in, over). ~**ant,** *a.*; ~**ancy,** *n.* **exūltā′tion,** *n.*

exū′viae, *n.pl.* animal's cast skin, shell, &c. ~**ial,** *a.*

exū′viāte, *v.t.* & *i.* shed exuviae; slough. ~**tion,** *n.*

eyas (ī′as), *n.* young hawk not yet completely trained.

eye (ī), *n.* organ of sight; iris of this; eye-like thing, a hole; observation, perception. *v.t.* observe, watch closely or suspiciously. ~**ball,** pupil of eye. ~**brow,** fringe of hair over eye. ~**glass,** lens for defective sight. ~**lash,** hair(s) on eyelid. ~**lid,** either cover of eye. ~**opener,** surprising fact, &c. ~**shot,** distance one can see. ~**sight,** faculty or strength of sight. ~**sore,** ugly mark or thing. ~**tooth,** canine tooth under eye. ~**wash,** (sl.) mere professions, humbug. ~**water,** lotion for the eye. ~**witness,** one who can testify from his own observation.

---

măte, mēte, mĭte, mōte, mūte, mōōt; răck, rĕck, rĭck, rŏck, rŭck, rōōk;

eye'let (-lĭt), *n.* small hole; loop-hole.

eyot (āt), *n.* small isle in river.

eyre (ār), *n.* circuit court.

eyrie. See aerie.

F

F (ĕf), (Mus.) fourth note in scale of C major.

Fā'bian, *a.* cautiously persistent.

fā'ble, *n.* story, esp. supernatural one, not based on fact; lie; short moral tale. *v.i. & t.* tell fictitious tales; celebrate in fable.

fǎb'ric, *n.* thing put together; building; woven material.

fǎb'ricate, *v.t.* invent (lie, &c.); forge (document); *make by plan. ~tion, ~tor, *nn.*

fǎb'ūlous, *a.* famed in fable; incredible. fǎbūlōs'ĭty, *n.*

façade' (-sahd), *n.* face of building towards street, &c.

fāce, *n.* front of head; expression, grimace; aspect; surface; front, right side, dial-plate of clock, &c. *v.t. & i.* meet firmly; be opposite to; (Mil.) turn, cause to turn, in some direction. ~ache, neuralgia. ~card, king, queen, or knave. ~value, that stated on coin, note, &c. ~r, *n.* blow in face; sudden difficulty.

fǎ'cet, *n.* one side of many-sided body, esp. cut gem.

facē'tiae (-shiē), *n.pl.* pleasantries.

facē'tious (-shus), *a.* given to or marked by pleasantry.

fā'cia (or fā-, -sha), *n.* plate over shop-front with name, &c.

fā'cial (-shl), *a.* of the face.

fā'cile, *a.* easy; working easily; fluent; flexible.

|| fā'cile prin'ceps, *pred.a.* easily first.

facǐl'ĭtāte, *v.t.* make easy, promote. ~tion, ~tor, *nn.*

facǐl'ĭty, *n.* absence of difficulty; dexterity; (usu. pl.) opportunity.

fā'cing, *n.* coating of different material; (pl.) cuffs, collar, &c. of soldier's jacket; turning in some direction.

fǎcsim'ĭle, *n.* exact copy of writing, picture, &c.

fǎct, *n.* a thing done; thing known to be true; act, event.

fǎc'tion, *n.* self-interested or unscrupulous party; prevalence of party spirit. fǎc'tious, *a.*

factĭ'tious (-shus), *a.* artificial, got-up.

fǎc'titive, *a.* ~verb, expressing idea of making to be something.

fǎc'tor, *n.* agent; (Sc.) land-steward; any of the numbers whose product is the given number; element in a result.

fǎc'tory, *n.* manufactory; company's foreign trading-station.

factō'tum, *n.* servant employed in all kinds of work.

fǎc'ulty, *n.* aptitude for particular action; physical or mental power; branch of science, &c.; (esp. eccl.) authorization. ~tative, *a.* permissive, optional.

fǎd, *n.* pet notion, craze. ~dish, ~dy, *aa.*; ~dist, *n.*

fāde, *v.i. & t.* droop, wither; (cause to) lose freshness or colour; disappear gradually. ~less, *a.*

fae'ces (-z), *n.pl.* sediment; excrement of bowels. faec'al, *a.*

Fā'erie, ~ry, *n.* the fairies.

fǎg, *v.i. & t.* toil; grow, make, weary; (School) do service for seniors. *n.* drudgery; junior liable to fag; (sl.) cigarette. ~end, inferior remnant; very end.

fǎg'ot, *n.* bundle of sticks for fuel; bundle of steel rods; dish of chopped liver.

Fahr'enheit (-hīt), *a.* ~thermometer, with 32° and 212° for freezing and boiling points.

|| faience (fah'yahns), *n.* decorated earthenware or porcelain.

fail, *v.i. & t.* be missing; be deficient; break down; not succeed; go bankrupt; disappoint; neglect. ~ing, *n.* deficiency; failure; foible, fault, weakness.

fail'ure, *n.* non-performance; ill success; bankruptcy; unsuccessful person or thing.

fain[1], *pred.a.* well-pleased; only too glad. *adv.* would ~, gladly.

fain², fains (-z), fĕn(s) (-z), child's formula claiming exemption.

‖ **fainéant** (fā'nāahň), a. idle, inactive. n. idler.

faint, a. feeble; inclined to swoon; dim, pale; timid. v.i. & n. swoon. ~-heart, n. coward. ~-hearted, a. timid.

fair¹ (fār), n. periodical gathering for sale of goods, often with shows and entertainments. ~-ground, enclosure for fair, &c.

fair², a. beautiful; blond, not dark; just, equitable; of moderate quality or amount; (of weather) favourable. adv. in fair manner. ~-piece, n. ball, baseball batted within foul lines. ~ play, equal opportunities, just treatment. ~ trade, free trade conditional on reciprocity.

fair'ing, n. present from fair.

fair'ly, adv. (esp.) utterly; rather.

fair'way, n. navigable channel; (Golf) the regular track.

fair'y, n. small supernatural being with magical powers. a. of fairies; fairy-like. ~ lamp, small kind used in outdoor festive illuminations. ~-land, home of fairies. ~ ring, ring of darker grass caused by fungi. ~-tale, tale of fairies; marvellous account.

‖ **fait accompli** (fāt ahkawn'plē), n. thing done and past arguing about.

faith, n. trust; belief in religious doctrine or divine truth; religion; loyalty, fidelity, confidence.

faith'ful, a. loyal, constant; true, accurate. ~ly, adv.

faith'less, a. perfidious, false.

fake, (sl.) v.t. do up, make specious. n. faking; faked-up thing. *fā'ker, pedlar at fair, &c.

fakir' (-ēr), n. Mohammedan or Hindu religious mendicant or naked ascetic.

falchion (fawl'chon), n. broad curved convex-edged sword.

falcon (faw'kn), n. small diurnal bird of prey, trained to hawk for sport. ~-er, one who trains hawks. ~ry, n. hawking; breeding of hawks.

falc'onet (fawk-), n. (hist.) light cannon; kind of shrike.

fal'deral, n. gewgaw, trifle.

fald'stool (fawl-), n. bishop's armless chair; small desk for kneeling at.

fall (fawl), v.i. descend freely, drop, come down, lose high position; abate, droop; collapse; sin, perish; lapse; occur. n. falling; amount that falls; *autumn; cataract (often pl.); descent; drop; downfall, ruin; kind of veil.

falla'cious (-shus), a. containing a fallacy; delusive.

fall'acy, n. misleading argument; delusiveness; flaw in syllogism.

fal-lal', n. piece of finery.

fall'ible, a. liable to err or be erroneous. ~bility, n.

fall'ing-sickness (fawl-), n. epilepsy.

fall'ow¹ (-ō), a. ploughed, &c. but left uncropped (often fig.); uncultivated. n. fallow ground. v.t. break up (land).

fall'ow² (-ō), a. of pale brownish or reddish yellow. ~-deer, kind smaller than red deer.

false (fawls), a. erroneous, deceptive; deceitful, lying; spurious. ~ bottom, horizontal partition above true bottom of ship or box. ~ quantity, blunder as to length of vowel. **fal'sity** (fawl-), n.

false'hood (fawls-h-), n. falseness, lying, lie(s).

falsett'o (fawl-), n. (pl. -os), voice above one's natural range.

fal'sify (fawl-), v.t. fraudulently alter; misrepresent, pervert; disappoint. ~fication, n.

fal'ter (fawl-), v.i. & t. stagger; say hesitatingly; flinch.

fame, n. public report, rumour; reputation. **famed** (-md), a. & p.p. famous; currently reported.

famil'iar (-lyar), a. intimate; well-known; common; unceremonious; amorously intimate with. n. intimate friend; demon attending witch, &c. **famili̇ā'rity**, n.

famil'iarize (-lya-), *v.t.* make familiar; accustom. **~zation**, *n.*

fam'ily, *n.* a household; set of parents and children or of relations; person's children; lineage; race; group of allied genera.

fam'ine, *n.* extreme scarcity of food, &c.; starvation.

fam'ish, *v.t.* & *i.* reduce, be reduced, to extreme hunger.

fā'mous, *a.* celebrated; (colloq.) very good, excellent.

fan¹, *n.* winnowing-machine; an instrument used by ladies to agitate the air and cool the face; ventilating apparatus. *v.t.* winnow; move air with fan; stimulate. **~light**, fan-shaped window over door. **~palm**, large palm with fan-shaped leaves. **~tail**, kind of pigeon.

*fan², *n.* enthusiast, esp. fanatical devotee of specified thing.

fanāt'ic, *a.* filled with mistaken enthusiasm, esp. in religion. *n.* fanatic person. **~ism**, *n.*

fan'cier, *n.* connoisseur.

fan'ciful, *a.* indulging in fancies; capricious; imaginary.

fan'cy, *n.* faculty of imagination; delusion; supposition; caprice; whim; taste. *a.* ornamental; not plain; of whimsical kind. *v.t.* conceive, imagine; (colloq.) have good conceit of (oneself); take a fancy to, like. **~dress**, masquerade costume. **~free**, not in love.

fandāng'ō (-ngg-), *n.* (pl. *-oes*), lively Spanish dance.

fāne, *n.* (poet.) temple.

fan'fāre, *n.* flourish of trumpets, bugles, &c.

fanfăronāde', *n.* brag; fanfare.

fāng, *n.* canine tooth; serpent's venom-tooth; prong of tooth.

fantasia (-azē'a, -ahz'ĭa), *n.* (Mus.) composition in which form is subservient to fancy.

fan'tast, *ph-*, *n.* visionary, dreamer.

fantăs'tic, *a.* extravagantly fanciful; grotesque, quaint. **~ăl'ĭty**, **~cism**, *nn.*

fan'tasy, *ph-*, *n.* faculty of imagi-

nation; mental image; fanciful design; fantasia.

fantocci'ni (-ochēnē), *n.pl.* mechanically worked puppets.

fär, *adv.* at or to a great distance; by much. *n.* great distance. *a.* distant, remote. **~fetched**, not obvious, forced. **~flung**, widely extended. **~sighted**, seeing distant things best; prudent.

fā'rad, *n.* electromagnetic unit of capacity.

fârce, *n.* dramatic piece intended to excite laughter; absurdly futile proceeding. **făr'cical**, *a.*

|| **fârceur'** (-sēr), *n.* person who indulges in mystifications.

fârd'el, *n.* (arch.) bundle, burden.

fāre, *n.* cost of passenger's conveyance; passenger; food. *v.i.* happen, turn out; get on; be fed.

fārewěll', *int.* good-bye. *n.* leave-taking; act of departure.

farī'na, *n.* flour or meal of corn, nuts, or starchy roots; powder. **fărinā'ceous** (-shus), *a.* of the nature of farina. **fā'rinōse**, *a.* mealy.

fârl, *n.* piece of thin oatcake.

fârm, *n.* tract of land cultivated by a tenant; dwelling-place on farm. *v.i.* & *t.* take proceeds of (tax, office) on payment of fixed sum; cultivate, till the soil. **~stead**, farm with buildings. **~yard**, yard of farm-house.

fârm'er, *n.* one who farms land.

fâr'ō, *n.* gambling card-game.

farra'gō (-rah-, -rā-), *n.* (pl. *-ōs*), medley, hotchpotch. **~ginous**, *a.*

fā'rrier, *n.* shoeing-smith; horse-doctor.

fā'rriery, *n.* farrier's work.

fā'rrow (-ō), *n.* giving birth to, litter of pigs. *v.t.* & *i.* bear (pigs), bear pigs.

fârth'er (-dh-), *adv.* more far; (usu. *fur-*) also, in addition. *a.* more distant or advanced; (usu. *fur-*) additional, more. **~most**, *a.* farthest. **fârth'est** (-dh-), *a.* most distant; *adv.* to, at, the greatest distance.

fârth'ing (-dh-), *n.* quarter of a penny.

fàrth'ingàle (-dhĭngg-), *n.* (hist.) hooped petticoat.

făs'cēs (-z), *n.* bundle of rods and an axe carried before Roman magistrate.

fă'scia (-shĭa), *n.* (Archit.) long flat surface of wood or stone; stripe, band.

făs'cicle (-cŭle, *n.* bunch; bundle; part of book.

făs'cināte, *v.t.* make (victim) powerless by one's presence or look; charm irresistibly. **~tion**, **~tor**, *nn.*

fascine' (-sēn), *n.* long faggot used for lining trenches.

făsc'ism (-sh-), *n.* principles and organization of Italian nationalist anti-communist corporative government or imitations of this. **fasc'ist**, *n. & a.*

făsh, *v.t., & n.* (Sc.) trouble, bother.

fă'shion (-shn), *n.* make, shape, style; way, manner; custom, esp. in dress. *v.t.* form, shape.

fă'shionable (-shon-), *a.* characteristic of persons of fashion.

fast¹ (fah-), *v.i.* go without food, esp. as religious observance. *n.* fasting; going without food.

fast² (fah-), *a.* firm, fixed, steady; rapid; pleasure-seeking. *adv.* firmly, tightly; quickly.

fasten (fah'sn), *v.t. & i.* attach, fix, secure; become fast.

fa'stener, **fa'stening** (fahsn-), *nn.* clasp, &c., to fasten thing with.

făs'ti, *n.pl.* records, annals.

fāstĭd'ious, *a.* squeamish, hard to please.

fast'ness (fah-), *n.* firmness, strength; stronghold; rapidity.

făt, *a.* well-fed, plump; greasy, oily; *resinous; fertile, profitable. *n.* fat part of thing; oily substance in animal bodies. *v.t. & i.* fatten. **~head**, dolt.

fā'tal, *a.* destructive, ruinous; deadly, ending in death.

fā'talism, *n.* belief that all is predetermined; submission to all that happens as inevitable. **~ist**, *n.*; **~istic**, *a.*

fătăl'ĭty, *n.* supremacy of fate; calamity; death by accident.

fă'ta mŏrga'na (fah-, -gah-), *n.* kind of mirage.

fāte, *n.* power predetermining events from eternity; what is destined; death, destruction. *v.t.* preordain; (*p.p.*) doomed.

fāte'ful (-tf-), *a.* fraught with destiny; decisive; fatal.

fa'ther (fahdh-), *n.* male parent; forefather; originator; priest of religious order, &c.; oldest member; (pl.) elders. *v.t.* beget; originate; pass as father or author of. **~-in-law**, *n.* wife's or husband's father. **~hood**, *n.*; **~less**, *a.*

fa'therland (fahdh-), *n.* one's country.

fa'therly (fahdh-), *a.* like a father.

făth'om (-dh-), *n.* measure of 6 ft., esp. in soundings. *v.t.* sound (water); comprehend. **~less**, *a.*

fatigue' (-ēg), *n.* weariness from exertion; wearying task. *v.t.* tire.

făt'ling, *n.* young fatted animal.

fătt'en, *v.t. & i.* make or grow fat; enrich (soil).

fătt'y̆, *a.* of or like fat. *n.* (usu. voc.) fat child, &c.

făt'ŭous, *a.* silly, senseless; impotent. **fatū'ity**, *n.*

fau'cet, *n.* tap for barrel, pipe, &c.; *tap of any kind.

fault, *n.* defect, blemish; offence, misdeed; (Tennis, &c.) ball wrongly served; (Hunt.) loss of scent, check; (Geol.) break in continuity of strata, &c. **~find-ing**, *a. & n.* querulous(ness), censorious(ness). **~less**, **faul'ty̆**, *aa.*

faun, *n.* Latin rural deity with horns and tail.

fau'na, *n.* (pl. **-ae**, **-as**), the animals of a region or epoch.

‖ fauteuil (fōtĕr'ē), *n.* theatre stall.

‖ faux pas (fō pah), *n.* act that compromises one's reputation.

fā'vour (-ver), *n.* liking, goodwill, approval; partiality; aid; thing given or worn as mark of favour; (arch.) looks. *v.t.* regard, treat, with favour; oblige; treat with partiality; resemble in features.

fā'vourable (-ver-), *a.* well disposed; commendatory; promising, auspicious, helpful, suitable.

---

fā′vourite (-ver-), a. habitually preferred. n. favourite person; horse, &c. expected to win contest.

fā′vouritism (-ver-), n. practice of having favourites.

fawn[1], n. fallow deer in first year; light yellowish brown. a. fawn-coloured. v.i. & t. bring forth.

fawn[2], v.i. (of dog, &c.) show affection by frisking, grovelling, &c.; lavish caresses upon; behave servilely.

fay, n. (poet.) fairy.

*****faze**, v.t. (sl.) discompose, disturb.

fē′alty, n. duty of a feudal vassal to his lord; faithful adherence.

fear, n. emotion caused by impending evil; alarm, dread. v.i. & t. be afraid; be anxious; hesitate; shrink from. fear′ful, a. terrible, afraid; (colloq.) annoying, &c. fear′less, a. feeling no fear; brave. fear′some, a. (usu. joc.) formidable.

feas′ible (-z-), a. practicable, possible; plausible. ~bility, n.

feast, n. religious anniversary; village festival; sumptuous entertainment; (fig.) gratification. v.i. & t.(cause to) partake of feast; fare sumptuously; regale.

feat, n. notable act, esp. of valour; surprising performance.

feath′er (fĕdh-), n. the plume or quill of birds; plume worn in hat, &c; (Rowing) action of feathering. v.t. & i. furnish, line, coat with feathers; enrich; turn oar so as to pass through air edgeways. ~brain(ed), ~head(ed), flighty or silly (person). ~weight, light person or thing; a boxing-weight (9 st.). feathered (fĕdh′erd), a.; feath′ery, a.

fea′ture, n. (usu. pl.) part(s) of the face, external appearance; characteristic part of thing. v.t. be a feature of; portray; make special display of, star. ~less, a. lacking distinct features.

fĕb′rifūge (or fē-), n. medicine to reduce fever; cooling drink.

fē′brile, a. of fever.

Fĕb′ruary, n. second month.

fĕck′less, a. (Sc.) lacking purpose or resource; helpless, futile.

fē′cŭlence, n. turbidness; dregs.

fē′cŭlent, a. turbid, fetid.

fē′cŭnd (or fē-), a. fertile; fertilizing. fĕcŭn′dity, n.

fē′cŭndāte (or fē-), v.t. make fecund; impregnate. ~tion, n.

fed. See **feed**; ~up, (sl.) tired, bored.

fĕd′eral, a. (of States) united, but independent in internal affairs. ~ism, ~ist, nn. ~ize, v.t.

fĕd′erāte, v.t. & i. unite on federal basis or for common object. a. (-at), so united. ~tion, n. federating; federal society. ~tive, a.

fee, n. sum payable to officials, professional men, &c. for their services; charge; gratuity; inherited estate. v.t. pay fee to; engage for fee.

fee′ble, a. weak; wanting in character or intelligence.

feed, v.t. & i. (p.t. fĕd), supply with food; graze; comfort, keep in hope; take food. n. feeding; (colloq.)meal; pasturage; fodder.

feed′er, n. one who eats; one who feeds a machine; child's bib; tributary; feeding-apparatus in machine.

feed′pipe, n. pipe carrying water, &c. to machine, &c.

feel, v.t. & i. (fĕlt), explore by touch; perceive by touch; experience; be affected by; have pity for. n. sense of touch.

feel′er, n. organ of touch in some animals; tentative suggestion.

feel′ing, n. sense of touch; physical sensation; emotion; (pl.) susceptibilities; consideration for others; conviction or opinion. a. sensitive; sympathetic.

feign (fān), v.t. & i. pretend, simulate; practise simulation; invent, forge, imagine.

feint (fā-), n. sham attack, blow, &c., meant to deceive opponent; pretence. v.i. make feint.

fĕld′spar, n. kinds of crystalline white or flesh-red mineral.

fĕli′citāte, v.t. (-table). congratulate. ~tion, n. (usu. in pl.).

---

fĕli'citous, *a.* apt, well-chosen, happy. **fĕli'cĭty**, *n.* great happiness; bliss; felicitous phrase.

fē'line, *a.* of cats; catlike.

fĕll[1], *n.* animal's hide or skin with the hair; thick matted wool.

fĕll[2], *n.* (in names) mountain; stretch of moorland.

fĕll[3], *a.* fierce; destructive.

fĕll[4], *v.t.* strike down; cut down (tree); stitch down (seam).

fĕll, *p.t.* of fall.

fĕll'ah (-a), *n.* (pl. *-aheen, -ahs*). Egyptian peasant.

fĕll'oe (-lĭ, -lō), **fĕll'ў**, *n.* (section of) circumference of wheel.

fĕll'ow (-ō), *n.* comrade, associate; counterpart, equal; co-opted graduate member of a college; member of some learned societies; (colloq.) man, boy. *a.* of same class; associated in joint action, &c. **~-feeling**, sympathy.

fĕll'owship (-lō-), *n.* sharing; companionship; body of associates; status of college fellow.

fĕlō dĕ sē, *n.* (pl. *-ōnēs, -os*), self-murderer; self-murder (no pl.).

fĕl'on, *n.* a criminal; small abscess. *a.* cruel, murderous.

fĕl'onÿ, *n.* crime graver than misdemeanour. **felō'nious**, *a.*

fĕlt[1], *n.* cloth of matted wool, &c.

fĕlt[2], *p.t.* of feel.

felūcc'a, *n.* coasting vessel with oars or lateen sails or both.

fē'male, *a.* of the offspring-bearing sex; (of plants) fruit-bearing, having pistil and no stamens. *n.* female person or animal.

fĕm'inine, *a.* of women; womanly. **fĕminē'itÿ**, **fĕminĭn'itÿ**, *nn.*

fĕm'inism, *n.* influence of women; belief in or advocacy of it. **~ist**, *n.* **fĕm'inīze**, *v.t. & i.* (*-zable*), make or become feminine.

fĕm'oral, *a.* of the thigh.

fĕn[1], *n.* low marshy tract of land.

fĕnn'ÿ, *a.* **fen**[2]. See fair[2].

fence, *n.* art of using sword; hedge, &c. enclosing field; guard in machine; receiver of stolen goods. *v.i. & t.* practise sword

play; (fig.) parry, evade; surround as with fence; deal in stolen goods. **~-month**, **~-time**, close time.

fĕn'cible, *n.* (hist.) soldier liable only for home defence.

fĕn'cing, *n.* art of sword-play; fences, material for fences.

fĕnd, *v.t. & i.* ward off; provide for.

fĕn'der, *n.* thing used to keep something off; frame round hearth to keep in falling coals.

Fē'nian, *n.* one of a league among Irish in U.S. for overthrowing English rule in Ireland. **~ism**, *n.*

fĕnn'el, *n.* yellow-flowered herb used in sauces.

fĕn'ūgreek, *n.* leguminous plant with seeds used in farriery.

feoff (fĕf), *n.* = feud[2].

feoff'ment (fĕf-), *n.* a mode of conveying freehold estate. **feoffee** (fĕfē'), **feoff'or**, **~er**, (fĕf-), *nn.* one to whom, one by whom, land is so conveyed.

fĕr'al, **fĕr'ine**, *aa.* wild; untamed; uncultivated; brutal.

|| **fĕrash'** (-ah-), *n.* (Anglo-Ind.) menial servant who spreads carpets, pitches tents, &c.

fĕr'etorÿ, *n.* shrine; tomb; bier; chapel for shrines.

fē'rial, *a.* (of day) not a festival or fast.

Fering'hee (-nggī), *n.* (Indian term for) European; now used chiefly of the Indian-born Portuguese.

ferment, *n.* (fĕrm'ĕnt), leaven, fermenting-agent; tumult. *v.i. & t.* (fermĕnt'), suffer, subject to, fermentation; excite, foment. **~able**, **~ative**, *aa.*

fĕrmĕntā'tion, *n.* process like that induced by leaven in dough, with effervescence, heat, and change of properties; excitement.

fern, *n.* kinds of vascular cryptogam with feathery fronds.

fĕrn'erÿ, *n.* place for growing ferns.

ferō'cious (-shus), *a.* fierce, cruel. **ferō'citÿ**, *n.*

fĕ'rreous, *a.* containing iron.

fĕ'rrĕt[1], *n.* kind of polecat used in catching rabbits, rats, &c. *v.i.* & *t.* hunt with ferrets; clear out, drive out, with ferrets; rummage about, search for.

fĕ'rrĕt[2], *n.* cotton or silk tape.

fĕ'rriage, *n.* conveyance by, charge for using, ferry.

fĕ'rric, **fĕ'rrous**, *aa.* of or containing iron.

fĕrrif'erous, *a.* iron-yielding.

fĕ'rrotype, *n.* positive photograph on thin iron plate; this process.

ferrous. See **ferric.**

ferru'ginous (-rōō-), *a.* of iron-rust; rust-coloured, reddish-brown.

fĕ'rrule, **~rel**, *n.* metal ring or cap at end of stick, &c.

fĕ'rry, *v.t.* & *i.* take or go in boat, work boat, over river, canal, or strait. *n.* place, provision, for ferrying. **~bridge**, large ferry transporting railway train. **~man**, one who ferries passengers.

fĕr'tile (*or* -īl), *a.* bearing abundantly; fruitful. **fertil'ity**, *n.*

fĕr'tilize, *v.t.* (*-zable*) make fertile, fecundate. **~zation**, **~zer**, *nn.*

fĕ'rule (-ōōl), *n.* flat ruler with pierced end for punishing boys.

fĕr'vent, *a.* hot, glowing; ardent, intense. **fĕr'vency**, **fĕr'vour** (*-er*), *nn.* **fĕr'vid**, *a.* ardent.

fĕs'cūe, *n.* small stick, teacher's pointer; kinds of grass.

fĕs'tal, *a.* of a feast; gay.

fĕs'ter, *v.i.* generate matter; cause suppuration; rankle; rot. *n.* festering condition.

fĕs'tival, *n.* festal day; celebration, merry-making.

fĕs'tive, *a.* of a feast; joyous.

fĕstiv'ity, *n.* gaiety, festive celebration; (pl.) festive proceedings.

fĕstoon', *n.* hanging chain of flowers, ribbons, &c. *v.t.* adorn with, form into, festoons.

fĕtch, *v.t.* & *i.* go for and bring back; draw forth; be sold for; deal (blow). *n.* trick.

fĕtch'ing, *a.* attractive.

fête (fāt), *n.* festival, entertainment. *v.t.* entertain; make much of. **~fête-champêtre** (fāt shahn-pātr'), outdoor fête.

fĕ'tid (*or* fē-), **foe'tid** (fē-), *a.* stinking.

fĕ'tish (*or* fē-), **-ch(e)** (-sh), *nn.* inanimate object worshipped by savages; principle, &c. irrationally reverenced. **~ism**, **~ist**, *nn.*

fĕt'lock, *n.* part of horse's leg where tuft of hair grows.

fĕt'ter, *n.* shackle for the feet; band; (pl.) captivity; restraint. *v.t.* bind as with fetters.

fĕt'tle, *n.* condition, trim.

feud[1], *n.* lasting mutual hostility between two tribes or families.

feud[2], *n.* fief, feudal benefice; territory held in fee.

feud'al, *a.* of a feud or fief, held of a lord on condition of service; of or like the feudal system. **~ism**, **~ist**, *nn.* **feud'atory**, *n.* feudally subject to; *a.* feudal vassal.

fē'ver, *n.* morbid condition with high temperature; nervous excitement. *v.t.* throw into fever; (*p.p.*, *fig.*) restless, agitated. **~ish**, *a.* having symptoms of fever; excited, restless.

fĕ'verfew, *n.* herb formerly used as a febrifuge.

few, *a.* not many. *n.* small number of persons or things; small number. **~ness**, *n.*

fey (fā), *a.* with the mind in abnormal state; fated to die.

fĕz, *n.* Turkish cap.

|| **fiancé** (fēahn'sā), *n.* (fem. *-ée*), one's betrothed.

fias'cō, *n.* (pl. *-os*), failure, breakdown.

fi'at, *n.* authorization; decree.

fib[1], *n.* trivial lie. *v.i.* tell fib. **fibb'er**, **fib'ster**, *nn.*

fib[2] (Boxing), *n.* blow. *v.t.* hit.

fi'bre (-ber), *n.* thread-like filament; substance formed of fibres; character; small root or twig. **~silk**, artificial silk. **fi'bred** (-berd), *a.* **fi'bril**, *n.* small fibre.

fi'brous, *a.*

zh. as (rou)ge; ě=ĭ; ĭĭ, ŭr, =ẽr; ȳ, ŷ, =ī, ĭ; and see p. 4. *=U.S.

3495 G

fi′brin, *n.* insoluble protein present in clotted blood or plasma.

fi′broid, *a.* fibre-like. *n.* fibroid uterine tumour.

fib′ula, *n.* (pl. -*ae*, -*as*), splint bone on outer side of leg; brooch.

fi′chu (-shŏŏ), *n.* shawl of lace, &c. for shoulders and neck.

fic′kle, *a.* inconstant, changeable.

fic′tile, *a.* made by potter; of pottery.

fic′tion, *n.* invention; invented statement or narrative. ~al, *a.*

ficti′tious (-shŭs), *a.* not genuine; assumed; imaginary.

fid′dle, *n.* violin; (Naut.) contrivance for stopping things from rolling off table. *v.i.* & *t.* play fiddle; potter, move aimlessly. ~stick, fiddle-bow; (as *int.*) nonsense. fidd′ler, *n.* fidd′ling, *a.* petty, trifling.

fidĕl′ĭty, *n.* faithfulness, loyalty; accuracy.

fidg′ĕt, *n.* restless state or mood; one who fidgets. *v.i.* & *t.* move restlessly; be or make uneasy; worry. fidg′ĕtỹ, *a.*

fidū′cial (-shl), *a.* having the nature of trust or reliance.

fidū′ciary (-shɑ-), *a.* held or given in trust. *n.* trustee.

fie (fī), *int.* expressing sense of outraged propriety.

fief, *n.* See feud².

field, *n.* ground, esp. for pasture or tillage; tract rich in some product; scene of battle; expanse of sea, snow, &c.; all competitors, or all except favourite; (Crick.) fieldsman, fielders. *v.i.* & *t.* act as fieldsman in cricket, &c.; stop and return ball. ~-cornet, magistrate of township in Cape Province, &c. ~-day, manoeuvring exercise or review, (fig., so ~*night*) great occasion, important debate; *athletic meeting. ~ events, sports other than races. ~fare, kind of thrush. ~-glass, binocular telescope for outdoor use. ~-hospital, ambulance; temporary hospital near field of battle. F. Marshal, general officer of the highest

rank. ~s′man, fielder at cricket. ~-sports, esp. hunting, shooting, and fishing.

field′er, *n.* fieldsman at cricket or *baseball.

fiend, *n.* the devil; superhumanly wicked (*or clever) person; (fig.) person addicted to some harmful practice. ~ish, *a.*

fierce, *a.* violent in hostility; raging, vehement; intense.

fier′ỹ (fīr-), *a.* consisting of fire, flaming; flashing; inflaming; irritable; spirited; (of cricket pitch) making ball rise dangerously.

fife, *n.* shrill flute; fifer. *v.i.* play fife. fi′fer, *n.* fife-player.

fif′teen′, *a.* & *n.* one more than fourteen, 15, XV; Rugby football side of fifteen players. ~th, *a.* & *n.*

fifth, *a.* & *n.* next after fourth.

fif′tỹ, *a.* & *n.* five times ten, 50, L. ~fif′tỹ-fif′tỹ, half and half, equal shares. fif′tieth, *a.* & *n.*

fig¹, *n.* soft pear-shaped many-seeded fruit; valueless thing. ~-leaf, device for concealing what is indecorous. ~wort, brown-flowered herb.

fig², *v.t.* ~ *out* (person), dress up, adorn. *n.* dress, condition.

fight (fīt), *v.i.* & *t.* (fought, pr. fawt), contend in battle or single combat or with the fists; maintain against opponent. *n.* fighting; battle; (fig.) strife, conflict. fight′er (fīt-), *n.*

fig′ment, *n.* invented statement; imaginary thing.

fig′urant, fem. -te, *n.* ballet-dancer.

figūra′tion (or -ger-), *n.* act of formation; form, shape.

fig′urative, *a.* metaphorical; emblematic; pictorial, plastic.

fig′ure (-ger), *n.* external form; bodily shape; image; emblem; type; diagram; illustration; evolution in dancing; a character denoting a number (0, 1, 2, &c.). *v.t.* & *i.* represent in diagram or picture; imagine; calculate, estimate, be estimated; make ap-

FIGURE [193] FINE

pearance. ~head, carved bust, &c. over ship's cutwater; merely nominal leader, &c.; (joc.) person's face.

figúrine' (-ēn), n. statuette.

fil'ament, n. thread-like body, fibre; part of stamen that supports anther. ~ary, ~ous, aa.

fil'ature, n. reeling silk from cocoons; establishment for reeling silk.

fil'bert, n. nut of the hazel.

filch, v.t. steal, pilfer.

file¹, n. instrument for reducing or smoothing objects. v.t. smooth, reduce, remove, with file; elaborate, polish. fi'lings, n.pl. particles rubbed off by file.

file², n. stiff pointed wire or other device for holding papers; (Mil.) front-rank man and his rear-rank man or men; row of persons, &c. one behind another. v.i. & t. march in file; place papers on file.

fil'ial (or fī-), a. of, befitting, a son or daughter.

filiā'tion (or fī-), n. parentage; descent; branch of a society.

fil'ibeg, phila-, n. (Sc.) kilt.

fil'ibŭster, n. one who wages unauthorized warfare against foreign State; *one who delays legislation. v.i. act as filibuster.

fil'igree, fil'a-, n. fine tracery of gold or other wire.

fill, v.t. & i. make or become full; spread over, pervade; satisfy, satiate (up). n. a full supply. fill'er, n. vessel, &c. for filling others. ~ing, n.

fill'ét, n. ribbon, &c. for binding hair or worn round head; (pl.) animal's loins; undercut of sirloin; boneless strip of fish, &c.; (Archit.) narrow flat band between mouldings. v.t. bind, encircle, with fillet; divide (fish) into fillets.

fill'ip, n. smart stroke given with the finger; stimulus; mere trifle. v.t. strike slightly and smartly; give fillip to.

fill'ÿ, n. female foal; (sl.) girl.

film, n. thin skin or layer; (Photog.) gelatin, &c. used instead of plate or spread on paper or plate; celluloid roll used in cinema, its contents as shown; dimness over eyes. v.t. & i. cover, become covered, with film; take picture of (scene) for the cinema. fil'mÿ, a.

fil'osĕlle, n. floss silk.

fil'ter, n. device for cleaning liquid from impurities. v.t. & i. (also fil'trāte), pass (liquid), flow, through filter. filtrā'tion, n.

filth, n. loathsome dirt; garbage; obscenity. fil'thÿ, a.

fin, n. fish's propelling and steering organ; (sl.) hand.

fi'nal, a. at the end, coming last; conclusive, decisive, n. final heat or game in athletics; (sing. or pl.) final examination.

finā'lē (-nah-), n. last movement of instrumental composition; close of opera, drama, &c.

finăl'itÿ, n. final act, state, or utterance; being final.

finance' (or fī-), n. management of money; (pl.) pecuniary resources. v.t. & i. find capital for; deal with money. finăn'cial (or fī- ; -shl), a. finăn'cier (or fī-), n. one skilled in finance; capitalist.

finch, n. kinds of small bird.

find, v.t. (found), come across, meet with, obtain; discover; ascertain; determine; supply. n. discovery of treasure, first-class player, &c.

fi'nder, n. discoverer.

fi'nding, n. verdict of jury.

‖ fin de siècle (făṅ de syăkl), a. advanced, modern; decadent.

fine¹, n. sum fixed as penalty; sum paid for privilege. v.i. & t. (-nable), punish by fine; pay consideration for privilege.

fine², a. of high quality; pure, refined; thin, in small particles; excellent; handsome, imposing; bright, free from rain; smart, showy; fastidious. n. fine weather. adv, finely. v.t. make (beer) clear; (of liquid) become clear; (with away, down, off) make or become finer. ~~draw, *v.t.* sew together with imperceptible join. ~~drawn, *a.* subtle, extremely thin. ~~spun, *a.* delicate, too subtle.

fi′nery, *n.* showy dress or decoration; hearth where cast iron is made malleable.

finesse′, *n.* subtle management; artfulness. *v.i. & t.* use finesse; manage by finesse.

fing′er (-ngg-), *n.* one of the four terminal members of the hand; finger-like object. *v.t.* touch, turn about, with the fingers; take (bribe, &c.). ~~post, signpost at turning of road. ~~print, impression of finger, esp. as used for identifying criminal. ~~stall, cover to protect finger.

fing′ering¹ (-ngg-), *n.* management of the fingers in playing upon an instrument.

fing′ering² (-ngg-), *n.* wool for stockings.

fi′nial, *n.* ornamental top to gable, canopy, &c.

fin′ical, fin′icking, *aa.* over-nice, fastidious; too much finished.

fi′nis, *n.* the end.

fin′ish, *v.t. & i.* bring to an end, come to the end; perfect, put final touches to. *n.* last stage, decisive result; completed state.

fin′isher, *n.* workman doing final operation; crushing blow, &c.

fi′nite, *a.* bounded, limited.

finn′an, *n.* (also ~~haddock), smoke-cured haddock.

finn′y, *a.* like or having fins.

fiord, fjord (fy-), *n.* narrow arm of the sea between cliffs.

fir, *n.* (also ~~tree), kinds of coniferous tree with needles placed singly on shoots; their wood. ~~cone, fruit of fir. fir′r′y, *a.*

fire, *n.* state of combustion; flame, glow; burning fuel; conflagration; burning heat; fervour, spirit. *v.t. & i.* set fire to; catch fire; *dismiss; become heated or excited; cause to explode; (of gun) go off; propel from gun. ~~arm, gun, pistol, &c. ~~brand, piece of burning

wood; kindler of strife. ~~brigade, organized body of firemen. *~~bug, incendiary. ~~damp, (miner's name for) carburetted hydrogen, explosive when mixed with air. ~~dog, andiron. ~~engine, for extinguishing fire. ~~escape, apparatus for escape from house on fire. ~~fly, insect emitting phosphorescent light. ~~irons, tongs, poker, and shovel. ~~man, man employed to extinguish fires; tender of furnace, &c. ~ out, (sl.) expel. ~~place, grate or hearth in room. ~~plug, (abbr. *F.P.*) connexion in water-main for hose. ~~side, space round fireplace. *~~warden, officer protecting forests against fire. *~~water, whisky. ~~work, device giving spectacular effect by use of combustibles; (fig., pl.) display of wit, &c. fire′less cook′er, apparatus cooking with heated plates.

fir′ing, *n.* fuel; act of discharging firearms; cauterizing.

firk′in, *n.* small cask; half kilderkin.

firm¹, *n.* partners in business.

firm², *a.* of solid structure; fixed, steady; steadfast, resolute; (of offer) not liable to cancellation after acceptance. *v.t. & i.* solidify; fix firmly.

firm′ament, *n.* vault of heaven.

firmamen′tal, *a.*

firm′an, *n.* Oriental sovereign's edict, passport, &c.

first, *a.* the ordinal of 1; earliest in time or order; of highest repute, &c. *n.* first-class honours at university, &c.; first prize at show. *adv.* before all or something else; for the first time. ~ aid, given before doctor comes. ~~fruits, season's products as offered to God; first results. first′lings (-z), *n.pl.* first-fruits. first′ly, *adv.* in the first place, first.

firth, frith, *n.* arm of the sea, estuary.

fis′cal, *a.* of public revenue. *n.* (hist.) legal official; (S.-Afr.) kind of shrike.

---

ah, awl, oil, boot, cow, dowry: chin, go, bang, so, ship, thin; dh, as th(e):

fish[1], *n.* vertebrate cold-blooded animal living in water; flesh of fish; (colloq.) person (usu. with *cool*, *queer*). *v.i. & t.* try to catch fish; try to get information indirectly. ~-ball, cake of shredded fish. ~-hook, for catching fish. ~-pond, a small pool for fish; (joc.) the sea. ~-story, extravagant or incredible tale. ~-wife, woman selling fish.

fish[2], *n.* piece of wood for strengthening mast; flat plate of iron, wood, &c. strengthening beam, &c. *v.t.* mend, join, &c. with fish.

fish[3], *n.* piece of ivory, &c. used as counter in games.

fish'er, *n.* animal or (arch.) person that fishes. ~-man, one who lives by fishing; angler.

fish'er, *n.* (sl.) currency note.

fish'ery, *n.* business of fishing; fishing-ground.

fish'ing, *n.* taking fish; angling. ~-line, ~-net, ~-rod, ~-tackle, used in fishing.

fish'y, *a.* of or like fish; (sl.) dubious, open to suspicion.

fiss'ile, *a.* tending to split.

fi'ssion (-shn), *n.* act of breaking up into parts.

fi'ssure (-sher), *n.* cleft, split; narrow opening; cleavage.

fist, *n.* clenched hand; (colloq.) hand, handwriting. *v.t.* strike with fist. **fis'tic(al)**, *aa.* (joc.) pugilistic. **fis'ticuffs**, *n.pl.* fighting with fists.

fis'tula, *n.* a pipe or spout; pipe-like ulcer.

fit[1], **fytte**, *n.* section of poem.

fit[2], *n.* sudden seizure of hysteria, apoplexy, fainting, paralysis, or epilepsy; sudden transitory state.

fit[3], *a.* qualified, competent, worthy; becoming, proper; in good health or condition. *v.t. & i.* be in harmony with, be of right size and shape; adapt; make competent; supply. *n.* way a garment fits.

fitch, *n.* polecat's hair; brush made of this.

fitch'ew (-ōō), *n.* polecat.

fit'ful, *a.* active by fits and starts; spasmodic, intermittent.

fit'ment, *n.* fitting.

fit'ter, *n.* one who fits, specially in various trades.

fitt'ing, *n.* (usu. pl.) fixture(s), apparatus. *a.* becoming proper.

five, *a. & n.* one more than four. (5, V). ~fold, *a. adv. & adv.* repeated five times.

fi'ver, *n.*(sl.) £5 note, ~-dollar bill.

fives (-vz), *n.* ball-game played with hands or bat in court.

fix, *v.t. & i.* fasten, secure; direct steadily (eyes, attention) on; attract and hold attention; identify, locate; settle, specify (price, date, &c.); ~(sl.) get the better of, win over, esp. by bribery, corruption, &c. *n.* (colloq.) dilemma, difficult position.

fixa'tion, *n.* fixing; process of combining gas with solid.

fix'edly, *adv.* intently. ~edness, *n.*

fix'er, *n.* one who arranges matters with officials, juries, &c. for the benefit of law-breakers.

fix'ings (-z), *n.pl.* equipment; trimmings of dress or dish.

fix'ity, *n.* fixed state; security.

fix'ture, *n.* thing fixed; (pl.) articles annexed to land or house; (date fixed for) match, race, &c.

fizz, *v.i.* hiss, splutter. *n.* hissing sound; (colloq.) champagne.

fiz'zle, *v.i.* hiss or splutter feebly. *n.* fizzling sound; fiasco.

fläbb'ergast (-gah-), *v.t.* overwhelm with astonishment.

fläbb'y, *a.* (of flesh, &c.) limp, not firm; (fig.) nerveless, feeble.

fläc'cid (-ks-), *a.* flabby.

fläg[1], *n.* kinds of plant, esp. of iris, with bladed leaf.

fläg[2], *n.* (also ~-stone), flat slab of rock; (pl.) pavement of flags. *v.t.* pave with flags.

fläg[3], *n.* piece of bunting attached to staff or halyard as standard, ensign, or signal. *v.t.* communicate, inform, by flag-signals. ~-day, day on which money is raised for a cause by sale to passers-by of small flags; *June

14th, anniversary of adoption of Stars and Stripes by Congress. ~-officer, (vice-, rear-) admiral. ~-ship, with admiral on board. ~-staff, pole on which flag is hung. ~-wagging, (sl.) signalling with flags held in hands.

flag², v.i. hang down; droop; fall off in interest.

flagell'ant, n. one who scourges himself. a. self-scourging; given to flogging. flä'gellate, v.t. scourge. ~tion, ~tor, nn.

flageolet' (-jol-), n. wind-instrument with mouthpiece at end.

flagi'tious (-shŭs), a. deeply criminal, heinous.

flag'on, n. vessel to hold liquor.

flā'grant, a. glaring, scandalous.

flail, n. hand threshing-implement with which grain is beaten out.

|| flair, n. selective instinct for what is good, paying, &c.

flāke, n. light fleecy tuft or piece, esp. snow; thin broad piece; layer. v.i. & t. fall in, sprinkle with, flakes; take, come (off, &c.), in flakes. flā'kỹ, a.

flăm, n. sham story, hoax.

flăm'beau (-bō), n. (pl. ~s or ~x, pr. -z), lighted torch.

flămboy'ant, a. florid, gorgeous. n. kinds of flame-coloured flower.

flāme, n. visible combustion; bright light; passion, esp. love; sweetheart. v.i. emit flames; break out into anger; shine, gleam.

flām'en, n. a god's priest.

flā'ming, a. very hot or bright.

flamin'gō (-ngg-), n. (pl. -oes), bird with long legs and neck.

|| flâneur (flah'nér), n. idler.

flănge (-j), n. projecting flat rim, collar, or rib.

flănk, n. side of body between ribs and hip; side of body of troops or fleet. v.t. guard or strengthen on the flank; attack on flank.

flănn'el, n. open woollen stuff, usu. napless; (pl.) (white) flannel trousers. a. made of flannel. flăn-nelĕtte', n. cotton fabric imitating flannel. flănn'elled (-ld), a. dressed in flannels.

flăp, v.t. & i. strike, drive (flies, &c.), with broad thing; (of bird) strike with flat of wing; sway about, flutter. n. light stroke of broad thing; broad hanging piece, e.g. table-leaf, pocket-cover. ~-jack, small cake of flour fried in grease.

flăpp'er, n. flat fly-killer; young wild-duck, &c.; (sl.) girl in late teens; (sl.) hand.

flāre, v.i. blaze with bright unsteady flame. n. bright unsteady light; outburst of flame.

flā'ring, a. flaming; gaudy.

flăsh, v.i. & t. break into flame or sparks; gleam; appear or occur suddenly; fill or flood (stream, &c.) with water. n. sudden short blaze; signal light used at sea; instant; sudden short access; rush of water let down weir to take boats over shallows; ostentation. a. gaudy, showy; counterfeit; slang. ~-light, used for signals, lighthouses, and night photography. ~-point, temperature at which vapour from oil, &c. ignites.

flăsh'ing, n. strip of metal to obviate flooding or soaking at joint of roofing, &c.

flăsh'ỹ, a. gaudy, tawdry.

flask (-ah-), n. pocket-bottle of metal or glass; gunpowder case. flask'et (-ah-), n. small flask; long shallow basket.

flăt, a. horizontal, level; prostrate; smooth; dull, lifeless; (Mus.) below the true pitch. n. plain, lowland, level ground; (Mus.) note a semitone below natural pitch; suite of rooms on one floor; (sl.) duffer, dupe. *~-car, railroad freight-car without sides or roof. ~-fish, sole, turbot, plaice, &c. ~-footed, with feet not normally arched; *(sl.) determined, blunt. ~-iron, for ironing linen, &c. ~-race, over level ground. ~ rate, the same in all cases, not proportional. flătt'en, v.t. & i. make or become flat.

flătt'er, v.t. fawn upon; overpraise; gratify self-esteem of; (of portrait) exaggerate good looks of. flătt'erer, flătt'erẙ, *nm.*

flăt'ūlent, *a.* generating gas in alimentary canal; inflated, pretentious. flăt'ūlence, ~ncẙ, *nm.*

flaunt, *v.i. & t.* wave proudly; display oneself.

flaut'ĭst, *n.* flute-player.

flā'vīn (or flă-), *n.* surgical antiseptic and yellow dye.

flā'vour (-ver), *n.* mixed sensation of smell and taste; distinctive taste. *v.t.* give flavour to, season. ~ing, *n.*; ~less, *a.*

flaw¹, *n.* crack, rent; blemish; defect in document, &c. *v.t. & i.* crack, damage, mar. ~less, *a.*

flaw², *n.* squall of wind.

flăx, *n.* plant grown for its textile fibre and its seeds. New Zealand ~ *Phormium tenax* (also called ~bush, ~lily, ~plant), a native of New Zealand, the leaves of which yield a textile fibre. flăx'en, *a.* of flax; (of hair) pale yellowish-brown.

flay, *v.t.* strip off skin or hide; peel off; criticize severely.

flea, *n.* small wingless jumping insect; small or contemptible creature. ~bane, kinds of plant. ~bite, bite of a flea; (fig.) mere trifle; trifling injury, &c.

fleck, *n.* skin-spot, freckle; patch of colour, &c.; speck. *v.t.* mark with flecks. fleck'er, *v.t.* dapple; scatter in flecks.

fled, *p.t. & p.p.* of flee.

fledge, *v.t.* provide with feathers or down. fledg(e)ling (-jl), *n.* young bird; callow person.

flee, *v.i. & t.* (fled), run away; take to flight; shun.

fleece, *n.* woolly covering, esp. of sheep; wool shorn from a sheep. *v.t.* strip, plunder. flee'cẙ, *a.*

fleer, *v.i.* laugh mockingly, jeer. *n.* mocking look or speech.

fleet, *v.i.* glide away, pass rapidly. *n.* naval armament; ships, boats, sailing in company; creek, inlet. *a.* swift of foot.

flench, ~nse, *v.t.* cut up (whale); flay (seal).

flesh, *n.* soft substance between the skin and the bones; animal food; the sensual appetites; near relations. *v.t.* incite by taste of blood; initiate in bloodshed. ~colour, yellowish-pink. ~pots, high living.

flesh'er, *n.* (Sc.) butcher.

flesh'ings (-z), *n.pl.* tight-fitting flesh-coloured garment.

flesh'lẙ, *a.* carnal, worldly.

flesh'ẙ, *a.* plump; of or like flesh.

fleur-de-lis (flĕr de lē'), *n.* (pl. *fleurs-*, pr. as sing.), iris flower; royal arms of France.

flew, *p.t.* of fly.

flews (-z), *n.pl.* hanging lips of bloodhound, &c.

flex, *n.* flexible insulated wire used in electric lighting, &c.

flex'ible, *a.* easily bent; pliable; supple. ~bility, *n.*

flē'xion (-kshn), *n.* bending, bent state; bent part; flexure.

flex'or, *n.* muscle that bends a part of the body.

flex'ūous, *a.* full of bends, winding. flexūos'itẙ, *n.*

flē'xure (-ksher), *n.* bending, bent state; bend, curve.

flick, *n.* light blow with whiplash, duster, &c.; jerk; (pl.) cinema. *v.t.* strike, dash off, with a flick.

flick'er, *v.i.* shine or burn unsteadily; show fitful vibration. *n.* flickering light or motion.

fli'er, *n.* one that flees or flies; airman; fast animal or vehicle.

flight¹ (-īt), *n.* act, mode, of flying through air; migrating body, flock, of birds or insects; swift passage of time; series (of stairs, hurdles for racing); volley of arrows. ~lieutenant, officer of R.A.F. below squadron-leader.

flight² (-īt), *n.* running away; hasty retreat.

flight'ẙ (-īt-), *a.* fickle, changeable; half-witted.

flim'sẙ (-z-), *a.* slight, frail; paltry, shallow. *n.* thin kind of paper; (sl.) banknote(s).

flinch, *v.i.* draw back, shrink.

fling, *v.i. & t.* (flŭng), rush, **go**

violently; throw, hurl. *n.* throw, cast; impetuous dance.

flint, *n.* hard stone found in steel-grey lumps; piece of flint used with steel to produce fire. ~lock, (lock of) gun discharged by spark from flint. flin′ty, *a.*

flip, *n.* fillip, flick; mixture of beer and spirits. *v.t. & i.* propel, strike, with flip; make a flick.

flip′-flap, *n.* kind of somersault; a cracker; noise of flapping.

flip′pant, *a.* treating serious things lightly; disrespectful. ~ncy, *n.*

flip′per, *n.* limb used by turtle, &c. in swimming.

flirt, *v.t. & i.* fillip, jerk; *n.* sudden jerk; woman who encourages man who pays, attentions for amusement. flirtā′tion, *n.* playing at courtship.

flit, *v. i.* migrate, depart· pass lightly or rapidly about.

flitch, *n.* side of hog cured.

*fliv′ver, *n.* (sl.) Ford motor-car.

float, *v.t. & i.* rest, drift, on surface of liquid; hover before eye or mind; (of water) support, bear along; circulate (rumour); launch (company, scheme). *n.* thing that floats, or rests, on surface of liquid; raft; low-bodied cart.

float′age, *n.* floating; flotsam; ships, &c, afloat on river.

floatā′tion, **flot~,** *n.* floating, esp. of company or scheme.

float′ing, *a.* that floats; variable.

floc′culent, *a.* like tufts of wool.

flock¹, *n.* lock, tuft, of wool, &c.; (pl.) wool-refuse, &c. ~bed, stuffed with flocks. flock′y, *a.*

flock², *n.* large number of people; animals of one kind feeding or kept together; congregation in relation to its pastor. *v.i.* congregate, go in flocks.

floe, *n.* sheet of floating ice.

flog, *v.t.* beat with whip, stick, &c.; cast fishing-line repeatedly over.

flood (flŭd), *n.* (also ~tide) inflow of tide; inundation; downpour. *v.t. & i.* inundate; irrigate; come in great quantities. ~gate, for admitting or excluding water.

flood′-light, *n. & v.t.* (illuminate with) copious artificial lighting directed on to building, &c.

floor (-ōr), *n.* lower surface of room; rooms on one level in house; story; level area. *v.t.* furnish with floor; knock down; confound, nonplus; overcome. ~cloth, substitute for carpet. *~walker, overseer in large retail store.

floor′er (-ōr-), *n.* knock-down blow; disconcerting news, &c.

flop, *v.i. & t.* sway about heavily; sit down in ungainly way; cause to fall with soft dull thud; (sl.) fail. *n.* flopping motion and sound; (sl.) failure. *adv.* with a flop. flŏpp′y, *a.*

flor′a, *n.* (pl. -ae, -as), (list of) plants of a region.

flor′al, *a.* of flowers or floras.

flores′cence, *n.* flowering time or state.

flor′et, *n.* any of the small flowers of a composite flower.

flor′iculture, *n.* cultivation of flowers. ~ral, *a.*; ~rist, *n.*

flor′id, *a.* ornate, flowery; ruddy, high-coloured. florid′ity, *n.*

flor′in, *n.* English silver coin (2s.); (hist.) English gold coin.

flor′ist (or flŏ′-), *n.* one who deals in, raises, or studies flowers.

flor′uit (-ōŏ-), *n.* period at which person lived.

floss, *n.* rough silk enveloping cocoon. floss′y, *a.*

flotill′a, *n.* small fleet.

flot′sam, *n.* floating wreckage.

flounce¹, *v.i.* go, move, abruptly or impatiently. *n.* fling, jerk.

flounce², *n.* ornamental strip round woman's skirt. *v.t.* trim with flounces.

floun′der¹, *n.* small flat-fish.

floun′der², *v.i.* struggle and plunge; proceed in bungling or struggling fashion.

flour (-owr), *n.* finer part of meal got by bolting. *v.t.* sprinkle with flour. flour′y (-owr-), *a.*

flou′rish (flŭ-), *v.i. & t.* grow vigorously; thrive, prosper; wave or throw about. *n.* ornamental curve in writing; waving of weapon, hand, &c.; florid passage; fanfare of horns, &c.

flout, *v.t. & i.* express contempt for by word or act; scoff at. *n.* mocking speech or act.

flow (-ō), *v.i.* glide along as a stream; circulate; (of talk, style, &c.) move easily; (of dress) hang easily; gush out; be in flood. *n.* flowing; rise of tide; copious supply.

flow'er, *n.* reproductive organ in plant; flowering plant; state of blooming; best part, pick of; prime of; (pl.) ornamental phrases. *v.i.* bloom, blossom.

flow'eret, *n.* small flower; floret.

flow'ery, *a.* abounding in flowers; full of fine words.

flown, *p.p.* of fly.

fluc'tuāte, *v.i.* vary, rise and fall; be unstable. **~tion**, *n.*

flue[1] (flōō), *n.* fluff of cotton, &c.

flue[2] (flōō), *n.* smoke-duct in chimney; tube for conducting heat.

flu(e)[3] (flōō), *n.* (colloq.) influenza.

flue[4] (flōō), *n.* fishing-net.

flu'ent, *a.* copious and ready, flowing. **flu'ency** (-ōō-), *n.*

fluff, *n.* feathery stuff given off by blankets, &c.; soft fur or down. **fluff'y**, *a.*

flu'id (flōō-), *a.* moving readily; not solid or rigid or stable. *n.* fluid substance, e.g. gas or liquid. **fluid'ity** (flōō-), *n.* **fluid'ify** (flōō-), *v.t.* make fluid.

fluke[1] (flōōk), *n.* parasitic worm in sheep's liver.

fluke[2] (flōōk), *n.* triangular plate on arm of anchor; barbed head of lance, &c.; (pl.) whale's tail.

fluke[3] (flōōk), *n.* lucky accidental stroke. *v.i. & t.* make fluke; get, hit, &c. by fluke. **fluk'y** (flōō-), *a.*

*flume (flōōm), *n.* artificial channel; ravine with stream.

flumm'ery, *n.* kinds of sweet dish; empty compliments; trifles.

flumm'ox, *v.t.* (sl.) bewilder.

flung, *p.t.* of fling.

flunk'ey, *n.* (pl. *-eys*) footman; toady, snob. **~ism**, *n.*

*flunk, *n.* failure in studies, esp. in examination. *v.i. & t.* fail, cause to fail.

fluor (flōō-), *n.* kinds of gem-like mineral containing fluorine.

fluores'cence (flōō-), *n.* coloured luminosity produced in a transparent body by direct action of light. **fluoresce'** (flōō-), *v.i.* exhibit fluorescence. **~nt**, *a.*

flu'orine (flōō-; *or* -īn), *n.* non-metallic element grouped with bromine, chlorine, and iodine.

flu'rry, *n.* nervous hurry, agitation; gust, squall. *v.t.* agitate.

flush[1], *v.i. & t.* spurt, rush out; cleanse (drain) by flow of water; glow, blush. *n.* rush of water; sudden abundance; rush of emotion, elation; flushing of drain; glow, blush, freshness, vigour. *a.* full, in flood; having plenty; (of money) abundant; level or even with.

flush[2], *n.* set of cards all of one suit.

flus'ter, *v.t. & i.* confuse, flurry; be in a flurry. *n.* flurry.

flute (flōōt), *n.* musical instrument with blow-hole and finger-holes or keys; semicylindrical vertical groove in pillar, &c. *v.i. & t.* play flute; make grooves in. **flu'tist** (flōō-), *n.* flute-player.

flutt'er, *v.i. & t.* flap wings without flying or in short flights; descend, &c. quiveringly; flit, hover; be agitated, agitate; move irregularly. *n.* fluttering; tremulous excitement; stir, sensation; (colloq.) speculation, gamble.

flu'ty (flōō-), *a.* soft and clear in tone.

flu'vial, flu'viatile (*or* -īl; flōō-), *aa.* of, found in, rivers.

flux, *n.* morbid discharge of blood, excrement, &c.; flowing; inflow of tide; continuous succession of changes; substance mixed with metal, &c. to help fusion; (Math.) continued motion. *v.i. & t.* issue in a flux; make fluid, fuse.

flux'ion (-kshn), *n.* (Math.) rate of change of a continuously varying quantity. **~al, ~ary,** *aa.*

fly[1], *n.* two-winged insect; kinds

of plant-disease caused by flies.
~blown, tainted. ~catcher,
kinds of bird. ~trap, trap for
flies ; kinds of plant.

fly², v.i. & t. (flew pr. floo, flown pr.
flōn), move through air with
wings or in aircraft ; jump clear
over (fence, &c.) ; set or keep
(flag) flying ; travel swiftly ;
hasten, rush ; flee. n. flying ; one-
horse hackney-carriage ; speed-
regulating device in machines ;
strip or lap on a garment to contain
or cover button-holes ; (Theatr.,
pl.) space over proscenium. ~
~leaf, blank leaf at beginning or end
of book. ~wheel, heavy wheel
regulating machine. ~weight,
boxing weight (8st.).

flŷ³, a. (sl.) knowing, wideawake.

flŷ'ing, a. & n. ~boat, form of
seaplane in which a boat serves
as both fuselage and float.
~buttress, from pier to wall on
a slant with open space below it.
~column, of troops for rapid
marching. ~fish, either of two
kinds of fish which are able to
rise in the air. ~fox, family of
fruit-eating bats, found only in
the East and in Australia.
~jump, leap, with running start.
~man, airman. ~officer, R.A.F.
rank below flight-lieutenant.
~start, passing starting-point
at full speed.

foal, n. young of horse, ass, &c.
v.i. & t. bear foal.

foam, n. froth formed in liquid ;
froth of saliva or perspiration.
v.i. emit foam ; froth, gather
foam. foam'y, a.

fŏb¹, n. (hist.) small pocket for
watch, &c. in men's breeches ;
*short chain or ribbon for watch,
usu. with seal attached.

fŏb², v.t. cheat, trick, palm off.

fō'cal, a. of, at, a focus. ~ize, v.t.
focus. ~ization, n.

fō'cus, n. (pl. -ci pr. -sī, -uses),
point at which rays meet after
reflection or refraction ; a central
point. v.i. & t. adjust focus of
(lens, eye) ; concentrate (mind,
&c.) on.

fŏdd'er, n. dried food, hay, &c. for
cattle. v.t. give fodder to.

foe, n. enemy ; opponent ; (arch.)
enemy in war ; also ~man.

foe'tus (fē-), fē'tus, n. developed
embryo in womb or egg. foe'tal
(fē-), a. foe'ticide (fē-), n. killing
of foetus.

fōg¹, n. aftermath ; rank grass.

fŏg², n. vapour suspended at or
near earth's surface ; thick mist.
v.t. envelop as in fog ; perplex.
fŏgg'y (-g-), a.

fō'gy, ~gey (-g-), n. old-fashioned
fellow (usu. old fogy).

foi'ble, n. weak point, fault ;
point half of sword or foil.

foil¹, n. thin sheet of metal ; thing
that sets another off by contrast.
v.t. set off by contrast.

foil², v.t. & i. baffle, parry ; spoil
scent. n. track of hunted animal.

foil³, n. blunt-edged sword with
button on point.

foist, v.t. introduce surreptitiously
or wrongfully ; palm off on.

Fŏkk'er, n. German aeroplane.

fōld¹, n. enclosure for sheep ;
church, body of believers. v.t.
enclose (sheep) in fold.

fōld², v.t. & i. double flexible thing
over upon itself ; be folded ;
clasp ; envelop, wrap. n. folding ;
line made by folding.

fō'lder, n. (pl.) folding eye-glasses ;
cover for holding loose papers.

fōliā'ceous (-shus), a. of or like
leaves ; laminated.

fō'liage, n. leaves, leafage.

fō'liate¹, a. leaf-like, having leaves.
fō'liate², v.t. & i. split into
laminae ; decorate with foils.
~tion, n.

fō'lio, n. (pl. -os), n. leaf of paper,
&c. numbered only on front ;
once-folded sheet of paper giving
two folios or four pages ; book of
the largest size. v.t. paginate.

folk (fōk), n. nation, race ; (pl.)
people in general ; people of
specified class ; relatives. ~cus-
tom, ~dance, ~song, of the
people. ~lore, traditional beliefs, &c. ; study of these.

---

māte, mēte, mǐte, mōte, mūte, mōōt : răck, rěck, rǐck, rŏck, rŭck, rōōk :

föll′icle, n. small sac or vesicle ; cocoon. föllic′ular, a.

föll′ow (-ō), v.t. & i. go or come after ; pursue ; take as guide ; be the necessary inference ; grasp meaning of. ~on, (Crick., of side) go in again out of turn ; n. doing this.

föll′ower (-ōer), n. adherent, admirer ; maidservant's admirer.

föll′owing (-ō-), n. body of adherents. a. about to be named.

föll′y, n. foolishness ; foolish act, conduct, idea, &c.

fömĕnt′, v.t. bathe with lotion ; foster. fömĕntā′tion, n.

fönd, a. tender, loving ; doting ; foolishly credulous.

fŏn′dant, n. kind of sweetmeat.

fŏn′dle, v.t. & i. caress.

fönt, n. receptacle for baptismal water ; oil reservoir of lamp.

fön′tal, a. original ; baptismal.

fōod, n. victuals, nourishment ; material for the mind.

fōol, n. silly person, simpleton ; unwise person ; (hist.) jester, clown ; dupe ; dish of stewed fruit. v.t. & i. play the fool ; trifle ; cheat, dupe. *~-duck, the ruddy duck. *~-hen, grouse, esp. young grouse, in the early part of the season. ~'s cap, ancient jester's cap with bells ; dunce's conical paper cap. ~'s errand, a fruitless one. ~'s paradise, illusory happiness.

fōol′erў, n. fooling ; foolish act or thing.

fōol′hardў, a. foolishly venturesome ; needlessly daring.

fōol′ish, a. void of understanding ; indiscreet ; stupid.

fōol′scap, n. long folio writing or printing paper.

fōot, n. (pl. feet), termination of leg ; step, pace, tread ; infantry ; metrical unit with one syllable accented ; linear measure of 12 in. ; lower part, base. v.t. (with up) add up (account) ; pay (bill) ; (with it) trip, dance. foot-and-mouth disease, a fever, esp. in horned cattle. ~fall, sound of footstep. ~guards, Grenadier,

Coldstream, Scots, Irish, and Welsh Guards. ~lights, along front of stage. ~man, liveried servant ; infantryman. ~note, at foot of page. ~pad, unmounted highwayman. ~pound, energy needed to raise 1 lb. one foot. ~print, impression left by foot. ~rule, rigid measure one foot long. ~sore, with sore feet, esp. from walking. ~stalk, stalk of leaf, &c.; attachment of barnacle, &c. ~step, tread, footprint. ~stool, for feet of persons sitting. ~warmer, thing to warm feet.

fōot′ball (-awl-), n. large round or elliptical inflated ball ; games played with football. fōot′-baller, player in game. fōot′er, (sl.) game of football.

fōot′ing, n. foothold ; secure position ; degree of intimacy ; admittance to trade, society, &c.

fōo′tle (colloq.), v.i. play the fool. n. twaddle, folly. fōot′ling, a.

fōo′zle, v.t. & i. (sl.) bungle.

fŏp, n. dandy, vain man. fŏpp′erў, n. conduct, &c. of fop. ~ish, a.

for (fer ; emphat. or at end of clause fōr ; fŏr chiefly before it), prep. in place of ; in defence or favour of ; with a view to ; as regards, in the direction of ; because of, on account of. conj. introducing new sentence. forasmŭch′ as, since, because.

fŏ′rage, n. food for horses and cattle ; foraging. v.i. & t. collect forage from ; rummage, search ; supply with forage. ~cap, infantry undress cap. fŏ′rager, n.

forā′men, n. (pl. -mina), (Anat., Zool.), orifice, hole. forăm′inate, ~ātĕd, aa. having foramina.

fŏ′ray, n. incursion, raid. v.i. make foray.

forbear[1] (fŏrb′ār, forbăr′), n. (usu. pl.) ancestor(s).

forbear[2] (-bār), v.t. & i. (forbōre, forbōrne), abstain from : not mention ; be patient. ~ance, n.

forbĭd′, v.t. (forbād(e) ; forbĭdden), command not to do ; oppose.

forbidd'ing, *a.* repellent, uninviting.

force[1] *n.* (north.) waterfall.

force[2] *n.* strength, violence, intense effort; body of men; (pl.) troops; compulsion; influence, effectiveness. *v.t.* constrain, compel; strain, urge; break open by force; ravish; drive, propel; artificially hasten maturity. ~-pump, forcing water beyond range of atmospheric pressure. for'cedly, *adv.*

force'ful (-sf-), *a.* forcible.

|| force majeure (fôrs mahzhĕr'), *n.* irresistible compulsion; circumstances beyond one's control.

force'-meat (-sm-), *n.* meat chopped, &c. for stuffing.

for'ceps, *n.* (pl. same), surgical pincers; (Zool.) forceps-like organ.

for'cible, *a.* done by or involving force; telling, effective.

ford, *n.* shallow place where river, &c. may be crossed. *v.t.* wade across river.

fordone' (-ŭn), *a.* utterly wearied.

fore, *adv.* in front. *a.* situated in front. *n.* fore part; bow of ship.

forearm[1] (fôr'ărm), *n.* the arm from elbow to wrist. forearm[2] (fôr-ărm'), *v.t.* arm beforehand.

forebode (forbōd'), *v.t.* betoken, portend; have presentiment of.

forebō'ding (forb-), *n.* presentiment, omen.

fore'-cabin (fôrk-), *n.* cabin in forepart of ship.

forecast[1] (fôrkahst'), *v.t.* (-cast or -ed), estimate or conjecture beforehand. forecast[2] (fôr'kahst), *n.* conjectural estimate.

forecastle, fo's'le (fōk's'l), *n.* (hist.) short raised deck at bow; forward part under deck in merchant-ship.

foreclose (fôrklōz'), *v.t. & i.* exclude, prevent; bar (person entitled to redeem mortgage) on non-payment of money due. foreclosure (fôrklōzh'er), *n.* (of mortgage).

forefather (fôr'fahdher), *n.* (pl.)

those from whom one's father or mother is descended; (loosely) the earlier generations of a family or race.

forefinger (fôr'fingger), *n.* finger next the thumb.

fore'foot (fôr'f-), *n.* front foot of beast; foremost piece of keel.

forefront (fôr'frŭnt), *n.* very front.

forego (fôrgō'), *v.t. & i.* (-wĕnt, -gone pr. -gawn), precede.

fore'ground (fôrg-), *n.* part of view nearest observer.

fore'hand (fôr-h-), *n.* part of horse before rider. *a.* (of stroke at tennis, &c.) not back-handed. *~-handed, thrifty.

forehead (fŏ'rĭd), *n.* part of face above the eyebrows.

fŏ'reign (-rĭn), *a.* not of or in one's own country; of another district, parish, &c.; alien, dissimilar, irrelevant. fŏ'reigner (-rĭn-), *n.* alien, stranger; foreign ship, &c.

forejudge (fôrj-), *v.t.* judge before hearing evidence.

foreknow (fôrnō'), *v.t.* (-knew, pr. nū, -known), know beforehand. foreknowledge (fôrnŏl'ij), *n.*

fore'land (fôrl-), *n.* promontory; land lying in front.

fore'leg (fôrl-), *n.* beast's front leg.

fore'lock (fôrl-), *n.* lock of hair just above the forehead.

fore'man (fôrm-), *n.* principal juror; workman superintending others.

fore'mast (fôrm-), *n.* forward lower mast.

fore'most (fôrm-), *a.* first in place or order; chief, best. *adv.* in the first place.

fore'noon (fôrn-), *n.* day till noon.

foren'sic, *a.* of courts of law.

foreordain' (fôrôr-), *v.t.* appoint beforehand. foreordina'tion, *n.*

fore-run' (fôr-r-), *v.t.* (-răn, -rŭn), be precursor of, foreshadow. forerun'ner (fôr-r-), *n.*

foresail (fôr'sl, -săl), *n.* principal sail on foremast.

foresee (fôrsē'), *v.t.* see beforehand.

foreshadow (fôrshăd'ō), *v.t.* prefigure, be a type of.

---

ah, awl, oil, boor, cow, dowry; chin, go, bang, so, ship, thin; dh, as th(e).

fore'shŏre (forsh-). *n.* shore between high and low water marks.

foreshŏrt'en (forsh-). *v.t.* (of visual perspective) cause apparent shortening in object; represent thus in drawing.

foreshow (forshō'). *v.t.* (p.p. -*shown*), foretell, foreshadow.

foresight (for'sit). *n.* foreseeing; provident care.

fore'skin (fors-). *n.* prepuce.

fŏ'rest, *n.* large tract covered chiefly with trees and undergrowth. *v.t.* plant with trees; make into forest. **fŏ'rester**, *n.* officer in charge of forest; dweller in forest. **fŏ'restry**, *n.* science and art of management of forests.

forestall (forstawl'). *v.t.* be beforehand with; anticipate.

fore'stay, *n.* stay from foremast-head to ship's stem.

foretaste, *n.* (for'tāst), partial enjoyment or suffering in advance. *v.t.* (fortāst'), have foretaste of.

foretell' (fort-). *v.t.* (-*told*), predict, prophesy; be precursor of.

forethought (for'thawt), *n.* provident care; deliberate intention.

foretoken, *n.* (for'tōkn), sign of thing to come. *v.t.* (fortō'kn), be such sign of.

fore'tŏp (fort-). *n.* top of foremast.

forewarn (forworn'), *v.t.* warn beforehand.

forewoman (for'woŏman), *n.* president of jury of matrons; female supervisor.

fore'word (for'werd), *n.* preface, introductory remarks in a book.

fŏrf'eit (-fit), *a.* lost owing to crime or fault. *n.* forfeited thing; fine, penalty; (pl.) game in which player redeems forfeit by performing ludicrous task. *v.t.* pay or surrender as penalty.

fŏrf'eiture (-fit-), *n.* forfeiting.

fŏrfend', *v.t.* avert.

fŏrgăth'er (-dh-), *v.i.* assemble, associate, converse.

forgave, *p.t.* of forgive.

fŏrge[1], *v.i.* advance gradually.

fŏrge[2], *n.* smithy; furnace or hearth for melting or refining

metal. *v.t. & i.* shape by heating in fire and hammering; invent (tale, lie); counterfeit.

fŏr'gery, *n.* forging or falsifying of document; forged thing.

forget' (-g-), *v.t. & i.* (-*gŏt*, -*gŏtten*), lose remembrance of; neglect, overlook. **forgĕt'-mė-nŏt**, plant with small blue flower.

forget'ful (-g-), *a.* apt to forget.

forgive' (-g-), *v.t.* (-*gāve*, -*given*), pardon; remit. ~ness, *n.* pardoning-party; desperate enterprise.

forgo', *v.t.* (-*wĕnt*, -*gone* pr. gawn), go without, relinquish.

fork, *n.* pronged implement for digging, &c.; pronged instrument used in eating; divergence into branches. *v.i. & t.* form fork; branch; dig with fork. ~ out, (sl.) pay up.

forlŏrn', *a.* forsaken; in pitiful condition. ~ hope, storming-party; desperate enterprise.

fŏrm, *n.* shape, arrangement of parts, visible aspect; class in school; set order of words; formality; behaviour according to rule or custom; (of horse, athlete, &c.) good condition or style; bench; hare's lair. *v.t. & i.* fashion, mould; take shape, become solid; make up, amount to; (Mil.) draw up in order.

fŏrm'al, *a.* done as a matter of form, perfunctory; prim, stiff, methodical. ~ism, ~ist, *nn.* strict observance, observer, of forms.

fŏrmăl'ity, *n.* formal act or conduct; primness, precision.

fŏrm'alize, *v.t.* (-*zable*), make formal; give definite form to.

fŏrm'at (-mah), *n.* shape and size of book.

fŏrmā'tion, *n.* forming; thing formed; parts formed into a body or group.

fŏrm'ative, *a.* serving to form; (of suffix, &c.) used in forming words. *n.* formative element.

fŏrme, *n.* body of type locked up in chase for printing.

fŏrm'er, *a.* of the past, earlier; first-named. *pron.* first-named person, thing, or fact.

form′erly, adv. in former times.

form′ic, a. ~ acid, acid contained in a fluid emitted by ants.

form′idable, a. causing dread.

form′less, a. without distinct or regular form.

form′ula, n. (pl. *-ae*, *-as*) systematic or set form of words or symbols ; recipe.

form′ulary, a. of formulas. n. collection of formulas.

form′ulate, v.t. express systematically. ~tion, ~tor, nn.

forn′icate, v.i. commit fornication. ~tion, n. sexual intercourse with an unmarried woman. ~tor, n.

forsake′, v.t. (-*sŏŏk*, -*sāken*), give up, renounce ; desert, abandon.

forsooth′, adv. no doubt, indeed.

forswear′ (-*swār*), v.t. (-*swōre*, -*sworn*), abjure, renounce ; perjure oneself ; (p.p.) perjured.

fort, n. fortified place ; trading-station. **fort′alice,** n. small fort.

forte¹, n. one's strong point.

fort′e³, (Mus. direction) loud. ~ forte, very loud. ~ piano, loud and then immediately soft.

forth, adv. forward ; out of doors ; onwards in time. prep. from out of. forth′com′ing, about to come forth ; approaching. ~right (arch.), adv. straight forward, straightway ; a. going straight, outspoken ; n. straight course. ~with, at once, without delay.

fortifica′tion, n. art of fortifying ; (usu. pl.) defensive work(s).

fort′ify, v.t. & i. (-*fiable*), strengthen ; provide with defensive works ; confirm (statement).

fortiss′imō, adv. (Mus.) very loud.

fort′itude, n. courage in pain or adversity.

fort′night (-nĭt), n. two weeks. ~ly, adv. once a fortnight ; a. appearing once a fortnight.

fort′ress, n. military stronghold.

fortū′itism, **fortū′itist,** nn. belief, believer, in chance, not design, as causing adaptations in nature.

fortū′itous, a. due to chance.

fortū′ity, n.

fort′ūnate, a. lucky, prosperous, auspicious.

fort′une (-chn, -tyŏŏn), n. chance as a power in men's affairs ; luck ; prosperity, wealth ; coming lot. v.i. happen ; come by chance upon. ~hunter, man seeking rich wife.

fort′y, a. & n. four times ten, 40, XL ; ~winks, short nap. ~fold, a. & adv. **fort′ieth,** a. & n.

for′um, n. place of public discussion ; the law courts.

for′ward, a. in front of one ; towards the front ; well-advanced ; ready, prompt ; pert. n. (Footb.) first-line player. adv. towards the future ; to the front ; progressively. v.t. help forward, promote ; send (letter, &c.) on ; dispatch. **for′warder,** n. one who helps forward or transmits. **for′wardly,** adv. pertly. ~ness, n. pertness.

forwōrn′, a. tired out.

fosse, n. canal, ditch, trench.

foss′il, n. petrified remains of plant or animal, fossil object or person. a. like a fossil ; (fig. of person) antiquated. **foss′ilate,** **foss′ilize,** vv.t. & i. turn into fossil.

fos′ter, v.t. encourage, harbour (feeling) ; cherish. ~brother, ~daughter, ~father, ~mother, &c., so related not by blood but in virtue of nursing or bringing up. **fos′terage,** n. fostering ; employment of foster-mothers. ~ling, n. foster-child.

fought, p.t. & p.p. of fight.

foul, a. offensive, loathsome, stinking ; dirty, soiled ; charged with noxious matter ; clogged, choked ; morally polluted ; obscene ; unfair, against rules ; (of weather) wet, rough ; in collision. n. collision, entanglement, in riding, rowing, &c. ; irregular stroke, &c. in game. adv. unfairly. v.i. & t. make or become foul ; entangle ; become entangled ; collide with ; block. ~mouthed, given to foul language.

---

māte, mēte, mīte, mōte, mūte, mŏŏt ; răck, rĕck, rĭck, rŏck, rŭck, rŏŏk

foulard (fōol'ard), *n.* thin flexible material for blouses, &c.

foul'ly (-l-li), *adv.* vilely.

foum'árt (fōo-), *n.* polecat.

found[1], *v.t. & i.* lay base of ; establish, originate ; base, build up ; rely upon. **foun'der**[1], ~**dress**, *nn.* one who founds an institution.

found[2], *v.t.* melt and mould (metal) ; fuse (materials for glass) ; make things thus. **foun'der**[2], *n.*

found[3], *p.t. & p.p.* of find.

founda'tion, *n.* origination ; endowed institution ; solid ground or base ; basis. ~**stone**, esp. one laid with ceremony. **founda'tioner** (-shon-), *n.* participant in the revenues of a foundation.

founder[1,2]. See found[1,2].

foun'der[3], *v.i. & t.* (of ship) fill with water and sink ; (Golf) hit (ball) into ground ; fall down, give way ; (of horse) collapse, fall lame.

found'ling, *n.* deserted infant of unknown parents.

foundress. See found[1].

foun'dry, *n.* founder's workshop for casting metals.

fount[1], *n.* complete set of printing types of one size and face.

fount[2], *n.* spring, source, fountain ; reservoir of oil in lamp or of ink in pen.

foun'tain (-tin), *n.* spring ; source ; artificial jet of water ; reservoir for oil, &c. in lamp, &c. ~**pen**, with ink fountain.

four (fôr), *a. & n.* one more than three, 4, IV ; four-oared boat or its crew ; (pl.) military formation four deep. *~**flusher**, bluffer. ~**fold**, *a. & adv.* ~**in-hand**, vehicle with four horses and no outrider ; kind of necktie ; ~**poster**, bed with four tall posts. ~**some**, (Golf) game between two pairs. ~**square**, firmly placed, steady. ~ **-wheeler**, four-wheeled cab.

fourteen' (fôr-), *a.* four and ten. ~**th**, *a. ; ~**ly**, *adv.*

fourth (fôr-), *a. & n.* next after the third ; quarter, one of four equal parts. ~**ly**, *adv.*

fowl, *n.* kinds of bird kept to supply eggs and flesh for food ; bird. *v.i.* hunt, shoot, or snare wildfowl. **fowl'er**, *n.* sportsman who pursues birds. **fowl'ing**-**piece**, *n.* light gun.

fox, *n.* red-furred quadruped preserved as beast of chase ; crafty person. *v.i. & t.* act craftily ; discolour with brown spots. ~**brush**, tail of fox. ~**glove**, tall plant with purple or white flowers. *~**hole**, (army sl.) small pit to shelter one or two men from artillery-fire. ~**hound**, bred to hunt foxes. ~**hunter**, one who joins in fox-chase. ~**tail**, kinds of grass. ~**terrier**, short-haired dog kept chiefly as pet. ~**trot**, an American dance. **fox'y**, *a.* fox-like ; crafty(-looking) ; reddish-brown ; foxed.

|| **foyer** (fwah'yā), *n.* large room in theatre, &c. for use in interval.

frā'cas (-kah), *n.* (pl. same), noisy quarrel.

frac'tion, *n.* numerical quantity that is not an integer ; small part, amount, &c. **frac'tional**, *a.*

frac'tious (-shus), *a.* unruly, peevish.

frac'ture, *n.* breakage, esp. of bone or cartilage. *v.t. & i.* cause fracture in ; crack.

frā'gile, *a.* easily broken ; of delicate constitution. **fragil'ity**, *n.*

frag'ment, *n.* part broken off ; an imperfect piece. ~**ary**, *a.*

frā'grance, *n.* sweetness of smell. **frā'grant**, *a.* sweet-smelling.

frail[1], *n.* rush basket for figs, raisins, &c.

frail[2], *a.* fragile, delicate ; morally weak, unchaste. **frail'ty**, *n.* liability to yield to temptation ; weakness, foible.

frame, *v.t. & i.* (-mable), shape, direct, dispose ; adapt, fit ; construct ; articulate (words) ; form in the mind ; set in frame ; serve as frame for. *n.* construction, make, build ; case, border, enclosing picture, &c. ~ **aerial**, an

---

aerial for wireless reception, consisting of a number of turns of wire supported on a wooden frame. *~**up**, (sl.) conspiracy. ~**work**, frame, substructure.

frānc, n. French, Belgian, and Swiss monetary unit.

frăn′chise (-z), n. right to vote; citizenship; (hist.) privilege.

Frăncis′can, n. grey friar, of the order of St. Francis.

frănc′olin, n. kind of partridge like pheasant.

|| **franc-tireur** (frahn tērēr′), n. man of irregular light-infantry.

frăn′gipāne, ~āni (-j-), n. perfume of red jasmine; pastry.

frănk, a. candid, open, sincere; undisguised. v.t. superscribe a letter ensuring free delivery. n. franking signature, franked cover.

frănk′incense, n. aromatic gum resin burnt as incense.

frănk′lin, n. (hist.) landowner of free but not noble birth.

frăn′tic, a. wildly excited by pain, joy, &c.; violent.

frā′ter, n. (hist.) refectory.

fratĕrn′al, a. of brothers, brotherly. ~**nity**, n. brotherliness; religious body; guild; *college or school society. frăt′**ernize**, v.i. associate, make friends with.

frā′tricide (or -āt-), n. killing, killer, of a brother or sister.

fraud, n. criminal deception; dishonest trick; disappointing person, &c. ~**ulence**, n.; ~**ulent**, a.

fraught (frawt), a. full of; destined to produce.

fray[1], n. fight, conflict; brawl.

fray[2], v.t. & i. rub; make or become ragged at edge.

***frăz′zle**, n. worn or exhausted state.

freak, n. caprice, vagary; monstrosity; eccentric person.

freck′le, n. light brown spot on skin. v.t. & i. spot, become spotted, with freckles.

free, a. (freer, freest, pr. -ĕer, -ēist), not in bondage; at liberty; (of translation) not literal; clear of obstructions; disengaged, available; spontaneous; lavish, unre-

served; not charged for. v.t. (freed), make free, set at liberty; disentangle. **F.** Church, Protestant church unconnected with the State. ~**hand**, (of drawing) done without ruler, compasses, &c. ~**lance**, politician, &c. with no strict party allegiance. ~**thinker**, rejector of authority in religious belief. ~ **trade**, commerce left to its natural course without customs duties. ~**wheel**, (in bicycle) driving-wheel able to revolve while pedals are at rest. ~**will**, power of directing one's actions voluntarily.

free′booter, n. pirate.

free′dom, n. personal or civil liberty; liberty of action; undue familiarity; franchise.

free′hold, n. tenure in fee simple or fee tail; estate so held. ~**er**, n. possessor of freehold.

free′man (-an), n. citizen of free State; holder of the freedom of a city, &c.

freemā′son (-sn), n. member of fraternity having elaborate ritual and secret signs. ~**ry**, n. system of the freemasons.

frees′ia (-z-), n. fragrant flowering plant of iris kind.

freeze, v.i. & t. (frōze, frōzen), (cause to) become, be covered with, ice; become rigid from frost. **freez′ing**, a. very cold; (of manners) chilling. ~**point**, temperature at which water freezes.

freight (frāt), n. hire or charge of ship for transport of goods; cargo; load; *(railroads) ordinary transport of goods. v.t. load ship. ~**age**, n. hiring of ship, cost of conveyance; cargo.

Frĕnch, a. of France or its people. n. the French language. ~ **bean**, kind of haricot bean. ~ **horn**, instrument of trumpet class. (take) ~ **leave**, depart, act, without asking leave. ~ **polish**, used for furniture. ~ **window**, glazed folding-door.

frĕn′zy, n. delirious fury; wild folly. v.t. drive to folly.

frē′quency, n. frequent occurrence; (Physics) rate of recurrence (of vibration, &c.); number of repetitions in given time.

fre′quent[1], a. often occurring, common; numerous; habitual.

frequent′[2], v.t. go often or habitually to. frequenta′tion, n. ~ative, a. expressing frequent repetition; n. such verb.

fres′co, n. method of painting in water-colour on fresh plaster.

fresh, a. new, novel; not stale or faded; vigorous; inexperienced; unsullied; refreshing; excited with drink; *(sl.) presumptuous, forward. adv. freshly. ~en, v.i. & t.

fresh′et, n. flood of river.

fresh′ly, adv. recently; vigorously; with fresh appearance.

fresh′man (-an), fresh′er (sl.), nn. first-year man at university.

fret[1], n. pattern of straight lines joined usu. at right angles. v.t. variegate, chequer; ornament. ~work, wood or stone cut in patterns.

fret[2], v.t. & i. gnaw; wear by rubbing; chafe, worry; waste away. n. irritation, vexation. ~ful, a. querulous.

fret[3], n. bar or ridge on fingerboard of guitar, &c.

Freud′ian (-oid-), a. of Freud's theory of psycho-analysis. n. disciple of Freud.

fri′able, a. easily crumbled.

fri′ar, n. member of a religious order. fri′ary, n. convent.

frib′ble, v.i. trifle. n. trifler.

fricassee′, n. meat cut up, cooked, and served with sauce.

fric′ative, a. made by friction of breath in narrow opening. n. fricative consonant.

fric′tion, n. rubbing of two bodies, (fig.) disagreement; attrition; medical chafing.

Fri′day, n. sixth day of week. Good ~, Friday before Easter.

friend (frĕnd), n. one joined to another in intimacy and affection; (pl.) one's relations; sympathizer, helper. ~less, a.

friend′ly (frĕ-). a. acting as a

friend; on amicable terms. n. native of friendly tribe. ~ Society, for mutual insurance.

friend′ship (frĕ-), n. friendly relation or feeling.

frieze[1], n. coarse woollen cloth with nap.

frieze[2], n. member of entablature between architrave and cornice; band of decoration.

frig′ate, n. (hist.) warship next in size to ships of the line; cruiser; (~bird), tropical bird of prey.

fright (frīt), n. sudden or violent fear; grotesque-looking person. v.t. frighten.

fright′en (-it-), v.t. throw into fright; terrify into doing; (p.p.) alarmed at, afraid of.

fright′ful (-it-), a. dreadful, shocking; ugly; (sl.) great. ~ness, n. terrorizing actions.

frig′id, a. cold; lacking ardour; repellent. frigid′ity, n.

frill, n. fluted strip of woven material gathered at one edge; (pl., colloq.) airs. ~ed, a.

frill′ies (-liz), n.pl. (colloq.) frilled petticoats, &c. frill′ing, n. frills; material for frills.

fringe (-j), n. bordering of loose threads, tassels, or twists; short front hair over forehead; border, outskirts. v.t. adorn with fringe; serve as fringe to.

fripp′ery, n. finery; showy ornament; knick-knacks.

frisk, v.i. move sportively, gambol. n. gambol. frisk′y, a. lively.

frith. See fern.

fritill′ary (or frit′-), n. plant of lily kind; kinds of butterfly.

fritt′er[1], n. fried batter, often containing sliced fruit, &c.

fritt′er[2], v.t. waste (time, &c.).

friv′olous, a. paltry, trifling; futile; silly. frivol′ity, n.

frizz[1], v.i. sputter in frying. friz′zle[1], v.i. & t. fry, toast, grill, with sputtering noise.

friz(z)[2], v.t. crisp hair, form into mass of small curls. n. frizzed hair or state. friz′zle[2], v.t. & i. frizz hair. n. frizzled hair.

frô, adv. away, backward.

frŏck, *n.* monk's gown, (fig.) priestly character; child's skirt and bodice; woman's dress. ~-coat, man's long-skirted coat.

frŏg¹, *n.* tailless amphibious animal developed from tadpole.

frŏg², *n.* elastic horny substance in middle of horse's sole.

frŏg³, *n.* attachment to waist-belt to support sword; military coat-fastening.

frŏl′ic, *a.* mirthful. *v.i.* (*-cking, -cked*), play pranks, gambol. *n.* prank, merry-making. ~**some**, *a.* sportive.

from (from, *emphat. or at end of clause* frŏm), *prep.* out of; because of; at a distance; since, ever since.

frŏnd, *n.* organ like leaf, esp. of ferns. ~**age**, *n.* the fronds of a plant. ~**ōse**, *a.* frond-like.

front (-ŭnt), *n.* forepart; forward position; false hair or curls. *a.* of or at the front. *v.i. & t.* face, look; confront, oppose; furnish with front.

frŏn′tage (-ŭn-), *n.* land abutting on street or water; extent of front; front of building.

frŏn′tal (-ŭn-), *a.* of or on front. *n.* covering for an altar-front; façade.

frŏn′tier (-ŭn-, -ŏn-), *n.* the boundary of any territory.

frŏn′tispiece (-ŭn-), *n.* illustration at beginning of a book.

front′let (-ŭn-), *n.* band worn on forehead; phylactery.

front′ward (-ŭn-), *a.* looking to the front. *adv.* towards front.

frost (-aw-), *n.* freezing; frozen dew or vapour; (sl.) failure, fiasco. *v.t.* injure with frost; cover as with rime; turn (hair) white. ~**bite**, inflammation of skin from frost. **frost′y̆** (-aw-), *a.* cold with frost; frigid.

froth (-aw-), *n.* foam; scum; idle talk. *v.i.* emit or gather foam. **froth′y̆** (-aw-), *a.*

frō′ward, *a.* perverse; refractory.

frown, *v.i. & t.* knit brows; express disapprobation. *n.* wrinkled brows; look of displeasure.

frowst (colloq.). *n.* fusty heat in room. **frows′ty̆**, *a.*

frowz′y̆, *a.* fusty; slatternly.

frōze(n), *p.t. & p.p.* of freeze.

fruc′tify̆, *v.i. & t.* (*-fiable*), bear fruit; make fruitful. ~**fication**, *n.* fructifying; the reproductive parts of fern, &c.

frug′al (frōō-), *a.* sparing, economical. **frugal′ity̆**, *n.*

fruit (frōōt), *n.* (usu. pl.) vegetable products fit for food; produce or seed of a plant; produce of action; result. *v.i. & t.* bear, cause to bear, fruit. ~**age**, *n.* fruit-bearing; fruits. ~**er**, *n.* dealer in fruit. ~**ful**, *a.* fertile, prolific; remunerative. ~**less**, *a.* not bearing fruit; useless.

fruï′tion (frōō-), *n.* enjoyment; realization of hopes.

fruit′y̆ (frōō′tĭ), *a.* of fruit; (of wine) tasting of the grape.

fru′menty̆ (frōō-), **fŭrm′ety̆**, *nn.* hulled wheat boiled in milk and sweetened.

frŭmp, *n.* old-fashioned woman; a dowdy. ~**ish**, ~**y̆**, *aa.*

frŭs′trāte′, *v.t.* (*-table*), baffle, counteract, disappoint. ~**tion**, *n.*

frŭs′tum, *n.* (pl. *-ta, -tums*), remainder of regular solid whose top is cut off by plane parallel to the base.

frutes′cent, **frut′icōse** (frōō-), *aa.* shrub-like, shrubby.

frȳ¹, *n.* young fishes fresh from spawn; insignificant beings.

frȳ², *v.i. & t.* (*-ier, -yable*), cook in fat. *n.* fried meat; internal parts of animals, usu. eaten fried.

fuchsia (fū′sha), *n.* drooping-flowered shrub.

fū′cus, *n.* (pl. *-cī* pr. *-sī*), kinds of seaweed with flat fronds.

fŭd′dle, *v.i. & t.* tipple; intoxicate. *n.* spell of drinking.

fŭdge, *v.t.* (*-geable*), patch up in makeshift way. *n.* piece of fudging; nonsense (often *as int.*); kind of soft toffee.

fū′el, *n.* material for fire; thing that feeds passion, &c.

fūgā′cious (-shŭs), *a.* fleeting, elusive. **fūgā′city̆**, *n.*

fū′gitive, a. flying; fleeting, transient. n. exile, refugee.

fū′gleman (-gel-), n. soldier placed before regiment at drill to show motions, &c.; leader.

fugue (fūg), n. musical composition on short themes. **fū′gal**, a.

ful′crum, n. (pl. -ra), point against or on which lever is placed to get support.

fulfil′ (fool-), v.t. bring to pass; carry out; satisfy; bring to an end. ~ment, n.

ful′gent, a. shining.

fūli′ginous, a. sooty, dusky.

full[1] (fool), a. (of vessel, &c.) holding all it can; replete; crowded; copious; swelling. adv. quite, exactly. ~ back, football player placed behind. ~blown, quite open. ~ stop, complete cessation; punctuation mark used at end of sentence.

full[2] (fool), v.t. clean and thicken cloth. **full′er** (foo-), n. one who fulls. ~′s earth, kind of clay used in fulling.

full′ness (fool-), n. being full.

full′y (foo-), adv. completely.

ful′mar (fool-), n. kind of petrel.

ful′minant, a. fulminating; (of disease) developing suddenly.

fūl′minate, v.i. & t. (-nable), flash, explode, detonate; (fig.) thunder forth, issue censures. ~tion, ~tor, nn.; ~tory, a.

fulness. See fullness.

ful′some (fū-, foō-), a. gross; disgusting by excess.

ful′vous, a. tawny.

fū′marôle, n. smoke-hole in volcano.

fum′ble, v.i. & t. grope about; handle awkwardly.

fume, n. odorous smoke, vapour, or exhalation; fit of anger. v.t. & i. subject to fumes; darken (oak, &c.) thus; chafe.

fū′migate, v.t. (-gable), subject to fumes, purify thus; perfume. ~tion, ~tor, nn.

fū′mitory, n. herb formerly used in medicine.

fun, n. sport, amusement.

fūnam′bŭlist, n. rope-walker.

fŭnc′tion, n. the work a thing is designed to do; official duty; public ceremony; duty; fulfil function; operate. ~al, a. pertaining to the functions of an organ, &c. ~ary, n. official.

fŭnd, n. permanently available stock; capital sum. v.t. make debt permanent at fixed interest.

fŭn′dament, n. buttocks.

fŭndamen′tal, a. of or serving as the base or foundation; essential, primary. n. fundamental rule, note, &c. ~ism, n. strict adherence to traditional orthodox Protestant beliefs. ~ist, a. & n. ~äl′ïty, n.

fū′neral, n. burial of the dead; burial procession. a. of, used at, funerals. **fūner′eal**, a. fit for a funeral; dismal, dark.

fŭn′gicide (-j-), n. fungus-destroying substance. **fung′oid** (-ngg-), a. fungus-like.

fŭng′us (-ngg-), n. (pl. -gi pr. -jī, -uses), mushroom, toadstool, or allied plant; morbid growth. **fung′ous** (-ngg-), a.

fūnic′ular, a. or rope or its tension. ~ railway, one worked by cable and stationary engine.

fŭnk (sl.), n. fear panic; coward. v.i. & t. show funk; evade, shirk; be afraid of. **fŭnk′y**, a.

fŭnn′el, n. tube for conducting liquids into small opening; chimney of steam-engine or ship.

fŭnn′y, a. amusing; queer. n. narrow boat for one sculler. ~bone, part of elbow over which ulnar nerve passes.

fŭr, n. coat of ermine, beaver, &c.; (usu. pl.) garments of fur; short fine hair of some animals; skins of these; coating, crust. **fŭrr′y**, a.

fŭrb′elow (-ō), n. flounce; pleated border; (pl.) showy ornaments.

fŭrb′ish, v.t. polish, burnish.

fŭrcate (fèrk′āt), a. forked, branched. **fŭrca′tion**, n.

fŭr′ious, a. raging, frantic, very angry; uproarious.

fŭrl, v.t. & i. roll up (sail); fold up, close; become furled.

fŭrl′ŏng, n. eighth of a mile.

---

mắre, mẽre, mĩre, mõre, mūre; pắrt, pĕtt, pŏrt; *italics*, vague sounds;

fŭr'lough (-ō), n. leave of absence.

furmety. See **frumenty.**

fŭr'nace (-Is), n. chamber for melting metals; hot place; closed fireplace for heating.

fŭr'nish, v.t. & i. provide; fit up with furniture.

fŭr'niture, n. movable contents of house or room; outfit.

fŭror'ē, n. enthusiasm; rage.

fŭr'rier, n. dealer in, dresser of, furs.

fŭr'row (-ō), n. narrow trench made by plough; rut; wrinkle. v.t. plough; make furrows in.

fŭrth'er (-dh-), adv. to a greater distance; in addition. a. more remote; additional. v.t. promote, favour. ~ance, n. ~more, adv. moreover. ~most, adv. most distant. **fŭrth'est**, a. & adv.

fŭrt'ive, a. sly, stealthy.

fŭr'y, n. fierce passion, wild anger; violence; angry woman.

fŭrze, n. spiny yellow-flowered shrub; gorse. **fŭrz'y**, a.

fŭs'cous, a. dark-coloured.

fūse¹ (-z), v.t. & i. melt with intense heat; blend by melting.

fūse² (-z), n. cord, casing, &c., filled or saturated with combustible matter for igniting explosive.

fūsee' (-z-), n. large-headed match.

fū'selage (-zellj), n. shuttle-shaped body of aeroplane.

fū'sel oil (-z-), n. mixture of alcohols formed in making some spirits.

fū'sible (-z-), a. that may be fused. **fūsibil'ity** (-z-), n.

fū'sil (-z-), n. light musket. **fūsilier'** (-z-), n. soldier of some regiments formerly armed with a fusil. **fūsilläde'** (-z-), n. continuous discharge of firearms.

fū'sion (-zhn), n. fusing; fused mass; coalition.

fŭss, n. bustle, excessive commotion. v.i. & t. make a fuss; bustle; worry. **fŭss'y**, a.

fŭs'tian, n. a twilled cotton cloth; bombast. a. made of fustian; bombastic, worthless.

fŭs'tic, n. wood yielding a yellow dye.

fūs'tigate, v.t. cudgel. ~tion, n.

fŭs'ty, a. stale-smelling, musty, stuffy; antiquated.

fū'tile, a. useless, frivolous, worthless. **fūtil'ity**, n.

fū'ture, a. about to happen or be or become. n. time to come; future condition.

fū'turism (-che-), n. recent artistic and literary development marked by violent departure from tradition. **fū'turist** (-che-), n. supporter of futurism; also, one believing that the prophecies of the Apocalypse, &c. are still to be fulfilled.

fūtūr'ity, n. future time, future events; the future life.

fŭzz, n. fluff; fluffy or frizzed hair. **fŭzz'y**, a.

fye, see fie. fytte see fit¹.

G

G (jē), (Mus.) fifth note in scale of C major.

găb, n. (colloq.) talk, chatter.

găb'ble, v.i. & t. talk inarticulately or too fast. n. rapid talk.

*găb'by, a. talkative.

găb'erdine (-ēn), n. loose upper garment of Jews, &c.; a fine hard-laid cloth.

gā'bion, n. cylinder of wicker or woven metal bands filled with earth in fortification.

gā'ble, n. triangular part of wall at end of ridged roof.

gā'by, n. simpleton.

găd, v.i. go about idly. ~about, n. gadding person.

găd'-fly, n. a cattle-biting fly.

găd'gĕt, n. small fitting or contrivance in machinery, &c.

gā'doid, n. of the cod kind. n. gadoid fish.

gā'dolinite (-ĭt), n. (Min.) silicate of yttrium.

Gael (gāl), n. Scottish Celt. **Gael'ic** (gāl-, găl-), a. of Gaels; n. their language.

găff¹, n. barbed fishing-spear; stick with hook for landing fish. v.t. seize with gaff.

gaff², *n.* (sl.) cheap place of amusement (usu. *penny gaff*).

gaff'er, *n.* old man; a master.

gag, *n.* thing thrust into mouth to prevent speech; (Parl.) closure; actor's interpolations. *v.t. & i.* apply gag to, silence; insert gag.

gage, *n.* pledge, security; challenge. *v.t.* (-*geable*), stake, offer as gage.

gai'ety, *n.* being gay, mirth; amusement, gay-making.

Gai'kwär, Gaek-, (gīk-) *n.* ruler of Baroda.

gain, *v.t. & i.* obtain, secure; win; reach; persuade. *n.* increase of wealth, profit; money-making. ~ful, *a.* paying. ~ings, *n.pl.* sum gained.

gainsay', *v.t.* (past -*said*, pr. -ād, -ĕd) deny, contradict.

gait, *n.* manner of, or carriage in, walking.

gait'er, *n.* covering of leather, &c. for leg or ankle; *kind of high shoe with elastic strips at side.

gā'la (*or* gah'-), *n.* festivity.

găl'antine (-ēn), *n.* white meat boned, spiced, and served cold.

galan'tỹ-show (-ō), *n.* shadow pantomime shown through screen.

găl'axỹ, *n.* irregular luminous band of stars encircling heavens; brilliant company.

găl'banum, *n.* gum resin.

gāle¹, *n.* bog-myrtle.

gāle², *n.* rather strong wind.

găl'Ilee, *n.* porch, chapel, at entrance of church.

gall¹ (gawl), *n.* bile; asperity, rancour; *assurance, impudence. ~-bladder, vessel containing gall. ~-stone, calculus in the gall-bladder. **gall'-less**, *a.*

gall² (gawl), *n.* painful swelling, blister, &c.; sore; *(southern U.S.) patch of barren soil. *v.t.* rub sore; vex, humiliate.

gall³ (gawl), *n.* excrescence caused by insect on trees.

gallant (gă'lant, *also* galănt'), *a.* fine, stately; brave; attentive to women. *n.* man of fashion; ladies' man. **găll'antrỹ**, *n.* bravery; devotion to women.

găll'ĕon, *n.* Spanish ship.

găll'erỹ, *n.* covered walk, colonnade; (southern U.S.) verandah; raised floor over part of area of church, &c.; passage, corridor; room for showing works of art.

găll'ey, *n.* (pl. -*eys*), low flat one-decked vessel, usu. rowed; large row-boat of man-of-war; ship's kitchen; tray for set-up type. ~proof, proof in slip form.

Găll'ic, *a.* of Gaul(s); (usu. joc.) French. **găll'icism**, *n.* French idiom. **găll'icize**, *v.t. & i.* French. **găll'ĭgaskins** (-z), *n. pl.* (joc.) breeches, trousers.

gallinā'ceous (-shŭs), *a.* of the order including domestic poultry.

găll'iot (-y-), *n.* Dutch cargo-boat or fishing-vessel; small galley.

găll'ipot, *n.* small earthen glazed pot.

găll'ium, *n.* a soft bluish-white metal.

găll'ivant, *v.i.* gad about.

găll'on, *n.* measure (four quarts) for liquids, corn, &c.

galloon', *n.* narrow close braid.

găll'op, *n.* horse's fastest pace. *v.i. & t.* go at a gallop; make (horse) gallop; read, &c. fast. ~āde', *n.* lively dance. ~er, *n.* aide-de-camp; light field-gun.

găll'oway, *n.* small breed of horse.

găll'ows (-ōz), *n.pl.* (usu. as sing.) structure for hanging criminals. *galōot'*, *n.* worthless person.

găl'op, *n.* lively dance.

galōre', *adv.* in plenty.

galōsh', go-, *n.* an overshoe.

gălvăn'ic, *a.* of galvanism; (of smile, &c.) sudden and forced. **găl'vanism**, *n.* electricity produced by chemical action. ~ize, *v.t.* (-*zable*), apply galvanism to; rouse by shock. ~ization, *n.* **gălvanŏm'ĕter**, *n.* instrument for measuring galvanism.

gămbāde', -ā'dō, *n.* (pl. -*s*, -*oes*), horse's leap; escapade.

găm'bier, *n.* astringent extract from an Eastern plant, largely used in tanning and dyeing.

găm'bĭt, *n.* (Chess) kinds of opening with sacrifice of piece.

găm'ble, *v.i.* play games of chance for money stake; (fig.) take great risks. *n.* risky undertaking.

gămb'ler, *n.*

gămboge' (-ōozh), *n.* gum-resin used as yellow pigment.

găm'bol, *n.* & *v.i.* caper, frisk.

găme¹, *n.* spell of play, pastime, sporting contest; jest; dodge, trick; subdivision of tennis set, whist rubber, &c.; score that wins the game; animals, birds, &c. hunted for sport or food. *a.* spirited; ready. *v.i.* gamble. ~ ball, state of game in fives, &c. at which one point may win. ~-cock, of kind bred for fighting. ~-keeper, man employed to breed game, prevent poaching, &c.

găme², *a.* (of leg, &c.) crippled.

găme'some, *a.* sportive.

găme'ster (-ms-), *n.* gambler.

|| gamin (găm'ăn), *n.* street arab.

gămm'a, *n.* Greek letter; kind of moth.

gămm'er, *n.* old woman.

gămm'on¹, *n.* bottom piece of flitch of bacon with hind leg.

gămm'on², *n.* complete victory at backgammon; humbug, deception. *v.t.* & *i.* defeat at backgammon; talk plausibly.

gămp, *n.* (colloq.) umbrella.

găm'ut, *n.* whole series of recognized notes in music; compass of voice; (fig.) entire range.

găn'der, *n.* male goose; fool.

găng, *n.* set of workmen, slaves, or prisoners; set of associates, esp. for criminal purposes.

găng'er, *n.* foreman of a gang.

găng'lion (-ngg-), *n.* (pl. -*ia*) knot on nerve from which nerve-fibres radiate; nerve-nucleus in central nervous system.

găng'rēne (-ngg-), *n.* mortification of part of body. ~nous, *a.*

găng'ster, *n.* member of a gang of roughs or criminals.

gangue (găng), *n.* earth or matrix in which ore is found.

găng'way, *n.* opening in ship's bulwarks; bridge; passage.

|| găn'ja, *n.* preparation of Indian hemp, strongly intoxicating and narcotic.

gănn'et, *n.* solan goose.

găn'oid, *a.* (of fish-scale) smooth and bright; (of fish) with ganoid scales. *n.* ganoid fish.

găn'try, gaun'-, *n.* stand for barrels; structure supporting travelling crane, railway signals, &c.

gaol (jāl), *n.* prison. *v.t.* put in prison. ~bird, *n.* habitual criminal. gaol'er (jāl-), *n.* warder in gaol.

găp, *n.* breach in hedge or wall; interval; wide divergence.

gāpe, *v.i.* open mouth wide; stare at; yawn. *n.* yawn; stare.

garage (gă'rĭj, gă'rahzh), *n.* building for storing motor-cars.

gărb, *n.* (characteristic) dress of nation, class). *v.t.* dress in this.

gărb'age, *n.* offal used as food; refuse; worthless reading.

găr'ble, *v.t.* make unfair selection.

|| gărçon (gă'sawn), *n.* waiter.

gărd'en, *n.* piece of ground for growing flowers, fruit, or vegetables; (pl.) pleasure-grounds. *v.i.* cultivate garden. gărd'ener, *n.* person who tends gardens.

găr'fish, *n.* a long-snouted green-boned fish.

gărgăn'tŭan, *a.* gigantic.

găr'gle, *v.t.* & *i.* wash throat with liquid. *n.* liquid so used.

gărg'oyle, *n.* grotesque gutter-spout.

gărĭbăl'dĭ, *n.* woman's or child's blouse; biscuit with currants.

găr'ish, *a.* obtrusively bright.

gărl'and, *n.* wreath or chaplet. *v.t.* crown or deck with garland.

gărl'ĭc, *n.* plant with bulbous strong-smelling pungent root.

gărm'ent, *n.* article of dress.

gărn'er, *n.* storehouse for corn, &c. *v.t.* store up (usu. fig.).

gărn'et, *n.* vitreous mineral, esp. red kind used as gem.

gărn'ish, *v.t.* decorate, esp. dish of food. *n.* materials for this.

gărn'iture, *n.* appurtenances; decoration, esp. of dish.

gă'rrét, *n.* room on top floor.

gă'rrison, *n.* troops stationed in

town. *v.t.* furnish with, occupy as, garrison; place on g. duty.

garrotte', *n.* (apparatus for) Spanish capital punishment by strangulation; highway robbery by throttling victim. *v.t.* execute, throttle, thus.

garrul'ity (-ōōl-), *n.* loquacity.

ga'rrulous (-ōōl-), *a.* talkative.

gat'er, *n.* band to keep stocking up; highest order of knighthood.

garth, *n.* close, garden, paddock.

gas, *n.* (pl. *gases*) any aeriform or completely elastic fluid; coalgas, used for light or heat; empty talk, boasting; *(sl.)* gasolene. ~**-fitter**, person installing and repairing gas-pipes, and ~**-meter**, registering amount consumed in house, &c. *v.t. & i.* talk emptily, vaguely, or boastfully; project poison-gas over (enemy); (*p.p.*) disabled by gas.

gasconáde', *n. & v.i.* boast, brag.

gasélier', *n.* gas-lamp with several burners.

gas'eous (or -ā-), *a.* of gas.

gash, *n.* long deep cut or wound. *v.t.* make gash in.

gas'ket, *n.* small cord securing furled sail to yard.

gas'olëne, -ine (-ēn), *n.* liquid got from petroleum; *petrol.

gasom'eter, *n.* reservoir from which gas is distributed; (Chem.) vessel for holding gas.

gasp (gahsp), *v.i.* catch breath with open mouth. *n.* convulsive catching of breath. **gas'per**, *n.* (sl.) bad cigarette.

gass'y, *a.* like gas; wordy.

gas'teropod, *n.* mollusc, e. g. snail. **gas'tric**, *a.* of the stomach.

gastron'omer, -mist, *nn.* judge of cookery. **gastron'omy**, *n.* science of good eating. ~**mical**, *a.*

gate, *n.* (also gate'way) opening in wall closable with barrier; barrier of wood, iron, &c.; contrivance regulating passage of water; number paying at gates to see football match, &c.

gath'er (-dh-), *v.t. & i.* bring or come together; collect; pluck; draw together in folds or wrinkles;

develop purulent swelling; pick up from ground; infer. ~**ing**, *n.* assembly; purulent swelling.

gath'ers (-dherz), *n.pl.* gathered-in part of dress.

Gat'ling, *n.* a machine gun.

‖ **gauche** (gōsh), *a.* tactless, socially awkward. ‖ **gaucherie** (gō-sherē') *n.*

gaud, *n.* showy ornament, gewgaw, jewel.

gaud'y, *n.* grand entertainment. *a.* tastelessly showy.

gauge (gāj), *n.* standard measure; capacity, extent; instrument for measuring or testing; criterion, test. *v.t.* (*-geable*), measure exactly, test dimensions of; measure contents of.

Gaul, *n.* inhabitant of ancient Gaul; (joc.) Frenchman.

gault, *n.* clay and marl beds.

gaunt, *a.* lean, haggard, grim.

gaunt'let, *n.* (hist.) armoured glove; glove with long loose wrist, esp. for driving, &c.,

gaunt'let, *n. Run the* ~, pass between rows of men, &c., who strike one with sticks, &c. as punishment (also fig.)

gauze, *n.* thin transparent fabric of silk, wire, &c. **gauz'y**, *a.*

*gav'el, *n.* auctioneer's or chairman's hammer

gav'elkind, *n.* land-tenure involving equal division of property.

gā'vial, *n.* kind of alligator inhabiting the Ganges.

gavotte', *n.* dance like minuet, but more lively; dance tune.

gawk, *n.* awkward or bashful person. **gawk'y**, *a.*

gay, *a.* light-hearted, mirthful; showy; dissolute.

gaze, *v.i.* look fixedly at. *n.* intent look.

gaze'bo, *n.* structure whence view may be had.

gazelle', *n.* small graceful soft-eyed kinds of antelope.

gazette', *n.* a newspaper, esp. an official journal. *v.t.* publish in official gazette.

gazetteer', *n.* geographical dictionary.

---

gáz'ogĕne, gás~, *n.* apparatus for making aerated waters.

gear (gēr), *n.* apparatus, tackle, tools; set of wheels, levers, &c. working together; harness; apparel, household utensils. *v.t.* harness; put in gear, provide with gear. ~**box**, ~**case**, *nn.* enclosing gear of machine.

gĕck'ō, *n.* a house-lizard found in warm climates.

*****gee**, *int.* of asseveration, discovery, &c.

geez'er (g-), *n.* (sl.) old person.

gei'sha (gā-), *n.* Japanese dancing-girl.

geist (gī-), *n.* sensibility; tendency to mental fervour.

gĕl'atin(e), *n.* transparent tasteless substance. **gĕlāt'inous**, *a.*

gĕld (g-), *v.t.* deprive of generative powers, castrate. **gĕl'ding** (g-), *n.* gelded horse, &c.

gĕl'id, *a.* ice-cold; cool.

gĕl'ignite, *n.* a nitro-glycerine explosive.

gĕm, *n.* precious stone; thing of great beauty or worth; a jewel. *v.t.* adorn as with gems.

gĕm'inate, *v.t.* (-āt), double, arrange in pairs. *a.* (-ĭt) arranged in pairs. ~**tion**, *n.*

gĕmma, *n.* (pl. -ae) leaf-bud; small cellular body; bud-like animal growth developing into individual. **gemmate**, *a.* (jĕ'-) having buds, reproducing by gemmae. *v.i.* (-ăt') reproduce thus. ~**tion**, *n.*

gĕmmif'erous, *a.* yielding gems; reproducing by gemmae.

gĕmmip'arous, *a.* reproducing by gemmae.

génáppe', *n.* kind of worsted.

‖ **gendarme** (zhŏn'därm), *n.* (pl. -es) French soldier employed in police duty. ‖ **gendarmerie** (zhŏn-därm'erē), *n.* force of gendarmes.

gĕn'der, *n.* any of the classes (*masculine, feminine, neuter gender*) corresponding to the two sexes and sexlessness.

gĕnéäl'ogy, *n.* pedigree; lineage, study of pedigrees. ~**óg'ical**, *a.* ~**gist**, *n.* student of genealogies.

gĕn'eral, *a.* applicable to all, not partial or particular; prevalent, usual; vague, lacking detail. *n.* an army officer; commander of army; strategist; (colloq.) general servant; the public.

generaliss'imō, *n.* (pl. -os) commander of combined forces.

gĕneral'ity, *n.* a general statement; vagueness; the majority of.

gĕn'eralize, *v.t. & i.* (-zable) reduce to general laws; base general statement on (facts, &c.); speak vaguely. ~**zation**, *n.*

gĕn'erally, *adv.* in a general sense; in most respects; usually.

gĕn'eralship, *n.* office of general; military skill; management.

gĕn'erāte, *v.t.* (-rable), bring into existence. ~**tive**, *a.* productive. ~**tor**, *n.* begetter; apparatus for producing steam, &c.

generā'tion, *n.* procreation, begetting; period of about 30 years.

gĕnĕ'ric, *a.* characteristic of a genus or class; not specific.

generos'ity, *n.* munificence.

gĕn'erous, *a.* noble-minded; not mean; munificent; abundant.

gĕn'esis, *n.* origin; mode of formation or generation.

gĕn'et, *n.* kind of civet; its fur.

genĕt'ic, *a.* of, in, origin; of genetics. **genĕt'ics**, *n.pl.* study of heredity and variation; (loosely) the physiology of reproduction.

genē'va, *n.* spirit flavoured with juniper berries; gin.

gē'nial, *a.* mild, warm; cheering; sociable. **genĭal'ity**, *n.*

gē'nie, *n.* (pl. usu. *gēnii*) sprite or goblin of Arabian tales.

gĕnis'ta, *n.* kinds of yellow-flowered shrub.

gĕn'ital, *a.* of generation. *n.pl.* external genital organs.

gĕn'itive, *a.* indicating source, origin or possession. *n.* (Gram.) genitive case. **genitī'val**, *a.*

gē'nius, *n.* (pl. -iuses, -iī) tutelary spirit; exalted intellectual power; person having this.

‖ **genre** (zhahnr), *n.* kind, style, of

art, &c.; portrayal of scenes from ordinary life.

gĕnt, *n.* (vulg.) gentleman.

gĕnteel', *a.* elegant, stylish; well-bred. gĕnteel'ly, *adv.*

gĕn'tian (-shn), *n.* kinds of usu. blue-flowered plant.

gĕn'tile, *a.* not of Jewish race; heathen. *n.* gentile person.

gentil'ity, *n.* gentle birth; social superiority; upper-class habits.

gĕn'tle, *a.* well-born; mild, quiet; not rough or severe. *n.* maggot as bait; (pl., vulg.) gentlefolk. ~folk(s), people of good family.

gĕn'tleman (-telm-), *n.* (pl. *-men*) chivalrous well-bred man; man of good social position; (pl.) male part of audience. ~like, ~ly, *aa.* behaving, looking, like a gentleman; befitting a gentleman.

gĕn'tleness (-tel-), *n.* kindliness, mildness; freedom from violence.

gĕn'tlewoman (-telwŏŏman), *n.* (pl. *-en*, pr. -wimin) woman of good birth or breeding; lady.

gĕn'tly, *adv.* mildly, kindly; quietly, softly, slowly.

gĕn'try, *n.* people next below nobility; (contempt.) people.

gĕn'uflĕct, *v.i.* bend the knee, esp. in worship. gĕnŭflĕx'ion, *n.*

gĕn'ūine, *a.* pure-bred; not sham; authentic.

gē'nus, *n.* (pl. *gĕn'era*) group of animals, plants, &c., containing several species; (loosely) kind, class.

gĕocĕn'tric, *a.* considered as viewed from earth's centre.

gē'ōde, *n.* (stone with) cavity lined with crystals.

gĕŏd'ĕsў, *n.* branch of mathematics, study of figure and area of the earth or large portions of it. gĕodĕs'ic, -ĕt'ic, *aa.*

gĕŏg'nosў, *n.* geology, esp. of district or particular rocks.

gĕŏg'raphў, *n.* science of earth's form, physical features, &c.; features of place; manual of geography. ~pher, *n.*; ~phical, *a.*

gĕŏl'ogў, *n.* science of earth's crust, its strata, and their rela-

tions. ~gical, *a.*; ~gist, *n.* ~gize, *v.i.* practise geology.

gĕŏm'etrў, *n.* science of properties and relations of magnitudes in space. gĕomĕt'ric(al), *aa.* of geometry. gĕŏm'eter, gĕomĕtri'cian (-shn), *nn.* one versed in geometry.

George (jorj), *n.* jewel forming part of Garter insignia. by~, oath or exclamation.

georgĕtte' (jorj-). *n.* a thin silk dress material.

Geor'gian (jor-), *a.* of time of George I–IV or of George V.

Geor'gic (jor-), *n.* any book of Virgil's husbandry poem.

gerā'nium, *n.* kind of wild plant with fruit like crane's bill; cultivated pelargonium.

gĕr'falcon (-awkn), *n.* Icelandic or any large northern falcon.

gĕrm, *n.* source, origin; rudiment of animal or plant; micro-organism or microbe.

gĕrm'an¹, *a.* closely related.

Gĕrm'an², *a.* of Germany. *n.* native, language, of Germany. ~ measles, disease like mild measles. ~ sausage, large kind with spiced meat. ~ silver, white alloy of nickel, &c. ~ text, Gothic black-letter.

gĕrmān'der, *n.* kinds of plant, esp. ~ *speedwell*.

germāne', *a.* relevant to a subject.

gĕrmā'nium, *n.* metallic element of greyish-white colour.

gĕrm'icide, *n.* destructive of germs. *n.* germicide substance.

gĕrm'inal, *a.* of germs; in earliest stage of development.

gĕrm'ināte, *v.i. & t.* sprout, bud; cause to shoot, produce. ~ant, *a.*; ~tion, ~tor, *nn.*

gĕrrў'mander (g-), *v.t.* manipulate (constituency, &c.) so as to give undue influence to some class.

gĕ'rund, *n.* cases of Latin infinitive constructed as noun but governing like verb; English verbal noun in *-ing*. gĕrun'dive, *n.* Latin verbal adjective from gerund stem; *a.* of, like, the gerund.

gĕss'ō, *n.* gypsum as used in painting and sculpture.

gh, as (*rou*)*ge*; ė=**i**; ū̆, ū̆, =ŏr; ў̆, ў̆, =ī, ĭ; and see p. 4. *=U.S.

gestā′tion, *n.* carrying in womb between conception and birth.

gestic′ūlāte, *v.i. & t.* use expressive motion of limbs, &c. with or instead of speech. ~**tion**, ~**tor**, *nn.*; ~**tive**, ~**tory**, *aa.*

ges′ture, *n.* significant movement of limb or body; step or move calculated to evoke response from another.

get (g-), *v.t. & i.* (past *got*; p.p. *got* & *gotten*), obtain, earn, gain, win, procure; fetch; learn; induce; beget; experience or suffer; catch or contract; have inflicted; arrive at; find the way; have recourse to. ~**at′-able**, accessible. ~**up**, style of arrangement or production.

gē′um, *n.* kinds of flowering plant.

gew′-gaw (g-), *n.* gaudy plaything or ornament.

gey′ser (gā-), *n.* hot spring; apparatus for heating water.

‖ **gharr′y̆**, *n.* (Anglo-Ind.) horsed vehicle resembling a bathing-machine.

ghast′ly̆ (gah-), *a.* horrible, frightful; deathlike, pallid.

‖ **gha(u)t** (gawt), *n.* (Ang.-Ind.) mountain pass; steps leading to river; landing-place.

gha′zi (gah-), *n.* fanatic Mohammedan fighter.

ghee (gē), *n.* Indian clarified buffalo-milk butter.

gherk′in (gẽr-), *n.* young or small cucumber for pickling.

ghett′o (gĕ-), *n.* (hist.; pl. *-os*) Jews' quarter in city.

ghost (gō-), *n.* dead person appearing to the living, spectre; emaciated or pale person; semblance.

ghost′ly̆ (gō-), *a.* spiritual; as of a ghost, spectral.

ghoul (gōōl), *n.* spirit said to prey on corpses. ~**ish**, *a.*

gi′ant, *n.* being of superhuman size; very tall person, animal, &c.; person of extraordinary ability. *a.* gigantic. ~**ess**, *n.* ~**'s-stride**, gymnastic apparatus enabling user to take huge strides round a pole.

giaour (jowr), *n.* Turkish name for infidel, esp. Christian.

gibb′er (j-, g-), *v.i.* chatter inarticulately. *n.* such chatter. ~**ish**, *n.* unintelligible speech.

gibb′et, *n.* post on which executed criminal was exposed. *v.t.* expose on gibbet; hold up to contempt.

gibb′on (g-), *n.* kinds of long-armed ape.

gibb′ous (g-), *a.* convex, protuberant; hunchbacked. **gibbŏs′ity** (g-), *n.*

gibe, jibe, *v.i. & t.*, & *n.* flout, jeer; mock, taunt.

gib′lets, *n.pl.* liver, &c. of bird removed before cooking.

gig′ (g-), *n.* crush hat.

gidd′y̆ (g-), *a.* dizzy, disposed to fall or stagger; frivolous.

gift (g-), *n.* thing given, present; natural endowment. *v.t.* endow with gifts; present.

gig (g-), *n.* light two-wheeled one-horse carriage; light ship's boat; rowing-boat, esp. for race.

gigăn′tic, *a.* huge, giant-like.

gig′gle (g-), *v.i. & n.* laugh affectedly, titter.

Gilbert′ian (g-), *a.* topsy-turvy, in vein of Gilbert & Sullivan opera.

gild¹ (g-), *v.t.* (p.p. *gilded*), cover thinly with gold; tinge with golden colour; make specious.

gild². See guild.

gill¹ (g-), *n.* (usu. pl.) respiratory organ(s) of fish, &c.; flesh below person's jaws and ears.

gill² (g-), *n.* deep wooded ravine; narrow mountain torrent.

gill³, *n.* quarter-pint measure.

gillarŏō′ (g-), *n.* Irish trout.

gill′ie (g-), *n.* sportsman's or (hist.) Highland chief's attendant.

gill′yflower, *n.* clove-scented pink; wallflower.

gilt¹ (g-), *n.* gilding. *a.* overlaid with gold.

gilt², *n.* young sow.

gim′bal, *n.* (pl.) contrivance of rings, &c. for keeping things horizontal at sea.

gim′crack, *n.* trumpery ornament, &c. *a.* flimsy, trumpery.

---

gim′let (-g-), *n.* small boring-tool.

gimp, **gymp** (g-), *n.* twist of silk, &c. interlaced with cord or wire.

gin[1], *n.* snare, trap; kinds of crane and windlass; machine separating cotton from seeds. *v.t.* trap; treat cotton in gin.

gin[2], *n.* spirit distilled from grain or malt, geneva.

|| **gin′gall**, **j-**, *n.* rest-musket or light swivel gun used in India and China.

gin′ger (-j-), *n.* hot spicy root; mettle, spirit; (sl.) stimulation; light reddish yellow. *v.t.* apply ginger to (horse) to produce show of spirit; stimulate. ~**ade**, ~**ale**, ~**beer**, ~**pop**, ~**wine**, ginger-flavoured drinks. ~**bread**, ginger-flavoured treacle cake.

gin′gerly (-j-), *a.* such as to avoid noise or injury to oneself. *adv. in* gingerly manner.

gingham (ging′am), *n.* a cotton or linen cloth; umbrella.

gin′nery, *n.* (S.-Afr.) cotton factory.

gip′sy, *n.* member of a wandering race; mischievous or dark-complexioned woman.

giraffe′ (-ahf), *n.* ruminant quadruped with long neck.

gi′randole, *n.* revolving firework or jet of water; branched candle bracket or candlestick.

gi′rasol(e) (or -sŏl), *n.* opal reflecting reddish glow.

gird[1] (g-), *v.t.* (*girded* or *girt*), encircle with waistbelt, &c.; equip; invest with strength, &c.; encircle.

gird[2] (g-), *v.i.*, & *n.* gibe.

gird′er (g-), *n.* beam supporting joists; iron or steel beam.

gir′dle[1] (g-), *n.* cord, belt, used to gird waist; thing that surrounds. *v.t.* surround with girdle.

gir′dle[2] (g-), *n.* round iron plate for cooking *girdle-cakes.*

girl (g-), *n.* female child; young unmarried woman; maid-servant; man's sweetheart. ~ **guides**, organization parallel to boy scouts. ~**hood**, *n.*; ~**ish**, *a.*

girt, *p.t.* of gird.

girth (g-), *n.* band round body of horse securing saddle; measurement round a thing. *v.t.* encircle (horse), secure (saddle), with girth.

gist (j-), *n.* substance, pith.

gitt′ern (g-), *n.* cithern.

give[1] (g-), *v.t.* & *i.* (*gāve*, *given*; -*vable*), bestow gratuitously; grant, accord; deliver, administer; consign, put; pledge; devote; present, offer (one's hand, arm, &c.); impart, be source of; assume, grant, specify; collapse, yield, shrink. ~ **away**, *n.* unwitting disclosure.

give[2] (g-), *n.* yielding to pressure; elasticity. ~**and-take**, mutual concession, exchange of talk.

gizz′ard (g-), *n.* bird's second stomach for grinding food.

glā′brous, *a.* smooth-skinned.

glā′cial (or glā′shl), *a.* of ice; (Chem.) crystallized.

glā′ciāted (or glā′-; -si-, -shi-), *a.* marked by ice-action; covered with glaciers. ~**tion**, *n.*

glā′cier, *n.* slowly moving river or mass of ice.

glā′cis (or glā′-, glahsē′), *n.* bank sloping down from fort.

glad, *a.* pleased; joyful, cheerful. **gladd′en**, *v.t.* make glad.

glāde, *n.* clear space in forest.

glad′iātor, *n.* trained fighter in ancient Roman shows. ~**ial**, *a.*

glad′iolus, *n.* (pl. -*li*) plant of iris kind with bright flower-spikes.

glad′some, *a.* joyful, cheerful.

glad′stone bāg′, *n.* portmanteau.

glair, *n.* white of egg. *v.t.* smear with glair. ~**eous**, ~**y**, *aa.*

glaive, *n.* a sword, falchion.

glam′our (-er), *n.* magic, enchantment; delusive or alluring beauty. **glam′orous**, *a.*

glance (-ah-), *v.i.* & *t.* glide off object; make brief allusion to; cast momentary look at. *n.* swift oblique movement or impact; flash, gleam; brief look.

gland, *n.* organ formed of cells secreting constituents of blood for use or ejection; secreting cells on surface of plant-structure.

---

mãre, mēre, mĩre, mŏre, mũre; pãrt, pĕrt, pŏrt; *italics*, vague sounds;

glän'diform, a. acorn-shaped. glän'dular, glän'dulous, aa.

glän'ders (-z), n.pl. contagious horse-disease. glän'dered (-erd), glän'derous, aa.

glāre, v.i. shine oppressively; look fiercely at. n. oppressive light; tawdry brilliance; fierce look.

glass (-ah-), n. siliceous substance, usu. transparent, lustrous, hard, and brittle; glass drinking-vessel; looking-glass; lens; (pl.) pair of spectacles. v.t. mirror, reflect; make (eye) glassy. ~-blower, one who blows and shapes glass. glass'ў (-ah-), a. like glass; (of eye) fixed, dull.

glaucō'ma, n. an eye-disease.

glauc'ous, a. of dull greyish green or blue.

glāze, v.t. & i. (-zable), fit with glass or windows; cover (pottery, &c.) with vitreous substance; (of eye) become glassy. n. substance used for, surface produced by, glazing.

glā'zier (-zher, -zier), n. one who glazes windows.

gleam, n. subdued or transient light. v.i. emit gleams.

glean, v.i. & i. gather corn left by reapers; pick up (facts, &c.). ~er, n.; ~ings, n.pl.

glëbe, n. land going with benefice; earth, land, field.

glee, n. composition for three or more voices; mirth, manifest joy. ~ful, a. joyful.

gleet, n. thin morbid discharge.

glën, n. narrow valley.

Glĕngä'rrŷ (-n-g-), n. kind of Highland cap.

glib, a. fluent, voluble.

glide, v.i. & t. pass, proceed, by smooth continuous movement; go stealthily. n. gliding motion.

glimm'er, v.i. shine faintly or intermittently. n. faint light.

glimpse, n. faint transient appearance; brief view. v.t. & i. see or be seen faintly or partly.

glint, v.i. & t. flash; glitter; reflect (light). n. flash, glitter.

glissade' (-ahd), n. slide down slope of ice, &c. v.i. slide thus.

glis'ten (-sn), v.i. & n. glitter, sparkle.

glis'ter, v.i. & n. glitter.

glitt'er, v.i. sparkle; shine with bright light. n. such light.

gloam'ing, n. evening twilight.

gloat, v.i. feast eyes or mind greedily, malignantly, &c. upon.

glō'bal, a. embracing totality of a group of items, &c.

globe, n. sphere; planet, star, sun; spherical chart of the earth; spherical lamp-shade.

globōse', a. like a globe; round. globōs'itŷ, n. roundness of form.

glŏb'ūlar, a. globe-shaped; composed of globules. ~ä'ritŷ, n.

glŏb'ūle, n. small globe, e.g. pill; round particle.

glŏb'ūlin, n. protein found in blood.

glŏm'erate, a. compactly clustered.

glōom, n. darkness; melancholy, depression. v.i. look or be sullen or depressed; be dull.

glōom'ў, a. dark, depressing.

glōr'ia, n. doxology; aureole.

glōr'ifŷ, v.t. (-iable), make glorious or radiant; extol. ~fication, n.

glōr'iōle, n. aureole, halo.

glōr'ious, a. possessing or conferring glory; splendid, excellent.

glōr'ў, n. renown, honourable fame; resplendent majesty, beauty, &c.; halo of saint. v.i. take a pride in.

glŏss[1], n. superficial lustre; specious appearance. v.t. give gloss to; make specious. glŏss'ў, a. shiny.

glŏss[2], n. marginal explanation; comment; specious interpretation. v.t. & i. insert glosses; make comments; explain away.

glŏss'arŷ, n. dictionary of technical or special words. ~rial, a. glŏssŏg'rapher, n. commentator.

glŏtt'is, n. opening at upper part of windpipe. ~tal, a. of, in, the glottis.

glove (-ŭv), n. hand-covering of leather, wool, &c.; boxer's glove. ~fight, with boxing-gloves.

glō'ver (-ŭv-), n. glove-maker.

glow (-ō), v.i. emit flameless light

and heat; burn with bodily heat or emotion. *n.* glowing state; ardour. **~-worm**, coleopterous insect female of which emits green light at tail.

glower (-owr), *v.i.* look angrily.

glôze, *v.i. & t.* (*-zable*), explain away; use fair words.

glu'côse (glōō-), *n.* fruit-sugar.

glue (glōō), *n.* hard gelatin used warm as cement. *v.t.* fasten with glue. **~-pot**, with outer coat holding water to heat glue.

gluey (glōō'ĭ), *a.*

glŭm, *a.* dejected, sullen.

glume (-ōōm), *n.* husk.

glŭt, *v.t.* feed to the full, sate. *n.* surfeit; excessive supply.

glu'tĕn (glōō-), *n.* sticky substance; viscid part of flour. **glu'tinous**, *a.*; **glutinŏs'itў**, *n.*

glŭtt'on, *n.* excessive eater; person insatiably eager. **~ous**, *a.*

glŭtt'onў, *n.* character, conduct, of a glutton.

glў'cerine, *n.* colourless sweet liquid got from any fatty substance.

glўp'tic, *a.* of carving, esp. on gems. **glўptŏg'raphy**, *n.* gemengraving.

gnarled (närld), *a.* knobby, rugged, twisted. **gnärl'ў**, *a.*

gnāsh (n-), *v.i. & t.* (of teeth) strike together; grind one's teeth.

gnăt (n-), *n.* small insect.

gnaw (n-), *v.t. & i.* (p.p. *gnawed*, *gnawn*), bite persistently; corrode, torture.

gneiss (gnīs, n-), *n.* laminated rock of quartz, feldspar, and mica.

gnome (nōm), *n.* maxim; goblin, dwarf. **gnō'mic** (n-), *a.* of maxims, sententious. **~ish**, *a.* of, like, a gnome (goblin).

gnō'mon (n-), *n.* rod, pin, &c. of sun-dial; geometrical figure.

gnō'sis (n-), *n.* knowledge of spiritual mysteries; gnosticism. **gnŏs'tic** (n-), *a.* of knowledge; having esoteric spiritual knowledge. *n.* early Christian heretic claiming gnosis. **~ism**, *n.*

gnu (nū), *n.* oxlike antelope.

gō, *v.i.* (*went*, *gone* pr. -awn), walk, travel, proceed; move, pass;

become; (of money) be spent in or on; collapse, give way, fail; extend, reach. *n.* (colloq.; pl. *goes*), act of going; animation, dash; (sl.) state of affairs; (Cribbage) inability to play. **~ahead**, enterprising. **~between**, an intermediary. **~by**, an evasion. **~cart**, wheeled frame for teaching child to walk; perambulator. **~dry**, (of State or locality) prohibit sale of intoxicants. **~getter**, (sl.) person who succeeds in his object. **~off**, a start. **~west**, (army sl.) be killed, die.

goad, *n.* spiked stick for urging cattle; thing that incites or torments. *v.t.* urge with goad.

goal, *n.* point where race ends; object of effort; destination; posts between which football, &c. is to be driven, points so won. **~keeper**, player protecting goal.

goat, *n.* horned ruminant quadruped; *(sl.)* butt. **~herd**, one who tends goats. **~ish**, **~ў**, *aa.*

goatee', *n.* beard like goat's.

goat'sucker, *n.* nightjar.

gōbăng', *n.* game played on chequer-board.

gŏbb'ĕt, *n.* lump of meat, &c.

gŏb'ble[1], *v.t. & i.* eat hurriedly and noisily. *n.* (Golf) rapid straight putt into hole. **gŏb'bler**, *n.* noisy ravenous eater.

gŏb'ble[2], *v.i.* (of turkey-cock) make gurgling sound in throat.

gŏb'elin, *n.* a rich French tapestry or an imitation of it.

gŏb'lĕt, *n.* bowl-shaped drinking-cup; glass with foot and stem.

gŏb'lin, *n.* mischievous demon.

gŏ'bў, *n.* kinds of small fish.

gŏd, *n.* (*God*) the Supreme Being; superhuman being worshipped as possessing divine power; a false god; image worshipped as symbol, an idol; adored person; (Theatr., pl.) occupants of the gallery. **~child**, baptized child in relation to his godparent. **~daughter**, female godchild. **~father**, **~mother**, male and female godparent. **~parent**, one's sponsor at baptism. **~son**,

---

zh, as (*rou*)*ge*; **ė** = **ĭ**; **ö**, **ür**, = **ĕr**; **ў̄**, **ў**, = **ī**, **ĭ**; and see p. 4. * = U.S.

male godchild. ~'s-acre, church-yard.

gŏdd'ess, n. female deity.

gŏdē'tia (-sha), n. a free-flowering hardy annual.

gŏd'fearing, a. religious.

gŏd'forsāken (also -ŏk'-), a. dismal.

gŏd'head (-ĕd), n. divine nature, deity.

gŏd'lĕss, a. not recognizing God; impious, wicked. **gŏd'līke,** a. like God; like that of a god. **gŏd'lў,** a. pious, devout.

|| **gŏ'down,** n. (Anglo-Ind.) warehouse.

gŏd'sĕnd, n. piece of luck.

gŏd'wit, n. marsh bird like curlew.

gō'er, n. one who goes; a runner or walker.

gof(f)'er, goph'er¹ (gŏ, gō-), v.t. make wavy, crimp, with hot irons. n. such iron; plating for frills, &c.

gŏg'gle, v.i. & t. roll eyes about; (of eyes) roll about, project. a. (of eyes) protuberant, rolling. n.pl. spectacles for protecting eyes from glare, dust, &c.

gō'ing, a. existing, available. n. the act of walking; departure; condition of ground for riding, &c. **gōings-ŏn'**, (colloq.) strange or wild conduct.

goi'tre (-ter), n. morbid enlargement of thyroid gland. **goi'tred** (-erd), a. having goitre.

Gŏlcŏn'da, n. mine of wealth.

gŏld, n. precious yellow metal; coins of this, wealth; colour of gold. a. of or coloured like gold. ~-**beater,** one who beats gold into gold-leaf. ~-**leaf,** gold beaten into thin sheet.

gō'lden, a. of gold; coloured or shining like gold; precious. ~-**mean,** neither too much nor too little. ~-**rod,** plant with yellow flower-spikes. ~-**syrup,** pale treacle. ~-**wedding,** 50th wedding anniversary.

gŏld'finch, n. song-bird with yellow on wings; (sl.) gold coin.

gŏld'fish, n. small red Chinese carp.

gŏld'smith, n. worker in gold.

gŏlf (or gŏf), n. game in which small hard ball is struck with club into hole on each of successive smooth greens separated by rough ground. v.i. play golf. ~-**club,** golf implement or society. **gŏl'fer** (also gŏf-), n.

gŏl'iwŏg, n. quaint black doll of formal pattern with fuzzy hair.

golosh. See galosh.

golŭp'tious (-shus), a. (joc.) delicious (esp. of food).

gŏmbeen', n. (Anglo-Ir.) usury. ~-**man,** money-lender.

|| **gŏm(b)rŏon',** n. Persian pottery, imitated in Chelsea ware.

gŏn'dola, n. light Venetian canal-boat; car suspended from air-ship; *flat-bottomed river-boat. **gŏndolier',** n. rower of gondola.

gone, p.p. of go.

gon'er (gaw-), n. (sl.) person or thing in desperate case.

gŏn'falon, n. banner, often with streamers, hung from cross-bar.

gŏng, n. resonant metal disk; saucer-shaped bell.

gŏnorrhœ'a (-rēa), n. inflammatory discharge from urethra or vagina.

good, a. having the right qualities, adequate; worthy; proper; well-behaved; benevolent; agreeable; suitable; considerable. n. profit, well-being; (pl.) movable property, merchandise; *(pl., sl.) resources. ~ **afternoon,** evening, salutations at meeting or parting. ~-**fellowship,** conviviality. ~-**for-nothing,** ne'er-do-well. ~-**looking,** having good looks. ~ **morning,** ~ **night** (as ~ **afternoon**). ~-**natured,** of kindly disposition. ~ **people,** the fairies.

good-bye', int. & n. farewell.

good'lў, a. handsome; of imposing size, &c.

good'nĕss, n. virtue; excellence; kindness; essence or nutriment.

good'wife, n. mistress of house.

goodwill', n. kindly feeling; heartiness; custom of a business.

good'ў, n. sweetmeat; old woman. a. (also goody'-goody) obtrusively, feebly, or sentimentally virtuous.

goo′ly, n. (Crick.) off-break ball with leg-break action.

goosan′der, n. duck-like bird.

goose, n. (pl. **geese** pr. gēs), web-footed bird between duck and swan in size; simpleton; tailor's smoothing-iron. ~**flesh,** ~**skin,** bristling state of skin due to cold or fright. ~**step,** army recruit's balancing-drill, also formal parade step, esp. as used in German army.

goose′berry (-zb-), n. a thorny shrub, its edible berry; wine made of gooseberries. **goose′gog** (-zg-), n. (colloq.) gooseberry.

gopher[1]. See got(f)er.

"go′pher", n. kinds of burrowing rodent. v.i. burrow; (Mining) dig haphazard.

‖ **gor′al,** n. an Indian antelope.

Gord′ian, a. Cut the ~ *knot,* solve problem by force or evasion.

gore[1], n. clotted blood.

gore[2], n. wedge-shaped piece inserted to narrow a garment. v.t. shape with gore.

gore[3], v.t. pierce with horn.

gorge, n. internal throat; contents of stomach; surfeit; narrow opening between hills. v.i. & t. (-*geable*) feed greedily; satiate.

gor′geous (-jus), a. richly coloured; splendid, dazzling.

gor′get, n. armour for throat; woman's wimple; necklace.

Gor′gon, n. terrible or repulsive woman. ~**ize,** v.t. petrify with stare. gorgō′nian, a.

gorgonzo′la, n. a rich cheese.

gorill′a, n. large ferocious anthropoid ape.

gorm′andize, v.i. eat like a glutton. **gorm′andizer,** n.

gorse, n. prickly yellow-flowered shrub; furze. **gors′y,** a.

gor′y, a. covered with blood.

gosh, int. of surprise, &c.

gos′hawk (-s-h-), n. a large short-winged hawk.

gos′ling (-z-), n. young goose.

gos′pel, n. Christian revelation; any of the records of the four evangelists; principle that one acts upon or preaches. ~**-pusher,** clergyman.

gos′peller, n. reader of gospel in the Communion service.

goss′amer, n. filmy substance of small spiders' webs; flimsy thing; delicate gauze; "thin waterproof garment. a. light, flimsy, as gossamer.

goss′ip, n. familiar acquaintance; tattler, esp. woman; idle talk; informal talk or writing. v.i. talk or write gossip.

gossoon′, n. (Anglo-Ir.) lad.

got, p.t. & p.p. of get.

Go′tha (-ta), n. (obs.) type of large German aeroplane.

Goth′ic, a. (Archit.) in the pointed-arch style; barbarous, uncouth; (of type) German, also black-letter. n. Gothic language, architecture, type.

gouge (gowj, gōōj), n. concave-bladed chisel; "groove; "(sl.) cheat. v.t. cut with gouge; force as with gouge.

"goulash (gōō′lahsh), n. ragout of steak and vegetables flavoured with peppers.

gourd (gōrd, goord), n. a trailing or climbing plant; dried rind of this used as bottle.

gourmand (goorm′and), a. gluttonous. n. lover of delicacies.

gourmet (goorm′ā), n. connoisseur of wine or table delicacies.

gout (gowt), n. disease with inflammation, esp. of great toe; drop, esp. of blood. **gout′y,** a.

go′vern (gǔ-), v.t. & i. rule with authority; conduct the policy and affairs of State, &c.; curb, control; sway, influence. ~**ance,** n. act of governing.

go′verness (gǔ-), n. female teacher, esp. in private household. ~ **car(t),** light two-wheeled cart.

go′vernment (gǔ-), n. form of polity; persons governing a State; the State as agent. ~**al,** a.

go′vernor (gǔ-), n. ruler; official governing province, town, &c.; executive head of each of the U.S.; one of a governing body of

---

māre, mēre, mīre, mōre, mūre; pårt, pêrt, pûrt; *italics,* vague sounds;

institution; (sl.) one's employer or father; sir. ~ general, representative of Crown in dominion.

gowk, *n.* fool; (dial.) cuckoo.

gown, *n.* a woman's upper garment, frock; robe of alderman, judge, clergyman, member of university, &c. ~s'man (-*an*), member of a university.

grăb, *v.t. & i.* seize suddenly; appropriate greedily; capture. *n.* sudden clutch or attempt to seize; rapacious proceedings.

grăbb'le, *v.i.* grope, sprawl.

grăbb'ў, *n.* (Naut. sl.) soldier.

grāce, *n.* charm; air, bearing; embellishment; goodwill; divine regenerating and inspiring influence; delay granted; thanksgiving at meals. *v.t.* add grace to, adorn; honour. ~ful, *a.* full of charm, attractive. ~less, *a.* shameless, depraved.

grā'cious (-shŭs), *a.* pleasing; condescending; kindly; merciful.

*grăd, *n.* (sl.) graduate.

gradāte', *v.t. & i.* (-*table*), (cause to) pass by gradations from one shade to another; arrange in gradations.

gradā'tion, *n.* each stage in transition or advance; series of degrees in rank, intensity, &c.; arrangement in grades. ~al, *a.*

grāde, *n.* degree in rank, merit, &c.; *gradient, slope. *v.t.* (-*dable*), arrange in grades; give gradations of colour to; blend so as to affect grade.

grā'dely (-dlĭ), *a.* (dial.) excellent, thorough; handsome; real, true.

grā'dient, *n.* amount of slope in road, railway, &c.

grăd'ūal, *a.* happening by degrees; not steep or abrupt. *n.* (also grail) antiphon sung between Epistle and Gospel.

grăd'ūate, *v.i. & t.* (-āt), take or admit to academic degree; arrange in gradations. *n.* (-ĭt), holder of academic degree or *(U.S.) one who has completed course of study at a school. ~tion, *n.*

grā'dus, *n.* dictionary for use in writing Latin verse.

graffi'tō (-fē-), *n.* (pl. -*ti*, pr. -tē), drawing or writing scratched on (esp. ancient) wall, &c.

graft¹ (grahft), *n.* shoot, scion, planted in slit of another stock; piece of transplanted living tissue. *v.t.* insert graft.

*graft² (grahft), *n.* (practices for securing) illicit political or business spoils. *v.i.* seek or make graft. *graft'er (-aht-), *n.*

grail¹. See gradual.

grail², *n.* platter used by Christ at the Last Supper.

grāllātŏr'ial, *a.* of the long-legged wading birds.

grain, *n.* a fruit or corn of a cereal; (collect.) wheat or allied foodgrass; corn; (pl.) refuse malt after brewing; particle, least possible amount; unit of weight; texture in skin, wood, stone, &c.; arrangement of lines of fibre in wood. *v.t. & i.* form into grains; dye in grain; paint in imitation of grain of wood. ~ing, *n.* grain-painting.

grăm¹, *n.* chick-pea; any pulse used as horse-fodder.

gram². See gramme.

*grā'ma, grămm'a, *n.* kinds of low pasture grasses in the western U.S.

gramĕr'cў, *int.* (arch.) thank you.

grāmĭnā'ceous (-shŭs), *a.* of or like grass.

grāmĭnĭv'orous (-shŭs), *a.* grass-eating.

grămm'alogue (-ŏg), *n.* (shorthand) word represented by single sign; such sign.

grămm'ar, *n.* science of the sounds, inflexions, and constructions used in a language; book on grammar. ~-school, founded for teaching Latin, now often of public-school type; *school between primary and high school. grammār'ian, *n.* one versed in grammar. grammăt'ical, *a.* according to grammar.

grămme, grăm, *n.* unit of weight in metric system.

grăm'ophŏne, *n.* phonograph, esp. of the kind reproducing music, speech, &c. from hard rubber or plastic records.

ăh, awl, oil, boor, cow, dowry; chin, go, bang, so, ship, thin; dh, as th(e).

grăm'pus, n. kinds of blowing and spouting cetacean.

grăn'ary, n. storehouse for grain; region producing grain.

grănd, a. (in titles) chief, of highest rank; of chief importance; imposing, lofty, noble; (colloq.) excellent. **~ piano**, grand piano. **gran'dad**, (fam. for) grandfather. **gran'dam(e)**, (arch. for) grandmother. **grand'child**, one's child's child. **~-daughter**, one's child's daughter. **~-father**, one's parent's father. **~-mother**, one's parent's mother. **~-parent**, one's parent's parent. **~ piano**, one with strings horizontal. **~sire**, grandfather. **~son**, one's child's son.

grăndee', n. foreign noble of high rank; great personage.

grăn'deur (-dyer), n. high rank, eminence; majesty, splendour.

grăndil'oquent, a. pompous, inflated, in language. **~nce**, n.

grăn'diose, a. imposing; planned on large scale. **grăndiŏs'ĭtў**, n.

grănge (-j), n. country-house with farm buildings; 'agricultural association.

grā'ngerize (-j-), v.t. illustrate book with extra prints, &c. gathered from other sources.

grăn'ite, n. granular crystalline rock of quartz, mica, &c.

grănn'ў, n. (colloq.) grandmother. **reef-knot crossed the wrong way.**

grant (-ah-), v.t. consent to give; concede, permit; transfer; admit. n. granting; thing or sum granted. **grantee', gran'tŏr**, nn. person to, or by, whom property, &c. is legally transferred.

grăn'ular, a. of or like grains.

grăn'ūlate, v.t. & i. (-lable), form into grains; roughen surface of. **~tion**, n.

grăn'ūle, n. small grain.

grāpe, n. green or purple berry growing in clusters on vine; grape-shot; diseased growth on pastern of horse, &c. **~-fruit**, fruit like a large orange, growing in clusters. **~-shot**, small balls as scattering charge for cannon.

grăph, n. symbolic diagram expressing a system of connexions.

grăph'ic, a. of drawing, painting, etching, &c.; vividly descriptive of writing; of symbolic curves.

grăph'ite, n. plumbago.

graphŏl'ogў, n. study of handwriting; use of graphs.

grăp'nel, n. a grappling-iron; small many-fluked anchor.

grăp'ple, n. clutching instrument; grip, of wrestler; close contest. v.t. & i. seize; grip with hands; come to close quarters with. **grappling-iron**, instrument by which one ship fastens to another in fighting.

grasp (-ah-), v.t. & i. clutch, seize greedily; hold firmly; understand, realize. n. fast hold, grip; mental hold, mastery. **~ing**, a. avaricious.

grass (-ah-), n. herbage; any species of this; grazing; pasture land. v.t. cover with turf; (sl.) knock down. **~hopper**, a jumping chirping insect. **~-tree**, kinds of Australasian tree. **~ widow**, (sl.) married woman whose husband is absent from her.

grass-cloth (grahs-clawth), fine light cloth, resembling linen, woven from vegetable fibres.

grāte[1], n. metal frame confining fuel in fireplace.

grāte[2], v.t. & i. (-lable), rub to small particles on rough surface; grind, creak; have irritating effect.

grāte'ful, a. thankful; feeling or showing gratitude.

grăt'ifў, v.t. (-lable), please, delight; indulge. **~fication**, n.

grā'ting, n. framework of parallel or crossed bars.

grā'tis, adv. & a. free of charge.

grăt'ĭtūde, n. being thankful for and ready to return kindness.

gratū'itous, a. got or done gratis; uncalled for, motiveless.

gratū'itў, n. money present for services, tip; bounty to soldier.

grăt'ŭlātorў, a. conveying congratulation.

gravā'měn, n. essence (of accusation); grievance.

grāve¹, n. hole dug for corpse; (fig.) receptacle of what is dead. ~clothes, wrappings of corpse. ~stone, inscribed stone over grave. ~yard, burial ground.

grāve², v.t. (p.p. ~en, -ed; -vable). engrave, carve; fix indelibly.

grāve³, a. serious, weighty; dignified, solemn; (of accent) lowpitched, not acute. n. grave accent (as è).

grāve⁴, v.t. clean (ship's bottom) by burning and tarring.

grăv'el, n. coarse sand and small stones; disease with aggregations of urinary crystals. v.t. lay with gravel; puzzle, nonplus.

grăv'id, a. pregnant.

grăv'itāte, v.i. move or tend towards the centre; sink as by gravity; (fig.) be attracted (towards). ~tion, n.; ~tional, a.

grăv'ity, n. solemnity; importance; weight; a body's attraction to the centre of the earth.

grā'vy, n. juices exuding from meat in and after cooking.

gray. See grey.

gray'ling, n. a silver-grey freshwater fish.

grāze¹, v.i. & t. touch lightly in passing; abrade skin, &c. in rubbing past. n. grazing; an abrasion.

grāze², v.i. & t. (-zable), feed on growing grass; pasture cattle. grā'zier (-zher), n. one who feeds cattle for market. grā'zing, n. pasture; grass feed.

grease, n. (-ēs), melted fat of dead animal; fatty or oily matter. v.t. (-ēz), lubricate or soil with grease; bribe. grea'ser (-z-), n. head fireman on steamer; *(sl.) native Mexican or SpanishAmerican. greas'y (-zī), a. of, like, or smeared with grease; slimy; too unctuous.

great (grāt), a. large in bulk or number; considerable in extent or time; important, pre-eminent; of great ability; familiar; pregnant; hard, difficult, grievous. n.pl. the Oxford final classical school. ~aunt, one's parent's aunt. ~nephew, ~niece, one's nephew's or niece's child. ~uncle, one's parent's uncle.

greatcoat' (grāt-), n. overcoat.

great'ly (grāt-), adv. much.

greave, n. armour for shins.

greaves (-vz), n.pl. tallow refuse.

grēbe, n. a diving bird.

Grē'cian (-shn), a. Greek. n. Greek scholar.

greed, n. insatiate desire for food or wealth. greed'y, a. gluttonous, avaricious.

Greek, n. native of Greece; Greek language. a. of Greece or its people, Hellenic.

green, a. of colour like grass; unripe, young; inexperienced; not seasoned or dried. n. green colour; green part of thing; (pl.) vegetables; a common; grassplot. v.i. & t. become or make green. ~ish, a.

*green'back, n. legal-tender note.

green'ery, n. vegetation.

green'finch, n. bird with gold and green plumage.

green'fly, n. aphis, plant louse.

green'gage, n. round green plum.

greengrō'cer, n. retailer of fruit and vegetables. ~y, n.

green'horn, n. simpleton, novice.

green'house, n. glass house for rearing plants.

green'ing, n. kind of apple green when ripe.

green'room, n. retiring room for actors off the stage.

green'-sickness, n. chlorosis.

green'stone, n. kind of jade found in New Zealand and much used for weapons and ornaments.

green'sward (-ŏrd), n. turf.

green'wood, n. woodlands in spring or summer.

greet¹, v.t. accost with salutation; salute, receive (with words, &c.); meet (eye, ear, &c.). ~ing, n.

greet², v.i. (Sc.) weep.

gregā'rious, a. living in flocks or communities; fond of company.

grège (-āzh), a. & n. (of) colour between grey and beige.

Grēgŏr'ian, a. of the ritual music

named after Pope Gregory I. ~ calendar, reformed calendar of Pope Gregory XIII.

grénade', n. explosive shell thrown by hand or shot from rifle-barrel; glass vessel thrown to disperse chemicals for extinguishing fires, &c.; **grénadier'**, n. soldier who threw grenades; (pl.) first regiment of household infantry.

grén'adïne, n. dish of fillets of veal, &c.; dress-fabric of open silk or silk and wool.

grew, p.t. of grow.

grey, gray (grā), a. coloured like ashes or lead; clouded, dull; white or hoary with old age. n. grey colour, pigment, or clothes; **grey horse**; cold sunless light. v.t. & i. make or become grey. ~beard, old man; stoneware spirit jug; kind of lichen. ~ friar, Franciscan monk. ~ hen, female of black grouse.

grey'hound (grā-), n. slender swift dog used in coursing. ~racing, sport in which mechanical hare is coursed by greyhounds.

grey'lág (grā-), n. grey goose.

grid, n. gridiron; (Electr.) part of amplifying valve; network of lines, railways, electric-power connexions, &c.

grid'dle, n. round iron plate for cooking cakes over fire.

gride, v.t. cut, scrape, with grating sound. n. such sound.

grid'iron (-ïrn), n. portable barred utensil for broiling; frame for supporting ship in dock; *(field for) American football.

grief, n. sorrow, deep trouble.

griev'ance, n. real or fancied ground of complaint.

grieve, v.t. & i. cause to feel grief; be in pain; mourn, sorrow.

griev'ous, a. oppressive, painful; flagrant, heinous.

griff'in¹, n. (Anglo-Ind.) newly-arrived European; greenhorn; *mulatto. ~age, n. one's first year in India.

griff'in², griff'on, gryph'on, n. fabulous creature with eagle's head and wings and lion's body;

(griffon) kind of vulture, coarse-haired terrier-like dog.

grig, n. small eel; cricket.

grill, n. gridiron; grilled food; (also ~room) room where food is served and grilled; (also grille) grating in door, latticed screen. v.t. & i. broil on grill (also fig. of great heat).

grilse, n. young salmon.

grim, a. stern, merciless; of harsh aspect; ghastly, joyless.

grimáce', n. wry face made in disgust or in jest; affected look; affectation. v.i. make grimace.

grimal'kin (-awl-), n. old she-cat; spiteful hag.

grime, n. dirt deeply ingrained. v.t. blacken, befoul. **grï'mý**, a.

grin, v.i. show teeth in pain or in smile. n. this act or aspect.

grind, v.t. & i. (ground), crush to small particles; harass with exactions; sharpen; study hard, toil; rub gratingly. n. grinding; hard dull work; walk, &c. for exercise; *plodding student; steeplechase.

grï'nder, n. molar tooth; grinding-machine; one who grinds.

grind'stöne, n. revolving disk for grinding and polishing.

grip, n. firm hold, grasp; mastery of subject. v.t. & i. grasp tightly; take firm hold. ~sack, or grip, handbag.

gripe, v.t. (-pable), clutch, grip; oppress; affect with colic pains. n. grip; hold, control; (pl.) colic pains.

grippe, n. influenza.

gris'kin, n. lean part of loin of bacon pig.

gris'lý (-z-), a. causing terror.

grist, n. corn to grind; malt crushed for brewing.

gris'tle (-sl), n. tough flexible tissue; cartilage. **gris'tlý** (-slï), a.

grit, n. particles of sand; (also grit'stone) coarse sandstone; (colloq.) pluck, endurance. v.i. & t. make grating sound. **grind. grit'tý**, a.

Grit², n. (Canadian pol.) member of the Liberal party.

grits, n.pl. oats husked but unground; coarse oatmeal.

griz'zled (-zeld), a. grizzly.

grizz'ly, a. grey, grey-haired. ~ bear, large fierce bear.

groan, v.i. & t. make deep sound expressing pain or the like; be oppressed. n. moaning sound.

groat, n. silver fourpenny piece.

groats, n.pl. hulled (and crushed) grain, esp. oats.

gro'cer, n. dealer in spices, tea, sugar, and domestic stores. ~y, n. grocer's trade or goods.

grog, n. drink of spirit and water.

grog'gy (-g-), a. drunk; unsteady, shaky.

grog'ram, n. coarse fabric of silk, mohair, &c.

groin, n. depression between belly and thigh; edge formed by intersecting vaults. v.t. build with groins.

groom, n. servant who tends horses; bridegroom. v.t. tend (horse). ~s'man, friend attending bridegroom at wedding.

groove, n. channel or hollow; routine. v.t. make groove in.

grope, v.i. feel about as in dark; search blindly.

gro'sbeak, n. kinds of small bird with large beak.

gross, a. luxuriant, rank; flagrant; total, not net; coarse; indecent. n. the bulk; twelve dozen.

grot, n. (poet.) grotto.

grotesque' (-sk), n. a style of decorative art; (pop.) distorted figure, &c. a. distorted; incongruous; absurd.

grott'o, n. (pl. -oes), picturesque cave; structure imitating cave.

*grouch, n. (sl.) peevish state of mind; ill-humour; habitually peevish person.

ground¹, n. surface of earth; bottom of sea or water; (pl.) dregs; land; (pl.) enclosed land attached to house; field or place of action; floor or level; (Painting, &c.) surface worked upon; foundation, motive. v.t. & i. fix or place on the ground; base upon cause or principle; in-

struct thoroughly; run ashore. ~bait, bait thrown to bottom to attract fish. ~floor, story of house on level of outside ground. ~game, hares, rabbits, &c. ~nut, (edible tuber of) N.-Amer. wild bean; also (W.-Ind. W.-Afr., &c.) pea with pod ripening underground. ~(s)man, man in charge of cricket-ground. ~rent, rent paid for ground leased for building. ~swell, heavy sea due to storm or earthquake. ~work, foundation, chief ingredient.

ground², p.t. & p.p. of grind.

groun'ding, n. drill in elements of subject.

ground'less, a. without motive or foundation.

ground'ling, n. kinds of fish living at bottom; ground plant; person of inferior taste.

ground'sel, n. kinds of weed.

group (-ōō-), n. number of persons or things near together, or belonging or classed together. v.t. & i. form, fall, into a group; classify. ~captain, R.A.F. officer.

grou'per (-ōō-), n. kinds of W.-Ind. and Austral. fish.

grouse¹, n. any gallinaceous bird with feathered feet.

grouse², v.i. & t. n. (sl.) grumble.

grout¹, n. thin fluid mortar; (pl.) dregs. v.t. apply grout to.

grout², v.i. & t. (of pigs) turn up earth, turn up with snout.

grove, n. small wood; group of trees.

grov'el, v.i. lie prone, abase oneself. grov'eller, n.

grow (-ō), v.i. & t. (grew pr. grōō, p.p. grown pr. -ō-), develop or exist as living plant; produce by cultivation; increase in size, height, amount, &c.; come by degrees; let grow; (pass.) be covered with growth. grow'er (-ōer), n. one who grows fruit, &c.

growl, n. guttural sound of anger; rumble; murmur, complaint. v.i. & t. make growl. growl'er, n. a grumbler; four-wheeled cab; *(sl.) beer-jug.

grown, *p.p.* of grow.

growth (-ōth), *n.* increase; what has grown or is growing.

groyne, *n.* structure run out to stop shifting of sea-beach.

grub, *v.i. & t.* dig superficially; clear ground of roots, &c.; rummage; plod, toil. *n.* larva of insect; (sl.) food; (Crick.) ball bowled along ground. **grub'b'y,** *a.* dirty.

grudge, *v.t.* (-geable), be unwilling to give or allow. *n.* resentment, ill-will.

gru'el (-ŏŏl), *n.* liquid food of oatmeal, &c.; (sl.) severe punishment. **gru'elling** (-ŏŏ-), *n.* severe treatment.

grue'some (-ŏŏs-), *a.* horrible.

gruff, *a.* surly; rough-voiced.

grum'ble, *n.* faint growl; murmur; complaint. *v.i. & t.* utter grumble; complain; murmur. **grum'bler,** *n.*

grum'py, *a.* ill-tempered.

grunt, *n.* low gruff sound characteristic of hog. *v.i. & t.* utter grunt. **grun'ter,** *n.* pig.

gru'yère (-yâr), *n.* Swiss pale cows'-milk cheese full of holes.

gry'sbok, *n.* small grey S.-Afr. antelope.

gua'na (gwah-), *n.* iguana; (Austral.) any large lizard.

gua'no (gwah-), *n.* excrement of sea-fowl used as manure.

guarantee' (gă-), *n.* giver of guaranty or security; guaranty; recipient of guaranty. *v.t.* be guarantee for; answer for; engage, secure. **~tor,** *n.* **gua'ranty** (gă-), *n.* written or other undertaking to answer for performance of obligation; ground of security.

guard (gärd), *n.* defensive posture; watch, vigilant state; protector; sentry; official in charge of train; soldiers protecting place or person; (pl.) household troops; device to prevent injury or accident. *v.t. & i.* protect, defend; take precautions; keep in check. **~s'man,** soldier of the Guards.

guard'ian (gär-), *n.* keeper, protector; custodian. **~ship,** *n.*

gua'va (gwah-), *n.* tropical tree with acid fruit used for jelly.

gudg'eon (-jon), *n.* small freshwater fish; credulous person; kinds of pivot and metal pin.

guel'der rose (gĕ-, -z), *n.* plant with balls of white flowers.

guerd'on (gĕr-), *n.* reward.

guernsey (gĕrn'zi), *n.* thick knitted woollen jersey.

guerill'a, guerill'a (ger-), *n.* irregular war waged independently by small bodies.

guess (gĕs), *v.t. & i.* conjecture, think likely; **I guess,* I know, am sure. *n.* rough estimate, conjecture. **~work,** *n.* guessing.

guest (gĕst), *n.* person entertained at one's house or table, or lodging at hotel, &c.

***guff,** *n.* (sl.) empty talk.

guffaw', *n.* boisterous laugh. *v.i.* make guffaw.

guid'ance (gī-), *n.* act of guiding; direction.

guide (gīd), *n.* one who shows the way; adviser; directing principle; (also **~book**) book of information about place, &c. *v.t.* (-dable), act as guide to; lead, direct. **~post,** finger-post.

guid'on (gī-), *n.* pennant narrowing to point at free end.

guild, gild (gi-), *n.* society for mutual aid or with common object. **~hall,** meeting-place of medieval guild; town hall.

guile (gīl), *n.* treachery, deceit. **~ful, ~less,** *aa.*

guill'émot (gī-), *n.* a sea-bird.

guilloche (gĭlōsh'), *n.* (Archit.) ornament like braided ribbons.

guillotine (gĭlotēn', *or* gĭ'-), *n.* beheading-machine; machine for cutting paper; (Parl.) closure.

guilt (gĭ-), *n.* the having committed an offence; culpability. **~less,** *a.* innocent.

guil'ty (gĭ-), *a.* having committed offence; culpable, criminal.

guinea (gĭn'ĭ), *n.* sum of 21*s.*; **~fowl,** gallinaceous bird with white-spotted slate plumage. **~pig,** small rodent now common as a pet; person receiving guinea fees, esp. **company director.** **~worm.** tropical parasite.

guipure (gē´poor), n. kind of lace; kind of gimp.

guise (gīz), n. external, esp. assumed, appearance; pretence.

guitar´ (gi-), n. six-stringed lute played with hand.

gulch, n. ravine, gully.

gul´den (gŏŏ-), n. Dutch and Austro-Hung. silver coin (1s. 8d.).

gules (-lz), n. & a. (Herald.) red.

gulf, n. piece of sea like a bay; deep hollow, chasm; impassable dividing line; whirlpool. v.t. engulf, swallow up. **~ stream,** oceanic warm current from Gulf of Mexico.

gull¹, n. kinds of long-winged web-footed mostly marine bird.

gull², n. & v.t. dupe, fool. **gull´ible,** a.; **gullibil´ity,** n.

gull´et, n. food-passage from mouth to stomach; throat.

gull´y, n. water-worn ravine; gutter, drain; (Crick.) part of ground behind batsman on off side.

gulp, v.t. & i. swallow hastily or with effort; gasp, choke. n. act of gulping; effort to swallow; large mouthful.

gum¹, n. firm flesh in which the teeth stand. **~boil,** small abscess on a gum.

gum², n. viscid secretion of some trees and shrubs, used as glue; (pl.) kinds of sweetmeat; (pl., sl.) rubber boots; gum-tree. v.t. apply gum to; fasten with gum.

***gum´bō,** n. a kind of soup.

gumm´y, a. sticky; exuding gum.

gump´tion, n. practical sense.

gun, n. general name for firearms, e.g. cannon, fowling-piece, rifle, carbine; *(sl.) revolver; member of shooting-party. **~boat,** small warship with heavy guns. **~cotton,** cotton steeped in nitric and sulphuric acids, used for blasting. **~man,** (esp.) armed civilian; *(sl.) armed robber. **~metal,** alloy of copper and tin or zinc. **~powder,** explosive of

saltpetre, sulphur, and charcoal. **~room,** in warship, for junior officers or as lieutenants' mess-rooms. **~shot,** range of gun. **~smith,** maker of small firearms. **gunnel.** See gunwale.

gunn´er, n. officer, man, of artillery; (Naut.) warrant officer in charge of battery, magazine, &c. **gunn´ery,** n. management of large guns.

gun´ny, n. a coarse material used chiefly for sacking and made from the fibres of jute; a sack made of this.

gun´ter, n. flat 2-ft. rule with scales, &c. for mechanically solving problems in navigation, &c.

gun´wale (-nal), **gunn´el,** n. upper edge of ship's or boat's side.

gun´yah, n. native Australian hut.

gurgita´tion, n. surging; bubbling motion or sound.

gur´gle, n. bubbling sound. v.i. & t. make, utter with, gurgles.

***gur´jun,** n. E.-Ind. tree yielding **~ balsam** or **oil.**

Gurkha (goork´a), n. member of ruling Hindu race in Nepal.

gur´nard, gurn´et, n. kinds of sea-fish with large head.

gu´rry, n. small Indian fort.

guru (gŏŏ´rŏŏ), goō´rŏŏ, n. Hindu spiritual teacher.

gush, n. sudden or copious stream; effusiveness. v.i. & t. flow with gush; emit gush of; speak or behave with gush. **gush´er,** n.

guss´et, n. triangle let into garment to strengthen or enlarge; strengthening iron bracket.

gust, n. sudden violent rush of wind; burst of rain, smoke, anger, &c. **gust´y,** a.

gusta´tion, n. tasting. **~tory,** a.

gus´tō, n. zest; enjoyment.

gut, n. (pl.) bowels or entrails; intestine; (pl., sl.) pluck; material for violin strings or fishing-line; narrow water-passage. v.t. remove guts of; remove, destroy, internal fittings of (house).

gutta-perch´a, n. horny flexible

---

māte, mēte, mite, mōte, mūte, mŏŏt : răck, rĕck, rick, rŏck, rŭck, rook :

substance of juice of some Malayan trees.

gŭtt'er, n. shallow trough below eaves, channel in street, carrying off water; channel, groove. *v.t. & i.* furrow; (of candle) melt away by becoming channelled.

gŭt'tural, a. of or produced in throat. n. guttural sound or letter.

gŭtt'y, n. (Golf) gutta-percha ball.

guy¹ (gī), n. rope, chain, to steady crane-load, &c., or secure tent. *v.t.* secure with guy.

guy² (gī), n. effigy of Guy Fawkes burnt on Nov. 5; grotesquely dressed person; *(sl.)* boy, fellow. *v.t.* treat as a guy, ridicule.

gŭz'zle, *v.i. & t.* drink, eat, greedily. **gŭzz'ler**, n.

gȳbe, *v.i. & t.* (of fore-and-aft sail or boom) swing to other side; (of boat, &c.) change course thus.

gym, n. (sl.) gymnasium.

gȳmkha'na (-kah-), n. place for display of athletics; athletic sports.

gȳmnā'sium (-z-), n. (pl. *-ums, -a*), room, &c. fitted up for gymnastics; higher-grade school in Germany, &c.

gym'nāst, n. expert in gymnastics.

gymnăs'tic, a. of gymnastics. n. course or mode of bodily or mental discipline; (pl.) muscular exercises, esp. as done in gymnasium.

gynaecŏl'ogy (or gī-), n. science of women's diseases.

gyp, n. college servant at Cambridge and Durham.

gyp'sum, n. mineral from which plaster of Paris is made.

gypsy. See gipsy.

gȳrāte', *v.i.* move in circle or spiral. ~tion, n. ~tory, a.

gȳr'ō, gyroscope. ~compass, gyroscope arranged to serve as compass when magnetic compass cannot be used.

gȳr'ograph (-ahf), n. instrument recording revolutions.

gȳr'oscope —stăt, nn. instruments illustrating dynamics of

rotating bodies; also (-*scope*) rapidly spinning wheel fixed in something, e.g. car on single rail, to keep it in equilibrium.

gyve, n. (usu. pl.), & *v.t.* fetter.

H

hā'bĕăs côr'pus, n. writ requiring person to be brought before judge, &c.

hăb'erdăsher, n. dealer in small articles of dress, &c. **hăb'erdăshery**, n. haberdasher's wares.

hăb'ergeon (-jon), n. (hist.) sleeveless coat of mail.

hăbil'iment, n. (pl.) dress; clothes.

hăb'it, n. settled tendency or practice; constitution (of body or mind); dress. *v.t.* clothe.

hăb'itable, a. that can be inhabited. **hăbitabil'itў**, n.

hăb'itant (or ăbētahn'), n. (descendant of) French settler in Canada or Louisiana.

hăb'ĭtăt, n. natural home of plant or animal. **hăbĭtā'tion**, n. inhabiting; place of abode.

habit'ūal, a. customary; given to some habit. **habit'ūate**, *v.t.* (-*uable*), accustom. ~**tion**, n.

hăb'itūde, n. customary mode of action; inveterate use.

‖ **habitué** (*habit'ūā*), n. habitual visitor or resident.

hacien'da (ăs- or ahth-), n. estate, plantation, with dwelling-house in Spain or Spanish colony.

hack¹, n. wound, esp. from kick; mattock, pick. *v.t. & i.* cut, mangle; kick; emit short dry cough. ~**saw**, saw for cutting metal.

hăck², n. hired horse; horse for ordinary riding; common drudge.

‖ **hăck'erў**, n. (Anglo-Ind.) bullock-cart.

hăc'kle¹, n. steel flax-comb; long feathers on neck of domestic cock, &c.; fishing-fly dressed with hackle. *v.t.* dress (flax, &c. or fly) with hackle.

hăc'kle², *v.t.* hack, mangle.

hăck'ney, n. (pl. -*eys*) horse for ordinary riding; drudge. *v.t.*

make common or trite. ~-coach, vehicle kept for hire.

had, p.t. & p.p. of have.

hăd'dock, n. fish allied to cod.

Hā'dēs (-z), n. abode of the dead.

Hădj'ī, Hăjj'ī, n. Mohammedan pilgrim who has been to Mecca.

haem'al, a. of the blood.

haemăt'ĭc, a. of or containing blood. n. medicine acting on blood.

haem'atīte (commerc. hĕm-), n. a red or brown iron oxide ore.

haemoglō'bin, n. colouring matter of red corpuscles of blood.

haemorrhage, hem- (hĕm'ŏrij), n. escape of blood from blood-vessels.

haemorrhoids, hem- (hĕm'oroidz), n.pl. piles.

hăf'nium, (Chem.) a rare metal.

haft (hahf-), n. handle of knife, &c.

hăg, n. ugly old woman. ~ridden, a. afflicted by nightmare.

hăgg'ard, a. wild-looking: (of hawk) untamed. n. haggard hawk.

hăgg'is, n. minced heart, &c. of sheep boiled in maw with oatmeal, &c.

hăg'gle, v.i., & n. dispute, esp. about price or terms.

hăgiŏg'rapha (-gi-), n.pl. Hebrew Scriptures not included under Law and Prophets.

ha-ha (hah'hah), n. sunk fence bounding garden, &c.

hail[1], n. frozen rain-drops falling as pellets of ice (hail-stones). v.i. & t. pour down hail; (fig.) pour down, come down, like hail.

hail[2], int. of greeting. v.t. & i. salute; greet as; call to; be come from. n. hailing.

hair, n. any or all of the fine filaments growing from the skin; hair-like thing. ~breadth, minute distance. ~dresser, one who dresses and cuts hair. ~net, ~oil, ~pin, used for the hair. ~splitting, a. & n. over-subtle(ty).

hair'ў, a. having hair; hirsute.

hāke, n. fish like the cod.

‖ hakeem, -kim[1] (hakēm'), n. a physician or doctor, in Mohammedan countries and in India.

‖ ha'kim[2] (hah-), n. a judge, ruler, or governor, in Mohammedan countries and in India.

hăl'berd, n. (hist.) combined spear and battle-axe. hălberdier', n. man armed with battle-axe.

hăl'cўon, n. bird fabled to calm the sea; Australasian kingfisher. a. peaceful, quiet.

hāle[1], a. robust, vigorous.

hāle[2], v.t. drag forcibly.

half (hahf), n. (pl. halves), either of two (esp. equal) parts into which a thing is divided; (colloq.) school term. a. amounting to half. adv. in part; equally. ~back, (Footb.) position or player next behind forwards, or in American game behind quarter-back. ~baked, (fig.) half-witted, incomplete, unfinished. ~breed, half-blooded person, one born of different races. ~brother, ~sister, by one parent. ~caste, half-breed. ~crown, coin worth 2s. 6d. ~hearted, lacking courage or zeal. ~moon, moon with disk half illuminated. ~pay, given to army or navy officer when retired or not in actual service. ~volley, n. striking of bouncing ball, ball easily hit, the instant it rises.

halfpenny (hā'pnĭ), n. bronze coin worth half of a penny.

hăl'ĭbut, hŏl~, n. a flat fish used as food.

hall (hawl), n. large room for public business; college dining-room; *building belonging to college or university; residence of landed proprietor; entrance-passage of house. ~mark, n. used at Goldsmiths' Hall for marking standard of gold and silver; v.t. stamp with this (often fig.).

hallelujah. See alleluia.

halliard. See halyard.

halloō', int. used to incite dogs to chase, call attention, or express surprise. v.i. & t. cry halloo; urge dogs thus; shout to call attention,

ah, awl, oil, boor, cow, dowry; chin, go, bang, so, ship, thin; dh, as th(e);

hăll'ow (-ō), *v.t.* make or honour as holy. **Hăll'owmas**, All Saints Day, 1 Nov. **~e'en**, (Sc. & U.S.), eve of All Hallows.

hallucinā'tion (-lōō-), *n.* illusion; apparent perception of object not present; mistake.

hăl'ma, *n.* game on board of 256 squares.

hā'lo, *n.* (pl. *-oes*), circle round sun, moon, &c.; disk of light round head of saint.

halt[1] (hawlt), *n.* stoppage on march or journey. *v.i. & t.* come, bring, to a stand.

halt[2] (hawlt), *a.* lame. *v.i.* hesitate; walk hesitatingly; limp.

hal'ter (hawl-), *n.* rope or strap with noose for horses or cattle; rope for hanging person.

halve (hahv), *v.t.* divide into halves; reduce to half.

hăl'yard, **hăll'iard**, *n.* tackle for raising and lowering sail, &c.

hăm[1], *n.* back of thigh; hog's thigh salted and cured.

hăm[2], *n.* town, village.

hămădry'ăd, *n.* wood nymph.

hăm'lĕt, *n.* small village.

hămm'er, *n.* instrument for driving nails, beating, breaking, &c. *v.t. & i.* strike or drive with or as with hammer. **~cloth**, cloth covering driver's seat in coach.

hămm'ock, *n.* bed of canvas, &c. hung by cords at ends.

hăm'per[1], *n.* basketwork packing-case; hamper of food.

hăm'per[2], *v.t.* obstruct movement of; impede, hinder.

hăm'shăckle, *v.t.* shackle with rope connecting head and foreleg.

hăm'ster, *n.* rodent like large rat.

hăm'string, *n.* any of five tendons at back of knee in man; quadruped's Achilles tendon. *v.t.* (*-inged* or *-ŭng*), cripple by cutting the hamstrings.

hănd, *n.* extremity of human arm comprising palm and fingers; manual worker in factory, &c.; style of writing; cards held by one person in play; index, pointer of clock, &c.; measure of horse's height (4 inches). *v.t.*

hold out hand to; give, transmit, with the hand. **~bill**, notice circulated by hand. **~book**, short treatise, guide-book. **~cuff**, *n.* (pl.) pair of metal rings joined by short chain; *v.t.* secure with handcuffs. **~gallop**, easy gallop. **~glass**, small mirror with handle. **~ over hand**, passing each hand in turn beyond the other, as in rope-climbing; (fig.) gaining rapidly in pursuit. **~rail**, rail along footbridge, &c. to hold on to. **~shake**, shaking of hands. **~spike**, iron-shod wooden lever. **hands down**, of winning race without effort. **~s off!** order not to touch. **~s up!** order to lift hands in sign of surrender.

hănd'ful (-ŏŏl), *n.* (pl. *-fuls*), enough to fill the hand; small number or quantity; (colloq.) troublesome person or task.

hăn'dĭcăp, *n.* race or contest in which competitors are equalized by start, difference in weight carried, &c. *v.t.* impose handicap on; (fig.) place at disadvantage.

hăn'dicraft (-ahft), *n.* manual art, trade, or skill. **~sman**, *n.*

hăn'diwork (-wĕrk), *n.* thing done or made by the hands or by any one's personal agency.

handkerchief (hăng'kerchif), *n.* square of linen, silk, &c., used to wipe the face or cover the neck.

hăn'dle, *n.* part of thing by which it is held. *v.t.* touch or feel with the hands; manage, deal with; treat in particular way.

Hăn'dley-Page, *n.* type of large aeroplane. P.

hănd'maid, **-en**, *n.* (arch.) female servant.

hănd'sel (-ns-), *n.* New-Year gift; earnest money; foretaste. *v.t.* give handsel to; be the first to try.

hănd'some (-ns-), *a.* of fine appearance; generous.

hănd'writing, *n.* way a person writes.

hăn'dy, *a.* ready to hand; convenient; clever with the hands.

hăng, *v.t.* & *i.* (*hŭng*; also *hanged* as below), cause thing to be supported by hooks, &c. from above; attach (wall-paper); fit up (bells in house); decorate (wall with drapery, &c.); (*hanged*) suspend on gibbet as capital punishment; droop; hover; rest upon. *n.* way a thing hangs; the imprecation *ḥáng*. *~bird*, Baltimore oriole. *~dog*, of sneaking shamefaced aspect. *~man*, executioner.

hăng'ar (or *-ngg-*), *n.* shed for housing aeroplane, &c

hăng'er¹, *n.* person or thing that hangs; that by which a thing hangs; short sword. *~ou*, follower, dependant. **hăng'ings** (-z), *n.pl.* drapery for walls, &c.

hăng'er², *n.* wood on hill-side.

hăng'nail, *n.* agnail.

hănk, *n.* parcel or skein of thread or wool.

hăn'ker, *v.i.* crave after.

hănk'y̆-pănk'y̆, *n.* trickery.

hăn'som, *n.* two-wheeled cab.

hăp, *n.* chance; luck; chance occurrence. *v.i.* happen.

hăphă'zard (-p-h-), *n.* mere chance. *a.* casual. *adv.* casually.

hăp'less, *a.* unlucky.

hăp'ly̆, *adv.* perhaps; by chance.

hăpp'en, *v.i.* come to pass, fall out, occur; come by chance.

hăpp'y̆, *a.* lucky, fortunate; content; glad; apt, felicitous. *~go-lucky*, *a.* haphazard.

hăra-kī'rī, *n.* suicide by disembowelment, happy dispatch.

harăngue' (-ng), *n.* speech to assembly; vehement address. *v.i.* & *t.* make speech (to).

hă'rass, *v.t.* worry, trouble; attack repeatedly.

hăr'binger (-j-), *n.* one who announces another's approach; forerunner.

hăr'bour (-ber), *n.* shelter for ships; shelter. *v.i.* & *t.* come to anchor in harbour; give shelter to; entertain. *~age*, *n.* shelter.

hărd, *a.* firm, solid; stern, unyielding, cruel; difficult to bear or do; inclement, severe; strenu-

ous; *(of liquor)* spirituous, strong. *adv.* strenuously, severely; with difficulty. *n.* beach or jetty for landing. *~bake*, almond toffee. *~favoured*, harshfeatured. *~headed*, proof against sentimental delusions. *~hearted*, unfeeling, merciless. *~lines*, worse fortune than one deserves. *~set*, rigid, tight. *~up*, short of money.

hărd'en, *v.t.* & *i.* make or grow hard, callous, or robust.

hărd'ihood, *n.* audacity.

hărd'ly̆, *adv.* with difficulty; scarcely; harshly, severely.

hărd'ship, *n.* hardness of fate; severe suffering or privation.

hărd'ware, *n.* ironmongery.

hărd'y̆, *a.* bold; robust; capable of resisting exposure.

hāre, *n.* speedy rodent with long ears, short tail, and divided upper lip. *~ and hounds*, paperchase. *~brained*, rash, wild. *~lip*, fissure of upper lip.

hāre'bell, *n.* round-leaved bellflower; also wild hyacinth.

hā'rem, *n.* women's part of Mohammedan dwelling; its occupants.

hă'ricot (-ō), *n.* ragout, usu. of mutton. *~bean*, French bean.

hărk, *v.i.* listen; (as call to hounds) go (*forward*, &c.). *int.* hear! listen! *~ back*, retrace course to find scent; (fig.) revert to subject.

hărl'equin, *n.* (in pantomime) mute character invisible to clown and pantaloon. **harlequināde'**, *n.* part of pantomime.

hărl'ot, *n.* prostitute. *~ry*, *n.*

hărm, *n.*, & *v.t.* damage, hurt. *~ful*, *a.* that does harm. *~less*, *a.* that does no harm.

harmŏn'ic, *a.* of or in harmony. *n.* harmonic tone. *~s*, *n.pl.* (Acoustics) frequencies which are multiples of another frequency.

harmŏn'ica, *-cŏn*, *nn.* kinds of musical instrument.

harmō'nious, *a.* in concord; free from dissent; tuneful.

hărm'onist, *n.* person skilled in harmony.

---

măte, mēte, mite, mōte, mūte, mōŏt; răck, réck, rĭck, rŏck, rŭck, rōŏk;

harmō′nium, *n.* keyboard instrument with metal reeds.

harm′onize, *v.t. & i.* (*-zable*), bring into, be in, harmony; form chords for melody; ~*zation*, *n.*

harm′ony, *n.* agreement, concord; combination of notes to form sound; melodious sound.

harn′ess, *n.* gear of draught horses, &c.; (hist.) defensive armour. *v.t.* put harness on (horse, &c.); (fig.) utilize (waterfall, &c.) for motive power.

harp, *n.* musical instrument with strings played by the fingers. *v.t.* play on harp; dwell tediously on subject. ~er, ~ist, *nn.* player on harp.

harpoon′, *n.* spear to strike whales, &c. *v.t.* strike with harpoon.

harp′sichord (-k-), *n.* stringed instrument with keyboard.

harp′y, *n.* monster with woman's face and bird's wings and claws; rapacious person.

harq′uebus, ar-, *n.* (hist.) portable gun supported on tripod.

hā′rridan, *n.* haggard old woman; vixen.

hā′rrier, *n.* hound used in hunting hare; (pl.) pack of hounds, hare-and-hounds club; kind of falcon.

hā′rrow (-ō), *n.* frame with iron teeth for breaking clods, &c. *v.t.* draw harrow over; distress, wound (feelings, &c.).

hā′rry, *v.t.* (*-iable*), ravage, spoil (land, people); harass.

harsh, *a.* severe, unfeeling; rough to the ear or taste.

hart, *n.* male of deer.

hart′al, *n.* form of boycott in India.

hart′(e)beest, *n.* (S.-Afr.) kind of antelope.

harts′horn (-s-h-), *n.* substance got from hart's horn.

hart′s-tongue (-tŭng), *n.* fern with long smooth fronds.

hăr′um-scăr′um, *n.* reckless.

hărv′est, *n.* season for reaping and storing of grain, &c.; a season's yield. *v.t.* reap and gather in. **hărv′ester**, *n.* reaper; reaping-machine.

has. See have.

---

hăsh, *v.t.* cut (meat) into small pieces and mingle. *n.* dish of hashed meat; repetition.

‖ **hăsh′ish, -eesh**, *n.* top leaves and tender parts of the Indian hemp, dried for smoking or chewing in Arabia, &c.

hăs′let, hăs′-, *n.* piece of meat for roasting, esp. pig's fry.

hasp (hah-), *n.* clasp passing over staple and secured by pin.

hăss′ock, *n.* kneeling-cushion.

hāste, *n.* urgency of movement hurry. *v.i.* hasten.

hā′sten (-sen), *v.t. & i.* proceed or go quickly; cause to hasten.

hā′sty, *a.* hurried; rash; quick-tempered. ~ **pudding**, batter; *Indian-meal mush.

hăt, *n.* outdoor head-covering. ~ **-band**, band round hat. ~**trick**, (Crick.) taking three wickets by successive balls.

hătch[1], *n.* lower half of divided door; hatchway, trap-door over it. ~**way**, opening in deck for lowering cargo, &c.

hătch[2], *v.t. & i.* bring or come forth from egg; incubate; form (plot). *n.* hatching; brood hatched.

hătch[3], *v.t.* engrave lines on. *n.* such line.

hătch′et, *n.* light short axe.

hătch′ment, *n.* escutcheon; armorial tablet of deceased person.

hāte, *v.t.* (*-table*), dislike strongly; bear malice to. *n.* hatred.

hāte′ful (-tf-), *a.* exciting hatred.

hā′tred, *n.* active dislike; ill-will.

hăt′ter, *n.* hat-maker or dealer.

hau′berk, *n.* (hist.) coat of mail.

haught′y (-awt-), *a.* proud, arrogant.

haul, *v.t. & i.* pull or drag forcibly; turn ship's course; (of wind) shift, veer. *n.* hauling; amount gained. **haul′age**, *n.* conveyance of loads, charge for it. **haul′ier**, *n.* one who hauls, esp. tubs in coal-mine; jobbing carter.

haulm (hawm, hahm), *n.* stalks of beans, peas, potatoes, &c.

haunch (haw-, hah-), *n.* part of body between ribs and thigh; leg and loin of deer, &c.

---

māre, mēre, mīre, mōre, mūre; părt, pĕrt, pŏrt; *italics*, vague sounds;

haunt, *v.t.* be persistently in or with. *n.* place of frequent resort.

hautboy, oboe (hō'boi, ō'-), *n.* high-pitched wind instrument.

hauteur (hōtér'), *n.* haughtiness.

have (hăv, hav), *v.t.* & *i.* & *aux.* (3rd sing. pres. *has* pr. hăz, haz; past & p.p. *had* pr. hăd, had), hold in possession; possess, contain; enjoy, suffer; be burdened with; (sl.) *be had* (cheated). *n.* (sl.) swindle, take-in.

hā'ven, *n.* harbour; refuge.

hăv'ersăck, *n.* soldier's canvas provision-bag.

‖ hăv'ildâr, *n.* (Anglo-Ind.) sepoy non-commissioned officer corresponding to sergeant.

hăv'oc, *n.* devastation.

haw, *n.* hawthorn berry.

haw'finch, *n.* grosbeak.

hawk¹, *n.* bird of prey used in falconry; rapacious person. *v.i.* & *t.* hunt with hawk.

hawk², *v.i.* & *t.* clear the throat noisily; bring phlegm, &c. up thus.

hawk³, *v.t.* carry about for sale. hawk'er, *n.* itinerant dealer.

hawse (-z), *n.* part of ship's bows in which *hawse-holes* are cut for cables. haws'er (-s-, -z-), *n.* large rope, small cable, often of steel.

haw'thôrn, *n.* thorny shrub bearing haws.

hay, *n.* grass mown and dried for fodder. ~cock, conical heap of hay. ~ fever, fever due to pollen or dust. ~loft, loft for hay in outbuilding. ~maker, one employed in drying grass for hay. ~stack, regular pile of hay.

hăz'ard, *n.* a game at dice; chance; danger, risk; (Tennis) winning opening; (Golf) bad ground. *v.t.* expose to hazard; run the hazard of; venture on (a guess, &c.). ~ous, *a.* risky.

hāze¹, *n.* fog, mist; mental obscurity. *v.t.* make hazy.

hāze², *v.t.* (Naut.) harass with overwork; *subject to horseplay; bully, ballyrag.

hā'zel, *n.* a bush; reddish-brown colour. ~nut, fruit of the hazel.

hā'zy, *a.* misty; vague.

hē, *pron.* (obj. *him*, poss. *his*; pl. *they*, obj. *them*, poss. *their*), the male person or animal in question. *n.* (pl. *hes*) & *a.* male. *~man*, masterful or virile man.

head (hĕd), *n.* upper part of man's, anterior part of animal's body; ruler, chief, principal person, head master; thing like head in form or position; source of a stream; division in discourse; culmination. *v.t.* & *i.* lead, influence, direct; put oneself, or be put, at the head; get ahead of; strike (football) with head. ~ache, pain in the head. ~dress, covering for head. ~master, ~mistress, chief master, mistress, of school. ~phone, telephone receiver attachable to listener's ears. ~piece, helmet; (colloq.) intellect. ~stall, part of bridle or halter fitting round head. ~work, mental work.

head'er (hĕd-), *n.* plunge into water head first.

head'ing (hĕd-), *n.* title, &c. at head of article or page.

head'land (hĕd-), *n.* promontory.

head'long (hĕd-), *a.* rash, precipitate. *adv.* rashly, precipitately.

headquart'ers (hĕdkwôrt'-), *n.pl.* centre of operations; commander-in-chief's residence.

heads'man (hĕdsman), *n.* executioner.

head'strong (hĕd-), *a.* self-willed.

head'way (hĕd-), *n.* progress.

head'y (hĕd-), *a.* impetuous; (of liquor) apt to intoxicate.

heal, *v.t.* & *i.* restore to health; cure; become sound. ~er, *n.*

health (hĕl-), *n.* soundness of body; condition of body; (fig.) soundness of mind. ~ful, *a.* health-giving.

health'y (hĕl-), *a.* having, or conducive to, good health.

heap, *n.* group of things lying one on another; (colloq.) large number or amount. *v.t.* pile in a heap; load; accumulate.

hear, *v.t.* & *i.* (*heard* pr. hĕrd), perceive with ear; listen, give

audience, to; be informed of.
~say, *n.* gossip. ~er, *n.* auditor.
~ing, *n.*

hark'en (här-), *v.i.* listen to.

hearse (hêrs), *n.* car for conveying coffin.

heart (härt), *n.* organ of circulation; seat of the emotions or affections; soul, mind; courage; central or vital part, essence; (pl.) suit of playing-cards marked with hearts. ~breaking, ~broken, causing, crushed by, great distress. ~burn, burning sensation in chest. ~burning, jealousy, grudge. ~disease, morbid condition of the heart. ~felt, sincere. ~ of oak, timber; (fig.) brave man. ~rending, distressing. ~sick, despondent. ~strings, one's deepest affections. ~whole, not in love.

heart'en (härt-), *v.t. & i.* inspirit, cheer.

hearth (härth), *n.* floor of fireplace. ~rug, rug laid before hearth. ~stone, slab forming hearth; stone for whitening hearth.

heart'ily (härt-), *adv.* in hearty manner; very.

heart'less (härt-), *a.* unfeeling, pitiless.

heartsease (härts'êz), *n.* pansy.

heart'y (härt-), *a.* vigorous; genial; sincere; (of meals) copious.

heat, *n.* hotness; hot weather; inflamed state of body; warmth of feeling; anger; course at a race. *v.t. & i.* make or become hot; inflame. ~wave, great heat in atmosphere viewed as passing from place to place.

heat'edly, *adv.* in irate words.

heath, *n.* flat waste tract of land; kinds of shrub. ~bell, flower of heath. ~cock, blackcock.

heath'en (-dh-), *a.* not Christian, Jewish, or Mohammedan. *n.* heathen person; unenlightened person. ~dom, ~ism, *nn.*; ~ish, *a.*

hea'ther (hêdh-), *n.* kinds of shrub; heath, ling. hea'thery, *a.*

heave, *v.t. & i.* (*heaved,* naut. also *hōve; -vable*), lift, raise; utter (sigh, groan) with effort; (Naut.) haul; (colloq.) throw; pull (rope); swell, rise; displace. *n.* heaving; displacement.

hea'ven (hê-), *n.* the sky; regions above; abode of God; place of bliss. hea'venly (hê-), *a.* of heaven, divine; of the sky; divine or (colloq.) great excellence.

hea'vily (hê-), *adv.* with ponderousness; sorrowfully, dejectedly.

hea'vy (hê-), *a.* of great weight, ponderous; of great specific gravity; abundant; striking or falling with force; hard to digest; (of ground) difficult to travel over; dull, tedious, oppressive, sad. ~weight, boxing weight, over 12 st. 7 lb.

hebdom'adal, *a.* weekly.

Hê'bê, *n.* goddess of youth; (joc.) waitress, barmaid.

Hê'braism, *n.* Hebrew idiom. ~ist, *n.* Hebrew scholar, adherent of Hebrew religion, &c.

hec'atomb (-ōm, -ōōm), *n.* great public sacrifice.

hec'kle, *v.t.* catechize (esp. candidate) severely. *n.* = hackle[1].

hec'tic, *a.* consumptive; (sl.) excited, wild. *n.* hectic fever.

hec'togram(me), *n.* weight of 100 grammes.

hec'tograph (-grahf, -âf), apparatus for multiplying copies.

hec'tolitre (-lêter), 100 litres.

hec'tometre (-ter), 100 metres.

hec'tor, *v.t. & i.* bluster, bully.

hedge, *n.* fence of bushes or low trees; barrier of turf, stone, &c. *v.t. & i.* surround with hedge; make or trim hedges; secure oneself against loss; avoid committing oneself. ~row (-ō), bushes forming hedge.

hedg'er, *n.* one who makes hedges.

hedge'hog, *n.* kinds of spiny animal; (U.S. & Canada) porcupine.

hedge'sparrow (-ō), *n.* a songbird.

hêdon'ic, *a.* of pleasure.

hê'donism, *n.* doctrine that pleasure is the chief good. ~ist, *n.*; ~istic, *a.*

---

gh, as (*rou*)*ge*; ô = ĭ: ŏ, ŏŏ, = ŏ̄; ŷ, ў, = ĭ, ĭ; and see p. 4. * = U.S.

heed, *v.t.* attend to; take notice of. *n.* care, attention. ~ful, *a.* ~less, *a.* negligent, inattentive.

heel¹, *n.* hinder part of human foot; quadruped's hind foot, (pop.) hinder part of hoof; part of sock, &c. that covers, or of boot, &c. that supports, the heel. *v.i.* & *t.* furnish with heel; *(p.p.*, sl.) supplied with money; (Footb.) heel out, pass ball out at back of scrummage with heel. ~ball, shoemaker's polishing mixture of wax, &c. ~taps, liquor left at bottom of glass.

heel², *v.i.* & *t.* (of ship) lean to one side; make heel. *n.* heeling.

*heel'er, *n.* hanger-on of political boss.

*heft, *n.* weight. *v.t.* lift, esp. to judge weight. hĕf'tў, *a.* sturdy, stalwart; *heavy.

hĕgĕm'on'ic (-g-), *a.* supreme.

hĕgĕm'onў (-g-), *n.* leadership.

hĕ'gira, -jira, *n.* Mohammedan era, dating from A. D. 622.

hei'fer (hĕf-), *n.* young cow that has not had calf.

heigh (hā), *int.* expr. encouragement or inquiry. ~-ho, expr. boredom, languor, &c.

height (hīt), *n.* measure from base to top; elevation above ground or sea level; high point; top; utmost degree.

height'en (hīt-), *v.t.* raise higher; intensify; exaggerate.

hei'nous (hān-), *a.* atrocious.

heir (ār), *n.* person entitled to property or rank as legal representative of former holder. ~ apparent, presumptive, whose claim cannot, may, be superseded by birth of nearer heir. ~ess, *n.* ~loom, piece of property that has been in family for generations.

hĕl'ical, *a.* spiral.

hĕl'icŏpter, *n.* flying-machine with horizontal air-screws.

hē'liograph, *n.* signalling apparatus reflecting sunlight. *v.t.* send message by this.

hĕliŏm'ēter, *n.* instrument for finding distance between stars.

hē'Hoscōpe, *n.* apparatus for observing the sun.

hē'liotrōpe (or hĕl'-), *n.* plant with small clustered purple flowers; colour or scent of these.

hĕliotrŏp'ic, *a.* (of plant) turning under influence of light.

hē'lium, *n.* a gas, first inferred in sun's atmosphere.

hē'lix (or hĕl'-), *n.* (pl. -icēs), spiral; rim of ear; snail-shell.

hĕll, *n.* abode of the dead or of the damned; state of misery; gaming-house.

hĕll'ebore, *n.* kinds of plant, including Christmas Rose.

Hĕll'ēne, *n.* ancient Greek of genuine Greek race; modern Greek subject. Hĕllē'nic, *a.* Hĕll'ĕnism, *n.* Greek idiom; Grecian culture. ~ist, *n.* non-Greek who used Greek language.

hĕll'ish, *a.* like or fit for hell.

hĕllō, *int.* hullo.

hĕlm¹, *n.* tiller or wheel for managing rudder; the steerage; guidance. ~s'man, steersman.

hĕlm², *n.* (arch.) helmet.

hĕl'met, *n.* defensive head-cover; upper part of retort.

hĕl'ot, *n.* Spartan slave; serf.

hĕlp, *v.t.* (helped) arch. past hŏlp, p.p. hŏlpen) aid, assist; remedy, prevent, avoid. *n.* aid; *domestic servant; remedy; helper.

hĕlp'ful, *a.* useful, serviceable.

hĕlp'ing, *n.* portion of food.

hĕlp'less, *a.* unable to help oneself; without help.

hĕlp'māte, -meet, *nn.* helpful companion, esp. husband or wife.

hĕl'ter-skĕl'ter, *adv.* in disordered haste.

hĕlve, *n.* handle of a tool.

Hĕlvē'tian (-shn), *n.* & *a.* Swiss.

hĕm¹, *n.* edge of a garment turned down and sewed. *v.t.* sew edge thus; enclose, confine. ~stitch, *n.* an ornamental stitch.

hĕm², *int.* expr. hesitation or calling attention.

hĕm'isphēre, *n.* half sphere; half the celestial sphere; half the earth. hĕmisphĕr'ic(al), *aa.*

hĕm'istich (-k), *n.* half line of verse.

hĕm′lŏck, *n.* a poisonous plant; poison, sedative, got from it.

hĕmp, *n.* herbaceous plant with fibre used for rope, &c. ~**en**, *a.*

hĕn, *n.* female of birds, esp. of the common domestic fowl. ~**-harrier**, kind of hawk. ~**-pecked**, domineered over by one's wife.

hĕn′bāne, *n.* narcotic and poisonous plant; drug from this.

hĕnce, *adv.* from here; from now; as result of or inference from this. ~**forth**, ~**forward**, from this time forward.

hĕnch′man, *n.* (hist.) squire, page; follower; political supporter.

hĕndĕc′agon, *n.* a plane figure of eleven sides or angles. ~**al**, *a.*

hĕndĕcasyll′able, *n.* verse or line of eleven syllables. ~**bic**, *a.*

hĕndī′adys, *n.* expression of complex idea by two words coupled with *and*.

hĕnn′a, *n.* Egyptian privet; dye made from it.

hĕn′rў, *n.* unit of inductance.

hėpăt′ic, *a.* of the liver.

hĕp′tad, *n.* set or group of seven.

hĕp′tagon, *n.* plane rectilineal figure of seven sides. ~**al**, *a.*

hĕptahē′dron (-a-h-), *n.* solid of seven faces.

hĕp′tărchў (-k-), *n.* period of many co-existing kingdoms of Angles and Saxons in Britain.

hĕptasyll′able, *n.* verse of seven syllables. **hĕptasyllăb′ic**, *a.*

hĕp′tateuch (-ūk), *n.* first seven books of the Bible.

her, *pron.*, objective case of *she*; also *poss. adj.* of *she*, with abs. and pred. form *hers*.

hĕ′rald, *n.* officer who made State proclamations, regulated armorial bearings, &c.; messenger; forerunner. *v.t.* proclaim approach of; usher in. **hėrăl′dic**, *a.* of heraldry. ~**ry**, *n.* science of heraldic bearings.

hĕrb, *n.* plant whose stem is soft and dies down to the ground after flowering; plant whose leaves, &c. are used for food, medicine, &c. ~**ā′ceous**, *a.* of or like herbs.

hĕrb′age, *n.* herbs; pasturage.

hĕrb′al, *a.* of herbs. *n.* book about herbs. ~**ist**, *n.* writer on herbs; dealer in medicinal herbs.

hėrbā′rium, *n.* collection of dried herbs.

hĕrb′ivorous, *a.* herb-eating.

hĕr′cūlē′an. *a.* strong as Hercules; (of task) of great difficulty.

hĕrd, *n.* number of cattle feeding or travelling together; (contemptuously) the common people; herdsman. *v.i. & t.* go in a herd; tend; drive or crowd. ~**s′man**, keeper of herds.

hĕre, *adv.* in, or to, this place; at this point. *n.* this place or point. ~**about(s)**, somewhere near here. ~**after**, in the future, in the next world. ~**at**, at this. ~**by**, by this means. ~**in**, in this book, place, &c. ~**inafter**, below (in document). ~**of**, of this. ~**to**, to this. ~**tofore**, formerly. ~**upon**, after or in consequence of this. ~**with**, with this.

hĕrĕd′itable, *a.* that can be inherited. ~**bility**, *n.*

hĕrĕd′itament (*or* hĕrĭdĭ′-), *n.* hereditable property; inheritance.

hĕrĕd′itarў, *a.* descending by heritance; transmitted from one generation to another.

hĕrĕd′itў, *n.* tendency of like to beget like.

hĕ′resў, *n.* opinion contrary to accepted doctrine.

hĕ′retic, *n.* holder of a heresy. **hėrĕt′ical**, *a.*

hĕ′riot, *n.* payment in money or kind to lord on tenant's decease.

hė′ritable, *a.* that can be inherited or inherit.

hĕ′ritage, *n.* what is or may be inherited; one's portion or lot.

hĕrmăph′rodīte, *n.* person, animal, or plant with characteristics of both sexes. ~**it′ic**, *a.*; ~**tism**, *n.*

hėrmĕt′ic, *a.* of alchemy. ~**seal**, air-tight closure by fusion, &c. ~**ally**, *adv.* so as to be air-tight.

hĕrm′it, *n.* person living in solitude. ~**age**, hermit's abode.

hĕrn′ia, *n.* rupture.

hē′rō, *n.* demigod; man admired

---

for great or noble deeds; chief man in poem, play, or story.

hĕrō′ĭc, *a*. of, fit for, worthy of, or having qualities of a hero; (of verse) dealing with heroes. *n*. heroic verse; (pl.) high-flown language.

hĕrō′ĭn, *n*. a morphia preparation.

hĕ′rōĭne, *n*. female hero.

hĕ′rōĭsm, *n*. heroic conduct.

hĕ′ron, *n*. a long-legged wading bird. **hĕ′ronrȳ**, *n*. place where herons breed.

hĕr′pes (-z), *n*. a skin disease.

hĕ′rring (-z), *n*. North-Atlantic fish used for food. **hĕ′rringbōne**, *n*. stitch suggesting bones of herring; *v.t.* work in herringbone.

hĕrsĕlf′, *pron*., emphat. & reflexive form of *she, her*.

hĕrtz, *n*. (Electr.) frequency of one cycle per second. **Hĕrt′zian télĕg′raphy**, wireless telegraphy. **~ waves**, electro-magnetic waves.

hĕs′ĭtancȳ (-z-), *n*. hesitation.

hĕs′ĭtant (-z-), *a*. hesitating.

hĕs′ĭtāte (-z-), *v.i.* feel or show indecision; scruple. **~tion**, *n*.

Hĕspĕr′ĭan, *a*. western.

Hĕs′perus, *n*. evening star.

Hĕ′ssian (-shn), *a*. of Hesse. *n*. a coarse cloth; Hessian boot. **~ boot**, high boot first worn by Hessian troops. **~ fly**, fly whose larva destroys wheat.

hĕtaer′ism (-ēr-), *n*. open concubinage; tribal communal marriage.

hĕt′erodŏx, *a*. not orthodox. **~y**, *n*.

hĕt′erodŷne, **~nĭng**, *n*. (in wireless reception) pulsation due to simultaneous sounding of waves that are nearly of same length.

hĕterogē′neous, *a*. diverse; composed of diverse elements.

hĕterogĕn′esis, *n*. birth other than from parent of same kind; spontaneous generation.

hĕt′man, *n*. Polish commander.

hew, *v.t.* & *i.* chop, cut, with axe, sword, &c.; cut into shape; cut coal from seam. **hew′er**, *n*.

hĕx′ad, *n*. set or group of six.

hĕx′agon, *n*. figure having six sides. **hĕxăg′onal**, *a*.

hĕxahĕd′ron (-a-h-), *n*. figure having six faces. **~hĕd′ral**, *a*.

hĕxăm′ēter, *n*. line of six metrical feet. **hĕxamĕt′rĭc(al)**, *aa*.

hey′day, *n*. bloom, prime.

hī, *int*. calling attention.

hiā′tus, *n*. (pl. *-uses*), gap in series; break between two vowels.

hī′bernāte, *v.i.* spend winter (of animals) in torpor or (of person) in mild climate. **~tion**, *n*.

Hībĕrn′ian, *a*. & *n*. Irish(man).

hicc′up, *n*. spasm of respiratory organs. *v.i.* & *t.* make hiccup; utter words with hiccup.

|| **hic jā′cĕt**, *n*. epitaph.

*hick (sl.), *n*. farmer, provincial.

hick′orȳ, *n*. N.-Amer. tree allied to walnut; its wood.

hid, hidden. See **hide²**.

hidăl′gō, *n*. (pl. *-ōs*), Spanish gentleman.

hide¹, *n*. animal's skin, raw or dressed; (joc.) person's skin. **~-bound**, (of cattle) with skin clinging close; narrow-minded.

hide², *v.t.* & *i.* (past *hid*, p.p. *hidden* and *hid*; *-dable*), put or keep (thing) out of sight; conceal oneself; conceal fact.

hide³, *n*. measure of land.

hid′eous, *a*. repulsive, revolting.

hī′dĭng, *n*. a thrashing.

hie, *v.i.* & *refl.* (poet.) go quickly.

hī′erärch (-k), *n*. chief priest.

hī′erärchȳ (-k-), *n*. each of three divisions of angels; graded priesthood or other organization.

hierăt′ic, *a*. of the priests (esp. of ancient Egyptian writing).

hī′eroglŷph, *n*. figure of an object standing for word or sound in ancient Egyptian writing. **hieroglŷph′ic**, *a*. & *n.pl.*

hig′gle, *v.i.* dispute about terms.

hig′gledy-pig′gledy (-geld-), *adv.* & *a*. in utter confusion.

high (hī), *a*. of great or specified upward extent; of exalted rank or superior quality; (of meat) slightly tainted; (of sound) acute in pitch; tempestuous; exorbitant in price. *n*. superior region, high place, elevation. *adv*. far up, aloft; in or to high degree; at high rate. °~ball, whisky and soda in tall glass. °~boy, tallboy. ~brow, person of superior intellectual views. ~ Church, party giving high place to authority of priesthood, &c. ~flown, extravagant, bombastic. ~handed, overbearing. ~ jump, athletic contest in clearing greatest height. ~minded, morally elevated; proud. ~ road, main road. ~ school, usu. the chief public school in a town providing a secondary education; °public school above elementary grammar school. ~seas, beyond 3-mile limit. ~spirited, of courageous spirit. ~strung, very sensitive. ~toned, lofty, noble. ~ water, high tide.

High′lander (hī-), n. inhabitant of the Scottish highlands.

high′lands (hī-), n. mountainous country, esp. of N. Scotland.

high′ly (hī-), adv. in a high degree, at a high rate.

high′ness (hīn-), n. title of princes; elevation above the surface.

high′way (hī-), n. public road, main route. ~man, man who robs on the highway.

°**hi′jacker**, n. (sl.) armed bandit who preys on bootleggers.

hike, n. & v.i. walk, tramp.

hilar′ious, a. cheerful, merry.

hila′rity, n. merriment.

hill, n. small mountain; heap, mound. **hill′y**, a.

hill′ock, n. small hill; mound.

hilt, n. handle of sword or dagger.

him, pron., objective (& colloq. subjective) case of he.

himself′, pron., emphatic & reflex. form of he.

hind¹, n. female of red deer.

hind², n. farm worker; rustic.

hind³, hind′er¹, aa. at the back, posterior. hind′most, a.

Hin′di (-ē), a. of N. India. n. Hindi vernacular language.

hin′drance, n. obstruction.

Hin′du, ~doo′ (-dō̄-; also hi′-), a. Indian. n. one who professes

Hinduism. ~**ism**, n. polytheistic religion of Hindus.

Hindusta′ni (-ōōstahnē), a. of Hindustan. n. Hindu, Mohammedan, of N. India; language of Hindustan, Urdu.

hing, n. the drug asafoetida.

hinge (-j), n. movable joint like that by which door is hung on post. v.t. & i. (-geable), attach with hinge; (fig.) turn.

hinn′y, n. offspring of she-ass by a stallion.

hint, n. covert suggestion; slight indication. v.t. & i. suggest covertly.

hin′terland (-ahnd), n. district behind coast or river's banks.

hip¹, n. projection of pelvis and upper part of thigh-bone.

hip², n. fruit of wild rose.

hip³, n. morbid depression. v.t. depress.

hip⁴, int. used in cheering.

hippocam′pus, n. (pl. -pī), kinds of small fish; sea-horse.

hipp′ocras, n. spiced wine.

hipp′odrome, n. course for chariot races, &c.; circus.

hipp′ogriff, ~**gryph**, n. griffin-like creature with horse's body.

hippopot′amus, n. (pl. -muses), -mī), African river-horse.

hire, n. payment for use of thing, labour, &c. v.t. (-rable), employ, procure, on hire. ~**ling**, n. (contempt.) one who works for hire.

hirs′ute, a. hairy.

his (hiz), possessive adj. of he.

hiss, n. sharp sound of s as sign of disapproval. v.i. & t. make hiss; express disapproval thus.

hist, int. used to call attention.

histol′ogy, n. science of organic tissues.

histō′rian, n. writer of history.

histō′ric, a. noted in history.

histō′rical, a. pertaining to history; belonging to the past. histori′city, n. being historical not legendary.

histōriog′rapher, -**phy**, nn. writer, writing, of history, esp. of official kind.

his′tory, n. methodical record of

public events ; past events, study of these ; eventful career.

histri͞on'ic, a. of acting, stagy. n.pl. theatricals ; stagy language ; pretence.

hit, v.t. & i. strike with blow or missile ; aim blow ; light upon, find ; suit ; *(sl.) arrive at. n. blow ; stroke of satire ; success.

hitch, v.t. & i. move with jerk ; fasten with loop, &c. ; become so fastened. n. jerk ; (Naut.) kinds of noose or half knot ; impediment.

hith'er (-dh-), adv. to this place. a. situated on this end.

hitherto' (-to͞o), adv. up to now.

hive, n. artificial home for bees ; busy swarming place. v.t. & i. (-vable), place in hive ; house.

hives (-vz) n.pl. skin eruption ; inflammation of bowels, larynx, &c.

hoar (hōr), a. grey with age ; white. n. hoar-frost. ~frost, white frost.

hoard (hōrd), n. stock, store. v.t. & i. amass or keep in hoard ; husband privily ; treasure up.

hoard'ing (hōr-), n. high board fence round building, &c.

hoarse (hōrs), a. (of voice) rough, husky ; having hoarse voice.

hoar'y (hōr-), a. white or grey with age ; venerable.

hoax, v.t. deceive by way of joke. n. such deception.

hob, n. flat iron shelf at side of grate. ~nail, heavy-headed nail for boot-sole.

hob'ble, v.i. & t. walk lamely, limp ; (also hopple) tie horse's legs together to keep it from straying. n. limping gait ; awkward situation.

hob'bledehoy' (-beldi-), n. awkward youth. ~hood, in fra.

hobb'y¹, n. favourite pursuit outside one's main occupation. ~-horse, wicker horse for morris-dance, &c. ; rocking-horse.

hobb'y², n. a small falcon.

hob'goblin, n. elf ; bogy.

hob'-nob, v.i. drink together ; hold familiar intercourse with.

*hō'bō, n. (pl. -os), wandering workman or tramp.

hock¹. See hough.

hock², n. kinds of white wine.

*hock³, (sl.) v.t. pawn, pledge.

hock'ey, n. game with ball and curved sticks between goals.

hō'cus, v.t. hoax ; drug.

hō'cus-pō'cus, n. jugglery.

hod, n. trough on staff for carrying mortar, &c. ~man, labourer carrying hod.

hodd'en, n. coarse woollen cloth.

Hodge, n. English farm-labourer.

hodge-podge. See hotch-potch.

hoe, n. tool for cutting up weeds, &c. v.t. loosen ground, remove weeds, with hoe.

hog, n. swine, esp. castrated boar ; young sheep before shearing ; greedy person. v.t. & i. raise (back, &c.), rise, archwise in centre ; cut short. ~back, sharply crested hill ridge. ~deer, (Anglo-Ind.) animal running with its head low, resembling a hog. ~fish, fish with bristles on head. ~ gum, kind of gum or resin obtained from various trees in the W. Indies, &c. ~like, greedy. ~mane, horse's mane clipped short. ~plum, fruit of species of Spondias, a common food for hogs in the West Indies, &c. ~'s pudding, hog's entrail variously stuffed. ~sty, pigsty. ~wash, swill given to pigs. hog'gish, a. greedy.

hogg'et (-g-), n. yearling sheep.

hog'manay (-anā), n. (Sc.) last day of year ; gift of cake, &c. demanded by children on that day.

hogs'head (-hĕd), n. large cask ; a measure (52½ galls.).

hoi(c)k, v.t. & i. force aeroplane to turn abruptly upward.

hoist, v.t. raise aloft ; raise with tackle, &c. n. hoisting ; elevator, lift.

hoit'y-toit'y, a. haughty. int. expressing surprise at person's airs, &c.

hō'key-pō'key, n. cheap ice-cream.

---

māte, mēte, mīte, mōte, mūte, mo͞ot ; răck, rĕck, rick, rŏck, rŭck, ro͞ok ;

hōld¹, v.t. & i. (*hĕld*; p.p. in formal reports *hōlden*), keep fast, grasp; possess; contain, have room for; observe, celebrate; restrain; think, believe. n. grasp; means of holding; place of custody; fortified place. ~**fast**, clamp securing thing to wall, &c. ~**hard !** (colloq.) stop ! wait. *~***up**, (sl.) assault on traveller, &c. for purpose of robbery.

hōld², n. cavity below deck for cargo.

hō'lder, n. one who holds anything ; tenant; possessor for the time ; device for holding.

hō'lding, n. tenure of land ; land or stocks, &c. held.

hōle, n. hollow place, gap ; cavity into which ball must be got in some games. (Golf) point scored by doing this in fewest strokes ; (colloq.) wretched place ; dilemma, fix. v.t. & i. make holes in ; drive golf-ball into hole.

hŏl'iday (-dĭ), n. day of cessation from work or of recreation ; (pl.) period of this.

hŏll'and, n. fine linen fabric made in Holland.

hŏll'ands (-z), n. spirit made in Holland ; kind of gin.

hŏll'ō, hŏlloa' (-ō), v.i. & t. shout, call out; call to hounds. n. shout, cry.

hŏll'ow (-ō), a. having a hole ; empty ; (fig.) false, unreal. n. hollow place ; hole ; valley. adv. completely. v.t. make a hollow in.

hŏll'y, n. evergreen shrub with red berries.

hŏll'yhŏck, n. tall plant with large showy flowers.

hŏlm¹ (hōm), n. islet, esp. in river ; flat ground by river.

hŏlm² (hōm), n. (usu. **holm-oak**), evergreen oak, ilex.

hŏl'ocaust, n. whole burnt-offering ; (fig.) wholesale sacrifice or destruction.

hŏl'ograph (-ahf), n. document wholly in handwriting of person in whose name it appears.

hŏl'ster, n. leather pistol-case.

hōlt, n. copse ; wooded hill.

hō'ly, a. belonging or devoted to God ; of high moral or spiritual excellence. ~**day**, day of some ecclesiastical festival. ~**Ghost**, ~**Spirit**, third person of the Godhead. ~**Thursday**, Ascension Day. ~**water**, water blessed by priest. ~**Week**. w. before Easter week. ~**Writ**, the Bible.

hō'lystōne, n. sandstone for scouring. v.t. scour with holystone.

hŏm'age, n. formal acknowledgement of allegiance ; (fig.) tribute paid to person or merit.

home, n. dwelling-place, residence ; native land ; institution ; (in games) goal. a. pertaining to home ; not foreign. adv. to or at one's home ; to the point aimed at. v.i. (of pigeon) make way home. ~**sick**, depressed by absence from home. ~**spun**, a. & n. cloth of homespun yarn. ~**stead**, house with outbuildings ; farm.

hōme'ly, (-mlĭ), a. plain ; unpretending ; not beautiful.

Homē'ric, a. of or in the style of Homer ; heroic.

hōme'ward(s) (-mw-, -z), a. & adv. towards home or one's native land.

hŏm'icide, n. killing, killer, of human being. **hŏmici'dal**, a.

hŏmilĕt'ic, a. of homilies. ~**s**, n.pl. art of preaching.

hŏm'ily, n. sermon ; discourse.

hŏm'iny, n. ground maize boiled in water or milk.

hŏ'moeopăth, -ist (-mǐ-), nn. one who practises homoeopathy.

hŏmoeopăth'ic (-mǐ-), a. of homoeopathy.

hŏmoeŏ'pathy (-mǐ-), n. treatment of diseases by drugs that in healthy persons would produce symptoms like those of the disease.

hŏmogēnē'ĭty, n. uniformity.

hŏmogē'neous, a. of the same kind or nature ; uniform.

homŏl'ŏgāte, v.t. admit, confirm (statement). ~**tion**, n.

homŏl'ogous, a. having the same relation or value ; corresponding.

---

hŏm'ologue (-ŏg), n. homologous thing. **homŏl'ogy̆**, n. homoiogous relation.

hŏm'ony̆m, n. word of same form as another but different sense; namesake. **homŏn'y̆mous**, a.

hŏm'ophône, n. one of two or more words sounding alike.

hŏmŏsĕx'ūal, a. with sexual propensity for one's own sex.

hône, n. whetstone, esp. for razor. v.t. whet on hone.

hon'ĕst (ŏ-), a. upright; not cheating or stealing; chaste.

hon'ĕsty̆ (ŏ-), n. uprightness; plant with purple flowers.

ho'ney (hŭ-), n. (pl. -eys), sweet fluid collected from flowers by bees, &c.; sweetness. ~comb, n. bees' wax structure of hexagonal cells for honey and eggs; v.t. fill with cavities, mark with honeycomb pattern. ~moon, holiday of newly married couple. ~suckle, climbing shrub with yellow fragrant flowers; woodbine. honeyed, -ied (hŭn'ĭd), a. sweet.

honorār'ium (hŏ-, ŏ-), n. (pl. -ums, -a), (voluntary) fee esp. for professional services.

hŏn'orary̆ (ŏ-), a. conferred by way of honour; unpaid.

hŏnorif'ĭc, a. implying respect.

hŏn'our (ŏ-), n. glory, high reputation; chastity; mark of respect; (pl.) distinction for proficiency in examination, &c. v.t. respect highly; confer honour on; accept or pay bill when due.

hŏn'ourable (ŏner-), a. deserving or bringing honour; generous, not base; applied as an official or courtesy title of honour or distinction.

hood, n. covering for head and neck; badge worn over gown to show university degree; hoodshaped thing. v.t. cover with ~.

****hood'lŭm**, n. (sl.) a rowdy.

****hoo'doo**, n. bad luck. v.t. bring bad luck to.

hood'wink, v.t. deceive, humbug.

hoof, n. (pl. -fs, -ves), horny casing of foot in horse, &c.; (joc.) human foot. v.t. strike with hoof. (sl.) kick.

hook, n. bent piece of wire, &c. for catching hold or for hanging things on; curved cutting instrument. v.t. & i. grasp, secure, fasten; catch with hook; (Golf) drive ball far to left; (Crick.) play ball round from off to on without hitting it at pitch. ~ and eye, small hook with loop as dress-fastener.

hook'ah (-a), n. smoking pipe with long flexible tube.

hook'er, v. kinds of small Dutch and Irish sailing-ship.

|| **hoo'lee**, **hō'lī** (-ē), n. Hindu festival in honour of Krishna and the milkmaids.

hoo'ligan, n. one of a gang of street roughs.

hoo'lŏck, n. the black gibbon, native of Assam.

hoop[1], n. band of metal for binding cask, &c.; wooden or iron circle trundled by child; iron arch used in croquet. v.t. bind with hoop.

hoop[2], n. sound heard in hoopingcough. hooping-cough, disease with convulsive cough.

hoop'oe (-ōō), n. bird with gay plumage and erectile crest.

****Hoo'sier** (-zher), n. & a. (native) of Indiana.

hoot, v.i. & t. make loud sounds, esp. of disapproval; utter cry; (of steam whistle, motor-car) sound. n. sound of derision, &c.; owl's cry. hoot'er, n. steam whistle.

****hootch**, n. (sl.) strong drink.

hop[1], n. plant with bitter cones used to flavour beer, &c.; (pl.) these cones. v.t. & i. bear, gather, hops; flavour with hops.

hop[2], v.i. & t. spring on one foot; jump. n. hopping; (sl.) a dance. ~scotch, child's game of hopping over lines (scotches).

hope, n. expectation and desire; trust. v.t. & i. expect and desire. feel hope. ~ful, a. feeling hope; promising. ~less, a.

hŏpp'er[1], n. person, &c. that hops; device for feeding grain into mill or similar purpose.

höpp'er[2], *n.* hop-picker.

höpp'er[3], *n.* (Anglo-Ind.) kind of cake, usually of rice-flour.

hopple. See hobble.

‖ hoppʻō, *n.* (in China) board of revenue or customs.

horde, *n.* troop of Tartars or other nomads; gang, troop.

hore'hound (hor-), *n.* herb with bitter juice used for coughs.

hori'zon, *n.* line at which earth and sky appear to meet; boundary of mental outlook, &c.

horizon'tal, *a.* parallel to plane of horizon; of or at the horizon. *n.* horizontal line, bar, &c.

hor'mōne, *n.* (Physiol.) kinds of internal secretion that pass into the blood and stimulate organs to action.

horn, *n.* excrescence, often curved and pointed, on head of cattle, &c.; horn-like projection; deer-antler; instrument or vessel made of horn; wind instrument. *v.t.* furnish with horns. ~beam, a hedgerow tree. ~bill, bird with horn-like excrescence on bill. ~book, child's alphabet, &c. on framed paper covered with thin horn. ~ in, (sl.) butt in, intrude.

horn'blende, *n.* a constituent of granite, &c.

horn'et, *n.* large species of wasp.

horn'pipe, *n.* lively dance esp. associated with sailors.

horn'ỹ, *a.* of or like horn; hard.

horol'ŏgy, *n.* clock-making.

hor'olŏge (-j), *n.* timepiece, clock.

hor'oscōpe, *n.* configuration of the heavens at certain moment, esp. one's birth. horoscŏp'ic(al), *aa.*; horŏs'copỹ, *n.*

hor'rible, *a.* exciting horror; hideous, shocking; unpleasant.

hor'rid, *a.* horrible; unpleasing.

horrif'ic, *a.* horrifying.

hor'rifỹ, *v.t.* (-fiable), excite horror in; shock.

hor'ror, *n.* terrified shuddering; terror; intense dislike or fear.

‖ hors de combat (ôrdekawm'bah), disabled.

‖ hors-d'œuvre (ôrdĕr'vr), *n.* extra dish as relish.

horse, *n.* solid-hoofed quadruped, used as beast of burden and draught; (collect.) cavalry; gymnastic vaulting-horse; frame for supporting things. *v.t.* provide with horse; carry (person) on one's back. ~artillery, of mounted gunners. ~box, stall for taking horses by rail or slinging horse into ship. ~breaker, one who trains or breaks in horses. ~chestnut, tree with conical clusters of white or pink flower; its fruit. ~cloth, for covering horses. ~coper, horse-dealer. ~Guards, cavalry brigade of English Household troops. ~hair, from mane or tail of horse. ~leech, a large kind of leech; insatiable person. ~play, boisterous play. ~power, 550 foot-pounds per second. ~race, race between mounted horses. ~radish, plant with pungent root. ~sense, (colloq.) strong common sense. ~shoe, iron shoe for horse. ~whip, whip for horse; *v.t.* chastise (person) with this.

horse'man (-an), *n.* rider on horse-back. ~ship, skill in riding.

horse'woman (-woŏ-), *n.* woman who rides horse.

hors'ỹ, *a.* affecting dress, &c. of groom or jockey.

hort'ative, *a.* of exhortation.

hort'atorỹ, *a.* exhorting.

hort'iculture, *n.* art of gardening. hŏrticul'tural, *a.*; ~rist, *n.*

hŏsänn'a (-z-), *n.* cry of adoration.

hose (hōz), *n.* stockings; flexible tube for watering plants, &c. ~tops, footless stockings.

hō'sier (-zher), *n.* dealer in hose, &c. hō'sierỹ, *n.* such goods.

hŏs'pice, *n.* travellers' house of rest kept by religious order, &c.; home for the destitute or sick.

hŏs'pitable, *a.* given to hospitality.

hŏs'pital, *n.* institution for care of the sick; charitable institution.

hŏspital'itỹ, *n.* friendly reception of guests or strangers.

hŏs'pitaller, *n.* member of charitable order; chaplain in hospital.

hōst[1], *n.* large number; army.

host[1], *n.* one who entertains another; landlord of an inn; animal having parasite. **hŏ'stĕss**, *n.*

host[3], *n.* bread, wafer, consecrated in the Eucharist.

hŏs'tage, *n.* person or thing given as pledge.

hŏs'tel, *n.* house of residence for students, &c.

hŏs'telry, *n.* an inn.

hŏs'tile, *a.* of an enemy; opposed.

hostil'ity, *n.* enmity; warfare; (pl.) hostile proceedings.

hostler. See ostler.

hot, *a.* of high temperature, very warm; giving or feeling heat; pungent; ardent; excited. *v.t.* heat (vulg., usu. *hot up*). ~**air**, (sl.) excited or boastful talk. ~**bed**, bed of earth heated by fermenting manure; place that promotes growth. ~**foot**, in hot haste. ~**head**, hasty person. ~**house**, building for forcing growing plants.

Hŏtch'kiss, *n.* kind of machine gun. P.

hŏtch'pŏtch, **-pŏt**, *n.* dish of many ingredients; medley.

hotel', *n.* house for travellers; large inn.

Hŏt'tentŏt, *n.* one of a S.-Afr. race formerly occupying a region near the Cape.

hough (hŏk), **hŏck**, *n.* joint of hind leg between true knee and fetlock. *v.t.* hamstring.

hound, *n.* dog for the chase; runner following scent in paper-chase; despicable man. *v.t.* chase, pursue; urge on.

hour (owr), *n.* 60 minutes; (pl.) fixed time for work, &c.; short (esp. present) time. ~**glass**, sand-glass running an hour.

houri (hoor'ĭ, howr'ĭ), *n.* nymph of Mohammedan paradise.

hour'ly (owr-), *adv.* every hour.

house, *n.* (pl. pron. -zĭz), building for habitation or for some specified purpose; an assembly, business firm, &c.; theatre or its audience; family. ~**boat**, kind of barge fitted up for living in. ~**breaker**, burglar. ~**hold**, in-

mates of house. ~**holder**, one who occupies house as his own dwelling. ~**keeper**, woman managing affairs of house. ~**leek**, pink-flowered plant on walls and roofs. ~**maid**, maid-servant in charge of house-cleaning, &c. ~**master**, keeper of school boarding-house. ~ **physician**, ~**surgeon**, resident doctor of hospital or institution. ~**warming**, party, &c. celebrating entry into new house. ~**wife**, mistress of house; (with *good*, *bad*, &c.) domestic manager; (pr. hŭz'ĭf) case for sewing requisites.

hous'ing (-z-), *n.* horse-cloth.

hove, *p.t.* of **heave**.

hŏv'el (*or* hŭ-), *n.* shed, outhouse; mean dwelling.

hŏv'er (*or* hŭ-), *v.i.* (of bird, &c.) hang in the air; loiter about.

how, *adv.* in what way; by what means; to what extent. ~**be'it**, *adv.* nevertheless. ~**ev'er**, *adv.* nevertheless; in or to whatever way or degree. ~**soev'er**, *adv.* in or to whatever manner or degree.

howd'ah (-ä), *n.* seat, usu. with canopy, on elephant's back.

how'itzer, *n.* short gun firing shell at high elevation.

howl, *v.i.* & *t.* (of animal) utter long loud cry; (of person) utter long cry of pain, derision, &c.; utter words thus. *n.* such cry.

howl'er, *n.* glaring blunder.

hoy[1], *n.* small coasting vessel, usu. rigged as sloop.

hoy[2], *int.* used to call attention.

hoyd'en, *n.* boisterous girl.

hŭb, *n.* central part of wheel, from which spokes radiate.

hŭb'ble-bŭb'ble, *n.* (Anglo-Ind.) form of hookah.

hŭbb'ŭb, *n.* din; tumult.

hŭck'abăck, *n.* rough linen fabric for towels, &c.

hŭc'kleberry (-kelb-), *n.* (fruit of) shrub common in N. Amer.

hŭc'kle-bŏne (-kelb-), *n.* hip or haunch bone; knuckle-bone.

hŭck'ster, *n.* hawker; mercenary person. *v.i.* & *t.* haggle; hawk.

---

măte, mēte, mǐte, mōte, mūte, mōot; răck, rĕck, rick, rŏck, rŭck, rōŏk;

hŭd′dle, v.t. & i. heap, crowd, or nestle promiscuously. n. confused heap, &c.; confusion.

hūe¹, n. colour, tint.

hūe², n. In phr. *hue and cry*, proclamation for capture of criminal; clamour of pursuit; outery.

hŭff, v.t. & i. bully; offend; take offence; (Draughts) remove opponent's man as forfeit. n. fit of petulance; (Draughts) huffing. ~ish, a. hŭff′y̆, a. offended; apt to take offence.

hŭg, v.t. squeeze in one's arms; keep close to (shore, &c.); cling to. n. clasp; wrestling grip.

hūge, a. very large. hūge′ly̆ (-jli), adv. very much.

hŭgg′er-mŭgg′er (-g-), n. secrecy; confusion. a. secret; confused.

hū′guenŏt (-ge-), n. (hist.) French Protestant.

hŭlk, n. body of dismantled ship; unwieldy vessel; big person or mass. ~ing, a. big, clumsy.

hŭll¹, n. outer covering or pod of beans, &c. v.t. remove hull of.

hŭll², n. frame of ship.

hŭllabaloo′, n. uproar.

hŭllo′, int. of surprise, &c.

hŭm, v.i. & t. murmur continuously like bee or top; sing with closed lips. n. humming sound. int. expr. doubt, &c.

hū′man, a. having the qualities of a man; belonging to the human race. ~kind, n. mankind.

hūmāne′, a. benevolent, compassionate; (of studies) refined.

hū′manism, n. devotion to human interests; literary culture. ~ist, n. student of human affairs; classical scholar.

hūmănĭtār′ian, n. one who rejects the supernatural and concerns himself chiefly with man's welfare; philanthropist. a. of or holding the views of humanitarians. ~ism, n.

hūmăn′ĭty̆, n. human nature or (pl.) qualities; the human race; humaneness; (pl.) polite scholarship; (Sc.) study of Latin.

hū′manĭze, v.t. & i. (-zable). make or become human or humane.

hŭm′ble, a. having or showing low estimate of one's importance; lowly, modest. v.t. abase, lower.

hŭm′ble-bee (-bel-), n. bumblebee.

hŭm′bŭg, n. sham, deception; impostor. v.t. delude, cheat.

hŭm′drŭm, a. dull, commonplace.

hū′meral, a. of the shoulder.

hū′merus, n. bone of upper arm.

hū′mĭd, a. damp. hūmĭd′ĭty̆, n.

hūmĭl′ĭāte, v.t. (-liable). humble, abase; mortify. ~tion, ~tor, nn.

hūmĭl′ĭty̆, n. humbleness; meekness.

hŭm′mock, n. hillock.

hū′moral, a. of the humours.

hū′morist, n. facetious talker, writer, &c. hū′morous, a. full of humour; funny.

hū′mour (-mer ; *also* ū-), n. state of mind, mood, inclination; facetiousness, comicality, jocose imagination; (Med.) fluid of the body. v.t. gratify, indulge.

hŭmp, n. normal or other protuberance, esp. on the back; (sl.) depression. v.t. & i. make hump-shaped; *(sl.) exert (oneself), hurry. ~back, (person having) back with hump. ~backed, a.

hū′mus, n. vegetable mould.

hŭnch, n. hump; thick piece; *(sl.) intuitive apprehension, suspicion. v.t. bend convexly; form hump. ~back, humpback.

hŭn′dred, n. ten times ten (100, C); subdivision of a county. ~fold, a. & adv.; hŭn′dredth, a. hun′dredweight, 112 lb. ; *100 lb.

hŭng, p.t. & p.p. of *hang*.

hŭng′er (-ngg-), n. craving for food; strong desire for. v.i. feel hunger; crave for. ~strike, prisoner's refusal to take food in order to secure release.

hŭn′gry̆ (-ngg-), a. feeling or showing hunger; eager; (of soil) poor, wanting manure.

hŭnk, n. large lump, hunch.

hŭnks, n. miser.

hŭnt, v.t. & i. pursue wild animals for food or sport; search for; drive away. n. hunting; hunting district or party. ~ball,

ball given by members of hunt.
~-the-slipper, a parlour game.

hŭn'ter, n. one who hunts; horse for hunting; watch with cover protecting glass. hŭn'tress, n.

hunts'man (-an), n. man in charge of pack of hounds.

hur'dle, n. portable frame with bars, &c.; frame to be jumped over in *hurdle-race.* hŭrd'ler, n. hurdle-maker; hurdle-racer.

hŭrd'ў-gŭrd'ў, n. musical instrument with droning sound.

hŭrl, v.t. throw violently. n. violent throw. ~er, n. thrower.

hŭrl'ey, hŭrl'ing, n. (Ir.) game similar to hockey.

hŭrl'ў-bŭrl'ў, n. commotion.

hurrah', ~ray' (hu-, hŏŏ-), int. expr. joy or approval. n. the cry hurrah. v.i. cry hurrah.

hŭ'ricane, n. violent storm.

hŭ'riedly (-id-), adv. in a hurried manner.

hŭ'rrў, n. undue haste; eagerness. v.t. & i. (-riable), move or act with great haste; cause to move with haste. ~-scurry, adv., a., & n. (in) disorderly haste.

hŭrst, n. wood, wooded eminence.

hurt, v.t. & i. injure, damage, pain; distress, wound; (colloq.) suffer harm or pain. n. wound, injury; harm. ~ful, a.

hŭr'tle, v.i. (of missile, &c.) go with rushing sound.

hŭs'band (-z-), n. man married to woman; (arch.) economist. v.t. economize. ~man, farmer. ~ry, farming; economy.

hush, v.t. & i. silence; be silent; (with *up*) suppress. n. silence. ~-money, sum paid to avoid exposure.

hŭsk, n. outer covering of fruit or seed. v.t. remove husk from.

hŭs'kў[1], a. full of, dry as, husks; hoarse; *[2](sl.) strong, powerful.

hŭs'kў[2], n. Eskimo dog; (H~) Eskimo person or language.

hussar' (hŏŏz-), n. light cavalry soldier.

hŭss'ў (~zzў, n. pert girl; worthless woman.

hŭs'tings (-z), n. platform for

nomination of candidates; (fig.) election proceedings; (hist.) court held in London Guildhall.

hŭs'tle (-sl), v.t. & i. push roughly, jostle; hurry; push one's way, bustle. n. hustling.

hŭt, n. small mean house; temporary wooden house.

hŭtch, n. pen for rabbits, &c.

huzza' (-ah), int. expr. joy or applause. n. the cry huzza. v.i. cry huzza.

hў'acinth, n. kinds of bulbous plant with bell-shaped flower; orange variety of zircon. ~'ine, a. resembling hyacinth.

hў'aline (or -in), a. crystal-clear; vitreous, transparent.

hў'aloid, a. glass-like.

hў'brid, a. offspring of two animals or plants of different species, &c.; cross-breed. a. crossbred, mongrel; heterogeneous. ~ism, n.

hў'dra, n. (Gk. myth.) snake whose many heads grew again when cut off; fresh-water polyp.

hўdrā'nga (or -ăn-; -ja), n. kinds of flowering shrub.

hў'drant, n. water-pipe with nozzle for hose.

hў'drate, n. compound of water with an element, &c.

hydraul'ic, a. of water conveyed through pipes, &c. n.pl. science of conveyance of liquids through pipes, &c., esp. as motive power.

hў'dric, a. of hydrogen.

hў'drō, n. (colloq.) hydropathic.

hydrocarb'on, n. compound of hydrogen and carbon.

hydrocĕph'alus, n. water on the brain. ~ăl'ic, ~lous, aa.

hydrocў̆ăn'ic, a. containing hydrogen and cyanogen.

hydrodў̆năm'ics, n.pl. science of forces exerted by liquids.

hў'drogen, n. colourless invisible odourless gas, an element forming two-thirds in volume of water.

hўdrŏg'raphў, n. description of the waters of the earth.

hydrokinĕt'ics, n.pl. science of motion of liquids.

---

ah, awl, oil, boor, cow, dowry; chin, go, bang, so, ship, thin; dh, as *th*(e):

hy̆drŏm′ĕter, n. instrument for finding densities of liquids.

hy̆drŏpăth′ĭc, a. of hydropathy. n. establishment for hydropathy.

hy̆drŏp′athy̆, n. treatment by external and internal application of water. hy̆drŏp′athist, n.

hy̆drŏphō′bĭa, n. aversion to water, esp. as symptom of rabies in man ; rabies.

hy̆′drŏphŏne, n. kinds of instrument for detecting sound in or through, or by aid of, water.

hy̆′drŏplāne, n. fin-like device enabling submarine to rise, &c.

hy̆drŏstăt′ĭc, a. of the equilibrium of liquids and the pressure exerted by liquids at rest. n.pl. hydrostatic science.

hy̆′drous, a. containing water.

hyē′na, hȳae′na, n. carnivorous quadruped allied to dog.

hy̆′giēne, n. principle of health ; sanitary science. hy̆giĕn′ĭc, a. ; ~nĭcs, n.pl. ; hy̆′gienist, n.

hy̆grŏm′ĕter, n. instrument measuring humidity of air, &c.

hy̆′groscŏpe, n. instrument showing humidity of air.

Hȳ′mĕn, n. god of marriage. hȳmĕnē′al, a.

hȳmĕnŏp′terous, a. (Zool.) with membranous wings.

hymn (him), n. sacred song of praise. v.t. praise in hymns.

hy̆m′nal, a. of hymns. n. hymn-book.

hy̆m′nŏdy̆, n. singing, making, of hymns. ~dist, n.

hy̆mnŏl′ogy̆, n. study of hymns. ~gist, n.

hy̆oscy̆′amĭne, hy̆′oscĭne, nn. alkaloids contained in henbane and used in medicine.

hȳpĕrb′ola, n. curve produced when cone is cut by plane making larger angle with base than side of cone makes. ~bŏl′ĭc, a.

hȳpĕrb′olē, n. rhetorical exaggeration. hȳpĕrbŏl′ĭcal, a.

hȳpĕrbor′ean, a. of the extreme north. n. dweller in this.

hy̆percrĭt′ĭcal, a. too critical.

hȳpĕrt′rophy̆, n. enlargement due to excessive nutrition. ~phied, a.

hy̆′phen, n. sign (-) used to join or divide words. v.t. join, divide, with hyphen. hy̆′phenātĕd, a. hyphened.

hy̆pnō′sĭs, n. (pl. -osēs) state like deep sleep in which the subject acts only on external suggestion ; artificial sleep.

hy̆pnŏt′ĭc, a. of hypnosis. n. person under hypnosis.

hy̆p′notĭsm, n. (production of) hypnosis. ~ĭst, n. ; ~ĭze, v.t.

hy̆′pocaust (or hy̆′-), n. hollow space under floor for heating house or bath from furnace.

hy̆pochŏn′drĭa (-k-), n. state of causeless depression. hy̆pochŏn′drĭăc (-k-), a. of hypochondria. n. sufferer from hypochondria.

hy̆poc′risy̆, n. simulation of virtue ; dissimulation, pretence.

hy̆p′ocrĭte, n. person guilty of hypocrisy ; dissembler. ~tĭcal, a.

hy̆podĕrm′ĭc (or hy̆′-), a. introduced beneath the skin.

hy̆pot′ĕnūse (or hy̆′-), n. side opposite right angle of triangle.

hy̆pŏth′ĕcāte (or hy̆′-), v.t. pledge, mortgage.

hy̆pŏth′ĕsĭs (or hy̆′-), n. (pl. -thesēs), supposition made as basis for reasoning, &c. hy̆pŏthĕt′ĭc(al) (or hy̆′-), a. of, resting on, hypothesis.

hy̆′son, n. a Chinese green tea.

hy̆′-spy̆, n. boys' hiding game.

hy̆ss′op, n. aromatic herb formerly used medicinally.

hy̆stĕr′ĭa, n. disturbance of (esp. woman's) nervous system ; morbid excitement. hy̆stĕr′ĭcal, a. of or affected with hysteria. hy̆stĕr′ĭcs, n.pl. fit of hysteria.

I

I (I), subjective case of 1st pers. pron. (objective me ; pl. we, obj. us). I spy n. children's guessing game.

ĭam′bus (pl. -buses), ī′amb, nn. metrical foot of one short and one long syllable. ĭăm′bĭc, a. of iambics. n. iambic line.

ī′bĕx, n. (pl. -exes), wild goat.

i'bis, n. (pl. *ibises*). stork-like bird.

ice, n. frozen water; (with pl.) frozen confection. v.t. cover with ice; cool (wine) in ice; cover with concreted sugar. ~berg, mass of floating ice at sea. ~cream, frozen cream or custard. ~field, expanse of ice in Polar regions. ~pack, drift ice.

Ice'land spar (isl-), n. transparent carbonate of lime.

ichneu'mon (-k-), n. weasel-like quadruped that destroys crocodiles' eggs.

i'chor (-k-), n. watery discharge from wound, &c.

ichthyŏl'ogy (-k-), n. study of fishes. ichthyŏsaur'us (-k-), n. extinct marine animal.

i'cicle, n. tapering spike of ice hanging from eaves, &c.

i'con, n. image, statue; sacred painting, mosaic, &c. icŏn'ic, a.

icŏn'oclăsm, n. breaking of images.

icŏn'oclăst, n. breaker of images; one who assails cherished beliefs.

iconŏg'raphy, n. picturing; description of ancient images or representations.

ic'tus, n. rhythmical or metrical stress.

i'cy, a. abounding in ice; very cold; (of manner) chilling.

id, n. (Biol.) unit of germ-plasm; (Psycho-anal.) instinctive impulses of the individual.

ide'a (-ia), n. notion conceived by the mind; vague belief, fancy; plan, intention, aim.

ide'al, a. perfect; existing only in idea; visionary. n. perfect type; actual thing as standard for imitation. ~ism, n. representation of things in ideal form; imaginative treatment. ~ist, n. idĕăl'ity, n. quality of being ideal.

ide'alize, v.t. (-zable). make or treat as ideal. ~zation, n.

iděn'tic, a. identical.

iden'tical, a. the same; agreeing in all details with

iděn'tify, v.t. (-fiable). treat as identical; associate oneself with (party, policy, &c.); establish identity of. ~fication, n.

iden'tity, n. absolute sameness; individuality.

i'deōgrăm, ~graph (or I-; -ahf-, -âf), nn. character indicating the idea of a thing without its name.

ideŏl'ogy, n. science of ideas; abstract speculation. ~gist, n. ∥ id ēst (abbr. i.e.) that is to say.

id'iocy, n. extreme imbecility.

id'iom, n. language of a people; form of expression peculiar to a language. idiomăt'ic, a.

idiosync'rasy, n. mental (also physical) constitution, view, or feeling peculiar to a person.

id'iot, n. person too deficient in mind to be capable of rational conduct. idiŏt'ic, a.

i'dle, a. lazy, indolent; unoccupied; useless, purposeless. v.i. & t. be idle; pass (time) thus. i'dler, n.; i'dly, adv.

i'dol, n. image as object of worship; false god; object of devotion.

idŏl'ater, n. worshipper of idols; devout admirer. ~tress, n.; ~trous, a.; ~try, n.

i'dolize, v.t. (-zable). make an idol of; venerate or love to excess. ~zation, n.

i'dyll (or i-), n. short description of picturesque scene or incident. idyll'ic, a.; i'dyllist, n.

i'dyllize (or i-), v.t. (-zable). make an idyll of.

if, conj. on the condition or supposition that; whenever; whether.

ig'neous, a. of fire; produced by volcanic action.

ig'nis făt'ūus, n. phosphorescent light seen on marshy ground; delusive hope.

ignite', v.t. & i. (-table). set fire to; take fire. igni'tion, n.

ignŏ'ble, a. of low birth or position; mean, base.

ignomin'ious, a. mean, shameful.

ig'nominy, n. dishonour, infamy.

ignorā'mus, n. (pl. -muses). ignorant person.

ig'norance, n. want of knowledge.

ig'norant, a. lacking knowledge; uninformed.

ignŏre', v.t. (-rable). refuse to take notice of.

Igua'na (-gwah-), *n.* large S.-Amer. tree lizard. **iguan'odon** (-gw-), *n.* huge fossil lizard.

i'lex *n.* (pl. *-exes*), holm-oak; (Bot.) genus including holly.

il'iac, *a.* of the flank.

ilk, *a.* (Sc.) same. **of that ilk**, said of a person when his name is the same as his estate; (vulg.) of that family, class, &c.

ill, *a.* out of health, sick; evil, harmful; faulty, deficient. *n.* evil; harm; (pl.) misfortunes. *adv.* badly, unfavourably; scarcely. **~-advised**, injudicious. **~-bred**, rude. **~-favoured**, uncomely. **~-omened**, attended by bad omens. **~-starred**, unlucky. **~-tempered**, morose. **~-timed**, unseasonable. **~-treat**, **~-use**, treat badly.

illa'tion, *n.* deduction, conclusion. **illa'tive**, *a.* inferential.

ille'gal, *a.* contrary to law. **illegal'ity**, *n.*

ille'gible, *a.* not legible, unreadable. **illegibil'ity**, *n.*

illegit'imacy, *n.* bastardy.

illegit'imate (-it), *a.* & *n.* not legitimate, bastard.

illib'eral, *a.* narrow-minded; sordid, stingy. **illiberal'ity**, *n.*

illic'it, *a.* unlawful.

illim'itable, *a.* boundless.

illit'eracy, *n.* want of learning.

illit'erate, *a.* unlearned; unable to read. *n.* such person.

ill'ness, *n.* ill health, sickness.

illog'ical, *a.* devoid of, contrary to, logic. **illogical'ity**, *n.*

illu'minant (-ōō-), *a.* serving to illuminate. *n.* agent of light.

illu'minate (-lōō-), *v.t.* (*-nable*), light up; throw light on; decorate with lights as sign of festivity; decorate (MS. &c.) with gold, &c. **~tion**, **~tor**, *nn.* ; **~tive**, *a.*

illu'mine (poet.) **illume'**, (-lōō-), *v.t.* light up; enlighten.

illu'sion (-lōōzhn), *n.* deceptive appearance, statement, or belief. **~ist**, *n.* **illu'sive** (-lōō-), *a.* deceptive.

illu'sory (-lōō-), *a.* deceptive.

ill'ustrate, *v.t.* (*-rable*), make clear,

esp. by examples or drawings; adorn with pictures. **~tion**, *n.* elucidation; drawing, &c. in book. **~tive**, *a.* explanatory. **~tor**, *n.*

illus'trious, *a.* distinguished.

im'age, *n.* imitation of object's external form, as a statue; idol; counterpart; simile, metaphor. *v.t.* (*-geable*), imagine; mirror.

im'agery (-ij-), *n.* statuary, images; figurative illustration.

ima'ginary, *a.* existing only in, due to, imagination.

imagina'tion, *n.* mental faculty forming images of objects not present; fancy. **imag'inative**, *a.* full of imagination.

ima'gine, *v.t.* (*-nable*), form mental image of, conceive; suppose, think; fancy.

imam', **imaun'**, (-ah-), *nn.* officiating priest of mosque.

im'becile (-ēl), *a.* mentally weak; idiotic. *n.* such person. **~lity**, *n.*

imbibe', *v.t.* (*-bable*), drink in; drink; inhale; absorb.

im'bricate, *v.t.* & *i.* (*-āt*), arrange, be arranged, so as to overlap. *a.* (*-at*), overlapping. **~tion**, *n.*

imbro'glio (-ōlyō), *n.* confused heap; complicated situation.

imbrue' (-ōō), *v.t.* stain.

imbue', *v.t.* (*-uable*), saturate, dye; inspire.

im'itable, *a.* worthy of imitation. **imitabil'ity**, *n.*

im'itate, *v.t.* follow; mimic; be like. **~tion**, *n.* ; **~tive**, *a.* ; **~tor**, *n.*

immac'ulate, *a.* pure, spotless.

imm'anent, *a.* inherent; (of God) pervading the universe.

immate'rial, *a.* incorporeal; unimportant. **immaterial'ity**, *n.*

immature', *a.* not mature. **~rity**, *n.*

immea'surable (-mĕzher-), *a.* not measurable; immense. **immeasurabil'ity**, *n.*

imme'diate, *a.* without intervening medium, direct; occurring at once. **~ly**, *adv.* without delay.

immemo'rial, *a.* beyond memory.

immense', *a.* vast, huge; (sl.) very good. **~ly**, *adv.* vastly; very.

immens'ity, *n.* vastness; infinity.

---

immerse', v.t. (-sable). dip, plunge ; put under water ; involve deeply. ~sion, n.

imm'igrant, a. immigrating. n. one who immigrates.

imm'igrate, v.i. (-rable). remove into a country. ~tion, n.

imm'inence, n. being imminent.

imm'inent, a. (of danger, &c.) about to happen soon.

immo'bile, a. immovable ; motionless. ~bility, n.

immod'erate, a. excessive.

immod'est, a. indecent, indelicate ; impudent. immod'esty, n.

imm'olate, v.t. (-lable), sacrifice ; kill in sacrifice. ~tion, ~tor, nn.

immo'ral, a. morally wrong or evil ; dissolute. immoral'ity, n.

immort'al, a. undying ; famous for all time. n. such being, esp. (pl.) gods of antiquity ; person, esp. author, of enduring fame. ~ity, n.

immort'alize, v.t. (-zable). make immortal, esp. in fame.

immortelle', n. flower retaining colour when dried.

immo'vable (-moo-), a. not movable ; unyielding. n.pl. (of property) fixtures. ~bility, n.

immune', a. exempt, secure. immu'nity, n. exemption.

immure', v.t. imprison, shut up.

immu'table, a. unchangeable ; unalterable. immutabil'ity, n.

imp, n. little devil ; mischievous child.

im'pact, n. collision, striking.

impair', v.t. damage, weaken. ~ment, n. deterioration ; injury.

impale', v.t. (-lable). transfix on a stake. ~ment, n.

impal'pable, a. not to be perceived by touch ; not easily grasped.

impart', v.t. give share of ; communicate to.

impar'tial (-shal), a. not partial ; fair. impartial'ity (-shi-), n.

impass'able (-pah-), a. that cannot be traversed. ~bility, n.

impasse' (-ahs), n. blind alley ; deadlock ; fix.

impass'ible, a. not liable to pain or injury. ~bility, n.

impa'ssioned (-shond), a. deeply moved ; ardent.

impass'ive, a. void of feeling or emotion ; serene. impassiv'ity, n.

impa'tient (-shent), a. not patient ; intolerant. ~tience (-shens), n.

impeach', v.t. call in question ; disparage ; accuse. ~ment, n.

impecc'able, a. not liable to sin ; faultless. ~bility, n.

impecu'nious, a. having no money. impecunios'ity, n.

impe'dance, n. (Electr.) virtual resistance due to self-induction in electrified body.

impede', v.t. retard ; hinder.

imped'iment, n. hindrance ; (pl., often -ta) baggage.

impel', v.t. drive, force ; propel.

impell'ent, a. impelling. n. impelling force, &c.

impend', v.i. hang over ; be imminent. ~ence, n.

impen'etrable, a. not penetrable ; impervious (to, by, ideas, &c.) ; inscrutable. ~bility, n.

impen'itent, a. not penitent ; obdurate. impen'itence, n.

imp'erative, a. expressing command ; peremptory ; necessary.

impercep'tible, a. not perceptible ; very slight or gradual.

imperf'ect, a. not perfect ; incomplete ; faulty. ~ec'tion, n.

imper'ial, a. of an empire, or sovereign State ranking with this ; of an emperor ; supreme ; majestic ; a large size of paper. n. small part of beard left beneath lower lip. ~ism, n. rule of emperor ; belief in value of colonies and extension of British empire. ~ist, n. advocate of imperialism or of imperial rule.

imper'il, v.t. endanger.

impe'rious, a. domineering ; commanding ; urgent.

impe'rishable, a. not perishable.

imperm'eable, a. impervious.

impers'onal, a. having no personality or personal reference.

impers'onate, v.t. personify ; play the part of. ~tion, ~tor, nn.

impert'inent, a. insolent, saucy ; irrelevant. impert'inence, n.

Imperturb′able, a. not excitable; calm. **~bility**, n.

Imperv′ious, a. unpassable; impenetrable; (fig.) inaccessible.

Impet′uous, a. moving violently or fast; acting rashly. **~ōs′ity**, n.

im′pĕtus, n. (pl. -uses), moving force; momentum; impulse.

im′pi, n. body of Kafir warriors.

impi′ety, n. lack of piety.

impinge′ (-j), v.i. & t. strike, dash against. **~ment**, n.

im′pious, a. not pious; wicked.

im′pish, a. of or like an imp.

implac′able, a. not appeasable; inexorable. **~bility**, n.

im′plant′ (-ahnt), v.t. insert, fix; instil; plant. **~ation**, n.

im′plĕment¹, n. tool, utensil.

im′plĕment², v.t. carry into effect.

im′plicate, v.t. (-cable), entwine, entangle; involve; imply. **~tion**, n. thing implied.

impli′cit, a. involved though not expressed; unquestioning.

implore′, v.t. (-rable), beg earnestly.

imply′, v.t. involve the truth of; mean; insinuate. **impli′edly**, adv.

impol′icy, n. injudiciousness.

impolite′, a. uncivil, rude.

impol′itic, a. injudicious.

impon′derable, a. without perceptible weight; very light.

import, v.t. (-port′), bring in, esp. foreign goods, from abroad; imply, mean. n. (im′pōrt), meaning, implication; importance; (usu. pl.) imported commodity. **~able**, a.; **~ation**, **~er**, nn. (all in first sense of the verb).

import′ance, n. being important.

import′ant, a. of great consequence; momentous; pompous.

import′ūnate, a. persistent in solicitation. **importū′nity**, n.

importūne′ (or impōr′-), v.t. solicit pressingly and repeatedly.

impose′ (-z), v.t. & i. (-sable), place (thing on); lay (tax) on; palm off on. **~ upon**, overawe; deceive.

Impo′sing (-z-), a. impressive, formidable, esp. in appearance.

imposi′tion (-z-), n. laying on; impost, tax; deception; over-

charge; work set as punishment at school.

imposs′ible, a. not possible; difficult. **~bility**, n.

im′pŏst, n. tax, duty; tribute; (sl.) horse's handicap. *v.t. classify (imported goods) for fixing duty.

impos′tor, n. one who assumes a false character; swindler.

impos′ture, n. deception, sham.

im′pŏt, n. (sch. sl.) imposition.

im′potent, a. powerless; decrepit; without sexual power. **~nce**, n.

impound′, v.t. shut up (cattle, &c.) in pound; confiscate.

impov′erish, v.t. make poor; exhaust strength of. **~ment**, n.

imprac′ticable, a. not practicable; unmanageable. **~bility**, n.

im′precate, v.t. (-cable), invoke evil upon. **~tion**, n.; **~tory**, a.

imprĕg′nable, a. proof against attack. **~bility**, n.

impreg′nāte, v.t. make pregnant; fill, saturate. **~tion**, n.

impresa′rĭō, n. (pl. -os), organizer of public entertainment.

imprescrip′tible, a. that cannot be legally taken away.

impress′¹, v.t. force into service. **~ment**, n.

impress′², v.t. (imprĕs′), imprint, stamp, by pressure; enforce, fix; affect deeply. n. (im′prĕs), mark impressed; (fig.) characteristic mark. **~ible**, a.; **~ibility**, n.

impre′ssion (-shn), n. impressing; mark impressed; print from type or engraving; effect produced on mind; belief. **~able**, a. easily influenced. **~ability**, n.

impre′ssionism (-shon-), n. method of painting or writing so as to give general effect without detail. **~ist**, n.; **~istic**, a.

impress′ive, a. solemn; affecting.

imprima′tŭr, n. licence to print.

|| impri′mis, adv. in the first place.

imprint, v.t. (-print′), impress mark on. n. (im′-), impression; printer's or publisher's name in book, &c.

impris′on (-z-), v.t. put into prison; confine. **~ment**, n.

improb′able, a. not likely; incredible. **~bility**, n.

imprŏb′ĭtў, n. wickedness.

imprŏmp′tū, adv. & a. extempore.

imprŏp′er, a. inaccurate, wrong; unseemly, indecent.

imprō′prĭāte, v.t. (-iable), place (tithes, benefice) in hands of layman. ~tion, ~tor, nn.

improve′ (-ōōv), v.t. & i. (-vable), make or become better; make good use of (occasion, opportunity). ~ability, ~ment, nn.

impro′ver (-ōōv-), n. one who improves anything; one who serves a further term of apprenticeship.

imprŏv′ĭdent, a. unforeseeing; thriftless. imprŏv′ĭdence, n.

im′provise (-z), v.t. (-sable), compose or utter extempore; provide or get up extempore. improvisā′tion, ~tor, nn.; ~tory, a.

imprūd′ent (-rōō-), a. rash, indiscreet. imprūd′ence (-rōō-), n.

im′pūdent, a. shameless; pert, insolent. im′pūdence, n.

impugn′ (-ūn), v.t. call in question, challenge. ~able, a.

im′pulse, n. impelling; impetus; sudden tendency to act without reflection. ~ive, a. apt to be moved by impulse.

impū′nĭtў, n. exemption from loss or punishment.

impūre′, a. dirty; unchaste; adulterated. impūr′ĭtў, n.

impūte′, v.t. (-table), attribute to; ascribe. ~tability, ~tation, nn.

in, prep. within; into; during. adv. within; in addition to.

ĭnabĭl′ĭtў, n. want of power.

ĭnacćess′ĭble (-ks-), a. not to be reached. ~bility, n.

ĭnăc′cūrate, a. not exact. ~acy, n.

ĭnăc′tion, n. absence of action; sluggishness, inertness. ~ive, a. not acting; inert. ~ivity, n.

ĭnăd′equate, a. insufficient. ~acy, ~ness, nn.

ĭnadmĭss′ĭble, a. not allowable. ~bility, n.

ĭnadvert′ent, a. inattentive; unintentional. ~nce, ~ncy, nn.

ĭnā′liĕnable, a. not transferable.

ĭnămorā′tō (-rah-), n. (fem. -ta, pr. -ta), lover.

ĭnāne′, a. empty, void; silly, senseless. ĭnăn′ĭtў, n.

ĭnăn′ĭmate, a. void of life; dull.

ĭnanĭ′tion, n. emptiness; exhaustion.

ĭnăpp′lĭcable, a. irrelevant; unsuitable. ~bility, n.

ĭnăpp′osĭte, a. not pertinent.

ĭnapprē′ciable (-sha-), a. not appreciable; not worth reckoning.

ĭnapprō′prĭate, a. unsuitable.

ĭnăpt′, a. unskilful. ~itude, n.

ĭnartĭc′ūlate, a. not jointed; not articulate, indistinct; dumb.

ĭnartifĭ′cial (-shal), a. artless; natural.

ĭnartĭs′tic, a. contrary to, unskilled in, art.

ĭnasmŭch′ as, adv. seeing that.

ĭnatten′tion, n. lack of attention; negligence. ~ive, a.

ĭnaud′ĭble, a. that cannot be heard. ~bility, n.

ĭnaug′ūrāte, v.t. (-rable), admit to office; begin undertaking; initiate, open. ~al, a.; ~ation, n.

ĭnauspĭ′cious (-shus), a. not of good omen; unlucky.

in′born, in′bred, aa. inherent by nature; produced within.

ĭncăl′cūlable, a. beyond calculation; uncertain. ~bility, n.

‖ in căm′era, in judge's private room, not in open court.

ĭncandĕsce′, v.i. & t. glow, cause to glow, with heat. ĭncandĕs′cent, a. glowing with heat; shining; (of artificial light) produced by glowing filament. ~nce, n.

ĭncantā′tion, n. spell, charm.

ĭncā′pable, a. not capable; unable to comprehend. ~bility, n.

ĭncapăc′ĭtāte, v.t. (-iable), make incapable or unfit.

ĭncapăc′ĭtў, n. inability; legal disqualification.

ĭncăr′cerāte, v.t. (-rable), imprison; confine. ~tion, ~tor, nn.

ĭncar′nadĭne (or -dīn), a. crimson. v.t. dye crimson.

ĭncar′nāte, v.t. (in′-kärnāt), embody in flesh; be living embodiment of. a. (in-kär′nat), embodied in flesh. ~tion, n.

ĭncau′tious, a. rash.

incen'diarism, n. incendiary practices.

incen'diary, a. of, or guilty of, the malicious setting on fire of property, &c.; (fig.) inflammatory. n. incendiary person.

incense'¹, v.t. (-sable), make angry.

in'cense², n. gum, spice, giving sweet smell when burned.

incen'tive, a. inciting. n. motive.

incep'tion, n. beginning. ~ive, a. beginning; initial.

incer'titude, n. uncertainty.

inces'sant, a. continual; repeated.

in'cest, n. sexual commerce of near kindred. inces'tuous, a.

inch, n. twelfth part of a foot.

in'choate (in-kō-), a. (-āt), begin, originate. a. (-at), just begun.

in'cidence, n. falling on a thing; range of influence.

in'cident, a. apt to occur; naturally attaching to. n. event, occurrence; episode.

inciden'tal, a. casual; not essential.

incin'erate, v.t. (-rable), consume by fire. ~tion, ~tor, nn.

incip'ient, a. beginning.

incise' (-z), v.t. (-sable), make a cut in; engrave. inci'sion, n.

inci'sive, a. sharp; trenchant.

inci'sor (-z-), n. a cutting-tooth.

incite', v.t. (-table), urge on, stir up. ~ment, n.

incivil'ity, n. rudeness.

inclem'ent, a. (of weather) severe; cold or stormy. ~ncy, n.

incli'nable, a. somewhat disposed.

inclina'tion, n. slope, slant; propensity; liking, affection.

incline', v.t. & i. lean, cause to lean; bend forward or downward; dispose, be disposed. n. inclined plane; slope.

include' (-lōō-), v.t. comprise, reckon in, as part of a whole. ~dible, a. inclu'sion (-lōōzhn), n. ~ive, a. including.

incog'nitō, colloq. incog', a. & adv. under false name; with identity concealed; in private.

incoher'ent, a. not coherent; inconsequential. ~nce, ~ncy, nn.

incombus'tible, a. not to be consumed by fire. ~bility, n.

in'come (-ŭm), n. receipts from one's work, investments, &c.

in'coming (-kŭ-), n. entrance, arrival; (pl.) income. a. coming in.

incommen'surable (-sher-), a. having no common measure; irrational. ~bility, n.

incommen'surate (-sher-), a. out of proportion; inadequate.

incommōde', v.t. (-dable), trouble, annoy; inconvenience. ~dious, a. not commodious; inconvenient.

incommu'nicable, a. that cannot be shared or told. ~bility, n.

incom'parable, a. matchless.

incompat'ible, a. opposed; discordant; inconsistent. ~bility, n.

incom'petent, a. not competent; not legally qualified. ~nce, n.

incomplete', a. not finished.

incomprehen'sible, a. that cannot be understood. ~bility, n.

incompress'ible, a. that cannot be compressed. ~bility, n.

incompu'table, a. incalculable.

inconceiv'able (-sēv-), a. that cannot be imagined. ~bility, n.

inconclu'sive (-klōō-), a. not convincing or decisive.

incong'ruous (-kŏnggrōō-), a. out of keeping; absurd. incongru'ity (-grōō-), n.

inconsec'utive, incon'sequent, inconsequen'tial (-shal), aa. wanting in sequence; irrelevant.

inconsid'erable, a. not worth considering; of small size, value, &c.

inconsid'erate, a. thoughtless; rash.

inconsis'tent, a. not in keeping; incompatible. inconsis'tency, n.

inconso'lable, a. not to be comforted.

incon'sonant, a. not harmonizing with. incon'sonance, n.

inconspic'uous, a. not noticeable.

incon'stant, a. fickle; variable; irregular. incon'stancy, n.

incontes'table, a. past dispute.

incon'tinent, a. lacking self-restraint; unchaste. incon'tinence, n.

Incŏn′tinently, *adv.* immediately.

Incŏntrovêrt′ible, *a.* indisputable.

Inconvē′nient, *a.* inopportune; troublesome. inconvē′nience, *n.*

Inconvêrt′ible, *a.* not to be changed. ~bility, *n.*

Incŏr′porate, *v.t.* & *i.* (-ăt), form into a corporation; unite. *a.* (-at), so united. ~tion, ~tor, *nn.*

Incŏrpôr′eal, *a.* not composed of matter; of immaterial beings.

Incŏrrĕct′, *a.* untrue; inaccurate.

Incŏr′rigible, *a.* past correction.

Incŏrrup′tible, *a.* that cannot decay. ~bility, ~ness, *nn.*

Increase, *v.i.* & *t.* (inkrēs′) (-sable), become, make, greater or more numerous; advance. *n.* (in′krēs), growth, enlargement; offspring.

Incrĕd′ible, *a.* that cannot be believed; surprising. ~bility, *n.*

Incrĕdū′lity, *n.* scepticism.

Incrĕd′ulous, *a.* unbelieving.

In′crement, *n.* increase; profit.

Incrim′inate, *v.t.* (-nable), charge with crime; accuse. ~tory, *a.*

Incrŭstā′tion, *n.* hard coating.

In′cubāte, *v.t.* & *i.* hatch; sit on eggs. ~tion, *n.* ~tor, *n.* apparatus for hatching birds, rearing children born prematurely, or developing bacteria.

In′cubus, *n.* nightmare; oppressive spirit or thing.

In′culcate, *v.t.* (-table), impress upon persistently. ~tion, *n.*

In′culpate, *v.t.* (-table), accuse, blame; involve in charge.

Incŭm′bent, *a.* resting upon. *n.* holder of benefice. incŭm′bency, *n.* office or tenure of incumbent.

Incunăb′ūla, *n.pl.* early printed books, esp. before 1501.

incŭr′ (-rrable), *v.t.* fall into; bring on oneself.

incŭr′able, *a.* past cure. *n.* incurable person. ~bility, *n.*

incŭr′ious, *a.* indifferent.

incŭr′sion (-shn), *n.* invasion; sudden attack.

Incûrve′, *v.t.* bend into curve; curve inwards. ~vation, *n.*

Ind′aba (-dah-), *n.* (S.-Afr.) council; conference between or with natives.

indĕbt′ĕd (-dĕt-), *a.* owing money to; obliged to.

Indē′cent, *a.* unbecoming; immodest. indē′cency, *n.*

Indēcī′pherable, *a.* illegible.

Indecī′sion (-zhn), *n.* want of decision. indēcī′sive, *a.*

Indēclī′nable, *a.* not inflected.

Indĕcôr′ous, *a.* unbecoming.

Indēcôr′um, *n.* lack of decorum.

Indeed′, *adv.* in truth; really.

Indĕfăt′igable, *a.* unwearying.

Indēfeas′ible (-z-), *a.* that cannot be lost or annulled. ~bility, *n.*

Indēfec′tible, *a.* unfailing.

Indēfen′sible, *a.* admitting of no defence. ~bility, *n.*

Indēfī′nable, *a.* unexplainable.

Indĕf′inite, *a.* vague, undefined.

Indēl′ible, *a.* that cannot be blotted out. ~bility, *n.*

Indĕl′icate, *a.* coarse, immodest; tactless. indĕl′icacy, *n.*

Indĕm′nify, *v.t.* (-fiable), secure against loss. ~fication, *n.*

Indĕm′nity, *n.* security against damage or loss; compensation.

Indĕnt′, *v.t.* make notches, dents, or recesses in. ~tation, *n.* indentation; indenture. ~ation, *n.* notch, dent; requisition.

Indĕn′ture, *n.* indented document; (pl.) sealed agreement, esp. binding apprentice to master. *v.t.* bind by indentures.

Indēpen′dence, *n.* freedom; exemption from control; independent income. *I~ Day,* U.S. holiday on 4th July, anniversary of Declaration of Independence. indēpen′dency, *n.* independent State; Congregationalism.

Indēpen′dent, *a.* not dependent; free; not supported by others. *n.* politician, &c. independent of any party; Congregationalist.

Indēscrī′bable, *a.* vague; beyond description. ~bility, *n.*

Indēstruc′tible, *a.* that cannot be destroyed. ~bility, *n.*

Indētêr′minable, *a.* that cannot be ascertained or settled.

Indētêr′minate, *a.* not fixed in extent, character, &c.; vague. ~tion, *n.* want of decision.

In´dĕx, n. (pl. -exes, -ĭcēs), forefinger; hand, pointer, on instruments; alphabetical list with references. v.t. furnish (book) with index; enter in index.

In´dia (I-), n. ~man, ship in Indian trade. ~paper, kind from China used for proofs of engravings; also a thin, opaque, featherweight paper used in printing. ~ rubber, rubber, esp. for rubbing out pencil-marks, &c.

In´dian (I-), a. of India or Amer. Indians, ~civilian, member of I.C.S. ~club, bottle-shaped implement for gymnast's use. ~ corn, maize. ~file, single file. ~ink, a black pigment. *~ summer, period of calm dry hazy weather in late autumn in northern U.S.

In´dicate, v.t. (-cable), point out, make known, show; be a sign of, betoken. ~tion, n.

Indic´ative, a. showing; pointing out; giving indication of.

In´dicātor, n. recording instrument on machine, &c.

Indict´ (-īt), v.t. accuse, esp. by legal process. ~able, a. ~ment, n. formal accusation.

Indiff´erence, n. absence of interest or attention; neutrality.

Indiff´erent, a. impartial; unconcerned; neither good nor bad.

In´digence, n. want, poverty.

Indi´genous, a. native; belonging naturally to the soil, &c.

In´digent, a. needy, poor.

Indiges´tion (-schon), n. difficulty in digesting food. ~ible, a.

Indig´nant, a. moved by anger and scorn or sense of injury. Indignā´tion, n. such feeling.

Indig´nity, n. unworthy treatment; contumely; insult.

In´digo, n. (pl. -os), blue powder from some plants, used as dye.

Indirect´, a. not direct; not done by direct means.

Indiscern´ible, a. imperceptible.

Indis´cipline, n. lack of discipline.

Indiscreet´, a. injudicious.

Indiscre´tion, n. imprudence; rashness; social transgression.

Indiscrim´inate, a. confused; undiscriminating. ~tion, n.

Indispen´sable, a. not to be dispensed with; necessary; that cannot be set aside. ~bility, n.

Indispose´ (-z), v.t. make unfit or unable; make averse to.

Indisposi´tion (-zi-), n. ill-health; disinclination, aversion.

Indis´putable, a. incontrovertible.

Indiss´oluble, a. not dissoluble.

Indistinct´, a. not distinct; confused; obscure. ~ive, a.

Indisting´uishable (-nggw-), a. not distinguishable.

Indite´, v.t. (-table), put into words; (joc.) write (letter, &c.).

In´dium, n. a rare metal of leadgrey colour occurring in zinc ores.

Indivi´dūal, a. single; particular; characteristic of particular person, &c. n. single person.

Indivi´dūalism, n. egoism; social theory favouring free action of individuals. ~ist, n.; ~istic, a.

Individūal´ity, n. individual existence; individual character.

Indivi´dūalize, v.t. (-zable), give individual character to; specify. ~zation, n.

Indivis´ible (-z-), a. not divisible. ~lity, n.

Indō´cīle, a. intractable. ~lity, n.

In´dolence, n. laziness, sloth.

In´dolent, a. lazy, slothful.

Indom´itable, a. unyielding.

In´door (-dōr), a. done within house or under cover; domestic.

Indoors´ (-ōrz), adv. within house.

Indorsee´, n. one in whose favour bill, &c. is endorsed.

Indu´bitable, a. beyond doubt.

Induce´, v.t. (-cible), prevail on, persuade; bring about. ~ment, n. attraction; motive.

Induct´, v.t. install; introduce.

Induc´tion, n. inducting; general inference from particular instances; (Electr.) the electrification of an uncharged body by the proximity of a charged one. ~ive, a. based on induction.

Indulge´ (-j), v.t. & i. (-geable), gratify; give free course to.

Indul´gence, n. habitual indulging of desire; privilege granted.

Indŭl'gent, *a.* gratifying; favouring; giving way to.

In'dūrāte, *v.t. & i.* (*-able*), make or become hard. ~**tion**, *n.*

Indūs'trial, *a.* of industries. ~**ism**, *n.* system involving, or prevalence of, industries.

Indūs'trious, *a.* diligent.

In'dŭstry, *n.* diligence; branch of trade or manufacture.

In'dwell'ing, *a.* dwelling within.

Inē'briate, *a.* (*-at*), drunken. *n.* (*-at*), drunkard. *v.t.* (*-āt*), make drunk. ~**tion**, *n.*

Inēbri'etў, *n.* drunkenness.

Inēd'ible, *a.* not edible.

Ineff'able, *a.* unspeakable.

Ineffec'tive, *a.* inefficient; useless.

Ineffec'tual, *a.* without effect.

Ineffi'cient (*-shent*), *a.* not fully capable; ineffective. ~**ncy**, *n.*

Inel'egant, *a.* ungraceful, unrefined; unpolished. ~**nce**, *n.*

Inel'igible, *a.* not qualified.

Inept', *a.* absurd, silly; out of place. ~**itude**, *n.*

Inequal'itў (*-ŏl-*), *n.* want of equality; variableness; unevenness.

Inēq'uitable, *a.* unfair, unjust.

Inērad'icable, *a.* that cannot be rooted out.

Inert', *a.* without inherent power of action; sluggish, slow.

Inēr'tia (*-shya*), *n.* inertness; sloth.

In ēss'é, in actual existence.

Inēs'timable, *a.* too good or too great to be estimated.

Inēv'itable, *a.* unavoidable; bound to happen or appear. ~**bility**, *n.*

Inĕxăct' (*-gz-*), *a.* not exact.

Inexhaus'tible (*-Igzaw-*), *a.* unfailing.

Inex'orable, *a.* relentless.

Inexpē'dient, *a.* not expedient.

Inexpĕn'sive, *a.* cheap.

Inexpēr'ience, *n.* want of experience.

Inexpĕrt', *a.* unskilled.

Inex'piable, *a.* that cannot be expiated; implacable.

Inex'plicable, *a.* that cannot be explained. ~**bility**, *n.*

Inexprĕss'ible, *a.* unutterable; not to be told. *n.pl.* (joc.) trousers.

In extĕn'sō, in unabridged form.

Inexting'uishable (*-nggw-*), *a.* unquenchable.

In extrē'mis, at point of death.

Inex'tricable, *a.* that cannot be loosed, solved, or escaped from.

Infall'ible, *a.* not liable to err; unfailing, sure. ~**bility**, *n.*

In'famous, *a.* of ill fame; vile.

In'famў, *n.* ill fame; vileness.

In'fancy, *n.* first stage of life.

In'fant, *n.* babe; child under 7; person under 21.

Infan'te, *-ta* (*-ahntā*, *-ta*), *nn.* Sp. or Port. prince, or princess, not being heir to throne.

Infan'ticide, *n.* murder of newborn child; person guilty of this.

In'fantile, *a.* of infancy.

In'fantrў, *n.* foot-soldiers.

Infat'ūāte, *v.t.* (*-uable*), affect with extreme folly; inspire with extravagant passion. ~**tion**, *n.*

Infĕct', *v.t.* affect with contagion; imbue with opinion, &c.

Infĕc'tion, *n.* communication of disease; diffusive influence.

Infĕc'tious (*-shŭs*), *a.* contagious; transmissible by infection.

Infēli'citous, *a.* not felicitous.

Infēli'citў, *n.* unhappiness.

Infĕr', *v.t.* deduce; conclude; imply. ~**able**, *a.* **In'ference**, *n.* **Inferĕn'tial**, *a.*

Infē'rior, *a.* situated below; lower in rank, &c.; of poor quality. *n.* one of lower rank. ~**ŏ'ritў**, *n.*

Infĕr'nal, *a.* of hell; hellish.

Infĕr'nō, *n.* (pl. *-os*), hell.

Infĕr'tile, *a.* unfruitful.

Infĕst', *v.t.* haunt, swarm in.

In'fidel, *n.* disbeliever in religion. *a.* unbelieving; of infidels.

Infidĕl'itў, *n.* disbelief in Christianity; disloyalty.

In'fight'ing, *n.* boxing at closer quarters than arm's length.

Infil'trāte, *v.t. & i.* (*-rable*), introduce (fluid) by filtration; permeate by filtration. ~**tion**, *n.*

In'finite, *a.* boundless; endless; very great or many.

Infinitĕs'imal, *a.* infinitely or very small. ~**calculus**, the differential and integral calculuses conceived as one.

---

infin'itive, *a.* (of verb form) expressing the verbal notion without predicating it of a subject. *n.* infinitive form.

infin'itude, infin'ity, *nn.* immensity; infinite number or extent.

infirm', *a.* physically weak; weak of mind; irresolute. ~ity, *n.*

infirm'ary, *n.* hospital; sickquarters in school, &c.

‖ **in flagran'tě delic'tō,** in the act of committing the offence.

inflame', *v.t. & i.* set ablaze; catch fire; raise to morbid heat, be so raised; excite.

inflamm'able, *a.* easily set on fire; easily excited. ~bility, *n.*

inflamma'tion, *n.* morbid process affecting part of body with heat, swelling, and redness.

inflamm'atory, *a.* having the power of inflaming.

inflate', *v.t.* (-table), distend with air or gas; puff up; raise (price) artificially; (*p.p.*) bombastic. ~tion, ~tor, *nn.*

inflect', *v.t.* bend, curve; modify to express grammatical relation.

inflex'ible, *a.* unbendable; unbending; unyielding. ~bility, *n.*

inflex'ion (-kshon), *n.* inflecting; inflected word, suffix, &c. used in this; modulation of voice.

inflict', *v.t.* deal forcibly (blow, &c.); impose as punishment.

inflic'tion, *n.* punishment; troublesome or boring experience.

inflores'cence, *n.* collective flowers of plant; flowering.

in'flow (-ō), *n.,* **in'flowing** (-ōing), *n. & a.* flowing in.

in'fluence (-lōō-), *n.* action invisibly exercised; ascendancy, moral power; thing or person exercising this. *v.t.* (-ceable), exert influence upon; affect.

influen'tial (-lōō-ěnshal), *a.* having great influence.

influen'za (-lōō-), *n.* contagious febrile disorder; severe catarrh.

in'flux, *n.* flowing in.

inform', *v.t. & i.* tell; instruct; inspire; bring charge against.

inform'al, *a.* not in due form; without formality. ~al'ity, *n.*

inform'ant, *n.* giver of information.

informa'tion, *n.* telling; what is told; knowledge; news; charge or accusation. inform'ative, *a.* giving information; instructive.

inform'er, *n.* one who informs against others.

‖ **in'fra,** *adv.* below or further on in book, &c. **in'fra dig.,** beneath one's dignity.

infrac'tion, *n.* infringement.

infre'quency, *n.* rarity.

infre'quent, *a.* not frequent.

infringe' (-j), *v.t.* (-geable), transgress (law, &c.). ~ment, *n.*

infu'riate, *v.t.* (-iable), enrage.

infuse' (-z), *v.t. & i.* (-sible), pour in; instil; steep, be steeped, in liquid to extract properties.

infu'sion (-zhn), *n.* infusing; liquid extract so obtained.

infuso'ria, *n.pl.* class of protozoa in infusions of decaying matter.

in'gathering (In-gădh-), *n.* a gathering in, esp. of harvest.

inge'nious (-j-), *a.* clever at contriving; cleverly contrived.

‖ **ingénue** (ăn'zhēnoo), *n.* artless girl, esp. as stage type.

ingenu'ity (-j-), *n.* ingeniousness.

ingen'uous (-j-), *a.* frank; artless.

ingle (Ing'gl), *n.* fire on hearth. ~nook, chimney-corner.

inglo'rious (In-g-), *a.* ignominious; obscure.

in'going (In-g-), *a. & n.* going in.

in'got (-ngg-), *n.* mass of metal, esp. gold, silver, or steel.

ingrain (*before noun* in'-grān, *else* in-grān'), *a.* dyed in grain; (fig.) inveterate. ~ed, *a.*

ingrate' (In-g-), *n.* ungrateful person.

ingra'tiate (In-grāshi-), *v.refl.* get into favour *with*.

ingrat'itude (In-g-), *n.* want of gratitude.

ingre'dient (In-g-), *n.* component part in mixture.

in'gress (In-g-), *n.* entrance.

inhab'it, *v.t.* dwell in, occupy.

inhab'itant, *n.* person, &c. who inhabits place.

inhale', *v.t.* (-lable), take into lungs; breathe in. **inhala'tion,** *n.*

inhắrmõ′nious, *a.* discordant.

inhẽre′, *v.t.* exist, abide, in; be vested in. ~nce, *n.* ; ~nt, *a.*

inhĕ′rit, *v.t.* receive as heir; derive from parents, &c. ~ance, *n.* inheriting; what is inherited. ~or, *n.* ; ~ress, ~trix, *nn. fem.*

inhĕ′sion (-zhn), *n.* inhering.

inhĭb′it, *v.t.* prohibit; hinder, restrain. inhibĭ′tion, *n.* ; ~ory, *a.*

inhŏs′pitable, *a.* affording no kindness or shelter.

inhū′man, *a.* brutal, unfeeling, barbarous. inhūmăn′ĭty, *n.*

inhūme′, *v.t.* (-mable), bury.

inĭm′ical, *a.* hostile; harmful.

inĭm′itable, *a.* defying imitation.

inĭq′uitous, *a.* unjust; wicked.

inĭq′uĭty, *n.* wickedness.

inĭ′tial (-shal), *a.* of, occurring at, the beginning. initial letter. *v.t.* mark, sign, with initials.

inĭ′tiate (-shĭ-), *v.t.* (-iable), originate, set on foot; admit, introduce. inĭ′tiate (-shĭ-), *n.* initiated person. ~tion, *n.* ; ~tory, *a.*

inĭ′tiative (-shya-), *n.* first step, lead. *a.* originating.

injĕct′, *v.t.* force into as by syringe; fill with fluid thus. ~ion, *n.* fluid, &c. injected.

injudĭ′cious (-jŏŏdishus), *a.* without judgement.

injŭnc′tion, *n.* command; order.

in′jure (-jer), *v.t.* do wrong to; harm, impair.

injur′ious (-joor-), *a.* wrongful, harmful; calumnious.

in′jury, *n.* wrong, damage.

injŭs′tice, *n.* unjust act.

ink, *n.* kinds of fluid for writing or printing. *v.t.* mark, cover, or smear with ink. ink′ỹ, *a.*

ink′ling, *n.* hint; slight knowledge or suspicion of.

in′land (-a-, -ă-), *n.* interior of country. *a.* within a country; remote from sea or border. *adv.* in, towards, the inland.

inlay′, *v.t.* (inlā′), embed thing in groundwork of another; ornament thus. *n.* (in′lā) inlaid work.

in′lĕt, *n.* small arm of sea.

in′lỹ, *adv.* inwardly.

in′māte, *n.* occupant of house.

‖ in mĕmŏ′rĭăm, in memory of.

in′most, *a.* most inward.

inn, *n.* public house for lodging, &c. of travellers. ~keeper, *n.*

innate (inăt′, ĭ′-), *a.* inborn.

inn′er, *a.* interior, internal. *n.* circle next bull's eye. ~most, *a.*

inn′ings (-z), *n.* (pl. same), (Crick., Baseball) time occupied in batting, by batsman or side; also freq. used *fig.*

inn′ocent, *a.* sinless; not guilty; guileless, harmless. *n.* simple person; idiot. inn′ocence, *n.*

innŏc′ūous, *a.* harmless.

inn′ovate, *v.i.* bring in novelties; make changes. ~tion, *n.* ; ~tor, *nn.*

innūen′dō, *n.* (pl. -oes), allusive (usu. depreciatory) remark.

innū′merable, *a.* countless.

innūtrĭ′tion, *n.* lack of nutrition.

innūtrĭ′tious (-shus), *a.* not nourishing.

inobsĕrv′ance (-z-), *n.* non-observance; inattention.

inŏc′ūlate, *v.t.* (-lable), impregnate with disease, &c. esp. as protective measure. ~tion, *n.* ; ~tor, *nn.*

inō′dorous, *a.* odourless.

inoffĕn′sive, *a.* unoffending; not objectionable.

inŏp′erative, *a.* not working or taking effect.

inŏppŏr′tūne, *a.* unseasonable.

inŏrd′inate, *a.* excessive.

inorgăn′ic, *a.* without organized physical structure.

inq′uest (in-kw-), *n.* legal or judicial inquiry into matter of fact.

inquiĕ′tūde (in-kw-), *n.* uneasiness.

inquĭre′ (in-kw-), *v.i. & t.* search; seek out; ask for.

inquĭr′ỹ (in-kw-), *n.* question; investigation.

inquisĭ′tion (in-kwiz-), *n.* investigation; official inquiry. ~al, *a.*

inquĭs′itive (in-kwiz-), *a.* curious, prying.

inquĭs′itor (in-kwiz-), *n.* investigator. ~ōr′ial, *a.* prying.

in′road, *n.* hostile incursion.

in′rush, *n.* violent influx.

insalū′brious (-lōō-), *a.* unhealthy.

insalūb′rĭty (-lōō-), *n.*

---

s.b. awl, oil, boor, cow, dowry; chin, go, bang, so, ship, thin; dh. as th(e)

insane', a. mad; senseless.

insan'itary, a. contrary to sanitary principles.

insan'ity, n. madness.

insa'tiable (-sha-), a. that cannot be sated; greedy. ~bility, n.

insa'tiate (-shyat), a. never satisfied.

inscribe', v.t. (-bable), write on stone, &c.; mark in writing.

inscrip'tion, n. inscribing; words inscribed on monument, coin, &c. ~tional, ~tive, aa.

inscru'table (-rōō-), a. mysterious, impenetrable. ~bility, n.

in'sect, n. small invertebrate animal. insectiv'orous, a. insect-eating. insectŏl'ogy, n.

insecure', a. unsafe.

insecu'rity, n. uncertainty.

insen'sate, a. without sensibility; stupid.

insen'sible, a. imperceptible; unconscious; void of feeling; unaware. ~bility, n.

insen'sibly, adv. imperceptibly.

insen'sitive, a. not sensitive.

insen'tient (-shi-), a. inanimate.

insep'arable, a. that cannot be separated. ~bility, n.

insert', v.t. place in or among other things; introduce; engraft; include. inser'tion, n. inserting; thing inserted.

in'set, n. extra piece inserted.

in'shore, adv. & a. close to shore.

inside', n. (in'sīd'), inner side or part; interior; (-īd'), inside passenger; (colloq.) stomach. a. (in'-), situated on or in the inside. adv. (-īd'), on or in the inside. prep. on the inside of.

insid'ious, a. treacherous, proceeding secretly or subtly.

in'sight (-īt), n. mental penetration.

insig'nia, n.pl. badges, marks of office, &c.

insignif'icant, a. unimportant; meaningless. insignif'icance, n.

insincere', a. not sincere; disingenuous. insince'rity, n.

insin'uate, v.t. (-uable), wheedle; introduce gradually or subtly; hint. ~tion, ~tor, nn.; ~tive, a.

insip'id, a. flavourless; dull, lifeless. insipid'ity, n.

insist', v.i. & t. emphasize; maintain; demand persistently. ~ence, ~ency, nn.; ~ent, a.

ǁ in si'tū, in its original place.

insobri'ety, n. intemperance.

in'solent, a. offensively contemptuous; insulting. in'solence, n.

insol'uble, a. not to be solved; not to be dissolved. ~bility, n.

insol'vent, a. unable to pay debts. n. such debtor. insol'vency, n.

insŏm'nia, n. sleeplessness.

insomuch', adv. to such a degree.

inspan', v.i. & t. (S.-Afr.) yoke (oxen, &c.) to vehicle; harness.

inspect', v.t. look closely into; examine officially. ~ion, ~or, ~orship, nn.; ~oral, ~ōr'ial, aa.

in'spirator, n. apparatus for drawing in air, &c.

inspi'ratory, a. of breathing in.

inspire', v.t. (-rable), breathe in; infuse thought or feeling into; animate. inspira'tion, n.

inspi'rit, v.t. put life into; animate; encourage.

inspiss'ate, v.t. thicken, condense.

instabil'ity, n. lack of (esp. moral) stability.

install' (-awl), v.t. place in office with ceremony; establish in place. installa'tion, n.

instal'ment (-awl-), n. part payment of a debt; part of a whole.

in'stance, n. example; particular case; request. v.t. (-ceable), cite (case) as instance; be an instance of.

in'stant, a. urgent, pressing; immediate. n. precise moment; short time. ~ly, adv. at once.

instantā'neous, a. occurring, done, in an instant.

ǁ in stā'tū quō (ǎntē), in same position as before.

instead' (-ĕd), adv. as a substitute; in place of.

in'step, n. top of foot between toes and ankle; part of shoe.

in'stigate, v.t. (-gable), incite to or bring about revolt, murder, &c. ~tion, ~tor, nn.

instil', v.t. put into by drops; put

(ideas) into the mind gradually. instillā'tion, n.

Instinct, n. (in'-), innate impulse; intuition. a. (-inkt'), filled, charged, with life, energy, &c. instinc'tive, a.

In'stitute, v.t. (-table), establish; set on foot; appoint. n. organized body for promotion of public object; its building.

Institū'tion, n. instituting; established law or custom; (colloq.) familiar object. ~al, a. ; ~tor, n.

Instruct', v.t. teach; inform; give information to; direct.

Instruc'tion, n. teaching; information; (esp. pl.) direction, orders.

Instruc'tive, a. enlightening.

Instruc'tor, n. teacher; *teacher ranking below professor. ~tress.

In'strument (-rōō-), n. tool, implement; contrivance producing musical sounds; legal document.

Instrumen'tal (-rōō-), a. conducive as means to some end; of, performed on, instruments.

Instrumen'talist (-rōō-), n. performer on instrument.

Instrumen'tality (-rōō-), n. agency.

Instrumentā'tion (-rōō-), n. arrangement of music for instruments.

Insubord'inate, a. disobedient; unruly. insubordinā'tion, n.

Insuff'erable, a. unbearable.

Insuffi'cient (-shent), a. not enough, inadequate. ~ncy, n.

In'sular, a. belonging to an island. ~ism, insulā'rity, nn.

In'sulāte, v.t. (-table), make into an island; isolate, esp. by non-conductors. ~tion, ~tor, nn.

In'sulin, n. a specific for diabetes extracted from the pancreas of animals.

Insult, n. (in'-), scornful abuse; affront. v.t. (-ŭlt'), treat with insult.

Insū'perable, a. that cannot be got over. ~bility, n.

Insuppŏrt'able, a. unbearable.

Insur'ance (-shoor-), n. contract to indemnify insured against loss or damage to property, &c., or

to pay fixed sum at the insurer's or another's death, or make payment to insured person in case of sickness, unemployment, &c.

Insure' (-shoor), v.t. & i. (-rable), issue, take out, insurance policy.

Insur'gent, a. in revolt; rebellious. n. rebel. insur'gency, n.

Insurmoun'table (-ser-), a. insuperable.

Insurrec'tion (-su-), n. incipient rebellion; rising. ~ary, a. ~ist, n. insurgent.

Insuscep'tible, a. not susceptible. ~bility, n.

Intact', a. untouched, unimpaired; entire.

Inta'glīātěd (-tāl-), a. carved on the surface. inta'glīō (-tāl-), n. engraved design; gem with incised design.

In'take, n. place of taking water into pipe, &c.; inlet.

Intan'gible (-j-), a. that cannot be touched. ~bility, n.

In'těger, n. whole number; thing complete in itself.

In'tĕgral, a. of or essential to a whole; complete, not fractional.

In'tĕgrant, a. component.

In'tĕgrāte, v.t. (-rable), complete, form into a whole; indicate average or sum of. ~tion, ~tor, nn. ~tive, a.

Integ'rity, n. entirety; honesty.

Intĕg'ument, n. skin, husk, rind, or the like. Intĕgūmen'tary, a.

In'tĕllect, n. faculty of knowing and reasoning; understanding. ~tion, n. process of understanding.

Intĕllec'tual, a. of the intellect; enlightened. n. such person. ~ism, n. doctrine that knowledge is mainly derived from pure reason. ~ist, ~al'ity, nn.

Intĕll'igence, n. intellect; quickness of understanding; news.

Intĕll'igent, a. having, showing, a good intelligence.

Intĕllĭgĕnt'sīa, n. class aspiring to independent thinking.

Intĕll'igible, a. that can be understood; comprehensible; clear. ~bility, n.

Intĕm'perate, a. immoderate; ex-

---

māte, mēte, mīte, mōte, mūte, mōōt ; rǎck, rěck, rick, rǒck, rǔck, rōōk ;

cessively indulgent of appetite; addicted to drinking. ~ance, a.

Inténd', v.t. purpose; design.

Inténse', a. existing in a high degree; vehement; strenuous; strained. inten'sity, n.

Inten'sify, v.t. & i. make or become intense. ~fication, n.

Inten'sion (-shn), n. high degree of quality.

Inten'sive, a. of or in intensity; forced; assiduous.

Inténtt', n. intention. a. resolved, bent on; absorbed; eager.

Inten'tion, n. intending; purpose, aim. inten'tional (-shon-), a. done on purpose.

Intér', v.t. place (corpse, &c.) in earth or tomb; bury.

Interáct', v.i. act reciprocally or on each other. interác'tion, n.

|| inter á'lia, among other things.

Interblénd', v.t. & i. blend with each other.

Interbreed', v.t. & i. crossbreed.

Intercal'ary, a. inserted to harmonize calendar with solar year.

Intér'calāte, v.t. (-lable), insert; interpose. ~tion, n.

Intercēde', v.i. plead; mediate.

Intercépt', v.t. seize, catch; stop in transit; cut off. ~ion, n.

Intercé'ssion (-shn), n. interceding. ~sor, n.; ~sory, a.

Interchánge (-j), v.t. (-ánj') (-geable), put (things) in each other's place; make an exchange of; alternate. n. (In'-), exchange between persons; alternation.

Intercolō'nial, a. existing, carried on, between colonies.

Intercommū'nicate, v.i. have intercourse with. ~tion, n.

Intercommū'nion (-yon), n. intimate intercourse; mutual relation.

Intercommū'nity, n. being, or having things, in common.

In'tercourse (-ōrs), n. social communication; trade between countries, &c.; sexual connexion.

Interdict', v.t. (-īkt'), forbid; prohibit; restrain. n. (In'-), authoritative prohibition. ~ion, n.

In'terest, n. legal concern, title,

right; advantage; personal influence; money paid for use of loan. v.t. excite interest of; cause to take interest in; (p.p.) having a private interest in, not impartial. in'teresting, a. exciting interest.

Interfēre', v.i. meddle; intervene; be an obstacle. interfēr'ence, n. intermeddling.

Interfūse' (-z), v.t. & i. (-sible), mix; blend. ~sion, n.

In'terim, n. meantime. a. intervening; provisional.

Intēr'ior, a. situated within; inland. n. inland part; inside.

Interjā'cent, a. lying between.

Intérjéct', v.t. utter (words) abruptly or parenthetically.

Interjéc'tion, n. exclamation, ejaculation. ~al, a.; ~tor, n.

Interlāce', v.t. & i. (-ceable), bind intricately together; interweave.

Interlárd', v.t. mix; diversify.

Interleave', v.t. insert blank leaves between printed leaves.

Interline', v.t. insert words between lines. ~lin'ear, a. so inserted. ~lineā'tion, n. such insertion.

Interlink', v.t. link closely.

Interlóck', v.t. & i. be locked together; lock or clasp together.

Interlōc'ūtor, n. one who takes part in conversation. ~ū'tion, n. dialogue. interlōc'ūtory, a.

Interlōpe', v.i. thrust oneself into others' affairs, esp. for gain. in'terlōper, n. intruder.

In'terlude (-lŏod), n. pause between acts of play; piece of music, event, &c. interposed.

Intermá'rry, v.i. become connected by marriage with members of different tribes, families, &c. ~má'rriage (-ij), n.

Intermé'ddle, v.i. interpose in others' concerns.

Intermē'diary, a. acting between parties. n. mediator.

Intermē'diate (-at), a. intervening; interposed. ~tion, n.

Intér'ment, n. burial.

Intér'minable, a. endless; tediously protracted.

intermingle (-mǐng'gl), *v.t.* & *i.* mix together.

intermi'ssion (-shn), *n.* pause; cessation for a time.

intermit', *v.t.* & *i.* suspend; stop for a time. ~**mitt'ent**, *a.*

intermix', *v.t.* & *i.* mix together. ~**ture**, *n.*

intern', *v.t.* confine within prescribed limits. ~**ment**, *n.*

intern'al, *a.* of or in the inside; intrinsic; inward. ~**ǎl'ǐty̆**, *n.*

interna'tional (-shon-), *a.* existing, carried on, between nations. *n.* one who takes part in an international match; (often as F. -*ale*) International Working Men's Associations for promoting joint political action of working classes in all countries. ~**ist**, *n.*

internationale' (-shonǎl), *n.* socialistic hymn (*the* ~) sung at demonstrations (see prec. *n.*).

interna'tionalize (-shon-), *v.t.* (-*zable*), make international; bring (territory) under joint protection. ~**zation**, *n.*

interne'cine, *a.* mutually destructive; deadly.

internŭn'cio (-shǐō), *n.* Pope's ambassador.

interp'ĕllate, *v.t.* interrupt to demand explanation. ~**tion**, *n.*

interpĕn'ĕtrate, *v.t.* & *i.* pervade; penetrate mutually. ~**tion**, *n.*

in'terplay, *n.* reciprocal action.

interplead', *v.i.* litigate with each other in order to settle a point in which a third party is concerned.

interp'olate, *v.t.* make (esp. misleading) insertions in; interject in talk. ~**tion**, *n.*

interpose' (-z), *v.t.* & *i.* (-*sable*), insert between others; interject remark; intervene. ~**si'tion**, *n.*

interp'rĕt, *v.t.* & *i.* explain; render, represent; translate. ~**ā'tion**, *n.*

interp'rĕter, *n.* an expositor; one who translates orally.

interrĕg'num, *n.* (pl. -*na*, -*nums*) interval between successive reigns; interval, pause.

inte'rrogate, *v.t.* (-*gable*), question closely or formally. ~**tion**, *n.*

interrŏg'ative, *a.* of, suited to, questions; *n.* such word. ~**tor**, *n.*

interrŏg'atory̆, *a.* of inquiry. *n.* question; set of questions put to accused person.

interrupt', *v.t.* break in upon; break the continuity of; obstruct (view, &c.). ~**ion**, *n.*

intersĕct', *v.t.* & *i.* divide (thing) by crossing it. **intersĕc'tion**, *n.* point, line, common to intersecting lines, planes.

in'terspace, *n.* intervening space.

interspĕrse', *v.t.* (-*sable*), scatter (things) between; diversify. **interspĕr'sion** (-shn), *n.*

intĕrs'tice, *n.* chink, crevice, gap. **intersti'tial** (-shl), *a.*

intertwine', *v.t.* & *i.* twine closely together.

in'terval, *n.* intervening time or space; pause; break.

intervene', *v.i.* occur in meantime; come between persons or things; interfere, mediate. **intervĕn'tion**, *n.* interference, mediation.

in'terview (-vū), *n.* meeting of persons face to face for purpose of discussion, business, &c.

interweave', *v.t.* weave together; blend intimately.

intĕs'tate, *a.* not having made a will. *n.* one who dies intestate. **intĕs'tacy̆**, *n.*

intĕs'tine, *a.* internal, domestic; wholly within a body. *n.* (usu. pl.) lower part of alimentary canal. **intĕs'tinal**, *a.* of the intestines.

in'timate¹, *a.* closely acquainted; familiar; close. *n.* intimate friend. **in'timacy̆**, *n.*

in'timate², *v.t.* (-*mable*), make known, state; imply. ~**tion**, *n.*

intim'idate, *v.t.* (-*dable*), frighten, cow. ~**tion**, ~**tor**, *nn.*

in'to (-tŏo), *prep.* expr. motion or direction to a point within, or change to a state.

intŏl'erable, *a.* not to be endured. ~**ance**, *n.* ; ~**ant**, *a.*

intŏne', **in'tonate**, *vv.t.* (-*nable*), recite in singing voice; utter with particular tone. **intonā'-**

tion, *n*. intoning; modulation of voice, accent, &c.

‖ in tō'tō, entirely.

intŏx'icant, *a*. intoxicating. *n*. intoxicating liquor.

intŏx'icāte, *v.t*. (*-cable*), make drunk; excite, elate, beyond self-control. intŏxicā'tion, *n*.

intrăc'table, *a*. not docile; refractory. ~bility, *n*.

intramūr'al, *a*. situated, done, within walls of city, house, &c.

intrăn'sigent (*-z-*), *a*. uncompromising in politics. *n*. uncompromising Republican.

intran'sitive (*-ahns-*), *a*. not taking direct object.

intrĕp'id, *a*. fearless; brave. intrĕpĭd'ĭtў, *n*.

in'tricate, *a*. entangled; involved; complicated. in'tricacў, *n*.

intrigue' (*-ēg*), *n*. plot; secret amour. *v.i*. & *t*. carry on intrigue; employ secret influence; rouse the interest or curiosity of.

intrĭn'sic, *a*. inherent; essential.

introdūce', *v.t*. (*-cible*), usher in, bring forward; make (person) known to another; bring into notice.

introdūc'tion, *n*. introducing; preliminary matter in book; presentation of person to another. introdŭc'torў, *a*.

intrō'it, *n*. psalm, &c. sung while priest approaches altar for mass or Communion.

intromĭt', *v.t*. admit into; insert. intromĭs'sion (*-shn*), *n*.

introspĕct', *v.i*. examine one's own thoughts. ~ion, *n*.; ~ive, *a*.

introvĕrt', *v.t*. (*-ĕrt'*), draw (organ, &c.) within its own tube or base; turn (mind) inwards. *n*. (In'-'). introversible organ, &c.; thing or person introverted. intrōvĕrs'ible, *a*.; intrōvĕr'sion, *n*.

intrūde' (*-rŏŏd*), *v.t*. & *i*. (*-dable*), thrust into; force upon.

intrū'sion (*-rōŏ-*), *n*. intruding; forcing in. ~ive, *a*.

intū̇i'tion, *n*. immediate apprehension by the mind without reasoning; immediate insight. intū̇i'tional, *a*.

intū̇i'tive, *a*. of, possessing, or perceived by intuition.

inŭndāte, *v.t*. (*-table*), flood, submerge. inŭndā'tion, *n*.

inūre', *v.t*. (*-rable*), habituate, accustom. ~ment, *n*.

inŭrn', *v.t*. put (ashes) in urn.

invāde', *v.t*. (*-dable*), make hostile inroad into; encroach on.

invăl'id[1] (*-ēd*), *a*. enfeebled or disabled by illness or injury. *n*. invalid person. *v.t*. remove from active service; send away as an invalid. ~ism, *n*.

invăl'id[2], *a*. not valid.

invăl'idāte, *v.t*. (*-dable*), make invalid. ~tion, invalĭd'ĭtў, *nn*.

invăl'uable, *a*. above price.

invâr'iable, *a*. always the same; (Math.) constant. ~bility, *n*.

invā'sion (*-zhn*), *n*. invading; encroachment. ~ive, *a*.

invĕc'tive, *n*. abusive speech.

inveigh' (*-vā*), *v.i*. speak violently, rail *against*.

invei'gle (*-vē-, -vā-*), *v.t*. entice, seduce; wheedle. ~ment, *n*.

invĕnt', *v.t*. devise, originate; fabricate. invĕn'tion, *n*. inventing; thing invented; inventiveness. ~ive, *a*.; ~or, ~ress, *nn*.

in'ventorў, *n*. list of goods, &c. *v.t*. enter in inventory.

invĕrness', *n*. kind of man's cloak with long removable cape.

invĕrse', *a*. inverted in position, order, or relation. ~sion, *n*. (esp.) reversal of natural order of words. ~sive, *a*.

invĕrt', *v.t*. reverse position, order, or relation of.

invĕr'tebrate, *a*. without backbone or spinal column; (fig.) weak-willed. *n*. invertebrate animal.

invĕst', *v.t*. & *i*. clothe, dress; endue with qualities, &c.; lay siege to; lay out money.

invĕs'tigāte, *v.t*. (*-gable*), examine, inquire into. ~tion, ~tor, *nn*.

invĕs'titure, *n*. formal investing of person with office.

invĕst'ment, *n*. investing; money invested. invĕs'tor, *n*.

invĕt'erate, *a*. deep-rooted, confirmed. invĕt'eracў, *n*.

invid'ious, *a.* giving offence; likely to provoke ill-will.

invi'gilate, *v.i.* maintain surveillance over examinees. ~**tor,** *n.*

invig'orate, *v.t.* (-*rable*), make vigorous. ~**tive,** *a.* ; ~**tor,** *n.*

invin'cible, *a.* unconquerable ; not to be subdued. ~**bility,** *n.*

invi'olable, *a.* not to be violated. ~**bility,** *n.* **invi'olacy,** *n.* state of being inviolate. **invi'olate,** *a.* not violated.

invis'ible (-z-), *a.* that cannot be seen. ~ **exports,** shipping services, foreign investments, and the like. ~**bility,** *n.*

invite', *v.t.* (-*table*), request courteously to come ; solicit courteously ; be attractive ; *n.* (colloq.) invitation. **invita'tion,** *n.* **invo'king,** *n.* invoking ; calling upon in prayer. **invoc'atory,** *a.*

invoca'tion, *n.* invoking ; calling upon in prayer. **invoc'atory,** *a.*

in'voice, *n.* list of goods sent, with prices. *v.t.* make invoice of.

invoke', *v.t.* call on in prayer ; appeal to ; ask earnestly for.

in'volucre (-lōōker), *n.* (Bot.) whorl of bracts round inflorescence ; (Anat.) covering, envelope.

invol'untary, *a.* unintentional.

in'volute (-lōōt), *a.* intricate ; curled spirally. ~**tion,** *n.* involving ; intricacy ; curling inwards, part so curled.

involve', *v.t.* (-*vable*), entangle ; implicate ; entail. ~**ment,** *n.* financial embarrassment.

invul'nerable, *a.* that cannot be hurt. ~**bility,** *n.*

in'ward, *a.* situated within ; mental, spiritual. *n.pl.* entrails.

in'wardly, *adv.* on the inside.

in'wardness, *n.* inner nature.

in'wards (-dz), -**rd,** *advv.* towards the inside.

inweave', *v.t.* (-*vable*), weave in.

inwrought (inrawt', before noun in'-), *a.* decorated ; wrought in.

inya'la (-ah-), *n.* S.-Afr. antelope.

i'odine (or -ēn), *n.* non-metallic element used in medicine and photography.

i'odize, *v.t.* impregnate with iodine.

io'doform, *n.* an antiseptic.

i'on, *n.* electrified particle formed when neutral atom or group of atoms loses or gains one or more electrons.

io'ta, *n.* Greek letter i ; jot.

I O U (ī ō ū), *n.* signed document acknowledging debt.

ipecacuān'ha (-na), *n.* root of S.Amer. plant used as emetic.

‖ **ip'se dix'it,** *n.* (pl. -*its*), dogmatic statement ; dictum.

‖ **ip'so fac'to,** *adv.* by that very fact.

iras'cible (or īr-), *a.* irritable ; hot-tempered. ~**bility,** *n.*

ire, *n.* anger. **īr'ate,** ~**ful,** *aa.*

irida'ceous (-shus), *a.* (of plants) of the iris kind.

irides'cent, *a.* showing rainbow-like colours. **irides'cence,** *a.*

irid'ium, *n.* a white metal.

ir'is, *n.* circle round the pupil of the eye ; kinds of plant.

Ir'ish (īr-), *a.* of Ireland. *n.* I. language. ~ **Free State,** part of Ireland separated from the U.K. and established as a British Dominion. ~**ism,** *n.* I. idiom.

irk, *v.t.* tire, bore. ~**some,** *a.*

iron (ī'ern), *n.* a metal much used for tools, &c. ; tool of iron, esp. one heated to smooth linen, &c. ; (pl.) fetters. ~ **of iron ;** robust ; unyielding. *v.t.* smooth with iron ; shackle with irons. ~**clad,** *a.* protected with iron ; *n.* ship cased with iron. ~**founder,** maker of iron castings. ~**man,** (sl.) silver dollar. ~**master,** manufacturer of iron. ~**monger,** dealer in iron goods. ~**mongery,** iron goods. ~**mould,** spot caused by rust or ink-stain. ~**stone,** ore of iron. ~**wood,** various species of trees. ~**works,** place where iron is smelted or iron goods made.

iron'ic, ~**al,** *aa.* of or addicted to irony.

ir'onist, *n.* one who uses irony.

ir'ony¹, *n.* expression of one's meaning by language of opposite or different tendency.

irony² (ī'rnī), *a.* of or like iron.

irra'diate, *v.t.* (*-iable*), shine upon ; throw light on ; light up (face). ~**tion**, ~**tor**, *nn.*

irra'tional (-shon-), *a.* unreasonable, illogical ; not endowed with reason. **irrationa'ity**, *n.*

irreclaim'able, *a.* not to be reclaimed or reformed.

irrec'oncilable, *a.* implacably hostile ; incompatible. ~**bility**, *n.*

irreco'verable (-kŭ-), *a.* that cannot be recovered or remedied.

irredeem'able, *a.* irreclaimable, hopeless ; not to be redeemed.

irredu'cible, *a.* not reducible.

irref'ragable, *a.* indisputable, unanswerable.

irrefran'gible, *a.* inviolable.

irref'utable, *a.* not to be refuted. ~**bility**, *n.*

irreg'ular, *a.* contrary to rule ; uneven, varying ; disorderly ; not in regular service. *n.pl.* troops not in regular service. **irregula'rity**, *n.*

irrel'evant, *a.* not relevant. **Irrel'evance**, *n.*

irreli'gion (-jn), *n.* hostility or indifference to religion ; impiety. **irreli'gious** (-jus), *a.*

irreme'diable, *a.* past remedy.

irremo'vable (-mŏŏ-), *a.* not removable. ~**bility**, *n.*

irrep'arable, *a.* that cannot be made good.

irrepla'ceable (-sa-), *a.* of which the loss cannot be supplied.

irrepress'ible, *a.* that cannot be repressed.

irreproach'able, *a.* faultless, blameless. ~**bility**, *n.*

irresis'tible (-zis-), *a.* too strong, convincing, charming, &c. to be resisted. ~**bility**, *n.*

irres'olute (-zolōt), *a.* hesitating ; wanting in resolution. ~**tion**, *n.*

irresol'vable (-zŏl-), *a.* that cannot be resolved into parts.

irrespec'tive, *a.* ~**of**, without reference to.

irrespon'sible, *a.* not responsible ; acting, done, without due sense of responsibility. ~**bility**, *n.*

irrespon'sive, *a.* not responsive to.

irretriev'able, *a.* not retrievable.

irrev'erent, *a.* wanting in reverence. **irrev'erence**, *n.*

irrevers'ible, *a.* that cannot be reversed. ~**bility**, *n.*

irrev'ocable, *a.* unalterable ; gone beyond recall. ~**bility**, *n.*

ir'rigate, *v.t.* (*-gable*), supply (land) with water ; water (land) with channels. ~**tion**, ~**tor**, *nn.*

ir'ritable, *a.* easily annoyed. ~**bility**, *n.*

ir'ritant, *a.* causing irritation. *n.* such substance or agency.

ir'ritate, *v.t.* excite to anger, annoy ; inflame. ~**tion**, *n.*

irrup'tion, *n.* invasion.

is, 3rd pers. sing. pres. of be.

isinglass (I'zingglahs), *n.* kind of gelatin got from sturgeon, &c.

Islam (iz-), *n.* Mohammedanism ; the body of Mohammedans or Mussulmans. ~**ism**, *n.*

island (I'l-), *n.* piece of land surrounded by water.

isle (il), *n.* island.

is'let (il-), *n.* small island.

i'sobar (or is-), *n.* isobaric line.

isobar'ic (or is-), *a.* on which the barometric pressure is equal.

isoch'ronous (or is- ; -kr-), *a.* occupying equal time.

isocli'nal (or is-), *a. & n.* (line) of equal magnetic dip.

i'solate, *v.t.* (*-lable*), place apart or alone. ~**tion**, *n.*

isoseis'mal (or is- ; -sIz-), *a. & n.* (line) of equal earthquake-shock intensity.

i'sotherm (or is'-), *n.*, **isother'mal** (or is-), *a.*, (line) of equal mean annual temperature.

iss'ue, *n.* outgoing, outflow ; result, outcome ; children ; question, dispute ; copies of journal, &c. issued at one time. *v.i. & t.* (*-uable*), go or come out, emerge ; be derived, result ; send forth ; publish, circulate.

isth'mus (or is'mus), *n.* (pl. *-muses*), neck of land ; narrow connecting part.

it, *pron. poss. its* (ö), pl. *they, obj. them, poss. their*), the thing named or in question.

Italian (Ĭtăl'yan), a. of Italy. n. native, language, of Italy.

ităl'ic, a. (I-) of ancient Italy. n.pl. (i-) italic type. ~ **type**, sloping type. **ităl'icīze**, v.t. (-zable), print in italics.

itch, n. irritation in skin; disease with itch; desire. v.i. feel itch; crave for; desire to do.

i'tĕm, n. any one of enumerated things. adv. also, likewise. *~**īze**, v.t. state in items.

it'erāte, v.t. (-rable), repeat; state repeatedly. ~**tion**, n.; ~**tive**, a.

itin'erant (or īt-), a. travelling from place to place. ~**ncy**, n.

itin'erary (or īt-), n. record of travel; guide-book; route. a. of roads or travelling.

itin'erāte (or īt-), v.i. be itinerant, esp. preach in circuit.

its, pron. possessive of it.

itsélf', pron. (pl. themselves), emphatic and refl. form of it.

i'vory, n. white substance of the tusks of elephants, &c.; (sl., pl.) dice, billiard-balls, teeth.

i'vy, n. climbing evergreen with shining leaves. **i'vied** (-īd), a. overgrown with ivy.

i'xia, n. S.-Afr. plant of iris kind with showy flowers.

J

jăb, v.t. poke roughly; thrust abruptly. n. abrupt blow.

jăbb'er, v.i. & t. chatter volubly; utter fast and indistinctly. n. chatter, gabble.

jabot (zhăbō'), n. frill on bodice.

jā'cinth (or jă-), n. a gem, reddish-orange kind of zircon.

jăck¹, n. machines for turning spit, lifting weights, &c.; a fish, the pike; ship's flag, esp. one flown from bow and showing nationality; (also black ~) leather vessel; the knave in cards; figure of man which strikes bell on the outside of a clock; small ball aimed at in bowls; *money. v.t. hoist with jack. ~**boot**, large boot coming above knee. J~**in-office**, fussy official. J~**in-the-**

green, in May-day sports man in framework covered with leaves. J~ **Ketch**, common hangman. ~**knife**, large pocket clasp-knife. ~**of-all-trades**, one who can turn his hand to anything. ~**o'-lantern**, will-o'-the-wisp; *pumpkin lantern. ~ **tar**, common sailor. ~**towel**, roller-towel.

jăck², n. fruit of an E.-Ind. tree, a large and coarse kind of bread-fruit; the tree itself.

jăck'al (-awl), n. animal of dog kind; a drudge for another.

jăck'anāpes, n. pert fellow.

jăck'ass, n. male ass; blockhead.

jăck'daw, n. daw.

jăck'et, n. sleeved outer garment; animal's coat; skin of potato; outside wrapper of book.

Jăcobē'an, a. of James I's reign; of St. James the Less.

Jăc'obin, n. Dominican friar; member of extreme democratic club established 1789 in Paris.

Jăc'obīte, n. adherent of the exiled Stuarts. **Jăcobīt'ical**, a.

jăc'onet, n. a cotton cloth of medium thickness.

jāde¹, n. poor or worn-out horse; (joc.) reprehensible woman or girl. **jā'dĕd**, a. tired out.

jāde², n. a hard green, blue, or white stone, silicate of lime and magnesia.

jā'deite (-dīt), n. silicate of sodium and aluminium.

jaeger (yā'ger), n. kinds of woollen clothing material from which vegetable fibres are excluded as unwholesome P.

Jăff'a (orange), n. large, usu. seedless, dessert orange.

jăg¹, n. sharp projection. v.t. make jags in. **jăgg'ĕd**, a.

*jăg², n. small load; have a ~ on, (sl.) be drunk.

‖ **jăgg'ery**, n. coarse dark brown sugar made in India by evaporation from palm sap.

‖ **jăghīre'**(-g-), n. (E.Indies) assignment of land and its rent as annuity; the district, or the income, so assigned.

---

ah, awl, oil, boor, cow, dowry; chin, go, bang, so, ship, thin; dh, as th(e);

jăg′uar (-gw-), n. large Amer. carnivorous spotted quadruped.

Jah, n. Jehovah.

jail, &c. See gaol, &c.

Jain, a. of a non-Brahminical E.-Ind. sect, with doctrines like those of Buddhism. n. member of this.

jăl′ap, n. a purgative drug.

jalousie (zhăl′ōoze), n. blind, shutter, with slats sloped upwards from without.

jăm¹, v.t. & i. squeeze; cause to get wedged; block (passage); (Wireless) make (message) unintelligible by operating elsewhere. n. squeeze; stoppage; conserve of boiled fruit and sugar.

Jam² (-ah-), n. a title given to certain native chiefs in Kutch, Kattywar, and the lower Indus.

jamb (jăm), n. side post, side of doorway, window, or fireplace.

jamboree′. n. (sl.) celebration; merrymaking; large rally of boy scouts.

jangle (jăng′gl), n. harsh noise, wrangle. v.i. & t. make, cause to make, a jangle; wrangle.

jăn′itor, n. doorkeeper; *caretaker of a building.

jăn′izary, n. (hist.) one of a body of Turkish infantry.

jănn′ock, a. (dial.) genuine.

Jăn′ūarў, n. first month of the year.

japăn′, n. hard varnish, esp. kind orig. from Japan. v.t. lacquer with japan; make black.

Japanese′ (-z), a. of Japan. n. native, language, of Japan.

japŏn′ica, n. kinds of plant, esp. pear or quince, from Japan.

jāpe, v.i., & n. jest.

jar¹, v.i. & t. strike discordantly, grate; wrangle. n. jarring sound, shock, or thrill; quarrel.

jar², n. kinds of round vessel with or without handles.

jar³, n. In phr. on the jar, ajar.

‖ jardinière (zhărdinyâr′), n. ornamental stand for flowers.

jär′gon, n. debased or unintelligible language; gibberish.

jär′gonelle′, n. kind of pear.

jär′vey, n. (pl. -eys), driver of Irish car.

jăs′min(e), jĕss′amin(e), n. shrub with white or yellow flowers.

jas′per (-ah-), n. red, yellow, or brown opaque quartz.

jaun′dice (jaw-, jah-), n. morbid state due to obstruction of bile; disordered (esp. mental) vision. v.t. affect with jaundice.

jaunt (jaw-, jah-), n. pleasure excursion. v.i. take a jaunt.

jaun′tў (jaw-, jah-), a. airily self-satisfied; sprightly.

jăv′elin (-vl-), n. spear; dart.

jaw, n. bone containing the teeth; (pl.) mouth; (colloq.) talk, lecture. v.i. & t. (sl.) talk tediously; lecture (person).

jay, n. a noisy bird of brilliant plumage; silly chatterer.

jăzz, n. syncopated music, and dancing, of U.S. negro origin; noisy proceedings. v.i. play, dance, indulge in, jazz. a. (sl.) discordant; loud in colour, &c. *~ up, agitate, excite, stir up.

jea′lous (jĕl-), a. watchfully tenacious; suspicious, resentful, of rivalry in the affections; envious of. jea′lousў (jĕlu-), n. being jealous.

jean (jān), n. a twilled cotton cloth, kind of fustian; *(pl.) garment of jean, short slacks.

jeer, v.i. & t. scoff at; deride. n. scoff, taunt.

jehad. See jihad.

Jĕhō′vah (-a-), n. Hebrew name of God.

jĕjune′ (-ōon), a. poor, barren.

jĕll′ў, n. semi-transparent food made with gelatin; fruit-juice, &c. of like consistence. ~-bag, jelly-like marine animal.

‖ jĕm′adār, n. (E.-Ind.) native officer in Sepoy regiment, corresponding to lieutenant; also, the head of a body of police, &c., or of servants.

jĕmm′ў, n. burglar's crowbar.

jĕnn′et, n. small Spanish horse.

jĕnn′ў, n. locomotive crane.

jeo′pardize (jĕp-), v.t. (-zable), endanger. jeo′pardў (jĕ-), n. danger.

jĕrbō′a, n. small African jumping rodent with long hind legs.

jĕrĕmī'ad, *n.* doleful complaint.

jĕrk¹, *n.* sharp sudden pull; spasmodic twitch of muscle; jerking throw. *v.t.* & *i.* move with a jerk; throw with suddenly arrested motion. **jĕrk'ў**, *a.*

jĕrk², *v.t.* cure (beef) by drying in long slices in sun.

jĕrk'in, *n.* (hist.) man's close-fitting jacket, often of leather.

jĕ'rry, *n.* ~-builder, ~-building, of flimsy houses with bad materials.

jĕr'sey (-zĭ), *n.* (pl. -*eys*), close woollen tunic or undervest.

jĕss, *n.* short strap round each leg of hawk (in falconry).

jessamine. See jasmine.

jĕst, *n.* joke; fun; object of derision. *v.i.* joke, make jests.

jĕs'ter, *n.* (esp.) professional joker of a court, &c.

Jĕs'ūit (-z-), *n.* member of Society of Jesus (R.C. order); (fig., hist.) deceitful person. **Jĕsūit'ical** (-z-), *a.* (hist.) crafty. **Jĕs'ūitism** (-z-), *n.* principles, practices, of Jesuits.

jĕt¹, *n.* hard black lignite taking brilliant polish. ~-**black**, black as jet.

jĕt², *n.* stream or shoot of water, steam, &c.; spout, nozzle, for emitting jet. *v.t.* & *i.* spurt forth.

jĕt'sam, *n.* goods thrown out of ship to lighten it and washed ashore. **jĕtt'ison**, *n.* such throwing out. *v.t.* throw out thus.

jĕtt'ў¹, *a.* black as jet.

jĕtt'ў², *n.* mole; landing-pier.

‖ jeu d'esprit (zhĕr dĕsprē'), witty or humorous trifle.

Jew (jōō), *n.* person of Hebrew race; (fig., hist.) unscrupulous usurer. **Jewry** (joor'ĭ). *n.* the Jews; (hist.) Jews' quarter in town. **Jew's harp**, small musical instrument held between the teeth.

jew'ĕl (jōō-), *n.* precious stone; ornament with jewels; precious thing. **jew'ĕller** (jōō-), *n.* dealer in jewels. **jew'ĕl(le)rў**, *n.*

Jĕz'ĕbel, *n.* shameless woman.

jĭb, *n.* triangular stay-sail from outer end of jib-boom to foretopmast head or from bowsprit

to masthead. *v.t.* & *i.* pull (sail) round to other side, (of sail) swing round; (of horse) stop and refuse to go on. ~-**boom**, spar from end of bowsprit.

jibe¹. See gibe.

jibe², *v.i.* agree.

jĭff' (ў), *n.* short time, moment.

jĭg, *n.* lively dance, music for it. *v.i.* & *t.* dance jig; move quickly up and down. *~-saw*, machine fret-saw.

jihad', je- (-ahd), *n.* religious war of Mohammedans against unbelievers; (fig.) crusade for or against a doctrine, &c.

jĭlt, *n.* woman who capriciously discards lover. *v.t.* treat thus.

*Jim Crow (-ō), *n.* negro.

jĭngle (jĭng'gl), *n.* mixed noise as of shaken keys; repetition of same sound in words. *v.i.* & *t.* make, cause to make, a jingle.

jĭng'ō (-ngg-), *n.* by ~, a form of asseveration; (*n.*, pl. -*oes*) a bellicose patriot. ~-**ism**, *n.*

jĭnrĭck'sha, -rĭk'isha, *n.* light two-wheeled hooded vehicle drawn by man or men.

*jĭt'ney, *n.* (sl.) five cents; motorbus carrying passengers at low rates.

jiu-jitsu. See ju-jutsu.

jŏb¹, *n.* piece of work; unscrupulous transaction; post, situation. *v.i.* & *t.* do jobs; hire, let out, for time or job; buy and sell as broker; handle corruptly. ~-**master**, one who lets out horses and carriages for hire. **jŏbb'er**, *n.* **jŏbb'erў**, *n.* corrupt dealing.

jŏb², *v.t.* & *i.* prod, thrust at; hurt (horse) with bit. *n.* prod; jerk at bit.

jobā'tion, *n.* reprimand.

Jŏck, *n.* (sl.) Scottish esp. Highland soldier.

jŏck'ey, *n.* (pl. -*eys*), rider in horse-races. *v.t.* cheat, trick.

jŏck'ō, *n.* (pl. -*os*), chimpanzee.

jocōse', **jŏc'ŭlar**, *aa.* waggish, humorous; given to joking. **jocōs'itў**, **jŏcŭlă'ritў**, *nn.*

jŏc'und, *n.* merry, sprightly. **jŏcun'ditў**, *n.*

jō′ey, n. (Austral.) young kangaroo ; young animal.

jŏg, v.t. & i. push ; nudge ; stimulate (memory) ; walk, trot, at slow pace. n. push, jerk, nudge ; slow walk or trot ; *irregularity of line or surface. ~trot, slow regular trot.

jŏg′gle¹, v.i. & t. move to and fro in jerks. n. slight jog.

jŏg′gle², n. key let into two stones, &c., to prevent their sliding on one another ; such or similar joint. v.t. join by joggle.

John (jŏn), n. ~ Barleycorn, malt liquor. ~ Bull, nickname for the English people or a typical Englishman. ~ Company, (nickname of) the E. India Company as governing India before 1858. ~ Dory, an edible sea-fish.

john′ny (jŏn-), n. (colloq.) fellow ; fashionable idler. ~cake, cake of (U.S.) maize-meal or (Austral.) wheat-meal.

join, v.t. & i. put together, fasten, unite ; unite, be united, in friendship, &c. ; take part with others. n. point, line, plane, of junction.

join′er, n. (esp.) maker of furniture and light woodwork. join′er′y, n. such work.

joint, a. combined ; shared by two or more in common. n. point at which two things join ; structure by which two bones fit together ; leg, loin, &c. of carcass as used for food. v.t. connect by joints ; fill up joints of (wall, &c.), point ; divide at a joint or into joints. ~ stock, common fund, share capital.

join′tress, n. widow holding jointure.

join′ture, n. estate settled on wife to be enjoyed by her after husband's death.

joist, n. any of the parallel timbers stretched from wall to wall to take ceiling laths or floor boards. jois′tĕd, a.

jōke, n. thing said or done to excite laughter. v.i. & t. (-kable), make jokes ; banter. jō′ker, n.

one who jokes ; highest trump card in some games.

jŏll′ify, v.i. & t. make merry ; tipple ; make jolly. ~fication, n.

jŏll′ity, n. merrymaking.

jŏll′y, a. joyful ; festive, jovial ; (colloq.) pleasant, delightful. n. (Nav. sl.) royal marine. *v.t. banter, talk into a good humour, flatter. adv. very. ~(-boat), clinker-built ship's boat smaller than cutter.

jŏlt, v.t. & i. jerk from seat, &c. ; move along with jerks. n. such jerk. jŏl′ty, a.

Jŏn′athan, n. (Brother) ~, personified people, typical citizen, of U.S.

jŏnq′uil (jŏ-, jŭ-), n. rush-leaved daffodil ; pale yellow.

Jor′dan alm′ond, n. fine almond, esp. from Malaga.

jō′rum, n. large drinking-bowl ; its contents, esp. punch.

*jŏsh, v.t. make fun of, banter. jŏsh′er, n. joker.

jŏs′kin, n. (sl.) bumpkin, rustic.

jŏss, n. Chinese idol. ~house, Chinese temple. ~stick, incense-stick of fragrant tinder.

jō′stle (-sl), v.i. & t. push against ; struggle with. n. jostling.

jŏt, n. small amount, whit. v.t. write briefly.

journ′al (jĕr-), n. daily record of events, &c. ; log-book ; daily newspaper or other periodical. ~ist, writer for public journal. ~ism, n. his work. ~istic, a.

journ′ey (jĕr-), n. (pl. -eys), travel ; going to a place. v.i. travel ; pass from place to place. ~man, qualified artisan.

joust (jōō-), jŭst, n. combat with lances between two mounted knights. v.i. engage in joust.

Jŏve, n. Jupiter.

jō′vial, a. merry, convivial. jōviǎl′ĭty, n.

jowl, n. jaw, jaw-bone ; cheek.

joy, n. gladness, pleasure. v.i. & t. rejoice. ~ride, (sl.) stolen or other pleasure-ride in motor, &c. ~stick, (sl.) control lever of aeroplane. ~ful, ~ous, aa.

---

ju'bilant (joō-), *a.* exultant.

jubilate (joō'bilāt), *v.i.* exult, manifest joy. ~**tion,** *n.*

ju'bilee (joō-), *n.* fiftieth anniversary; public rejoicing.

Judā'ic (joō-), *a.* Jewish.

Ju'dāize (joō-), *v.t. & i.* (-zable) make Jewish, follow Jewish customs. **Ju'dāism** (joō-), *n.*

judge, *n.* officer appointed to try causes in court of justice; (of God) supreme arbiter; one appointed to decide dispute or contest. *v.t. & i.* (-geable), pass sentence upon; try cause; decide question; award.

judge'ment, -dgment (-jm-), *n.* sentence of court of justice, &c.; misfortune as sign of divine displeasure; opinion; sagacity.

ju'dicature (joō-), *n.* administration of justice; body of judges.

judicial (joōdish'al), *a.* of or by a court of law; of, or proper to, a judge; impartial.

judiciary (joōdish'ari), *n.* the judges of a State collectively.

judicious (joōdish'us), *a.* sensible, prudent; skilful.

jug, *n.* deep vessel for liquids with handle; (sl.) prison. *v.t.* stew (hare) in jug or jar.

Jugg'ernaut (-g-), *n.* idol of Krishna dragged yearly in procession on car under whose wheels devotees formerly threw themselves.

jugg'ins (-ginz), *n.* (sl.) fool.

jug'gle, *v.i. & t.* play conjuring tricks; trick, cheat. *n.* trick, fraud. **jug'gler,** *n.* conjurer; cheat. **jug'glery,** *n.*

Jugoslav (ū'goslahv), *a.* of the State, including Serbia, called *Jugoslavia.* ~**n.** J. person.

jug'ular, *a.* of neck or throat. *n.* jugular vein.

juice (joōs), *n.* liquid part of vegetable or fruit; fluid part of animal body; (sl.) petrol. **jui'cy** (joō-), *a.* full of juice.

ju-ju (joō-joō), *n.* (W.-Afr.) charm or fetish; ban effected by this.

ju'jube (-oō-), *n.* a kernel-fruit; lozenge of gelatine, &c.

ju-jutsu, jiu-jitsu (joō'jutsoō'), *n.* Japanese art of wrestling, &c.

jul'ep (joō-), *n.* sweet drink; medicated drink; *iced and spiced spirit and water.

July' (joō-), *n.* seventh month.

jum'bal, *n.* thin crisp cake of flour, sugar, butter, &c.

jum'ble, *v.t. & i.* move about in disorder; mix confusedly. *n.* confused heap, &c.; muddle.

jum'bō, *n.* (pl. -os), big clumsy person, animal, or thing.

jump, *v.i. & t.* leap, spring from ground; rise or move with a sudden start; skip (book, &c.). *n.* leap; start caused by shock, &c.; sudden rise in price, &c.

jum'per¹, *n.* one who jumps; jumping insect; quarrying-drill.

jum'per², *n.* loose jacket of sailors, &c.; outer woollen garment slipped on over head and reaching to hips.

jum'py, *a.* nervous, panicky.

junc'tion, *n.* joining-point; station where railway lines meet.

junc'ture, *n.* joining-point; state of affairs, critical point.

June (joōn), *n.* sixth month.

jungle (jŭng'gl), *n.* land covered with tangled vegetation; tangled mass. ~**fowl,** an E.-Ind. bird of the genus *Gallus*; a mound-bird of Australia. ~**rice,** millet-rice. ~**sheep,** an Indian ruminant.

jun'ior (joō-), *a.* the younger; of less standing. *n.* junior person.

jun'iper (joō-), *n.* coniferous evergreen shrub.

junk¹, *n.* lump, chunk; (Naut.) salt meat; piece of old cable; *scrap metal, rubbish.

junk², *n.* flat-bottomed sailing-vessel in Chinese seas.

‖ **junker** (yŏŏng'ker), *n.* member of the exclusive land-owning aristocracy in Prussia.

junk'et, *n.* dish of milk curdled by rennet; feast. *v.i.* feast, picnic.

jun'ta, *n.* deliberative or administrative council in Spain or Italy; (also -tō) clique, faction.

Ju'piter (joō-), *n.* (Myth.) king of gods; largest of the planets.

---

jurass´ic (joor-), *a.* of the Jura mountains; marked by prevalence of oolitic limestone.

jurid´ical (joor-), *a.* of judicial proceedings; legal.

jurisconsült´ (joor-), *n.* one learned in law.

jurisdic´tion (joor-), *n.* administration of justice; legal authority; territory it extends over.

jurisprud´ence (joorisproō-), *n.* science of skill in law.

jur´ist (joor-), *n.* one versed in law; writer on law. ~ic(al), *aa.*

jur´or (joor-), *n.* member of jury; one who takes oath.

jur´ȳ (joor-), *n.* body of persons sworn to render verdict in court of justice; judges in a competition. ~man, juror.

jury-mast (joor´imahst), *n.* temporary mast.

jüss´ive, *a.* (Gram.) expressing a command.

jüst, *a.* upright, fair; correct, due, proper, right. *adv.* exactly; barely; not long ago.

jüs´tice, *n.* justness, fairness; judicial proceedings; judge; magistrate. ~ship, *n.*

justi´ciar(ȳ) (-shya-), *nn.* administrator of justice.

jüs´tifȳ, *v.t.* (-*fiable*), show the justice or truth of; clear from imputed guilt; warrant; adjust. ~fiability, ~fication, *nn.*; ~ficatory, *a.*

jüt, *v.i.* project. *n.* projection.

jute (joŏt), *n.* fibre from some plants, used for sacking, &c.

juvenes´cence (joō-), *n.* being juvenile; youth. ~nt, *a.*

juv´enile (joō-), *a.* youthful; of, for, young persons. *n.* young person. juvenil´itȳ (joō-), *n.*

jüx´tapöse (-z), *v.t.* (-*sable*), put side by side. jüxtaposi´tion, *n.*

K

Kǎf´ir, Kǎff´ir, Cǎf´fre (-*fer*), *n.* member of a S.-Afr. race of Bantu family.

kai´ser (kīz-), *n.* emperor.

ka´ka, ka´kapo (kah-), *nn.* kinds of New Zealand parrot.

kāle, kail, *n.* cabbage, esp. borecole; broth of kale, &c. ~yard, kitchen-garden.

kaleid´oscöpe (-līd-), *n.* tube in which figures are produced by reflections of pieces of coloured glass and varied by rotation of the tube.

kämptü´licön, *n.* floor-cloth of rubber, cork, &c., on canvas.

kǎn´aka, *n.* South Sea islander, esp. on Queensland sugar plantation.

kängaröō´ (-ngg-), *n.* Austral. marsupial, with hind-quarters strongly developed for jumping; (sl., pl.) W.-Austral. mine-shares; dealers in these. ~rat, small Austral. marsupial.

ka´olin (kah-, kā-), *n.* fine white clay used for porcelain.

käp´je (-pī), *n.* (S.-Afr.) woman's cape.

ka´pŏk (kah-), *n.* kind of tree-cotton used to stuff cushions.

‖ **kärm´a,** *n.* (Buddhism) sum of person's actions in one of his successive states of existence viewed as deciding his fate in the next; destiny.

kar(r)ōō´, *n.* S.-Afr. high plateau waterless in dry season.

karöss´, *n.* (S.-Afr.) mantle (or sleeveless jacket) of animals' skins with the hair on, worn by natives.

kärr´i, *n.* an Australian tree, one of the 'blue gums'; also, its hard red timber, used in street paving.

kät´tel (-tl), *n.* (S.-Afr.) wooden bed or hammock in an ox-wagon.

käsh´a, *n.* ladies' dress-fabric.

kä´tydid, large green American insect of locust family making characteristic sound.

kauri (kowr´i), *n.* coniferous tree of New Zealand, furnishing valuable timber and a resin.

kavass´, *n.* Turkish armed constable or servant.

kea (kā´a), *n.* green Alpine parrot of New Zealand which kills sheep for their kidney-fat.

keck, *v.i.* make sound as if about to vomit.

kedge, *v.t. & i.* warp ship, (of ship) move, by hawser attached to small anchor. *n.* such anchor.

kedg′eree, *n.* dish of fish, rice, eggs, &c.

keel[1], *n.* lowest longitudinal timber on which ship's framework is built up. *v.t.* turn (ship) keel upwards. ~ **over**, upset, capsize.

keel[2], *n.* flat-bottomed boat on Tyne, &c. for loading colliers.

keen[1], *a.* sharp; strong, acute, penetrating; eager, ardent.

keen[2], Irish funeral song accompanied with wailing. *v.i. & t.* bewail person; utter in wailing tone.

keep, *v.t. & i.* (kĕpt), pay due regard to, observe; protect, have charge of; retain possession of; maintain; reserve for future use; remain in same state; conduct, maintain, for profit; reside, lodge (esp. Cambridge Univ. & U.S.). *n.* maintenance, food; (hist.) tower, citadel. ~ **goal**, be goal-keeper. ~ **wicket**, be wicket-keeper. *for keeps, for good, permanently.

keep′er, *n.* one who has superintendence or care of anything; ring to keep another on finger.

keep′ing, *n.* holding; custody; harmony. *~-room, sitting-room.

keep′sake, *n.* thing treasured for sake of the giver.

keg, *n.* small cask or barrel.

kelp, *n.* a seaweed; calcined ashes of kelp yielding iodine, &c.

kel′pie, *n.* malevolent water-spirit, usu. in form of a horse.

kel′son, *n.* line of timber fixing floor-timbers to keel.

kelt[1], *n.* a spent salmon.

Kelt[2], &c. See Celt, &c.

ken, *v.t.* (Sc.) know. *n.* range of knowledge or sight.

kenn′el[1], *n.* house for shelter of house-dog or hounds. *v.t. & i.* put or be put into kennel.

kenn′el[2], *n.* gutter.

kept, *p.t.* of keep.

kerb, *n.* stone edging to pavement or raised path.

ketch′ief (-tf), *n.* cloth used to cover head.

kerf, *n.* slit made in cutting; cut end of felled tree.

kerm′es (-ēz), *n.* pregnant female of an insect; red dye-stuff made of its dried body.

kern, *n.* (hist.) light-armed Irish foot-soldier; peasant.

kern′el, *n.* part within hard shell of nut or stone fruit; central or essential part.

ke′rosēne, *n.* lamp-oil got by distillation of petroleum, &c.

kers′ey (-zĭ), *n.* (pl. -*eys*), coarse cloth woven from wool.

kers′eymēre (-zĭ-), *n.* twilled fine woollen cloth.

kes′trel, *n.* kind of small hawk.

ketch, *n.* small two-masted or cutter-rigged coasting vessel.

ketch′up, *n.* sauce made of mushrooms, tomatoes, &c.

ket′tle, *n.* metal vessel with spout and handle for boiling.

ket′tledrum, *n.* a drum with parchment spread over a brass hemisphere; (colloq.) tea-party.

key[1] (kē), *n.* instrument for turning bolt of lock; solution; code, crib, manual; (Mus.) set of notes definitely related and based on particular note; (pl.) levers for the fingers in piano, typewriter, &c.; instrument for winding clock, &c. *v.t.* fasten with wedge, bolt, &c.; regulate pitch of strings of (piano, &c.); brace up, raise. ~**board**, set of keys on piano, type-setting machine, &c. ~**hole**, that by which key enters lock. ~**note**, note on which key is based, (fig.) dominant idea. *~**noter**, (sl.) one who outlines the policy of a campaign. ~**stone**, central stone of arch, (fig.) central principle.

key[2] (kē), *n.* reef, low island.

key′less (kē-), *a.* without a key, esp. of watch.

kha′ki (kah-), *a.* dull-yellow. *n.* khaki cloth, esp. as used for service uniforms.

Khal'ifa (kă-), n. Caliph.

Khal'ifat (kă-), n. Caliphate. ~ agitation, &c., anti-British movement in India based on Moslem resentment of the loss of power by Islam.

khan[1] (kän, kahn), n. ruler, official, in Central Asia, &c. khan'ate, n. khan's rule or district.

khan[2] (kän, kahn), n. caravanserai.

|| kheda (kā-), n. (hist.) stockade, enclosure used in Bengal, &c., to catch elephants.

Khedive (kĭdēv'), n. (hist.) Viceroy of Egypt. Khedi'val (kĭdē-), a.

|| khid'mutgar (kĭ-), n. male table-servant in India.

|| khud (kŭd), n. (E.-Ind.) a deep ravine or chasm.

kibe, n. ulcerated chilblain.

kibosh (kī'bŏsh, kĭbŏsh'), (sl.) n. put ~ on, do for. v.t. dispose of.

kick, v.i. & t. strike or move with the foot; score (goal) by kicking ball. n. kicking; blow given with foot; recoil of gun; reacting power; *(sl.) protest, complaint; (Footb.) kicker. kick'er, n. one that kicks; horse apt to kick.

kick'shaw, n. fancy dish of food; toy, trifle.

kid, n. young goat; kid-skin leather; (sl.) child; (sl.) hoax. v.t. & i. give birth to kid; (sl.) hoax. kidd'y, n. child.

kid'nap, v.t. steal (child); carry off (person) illegally. ~per, n.

kid'ney, n. (pl. -eys), either of a pair of glandular organs serving to excrete urine; nature, kind. ~bean, n. kidney-shaped bean, esp. scarlet-runner.

*kike, n. (sl.) Jew.

kie-kie (kē'kē), n. New Zealand climbing plant with leaves used for baskets, &c.

kil'derkin, n. (cask holding) 18 or 16 gallons.

kill, v.t. & i. put to death, slay; cause the death of; destroy, make useless. n. killing; animal(s) killed by sportsman. ~joy, depressing person.

|| kill'adar, n. (E.-Ind.) the governor of a fort or castle.

kiln (kĭln, kĭl), n. furnace, oven, esp. for calcining lime or baking bricks.

kilo- in comb. = 1,000. kil'ocycle, unit of frequency (1,000 alternations per second) used in distinguishing wave-length metres in distinguishing wave-length metres in distinguishing wave-length metres in distin-guishing wave-length metres in distin-guishing wave-length metres. ~gram-(me), weight of 1,000 grammes (2·205 lb. avoird.). ~litre (-lēter), measure of 1,000 litres (35·31 cub. ft.). ~metre (-ter), measure of 1,000 metres (3280·89 ft.). ~watt (-wŏt), 1,000 watts.

kilt, n. Highlander's skirt from waist to knee. v.t. tuck up (skirts) round body; gather in vertical pleats.

kin, n. ancestral stock, family; one's relative. pred.a. related.

kin'chin, n. (sl.) child.

kin'cob (-ngk-), n. rich Indian stuff embroidered with gold or silver.

kind, n. race of animals, &c.; class, sort. a. gentle, benevolent, friendly, considerate.

kin'dergarten, n. school for educating young children by object lessons, games, &c.

kin'dle, v.t. & i. set on fire, light; inspire; become kindled; glow. kind'ling, n. setting on fire; small wood, &c. for lighting fires.

kind'ly, a. kind, sympathetic. adv. in a kind manner.

kin'dred, n. blood relationship; one's relations. a. related by blood; similar.

kine. See cow.

kinema, &c. See cinema, &c.

kinemat'ic, a. of motion viewed without reference to force. n.pl. science of this.

kinet'ic, a. of motion in relation to force. n.pl. science of this.

king, n. sovereign ruler of independent State; piece in chess; card with king on it. ~craft, able exercise of royalty. ~ Emperor, the King of Great Britain, Ireland, and the British Dominions beyond the Seas, Emperor of India. ~ship, n. state.

dignity, of a king. ~'s Bench, a division of the High Court of Justice. ~'s Counsel (abbr. K.C.), practising barrister appointed as counsel to the Crown. ~'s evil, scrofula, formerly held curable by king's touch.

king'cup, n. marsh marigold.

king'dom, n. State, territory, ruled by king.

king'fisher, n. small brilliant-plumaged bird diving for fish.

king'let, -ling, nn. petty king.

king'-pin, n. central pin in game of bowls or ninepins; (colloq.) most important person.

king'post, n. upright from tie-beam to rafter-top.

kink, n. back-twist in wire, chain, or rope; (fig.) mental twist. v.i. & t. form, cause (wire, &c.) to form, a kink.

kink'ajou (-ōō), n. nocturnal racoon-like animal.

kins'folk, -man, -woman, nn. blood relation(s).

kin'ship, n. relationship.

kiosk', n. light open pavilion; structure for sale of newspapers, bandstand, &c.

kipp'er, v.t. cure (herring, salmon, &c.) by splitting open, salting, drying, and smoking. n. kippered fish, esp. herring; male salmon in spawning season.

kirk, n. (Sc.) church. ~ session, governing body of a particular congregation. ~yard, graveyard.

kir'tle, n. gown or outer petticoat; man's tunic or coat.

‖ kis'met, n. destiny, fate.

kiss, n. caress given with lips. v.t. touch with the lips as sign of affection, reverence, &c.

kit¹, n. wooden tub; contents of soldier's valise or knapsack; personal equipment; outfit. ~bag, for soldier's or traveller's outfit.

kit², n. small fiddle.

kit'-cat, n. portrait, less than half-length but including hands.

kitch'en, n. room used for cook-

ing. ~ garden, for fruit and vegetables.

kitch'ener, n. cooking-range.

kitchenette', n. small combination kitchen and pantry.

kite, n. bird of prey of falcon family; rapacious person; child's toy flown in wind; (sl.) accommodation bill. ~ balloon, captive balloon for military observations.

kith, n. acquaintance.

kitt'en, n. young of cat; playful girl. v.i. bring forth kittens.

kitteree'n, n. W.-Ind. one-horse chaise.

kitt'iwake, n. kind of seagull.

ki'wi (kē-), n. New Zealand bird with rudimentary wings and no tail.

kleptoma'nia, n. morbid tendency to theft. ~niac, n. person subject to kleptomania.

klip'springer (-nger), n. small S.-Afr. antelope.

kloof, n. (S.-Afr.) ravine.

knack, n. acquired dexterity; trick, habit. knack'y, a.

knack'er, n. buyer of useless horses for slaughter, or of old houses, &c. for the materials.

knag, n. knot in wood. knagg'y (-g-), a. knotty.

knap, v.t. break (flints) with hammer; break, snap. knapp'er, n.

knap'sack, n. soldier's or traveller's bag for necessaries.

knap'weed, n. weed with purple flowers on globular head.

knar, n. knot in wood.

knave, n. unprincipled man, rogue; lowest court card. kna'very, n.; kna'vish, a.

knead, v.t. work up into dough or paste; make (loaf, pottery) thus; massage.

knee, n. joint between thigh and lower leg; angular piece of iron, &c. ~cap, bone in front of knee-joint; cap used to protect knee.

kneel, v.i. (knelt), fall, rest, on the knees, esp. in reverence.

knell, n. sound of bell, esp. at

In words beginning kn-, k is silent.

---

funeral or after a death; doom
of. *v.t.* & *i.* ring a knell.

knelt, *p.t.* & *p.p.* of kneel.

knew, *p.t.* of know.

knick′erbockers, *n.pl.* loose-fitting
breeches gathered in at knee;
knick′ers, *n.pl.* (colloq.) knickerbockers; woman's drawers of
knickerbocker shape.

knick′-knack, **nick′-nack**, *n.* light
dainty article of furniture, dress,
or food; gimcrack. **knick-
knack′ery**, *n.*

knife, *n.* (pl. *-ives*), blade with long
sharpened edge used for cutting;
blade in cutting-machine. *v.t.*
(*knifed*; *-fable*), cut, stab, with
knife.

knight (nīt), *n.* person raised to
rank below baronetcy; (hist.)
person raised to honourable
military rank; piece in the game
of chess. *v.t.* make (person) a
knight. **~age**, *n.* (list of) the
knights. **~hood**, *n.*; **~ly**, *a.*

knit, *v.t.* & *i.* (*knitted* or *knit*), form
(texture, garment) of interloop-
ing yarn or thread; wrinkle (brow);
make or become compact;
unite together.

knob, *n.* rounded protuberance;
small lump of coal, &c. **~kĕ′rrie**,
short knob-headed stick of
S.-Afr. tribes. **~stick**, knobbed
stick; blackleg (workman).
knŏb′ble, *n.* small knob. **knŏb-
b′ly**, **knŏbb′y**, *aa.*

knŏck, *v.t.* & *i.* strike, esp. with
hard blow; collide with or be
driven against; (sl.) amaze,
stupefy; *(sl.) depreciate, disparage. *n.* blow; rap, esp. at
door; (Cricket sl.) innings.
~out, plot between buyers at
auction to secure lot cheap by
avoiding competition; finishing
blow; (sl.) paragon.

knŏck′er, *n.* metal appendage
hinged to door for knocking
with.

knŏll, *n.* small hill, mound.

knŏp, *n.* (arch.) knob; bud.

knŏt, *n.* intertwining of parts of

one or more strings, &c. to
fasten them together; tangled
mass, cluster; hard mass in
trunk at insertion of branch;
(Naut.) division marked by
knots in log-line, (loosely) nautical mile; difficulty. *v.t.* & *i.* tie
knot in (string, &c.); entangle.
~grass, weed with intricate
stems and pink flowers. **knŏtt′y**,
a. full of knots; puzzling.

knout (n-, kn-), *n.* scourge formerly
used in Russia. *v.t.* flog.

know (nō), *v.t.* & *i.* (*knew* pr. nū,
known), be aware of; perceive
with certainty; be acquainted
with; recognize. **know′ing** (nōi-),
a. (esp.) cunning, wide awake;
(of hat, &c.) stylish, smart.
know′ingly (nōi-), *adv.* in a
knowing manner; consciously.

knowl′edge (nŏl-), *n.* knowing;
what one knows; all that is or
may be known. **~able**, *a.* intelligent or well-informed.

knŭc′kle, *n.* bone at finger-joint;
projection of knee- or ankle-
joints of quadruped. *v.t.* & *i.*
strike, rub, &c. with knuckles;
(with *down*) give in, submit.
~bone, game played with sheep's
knuckle-bones. **~duster**, metal
instrument to protect knuckles.

knŭr, *n.* knot on tree-trunk; hard
concretion; wooden ball in game
like trap-ball.

kō′ala (-ä-), *n.* arboreal mammal
of Australia, like sloth in form.

kō′dăk, *n.* kind of camera. **P.**

kohl (kōl), *n.* powder used in the
East to darken eyelids.

kohlra′bi (kōlrah-), *n.* cabbage
with turnip-like stem.

kolin′skў, *n.* fur of Siberian mink.

koodoo, kudu (kōō′dōō), *n.* large
white-striped South African
antelope.

kŏp′je (-pi), *n.* (S.-Afr.) small hill.

Koran′ (kŏr′an, korahn′), *n.* sacred
book of Mohammedans.

koran′ (korahn′), *n.* a S.-Afr. bus-
tard.

kō′sher, *a.* (of food **or** food-shop)

In words beginning kn-, k is silent.

fulfilling requirements of Jewish law. *n.* kosher food or shop.

kŏtow′, *n.* Chinese custom of touching ground with forehead as sign of submission, &c. *v.i.* perform the kotow; act obsequiously.

koum′iss (kōō-), *n.* fermented liquor of mare's milk.

kourb′äsh (-oor-), *n.* hide whip as scourge.

kraal (krahl), *n.* S.-Afr. village within fence; cattle enclosure.

kra′ken (-ah-), *n.* mythical Norwegian sea-monster.

krán(t)z, *n.* (S.-Afr.) precipitous or overhanging wall of rocks.

krĕm′lin, *n.* citadel in a Russian town esp. (*K-*) that of Moscow.

krieg′spiel, *n.* war-game on maps, with blocks for troops, &c.

Krish′naism (-oi-), *n.* worship of Krishna, great deity of later Hinduism.

kromĕs′ky̆, *n.* small fried roll of minced chicken, &c.

krō′ne (-*e*), *n.* silver coin of Austria (10*d.*) or Denmark, Norway, and Sweden (1*s.* 1½*d.*); German 10-mark gold piece.

kŭ′dŏs, *n.* (sl.) glory, renown.

***Kŭ′-Klŭx**(-Klăn), *n.* secret society hostile to negroes formed in Southern States after the civil war; similar organization throughout U.S. to combat alien influences after the great war.

kuk′rĭ (kōō-), *n.* heavy curved knife as Gurkha weapon.

kultur (kōōltoor′), *n.* civilization as conceived by the Germans.

ku′mara (kōō-), *n.* (New Zealand) sweet potato.

‖ **kŭn′kur** (-ngg-), *n.* large coarse kind of limestone found in India.

kursaal (koor′zahl), *n.* building for visitors at health resort.

ky̆′lōe, *n.* one of small breed of long-horned Scotch cattle.

ky̆′mograph, *n.* instrument recording curves of pressure, pulsations, sound-waves, &c.

kyr′ĭē (ĕlē′ĭson) (kēr-, -lĭ-), *n.* the 'Lord have mercy upon us' or a musical setting of it.

L

la (lah), *n.* sixth note of scale.

laag′er (lahg-), *n.* encampment, esp. in circle, of wagons. *v.i. & t.* make laager; place in laager.

lā′bel, *n.* slip attached to an object to give some information about it. *v.t.* attach label to.

lā′bial, *a.* of the lips; (Phonet.) pronounced with the lips. *n.* (Phonet.) labial sound.

lăb′oratory, *n.* place used for scientific experiments; (obs.) for manufacture of chemicals.

labŏr′ious, *a.* hard-working, toilsome; (of style) laboured.

lā′bour (-ber), *n.* exertion of body or mind; task; pains of childbirth; labourers. *v.i. & t.* exert oneself; work hard; strive; elaborate, work out in detail. **~ Party**, that representing labourers and artisans; M.P.s belonging to it. **lā′bourer** (-ber-), *n.* (esp.) man doing unskilled work. **lā′bourite**, *n.* member or adherent of labour party.

labŭr′num, *n.* tree with yellow hanging flowers.

lăb′yrinth, *n.* network of winding passages; maze; tangled affairs. **lăbyrĭn′thine**, *a.*

lăc[1], *n.* dark-red resin used as scarlet dye; basis of shellac.

lăc[2], **lăkh** (-k), *n.* (Anglo-Ind.) 100,000 (esp. *lac* of rupees).

lāce, *n.* cord, &c. passed through eyelets or hooks to fasten or tighten boots, stays, &c.; trimming-braid; kinds of fine open fabric. *v.t. & i.* (-*ceable*), fasten, tighten, compress, trim, with lace; flavour (milk, beer, &c.) with spirit. **lā′cy̆**, *a.*

lā′cerāte, *v.t.* (-*rable*), tear, rend; wound feelings, &c. **~ā′tion**, *n.*

lăch′es (-ĭz), *n.* negligence in performance, &c.

lăc′hrymal (-k-), *a.* of tears.

lăc′hrymatory (-k-), *n.* one of the phials found in ancient-Roman tombs and conjectured to be tear-bottles. *a.* of or causing

---

māte, mēte, mīte, mōte, mūte, mōōt ; răck, rĕck, rĭck, rōck, rŭck, rōōk.

tears. **lăc'hrўmōse** (-k-). *a.* tearful.

lăck, *n.* deficiency or want. *v.t.* & *i.* need; be without.

lăckadais'ical (-z-), *a.* languidly superior; eschewing enthusiasm.

lăck'ey, *n.* (pl. *-eys*), footman; obsequious person. *v.t.* play lackey to; wait upon.

lacŏn'ic, *a.* using, expressed in, few words. **lacŏn'icism**, *n.*

lăcq'uer (-ker), *n.* kinds of varnish, esp. that made of shellac and alcohol. *v.t.* coat with lacquer.

lacrosse' (-kraws), *n.* N.-Amer. ball-game.

lactā'tion, *n.* suckling; secreting of milk. **lăc'tĕal**, *a.* of milk; conveying chyle; *n.pl.* chyle-conveying vessels. **lăctĕs'cent**, *a.* looking like milk or yielding milky juice. **lăctĕs'cence**, *n.* **lăc'tic**, *a.* of milk. **lăctĭf'erous**, *a.* yielding milk or milky juice. **lăctŏm'ēter**, *n.* instrument for testing purity of milk.

lacū'na, *n.* (pl. *-ae*), gap in MS.; missing link in argument; vacant interval; interstice.

lacŭs'trine (*or* -in), *a.* of lakes.

lăd, *n.* boy, young fellow.

lădd'er, *n.* frame with cross-bars (rungs) used as means of ascent; vertical flaw in stocking, &c.; (fig.) means of rising.

lāde, *v.t.* (p.p. *lāden*; *-dable*), load (ship); ship (goods); (*p.p.*) loaded or burdened (*with*). **lā'ding**, *n.* load; cargo.

lā'dle, *n.* long-handled large-bowled spoon for transferring liquids. *v.t.* transfer with ladle. **lā'dleful** (-dĭfool), *n.*

lā'dў, *n.* gentlewoman, woman of good birth or breeding; (prefixed to name) woman of title below duchess, daughter of duke, marquis, or earl; mistress of a house; wife; (esp. in pl.) complimentary term applied to women in general. **~bird**, ***~bug**, winged insect, usu. reddish-brown with black spots. **~ Day**, the Annunciation, 25th Mar., a quarter-day. **~ help**, gentlewoman ser-

vant. **~killer**, male flirt. **~love**, man's sweetheart. **~'s bedstraw**, a plant. **~'s-maid**, in charge of lady's toilet. **~smock**, cuckoo-flower. **~'s slipper**, calceolaria.

lā'dўlīke, *a.* behaving as or befitting a lady.

lā'dўship, *n.* used as substitute for titled lady's name.

lăg, *v.i.* & *t.* go too slow, fall behind; (sl.) take into custody. *n.* (sl.) a convict. **lăgg'ard**, *n.* person who lags behind.

lā'ger (beer) (lahg-), *n.* light beer of the German kind.

lagoon', *n.* salt-water lake parted from sea by sand-bank.

lā'ic, *a.* non-clerical. *n.* layman. non-ecclesiastic.

lā'icize, *v.t.* (*-zable*), rid of priestly control; throw open (office) to laymen. **~zation**, *n.*

laid, *p.t.* of lay.

lain, *p.p.* of lie.

lair, *n.* beast's lying-place.

laird, *n.* Scotch landowner.

∥laiss'ez faire (-sā), *n.* government abstention from interference with individual action.

lā'itў, *n.* laymen.

lāke¹, *n.* large body of water surrounded by land. **~let**, *n.*

lāke², *n.* a crimson pigment.

lakh. See lac².

lăm, *v.t.* & *i.* (sl.) hit, thrash.

lā'ma¹ (lah-), *n.* Thibetan or Mongolian Buddhist monk.

lama². See llama.

lămb (-m), *n.* young sheep, its meat; innocent child, helpless person. *v.i.* & *t.* (of sheep) give birth (to). **~kin**, *n.* little lamb. **~like**, *a.* (esp.) meek.

lăm'bent, *a.* (of flame, &c.) playing about a surface; gently brilliant. **lăm'bencў**, *n.*

lāme, *a.* crippled by injury or defect; limping or unable to walk; (of metre) halting. *v.t.* (*-mable*), make lame; disable. **~ duck**, disabled or weak person; defaulter on Stock Exchange; *****official not re-elected.

lament', *n.* passionate expression

---

māre, mĕre, mīre, mŏre, mūre; părt, pĕrt, pŏrt; *italics,* **vague sounds;**

of grief; elegy. *v.i. & t.* utter lament; express or feel grief for; (*p.p.*) mourned for. **lăm'ént**-**able**, *a.* deplorable, regrettable. **~ā'tion**, *n.* lament, lamenting.

lăm'ĭna, *n.* (Geol., &c.; pl. *-ae*), thin plate or flake or layer. **lăm'ĭnāte**, *v.t. & i.* (*-nable*), beat or roll metal into laminae; split into layers; overlay with metal plates. **lăm'ĭnated** (*-ātĭd*), **lăm'ĭnar**, **lăm'ĭnōse**, *aa.* in plates.

Lămm'as, *n.* 1st August, formerly kept as harvest festival.

lămp, *n.* vessel with oil and wick for giving light; glass vessel enclosing gas-jet or other illuminant; (fig.) source of spiritual or intellectual light. **~black**, *n.* pigment made from soot.

lăm'pĭon, *n.* glass pot holding light for illuminations.

lămpoōn', *n.* piece of virulent satire. *v.t.* write lampoon against.

lăm'prey, *n.* (pl. *-eys*). eel-like fish with sucker mouth.

lance (*-ah-*), *n.* horseman's long spear. *v.t.* (*-ceable*), prick or open with lancet. **~corporal**, N.C.O. below corporal.

lance'lét (*-ahnsl-*), *n.* a small fish.

lăn'céolate, *a.* shaped like spearhead, tapering to each end.

la'ncer (*-ah-*), *n.* soldier of cavalry regiment armed with lances; (pl.) kind of quadrille.

la'ncĕt (*-ah-*), *n.* pointed and two-edged surgical instrument; arch or window with pointed head.

lăn'cĭnātĭng, *a.* (of pain) shooting.

lănd, *n.* solid part of earth's surface; ground, soil, expanse of country; country, State; landed property, (pl.) estates. *v.t. & i.* disembark, go or put ashore; catch (fish), win (prize). **~bank**, bank issuing notes on security of landed property. **~holder**, proprietor or (usu.) tenant of land. **~lady**, woman keeping inn or lodgings; woman having tenants. **~locked**, almost or quite enclosed by land. **~lord**, person of whom another holds any tene-

ment; keeper of inn or lodgings. **~mark**, boundary mark; conspicuous object; notable event. **~rail**, corncrake. **~slide**, overwhelming political victory; **landslip**, slip, sliding down of mass of land from cliff, &c. **~ward**, *a.*, *adv. & n.*; **~wards**, *adv.*

lăn'dau, *n.* four-wheeled carriage with top whose back and front can be raised and lowered. **lăndaulĕt(te)'**, *n.* coupé with landau top.

lăn'dĕd, *a.* possessing, consisting of, land.

lănd'gräve, *n.* title of certain German potentates.

lăn'dĭng, *n.* place for disembarking; platform at head of stairs. **~net**, net for landing large fish.

lănd'scāpe (*-ns-*), *n.* piece of inland scenery; picture of it.

lāne, *n.* narrow road between hedges; narrow street; passage.

lăng sȳne, *adv. & n.* (Sc.) (in) the old days.

lăng'uage (*-nggw-*), *n.* words and their use; speech; form of speech used by a people; style; expression.

lăng'uĭd (*-nggw-*), *a.* suffering from or seeming to be affected by languor.

lăng'uĭsh (*-nggw-*), *v.i.* lose or lack vitality; lose intensity; droop; pine for. **~ment**, *n.*

lang'uor (*-ngger*), *n.* faintness; lassitude; soft or tender mood. **~ous**, *a.* indulging in languor.

lănk, *a.* lean and tall; long; (of grass, hair, &c.) long and limp. **lănk'ȳ**, *a.* tall, long.

lăn'olin, *n.* fat permeating sheep's wool, used as basis of ointments.

lăns'quenĕt (*-kĭ-*), *n.* a card game.

lăn'tern, *n.* case for a light to be used out of doors; erection on top of dome or room with glazed sides.

lăn'yard, *n.* (Naut.) short cord for fastening or holding something.

Lāodicē'an, *n.* person lacking zeal, esp. in religion or politics.

lăp', *v.i. & t.* drink by scooping with the tongue; drink greedily; (of waves, &c.) make lapping sound. *n.* liquid food; (sl.) weak beverage; sound of wavelets.

lăp², *n.* tail or skirt of coat; front of woman's skirt held up as a receptacle; thighs of sitting person; one circuit of course in a race. *v.t. & i.* swathe, enfold; arrange so as to overlap. **~dog**, small enough to be held in the lap. **~ful**, *a.*

lapél', *n.* part of coat-breast folded back. **lapélled'** (-ld), *a.*

lăp'idáry, *a.* of stones; engraved on stone. *n.* engraver of gems.

lăp'is lăz'ŭlī, *n.* a bright blue pigment; a rich blue silicate.

lăpp'ét, *n.* flap or fold of garment, &c. or flesh.

lăpse, *n.* slip of memory, &c.; slight mistake; backsliding; coming to an end; elapsing. *v.i.* fall back or away; become void, fall in; elapse.

‖ **lăp'sus ling'uae** (-nggwē), slip of the tongue. ‖ **~ căl'ami**, slip of the pen.

lăp'wing, *n.* pewit.

lăr'board (-berd), *n.* older term (now rare) for port.

lăr'céný, *n.* theft. **larcénous**, *a.*

lărch, *n.* bright-foliaged tree of pine kind; its timber.

lărd, *n.* pig fat prepared for cooking, &c. *v.t.* smear with lard; garnish. **lărdā'ceous** (-shŭs), *a.* lard-like. **lărd'ý**, *a.*

lărd'er, *n.* room or cupboard for meat, &c.

lăr'ēs (-z), *n.pl.* household gods.

lărge, *a.* of considerable or relatively great magnitude; of wide range, comprehensive; liberal, generous. *n.* (only with *at* or *in*): at **~**, not in custody; at full length; as a whole; broadcast. in **~**, without reduction of scale. **large'lý**, *adv.* to a great or preponderating extent.

lăr'gésse, *n.* money or gifts scattered on occasions of rejoicing.

*****lăr'iat**, *n.* picketing-rope, lasso.

lărk¹, *n.* kinds of small bird including the skylark.

lărk², *n.* frolic, spree; amusing incident. *v.i.* indulge in lark.

lărk'spur, *n.* plant with spur-shaped calyx.

lă'rrikin, *n.* rowdy street boy.

lărv'a, *n.* (pl. *-ae*), insect in caterpillar stage. **lărv'al**, *a.*

laryng'oscōpe (-ngg-), *n.* instrument for inspecting larynx.

lăryngŏt'omý (-ngg-), *n.* making of the incision into larynx.

lă'rynx, *n.* cavity in throat holding vocal chords. **laryn'géal** (-j-), *a.* **lăryngi'tis** (-j-), *n.* inflammation of larynx.

Lăs'cár, *n.* E.-Indian seaman.

lasciv'ious, *a.* lustful.

lăsh, *v.i. & t.* make sudden movement of tail, limb, &c.; pour, rush; beat with thong, &c.; urge as with whip; castigate; tie tightly. *n.* stroke given with thong, &c.; flexible part of whip. **lăsh'ing**, *n.* a flogging; cord used in making fast. **lăsh'ings** *n.pl.* (sl.) plenty.

lăsh'er, *n.* weir; pool below it.

lăsh'kar, *n.* body of armed Indian tribesmen.

lăss, **lăss'ie**, *nn.* girl.

lăss'ĭtŭde, *n.* languor; disinclination to exert oneself.

lăss'ō (or **lasō̆'**), *n.* (pl. *-os*), noosed rope for catching cattle. *v.t.* catch with lasso.

last¹ (-ah-), *n.* shoemaker's model for shaping shoe on.

last² (-ah-), *n.* a load; cargo; a large quantity or amount varying with the class of goods.

last³ (-ah-), *a.* after all others; coming at the end; most recent; utmost. *adv.* on the last occasion before the present. *n.* most recent letter, &c.; last performance of certain acts; end.

last⁴ (-ah-), *v.i.* go on; remain unexhausted or adequate or alive. **last'ing** (-ah-), *a.* permanent; durable. *n.* kind of hard cloth used for boot-tops, &c.

last'lý (-ah-), *adv.* finally.

lătch, *n.* bar with catch as fastening of gate, &c.; small spring lock as fastening of outer door. *v.t.* fasten with latch.

lătch'ét, *n.* (arch.) thong for fastening shoe.

lāte, *a.* after the right time; far on in day or night or period; backward; now dead; that occurred lately. *adv.* after right time; far on in time. *n.* of ~, recently.

lateen' (-ah-), *a.* ~ sail, triangular sail on long yard at angle of 45° to mast. ~ ship, so rigged.

lāte'ly (-tl-), *adv.* not long ago; in recent times.

lā'tent, *a.* concealed; dormant; existing but not developed or manifest. lā'tency, *n.*

lăt'eral, *a.* of, at, toward, or from the side(s). *n.* a lateral shoot or branch.

lath (-ah-), *n.* (pl. pr. -dhz), thin strip of wood. la'thy (-ah-), *a.*

lāthe (-dh), *n.* kinds of machine used in turnery and pottery.

lathee (lahtē'), *n.* (Anglo-Ind.) long heavy stick, usu. of bamboo.

lăth'er (-dh-), *n.* froth of soap and water; frothy sweat of horse. *v.i.* & *t.* form lather; cover (chin) with lather; (sl.) thrash.

Lăt'in, *n.* language of ancient Rome; inhabitant of ancient Latium. *a.* of or in Latin; of Latium or ancient Rome. Lăt'inism (-izm), *n.* idiom or construction imitating Latin. ~ist, *n.* person knowing Latin. ~ity, *n.* Latin style. ~ize, *v.t.* & *i.* (-zable), give Latin form to; use latinisms. ~ization, *n.*

lăt'itude, *n.* scope, full extent; freedom from restriction in action or opinion; angular distance N. or S. of the equator; (usu. pl.) regions, climes.

lătitūdinā'rian, *a.* claiming or allowing freedom of interpretation in religion. *n.* person of such views. ~ism, *n.*

latrine' (-ēn), *n.* place for evacuation of bowels or bladder.

lătt'er, *a.* recent; mentioned later of the two. ~ly, *adv.* of late; in later part of.

lătt'ice, *n.* structure of laths or bars crossing each other with interstices. ~ window, window so made, with small panes set in lead. lătt'iced (-st), *a.*

laud, *n.* praise; song of praise. *v.t.* praise, extol. laud'able, *a.* commendable. ~ability, *n.*

laudanum (lŏd'num), *n.* tincture of opium.

laudā'tion, *n.* praising; a panegyric. laud'atory, *a.*

laugh (lahf), *v.i.* & *t.* make the sounds usual in expressing amusement, exultation, and scorn; utter with a laugh. *n.* sound or act of laughing.

laugh'able (-ahf-), *a.* exciting laughter; amusing.

laugh'ing (-ahf-), *a.* indulging in laughter. *n.* a laugh. ~-gas, nitrous oxide as anaesthetic. ~-stock, object of general derision.

laugh'ter (-ahf-), *n.* laughing.

launch¹ (-ah-, -aw-), *v.t.* & *i.* hurl, discharge, send forth; start on a course; set vessel afloat. *n.* launching of ship.

launch² (-ah-, -aw-), *n.* man-of-war's largest vessel; large mechanically propelled boat.

laun'dress, *n.* woman who washes and gets up linen. laun'dry, *n.* establishment for washing clothes; linen for washing.

laur'eate, *a.* wreathed with laurel. *n.* poet laureate. ~ship, *n.*

lau'rel (lŏ-), *n.* kinds of glossy-leaved shrub; (sing. or pl.) wreath of bay-leaves as emblem of victory or poetic merit. lau'relled (-ŏreld), *a.* wreathed with laurel.

laurusti'nus (lŏ-), *n.* an evergreen flowering shrub.

lā'va (lah-), *n.* matter discharged in fluid form by volcano.

lăv'atory, *n.* room, &c. for washing hands and face; (euphem.) water-closet(s) and urinal.

lāve, *v.t.* (-vable), wash, bathe; wash against, flow along.

lăv'ender, *n.* a fragrant-flowered shrub, its flowers and stalks used to perfume linen; colour of its flower. ~-water, a scent.

lā'ver, *n.* vessel for ablutions; font; spiritual cleansing.

lăv'erock (-vr-), *n.* lark.

lăv′ish, *a.* profuse, prodigal; overabundant. *v.t.* bestow or spend lavishly. ~ment, *n.*

law, *n.* a rule established among a community and enjoining or prohibiting certain action; the system made up of these rules; any rule of procedure. ~abiding, obedient to the laws. ~court, court of law. ~giver, author of code of laws. ~merchant, laws regulating trade and commerce. ~officer, (esp.) Attorney or Solicitor General. ~suit, prosecution of claim in lawcourt.

law′ful, *a.* permitted or appointed by law; not illegal.

law′less, *a.* having no laws; disobedient to law; unbridled.

lawn¹, *n.* kind of fine linen.

lawn², *n.* close-mown piece of turf in gardens, &c. ~mower, lawn-mowing machine. ~tennis, modification of tennis played on level ground without walls.

law′yer, *n.* person pursuing law as a profession.

lăx¹, *a.* negligent; not strict; loose; vague. lăx′ĭtў, *n.*

lăx², *n.* Swedish or Norwegian salmon.

lăx′ative, *a.* loosening the bowels. *n.* laxative drug.

lay¹, *p.t.* of lie.

lay², *n.* minstrel's song, ballad.

lay³, *a.* non-clerical; non-professional; amateur. ~brother, sister, member of religious order employed in manual labour. ~clerk, chairman in cathedral, &c. ~man, person not in orders; person without professional or special knowledge of a subject. ~reader, layman licensed to conduct religious services.

lay⁴, *v.t.* (laid), deposit on a surface; lay in specified position; put or bring into specified state; impose, enjoin; bury; calm, allay; make subside; beat down (crop); set (trap) in readiness; set on table; wager; produce (egg).

lay′er, *n.* person, &c. that lays; a thickness of matter laid over a surface; a shoot fastened down to take root. *v.t.* propagate (plant) by layer.

layĕtte′, *n.* clothes, &c. needed for new-born child.

lay fĭg′ure (-ger), *n.* jointed figure used by artists for arranging draperies, &c. on; unreal character in novel, &c.

lăz′ar, *n.* (hist.) beggar with leprosy, &c. lăzarĕtt′ō, *n.* (pl. -os), hospital for lepers.

lā′zў, *a.* averse to work; indolent; inducing indolence. **lāze**, *v.i.* & *n.* (colloq.) (indulge in) laziness.

lăzzarō′nē, *n.* (pl. -*nī*), Neapolitan street-lounger and beggar.

lea, *n.* piece of meadow or arable or pasture land.

lead¹ (lēd), *v.t.* & *i.* (lĕd), force to go with one; conduct, guide; (of commander or conductor) direct movements of; guide by persuasion; guide actions or opinions of; show the way towards; play (card) as first player; experience a life of specified kind. *n.* performance done as example; leader's place; right of playing first at cards, suit led from; string, &c. for leading dog; (Electr.) conductor conveying current from source to place of use.

lead² (lĕd), *n.* a heavy soft grey metal; stick of plumbago in pencil; bullets; lump of lead used in sounding water; (pl.) piece of usu. flat roof covered with lead. *v.t.* cover, weight, with lead.

lea′den (lĕd-), *a.* consisting of lead; heavy; sombre.

lead′er (lēd-), *n.* one who leads or conducts; a commander; leading article; *line of gut to which snell of fishing-fly is attached. **leaderĕtte′**, *n.* short editorial note.

lead′ing (lēd-), *a.* chief; of most importance; giving guidance. *n.* guidance. ~article, editorial pronouncement at full length. ~question, one so framed as to prompt the answer desired. ~strings, strings with which children are taught to walk.

---

leaf, *n.* (pl. *-ves*), (pl.) the parts that give trees and other plants their green appearance; foliage: (sing.) single member of plant's foliage; section of sheet of paper of which each side is a page; hinged flap of table, &c. leaf′age, *n.* foliage. leaf′let, *n.* printed paper, single or folded, for distribution. leaf′y, *a.*

league¹ (-g), *n.* varying measure of distance, usu. about 3 miles.

league² (-g), *n.* compact for mutual help; the parties to it; association for common interests. *v.t. & i.* combine in league. ~ match, (Crick., Footb.) match for championship between clubs belonging to same League. ~ of Nations, established by the treaty of peace of 1919 for the prevention of war. leag′uer¹ (-ger), *n.* member of league.

leag′uer² (-ger), *n.* siege; besiegers' camp.

leak, *n.* hole or passage through which liquid, &c. makes its way in or out. *v.i.* pass, let water, &c. pass, through leak. ~age, *n.* what leaks out or in. leak′y, *a.* having leaks.

leal, *a.* loyal; honest.

lean¹, *a.* having no superfluous fat; thin; (of meat) not fat. *n.* the lean part of meat.

lean², *v.i. & t.* (*leant* pr. lĕnt, or *leaned*), be in or put in a sloping position; be inclined or partial to. ~to, shed, &c., with roof leaning against wall of larger building. lean′ing, *n.* tendency or inclination.

leap, *v.i. & t.* (*leapt* pr. lĕpt, or *leaped*) & *n.* jump. ~frog, game in which players vault over others bending down. ~year, with 29th Feb. as intercalary day.

learn (lĕrn), *v.t. & t.* (*learnt*, or *learned* pr. -nd), get knowledge of, or skill in, by study, experience, or being taught; find out; (vulg.) teach. learn′ed pr. -nd), deeply read, erudite. learn′er (lĕr-), *n.* person learning; esp.

tiro. learn′ing (lĕr-), *n.* knowledge got by study; erudition.

lease, *n.* contract by which land or tenement is conveyed for a term by its owner (the *lessor*) to a tenant (the *lessee*), usu. for a rent. *v.t.* (*-sable*), grant or take on lease. ~hold, tenure or tenement on lease. ~holder, tenant on lease.

leash, *n.* thong for holding dogs; three dogs, hares, &c. *v.t.* put leash on; hold in leash.

leas′ing (-z-), *n.* (Bibl.) falsehood.

least, *a.* smallest. *n.* least amount. *adv.* in the least degree.

lea′ther (lĕdh-), *n.* material made by tanning or otherwise dressing hides. *v.t.* cover, &c. with leather; flog. ~hunting, (sl.) fielding at cricket. ~jacket, a land pest, the larval stage of daddy-long-legs. leatherĕtte′ (lĕdh-), *n.* imitation leather. lea′thering (lĕdh-), *n.* flogging. lea′thern (lĕdh-), *a.* made of leather. lea′thery (lĕdh-), *a.* like leather, esp. in toughness.

leave¹, *n.* permission; permission to be absent from duty or to withdraw.

leave², *v.t. & i.* (*lĕft*: *-vable*), let remain; bequeath; abstain from; go away (from); cease to reside at or belong to; trust or commit to another; abandon.

lea′ven (lĕ-), *n.* substance used to make dough ferment and rise; admixture of some quality. *v.t.* treat with leaven; act as leaven upon.

leav′ings (-z), *n.pl.* what some one has left as worthless, &c.

lĕch′er, *n.* (arch.) fornicator. ~ous, *a.* lustful. lĕch′ery, *n.*

lĕc′tern, *n.* reading or singing desk in church. lĕc′tionary (-sho-), *n.* portions of Scripture appointed to be read in churches.

lĕc′ture, *n.* discourse delivered to a class or other audience; piece of admonition. *v.i. & t.* deliver lecture; admonish. lĕc′turer (-kche-), *n.* lĕc′tureship (-kcher-), *n.* appointment as lecturer.

led, *p.t.* & *p.p.* of lead.[1]

lödge, *n.* narrow shelf or projection; rock-ridge below sea-level.

lẽdg'er, *n.* book in which a firm's debtor-and-creditor accounts are kept. ~-line, (*mus.*) short line added above or below stave.

lee, *n.* shelter given by neighbouring object; side of something away from the wind. lee'ward (lū'ard), *a.* & *adv.* on or towards the side turned from the wind. *n.* leeward direction or region. ~way, drift of ship to leeward.

leech[1], *n.* physician; blood-sucking worm used in bleeding.

leech[2], *n.* edge of sail.

laek, *n.* onion-like herb.

leer, *n.* & *v.i.* glance with lascivious or malign expression. leer'ÿ, *a.* knowing; sly.

lees (-z), *n.pl.* sediment of wine, &c.; worst part after best is gone.

left[1], *p.t.* & *p.p.* of leave.[2]

left[2], *a.* of, or situated on, the side opposite to the right. *n.* the left side; *the* ~, in politics, the advanced or radical party. ~ward, *a.* & *adv.*; ~wards, *adv.*

lẽg, *n.* one of the limbs on which person or animal walks and stands; artificial leg; support of chair or other piece of furniture; *(colloq.)* section of journey, &c.; (Crick.) that part of the 'on' side of the field which is behind, or about in a line with, the playing batsman. ~-bail', making off, decamping.

lẽg'acÿ, *n.* gift left by will; (*fig.*) something handed down by predecessor.

lẽ'gal, *a.* of or based on law; appointed or required or permitted by law. lẽ'galism, *n.* exaltation of law or formula. lẽ'galist, *n.* lẽgal'itÿ, *n.* lawfulness. lẽ'galize, *v.t.* (~zable), make lawful; bring into harmony with law. ~ization, *n.*

lẽg'ate, *n.* papal ambassador.

lẽgatee', *n.* recipient of legacy.

lẽga'tion, *n.* body of deputies; diplomatic minister and his suite; his residence.

lẽ'gend, *n.* traditional story, myth; inscription or motto on coin, &c. lẽ'gendarÿ, *a.* famous, existing only, in legend.

lẽ'gerdemain', *n.* sleight of hand, juggling; sophistry.

lẽgg'ing (-g-), *n.* (usu. in pl.) outer covering of leather, &c., usu. for lower leg; cricket-pad.

lẽghorn' (-gôrn), *n.* kind of plaited straw for hats; hat of it; breed of fowls.

lẽ'gible, *a.* easily read (of handwriting, &c.). ~bility, *n.*

lẽ'gion (-jn), *n.* a division of 3,000–6,000 men in the armies of ancient Rome; great number. British ~, national association of ex-service men. lẽ'gionarÿ (-jo-), *a.* of legion or legions; *n.* soldier of legion.

lẽ'gislate, *v.i.* make laws. ~tion, *n.* law-making; laws made. ~tive, *a.*; ~tor, *n.* ~ture, *n.* legislative body of a State.

lẽgit'imacÿ (-sî), *n.* being legitimate.

lẽgit'imate, *a.* lawful; regular, proper. *v.t.* (-āt), legitimatize.

lẽgit'imatize, lẽgit'imize, *vv.t.* (~zable), make legitimate by decree or enactment; prove legitimate. ~zation, *n.*

lẽgit'imism, *n.* adherence to sovereign or pretender whose claim is based on direct descent. lẽgit'imist, *n.*

lẽgū'minous, *a.* bearing seed in valved pods (beans, peas, &c.).

leisure (lẽzh'er), *n.* spare time; freedom from pressing business. leisured (lẽzh'erd), *a.* having plenty of leisure. lei'surelÿ (lẽzher-), *a.* deliberate, not hurried. *adv.* without hurry.

‖ leit-motif, -iv (lī'tmōtē'f), *n.* (Mus.) theme associated throughout piece with some person, situation, or sentiment.

lẽm'an, *n.* (arch.) sweetheart, paramour; illicit mistress.

lẽmm'ing, *n.* arctic rodent.

lẽm'on, *n.* pale-yellow acid fruit; its colour; tree bearing it; *(sl.)* unattractive girl, any person or thing suggestive of sour fruit. **~grass**, fragrant E.-Ind. grass yielding the grass oil used in perfumery. **~squash**, drink of squeezed lemon and soda-water. **~wood**, New Zealand tree, the Tarata. **lĕmŏnāde´**, *n.* drink made from or flavoured like lemon-juice.

lĕm´ūr, *n.* kind of nocturnal mammal allied to monkeys.

lĕnd, *v.t.* (*lĕnt*), grant temporary use of (thing); let out at interest or for hire; bestow, contribute; accommodate (oneself) to.

lĕngth, *n.* measurement from end to end in space or time; vowel quantity. **lĕng´then**, *v.i. & t.* make or become longer. **lĕngth´ways** (-z), *adv.*; **~wise** (-z), *adv. & a.* **lĕng´thў**, *a.* of unusual or undue length.

lē´nient (-nye-), *a.* indisposed to, marked by absence of, severity. **lē´nience, -cў, lĕn´itў**, *nn.*

lĕn´itive, *a. & n.* soothing or gently laxative (drug).

lĕns (-z), *n.* piece of glass spherically convex on one or both sides, used in spectacles, &c.

lent¹, *p.t. & p.p.* of lend.

Lĕnt², *n.* period of fasting and penitence from Ash Wednesday to Easter Eve. **lĕn´ten**, *a.* of or in or suited to Lent.

lĕn´til, *n.* edible seed, shaped like double-convex lens, of a leguminous plant. **lĕntic´ūlar**, *a.* lentil-shaped.

lĕn´tisk, *n.* mastic-yielding tree.

Lē´ō, *n.* sign of zodiac.

lē´onine¹, *a.* lionlike.

lē´onine², *a. & n.* **~verse** or *leonine*, Latin hexameter or elegiac couplet with internal rhyme(s).

lĕo´pard (lĕp-), *n.* large carnivorous beast with dark-spotted fawn coat; panther. **~ess**, *n.*

lĕp´er, *n.* person with leprosy.

lĕpidŏp´terous, *a.* of the *Lepidoptera* or insects with four scale-covered wings, such as moths and butterflies.

lĕp´orine, *a.* of the hare kind.

lĕp´rosў, *n.* (Path.) an endemic chronic constitutional disease, varying in manifestations as the skin, nerves, or other tissues are affected; (pop.) loathsome disease of the skin, eating away the parts affected. **lĕp´rous**, *a.*

lese-mäj´estў (lēz-), *n.* treason.

lē´sion (-zhn), *n.* (Med.) injurious change in the action or texture of an organ.

lĕss, *a.* smaller; of lower rank or degree; a lesser quantity of, fewer. *n.* a less amount; a less quantity or number. *adv.* to a less degree or extent or amount. *prep.* minus; with the deduction of.

lĕssee´. See lease.

lĕss´en, *v.i. & t.* diminish.

lĕss´er, *a.* not so great as the other or the rest; minor.

lĕss´on, *n.* one of two readings at matins and evensong; thing to be learnt by pupil; spell of teaching; a warning experience; example. *v.t.* discipline.

lĕss´ôr. See lease.

lĕst, *conj.* in order that — not; for fear that.

lĕt¹, *v.t.* (*lĕtted* or *lĕt*), hinder, obstruct. *n.* a hindrance; (Rackets, &c.) accidental obstruction of ball or player, annulling the round.

lĕt², *v.t. & i.* (*lĕt*), allow or enable or cause to; grant use of for rent or hire; cause or allow to escape.

lē´thal, *a.* causing or designed to cause death.

lĕth´argў, *n.* torpid or apathetic state. **lĕthär´gic**, *a.*

Lē´thē, *n.* river in Hades producing forgetfulness of the past. **Lēthē´an**, *a.*

lĕtt´er, *n.* any of the symbols of which written words are composed; written message, epistle; literal meaning; (pl.) kinds of legal or formal letter; type used in printing; (pl.) literature, authorship as a profession. *v.t.* impress title, &c. on (book-cover); classify with letters. **~perfect**, (Theatr.) knowing

---

māte, mĕte, mīte, mōte, mūte, mōŏt; răck, rĕck, rick, rŏck, rŭck, rōōk;

one's part perfectly. ~press, matter printed from type. ~weight, balance for weighing postal letters; thing used to keep papers still on table. **letters patent**, see patent.

lẽtt'ered (-erd), a. well-read.

lẽtt'uce (-tis), n. herb grown for salad.

leuc'ocyte, n. colourless blood-corpuscle.

lẽvant'[1], v.i. abscond without paying one's debts.

Lẽvant'[2], n. the East Mediterranean region. **Lẽvan'ter**, n. easterly wind in the Levant. **Lẽvan'tine**, a. of the Levant; n. native of the Levant.

lẽv'ee'[1] (-vi), n. sovereign's reception for men only; any gathering of visitors.

"levee'[2] (lĩvē', lẽ'vī), n. embankment to prevent overflow of river; landing-place.

lẽv'el, n. instrument for giving or testing a horizontal line or plane; such line or plane; a social or intellectual standard; flat country. a. horizontal; on an equality with; even; in the same line with anything. v.t. & i. make level, even, or uniform; place on same level; lay low, raze, abolish; take aim at. ~ **crossing**, intersection of road and railway, &c. without bridge. **lẽv'eller**, n. person who would abolish social distinctions.

lẽ'ver, n. a bar or other rigid structure used as a mechanical aid to raise a weight; tool used in prizing. v.t. move with lever. **lẽ'verage**, n. advantage given by use of lever.

lẽv'erět, n. young hare.

lẽvi'athan, n. sea monster; huge ship; anything large of its kind.

lẽv'igāte, v.t. (-gable), rub down into powder or paste.

lẽv'in, n. (poet.) lightning.

lẽvitā'tion, n. power or act of rising or raising (body) into the air by spiritualism.

Lẽ'vite, n. member of the tribe of Levi; priests' assistant in Jewish temple-worship. **Lẽvit'ical**, a. of the Levites or their duties.

lẽv'itỹ, n. disposition to make light of weighty matters; unseasonable jocularity; frivolity.

lẽv'ỹ, n. collecting of tax or compulsory payment, enrolling of soldiers, &c.; amount or number levied. v.t. raise or impose compulsorily.

lewd, a. lustful, indecent.

Lew'is gun (lōō-), n. kind of machine-gun.

lẽxicŏg'rapher, lẽxicŏg'raphỹ, nn. maker, making, of dictionaries. **lẽx'icon**, n. dictionary.

Ley'den jãr (lī-), n. kind of electrical condenser.

liabil'itỹ, n. being liable; (pl.) debts, &c. for which one is liable.

li'able, a. legally bound, subject to, answerable for; exposed to.

liais'on (-zn), n. illicit amour; (Mil.) connexion, touch.

lia'na (-ah-), n. kinds of twining plant in tropical forests.

li'ar, n. person who utters an intentionally false statement.

li'as, n. a blue limestone rich in fossils.

libā'tion (or lī-), n. drink-offering; (joc.) toast-drinking, &c.

li'bel, n. published statement damaging to person's reputation; false defamatory statement. v.t. defame falsely, misrepresent maliciously. **li'bellous**, a.

lib'eral, a. open-handed, generous; abundant; open-minded, unprejudiced; (Pol.) of the Liberal party. n. advocate of democratic reform, member of the Liberal party. **lib'eralism**, n. principles of Liberal party. **liberal'itỹ**, n. munificence; freedom from narrow views. **lib'eralize**, v.t. (-zable), free from narrowness. ~**ization**, n.

lib'erāte, v.t. (-table), set at liberty, release. ~**tion**, ~**tor**, nn. **liberā'tionism** (-sho-), n. policy of freeing religion from State control by disestablishment.

lib'ertine, n. licentious man.

~nism, n.

lib'erty, n. being free, freedom; right or power to do as one pleases; piece of presumption; (pl.) privileges enjoyed by prescription or grant. ~man, sailor ashore on leave.

libi'dinous, a. lustful.

li'brary, n. collection of books or place in which it is kept; reading and writing room in house. librar'ian (or li-), n. custodian of library.

librett'o, n. (pl. -ti, pr. -ē), book of the words of an opera or long musical work. librett'ist, n.

lice. See louse.

li'cence, n. permission to do something otherwise prohibited; document conveying it; excessive liberty of action; licentiousness. li'cense, v.t. (-sable), authorize; grant licence to or for. licensed victualler, n. innkeeper with licence to sell alcohol. licensee', n. holder of a licence. li'censer, n. official granting licences.

licen'tiate (or li-; -shi-), n. holder of a certificate from a collegiate or examining body.

licen'tious (or li-; -shus), a. immoral in sexual relations.

li'chen (-k-), n. kinds of flowerless plant forming a crust on stones, tree-trunks, &c.

lich'gate, n. roofed gateway of churchyard.

lick, v.t. pass tongue over; take up by licking; play lightly over; (sl.) thrash, defeat. n. act of licking; smart blow; small quantity. lick'spittle, n. toady.

lick'erish (-ke-), a. fond of dainty fare; greedy; lecherous.

lick'ing, n. thrashing, defeat.

lic'tor, n. Roman official bearing axe and rods before magistrate.

lid, n. cover fitting an aperture.

lie[1], n. intentional false statement; imposture; false belief. v.i. (lying), tell lie(s); be deceptive.

lie[2], v.i. (past lay; p.p. lain), be in or assume a horizontal position on a supporting surface; be at rest on something; be spread out to view; be comprised; (Law) be sustainable or admissible. n. way thing lies.

lief, adv. as ~, liefer, with as much, more, willingness.

liege, a. (arch.) entitled to receive or bound to give feudal service or allegiance. n. one's liege lord; vassal or subject.

lien (lē'en), n. right to hold another's property till debt on it is paid.

lieu (lū), n. in ~, instead.

lieuten'ant (lěft-, left-, in navy lėt-), n. vicegerent or deputy or subordinate commander; a navy or army officer. ~colonel, ~commander, ~general, officers of navy and army. lieuten'ancy, n. lieutenant's rank.

life, n. (pl. -ves), the active principle peculiar to animals and plants; living state; living things and their movements; energy or vivacity; events of individual's existence or written story of them; the business and pleasures of the world. ~ assurance, insurance of one's life. ~belt, belt of buoyant material to support body in water. ~blood, blood necessary to life; (fig.) vitalizing influence. ~boat, boat for saving life in storms. ~buoy, appliance for keeping person afloat. ~ Guards, two Household-Cavalry regiments. ~preserver, short stick with loaded end. ~time, duration of person's life.

life'less (-fl-), a. dead; lacking in animation.

life'like (-fl-), a. realistic or vivid.

lift, v.t. & i. raise to higher level; take up; hoist, elevate; steal, plagiarize; (of cloud, darkness, &c.) cease to obstruct view; *pay (mortgage) and so take up. n. lifting; apparatus for raising and lowering people, &c., from floor to floor.

lig'ament, n. tough fibrous tissue binding bones together.

lig'ature, n. a tie or bandage; (Mus.) slur or tie; (Print.) two or more letters joined (æ, fl, ffl, &c.). *v.t.* bind or connect with or in ligature.

light¹ (līt), *n.* the natural agent that makes things visible; presence or effect of this; any source of light such as the sun or a burning candle; means of procuring fire such as match or taper; brightness of eyes or aspect; mental illumination; way thing presents itself to the mind. *a.* (of place) having plenty of light; (of colours) pale, not deep. *v.t. & i.* (*lit* or lighted) set burning; begin burning; show the way with a light; brighten with animation. ~house, structure with beacon light for guiding or warning ships. ~ship, anchored ship with beacon light. *lit up, drunk.

light² (līt), *a.* not heavy; of little weight or low specific gravity; deficient in weight; easy to wield or digest or do; not ponderous; elegant; not grave or important; trivial; inconstant; loose; not dense or tenacious. *adv.* lightly. *v.i.* (*lit* or lighted), come by chance upon; (arch.) alight. ~armed, with light equipment and weapons. ~fingered, said of pickpockets, &c. ~handed, adroit at managing others. ~headed, delirious; thoughtless. ~hearted, gay, untroubled. ~horse, light-armed cavalry. ~ infantry, light-armed footsoldiers. ~minded, flighty, frivolous, irresponsible. ~o'-love, wanton woman. ~weight, person under average weight (and see boxing-weights).

light'en¹ (līt-), *v.t. & i.* make or grow lighter; reduce weight of; relieve of care; mitigate.

light'en² (līt-), *v.t. & i.* suffuse with light or shed light on; emit lightning; (of eyes) flash.

light'er (līt-), *n.* flat-bottomed or other boat for shifting goods between ship and land, &c. ~age, *n.* fees for such shifting.

light'ning (līt-), *n.* discharging of electricity from cloud to cloud or ground. ~conductor, ~rod, metal rod or wire fixed to building to divert lightning to earth. ~ strike, labour strike without legal notice by way of surprise.

lights (līts), *n.pl.* lungs of animals as food.

light'some (līt-), *a.* gracefully light; merry, agile.

lig'neous, *a.* of the nature of wood; (of plants) having wood.

lig'nite, *n.* brown coal of woody texture.

lig'num vi'tae, *n.* a hard-wooded tree.

like, *a.* resembling another or the original; such as, characteristic of. *prep.* in the manner of; to the same degree as. *adv.* in the same manner. *n.* counterpart, equal; like thing or person; (pl.) likings. *v.t.* (-kable), find agreeable or satisfactory; feel attracted by. ~minded, agreeing in tastes or opinions.

like'lihood (-kl-), *n.* probability.

like'ly (-kl-), *a.* probable; such as may well happen or prove to be true; promising, apparently suitable. *adv.* probably.

li'ken, *v.t.* represent as comparable or similar to.

like'ness (-kn-), *n.* resemblance; semblance; portrait.

like'wise (-kwīz), *adv. & conj.* similarly; also, moreover.

likin (lē'kēn'), *n.* provincial transit duty in China.

li'king, *n.* one's taste; regard or taste or predilection for.

li'lac, *n.* a flowering shrub; the more usual colour of the flower, a pale violet. *a.* lilac-coloured.

Lilliputian (-shn), *a. & n.* pygmy, dwarf.

lilt, *v.t. & i.* sing with rhythmical effect. *n.* such effect; song marked by it.

lil'y, *n.* kinds of plant with showy flower; the fleur-de-lis. ~ of the valley, spring flower with small fragrant white bells.

limb¹ (-m), *n.* (Astr.) specified edge of sun, moon, &c.

limb² (-m). *n.* leg, arm, or wing; main branch of a tree. *v.t.* disable, pull to pieces.

lim'ber¹, *n.* detachable front of gun-carriage. *v.t.* attach limber to gun.

lim'ber², *a.* flexible; lithe, agile. *\~-neck*, *n.* disease of poultry.

lim'bō, *n.* (pl. *-ōs*), region on border of hell assigned to those who have failed to be Christians because they have not had the chance; a prison.

lime¹, *n.* white caustic substance got by burning kinds of rock. *v.t.* smear (twigs) with birdlime; snare (birds) thus; treat with lime. *\~kiln*, furnace for making lime. *\~light*, intense light given by heating lime in oxyhydrogen flame; (fig.) glare of publicity. *\~stone* (-stŏn), kinds of rock with much lime.

lime², *n.* fruit of lemon kind. *\~juice*, antiscorbutic drink. **li'mey*, *n.* (sl.) English sailor.

lime³, *n.* a garden tree (often *limetree*); **tupelo.*

lim'erick, *n.* five-line stanza of kind of nonsense-verse.

lim'it, *n.* bounding line; terminal point; bound that may not or cannot be passed. *v.t.* set limits to; serve as limit to; restrict; (*p.p.*) scanty. *\~ man*, competitor receiving maximum start in handicap. **lim'itary**, *a.* restrictive. *\~ā'tion*, *n.* limiting; limited condition or disability.

limn (-m), *v.t.* paint (picture); portray. **lim'ner**, *n.*

lim'ousine (-ōōzĕn), *n.* motor-car with closed body and roof over the driver.

limp¹, *v.i.* go with lame gait; halt. *n.* limping gait.

limp², *a.* neither stiff nor springy; without energy.

lim'pet, *n.* tent-shaped shell-fish sticking tight to rock.

lim'pid, *a.* transparently clear. **limpid'ity**, *n.*

linch'pin, *n.* pin passed through axle-end to keep wheel on.

lin'den, *n.* the lime-tree.

line, *n.* a piece of cord serving some purpose; wire over which telegraphic, &c. messages travel; **(pl.)* driving reins; long narrow mark; row of persons or things; lineage; series of things, esp. ships following same route; track or course or direction; limit or boundary; contour or outline; the equator; measure of one-twelfth of an inch; (pl., Mil.) set of field-works or boundaries of encampment; regular regiments, esp. infantry. *v.t. & i.* (*-nable*), mark with lines; post men or take post or stand at intervals along a road, hedge, &c.; put lining into, serve as lining of. *\~ engraving*, done with incised lines. *\~'s'man*, soldier of line regiment; umpire's assistant in some games with boundary lines.

lin'eage, *n.* descent, pedigree.

lin'eal, *a.* in the direct line of descent or ancestry.

lin'eament, *n.* (usu. pl.) distinctive feature(s) or characteristic(s), esp. of the face.

lin'ear, *a.* of or in lines; long and narrow and of uniform breadth.

lin'en, *a.* made of flax. *n.* linen cloth; articles made of this or of calico. *\~draper*, dealer in linen, calico, &c.

li'ner, *n.* ship of a line of passenger-ships.

ling¹, *n.* a sea-fish.

ling², *n.* kinds of heather.

ling'er (-ngg-), *v.i.* be slow to depart; seem long; stay about, daily; be protracted.

|| **lingerie**, (lă'nzhĕrē), *n.* linen articles; women's underclothing.

ling'ō (-ngg-), *n.* (pl. *-ōes*), foreign language; queer way of talking.

ling'ual (-nggw-), *a.* of the tongue, of speech.

lin'guist (-nggw-), *n.* person skilled in foreign languages. **linguis'tic**, *a.* of the study of languages; of speech. *\~ics*, *n.*

lin'iment, *n.* liquid for rubbing into affected part.

li'ning, *n.* layer of material applied to the inside of a garment, box, vessel, &c.

link, *n.* one loop or ring of a chain or of knitted work, &c.; thing or person that unites; member of series; measure of 7·92 in.; (hist.) torch made of tow and pitch. *v.t. & i.* connect, join together; clasp or intertwine.

links, *n.pl.* ground on which golf is played.

Linnæ'an (-nēan), *a.* of Linnæus or his classification of plants.

linn'et, *n.* a songbird.

lino'leum, *n.* floor-covering of canvas thickly coated with a preparation of linseed.

Li'notype, *n.* machine producing stereotyped lines of type.

lin'seed, *n.* seed of flax.

linsey-wool'sey (-z-, -z-), *n.* fabric of coarse wool and cotton.

lin'stock, *n.* (hist.) staff holding match for firing gun.

lint, *n.* linen with one side made fluffy by scraping.

lin'tel, *n.* wood or stone across top of door or window.

li'on, *n.* large carnivorous beast noted for his courage; courageous person; celebrity. **li'oness,** *n.* **li'onize,** *v.t. & i.* (-*zable*), treat (person) as a celebrity.

lip, *n.* either edge of the opening into the mouth; brim of vessel; (sl.) saucy talk. ~**stick,** stick of cosmetic for rouging lips.

liq'uefy, *v.t. & i.* (-*iable*), make or become liquid. ~**fac'tion,** *n.*

liques'cent, *a.* becoming liquid.

liqueur' (-kūr), *n.* kinds of strong alcoholic liquor.

liq'uid, *a.* having a consistence like that of water or oil; neither solid nor gaseous; having the clearness of water; (of sounds) flowing, clear, pure. *n.* a liquid substance; either of the letters *l, r.*

liq'uidate, *v.t. & i.* (-*dable*), pay off (debt), wind up the affairs of (company, &c.). ~**tion,** *n.* process of winding up affairs. ~**tor,** *n.* official appointed to liquidate company, &c.

liq'uor (-ker), *n.* alcoholic or other drink; liquid used in or resulting from some process.

liq'uorice (-ko-), *n.* black substance used in medicine and as sweetmeat; plant from whose root it is obtained.

lira (lēr'a), *n.* (pl. -*re*, pr. -rā), Italian franc.

lisp, *v.i. & t.* fail to pronounce the sibilants (s, z, sh) clearly; say lispingly. *n.* lisping pronunciation.

liss'om, *a.* lithe, agile.

list[1], *n.* selvedge; (pl.) palisades enclosing tilting-ground (often used fig.); roll or catalogue or inventory. *v.t. & i.* enter in a list; (vulg.) enlist as a soldier.

list[2], *v.t. & i.* (3 sing. pres. *list* or *listeth*; past *list* or *listed*), be pleasing to; be inclined to do; (of ship, wall, &c.) lean over to one side. *n.* listing of ship, &c.

list[3], *v.i. & t.* (arch.) listen, listen to.

li'sten (-sn), *v.i.* make effort to hear something; give ear to: ~ *in,* tap telephonic communication; listen to broadcast programmes by using receiver.

list'less, *a.* without inclination or energy; languid.

lit, *p.t. & p.p.* of **light[1,2].**

lit'any, *n.* series of petitions for use in church services.

‖ **litchi** (lētshē'), *n.* tree, or its fruit, orig. from China, grown in Bengal.

lit'eracy, *n.* ability to read and write.

lit'eral, *a.* of the letters or a letter; exactly corresponding to the original; giving words their ordinary sense. ~**ism,** *n.* adherence to the letter.

lit'erary, *a.* of or constituting or concerned with literature.

lit'erate, *a.* able to read and write. *n.* literate person.

litera'ti, *n.pl.* the lettered or learned.

litera'tim, *adv.* letter for letter.

lit'erature, *n.* books and written composition valued for form and style; the realm of letters; (colloq.) printed matter.

lithe (-dh), *a.* pliant, supple; easily bent. ~**some**, *n.*

lith′ium, *n.* a metallic element. **lith′ia**, *n.* oxide of lithium.

lith′ograph (-ah-), *v.t.* engrave or draw on stone and print impressions from it. *n.* such impression. **lithŏg′rapher**, *n.*; **lithŏgrăph′ic**, *a.* **lithŏg′raphȳ**, *n.* the art or process.

lithŏt′omȳ, *n.* (surg.) cutting operation for stone.

lit′igant, *a.* engaged in lawsuit. *n.* party to lawsuit.

lit′igāte, *v.i. & t.* (-*gable*), go to law; contest at law. **litigā′tion**, *n.*

liti′gious (-jus), *a.* fond of litigation; contentious.

lit′mus, *n.* blue colouring-matter got from lichens.

litre (lē′ter), *n.* unit of capacity in metric system (about 1¾ pints).

litt′er, *n.* carrying-couch formerly used as a carriage; kind of stretcher for the wounded; bedding for beasts; odds and ends lying about; the young brought forth at a birth. *v.t. & i.* provide (horse, &c.) with litter; make (place) untidy; bring forth young.

‖ **littérateur** (lĕtĕrahtĕr′), *n.* man of letters.

lit′tle, *a.* not great or big; small in quantity; short in stature or distance or time; unimportant; paltry or mean. *n.* or *pron.* only a small amount; such amount of something. *adv.* to a small extent only; not at all. ~**people**, fairies.

litt′oral, *a.* of or on the shore; close to the sea. *n.* littoral district of a country.

lit′urgȳ (-ter-), *n.* a Church's formularies for public worship. **litŭr′gical**, *a.*

liv′able, *a.* worth living; fit to live in or with.

live, *v.i. & t.* (lĭv), have life; be or continue alive; subsist; conduct oneself in specified way; enjoy life to the full; pass or spend; dwell. *a.* (līv), that is alive or real or active: not dead or fictitious or exhausted; *lively, wideawake, energetic. *~**stock**, animals kept for use or profit. ~ **wire**, wire with electric current running through it.

live′lihŏŏd (-vl-), *n.* means of living; sustenance.

live′long (-vl-), *a.* the whole (tedious or delightful) length of.

live′lȳ (-vl-), *a.* lifelike or realistic; full of life or energy; gay; (joc.) exciting or dangerous.

li′ven, *v.t. & i.* brighten up.

liv′er[1], *n.* person who lives in specified way (*good, clean,* &c.).

liv′er[2], *n.* organ secreting bile and purifying the blood; flesh of animal's liver as food.

liv′erwort (-wĕrt), *n.* kinds of plant.

liv′erȳ, *n.* allowance of provender for horses; distinctive clothes worn by members of city company or person's servant; *livery stables. ~ **company**, one of the London city companies that formerly wore livery. ~**man**, member of livery company or keeper of livery stables. ~ **stables**, stables where horses are kept at livery or let out for hire.

liv′id, *a.* of bluish leaden colour.

liv′ing[1], *n.* livelihood; a benefice.

liv′ing[2], *a.* now alive; (of likeness) lifelike, exact.

liz′ard, *n.* kinds of four-legged reptile.

lla′ma, **la′ma** (lah-), *n.* woolly ruminant used in S. America as beast of burden.

Lloyd′s (loidz), *n.* incorporated society of marine underwriters.

lō, *int.* (arch.) look, behold.

loach, *n.* small fresh-water fish.

load, *n.* what is carried or borne; amount that cart, &c. can carry. *v.t. & i.* put load on; (goods, &c.) aboard or on vehicle, &c.; burden; charge (gun, &c.). ~**line**, ship's waterline when laden.

load′stŏne, **lōde′~**, *n.* magnetic oxide of iron; piece of it used as magnet; also fig.

loaf[1], *n.* (pl. -*ves*), piece of bread baked alone or as part of a batch.

---

ah, awl, oil, boor, cow, dowry; chin, go, bang, so, ship, thin; dh, as th(e).

~ **sugar**, sugar in the lump or in small lumps cut from it.

loaf², v.i. spend time idly; hang about. **loaf'er**, n.

loam, n. rich soil of clay, sand, and decayed vegetable matter; clay paste for brickmaking, &c. **loam'ȳ**, a.

loan, n. thing lent; sum to be returned with or without interest. v.t. grant loan of.

loath, lōth, a. disinclined, reluctant, unwilling.

loathe (-dh), v.t. (-thable), regard with disgust. **loath'ing** (-dh-), n. **loath'some**, a. exciting nausea or disgust; odious.

lob, v.t. & i. toss, bowl, or send ball with slow or high-pitched motion. n. ball bowled slow underhand at cricket or sent high in air at lawn-tennis. ~**worm**, kinds of worm used as bait.

lō'bāte, a. lobed.

lobb'ȳ, n. porch, entrance-hall; ante-room or corridor; (in legislative buildings) hall open to outsiders as well as members; *persons frequenting this to influence votes. **lobb'ȳing**, n. frequenting of parliamentary lobby to solicit votes, &c.

lōbe, n. lower pendulous part of outer ear; similar flap of other natural objects. **lōbed** (-bd), a.

lobe'lia, n. garden flower used esp. as edging.

lob'ster, n. long-tailed clawed shellfish; its flesh.

lob'ūlar, a. lobe-shaped.

lob'ūle, n. small lobe.

lō'cal, a. of place; belonging to or peculiar to some place or places. ~ **examination** (colloq. local), examinations held by universities at centres convenient for candidates. ~ **option**, right given to a district to prohibit local sale of alcoholic liquor.

locale' (-ahl), n. scene or locality of operations or events.

lō'calism, n. attachment to a place; a local idiom, &c.

local'itȳ, n. thing's position; site or scene of something.

lō'calize, v.t. (-zable), make local; decentralize. **lōcalizā'tion**, n.

locāte', v.t. & i. (-table), state locality of; discover exact place of; establish in a place; *(colloq.) establish oneself. **locā'tion**, n.

lō'cative, a. (Gram.) denoting place where. n. locative case.

loch (-ch soft guttural), n. Scotch lake or arm of the sea.

lock¹, n. a tuft of hair or wool; (pl.) the hair.

lock², n. fastening for a door, &c.; mechanism by which gun is fired; section of river or canal confined within sluiced gates. v.t. & i. fasten with lock; bring or come into rigidly fixed position; jam or catch or make catch. ~**jaw**, kind of tetanus in which the jaws are rigidly closed. ~**keeper**, custodian of river or canal lock. ~**out**, exclusion of workmen by an employer in a dispute as to wages, &c. ~**smith**, maker and mender of locks. ~**up**, (time of) locking up school, &c. for the night; room, &c. for detention of prisoners.

lock'er, n. small cupboard, esp. one reserved for individual in public room.

lock'et, n. small gold or silver case for portrait, &c.

locomō'tion, n. going from one place to another; power of accomplishing this. **lō'comōtive**, a. of or having or effecting locomotion; not stationary. n. locomotive engine.

lō'cum tē'nēns (-z), n. deputy acting for clergyman, doctor, &c. in his absence.

lō'cus, n. (pl. -cī, pr. -sī) exact place of something; (Math.) curve, &c. made by all the points satisfying certain conditions, or by the defined motion of a point or line or surface.

lō'cust, n. destructive winged insect migrating in swarms; kinds of tree and their fruit.

locū'tion, n. style of speech; a phrase or idiom.

lōde, n. vein of metal ore. ~**star**,

the pole-star; guiding principle or object. **~stone**, see loadstone.

lŏdge, *n.* small house (arch.); gatekeeper's cottage or porter's room; (of freemasons, friendly societies, &c.) members of branch, or place where they meet. *v.t. & i.* (*-eable*), provide with sleepingquarters; reside as lodger; deposit for security or attention; fix in; settle; place. **lŏdg'er**, *n.* person paying for accommodation in another's house. **lŏdg'ing**, *n.* place where one lodges. **lŏdge'ment** (*-jm-*), *n.* stable position gained, foothold; accumulation of intercepted matter.

loft (*-aw-*), *n.* upper room directly covered by roof; gallery in church or hall. *v.t.* send (golfball) high. **lof'ter** (*-aw-*), *n.* golfclub for lofting. **lof'ty** (*-aw-*), *a.* of imposing height; haughty; exalted, high-flown.

lŏg, *n.* unhewn piece of felled tree; any large rough piece of wood; apparatus for gauging ship's speed. **~book**, book containing daily record of ship's rate of progress, &c. **~rolling**, *n.* mutual puffery. **~wood**, a tree yielding dye.

lŏ'ganberry, *n.* fruit got by cross between raspberry and blackberry.

lŏg'an(-stōne), *n.* poised heavy stone rocking at a touch.

lŏg'arithm, *n.* one of a series of reckoning-numbers tabulated for simplifying computation. **lŏgarith'mic**, *a.*

lŏgg'erhead, *n.* at **~s**, engaged in dispute, or bad terms.

lŏgg'ia (*-jya*), *n.* open-sided gallery or arcade.

lŏ'gic, *n.* the science of reasoning; power of convincing. **lŏ'gical**, *a.* of logic; in conformity with the laws of logic; defensible on the ground of consistency. **logi'cian** (*-shn*), *n.*

logŏm'achy (*-k-*), *n.* dispute about words.

loin, *n.* (pl.) the back part between the hip-bone and the ribs; (sing.) joint of meat cut from the loins.

loit'er, *v.i.* linger on the way; hang about; be dilatory.

lŏll, *v.i. & t.* recline or stand in lazy attitude; hang out (the tongue); (of tongue) hang out.

Lŏll'ard, *n.* one of the 14th-cent. heretics holding views like those of Wyclif. **~ism**, **~ry**, *nn.*

lŏll'ipŏp, *n.* sugar-plum, bon-bon.

Lo'ndon pride (*lŭ-*), *n.* a saxifrage.

lōne, *a.* companionless; unfrequented, uninhabited; lonely. **lone'ly** (*-nl-*), *a.* solitary, isolated, unfrequented; companionless. **~some**, *a.* feeling or making feel lonely.

lŏng, *a.* measuring much from end to end in space or time; tall (colloq.); protracted; dilatory; of specified length; the whole length of. *n.* a long interval or period; long vowel or syllable. *adv.* for a long time; by a long time; (*comp.*) beyond the present or some other point of time. *v.i.* yearn or wish vehemently. **~boat**, sailing-ship's largest boat. **~bow**, bow drawn by hand and discharging arrow. **~cloth**, kind of calico. **~clothes**, **~coats** (arch.), clothes of baby in arms. **~field**, same as *long-off* or *long-on* (see below). **~firm**, set of swindlers who obtain goods and do not pay. **~headed**, sagacious. **~hop**, short-pitched ball in cricket. **~jump**, jump measured along the ground in athletic sports. **~off** (or *-on*), man fielding at bowler's left (or right) rear. **~shanks**, kind of plover. **~shore**, found or employed on or frequenting the shore. **~sight**, vision that sees distant objects. **~sighted**, having long sight; having prevision, sagacious. **~stop**, man fielding straight behind wicket-keeper. **~suffering**, *n. & a.* bearing provocation patiently. **~wind**, capacity for running far without resting.

~-winded, long-breathed; tedious, prolix. **~ways, ~wise,** *adv.* in a direction parallel with a thing's length.

lŏn´geron (-j-), *n.* (usu. in pl.) longitudinal member(s) of aeroplane's fuselage or nacelle.

lŏngĕv´ity (-j-), *n.* long life.

lŏng´ing, *n.* vehement desire.

lŏn´gĭtūde (-j-), *n.* angular distance east or west from the meridian of Greenwich or other standard meridian to that of any place. **lŏngĭtū´dinal** (-ji-), *a.* of or in length; lying longways; of longitude.

lŏo, *n.* a card game.

lŏob´y, *n.* silly fellow.

lŏof´ah (-ä), *n.* pod of a plant used as flesh-brush.

lŏok, *v.i.* & *t.* use or direct one's eyes; make an effort to see; make search; express by the eyes; have specified appearance or aspect; face or be turned in specified direction. *n.* act of looking; gaze or glance; expression of the eyes; appearance or aspect; (pl.) personal appearance. **looker-on´** (pl. *-rson*), spectators. **look-in´,** casual visit (*have a ~,* come near winning, have a chance). **looking-glass,** mirror, quick-silvered glass. **look´it,* (sl.) listen to me. **look´-out´,** watch; post of observation; man, &c. stationed to watch; view; prospect of luck; person's own concern.

lŏom¹, *n.* weaving-machine.

lŏom², *v.i.* appear dimly; be seen in vague magnified shape.

lŏon¹, *n.* (Sc.) scamp, fellow.

lŏon², *n.* kinds of diving bird.

lŏon´y, *n.* (sl.) lunatic.

lŏop, *n.* figure made by a curve that crosses itself; similarly shaped part of a cord so crossing or meeting. *v.t.* & *i.* make loop or loops in; form loop; fasten with loop or loops. **~line,** piece of railway or telegraph that leaves main line and joins it again. **~ the loop,** (of airman) execute somersault.

lŏop´-hōle, *n.* narrow slit in wall; (fig.) means of evasion.

lŏose, *a.* released from bonds or restraint; not fixed or tight; not close-fitting; not exact or literal; careless; wanton, incontinent. *v.t.* let loose, untie; free from constraint; detach from moorings, &c. *n.* freedom from restraint. **~ ball, ~ bowling,** (Crick.) ball inaccurately pitched, sending of loose balls. **~ box,** stall in which horse can move about. **~ end,** want of occupation. **~ fielding,** careless fielding.

lŏos´en, *v.t.* & *i.* make or become less tight or firm; relax. **~ up,* (sl.) throw off constraint, show generosity.

lŏose´strife, *n.* kinds of flowering plant.

lŏot, *n.* booty, spoil. *v.t.* & *i.* take loot from; carry off loot.

lŏp¹, *v.t.* cut away branches or twigs of trees; cut off.

lŏp², *v.i.* hang limply. **~-ear,** drooping ear; rabbit with such ears. **~-sided,** with one side lower, &c.; unevenly balanced.

lōpe, *n.* & *v.i.* (run with) long bounding stride.

lŏquā´cious (-shus), *a.* talkative, babbling. **lŏquā´city,** *n.*

lō´quăt, *n.* Chinese and Japanese tree or its fruit, naturalized in S. Europe, India, and Australia.

lôrd, *n.* feudal superior, master, owner, husband; God or Christ; a nobleman; first word of the personal style of a marquis, earl, viscount, or baron, or courtesy title prefixed to Christian name to denote the younger son of a duke or a marquis; honorary title applied to offices, e.g. a bishop, Lord Mayor, or judges of the supreme court. *int.* expressing wonder, &c. *v.t.* & *i.* play the lord over; domineer. **lôrd´ling,** *n.* young or petty lord. **lôrd´ly,** *a.* as of, or beseeming, a lord. **lôrd´ship,** *n.* rule over, ownership of; domain or manor; lord's personality. **lords and ladies,** wild arum. **Lord's day,**

Sunday. Lord's prayer, the Our Father. Lord's Supper, Eucharist. Lord's table, communion table.

lŏre, n. erudition ; body of tradition and facts.

lorgnette (lôrnyĕt'), n. pair of glasses held up with long handle ; opera-glass.

lŏrn, a. desolate, forlorn.

lŏ'rry, n. long low sideless wagon ; large truck.

lŏr'y, n. kinds of parrot-like bird.

lose (lōōz), v.t. & i. (lost pr. law- or lô- ; -sable), be deprived of ; cease to have ; let pass from one's control ; get rid of ; forfeit ; be worsted in ; suffer detriment ; cause the loss of to ; (p.p.) vanished ; not to be found ; deprived of help or salvation ; astray. los'er (lōōz-), n. one who is deprived of anything ; not a winner.

loss (-aw-), n. losing ; what is lost ; detriment resulting from losing.

lost. See lose.

lŏt, n. one of a set of objects used in securing a chance selection ; this method, or a share or office given by it ; share, fortune, destiny ; appointed task ; piece of land allotted to a person ; article or set of articles put up for sale at auction, &c. ; (colloq.) a considerable number or amount.

loth. See loath.

Lothā'rĭŏ, n. (pl. -os), libertine.

lŏ'tion, n. wash for wounds or the skin.

lŏtt'ery, n. gamble in which part of money paid for tickets is distributed by lot among some of the holders.

lŏtt'ō, n. game of chance with drawing of numbers as in lottery.

lŏ'tus, n. legendary plant possessing the eater with luxurious languor ; kinds of water-lily, &c.

loud, a. strongly audible, sonorous ; noisy ; (of colour, dress, manners) obtrusive. adv. with loud voice. ~speaker, wireless receiver loud enough to be heard without head-phones.

lough (lŏch, soft guttural), n. Irish lake or arm of sea.

lounge (-j), v.i. loll, recline ; stand about lazily ; idle. n. spell of, place for, lounging ; sofa or deep chair. *~-lizard, fashionable idler. ~-suit, man's suit with tailless jacket.

lour, lower (lour), v.i. frown, look sullen ; (of sky, &c.) look dark and threatening. n. a scowl ; gloominess of clouds, &c.

louse, n. (pl. lice), kinds of parasitic insect. lous'y (-z-), a. infested with lice.

lout, n. hulking or rough-mannered fellow. lout'ish, a.

louver, -vre (lōōv'er), n. erection on roof with unglazed side-openings for ventilation, &c. ; set of boards or glass slips set like slats of Venetian blinds to admit air.

lo'vable (lŭ-), a. inspiring affection.

love (lŭv), n. fondness, warm affection ; sexual passion ; sweetheart or object beloved ; (Games) no score, nil. v.t. & i. be in love (with) ; feel affection for ; delight in ; admire ; like to see. ~all, state of game before either side has scored. ~-bird, kind of small parrot. ~-child, illegitimate child. ~-in-a-mist, blue-flowered garden plant. ~-lies-bleeding, garden plant with drooping red spike. ~-sick, languishing with love.

love'less (lŭv'l-), a. unloving or unloved or both.

love'ly (lŭv'l-), a. exquisitely beautiful ; (colloq.) delightful.

lo'ver (lŭ-), n. woman's suitor or sweetheart ; (pl.) pair in love ; admirer or devotee of something.

lo'ving (lŭ-), a. kind, affectionate. ~-cup, bowl passed round at banquet.

low¹ (lō), n. the sound made by cows. v.i. utter low.

low² (lō), a. not placed high or reaching far up ; not attaining a high degree ; of humble rank ; no longer full or abundant ; lacking in vigour ; degraded or vulgar or rascally. adv. in or to low place on low diet; for low stakes; in low voice. *~boy, chest of drawers on short legs. *~brow, (sl.) unintellectual. ~ Church, the Evangelical party in the Church of England. ~ pressure, atmospheric condition sending barometer down. ~ tide, level of sea between ebb and flow; time of extreme ebb. ~ water, low tide; (fig., with in) out of funds.

lower[1] (lō'er), v.t. & i. let or haul down; make or become lower; be degrading to; reduce bodily condition of. ~class, of the lower orders. ~deck, petty officers and men of the Navy or of a ship. ~ orders, people of inferior social status. ~ world, Hades, hell.

lower[2]. See lour.

lowermost (lō'er-), a. very lowest.

low'land (-and), n. low-lying country. a. of or in such country or the Lowlands. **Low'lands** (-andz), n. less mountainous part of Scotland. **Low'lander**, n. inhabitant of Lowlands.

low'ly (lō-), a. humble, unpretending.

loy'al, a. faithful; true to allegiance; devoted to the sovereign. ~ism, n. adherence to the sovereign. ~ist, ~ty, nn.

lŏz'enge (-j), n. rhombus or diamond figure, esp. as heraldic bearing; shield or small pane of glass of this shape; small tablet of medicine, food, or sweet stuff.

lŭbb'er, n. clumsy fellow, lout. ~ly, a. awkward, unskilful.

lu'bricant (loo-), n. substance used to oil machinery.

lu'bricate (loo-), v.t. (-cable), oil or grease (machinery); make slippery. ~tion, ~tor, nn.

lubri'city (loo-), n. slipperiness; skill in evasion; lewdness.

lucerne' (loo-), n. a clover-like fodder-plant.

lu'cid (loo-), a. free from obscurity; clearly expressed or arranged; bright. lucid'ity, n.

Lu'cifer (loo-), n. the morning star; Satan; (l-) match.

lŭck, n. good or ill fortune. ~less, a. unfortunate; unhappy.

lŭck'y, a. favoured by fortune; in luck; due to luck rather than skill or merit. ~bag or ~tub, of hidden toys, &c. into which each comer dips.

lu'crative (loo-), a. yielding considerable profits.

lucre (loo'ker), n. pecuniary gain as a motive.

lucu̇bra'tion (loo-), n. nocturnal study; essay or dissertation.

lu'cu̇lent (loo-), a. clear; lucid.

lu'dicrous (loo-), a. absurd, ridiculous; laughable.

lŭff, v.i. bring ship's head nearer the wind.

lŭg[1], v.t. & i. drag with effort or violence; pull hard at. n. act of lugging.

lŭg[2], n. (north.) ear; (Mech.) projection from a casting, &c. by which it may be fixed in place.

lŭgg'age, n. traveller's baggage.

lŭgg'er (-g-), n. small ship with four-cornered sails set fore and aft. **lŭg'sail** (-sl), n. four-cornered sail bent on an unequally slung yard.

lugu̇'brious (loo-), a. doleful.

lukewarm (look'wawm), a. neither hot nor cold; half-hearted.

lŭll, v.t. & i. send to sleep; soothe; hoodwink; allay; (of storm or noise) lessen, fall quiet. n. intermission in storm or pain. **lŭll'aby**, n. lulling song or sounds.

lŭmbā'go, n. (pl. -os), rheumatism in loins. **lŭmbā'ginous**, a.

lŭm'bar, a. of the loins.

lŭm'ber, n. disused articles; useless stuff; roughly prepared timber. v.t. & i. cumber or obstruct; go heavily and noisily.

Lumière (loo'miar), n. ~ process, a colour-photography method.

lu'minary (loo-), n. shedder of light, esp. sun or moon; person noted for learning, &c. **lu'minous** (loo-), a. shedding light. **luminos'ity** (loo-), n.

lŭmp, n. compact shapeless mass; the whole taken together; protuberance or swelling; heavy ungainly person. *v.t.* & *i.* class together; take in the lump; go heavily; dump down in a mass. ~fish, fish clinging to objects by means of sucking-disk on belly. ~ sugar, loaf-sugar cut into cubes. ~ sum, single sum in lieu of instalments.

lŭm′pish, *a.* heavy; clumsy; dull.

lŭm′pў, *a.* full of or covered with lumps; (of water) choppy.

lu′nacў (lōō-), *n.* insanity; folly.

lu′nar (lōō-), *a.* of, in, depending on or caused by, the moon.

lu′nāte (lōō-), *a.* crescent-shaped.

lu′natic (lōō-), *a.* insane; outrageously foolish. *n.* lunatic person.

lunā′tion (lōō-), *n.* moon's changes from one new moon to next.

lunch, *n.* midday meal; light refreshment taken between breakfast and dinner. *v.i.* & *t.* take lunch; provide lunch for.

lŭn′cheon (-chn), *n.* lunch; a midday banquet.

lunětte′ (lōō-), *n.* arched aperture in concave ceiling to admit light.

lŭng, *n.* either of the pair of air-breathing organs. *lŭng′er (-ngg-),* *n.* (sl.) consumptive.

lŭnge (-j), *n.* thrust with sword, &c.; sudden delivery of blow or kick; plunge. *v.i.* & *t.* make a lunge; shoot out in a lunge.

lŭnk′ah (-a), *n.* Indian cheroot.

lupine, *a.* (lōō′pīn), of or like wolves. *n.* (lōō′pĭn), a leguminous garden and fodder plant; (pl.) its seeds.

lu′pus (lōō-), *n.* an ulcerous skin-disease. **lu′pous (lōō-),** *a.*

lŭrch¹, *n.* In phr. *leave in the ~,* desert one in difficulties.

lŭrch², *n.* sudden shifting of the weight to one side. *v.i.* make a lurch; go with lurches.

lŭrch′er, *n.* cross-bred dog between collie and greyhound.

lūre, *n.* falconer's apparatus for recalling hawk; something used to entice; enticing quality. *v.t.* (-rable), recall with lure; entice.

lū′rid, *a.* ghastly, glaring, or terrible in colour, &c.

---

lŭrk, *v.i.* keep out of sight; be hidden; be latent or elusive.

lŭ′scious (-shus), *a.* richly sweet in taste or smell; cloying.

lŭsh, *a.* luxuriant, succulent.

lŭst, *n.* passionate enjoyment or desire; lascivious passion. *v.i.* have passionate longing. **lŭst′ful,** *a.* lascivious.

lŭstrā′tion, *n.* ceremonial washing or other rite of purification. **lŭs′tral,** *a.* used in lustration.

lŭs′tre¹ (-ter), *n.* gloss, shining surface; brilliance, splendour.

lŭstre². See lustrum.

lŭs′trine, lŭs′tring (lōōts-), *nn.* a glossy silk fabric.

lŭs′trous, *a.* shining; luminous.

lŭs′trum, lŭs′tre² (-ter), *n.* (pl. *-tra, -trums, -tres),* period of five years.

lŭs′tў, *a.* healthy and strong; vigorous, lively. **lŭs′tihŏŏd,** *n.*

lute¹ (lōōt), *n.* guitar-like instrument of 14th-17th cc. **lu′tanist (lōō-),** *n.* lute-player.

lute² (lōōt), *n.* composition for making joints airtight, &c.

lutestring. See lustrine.

Lu′theran (lōō-), *a.* relating to Martin Luther. *n.* member of the Lutheran Church. **~ism,** *n.*

lŭxūr′iant, *a.* profuse; (of style) florid. **lŭxūr′iance,** *n.*

lŭxūr′iāte, *v.i.* feel keen delight in; grow profusely.

lŭxūr′ious, *a.* fond of luxury; self-indulgent; exuberant.

lŭx′urў (-ksher-), *n.* gratification of the senses; desirable thing that can be done without.

Lўcē′um, *n.* garden in which Aristotle taught; lecture-hall.

lўdd′īte, *n.* explosive for shells.

lўe, *n.* water alkalized with wood ashes, &c. for washing.

lÿ′ing. See lie¹,².

lўke′-wăke, *n.* watch kept at night over dead body.

lўmph, *n.* pure water; colourless fluid from organs of the body; matter from cowpox vesicles used in vaccination. **lўmphăt′ic,** *a.* of or secreting lymph. *n.* vein-like vessel conveying lymph.

lўnch, *v.t.* execute by lynch law.

---

māte, mēte, mīte, mōte, mūte, mōōt; răck, rĕck, rick, rŏck, rŭck, rōōk;

~law, procedure of a self-constituted court that summarily executes offender.

lynx, n. feline wild beast noted for keen sight.

lyre (līr), n. obsolete U-shaped stringed instrument. ~**bird**, bird with lyre-shaped tail.

ly´ric, a. of or for the lyre; of the nature of song. lyric poem; (pl.) lyric verses. **ly´rical**, a. resembling lyric poetry; highflown. **lyr´ist** (līr-), n.

M

maca´bre (-ahbr), a. gruesomely imaginative.

macad´am, n. road-surface got by compacting stone broken small. ~**ize**, v.t. ~**ization**, n.

mácaro´ni, n. wheaten paste formed into long tubes for cooking; 18th-cent. dandy. **mácarōn´ic**, a. (of verse) containing Latin or other foreign words, native words with Latin endings, &c. **mácarōn´ics**, n.pl. macaronic verse.

mácaroōn´, n. biscuit of ground almonds, &c.

macáss´ar-oil, n. a hair-oil.

macaw´, n. kinds of parrot.

mâce[1], n. medieval hammer-like weapon; large-headed staff of office; headed cue used in bagatelle.

mâce[2], n. nutmeg-husks dried and used as spice.

má´cerāte, v.t. & i. (-rable), make or become soft by soaking; make lean by fasting. ~**tion**, n.

Măchiavell´ian (-kī-), a. unscrupulous, crafty; deep-laid.

măchinā´tion (-kī-), n. (usu. pl.) intrigue; underhand devices.

machine´ (-shēn), n. apparatus in which the action of several parts is combined for the applying of mechanical force to a purpose; controlling organization in politics, &c.; bicycle, motor-car, vehicle. v.t. print, sew, &c. with machine. ~**gun**, gun with load-ing and firing mechanism, maintaining continuous fire.

machi´nery (-shē-), n. machines; mechanism; organization.

machi´nist (-shē-), n. maker of machinery; worker of machine.

măck´erel, n. a sea fish barred with blue and silver.

măck´inăc, -naw, (~ **blanket**), n. (U.S. & Canada) heavy blanket. ~ **coat**, coat made of this.

măck´intōsh, n. cloth waterproofed with rubber; coat or sheet of this.

macō´nochie (-kǐ), n. tinned stew as part of army rations.

măc´rocōsm, n. the great world, the universe; any great whole.

măc´ūla, n. (pl. -lae), spot of different colour from its surroundings. **măc´ūlātĕd**, a.

măd, a. of disordered mind, insane; rabid; wildly foolish (colloq.) annoyed. ~**cap**, reckless person. ~**man**, ~**woman**, nn.

măd´am, ma'am (mahm, măm), n. polite form of address to women. **măd´ame** (pl. **mesdames** pr. **mādahm´**), n. title prefixed like **Mrs**. to foreign lady's name.

mădd´en, v.t. & i. make mad; irritate; grow mad, chafe.

mădd´er, n. kinds of red dye and plants yielding them.

Madeir´a (-dēra), n. (or M. **wine**) a white wine like sherry.

mademoiselle (mădmwăzĕl´), n. (pl. **mesdemoiselles** pr. mādmwăzĕl´), title prefixed like **Miss** to foreign lady's name or used alone as vocative.

mădonn´a, n. (picture or statue of) the Virgin Mary.

Madras´ (-ahs), n. city and province of India, used attrib. in names of things produced there or orig. connected therewith. ~ **handkerchief** (also **Madras**), brightcoloured handkerchief of silk and cotton worn by the negroes of the W. Indies as a headdress. ~ (**net**) muslin, handsome but coarse kind of muslin. ~ **work**, work executed upon Madras handkerchiefs.

măd'rigal, *n.* love song; part-song, usu. of five or six parts for voices only.

mael'strom (māl-), *n.* whirlpool; whirl or rush of affairs.

măgazine' (-zēn), *n.* store for explosives, arms, or military provisions; literary miscellany.

Măg'dalen, *n.* reformed prostitute.

magĕn'ta, *n.* a crimson aniline dye. *a.* coloured like magenta.

măgg'ot, *n.* grub or larva, esp. of the blue-bottle or cheese-fly.

Mā'gi, *n.pl.* priests of ancient Persia, the 'wise men from the east'. **Mā'gian**, *a. & n.* (one) of the Magi.

mă'gic, *n.* art of influencing events by occult control of nature or spirits; witchcraft; mysterious agency or power. ~ **lantern**, apparatus for projecting pictures on screen. **măg'ical**, *a.* of, like, or affected by magic. **măg'cian** (-shn), *n.* one skilled in magic; necromancer.

măgistēr'ial, *a.* of a magistrate; dictatorial.

mă'gistracy, *n.* the magistrates; a magisterial office.

mă'gistrate, *n.* civil officer administering law; a justice.

măgnăn'imous, *a.* high-souled; not petty. **măgnanim'ity**, *n.*

măg'nate, *n.* person influential by wealth or position.

măgnē'sia (-sha), *n.* oxide of magnesium; also, a carbonate of magnesium used in medicine. **măgnē'sian** (-shn), *a.* of magnesia.

măgnē'sium, *n.* a chemical element, base of magnesia.

măg'net, *n.* piece of iron having the property of attracting iron and of pointing north; thing that attracts. **măgnet'ic**, *a.* of or like or acting as a magnet; exercising attraction; mesmeric.

măg'netism, *n.* magnetic phenomena; science of these; personal charm.

măg'netize, *v.t.* (- *zable*), make into a magnet; attract like a magnet. ~**zation**, *n.*

măgnē'to, *n.* (pl. -os), igniting-apparatus of petrol engine.

măgnif'icent, *a.* splendid; imposing; first-class. **măgnif'icence**, *n.*

măg'nifier, *n.* magnifying lens.

măg'nify, *v.t.* (-*iable*), show on enlarged scale; extol, exalt.

măgnil'oquence, *n.* high-flown words or style. **măgnil'oquent**, *a.*

măg'nitude, *n.* size, bulk.

măgnō'lia, *n.* a flowering tree.

măg'num, *n.* two-quart bottle.

măg'pie, *n.* black and white chattering bird; chatterer; hit in rifle-shooting counting 2.

Magyar (mŏd'yar), *n. & a.* (member, language) of the Mongol race predominant in Hungary. ~ **blouse**, with sleeves cut in one piece with bodice.

Mahabharata (mah-hahbah'rata), *n.* an ancient Hindu epic.

Maharanee (mah-arahn'ī), *n.* Maharajah's wife.

Maharaja(h) (mah-arahj'a), *n.* title of some Indian princes.

mahăt'ma (ma-h-), *n.* person of preternatural powers in esoteric Buddhism.

Mahd'i, *n.* leader whose coming is looked for by Mohammedans.

mah-jŏngg', *n.* a Chinese game for four played with 144 pieces called tiles, recently adopted in Europe and America.

mahŏg'any (ma-h-), *n.* reddish-brown wood used for furniture; mahogany colour.

Mahometan. See Mohammedan.

mahout (ma-howt'), *n.* elephant-driver.

Mahrăt'ta (mar-),**Marăt'ha** (-ta), *n.* member of warlike Indian race.

mah'seer, *n.* large Indian fresh-water cyprinoid fish.

maid, *n.* virgin; spinster; young girl; female servant.

maidan (mīdahn'), (Anglo-Ind.) parade-ground.

maid'en, *n.* virgin; spinster (usu. joc.); (hist.) kind of guillotine; (Crick.) maiden over (see below); (attrib) unmarried, untried; with blank record. ~**hair**, a delicate fern. ~**head**, ~**hood**, virginity. ~ish, ~like, ~ly, aa. ~ name, married woman's previous surname. ~ over, one in which no runs are scored. ~ speech, person's first speech in an assembly.

mail¹, n. armour of metal rings or plates. mailed (-ld), a. clad in mail.

mail², n. bag or case of postal letters, &c.; the (esp. oversea) post, what is conveyed by it. v.t. send by mail.

maim, v.t. cripple; mutilate.

main¹, a. chief, principal. n. the gross; chief part; the high sea; main pipe or channel for water, gas, &c. ~land (-and), a country or continent without its adjacent islands. ~mast (-ast), principal mast. ~sail (-sl), lowest sail of mainmast. ~spring, chief spring of watch or clock (also fig.). ~stay, from maintop to foot of foremast; (fig.) chief support or helper. ~top, platform at head of lower mainmast. ~yard, yard supporting mainsail.

main², n. number called in hazard before throwing of dice; match between fighting-cocks.

main'ly, adv. in the main.

maintain' (měn-, man-), v.t. keep up; keep going; keep in repair; support; assert as true. main'ténance, n. maintaining; a subsistence; (Law) offence of aiding a party in litigation without lawful cause.

maize, n. Indian corn.

maj'esty, n. stateliness of aspect, manner, language, &c. majes'tic, a. stately.

majol'ica, n. Italian pottery.

ma'jor, a. greater of two units or sets; senior. n. person no longer a minor; major premise; army officer ranking above captain; (army sl.) sergeant-major. ~dō'mō (pl. -os), (loosely) housesteward. ~ general, army officer ranking next to lieutenant general.

majō'rity, n. the greater number, more than half; number by which the winning vote exceeds the next; coming or being of age; rank of major.

māke, v.t. & i. (māde; -kable), create, manufacture; cause to exist, bring about; amount to, constitute; bring up total to; represent to be or to do; take specified direction; acquire by effort, earn; win (trick); score (runs); produce by cookery; perform or execute; utter or put on record. n. way thing is made; figure or shape. ~believe, pretence. ~ good, fulfil promise, &c.; pay expense; prove statement; (colloq.) succeed in undertaking. ~ out, draw up or write out (list, &c.); prove; represent; understand; *extend; *(sl.) succeed. ~shift, method, tool, &c. used for want of a better. ~ up, supply deficiency; complete; (of actor) adapt face, &c. for his part. ~-up, way actor is made up; way type is made up into pages; a fabrication; materials used for making up, cosmetics. ~weight, small quantity added to make up weight.

mā'ker, n. one who makes anything; the Creator.

*mā'kings, n.pl. materials for rolling cigarettes.

Malacc'a cāne, n. rich-brown walking-cane.

mal'achite (-kīt), n. a green mineral.

maladjust'ment, n. faulty adjustment.

maladministrā'tion, n. faulty administration.

mal'adroit, a. bungling, tactless.

mal'ady, n. ailment, disease.

Malagās'y, a. of Madagascar. n. Malagasy language or person.

mal'aise (-z), n. feeling of illness or uneasiness.

mal'apert, a. (arch.) saucy; forward.

mal'apropism, n. ludicrous confusion between words.

malàpropos' (-pō), adv. inopportunely. a. said or done or happening inopportunely. n. inopportune thing.

malā´ria, *n.* fever due to mosquito bites. **malā´rial, ~ious,** *aa.*

Malay´, *n.* native, language, of Malay Peninsula.

mal´content, *n.* disaffected person.

māle, *a.* of the impregnating sex; (of plants) having stamens but no pistil. *n.* a male person or animal.

malēdic´tion, *n.* imprecation or curse. **malēdic´tory,** *a.*

mal´efactor, *n.* criminal.

malē´fic, malē´ficent, *aa.* hurtful; noxious. **malē´ficence,** *n.*

malēv´olent, *a.* wishing ill to others. **malēv´olence,** *n.*

māl´feas´ance (-z-), *n.* official misconduct.

mālförmā´tion, *n.* faulty formation. **mal´förmed´** (-md), *a.*

mal´ice, *n.* ill-will; desire to do harm. **mali´cious** (-shŭs), *a.*

malign´ (-līn), *a.* maleficent; (of disease) malignant. *v.t.* slander, misrepresent.

malig´nant, *a.* outrageously malevolent; (of disease) of the more virulent type. *n.* (hist.) supporter of Charles I against Parliament. **malig´nancy,** *n.*

malig´nity, *n.* malignant disposition or properties.

maling´er (-ngg-), *v.i.* pretend illness to escape duty.

mal´ison (-zn), *n.* (arch.) curse.

mall´ard, *n.* wild duck.

mall´eable, *a.* that can be shaped by hammering; educable, pliable. **mālléabil´ity,** *n.*

mall´et, *n.* hammer with large wooden head; forms of this used in croquet and polo.

mall´ow (-ō), *n.* kinds of plant.

malmsey (mahm´zi), *n.* a strong sweet wine.

mālnūtri´tion, *n.* underfeeding.

malō´dorous, *a.* stinking.

mālprāc´tice, *n.* wrongdoing (usu. in pl.); wrongful procedure.

malt (mawlt), *n.* barley or other grain prepared for brewing. *v.t.* convert grain into malt.

Maltese (mawltēz´), *a.* of Malta. *n.* Maltese person; the M. language. **~ cat,** a short-haired blue-coloured variety of the domestic

cat. **~ cross,** badge of the Knights of Malta. **~ dog,** small kind of spaniel, with roundish muzzle and long silky hair.

māltreat´, *v.t.* handle roughly; use badly. **~ment,** *n.*

maltster (mawl´ster), *n.* one who makes malt.

māl´va´ceous (-shŭs), *a.* of mallows.

mālversā´tion, *n.* corrupt handling of public or trust money.

mamma (´-ah), *n.* mother.

mämm´al, *n.* member of the *Mammalia* or animals that give suck. **mammā´lian,** *a.* **mäm´mary,** *a.* of the breasts. **mammif´erous,** *a.* having breasts.

mämm´on, *n.* wealth as an object of pursuit or evil influence; the purse-proud.

mämm´oth, *n.* an extinct elephant; (attrib.) huge.

mämm´y, *n.* mother (in nursery and derisive use); *coloured woman having the care of white children.

man, *n.* (pl. **men**), human being; the human race; male and usu. adult person; husband; male servant, workman, ordinary soldier or sailor; piece at draughts. *v.t.* supply with men; guard, fortify. **~-at-arms,** soldier, esp. medieval. **~-eater,** man-eating tiger; biting horse. **~-hole,** aperture in floor, sewer, &c., for man to pass through. **~-o'-war,** armed navy ship. **~-power,** amount of men available for State or other service. **~-slaughter,** criminal homicide without malice aforethought. **~-trap,** (esp.) trap set to catch trespassers.

man´acle, *n.* (usu. pl.) fetter(s). *v.t.* put manacles on.

man´age, *v.t. & i.* (-*geable*), conduct the working of; have effective control of; bend to one's will; cajole; contrive.

man´agement (-ijm-), *n.* administration; skilful handling; manager(s) of a concern.

man´ager (-nij-), *n.* one who has direction or control. **~ess,** *n.* woman manager of hotel, &c.

---

māte, mēte, mīte, mōte, mūte, mōōt : răck, rĕck, rick, rŏck, rŭck, rŏŏk

manatee′, *n*. an aquatic animal, the sea-cow.

man′ciple, *n*. a steward or catering official in colleges, &c.

mandā′mus, *n*. superior court's writ conveying command to lower one.

man′darin, *n*. Chinese official; party leader who lags behind the times; small orange.

man′date, *n*. authoritative command; commission to act for another (esp. one from the League of Nations); instruction from electorate, as inferred by its votes. **man′datarȳ**, *n*. receiver or holder of a mandate. —tory, *a*.

man′dible, *n*. lower jaw-bone; either part of bird's beak; either half of insect's jaw.

man′dolin, *n*. kind of lute.

mandrā′gora, **man′drāke**, *nn*. a narcotic plant.

man′drel, *n*. axis on which material revolves in lathe; rod round which metal, &c. is forged, cast, &c.

man′drill, *n*. large baboon.

māne, *n*. long hair of horse's or lion's neck.

‖manēge (manäzh′), *n*. riding-school; horsemanship.

mā′nēs (-z), *n.pl.* souls of ancestors; spirit of dead person.

man′ful, *a*. brave, resolute.

măng′anese (-nganēz), *n*. a metal; an oxide of this.

mānge (-j), *n*. a skin-disease of dogs, &c. **măn′gy** (-ji), *a*.

măng′el-wŭrz′el, **măng′old** (-wŭrz′el), (-ngg-). *n*. kind of beet for cattle.

man′ger (-j-), *n*. eating-trough in stable.

mangle[1] (măng′gl), *n*. laundry machine for pressing and smoothing linen, &c. *v.t.* put through mangle.

mangle[2] (măng′gl), *v.t.* hack, cut about, mutilate; spoil.

mango′ (-nggō), *n*. (pl. -oes), an Indian fruit and tree. **~bird**, an oriole, native of India; a humming-bird, native of Ja-

maica. **~fish**, golden-coloured Indian fish. **~(tree) trick**, Indian juggling trick in which a mango-tree appears to spring up and bear fruit within an hour or two.

măng′ōsteen (-ngg-), *n*. E.-Ind. tree and its fruit.

măng′rōve (-ngg-), *n*. a tropical tree growing in swamps with interlacing roots above ground.

măn′hood, *n*. men of a country; adult age in males; manliness.

mā′nia, *n*. madness; prevailing craze; devotion to a hobby. **mā′niäc**, *n*. raving madman.

măn′icure, *n*. person undertaking the treatment of finger-nails and hands; such treatment. *v.t.* apply such treatment to. **~rist**, *n*.

man′ifest, *a*. clear to sight or mind; indubitable. *v.t.* make manifest; betray. *n*. list of cargo for the Customs. **~ation**, *n*.

manifes′tō, *n*. (pl. -os) declaration of policy or intentions issued by a sovereign or leader(s).

man′ifōld, *a*. of various forms, origins, functions, &c.; many and diverse. *v.t.* multiply copies of (letters, &c.).

măn′ikin, *n*. little man; lay figure.

manill′a, *n*. fibre used for ropes, &c.; Manilla cheroot.

manip′ūlāte (-lable), *v.t.* handle; deal skilfully with; manage craftily. **~tion**, **~tor**, *nn*.

mankind′, *n*. (mănkīnd′) the human species; (măn′kīnd) males, esp. those of a household, &c.

măn′līke, *a*. of or like a man; (of woman) mannish.

măn′lȳ, *a*. having the qualities or bearing of a man; firm.

mănn′a, *n*. food of Israelites in the wilderness; spiritual food; sweet juice used in medicine.

mănn′equin (or -kin), *n*. person employed by dressmakers, &c. to show off costumes.

mănn′er, *n*. way thing is done or happens; sort or kind; style; (pl.) social bearing. **~ism**, *n*. addiction to a literary or artistic manner; a recurrent trick of style or behaviour. ~ist, n.; ~istic, a. ~less, a. unmannerly. ~ly, a. well-behaved.

mann´ish, a. like a man; (of women) lacking feminine qualities.

manœu´vre (-nōōver), n. strategical or tactical movement; skilful or crafty plan. v.i. & t. perform, make (troops, ship) perform, manœuvre(s); adroitly work oneself or others into or out of a position.

man´or, n. a territorial unit of the feudal period; the (land and) rights of such unit that are still held by the lord of the manor. ~house, lord of the manor's residence. manor´ial, a.

man´sard, n. roof with faces of two slopes, the steeper below.

manse, n. minister's house.

man´sion (-shn), n. large dwelling-house.

man´suetude (-swi-), n. gentleness, mild temper.

man´tel, n. structure enclosing fireplace. ~board, ~shelf, shelf at top of mantel. ~piece, mantel or mantelshelf.

Mantill´a, n. Spanish woman's lace veil used as headdress and covering shoulders.

man´tle, n. loose sleeveless cloak; hood fixed round gas-jet to give incandescent light. v.t. & i. envelop, cover as with mantle; (of liquids) form a scum; (of blood) suffuse cheeks; (of face) blush.

mant´let, n. short mantle; movable bullet-proof screen.

man´ual, a. of or done with the hands. n. handbook, primer, textbook; organ keyboard.

manufac´ture, n. making of articles or material, esp. in large quantities. v.t. produce by labour; work up materials into finished articles. ~tory, n. factory, workshop.

manumit´, v.t. give freedom to slave. ~mis´sion, n. setting free.

manure´, n. dung or other substance used for fertilizing soil. v.t. (-rable), treat with manure.

man´uscript, a. handwritten. n. (abbrev. MS., pl. MSS.), manuscript book or roll or document; copy of matter to be printed.

Manx, a. of the Isle of Man. n. the Manx language.

ma´ny (mě-), a. numerous, much more than one. n. a multitude, great number; the populace.

Mao´ri (mowr´ĭ), n. member, language, of New Zealand race.

map, n. flat representation of the earth or some part of it. v.t. make map of; (with out) plan arrangement of.

ma´ple, n. kinds of tree. ~ leaf, emblem of Canada. ~ sugar, sugar got from kind of maple.

mar, v.t. impair, spoil. ~plot, officious frustrator of plans.

ma´rabou (-bōō), n. kind of stork; its down as trimming, &c.

ma´rabout (-bōōt), n. Mohammedan hermit or monk.

maraschi´no (-kē-), n. a liqueur.

Maratha. See Mahratta.

maraud´, v.i. make raid, pillage. maraud´er, n.

mar´ble, n. kinds of limestone used in sculpture and architecture; (pl.) collection of sculpture; small ball of stone used in child's game, (pl.) the game. v.t. stain like marble.

marcel´ ~ wave, nn. kind of artificial wave in hair. ~wave, v.t. produce marcel wave in.

March¹, n. third month of year. ~ hare, hare in breeding season.

march², v.i. & t. (cause to) walk in military manner or with regular paces; (of events) go steadily on. n. action or piece of marching; progress; musical composition adapted for marching to.

march³, n. (usu. pl.) boundary or debatable strip between countries. v.i. have common boundary (with).

mar´chioness (-sho-), n. wife of a marquis.

marco´ni, n. marconigram. v.i. & t. send marconigram; send (message, &c.).

marco´nigram, n. wireless message.

māre, n. female horse or other equine animal. ~'s-nest, fancied discovery.

mārg'arine (-g- or -j-), n. imitation butter.

mar'gin, n. border; strip near the edge of something; unprinted space round printed page; extra amount over what is necessary. mar'ginal, a. written or printed in the margin. marginā'lia, n.pl. marginal notes.

mārg'rāve, n. title of certain princes of the Holy Roman Empire. ~vine (-ēn), n. margrave's wife.

marg'uerite (-gerēt), n. kinds of large daisy.

mā'rigold, n. kinds of yellow-flowered plant.

marine' (-ēn), a. of, from, or beside the sea; for use on the sea; of shipping. n. shipping; soldier serving on board ship. mā'riner, n. sailor.

Mariol'atry, n. worship of the Virgin.

mā'rionĕtte', n. puppet worked with strings.

mar'ital (mǎ'rǐ-, marǐt'-), a. of a husband; of or between husband and wife.

mǎ'ritime, a. situated, dwelling, or found near the sea; connected with seafaring.

marj'oram, n. kinds of herb.

mark[1], n. German coin (about 1s.).

mark[2], n. target; thing aimed at; normal standard; indication of or trace left by something; visible sign, stain, spot, or dent on something; merit of work; heel-mark for fair catch in Rugby football. v.t. & i. distinguish with a mark; characterize or serve as mark of; assign marks of merit to; notice, observe, watch; record as score or act as scorer in games. mark'edly, adv. unmistakably.

mark'er, n. scorer at billiards; man employed to mark game-birds; thing used to mark place in book.

mark'ĕt, n. gathering for sale of commodities or live-stock; space or building used for it; seat of or facilities for trade. v.t. & i. bring or send to or sell in market; buy goods in market. ~ cross, cross in market-place. ~ garden(er), growing vegetables for sale. ~-place, square in which market is held. ~ price, prevailing price resulting from supply and demand. ~ town, town having fixed market day(s). ~able, a. fit for sale; in demand.

mark'ing, n. variegated colours of feathers, skin, &c. ~-ink, ink for marking linen.

marks'man, n. (pl. -men), skilled shot, esp. with rifle. ~ship, n.

marl, n. kind of rich soil often used as manure. marl'y, a.

marl'ine, n. (Naut.) two-strand cord. ~spike, pointed tool for unravelling rope to be spliced.

marm'alāde, n. orange jam.

marmor'ėal, a. of marble; white or cold or polished as marble.

marm'osĕt (-z-), n. small bushy-tailed monkey.

marm'ot, n. rodent allied to the squirrel.

mar'ocain, n. a dress-fabric of wool, silk, or cotton, with a wavy texture.

maroon'[1], n. brownish-crimson colour; kind of firework. a. maroon-coloured.

maroon'[2], n. one of the wild negroes of the W. Indies; marooned person. v.t. put and leave ashore on a desert island.

marque (-k), n. In phr. letters of ~, licence to act as privateer.

marquee' (-kē), n. large tent.

marq'uetry (-kǐ-), n. inlaid work.

marq'uis, ~quess, n. peer ranking between duke and earl.

marq'uisate, n. marquis's patent.

mā'rriage (-rǐj), n. act, ceremony, or state of being married; (fig.) union; wedding or wedlock. ~able, a. old enough for marriage.

mǎ'rrow[1] (-ō), n. fatty substance in cavity of bones; kind of gourd cooked as table vegetable.

~bone, bone with edible marrow; (pl., joc.) the knees. ~-fat, kind of large pea. ~-y (-ōī), a.

mă'trow² (-ō), n. (dial.) mate, consort, match; very image of.

mă'rry, v.t. & i. (-iable), unite, give, or take in wedlock; take a wife or husband.

Mars (-z), n. Roman god of war; (poet.) war, armies; a planet.

mārsa'la (-sah-), n. Sicilian wine like sherry.

Marseillaise (marselāz'), n. national anthem of France.

mărsh, n. piece of low watery ground. mărsh'ȳ, a.

mărsh'al, n. kinds of official (now chiefly in comb., as air, field, provost ~); master of ceremonies; steward at assemblies; foreign field marshal. v.t. arrange in due order; conduct.

mărsū'pial, a. of the class of animals that carry their young in a pouch. n. a marsupial animal.

mart, n. place of trade.

mărtellō, n. (hist.; pl. -os). ~-tower, circular fort for coast defence.

mărt'en, n. kind of weasel with valuable fur.

mār'tial (-shl), a. warlike; suited to or loving war.

mărt'in, n. bird of swallow kind.

mărtinět', n. strict disciplinarian.

mărt'ingale (-ngg-), n. check-strap preventing horse from rearing or throwing up head; gambling system of doubling the stakes at each venture.

mărti'ni (-ēnī), n. the Martini-Henry rifle.

Mărt'inmas, n. St. Martin's day, 11th November.

mărt'let, n. the swift; footless heraldic bird.

mărt'yr (-er), n. person put to death for adherence to a cause; one who is victimized. v.t. put to death as martyr; make a martyr of. ~dom, n. martyr's death; sufferings or discomfort. ~ŏ'logy, n. history, collection of tales, of the Christian martyrs.

mărv'el, n. wonderful thing. v.i. feel surprise, wonder. mărv'-

ellous, a. astonishing, extraordinary, preternatural.

Mărx'ian, a. & n. (follower) of the German socialist Karl Marx.

mărzipăn', n. sweet confection of ground almonds.

măs'cot, n. luck-bringer.

măs'culine (mah-), a. (Gram.) of the male gender; male, manly; vigorous; mannish. n. masculine gender. măsculin'itȳ, n.

măsh, n. malt, bran, or other substance, mixed with water into a thick liquid for brewing. horse-fodder, &c.; (sl.) mashed potatoes. v.t. make into mash; crush to pulp; (sl., of lady-killer) practise fascination on. măsh'er, n. (sl.) lady-killer; dandy.

măsh'ie, n. short-headed iron golf-club.

mask, n. artificial face worn as disguise; face-covering of velvet, &c. to hide identity, or of wire, &c. to serve as protection; likeness of face only in wax, clay, or stone. v.t. cover with mask; disguise, hide, or screen as with mask.

mā'son, n. builder in and dresser of stone; freemason. măson'ic, a. of freemasons. mā'sonrȳ, n. stonework; built-up stones.

măsque (-k), n. kind of poetic drama with pageantry. măs'quer (-ker), n. person taking part in masque or masquerade. măsquerāde' (-ke-), n. ball, &c. at which masks or fancy dresses are worn. v.i. appear in disguise.

măss¹, n. the Eucharist or a celebration of it.

măss², n. large body of matter; dense aggregation of objects; (pl.) the general body of the people. v.t. & i. gather into a mass.

măss'acre (-ker), n. general slaughter, esp. of unresisting persons. v.t. make massacre of.

massage' (-ahzh), n. kneading and rubbing of the muscles, &c. as curative treatment. v.t. apply massage to. măsseur', (-êr), -euse' (-êrz), nn.

mäss´if, n. mountain heights forming a compact group.

mäss´ive, a. large and heavy or solid; (fig.) substantial.

mäss´y, a. solid, weighty.

mast¹ (mahst), n. fruit of beech, oak, &c. as food for pigs.

mast² (mahst), n. upright to which ship's yards and sails are attached; upright for decorations, wireless telegraphy, &c.

ma´ster (mah-), n. man who has authority over or teaches others; employer; skilled artist or expert; (Sc.) heir apparent of peerage below earldom. v.t. acquire complete knowledge of; master or reduce to subjection. ~ful, a. imperious. ~ly, a. of consummate skill. ~piece, n. best or very fine specimen of an artist's work. ~y, n. masterly skill, dominion, superiority.

mäs´tic, n. kind of resin.

mäs´ticäte, v.t. (-cable) reduce (food) to pulp by chewing. ~tion, ~tor, nn.

ma´stiff (mah-), n. dog of a powerful breed.

mäs´todon, n. extinct animal allied to elephant.

mäs´turbäte, v.i. practise self-abuse. ~tion, n.

mät¹, mätt, a. (of surface) dull.

mät², n. coarse fabric of plaited fibre; piece of material laid on floor or table, &c. to protect surface. v.t. & i. bring or come into a thickly tangled state.

mät´adór, n. man whose task is to kill bull in bull-fight.

mätch¹, n. slip of wood, wax, &c. with head that ignites when rubbed; fuse. ~lock, obsolete musket fired with fuse.

mätch², n. person or thing nearly resembling or corresponding to another; marriage; a contest, game. v.t. & i. find or be a match for; show similarity. mätch´less, a. incomparable.

mäte¹, n. & v.t. (-table), checkmate in chess.

mäte², n. one of a pair of birds, lovers, or married people; fellow

workman; subordinate officer of merchant-ship. v.t. & i. (-table), pair, marry or mate.

ma´ter, n. (school sl.) mother.

matér´ial, a. composed of or connected with matter; unspiritual; considerable, essential. n. that from which something is made; textile fabric.

matér´ialism, n. belief that nothing exists but matter and its manifestations; exclusive attention to material prosperity. ~ist, n. & a.; matérialis´tic, a.

matér´ialize, v.t. & i. (-zable), make materialistic; be fulfilled.

matérn´al, a. of a mother; from, on the side of, one's mother.

matérn´ity, n. motherhood.

mäthémät´ics, n. science of space and number. mäthémät´ical, a. mäthémäti´cian (-shn), n.

mät´in, n. (pl.) morning prayer. a. of the morning.

matinée (mät´inā), n. theatrical performance in afternoon.

mä´tricide, n. killing of one's mother; person guilty of it.

matric´uläte, v.t. & i. (-lable), admit, be admitted, as student in a university. matricülä´tion, n.

mät´rimony, n. state of having a husband or wife. ~ō´nial, a.

ma´trix, n. (pl. -ices pr. -isēz, -ixes), mould in which a cast is made; substance in which mineral is found embedded.

ma´tron, n. married woman, esp. elderly one; woman in charge of hospital; housekeeper in school or institution.

mätt´er, n. physical substance; objects of specified kind; material; affair, concern; purulent discharge. v.i. be of importance; make a difference (to).

mätt´ing, n. fabric used for mats.

mätt´ock, n. tool like pickaxe.

mätt´ress, n. large cushion on which bed-clothes rest.

mät´ūräte, v.i. (of pustule, &c.) come to maturation. ~tion, n. ripening of morbific matter.

matūre´, a. fully developed; ripe; adult. v.t. & i. bring to or reach

maturity; ripen; develop fully.
matūr′lty, n.

matūti′nal, a. of or in the morning.

maud, n. grey striped plaid.

maud′lin, a. weakly sentimental.

mau′gre (-ger), prep. in spite of.

maul, n. heavy hammer for pile-driving, &c. v.t. beat and bruise; handle roughly; *split (rail, &c.) with wedge and maul.

maul′stick, n. stick used to steady the hand in painting.

maund, n. (Anglo-Ind.) measure of weight, varying in different places from about 25 lb. to 82 lb.

maun′der, v.i. talk ramblingly.

maun′dy, n. footwashing ceremony on Thursday before Easter; royal alms given on that day.

Mau′ser (mow-), n. a magazine rifle.

mausolē′um, n. building erected as tomb and monument.

mauve (mōv), n. & a. pale purple.

mā′vis, n. song-thrush.

maw, n. gullet or stomach of an animal; also used fig.

mawk′ish, a. of faint sickly flavour; feebly sentimental.

māxill′ary, a. of the jaw.

max′im¹, n. a machine gun.

max′im², n. piece of wisdom or advice expressed in a sentence.

max′imalist, n. person who holds out for the maximum of his demands and rejects compromises.

max′imum, n. (pl. -ima), highest recorded or highest possible degree.

max′imus, a. eldest of the name.

may¹, v.aux. (3rd sing. may; past might pr. mīt) expressing possibility, permission, request, wish, &c. ~be, perhaps.

May², n. a month associated with greenery; hawthorn blossom. ~day, 1st of May as country festival. ~fly, ephemeral insect. ~pole, flower-decked pole danced round on May-day. ~ queen, girl chosen as queen of May-day games. ~tree, hawthorn. may′ing, n. picking of May flowers.

mayor (mār), n. head of town corporation. ~ess, n. mayor's wife or female mayor. may′oralty, n. mayor's office or tenure.

māzarine′ (-ēn), n. & a. deep blue.

māze, n. labyrinth; network of paths or lines; tangle of facts, &c. v.t. bewilder, stupefy.

mazūrk′a, n. a dance in triple time; music for it.

me (mē, mi), pron., obj. case of I.

mead¹, n. fermented honey and water as alcoholic drink.

mead², meadow (mĕd′ō), nn. piece of grass land esp. used for hay.

mea′gre (-ger), a. lean, scanty, insufficient; jejune.

meal¹, n. grain or pulse ground to powder.

meal², n. taking of food, esp. at table at a certain time.

meal′ie, n. (S.-Afr.) maize (used chiefly in pl.) ~cob, seeding head of mealie.

meal′y, a. of, like, or containing meal. ~mouthed, not outspoken.

mean¹, a. low in the scale; of low degree or poor quality; ignoble; ungenerous; stingy.

mean², v.t. & i. (meant pr. mĕnt). purpose, design; be resolved; intend; signify. mean′ing, n. what is meant, significance. a. full of meaning, significant.

mean³, a. equidistant from both extremes; intermediate. n. mean degree or state or course; (pl.) intermediate steps to an end; resources; money. ~time, ~while, adv. in the intervening time.

meăn′der, n. departure from straight course. v.i. wind about; go deviously.

mea′sles (-zlz), n.pl. infectious human disease with red rash; a swine-disease. meas′ly (-z-), a. of, like, having, measles. (sl.) scanty, worthless.

measure (mĕzh′er), n. size or quantity in relation to a standard; appliance for ascertaining or testing this; prescribed amount; limit; rhythm, metre, musical

time; expedient, calculated action; parliamentary bill or act. *v.t.* (*-rable*), ascertain size, quantity, &c. with measure; amount to; estimate. ~ment, *n.* act of measuring; (*pl.*) detailed dimensions.

meat, *n.* flesh of beasts as food. **meat′y**, *a.* full of meat.

méchăn′ĭc (-k-), *n.* skilled artisan who works with tools.

méchăn′ĭcal (-k-), *a.* of machines or mechanism; automatic.

mĕchani′cian (-kanĭshn), *n.* one skilled in constructing machines.

mĕchăn′ĭcs (-k-), *n.pl.* (usu. with sing. vb.), science of motion; science of machinery.

mĕc′hanism (-k-), *n.* way a machine works; piece of machinery; framework of story.

mĕc′hanist (-k-), *n.* mechanician, expert in mechanics. ~ĭc, *a.*

mĕc′hanize (-k-), *v.t.* (*-zable*), make mechanical.

Mĕc′hlin (-k-), *n.* kind of lace.

mĕd′al, *n.* coinlike metal disk with device, &c. **mĕdăl′lion** (-yon), *n.* large medal; circular picture or decorative panel. **mĕd′allist**, *n.* winner of prize-medal.

mĕd′dle, *v.i.* busy oneself unduly *with*; interfere *in*. ~some, *a.* given to meddling.

mē′dial, *-an*, *aa.* in the middle.

mē′dĭate, *a.* involving an intermediary; without direct connexion. *v.i.* (*-iāt*), act as go-between or peace-maker. ~tion, ~tor, *nn.*; mĕdiātŏr′ial, mē′dĭātory, *aa.*; mē′dĭātrĭx, *n.*

mĕd′ĭcal, *a.* of medicine.

mĕd′ĭcament, *n.* thing used as medicine.

mĕd′ĭcāte, *v.t.* (*-cable*), impregnate with medicinal substance.

mĕdĭ′cinal, *a.* healing or curative.

medicine (mĕd′sn), *n.* the art of preserving and restoring health; drugs, potions, &c., used in this. *v.t.* administer drugs to.

mĕdĭ′eval, *-iae′val*, *a.* of the middle ages. ~ism, ~ist, *nn.*

mē′dĭŏcre (-ker), *a.* middling, second-rate. **mĕdĭŏc′rĭty** (or mē-), *n.* mediocre person.

mĕd′ĭtāte, *v.t. & i.* (*-itable*), plan, scheme; ponder over. ~tion, *n.* reflection. ~tive, *a.*

Mĕdĭterrā′nean, *n.* sea enclosed by Europe, Asia, and Africa.

mē′dĭum, *n.* (*pl. -ums, -a*), middle quantity or degree; means or agency; person serving as go-between in spiritualism. *a.* remote from either extreme.

mĕd′lar, *n.* a tree-fruit eaten when decayed.

mĕd′ley, *n.* (*pl. -eys*), heterogeneous mixture; miscellany.

mĕdŭll′ary, *a.* of marrow or pith.

meed, *n.* reward; recompense.

meek, *a.* submissive; gentle.

meer′kăt, *n.* either of two small S.-Afr. mammals.

meer′schaum (-shm), *n.* creamy clay used esp. for pipe-bowls; pipe with meerschaum bowl.

meet[1], *a.* fitting, proper.

meet[2], *v.t. & i.* (*mĕt*), come into contact or company (with); confront; become perceptible to; satisfy the claims of. *n.* assembly preparatory to starting hunt.

meet′ing, *n.* duel; contest, sporting event; assembly. ~house, *n.* nonconformist place of worship.

mĕgalomā′nia, *n.* insane self-exaltation; mania for big things.

mĕgalosaur′us, *n.* huge extinct lizard.

mĕg′aphŏne, *n.* speaking-trumpet.

mĕg′ohm (-ōm), *n.* (elect.) one million ohms.

mē′grim[1], *n.* brow-ague; (*pl.*) low spirits; (*pl.*) staggers in horses.

mē′grim[2], *n.* a flat-fish, the smooth sole.

mĕlanchō′lia (-k-), *n.* mental disease marked by melancholy.

mĕlanchŏl′ic (-k-), *a.* of or liable to melancholia.

mĕl′ancholy (-k-), *n.* mental depression; lack of cheerfulness. *a.* sad, depressed.

mê′lée (mĕl′ā), *n.* confused fight or struggle or crowd.

mĕl′inĭte, *n.* an explosive.

mē'liorāte, *v.t.* make better, improve. ~tion, *n.*

méllif'luent, -luous (-lŏŏ-), *aa.* (of words, &c.) honey-sweet.

mėll'ow (-ō), *a.* soft and rich in flavour, colour, or sound. *v.t. & i.* make or grow mellow; ripen.

mėlō'dėon, *n.* kind of accordion.

mėlō'dious, *a.* full of melody.

mėl'odist, *n.* artist in melody.

mėlodra'ma (-rah-), *n.* drama marked by crude appeals to emotion. ~dramāt'ic, *a.* theatrical.

mėl'odÿ, *n.* sweetness of sound; songs or music; the air in harmonized music.

mėl'on, *n.* kinds of gourd eaten as fruit.

mėlt, *v.t. & i.* (p.p. melted, and, as adj., mō'lten), pass or convert from solid to liquid form under heat; dissolve, dwindle, vanish.

mėl'ton, *n.* kind of cloth for men's clothes.

mėm'ber, *n.* limb or other bodily organ; distinct part of complex structure; one of a society.

mėm'brāne, *n.* pliable sheet-like tissue lining or connecting parts of animal or vegetable body; piece of parchment or similar material. mėmbrā'ceous (-shŭs), mėmbrā'nėous, *aa.*

mėmen'tō, *n.* (pl. -os) object serving as a memorial; keepsake.

mėm'oir (-wǎr), *n.* brief biography; (pl.) account of one's life or experiences; scientific paper.

mėm'orable, *a.* likely or worthy to be remembered. mėmorabil'ia, *n.pl.* memorable things.

mėmoran'dum, *n.* (pl. -da) note made for future use; informal business communication.

mėmōr'ial, *a.* commemorative. *n.* commemorative monument; (usu. pl.) chronicles; written representation made to authorities. ~ist, *n.* signatory of memorial. ~ize, *v.t.* address memorial to. *'M~* Day, 30th May or other day to commemorate those who fell in the U.S. Civil War.

mėm'orīze, *v.t.* learn by heart.

mėm'orÿ, *n.* faculty by which things are recalled to or kept in the mind; posthumous repute.

mėm'sahib (-sah-ĭb), *n.* used by the natives of India in addressing European women.

mėn'ace, *n.* threat; apparent danger. *v.t.* (-ceable), threaten.

|| ménage (mėnahzh'), *n.* household or its management.

ménā'gerie, *n.* show of caged wild animals.

mėnd, *v.t. & i.* repair, patch; put right; improve; rectify. *n.* mended hole or crack.

mėndā'cious (-shŭs), *a.* lying, given to lying. mėndăc'itÿ, *n.*

Mėn'delism, *n.* theory of heredity tending to reduce to numerical law the recurrence of inherited characters. Mėndē'lian, *a. & n.*

mėn'dicant, *n.* beggar (often attrib.). ~ncÿ, mėndĭc'itÿ, *nn.*

mė'nial, *n.* household servant. *a.* fit only for a menial.

mėningī'tis (-j-), *n.* inflammation of membrane enclosing the brain.

mėn'sēs (-z), *n.pl.* monthly discharge from the womb.

Mėn'shėvĭk, *n.* Russian socialist of the more moderate party.

mėn'strual (-ŏŏ-), *a.* monthly; of the menses. mėn'struāte (-ŏŏ-), *v.i.* discharge the menses. mėnstruā'tion (-ŏŏ), *n.*

mėn'struum (-ŏŏ-), *n.* (pl. -rua) solvent liquid.

mėn'sūrable, *a.* measurable.

mėnsūrā'tion, *n.* the art or practice of computing measurements.

mėn'tal, *a.* of or in the mind. mėntăl'itÿ, *n.* character of a person's mind; idiosyncrasy.

mėn'thol, *n.* camphor-like substance used in relieving pain.

mėn'tion, *v.t.* speak of; call attention to. *n.* a mentioning.

mėn'tŏr, *n.* adviser, counsellor.

mėn'ū (or -ōō'), *n.* bill of fare.

mėphī'tis, *n.* noxious emanation from below ground. ~it'ic, *a.*

mėrc'antile, *a.* trading; of trade or merchants.

mėr'cenarÿ, *a.* working for money

or reward; not disinterested. *n.* hired soldier.

mer´cer, *n.* dealer in silk, velvet, and such fabrics. **mer´cery,** *n.*

merch´andise (-z), *n.* mercantile commodities; goods for sale.

merch´ant, *n.* wholesale trader, esp. with foreign countries; dealer; (U.S. & Sc.) shopkeeper. ~**able,** *a.* salable; in demand.

mer´ciful, *a.* disposed to mercy; compassionate; kind.

mer´ciless, *a.* cruel, pitiless.

mercur´ial, *a.* of lively temperament; of or containing mercury.

mer´cury, *n.* a white normally liquid metal, quicksilver; (**M~**) Roman god, messenger of Jove; messenger (joc.).

mer´cy, *n.* abstention from the infliction of suffering or punishment; compassionateness; piece of good fortune.

mere¹, *n.* lake.

mere², *a.* neither more nor less than; bare, undiluted.

merely (mēr´li), *adv.* just, only.

meretri´cious (-shus), *a.* showily attractive; flashy.

mergan´ser, *n.* a diving bird.

merge, *v.t. & i.* (-*geable*), lose or cause to lose identity by absorption. **mer´ger,** *n.* absorption in a greater whole.

merid´ian, *n.* sun's position at noon; stars highest altitude; circle passing through a place and the N. & S. poles; (attrib.) culminating. **merid´ional,** *a.* of the south; of a meridian.

meringue´ (-răng), *n.* sweet made with white of egg, sugar, &c.

meri´no (-rē-), *n.* (pl. -os), kind of sheep; fine yarn or soft fabric of its wool; fine woollen yarn.

mer´it, *n.* commendable quality; goodness; (pl.) deserts. *v.t.* deserve. **merĭtŏr´ious,** *a.* praiseworthy.

merle, *n.* blackbird.

mer´lin, *n.* kind of falcon.

merm´aid, merm´an, *nn.* woman, man, of the sea with fish-tail.

mer´riment, *n.* amused enjoyment; mirth.

mer´ry, *a.* laughing, given to laughter; full of fun. ~**making,** festivity. ~**thought,** the forked bone of a bird's breast.

‖ **mésalliance** (mězăl´iahns), *n.* a lowering marriage.

mesh, *n.* one of the spaces between the threads of a net; (pl.) net. *v.t.* catch in a net.

mes´merism (měz-), *n.* hypnotic state induced in a person by the exercise of another's will-power. **mésmě´ric** (-z-), *a.* ; ~**ist,** *n.* **més´merize** (měz-), *v.t.* (-*zable*), subject to mesmerism.

mesozo´ic, *a.* of the second geological period.

mess, *n.* portion of food; spilt liquid, &c.; untidyness, dirty state; company, esp. in army or navy, feeding together; its meal or mess-room. ~**mate,** member of same mess, esp. on ship. *v.t. & i.* make dirty or untidy; bungle; take meals *with.*

mess´age, *n.* communication sent; what a prophet or moralist is inspired to say.

mess´enger (-j-), *n.* bearer of message.

Messi´ah (-*a*), *n.* deliverer expected by the Jews; Christ in that character. **Messiăn´ic,** *a.*

Mess´rs (-*erz*), *n.* title prefixed to name of firm or to list of gentlemen.

mess´uage, *n.* dwelling-house with outbuildings and land.

metáb´olism, *n.* the changes undergone by nutritive material in the body. **metăbŏl´ic,** *a.*

metacărp´us, *n.* hand from wrist to finger-roots.

mĕt´al, *n.* any of a class of substances represented by gold, silver, copper, iron, lead, and tin; stone for road-making; (pl.) the rails of a railway. *v.t.* fit, &c. with metal; make or mend (road) with metal. **metăll´ic,** of, or as of, metal. **metallif´erous,** *a.* **mĕt´alline,** *a.* of the nature of or yielding metal. **mĕt´allize,** *v.t.* (-*zable*), give metallic qualities to. **metăll´urgy** (-ler-), *n.* art of ex-

---

tracting metal from ore and of working in metal. ~gist, *n.*

mĕtamōrph′ic, *a.* (of rocks) changed in structure by volcanic or other natural agency. **mĕtamōrph′ism,** *n.*

mĕtamōrph′ōse (-z), *v.t.* (*-sable*), subject to metamorphosis.

mĕtamōrph′osis, *n.* (pl. *-oses* pr. -ēz), change of form, esp. magic transformation; change of character, circumstances, &c.

mĕt′aphor, *n.* application of name or descriptive term to an object to which it is not literally applicable. **mĕtaphŏr′ical,** *a.*

mĕtaphŷs′ics (-z-), *n.pl.* (often with sing. vb.), speculations on the nature of being, truth, and knowledge; (pop.) abstract or subtle talk. **~cal,** *a.* ; **~cian,** *n.*

mĕtatār′sus, *n.* bones between tarsus and toes. **~tārs′al,** *a.*

mĕtăth′esis, *n.* (pl. *-eses* pr. -ēz), transposition of the letters or sounds in a word.

mēte, *v.t.* (*-table*), measure.

mĕtĕmpsy̆chō′sis (-k-), *n.* (pl. *-oses* pr. -ēz), migration of soul at death into another body.

mē′teor, *n.* any atmospheric phenomenon, esp. shooting star. **mĕtĕŏr′ic,** *a.* brilliant and transitory as a meteor; of meteors. **mē′teorite,** *n.* fallen meteor; meteoric stone.

mĕteōrŏl′ogy, *n.* science of the weather. **~ŏ′gical,** *a.* ; **~gist,** *n.*

mē′ter, *n.* apparatus registering the amount of gas or other fluid that passes through it.

mĕthinks′, *v.impers.* it seems to me.

mĕth′od, *n.* way of doing something; orderliness. **mĕthŏd′ical,** *a.* orderly, systematic.

Mĕth′odist, *n.* member of any of the religious bodies owing their origin to the Wesleys and Whitefield. **~ism,** *n.* ; **~istical,** *a.*

mĕth′odize, *v.t.* (*-zable*), introduce method into.

mĕth′yl, *n.* the base of wood spirit. **mĕth′ŷlāte,** *v.t.* mix with methyl (as *methylated spirit*).

mĕtic′ulous, *a.* slavishly accurate or correct or proper.

‖ **mĕtier** (mĕt′yā), *n.* one's line or forte.

mĕtŏn′ymy̆, *n.* substitution of an attribute for the name of the thing meant.

mē′tre (-ter), *n.* verse rhythm; unit of length (39·37 in.) in metric system.

mĕt′ric, -al, *aa.* of or in metre; involving measurement. **~ system,** decimal system of weights and measures.

mĕtrŏl′ogy̆, *n.* science of measures. **~gist,** *n.*

mĕt′ronōme, *n.* musician's pendulum giving regular beat at required pace. **~nŏm′ic,** *a.*

mĕtrŏp′olis, *n.* chief city of a State; (Eccl.) metropolitan's see.

mĕtropŏl′itan, *a.* of a metropolis. *n.* archbishop or other bishop having authority over bishops of a province.

mĕt′tle, *n.* spirit, courage, endurance. **~some, mĕt′tled** (-ld), *aa.* spirited.

mew[1], *n.* sea-gull.

mew[2], *v.i.* & *t.* (of hawk) moult; shut up hawk in mew; shut up in school, office, &c. *n.* cage for hawks; (pl., as sing.) stable-yard and stables; livery stable.

mew[3], **mewl, miaow** (mīow′), *miaul, v.i.* cry like cat or (mewl, miaul) baby. *n.* such sound.

mĕz′zotint (-dz-), *n.* method of engraving; a print so produced.

miăs′ma (-z-), *n.* (pl. *-ata*), noxious exhalation from marshes, putrid matter, &c.

mi′ca, *n.* kinds of mineral found as small glittering scales in granite, &c., and as crystals separable into thin plates.

Mic′haelmas (-kal-), *n.* feast of St. Michael, 29 Sept.

*Mick, *n.* an Irishman.

mic′kle, *n.* (Sc.) large amount.

mi′crōbe, *n.* minute plant or animal, esp. as cause of disease.

mi′crocŏsm, *n.* man as an epitome of the universe; analogue on small scale of something.

---

ah, awl, oil, boor, cow, dowry ; chin, go, bang, so, ship, thin ; dh, as th(e)

mi′cron, n. millionth of a metre.

mi′crophone, n. device for making faint sounds louder.

mi′croscope, n. lens or arrangement of lenses, &c. by which minute objects are made visible. **microscop′ic**, a. of, with, like, the microscope. **microscop′ical**, a.; **micros′copy**, n.

mictūri′tion, n. passing of urine.

mid, a. that is in the middle; intermediate. prep. amid. **~day**, noon or thereabouts. **~night**, twelve o'clock at night. **~off**, **~on**, fielders nearer batsman than long-off and long-on.

mid′den, n. dung-hill; refuse-heap.

mid′dle, a. equidistant from extremities; intermediate in rank, quality, &c. n. middle point or position; the waist. **~ages**, about A.D. 1000–1400. **~man**, dealer intervening between producer and consumer. **~weight**, boxing weight (from 11 st. 6 lb. to 10 st. 7 lb.).

mid′dling, a. moderately good; fairly well in health. adv. fairly or moderately.

midge, n. gnat; small fly.

midg′et, n. diminutive person; photograph of small size.

mid′land (-and), a. remote from the sea or border.

mid′riff, n. the diaphragm.

mid′shipman (-an; abbr. *midd′y*), n. rank between naval cadet and sub-lieutenant.

midst, n. middle. prep. amidst.

mid′summer, n. summer solstice, about 21 June.

mid′wife, n. (pl. -ives), woman who assists others in childbirth. **mid′wifery** (-difrĭ, -dwifrĭ), n. obstetrics.

mien (mēn), n. person's bearing or look.

might¹, p.t of may.

might² (mīt), n. great power of strength or resources. **might′y** (-ĭt-), a. having might; massive or huge. adv. (colloq., iron.) very, quite.

mignonette′ (mĭnyo-), n. a fragrant-flowered plant.

mi′grant, a. that migrates. n. migrant bird, &c.

mi′grate, v.i. change one's abode; (of birds, &c.) come and go with the seasons. **~tion**, n.; **~tory**, a.

mika′dō (-kah-), n. (pl. -os), Emperor of Japan.

mike (sl.), v.i. shirk work; idle. n. idling or a spell of it.

milch, a. giving, kept for, milk.

mild, a. gentle; not severe or harsh or drastic; not bitter.

mil′dew, n. growth of minute fungi on plants, or on leather, &c., exposed to damp. v.t. & i. taint, be tainted, with mildew.

mile, n. linear measure, 1,760 yards. **~stone**, roadside pillar stating milage. **mi′lage**, n. distance reckoned in miles; cost per mile; *travelling allowance to member of legislature, &c.; *book of railroad tickets each good for one mile.

mil′foil, n. kinds of plant with minute leaf-divisions.

mil′itant, a. engaged in warfare; combative. n. combative person.

mil′itarism, n. exaltation of or reliance on military force or methods. **mil′itarist**, n.

mil′itary, a. pertaining to soldiers or army or land warfare. n. the soldiery.

mil′itāte, v.i. serve as an argument or influence against.

milī′tia (-sha), n. (hist.) branch of British military service enlisted for home defence, since 1908 absorbed in Special Reserve. **~man**, n.

milk, n. liquid with which mammals feed their young; cow's milk as article of food. v.t. draw milk from. **~maid**, woman milking cows or working in dairy. **~man**, seller of milk. **~sop**, unmanly fellow. **mil′ky**, a.

mill, n. building in which corn is ground; grinding-machine; factory; kinds of manufacturing machine. v.t. grind or treat in mill. **~board**, stout paste-board. **~hand**, factory worker.

millenā′rian, a. of, expecting, the

millennium. *n.* believer in the millennium. **mill´énary**, *a.* consisting of a thousand (esp. years).

millénn´ium, *n.* thousand-year period; coming time of happiness on earth. **millénn´ial,** *a.*

mill´épède, *n.* many-legged creature; wood-louse, &c.

mill´er, *n.* one whose business is to grind corn. **~'s** thumb, kinds of small fish.

milles´imal, *a.* thousandth.

mill´et, *n.* a cereal with minute seeds.

mill´i-, in comb. = one-thousandth of a — (in metric system), as: **~gramme** (·0154 of English grain), **~litre** (·061 cub. in.), **~metre** (·0393 in.).

mill´iard (*-yard*), *n.* a thousand millions; this number of francs.

mill´iner, *n.* maker-up of or dealer in women's hats, ribbons, &c. **mill´inery,** *n.*

mill´ion (*-yon*), *n.* ten hundred thousand; a million pounds, dollars, &c. **millionaire´** (*-yon-*), *n.* possessor of a million of money or more; rich person.

mill´stone, *n.* one of stones between which corn is ground.

milt, *n.* spawn of male fish. *v.t.* impregnate (female roe).

mime, *n.* dramatic scene of ancient Greek or Italian common life with mimicry; performer in it. **mime´sis,** *n.* close resemblance in markings, &c. of an animal to its habitat or other animal. **mimet´ic,** *a.* of or showing mimesis; given to mimicry.

mim´ic, *a.* feigned, esp. to amuse; sham; imitative. *n.* person who mimics others. *v.t.* copy the speech or gestures of, esp. to amuse others; closely imitate. **mim´icry,** *n.* mimicking; imitative action or objects.

mimo´sa (*-z-*), *n.* kinds of plant, including Sensitive Plant.

mi´na, *n.* kinds of Eastern passerine bird.

min´arêt, *n.* turret of mosque.

min´atory, *a.* threatening.

mince, *v.t. & i.* (*-ceable*), cut (meat, &c.) quite small; walk with affectedly short steps. *n.* minced meat. **~meat,** mixture of minced currants, spices, suet, &c. **~pie,** patty of mincemeat.

mind, *n.* the seat of consciousness, thought, volition, and feeling; intellectual powers; memory; opinion. *v.t.* bear in mind; heed; take charge of; have any objection. **mind´ed,** *a.* disposed, inclined. **mind´ful,** *a.* not forgetful.

mine¹, *pron.* the one(s) belonging to me. *a.* belonging to me.

mine², *n.* excavation from which minerals are extracted; explosive charge placed ready to go off when required. *v.t. & i.* (*-nable*), dig for minerals; burrow or make subterraneous passages in; lay explosive charges under or in. **~layer,** vessel for laying mines. **mi´ner,** *n.* worker in mine; soldier who lays mines.

min´eral, *a.* inorganic, not animal or vegetable; got from the earth by mining. *n.* a mineral substance. **~(water),** water naturally or artificially impregnated with some mineral.

mineral´ogy, *n.* the science of minerals. **~ó´gical,** *a.* **~gist,** *n.*

mingle (*ming´gl*), *v.i. & t.* be mixed; be united with; mix, blend.

min´iature, *n.* painted portrait on small scale; small-scale representation. *a.* small-scale, diminutive. **min´iatûrist** (*-ya-*), *n.* painter of miniatures.

min´im, *n.* a musical note, half a semibreve; 1/60 of a fluid drachm.

min´imalist, *n.* person ready to accept a minimum provisionally. **min´imize,** *v.t.* (*-zable*), reduce to or estimate at the minimum. **min´imum,** *n.* (pl. *-ima*), least possible or recorded amount.

min´ion (*-yon*), *n.* spoilt darling, favourite; mere dependant.

min´ister, *n.* executive agent; person in charge of State department; ambassador or State envoy; clergyman. *v.i.*

---

māte, mēte, mīte, mōte, mūte, mōōt : răck, rĕck, rick, rŏck, rŭck, rōōk ·

(-*trable*), be serviceable or contributory; officiate as minister of religion.

minister'ial, *a.* of a minister of religion or his office; of or on the side of the Government. ~ist, *n.* Government supporter.

min'ister, *a.* ministering. *n.* one who ministers.

ministra'tion, *n.* rendering of help; priestly service.

min'istry, *n.* priestly office; ministers of a church; office of a State minister; the ministers forming a Government.

min'iver, *n.* plain white fur in robes of peers, &c.

mink, *n.* kinds of small animal; their fur.

minn'esinger, *n.* medieval German lyric poet.

minn'ow (-ō), *n.* small freshwater fish.

Mino'an (or Mi-), *a.* of the recently discovered prehistoric culture (3000-1500 B.C.) of Crete.

mi'nor, *a.* lesser of two units or sets; of the lesser kind. *n.* person under age (21).

mino'rity (or mi-), *n.* being a minor; period of this; smaller of two sets; the smaller number.

Min'otaur (-tŏr), *n.* bull-headed man of Greek legend.

min'ster, *n.* a large church.

min'strel, *n.* medieval singer or musician; poet; (pl.) performers of nigger songs. min'strelsy, *n.* minstrel's art; poetry.

mint[1], *n.* aromatic herb.

mint[2], *n.* place where money is coined. *v.t.* coin money; invent. min'tage, *n.* what is minted; duty paid for minting.

minuet', *n.* slow stately dance or music for it.

mi'nus, *prep.* less, with the deduction of (symbol, -).

min'ute[1] (-nit), *n.* sixtieth of an hour; a short time; sixtieth of a degree; an official paper; (pl.) summary of proceedings. *v.t.* draft; note down.

minute'[2] (or mī-), *a.* very small; precise, going into details.

minū'tia (-shīa), *n.* (pl. -*ae*), trivial point; small detail.

minx, *n.* sly girl, hussy.

mi'ocene, *a.* of the middle division of tertiary strata.

mi'racle, *n.* event due to supernatural agency; remarkable event, mirāc'ūlous, *a.* supernatural; wonderful.

mirage' (-ahzh), *n.* illusion produced by atmospheric conditions.

mire, *n.* swampy ground; mud. *v.t.* entangle in mud; soil.

mi'rror, *n.* image-reflecting surface; a looking-glass. *v.t.* reflect image of.

mirth, *n.* being merry.

mir'ȳ, *a.* muddy.

misadven'ture, *n.* undesigned evil result; unlucky accident.

misalli'ance, *n.* unsuitable marriage.

mis'anthrope, *n.* hater of mankind. misanthrop'ic, *a.* misăn'thropy, *n.* misanthrope's temper.

misapply', *v.t.* apply wrongly.

misapprehend', *v.t.* misunderstand. ~nsion, *n.*; ~nsive, *a.*

misappro'priate, *v.t.* use (others' money) as one's own. ~tion, *n.*

misbecome' (-ŭm), *v.t.* suit ill.

misbegot'ten, *a.* illegitimate.

misbehave', *v.i.* & *refl.* behave improperly. ~viour, *n.*

misbelief' (-ēf), *n.* wrong belief; false opinion. ~believer, *n.*

miscal'cūlate, *v.t.* & *i.* calculate wrongly. ~tion, *n.*

miscall' (-awl), *v.t.* call by wrong name; abuse.

miscă'rriage (-rĭj), *n.* miscarrying; woman's untimely delivery.

miscă'rrȳ, *v.i.* fail of success; (of letter, &c.) not reach destination; (of woman) have miscarriage.

miscĕgēnā'tion, *n.* interbreeding between races, esp. of whites and negroes.

miscella'nea, *n.pl.* odds and ends; stray items.

miscellā'neous, *a.* consisting of various kinds. mis'cellany, *n.* literary or other medley.

mischance' (-ahns), *n.* unlucky event.

mis'chief (-chif), *n.* harm, injury, wrought by person or other agent; discord; childish scrapes. **mis'chievous** (-chiv-), *a.* tending to harm; full of mischief.

misconceive' (-sev), *v.i. & t.* have wrong idea of; misunderstand. **misconcep'tion**, *n.*

miscon'duct, *n.* improper conduct, esp. adultery. **~conduct'**, *v.t.*

miscon'strue (-ōō), *v.t.* put wrong construction on. **~struc'tion**, *n.*

miscount', *n.* wrong count, esp. of votes. *v.t.* count wrongly.

mis'creant, *n.* wicked person.

misdate', *v.t.* date wrongly.

misdeal', *v.i.* make mistake in dealing cards. *n.* wrong deal.

misdeed', *n.* sinful act.

misdemean'ant, *n.* person convicted of misdemeanour.

misdemean'our (-nor), *n.* indictable but not felonious offence.

misdirect', *v.t.* direct (person, letter, &c.) wrongly. **~ion**, *n.*

misdo'ing (-dōō-), *n.* misdeed.

misdoubt' (-owt), *v.t.* have doubts or suspicions; be apprehensive.

‖ **mise en scène** (mēz ahn sān'), *n.* staging of a play; surroundings.

mi'ser (-z-), *n.* avaricious person; hoarder of money. **~ly**, *a.*

mis'erable (-z-), *a.* pitiable; very unhappy; contemptible; mean.

misé'ricord (-z-), *n.* hinged seat in choir stall.

mis'ery (-z-), *n.* acute unhappiness; distressing poverty.

misfeas'ance (-z-), *n.* wrongful exercise of lawful authority.

misfire', *v.i. & n.* (of gun, motor engine, &c.) fail(ure) to act.

mis'fit, *n.* garment, &c., that does not fit.

misfor'tune (-chn, -tyōōn), *n.* calamity; bad luck.

misgive', *v.t.* (-*gāve*, -*given*), (of one's mind, &c.) suggest misgivings to. **misgiv'ing**, *n.* apprehension; uneasy doubt.

misgo'vern (-gŭ-), *v.t.* govern (State, &c.) badly. **~ment**, *n.*

misguide' (-gīd), *v.t.* mislead.

mishan'dle, *v.t.* ill-treat.

mishap', *n.* minor calamity.

misinform', *v.t.* give wrong information to. **misinforma'tion**, *n.*

misinter'pret, *v.t.* give wrong interpretation to; make wrong inference from. **~a'tion**, *n.*

misjudge', *v.t.* judge wrongly; have wrong opinion of.

mislay', *v.t.* so place (thing) as to be unable to find it.

mislead' (-lēd), *v.t.* lead astray; give wrong impression to.

misman'age, *v.t.* manage badly or wrongly. **~ment**, *n.*

misname', *v.t.* call by wrong name.

misno'mer, *n.* name applied wrongly; wrong use of term.

misog'amy (-g-), *n.* hatred of marriage. **misog'amist**, *n.*

misog'yny (-g-), *n.* hatred of women. **misog'ynist**, *n.*

misplace', *v.t.* (-*ceable*), put in wrong place; bestow (love, &c.) on ill-chosen object. **~ment**, *n.*

misprint', *n.* error in printing. *v.t.* make error in printing.

mispri'sion (-zhn), *n.* wrong action or omission.

misprize', *v.t.* scorn, undervalue.

mispronounce', *v.t.* pronounce wrongly. **~nuncia'tion**, *n.*

misquote', *v.t.* quote wrongly. **misquota'tion**, *n.*

misread', *v.t.* (past -*read* pr. -rĕd), read or interpret wrongly.

misrepresent' (-z-), *v.t.* represent wrongly; falsify. **~a'tion**, *n.*

misrule' (-rōōl), *v.t.* rule badly. *n.* bad government.

miss¹, *v.t. & i.* fail to hit, reach, meet, find, catch, or perceive; pass over; regret absence of; have a failure. *n.* fact of missing.

miss², *n.* unmarried woman or girl. **~ish**, *a.* like a schoolgirl.

miss'al, *n.* R.C. mass-book.

miss'el, *n.* large kind of thrush.

mis-shā'pen, *a.* deformed.

miss'ile, *n.* thing that can be thrown to do damage.

miss'ing, *a.* not to be found.

miss'ion (-shn), *n.* persons sent

out as envoys or evangelists ; their task or operations.

mi'ssionary (-sho-), *a.* of, concerned with, religious missions. *n.* person who goes on missionary work ; person attached to police-court to help offenders or applicants.

miss'is, *n.* (vulg.) mistress ; (joc.) wife.

miss'ive, *n.* letter, esp. official one.

mis-spell', *v.t.* spell wrongly.

mis-spend', *v.t.* (-spent), spend amiss or wastefully.

mis-state', *v.t.* state wrongly. ~ment, *n.*

mist, *n.* water-vapour in drops smaller than rain ; bleared effect given by tears in the eyes, &c.

mistake', *v.t. & i.* (-took, -taken ; -kable), come to wrong conclusion about, misinterpret ; erroneously take person or thing for another ; (*p.p.*) due to error, ill-judged. *n.* error, blunder ; mistaken opinion or act.

Mis'ter (*Mr.*), *n.* master, sir.

mistime', *v.t.* judge time of wrongly.

mis'tletoe (-sltō), *n.* parasitic white-berried plant.

mistranslate' (-nz-), *v.t.* translate incorrectly. ~tion, *n.*

mis'tress, *n.* woman in relation to servants ; woman having control ; female teacher ; man's paramour ; (arch.) = *Mrs.*

mistrust', *v.t.* feel no confidence in. *n.* lack of confidence ; uneasy doubts. ~ful, *a.*

mis'ty, *a.* of, in, or like mist ; of dim outline ; obscure.

misunderstand', *v.t. & i.* (-stood), take in wrong sense ; come to false conclusion about. ~ing, *n.*

misuse', *v.t.* (-z), apply to wrong use ; ill-treat. *n.* (-s), ill-treatment ; wrong use.

mite, *n.* anything very small ; small child or person ; small insect found in cheese. **mi'ty**, *a.* (of cheese) full of mites.

mit'igate, *v.t.* (-gable), appease, alleviate ; reduce severity of. ~tion, ~tor, *nn.* ; ~tory, *a.*

mi'tre (-ter), *n.* tall cap worn by

bishops ; episcopal rank ; joint between boards, &c. meeting at right angles. *v.t.* (-trable), put or bestow mitre on ; join with or shape for a mitre-joint.

mitt, **-en**, *nn.* glove leaving fingers and thumb-tip bare ; (pl., sl.) boxing-gloves ; *(sl., mitt)* hand, fist.

mix, *v.t. & i.* unite or blend into one mass ; compound together ; become united, mingle. **mixed** (-kst), *a.* of diverse qualities or elements ; of both sexes ; confused. *mix'er, n.* (with *good, bad*) person sociably, unsociably, inclined with casual acquaintances. **mix'ture**, *n.* mixing ; compound, esp. a medicinal draught.

miz(z)'en, *n.* lowest fore-and-aft sail of full-rigged ship's ~-mast (aftermost mast of three-masted ship) ; (loosely) spanker.

mnemon'ic (n-), *a.* of, designed to aid, the memory. ~s, *n.pl.* mnemonic art or system.

mō'a, *n.* large extinct flightless bird of New Zealand, resembling ostrich.

moan, *n.* low inarticulate sound expressing pain or grief. *v.i. & t.* utter moan ; lament, deplore.

moat, *n.* defensive ditch round castle, town, &c. ~ed, *a.*

mob, *n.* a riotous crowd ; a promiscuous gathering. *v.t.* crowd upon and hustle or ill-treat.

mob'-cap, *n.* woman's indoor cap.

mō'bile, *a.* shifting position readily ; not fixed. **mobil'ity**, *n.*

mō'bilize, *v.t. & i.* (-zable), render movable ; prepare (forces) for active service. ~zation, *n.*

mŏcc'asin, *n.* Amer.-Ind. soft shoe of deerskin, &c.

mŏck, *v.t. & i.* scoff at, ridicule, mimic ; tantalize with illusion. *n.* laughing-stock, mocking. *a.* (attrib. only) sham, mimic, counterfeit. ~heroic, *a. & n.* burlesquing, burlesque imitation of, the heroic style. **mŏck'ery**, *n.* derision, laughing-stock ; futile action. **mocking-bird**, kinds that mimic other birds' notes.

---

mō′dal, *a.* of mode or form and not of substance. **modál′ity**, *n.* (esp.) method laid down for discharge of obligation, &c.

mōde, *n.* way in which thing is done; current fashion.

mŏd′el, *n.* representation of designed or actual object; design or style to be followed; person employed by artist to pose, or by draper, &c. to show off clothes. *v.t.* mould, fashion; give shape to, form.

mŏd′erate, *a.* (-ĭt), not given to extremes; (of cost, &c.) not excessive; middling in quantity or quality. *n.* (-ĭt), politician of moderate views. *v.t. & i.* (-āt), make or become less violent or excessive; act as moderator. ~ā′tion, *n.* moderating; moderateness. **mŏd′erātor**, *n.* mediator; president of presbytery or any Presbyterian body; kind of oil lamp.

mŏd′ern, *a.* of the present and recent times; new-fashioned. *n.* (esp. in pl.) person living in modern times. ~ity, *n.*

mŏd′ernism, *n.* tendency to subordinate tradition to harmony with modern thought. ~ist, *n.*

mŏd′ernize, *v.t. & i.* (-zable), assimilate to modern needs; adopt modern views. ~zation, *n.*

mŏd′est, *a.* not overrating one's own merit; unassuming; not excessive; pure-minded, decorous. **mŏd′esty**, *n.* modestness.

mŏd′icum, *n.* what is barely enough; small quantity.

mŏd′ify, *v.t.* (-iable), tone down, qualify; make less severe; change form of. ~fication, *n.*

mō′dish, *a.* fashionable.

modiste′ (-ēst), *n.* milliner or dressmaker.

mŏd′ulate, *v.t. & i.* (-lable), vary or regulate the pitch; attune; (Mus.) change key. ~tion, *n.*

‖ **mō′dus ŏperan′dī**, method of procedure. ‖ **mō′dus vīvĕn′dī**, compromise pending settlement of dispute.

mofŭss′il, *n.* (Anglo-Ind.) in India,

the country as distinct from the 'Presidency'; rural localities as distinct from the chief station.

Mogŭl′, *n.* a Mongol or Mongolian; *Great ~, Grand ~, the ~,* emperor of Delhi; (transf.) a great personage; (pl.) playing cards of the best quality.

mō′hair, *n.* hair of Angora goat; yarn or fabric of it.

Mohămm′édan, **Mahŏm′étan** (ma-h-), *a.* of Mohammed or the religion founded by him. *n.* believer in Mohammed. **Mohăm′-médanism**, *n.*

mō′hur, *n.* gold coin of British India (15 rupees).

moid′ōre, *n.* Portuguese gold coin (27s.).

moi′ety, *n.* a half.

moil, *v.i.* drudge.

moire (mwahr), *n.* watered fabric, usu. silk. **moiré** (mwahr′ā), *a.* having watered surface.

moist, *a.* slightly wet, humid. **moi′sten** (-sn), *v.t. & i.* make, become, moist. **mois′ture**, *n.* liquid in a diffused or absorbed state.

mōke, *n.* (sl.) donkey; *negro.

mō′lar, *a.* (of teeth) serving to grind. *n.* a molar tooth.

molăss′es (-z), *n.* drainings of raw sugar; treacle.

mōle¹, *n.* permanent dark excrescence on the skin.

mōle², *n.* small burrowing animal with short dark fur. ~hill, mound thrown up by mole. ~skin, mole's fur; kind of fustian like it.

mōle³, *n.* stone pier, breakwater, or causeway.

mŏ′lécule (*or* mō-), *n.* one of the uniform particles of which a homogeneous substance is composed. **molĕc′ūlar**, *a.*

molĕst′, *v.t.* subject to intentional annoyance. **mŏlĕstā′tion**, *n.*

mŏll′ify, *v.t.* (-fiable), soften, calm down. ~fication, *n.*

mŏll′usc, *n.* one of the *Mollusca,* a sub-kingdom of soft-bodied animals, often with hard shells, including snails, oysters, &c.

---

mäte, mēte, mīte, mōte, mūte, mōōt; răck, rĕck, rick, rŏck, rŭck, rōōk;

mŏll'ў̌cŏddle, *n.* effeminate creature. *v.t. & i.* coddle, coddle oneself.

Mŏ'loch (-k), *n.* Canaanite idol to which children were sacrificed (often used fig.); the thornlizard or thorn-devil, a hideous Australian reptile.

mŏlÿbdē'nŭm, *n.* a rare silverywhite metallic element.

molten, *p.p.* of melt.

mō'ment, *n.* point or brief space of time. **~ary**, *a.* lasting only a moment. **momĕn'tous**, *a.* of great importance.

momĕn'tum, *n.* (pl. *-ta*), quantity of motion of a moving body; (pop.) impetus gained by movement.

mŏn'achal (-k-), *a.* monastic. **mŏn'achism** (-k-), *n.*

mŏn'ad, *n.* a unit; a simple organism assumed as the first term in evolution. **monăd'ic**, *a.*

mŏn'arch (-k-), *n.* imperial or royal ruler of a State. **monărc'hal**, **~arc'hic(al**, *aa.*); **~ism**, **~ist**, *nn.* **mŏn'archÿ** (-k-), *n.* monarchical system or State.

mŏn'astery, *n.* residence of community of monks. **monăs'tic**, *a.* of monks or monasteries. **~ticism**, *n.* life in monasteries.

Monday (mŭn'dǐ), *n.* second day of the week, sacred to the Moon.

mo'nětarÿ (mŭn-), *a.* of coinage or money.

mo'nětize (mŭn-), *v.t.* make into or recognize or put into circulation as money. **~zation**, *n.*

mo'ney (mŭ-), *n.* (pl. *-eys*), current coin; banknotes or other documents representing it; wealth. **~changer**, person giving the equivalent of money in another coinage. **~lender**, usurer. **~market**, haunts and operations of dealers in stocks and bills. **~spinner**, kind of small spider.

moneyed (mŭn'ǐd), *a.* wealthy.

Mŏng'ol, Mŏngō'lian (-ngg-), *aa.* of a race now inhabiting Mongolia. *nn.* a Mongol person; the Mongolian language.

mŏng'ōōse (-ngg-), *n.* E.-Ind. ichneumon, noted for killing venomous snakes.

mo'ngrel (mŭngg-), *a.* of mixed breed or type. *n.* a mongrel animal; hybrid plant or person.

mŏn'ism, *n.* forms of doctrine maintaining that there is only one kind of being. **mŏn'ist**, *n.*

moni'tion, *n.* admonition; legal or official notice to do or refrain from doing something.

mŏn'ĭtor, *n.* person who gives advice or admonishes; senior schoolboy placed in authority; ironclad with revolving gun-turrets. **monĭtō'rial**, *a.* (esp. in school sense). **mŏn'ĭtress**, *n.* **mŏn'ĭtorÿ**, *a.* giving or serving as warning.

monk (mŭ-), *n.* member of male community living apart under religious vows. **~'s-hood**, kinds of flowering plant, aconite.

mo'nkey (mŭ-), *n.* (pl. *-eys*), kinds of mammal closely allied to man; (sl.) temper; (sl.) £500. *v.i.* play tricks (*with*). **~bread**, fruit of baobab tree. **~nut**, peanut. **~puzzle**, kind of prickly tree. **~shines**, monkey-like tricks. **~tricks**, mischievous tricks.

monk'ish (mŭ-), *a.* of monks.

mŏn'ochord (-k-), *n.* one-stringed musical instrument; one-stringed appliance for determining musical intervals.

mŏn'ochrōme (-k-), *n.* one-colour picture or design. **~măt'ic**, *a.*

mŏn'ocle, *n.* single eye-glass.

mŏnocŏtyle'don, *n.* member of the single-cotyledon division of flowering plants. **~ous**, *a.*

monŏc'ūlar, *a.* one-eyed.

mŏn'odÿ, *n.* dirge or elegy.

monŏg'amÿ, *n.* custom by which one man or male has one wife or mate. **~mist**, *n.*; **~mous**, *a.*

mŏn'ogram, *n.* set of letters interwoven in one design.

mŏn'ograph (-ahf), *n.* treatise on a single subject. **~ic**, *a.*; **~ist**, *n.*

mŏn'olith, *n.* single block of stone as pillar, &c. **mŏnolĭth'ic**, *a.*

mŏn'ologue (-g), *n.* soliloquy;

---

mãre, mēre, mīre, mõre, mūre; pãrt, pãrt, põrt; *italics*, vague sounds;

dramatic composition in which only one person speaks.

mŏnomā'nia, *n.* madness on a single subject. ~**mā'niăc**, *n.*

mŏnomét'allism, *n.* use of one metal as standard of currency.

mŏn'oplāne, *n.* aeroplane with one plane.

monŏp'olist, *n.* one who holds or favours a monopoly.

monŏp'olize, *v.t.* (-zable), secure monopoly of. ~**zation**, *n.*

mŏnŏp'olў, *n.* exclusive privilege of the trade in something; sole possession or control of.

mŏn'orail, *n.* railway with cars running on a single rail.

mŏnosyll'able, *n.* word of one syllable. **mŏnosўllăb'ic**, *a.*

mŏn'othēism, *n.* doctrine that there is only one God. ~**thēist**, *n.*; ~**thēis'tic**, *a.*

mŏn'otōne, *n.* successive sounds or utterance without change of pitch. *v.t. & i.* recite in monotone. **monŏt'onous**, *a.* unvarying in tone; wearisome. **monŏt'onў**, *n.* monotonousness.

mŏn'otype, *n.* method of producing single letters of movable type, and assembling them into readable matter, by means of composing and casting machines; also used *attrib.* P.

monseigneur (mɔ̃wnsěnyĕr'), *n.* French title for dignitaries.

monsieur (mesyĕr'), *n.* (pl. *messieurs*), (as French title, abbr. *M.*) Mr.; sir; Frenchman.

mŏnsoon', *n.* seasonal wind, esp. those blowing in Indian Ocean from SW. in summer and from NE. in winter.

mŏn'ster, *n.* mis-shapen creature; person or thing of portentous appearance or size; miscreant.

mŏn'strance, *n.* vessel in which the Host is exposed.

mŏnstrŏs'itў, *n.* monstrousness; mis-shapen or outrageous thing.

mŏn'strous, *a.* of the nature of a monster; huge; outrageous.

month (mŭ-), *n.* period of moon's revolution; any of the twelve divisions of a year. **month'lў**

(mŭn-), *a.* recurring, payable, &c. once a month; *n.* monthly magazine; *adv.* once a month.

mŏn'ūment, *n.* anything designed or serving to commemorate something. **mŏnūmen'tal**, *a.* of or serving as monument; colossal or stupendous.

mōoch, *v.i.* (colloq.) slouch along, loiter about.

mōod¹, *n.* any of the groups of forms in conjugation of verb that serves to indicate its function.

mōod², *n.* state of mind or feeling. **mōod'ў**, *a.* subject to changes of mood; depressed, sullen.

mōol'vee, *n.* Mohammedan doctor of the law; in India, a complimentary term for a teacher of Arabic, or any learned man.

mōon, *n.* satellite revolving round earth in lunar month and reflecting light from sun; (poet.) month. *v.i.* go dreamily or listlessly about. ~**calf**, born fool. ~**light**, light of moon; ; ~**light** flitting, removal by night to avoid payment of rent. ~**lighter**, committer of agrarian outrages by night in Ireland. ~**shine**, visionary stuff; *(sl.)* illicitly distilled spirits. *~**shiner**, (sl.) illicit distiller, spirit-smuggler. ~**stone**, pearly feldspar. ~**struck**, lunatic. **mōon'ў**, *a.* dreamy.

mōon'shee, **mun'shi** (-ō-), *n.* native secretary or language teacher in India.

moor¹, *n.* tract of uncultivated and often heather-clad ground. ~**cock**, cock grouse. ~**hen**, water-hen. ~**land**, *n.*

Moor², *n.* one of a Mohammedan race of N.W. Africa. ~**ish**, *a.*

moor³, *v.t.* attach (boat, &c.) by rope to shore or something fixed. ~**age**, *n.* place, charge made, for mooring. ~**ing**, *n.* (usu. pl.) anchored chains, &c. to which boat, &c. is moored.

mōose, *n.* N.-Amer. elk.

mōot, *n.* (hist.) meeting, esp. of legislative or judicial kind. *v.t.*

raise (question) for discussion. ~ case or point, matter on which opinions differ.

mŏp, n. bundle of yarn, &c. fixed to stick for use in cleaning. v.t. clean or wipe with mop-head or absorbent stuff.

mōpe, v.i. be in depressed spiritless state. n. person given to moping; (pl.) dumps. **mō'pish**, a. inclined to mope.

mopoke. See morepork.

moraine', n. débris deposited by glacier.

mŏ'ral, a. concerned with right and wrong conduct; practising virtue. n. the guidance deducible from a fable, incident, &c.; (pl.) conduct of person, nation, &c., as compared with the moral law.

morale' (-ahl), n. discipline and spirit pervading an army or other body of persons.

mŏ'ralist, n. person given to moralizing; person for whom morality requires no religious sanction. **moralist'ic**, a.

morăl'ĭty, n. ethics; morals; moral conduct; kind of moralizing drama.

mŏ'ralize, v.i. & t. (-zable). talk on the moral aspect of things; draw the moral of.

morăss', n. marsh, slough.

morātō'rium, n. legal authorization to defer payment.

Morā'vian, n. native of Moravia; member of a Hussite protestant sect.

morb'ĭd, a. not natural and healthy; diseased.

morbif'ĭc, a. causing disease.

mŏrd'ant, a. (of wit, &c.) biting, stinging; (of pain) acute; (of acids, &c.) corrosive or cleansing. n. mordant substance. ~ncy, n.

mōre, a. & pron. a greater or additional quantity or number (of). adv. to a greater degree or extent or amount. ~ō'ver, adv. besides what has been already said; and further.

moreen', n. a stuff for curtains.

mōre'pŏrk, mō'pōke, n. in New

Zealand, an owl; in Tasmania night-jar; in Australia, various birds.

Morĕsque' (-k), a. Moorish in style.

mŏrganăt'ic, a. ~ marriage, one between man of exalted rank and woman of lower rank, who remains in her former station.

mŏrgue (-g), n. identification mortuary in Paris.

mŏ'ribund, a. at the point of death; likely soon to perish.

mŏ'rion, n. (hist.) steel cap.

Mŏrm'on, n. member of a U.S. Christian sect that formerly practised polygamy. ~ism, n.

mŏrn, n. (poet.) morning.

mŏrn'ing, n. the day from dawn till noon or the midday meal. ~ watch, (Naut.) 4-8 a.m.

morŏcc'ō, n. (pl. -os), leather of goatskin tanned with sumac.

morōse', a. of bitter unsociable temper; sullen.

Mŏrph'eus, n. God of dreams.

mŏrph'ia, mŏrph'ine, nn. narcotic principle of opium. **mŏrph'inism**, n. state induced by excessive use of morphia.

mŏrphŏl'ogy, n. branch of biology, or of philology, dealing with forms. ~gical, a.; ~gist, n.

mŏ'rris, or ~ dance, nn. kinds of dance, with bells, cudgels, &c.

mŏ'rris tūbe, n. appliance by which rifle is adapted for practice on miniature range.

mŏ'rrow (-ō), n. day that follows a day or event.

mŏrse[1], n. walrus.

Mŏrse[2], n. ~ alphabet, code, signals, &c. for use in telegraphy, signalling, &c.

mŏrs'el, n. mouthful, bit; small quantity.

mŏrt'al, a. subject to or causing death; (sl.) very great. n. human being. **mŏrtăl'ĭty**, n. being mortal; human beings; death-rate.

mŏrt'ar, n. vessel in which drugs, food, &c. are pounded with a pestle; short gun throwing shells; mixture of lime, water,

zh, as (rou)ge : ŏ = 1 ; ŏ, ŏ, = ŏr ; ȳ, ẏ, = 1, ĭ ; and see p. 4. * = U.S.

3495 L

&c. used in building. ~board, on which building mortar is held for use; square college cap.

mortgage (morˈgij), *n.* conveyance of property as security for debt until money is repaid. *v.t.* make over by mortgage; pledge. **mortgagor** (morgˈajor); *n.* person who mortgages. **mortgagee'** (morg-), *n.* person to whom mortgage is given.

morˈtify, *v.t. & i.* (-fiable), chasten (flesh, &c.) by repression; humiliate, chagrin; be affected with gangrene. ~fication, *n.*

morˈtise, **-ice**, *n.* hole made in piece of wood, &c. to receive the end of another piece. *v.t.* (-sable), make mortise in; join by mortise.

mortˈmain, *n.* condition of land, &c. held inalienably by a corporation.

mortˈuary, *a.* of or for burial. *n.* building for temporary keeping of corpses.

mosaˈic¹ (-z-), *n.* picture or pattern made with small coloured pieces of stone or glass.

Mosaˈic² (-z-), *a.* of Moses.

noselle' (-z-), *n.* a white wine.

*moˈsey (-zi), *v.i.* (sl.) go away (in a specified manner).

Mosˈlem, **Musˈlim** (-z-), *a. & n.* Mohammedan.

mosque (-k), *n.* Mohammedan place of worship.

mosquiˈto (-kē-), *n.* (pl. *-oes*), kinds of gnat, some biting severely, some carrying malaria.

moss, *n.* swamp, peat-bog; kinds of small plant growing on moist surfaces. ~rose, with moss-like growth on calyx and stalk. ~trooper, 17th-c. border freebooter. **mossˈy**, *a.* moss-grown.

most, *a.* the greatest number or quantity of. *pron.* the greatest amount; the greater part of. *adv.* to a great or the greatest degree or extent or amount. **mostˈly**, *adv.* for the most part.

‖ **mot** (mō). *n.* (pl. *-s* pr. mōz), witty saying.

mote, *n.* particle of dust.

moth, *n.* kinds of winged insect

resembling butterflies. ~eaten, injured by moths; antiquated. **mothˈy**, *a.* infested with moths.

moˈther (mŭdh-), *n.* female parent; head of nunnery, &c.; old woman. *v.t.* be mother of (usu. fig.); act as mother to. ~in-law, a wife's or husband's mother. ~ of pearl, iridescent lining of oyster and other shells. "M~'s Day, day for honouring motherhood, second Sunday in May. ~ tongue, one's native language. **moˈtherhood**, *n.* office or state of a mother. **moˈthering** (mŭdh-), *n.* custom of visiting parents and giving or receiving presents on Mid-lent Sunday (called *Mothering Sunday*). **moˈtherless**, ~ly, *aa.*

‖ **motif'** (-ēf), *n.* a distinct element or feature in a composition; lace, &c., ornament on dress, &c.

moˈtion, *n.* moving; a gesture; proposal for action to be taken. *v.i. & t.* make significant gestures; direct by gesture. ~less, *a.*

moˈtive, *a.* productive of motion or action. *n.* what impels a person to action. *v.t.* (alsomoˈtivate), supply a motive to; be the motive or motif of. ~vation, *n.* **moˈtivity**, *n.* motive quality.

motˈley, *a.* parti-coloured; heterogeneous. *n.* fool's motley garb.

moˈtor. *n.* what imparts motion; machine supplying motive power, internal-combustion engine, (attrib.) propelled by such machine, as ~ *bicycle, -boat, -car*; (Anat.) muscle or nerve producing motion. *v.i. & t.* go, convey, by motor-car. ~car, motor-carriage for use on roads. ~man, (U.S. & Canada) driver of electric street-car or locomotive. **moˈtorist**, *n.* user of motor-car.

motˈtle, *v.t.* make mottled. *n.* mottled surface. **motˈtled** (-tld), *a.* showing colours in blotches.

motˈto, *n.* (pl. *-oes*), a saying chosen for inscription or quotation.

mouˈjik (mōōzh-), *n.* Russian peasant.

---

māte, mēte, mite, mŏte, mŭte, mŏŏt ; rāck, rĕck, rick, rŏck, rŭck, rŏŏk

mould[1] (mōld), *n.* loose earth ; soil rich in organic matter.

mould[2] (mōld), *n.* woolly fungous growth formed on moist surfaces.

mould[3] (mōld), *n.* matrix in which metal is cast ; vessel used to give shape to metal, &c. ; form or character ; gauge or pattern used in making mouldings. *v.t.* form or shape according to a pattern.

moul′der (mōl-), *v.i.* decay to dust ; crumble away.

mould′ing (mōl-), *n.* piece of ornament running along some line in a building.

mould′y (mōl-), *a.* covered with mould ; (fig.) stale, antiquated.

moult (mōlt), *v.i. & t.* shed feathers ; shed (feathers) in changing plumage. *n.* moulting.

mound, *n.* heap or bank of earth ; *(Baseball)* pitcher's box.

mount, *n.* mountain or hill ; card, &c. on which photograph, &c. is mounted ; horse, &c. on which person is or to be mounted. *v.i. & t.* ascend, go upwards ; climb on to ; put upon or provide with horse, &c. ; provide with supports or setting.

moun′tain (-tĭn), *n.* hill of impressive height ; large heap of something. ~**eer,** *n.* dweller in mountains ; mountain-climber. *v.i.* climb mountains as a recreation. ~**ous,** *a.* abounding in mountains ; huge.

moun′tebank, *n.* quack discoursing and dispensing on platform in street, &c. ; a charlatan.

mourn (mōrn), *v.i. & t.* be sorrowful or distressed ; grieve for the loss of. ~**er,** *n.* one who mourns ; person attending funeral. ~**ing,** *n.* lamentation ; clothes worn in sign of bereavement. ~**ful,** *a.*

mouse, *n.* (mows), (pl. *mīce*), kinds of small rodent. *v.i.* (-z), hunt mice. **mous′er** (-z-), *n.* mousecatcher, esp. cat.

mousse (mōōs), *n.* dish of flavoured cream whipped and frozen.

moustache (mustahsh′), *n.* the hair of the upper lip.

mouth, *n.* (pl. pr. -dhz), the cavity of the head used in eating and speaking ; opening at which anything enters ; outfall of river ; (sl.) impudent talk. *v.t. & i.* (mowdh), grimace in speaking ; touch with the mouth. ~**organ,** kinds of musical instrument. ~**piece,** part of musical instrument or tobacco or tobacco pipe placed between lips ; person commissioned to speak for others.

move (mōōv), *v.t. & i.* (-vable), change position, posture, place, or abode ; stir or rouse ; affect with emotion ; propose as a resolution. *n.* moving of piece at chess, &c. ; (fig.) step or proceeding. **movables** (mōōv′ablz), *n.pl.* personal property. **move′ment** (mōōvm-), *n.* moving ; combined endeavour ; main division of a musical work. **mo′ver** (mōō-), *n.* source of motion ; originator ; proposer of motion. *movies* (mōō′ĭz), *n.pl.* (sl.) cinema pictures.

mo′ving (mōō-), *a.* ~**pictures,** movies. ~**staircase,** made on endless chain principle, with steps moving up or down continuously.

mow, *n.* stack of hay, corn, &c.

mow[2] (mō), *v.t. & i.* (p.p. *mown* pr. mōn), cut grass, &c. with scythe or machine.

Mr. (mĭs′ter), **Mrs.** (mĭs′ĭz), titles prefixed to name of man or of married woman. **Mrs. Grŭn′dy,** conventional propriety personified.

MS. (ĕm′ĕs′), *n.* manuscript.

much, *a.* a great amount of ; *pron.* a great deal ; a great amount of something. *adv.* to a great degree ; by a great deal. ~**ly,** *adv.* (joc. only). ~**ness,** *n.*

mu′cilage, *n.* viscous substance extracted from plants ; *adhesive gum.* **mucilag′inous,** *a.*

muck, *n.* manure, dirt ; dirty state. *v.t. & i.* make dirty ; (sl.) bungle ; potter. **muck′er,** *n.* (sl.) heavy fall ; bungler ; **muck′y,** *a.*

mū'cus, *n.* thick fluid secreted by mucous membrane. **mū'cous**, *a.*

mŭd, *n.* mixture of dust or earth with water. **~guard**, appliance protecting cyclist, &c., from mud. **~lark**, street arab. **mŭdd'y̆**, *a.* dirty with mud; (of water) turbid; *v.t.* spatter with mud.

mudar', *n.* E.-Ind. shrub.

mŭd'dle, *v.t. & i.* bewilder; bungle, mix up; carry on or put things through in haphazard way. *n.* confused state.

muĕzz'in (moo-), *n.* Mohammedan crier who proclaims hours of prayer from minaret.

mŭff[1], *n.* cover of fur, &c. for the hands carried by women.

mŭff[2], *n.* unenterprising person; bungler. *v.t.* fail in, bungle; miss (catch, ball, chance, &c.).

mŭff'in, *n.* kind of tea-cake eaten hot with butter. **mŭffineer'**, *n.* castor for sprinkling muffins with salt or sugar.

mŭf'fle, *v.t.* wrap up for warmth; deaden sound by wrapping up.

mŭf'fler, *n.* neck-wrap.

mŭf'ti, *n.* plain clothes worn by official off duty.

mŭg, *n.* drinking-vessel; (sl.) mouth or face; (sl.) person who mugs; (sl.) fool or gullible person. *v.i. & t.* (sl.) study hard.

mŭgg'er, *n.* the broad-nosed crocodile of India.

mŭgg'y̆ (-g-), *a.* (of weather, &c.) warm and moist; oppressive.

*mŭg'wŭmp, *n.* great man, boss; one who holds aloof from party politics.

mŭlătt'ō, *n.* (pl. -os), person of mixed negro and white blood.

mŭl'berry, *n.* a dark-red oval compound fruit; tree bearing it.

mŭlch, *n.* wet straw, leaves, &c., put round plant's roots.

mŭlct, *v.t.* fine as a punishment; deprive of, *n.* a fine.

mūle, *n.* offspring of mare by he-ass; any hybrid; obstinate person; kind of spinning-machine. **mūleteer'**, *n.* mule-driver. **mū'lish**, *a.* obstinate, intractable.

mŭll, *v.t.* heat and spice (wine,

beer); make a mess of. *n.* a bungle or failure.

mull'ah, **moo'lah**, *n.* Mohammedan theologian.

mŭll'ein (-in), *n.* kinds of woolly-leaved herb.

mŭll'ĕt, *n.* kinds of sea-fish.

mŭlligatawn'y̆, *n.* E.-Ind. soup made with curry-paste.

mŭll'igrubs (-z), *n.pl.* dumps, low spirits; colic.

mŭll'ion (-yon), *n.* upright separating the lights of a divided window. **~ed**, *a.*

mŭll'ock, *n.* (Austral.) rock which does not contain gold; also, refuse from which gold has been extracted.

mŭltifār'ious, *a.* of many kinds.

mŭl'tiform, *a.* of many forms.

mŭltimillionaire' (-yon-), *n.* person with two or more millions of money.

mŭltinō'mial, *a. & n.* (expression) of more than two terms.

mŭl'tiple, *a.* of many parts, components, origins, &c.; (with pl. n.) more than one. *n.* quantity exactly divisible by another.

mŭl'tiplex, *a.* manifold.

mŭltiplicand', *n.* quantity to be multiplied.

mŭltiplicā'tion, *n.* multiplying, esp. the arithmetical process.

mŭltiplic'ity, *n.* being multiplied.

mŭl'tiplier, *n.* number by which multiplicand is multiplied.

mŭl'tiply, *v.t. & i.* (-cable), make or become many; perform, subject to, multiplication.

mŭl'titūde, *n.* great number; crowd of people. **~u'dinous**, *a.*

‖ **mŭl'tum in pār'vō**, *n.* much in small compass.

mŭm, *int.* enjoining silence or secrecy. *a.* silent. *v.i.* act in dumb show.

mŭm'ble, *v.i. & t.* pronounce, chew (food), like a toothless person. *n.* indistinct talk.

Mŭm'bō Jŭm'bō, *n.* (pl. -os), supposed African idol; any object of senseless veneration.

mŭmm'er, *n*. actor in dumb show; (contempt.) play-actor. **mŭmm'-ery**, *n*. buffoonery; ridiculous ceremonial.

mŭmm'ĭfy, *v.t.* (*-fiable*), make into a mummy. **~fication**, *n*.

mŭmm'y, *n*. embalmed corpse.

mŭmp, *v.i.* be sullen and silent.

mŭmps, *n.pl.* contagious disease with swollen neck and face.

mŭnch, *v.t. & i.* chew steadily.

mŭn'dāne, *a.* worldly; earthly.

mŭnĭ'cipal, *a.* of or carried on by a municipality.

mŭnĭcĭpăl'ĭty, *n*. town or district with local self-government; its governing body.

mŭnĭ'cipalize, *v.t.* bring under municipal control. **~zation**, *n*.

mŭnĭf'ĭcent, *a.* a splendidly generous. **mŭnĭf'ĭcence**, *n*. liberality.

mū'nĭments, *n.pl.* title-deeds and similar records.

mūnĭ'tion, *n*. (sing. only in comb.), (pl.) military weapons, ammunition, equipment, and stores.

mŭnjeet', *n*. Bengal madder; roots of this plant used in dyeing.

munshi. See moonshi.

munt'jac, *n*. small Asiatic deer.

mūr'al, *a.* of, in, on, a wall.

mûr'der, *n*. unlawful killing of person with malice aforethought. *v.t.* kill (human being) unlawfully; spoil by bad execution. &c. **~er**, **~eress**, *nn.*; **~ous**, *a*.

mûr'ex, *n*. shell-fish from which Tyrian purple was got.

mûrk'y, *a.* full of or thick with darkness.

mûrm'ur (*-er*), *n*. subdued continuous sound; subdued expression of discontent; hushed speech. *v.i. & t.* make or utter murmur; utter softly. **~ous**, *a*.

mûrph'y, *n*. (sl.) potato.

mû'rrain (*-rĭn*), *n.* a cattle-disease; (arch.) plague.

mŭs'cadine (*or -ĭn*), *n*. grape tasting or smelling of musk. **mŭsca-dĕl'**, **-'căt**, **-catĕl'**, *nn.* muscadine or wine made from it.

mŭs'cle (*-sl*), *n*. contractile fibrous band or bundle producing

motion in animal body; lean flesh or meat; muscular strength.

Mŭs'covite, *n. & a.* Russian.

mŭs'cūlar, *a.* of, in, the muscles; having much muscle. **~ăr'ĭty**, *n*.

mūse¹ (*-z*), *v.i.* ponder, meditate.

mūse², *n*. The *Muses*, nine sister goddesses to whom inspiration in learning and art was attributed; *the muse*, poet's inspiration or genius.

mūse'um (*-z-*), *n*. building in which objects illustrating art or science are kept for show.

mush¹, *n*. soft pulp; *porridge of (esp. Indian) meal boiled in water. **mush'y**, *a.* soft; (sl.) sentimental.

mush² (U.S. & Canada), *n*. journey across snow with dog-sledge. *v.i.* go on mush.

mush'room, *n*. kinds of edible fungus noted for rapidity of growth; upstart person or thing.

mū'sic (*-z-*), *n*. art of expressing or stirring emotion by harmonious combination of sounds; sounds so combined; record or score of these for reproduction; any pleasant sound. **~hall**, variety theatre. **mū'sical** (*-z-*), *a.* fond of or skilled in music; sweet-sounding. *musicale (zikahl)*, *n.* musical party. **mūsĭ'cian** (*-zĭshn*), *n*.

mŭsk, *n*. substance secreted by male musk-deer used as basis of perfumes; kind of plant. **~deer**, small hornless ruminant of Central Asia. **~rat**, large North-American aquatic rodent; its fur. **~rose**, rambling rose with large fragrant white flowers. **~tree**, various musky-smelling trees.

mŭs'kĕt, *n*. infantryman's gun, esp. of unrifled types. **mŭskĕteer'**, *n*. (hist.) soldier with musket. **mŭs'kĕtry**, *n*. smallarm fire; (Mil.) rifle-firing instruction.

mŭs'ky, *a.* smelling like musk.

mŭs'lin (*-z-*), *n*. cotton gauze for dresses, curtains, &c.; *cotton cloth of coarse heavy kinds.

mŭs'quash (-ŏsh), n. fur of the musk-rat.

*mŭss, v.t. (with *up*) disarrange, throw into disorder. n. state of confusion, untidiness. **'mŭss'ў,** a. untidy, rumpled, tousled.

mŭss'el, n. kinds of bivalve mollusc.

mŭss'uck, n. (Anglo-Ind.) leather water-bag.

Mŭss'ulman, a. & n. Mohammedan.

must¹, n. grape-juice before or during fermentation; new wine.

mŭst², a. (of male elephant or camel) affected by dangerous periodical excitement. n. this state.

must³ (mŭ-, emph. mŭ-), v. aux. be obliged to; be certain to.

mŭs'tăng, n. Mexican wild horse.

mŭs'tard, n. kinds of plant; the ground seeds of some of them; hot condiment made of this.

mŭs'ter, n. assembling of men for inspection, &c. v.t. & i. hold muster of; bring or come together; collect. ~-roll, official list, esp. of officers and men.

mŭs'tў, a. mouldy, antiquated.

mū'table, a. liable to change; fickle. **mūtabĭl'itў,** n.

mūtā'tion, n. change that befalls something.

‖ **mūtā'tis mūtān'dis,** adv. with due alteration of details.

mŭtch, n. (Sc.) woman's or child's linen cap.

mūte¹, a. silent; without speech, dumb; soundless. n. a mute consonant; dumb person; instrument to deaden sound.

mūte², v.i. (of birds) void dung.

mū'tilate, v.t. (-lable), injure, make imperfect, by depriving of a part. ~tion, ~tor, nn.

mūtineer', n. partaker in mutiny.

mū'tinous, a. rebellious.

mū'tinў, n. refusal of body of persons under discipline to obey orders. v.i. engage in mutiny.

*mŭtt, n. (sl.) fool.

mŭtt'er, v.i. & t. speak in low tone; talk covertly. n. muttering.

mŭtt'on, n. sheep's meat.

mū'tūal, a. felt or done by each to the other; bearing the same relation to each other; (improp.) common to two or more.

mŭz'zle, n. beast's nose and mouth; open end of gun-barrel; cage, &c. put on animal's muzzle. v.t. put muzzle on; impose silence on.

mŭzz'ў, a. stupid with drink.

my (mī, mĭ), a. (attrib. only) of, belonging to, affecting, me. int. of surprise (vulg.).

myăl'gia (-ja), n. muscular rheumatism.

my'all, n. Australian acacia.

mўcŏl'ogў, n. study of fungi.

my'ōpe, n. short-sighted person.

mўō'pia, mў'opў, nn. short sight. **mўōp'ic,** a.

mў'riad, n. vast number; (rare) ten thousand. a. vastly or indefinitely numerous.

myrm'idon (mêr-), n. member of person's retinue or following.

myrrh (mêr), n. gum-resin used in perfumes, medicine, &c.

myr'tle (mêr-), n. kinds of plant, esp. a shiny evergreen shrub with fragrant white flowers; *kind of trailing periwinkle.

mўsĕlf' (or mў-), pron. used as refl. form of *me* and as emphatic addition to or substitute for *I* and *me*.

mystē'rious, a. full of, wrapt in, or affecting mystery.

mўs'terў, n. revealed religious truth, esp. one beyond human intelligence; symbolic rite; miracle-play; secrecy; obscurity. n. (arch.) handicraft.

mўs'tic, a. spiritually symbolic; esoteric; of hidden meaning, mysterious. n. holder of mystic view, &c. a. **mўs'ticism,** n.

mўs'tifў, v.t. (-fiable), hoax, bewilder. **mystifica'tion,** n.

myth (or mў-), n. primitive tale imaginatively describing natural phenomena, esp. by personification; fictitious person or thing. **mўth'ic, ~ical,** aa.

mўthŏl'ogў (or mī-), n. body of myths; study of myths. **mўthŏlŏ'gical,** a.; **mўthŏl'ogist,** n.

N

năb, *v.t.* (sl.) catch unexpectedly.

nā′bŏb, *n.* official of Mogul Empire; rich retired Anglo-Indian.

nacĕlle′, *n.* body of pusher aeroplane; car of airship.

nā′cre (-ker), *n.* mother of pearl or shell yielding it.

nā′dir, *n.* point opposite zenith; lowest point; state or time of greatest depression.

năg′, *n.* horse, esp. saddle-horse.

năg², *v.i. & t.* indulge in wearisome fault-finding; worry thus.

nā′gŏr, *n.* Senegal antelope.

naï′ad (nī-), *n.* (pl. *-ds* or *-des* -dēz), water nymph.

nail, *n.* horny growth covering outer tip of human finger or toe; bird's or beast's claw; spike of metal. *v.t.* fasten with nail(s); fix or hold tight; secure, catch. **nail′er**, *n.* nail-maker; (sl.) excellent specimen.

nain′sŏŏk, *n.* fine cotton fabric, orig. Indian.

naïve (nah-ēv′), **naïve**, *a.* artless, unaffected; amusingly simple. **naïveté** (nah-ēv′tā) or **naïv′ĕty**, *n.*

nā′kĕd, *a.* unclothed, nude; defenceless; bare, uncovered; without ornament, addition, support, comment, &c.

năm′bў-păm′bў, *a.* insipidly pretty; mildly sentimental. *n.* namby-pamby stuff or manners.

nāme, *n.* word by which individual person, animal, place, or thing is spoken of or to; family, clan; reputation, fame. *v.t.* (-mable), give a name to; speak of or to by name; nominate; specify. ~**less**, *a.* obscure; left unnamed; unmentionable. ~**ly**, *adv.* that is to say, videlicet. ~**sake**, *n.* person with same name as another.

nänkeen′, *n.* a yellowish-buff cotton cloth; (pl.) trousers of it.

nănn′ў(-goat), *n.* she-goat.

năp′, *v.i.* take short sleep, esp. by day. *n.* spell of such sleep.

năp², *n.* woolly substance on the surface of cloth; pile of hat.

năp³, *n.* a card-game. go ~, take highest risk in this.

nāpe, *n.* back of the neck.

nā′perў, *n.* table-linen.

năph′tha, *n.* inflammable oil distilled from coal, &c. ~**line**, *n.* disinfectant got from coal-tar.

năp′kin, *n.* piece of linen for wiping lips, &c. at table; sanitary towel.

napō′leon, *n.* French gold 20-franc piece; kind of top-boot.

napŏŏ′ (nah-), *int.* (army sl.) vanished !, lost !, finished !

nar′cĕine (or -ĭn), *n.* a sedative got from opium.

narcĭss′us, *n.* (pl. *-ssuses, -ssī*), kinds of flowering bulb.

narcō′sis, *n.* narcotic action, insensible state.

narcŏt′ic, *a.* inducing drowsiness, sleep, or insensibility. *n.* narcotic drug or influence.

narc′otize, *v.t.* (-zable), subject to narcotics. **narcotizā′tion**, **narc′otism**, *nn.* morbid dependence on narcotics.

nard, *n.* aromatic balsam.

nar′ghilĕ (-gǐ-), *n.* Oriental tobacco-pipe, hookah.

narrāte′, *v.t.* (-table), recount, rehearse the facts of; relate in the form of a story. ~**tion**, ~**tor**, ~**tress**, *nn.* **nā′rrative**, *n.* spoken or written recital of connected events; *a.* of, in, by, &c. narration.

nă′rrow (-ō), *a.* of small width in proportion to length; with little margin; illiberal, prejudiced, exclusive. *n.* (usu. pl.) the narrow part of a sound, strait, river, or pass. *v.i. & t.* make or become narrower; lessen, contract. ~**minded**, *a.* nă′rrowlỹ (-ōl-), *adv.* closely; vigilantly.

nar′whal (-wal), *n.* sea-unicorn with tusk developed into horn.

nā′sal (-zl), *a.* of the nose; (of speech) sounded through the nose. *n.* a nasal letter. **nā′salize**, *v.i. & t.* speak nasally; give nasal sound to. ~**zation**, *n.*

năs′cent, *a.* in process of birth; not mature. **nas′cencў**, *n.*

---

māre, mēre, mĭre, mōre, mūre; part, pĕrt, pŭrt; *italics,* **vague sounds;**

nastūr′tium (-shm), *n.* trailing yellow-flowered garden plant.

nas′ty (nah-), *a.* repulsively dirty; obscene; ill-natured, spiteful; unpleasant; disagreeable.

nā′tal, *a.* of birth. **natāl′ity**, *n.* birth-rate.

natā′tion, *n.* act or art of swimming. **nātatōr′ial**, **nā′tatory**, *aa.*

nā′tion, *n.* a people or race distinguished by community of descent, language, history, or political institutions.

nā′tional (-sho-), *a.* of a, or the, nation; common to or characteristic of a whole nation. *n.pl.* one's fellow-countrymen. **nā′tionalism** (-sho-), *n.* patriotic feeling or efforts on behalf of one's country; policy of nationalizing industry. **~ist**, *n.* **nā′tionalism** (-sho-), *n.* national existence; membership of a nation. **nā′tionalize** (-sho-), *v.t.* (-zable), make national; naturalize (foreigner); convert (land, railways, &c.) into national property. **~zation**, *n.*

nā′tive, *a.* inborn, innate; derived from one's country or parents; born in a place, indigenous. *n.* one born in a place; indigenous animal or plant. **nativ′ity**, *n.* birth; horoscope.

nā′tron, *n.* a native carbonate of soda.

nătt′erjack, *n.* kind of toad.

nătt′y, *a.* spruce, trim; deft.

nā′tural (-cher-), *a.* of, according to, or provided by nature; physically existing; not artificial or conventional; (Mus.) not flat or sharp. *n.* half-witted person; (sign indicating) natural note.

nā′turalism (-cher-), *n.* action, morality, religion, or philosophy based on nature alone; realism.

nā′turalist (-cher-), *n.* adherent of naturalism; student of natural history; taxidermist. **~ic**, *a.*

nā′turalize (-cher-), *v.t.* (-zable), admit alien to citizenship; adopt or introduce foreign word, custom, animal, or plant; rationalize. **~zation**, *n.*

nā′turally (-cher-), *adv.* according to nature; without affectation.

nā′ture, *n.* thing's essential qualities; person's or animal's innate character; general characteristics and feelings of mankind; kind, sort, class; physical power causing phenomena of material world; fidelity in art.

naught (nawt), *n.* nothing. *a.* worthless. **naught′y** (nawt-), *a.* badly behaved; disobedient; wicked.

naus′ea, *n.* inclination to vomit; loathing. **naus′eāte**, *v.t. & i.* (-tate), disgust; loathe; feel nausea. **naus′eous**, *a.* loathsome.

nautch, *n.* performance of E.-Ind. dancing-girls. **~girl**, *n.* professional dancing-girl.

naut′ical, *a.* of sailors or navigation.

naut′ilus, *n.* (pl. *-luses*, *-li*), mollusc formerly supposed to sail on sea.

nā′val, *a.* of the navy; of warships; of ships.

nāve¹, *n.* body of church apart from chancel and aisles.

nāve², *n.* central block of wheel; hub.

nā′vel, *n.* pit on belly left by severing of umbilical cord; central point of anything.

nāv′igable, *a.* affording passage for ships; seaworthy; (of balloon) steerable. **~bility**, *n.*

nāv′igāte, *v.i. & t.* voyage, sail ship; sail or steam on or through (sea, river, air); manage, direct course of. **~tion**, **~tor**, *nn.*

năvv′y, *n.* labourer digging, &c. for canals, roads, and railways.

nā′vy, *n.* war-ships with their crews and organization; officers and men of the navy; fleet.

nawab′ (-wawb), *n.* native governor or nobleman in India.

nay, *particle.* no; or rather; and even; why. *n.* a refusal.

Năzarēne′, *a.* of Nazareth; of an early Jewish-Christian sect.

Năz′arīte, *n.* Hebrew under vow of abstinence.

nāze, *n.* headland.

---

ah, awl, oil, boor, cow, dowry; chin, go, bang, so, ship, thin; dh, as th(e)

Neăn'dĕrthal (-tahl), a. ~ man, race, &c., applied to a people inhabiting Europe in the Stone Age.

neap, a. low (applied only to a tide. v.i. (of tides) tend towards neap; (of tide) reach highest point of neap. ~tide or neap, n. tide in which high-water level is at lowest.

Neăpŏl'itan, a. of Naples. n. a Neapolitan person.

near, adv. in proximity in space or time; nearly; closely. prep. near to in space, time, condition, or semblance. a. closely related; close or close to; (of way) direct, short; with little difference; parsimonious; (riding or driving) on the left. v.t. & i. approach. **near'ly**, adv. almost; closely.

neat¹, n. (pl. neat), ox, cow; cattle. ~herd, cowherd.

neat², a. undiluted (of alcoholic drinks); nicely arranged; cleverly phrased; deft, dextrous.

něb, n. (Sc.) beak, nose; tip.

něb'ūla, n. (pl. -ae), luminous patch in sky made by distant star-cluster or gaseous matter něb'ūlar, a. of nebula(e). něb'ūlous, a. cloudlike, hazy, indistinct; vague; formless.

nebū'lium, n. (obs.) element known only as producing green line in spectrum of gaseous nebulae.

ně'cessarў, a. indispensable; that must be done; inevitable. n. thing without which life cannot be maintained; (loosely) something not a luxury that one needs.

necessitār'ian, n. person denying freedom of will. a. pertaining to the doctrine of fatalism. ~ism, n.

necěssĭ'tāte, v.t. render necessary; involve as condition or result.

necěs'sĭtous, a. poor, needy.

necěs'sĭtў, n. constraint or compulsion regarded as a law and governing human action; imperative need; indispensable thing; (usu. pl.) pressing need.

neck, n. part of body connecting head with shoulders; contracted part of anything between wider parts. ~cloth, necktie. ~lace,

ornament round neck. ~let, neck ornament or boa. ~tie, band of silk, &c. tying shirt-collar. ~wear, collars and ties.

něck'ling, n. part of column between shaft and capital.

něc'rŏmancer, n. wizard.

něc'rŏmancў, n. dealings with the dead as means of divination; magic. **něcrŏmān'tic**, a.

necrŏp'ŏlis, n. cemetery, esp. in or for great town.

necrō'sis, n. (pl. -osēs), mortification of piece of bone or tissue. **necrŏt'ic**, a.

něc'tar, n. sweet fluid yielded by plants; kind of aerated water. **něc'tarine**, n. downless kind of peach. **něc'tarous**, a. sweet. **něc'tarў**, n. plant's nectar-producing organ.

║ née (nā), a. fem. having had — as maiden name.

need, n. a want, a requirement; time of difficulty; destitution, poverty. v.i. & t. stand in need of, require; be under necessity to do something. ~ful, a. requisite. ~less, a. uncalled for.

nee'dle, n. pointed headless pin, pierced with eye for thread, &c.; bar of mariner's compass; indicator on dial, esp. in telegraphy; pointed instrument in etching, surgery, &c.; obelisk; sharp rock, peak; slender crystal; leaf of fir or pine. ~fish, garfish. ~gun, with needle exploding cartridge. ~woman, sempstress. ~work, sewing, &c.

needs (-z), adv. of necessity. **need'ў**, a. necessitous.

neem, n. an E.-Ind. tree, the margosa.

ne'er (nār), adv. (poet.) never. ~do-well, good-for-nothing person.

nefār'ious, a. wicked.

negā'tion, n. denying; negative statement; negative or unreal thing. ~ist, n. merely destructive critic, &c.; sceptic.

neg'ative, a. expressing or implying denial, prohibition, or refusal;

wanting positive attributes; opposite to positive. *n.* a negative statement, fact, reply, or word; negative photographic print from which positive prints are taken. *v.t.* (-vable), veto; serve to disprove; contradict; neutralize.

nĕg´atorў, *a.* of the nature of negation.

neglĕct´, *v.t.* slight, not pay attentions to; leave uncared for; leave undone. *n.* neglecting or being neglected; careless treatment; negligence. ~**ful**, *a.*

|| **négligé** (nĕg´lĭzha), *n.* free and easy attire.

nĕg´lĭgence, *n.* want of proper care; heedlessness. nĕg´lĭgent, *a.*

nĕg´lĭgĭble, *a.* that need not be taken account of.

nėgō´tĭable (-sha-), *a.* capable of being negotiated. nĕgō´tĭant (-shi-), *n.* one who negotiates.

nėgō´tĭāte (-shi-), *v.i. & t.* confer with a view to finding terms of agreement; get or give money value for (bill, cheque); deal successfully with. ~**tion**, ~**tor**, ~**tress** *or* ~**trix**, *nn.*

nē´grō, *n.* (pl. *-oes ; fem. negress*), member of black woolly-haired flat-nosed thick-lipped African race. nē´groid, *a. & n.* (person) of a partly negro type.

Nĕ´gus¹, *n.* ruler of Abyssinia.

nē´gus², *n.* hot wine and water.

neigh (nā), *v.i.* utter neigh. *n.* horse's usual cry.

neighbour (nā´ber), *n.* dweller next door, near, in same district, or in adjacent country; person or thing near or next another. ~**hood**, *n.* district; people of a district; vicinity. ~**ing**, *a.* situated close by. ~**ly**, *a.* acting as a neighbour should.

neith´er (nīdh-, nēdh-), *adv.* not either. *conj.* nor; nor yet. *adj. & pron.* not one nor the other.

nĕk, *n.* (S.-Afr.) depression in mountain-chain.

nĕm´esĭs, *n.* retributive justice.

nēō-Hĕll´ēnĭsm, *n.* reversion to Greek ideas.

nēolĭth´ĭc, *a.* of the later Stone Age.

nēŏl´ogĭsm, nēŏl´ogў, *nn.* wordcoining; coined word; theological rationalizing. ~**gist**, *n.* ~**gize**, *v.i.* nēōlō´gĭan, *n. & a.* rationalist(ic) in theology.

nēō-pā´ganism, *n.* reversion to pagan ideas.

nē´ophyte, *n.* new convert; religious novice; beginner, tiro.

nēō-Plā´tonĭsm, *n.* 3rd-century mixture of Platonic ideas with Oriental mysticism.

nēotrŏp´ical, *a.* of, found in, tropical and subtropical parts of S. America.

nėpĕn´the, **-s** (-I-, -ĕz), *n.* carekilling drug; the Pitcher-plant.

nĕ´phew (-v-), *n.* brother's or sister's son.

nephŏl´ogў, *n.* study of the clouds.

nephrĭt´ĭc, *a.* of the kidneys; of or for nephritis. nĕphrī´tis, *n.* inflammation of the kidneys.

|| **nē plūs ŭl´tra**, *n.* farthest attainable point; acme.

nĕp´otĭsm, *n.* favouritism to relatives in bestowing offices.

Nĕp´tūne, *n.* god of the sea; the sea; a planet.

nē´reĭd, *n.* sea nymph; (Zool.) sea centipede.

nerve, *n.* sinew, tendon; (Bot.) rib of leaf; (Anat.) fibrous connexion conveying impulses of sensation or motion between the brain and other parts; (pl.) bodily state as conditioned by relation between brain and other parts; abnormal sensitiveness to annoyance, &c.; presence of mind; coolness in danger; assurance. *v.t.* give strength, vigour, or courage to. nĕrve´less (-vl-), *a.* wanting in vigour; (of style) diffuse.

nĕrv´ous, *a.* sinewy; (of style) terse; of the nerves; full of nerves; excitable, agitated.

nĕrv´ў, *a.* sinewy; impudent; (colloq.) in nervous state.

nescient (nĕsh´yent), *a.* not having knowledge; agnostic. *n.* an agnostic. nescience (nĕsh´yens), *n.*

ness, n. headland.

nest, n. receptacle in which bird lays and hatches; breeding-place or lair; snug retreat, shelter, bed, haunt; brood, swarm; cluster of similar things. v.i. make or have nest in specified place.

ne′stle (-sl), v.i. & t. settle oneself, be settled, comfortably somewhere; lie embedded.

ne′stling (-sl-), n. bird too young to leave nest.

Nes′tor, n. wise old man.

net¹, n. meshed fabric of cord, twine, thread, hair, &c.; piece of this used for catching fish or birds, or for other purposes. v.t. & i. cover, confine, catch, with net; make net; make by netting. ~work, intersecting lines; material formed like net.

net², a. left after all deductions; subject to no deduction. v.t. yield (sum) as net profit.

neth′er (-dh-), a. lower.

‖ **net′suke** (-ooka), n. carved buttonlike ornament worn by Japanese.

nett′ing, n. netted string, &c.

net′tle, n. plant with stinging hairs on leaves. v.t. irritate, provoke. ~-rash, skin-eruption like nettle-stings.

newt, n. a water lizard.

neur′al (nūr-), a. of the nerves. **neuralgia** (nūrăl′ja), n. intermittent neural pain, esp. in face and head. ~ic, a.

neurasthē′nia (nūr-; or -thē-), n. nervous debility. ~ic, a.

neuri′tis (nūr-), n. inflammation of a nerve.

neuro′sis (nūr-), n. (pl. -ōsēs), neurotic action or disorder.

neurot′ic (nūr-), a. suffering from nervous disorder; of abnormal sensibility. n. neurotic person.

neut′er, a. (Gram.) neither masculine nor feminine; (of verb) intransitive; neutral; (Bot.) asexual. n. neuter word, a neuter gender.

neut′ral, a. taking neither side; impartial; indeterminate. n. neutral State or person. **neu-**

trăl′ĭty, n. neut′ralize (-zable), v.t. exempt or exclude by agreement from hostilities; counterbalance; render ineffective. ~zation, n.

nĕv′er, adv. at no time, not ever; (colloq.) surely not. ~more, never again. ~theless, for all that; notwithstanding.

new, a. now first introduced or discovered; fresh, additional; different, changed; recent; not worn.

new′el, n. core of winding stairs; post of stair-rail.

newfăng′led (-nggld), a. different from the old fashion; novel.

Newfound′land, n. large breed of dog noted for swimming.

new′ly, adv. recently, afresh.

New′market, n. close-fitting overcoat; a card-game.

news (-z), n.pl. (usu. with sing. vb. &c.), tidings; fresh events reported. ~agent, dealer in newspapers. ~monger, a gossip. ~paper, periodical publication with the latest news. ~reel, cinema film giving news.

Newtō′nian, a. & n. of, adherent of, Sir Isaac Newton's doctrines.

next, a. nearest; immediately following or preceding. adv. in the next place or degree. prep. in or into the next place or degree. n. the next person or thing.

nex′us, n. bond of connexion.

nib, n. split pen-point; (pl.) crushed cocoa-beans. v.t. mend, insert, nib of pen.

nib′ble, v.t. & i. take small bites at; dally with. n. nibbling.

nib′lick, n. kind of golf club.

nice, a. fastidious; punctilious; subtle, fine; agreeable; kind, friendly, considerate. ~-looking, pretty or engaging.

ni′cĕty, n. precision; minute distinction; unimportant detail.

niche, n. shallow recess for statue or other ornament.

nick, n. notch serving as catch, guide, mark, &c.; critical or opportune moment. v.t. indent;

---

māre, mēre, mĭre, mōre, mūre; part, pert, port; italics, vague sounds;

make a nick in; just catch in time; nab.

nick'el, n. silver-white metallic element used esp. in alloys and as plating; *5 cent coin of nickel alloy. v.t. coat with nickel.

nick'name, n. name added to or substituted for regular name. v.t. call by nickname.

nic'otine (-tēn), n. poisonous oily liquid from tobacco. **nic'otinism,** n. tobacco-poisoning.

nic'tate, nic'titate, vv.i. blink, wink. ~**tion, ~titation,** n.

nid'ificate, nid'ify, vv.i. build nest. ~**fication,** n.

ni'dus, n. (pl. -di, -duses), developing-place of spores, seeds, germs, insects' eggs, &c.; accumulation of eggs, tubercles, &c.

niece, n. one's brother's or sister's daughter.

niell'o, n. (pl. -lli pr. -lē, or -llos), black alloy for filling designs engraved on silver, &c.; piece of niello-work.

*nif'ty, a. (sl.) neat, fashionable.

nigg'ard, n. stingy person; grudging giver. ~**ly,** a. parsimonious.

nigg'er (-g-), n. negro; (loosely) member of other dark-skinned race; (dress, &c.) very deep brown. ~ **heaven,** highest gallery in theatre. ~**minstrels,** singing troupe of sham negroes.

nig'gle, v.i. fiddle; prefer petty detail to broad effects. **nigg'ling,** a. petty; cramped.

nigh (nī), adv. & prep. near.

night (nīt), n. time from sunset to sunrise; the dark. ~**bird,** owl, nightingale; person who goes about by night. ~**club, club** open through night. ~**dress, ~gown,** woman's or child's night attire. ~**fall,** end of daylight. ~**ingale,** small bird singing much by night. ~**jar,** the goatsucker. ~**mare,** horrible dream; any haunting fear. ~**shade,** kinds of plant.

night'ly (nīt-), a. existing or done in the night; recurring every night. adv. every night.

nigres'cent, a. blackish.

nig'ritude, n. blackness.

ni'hilism (nī-), n. philosophic doctrine that nothing has real existence; a form of scepticism; views of Russian revolutionaries opposed to all constituted authority. **ni'hilist** (nī-), n.

nil, n. nothing; no number or amount.

nim'ble, a. agile, swift; (of mind, &c.) quick, clever.

nim'bus, n. (pl. -bi, -buses), cloud of glory, halo, aureole; (Meteor.) storm-cloud.

nim'iny-pim'iny, a. mincing.

Nim'rod, n. hunter, sportsman.

nin'compoop, n. feeble person.

nine, a. & n. one more than eight, 9, IX. ~**fold,** a. & adv. ~**pins,** kind of skittles. **ninth,** a. next after eighth; n. ninth part. **ninth'ly,** adv. in the ninth place.

nine'teen, a. & n. nine and ten, 19, XIX. ~**th,** a. & n.

nine'ty, a. & n. nine times ten, 90, XC. ~**tieth,** a. & n.

nin'ny, n. weak foolish person.

ninon (nē'nawn), n. light-weight silk dress fabric.

nio'bium (= columbium), n. a rare steel-grey metallic element.

nip, v.t. & i. pinch, squeeze sharply; check growth of; (sl.) go nimbly; indulge in drams of spirit. n. pinch, sharp squeeze; cold blast checking growth; dram of spirit. ~ **and tuck,** neck and neck.

nip'per, n. (pl.) forceps or gripping tool; (pl.) pincenez; claw of crab, &c.; a boy.

nip'ple, n. point of mammal's breast; teat of baby's bottle; nipple-like protuberance.

nip'py, a. cold; (sl.) nimble.

nirva'na (-ah-), n. extinction of individuality and absorption into the supreme spirit as the Buddhist highest goal.

nit, n. egg of louse or other parasite; *insignificant person.

ni'trate, n. compound of nitric acid with alkali, &c.

ni'tre (-ter), n. potassium nitrate or saltpetre. **ni'tric,** a.

ni′trify, v.t. & i. make or become nitrous.

ni′trogen, n. an atmospheric gas. nitró′genous, a.

nitrogly′cerine, n. explosive liquid made by adding glycerine to mixture of nitric and sulphuric acids.

ni′trous, a. of, like, or impregnated with nitre.

nit′wit, n. (sl.) fool, idiot.

nix¹, int. (sl.) = cave².

nix², n. (fem. nixie), water elf.

nix³, n. (sl.) nothing.

Nizam′ (-ahm), n. ruler of Hyderabad; Turkish regular army, soldier in it.

no̱, a. not any, not one; nonexistent. adv. not; by no amount; not at all. n. (pl. noes), the word no, a denial or refusal; (pl.) voters against a motion. ~ ball, unlawfully delivered ball in cricket; v.t. (noball) pronounce bowler to have delivered a no ball. ~body, no person; person of no importance. ~how, in no way. ~where, in, at, or to no place. ~wise, in no manner or degree.

No̱′ah (-a). ~'s ark, n. the ark of the Flood; child's toy containing animals, &c. No̱ā′chian, No̱ā′chic (-k-), aa. of (time of) Noah.

nob¹, n. head; (Cribbage) knave of same suit as turn-up.

nob², n. (sl.) member of the upper classes.

nob′ble, v.t. (sl.) tamper successfully with (racehorse, &c.); dishonestly get possession of.

nobb′y, a. (sl.) smart; fine.

nobil′iary (-lya-), a. of nobility.

nobil′ity, n. the noble class; noble character or rank.

no̱′ble, a. illustrious by rank, title, or birth; of lofty character; magnanimous; of imposing appearance. n. member of the nobility; obsolete coin, 6s. 8d. ~man, peer.

‖ noblêsse′, n. the nobility of a foreign country. ‖ ~ oblige (ŏblēzh′), privilege entails responsibility.

nŏctûrn′al, a. of the night.

nŏc′tûrne, n. dreamy musical piece; picture of night scene.

nŏd, n.v.i. & t. incline head slightly and quickly; let head droop, be drowsy; make mistake; (of plumes) dance. n. nodding of head; sign of assent.

nŏd′dle, n. (colloq.) head, pate.

nŏdd′y, n. simpleton; tropical seabird.

no̱de, n. knob on root or branch; hard tumour on joint; intersecting point of planet's orbit and ecliptic; central point of system. no̱′dal, a. no̱′dical, a. (Astron.). no̱dō̱se′, a. knotty, knobbed. no̱dŏs′ity, n.

nŏd′ule, n. small rounded lump of anything; small knotty tumour, ganglion. ~lā′tion, n. arrangement of nodules.

no̱′dus, n. (pl. -dī), knotty point, difficulty; complication.

nŏg, n. small block or peg.

nŏgg′in (-g-), n. small mug.

nŏgg′ing (-g-), n. brickwork, stone, or concrete in timber framing.

noise (-z), n. clamour, din; any sound. v.t. make public, spread abroad. ~less, a.

noisette′¹ (nwahz-), n. kind of rose. noisette′² (nwahz-), n. (usu. pl.) small piece(s) of cooked meat.

nois′ome, a. noxious, disgusting.

nois′y (-zi), a. loud-sounding, clamorous; self-assertive.

‖ no̱lens vo̱lens (-z), adv. willy-nilly, willing or unwilling.

no̱m′ad (or nŏ-), a. roaming from pasture to pasture. n. member of a nomad tribe; wanderer. no̱mad′ic, a.; no̱m′adism, n.

‖ nom de guerre (nŏm de gār′), n. assumed name under which person fights, writes, &c. ‖ ~ de plume (nŏm de ploom′), n. a writer's assumed name.

no̱′menclā̱tor, n. giver of names, esp. in classification.

no̱′menclā̱ture, n. system of names or naming; terminology.

no̱m′inal, a. existing in name or word only. ~ism, n. doctrine that abstract concepts are mere names. ~ist, n.

nŏm′ĭnāte, v.t. (-nable), appoint, propose for election, to office. **~tion**, n. act or power of nominating. **~tor**, n. **nŏminee**′, n. one who is nominated.

nŏm′inative, a. (Gram.) (of case) used as subject ; or in this case. n. nominative case ; a word in the nominative.

nŏn-, pref. negativing the sense of words with which it is combined. For the meanings of such combinations not given below the main word should be consulted.

nŏn′age, n. being under age.

nŏnagēnār′ian, n. person between 89 and 100 years old.

nŏnce, n. In phr. for the ~, for the occasion only.

nŏn′chalant (-sh-), a. unmoved ; indifferent ; cool. **~nce**, n.

nŏn-collē′giate, a. (of student) not belonging to a college ; (of university) not having colleges.

nŏn-commi′ssioned off′icer (-shn-), n. officer of grade below those with commissions.

nŏn-committ′al, a. keeping alternative courses open.

|| **nŏn cŏm′pŏs** (mĕn′tĭs), mad, not responsible.

nŏn-conduc′tor, n. substance or object that does not conduct electricity or heat.

nŏnconform′ist, n. Protestant dissenter. **~ity**, n. nonconformists or their principles, &c. ; failure to conform ; irregularity.

nŏncontĕnt′, n. negative vote(r).

nŏn′descript, a. hard to classify ; indeterminate. n. a nondescript person or thing.

none (nŭn), pron. no person or persons ; no amount. a. no ; not any. adv. by no amount.

nŏnĕn′tity, n. non-existent thing ; person of no account.

nŏnes (-nz), n.pl. (Eccl.) an office originally said at the ninth hour.

nonesuch. See nonsuch.

nŏn-feasance (-fē′zans), n. omission of obligatory act.

nŏn-interven′tion, n. keeping aloof from others′ disputes.

nŏn-jur′or (-joor-), n. one who refused the oath of allegiance to William and Mary. **~jur′ing**, a.

nŏnpareil′ (-rĕl), a. unrivalled, unique. n. person or thing that is unrivalled ; type (6-point) a size larger than that here used.

|| **nŏn plā′cĕt**, n. negative voting form at universities, &c.

nŏnplŭs′, n. perplexity ; standstill. v.t. reduce to a nonplus.

|| **nŏn pŏss′ŭmus**, plea of inability ; refusal to act or permit action.

nŏn-resis′tance, n. 17th-cent. principle that authority must be submitted to however exercised.

nŏn′sense, n. absurd or meaningless words or ideas ; foolish conduct. int. you are talking nonsense. **nŏnsĕn′sical**, a.

|| **nŏn sĕq′uitur** (-er), n. an illogical inference.

nŏn′such, none′such (nŭns-), n. unrivalled person or thing ; paragon ; kind of lucerne.

nŏn′suit (-ūt), n. stoppage of a suit by judge as unsustainable. v.t. subject (plaintiff) to nonsuit.

nŏn-ū′nion (-yon), a. not belonging to a trade-union.

nŏn-ū′ser (-z-), n. failure to exercise a right or duty.

nŏo′dle, n. simpleton.

nŏŏk, n. secluded corner.

nōōn, n. twelve o′clock in the day. **~day, ~tide**, the time about noon.

nōōse, n. cord with running loop at end ; snare. v.t. catch with or enclose in noose.

nor (nôr, nor), adv. neither. conj. and not ; neither.

Nôrd′enfĕlt, n. a machine gun.

Nŏrd′ic, a. of the tall blond dolichocephalic race found esp. in Scandinavia and in northern Britain.

norm, n. recognized type.

nôrm′al, a. (Geom.) at right angles, perpendicular ; illustrating the type ; regular, ordinary. n. (Geom.) normal line ; usual state, level, &c. **nŏrmăl′ity**, n. **~ize**, v.t. ; **~ization**, n.

Nôrm′an, n. native of Normandy.

a. of the Normans. ~esque, *a.* in the Norman style of architecture.

Norse, *n.* the Norwegian language. *a.* Norwegian. ~ma.., *n.*

north, *n.* the point opposite the sun at noon; northern part of a country. *adv.* towards or in the north. *a.* situated, &c. in or towards the north; facing north; coming from north. ~east, region halfway between north and east. ~easter, north-east wind. ~easterly, towards or coming from the north-east. ~eastern, belonging to the north-east, or in that direction. ~eastwards, towards or in the north-east. ~polar, of the north pole. ~ pole, see pole². ~ star, the polar star. ~west, &c., like *north-east*, &c. ~nŏrth′er (-dh-), *n.* wind or storm from the north. north′erly̆ (-dh-), *a.* & *adv.* (of direction) towards; (of wind) from, north or thereabouts. north′ern (-dh-), *a.* situated in or belonging to or characteristic of the north (~ *lights*, Aurora Borealis). north′erner (-dh-), *n.* native of the north. north′ward, *a.*, *adv.*, & *n.* ; ~wards, *adv.*

Norwe′gian (-jn), *a.* of Norway. *n.* N. person or language.

nŏr′-wĕst′er, *n.* north-wester; glass of strong liquor; oilskin hat.

nose, *n.* member of face or head placed above mouth; sense of smell; open end of nozzle of pipe, &c. ; prow; projecting part. *v.t.* & *i.* perceive smell of, discover by smell; detect; thrust nose into; pry or search after. ~bag, bag hung to horse's head with fodder. ~dive, *n.* aeroplane's downward plunge; *v.i.* make nose-dive. ~gay, bunch of flowers. ~ring, ring fixed in nose of bull, &c. for leading; ornament worn by savages.

nō′sing (-z-), *n.* edge of step, &c., or shield for it.

nosŏl′ogy̆, *n.* the classification of diseases.

nŏstăl′gia (-ja), *n.* home-sickness. nŏstăl′gĭc, *a.*

nŏs′tril, *n.* opening in nose.

nŏs′trum, *n.* quack remedy, patent medicine; pet scheme.

nō′sy̆ (-z-), *a.* large-nosed (sl.) ; inquisitive (sl.) ; ill-smelling.

nŏt, *adv.* expressing negation, refusal, or denial. ~ half, (sl.) very, very much.

|| nō′ta bē′nē, *v.imperat.* observe, note this (abbrev. N.B.).

nō′table, *a.* worthy of note, striking. *n.* eminent person. ~bility, *n.* notable person or thing.

nō′tary̆, *n.* person with authority to draw up deeds and perform other formalities. notăr′ial, *a.*

notā′tion, *n.* representing of numbers, quantities, &c. by symbols; any set of such symbols.

notch, *n.* V-shaped indentation on edge or convex surface; run scored at cricket. *v.t.* make notches in ; make (specified score) at cricket. nŏtch′y̆, *a.*

note, *n.* written sign representing single sound in music; single tone of definite pitch made by instrument, voice, &c. ; sign, characteristic; brief record of facts, &c. for speech, &c. (usu. pl.) ; comment on passage in book; short letter; formal diplomatic communication. *v.t.* observe, notice; set down as thing to be remembered; (*p.p.*) celebrated, well known. ~book, book in which memoranda are set down. ~paper, letter-paper.

note′worthy̆ (-twĕrdh-), *a.* worth remembering; remarkable.

nŏ′thing (nŭ-), *n.* not anything; naught; no amount, nought; thing of no importance; (with pl.) trifling thing or remark. *adv.* not at all ; in no way. ~ness, *n.* non-existence; worthlessness.

nō′tice, *n.* intimation, warning, announcement; newspaper review or comment. *v.t.* (-ceable) perceive, take notice of; remark upon. ~board, board for posting notices on.

nō′tify̆, *v.t.* report, give notice of;

inform. ~fiable, *a*. that must be notified. ~fication, *n*.

nō′tion, *n*. concept; idea, conception; view, opinion; *an appliance, useful article. ~al, *a*.

Nōtogaea′ (-jēa), *n*. large zoological region, comprising the Australian, New Zealand, and Neotropical regions.

notōr′ious, *a*. known and talked of; known to deserve an ill name. nōtori′ety, *n*.

nōtwithstand′ing, *prep*. in spite of. *adv*. nevertheless.

nought (nawt), *n*. figure 0; no number or quantity. (Usu. *naught* in other senses.)

noumē′non, *n*. (pl. -*ena*), object of intellectual intuition.

noun, *n*. word used as name of person or thing; substantive.

nou′rish (nŭ-), *v.t.* sustain with food (lit. & fig.); keep up (hope, resentment, &c.). ~ing, *a*. containing nourishment. ~ment, *n*. sustenance, food, nutrition.

nous, *n*. the pure intellect; (sl.) common sense, gumption.

nŏv′el, *a*. of new kind; strange; hitherto unknown. *n*. a fictitious prose tale of considerable length. nŏvelětte′, *n*. a short novel. nŏv′elist, *n*. writer of novels. nŏv′elty, *n*. a novel thing or occurrence.

Nověm′ber, *n*. eleventh month.

nŏv′ice, *n*. probationary member of religious order; beginner, tiro. novic′iate, -tiate (-shi-), *n*. period of being a novice; a novice; novice's quarters.

now, *adv*. at the present time; in the immediate past. *n*. this time; the present. ~aday, *a*. of nowadays. ~adays, *adv*. in our time; as things are now; *n*. these times.

noways, -where, -wise. See *no*.

nŏ′xious (-kshŭs), *a*. harmful; unwholesome.

nŏz′zle, *n*. pointed and bored piece attached to hose, &c.

nuance (nū′ahns), *n*. delicate difference in shade of meaning, feeling, colour, &c.

*nŭbb′in, *n*. small imperfect ear of maize.

nū′bile, *a*. marriageable (of women), nūbil′ity, *n*.

nū′cleus, *n*. (pl. -*ei*), central part or thing around which others collect; kernel. nū′clear, *a*.

nūde, *a*. naked, unclothed. *n*. picture or sculpture of the nude. nū′dity, *n*. nakedness; specimen of the nude.

nūdge, *v.t.* & *n*. push with elbow to bespeak attention.

nū′gatory, *a*. futile, trifling; inoperative, not valid.

nŭgg′et (-g-), *n*. lump of gold.

nuis′ance (nū-), *n*. source of annoyance; obnoxious act, circumstance, thing, or person.

null, *a*. void, not valid; expressionless; non-existent.

nŭll′ah (-*a*), *n*. stream, watercourse, ravine, in India.

nŭll′ify, *v.t.* neutralize; make invalid. ~fication, *n*.

nŭll′ity, *n*. lack of force or efficacy; a nonentity.

numb (-m), *a*. torpid; deprived of sensation. *v.t.* make numb.

nŭm′ber, *n*. aggregate of units, sum, company; word or symbol stating how many; numbered issue of periodical, &c.; (pl.) groups of musical notes; metrical feet; verses. *v.t.* count; mark or distinguish with a number; have or amount to specified number. ~less, *a*. innumerable.

nŭm′dah, nŭm′nah, *n*. (Anglo-Ind.), kind of felt or coarse woollen cloth; saddle-cloth or pad made of this.

nū′merable, *a*. countable.

nū′meral, *a*. of number; denoting a number. *n*. word or figure denoting a number.

nŭmerā′tion, *n*. numbering; conversion of numerals from symbols into words. nū′merātor, *n*. one who counts; number above the line in vulgar fractions.

nŭmě′rical, *a*. of, in, or denoting number.

nū′merous, *a*. comprising many units; (with pl. noun) many.

numismăt'ic (-z-), a. of coins or coinage. numismăt'ics, n. science and study of coins and medals. numis'matist, numismatŏl'ogy (-z-), nn.

numm'ary, numm'ulary, aa. of, in, coin. numm'ulite, n. coin-shaped fossil shell.

num'met, n. (dial.) lunch.

numnah. See numdah.

num'skull, n. dolt or his head.

nun, n. woman living in convent under religious vow; kinds of bird and moth.

nun'cio (-shi-), n. (pl. -os), Pope's envoy. nun'ciature (-shatūr), n. nuncio's office; tenure of it.

nunc'ūpate, v.t. declare, make will, by word of mouth only. ~tion, ~tor, nn.; ~tive, a.

nunn'ery, n. convent of nuns.

nup'tial (-shl), a. of wedlock or wedding. n.pl. wedding.

nurse, n. woman who suckles another's child, or has charge of child; person trained for care of the sick. v.t. & i. suckle, give suck; act as nurse, to be a nurse; foment, encourage. nurse'ling (-sl-), n. infant in relation to its nurse. nurs'ery, n. children's quarters.

nur'ture, n. bringing up, fostering care; food. v.t. (-rable), bring up, rear.

nut, n. fruit consisting of hard shell enclosing edible kernel; (sl.) head; (sl.) dandified young man; *blockhead, lunatic; piece screwed on at end of bolt to secure it; (pl.) small lumps of coal. v.i. seek or gather nuts. ~brown, brown as a nut. ~cracker, a bird. ~crackers, instrument for cracking nuts. ~gall, gall of dyer's-oak used in dyeing. ~hatch, a bird. ~tree, esp. the hazel.

nutā'tion, n. nodding; oscillation of the earth's axis.

nut'meg, n. hard aromatic seed of an Indian tree used as spice, &c. ~grater, appliance for grating nutmeg.

nū'tria, n. fur of a S.-Amer. rodent.

nū'trient, a. serving as or conveying nourishment. nū'triment (-ent), n. nourishing food. nutri'tion, n. food; nourishing. nutri'tious (-shus), a. efficient as food. nū'tritive, a. nutritious.

nutt'y, a. tasting of nuts; *(sl.) crazy.

nux vŏm'ica, n. seed yielding strychnine.

nuz'zle, v.i. & t. nose; burrow, press, rub, or sniff with the nose; nestle, lie snug.

nyl'ghau (-gaw), n. short-horned Indian antelope.

nymph, n. (Mythol.) semi-divine maiden of sea, mountain, wood, &c.; (poet.) maiden.

nym'pholepsy, n. rapt state induced by craving for the unattainable. nym'pholept, n.

nystăg'mus, n. disease with spasmodic movements of eyeballs.

O

O, oh (ō), int. prefixed to vocative name (O); or expressing various emotions (usu. oh if separated by punctuation).

oaf, n. (pl. -s, oaves), awkward lout. oaf'ish, a.

oak, n. forest tree with hard wood, acorns, and jagged leaves; its wood. ~apple, ~gall, ~wart, kinds of excrescence produced on oak by gall-flies. oak'en, a. made of oak.

oak'um, n. caulking-fibre got by picking rope to pieces.

oar (ōr), n. bladed pole worked with both hands by one of the rowers of a boat; (with good, &c.) oarsman. v.t. & i. row. oars'man, ~woman, rower. oars'manship, skill in rowing.

ōā'sis, n. (pl. oasēs), fertile spot in desert.

oast, n. kiln for hops. ~house, a building with oast.

oat, n. (pl.) a grain grown for food; an oat-stem used as shepherd's pipe. ~cake, thin unleavened cake of oatmeal. ~meal, used for oatcake and porridge.

oat'en, _a._ made of oats or an oat-stem.

oath, _n._ (_pl._ pr. ŏdhz), confirmation of statement by naming of God or other power; name of God, &c. used profanely.

ŏbbliga'to (-ah-), _a._ (Mus.) forming an integral part of the composition. _n._ (_pl._ -os), an obbligato part or accompaniment.

ob'dūrate, _a._ hardened; stubborn. **ob'dūracy**, _n._

ō'beah (-a), **ō'bi**, _n._ (W.Afr.) kind of sorcery practised by negroes.

obē'dience, _n._ obeying; submission; complying.

obē'dient, _a._ submissive to superior's will.

obeis'ance (-bās-), _n._ bow or curtsy; homage.

ob'elisk, _n._ tapering stone shaft of rectangular section; obelus (mark in MS. or book).

ob'elize, _v.t._ mark with obelus.

ob'elus, _n._ (_pl._ -lī), mark placed against spurious word, &c.; mark of reference (†).

obēse', _a._ corpulent. **obē'sitў**, _n._

obey' (-bā), _v.t._ & _i._ perform bidding of; be obedient to.

ŏb'fuscāte, _v.t._ (-table), darken; stupefy, bewilder. **~tion**, _n._

|| **ŏb'iit**, died (abbr. _ob._).

|| **ŏb'iter dic'tum**, _n._ (_pl._ -ta), casual remark, esp. judge's opinion expressed incidentally.

obit'uarў, _n._ record of death(s); account of deceased person.

object, _n._ (ŏb'jĭkt), material thing; thing aimed at; end, purpose; (Gram.) word governed by transitive verb or preposition. _v.t._ & _i._ (objĕkt'), state reason against; announce opposition or feel dislike or reluctance to.

objec'tion, _n._ objecting; thing objected; adverse reason; expression of disapproval. **~able**, _a._ open to objection; offensive.

objec'tive, _a._ external to the mind; actually existing; dealing with outward things; (Gram.) constructed as or appropriate to the object. **~tivism**, _n._ tendency to exalt the objective. **~tivity**, _n._

objec'tor, _n._ one who objects; _conscientious ~_, one who pleads conscience in order to be exempted from compulsory service, vaccination, &c.

ŏb'jūrgāte, _v.t._ chide, scold. **~tion**, _n._; _tor_, _nn._; _~tory_, _a._

ŏb'lāte[1], _n._ dedicated person.

oblāte'[2], _a._ (Geom.) (of sphere) flattened at poles.

oblā'tion, _n._ thing offered to God; pious donation. **~al**, _a._

ŏb'ligāte, _v.t._ put under legal obligation.

obligā'tion, _n._ binding agreement; written contract or bond; service or benefit received. **oblig'atorў**, _a._ binding; not optional.

oblige', _v.t._ (-geable), constrain, compel, require; be binding on; confer favour on; (pass.) express gratitude. **obligee'**, _n._ person in whose favour obligor is bound. **obli'ging**, _a._ ready to serve others; accommodating.

ŏb'ligor, _n._ person legally bound to another.

oblique' (-ēk), _a._ slanting; diverging from straight line or course; indirect.

obliq'uitў, _n._ (esp.) moral perversity.

oblit'erate, _v.t._ (-rable), make illegible; efface. **~tion**, _n._

obliv'ion, _n._ state of having or being forgotten. **obliv'ious**, _a._

ŏb'long, _a._ greater in breadth than height. _n._ an oblong figure or object.

ŏb'loquў, _n._ abuse, detraction.

obnō'xious (-kshus), _a._ offensive, objectionable; disliked.

ō'boe (-bo), _n._ hautboy.

ŏ'bol, _n._ anc.-Greek silver coin.

obscēne', _a._ indecent; lewd. **obscē'nitў**, _n._

obscūr'ant, _n._ opponent of enlightenment. **~ism**, **~ist**, _nn._

obscūrā'tion, _n._ act of darkening; (Astron.) occultation, eclipse.

obscūre', _a._ dark, indistinct; hidden, undistinguished; not conspicuous. _v.t._ (-rable), make obscure or invisible. **obscūr'itў**, _n._

ŏbsecrā'tion, _n._ entreaty.

ŏb'sĕquies (-ĭz), n. funeral.

obsē'quious, a. fawning, servile.

observ'ance (-z-), n. keeping or performance (of law, occasion, &c.); rite, ceremonial act.

observ'ant (-z-), a. good at observing or observation.

observā'tion (-z-), n. noticing or being noticed; comment, remark, statement. ~car, ~ platform, in train, esp. in U.S., so built as to give good views.

observ'atory (-z-), n. building for astronomical observation.

observe' (-z-), v.t. & i. (-vable), keep, follow, adhere to; perceive, watch, take notice of; say by way of comment. observ'er (-z-), n. one who observes; person carried in aeroplane to note enemy's position, &c.

obsess', v.t. haunt; fill mind of. obsĕ'ssion (-shn), n.

obsid'ian, n. a vitreous lava.

obsolĕs'cent, a. becoming obsolete. obsolĕs'cence, n.

ŏb'solēte, a. disused, discarded.

ŏb'stacle, n. hindrance, impediment, obstruction.

obstĕt'ric, -ical, a. of child-birth as a branch of medicine and surgery. obstĕt'rics, n.

ŏb'stinate, a. stubborn, intractable. ŏb'stinacy, n.

obstrĕp'erous, a. noisy, wild.

obstruct', v.t. & i. block up; retard or prevent progress of.

obstruc'tion, n. hindrance, obstacle. ~ist, n.

obstruc'tive, a. causing delay. n. obstructionist. ~tor, n.

obtain', v.i. & t. acquire; get; have granted; be in vogue.

obtrude' (-ōōd), v.t. (-dable), thrust importunately forward. obtru'sion (-ōōzhn), n. ~sive, a.

ŏb'tūrate, v.t. stop up, seal. ~tor, n. obturating appliance.

obtūse', a. of blunt form; not pointed; greater than one right angle and less than two; dull, slow of perception.

ŏb'vĕrse, n. side of coin or medal that bears the head or principal design; front or top side of a thing.

ŏb'viāte, v.t. (-viable), clear away, get rid of; prevent.

ŏb'vious, a. seen or realized at the first glance; evident.

ŏcarī'na (-rē), n. egg-shaped musical wind-instrument.

occā'sion (-zhn), n. suitable juncture, opportunity; reason; time marked by a special occurrence. v.t. cause, esp. incidentally. occā'sional (-zho-), a. not regular; incidental. ~ally, adv. sometimes; intermittently.

ŏc'cident (-ks-), n. the west; the O~, Europe (and America). ŏccident'al, a. ~alism, n.

ŏc'ciput (-ks-), n. back of head. occip'ital (-ks-), a.

occult', a. esoteric; recondite; mystical, magical; hidden. v.t. (Astron.) hide by passing in front of. occultā'tion, n. (Astron.).

ŏc'cupant (-ks-), n. person holding piece of property or office; one who resides in, or is in, a place. ŏc'cupancy, n.

occupā'tion, n. a calling or employment; possession.

ŏc'cupier, n. person in possession of land, house, &c.

ŏc'cupy, v.t. (-iable), take military possession of; reside in; hold (office); take up, fill, be in; busy, keep engaged.

occur', v.i. be found here and there; come into one's mind; take place, happen. occu'rrence, n. happening; incident.

ocean (ō'shn), n. great body of water surrounding the land of the globe; the sea; immense quantity of. oceān'ic, a. of the ocean. ~ō'graphy, n. physical geography of the ocean.

ŏc'elot, n. S.-Amer. feline animal resembling leopard.

ochre (ō'ker), n. kinds of earth used as pigments; pale brownish-yellow colour. ō'chrous (-kr-), a.

ŏc'tagon, n. plane figure with eight angles and sides. ~al, a.

octahĕd'ron, n. solid figure contained by eight plane faces, and usu. by eight triangles. ~ral, a.

ŏc'tant, n. half-quadrant.

ŏc′tave (-īv), *n.* the day week of a festival, the eight days including festival and the eight days week; (Mus.) an eighth or an interval of eight sounds.

ŏctā′vŏ, (*abbr.* 8vo), *n.* book of which each sheet is folded into 8 leaves or 16 pages.

ŏctĕn′nial, *a.* lasting, recurring every, eight years.

ŏctĕt′, *n.* (composition for) eight singers or players.

Octō′ber (ŏ-), *n.* tenth month of year (or eighth in the old style).

ŏctōdē′cimō (*abbr.* 18mo), *n.* book of which each sheet is folded into 18 leaves or 36 pages.

ŏctogĕnā′rian, *a. & n.* eighty-year-old (person).

ŏc′tŏpus, *n.* (pl. *-uses*), mollusc with eight suckered arms round mouth; (fig.) formidable power.

ŏctorōōn′, *n.* offspring of quadroon and white; person of one-eighth negro blood.

ŏctosyll′able, *n.* verse of eight syllables. **ŏctŏsyllăb′ic**, *a.*

ŏc′ūlar, *a.* of, for, by, with, the eyes or sight; visual. **ŏc′ūlist**, *n.* eye-specialist.

ŏdd, *a.* not even; not divisible by two; additional; casual; extraordinary, strange. *n.pl.* (often treated as sing.) inequalities; difference; variance, strife; ratio between amounts staked by parties to bet; chances in favour of some result.

Odd′fellow (ŏ-, -ō), *n.* member of friendly society of Oddfellows.

ŏdd′ity, *n.* strangeness; peculiar trait; queer person.

ŏdd′ments, *n.pl.* odds and ends.

ŏde, *n.* lyric poem of exalted style and tone.

ŏ′dious, *a.* hateful, repulsive.

ŏ′dium, *n.* widespread dislike or reprobation.

odŏn′toglŏss′um, *n.* kinds of large-flowered orchid.

ŏdontŏl′ogў, *n.* science dealing with the teeth.

ŏdorif′erous, *a.* diffusing odour; fragrant or fetid. **ŏ′dorous**, *a.*

ŏ′dour (-der), *n.* pleasant or unpleasant smell; fragrance.

Oed′ipus (ēd-), *n.* solver of riddles. ~ complex, psycho-analyst's term for an infantile fixation on the mother.

oecūmĕn′ical (ēk-), *a.* of the whole Christian Church; universal.

o′er (ŏr), poetic form of over.

oesŏph′agus (ēs-), *n.* canal from mouth to stomach; gullet.

oes′trum, **-us** (ēs-), *n.* gadfly; stimulus; vehement impulse.

of (ov, ŏv), *prep.* from; concerning; out of; among; relating to.

off (awf), *adv.* away; at or to a distance; out of position; loose, separate, gone; discontinued, stopped. *prep.* from; no longer upon. *a.* farther; far; (of horses, &c. or vehicles) right; (Crick.) coming from or going towards the right-hand front side of the wicket-keeper (*off drive*, *stump*, *break*). *n.* (Crick.) the 'off' side. **~-hand**, *adv.* extempore, without preparation; *a.* brusque, curt. **~-licence**, licence to sell beer, &c. for consumption off the premises. **~-print**, reprint of part of a publication. **~-scourings**, worst part of dregs. ~ side, (Crick.) the ground on the right front of the wicket-keeper; (Footb.) illegally between ball and opponents' goal.

off′al, *n.* refuse, waste stuff, garbage, scraps; bran or other by-product of grain; carrion.

offence′, *n.* transgression; misdemeanour; illegal act; aggressive action; displeasure.

offend′, *v.i. & t.* transgress; hurt feelings of; outrage. **offen′der**, *n.* guilty person; one who has done an injury.

offen′sive, *a.* aggressive; insulting; disgusting; ill-smelling. *n.* offensive campaign or stroke.

off′er, *v.t. & i.* present by way of sacrifice; tender for acceptance or refusal; express readiness; attempt. *n.* expression of readiness to do or give or sell; proposal, esp. of marriage; price bid. **öff'ering,** n. thing offered as sacrifice or in sign of devotion.

öff'ertory, n. collection of money at religious service.

öff'ice, n. duty, task, function; position with duties attached to it; authorized form of worship; place for transacting business; (pl.) parts of house devoted to household work, storage, &c. **~bearer,** official or officer.

öff'icer, n. functionary of State; holder of authority in army, navy, air force, or mercantile marine; functionary in some public office; president, treasurer, &c. of a society, &c.

offi'cial (-shl), a. of an office or its tenure; properly authorized. n. person holding public office or engaged in official duties. **~dom,** **~ism,** nn.

offi'ciant (-shnt), n. officiating clergyman.

offi'ciate (-shi-), v.i. perform divine service; act in some official capacity. **~tor,** n.

offi'cinal, a. (of herb or drug) used in medicine or the arts.

offi'cious (-shŭs), a. intrusively kind; meddling.

öff'ing, n. more distant part of sea visible to observer on shore or ship; position at distance from shore.

öff'ish (aw-), a. (colloq.) distant or stiff in manner.

öff'set (aw-), n. lateral branch, esp. as used for propagation; sloping ledge; a set-off.

öff'shoot (aw-), n. side shoot of branch (lit. & fig.).

öff'spring (aw-), n. progeny, issue; (fig.) result.

oft, oft-times (aw-), advv. often.

often (aw'fn), adv. frequently; many times; at short intervals.

ögee', n. sinuous line of two opposite curves as in S; moulding with such section.

ogham, ogam (ŏg'am), n. ancient British and Irish alphabet; inscription in, letter of, this.

ögive', n. diagonal rib of vault; pointed arch. ogi'val, a.

ö'gle, v.i. & t. make eyes; make eyes at. n. amorous glance.

Og'pu (-ōō), n. organization for combating counter-revolutionary activities in Soviet Russia.

ö'gre (-ger), n. man-eating giant. **ö'gress,** n.; **ö'grish,** a.

oh. See O.

ohm (ōm), n. unit of electrical resistance.

oil, n. liquid pressed from olives; kinds of vegetable or animal or mineral liquid; oil-colour (usu. pl.). v.t. apply oil to; lubricate. **~cake,** compressed linseed as cattle-food or manure. **~cloth,** canvas used as floor-covering, &c. **~colour,** paint or pigment ground in oil. **~man,** maker or seller of oils. **~painting,** use of, picture in, oil-colours. **~skin,** cloth waterproofed with oil; garment or (pl.) suit of it. **oil'er,** n. one who oils, (sl.) unctuous person; lubricating can. **oil'y,** a. of, like, covered or soaked with, oil; (fig.) unctuous.

oint'ment, n. unctuous healing or beautifying preparation for the skin.

Oireachtas (ēr'áchtăs), n. legislature of the Irish Free State.

***O.K., ö'keh'** (-kā), adv. & a. all right. v.t. pass (thing) as O.K.

oka'pi (-ah-), n. African ruminant with resemblances to giraffe, deer, and zebra.

öld, a. advanced in age; not young or near its beginning; dating from far back; long established; former. n. old time. **~age** pensions, weekly State payments to persons over 70, and contributory pensions for insured persons over 65. **~bean,** **~cock,** slangy address to familiars. **~fashioned,** antiquated; not new-fangled. **~Glory,** the Stars and Stripes. **~hand,** person of experience in something. **~Harry,** the devil. **~maid,** confirmed spinster. **~man's-beard,** a moss, wild clematis. **~Nick,** the devil. ***~stuff,** (sl.) stale news, hackneyed material. **~ thing**, (*sl.*) address of familiarity, &c., to a person. ***~timer,** person whose experience goes back to old times. **~ woman**, fussy or timid man; one's wife (colloq.).

ŏ'lden, *a.* of an earlier period.

ŏ'lster, *n.* one no longer young.

ŏleă'ginous, *a.* having properties of or producing oil.

ŏ'leănder, *n.* evergreen poisonous flowering shrub.

ŏ'leăster, *n.* wild olive.

ŏ'leograph (-ahf), *n.* picture printed in oils.

ŏlfăc'tory, *a.* concerned with smelling.

ŏl'igarchy (-kĭ), *n.* government, State governed, by the few; members of such government. **ŏl'igărch** (-k), *n.* member of oligarchy. **~ĭc, ~ical,** *aa.*

|| **ŏ'lĭō**, *n.* (*pl.* -os), mixed dish, hotchpotch; miscellany.

ŏlivă'ceous (-shŭs), *a.* olive-green.

ŏl'ĭve, *n.* oval hard-stoned fruit yielding oil; tree bearing it; shade of green. *a.* of olive colour. **~branch**, (*fig.*) overture for peace or reconciliation. ***~drab**, (official name of) colour of U.S. army service uniform. **~oil**, *n.*

ŏl'ĭver, *n.* small lift hammer.

ŏlĭvĕt', *n.* an imitation pearl.

ŏl'ĭvĭne (*or* -ĭn), *n.* olive-coloured chrysoprase.

ŏll'a podri'da (-rē-), *n.* = olio.

ŏlÿm'pĭăd, *n.* period of four years between Olympic games.

ŏlÿm'pĭan, *a.* of Olympus; celestial; (of manners, &c.) magnificent, condescending.

ŏlÿm'pĭc, *a.* of Olympia. **~ games**, four-yearly anc.-Gk. festival; modern quadrennial international athletic meeting.

ŏm'bre (-er), *n.* card game for three (17th & 18th cc.).

ŏ'mēga, *n.* last letter of Greek alphabet; last of series.

ŏm'elĕt, -ĕtte (-ml-), *n.* eggs fried and folded or rolled.

ŏ'men, *n.* a sign portending good or evil; presage. **ŏm'inous**, *a.* of evil omen; inauspicious.

omĭ'ssion (-shn), *n.* omitting, non-inclusion; neglect of duty.

omĭt', *v.t.* leave out, not include; leave undone, neglect doing.

ŏm'lah (-*a*), *n.* in northern India, a body or staff of native officials in a civil court.

ŏm'nibus, *n.* (*pl.* -uses; abbr. *bus*). road vehicle plying on fixed route or in the service of hotels, &c. *a.* serving several objects at once; comprising several items.

ŏmnĭp'otent, *a.* all-powerful. **ŏmnĭp'otence**, *n.* infinite power.

ŏmnĭprĕs'ent (-z-), *a.* ubiquitous, present everywhere. **ŏmnĭprĕs'ence**, *n.*

ŏmnĭs'cient (-shyent), *a.* knowing everything (often hyperbolical). **ŏmnĭs'cience** (-shns), *n.*

ŏm'nĭum găth'erum (-dh-), *n.* queer mixture; miscellaneous party.

ŏmnĭv'orous, *a.* devouring all things; not fastidious.

ŏm'phalŏs, *n.* central point of a system, &c.; hub; nucleus.

ŏm'rah (-*a*), *n.* lord or grandee of a Mohammedan court, esp. that of the Great Mogul.

on, *prep.* (on, ŏn), upon; close to, in the direction of; at, near; concerning, about; added to. *adv.* (ŏn), on something (*play on*, let ball hit wicket off one's bat); in some direction, forward; (Crick.) in advance of the opposite side (50 *runs on*). *n.* (ŏn), in cricket, the 'on' side. *int.* go on, advance. **~ side**, (Crick.) the ground on the left front of the wicket-keeper.

ŏn'ager, *n.* wild ass.

once (wŭns), *adv.* for one time or one occasion only; formerly; (with *at*) without delay. *conj.* as soon as; when once. *n.* one time, performance, &c. ***the ~-over,** a preliminary survey.

ŏn'coming (-n-kŭ-), *n.* & *a.* approach, approaching.

|| **on dit** (ŏn dē'), *n.* piece of hearsay.

one (wŭn), *a.* single and integral; only, without others; identical, the same. *n.* the number or

figure 1, unit, unity; single specimen. *pron.* a particular but unspecified person; a person or
thing of specified kind. ~eyed,
(sl.) unfair. ~man show, requiring, concerning, one man
only. ~sided, lopsided; partial,
unfair, prejudiced.

one′ness (wŭn-n-), *n.* singleness;
uniqueness; concord; sameness.

on′er (wŭ-), (sl.), *n.* remarkable
person or thing; severe blow.

o′nerous, *a.* burdensome.

oneself′ (wŭ-), refl. and emphatic
form of *one* as a generalizing
pronoun.

on′fall (-awl), *n.* assault.

on′flow (-ō), *n.* onward flow.

on′goings (-n-g-, -z), *n.pl.* strange
or improper proceedings.

onion (ŭn′yon), *n.* edible bulb of
pungent smell and flavour; (sl.)
native of Bermuda.

on′looker, *n.* one who looks on.

o′nly, *a.* single, sole; that is pre-
eminent of its kind. *adv.* solely,
merely, exclusively. *conj.* but
then; with the exception.

onomatopoe′ia (-pē-a), *n.* formation of names or words from
sounds that resemble those
associated with the object or
action to be named; such word.

on′rush, *n.* rapid or tumultuous
advance; spurt.

on′set, *n.* attack; impetuous beginning.

on′slaught (-awt), *n.* fierce attack.

ontol′ogy, *n.* department of metaphysics concerned with the
essence of things or being in
general. ~ōgical, *a.* ~gist, *n.*

o′nus, *n.* the responsibility for or
burden of doing something.

‖ **onus proban′di**, obligation to
prove resting on opponent of the
orthodox or established.

on′ward, *a.* directed onwards.

on′ward(s) (-z), *adv.* further on;
towards the front; progressively.

on′yx, *n.* kinds of quartz with
colour layers.

oof, *n.* (sl.) money, wealth.

o′olite, *n.* granular limestone.
~ōlit′ic, *a.*

ōōm, *n.* (S.-Afr.) uncle.

ōōnt, *n.* (Anglo-Ind. sl.) camel.

ōōze, *n.* wet mud, slime; sluggish
flow, exudation. *v.i.* pass slowly
through pores, *&c.*; (fig.) leak
out or away. **ōōz′y**, *a.*

opā′city, *n.* opaqueness.

o′pal, *n.* milk-white or bluish
stone with iridescent reflections.
~ĕs′cent, ~ine, *a.* iridescent.

opāque′ (-k), *a.* not transmitting
light, not transparent; not lucid,
obscure; obtuse.

ōpe, *v.t. & i.* (poet.) open.

o′pen, *a.* not closed or blocked
up; unlocked; unconfined, uncovered; exposed, manifest;
public; clear; expanded, spread
out; not close, unfolded; com-
municative, frank. *v.t. & i.* make
or become open or more open;
unclose, unlock; begin, make a
start. ~ open space or country
or air. ~eyed, vigilant, watchful. ~faced, ingenuous-looking.
~handed, generous, liberal.
~hearted, frank, generous.
~ letter, esp. protest, *&c.* printed
in newspaper, *&c.* but addressing
individual. ~minded, unprejudiced, accessible to new ideas.

o′pening (-pn-), *n.* gap, aperture;
commencement; preliminary
statement. *a.* initial; first.

o′penly, *adv.* publicly; frankly.

op′era, *n.* drama of vocal and
instrumental music. ~cloak,
lady's cloak for the opera or
evening parties. ~glass(es),
small binocular used in theatres,
&c. ~hat, man's collapsible
high hat. ~house, theatre for
operas.

op′erāte, *v.i. & t.* (-rable), be in
action; bring influence to bear;
perform operations; work (machine, *&c.*).

operā′tic, *a.* of or like opera.

operā′tion, *n.* action, working;
financial transaction; piece of
surgery; strategic manœuvre.

op′erative, *a.* in operation;
having effect; of or by surgery;
n. artisan, workman. ~tor, *n.*

operc′ulum, *n.* (pl. *-la*), fish's gill-

---

māre, mēre, mîre, mōre, mūre; părt, pĕrt, pŏrt; *italics,* **vague sounds;**

cover; valve closing mouth of shell.

op̆erĕt'ta, n. short light opera.

ŏph'icleïde (-līd), n. keyed brass wind-instrument.

ŏphid'ian (-dyan), a. of the reptile order that includes snakes. n. such reptile.

ŏphthăl'mia, n. inflammation of the eye. **~ic,** a. of or for the eye; affected with ophthalmia. **ŏphthăl'moscōpe,** n. instrument for examining the eye.

o͞o'piate, (o.t. (-āt), mix with opium. n. (-at), drug for easing pain or inducing sleep. a. (-at), inducing drowsiness.

opīne', v.t. (-nable), express or hold the opinion.

opin'ion (-yon), n. belief based on grounds short of proof; view; piece of professional advice. **~ātĕd,** a. unduly confident in one's opinions; stubborn.

o͞o'pium, n. drug made from poppy and used as a stimulant.

op̄op'anăx, n. a gum-resin used in perfumery.

opŏss'um, n. Amer. marsupial.

Opp'idan, n. member of Eton College not on the foundation.

oppo'nent, n. adversary, rival.

opp'ortūne, a. at an especially favourable time; well-timed. **~nism,** adaptation of policy or method to circumstances; time-serving. **~nist,** n. & a.

op̄portū'nĭty, n. favourable juncture; good chance; opening.

oppōse' (-z), v.t. place in opposition or contrast; set oneself against; resist; (p.p.) contrary, adverse, (to).

opp'osite (-z-), a. contrary in position or kind; facing each other; diametrically different. n. opposite thing or term. adv. in opposite position. prep. opposite to.

opposi'tion (-z-), n. antagonism, resistance; party of opponents opposed to party in office; contrast; (Astron.) diametrically opposite position of two heavenly bodies.

oppress', v.t. govern tyrannically; treat with gross harshness or injustice; weigh down. **~ion,** n. **~ive,** a. (esp., of weather, &c.) sultry, close. **~or,** n.

oppro'brious, a. (of language) vituperative, abusive.

oppro'brium, n. reproachful language; being in disgrace.

oppugn' (-ūn), v.t. controvert; not admit; resist.

ŏpsōn'ic, a. making bacteria easier of consumption by phagocytes.

ŏp'tative (or ŏptā'-), a. (Gram.) expressing wish. n. the optative mood.

ŏp'tic, a. of eye or sight. n. (now joc.) eye. **ŏp'tical,** a. visual; aiding sight; or according to optics. **ŏpti'cian** (-shn), n. maker or seller of optical instruments. **ŏp'tics,** n.pl. (usu. treated as sing.) science of sight and the laws of light.

ŏp'timism, n. view that good must ultimately prevail; sanguine disposition. **~ist,** n.; **~istic,** a.

ŏp'tion, n. choice, choosing; thing that is or may be chosen. **ŏp'tional** (-sho-), a. not obligatory.

ŏp'tophone, n. instrument converting light into sound, and so enabling the blind to read print, &c. by ear.

ŏp'ulent, a. wealthy; well stored; abundant. **ŏp'ulence,** n.

‖ **ŏp'us** (or ō-), n. musician's separate composition (abbr. op.).

opŭs'cūle, -cūlum (pl. -la), nn. minor composition.

ŏr¹, n. gold or yellow in heraldry.

ŏr², prep. & conj. ere, before.

or³ (ŏr, or), conj. introducing second of two alternatives.

o͞o'racle, n. place at which ancient Greeks, &c. consulted their deities; a divine revelation; person or thing serving as infallible guide. orăc'ūlar, a. (esp.) dogmatic; of doubtful meaning.

ŏr'al, a. spoken; by word of mouth; (Anat.) of the mouth.

ŏr'ange¹ (-inj), n. globular reddish-yellow fruit; tree bearing it; its colour. a. orange-coloured.

ŏ'rangerỹ (-ĭnj-), n. orange plantation or house.

Orange² (ŏ'rĭnj), n. (attrib. & in comb.) of the Irish ultra-protestant party. ~man, member of Orange society. O'rangism (ŏ'rĭnj-), n.

ŏrangeade' (-ĭnjăd), n. orange-flavoured aerated water.

orăng'-outăng' (-ŏot-), n. large anthropoid ape.

orāte', v.i. (joc.) speechify.

orā'tion, n. a speech, esp. of a ceremonial kind.

ŏ'rator, n. maker of a speech; skilful speaker. ŏ'ratrĕss, n.

ŏratŏr'ĭō, n. (pl. -os), musical composition on sacred theme.

ŏ'ratorỹ¹, n. small chapel; place for private worship.

ŏ'ratorỹ², n. rhetoric; speeches; eloquent language. ~orĭcal, a.

orb, n. sphere, globe; part of regalia; (poet.) eyeball. orbed (ŏrbd, ŏrb'ĭd), a. rounded; bearing an orb. ŏrbĭc'ŭlar, a. spherical or circular.

ŏrb'ĭt, n. eye-socket; curved course of planet, comet, or satellite. ŏrb'ĭtal, a.

Orcā'dian (ŏr-), a. of Orkney. n. native of Orkney.

ŏrch'ard, n. enclosure with fruit-trees.

ŏrch'ĕstra (-k-), n. place occupied by band or chorus in theatre or concert-room; such band or its music. ŏrchĕs'tral (-k-), a. for, of, performed by, the band. ŏrch'ĕstrāte (-k-), v.t. (-table), arrange or score for orchestral performance. ~tion, n.

ŏrc'hĭd, ŏrc'hĭs (-k-), nn. kinds of flowering plant (-is is usual for wild British kinds, -id for hot-house exotics). ~dā'ceous, a.

ŏrdain', v.t. confer holy orders upon; appoint; enact.

ordeal', n. experience that tests character or endurance.

ŏrd'er, n. social class or rank; grade of Christian ministry; religious fraternity; company to which distinguished persons are admitted as an honour or reward, insignia worn by its members; friendly society; (Nat. Hist.) classification; division of class, subdivided into genera or families; sequence, succession; method; tidiness; efficient state; stated form of divine service; law-abiding state; injunction; authoritative direction or instruction. v.t. put in order; ordain; command, prescribe; direct tradesman, &c. to supply.

ŏrd'erlỹ, a. methodically arranged, tidy; not unruly; (Mil.) of or for orders. n. soldier in attendance on officer; hospital attendant.

ŏrd'ĭnal, a. of or defining a thing's place in a series. n. an ordinal number; service-book used at ordinations.

ŏrd'ĭnance, n. authoritative direction; decree; religious rite.

ŏrd'ĭnarỹ, a. normal; not exceptional; commonplace. n. (Eccl.) the O~, bishop in his diocese, archbishop in his province; the common run of things.

ŏrdĭnā'tion, n. ordaining; conferring of holy orders.

ŏrd'nance, n. mounted guns; department for military stores.

ŏrd'ure (-dyer), n. dung.

ōre, n. native mineral yielding metal.

ōr'ĕăd, n. mountain nymph.

ŏr'gan, n. musical instrument of or, pipes supplied with wind by bellows and sounded by keys; part of body serving some vital function; a medium of opinion.

ŏrgăn'ĭc, a. of the bodily organs; (of disease) affecting structure of an organ; (Chem...of substances) derived from or belonging to the animal and vegetable kingdom; structural; organized.

ŏrg'anism, n. organized body; individual animal or plant.

ŏrg'anist, n. player of organ, esp. as director of church choir.

ŏrg'anīze, v.t. (-zable), furnish with vital organs; give orderly structure to; bring into working order. ~zation, n. (esp.) organized body or system.

ōrg′anŏn, -anum, n. instrument of thought; system of logic.

ōr′ğăsm, n. paroxysm of desire or rage or other passion.

ōr′ğў, n. drunken or licentious revel; (pl.) revelry, debauchery.

ōr′ĭel, n. projecting part of upper room containing window; such window.

orient (ōr′ĭent), n. the eastward part of sky or earth; countries east of Mediterranean and S. Europe. a. (of sun, &c.) rising, nascent; oriental. v.t. (ōr′ĭĕnt′), place church with chancel end eastwards; ascertain the compass-bearings of. ~ā′tion, n.

ōrĭen′tal, a. of the eastern or Asiatic world or its civilization. n. native of the East. ~ĭsm, n. ~ĭst, n. expert in oriental languages and history. ~ĭze, v.t. & i.

ō′rĭfĭce, n. mouth of cavity.

ō′rĭflămme, n. sacred red banner of old French kings; any party symbol; blaze of colour.

ō′rĭġĭn, n. source; parentage.

orĭ′ġĭnal, a. existent from the first; primitive; earliest; not imitative or derived; creative. n. pattern, archetype; thing from which another is copied; eccentric person. orĭġĭnăl′ĭtў, n.

orĭ′ğĭnāte, v.t. & i. initiate or give origin to, or be the origin of; have origin; take rise. ~tĭon, ~tor, nn. ~tĭve, a.

ōr′ĭōle, n. kinds of bird with black and yellow plumage.

Orī′on, n. a constellation.

ō′rĭson (-zn), n. a prayer.

ōr′lŏp, n. lowest deck of ship with three or more decks.

ōrm′olu (-loō), n. gilded bronze; a gold-coloured alloy; articles made of these.

ornament, n. (ōrn′ament), thing that adorns; person whose presence confers grace or honour; decorative work. v.t. (ōrna-mĕnt′), adorn, beautify. ornamĕn′tal, a. ~ātĭon, n.

ōrnāte′, a. much adorned.

ōrnĭthŏl′oğў, n. study of birds. ōrnĭthŏlŏ′ğĭcal, a.; ~ŏl′ŏğĭst, n.

ornĭthōrhўnc′us (-rī-), n. Australian aquatic furred mammal with duck's bill and webbed feet.

ōr′ŏtŭnd, a. magniloquent.

ōrph′an, a. bereaved of parent(s). n. an orphan child. ~age, n. institution for orphans.

Orph′ĭc, Orphē′an (ōr-), aa. of Orpheus or his mystic doctrines (usu. -ĭc); like Orpheus's music (usu. -ean).

ōrp′ĭment, n. a yellow mineral pigment.

ōrp′ĭne, n. a purple-flowered plant.

ō′rrerў, n. clock-work model of planetary system.

ō′rrĭs, n. kind of iris (rare); orris-root or powder. ~~powder, ~~root, nn. perfume from root of kinds of iris.

ōrth′odox, a. holding correct or accepted views; not heretical. ōrth′odoxў, n. adherence to the orthodox; orthodox views.

ōrthō′ĕpў, n. science of pronunciation. ōrthōĕp′ĭc, a.

ōrthogĕn′esĭs, n. a view of evolution according to which variations follow a defined direction and are not merely sporadic and fortuitous.

ōrthŏg′raphў, n. spelling. ōrthŏ-grăph′ĭc, ~al, aa.

ōrthopaed′ĭc, a. for cure of deformities, esp. in children.

ōrt′olan, n. the garden bunting, esp. as table dainty; *bobolink.

ŏs′cĭllāte, v.i. swing to and fro; vacillate. ~tĭon, n. ~tor, n. (esp.) instrument for producing oscillation. ~torў, a.

ŏs′cŭlāte, v.i. kiss (joc.); have points of contact or coincidence. ŏs′cŭlant, a. osculating. ŏscŭlā′tĭon, n. ~torў, a.

ō′sĭer (-zher), n. willow used in basketwork; shoot of it.

Osmān′lĭ (ŏs-), a. & n. Ottoman.

ŏs′mĭum (-z-), n. a metal.

ŏs′mōse (-z-), ŏsmō′sĭs (-zm-), n. tendency of fluids separated by membrane or other porous sub-

stance to percolate and mix.
osmŏt'lo (-z-), a.

ŏs'mund (-z-), n. flowering fern.

ŏs'prey, n. (pl. -eys), the fishing-eagle; name for egret-plume.

ŏss'éous, a. bony; having bones.

ŏss'icle, n. small bone or hard substance in animal structure.

ŏss'ifrage, n. osprey or some kind of eagle.

ŏss'ify, v.t. & i. (-iable), turn into bone; harden; make or become rigid. ~fication, n.

ŏss'úary, n. charnel-house; bone-urn; cave with ancient bones.

ŏsten'sible, a. professed; used as a blind. ~bility, n.

ŏsten'sory, n. receptacle for displaying the Host; monstrance.

ŏstentā'tion, n. pretentious display; showing off. ~tious, a.

ŏsteŏl'ogy, n. science of bones; branch of anatomy dealing with bones. ŏstéolŏ'gical, a.; ŏsteŏl'ogist, n.

ŏsteŏp'athy, n. disease of the bones; cure of disease by manipulation of the bones. ŏs'teŏpăth, n. one who practises osteopathy.

ŏs'tler (-sl-), n. stableman at inn.

ŏs'tracize, v.t. (-zable), exclude from society; send to Coventry. ~ism, n. being ostracized.

ŏs'trich, n. large swift-running bird valued for its feathers.

o'ther (ŭdh-), a. not the same; separate in identity; distinct in kind; alternative, additional. pron. other person, thing, specimen, &c.

otherwise (ŭdh'erwiz), adv. in a different way; in other respects; else; or; but for this.

ōtiōse' (-shi-), a. not required; serving no practical purpose.

ŏtŏl'ogy, ō'toscŏpe, nn. science of, instrument for inspecting, the ear.

ŏtt'er, n. furred aquatic fish-eating mammal; its fur; kinds of fishing tackle.

ŏtt'ō, n. ~ of roses, attar.

Ŏtt'oman, o- (ŏ-), a. of the Turkish empire. n. (pl. -ans), a

Turk; (o-) cushioned seat without back or arms.

oubliĕtte' (ōō-), n. secret dungeon with trapdoor entrance.

ŏuch[1], n. (arch.) setting of gem; clasp.

*ŏuch[2], int. expr. annoyance or pain.

ought[1] (awt), n. (vulg.) figure 0, nought.

ought[2] (awt), v.i. to be obliged to; be bound in duty.

ounce[1], n. (abbr. oz.) unit of weight, one-twelfth lb. in Troy weight, one-sixteenth lb. in avoirdupois; (fig.) small amount.

ounce[2], n. (poet.) lynx or other feline beast of medium size; (Zool.) the snow-leopard.

our (owr), a. of or belonging to us.

ours (owrz), pron. the one(s) belonging to us.

 oursĕlf', pron. myself (used with royal or editorial we). (pl.) ~selves, we or us; not others.

ousel. See ouzel.

oust, v.t. put out of possession; eject; seize the place of.

out, adv. away from a place, not within; no longer in possession; in the open; at an end. n. (pl.) the party out of office. int. begone! ~fighting, boxing at arm's length.

outbăl'ance, v.t. outweigh.

outbĭd', v.t. bid higher than.

outbrāve', v.t. defy.

out'break (-āk), n. breaking out of anger, war, disease, fire, &c.

out'building (-bĭl-), n. outhouse.

out'burst, n. bursting out, esp. of emotion in vehement words.

out'cast (-ah-), a. cast out from home and friends. n. homeless and friendless person.

outclass' (-ah-), v.t. surpass by a wide difference.

out'come (-kŭm), n. result, issue.

out'crop, n. emergence of stratum, &c. at surface; stratum, &c. that emerges.

out'cry, n. clamour; loud cry.

out-dis'tance, v.t. get far ahead of.

outdō' (-ōō), v.t. surpass, excel.

out'door (-dŏr), a. done or used or

māre, mēre, mīre, mŏre, mūre; părt, pĕrt, pŭrt; italics, vague sounds;

existing outdoors. **~doors,** *adv.* in the open air.

out'er, *a.* farther from centre or inside ; on the outside. *n.* hit on outer circle of target.

outface', *v.t.* look (person) out of countenance (lit. & fig.).

out'fall (-fawl), *n.* mouth of river.

out'field, *n.* outlying land ; (Crick.) part remote from pitch.

out'fit, *n.* equipment ; *(colloq.) force of workmen ; *(army sl.) company, battalion, &c. **out'fitter,** *n.* supplier of equipment.

outflank', *v.t.* extend beyond flank of enemy.

out'flow (-flō), *n.* what flows out.

outgen'eral, *v.t.* defeat by superior generalship.

outgo', *v.t.* surpass, excel.

out'goings (-z), *n.pl.* expenditure.

outgrow' (-ō), *v.t.* grow faster or get taller than ; get rid of with advancing age ; get too big for (clothes, &c.).

out'growth (-ōth), *n.* offshoot.

out'house, *n.* shed, &c. adjoining main house.

out'ing, *n.* pleasure-trip.

out-jock'ey, *v.t.* overreach.

outland'ish, *a.* foreign looking or sounding ; unfamiliar.

outlast' (-ah-), *v.t.* last longer than.

out'law, *n.* person deprived of the protection of the law. *v.t.* proscribe ; declare outlaw. **~ry,** *n.* condemnation as an outlaw.

out'lay, *n.* expenses.

out'let, *n.* means of exit ; vent.

out'lier, *n.* outlying part.

out'line, *n.* external boundary ; lines enclosing visible object ; contour ; rough draft, summary ; (pl.) main features. *v.t.* draw or describe in outline.

outlive' (-lïv-), *v.t.* live longer than or beyond.

out'look, *n.* view, prospect ; what seems likely to happen.

out'lying, *a.* far from a centre ; detached ; remote.

outmanœu'vre (-nōōver), *v.t.* defeat by superior manœuvring.

outmatch', *v.t.* march faster or farther than.

outmatch', *v.t.* be more than a match for.

outnum'ber, *v.t.* be more numerous than.

outpace', *v.t.* be quicker than.

out'patient (-shnt), *n.* patient not lodged in hospital, &c.

out'post, *n.* detachment on guard at some distance from army.

out'pouring (-pōr-), *n.* effusion ; expression of emotion.

out'put (-pŏot), *n.* amount produced by manufacture, &c.

out'rage, *n.* (-ij), forcible violation of others' rights, sentiments, &c. ; gross offence or indignity. *v.t.* (-āj), subject to outrage ; insult ; ravish. **outrā'geous** (-jus), *a.* immoderate ; violent ; grossly cruel ; abusive.

outrange' (-j), *v.t.* (of gun or its user) have a longer range than.

|| **outré** (ōōt'rā), *a.* eccentric ; outraging decorum.

out'-relief, *n.* relief given to person not resident in workhouse.

outride', *v.t.* ride faster or farther than ; keep afloat in gale.

out'rider, *n.* mounted attendant of person in carriage ; commercial traveller.

out'rigger, *n.* spar or framework projecting from or over ship's side ; iron bracket bearing rowlock outside boat, boat with these.

outright', *adv.* altogether, entirely ; once for all ; without reservation.

outri'val, *v.t.* surpass.

outrun', *v.t.* run faster or farther than ; pass the limit of.

out'runner, *n.* running attendant on carriage ; horse in traces outside shafts.

outsail', *v.t.* sail faster than.

out'set, *n.* start.

outshine', *v.t.* be more brilliant than.

outside', *n.* external surface, outer parts ; external appearance ; position without ; highest computation. *a.* of, on, or nearer the outside ; greatest existent or possible. *adv.* on or to the outside ; not within. *prep.* external to ; beyond the limits of ; without.

outsi'der, n. non-member of some circle, party, &c.; horse or person not known to have a chance in race or competition.

outsit', v.t. stay longer than.

out'skirts, n.pl. outer border of city, &c.; fringe of subject.

*outsmart', v.t. outdo.

out'span, v.i. & t. (S.-Afr.) unyoke or unharness.

outspo'ken, a. frank, unreserved.

out'spread' (-ĕd), a. spread out.

outstand'ing, a. prominent, conspicuous; still unsettled.

outstay', v.t. stay longer than.

outstep', v.t. transgress; pass beyond bounds of.

out'stretched', a. stretched out.

outstrip', v.t. pass in progression or progress.

out-thrust', n. outward pressure of some part in architecture.

outval'ūe, v.t. surpass in value.

outvie', v.t. surpass in competition.

outvote', v.t. defeat by number of votes. out'vōter, n. non-resident voter.

out'ward, a. directed towards the outside; bodily; external, superficial. adv. outwards. ~ly, adv. in outward appearance; on the surface. ~ness, n. objectivity; external existence.

out'wards (-z), adv. towards what is outside.

outweigh' (-wā), v.t. exceed in weight, value, or influence.

outwit', v.t. prove too clever for; overreach.

out'work, n. advanced or detached part of fortress, &c.; work done outside shop or house. ~er, n. one who does outwork.

out'worn', a. worn out.

ouzel, -sel (ōō'zl), n. kinds of small bird.

o'val, a. shaped like an egg. n. egg-shaped or elliptical closed curve; thing with oval outline.

o'vary, n. ovum-producing organ in female; seed-vessel in plant. ovār'ian, a.

o'vāte, n. (Nat. Hist.) oval.

ovā'tion, n. enthusiastic reception; general applause.

o'ven (ŭ-), n. receptacle for baking in.

o'ver, adv. above in place or position; more than a specified number or quantity; covering the whole surface; from one side to the other (Crick., as umpire's direction) change ends or position for bowling, &c.; from beginning to end; at an end; done with. n. (Crick.) number of deliveries allowed to bowler between two calls of over and the resulting play. prep. above; concerning; across; on or to the other side.

overact', v.t. & i. act, act rôle, with exaggeration.

o'verall (-awl), n. woman's loose work garment; (pl.) protective trousers or suit; (Mil., pl.) officer's full-dress tight trousers.

overawe', v.t. awe into submission.

overbal'ance, v.t. & i. lose balance and fall; cause to do this; outweigh. o'verbālance, n. excess; its amount.

overbear' (-bār), v.t. bear down by weight or force; repress; outweigh. ~ing, a. domineering.

o'verboard (-bōrd), adv. from within ship into water.

overbur'den, v.t. load too heavily.

over-cap'italize (-z), v.t. fix or estimate capital of (company, &c.) too high.

overcast' (-ah-), v.t. cover (sky) with clouds or darkness.

overcharge', v.t. & i. put excessive charge into (gun, &c.); use too much detail or rate too high; charge too much. o'vercharge, n. sum beyond the right price.

overcloud', v.t. cloud over.

o'vercoat, n. coat worn over another.

overcol'our (-kŭler), v.t. exaggerate details of.

overcome' (-kŭm), v.t. prevail over; get the better of; master.

overcrop', v.t. exhaust (land) by continuous cropping.

overdo' (-dōō), v.t. carry to excess; cook too much; overtax strength of. ~done, a. (esp.) over-acted.

ō'verdōse, n. excessive dose.

ō'verdraft (-ah-), n. overdrawing of bank account; amount by which balance is overdrawn.

overdraw', v.t. & i. draw cheque in excess of; make an overdraft; exaggerate in describing.

overdréss', v.t. & i. adorn with, wear, ostentatious finery.

overdrive', v.t. drive (animal), work (person), to exhaustion.

overdūe', a. more than due; in arrear.

ōver-ĕs'tĭmāte, v.t. put value or amount of too high.

overflow (-ō) v.t. & i. (-flow'), flow over, flood; extend beyond limits or capacity of. n. (ō'-), process of overflowing; what flows over or is in excess.

overgrow' (-ō), v.t. & i. grow too fast or beyond natural size; (of plants) grow over. ō'vergrowth', n.

ō'verhănd, a. & adv. with hand above object held; above the shoulder.

overhăng', v.t. & i. jut out over, jut out; impend over, impend.

overhaul', v.t. pull to pieces for inspection; catch up, overtake.

overhead, adv. (-hĕd), on high, in the sky; in the story above. a. (ō'-), placed overhead; (of charges, &c.) due to office expenses, interest on capital, &c.

overhear', v.t. hear as eavesdropper or involuntary listener.

overjoyed', a. transported with joy; ravished.

overlā'den, a. too heavily loaded.

overländ', adv. (-land'), by land and not sea. a. (ō'-), entirely or partly by land.

overlăp', v.t. & i. partly cover; cover and extend beyond.

overlay', v.t. cover surface of with coating, &c.; overlie (incorrectly).

overleaf', adv. on other side of leaf of book.

overlie' (-ī), v.t. lie on top of; smother (baby) thus.

overlook', v.t. have prospect of from above; take no notice of; condone; superintend.

ō'verlŏrd, n. supreme lord.

ō'vermăntel, n. ornamental shelves, &c. above mantelpiece.

overmas'ter (-mah-), v.t. get complete victory or control over.

overmătch', v.t. be too strong for.

overmŭch', a., n., & adv. too much.

over-nīce', a. too fastidious.

over-nīght', adv. on the preceding evening.

overpass' (-ah-), v.t. pass over or beyond; surmount, surpass. ~passad' (?), ~past', a. gone by.

overpĭtch', v.t. bowl so that ball pitches too near wicket.

ō'verplŭs, n. surplus.

overpoise' (-z), v.t. outweigh.

overpow'er, v.t. reduce to submission; subdue; overwhelm.

overpréss'ure (-sher), n. pressing or being pressed too hard.

overprodūc'tion, n. production in excess of the demand.

overrāte', v.t. estimate too high.

overreach', v.t. & i. circumvent, outwit; (of horse) strike forefoot with hind hoof.

override', v.t. trample (person) under one's horse's hoofs; (fig.) trample on, set aside, annul.

overrule' (-ōōl), v.t. set aside by superior authority; reject.

overrŭn', v.t. harry and spoil; swarm or spread over; exceed.

oversea', a. & adv. overseas', adv. across or beyond sea.

oversee', v.t. superintend. ō'verseer, n. superintendent.

oversĕt', v.t. upset, capsize.

overshăd'ow (-dō), v.t. shelter from sun; throw into the shade.

ō'vershoe (-ōō), n. shoe of rubber or felt for wearing over another.

overshōōt', v.t. shoot beyond the mark; assert too much.

ō'versight, n. omission to notice; inadvertence; supervision.

oversleep', v.i. or refl. sleep beyond time of rising.

overspread' (-ĕd), v.t. cover surface of; become diffused over.

overstāte', v.t. state too strongly; exaggerate. ~ment, n.

overstrain', v.t. damage by exertion; stretch too far. n. (ō'-), injurious bodily or mental strain.

---

mäte, mēte, mīte, mōte, mūte, mōōt; răck, rĕck, rick, rŏck, rŭck, rōōk ōverstrŭng´, a. intensely strained or wound up.

ōvert´, a. openly done, patent.

ōvertāke´, v.t. come up with, catch up; come suddenly upon.

ōvertask´ (-tahˈ-), v.t. burden too heavily.

ōvertăx´, v.t. make excessive demand on; burden with taxes.

ōverthrow (-ō), v.t. (-throw´), upset, knock down; vanquish. n. (ō´-), defeat, subversion; (Crick., Baseball) fielder's return not stopped near wicket (base) and so allowing further run(s).

ōvertīme, adv. (-timeˈ), beyond regular hours of work. n. (ō´-), extra time worked.

ōvertŏp´, v.t. be or become higher than.

ōvertrāin´, v.i. & t. lose condition, spoil condition of, by too severe athletic training.

ōvertrŭmp´, v.t. play higher trump than.

o´verture, n. opening of negotiations; formal proposal or offer; (Mus.) orchestral prelude.

ōvertŭrn´, v.t. & i. (-turnˈ), upset, overthrow; fall down or over. n. (ō´-), upsetting; revolution.

ōverween´ing, a. arrogant.

o´verweight (-wātˈ), n. excessive weight. ōverweight´ed, a. unduly burdened.

ōverwhĕlm´, v.t. bury beneath; submerge utterly; crush; overpower. ~ing, a. irresistible by numbers, weight, &c.

ōverwind´, v.t. injure (watch, &c.) by winding too tight.

ōverwork´ (-wĕrkˈ), v.t. & i. work too hard; exhaust with work. n. injurious amount of work.

ōverwrought´ (-rawtˈ), a. suffering from excitement; too elaborate.

ō´vifŏrm, a. egg-shaped.

ō´vine, a. of or like sheep.

ōvip´arous, a. producing young in eggs.

ōvipŏs´tor (-z-), n. tube with which insect deposits eggs.

ō´void, a. egg-shaped.

ō´vum, n. (pl. -a), germ in female

animal from which the young is developed.

owe (ō), v.t. be in debt to; be indebted for. ow´ing (ōī-), a. yet to be paid; due.

owl, n. night bird of prey; wise-looking dullard. owl´ĕt, n. young owl. owl´ish, a. like an owl.

own (ōn), a. (after possessive) and not another's; for one's unaided self; (abs.) what is one's own. v.t. & i. have as property, possess; acknowledge authorship or paternity; admit as valid, true, &c. own´er (ōn-), n. possessor; (Naut. sl.) ship's captain or master. ~ship, n. possessing; identity of owner.

ŏx, n. (pl. oxen), kinds of large horned ruminant quadruped; castrated male of domestic species. ~bow, U-shaped collar of ox-yoke; *horse-shoe bend in river. ~eye, large eye. ~lip, hybrid between primrose and cowslip.

ŏxăl´ic, a. of wood-sorrel.

Ŏx´ford (ō-), ~ bags, very wide trousers. ~ frame, picture-frame with cross at each corner. ~ mixture, dark-grey cloth. ~ shoes, *oxfords, low shoes, laced over instep.

ŏx´īde, n. compound of oxygen with an element or organic radical. ŏx´idize, v.t. & i. (-zableˈ), cause to combine with oxygen; cover with oxide, make rusty; combine with oxygen; rust. ŏxīdīzā´tion, n.

Ŏxō´nian (ō´-), a. of Oxford. n. an Oxford man.

ŏx´ygen, n. a colourless scentless tasteless gas essential to animal and vegetable life. ŏx´ygēnāte (-tableˈ), ~nīze (-zableˈ), vv.t. supply or treat our mix with oxygen; oxidize. ŏxy´gĕnous, a.

ŏxyhy´drogen, n. gaseous mixture of oxygen and hydrogen.

ŏxymŏr´on, n. figure of speech with pointed conjunction of seeming contradictories.

ŏx´ytone, n. (Gk. gram.) with acute accent on last syllable.

---

oys'ter, n. kinds of bivalve mollusc usually eaten alive.

ozō'cerite, ozŏk'erite, n. wax-like fossil resin.

ozōne', n. condensed form of oxygen with refreshing odour.

P

pāb'ūlum, n. food.

pace¹, n. a step with the foot; any special gait; speed, rate of progression. v.t. & i. (-ceable), walk with slow regular step; set the pace for (runner in race, &c.). ~maker, one who sets the pace. pā'cer, n. pace-maker; pacing horse.

‖ **pā'cē²**, prep. by leave of; with all due deference to.

pac'hȳderm (-k-), n. thick-skinned quadruped; (fig.) thick-skinned person. **pachȳderm'atous** (-k-), a. thick-skinned; (fig.) lacking in sensitiveness.

pacif'ic, a. fond of, tending to, peace. ~ation, n.; ~atory, a.

pacif'icist, ~ism, and (incorrect but usual) pā'cifist, ~ism, nn. advocate, advocacy, of the abolition of war.

pā'cify, v.t. (-iable), appease; reduce to quiet.

pack, n. bundle made to be carried by man or beast; bale of goods; lot, set; hounds of a hunt; forwards of a Rugby-football team; set of playing-cards. v.t. & i. form into a pack for transport or storage; dispose clothes, &c. in bag or other receptacle; fill (jury, meeting) with partisans. ~horse, horse used for carrying packs. ~man, pedlar with pack. ~thread, stout thread. **păck'age**, n. parcel, bale. **păck'ĕt**, n. small package; mailboat (also **păcket-boat**); large sum lost or won.

păct, n. covenant; compact.

păd, n. soft saddle; piece of soft stuff used to raise surface, improve shape, &c.; leg-guard in games; sheets of blotting or writing paper in a block. v.t. make soft; improve shape of, fill

out, protect, with pads or padding. **pădd'ing**, n. (esp.) literary matter inserted merely to increase quantity.

păd'dle, n. paddling-implement with broad blade at one or each end; striking-board in paddle-wheel; (Zool.) fin or flipper; action or spell of paddling. v.i. & t. play with paddle or paddles; row gently; walk with bare feet in the sea, &c. ~wheel, wheel with transverse boards successively striking water and so propelling ship.

pădd'ock¹, n. small field or enclosure; in Australia, &c., any enclosed piece of land.

pădd'ock², (arch., dial.) frog or toad.

Pădd'ȳ¹, p-, n. (colloq.) Irishman; (sl., p-), rage, temper.

pădd'ȳ², n. rice growing or in the husk. ~bird (Anglo-Ind.), species of white egret which frequent the paddy-fields. ~field, a rice-field.

pădd'ȳwhack, n. (colloq.) a rage, fit of temper.

‖ **păd'ishah, pad'shah** (pah-), n. title in Persia of the Shah, in Europe formerly of the Sultan of Turkey, in India of the British sovereign.

păd'lock, n. detachable lock with pivoted hoop to pass through staple or ring. v.t. secure with padlock.

padre (pahd'rā), n. in India, a minister or priest of any Christian Church; (sl.) chaplain in navy or army.

pae'an, n. song of triumph or thanksgiving.

pā'gan, a. acknowledging neither Jehovah, Christ, nor Allah; non-Christian. n. a pagan person. ~ish, a.; ~ism, n.; ~ize, v.t.

pāge¹, n. boy employed as liveried servant or personal attendant. v.t. attend on as page; °call or summon by page.

pāge², n. one side of leaf of book. v.t. number pages of (book); make up into pages.

---

pā′geant (-jnt), *n.* spectacular performance, usu. illustrative of historical events; any brilliant show. **pā′geantry,** *n.* what serves to make a pageant.

pā′ginate, *v.t.* number pages of book. **~tion,** *n.*

pagō′da, *n.* a sacred tower of Chinese or Indian type; obsolete Indian coin. **~tree,** species of trees cultivated in China, India and Japan; (fig.) mythical tree feigned to produce pagodas (coin).

pah (earlier **hippah**), *n.* Maori village or fort.

paid, *p.t.* & *p.p.* of pay.

pail, *n.* round open-topped vessel for carrying water, milk, &c.

pain, *n.* bodily or mental suffering; (pl.) endeavours; (pl.) throes of childbirth. *v.t.* inflict pain on. **~ful,** *a.* giving or involving pain. **~less,** *a.*

paint, *n.* colouring-matter prepared for application to surface. *v.t.* & *i.* portray or make pictures in colours; coat with paint; depict in words. **paint′er¹,** *n.* an artist; painter of woodwork, &c. **paint′ing,** *n.* (esp.) a painted picture.

paint′er², *n.* rope attaching boat to ship, &c.

pair, *n.* set of two; thing with two similar parts not used apart; engaged or married or mated couple. *v.t.* & *i.* arrange or unite as pair or in pairs; mate.

pajamas. See pyjamas.

pa′kēha (pah-), *n.* in New Zealand, a white man, European.

pāl, *n.* (sl.) comrade. *v.i.* make friends with.

pal′ace, *n.* official residence of sovereign, archbishop, or bishop; stately mansion or building.

pal′adin, *n.* peer of Charlemagne's court; knight-errant.

palæog′raphy, *n.* study of ancient writings and inscriptions.

palæolith′ic, *a.* of, using, &c. the earliest stone implements.

palæontol′ogy, *n.* study of extinct organisms.

palæozō′ic, *a.* of, containing, ancient forms of life.

palanquin′, -keen (-kēn), *n.* eastern covered litter.

pal′ate, *n.* roof of mouth; sense of taste or appetite. **~table,** *a.* pleasant to the taste; agreeable.

pal′atal, *a.* of the palate; (of sounds) made with tongue and palate. *n.* palatal sound or letter.

palā′tial (-shl), *a.* of or like a palace.

pal′atine, *a.* having local jurisdiction exclusive of the royal or imperial courts. **palat′inate,** *n.* count palatine's territory.

pala′ver (-ahv-), *n.* conference; empty words; cajolery. *v.i.* & *i.* use many words; cajole.

pāle¹, *n.* stake or lath serving as part of fence; boundary.

pāle², *a.* (of complexion) whitish, not ruddy; faintly coloured; (of colour) faint, (of light) dim. *v.t.* & *i.* grow or make pale.

pal′etot (-tō), *n.* loose outer garment.

pal′ette, *n.* artist's flat tablet for mixing colours on.

pa′lfrey (pawl-), *n.* saddle-horse for lady's or quiet use.

Pa′li (pah-), *n.* language used in canonical books of Buddhists.

pal′impsest, *n.* parchment, &c. used for second time after original writing has been erased.

pal′indrome, *n.* word, line, &c. that reads the same backwards as forwards. **palindrōm′ic,** *a.*

pā′ling, *n.* fence of pales.

palingen′esis (-nj-), *n.* regeneration; revival; resurrection.

pal′inode, *n.* recantation; poem containing it.

palisāde′, *n.* fence of stakes; a stake. *v.t.* enclose with palisade.

pall¹ (pawl), *n.* cloth spread over coffin, &c.; ecclesiastical vestment; (fig.) cloak (of darkness). **~bearer,** mourner holding edge of pall.

pall² (pawl), *v.i.* become tiresome.

Pallā′dian, *a.* (Archit.) in the pseudo-classical style of the 16th-c. Italian Palladio.

zh, as (rou)ge; ē=I; ñ, ūr, =ēr; ȳ, y̆, =I, ĭ; and see p. 4. * =U.S.

3495   M

pallā′dium, *n.* (pl. -*ia*), object or principle with which the safety of something is regarded as bound up; a rare metallic element.

pall′et, *n.* straw bed.

palliásse′, *n.* hard mattress.

pall′iāte, *v.t.* (-*liable*), alleviate without curing; excuse, extenuate. ~tion, ~tor, *nn.* pall′iātive, *a.* & *n.* giving, thing giving, temporary or partial relief.

pall′id, *a.* pale; sickly-looking.

pall′ium, *n.* archbishop's pall.

pall′or, *n.* pallidness.

palm (pahm), *n.* inner surface of hand between wrist and fingers; kinds of chiefly tropical tree; branch of this as symbol. *v.t.* (with *off*, *off on*) foist; pass off as superior. ~oil, oil from kinds of palm-tree; money given as bribe. ~ Sunday, Sunday before Easter. pál′mar, *a.* of or in palm of hand. pál′mary, *a.* deserving the palm; of highest excellence. pál′māte, ~d (-t, -id), *aa.* shaped like palm of hand; web-footed.

pa′lmer (pahm-), *n.* pilgrim from Holy Land with palm-branch. ~worm, kind of caterpillar.

pălmétt′ō, *n.* (pl. -*os*), dwarf fan-palm.

pál′mipěd, *a.* & *n.* web-footed (bird).

pa′lmist (pahm-), *n.* practiser of palmistry. ~ry, *n.* divination from lines in palm of hand.

pa′lmy (pahm-), *a.* bearing palm-trees; flourishing.

palmŷr′a, *n.* kind of palm cultivated in India and Ceylon, with fan-shaped leaves, used for thatch, matting, hats, &c.

pál′pable, *a.* that can be touched; that can be verified. ~bility, *n.*

pál′pitāte, *v.i.* pulsate, throb. ~tion, *n.* (esp.) abnormal throbbing of the heart in disease.

palsy (pawl′zi), *n.* paralysis; paralytic trembling. *v.t.* (usu. in *p.p.*) paralyse, make helpless.

pa′lter (pawl-), *v.i.* equivocate, shuffle.

pa′ltry (pawl-), *a.* petty, contemptible, trifling.

păm′pas (-z), *n.* S.-Amer. plains.

păm′per, *v.t.* over-indulge.

pămph′lět, *n.* thin paper-covered book, usu. controversial. ~eer′, *n.* writer of pamphlets.

pän[1], *n.* shallow vessel used in cooking, &c.; shallow receptacle or tray; hollow or depression in the ground, esp. a *salt-pan*; (S.-Afr.) dried-up salt-marsh or pool-bed. *v.i.* (with *out*) yield much or little gold; (fig.) turn out (well, &c.). păn′cāke, thin flat fried battercake.

*păn[2], *v.t.* (sl.) decry, disparage, find fault with. *păn′er, *n.* fault-finder.

Pän[3], *n.* the spirit of nature; paganism. ~pipe, set of reeds played on with the mouth.

|| pan[4] (pahn), *n.* (E.-Ind.) betel-leaf; combination of betel-leaf, areca-nut, lime, &c., used as a masticatory.

păn-, *pref.* = all, united, in comb.: ~-African, of, for, all Africans. ~-American, of N. & S. America. ~-Anglican, of the Anglican Church and its branches. ~-German, of all the Germans in political union. ~-Hellenism, political union of all Greeks. ~-Islam, union of Mohammedan world. ~-Slavism, movement for union of all Slavs.

panacë′a, *n.* universal remedy.

Pánama′ (-ah), *n.* (also *P.* hat), light hat of straw-like material.

|| panchayat, punchayet (pŭnchah′yat), *n.* (E.-Ind.) council of five (or now usually more) persons, assembled as jury or arbitrators, or as a committee to decide on matters affecting a village, community, or body.

pănc′rëas, *n.* gland near stomach supplying a digestive fluid.

păn′da, *n.* Indian racoon-like animal, the red bear-cat.

păn′dal, *n.* (Anglo-Ind.) shed, booth, or arbour.

păn′děcts, *n.pl.* Justinian's compendium of Roman civil law.

pănděmō′nium, *n.* scene of anarchy; confusion and din.

---

māte, mēte, mīte, mōte, mūte, mōōt; răck, rěck, rĭck, rŏck, rŭck, rōōk;

pan′der, n. go-between in illicit amours; procurer. v.i. basely minister to evil passions, &c.

pāne, n. single piece of glass in window.

panegy′ric, n. laudatory discourse; eulogy. ~al, a. panĕgȳ′rist, n. speaker or writer of panegyrics. ~ize, v.t. laud.

pan′el, n. distinct compartment inserted in door, wainscot, &c.; vertical strip of material in dress; thin board with picture on it; list of jurors, jury; list of Health Insurance doctors for a district, a doctor's list of insured persons. v.t. adorn with panels, **pan′elling,** n.

pāng, n. sudden sharp pain.

pangō′lin (-ngg-), n. scaly ant-eater.

pan′ic, a. (of fear, &c.) unreasoning, excessive. n. sudden and infectious fright.

pan′icle, n. (Bot.) an irregular raceme as in oats and many grasses. **panic′ular,** ~late(d), aa.

panne, n. a soft long-napped cloth used as dress-material.

pann′ier (-nyer), n. basket carried by beast of burden, or by person on shoulders; part of skirt looped up round hips.

pan′oplỹ, n. full armour (now usu. fig.). **pan′oplied** (-līd), a.

panora′ma (-ah-), n. cylindrical surface painted with scenery and unrolled before spectators; continuous revolving landscape; wide prospect. **panoram′ic,** a.

pan′sỹ (-z-), n. a flowering plant, the heartsease.

pant, v.i. & t. breathe quickly and audibly; throb; yearn. n. a panting respiration; a throb.

pantalettes′ (-ts), n.pl. child's frilled drawers; woman's knickerbockers, &c.

pantaloon′, n. pantomime character serving as butt to clown; (pl.: chiefly U.S.) trousers, pants.

pantec′hnicon (-kn-), n. place for storing or van for removing furniture.

pan′theism, n. identification of

God with the universe. ~ist, n.; ~is′tic, ~ist′ical, aa.

panthe′on, n. temple of all the gods; building with memorials of a nation's great dead.

pan′ther, n. leopard; *cougar, puma. ~ess, n.

pan′tile, n. curved roof-tile.

pan′tograph (-ahf), n. instrument for copying diagrams to any scale.

pan′tomime, n. dumb show; dramatic performance for children; dumb-show actor.

pan′trỹ, n. room in which provisions, &c. are kept.

pants, n.pl. trousers (chiefly U.S.); long tight drawers.

pāp, n. nipple of breast; soft or semi-liquid food for infants.

papa′ (-ah), n. father.

pā′pacỹ, n. Pope's office and dignity; the papal system.

pā′pal, a. of the Pope or his office.

papāverā′ceous (-shus), a. of the poppy family.

pā′per, n. substance made of pulp of rags, straw, wood, &c.; banknotes, negotiable documents; set of examination questions; newspaper; essay, memorandum. v.t. paste paper on wall, &c.; wrap up in paper. ~chase, cross-country run on scent laid by scattering small pieces of paper. ~hanger, wall-paperer. ~hanging, decorating with wallpaper; occupation of a paperhanger. ~money, bank-notes.

papier mâché (păp′yă măsh′ā), n. moulded paper pulp made into solid objects.

papiliona′ceous (-yonāshus), a. (Bot.) butterfly-shaped.

papill′a, n. (pl. -ae), nipple-shaped protuberance. **păp′illarỹ,** a. = papilla-shaped. **păp′illāte, păp′il-lōse,** aa. having papillae.

pā′pist, n. adherent of the Pope or papal power; Roman Catholic. **papis′tical,** a.; **pā′pistrỹ,** n. = Popery.

papoose′, n. Red-Indian child.

păpp′ỹ, a. like pap.

papyr′us (-ī-), n. the paper reed;

---

māre, mĕre, mīre, mōre, mūre; părt, pĕrt, pŏrt; italics, vague sounds;

M 2

ancient writing-material made from its stem.

pãr, *n.* equal footing; average or normal value or degree.

pã'rable, *n.* narrative used to typify some moral or spiritual truth; apologue, allegory.

parãb'ola, *n.* plane curve formed by intersection of cone with plane parallel to its side.

parabõl'ĭc, *aa.* expressed by parable (usu. *-ical*); of the nature of a parabola (usu. *-ic*).

pãrachute' (-shōōt), *n.* apparatus expanding like umbrella for enabling balloonist, &c. to descend to earth from a great height.

pã'raclête, *n.* advocate (as title of Holy Ghost).

parade', *n.* display, ostentation; muster of troops for inspection; ground used for this; public promenade. *v.t. & i.* (*-dable*). assemble for parade; display ostentatiously; promenade.

pã'radigm (-ĭm), *n.* tabulated inflexions of a word.

pã'radise, *n.* garden of Eden; heaven; region or state of felicity. **pãradis'ĭac** (-z-), **~al,** *aa.*

pã'radox, *n.* statement contrary to received opinion; person or thing conflicting with preconceived notions. **paradox'ical,** *a.*

pã'raffin, *n.* waxy substance distilled from shale, wood, &c.; oil of similar origin.

pã'ragon, *n.* model of excellence; excellent person or thing.

pã'ragraph (-ahf), *n.* distinct passage in book usually marked by indentation of first line; symbol (¶); detached item of news in newspaper.

pã'rakeet, pã'roquet (-kĕt), *n.* small long-tailed parrot.

pã'rallax, *n.* (Astron.) apparent displacement of object due to different position of observer; angular amount of this.

pã'rallel, *a.* (of lines) continuously equidistant; precisely analogous or corresponding to. *n.* imaginary line on earth's surface, line on map, marking degree of lati-

tude; comparison, analogy; mark (‖) of reference. *v.t.* represent as similar; compare; be parallel or correspond to.

pã'rallelepĭped, *n.* solid contained by parallelograms.

pã'rallelism, *n.* being parallel.

pã'rallel'ogram, *n.* four-sided rectilineal figure whose opposite sides are parallel.

parãl'ogism, *n.* violation of logic; false reasoning; a fallacy.

pã'ralÿse (-z), *v.t.* (*-sable*), affect with paralysis; make helpless or ineffectual; cripple.

parãl'ÿsis, *n.* partial incapacity to move or feel.

parãlÿt'ic, *a.* of or affected with paralysis. *n.* paralysed person.

pãramãtt'a, *n.* dress-fabric of merino and cotton.

pã'ramount, *a.* supreme; superior.

pã'ramour (-oor), *n.* illicit lover.

par'ang (pah-), *n.* large heavy sheath-knife used by Malays as weapon, &c.

pã'rapet, *n.* low wall at edge of roof, balcony, bridge, &c.; (Mil.) mound along front of trench.

pã'rapherna'lia, *n.pl.* personal belongings; accessories.

pã'raphrase (-z), *n.* restatement of the sense of a passage in other words. *v.t.* (*-sable*), render in paraphrase. **pãraphrãs'tic,** *a.*

pã'rasite, *n.* interested hanger-on; sycophant; animal or plant living in or on another. **parasĭt'ic,** *a.*; **pã'rasitism,** *n.*

pã'rasol', *n.* small sun-umbrella.

parãtax'is, *n.* use of separate sentences, &c. one after another without grammatical subordination.

pãratÿ'phoid, *n.* kinds of fever distinguishable from typhoid only by bacteriological examination.

parb'oil, *v.t.* scald surface of in boiling water; scorch.

pãrb'uckle, *n.* rope for raising or lowering casks, &c.

pãr'cel, *n.* package of goods, &c.;

portion; piece of land. *v.t.* divide into portions. **~gilt,** partly gilded.

pār′cenarẏ, pār′cener, *nn.* jointheirship, joint heir.

pārch, *v.t. & i.* dry by exposure to heat; roast; make dry.

pārch′ment, *n.* skin prepared for writing, &c.; MS. on this.

pārd[1], *n.* (arch.) leopard.

pārd[2], *n.* (sl., esp. U.S.) partner.

pārd′on, *n.* forgiveness; remission of punishment. *v.t.* forgive; abstain from punishing. **~able,** *a.* easily excused.

pāre, *v.t.* (-*rable*), trim or reduce by cutting away edge or surface of; whittle away. **pār′ing,** *n.* that pared off; the rind.

pāregō′ric, *n.* a tincture of opium.

pār′ent, *n.* father or mother; forefather; source, origin. **~age,** *n.* lineage; descent. **~hood,** *n.*; **parén′tal,** *a.*

parén′thesis, *n.* (pl. -*theses*), word, clause, or sentence inserted into a passage independently of the grammatical sequence; (sing. or pl.) round brackets used for this; (fig.) interlude. **parénthĕt′ic,** *a.* inserted as parenthesis.

‖ **par excellence** (pär ĕ′kselahns), *adv.* by virtue of special excellence.

pār′gĕt (-j-), *v.t. & n.* rough-cast; plaster.

parhē′lion (-lyon), *n.* (pl. -*ia*), bright spot in solar halo.

pā′riah, *n.* Indian of a low or no caste; social outcast. **~dog,** vagabond dog of low breed which frequents towns and villages in India and the East. **~kite,** the scavenger-kite of India.

Pār′ian, *a.* from Paros. *n.* kind of fine white porcelain.

pari′ĕtal, *a.* of the wall of the body or any of its cavities.

pā′ri mūtüĕl′ (-rē), *n.* form of betting in which those who have staked on winning horse divide the stakes on the rest.

‖ **pār′ī pāss′ū,** *adv.* with simultaneous progress.

pā′rish, *n.* ecclesiastical division

having its own church and clergyman; poor-law district; inhabitants of parish. **parish′ioner** (-sho-), *n.* inhabitant of parish.

pā′rity, *n.* being on a par; equivalence; parallelism.

pārk, *n.* large enclosed piece of ground attached to country house or devoted to public use; artillery, space in camp occupied by it; place assigned for storing motor-cars, aeroplanes, &c. *v.t.* enclose as a park; arrange compactly in place assigned.

pārk′ẏ, *a.* (sl.) chilly.

pārl′ance, *n.* way of speaking.

pārl′ey, *n.* (pl. -*eys*), meeting between representatives of opposed forces to discuss terms. *v.i.* hold discussion on terms.

pārl′iament (-la-), *n.* deliberative body consisting of House of Commons and House of Lords and forming with the sovereign the legislature of the United Kingdom; legislative assembly in other countries. **~ār′ian,** *n.* skilled parliamentary debater. **~ary,** *a.* of, in, concerned with, or enacted by parliament.

pārl′our (-ler), *n.* sitting-room in a small house; private room in inn. **~maid,** maid waiting at table.

pārl′ous, *a.* hard to escape from or deal with; embarrassing.

Pārmēsăn′ (-z-), *n.* hard cheese of the kind made at Parma.

Pārnăss′us, *n.* the realm of poetry; poetic fame.

parō′chial (-k-), *a.* of a or the parish; of narrow range, merely local. **~ism,** *n.*

pā′rodẏ, *n.* composition in which an author's characteristics are ridiculed by imitation; travesty. *v.t.* write parody of; caricature. **pā′rodist,** *n.*

parōle′, *n.* word of honour engaging giver to abstain from attempting escape or from resuming hostilities. (Mil.) password.

păronomā′sia (-zya), *n.* play on words; pun.

paroquet. See parakeet.

parŏt'id, a. near the ear. n. a parotid gland.

pă'roxy̆sm, n. sudden violent access of pain, rage, &c.

parq'uet (-kĭt), n. flooring of wooden blocks arranged in a pattern; *ground floor of theatre auditorium, esp. from front of stage to beneath gallery. v.t. lay with parquet. ~ing, ~ry, nn. parquet-work.

parr, n. young salmon.

pă'rricide, n. murder or murderer of father, parent, or person entitled to veneration. ~'dal, a.

pă'rrot, n. kinds of bird with hooked bill, some of which can imitate speech; unintelligent imitator or chatterer.

pă'rry, v.t. (-iable), ward off by interposing arm, sword, &c. n. act of parrying.

parse (-z), v.t. (-sable), describe (word), analyse (sentence), in terms of grammar.

Parsee', n. Indian adherent of Zoroastrianism. ~ism, n.

Pars'eval, n. type of non-rigid German airship.

pars'imony, n. avoidance of waste; economy, frugality; stinginess. parsimo'nious, a.

pars'ley, n. herb used for seasoning and garnishing.

pars'nip, n. plant with yellow root cooked for food.

pars'on, n. the clergyman of a parish; (colloq.) clergyman. ~age, n. parson's house.

part, n. some but not all; share, allotted portion; assigned character or rôle; one of the melodies making up the harmony of a concerted piece; region, direction, way; side in dispute or dealing; (pl.) ability. adv. partly, in part. v.t. & i. divide into parts; separate (friends, combatants, &c.); quit one another's company; distribute in shares; (sl.) pay money. ~owner, sharer of ownership. ~song, song for three or more voice-parts.

partake', v.i. (-tŏŏk, -tāken), take a share of or with; eat or drink some of; have something of the character of.

parterre' (-tār), n. space filled with flower-beds and the paths between them; *ground floor of theatre auditorium, esp. part beneath gallery.

parti' (-ē), n. person regarded as eligible or in specified light in the marriage market.

par'tial (-shl), a. biased in favour of one side; not total or complete. partial'ity (-shi-), n. bias; liking for.

parti'cipant, n. one who shares.

parti'cipate, v.t. & i. (-pable), share in by common action; have a share in. ~tion, ~tor, nn.

par'ticiple (-ts-), n. adjective formed by inflexion from a verb. particip'ial, a.

par'ticle, n. minute portion of matter; uninflected word.

par'ticoloured (-ŭlerd), a. differently coloured; variegated.

partic'ular, a. relating to one as distinguished from others; peculiar; scrupulously exact; fastidious. n. detail, item; (pl.) detailed account.

partic'ularism, n. exclusive devotion to a party, sect, &c.

particulă'rity, n. fullness or minuteness of detail.

partic'ularize, v.t. & i. (-zable), mention one by one; go into particulars. ~zation, n.

partic'ularly, adv. very; to an especial extent; in detail.

part'ing, n. leave-taking; division; dividing-line.

part'isan¹ (-zn), n. (hist.) kind of halberd.

partisan'² (-z-), n. adherent of a party or side or cause. ~ship, n. strong party spirit.

parti'tion, n. division into parts; structure effecting a division; receptacle or cell so made. v.t. divide into distinct parts.

par'titive, a. (Gram.) denoting partition or a part. n. a partitive word.

---

māte, mēte, mīte, mōte, mūte, mōōt; răck, rĕck, rĭck, rŏck, rŭck, rŏŏk,

pärt′ly, *adv.* in part; in some degree; not wholly.

pärt′ner, *n.* sharer; one who shares in a business; either of a pair in marriage or dancing or a game. *v.t.* arrange as partners, or as partner with; be partner to. ∼**ship**, *n.*

pärt′ridge, *n.* kinds of game-bird; its flesh; *other birds resembling this, as (Northern U.S.) ruffled grouse, (Southern U.S.) bob-white.

pārtūr′ient, *a.* about to give birth.

pārtūri′tion, *n.* child-birth.

pär′ty, *n.* body of persons united in a cause or in opposition to another party; body of persons travelling or engaged together; social reception; person consenting or contributing to an affair; either side in lawsuit, contract, or other transaction.

pärv′enu (-ōō), *n.* person who has risen from obscurity; upstart.

pärv′is, *n.* enclosed area or court in front of cathedral, &c.

|| **pas** (pah), *n.* precedence.

päsc′hal (-k-), *a.* of the Passover; of Easter.

pasha (pah′sha, pashah′), *n.* Turkish or Egyptian officer of high rank. **pa′shalic** (pah-), *n.* pasha's district or jurisdiction.

päsque′-flower (-skf-), *n.* kind of anemone.

päsquinäde′, *n.* lampoon.

pass (-ah-), *v.t. & i.* (p.p. *passed*, or as adj. *past*), move onward, proceed; be current; change into; die; go by; come to an end; percolate; be accepted as adequate; be sanctioned; satisfy examiner; happen; go across; outstrip; surpass; spend; hand round; give currency to; utter. *n.* passing, esp. of examination; standard that satisfies examiners without entitling to honours; state, critical position; written permission or ticket or order; thrust in fencing; (Footb.) passing of ball from one player to another; narrow passage through mountains, &c. *∼ out,* (sl.)

lose consciousness. *∼ the buck,* (sl.) shift responsibility. *∼ up,* (sl.) let go by.

pa′ssable (-ah-), *a.* that will pass muster; fairly good; (of river, &c.) that can be crossed.

päss′age, *n.* passing, transit; crossing, being conveyed, from port to port; corridor; (pl.) what passes between two persons; part of a speech or literary work.

päss′ant, *a.* (Herald.) walking sideways as walking past.

|| **passé** (pä′sā), *a.* (fem. **-ée**), past his, her, or its prime; gone off, out of date.

päss′enger (-j-), *n.* traveller by public conveyance.

pa′sser (-ah-), ∼**by**, *nn.* one who happens to be passing.

päss′erine, *a.* of the sparrow kind.

|| **päss′im**, *adv.* every here and there; all over the place.

pa′ssing (-ah-), *n.* act of moving on or by; dying. ∼**-bell**, bell rung immediately after a death.

pä′ssion (-shn), *n.* strong emotion; anger; sexual love; (usu. **P∼**) the sufferings of Christ on the cross. ∼**-flower**, plant with flower suggesting instruments of the Passion. ∼**-play**, mystery play of the Passion. ∼ **Week**, week before Holy Week.

pä′ssionate (-sho-), *a.* prone to passion; lacking self-control.

päss′ive, *a.* acted upon, not acting; inert; submissive; of, in, the passive voice. *n.* passive voice or form. ∼ **voice**, of verb, indicating that subj. suffers the action of the verb. **passiv′ity**, *n.*

Pass′over (-ah-), *n.* Jewish commemoration or lamb sacrificed at it.

pass′port (-ah-), *n.* official document showing traveller's identity.

pass′word (-ah-), *n.* selected word or phrase distinguishing friend from enemies; countersign.

past (-ah-), *a.* gone by, just over. *n.* past time; person's past life or career. *prep.* beyond. *adv.* by.

päste, *n.* flour kneaded with water, suet, butter, &c. as material for pastry ; flour and water as adhesive mixture ; relish of pounded fish, &c. ; material of imitation gems. *v.t.* (-*table*), fasten with paste ; cover by pasting. ~board, cardboard ; (sl.) visiting or playing card.

pās'tel, *n.* dry pigment-paste used for crayons, a drawing in this ; woad. pās'telist, *n.* artist drawing in pastel.

pās'tern, *n.* part of horse's foot between fetlock and hoof.

pās'teurism (-ter-), *n.* Pasteur's method of inoculation with virus as preventive or cure of hydrophobia, &c. pās'teurize (-ter-), *v.t.* (-*zable*), apply pasteurism to ; sterilize (milk, &c.) by exposure to high temperature.

pastiche' (-ēsh), *n.* musical or other medley of borrowings.

pās'til, -ille (pāstēl'), *n.* roll of aromatic paste ; a lozenge.

pa'stime (-ah-), *n.* recreation ; a sport or game.

pa'stor (-ah-), *n.* minister of a congregation ; spiritual adviser. pas'torate (-ah-), *n.* pastor's office or tenure of it ; the body of pastors. *pastor'ium, n.* parsonage.

pa'storal (-ah-), *a.* of shepherds ; of rural life ; of a pastor. *n.* pastoral poem or picture ; letter from bishop or other pastor to clergy or people.

pā'stry, *n.* baked flour-paste ; food made of or with it.

pa'sture (-ah-), *n.* herbage for cattle to eat ; land or field under such crop. *v.t. & i.* put cattle to pasture ; graze on land. pa'sturage (-ahscher-), *n.* business of pasturing ; pasture.

pa'sty¹ (pah-), *n.* venison, &c. enclosed in paste without pie-dish and baked. pā'sty², *a.* like paste, doughy ; pallid.

pāt, *v.t.* strike gently with open hand or other flat surface. *n.* patting touch or sound ; small lump of butter. *a.* opportune. ~ball, game of rounders ; poor or feeble lawn-tennis.

pătch, *n.* piece put on in mending ; piece of plaster over wound ; irregular stain on surface ; small plot of ground. *v.t.* mend with patch(es) ; piece together ; (with *up*) patch sufficiently to serve ; set (quarrel, &c.) to rights for the time. ~work, patching ; thing made up of odds and ends. pātch'y, *a.*

pătch'ouli (-ōōl-), *n.* an Indian perfume.

pāte, *n.* (*arch., joc.*) head.

pāt'en, *n.* plate for eucharist bread, usu. of silver.

pā'tent, *a.* obvious, unconcealed ; patented ; *letters* ~, open letter from sovereign, &c. conferring some privilege, e.g. a title, or the sole right for a term to make or sell something. *n.* (*often* pā-), letters patent ; grant of sole right to make or sell, invention or process protected by this. *v.t.* (*often* pā-), obtain patent for (invention). pātentee' (*or* pā-), *n.* holder of a patent.

pā'ter, *n.* (sl.) father. pāterfamil'iās, *n.* father of a family.

patern'al, *a.* of a father ; fatherly. patern'ity, *n.* fatherhood ; paternal descent.

păt'ernoster, *n.* the Lord's prayer in Latin, bead for it at intervals in rosary ; fishing-line with hooks at intervals.

path (pahth, *pl.* pahdhz), *n.* footway ; track ; line along which person or thing moves.

Pathan' (-tahn), *n.* member of Afghan tribes in, or on frontier of, India.

pathět'ic, *a.* exciting or appealing to compassion ; of the emotions.

pathŏl'ogy, *n.* the study of disease. pătholŏg'ical, *a.* ; ~gist, *n.*

pā'thŏs, *n.* pathetic quality.

pā'tience (-shns), *n.* endurance under pain, weariness, &c. ; perseverance ; card-game for one.

pā'tient (-shnt), *a.* endowed with or showing patience. *n.* person under medical treatment.

păt'ois (-twah), *n.* regional dialect of common people.

---

ah, awl, oil, boor, cow, dowry ; chin, go, bang, so, ship, thin ; dh, as *th*(e) ;

pā´triärch (-k), *n.* father and ruler of family or tribe; bishop of certain sees in the Eastern and R.-C. Churches; venerable old man. **pātriär´chal** (*or* pă- ; -k-), *a.* **pā´triärchate** (*or* pă- ; -k-), *n.* office or rank of ecclesiastical or tribal patriarch. **pā´triärchy** (*or* pă- ; -k-), *n.* tribal system or community under patriarchs.

patri´cian (-shn), *n.* person of noble birth. *a.* of the nobility.

păt´ricide, *n.* murder(er) of a father. **pătrici´dal**, *a.*

păt´rimony, *n.* property inherited from father or ancestors.

pā´triot (*or* pă-), *n.* champion or lover of his country. **pātriŏt´ic**, *a.* ; **pā´triotism** (*or* pă-), *n.*

patris´tic, *a.* of the Fathers of the Church.

patrōl´, *n.* going the rounds to see that all is right; man or party or ship(s) charged with this. *v.i.* & *t.* act as patrol; go the rounds as patrol.

pā´tron (*or* pă-), *n.* one who countenances, protects, or employs a person, cause, art, &c.; tutelary saint; person having right of presentation to a benefice. **patrō´nal**, *a.* of a patron saint. **~ess**, *n.*

pā´tronage (*or* pă-), *n.* patron's help; dispensing of appointments; patronizing airs. **pā´tronize** (*or* pă-), *v.t.* (*-zable*), act as patron to; support, encourage; treat condescendingly.

pătronym´ic, *a.* (of name) indicating one's father or descent. *n.* patronymic name; surname.

‖ **pătt(ī)´amár**, *n.* (E.-Ind.) courier; Indian advice-boat or dispatch-boat; lateen-rigged sailing-boat of west coast of India.

păt´ten, *n.* wooden sole mounted on iron ring for raising wearer's shoe above mud, &c.

păt´ter¹, *v.i.* & *t.* say, talk, with rapid utterance. *n.* rapid talk; piece of this introduced into a song; (sl.) lingo of a class.

păt´ter², *v.i.* (of rain, &c.) make tapping sound; (of child, &c.)

run with quick audible steps. *n.* sound of pattering.

păt´tern, *n.* excellent example; model; sample of cloth, &c.; decorative design on surface.

păt´ty, *n.* pie or pasty to be served to one person.

pau´city, *n.* fewness; smallness of amount.

paunch, *n.* belly, stomach.

paup´er, *n.* a poor person; recipient of poor-law relief. **~ism**, *n.* being a pauper. **~ize**, *v.t.* (*-zable*). reduce to pauperism, esp. by doles, &c. **~ization**, *n.*

pause (-z), *n.* interval of inaction or silence; break made in speech or reading; (Mus.) mark (⌢ or ⌣) denoting lengthening of note or rest. *v.i.* make a pause; wait.

pāve, *v.t.* (*-vable*), cover with pavement; (fig.) lead up to, make easy. **pā´vement** (-vm-), *n.* layer of flat stones, tiles, asphalt, &c., as surface of road or floor; paved footway.

pavil´ion (-lyon), *n.* large tent; building for spectators or players of outdoor game; projecting subdivision of building. *v.t.* serve as, enclose like, pavilion.

pā´viour (-vyer), *n.* workman employed in paving.

paw, *n.* foot of beast with claws; (sl.) hand. *v.t.* & *i.* touch with paw; (sl.) handle] with dirty or clumsy hands; (of horse) strike ground with hoof in impatience.

pawk´y, *a.* (of humour, esp. when Scotch) sly, arch quiet, dry.

pawl, *n.* lever with catch for teeth of wheel or bar, bar to prevent capstan, &c. from recoiling.

pawn¹, *n.* piece of least value in chess; (fig.) a mere tool.

pawn², *n.* thing handed over as pledge or security (now chiefly fig.); state of being pledged. *v.t.* deposit as security; borrow money on security of thing deposited; offer (one's life, &c.) as pledge. **~broker**, keeper of shop where money is lent on security of pawned goods.

---

zh, as (*rou*)ge; ē=I; ĭr, ūr,=ẽr; ȳ, ȳ,=I, ĭ; and see p. 4. *=U.S.

păx, *int.* used by schoolboys in demanding a truce.

pay, *v.t. & i.* give as due; discharge debt to; bear the cost; suffer the penalty of; render, bestow (attention, &c.); yield adequate return; (with *out*) let out rope by slackening it. *n.* money paid as wages. **~able**, *a.* that must be paid, due; likely to be profitable. **payee'**, *n.* person to whom money is to be or is paid. **pay'ment**, *n.* paying; sum paid; recompense.

pay'nim, *n.* (arch.) pagan.

pea, *n.* kinds of plant bearing round seeds in pods and cultivated for food; one of its seeds.

peace, *n.* freedom from or cessation of war; treaty securing this; civil order; quiet, calm; harmonious relations. **~maker**, reconciler. **~-offering**, propitiatory gift. **peace'able** (-sa-), *a.* disposed or leading to peace. **peace'ful** (-sf-), *a.* having or marked by peace.

peach¹, *v.i.* (sl.) turn informer.

peach², *n.* a stone-fruit of downy delicately coloured skin. **peach'y**, *a.* like a peach.

pea'cock, *n.* male bird with splendid plumage and fanlike tail; vain person. **~-fowl**, peacock or pea-hen. **~-hen**, female of pea-fowl.

pea'-jăcket, *n.* double-breasted jacket of thick cloth.

peak¹, *v.i.* waste away.

peak², *n.* pointed top, esp. of mountain; highest point in curve or record of fluctuations; projecting part of cap; narrow part of ship's hold at bow or stern. **peaked** (-kt), *a.*

peal, *n.* loud ringing of bell(s); set of bells; outburst of sound. *v.i. & t.* sound forth, ring (bells), in a peal.

pear (pār), *n.* a fruit of tapering shape. **~-shaped**, *a.*; **~-tree**, *n.*

pearl (pěrl), *n.* lustrous concretion found in oyster and other shells and prized as gem; a size of type (5 point) smaller than this. *v.i.*

& *t.* fish for pearls; (of moisture) form drops, form drops on. **pearl'ý** (pěr-), *a.*

pea'sant (pěz-), *n.* countryman, rustic. **~ry**, *n.* peasants collectively.

pease (-z), *n.* (arch.) = peas.

peat, *n.* vegetable matter decomposed by water and partly carbonized; piece of this as fuel.

pěb'ble, *n.* small water-rounded stone; rock-crystal used for spectacles, lens of this; kinds of agate. **pěbb'lý**, *a.*

pěc'cable, *a.* liable to sin. **pěccadill'ō**, *n.* (pl. *-oes*) venial sin that person is prone to.

pěcc'ant, *a.* offending; corrupt; morbid; ill-disposed. **pěcc'ancy**, *n.* sinfulness; a sin, offence.

pěcc'arý, *n.* American gregarious wild animal of pig kind.

| **pěccā'vī**, *sent. & n.* I have sinned; confession of fault.

pěck¹, *n.* dry measure, 2 gallons.

pěck², *v.t. & i.* strike (thing) or pick up (food) with the beak, as a bird; make dab(s) at; eat fastidiously; break (ground, &c.) with a pointed tool. *n.* stroke given with beak; (joc.) light kiss; (sl.) food. **pěck'er**, *n.* (sl.) nose. **~ish**, *a.* (sl.) hungry.

pěc'toral, *a.* of or for the chest. *n.* ornamental breastplate.

pěc'ūlāte, *v.t. & i.* (-lable), embezzle. **~tion**, **~tor**, *nn.*

pěcū'liar, *a.* belonging to the individual; exclusive; particular, special; odd. **pěcūliā'ritý**, *n.* individual characteristic; oddity.

pěcū'niarý, *a.* of or in money.

pěd'agōgue (-g), *n.* schoolmaster; pedant. **pěd'agogy** (-ŏg-), **~gics** (-ŏj-), *nn.* science of teaching.

pěd'al, *n.* of the foot. *n.* wooden key of organ played with feet; foot-lever in organ, piano, cycle, &c. *v.i. & t.* work pedals.

pěd'ant, *n.* one who insists on strict adherence to formal rules; doctrinaire. **~ic**, *a.*; **~ry**, *n.*

pěd'dle, *v.i. & t.* be a pedlar; potter. **pědd'ling**, *a.* petty.

pěd'ěstal, *n.* base of column;

block on which something stands.

pédes'trian, *a*. going or performed on foot ; prosaic, dull. *n*. walker, traveller on foot. ~**ism**, *n*.

pĕd'icel, **pĕd'icle**, *n*. stalk-like structure in plant or animal.

pĕd'igree, *n*. genealogical table ; ancestral line ; ancient descent.

pĕd'iment, *n*. triangular part crowning front of building.

pĕd'lar, *n*. travelling vendor of small wares. **pĕd'lary**, *n*.

pĕdŏm'eter, *n*. machine enabling one to estimate distance walked.

peduncle (pĭdŭng'kl), *n*. stem of cluster or flower or fruit.

peel[1], *n*. rind of fruit, thin soft bark of young shoots, &c. *v.t.* & *i*. strip of peel ; take off (skin, bark, &c.) ; shed bark or skin or paper or paint ; (of athlete, &c.) strip for race or game.

peel[2], *n*. small square defensible tower on the Scottish border.

peel'er, *n*. (sl.) policeman.

peel'ing, *n*. piece peeled off.

peep[1], *v.i.* look through half-closed eyelids or narrow aperture ; look furtively ; come cautiously into view, emerge. *n*. furtive or peering glance ; first light (of day). **peep'er**, *n*. (sl.) eye.

peep[2], *n*. & *v.i.* (of chick, mouse, &c.) chirp or squeak.

pee'pŭl, **pi'pal** (pē-), *n*. one of the great fig-trees of India, reverenced by Buddhists.

peer[1], *v.i.* look narrowly ; look into darkness or with short sight ; (of sun, &c.) become partly visible.

peer[2], *n*. person's equal in rank or merit ; duke, earl, marquis, viscount, or baron. ~**ess**, peer's wife or female holder of peerage. **peer'age**, *n*. the peers ; rank of a peer. **peer'less**, *a*. unequalled.

*peeve, *v.t.* (sl.) make peevish. ***peeved** (-vd), *a*. irritated, sulky. **peev'ish**, *a*. querulous, cross.

peg, *n*. wooden or metal bolt or pin for holding together parts of framework, hanging things on,

stopping cask-vent, marking cribbage-score, &c. *v.t.* & *i*. fix with peg ; mark score with pegs on cribbage-board. ~ **away**, persevere. ~ **out**, mark boundary of ; (Croquet) hit peg as final stroke ; (sl.) die. ~**top**, boy's wooden top with peg.

peg'amoid, *n*. kind of imitation leather used in coach-building,&c.

pē'kin' (*or* -ing), *n*. kind of silk stuff.

Pĕkinēse' (-z), *n*. Chinese pug.

pĕk'ōe, *n*. a kind of black tea.

pĕlārgō'nium, *n*. geranium.

pĕl'erine, *n*. woman's tippet.

pĕlf, *n*. money, wealth.

pĕl'ican, *n*. water-fowl with pouch for storing fish.

pélisse' (-ēs), *n*. woman's long mantle with sleeves or armholes ; child's outdoor garment.

pĕll'et, *n*. small rolled-up ball of paper, &c. ; pill ; small shot.

pĕll'icle, *n*. a thin skin or membrane or film.

pĕll-mĕll', *adv*. in disorder.

pĕllu'cid (-ōō-), *a*. transparent, clear ; free from obscurity.

Pĕl'manism (-an-), *n*. a 20th-c. memory-training system. **P.**

pĕlt[1], *v.t.* & *i*. assail with mud, abuse, &c. ; (of rain) come down hard. *n*. (sl.) violent temper.

pĕlt[2], *n*. undressed skin of sheep, goat, or fur-bearing animal. **pĕl'try**, *n*. furs and skins.

pĕl'vis, *n*. lower abdominal cavity formed by the haunch and other bones. **pĕl'vic**, *a*.

pĕmm'ican, *n*. preparation of dried and pounded meat.

pĕn[1], *n*. implement of quill, metal, &c., for writing with ink ; writing or literary style ; female swan. *v.t.* compose and write letter, &c. ~**knife**, small pocket-knife. ~**man**, performer with the pen. ~**name**, literary pseudonym.

pĕn[2], *n*. small enclosure for cows, sheep, poultry, &c. *v.t.* enclose ; put or keep in confined space.

pē'nal, *a*. of or involving punishment ; punitive. ~**ize**, *v.t.* (-*zable*), make (action) punishable; subject (competitor) to penalty.

pēn'altў, *n.* fine or other punishment; disadvantage imposed on previous winner in competition.

pĕn'ance, *n.* punishment suffered as an expression of penitence.

|| **penchant** (pahn'shahn), *n.* inclination or liking *for.*

pĕn'cil, *n.* writing-implement of black lead, &c.; artist's fine paint-brush or style; (Opt.) set of convergent rays. *v.t.* mark, jot down, with writing-pencil.

pĕn'dant, -dent, *a.* (usu. *-ent*), hanging, overhanging; awaiting decision. *n.* (usu. *-ant*), ornament hung from necklace, &c.; thing serving as complement to something else.

pĕnd'ing, *a.* awaiting settlement; in process. *prep.* during the unsettled state of.

pĕn'dūlous, *a.* hanging, swinging.

pĕn'dūlum, *n.* suspended body swinging to and fro by force of gravity, esp. in a clock.

pĕn'ĕtrāte, *v.t. & i.* (*-trable*), find access or pass into or through; find out, discern, make a way. **~ability,** *n.* **pĕn'ĕtrāting,** *a.* discerning, gifted with insight; (of voice, &c.) piercing, easily heard. **pĕnĕtrā'tion,** *n.* (esp.) acute insight. **pĕn'ĕtrātive,** *a.*

pĕng'ūin (-nggw-), *n.* sea-fowl with wings as swimming-paddles.

pĕnin'sūla, *n.* piece of land almost surrounded by water. **pĕnin'sūlar,** *a.* of a peninsula.

pĕn'itent, *a.* repentant for sin, contrite. *n.* a penitent person; one who is doing penance. **pĕn'itence,** *n.*

pĕnitĕn'tial (-nshl), *a.* of penitence or penance.

pĕnitĕn'tiarў (-sha-), *n.* papal office regulating penance; reformatory institution; *prison. a.* of penance or reformatory treatment; *(of crime) punishable by term in penitentiary.

pĕnn'ant, *n.* tapering flag, esp. that at mast-head of ship in commission; pennon.

pĕnn'ĭless, *a.* destitute.

pĕnn'on, *n.* long narrow triangular or swallow-tailed flag; long streamer of ship.

pĕnn'ў, *n.* (pl. *pence, pennies*), bronze coin worth one-twelfth of a shilling. **~worth,** what can be got for a penny.

pĕnnўroy'al, *n.* kind of mint formerly used in medicine.

pĕnn'ўweight (-wāt; abbr. *dwt.*), the 20th part of 1 oz. Troy.

pĕnn'ўwort (-ĕrt), kinds of plant with rounded leaves.

pēnŏl'ogў, *n.* study of punishment and prison discipline.

pĕn'sile (*or* -sĭl), *a.* hanging.

pĕn'sion (-shn), *n.* periodical payment made to person in consideration of past service, &c. **pĕn'sionarў** (-sho-), *a.* by way of pension; *n.* pensioner. **pĕn'sioner** (-sho-), *n.* pensioned person.

pĕn'sive, *a.* plunged in thought.

pĕnt, *a.* closely confined; not allowed to issue; shut up.

pĕn'tachŏrd (-k-), *n.* musical instrument of five strings; series of five notes. **pĕn'tacle,** *n.* figure of five-pointed star used in magic. **pĕn'tad,** *n.* the number 5; group of five. **pĕn'tagon,** *n.* five-sided (usu. plane rectilinear) figure; **~al,** *a.* **pĕntahĕd'ron,** *n.* solid figure of five faces. **~ral,** *a.*

pĕntăm'ĕter, *n.* Greek and Latin verse of five feet.

Pĕn'tateuch (-k), *n.* the first five Old Testament books.

Pĕn'tĕcŏst, *n.* Jewish harvest festival fifty days after Passover; Whitsunday. **pĕntĕcŏs'tal,** *a.*

pĕnt'house (-t-h-), *n.* sloping roof supported against wall of building.

pēnult (pĕnŭlt', pē'nŭlt), *n.* last syllable but one of a word. **pĕnŭl'timate,** *a.* last but one; *n.* penult.

pēnŭm'bra, *n.* partly lighted shadow on the skirts of a total shadow. **pēnŭm'bral,** *a.*

pēnū'rious, *a.* mean, stingy.

pĕn'ūrў, *n.* destitution, poverty.

pĕ″onў, n. garden plant with double red or white flower.

people (pē′pl), n. (as sing.) a race or nation; (as pl.) persons in general; the commonalty. v.t. fill with people; populate; inhabit.

*pĕp, n. (sl.) vigour, go, spirit. *pĕpp′ў, a. full of life.

pĕpp′er, n. hot-flavoured berries of certain plants used usu. in powdered form, as seasoning. v.t. sprinkle or flavour with pepper; besprinkle; hit with missiles. ~box, ~castor, box or castor with perforated top for sprinkling pepper. ~corn, dried pepper berry, often specified as nominal rent. ~mint, kind of mint grown for its essential oil, this oil; lozenge flavoured with it. pĕpp′erў, a. like pepper; hot-tempered.

pĕp′sin, n. constituent of gastric juice. pĕp′tic, a. digestive.

pĕr, prep. by, by means or instrumentality of (per post, rail, &c.); for each (per man). ~ annum (ăn′um), (so much) by the year, yearly. ~ cent, in every hundred. ~ contra (kŏn′tra), on the other side of the account; on the other hand. ~ di′ĕm, ~ mĕn′sĕm, (so much) by the day, month. ‖ ~ sē, by its very nature; intrinsically.

pĕradvĕn′ture, adv. (arch.) perhaps, perchance; by chance.

pĕram′bŭlāte, v.t. & i. (-lable), walk up and down; go from place to place. pĕrambŭlā′tion, n.

pĕram′bŭlātor, n. one who perambulates; child's carriage.

perceive′ (-sēv′), v.t. (-vable), become aware of by one of the senses; apprehend; understand.

percen′tage, n. rate per cent.; number of in every hundred.

pĕr′cĕpt, n. (Philos.) object or product of perception.

percĕp′tible, a. such as can be perceived. ~bility, n.

percĕp′tion, n. act or faculty of perceiving. ~al, a.

percĕp′tive, a. having or concerned in perception. pĕrcĕptiv′itў, n.

pĕrch[1], n. bird's resting place; elevated position; measure of length, 5½ yds. v.i. & t. (of bird) alight or rest on perch; put on a high place.

pĕrch[2], n. a fresh-water fish.

perchance′ (-ah-), adv. by chance; maybe.

percip′ient, a. having perception. n. person who perceives.

pĕrc′olāte, v.i. & t. (-lable), make way through pores or perforations; cause to percolate. ~tion, n. ~tor, n. strainer of coffee-pot.

percŭs′sion (-shn), n. striking of a body against another; sound so made. percŭss′ive, a.

perdi′tion, n. damnation; ruin.

pĕrdū(e)′, pred.a. in ambush; out of sight; hidden.

pĕ′rĕgrināte, v.i. & t. wander. wander through. ~tion, n.

pĕ′rĕgrine (or -in), n. kind of falcon used in hawking.

pĕ′rĕmptory (-mt-), a. imperious; urgent.

perĕnn′ial (-nyal), a. not coming to an end; (of plant) coming up year after year. n. a perennial plant.

perfect, a. (pĕr′fĭkt), complete, not deficient; faultless; thoroughly learned; exact, precise; entire, unqualified; thoroughly trained; (of tense) expressing action completed. n. (pĕr′fĭkt), the perfect tense. v.t. (perfĕkt′), make perfect. perfĕctibil′itў, n.

perfec′tion, n. being perfect; perfect state; highest manifestation; (pl.) accomplishments, beauties.

perfect′lў, adv. quite, quite well.

*perfĕc′to, n. medium-sized cigar tapered at both ends.

pĕr′fidў, n. breach of faith; treachery. perfid′ious, a.

pĕr′forāte, v.t. & i. (-rable), pierce, make hole(s) through. ~tion, n. ~tor, n. instrument for perforating.

perforce′, adv. of necessity.

perform′, v.t. & i. carry into effect; accomplish; go through, execute; act. ~ance, n. thing accomplished; single presentation of play, &c. ~er, n. (esp.) one who performs before an audience.

perfume, n. (pĕr'ūm), sweet smell; scent; fragrance. v.t. (perfūm'), impart fragrance to. perfū'mer, n. maker or seller of perfumes. perfū'mery, n. &c.

perfūnc'tory, a. done merely to pass muster; superficial.

pĕrg'ola, n. arbour or garden-walk arched with climbing plants.

pergun'nah, -gan'a (-gŭ-), n. division of territory in India, comprising a group of villages.

perhaps', adv. it may be.

pĕr'i, n. fairy of Persian mythology; beautiful girl or woman.

pĕ'rianth, n. outer part of flower, calyx and corolla.

pĕricard'ium, n. (pl. -ia), membranous sac enclosing the heart. pĕricard'iac, ~dial, aa.

pĕ'ricarp, n. seed-vessel of plant.

pĕricra'nium, n. membrane enclosing the skull; (joc.) skull.

pĕ'rigee, n. point of moon's orbit nearest the earth.

pĕrihē'lion (-lyon), n. point in planet's orbit nearest the sun.

pĕ'ril, n. danger, risk. v.t. put in peril; imperil. ~ous, a.

perim'eter, n. line or set of lines bounding a closed figure.

pĕr'iod, n. amount of time during which something runs its course; a complete sentence; full-stop symbol (.). pĕriŏd'ic, a. recurring at regular intervals. pĕriod'ical, a. coming at fixed times; cyclical; n. publication issued at fixed intervals. pĕriod'icity, n.

pĕripatĕt'ic, a. itinerant, going from place to place; of the school of Aristotle. n. follower of Aristotle; (joc.) walker.

pĕriph'ery, n. bounding line, esp. of round surface.

pĕriph'rasis, n. (pl. -asēs), round-about speech or phrase, circumlocution. pĕriphras'tic, a.

pĕ'riscope, n. kinds of mirror apparatus giving view of things above surface to observer in submarine or trench.

pĕ'rish, v.i. & t. suffer destruction; lose life; come to an untimely end; fail to last; (of cold) reduce to distress. ~able, a. that will not last long; n. (usu. in pl.) perishable thing(s).

pĕ'ristyle, n. row of columns round temple, cloister, &c.; space surrounded with this.

pĕritonē'um, n. membrane lining the abdomen. pĕritoni'tis, n. inflammation of the peritoneum.

pĕ'riwig, n. wig.

pĕ'riwinkle[1], n. evergreen trailing plant with light-blue flower.

pĕ'riwinkle[2], n. edible shell-fish like small snail.

pĕrj'ure (-jer), v.refl. swear falsely, give false evidence on oath. pĕrj'ured (-erd), a. guilty of perjury. pĕrj'urer (-jer-), n. pĕr'jury (-jer-), n. act of perjuring oneself.

pĕrk, v.i. & t. (colloq.) (with up) recover self-confidence; behave jauntily; lift up (one's head, nose, ears, &c.). pĕrk'y, a.

pĕrm'anence, n. duration or permanent quality. pĕrm'anency, n. permanent occupation.

pĕrm'anent, a. lasting or meant to last; not temporary.

pĕrm'eable, a. admitting the passage of fluid, &c. ~bility, n.

pĕrm'eāte, v.t. & i. make way throughout, pervade; be diffused. pĕrmeā'tion, n.

permiss'ible, a. allowable, that may be permitted. ~bility, n.

permi'ssion (-shn), n. leave, licence. permiss'ive, a. licensing but not enjoining something.

permit', v.t. & i. (permit'), allow, give leave for; admit of. n. (pĕrm'it), written order for permitting entry, &c.

pĕrmūtā'tion, n. (Math.) variation of the order of a series.

perni'cious (-shus), a. destructive, injurious.

pernick'ety, a. (colloq.) fastidious; ticklish.

pĕ'rorāte, v.i. indulge in rhetoric; make a peroration. pĕrorā'tion, n. passage closing a speech.

perpend', *v.t.* & *i.* (arch., joc.) ponder, reflect upon.

perpendic'ular, *a.* at right angles to plane of horizon, vertical; erect, upright; very steep. *n.* a perpendicular line.

perp'etrate, *v.t.* (*-trable*) be guilty of; commit. ~tion, ~tor, *nn.*

perpet'ual, *a.* eternal; held or holding for life; continuous.

perpet'uate, *v.t.* (*-uable*) make perpetual; not allow to go out of use or memory. ~tion, ~tor, *nn.*

perpetu'ity, *n.* perpetual continuance or possession.

perplex', *v.t.* bewilder, puzzle; complicate, tangle. **perplex'ity**, *n.* puzzled state; being at a loss.

perq'uisite (*-z-*), *n.* casual emolument, &c. attached to an employment beyond salary or wages.

pe'rry, *n.* fermented drink made from pears.

pers'ecute, *v.t.* (*-table*) subject to ill-treatment; harass for heresy; worry. **persecu'tion**, ~tor, *nn.*

persevere', *v.i.* be steadfast; persist. **persever'ance**, *n.*

persiflage (pârs'iflahzh), *n.* light irony, raillery.

persimm'on, *n.* a date-plum.

persist', *v.i.* continue to exist or do something in spite of obstacles. ~ence, ~ency, *nn.*; ~ent, *a.*

pers'on, *n.* individual human or divine being; one's body or bodily presence; character in a play; (Gram.) one of the classes of pronouns and verb forms appropriated to the person speaking, spoken to, or spoken of. ~able, *a.* good-looking. ~age, *n.* eminent character; character in a play.

‖ **perso'na gra'ta**, *n.* envoy in whose favour the power to which he goes is predisposed.

pers'onal, *a.* one's own; individual, private; done, &c. in person; directed against or referring to an individual. *n.pl.* paragraphs in newspaper relating to individual persons.

personal'ity, *n.* existence or distinctive character of any one; personage; (pl.) remarks aimed at an individual.

pers'onally, *adv.* in person.

pers'onalty, *n.* personal property.

pers'onate, *v.t.* (*-nable*), play the part of; pretend to be (another). **persona'tion**, ~tor, *nn.*

person'ify, *v.t.* (*-fiable*), attribute personal nature to; symbolize by human figure. ~fica'tion, *n.*

personnel', *n.* staff or hands of a business, &c. as opposed to its equipment or plant.

perspec'tive, *n.* art of drawing so as to give the effect of solidity and relative distance and size; relation or proportion between the parts of a subject; vista, view. *a.* of or in perspective.

perspica'cious (*-shus*), *a.* having insight; penetrating, discerning. **perspica'city**, *n.*

perspic'uous, *a.* expressed with clearness; lucid. **perspicu'ity**, *n.*

perspire', *v.i.* & *t.* (*-rable*), sweat. **perspira'tion**, *n.* sweat, sweating.

persuade' (*-sw-*), *v.t.* (*-dable*), convince; impel by argument, expostulation, &c. **persua'der** (*-sw-*), *n.* person or thing that persuades.

persua'sion (*-wâzhn*), *n.* act of persuading; particular religious belief or sect; (joc.) sort or class.

persua'sive (*-sw-*), *a.* efficacious in persuading. *n.* inducement.

pert, *a.* forward, saucy.

pertain', *v.i.* belong, relate.

pertina'cious (*-shus*), *a.* persistent, resolute. **pertina'city**, *n.*

pert'inent, *a.* to the point, have a real relation to. ~nce, *n.*

perturb', *v.t.* disquiet; throw into agitation. **perturba'tion**, *n.*

peruke' (*-ōōk*), *n.* wig.

peruse' (*-ōōz*), *v.t.* (*-sable*), read; scan (features, &c.). **peru'sal**, *n.*

Peru'vian (*-ōō-*), *a.* of Peru. ~ bark, bark of cinchona tree.

pervade', *v.t.* (*-dable*), spread through; be rife among or through. **perva'sive**, *a.*

perverse', *a.* obstinately or wil-

fully in the wrong; wayward;
peevish; wicked. **pĕrvers´ity**,
~sion, *nn.* : ~sive, *a.*

pervert, *v.t.* (pĕrvĕrt´), turn to
wrong use; interpret wrongly;
lead astray. *n.* (pĕr´vĕrt), person
who adopts another religion;
perverted person. ~ible, *a.*

pĕr´vious, *a.* allowing passage or
access; not impervious.

pĕse´ta (-sā-), *n.* Spanish silver
coin, 10*d.*

*pĕs´ky, *a.* vexatious, annoying.

peso (pā´sō), *n.* S.-Amer. silver
coin worth about 4*s.*

pĕss´imism, *n.* tendency to look at
the worst aspect of things. ~ist,
n.; pĕssimist´ic, *a.*

pĕst, *n.* troublesome or noxious
person, animal, or thing.

pĕs´ter, *v.t.* plague, importune.

pĕstif´erous, *a.* noxious; spreading
infection; foul.

pĕs´tilence, *n.* fatal epidemic
disease, esp. bubonic plague.

pĕs´tilent, *a.* deadly or pestiferous;
troublesome; obnoxious.

pĕstilĕn´tial (-shl), *a.* causing or
of the nature of pestilence.

pĕs´tle (-sl), *n.* instrument for
pounding in a mortar.

pĕstŏl´ogy, *n.* study of (esp. insect)
pests.

pĕt, *n.* animal or person on which
affection is lavished; favourite;
fit of sulks. *v.t.* make a pet of;
fondle.

pĕt´al, *n.* coloured leaf of a flower.

pĕtard´, *n.* (hist.) small bomb for
attaching to door, &c., to burst it
open; kind of firework.

pĕ´ter, *v.i.* (sl.), (with *out*) give out,
come to an end.

pĕ´tersham, *n.* thick ribbed ribbon
used for belts, &c.

pĕt´iole, *n.* leaf-stalk.

pĕti´tion, *n.* request, supplication,
esp. written. *v.t.* & *i.* make
petition (to); ask humbly. ~er,
n. one who offers a petition.

‖ pĕti´tio princip´ii (-shl-), *n.* begging of the question.

pĕt´rel, *n.* a small sea-bird associated with storms.

pĕt´rify, *v.t.* & *i.* (-*iable*), turn into

stone; paralyse with terror;
become rigid. ~fac´tion, *n.*

pĕt´rol, *n.* refined petroleum as
used in motor-cars, &c.

pĕtrō´leum, *n.* mineral oil.

pĕtt´icoat, *n.* woman's garment
worn immediately beneath dress.

pĕt´tifog, *v.i.* be or act like a petti-
fogger. ~ger, *n.* lawyer of low
class; mean or crooked dealer.
~ging, *a.* mean, quibbling.

pĕt´tish, *a.* fretful, peevish.

pĕt´titoes (-ōz), *n.* (*pl.*) pig's feet.

pĕt´ty, *a.* unimportant, trivial;
little-minded; minor, inferior.

pĕt´ulant, *a.* out of temper;
touchy. pĕt´ulance, *n.*

pĕtū´nia, *n.* plant with vivid
funnel-shaped flowers.

pew, *n.* enclosed seat in a church
for worshippers.

pē´wit, pee-, *n.* kind of plover
named from its cry; lapwing.

pew´ter, *n.* grey alloy of tin and
other metals; utensils of pewter.

pfenn´ig, *n.* small German coin,
1/100 of a mark.

phā´eton, *n.* light four-wheeled
open carriage, usu. pair-horsed.

phăl´anx, *n.* body of infantry in
solid oblong formation; united
or organized party or company.

phăn´erogăm, *n.* plant with pistils
and stamens; flowering plant.
~ic, phănerŏg´amous, *aa.*

phăn´tasm, *n.* illusion, phantom;
vision of absent person.

phăntasmagō´ria (-z-), *n.* crowd or
succession of dim or doubtfully
real persons. ~gō´ric, *a.*

phăn´tom, *n.* spectre, apparition;
dim image; (attrib.) unreal.

phă´risee, *n.* formalist; self-
righteous person; hypocrite.
~sā´ic(al), *aa.* : ~saïsm, *n.*

phârmaceut´ical, *a.* of pharmacy,
of the use or sale of medicinal
drugs. ~ics, ~ist, *nn.*

phârmacŏl´ogy, *n.* theory of pharmacy. ~gist, *n.*

phârmacopœ´ia (-pēa), *n.* book
with list and directions for use of
drugs; stock of drugs.

phârm´acy, *n.* the art of dispensing drugs; a drug-store.

phăr'ŏs, n. lighthouse; beacon.

phă'rynx, n. cavity behind mouth and nose. pharyn'gěal (-j-), a.

phāse (-z), n. aspect of moon or planet at a certain time; stage of development or process.

phea'sant (fěz-), n. a game-bird of handsome plumage.

phěnŏm'ěnal, a. concerned with phenomena; out of the common; remarkable.

phěnŏm'ěnon, n. (pl. -ena), observed or apparent object or fact or occurrence; remarkable person or thing; a wonder.

phī'al, n. small bottle.

philăn'der, v.i. amuse oneself with love-making.

philăn'thropy, n. doing good to one's fellow men. philanthrŏp'ic, a.; philăn'thropist, n.

philăt'ely, n. stamp-collecting. philatěl'ic, a.; philăt'elist, n.

philharmŏn'ic (-lär-), a. musical (only in titles of societies).

phil'hellēne (-lel-), n. lover of Greece. ~hellē'nic, a.; ~hell'ēnism, ~ist, nn.

philip'pic, n. an invective.

phil'ippine (-ēn), n. almond or other nut with double kernel.

Phil'istine (or -īn), n. uncultured person. a. uncultured. ~nism, n.

philŏl'ogy, n. science of the structure and development of language. ~ŏg'ical, a.; ~gist, n.

philoprogē'nitive, a. prolific; fond of one's offspring.

philŏs'opher, n. student or possessor of philosophy.

philŏsŏph'ic(al), aa. of, consonant with, showing, philosophy.

philŏs'ophize, v.i. play the philosopher; speculate, moralize.

philŏs'ophy, n. pursuit of wisdom or of the knowledge of things and their causes; equanimity.

phil'tre (-ter), n. love-potion.

phiz, n. (colloq.) person's face with regard to its looks.

phlěbŏt'omy, n. blood-letting as medical operation.

phlegm (flěm), n. bronchial mucus ejected by coughing; coolness of character or temper; impassive-ness; phlěgmăt'ic, a. not easily agitated; sluggish.

phlox, n. plant with salver-shaped flower.

Phoe'bus (fē-), n. Greek sun-god; (poet.) the sun.

phœn'ix (fē-), n. bird fabled to burn itself and rise renewed from its ashes; unique thing.

phōne, n. & v. (colloq.) telephone.

phonět'ic, a. of, in, corresponding to vocal sound. phonět'ics, n. study of phonetic phenomena.

*phō'ney, a. (sl.) false, bogus, counterfeit.

phō'nic, a. acoustic, phonetic. phō'nics, n. phonetics.

phō'nogram, n. sound-record made by phonograph; sound-symbol in shorthand.

phō'nograph (-ahf), n. instrument automatically recording and reproducing sounds. phonŏg'rapher, ~raphist, nn. phonŏg'raphy, n. sound-recording by the phonograph; kind of shorthand.

phonŏl'ogy, n. science of vocal sounds. phŏnŏlŏg'ical, a.

phō'notype, n. phonetic printing-type.

phŏs'gēne, n. a poison gas, carbon oxychloride, used in the 1914–18 war.

phŏs'phāte, n. a salt of phosphoric acid. phŏs'phīde, n. a combination of phosphorus with an element or radical. phŏs'phīte, n. a salt of phosphorous acid.

phŏs'phor-bronze, n. tough bronze alloy containing phosphorus.

phŏsphorěsce', v.i. show phosphorescence. phŏsphorěs'cence, n. faint luminosity in the dark. phŏsphorěs'cent, a.

phŏsphŏr'ic, phŏs'phorous, aa. having phosphorus in lower, higher, proportion.

phŏs'phorus, n. a non-metallic element; a yellowish wax-like substance appearing luminous in the dark.

phō'tō, n. (pl. -os), & v.t. & i. photograph (colloq.). *~stăt.

PHOTO [368] PICK

apparatus for making direct fac-simile reproductions. P.

phō′tograph (-ahf), *n.* picture taken by means of light on sensitive film. *v.t. & i.* take photograph of ; admit of being photographed. **photog′rapher, ~phy, *nn.* ~ic, *a.***

phōtogravūre′, *n.* photograph reproduced by etching on metal.

photŏm′eter, *n.* instrument for measuring the intensity of light. **photŏmĕt′ric**, *a.* ; **photŏm′ĕtrў**, *n.*

phō′tophōne, *n.* instrument for transmitting sounds by means of light.

phō′tosphēre, *n.* sun's or star's luminous envelope.

phŏto-tĕlĕg′raphў, *n.* electric reproduction of pictures, writing, &c. at a distance.

phōtŏthĕ′rapў, *n.* treatment of disease by the influence of light.

phrāse (-z), *n.* mode of expression, diction ; small group of words ; (Mus.) short sequence of notes. *v.t.*(-*sable*), choose phrases for ; term.

phrāsĕŏl′ogў (-z-), *n.* choice of words, diction. **~ŏ′gical**, *a.*

phrĕnŏl′ogў, *n.* study of external cranium as indicative of the affections and mental faculties. **~gist**, *n.*

phthī′sis (fth- or th- ; or -I-), *n.* pulmonary consumption ; progressive wasting disease. **phthis′ical** (fthĭz-, tĭz-), *a.* of phthisis.

phylăc′terў, *n.* small leather box containing Hebrew texts on vellum, worn by Jews ; amulet.

phyllŏxēr′a, *n.* plant-louse injurious to vines.

phys′ic (-z-), *n.* the medical art or profession ; (colloq.) drugs. *v.t.* dose ; (sl.) handle severely.

phys′ical (-z-), *a.* of nature or according to its laws ; of physics.

physi′cian (-zĭshn), *n.* healer ; qualified medical practitioner.

phys′icĭst (-z-), *n.* student of physics or of natural science.

phys′ics (-z-), *n.pl.* science of the properties and inter-relations of matter and energy.

physiŏg′nomў (-zĭŏn-), *n.* face as index of character ; art of judging character from face and form. **~mist**, *n.*

physiŏg′raphў (-z-), *n.* description of natural phenomena ; physical geography. **physiŏgrăph′ical**, *a.*

physiŏl′ogў (-z-), *n.* science of the functions and phenomena of living things. **physiŏlŏ′gical**, *a.* **physiŏl′ogist**, *n.*

physĭque′ (-zēk), *n.* bodily structure and development.

pi′a mā′ter, *n.* inner membrane enveloping brain and spinal cord ; one's brain or wits.

‖ **pianĭss′imo**, *adv. & n.* (Mus.) (passage to be played) very softly.

pi′anist (pēa-), *n.* performer on piano.

‖ **pia′nō**[1] (-ah-), *adv. & n.* (passage to be played) softly.

piă′nō[2] (pl. -os), **piănofŏrt′e**, *n.* metal-stringed keyboard musical instrument.

piano′la (pēa-), *n.* kind of mechanical pianoforte-player. *P.*

piăs′tre (-ter), *n.* Spanish or Egyptian or Turkish coin.

piăzz′a (-tza), *n.* square or market-place in Italian town.

pībroch (pē′brŏk), *n.* form of bag-pipe music.

pī′ca, *n.* size of type (12-point).

pic′adŏr, *n.* mounted man with lance in bull-fight.

picarĕsque′ (-k), *a.* (of fiction) relating to rogues.

picaroon′, *n.* rogue, pirate.

*****picayune** (-ayōōn′), *n.* small coin, esp. 5-cent piece or Spanish half-real ; trifle. *a.* petty, mean.

picann′ny, *n.* negro child.

picc′olō, *n.* (pl. -os), small high-pitched flute.

pice, *n.* E.-Ind. coin, ¼ anna.

pick, *n.* implement with sharp-pointed iron cross-bar for breaking up ground ; small pointed instrument ; the best. *v.t. & i.* break up ground, &c. ; probe teeth ; open lock ; pluck (feathers) ; rifle pocket by stealth ; pluck, gather (flower,

---

fruit, &c.); select (one's words, way, &c.). ~axe, pick (first sense). ~pocket, person who picks pockets.

pick'erel, n. young pike.

pick'et, n. peg or pointed stake; small body of men on military police duty; man or party stationed to deter would-be workers during strike. v.t. set with stakes; tether to peg; post as picket; beset with pickets.

pick'ings (-z), n.pl. odds and ends of profits made by agents, &c.

pic'kle, n. brine or other liquor for preserving food, &c.; sorry plight or dirty state; (usu. pl.) vegetables in vinegar, &c.; young rascal. v.t. preserve in or treat with pickle. *pic'kled (-ld), a. drunk.

pic'nic, n. pleasure excursion including outdoor meal. v.i. (-ck-), take part in picnic.

picotee', n. carnation with dark-edged petals.

pi'cric, a. ~ acid, bitter yellow substance used in dyes and explosives.

pic'tor'ial, a. of, in, by, or with painting or pictures.

pic'ture, n. painting or drawing of objects, esp. as work of art; portrait; beautiful object; *the pictures*, cinema-show. v.t. (-rable), depict in painting, &c.; represent to others in words or to oneself in imagination. ~gallery, building for exhibition of pictures. ~palace, ~theatre, cinema.

picturesque' (-kcherésk), a. such as would be effective in a picture; (of language) graphic.

pidg'in, a. ~ English, jargon used in dealings with Chinese.

pie¹, n. kinds of bird, esp. woodpecker.

pie², n. dish of meat or fruit covered in with paste. ~crust, baked paste of this. ~man, seller of pies. *~plant, garden rhubarb.

pie³, n. (Anglo-Ind.) small copper coin, the twelfth part of an anna.

piebald (pī'bawld), a. having white and black in irregular patches; motley, heterogeneous. n. a piebald horse or other animal.

piece, n. one of the distinct parts of a composite whole; fragment; specimen; example; picture, drama, or literary or musical composition. v.t. (-ceable), make of pieces; put together or mend; make out. ~goods, textile fabrics woven in recognized lengths. ~work, work paid for by the piece. ‖ **pièce de résistance** (pĕ'ǎs de rēzē'stahns), most substantial dish; most important item.

piece'meal (-sm-), adv. part at a time. a. done piecemeal.

pied (pīd), a. of black and white or of mixed colours.

pier, n. support of spans of bridge; pillar; solid part of wall between windows, &c.; structure running out into the sea; breakwater. ~glass, large mirror.

pierce, v.t. & i. (-ceable), go through or into like a spear or needle; penetrate; bore.

Piē'rian, a. of the Muses.

pierrot (pěr'-, pyar'ō), n. (fem. -rrètte), minstrel with whitened face and loose white dress.

pi'etism, n. exaggeration or affectation of piety. **pi'etist**, n.

pi'ety, n. piousness.

pif'fle, n. (sl.) silly stuff.

pig, n. swine, hog; person like pig in greed, dirt, or perversity; oblong mass of smelted iron or other metal. v.i. (of sow) produce litter; live in dirty untidy way. ~headed, obstinate. ~iron, iron in pigs or rough bars. ~nut, kind of earth-nut. ~skin, leather used for saddles, &c.; *(sl.) football. ~sticking, hunting of wild boar with spear, esp. in India; butchering of swine. ~sty, sty for pigs, (fig.) dirty hovel. ~tail, plait of hair hanging from back of head.

pi'geon (-jn), n. bird with many varieties, wild and domesticated; the dove; person who is rooked or plucked. ~hole, n. one of the compartments in a cabinet, &c.; *v.t.* deposit in a pigeon-hole. **pi′geonry** (-jn-), *n.* pigeon-house, dove-cot.

pigg′ery (-g-), *n.* place for pigs; dirty place. **pigg′ish** (-g-), *a.*

pig′ment, *n.* colouring-matter.

pigmy. See pygmy.

pike, *n.* spear formerly used by infantry; large voracious fresh-water fish. ~**staff**, shaft of pike.

pike′let, *n.* crumpet.

*'**pi′ker**, *n.* low-down untrust-worthy person.

pilas′ter, *n.* rectangular pillar, esp. one set in a wall.

pilau′, -aw, -aff, *n.* Oriental dish of rice with meat, spices, &c.

pil′chard, *n.* small sea-fish allied to herring.

pile[1], *n.* heap, esp. of flat things laid on one another; (Electr.) plates of dissimilar metals laid alternately for producing current; building of imposing height; (sl.) a fortune. *v.t.* (-*lable*), lay or throw in a pile; load.

pile[2], *n.* (usu. pl.) piece(s) of timber driven into ground as foundation for building.

pile[3], *n.* nap of velvet, plush, carpet, &c.

pile[4], *n.* (pl.) disease with tumours of the rectal veins, haemorrhoids; (sing.) such tumour.

pil′fer, *v.t.* & *i.* steal or thieve in a petty way. ~**age**, *n.*

pil′grim, *n.* person who journeys to sacred place; a wanderer. ~**age**, *n.* pilgrim's journey.

pill, *n.* small ball of medicine to be swallowed whole. *v.t.* administer pill to; (sl.) blackball.

pill′age, *n.* forcible seizure of others' goods; things so seized. *v.t.* & *i.* (-*geable*), subject to or indulge in pillage.

pill′ar, *n.* slender upright structure serving to support arch or other architectural weight; a column. ~**box**, hollow pillar for posting letters in.

pill′ion (-lyon), *n.* cushion on which woman formerly sat when riding behind man on horse;

seat for passenger behind motor-cyclist, &c.

pill′ory, *n.* frame with holes for head and hands in which offender was placed. *v.t.* set in pillory; expose to ridicule.

pill′ow (-ō), *n.* cushion on which head rests. *v.t.* serve as pillow to. ~**fight**, belabouring of each other with pillows.

pi′lose, **pi′lous**, *aa.* hairy.

pi′lot, *n.* person in charge of ships entering or leaving a harbour; steersman; (Aeronaut.) person navigating aeroplane; guide. *v.t.* act as pilot to; guide course of. ~**cloth**, blue woollen great-coat cloth. ~**fish**, small fish said to guide shark to prey. **pi′lotage**, *n.* pilot's function or fee.

pil′ule, *n.* small pill.

pimen′to, *n.* Jamaica pepper.

pimp, *n.* & *v.i.* pander.

pim′pernel, *n.* plant with small scarlet or blue or white flower, closing in dull weather.

pim′ple, *n.* small tumour of the skin. **pim′pled** (-ld), ~**ly**, *aa.*

pin, *n.* piece of thin stiff wire with point and head used as fastening; wooden or metal peg, rivet, &c.; (pl., sl.) legs. *v.t.* fasten with pin or pins. ~**money**, allowance made to woman for dress, &c. ~**prick**, act or remark intended to annoy.

pin′afore, *n.* child's or woman's washable overall.

pince-nez (păns′nā), *n.* pair of eye-glasses with clip.

pin′cers (-z), *n.pl.* gripping tool.

pinch, *v.t.* & *i.* nip with finger and thumb; pain or injure by squeezing; stint, be niggardly; (sl.) steal, arrest. *n.* a nip, squeeze; stress of want, &c.; smallamount; emergency.

pinch′beck, *n.* copper and zinc alloy; cheap jewellery, counterfeit stuff. *a.* counterfeit, flashy.

pine[1], *v.i.* waste away with grief, want, &c.; long for, languish.

pine[2], *n.* kinds of evergreen needle-leaved coniferous tree; pine-apple. ~**apple**, large exotic fruit

---

ah, awl, oil, boor, cow, dowry; chin, go, bang, so, ship, thin; dh, as th(e)

resembling pine-cone in shape.
~cone, fruit of pine. pi′nery, n. pine-apple house.

pin′fold, n. pound for cattle.

pin′ion¹ (-nyon), n. outer joint of bird's wing; (poet.) wing; flight-feather. v.t. cut off pinion to prevent flight; restrain by binding arms to side.

pin′ion² (-nyon), n. smaller wheel engaging cog-wheel.

pink¹, v.t. run through with sword; ornament with perforations.

pink², n. garden plant with clove-scented flowers; pale-red colour; fox-hunter's red coat; point of perfection or excellence. a. pink-coloured. ~eye, kind of horse fever; kind of ophthalmia.

*pink′ster, n. Whitsuntide. *~flower, the pink azalea.

pinn′ace, n. man-of-war's double-banked boat; (hist.) small ship in attendance on larger one.

pinn′acle, n. pointed turret crowning a buttress or roof; culmination or climax.

pinn′ate (-at), a. with leaflets, tentacles, &c., on each side of petiole or axis.

*pin′och(l)e (-okl; or pē-), n. game like bezique.

pint, n. measure of capacity, one-eighth of a gallon.

pin′tle, n. bolt or pin, esp. that on which rudder hangs.

pioneer′, n. one of advance corps preparing road for troops; explorer; one who originates any enterprise. v.i. act as pioneer.

pi′ous, a. devout, religious.

pip¹, n. seed of apple, pear, orange, &c. pip², n. spot on domino, die, or playing-card; star on army officer's shoulder. pip³, n. a bird disease; (sl.) have the pip, be out of sorts or temper. pip⁴, v.t. (sl.) blackball; frustrate.

pipal. See peepul.

pipe, n. tube of earthenware, metal, &c., for conveying gas, water, &c.; musical instrument, boatswain's whistle, (pl.) bagpipes; bird's note; appliance used in tobacco-smoking; 105-gall.

wine-cask. v.i. & t. (-pable), play on pipe; summon by sound of pipe or whistle; utter shrilly; (of birds) sing; (colloq.) weep, blubber. ~clay, n. clay used for tobacco-pipes and for whitening soldiers' belts, &c.; v.t. whiten with pipeclay.

pi′per, n. (esp.) bagpiper.

pi′ping, n. pipe-like ornament along seams of clothes.

pip′it, n. kinds of small bird.

pip′kin, n. small earthenware pot.

pipp′in, n. kinds of apple.

piquant (pē′knt), n. pungent, sharp, appetizing, stimulating.

pi′quancy (pēkn-), n.

pique (pēk), v.t. (-quable), wound the pride or stir the curiosity; plume oneself on. n. pettishness.

piqué (pē′kā), n. stiff ribbed cotton fabric.

piquet′ (-kĕt), n. a card-game for two.

pir′ate (-at), n. sea-robber; publisher, &c. who infringes copyright. v.t. publish regardless of copyright. pir′acy, n.; pirăt′ic(al), aa.

pirouette′ (-rōō-), n. & v.i. (ballet-dancer's) spin round on toe.

‖ pis aller (pēzăl′ā), n. course adopted for want of a better.

pis′catory, piscatôr′ial, aa. of fishing.

Pis′ces (-z), n.pl. the Fishes; twelfth sign of the zodiac.

pis′ciculture, n. fish-rearing.

pisci′na (-sē-, -sī-), n. (pl. -ae, -as) stone basin in niche on south side of altar.

pis′cine, a. of fish.

pisciv′orous, a. fish-eating.

pis′mire, n. ant.

pistă′chio (-shiō, -shō, -shah), n. (pl. -os), kind of nut with green kernel.

pis′til, n. seed-bearing organ in flowers. pis′tillate, a.

pis′tol, n. small fire-arm used with one hand.

pistôle′, n. Spanish coin, 18s.

pis′ton, n. plug fitting the bore of a hollow cylinder in which it moves up and down.

pit[1], *n*. natural hole in ground ; hole made in digging for minerals, &c. ; depression in skin or any surface ; floor of theatre auditorium ; *part of exchange devoted to special business. *v.t.* make pits in ; store in pit ; match against another. ~**fall**, covered pit as trap ; also *fig.* ~**man**, miner ; *connecting-rod.

pit[2], *n*. stone of peach, plum, cherry, &c.

pit'-(a-)pāt, *adv.* with palpitations ; with light quick steps.

pitch[1], *n*. dark resinous substance for caulking ships, &c. *v.t.* coat with pitch. ~**pine**, resinous kinds of pine.

pitch[2], *v.t. & i.* set up in chosen position ; encamp ; give a chosen altitude or gradient to ; throw, fling, fall. *n.* act or process of pitching ; height, degree, intensity, gradient ; acuteness of tone ; part of ground where wickets are pitched. ~**fork**, *n.* implement for pitching hay ; *v.t.* toss with pitchfork ; thrust into office, &c. ~**pipe**, small pipe blown to set pitch.

pitch'er[1], *n.* (esp.) baseball player who delivers the ball.

pitch'er[2], *n.* large jug, ewer. ~**plant**, plant with pitcher-shaped leaves.

pit'eous, *a.* deplorable ; stirring or claiming pity.

pith, *n.* spongy cellular tissue in stems of plants ; chief part ; vigour, energy. ~**less**, *a.* flaccid. **pith'ȳ**, *a.* concise, terse.

pit'iable, *a.* deserving of pity.

pit'iful, *a.* compassionate ; stirring pity ; contemptible.

pit'iless, *a.* feeling no pity.

pitt'ance, *n.* scanty allowance.

pitū'itarȳ, *a.* of or secreting phlegm or mucus.

pit'ȳ, *n.* sorrow for another's suffering ; regrettable fact, regrettableness. *v.t.* feel pity for.

piv'ot, *n.* pin on which something turns ; cardinal point in discussion. **piv'otal**, *a.*

pix'ȳ, *n.* fairy.

plāc'able, *a.* easily appeased ; mild-tempered. ~**bility**, *n.*

placard, *n.* (plăk'ärd), paper with announcement for posting up. *v.t.* (plăkärd'), post placards on wall, &c. ; advertise by placards.

placāte', *v.t.* (-*table*), conciliate, propitiate ; *purchase the connivance, &c. of opponents.

plāce, *n.* particular part of space ; city, town, village, residence, building ; situation as public or other servant ; (also *place-kick*) kicking of football laid by another player for the purpose. *v.t.* (-*ceable*), put or dispose in place ; assign rank or order to ; put order for goods into the hands of ; kick (goal) with place-kick. ~**man**, holder of public office.

placen'ta, *n.* (pl. -*ae*) spongy organ nourishing the foetus in mammals ; (Bot.) part of carpel to which seeds are attached. **placen'tal**, *a.*

plā'cid, *a.* calm, unruffled ; not easily disturbed. **placid'itȳ**, *n.*

plăck'ĕt, *n.* slit in woman's skirt or petticoat.

plā'giarize, *v.i. & t.* (-*zable*), publish borrowed thoughts, &c. as original ; steal from thus. ~**ism**, ~**ist**, *nn.*

plāgue (-g), *n.* pestilence ; prevalence of some pest ; (colloq.) nuisance. *v.t.* (-*guable*), pester, worry. **plā'guy** (-gi), *a.* annoying.

plaice, *n.* kind of flat-fish.

plaid (plăd), *n.* long shawl used by Highlanders ; tartan rug.

plain, *a.* clear, evident ; straightforward ; ordinary, homely ; not luxurious ; not good-looking. *adv.* intelligibly, clearly. *n.* level tract of country. ~**song**, unison singing with free rhythm as in Gregorian chants. ~**spoken**, frank.

plaint, *n.* statement of grievance in court ; lamentation. **plain'tiff**, *n.* prosecutor in lawsuit.

plain'tive, *a.* mournful-sounding.

plait (plăt), *n.* tress of hair or band of straw, &c. made by interlacing. *v.t.* form into plait.

---

māte, mēte, mīte, mōte, mūte, mōōt ; răck, rĕck, rick, rŏck, rŭck, rook ;

plān, n. drawing exhibiting the relative position and size of the represented thing's parts; diagram, map; project, design. v.t. & i. make plan of; make design for; arrange beforehand.

plănchétte (-sh-), n. small board used in psychical experiments.

plāne[1], n. a tall spreading broadleaved tree.

plāne[2], n. a level surface; supporting-part of aeroplane; (esp. in pl.) aeroplane(s); level of attainment; paring-tool for smoothing surface of wood or metal. a. forming level or lying in a plane. v.t. & i. (-nable), smooth or pare away with plane; travel, glide, in aeroplane.

plăn′ét, n. heavenly body revolving round the sun. ~ary, a.

plank, n. long flat piece of smoothed timber; item of party programme. v.t. lay, &c. with planks; (sl.) ~ down, pay.

plant (-ah-), n. member of the vegetable kingdom; equipment for a manufacture; (sl.) hoax. v.t. place (seed, &c.) in the ground to grow; furnish (land) with people or settlers; fix firmly, establish; deliver (blow).

plăn′tain[1] (-tǐn), n. herb yielding seed used as food for cage-birds.

plăn′tain[2] (-tǐn), n. tropical tree and fruit like banana.

plăntā′tion, n. number of trees planted together; estate for cultivation of cotton, &c.; colony.

plā′nter (-ah-), n. grower of tropical produce.

plaque (plahk), n. ornamental tablet of metal, porcelain, &c.

plăsh[1], n. sound of plunging into water. v.i. make plash.

plăsh[2], v.t. bend down and interweave hedge-growth.

plăsm, ~ma (-z-), nn. living matter of a cell; colourless liquid part of milk, blood, or lymph.

plā′ster (-ah-), n. fabric spread with medicinal or adhesive substance for application to the body; plastic mixture spread on walls, &c.; preparation of gypsum. v.t. apply plaster to; bedaub. **plās′terer** (-ah-), n. workman plastering walls.

plăs′tic, a. moulding; giving form to clay, wax, &c.; easily moulded, pliant. **plăsti′cĭty,** n.

plăs′tron, n. fencer's chest-pad; Lancers' breast-cloth; woman's ornamental bodice-front.

plāte, n. flat thin sheet of metal, glass, &c.; engraved piece of metal; illustration printed from engraved plate, &c.; (collect.) table utensils of gold, silver, or other metal; shallow circular food vessel. v.t. (-table), cover ship with metal plates; coat (metal) with deposit of silver, gold, or tin.

plā′teau (-tō), n. (pl. -s, -x, pr. -z), table-land; tract of high ground.

plăt′en (-tn), n. plate in printingpress by which paper is pressed against type; corresponding part in type-writers, &c.

plăt′fórm, n. level surface raised above the surrounding ground or floor; party programme.

plăt′inotype, n. photograph process or picture done with platinum.

plăt′inum, n. white heavy ductile malleable metal.

plăt′itūde, n. trite remark.

Platŏn′ic, a. of Plato or his doctrines; (pop.) confined to words or theory; harmless or ineffectual.

platŏōn′, n. the quarter of an infantry company, each containing four sections.

plătt′er, n. dish or plate.

plaud′ĭt, n. (usu. in pl.) round of applause; commendation.

plaus′ible (-z-), a. specious; clever at making out a case. ~bĭlity, n.

play, v.i. shift about; have free movement; sport, trifle, amuse oneself; engage in games, gambling, acting, or make-believe; perform on musical instrument. v.t. take part in game; have as opponent in game; (Crick.) strike ball defensively; act in drama, &c.; perform on musical instrument; keep (fish, dupe) lightly in hand till secure. **n.** fitful or light movement; recreation; trifling; playing of game; dramatic piece; gambling. ~**bill**, theatre programme or poster. ~**fellow**, companion in childhood. ~**ground**, school recreation-ground. ~**house**, theatre. ~**mate**, playfellow. ~**thing**, toy. ~**wright**, dramatist. **play'er, n.** (esp.) actor; professional at cricket, &c. player piano, self-playing piano. **play'ful,** a. frolicsome, sportive.

plea, n. excuse; defence; defendant's or prisoner's statement.

plead, v.i. & t. address court as advocate or party; allege as plea; make earnest appeal. ~**er, n.** professional advocate. ~**ing, n.** formal statement of charge or defence.

plea'sance (-lĕz-), **n.** pleasure-ground.

plea'sant (-lĕz-), a. agreeable; giving pleasure. ~**ry, n.** a jest.

please (-z), v.t. & i. (-sable), be agreeable or give joy or gratification to; choose, be willing.

pleasure (plĕzh'er), **n.** satisfaction; delight; sensuous enjoyment; will, discretion, choice; (attrib.) designed, &c., for pleasure and not for business (~ **boat**, &c.). ~**rable,** a. affording pleasure.

pleat, n. band of triple thickness on garment, &c. made by folding. **v.t.** make pleat in.

****plebe,** n. (sl.) member of lowest class at U.S. Naval or Military Academy.

plèbei'an (-bēan), a. belonging to the common people; of low birth. **n.** a plebeian person.

plĕb'iscite, n. decision of a whole people by direct voting.

plĕc'trum, n. (pl. -**ra**), implement of ivory, &c. for plucking strings of lyre, &c.

plēdge, n. thing deposited as security; thing pawned; token, earnest, proof; toast; solemn promise. **v.t.** (-**geable**), deposit as pledge; pawn; bind (oneself); drink to health of.

plědg'ĕt, n. small mass of lint, &c. for wound, &c.

Pleiads (plī'adz) or **Pleiades** (-ēz), n.pl. seven stars closely grouped in Taurus.

pleis'tocēne (-lĭs-), a. (Geol.) of the division immediately overlying the pliocene formation.

plē'nary, a. not subject to limitation or exceptions; complete.

plĕnipotĕn'tiary (-sha-), n. envoy or commissioner appointed to act according to his own discretion. **a.** having full powers.

plĕn'itŭde, n. abundance; fullness; completeness.

plĕn'tèous, plĕn'tiful, aa. copious, abundant.

plĕn'ty, n. abundance; quite enough. **adv.** (colloq.) quite.

plē'onăsm, n. (Gram.) use of more words than are needed to give the sense. **plèonăs'tic,** a.

plĕth'ora, n. excess of red corpuscles in the blood; over-supply, glut. **plĕthō'ric,** a.

pleur'isy (ploor-), n. inflammation of the membrane enclosing the lung. **pleurit'ic,** a.

pleuropneumō'nia (plooron-), n. pleurisy and pneumonia.

plĕx'us, n. network, esp. (Anat.) of fibres, &c.

plī'able, plī'ant, aa. easily bent or influenced; supple; yielding; accommodating. **pliabil'itў, plī'ancў,** nn.

plī'ers (-z), n.pl. pincers with flat grip for bending wire, &c.

plīght¹ (plīt), v.t. pledge, give as surety; engage (oneself).

plīght² (plīt), n. condition, state; predicament.

plinth, n. slab or course between ground or floor and pedestal, pillar, wall, &c.

plī'ocēne, a. (Geol.) of the newest division of Tertiary formations.

plŏd, v.i. walk or work doggedly.

plŏt, n. small piece of land; plan or essential facts of a tale; conspiracy. **v.t. & i.** devise secretly; hatch secret plans; represent by chart or map or diagram.

plough (plow), **n.** implement for

---

furrowing and turning up the soil. *v.t. & i.* turn up (land) with plough; furrow, make furrow; (sl.) reject candidate in examination. ~man, guider of plough. ~share, blade of plough.

plo'ver (-ŭv-), *n.* kinds of shore bird.

ploy, *n.* (north.) expedition, undertaking, occupation, job.

pluck, *v.t. & i.* strip (bird) of feathers; plunder or swindle; summon up; pick or gather; snatch at; (sl.) reject candidate in examination. *n.* beast's heart, liver, and lungs; courage. pluck'y, *a.* brave, spirited.

plug, *n.* something fitting into and stopping or filling a hole or cavity; hard-pressed tobacco; *(sl.)* worn-out horse. *v.t. & i.* stop with plug; put plug into; (sl.) work hard.

plum, *n.* kinds of stone-fruit and tree; currant or raisin; fortune of £100,000; good thing. ~ cake, ~ duff, ~ pudding, cake or pudding containing raisins, currants, &c.

plu'mage (-ōo-), *n.* bird's feathers.

plumb (-m), *n.* ball of lead attached to string for testing perpendicularity of walls, &c.; perpendicularity; sounding-lead. *a.* vertical; level, true. *adv.* vertically; exactly; *(sl.)* quite, utterly. *v.t. & i.* sound (water); measure (depth); ascertain depth or get to the bottom of; make vertical; work as plumber. ~line, string with plumb attached.

plumbä'gō, *n.* black lead, the material of pencils; the plant leadwort. plumbä'ginous, *a.*

plum'beous, *a.* like lead, esp. in colour.

plumb'er (-mer), *n.* artisan who fits and repairs pipes, &c. with lead, &c. plumb'ery (-mer-), *n.*

plume (-ōo-), *n.* feather, esp. of the showy sort; feathery ornament in hat, helmet, hair, &c. *v.t.* furnish with plume; pride (oneself); (of bird) trim (feathers). ~let, *n.*

plumōse' (-ōo-), *a.* with feathery filaments.

plumm'et, *n.* plumb or plumb-line; sounding-lead.

plump, *a.* rounded with sufficient flesh or fat; (of statement, &c.) direct, uncompromising. *v.t. & i.* deposit or fall or sit abruptly; come unexpectedly upon; vote only for one candidate; express unhesitating preference for. *adv.* abruptly, bluntly. plum'per, *n.* unsplit vote or its giver.

plun'der, *v.t. & i.* carry off goods by open force; rob, steal, embezzle. *n.* pillage, spoils.

plunge (-j), *v.t. & i.* (-geable), immerse completely; (fig.) put into any state suddenly; dive or throw oneself impetuously into; (of horse) start violently forward; (sl.) gamble, run into debt. *n.* plunging action; dive.

plun'ger (-j-), *n.* (esp.) pump-piston; (sl.) gambler or speculator.

*plunk, *v.t. & i.* throw or fall heavily or abruptly. *n.* dull hard blow; (sl.) dollar.

plu'per'fect (-ōo-), *or* ~ tense, tense expressing action completed before a past point of time.

plu'ral (-oor-), *a.* more than one in number. *n.* the plural number; a plural word or form. ~ism, *n.* holding of plural offices or votes. ~ist, *n.*; ~istic, *a.* plural'ity (-oor-), *n.* being plural; pluralism; majority of votes.

plus, *prep.* with the addition of. *a.* to be added. *n.* (pl. *-sses*), symbol of addition (+). ~fours, a style of men's knickerbockers.

plush, *n.* cloth of silk or cotton with long soft nap.

plutoc'racy (-ōo-), *n.* State in which power belongs to the rich; the wealthy class. plu'tocrat (-ōo-), *n.* member of plutocracy; rich man. plutocrat'ic, *a.*

Pluto'nic, Plutō'nian (-ōo-), *aa.* of Pluto, the God of Hades; (Geol.) igneous; volcanic.

plu'vial (-ōo-), *a.* (Geol.) of or caused by rain.

---

pluviŏm´éter (-ō-), n. rain gauge. pluviomĕt´ric, a.

plȳ¹, n. one thickness or strand; bent, bias.

plȳ², v.t. & i. wield vigorously; work diligently; supply pressingly; (of ship, vehicle, &c.) go to and fro between places.

pneumăt´ic (n-), a. of, acting by, wind or air. pneumăt´ics (n-), n.pl. science of mechanical properties of elastic fluids.

pneumō´nia (n-), n. inflammation of the lungs. pneumŏn´ic, a.

pō´a, pō´a-grass, meadow-grass.

poach¹, v.t. cook (egg) by boiling without the shell.

poach², v.i. & t. take game or fish illegally; trespass for this purpose; be an interloper.

poach´er, nn. person who poaches; egg-poaching appliance.

pō´chard, n. a diving bird.

pŏck, n. eruptive spot in smallpox, &c. ~marked, a.

pŏck´et, n. small bag inserted in garments; sack of hops or wool; billiard-table bag; cavity in earth or rock. v.t. put into pocket; appropriate; conceal (feelings). ~book, note-book; small case for papers. ~money, allowance for occasional expenses, &c.

pōcocūrăn´té, a. without enthusiasms, indifferent. n. a pococurante person. ~tism, n.

pŏd, n. long seed-vessel of pea, bean, &c. v.i. & t. form pods; take from pods, shell.

pŏd´agra, n. gout. podăg´ric, a.

pŏdg´y, a. short and fat.

pō´ĕm, n. a metrical composition, esp. of elevated tone.

pō´ĕsy, n. poems or the art of making them.

pō´ĕt, n. maker of poems; writer of (esp. elevated) verse. ~ess, n.

pō´ĕtáster, n. petty versifier.

pŏĕt´ic, -al, aa. of poets or poetry; suitable to or having the qualities of poetry. pŏĕt´ics, n.pl. the science of or a treatise on poetry.

pō´ĕtrȳ, n. the poet's art or work; expression, esp. in metrical

form, of elevated thought or feeling.

pō´gŏ, n. (pl. -os), (game with) toy like one stilt with a spring on which user jumps about.

pogrŏm´, n. riot against Jews or other class in Russia.

poign´ant (poin-), a. pungent, stinging; keen, penetrating; moving, vivid. poign´ancy, n.

poilu (pwah´lōō), n. (sl.) modern French soldier.

point, n. dot; particular place or spot; exact moment; degree of measurement; item, detail; thing that counts; sharp end, tip; projection, promontory; (pl.) on railway, tapering movable rails for directing train on to another line; fielder at cricket, named from nearness to point of bat. v.t. & i. sharpen, furnish with point; punctuate; give point to by illustration; hold (finger, pistol, stick, &c.) directed at; (of dogs) indicate where game is. ~blank, with aim level and not above the object; (fig.) flatly or uncompromisingly. ~duty, of constable stationed at particular spot to direct traffic, &c.

point´ĕd, a. sharp; emphatic; epigrammatic. ~ly, adv.

point´er, n. anything that points; indicating-rod used at blackboard, &c.; breed of dog trained to point at game.

point´less, a. blunt, not sharp; obtuse, lacking point; not having scored a point.

points´man (-an), n. man working railway points.

poise (-z), v.t. & i. (-sable), hold in a balanced or steady position; be balanced; hover; hang suspended. n. equilibrium; way thing hangs or balances.

pois´on (-zn), n. substance that when absorbed by a living organism kills or injures it; harmful principle, influence, &c. v.t. administer poison to; fill with prejudice; spoil. ~er, n.; ~ous, a.

---

măte, mēte, mĭte, mōte, mūte, mōōt; răck, rĕck, rick, rŏck, rŭck, rōōk;

pŏke, v.t. & i. (-kable), push the end of a finger, stick, &c. against; make thrusts at; thrust forward. n. thrust with finger-end, &c.; projecting front of bonnet.

pō'ker, n. metal rod for poking fire; an American card-game.

pŏ'ky, a. (of room, &c.) confined; (of occupation, &c.) petty, obscure.

pō'lar, a. of or near either pole of the earth; having polarity, magnetic; having positive and negative electricity. polā'rity, n. tendency to point to the magnetic poles of earth. ~ization, n.

pōle[1], n. long slender rounded piece of wood used as support for scaffolding, tent, &c.; flagstaff; (measure) rod or perch, 5½ yards. ~jump, jump with aid of pole carried in the hands.

pōle[2], n. North, South, ~, the two points in the celestial sphere about which the stars appear to revolve; also, N. & S. extremities of earth's axis; each of the two opposite points on surface of magnet at which magnetic forces are manifested; each of two opposed principles, &c. ~star, a star near North Pole of the heavens; (fig.) thing serving as guide, lodestar.

Pōle[3], n. native of Poland.

pōle-axe (-lǎ-), n. battle-axe; butcher's slaughtering axe. v.t. kill or strike with pole-axe.

pōle'căt (-lk-), n. small fetid animal like a weasel; *skunk.

polĕm'ic, a. of controversy or wordy warfare. n. a controversy or controversialist; (pl.) controversy.

polĕn'ta, n. Italian porridge of chestnuts, maize, &c.

police' (-ēs), n. public order; the civil force charged with keeping order. v.t. (-ceable), control or furnish with police; act as police in; *(Mil.) clean up, put (barrack, camp, &c.) in order. ~man, member of the police force.

pŏl'icy[1], n. statecraft; course of action; sagacious procedure.

pŏl'icy[2], n. document containing contract of insurance.

pŏl'igar, n. (S.-India) subordinate feudal chief; head of a village or district. ~dog, large breed of dogs in S. India.

pŏl'ish[1], v.t. & i. make or become smooth or glossy by friction; make cultured; smarten up. n. smoothness, glossiness; substance used to give polished surface; refinement.

Pō'lish[2], a. of Poland or the Poles.

polite', a. cultivated, well-bred; courteous. ~ness, n. courtesy.

pŏl'itic, a. judicious, expedient; sagacious, prudent.

polit'ical, a. of the State or its affairs; of politics. ~ agent, resident, official of Indian Government advising ruler of native State. ~ economy, theory of the production and distribution of wealth.

politi'cian (-shn), n. person engaged or interested in politics.

pŏl'itics, n.pl. science of government; affairs of State; questions of policy; strife of parties.

pŏl'ity, n. form of civil government; an organized State.

pō'lka, n. kind of dance.

pŏll[1], n. the head; counting of voters, voting, number of votes. v.t. & i. crop hair of; cut off top of tree or horns of beast; count votes of, vote, receive votes of.

Pŏll[2], n. parrot. ~-parrot, parrot; silly babbler.

pŏll'ack, -ock, n. sea-fish allied to cod.

pŏl'lam, n. (S. India) district held by a poligar.

pŏll'ard, n. tree made by polling to produce a close head of young shoots; hornless animal. v.t. make pollard of (tree).

pŏll'en, n. fertilizing powder discharged from flower's anther.

pŏll'inate, v.t. fertilize with pollen. pollinā'tion, n.

pollute' (-ōot), v.t. (-table), destroy the purity of. ~tion, n.

pō′lō, *n.* game like hockey played by men on ponies.

pŏlonaise′ (-z), *n.* form of woman's dress ; kind of dance.

polō′nĭum, *n.* a highly radio-active element.

pŏlō′nў, *n.* kind of sausage.

pŏl′tergeist (-gīst), *n.* spirit announcing its presence by raps or other sound.

pŏltrōōn′, *n.* coward. **~ery,** *n.*

pŏl′ўǎndrў, *n.* polygamy in which one woman has more than one husband. **~rous,** *a.*

pŏlўǎn′thus, *n.* kinds of cultivated primula.

pŏlўchrōmăt′ĭc (-kr-), *a.* many-coloured. **pŏl′ўchrōme** (-kr-), *n.* polychromatic work of art.

pŏlўg′amў, *n.* having more than one wife or more than one husband. **~mist,** *n.* ; **~mous,** *a.*

pŏl′ўglŏt, *a.* of or in several languages. *n.* polyglot book.

pŏl′ўgŏn, *n.* figure with many angles or sides. **pŏlўg′onal,** *a.*

pŏlўhḗd′ron, *n.* many-sided solid. **~ral,** *a.*

pŏl′ўp, *n.* kinds of animal of low organization, as sea-anemones.

pŏlўph′onў, *n.* harmonizing of separate simultaneous melodies.

pŏl′ўpodў, *n.* fern growing on rocks, walls, &c.

pŏl′ўpus, *n.* (pl. -pī, -puses), kinds of tumour, esp. of nose.

pŏl′ўsyllable, *n.* word having many syllables. **~ăb′ic,** *a.*

pŏlўtĕc′hnic (-k-), *a.* dealing with, devoted to, various arts. *n.* technical school.

pŏl′ўthēism, *n.* belief in more than one god. **~ist,** *n.* ; **~istic,** *a.*

pomace (pŭm′ĭs), *n.* crushed apples in cider-making.

pomade′ (-ahd), **pomā′tum,** *nn.* scented ointment for the hair.

pŏme′grănate (-mg-), *n.* a large tough-rinded fruit.

Pŏmerā′nian, *n.* a breed of small dogs.

pŏm′frĕt, *n.* fish found in Indian and Pacific Oceans, used as food.

po′mmel (pŭ-), *n.* knob of sword-hilt ; front of saddle ; horn of

side-saddle. *v.t.* strike with sword-pommel or with fists.

pŏmp, *n.* splendid display ; splendour, grandeur.

pŏm′-pŏm, *n.* quick-firing gun.

pŏm′pŏn, *n.* tuft of ribbon, &c. on hat, shoe, &c.

pŏm′pous, *a.* magnificent, splendid ; showing self-importance ; (of language) inflated. **pŏm-pŏs′itў,** *n.*

pŏn′chō, *n.* (pl. -os), cloak or cape made of a piece of cloth, &c. with opening for the head.

pŏnd, *n.* small body of still water artificially formed.

pŏn′der, *v.t. & i.* think over, muse.

pŏn′derable, *a.* of appreciable weight ; material. *n.* (esp. in pl.) material thing(s). **~bility,** *n.*

pŏn′derous, *a.* unwieldy by weight ; heavy, dull. **pŏnderŏs′itў,** *n.*

pŏn′iard (-yard), *n.* dagger. *v.t.* stab with poniard.

pŏn′tiff, *n.* the Pope ; bishop ; chief priest. **pŏntĭf′ical,** *a.* episcopal, papal ; (of manner, &c.) as of a pontiff ; *n.* book of episcopal rites ; (pl.) episcopal vestments.

pontōōn′, *n.* flat-bottomed boat for use with others as supports of temporary bridge ; punt game.

pō′nў, *n.* horse of any small breed ; (sl.) £25 ; *(sl.) translation, crib.

pōōd, *n.* a Russian weight (36 lb.).

pōō′dle, *n.* kinds of pet dog with long curling hair.

‖ **pōō′gye** (-gē), *n.* Hindu nose-flute.

pooh (pōō, pŏŏ), *int.* of contempt. **pooh-pooh′,** *v.t.* ridicule.

‖ **pōōj′a,** (E.-Ind.) rites performed in Hindu idol-worship ; any Hindu religious ceremony or rite.

pōō′kōō, puku (pōō′kōō), *n.* red antelope of Central Africa.

pōōl[1], *n.* small body of still water ; puddle ; deep place in river.

pōōl[2], *n.* collective stakes in cards or betting ; game for several players on billiard-table with pool taken by winner ; combination of manufacturers, &c. *v.t.* throw into common fund.

pōōn, *n.* E.-Ind. tree. **~-oil,** oil

from seeds of this, used in medicine and for lamps.

poon'ah, *a.* ~ painting, painting on rice or other thin paper in imitation of oriental work. ~brush, ~ paper, brush, paper, used for this.

poop, *n.* stern of ship; aftermost and highest deck.

poor, *a.* having little money or means; (of soil) unproductive; inadequate; despicable, insignificant; deserving pity. ~law, ~rate, providing for support of paupers. ~spirited, meek, cowardly.

poor'ness, *n.* unproductiveness; lack of some good quality or constituent.

poor'ly, *adv.* insufficiently, with little success. *pred.a.* out of sorts, not in good health.

pop[1], *n.* abrupt explosive sound; (colloq.) champagne, gingerbeer. *v.i. & t.* make pop; (colloq.) let off (pistol, &c.); go or come unexpectedly or suddenly; put quickly in, down, &c. *adv.* with a pop; suddenly.

***pop**[2], *n.* (colloq.) father.

pope, *n.* bishop of Rome as head of R.-C. church. ~dom, *n.*

po'pery, *n.* (contempt.) the papal system; Romanizing tendencies.

pop'injay, *n.* fop, coxcomb.

po'pish, *a.* of popery; papistical.

pop'lar, *n.* kinds of tree noted for tallness and slenderness.

pop'lin, *n.* corded fabric of silk and worsted.

***popp'a**, *n.* papa.

popp'et, *n.* darling; lathe-head.

popp'ied (-pĭd), *a.* having poppies; drugged with opium.

popp'ing-crease, *n.* white line marking front of batsman's ground.

popp'y, *n.* kinds of plant with bright flowers.

***popp'ycock**, *n.* (sl.) nonsense.

pop'ulace, *n.* the common people.

pop'ular, *a.* of the people; generally liked or admired. ~a'rity, *n.* being generally liked. ~ize, *v.t.* (-*zable*), make popular.

pop'ulate, *v.t.* (-*lable*), fill with inhabitants. **popula'tion**, *n.* the inhabitants; the number of them. ~tor, *n.* **pop'ulous**, *a.* thickly populated.

***pop'ulist**, *n.* member of U.S. political party advocating public control of railroads, graduated income-tax, &c.

porce'lain (-slĭn), *n.* fine kind of earthenware; china.

porch, *n.* covered approach to entrance of building.

por'cine, *a.* of or like pigs.

porc'upine, *n.* beast armed with pointed quills.

pore[1], *n.* one of the small openings making skin, wood, brick, &c. permeable to fluids.

pore[2], *v.i.* have the eyes or mind intent upon.

pork, *n.* pigs' flesh. *~barrel*, (colloq.) congressional grant of money for local public works. **pork'er**, *n.* young fattened hog.

pornog'raphy, *n.* obscene writing.

por'ous, *a.* having pores; permeable. **poros'ity**, *n.*

porph'yry, *n.* kinds of rock with crystals embedded in a red or other ground-mass.

porp'oise (-*pus*), *n.* blunt-snouted marine mammal 5 ft. long.

po'rridge, *n.* oatmeal or other meal boiled in water or milk.

po'rringer (-j-), *n.* small basin for portion of porridge, &c.

port[1], *n.* harbour; town or place possessing harbour.

port[2], *n.* opening in ship's side for entrance, &c.; (also *port-hole*) aperture in ship's side to admit light and air.

port[3], *v.t.* hold (rifle, sword) diagonally in front of body. *n.* bearing, deportment.

port[4], *n.* left of ship looking forward. *v.t. & i.* turn (helm, ship) to port; (of ship) turn to port.

port[5], *n.* a strong sweet red wine.

port'able, *a.* that can be carried about; movable.

port'age, *n.* transport of goods or its cost; carrying necessary between two navigable rivers.

pŏrt'al, n. doorway, gateway.

pŏrtcŭll'is, n. grating raised and lowered in grooves as defence of gateway. ~ed, a.

portĕnd', v.t. foreshadow; be an omen or presage of.

pŏrt'ĕnt, n. thing that portends something; significant sign; a prodigy. **pŏrtĕn'tous**, a. of the nature of a portent; solemn.

pŏrt'er¹, n. attendant at door or gate; *attendant in Pullman or sleeping car.

pŏrt'er², n. person employed to carry burdens; ˢ dark-brown bitter beer. ~-house, tavern restaurant. *~-house steak, a choice cut of beef. **pŏrt'erage**, n. hire of porters.

pŏrt'fīre, n. appliance for igniting fireworks or explosives.

pŏrtfō'lĭō, n. (pl. -os). case for loose drawings or sheets of paper; office of minister of State.

pŏrt'ĭcō, n. (pl. -os). colonnade serving as porch to a building.

portière (pŏrt'yār), n. curtain over door or doorway.

pŏr'tion, n. part allotted; share; helping; dowry; destiny or lot; part, some. v.t. divide into shares or lots; give dowry to. ~less, a. without dowry.

pŏrt'lȳ, a. bulky, corpulent; of stately appearance.

pŏrtmăn'teau (-tō), n. (pl. -s, -x), leather trunk for clothes, &c.

pŏrt'rait (-rĭt), n. likeness of person or animal; description. ~ure, n. portraying; portrait(s).

pŏrtrāy', v.t. paint or draw likeness of; describe. ~al, n.

pŏrt'reeve, n. officer inferior to mayor in some towns.

pŏrt'ress, n. female porter.

pōse (-z), v.t. & i. (-sable), propound for solution; arrange in required attitude; set up, give oneself out, as; puzzle (person) with question or problem. n. attitude of body or mind, esp. one assumed for effect. **pō'ser** (-z-), n. a difficult question.

pŏs'it (-z-), v.t. lay down as basis of argument or inference.

posi'tion (-z-), n. way thing is placed; state of affairs; mental attitude; situation; rank or status; an office; strategic point.

pŏs'itive (-z-), a. formally or explicitly laid down; definite; unquestionable; absolute; confident in opinion, cocksure; not negative; greater than zero; (Gram., ~ adjective, degree) stating simply the existence of the quality without comparison; (Photog.) showing lights and shades as seen in nature. n. positive degree, adjective, quantity, photograph, &c.

pŏs'itivism (-z-), n. philosophy of Comte recognizing only positive facts and ᵃ observable phenomena; religion founded on this. ~ist, n.

pŏss'é, body of police or of men summoned to aid sheriff.

possĕss' (-z-), v.t. hold as property; own, have; have the mastery of; influence; seize.

posse'ssion (-zĕshn), n. possessing or being possessed; occupancy; thing possessed; (pl.) property.

possĕss'ive (-oz-), a. of or indicating possession. n. possessive pronoun or case.

possĕss'or (-zĕs-), n. owner; proprietor. ~y, a. of or as of, a possessor.

pŏss'ĕt, n. hot drink of milk with wine, spice, &c.

pŏss'ible, a. that can exist, be done, or happen. n. full marks, highest possible score. **possĭbil'itȳ**, n. what is possible; possible occurrence. **pŏss'iblȳ**, adv. perhaps.

pŏss'um, n. (colloq. for) opossum; play ~, feign illness or death.

pōst¹, n. upright of timber or metal fixed in ground, &c.; the ~, winning-post. v.t. display (notice, &c.) on a post or notice-board.

pōst², n. official conveying of letters and parcels; appointed station; place of duty; appointment; fort; trading-station; size of paper. v.t. & i. put (letter, &c.) into official receptacle for

---

māte, mēte, mīte, mōte, mūte, mōŏt; răck, rĕck, rick, rŏck, rŭck, rōŏk;

transmission by post; travel with post-horses; hurry; station in particular spot; enter in ledger; supply with latest information. *adv.* with post-horses; express, in haste. ~boy, postilion. ~card, card conveying message by post. ~chaise, (hist.) travelling carriage. ~ -haste, with all speed. ~horses, formerly used in relays by the post or by travellers. ~man, man who delivers or collects the post. ~mark, official mark stamped on letters. ~master, official in charge of a post office. ~ office, any building in which postal business is carried on.

|| pŏst³, Latin *prep.* after.

pō′stage, *n.* charge for carriage of letter, &c. by post.

pō′stal, *a.* of the post office.

pŏst-dāte′, *v.t.* affix or assign a later date than the real one.

pŏst-dǐlū′vǐan (*or* dĭ-; -ōō-), *a.* after the Flood.

|| pŏstēen′, *n.* Afghan leathern pelisse.

pō′ster, *n.* posted placard; (Rugby footb.) attempt at goal that passes straight over a post.

pŏstēr′ǐor, *a.* hinder; later in time or order. *n.* the buttocks.

pŏstē′rǐty, *n.* person's descendants; later generations.

pō′stern (*or* pŏ-), *n.* back or side entrance; private door.

pŏst′humous (-tū-), *a.* born or published after the father's or author's death; occurring after death.

postĭl′ion (-lyon), *n.* man riding one of the horses that draw a carriage and guiding the team.

|| pŏst merid′iĕm, *adv.* (abbr. *p.m.*), after noon.

pŏst-mŏrt′ĕm, *a.* after death. *n.* examination made after death.

pŏst-ŏb′ĭt, *n.* bond given by expectant heir for money to be paid on succession to the property.

postpōne′, *v.t.* (-nable), defer, put off for later time. ~ment, *n.*

pŏst-prăn′dǐal, *a.* (of speech, &c.) after-dinner.

post′script (pōsk-), *n.* addition made at end of letter, &c.

pŏs′tŭlāte, *v.t.* (-āt), demand as a pre-requisite or basis; lay down as indisputable. *n.* (-ĭt), thing postulated.

pŏs′tŭre, *n.* carriage; attitude of body or mind; condition, state. *v.i.* (-rable), take up a posture for effect; pose.

pō′sy̆ (-z-), *n.* bunch of flowers; inscribed motto on ring, &c.

pŏt, *n.* vessel of earthenware, metal, or glass; (usu. *pott*) a size of paper. *v.t.* put into pot for preservation; plant in flowerpot. ~hole, deep hole worn in rock &c. by water; depression in road surface. ~hook, hook for hanging pots over fire, &c.; curved stroke used in learning to write. ~hunter, competitor seeking to add to his number of prizes; *person killing game to sell to market. ~sherd, piece of broken earthenware.

pō′table, *a.* drinkable.

pŏt′ash, *n.* an alkali used in soap, &c.

potăss′ĭum, *n.* a white metal.

potā′tion, *n.* drinking; draught.

potā′tō, *n.* (pl. *-oes*), plant with tubers used as food; its tuber.

poteen′, potheen′ (-t-h-), *n.* Irish whisky from illicit still.

pō′tent, *a.* powerful; cogent; strong; influential. pō′tency, *n.*

pō′tentāte, *n.* ruler, king, &c.

potĕn′tial (-shl), *a.* capable of coming into being, latent; (Gram., of mood, &c.) expressing possibility. *n.* potential mood; potential function or amount of energy or work denoted by it. potĕntǐal′ity (-shǐ-), *n.* possibility.

pŏth′er (-dh-), *n.* disturbance; din.

pō′tion, *n.* draught of medicine or poison.

pot-pourri (pō′pōō′rǐ), *n.* mixture of rose petals, spices, &c.; musical or literary medley.

pŏtt′age, *n.* soup or stew.

pŏtt′er¹, *v.i.* work in feeble manner.

pŏtt′er², *n.* maker of earthenware

---

māre, mĕre, mīre, mŏre, mūre; pärt, pĕt, pôrt; *italics*, vague sounds;

vessels. **pŏtt'erў**, *n.* potter's work or workshop.

pŏt'tle, *n.* liquid measure (half gallon), pot containing it.

pŏtt'ў, *a.* (sl.) insignificant; crazy.

pouch, *n.* small bag; detachable pocket. *v.t. & i.* put into pouch; take shape of or hang like pouch.

poult (pōlt), *n.* young fowl, turkey, or game-bird. **poul'terer** (pōl-), *n.* dealer in poultry.

poul'tice (pōl-), *n.* soft dressing applied to sore or inflamed part. *v.t.* apply poultice to.

poul'trў (pōl-), *n.* barndoor and other fowls reared for food.

pounce¹, *v.i.* swoop, come suddenly down, upon. *n.* sudden descent upon something; (arch.) talon.

pounce², *n.* fine powder used in pattern-tracing, or to prevent ink from spreading on unsized paper.

pound¹, *v.t. & i.* crush to pieces or powder or shapelessness; thump, pummel; make continued efforts.

pound², *n.* enclosure for detention of stray cattle.

pound³, *n.* a measure of weight (abbr. *lb.*), 16 oz. avoirdupois, 12 oz. troy; a money of account (symbol £ or *l.*), 20 shillings; (hist.) pound Scots, 1s. 8*d.* **poun'dage**, *n.* commission or fee of so much per £; payment of so much per lb.; (hist.) customs-duty on pound's-worth of imports and exports.

pour (pōr), *v.t. & i.* issue or make issue in a stream or shower; discharge; send forth.

‖ **pourparler** (poorpärl'ā), *n.* (usu. in pl.) informal opening of a question between diplomatists.

poussëtte' (pōō-), *n. & v.i.* swing round with joined hands in country dance.

pout, *v.i. & t.* thrust out the lips; protrude (lips). *n.* act or fact of pouting; kinds of fish. **pout'er**, *n.* (esp.) pigeon with prominent crop.

pŏv'ertў, *n.* want of means, indigence; the poor; poorness.

powd'er, *n.* mass of fine dry particles; cosmetic or a dose of medicine in this form; gunpowder. *v.t. & i.* reduce to powder; sprinkle with powder. **~-flask**, **~-horn**, **~-magazine**, for carrying or storing gunpowder. **~-monkey**, (hist.) boy carrying gunpowder on ship during fight. **powd'erў**, *a.* consisting of or covered with powder.

pow'er, *n.* ability to do or act; delegated authority; control, influence, ascendancy; mechanical energy applicable to work. **~-house**, **~-station**, house or station for generating and distributing electric power.

pow'erful, *a.* having great power. **~less**, *a.* without power; helpless.

pow'-wow, *n.* meeting of N.-Amer. Indians for conference, &c.; (joc.) conference, palaver.

prăc'ticable, *a.* that can be done; feasible. **~bility**, *n.*

prăc'tical, *a.* of, concerned with, shown in, action rather than theory or words. **~al'itў**, *n.*

prăc'tically, *adv.* virtually.

prăc'tice, *n.* action as opposed to theory; established method; exercise to improve skill; lawyer's or doctor's professional business; (Arith.) mode of multiplying together expressions of several denominations.

prăc'tise, *v.t. & i.* (*-sable*), put in practice; pursue profession; exercise oneself in; impose upon.

prăcti'tioner (-sho-), *n.* practising doctor or lawyer.

praepŏs'tor (prip-), *n.* prefect or monitor in school. **~ōr'ial**, *a.*

prae'tor, *n.* ancient-Roman magistrate of lower rank than consul. **praetōr'ian**, *a.* of a praetor; of the bodyguard of Roman emperor or general. *n.* man of praetorian rank; praetorian soldier.

prăgmăt'ic, **~al**, *aa.* (usu. *-al*) meddlesome; positive, dictatorial; (usu. *-ic*) treating facts of history with reference to their practical lessons; of State affairs. **prăg'matism**, *n.* pragmatical behaviour or tendencies ; (Philos.) doctrine that estimates any assertion solely by its practical bearing upon human interests. ~ist, n. ~istic, a.

prair′ie, n. large treeless tract of grass-land.

praise (-z), v.t. (-sable), express approbation of ; commend ; glorify. n. commendation, glorification ; praising. **praise′worthy** (-zwėr′dhi), a. meritorious.

Prak′rit (prah-), n. any of the dialects of N. and Central India existing alongside of or growing out of Sanskrit.

pra′line (prah-), n. sweetmeat of nuts and sugar.

prām, n. perambulator.

prance (-ah-), v.i. (of horse) spring from hind legs ; walk, move, in elated or arrogant manner. ~. spring, caper.

prān′dial, a. of or at dinner.

prank, v.t. & t. deck, adorn, spangle ; show oneself off. n. gambol, frolic, escapade.

prāse, n. a green quartz.

prāte, v.i. discourse foolishly ; talk solemn nonsense. n. idle talk.

prāt′tle, v.i. talk in childish or artless way. n. prattling talk. **prātt′ler**, n. (esp.) young child.

prawn, n. crustacean like large shrimp.

pray, v.i. & t. offer prayers, make supplication (to God or person) ; ask earnestly ; beg for.

prayer (prār), n. petition made to God ; praying ; entreaty. ~book, (esp.) Book of Common Prayer. **prayer′ful** (-ārf-), a. not without prayer ; given to prayer.

pre-, pref. before in (time, place, order, or importance), freely used with Eng. words, only the more important of which are given below.

preach, v.i. & t. deliver sermon ; talk like preacher of sermon ; give obtrusive advice. ~er, n. ~ment, n. (colloq.) intrusive moralizing.

preām′ble, n. part of a document, &c. serving as introduction.

prē-arrānge′, v.t. & t. arrange beforehand. ~ment, n.

prēb′end, n. stipend of canon or member of chapter. ~al, a. ~ary, n. holder of a prebend.

precār′ious, a. dependent on chance ; uncertain, risky.

precau′tion, n. thing done beforehand to prevent an apprehended evil. ~ary, a.

prēcēde′, v.t. & i. (-dable), come or go before in place or time.

prēce′dence, n. priority in time or succession ; superiority, higher position. **prēce′dent**, n. previous case taken as example or justification of rule. ~, preceding.

prēcen′tor, n. leader of choir's or congregation's singing.

prē′cept, n. rule for action or conduct ; kinds of writ or warrant. **prēcep′tor**, n. teacher, instructor. ~tress, n.

prēce′ssion (-shn), n. change by which the equinoxes occur earlier in each successive sidereal year.

prē′cinct, n. ground pertaining to a sacred or official building or place ; (pl.) environs ; *police- or election-district.

prēcios′ity (-shi-), n. over-refinement in art, esp. in choice of words.

prē′cious (-shŭs), a. of great value, valuable ; highly valued ; (colloq. usu. in irony) great, fine.

prē′cipice, n. vertical steep face of rock, cliff, mountain, &c.

prēcip′itance, ~cy, nn. rash haste ; headlong hurry.

prēcip′itate (-tlable), v.t. (-āt), throw headlong down ; cause to go hurriedly or violently ; cause (solid matter in solution) to be deposited. a. (-lt), headlong ; rash ; done too soon. n. (-lt), solid matter precipitated. ~tion, n. rash haste ; depositing of solid matter from solution.

prēcip′itous, a. of the nature of a precipice.

prē′cis (prēs′ē), n. summary.

prēcise′, a. strictly worded ; definite, exact, particular. ~ly, adv. exactly ; just so.

---

zh, as (rou)ge ; ē=1 ; ĭr, ūr,=ėr ; ỹ, ỹ,=ĭ, ĭ ; and see p. 4. *=U.S.

8495 N

prĕcī'sian (-zhn), n. punctilious or formal person.

prĕcī'sion (-zhn), n. accuracy.

prĕclúde' (-ōōd), v.t. (-dable), prevent; make impracticable.

prĕcō'cious (-shus), a. remarkable for early development; too forward. prĕcō'city, n.

prĕcŏgni'tion, n. foreknowledge; preliminary examination.

prĕconcēive' (-sēv), v.t. form an opinion beforehand.

prĕconcĕp'tion, n. preconceived notion.

prĕconcērt', v.t. agree upon beforehand.

prĕcūr'sor, n. person or thing serving to herald the coming of another. prĕcūr'sory, a.

prĕdā'cious (-shus), a. subsisting by the capture of living prey; of predacious animals.

prĕd'atory, a. of, addicted to, plunder or robbery.

prĕdecease', v.t. die before another. n. death before another's.

prĕ'decĕssor, n. former holder of any office or position.

prĕdĕs'tine, v.t. appoint or ordain beforehand. ∼nation, n. God's appointment from eternity of those who shall be saved.

prĕdĕtĕr'mine, v.t. determine beforehand, predestine. ∼nate, a.; ∼nation, n.

prĕ'dicable, a. that can be predicated or affirmed. n. predicable thing. ∼bility, n.

prĕdic'ament, n. unpleasant, trying, or dangerous situation.

prĕd'icate, v.t. (-āt), state as true of or pertaining to something. n. (-it), that which is predicated; (Gram.) what is said of the subject, including the copula. ∼tion, n. act of predicating. prĕdic'ative, a. making a predication. (Gram.) forming part or the whole of the predicate.

prĕdict', v.t. & i. foretell; prophesy. ∼ability, n. ∼ion, n. foretelling; a prophecy. ∼ive, a.; ∼or, n.

prĕdilec'tion, n. mental preference, partiality, (for).

prĕdispose' (-z), v.t. render liable, subject, or inclined beforehand.

prĕdisposition, n. antecedent state favourable to ailment, purpose, &c.

prĕdŏm'inate, v.i. have the chief power or influence; prevail; preponderate. ∼ance, n.: ∼ant, a.

prĕ-ĕm'inent, a. excelling all others. ∼nce, n. superiority.

prĕ-ĕmp'tion, n. purchase of a thing before it is offered to others; right to first refusal.

preen, v.t. trim (feathers) with beak; (fig.) smarten oneself.

prĕf'ace, n. introductory remarks prefixed to a book; preamble of speech, &c. v.t. (-ceable), introduce or begin as with a preface. prĕf'atory, a.

prĕf'ĕct, n. person put in authority; senior scholar entrusted with maintaining discipline. ∼ure, n. prefect's office, residence, district, or tenure.

prĕfĕr', v.t. hold superior, like better; bring forward (claim, &c.); promote to office. prĕf'erable, a. deserving preference; superior to. ∼bly, adv. for choice. prĕf'erence, n. liking of one thing more than another; prior right; favoured position. prĕferĕn'tial a. (-shl), of, giving, or receiving preference. prĕfĕr'ment, n. promotion; ecclesiastical or other post.

prĕfig'ure (-ger), v.t. be a type of; foreshadow. ∼ment, n.

prĕfix', v.t. add at the beginning. prĕ'fix', n. preposition or particle prefixed to a word; title or particle prefixed to names.

prĕg'nant, a. with child; fruitful in results; big with consequences; suggestive. prĕg'nancy, n.

prĕhĕn'sile (or -il), a. (of tail, foot, &c.) capable of grasping. ∼sion, n. power of grasping.

prĕhistŏ'ric, a. before the days recorded by history.

prĕjūdge', v.t. pass judgement on before hearing the evidence.

prĕj'udice (-jŏō-), n. preconceived

opinion, bias; injury or detriment that results from some action. *v.t.* (*-ceable*), impair the validity or prospects of; inspire with prejudice. **prejudi'cial** (-jŏŏdĭshl), *a.* detrimental.

prel'acy, *n.* Church government by prelates; the prelates; the dignity of a prelate. **prel'ate,** *n.* bishop or ecclesiastic of equal or higher rank. **prelat'ical,** *a.*

prelect', *v.i.* lecture, esp. as prelector. **~ion,** *n.* lecture. **~or,** *n.* public lecturer.

prelim'inary, *a.* preceding and leading up to the main business; introductory. *n.* preliminary step or arrangement.

prel'ude, *n.* that which serves as introduction. *v.t. & i.* serve as prelude to; play musical prelude. **prelu'sive** (-lōō-), *a.* introductory.

prematu're', *a.* occurring or done before the right or usual time; hasty.

premed'itate (prī-), *v.t.* think out beforehand. **~tion,** *n.*

prem'ier, *a.* foremost, leading; having precedence of all others. *n.* prime minister. **~ship,** *n.*

prem'ise, *n.* (prĕm'ĭs), proposition from which an inference is drawn; (pl.) beginning of a deed specifying names of parties, property, &c.; (pl.) any house or building with its belongings. *v.t.* (primīz'), say or write by way of introduction.

pre'mium, *n.* reward; amount or instalment payable for an insurance policy; fee for instruction in profession, &c.; a bonus.

premoni'tion, *n.* forewarning. **premon'itory,** *a.* serving to warn.

preoccupa'tion, *n.* occupying beforehand; business that takes precedence; mental absorption. **preocc'upy,** *v.t.* occupy beforehand; prevent from attending to other things.

preordain', *v.t.* decree beforehand.

prepara'tion, *n.* preparing; (usu. pl.) thing(s) done to make ready; time devoted to school lessons (abbrev. **prep.**); medicine.

prepa'rative, *a.* preparatory.

prepa'ratory, *a.* serving to prepare; introductory to.

prepare', *v.t. & i.* (*-rable*), make ready; get into train or proper state; make preparations.

prepay', *v.t.* pay in advance.

prepense', *a.* (placed after *n.*) deliberate, intentional.

prepon'derate, *v.i.* be heavier; be superior in influence, quantity, or number. **~ance,** *n.*; **~ant,** *a.*

preposi'tion (-z-), *n.* indeclinable word serving to mark relation between the noun or pronoun it governs and another word. **~al,** *a.*

prepossess', *v.t.* imbue with some sentiment; take possession of. **~ion,** *n.* prejudice, esp. in favour of person or thing.

prepos'terous, *a.* utterly absurd; perverse; contrary to reason.

prerog'ative, *n.* the power vested in a sovereign in virtue of his office; peculiar right or privilege.

presage, *n.* (prĕs'ĭj), omen, presentiment. *v.t.* (prĭsāj'), foreshadow, foretell, foresee.

presby'opia (-z-), *n.* long-sightedness incident to old age.

pres'byter (-z-), *n.* officer of the early Church; priest of Episcopal Church; elder of Presbyterian Church; member of presbytery. **presbytē'rian** (-z-), *a.* (of Church) governed by presbyteries; *n.* member of a Presbyterian Church. **~ianism,** *n.* **pres'bytery** (-z-), *n.* ecclesiastical court in Presbyterian Church; sanctuary or eastern part of chancel.

pre'scient (-shyĕnt), *a.* having foreknowledge or foresight. **pre'science** (-shyĕns), *n.*

prescribe', *v.t. & i.* (*-bable*), lay down authoritatively; advise use of; suggest remedy *for*. **pre'script,** *n.* an ordinance or decree. **prescrip'tion,** *n.* prescribing; thing prescribed, esp. by physician; written statement of this; uninterrupted use as

---

basis of a right. **~ive**, *a.* that ordains or gives directions; based on prescription or custom.

prés'ence (-z-), *n.* being present; place where person is; personal appearance; readiness at need. **~-chamber**, great person's reception-room.

prés'ent[1] (-z-), *a.* on the spot, here; now existing, occurring, being dealt with. *n.* the present time; present tense.

prés'ent[2] (-z-), *n.* gift.

présent'[3] (-z-), *v.t.* set in conspicuous position; introduce; exhibit; hold out; offer, deliver, give; hold (rifle) in position for shooting. *n.* (Mil.) attitude of presenting rifle. **~able**, *a.* of decent appearance; fit to be shown. **~ability**, *n.* **présentā'tion**, *n.* presenting; right of presenting to a benefice.

présen'timent (-z-), *n.* vague expectation; foreboding.

prés'ently (-z-), *adv.* before long.

présent'ment (-z-), *n.* laying of a formal statement before a court, &c.; performance of play, &c.

préservā'tion (-z-), *n.* preserving; being preserved.

préserv'ative (-z-), *a.* tending to preserve. *n.* drug, &c. for preserving.

préserve' (-z-), *v.t.* (-vable), keep safe; keep alive; maintain; prepare so as to keep fit for food. *n.* jam; place where game is preserved.

préside' (-z-), *v.i.* be chairman or president. **prés'idency** (-z-), *n.* office of president; district in India (*Bengal, Madras, Bombay, Presidency*, not now official). **prés'ident** (-z-), *n.* head of a company of persons; elected head of a republic. **présiden'tial**, *a.*

press[1], *v.t. & i.* subject to a steady push or squeeze; exert pressure; smooth (clothes, &c.). *n.* crowding; pressure; machine for pressing; printing-press, the newspapers; cupboard for clothes, &c.; set of shelves for books. **~-man**, operator of printing-press; journalist or reporter. **~-mark**, library shelf-mark.

press[2], *v.t.* force to serve in army or navy. **~-gang**, body employed to press men for the navy.

prés'sure (-*sher*), *n.* the force exerted by one body acting on another; urgency; constraining influence.

prestidigitā'tion (-z-), *n.* sleight of hand. **préstídí'gitātor**, *n.*

prestige' (-ēzh), *n.* influence or reputation.

prés'tō, *adv.* (used in conjuring) quickly. *a.* rapid, juggling.

présume' (-z-), *v.t. & i.* (-mable), take for granted; take the liberty, venture. **présu'mably**, *~mēdiў* (-z-), *adv.* as may fairly be or is presumed. **présu'ming**, *a.* presumptuous.

présump'tion (-z-), *n.* supposition; balance of probability; arrogance, assurance.

présump'tive (-z-), *a.* that may be assumed to be such till the contrary is proved; supposed.

présump'tuous (-z-), *a.* presuming; forward; arrogant.

présuppōse' (-z-), *v.t.* take for granted; imply the existence of. **~sition**, *n.* thing assumed as basis for argument, &c.

prétence' (-z-), *n.* pretending, make-believe; pretext; claim.

prétend', *v.t. & i.* lay claim; feign; profess falsely. **préten'der**, *n.* claimant to title, &c.

préten'sion (-shn), *n.* assertion of a claim; pretentiousness.

préten'tious (-shus), *a.* making claim to great merit; ostentatious; lacking in modesty.

prét'erite, *a. & n.* past (tense).

prétermit', *v.t.* pass over without mention; omit to do or perform; leave off for a time.

prē'text, *n.* ostensible reason; excuse.

prê'tty (-i-), *a.* attractive to eye, ear, or aesthetic sense; fine or commendable. *adv.* tolerably, fairly.

prévail', *v.i.* gain the mastery; attain one's object; predominate; be current.

prev'alent, *a.* in general operation; generally experienced at a time or place. **prév'alence**, *n.*

prevar'icate, *v.i.* make evasive or misleading statements; quibble; equivocate. **~tion, ~tor**, *nn.*

preve'nient, *a.* anticipatory; preceding something else.

prevent', *v.t.* hinder, stop; secure the non-occurrence of. **~ion**, *n.* **~ive**, *a.* serving to prevent something, esp. disease; *n.* preventive agent, drug, measure, &c.

pre'vious, *a.* coming before in time or order; prior to; (sl.) done or acting hastily.

previ'sion (-zhn), *n.* foresight; foreknowledge.

prey (prā), *n.* animal hunted and killed by carnivorous animals for food; person's victim. *v.i.* (with *upon*) habitually devour or plunder; exert baneful influence.

price, *n.* money for which thing is bought or sold; (fig.) consideration or sacrifice necessary to obtain a thing. *v.t.* (-ceable), state the price of; affix the price to. **~less**, *a.* too precious to be priced; invaluable; (sl.) ineffably amusing or delightful.

prick, *v.t. & i.* pierce slightly, make minute hole in; pain sharply, feel sharp pain; spur, goad. *n.* pricking, mark of it; goad.

prick'er, *n.* pricking instrument.

prick'le, *n.* sharp growth such as thorn or hedgehog's spine. *v.i.* feel or give a pricking sensation.

prick'ly, *a.* having prickles; **~ heat**, inflammation of sweat glands with eruption of vesicles and prickly sensation, common in hot countries. **~ pear**, name given to various species of prickly plants with pear-shaped edible fruit.

pride, *n.* inordinate self-esteem; feeling of elation and pleasure; arrogant bearing. *v.refl.* (with *on*) be proud of.

prie-dieu (prēdyér'), *n.* kneeling-desk.

priest, *n.* minister of religious worship; clergyman belonging to

the order between deacons and bishops. **~craft**, arts used by ecclesiastics to extend their influence. **~ess**, *n.* female priest of non-Christian religion. **~hood**, *n.* office of a priest; priests.

prig, *n.* precisian in speech or manners; conceited person; (sl.) thief. *v.t.* (sl.) steal. **prigg'ish** (-g-), *a.* conceited; straitlaced.

prim, *a.* formal; prudish.

pri'macy, *n.* office of primate; pre-eminence.

pri'ma donn'a (prē-), *n.* chief female singer in opera.

|| **pri'ma fa'cie** (-shiē), *adv.* at first considering; at first sight.

pri'mal, *a.* primitive or primeval; fundamental.

pri'mary, *a.* original; holding or sharing the first place in time or importance or development. *n.* primary colour, planet, &c.; *(Pol.) meeting or balloting of voters of a party for choosing delegates to a convention or nominating candidates for office.

pri'mate, *n.* archbishop of a province. **prima'tes** (-z), *n.pl.* highest order of mammals.

prime, *a.* chief, most important; primary, fundamental; of highest quality. *n.* the first of the divine offices; first or best part of something; state of highest perfection. *v.t.* (-mable), prepare (old gun, &c., explosive charge) for being let off; equip with facts; ply with liquor; prepare (wood) for paint. **~ minister**, head of the Government; **~ number**, an integer which has no factors.

pri'mer (or prī-), *n.* elementary schoolbook; manual.

prime'val, *a.* of the first age of the world; primitive.

pri'ming, *n.* (esp.) powder, mixture, to prime explosive or wood.

prim'itive, *a.* ancient; of an early, simple, or old-fashioned kind; original. *n.* painter or picture of pre-Renaissance period; word of colour not derived.

primogen'iture, *n.* principle by

which property descends to eldest son or child.

prĭmŏrd'ĭal, *a.* existing at or from the beginning.

prĭm'rōse (-z), *n.* pale-yellow spring flower; plant bearing it; (attrib.) primrose-coloured.

prĭm'ūla, *n.* kinds of flowering plant including primrose.

prī'mus[1], *a.* the first.

prī'mus[2], *n.* kind of stove burning vaporized oil. **P.**

prince, *n.* sovereign; ruler of feudatory State; male member of royal family; (in some foreign titles) noble of high rank. ~**ly**, *a.* becoming a prince; sumptuous, grand.

prin'cess, *n.* prince's wife; female member of royal family.

prin'cĭpal, *a.* first in importance; chief, leading. *n.* head of some institutions; person for whom another is an agent; capital sum originally lent or invested.

principăl'ĭtў, *n.* rule by, or State ruled by, a prince.

prin'cĭple, *n.* primary source or element; fundamental truth; rule by which conduct may be guided.

prink, *v.t.* smarten; preen.

print, *n.* mark left on a surface by pressure; impression left on paper by inked type or photography; reading-matter produced from type; engraving, newspaper, photograph; cotton fabric stamped in colours. *v.t.* stamp or impress; produce by means of printing-types; stamp (fabric) in colours. **prin'ter**, *n.* workman employed as a compositor, pressman, or machine-minder; employer or overseer of these. **print'ing**, *n.* (esp.) the process of impressing words from type; typography.

prī'or, *n.* superior of religious house; (in abbey) abbot's deputy. *a.* earlier; antecedent. ~**ess**, *n.* **prī'ŏrĭtў**, *n.* being earlier; precedence. **prī'ŏrў**, *n.* religious house governed by prior(ess).

prĭ'sm, *n.* solid figure whose two ends are similar, equal, and parallel rectilineal figures, and whose sides are parallelograms; transparent body of this form with refracting surfaces. **prĭs-măt'ĭc** (-z-), *a.* of prism shape; (of colour) such as is produced by refraction through prism; rainbow-like.

prĭs'on (-zn), *n.* place of captivity for law-breakers.

prĭs'oner (-zn-), *n.* person kept in prison; war captive.

prĭs'tĭne, *a.* primitive; unspoiled by modern tendencies.

prĭth'ee (-dhĭ), *int.* (arch.) accompanying a request or question.

prĭv'acў, *n.* seclusion.

prī'vate, *a.* not public; secret, confidential; not official; reserved, secluded. *n.* a private soldier (ranking below non-commissioned officers). ~**ly**, *adv.*

privateer', *n.* ship having letters of marque; its captain. *a.* acting as privateer.

privā'tion, *n.* want of necessaries or comforts; hardship.

prĭv'ative, *a.* denoting the absence of something usually present.

prĭv'et, *n.* a white-flowered evergreen used for hedges.

prĭv'ĭlĕge, *n.* right, advantage, or immunity belonging to a person, class, or office. *v.t.* invest with privilege; exempt from burden. **prĭv'ĭlĕged** (-jd), *a.*

prĭv'ĭtў, *n.* being privy to; knowledge shared with another of something kept private.

prĭv'ў, *a.* hidden, secret, private, confidential. *n.* place for easing nature. ~ **purse**, allowance from public revenue for monarch's private expenses. ~ **seal**, State seal affixed to documents of minor importance.

prize[1], *n.* reward given as symbol of victory or superiority; thing to be striven for; reward in lottery, competition, &c. *v.t.* value highly. ~**fight**, boxing-match for money. ~**fighter**, professional pugilist. ~**man**, winner of prize. ~**ring**, area assigned to

---

māte, mēte, mīte, mōte, mūte, mŏŏt; răck, rĕck, rĭck, rŏck, rŭck, rŏŏk;

prize-fighters; **pugilism** as an institution.

prize[2], *n.* ship or property captured in naval warfare.

prize[3], *v.t.* (*-zable*), force open or up by leverage.

prō′a, *n.* kinds of Malay boat, esp. a type of sailing-boat.

prō and cŏn, *adv.* for and against. *n.pl.* (**pros and cons**) the reasons for and against.

prŏbabil′ity, *n.* being probable; likelihood; what is probable.

prŏb′able, *a.* that may be expected to happen or prove true or correct; likely. **prŏb′ably**, *adv.* most likely.

prō′bate, *n.* official proving of will. **v.t.* (*-āt*), prove (will).

grobā′tion, *n.* testing of person's conduct or character; noviciate. ~**ary**, *a.*; ~**er**, *n.*

probe, *n.* blunt-ended surgical instrument for exploring wound, &c. *v.t.* (*-bable*), explore with probe; examine closely.

prŏb′ity, *n.* uprightness, integrity, incorruptibility.

prŏb′lem, *n.* question or difficulty in need of solution. **prŏblĕmăt′ic(al)**, *aa.* presenting a problem; disputable; unsettled.

probŏs′cis, *n.* elephant's trunk; snout; insect's sucking-tube.

procē′dure (*-dyer*), *n.* mode of conducting business.

proceed′, *v.i.* go on; continue or resume; take legal proceedings. ~**ing**, *n.* piece of conduct; (pl.) business done at a meeting; (pl.) legal steps. **prō′ceeds**, *n.pl.* the produce in money of a sale, &c.

prō′cĕss, *n.* state of going on or being carried on; method of operation in manufacture, &c.; an action at law; summons or writ; projection from a bone, &c. *v.t.* subject to a legal or manufacturing process.

procĕs′sion (*-shn*), *n.* array of persons going along in fixed order. ~**al**, *a.* of, in, for processions; *n.* processional hymn.

‖ **procès-verbal** (*prōsā′ vărbahl*), *n.* detailed report; minutes.

proclaim′, *v.t.* announce publicly and officially; tell openly; prohibit (meeting). **prŏclamā′tion**, *n.* proclaiming; formula or document that proclaims.

procliv′ity, *n.* natural leaning or tendency to.

prōcŏn′sul, *n.* ancient-Roman provincial governor; (rhet.) modern colonial governor. ~**sŭlar**, *a.*

procrás′tinate, *v.i.* put off doing things; leave things undone as long as possible. ~**tion**, *n.*

prō′crēate, *v.i.* produce offspring. ~**tion**, ~**tor**, *nn.*; ~**tive**, *a.*

prŏc′tor, *n.* University official with disciplinary powers; an attorney in ecclesiastical courts.

procŭm′bent, *a.* prone, lying down; (Bot.) trailing.

prŏcŭrā′tion, *n.* procuring, bringing about; acting as another's agent. **prŏc′ŭrātor**, *n.* person's proxy or agent; holder of power of attorney.

procūre′, *v.t.* (*-rable*), succeed in getting; bring about or cause by others' agency. ~**ment**, *n.* ~**er**, ~**ess**, *nn.* (esp.) one who procures women as prostitutes.

prŏd, *v.t.* poke with stick, &c., esp. to arouse or urge on. *n.* prodding touch.

prŏd′igal, *a.* wasteful, lavish. *n.* spendthrift. **prŏdigăl′ity**, *n.*

prŏd′igy, *n.* marvellous thing; wonderful person. **prŏd′igious** (*-jus*), *a.* marvellous, enormous.

produce′, *v.t.* (*prŏdūs*), bring forward or show for examination; yield, give birth to; cause or bring about; make or manufacture. *n.* (*prŏd′ūs*), yield, amount produced; agricultural or natural products. **prodū′cer**, *n.* in vbl. senses, esp. person producing articles of consumption or manufacture. **prodū′cible**, *a.*; ~**bility**, *n.*

prŏd′uct, *n.* thing produced by natural process or manufacture; (Math.) quantity given by multiplication of quantities together.

prodŭc′tion, *n.* producing; products; a thing produced by human activity. ~ive, a. tending to production; fertile. ~ivity, n.

pro'ĕm, n. prefatory discourse.

profănā'tion, n. profaning.

profāne', a. secular; heathen, unhallowed; irreverent, blasphemous. ~ly, (-nable), pollute, violate; treat with irreverence.

profān'itý, n. blasphemy; profane swearing; irreverent speech or behaviour.

profĕss', v.t. represent oneself to feel or believe in; declare oneself to be or do; have as one's trade or art or profession. profĕss'ĕdly, adv. according to one's account.

profĕs'sion (-shn), n. declaration, avowal; vocation or calling, esp. of learned or scientific or artistic kind.

profĕs'sional (-sho-), a. of the vocations called professions; practising for a livelihood or money; (of game, &c.) played by professionals. n. professional man (abbr. pro) paid performer at cricket, football, &c. ~ism, n. (esp.) practice of employing professionals in games.

profĕss'or, n. person who makes profession (of religion, &c.); holder of a university chair or other teacher of high rank. ~ship, n. profĕssŏr'ial, a. ~iate, n. the professors of a university.

proff'er, v.t. offer spontaneously. n. spontaneous offer.

profi'cient (-shnt), a. & n. expert, adept. profi'ciency, n.

pro'file (-fēl), n. outline of the face as seen from the side; any edge outlined against the sky or other background.

prof'it, n. advantage, benefit; (pl. or sing.) pecuniary gain, excess of returns over outlay. v.t. & i. bring advantage to; get good; make gains. ~able, beneficial, lucrative. profiteer', v.i. make inordinate profit out of the State's or the consumer's necessities; n. one who profits thus.

prof'ligate, a. licentious, dissolute; reckless. n. profligate person. prof'ligacý, n. evil courses.

profound', a. deep; of great insight or knowledge; hard to penetrate or unravel; heartfelt. profŭn'ditý, n.

profūse', a. lavish, extravagant, copious, excessive. ~sion (-zhn), n. profuseness; great quantity.

prŏg, n. (sl.) food, grub.

prŏgĕn'itor, n. person or animal in relation to his descendants. ~tress, n. pro'gĕný, n. offspring or descendants.

prŏg'nathous, a. with projecting jaws as in negroes.

prŏgnō'sis, n. (pl. -ōsēs) forecast of course of disease.

prŏgnŏs'tic, n. indication that something is likely to happen. prŏgnŏs'ticāte, v.t. (-cable), foreshow, foresee, foretell. ~tion, ~tor, nn.; ~tive, a.

pro'grămme, n. plan of intended proceedings; printed list.

prŏg'ress, n. (prō'grĕs, -ĕs) forward movement; advance; improvement; increase; a journey of state. v.i. (prŏgrĕs') make progress.

prŏgrĕs'sion (-shn), n. physical onward movement; (Math.) series of quantities each in the same relation to preceding one.

prŏgrĕss'ive, a. forward; increasing; favouring progress or reform. n. progressive politician.

prŏhib'it, v.t. forbid the doing, making, practice, or use of; debar, prevent. prohibi'tion (-ŏī-), n. forbidding; order that forbids something; legislation making sale of intoxicants illegal. ~ist, n. advocate of such legislation. prŏhib'itive, ~tory, aa. that prohibits; (of price) high enough to prevent purchase.

prŏjĕct, v.t. & i. (projĕkt'), make plans for; hurl, send forth into space; represent as plane surface; protrude, stick out. n. (prŏj'ĕkt), scheme or plan.

projĕc'tile, a. (projĕk'tĭl or -īl), impelling. n. (prŏj'ĭktĭl, -ojĕk'tĭl or -īl), heavy missile; shell, cannonball.

projec′tion, n. projecting; part that protrudes; map. &c. made by projecting.

projec′tor, n. one who forms schemes; a company promoter.

prolǎp′sus, n. forward or downward displacement of an internal organ.

prō′late, a. (of sphere) lengthened in the direction of the polar diameter.

prolego̅m′ena, n.pl. preliminary remarks or dissertation.

prolē′psis (or -ĕ-), n. (pl. -psēs), assumption that something is done or true before it is so. prolĕp′tic (or -ĕ-), a.

prolētā′rian, n. & n. of, member of, the proletariate.

prolētā′riat(e), n. the lowest classes; the common people.

prolif′ic, a. producing offspring; fruitful; abundantly productive.

prō′lix, a. lengthy; long-winded; tedious. prolix′ity, n.

prō′locutor, n. chairman, esp. of lower house of convocation.

prō′logue (-g), n. poem recited before first part of a play; first of a series of events, &c.

prolong′, v.t. make longer; cause to continue; (p.p.) long. prolongā′tion (-ngg-), n.

promenade′ (-ahd), n. a going up and down in a public place; place used for this. v.i. & t. take promenade; lead (person, &c.) up and down for show.

prom′inence, n. being prominent; a protuberance. prom′inency, n.

prom′inent, a. projecting; conspicuous; distinguished.

promis′cuous, a. of mixed and disorderly composition; unsorted; indiscriminate. promiscu′ity, n.

prom′ise, n. explicit undertaking to do or not to do something; favourable indications. v.t. & i. (-sable), undertake to give or procure; foretell; show promise. prom′issory, a. of the nature of or containing a promise.

prom′ontory, n. headland; high land jutting out into sea. &c.

promote′, v.t. (-table), move up to a higher office or position; help forward or initiate the process or formation of. promo′ter, encourager; person who promotes companies. promo′tion, n.

prompt, a. done at once or without delay; ready in action. v.t. incite, prime, inspire; help out (actor, speaker) by reading next words of part. promp′ter, n. (esp.) person stationed to prompt actors. promp′ting, n. incitement. promp′titude, n. promptness.

prom′ulgate, v.t. publish as coming into force or having authority. ∼tion, ∼tor, nn.

prone, a. lying face or front downwards; (loosely) prostrate; inclined, disposed.

prong, n. spike of a fork.

pronom′inal, a. of, or of the nature of, a pronoun.

prō′noun, n. word serving as substitute for a noun.

pronounce′, v.t. & i. utter formally; pass judgement, give one's opinion; articulate. ∼able, a. ∼ment, n. declaration of opinion or judgement. pronounced′ (-st), a. strongly marked; decided. pronuncia′tion, n. way word, &c. is pronounced.

proof, n. fact, evidence, or reasoning that proves the truth of something; test or trial; impression from type subject to correction before final printing; careful impression of engraved plate before printing of ordinary issue. a. (of armour) of proved strength; giving or having an impenetrable defence. ∼reader, press-corrector. ∼sheet, printing-proof.

prop, n. thing used to support something or keep it upright; supporter of cause, &c. v.i. be a prop to; uphold; hold up.

propagan′da, n. means for propagating a doctrine or practice. ∼dist, n. agent of a propaganda.

prop′agate, v.t. & i. (-gable), multiply or reproduce by sowing.

grafting, breeding, &c.; spread or disseminate. ~tion, ~tor, nn.

propel', v.t. drive or push forward; give forward motion to. pro-pĕll'er, n. revolving shaft with blades for propelling steamer or aircraft.

propen'sitỹ, n. inclination; pre-disposition to anything.

prŏp'er, a. one's own; suitable, appropriate; right; decent, decorous; (arch.) handsome; (colloq.) thorough.

prŏp'erlỹ, adv. in the right way; justifiably; with decency or good manners; thoroughly.

prŏp'ertỹ, n. owning; things or thing owned; a landed estate; attribute or quality; (usu. pl.) stage appurtenance(s).

prŏph'ecỹ, n. prophesying; pro-phetic utterance; a prediction.

prŏph'esỹ, v.i. & t. (-siable), speak as a prophet; predict the future.

prŏph'ĕt, n. inspired teacher; re-vealer or interpreter of God's will; person who predicts. ~ess, n. prophĕt'ic(al), aa. of or like a prophet; predicting; serving as a prediction.

prŏphylăc'tic, a. done or used as preventive. n. a prophylactic medicine or measure.

propĭnq'uitỹ, n. nearness, esp. in blood.

propi'tiāte (-shi-), v.t. (-iable), ap-pease; gain the forgiveness or favour of. ~ātion, n. propitiating; gift or act meant to pro-pitiate. ~torỹ, a. meant to pro-pitiate. propi'tious (-shus), a. inclined to show favour; favour-ing; of good omen.

propŏr'tion, n. comparative part; part bearing a definite relation to the whole; comparative re-lation, ratio; symmetry; (Arith.) rule of three. v.t. make propor-tionate; arrange the propor-tions of. ~able, a. proportionable. ~al, a. of proportion; aiming or aimed at due proportions. n. one of the terms of a proportion. ~ate, a. that is in due propor-tion; proportionally adjusted to.

propō'sal (-zl), n. scheme put for-ward; offer of marriage.

propōse' (-z), v.t. & i. (-sable), put forward as a problem, object, plan, intention, candidate, or toast; offer marriage.

prŏposi'tion (-z-), n. statement, assertion; predication; (Math.) formal statement of theorem or problem; proposal; offer of terms; (sl.) task, job, problem, opponent, prospect, &c.

propound', v.t. put forth for con-sideration or solution.

propri'ĕtarỹ, a. of a proprietor; held as property. n. proprietor-ship; proprietors.

propri'ĕtor, n. person having pro-perty; owner. ~tress, n.

propri'ĕtỹ, n. fitness; rightness; suitability; correct conduct.

propŭl'sion (-shn), n. propelling; impelling influence. ~ive, a.

prorögue' (-g), v.t. & i. (-gable), discontinue meetings of parlia-ment at end of session; be pro-rogued. prŏrogā'tion, n.

prosā'ic (-z-), a. like prose; un-poetical; commonplace.

prosce'nium, n. part of theatre stage in front of curtain.

proscrībe', v.t. (-bable), publish the name of as outlawed or con-demned; exile; ostracize. pro-scrip'tion, n.; ~ive, a.

prōse (-z), n. unversified language, esp. as a form of literature; plain speech. v.i. talk tediously.

prŏs'ĕcūte, v.t. (-table), pursue or carry on; institute legal proceed-ings. ~tion, n. prosecuting; the prosecuting party in a lawsuit. ~tor, n. bringer of suit in criminal court. ~trix, n. female prosecutor.

prŏs'elỹte, n. Gentile convert to Jewish faith; any convert. ~tism, n. practice of proselyti-zing. ~tize, v.i. & t. seek proselytes; make a proselyte of.

pros'odỹ, n. science of versifica-tion and vowel quantity. pro-sō'dial, prosŏd'ic, aa.

prospect, n. (prŏs'pĕkt), what is spread out before the eyes, a view; mental view; expectation.

v.i. & t. (prospĕkt'), go on exploring expedition; institute search; explore. **prospec'tive**, a. concerned with or applying to the future only; expected. **~tor**, n. person who prospects for gold, &c. **~tus**, n. circular describing chief features of company, book, school, &c.

pros'per, v.i. & t. get or go on well; (cause to) thrive. **prosper'ity**, n. state of prospering; auspicious. **~ous**, a. prospering; auspicious.

pros'titute, n. a harlot. v.t. (-table), make a prostitute of; sell for base gain; put to infamous use. **prostitu'tion**, n. **~tor**, nn.

prostrate, a. (prŏs'trāt), stretched on the ground; overcome, exhausted. v.t. (prostrāt'), throw flat on ground; reduce to exhaustion or despair. **~tion**, n.

pro'sy (-z-), a. tedious, commonplace.

protag'onist, n. the chief person in a drama, &c.; champion.

pro'tean, a. of or as of Proteus; versatile; variable.

protect', v.t. keep safe; shield; secure. **~ion**, n. protecting care; defence; system of protecting home industries by taxing imports; *certificate of American citizenship issued to seamen. **~ionism, ~ionist**, nn. principle or practice, advocate, of economic protection. **~ive**, a. **~or, ~ress**, n. person who protects; appliance for protecting something; (hist.) regent of State. **~orate**, n. office of protector of State; a State or territory protected or controlled by another State. **~orship**, n.; **~ress**, n.

protégé (prŏt'ĕzhā), n. (fem. -gée), person to whom another is patron or protector.

pro'tein, n. kinds of organic compound forming the most essential part of food of animals.

protest, v.t. & i. (protĕst'), affirm solemnly; make a protest (against). n. (prō'tĕst), formal statement of dissent or disapproval; remonstrance.

prot'estant, a. of or belonging to any of the Christian bodies separated from the Roman communion in the Reformation. n. member of such body. **~ism**, n.; **~ize**, v.t. & i. **protesta'tion**, n. solemn affirmation or the making of it.

pro'tocol, n. draught of terms agreed upon as the basis of a formal treaty.

pro'tomartyr (-ter), n. first person martyred for a cause.

pro'ton, n. positively charged particle, forming part (or, in hydrogen, whole) of the nucleus of the atom.

pro'toplasm, n. the semi-fluid substance constituting the basis of life in plants and animals.

pro'totype, n. first or primary type in relation to any copy, imitation, representation, &c.

protract', v.t. lengthen duration of; be dilatory with; (p.p.) long-drawn-out; draw to scale. **~ion**, n. **protrac'tor**, n. instrument for measuring angles.

protrude' (-ōōd), v.i. & t. (-dable). stick out; thrust out. **protru'sion** (-ōōzhn), n.; **~sive**, a.

protu'berance, n. bulging shape; a swelling or lump. **protu'berant**, a. bulging out; prominent.

proud, a. setting too high a value on oneself; arrogant; haughty; resolute to avoid dependence, humiliation, &c.; self-respecting; reserved; feeling honoured by something.

prove (prōōv), v.t. & i. (-vable). p.p. proved and arch. proven). give proof of; demonstrate; ascertain by experience; establish validity of (will); turn out to be; test, put to the proof.

prov'enance, n. what source something comes from.

prov'ender, n. fodder; (joc.) human food.

prov'erb, n. short pithy saying in general use; adage, saw; notoriety, byword; (pl.) round game played with proverbs. **prover'bial**, a. of proverbs; notorious or constantly spoken of.

provide', *v.i. & t.* (-*dable*), make due preparation; take precautions; equip, supply. **provi·déd**, *a.* in vbl. senses. *conj.* on the condition or understanding that.

prov'idence, *n.* timely care; thrift; beneficent care of God.

prov'ident, *a.* showing foresight; thrifty. **providén'tial** (-shl), *a.* arranged by Providence; strikingly opportune. **provi'der**, *n.* (esp.) purveyor.

prov'ince, *n.* large division of a country; (pl.) whole of a country except the capital; archbishop's or metropolitan's district; sphere of action; one's concern.

provin'cial (-shl), *a.* of a province; having the speech or manners of the provinces. *n.* inhabitant of the provinces. **~ism**, *n.* being provincial; a provincial word or phrase. **provin'cial·ity**, *n.*

provi'sion (-zhn), *n.* providing; amount of something provided; statement providing for something; (pl.) eatables. *v.t.* supply with a store of provisions.

provi'sional (-zho-), *a.* temporary; subject to revision.

provi'so (-zō), *n.* (pl. -*os*), a stipulation; a limiting clause.

provocá'tion, *n.* an act by which anger is roused. **provóc'ative**, *a.* adapted for the provoking of anger; intentionally irritating; *n.* thing that excites appetite.

provoke', *v.t.* rouse the anger of; call forth or give rise to.

próv'ost, *n.* head of certain colleges; Scottish official corresponding to mayor; officer of military police (provō').

prow, *n.* part of ship or boat immediately about its stem.

prow'ess, *n.* valour; gallantry.

prowl, *v.i.* go about furtively in search of prey or plunder.

próx'imate, *a.* nearest; next before or after.

‖ **proxime** (accéss'it) (prŏk'sĭmĭ aks-), *n.* person posted as coming next to winner of prize, &c.

proxim'ity, *n.* closeness; near neighbourhood or approach.

próx'ĭmo, *a.* of next month.

próx'y, *n.* agency of substitute; authorized agent; document authorizing one to vote on another's behalf; vote so given.

prude (prood), *n.* woman of squeamish propriety.

pru'dence (-ōō-), *n.* being prudent; discretion.

pru'dent (-ōō-), *a.* avoiding rashness; discreet. **prudén'tial** (-ōō--shl), *a.* dictated by prudence.

pru'dery (-ōō-), *n.* conduct or notions of prudes. **pru'dish**, *a.*

prune¹ (proon), *n.* dried plum; the colour of its juice.

prune² (proon), *v.t.* (-*nable*), rid of dead or overgrown parts; reduce the luxuriance of.

prunell'a (proo-), *n.* a strong silk or worsted stuff.

pru'rient (-oor-), *a.* given to or springing from lascivious thoughts. **prur'ience** (-oor-), *n.*

Prū'ssian (-shn), *a.* of or from Prussia. *n.* native of Prussia. **Prūss'ic a'cid**, *n.* hydrocyanic acid.

prý, *v.i.* make furtive search or inquiries (*into*).

psalm (sahm), *n.* one of the songs in the Book of Psalms; sacred song, hymn. **~ist**, *n.* author of a psalm. **~ody**, *n.* practice of singing psalms, anthems, &c.

psal'ter (sawl-), *n.* the Book of Psalms; volume of psalms.

psal'tery (sawl-), *n.* an obsolete stringed instrument.

pseudo- (or s-), *pref.* sham.

pseud'onym (or s-), *n.* fictitious name assumed by an author.

pshaw (shaw, -ah), *int.* putting thing aside as absurd, &c.

psilō'sis, *n.* stripping bare, e. g. of hair or flesh.

psych'ic, -**al** (psīk-, sīk-), *aa.* of the soul or mind; of what appears to be outside the domain of physical law.

psycho-anál'ysis (psīk-, sīk-), *n.* a psycho-therapeutic system aiming at revealing the subject's unconscious mind, or repressed wishes, thoughts, &c., to his consciousness.

---

ah, awl, oil, boor, cow, dowry; chin, go, bang, so, ship, thin; dh, as th(e);

psychol'ogy (psĭk-, sĭk-), n. the study of the human soul or mind.

psycho'logical, a.; psychol'ogist, n.

ptarm'igan (t-), n. kind of grouse changing to white in winter.

ptomaine (tō'mān), n. kinds of often poisonous substances found in putrefying matter.

pub, n. (colloq.) public-house.

pu'berty, n. sexual maturity.

pubes'cent, a. reaching puberty; (of plants, &c.) downy. ~nce, n.

pub'lic, a. of, concerning, the people as a whole; open to, shared by, the people in general; visible, generally known. n. the community, or a specified part of it. ~house, house licensed to sell alcoholic liquor. ~ school, grammar school endowed for public use; large boarding-school in which the monitorial system prevails; school provided and carried on at the public expense.

pub'lican, n. keeper of public-house; (Bibl.) tax-farmer.

publica'tion, n. publishing; a published book, periodical, &c.

pub'licist, n. writer on public concerns; political journalist.

publi'city, n. openness to general observation; notoriety.

pub'licly, adv. in public; without concealment; openly.

pub'lish, v.t. make generally known; formally announce; prepare and issue copies of book, &c. for sale or publication. ~er, n. person whose trade is the publishing of books, &c.

puce, a. & n. flea-colour, purplish-brown.

Puck[1], n. a mischievous sprite.

puck[2], n. rubber disk used for ice-hockey in Canada.

puck'a, a. (Anglo-Ind.) regular, good; sound, reliable.

puck'er, v.t. & i. contract or gather into wrinkles or folds. n. wrinkle, fold, bulge.

pu'dding (pŏŏ-), n. kinds of food made of ingredients mixed in a soft mass. ~cloth, cloth in which pudding is boiled.

pud'dle, n. small dirty pool; kind of rough cement of kneaded clay. v.t. & i. work (clay) into puddle; stir (molten iron); dabble in water or mud. pudd'ly, a. (of road, &c.) with many puddles.

pu'dency, n. modest instincts.

pueb'lo (pwĕb-), n. communal native house of adobe or stone in New Mexico, Arizona, &c.

pu'erile, a. childish; trivial. pu'eril'ity, n. childishness.

puer'peral, a. of or due to childbirth.

puff, n. short quick blast of breath or wind; smoke or vapour sent out by it; ball of down used for applying powder to skin; piece of pastry; laudatory notice. v.i. & t. emit puff or puffs; pant; advertise in laudatory manner. puff'ery, n. inflated praise. puff'y, a. of inflated appearance; short-winded.

puff'in, n. a large-billed sea-bird.

pug[1], n. snub-nosed breed of dog. ~nosed, having snub nose.

pug[2], n. (Anglo-Ind.) the footprint of a beast. v.t. track by pugs.

pugg'(a)ree (-rĭ), n. Indian's light turban; scarf of muslin, &c., worn round hat as protection against sun.

pu'gilism, n. boxing. ~ist, n. boxer, prize-fighter. ~istic, a.

pugna'cious (-shus), a. given to fighting. pugna'city, n.

puisne (pū'nĭ), a. later, subsequent to; petty. ~ judge, inferior or junior judge.

puiss'ant (pw-), a. wielding great power; potent. ~nce, n.

puke, v.i. & t. vomit.

pule, v.i. whine; be querulous.

pu'keko, pu'kaki (pŏŏ-), n. (New Zealand) swamp-hen.

pull (pŏŏl), v.t. & i. draw forcibly towards one; exert pulling force; pluck, gather; propel boat by pulling oars or sculls; make (face) by contorting muscles. n. act of pulling; spell of rowing; draught of liquor; unfair advantage.

pu'llet (pŏŏ-), n. young domestic fowl before moulting.

pu'lley (pŏŏ-), *n.* (pl. -*eys*), grooved wheel fixed in block enabling weights to be raised by downward pull of the cord running in the groove.

Pu'lliman-car (pŏŏ-), *n.* railway saloon-carriage.

pŭl'monary, *a.* of the lungs; affected with pulmonary disease.

pŭlp, *n.* the flesh of soft fruits; soft formless mass, esp. of materials for paper-making. *v.t. & i.* reduce to or rid of pulp; become pulpy. *pŭl'pў*, *a.* of like pulp.

pu'lpit (pŏŏl-), *n.* erection for preaching from; (fig.) preaching.

pŭlsate', *v.i.* expand and contract rhythmically; throb, vibrate, quiver. ~tion, *n.*; pŭl'sator̄ў, *a.*

pŭl'satile (*or* -ĭl), *a.* pulsatory; (Mus.) played by beating.

pŭlsatill'a, *n.* the pasque-flower; its extract used in pharmacy.

pŭlse¹, *n.* throbbing of the arteries as blood is poured through them; point where this can be felt externally as in the wrist; throb of feeling. *v.i.* pulsate.

pŭlse², *n.* edible seeds of peas, beans, lentils, &c.

‖ **pŭl'tŭn**, -an, -oon, *n.* regiment of infantry in India.

pŭl'verize, *v.t. & i.* (-*zable*), reduce to powder or dust; crumble; demolish (argument, opponent). ~zation, *n.* ~zer, *n.* machine for pulverizing.

‖ **pŭl'wār**, -wah, *n.* light keelless native boat used on the rivers of Bengal.

pū'ma, *n.* large tawny American carnivorous beast.

pŭm'ice, ~stone, *nn.* light kind of porous lava used for rubbing off stains, polishing, &c.

pŭmm'el, *v.t.* strike repeatedly with the fists.

pŭmp¹, *n.* machine used for raising water from a well or to a higher level; kinds of machine for raising or moving liquids, &c. *v.i. & t.* work pump; procure water; bring or send liquid out or up; (sl.) exhaust breath of; (colloq.) get information out of, interro-

gate. ~room, room at spa where medicinal water is sold.

pŭmp², *n.* light patent-leather shoe for dancing, &c.

pŭmp'kin, *n.* kind of gourd.

pŭn, *n.* jest consisting of a play on words with more than one meaning. *v.i.* make pun.

pŭnch¹, *v.t.* strike with fist; bore or perforate with a punch; drive (nail, &c.) in or out with a punch. *n.* blow with fist; tool hammered or pressed against a surface that is to be pierced or stamped, or a bolt or nail that is to be driven in or out; (sl.) vigour, effective force, momentum.

pŭnch², *n.* mixture of spirit or wine with water or milk, lemon, spice, &c. ~bowl, bowl in which punch is mixed. ~house, tavern where punch is supplied; in India, inn or tavern frequented by natives.

pŭnch³, *n.* short-legged thickset draught horse.

Pŭnch⁴, *n.* humpbacked figure in puppet-show called ~ *and Judy*.

pŭnch⁵, *n.* (E.-Ind.) council of five persons; short for *panchayat*, q.v.

pŭn'cheon (-chn), *n.* large cask.

Pŭnchinĕll'ō, *n.* (pl. -*os*), chief character in Italian puppet-show; fat person of comical appearance.

pŭnc'tate, *a.* spotted, dotted.

pŭnctil'io (-lyō), *n.* (pl. -*os*), nice point of ceremony; a mere form. **pŭnctil'ious** (-lyus), *a.* laying stress on punctilios.

pŭnc'tual, *a.* observant of appointed time; not late. ~ity, *n.*

pŭnc'tuāte, *v.t.* mark or divide with stops; diversify with recurrent interruption. ~tion, *n.*

pŭnc'ture, *n.* pricking; hole made by it. *v.t. & i.* make puncture in; suffer a puncture.

pŭn'dit, *n.* learned Hindu; (joc.) an authority on a subject.

pŭn'gent (-j-), *a.* stinging, caustic, biting, sharp. **pŭn'gency** (-j-), *n.*

pŭn'ish, *v.t.* subject to retributive

or disciplinary suffering; inflict penalty; (colloq.) handle or test severely. ~ment, n. penalty.

pū´nitive, a. that punishes or is designed to punish.

*pŭnk, n. rotten wood. a. (sl.; of bodily condition) seedy; (of things) poor, worthless.

pŭnk´a(h) (-ka), n. (E.-Ind.) large swinging fan to mitigate heat.

*pŭnk´ie, n. kind of small biting fly.

pŭnn´et, n. chip basket for fruit, &c.

pŭn´ster, n. person given to punning.

pŭnt¹, n. flat-bottomed boat propelled by pole. v.t. & i. propel with or use punt-pole.

pŭnt², v.t. & i. kick football on its way from one's hands to the ground. n. such kick.

pŭnt³, v.i. lay a stake against the bank in some card-games; bet on a horse.

pū´ny, a. undersized, feeble.

pŭp, n. puppy. v.t. & i. bring forth pups; give birth to.

pū´pa, n. (pl. -ae), chrysalis.

pū´pil, n. person being taught; child under guardianship; opening in middle of the iris of the eye. pū´pillage, n. nonage; minority; being a pupil. pū´pillary, a. under guardianship; of a pupil or pupils; of the pupil of the eye.

pŭpp´et, n. figure of a person worked by wires, &c.; person controlled by another. ~play, ~show, play or show with puppets.

pŭpp´y, n. young dog; vain young man, coxcomb. ~dom, ~hood, ~ism, nm.

pura´na (poorah-), n. one of a class of Sanskrit sacred poems, containing the mythology of the Hindus.

pŭrb´lind, a. dim-sighted; lacking discernment; obtuse, dull.

pŭrch´ase, v.t. (-sable), acquire at a cost; buy; raise by means of lever, &c. n. purchasing, thing purchased; leverage, grip.

pŭrd´ah (-da), n. curtain with which Indian women of rank are screened from strangers; (fig.) Indian system of secluding women of rank or other cloth for curtains.

pūre, a. without admixture; unadulterated; chaste, innocent; mere. ~ly, adv. solely, entirely.

pūr´fle, n. ornamental border of dress, &c. v.t. adorn with purfle.

pûrf´ling, n. purfle on violin.

pûrga´tion, n. act of cleansing or purifying. pûrg´ative, a. that tends to purge; n. purgative thing, esp. medicine. pûrg´atory, n. condition or place of spiritual purging or expiation; state of pain or distress. pûrgatôr´ial, a.

pûrge, v.t. (-geable), make physically or spiritually clean; clear (bowels) by aperient; atone by expiation; clear of charge, &c. n. an aperient.

pūrifica´tion, n. purifying; ritual cleansing. ~tory, a.

pûr´ifier, n. kinds of apparatus for purifying gas, flour, &c.

pūr´ify, v.t. (-fiable), make pure or cleanse; clear of foreign elements.

pūr´ist, n. stickler for correctness in the use of words. ~ism, n.

pūr´itan, n. (hist.) member of the protestant party who sought to expel unscriptural and corrupt ceremonies from the Church; person of professed strictness in religion or morals. a. of or like a puritan. ~ic(al), aa.; ~ism, n.

pūr´ity, n. freedom from physical or moral pollution.

pûrl¹, v.i. flow with babbling sound.

pûrl², n. edging of gold or silver wire or of small loops; ribbing in knitted work; inversion of stitches. v.t. adorn with purl.

pûrl´er, n. headlong fall.

pûrl´ieu (-lū), n. (usu. pl.) ground bordering on something; outskirts, suburbs.

purloin´ (per-), v.t. steal; make off with.

pûr´ple, n. colour between crimson and violet; purple robe or the imperial or cardinal's rank denoted by it. *a.* purple-coloured. *v.t. & i.* make or grow purple.

purport, *v.t.* (perport'), profess, be intended to seem; have as its meaning. *n.* (pér̃p'ŏrt), tenor or apparent meaning or substance. *v.t.*

pũrp'ose, *n.* design of effecting something; thing that it is designed to effect; fact or faculty of resolving on something. *v.t.* have as a purpose; intend. ~ful, *a.* having a purpose; intentional. ~less, *a.* given to drifting; answering no purpose. ~ly, *adv.* on purpose; intentionally.

purr, *n.* vibrating sound with which cat expresses pleasure. *v.i. & t.* emit purr; express by purring.

pũr'ree, *n.* yellow colouring matter from India and China.

pũrse, *n.* small pouch for carrying money; funds; sum given as testimonial or prize. *v.t. & i.* (-*sable*), contract (lips, brow, &c.) in wrinkles; become so contracted. pũrs'er, *n.* officer keeping the accounts, &c. on a ship. **pũrs'lane** (-ĭn), *n.* a herb formerly much used in salads.

pursũ'ance (per-), *n.* carrying out, pursuing (of object, &c.).

pursũ'ant (per-), *adv.* conformably to; in pursuance of.

pursũe' (per-), *v.t. & i.* (-*uable*), follow with intent to kill, capture, or overtake; persistently assail; proceed along; continue; follow (profession, &c.). pur-sũ'er (per-), *n.* in vbl. senses; also (Law) prosecutor. pursuit (persũt'), *n.* pursuing; employment or study.

pũrs'uivant (-sw-), *n.* officer of College of Arms below herald.

pũrs'ỹ, *a.* short-winded; fat.

pũr'ulent (-rōō-), *a.* of, containing, or discharging pus.

purvey (pervā'), *v.t. & i.* procure and supply (provisions); act as purveyor. ~ance, *n.* purveying.

~or, *n.* one whose business it is to supply provisions on a large scale.

pũrv'iew (-vū), *n.* providing clause; range or province.

‖ **purwan(n)ah, parwanah** (pũr-wah'na), *n.* (E.-Ind.) letter of authority; order, licence, pass.

pũs, *n.* matter produced by festering or inflammation.

Pũ'seyism (-zĭ-), ~**ite,** *nn.* hostile terms for Tractarianism and its upholders.

push (pŏŏsh), *v.t. & i.* move by the exertion of force; shove, propel, impel, urge. *n.* act of pushing; application of propelling force; shove; (Mil.) attack in force; enterprise, self-assertion. ~bike, bicycle worked by pedalling. ~ful, *a.* inclined to push oneself; bustling.

pu'sher (pŏŏ-), *n.* (esp.) aeroplane with airscrew behind.

Pūsh'tōō, -tu (-ōō), *n.* Afghan language.

pũsillan'imous (-z-), *a.* lacking courage; faint-hearted; mean-spirited. pũsillanim'ĭtỹ (-z-), *n.*

puss (pŏŏs), *n.* cat; hare; playful or coquettish girl. **pu'ssỹ** (-ōō-), *n.* cat; soft furry object; catkin, &c. ~foot, advocate of prohibitionist legislation.

pũs'tule, *n.* pimple. ~lar, ~lous, *aa.* pũs'tulate, *v.i.* form pimples.

put (pŏŏt), *v.t. & i.* (past & p.p. *put*), transfer to specified place; set in specified position; cause to be in specified state; express in words; (pr. pŭt, past & p.p. *pŭtted*) propel golf-ball with gentle stroke towards hole; (pŭt or pŏŏt, in athletics) cast weight. *n.* ~ over, succeed in, carry through. *n.* ~ wise, (sl.) disabuse or enlighten. *n.* putting-stroke at golf (pŭt); single cast in putting the weight (pŭt, pŏŏt).

pū'tative, *a.* supposed; reputed.

pū'trefỹ, *v.i. & t.* (-*uable*), become putrid; go bad; rot; fester. ~făc'tion, *n.*; ~factive, *a.*

pūtrĕs'cent, *a.* in process of rotting. pūtrĕs'cence, *n.*

---

pū′trid, a. decomposed, rotten; stinking. **pŭtrid′ĭtý**, n.

pŭtt′ee (-ī), n. long strip of cloth wound spirally round leg and serving as gaiter.

pŭtt′er, n. golf-club for putting. **pŭtt′ing-green**, n. smooth ground round each hole of golf-links. See put.

‖ **pŭtt′oo**, n. (E.-Ind.) fabric made of the coarse refuse hair of the Cashmere goat.

pŭtt′ý, n. paste of whiting and linseed oil used by glaziers; polishing powder used by jewellers. v.t. cement with putty.

pŭz′zle, n. perplexing question; problem or toy designed to test ingenuity. v.t. & i. perplex; cudgel one's brains or pore over. ~ment, n. **pŭzz′ler**, n. (esp.) difficult question or problem.

pȳaem′ia, n. blood-poisoning.

pȳg′mȳ, n. member of a diminutive race; very small person or thing; elf, pixy. **pȳgmē′an**, a.

pȳja′mas (-ahmaz), **paja′mas** (-ahmaz), n.pl. loose silk or cotton trousers tied round waist, worn by both sexes among Mohammedans; (pop.) sleeping-suit of loose trousers and jacket.

pȳe′dog, **pie-**, (Anglo-Ind.) an ownerless dog; pariah dog.

pȳ′lŏn, n. gateway flanked by towers as in Egyptian temples.

pȳlŏr′us, n. opening from stomach into bowels.

pȳorrhoe′a (-rēa), n. purulent discharge (esp. in a dental disease).

pȳr′amid, n. solid figure with triangular or square or polygonal base and sloping sides meeting at apex; monumental stone structure of this shape; (pl.) a billiard-table game. **pȳrăm′idal**, a. shaped or arranged like a pyramid.

pyre (pīr), n. pile of combustibles for burning a corpse.

pyrī′tēs (-z), n. sulphide of iron or copper.

pyrŏm′ėter (pīr-), n. instrument for measuring high temperatures.

pyrotec′hnic, -al (pīrŏtĕk-), aa. of

or like fireworks. ~tĕc′hnics, ~tĕchný, nn. art of making or using fireworks; pyrotechnic display. ~tĕc′hnist, n.

Pyr′rhic (-rĭk), a. ~ dance, ancient-Greek war-dance. ~ foot, metrical foot of two short syllables. n. Pyrrhic dance; Pyrrhic foot. ~ victory, victory that is as bad as a defeat.

Pyr′rhonism (-ro-), n. doctrine that certainty of knowledge is unattainable; philosophic doubt.

Pȳthăgŏrē′an (or -ȳ-), a. of Pythagoras or his doctrines, esp. the transmigration of souls. n. follower of Pythagoras.

Pȳth′ian (-dh-), a. of Delphi or the oracle or priestess of Apollo there.

pȳ′thon, n. large non-venomous snake that crushes its prey; familiar spirit, soothsayer. ~ess, n. woman having familiar spirit.

pȳx, n. vessel in which the Host is reserved; box in which specimen coins are deposited at the mint. v.t. test coin by weight and assay.

Q

‖ **quā**, conj. in the capacity of.

quăck, n. harsh sound made by ducks; pretender to medical or other skill, charlatan. v.i. utter quack; talk loudly and foolishly; play the quack. **quăck′erý**, n. quack methods.

Quadrăgěs′ima (-ŏd-), n. first Sunday in Lent. **quadrăgěs′imal** (-ŏd-), a. lasting 40 days; Lenten.

quadrangle (kwŏd′rănggl), n. four-sided figure, esp. square or rectangle; (also quad) four-sided court, esp. in colleges. **quadrăng′ular** (-ngg-), a.

qua′drant (-ŏd-), n. quarter of circle's circumference; instrument for taking angular measurements.

quadrat (kwŏd′rĭt), n. square or rectangular block, esp. (abbr. quad) small one used by printers in spacing. **quadrate**, v.t. & i. (kwädrāt′), square or agree with.

a. (kwŏd'rĭt), square or rectangular. **quadrat'ic,** *a.* involving the square and no higher power of unknown quantity or variable; *n.* quadratic equation; (pl.) algebra dealing with these. **qua'drature** (-ŏd-), *n.* finding a square with area precisely equal to that of a given figure; position of heavenly body in relation to another 90 degrees away.

quadrĕnn'ial, *a.* occurring every, lasting, four years.

quadrilāt'eral (-ŏd-), *a.* four-sided. *n.* a quadrilateral figure or area.

quadrille' (kăd-), *n.* a square dance, music for it; an old card game for four persons.

quadrillion (kwŏdrĭl'yon), *n.* fourth power of a million.

quadrino'mial (-ŏd-), *a.* consisting of four algebraic terms.

quadripart'ite (-ŏd-), *a.* consisting of four parts; shared by or involving four people.

quadroon', *n.* offspring of white and mulatto; person of quarter-negro blood.

qua'druped (-ŏdrŏŏ-), *n.* four-footed animal (usu. of mammals). **quadru'pedal** (-rŏŏ-), *a.*

qua'druple (-ŏdrŏŏ-), *a.* fourfold; of four parts or parties; four times greater than. *n.* number or amount four times greater than another. *v.t. & i.* multiply, increase, four times. **quadru'plicate** (-ŏŏ-), *v.t.* (-ăt), multiply by four; make four specimens of; *a.* (-ĭt), quadruplicated; *n.* (-ĭt), quadruplicated state; (pl.) four similar specimens.

quaes'tor, *n.* ancient-Roman official with financial and other duties. **~ship,** *n.*

quaff (-ah-), *v.t. & i.* drink in copious draughts.

quăgg'a, *n.* S.-Afr. animal related to ass and zebra.

quăg'mīre, also quăg, *nn.* quaking bog; marsh, slough.

quail[1], *n.* bird allied to partridge.

quail[2], *v.i.* flinch, show fear.

quaint, *a.* unfamiliar or old-fashioned; daintily odd.

quāke, *v.i.* tremble; rock to and fro. **quā'ky,** *a.* quaking.

quā'ker, *n.* member of the religious Society of Friends; *dummy gun in ship or fort. **~ess,** *n.*; **~ish,** *a.*; **~ism,** *n.*

qualificā'tion (-ŏl-), *n.* qualifying; thing that qualifies; modification. **qual'ificatory,** *a.*

qua'lify (-ŏl-), *v.t. & i.* (-*iable*), attribute a quality to, describe *as*; make or become competent; fulfil conditions; modify, limit, moderate, mitigate.

qua'litative (-ŏl-), *a.* concerned with or depending on quality.

qua'lity (-ŏl-), *n.* degree of excellence; relative nature; attribute, trait, faculty.

qualm (-ahm), *n.* momentary faint or sick feeling; misgiving; scruple of conscience. **~ish,** *a.*

quandār'y (-ŏn-), *n.* perplexed state; practical dilemma.

qua'ntify (-ŏn-), *v.t.* (-*fiable*), express as a quantity.

qua'ntitative (-ŏn-), *a.* of or measured or measurable by quantity; based on vowel quantity.

qua'ntity (-ŏn-), *n.* how-muchness; specified or considerable amount; any indeterminate weight or amount or number; length or shortness of vowel sounds.

qua'ntum (-ŏn-), *n.* required or desired or allowed amount.

quarantine (kwŏ'rantēn), *n.* isolation imposed on ship or person. *v.t.* put in quarantine.

qua'renden, -der (kwŏ-), *n.* kind of apple.

qua'rrel[1] (kwŏ-), *n.* (hist.) crossbow bolt.

qua'rrel[2] (kwŏ-), *n.* occasion of complaint; violent contention; rupture of friendly relations. *v.i.* find fault *with*; contend violently; fall out *with*. **~some,** *a.*

qua'rry[1] (kwŏ-), *n.* intended prey; object of pursuit.

qua'rry[2] (kwŏ-), *n.* place from which stone is extracted for building, &c. *v.t. & i.* extract from quarry. **~man,** *n.*

quart (kwŏrt), *n.* quarter of a gallon, two pints; pot or bottle (usu. **~-bottle**) containing it.

quar'tan (-ŏr-), *n.* ague or fever with paroxysm every third day.

quar'ter (kwŏr-), *n.* fourth part; one of four equal or corresponding parts; grain-measure of 8 bushels; quarter of cwt., 28 lb., (U.S.) 25 lb.; period ending at each quarter-day; point of time 15 min. before or after an hour; (U.S., Can.) 25 cents; quarter-mile race; point of compass, direction; district, locality; source of supply, help, or information; (pl.) lodgings, abode, station; mercy shown to enemy in battle. *v.t.* divide into quarters; divide by 4; put (troops, &c.) into quarters; provide with lodgings; (Herald.) bear quarterly or among the quarterings on shield. **~-day**, day on which quarterly payments are due. **~-deck**, part of upper deck between stern and after-mast. **~-master**, (Naut.) rating in charge of steering, hold-stowing, &c.; (Mil.) regimental officer in charge of quartering, rations, ammunition, &c. **~-staff**, long straight staff wielded with both hands in an old kind of fencing.

quar'tering (-ŏr-), *n.* division into quarters; (Herald., pl.) various coats marshalled on shield to denote alliance with other families.

quar'terly (-ŏr-), *a.* occurring, due, in each quarter of the year. *n.* quarterly magazine. *adv.* once a quarter; (Herald.) in the four, or in two diagonally opposite, quarters of a shield.

quar'tern (-ŏr-), *n.* fourth part of a pint or peck; 4 lb. loaf (usu. **~-loaf**).

quartet'(te) (-ŏr-), *n.* musical composition for four voices or instruments; players or singers rendering this; set of four.

quar'to (-ŏr-), *n.* (pl. **-os**). size given by folding sheet of paper twice; book of sheets so folded.

quartz(-ŏr-), *n.* kinds of siliciousmineral sometimes containing gold.

quash (kwŏsh), *v.t.* annul; reject as not valid.

quā'si, *conj.* as if. **quā'si-,** *pref.* seeming(ly), almost.

qua'ssia (-ŏsha), *n.* S.-Amer. tree; its wood or bark or root; bitter decoction made from these.

quăt'er-cen'tenary, *n.* four hundredth anniversary.

quatern'ary, *a.* having four parts; (Geol.) belonging to period subsequent to Tertiary. *n.* set of four things; the number four.

quatern'ion, *n.* set of four; (pl.) a calculus named as depending on four geometrical elements.

quatrain (kwŏt'rin), *n.* four-line stanza.

quat'refoil (kă-), *n.* four-cusped figure resembling symmetrical four-lobed leaf or flower.

quā'ver, *v.i.* & *t.* vibrate, shake, tremble, trill (esp. of voice or musical sound); say in trembling tones. *n.* trill; tremulousness in speech; (Mus.) note equal in length to half crotchet.

quay (kē), *n.* artificial landing-place for loading or unloading ships. **~-age**, *n.* quay dues.

quean, *n.* (arch.) bold girl or woman; hussy.

queas'y (-z-), *a.* (of digestion) easily upset; feeling or liable to qualms or scruples.

queen, *n.* king's wife; female sovereign of kingdom; woman, country, &c., supreme in specified sphere; *(sl.)* lady; perfect female of bee, wasp, ant, &c. *v.t.* & *i.* make (woman) queen; play the queen. **~-dowager,** late king's wife. **~-mother,** queen-dowager who is mother of king or queen. **queen'ly,** *a.* like a queen.

queen'ing, *n.* kind of apple.

queer, *a.* strange, odd, eccentric; of questionable character; out of sorts. *v.t.* (sl.) put out of order.

quĕll, *v.t.* suppress, crush.

quench, *v.t.* slake thirst; extinguish fire; cool; stifle or suppress.

~er, n. something to drink.
~less, a. unquenchable.

quenelle' (ke-), n. ball of fish or meat pounded and seasoned.

quer'ist, n. questioner.

quern, n. hand-mill for grinding corn, &c.

que'rulous (-rŏŏ-), a. complaining; peevish.

quer'y, n. question, esp. one disputing a fact, &c.; a mark of interrogation. v.t. (-iable), ask, inquire; dispute accuracy of.

quest, n. seeking; thing sought; inquiry or search.

ques'tion (-chn), n. sentence put in interrogative form; problem, concern, matter; subject of discussion or voting; doubt about a thing. v.t. ask questions of, interrogate; throw doubt upon. ~able, a. doubtfully true; not clearly consistent with honesty or wisdom. ~less, adv. indubitably.

questionnaire' (kĕ-), n. formulated series of questions.

queue (kū), n. hanging plaited tail of hair, pigtail; line of persons or vehicles awaiting their turns. v.i. stand in queue.

quib'ble, n. play on words; equivocation, evasion. v.i. use quibbles.

quick, a. living; lively; prompt; sensitive, intelligent; swift. n. sensitive flesh below nails or skin, or a sore; seat of feeling or emotion. adv. quickly. ~lime, unslaked lime. ~sand, loose wet sand readily swallowing up ships and animals. ~set, a. formed of living plants, esp. hawthorn; n. live slips, esp. of hawthorn; hedge of these. ~silver, mercury.

quick'en, v.t. & i. give life to; come to life; animate, inspire, kindle; accelerate; make or become quicker. ~ing, a.

quid¹, n. (sl.) a sovereign, £1.

quid², n. lump of tobacco for chewing.

quidd'ity, n. essence; what makes a thing what it is; quibble.

quid'nunc, n. newsmonger; person given to gossip.

|| quid pro quo, n. thing given as compensation.

quies'cent, a. inert, dormant; silent. ~nce, ~ncy, nn.

qui'et, n. undisturbed state; tranquillity, repose; calm, silence. a. with little or no sound or motion; of gentle disposition; (of colour, &c.) unobtrusive; tranquil. v.t. & i. soothe, calm, reduce to quiet; become quiet.

qui'etism, n. passive attitude towards life, esp. as a form of religious mysticism. ~ist, n. & a.

qui'etude, n. quietness.

quie'tus, n. receipt for bill; release from life; being got rid of.

quiff, n. curl plastered down on forehead.

|| Qui'hi(a)i (-hī), n. European who has lived a long time in India.

quill, n. large feather of wing or tail; hollow stem of feather; pen, fishing-float, plectrum, or tooth-pick made of quill; porcupine's spine(s); hollow reed used as bobbin or musical pipe. v.t. goffer; wind on bobbin.

quill'et, n. quibble.

quill'ing, n. goffered edging.

quilt, n. coverlet, esp. of quilted material. v.t. make (coverlet, garment) of padding held between two layers of linen, &c. by cross rows of sewing; (sl.) thrash.

qui'nary, a. consisting of five.

quince, n. acid pear-shaped fruit used in jams, &c.

quincenté'nary, n. 500th anniversary.

quinc'unx, n. the central and the four corner points of a square or rectangle.

quinine' (-ēn), n. a bitter drug got from cinchona bark.

Quinquagês'ima, or ~ Sunday, n. Sunday before Lent.

quinquenn'ial, a. five-year-long; five-yearly. ~ium, n.

quin'sy (-z-), n. inflammation of throat or tonsils.

quin'tain (-tǐn), n. (hist.) mark set up to be tilted at, with sandbag on pivoted bar.

quin'tal, n. 100 lb.; 112 lb. or cwt.

ah, awl, oil, boor, cow, dowry; chin, go, bang, so, ship, thin; dh, as th(e);

quin′tan, *a.* & *n.* (ague or fever) with paroxysm every fourth day.

quintess′ence, *n.* purest form or manifestation of some quality, &c.; highly refined extract.

quintet′(te), *n.* (performers of) piece for five voices or instruments; set of five.

quin′tuple, *a.* fivefold.

quip, *n.* verbal conceit; epigram.

quire¹, *n.* 24 sheets of writing-paper; one of the folded sheets that are sewn together in book-binding.

quire². See choir.

Quir′inal, *n.* the Italian Government or Court.

quirk, *n.* quip; trick of gesture, &c.; flourish in writing.

*****quirt** (western U.S.), *n.* riding-whip with long lash of braided leather. *v.t.* lash with quirt.

quit, *v.t.* & *i.* (quitted, rarely quit), give up, let go, abandon; depart from. *pred.a.* rid of; absolved. ~**rent**, rent paid by freeholder or copyholder in lieu of service.

quitch, *n.* couch-grass.

quite, *adv.* completely, altogether, absolutely; noticeably.

quits, *pred.a.* on even terms by retaliation or repayment.

quitt′ance, *n.* release from obligation; receipt for payment.

*****quitt′er**, *n.* (colloq.) person lacking in determination or strength of will.

quiv′er¹, *n.* case for arrows.

quiv′er², *v.i.* tremble or vibrate with slight rapid motion. *n.* quivering motion or sound.

‖ **qui vive** (kē′vēv′). On the ~, on the alert.

Quix′ote, *n.* person who neglects his interests in comparison with honour or devotion. **quixŏt′ic**, *a.*

quiz, *v.t.* make sport of; regard with mocking air; chaff; *****examine or coach (pupil, class, &c.) by questioning. *n.* person given to quizzing. **quizz′ical**, *a.*

quŏd, *n.* (sl.) prison.

‖ **quŏd vi′de** (abbr. *q.v.*), which see (used in references).

quoin (koin), *n.* angle or corner of building, corner-stone; wedge used in printing or gunnery.

quoit (koit), *n.* sharp-edged iron ring for throwing at a mark in the game of *quoits.*

quŏn′dam, *a.* that was; former.

quŏr′um, *n.* number of members that must be present to constitute a valid meeting.

quŏ′ta, *a.* share to be contributed to or received from a total by one of the parties concerned.

quŏ′table, *a.* worth quoting from or quoting. ~**bility**, *n.*

quotā′tion, *n.* quoting; passage or price quoted. ~**marks** (‘ ’ or " "), used at beginning and end of quoted passages or words.

quote, *v.t.* & *i.* cite or appeal to (author, book) in confirmation of some view; state price of. *n.* (colloq.) passage quoted; (usu. pl.) quotation-mark(s).

quoth (kwōth, -ōth), *v.t.* (arch.) ~**I**, *he, Tom,* said I, &c.

quotid′ian, *a.* daily; (of intermittent fever or ague) with a paroxysm every day. *n.* a quotidian ague or fever.

quō′tient (-shnt), *n.* result of a division sum.

quot′ety, *n.* number as a category.

R

răbb′et, *n.* groove or notch cut along edge or face of wood, &c. to receive corresponding projection of another piece. *v.t.* cut rabbet in.

răbb′i, *n.* Jewish doctor of the law. **răbb′in**, *n.* rabbi. ~**ic**, ~**ical**, *aa.* of the rabbins. ~**ism**, *n.* doctrines, &c. of the rabbins.

răbb′it, *n.* wild and domesticated rodent of hare family; (sl.) feeble player or person. ~**ing**, *n.* hunting of rabbits.

răb′ble, *n.* disorderly crowd, mob; lower part of the populace.

Răbelais′ian (-zyan), *a.* as of Rabelais, exuberantly and coarsely humorous.

răb′id, *a.* furious; unreasoning;

headstrong; (of dog) affected with rabies, mad. **rabid'ity**, n.

ra'bies (-z), n. canine madness.

race[1], n. contest of speed; course of life; strong current in sea, &c.; channel of stream. v.i. & t. go at full speed; compete in speed with; indulge in horse-racing. ~course, ground for horse-races. ~horse, horse bred or kept for racing. ~meeting, horse-racing fixture.

race[2], n. group of persons having common ancestor; the posterity of; family; kindred people; a particular breed of animals; genus or species of plants.

raceme', n. an inflorescence in which separate flowers are attached by short stalks along central stem. **ra'cemose**, a.

ra'cer, n. runner; race-horse or yacht or vehicle kept for racing.

ra'cial (-shl), a. of a race or races.

rack[1], n. kinds of wooden or metal framework (1) for holding fodder, (2) for keeping various articles on or in, (3) for adjusting the position of something by use of cogs or pegs, (4) for torturing victims by stretching their joints. v.t. & i. torture on the rack; (of disease, &c.) inflict torture or strain. ~rent, n. highest rent that can be exacted; v.t. extort this from tenant.

rack[2], n. driving clouds; destruction (esp. ~ and ruin).

rack[3], v.t. draw off (wine, cider, &c.) from the lees.

rack'et[1], -cquet (-kĭt), n. cat-gutted bat used in tennis, rackets, &c.; (pl.) a ball-game for two or four with rackets in a court of four plain walls; racket-like snow-shoe.

rack'et[2], n. uproar, din; bustle, hurry. v.i. live gay life; be much on the move. ~y, a. noisy; dissipated.

raconteur (răkôntěr'), fem. ~euse (-ěrz'), nn. teller of anecdotes.

racoon', n. a bushy-tailed American carnivorous animal.

ra'cy, a. of distinctive quality or vigour; vernacular.

rad'dle, n. red ochre. v.t. plaster with raddle; plaster with rouge.

ra'dial, a. of, in, or having rays of a ray; of a or the radius; of radius.

ra'dian, n. angle at centre of circle subtending arc whose length is equal to the radius.

ra'diance, n. brilliant light; dazzling looks or beauty.

ra'diant, a. emitting rays; issuing or operating radially; beaming with joy, &c.; bright or dazzling. n. point from which heat or light radiates.

ra'diate, v.t. & i. (-āt), diverge or emit from a centre; emit rays of light or heat; send or broadcast by wireless; be arranged like spokes; disseminate (joy, &c.). **radia'tion**, n.; **ra'diative**, a. **radiator**, n. (esp.) apparatus for warming room, &c. by radiation of heat; engine-cooling apparatus in motor-car.

rad'ical, a. of, from, or going to the root; fundamental, inherent, essential; primary; thorough. n. one desiring radical reforms; a word that is itself a root, not a derivative. ~ism, n. radical politics.

rad'icle, n. part of seed that develops into the root; root-like subdivision of nerve or vein.

ra'dio, n. wireless telegraphy and telephony; X-rays, Hertzian rays, and their applications. v.t. & i. telegraph or broadcast by wireless; photograph by X-rays; treat with radium. ~phare, wireless signalling station. ~station, wireless transmitting station.

radio-, of rays or radiation; of radium. **radio-ac'tive**, a. exercising radiation; emitting invisible rays that penetrate opaque matter and produce electrical effects. ~activity, n. **ra'diograph** (-ahf), n. instrument recording sunshine; image on sensitive plate given by Röntgen rays; *v.t.* secure such image of.

radiom'eter, *n.* instrument showing conversion of radiant energy into mechanical force. **radios'-copy**, *n.* examination by Röntgen rays.

rad'ish, *n.* plant with fleshy pungent root eaten raw.

ra'dium, *n.* a metal yielded by pitchblende and named from its radio-active power.

ra'dius, *n.* (pl. *-ii*), straight line from centre to circumference of circle or sphere; any of a set of spokes or other objects diverging from a point like radii of a circle; the thicker and shorter bone of the forearm.

ra'dix, *n.* (pl. *-ices* pr. *-ĭsēz*), number or symbol used as basis of numeration scale.

raff, *n.* riff-raff. ~**ish**, *a.* of dissipated appearance; disreputable.

raff'ia, *n.* kind of palm; fibre from its leaves.

raf'fle, *n.* lottery in which article is assigned by drawing lots or throw of dice. *v.t.* & *i.* sell by raffle; compete in raffle.

raft (-ah-), *n.* collection of logs, casks, &c., fastened together in the water for transportation; flat floating structure of timber.

raf'ter (-ah-), *n.* one of the sloping beams of a roof.

rag[1], *n.* torn or frayed piece of woven material; remnant; (contempt.) flag or handkerchief or newspaper. ~**time**, music with much syncopation as in negro melodies. ~**wort**, a yellow-flowered wild plant.

rag[2], *n.* kinds of hard coarse stone breaking in slabs.

rag[3], *v.t.* & *i.* (sl.) scold; torment, tease; play rough jokes on; engage in rag. *n.* (sl.) noisy disorderly conduct or scene; spree, lark.

rag'amuffin, *n.* ragged dirty fellow.

rage, *n.* violent anger; a fit of this; object of widespread temporary popularity. *v.i.* rave, storm; be violent; be madly angry.

ragg'ed (-g-), *a.* shaggy, hanging in tufts; torn or frayed; wearing rags. ~**robin**, a crimson-flowered wild plant.

Rag'lan (coat), *n.* coat with no shoulder-seams, the sleeves running up to the neck.

ragout' (-ōō-), *n.* meat in small pieces stewed with vegetables and highly seasoned.

raid, *n.* sudden incursion to secure military advantage, booty, &c.; surprise visit by police. *v.t.* & *i.* make raid upon; make raid(into).

rail, *n.* level or sloping bar as part of fence or gate, &c.; iron bar making part of the track of a railway or tramway. *v.t.* furnish or enclose with rails. *~road*, *n.* railway; *v.t.* & *i.* transport or travel by rail, (colloq.) send or put through with great speed. ~**way**, road laid with rails for the transit of trains with passengers and goods; *light railroad.

rail[2], *n.* kinds of bird.

rail[3], *v.i.* use abusive language. **rail'ery**, *n.* banter.

rail'ing, *n.* fence or barrier.

raim'ent, *n.* clothing, apparel.

rain, *n.* condensed moisture of atmosphere falling visibly in separate drops; (pl.) *the rains*, (Anglo-Ind. colloq.) the rainy season. *v.i.* & *t.* send down rain; fall or send down in showers. ~**bow**, arch of prismatic colours formed in rain or spray by the sun's rays. ~**fall**, quantity of rain that falls within given area in given time. ~**gauge**, instrument for measuring rainfall. **rain'y**, *a.* in or on which rain falls; showery.

raise (-z), *v.t.* (-*sable*), set upright; make stand up; rouse; build up; breed; utter; put or take into higher position; extract from earth; increase amount or heighten level of; levy, collect, procure. *n.* increase in wages, a rise.

rais'in (-zn), *n.* dried grape.

|| **raison d'être** (rā'zawn dā'tr), *n.*

what accounts for or justifies or has caused a thing's existence.

raj (rahj), *n.* (Anglo-Ind.) sovereignty. **rajah** (rah´ja), *n.* E.-Ind. king or prince or noble.

Ra´jpŏŏt (rah-), *n.* member of a Hindu soldier caste.

rāke[1], *n.* pole with comb-like cross-bar for drawing hay, &c. together or smoothing loose soil; croupier's money-raking implement; dissipated or immoral man. *v.t. & i.* (-*kable*), use rake; collect, draw together, as with rake; ransack, search over; sweep with shot, enfilade.

rāke[2], *v.t. & t.* (of ship) project at upper part of bow or stern; (of mast, funnel, &c.) incline towards stern or rear; give backward inclination to (mast, &c.). *n.* amount to which thing rakes; raking position or build.

rā´kish, *a.* of dissolute appearance or manners, fast; (of ship) smart, seeming to be built for speed.

rāll´1 cār(t), *n.* light two-wheeled driving-trap for four.

rāll´y[1], *v.t. & i.* (-*iable*), bring or come together for a united effort; revive by effort of will; throw off illness; (of prices) recover from depression. *n.* act of rallying; recovery of energy or spirit; coming together in support of a cause, &c.; (in tennis, &c.) strokes quickly exchanged.

rāll´y[2], *v.t.* banter, chaff.

rām, *n.* uncastrated male sheep; thing used for ramming, e.g. battering-ram; ship's charging-beak or ship having one; pile-driving or hydraulic or pumping-machine or parts of them. *v.t.* beat firm; squeeze tight; pack closely; butt; (of ship) strike with ram; impress by repetition. **~rod**, for ramming home charge of muzzle-loader. **rämm´er**, *n.* (esp.) block of wood used for ramming soil.

Rämadän´, *n.* ninth month of Mohammedan year, during all daylight hours of which rigid fasting is observed.

räm´ble, *v.i.* walk without definite route; talk in desultory or irrelevant way. *n.* a rambling excursion.

räm´bler, *n.* (esp.) kinds of climbing rose. **räm´bling**, *a.* (esp. of street, &c.) irregularly arranged, straggling.

räm´ekin, *n.* savoury baked in a small mould.

räm´ify, *v.i. & t.* form branches or subdivisions; develop into a complicated system. **~fication**, *n.*

ramōse´, *a.* (Bot.) branched.

rämp[1], *v.i. & t.* (of lion, &c.) stand on hind legs with fore-paws in air; (of wall, &c.) ascend or descend to different level; furnish or build (wall, earthwork) with ramp; rampage. *n.* inclined plane joining two levels of earthwork or wall; upward bend in stair-rail.

rämp[2], *(sl.) n.* attempt to extort payment of fictitious debt; levying of exorbitant prices.

rämpage´, *v.i.* (joc.) rage, storm, rush about. **~ous**, *a.*

rämp´ant, *a.* (Herald.) ramping; arrant; rank; aggressive; unchecked; (of arch, &c.) having one abutment higher, climbing. **~ncy**, *n.*

rämp´ärt, *n.* defensive mound of earth; (fig.) defence, protection.

räm´shäckle, *a.* rickety.

ran, *p.t.* of **run**.

ränch, *n.* American cattle-farm; (western U.S., colloq.) farm of any sort. *v.i.* keep ranch.

rän´cid, *a.* smelling or tasting like rank stale fat. **răncid´ity**, *n.*

ränc´our (-ker), *n.* malignant hate; bitterness. **ränc´orous**, *a.*

ränd, *n.* (S.-Afr.) highlands on either side of river valley; *the Rand,* Johannesburg.

rän´dan, *n.* boat for one sculler and two oarsmen.

rän´dom, *n. At* **~,** haphazard; without aim or purpose. *a.* made, done, &c. at random.

rän´dy, *a.* having a rude aggressive manner; loud-tongued. *n.* loud-tongued coarse-mannered woman; a scold.

---

ah, awl, oil, *boor*, cow, *dowry*; *chin*, go, *bang*, so, *ship*, thin; dh, as *th*(e);

ranee (rahn'î), *n.* Hindu queen.

rang, *p.t.* of ring².

range (-j), *n.* row, line, tier, or series of things; piece of ground with targets for shooting; sphere; scope; compass; register; distance passed over by gun or projectile; cooking fireplace. *v.t. & i.* (-geable), place or arrange in a row or ranks or in specified situation or order; extend, reach; vary between limits; rove, wander. ~-finder, instrument for finding distance of object to be shot at.

ra'nger (-j-), *n.* (esp.) keeper of a royal park; (pl.) mounted force; senior girl guide.

ra'ngy (-ji), *a.* (colloq.) capable of ranging; of long slender form.

rank¹, *n.* row, queue; soldiers in single line abreast; (pl.) common soldiers; distinct social class; station; place in a scale. *v.t. & i.* arrange in rank; assign a rank to; have relative rank. rank'er, *n.* soldier of, or who has risen from, the ranks.

rank², *a.* too luxuriant; coarse; loathsome; flagrant; gross.

rankle (răng'kl), *v.i.* gnaw at the heart; cause recurring pangs.

ran'sack, *v.t.* search the recesses of; pillage.

ran'som, *n.* redeeming of a captive; money or other consideration paid for it; blackmail. *v.t.* secure release of by paying ransom; redeem; expiate.

rant, *v.i. & t.* use bombastic language; preach noisily. rant'er, *n.* noisy preacher.

ranunc'ulus, *n.* (pl. *-luses*, *-li*), kinds of plant including buttercup.

rap, *n.* smart slight blow; sound of this, esp. on door. *v.t. & i.* deal a rap to; make the sound of a rap.

rapa'cious (-shŭs), *a.* grasping; greedy; extortionate; predatory. rapac'ity, *n.*

rape¹, *v.t.* (-pable), carry off by force; violate chastity of; ravish. *n.* act of raping.

rape², *n.* plant used as food for sheep; plant with oil-yielding seed.

rap'id, *a.* speedy; swift. *n.* steep descent in river-bed causing swift current. rapid'ity, *n.*

ra'pier, *n.* light slender sword for thrusting only.

rap'ine, *n.* plundering.

rappee', *n.* kind of snuff.

|| **rapprochement** (răprôsh'mahn), *n.* recommencement of harmonious relations.

răpscăll'ion (-lyon), *n.* rascal.

rapt, *a.* carried away in spirit; absorbed; enraptured.

răptor'ial, *a.* predatory; (Zool.) of the *Raptores*, an order of birds of prey.

rap'ture, *n.* ecstatic delight or the expression of it. ~rous, *a.*

|| **rar'a a'vis**, *n.* kind of person or thing rarely met with.

rare, *a.* thin, not dense; scarce, uncommon; of uncommon excellence, remarkably good; *(of meat) underdone.

rar'efy, *v.t. & i.* lessen the density of (air, &c.); refine; become less dense. rărĕfăc'tion, *n.*

rare'ly (-ârl-), *adv.* seldom, not often; in an unusual degree.

rar'ity, *n.* rareness; rare thing.

ra'scal (rah-), *n.* rogue, knave. ~dom, rascal'ity, *nn.*; ~ly, *a.*

răsh¹, *n.* skin eruption in spots or patches.

răsh², *a.* hasty, impetuous; overbold; reckless.

răsh'er, *n.* thin slice of bacon or ham.

rasp (-ah-), *n.* coarse file with raised teeth. *v.t. & i.* scrape with rasp; scrape roughly; grate upon; make grating sound.

ra'spberry (-ahzb-), *n.* (garden shrub with) red or yellow fruit resembling blackberry.

răt, *n.* kinds of rodent resembling but larger than the mouse; person who deserts his party or his union. *v.i.* hunt or kill rats; (Pol.) desert one's party.

ra'ta, *n.* large handsome New Zealand tree with crimson flowers and hard red wood.

---

ratafi′a, -fee′ (-fēa, -fē), n. liqueur flavoured with almonds, &c.; biscuit so flavoured.

rataplan′, n. drumming sound.

ratch′et, ratch, nn. set of teeth in edge of bar or wheel with catch allowing motion in one direction only.

rate¹, n. statement of numerical proportion between two sets of things; standard or way of reckoning; (measure of) value, tariff charge, cost, relative speed; assessment levied by local authorities. v.t. & i. estimate worth or value of; consider, regard as; subject to payment of a local rate (Naut.) class under a certain rating. ~payer, person liable to pay local rates.

rate², v.t. scold angrily.

ra′teable, a. liable to payment of municipal rates. ~bility, n.

ra′tel (rahtl), n.S.-Afr. carnivorous quadruped.

rathe (-dh), a. (arch.) coming or blooming early.

ra′ther (-ahdh-), adv. more truly; to a greater extent; somewhat; for choice; sooner; (colloq., in answers) most emphatically, assuredly.

rat′ify, v.t. (-fiable) confirm or accept by signature or other formality. ratifica′tion, n.

ra′ting¹, n. amount fixed as local rate (Naut.) person's class in ship's books; tonnage-class of racing-yacht.

ra′ting², n. angry scolding.

ra′tio (-shi-), n. (pl. -os), the relation or proportion of one thing to another.

ratio′cinate, v.i. reason formally; use syllogisms. ~tion, ~tor, nn. ~tive, a.

ra′tion (or rā-), n. fixed daily allowance of food served out. v.t. limit (person, food) to rations.

ra′tional (-sho-), a. able to reason or sensible; sane; moderate; of or based on reasoning. ~ism, n. the rejection of doctrines not consonant with reason. ~ist, n. & a.; ~istic, a.; ~ity, n.

rationā′le (-sho-), n. fundamental reason or logical basis.

ra′tionalize (-sho-), v.t. (-zable), bring into conformity with reason. ~zation, n. (esp.) co-operative and scientific organization in industry.

rat′lin(e), -ling, n. (usu. pl.) small line(s) fastened across ship's shrouds like ladder-rungs.

rattan′, n. palm with long thin many-jointed stems; cane of this.

ratt′en, v.t. molest (workman or employer) by abstracting or injuring tools or machinery.

rat′tle, v.i. & t. give out rapid succession of short sharp sounds; cause such sounds by shaking something; move or fall with rattling noise; say or recite rapidly; make move quickly; (sl.) shake nerves of, hustle, frighten. n. instrument or plaything made to rattle; set of horny rings in rattlesnake's tail; rattling sound; incessant talker. ~snake, venomous snake with rattle. rātt′ler, n. (sl.) first-class specimen; *rattlesnake.

ratt′y, a. (sl.) irritable, touchy.

rauc′ous, a. hoarse; harsh-sounding.

rau′pō (row-), n. New Zealand bulrush used for thatching roofs, &c.

rav′age, v.t. & i. (-geable), lay waste, plunder; make havoc. n. (usu. pl.) devastation.

rave, v.i. & refl. talk wildly or deliriously or enthusiastically; (of sea or wind) howl or roar.

rav′el, v.t. & i. entangle or disentangle; separate into strands. n. tangle; complication.

rav′elin (-vl-), n. (fortif.) outwork of two faces forming salient angle outside main ditch in front of the curtain.

ra′ven¹, n. large black bird of crow kind; (attrib.) black.

ra′ven², v.i. & t. seek prey or plunder; devour voraciously. ~ous, a. voracious; famishing.

ravine′ (-ēn), n. deep narrow

gorge; mountain-cleft. ~buck, ~deer, the Indian gazelle.

rav´ish, v.t. carry off by force; commit rape upon; enrapture, fill with delight. ~ment, n.

raw, a. uncooked; unwrought; crude, inexperienced, unskilled; stripped of skin; sore, sensitive to touch; (of weather) damp and chilly. n. a raw place on the skin. ~boned, gaunt.

ray[1], n. single line or narrow beam of light; beginning of enlightening influence; marginal part of daisy, &c. v.i. & t. come or send out in or like rays.

ray[2], n. kinds of edible sea-fish allied to shark.

ray´on, n. artificial silk. P.

raze, ráse (-z), v.t. (-zable, -sable), completely destroy; wipe out.

rā´zor, n. instrument for shaving. ~back, sharp ridge; *kind of half-wild hog. ~bill, kinds of bird. ~fish, ~shell, bivalves with shell like razor-handle.

răz´zle (-dăzzle), n. (sl.) excitement, bustle; spree; undulating merry-go-round.

∥ rē, prep. in the matter of.

re-, pref. attachable to any verb or verbal derivative with the senses *once more, again, anew, afresh, repeated, back*. For words with this prefix, if not found below, the root-words should be consulted.

reach, v.t. & i. stretch out, extend; stretch out the hand, &c.; get as far as, attain to, arrive at; amount to; pass or take with outstretched hand. n. act of reaching; range of the hand; power of the mind; compass, scope; continuous extent, esp. a straight stretch of river.

reăct´, v.i. produce reciprocal or responsive effect; respond to stimulus; undergo change due to some influence.

reăc´tion, n. return of previous condition emphasized by interval of the opposite; response to stimulus; retrograde tendency in politics, &c.; (Chem.) action set up by one substance in another. ~ary, a. retrograde; recoiling from progress; n. retrograde person. ~ist, n.

read, v.t. & i. (read pr. rĕd), interpret mentally; divine; peruse and reproduce mentally or vocally written or printed words; study by reading; find (thing) stated, find statement, in print, interpret in certain sense. ~able, a. interestingly written; legible. ~ability, n.

read´er, n. (esp.) publisher's private critic; printer's proof-corrector; university lecturer; book of selections for educational purposes. ~ship, n. office of university reader.

read´ing, n. perusal of books; literary knowledge; entertainment at which something is read; variation found in another MS. or book; interpretation or view taken of; one of the three stages of a Bill in each House of Parliament. ~desk, desk for supporting book, &c. ~room, room in club, &c. for persons wishing to read.

rea´dily (rĕd-), adv. without reluctance; willingly; easily.

rea´diness (rĕd-), n. prompt compliance; quickness in argument or action; prepared state.

rea´dy (rĕd-), a. with preparations complete; in fit state; willing; quick; facile; within reach; unreluctant; fit for immediate use or action. adv. beforehand; in readiness. n. position in which rifle is held before the present; (sl.) ready money. ~made, (of clothes) made to standard sizes.

~ money, actual coin; payment on the spot. ~ reckoner, book of tables for use in commerce, &c.

reā´gent, n. (Chem.) substance used to detect presence of another by reaction.

real[1] (rǐ´ăl), n. Spanish monetary unit (about 2½d.).

real[2] (rē´ăl), a. actually existing or occurring; objective; genuine; consisting of immovable property such as land or houses.

rē′alism, n. fidelity of representation; truth to nature; doctrine that general ideas have objective existence. **rē′alist**, n. & a.; **∼ic**, a.

rēal′ity, n. being real; likeness to the original; existent thing; real existence; the real nature of.

rē′alize, v.t. (-*zable*), convert (hope, plan, &c.) into fact; make realistic; apprehend clearly; convert into money; fetch as price. **∼zā′tion**, n.

rē′ally (ria-), adv. in fact; positively; *really?* is that so?

rē′alty, n. real estate.

realm (rĕlm), n. kingdom; sphere; domain.

ream, n. twenty quires or 480–500 sheets of paper.

reap, v.i. & t. cut grain, &c. with sickle or machine; gather harvest from field; gather in as harvest or reward. **reap′er**, n. person or machine employed to reap.

rear[1], v.t. & i. raise, build; bring up, breed, cultivate; (of horse, &c.) stand upright on hind legs.

rear[2], n. back part of anything, esp. an army or fleet; space or position at the back; (attrib.) hinder, back. **∼-admiral**, flag officer below vice-admiral. **∼-guard**, troops detached to protect rear. **∼most**, a. furthest back. **∼ward**, a., adv., & n.; **∼wards**, adv.

reas′on (-z-), n. fact adduced or serving as argument, motive, cause, or justification; the intellectual faculty by which things are judged; sanity; sensible conduct; moderation. v.i. & t. use argument *with* person by way of persuasion; form or try to reach conclusions by connected thought; think out (consequences, &c.). **∼able**, a. sound of judgement; moderate; inexpensive; not extortionate.

reassure′ (-shoor), v.t. (-*rable*), restore to confidence; dispel apprehensions of.

reave, reive (rēv), v.i. & t. commit ravages (usu. *reive*); take by

force; carry off. **reiv′er** (rēv-), n. robber.

rēbāte′, v.t. diminish; reduce force or effect of; blunt, dull. n. (usu. rē′-) deduction from sum to be paid, discount.

rē′bĕck (or rē-), n. early form of fiddle with three strings.

rebel′, n. (rĕ′bl), person who rises in arms against established government; person who resists authority or control. v.i. (rĭbĕl′), act as rebel (*against*); manifest repugnance to some custom, &c.

rebĕll′ion (-lyon), n. armed resistance to established government; resistance to authority.

rebĕll′ious (-lyus), a. in rebellion; disposed to defy authority.

rēbound′, v.i. & n. spring back after impact; recoil.

rēbŭff′, n. & v.t. check, snub, repulse.

rēbūke′, v.t. (-*kable*), & n. reprimand, reprove, reproof.

rē′bus, n. enigmatic representation of name, word, &c. by pictures, &c. suggesting its syllables.

rēbŭt′, v.t. force back; refute, disprove. **∼ment**, **∼tal**, nn.

recăl′citrant, a. refusing compliance; refractory. n. a recalcitrant person. **∼nce**, n.

recall′ (-awl), v.t. summon back; cancel appointment of; bring back to memory; remember; revive, resuscitate; revoke, annul. n. summons to come back; *(pol.)* removal of public official from office before expiration of his term by popular vote.

recănt′, v.t. & i. renounce as erroneous or heretical; disavow former opinion. **∼ation**, n.

rēcapĭt′ulāte, v.t. & i. (-*lable*), summarize; go quickly through again; give an epitome. **∼tion**, **∼tor**, nn.; **∼tive**, **∼tory**, aa.

rēcăst′ (-ah-), v.t. put into new shape; amend form of.

recēde′, v.i. & go or shrink back; slope backwards; withdraw, retreat; decline in value, &c.

receipt′ (-sĕt), n. recipe; amount of money received (usu. in pl.);

written acknowledgement of money received. *v.t.* give receipt for.

recei've (-sēv), *v.t. & i. (-vable),* accept delivery of; take into one's hands or possession; allow, admit; entertain as guest; welcome; accept as true. recei'ver (-sēv-), *n.* (esp.) person appointed to administer debtor's or disputed property; one who receives stolen goods; receptacle in machine; earpiece of telephone; apparatus designed to receive wireless messages, &c. (also *receiving-set*).

recen'sion (-shn), *n.* revision of text; revised text.

re'cent, *a.* not long past, late; not long established, modern.

recep'tacle, *n.* vessel, space, or place for containing things.

recep'tion, *n.* receiving or being received into a place or company; welcome of specified kind.

recep'tive, *a.* able or quick to receive ideas, &c. ~vity, *n.*

recess', *n.* vacation; niche or alcove; retired or secret place.

reces'sion (-shn), *n.* receding, withdrawal. ~al, *a.* (of hymn) sung while clergy and choir withdraw after service; *n.* recessional hymn. ~ive, *a.* receding.

‖ réchauffé (rāshō'fā), *n.* warmed-up dish; rehash.

‖ recherché (reshārsh'ā), *a.* choice; far-fetched; carefully thought out.

recid'ivism, *n.* habitual relapse into crime. ~vist, *n.*

re'cipe, *n.* statement of ingredients and procedure for a medicine or dish; nostrum.

recip'ient, *n.* one who receives.

recip'rocal, *a.* in return; mutual; expressing mutual relation; *n.* (Math.) expression so related to another that their product is 1.

recip'rocate, *v.t. & i. (-cable),* interchange; requite in kind; (Mech.) go with backward and forward motion. ~tor, *n.*

recipro'city, *n.* reciprocal condition; mutual action.

reci'tal, *n.* detailed account or narration of facts; instrumental, musical, dramatic, performance by one person.

recita'tion, *n.* (esp.) reciting as entertainment; piece recited.

rec'itative (-ēv), *n.* musical declamation as in narrative and dialogue of opera and oratorio.

recite', *v.t. & i. (-table),* repeat aloud; declaim from memory; rehearse facts; enumerate. reci'ter, *n.* (esp.) book of pieces for recitation.

reck, *v.i. & t.* care; take account of. reck'less, *a.* regardless of consequences; rash; heedless.

reck'on, *v.t. & i.* ascertain number or amount of by counting or calculation; compute; settle accounts *with* person; rely or base plans *upon*; *(chiefly southern U.S.)* think, suppose. reck'oning (-kn-), *n.* tavern bill (arch.); account of time; accounts of debtor and creditor; calculation.

reclaim', *v.t.* win from vice or error; reform; civilize; bring (waste land) under cultivation. reclama'tion, *n.*

recline', *v.t. & i.* assume or be in recumbent position; lean back or sideways; rely *upon.*

recluse' (-ōōs), *a.* living in retirement or isolation. *n.* a recluse person; hermit.

recogni'tion, *n.* act of recognizing; acknowledgement.

rec'ognizable, *a.* that can be identified or detected. ~bility, *n.*

recogn'izance (-kŏn-), *n.* bond by which person engages before court or magistrate to observe some condition; sum pledged as surety of such observance.

rec'ognizant (-kŏn-), *a.* showing recognition or consciousness of.

rec'ognize, *v.t.* know again, identify as known before; accord notice or consideration to; realize or admit that.

recoil', *v.i.* start back, shrink, in horror or disgust or fear; rebound; (of fire-arms) kick. *n.* fact or sensation of recoiling.

---

zh, as (*rou*)*ge*; ė=ĭ; ȵ, ṻr,=ēr; y̆, y̆,=ĭ, ī; and see p. 4. *=U.S.

recollect′, *v.t.* succeed in remembering; call to mind. **~ion**, *n.* person's memory or time over which it extends; remembrance.

recommend′, *v.t.* commit to the care of; commend as fit for employment, &c.; advise (course of action, &c.). **~ā′tion**, *n.* statement meant to recommend; quality that recommends something. **~atory**, *a.*

recommit′, *v.t.* commit anew; refer back for further consideration. **~ment**, **~tal**, *nn.*

recompense, *v.t.* (*-sable*) requite; make amends for; compensate. *n.* reward; requital; compensation.

reconcile, *v.t.* (*-lable*) make friendly after estrangement; make resigned; harmonize; make compatible; show compatibility of. **~ment**, *n.* **reconcilia′tion**, *n.*

recondite, *a.* abstruse; obscure.

recondi′tion, *v.t.* overhaul and refit ship, &c.

reconnaissance (-nĭs-), *n.* reconnoitring survey or party.

reconnoi′tre (-ter), *v.t. & i.* (*-tring*), approach and try to learn position and condition or strategic features of (enemy, district); make reconnaissance.

recon′stitute, *v.t.* (*-utable*), place together into an intelligible whole; constitute again. **~tion**, *n.*

record, *v.t.* (rĭkôrd′), register; put in writing or other legible shape; celebrate. *n.* (rĕk′ôrd), recorded state; register; report of proceedings; document or object that records (e.g. gramophone disk); facts known about a person's past; best performance on record; limit hitherto attained.

record′er, *n.* chief judicial officer of city or borough holding court of quarter sessions; (hist., usu. pl.) a kind of flute.

recount′, *v.t.* narrate; tell in detail. **~al**, *n.*

recoup′ (-ōōp), *v.t.* compensate, indemnify. **~ment**, *n.*

recourse (-ōrs), *n.* resorting to some source of help.

recov′er (-kŭ-), *v.t. & i.* regain possession or use or control of; reclaim; secure restitution or compensation by legal process; bring or come back to life, health, or normal state or position; get over, cease to feel effects of; retrieve. **recov′ery** (-kŭ-), *n.* act or process of recovering.

recreant, *a.* craven, cowardly, apostate. *n.* a recreant person. **rec′reancy**, *n.* apostasy.

recreate[1], *v.t. & i.* refresh, entertain; indulge in recreation. **~tion**, *n.* pastime; relaxation; amusement. **~tive**, *a.*

re-create[2], *v.t.* create over again.

recrim′inate, *v.i.* indulge in mutual or counter charges; retort accusation. **~tion**, *n.* **~tive**, **~tory**, *aa.*

recrudesce (-ōō-), *v.i.* (of sore, disease, discontent, &c.) break out again. **~dĕs′cence**, *n.* fresh outbreak. **~des′cent**, *a.*

recruit′ (-rōōt), *n.* newly enlisted soldier; person who joins a society, &c. *v.t. & i.* enlist recruits; replenish, reinvigorate; recover health. **~ment**, *n.*

rec′tal, *a.* of the rectum.

rec′tangle (-nggl), *n.* plane rectilinear four-sided figure with four right angles. **rectang′ular**, *a.* shaped like rectangle; placed at right angles. **rectangūla′rity**, *n.*

rec′tify, *v.t.* (*-fiable*), put right; correct; exchange for what is right; (Chem.) refine, purify. **~fication**, *n.*

rectilin′ear, **-ēal**, *aa.* in or forming a straight line; bounded or characterized by straight lines.

rec′titude, *n.* moral uprightness.

rec′to, *n.* right-hand page of open book; front of leaf.

rec′tor, *n.* parson of parish retaining tithe; head of some educational or religious institutions; *clergyman of Protestant Episcopal Church in charge of parish. **~ial**, *a.*; **~ship**, *n.* **rec′tory**, *n.* parish rector's benefice or house.

rec′tum, *n.* final section of the large intestine.

---

recum'bent, *a.* lying, reclining. **recum'bency**, *n.*

recu'perate, *v.t. & i.* (*-rable*), restore, be restored or recover, from exhaustion, illness, loss, &c. **~tion**, **~tor**, *nn.* **~tive**, *a.*

recur', *v.i.* go back in thought or speech; return to mind; occur again; be repeated. **recu'rrence**, *n.* return. **~rent**, *a.* recurring.

recurve', *v.i. & t.* (*-vable*), bend backwards. **~vate**, *a.* recurved.

recu'sant (-z-), *n.* person who refuses submission or compliance, esp. (hist.) one who would not attend Anglican services. **recu'sancy** (-z-), *n.*

red, *a.* of a colour varying from crimson to orange; having to do with bloodshed, burning, violence, or revolution. *n.* red colour; red cloth or clothes; red ball at billiards. **~ admiral**, a butterfly. **~breast**, the robin. **~ cent**, copper cent. **~coat**, British soldier. **~ cross**, St. George's cross, emblem of England; (emblem of) ambulance service in war. **~ ensign**, flag of British merchant-ships. **~ flag**, symbol of revolution; battle-signal, danger-signal. **~handed**, in the act of crime. **~ herring**, smoked herring; subject raised to distract attention from the point in hand. **~hot**, heated to redness; (fig.) furious, excited. **~ lead**, a pigment. **~ light**, danger signal on railways, &c. **~poll**, kinds of bird. **~shank**, kind of snipe. **~skin**, American Indian. **~start**, a song-bird. **~ tape**, excessive adherence to forms in official transactions. **~ triangle**, emblem of the Y.M.C.A. **~wing**, kinds of bird.

redac'tion, *n.* putting into literary form; editing or re-editing; new edition. **~tor**, *n.*

redan', *n.* field-work with two faces forming salient angle.

redd, *v.t.* (Sc.) clear up, arrange, tidy, put right.

redd'en, *v.t. & i.* make or grow red. **redd'ish**, *a.* rather red.

rede, *v.t.* (arch.) advise; read (riddle). *n.* (arch.) advice; tale.

redeem', *v.t.* buy back; recover by expenditure of effort; compound for by payment; save, rescue, reclaim; deliver from sin; make amends for, compensate. **re-deem'er**, *n.* one who ransoms or redeems; title of Christ. **redemp'tion**, *n.* redeeming or being redeemed.

redin'tegrate, *v.t.* (*-grable*), restore to wholeness or unity; re-establish. **~tion**, **~tor**, *nn.*

red'olent, *a.* smelling strongly of; suggestive of. **~nce**, *n.*

redou'ble (-dŭbl), *v.t. & i.* intensify; increase, multiply.

redoubt' (-owt), *n.* detached outwork without flanking defences.

redoubt'able (-owt-), *a.* (of opponent, &c.) formidable.

redound', *v.i.* contribute in the end (to one's advantage, &c.).

redress', *v.t.* put right again; remedy; make up for. *n.* redressing; compensation, reparation.

reduce', *v.t.* bring down; lower; weaken; impoverish; diminish; subdue; convert to other form; suit or adapt to. **~cible**, *a.*

reduc'tion, *n.* reducing or being reduced; a rule in arithmetic.

redun'dant, *a.* superfluous; excessive; pleonastic; copious; luxuriant. **redun'dancy**, *n.*

redu'plicate, *v.t.* (*-cable*), make double; repeat. **~a'tion**, *n.* repetition. **~tive**, *a.*

reebok, rhee- (or rā-), *n.* a S.-Afr. antelope.

re-ẽc'ho (-k-), *v.t. & i.* echo; go on echoing.

reed, *n.* kinds of water or marsh plant with tall straight stalk; vibrating part of some musical instruments; a weaver's instrument. **reed'ed**, *a.* (esp.) with vibrating reeds.

re-ẽd'ify, *v.t.* (*-iable*), build up again (usu. fig.).

reed'y, *a.* abounding in reeds; like a reed; (of voice) scratchy like a reed-instrument.

---

māre, mēre, mīre, mōre, mūre; pärt, pĕtt, pört; *italics*, vague sounds;

reef, n. one of several strips along top or bottom of sail that can be taken in ; ridge of rock, sand, &c., about the level of the water's surface ; lode or vein of auriferous quartz ; bed-rock. v.t. take in reef(s) of (sail). **reef′er**, n. one double-breasted stout jacket ; (sl.) midshipman.

reek, n. foul or stale smell ; smoke, vapour, exhalation. v.i. smell unpleasantly ; emit vapour, steam ; emit smoke.

reel, n. kinds of winding-apparatus ; cylinder for holding wound cotton, &c. ; staggering motion ; a Scottish dance. v.t. & i. wind on reel ; rattle off without pause ; sway, stagger ; be shaken ; be in a whirl ; be dizzy.

reeve¹, n. (hist.) magistrate of town or district ; (Canada) president of village or town council.

reeve², v.t. (Naut.) pass rope, &c. through ring, &c.

reeve³, n. female of the ruff.

refec′tion, n. slight meal ; refreshment by food or drink.

refec′tory (or ref′i-), n. room for meals in monastery, &c.

refer′, v.t. & i. trace or ascribe to ; assign to ; send on or direct to some authority or source of information ; make allusion to. **ref′erable**, a.

referee′, n. arbitrator ; person chosen to decide between opposing parties ; umpire. v.i. act as referee.

ref′erence, n. referring of something to another authority ; allusion ; direction to page, book, &c. where information may be found ; person vouching for another. ~ library, library of books that can be consulted but not taken away.

referen′dum, n. system by which a question is submitted to the direct vote of the electorate.

refine′, v.t. & i. (-nable) free from impurities or defects ; purify, clarify ; make elegant or cultured ; employ subtlety of thought or language. ~ment, n.

fineness of taste or feeling or manners ; subtle piece of arrangement or reasoning.

refi′ner, n. purifier, (esp.) person who refines sugar, metal, &c. **refi′nery**, n. place where sugar, &c. is refined.

refit′, v.t. & i. renew or repair ship ; (of ship) undergo refitting. n. process of refitting. ~ment, n.

reflect′, v.t. & i. throw back (light, heat, sound) ; (of mirror) show image of ; reproduce to eye or mind ; throw discredit on ; meditate, consider ; make disparaging remarks on. **reflec′tion**, n. reflected light, heat, colour, or image ; thing that brings discredit on ; a thought. ~ive, a. throwing back images ; meditative. ~or, n. (esp.) appliance for reflecting light or for reflecting image in telescope.

reflex, n. reflected light or colour or glory ; image in mirror, &c. ; a reflex action. a. reactive ; recoiling ; introspective. ~ive, a. (Gram.) implying agent's action upon himself ; n. a reflexive word or form.

ref′luent (-ōō-), a. back-flowing (of tide, blood, &c.). **re′flux**, n. backward flow.

reform′, v.t. & i. make or become better ; abolish or cure abuses. n. removal of abuses ; amendment ; improvement.

reforma′tion, n. change for the better, esp. in political or religious or social affairs. **reform′ative**, a. tending to reform.

reform′atory, a. reformative. n. type of school for juvenile offenders abolished 1933.

reform′er, n. an advocate of reform ; leader in the Reformation.

refract′, v.t. (of water, air, glass, &c.) deflect (light) where it enters obliquely from a medium of different density. ~able, a. ; ~ion, n. ; ~ional, ~ive, aa. re**frac′tor**, n. refracting medium or lens or telescope.

refrac′tory, a. stubborn ; unmanageable ; rebellious.

---

ah, awl, oil, boor, cow, dowry ; chin, go, bang, so, ship, thin ; dh, as th(e)

refrain'¹, n. recurring phrase or line, esp. at end of stanzas.

refrain'², v.i. & t. abstain from doing something; keep oneself aloof; check oneself (from).

refrān'gible (-j-), a. refractable.

refresh', v.t. & i. reanimate, reinvigorate; freshen up (memory); (sl.) take drink or food. ~er, n. extra fee to counsel in prolonged case; (sl.) a drink. ~ment, n. thing that refreshes; (usu. pl.) food.

refri'gerant, a. & n. (substance) serving to refrigerate.

refri'gerāte, v.t. (-rable), make cool or cold; freeze or preserve (food, &c.) by exposure to extreme cold. ~tion, n. ~tor, n. refrigerating apparatus.

ref'uge, n. shelter from pursuit or danger or trouble; person or thing that provides it. refū'gee, n. person taking refuge abroad to escape persecution.

reful'gent, a. shining, gloriously bright. reful'gence, n.

refund', v.t. & i. pay back; reimburse. ~ment, n.

refu'sal (-z-), n. act of refusing; chance of taking a thing before it is offered to others.

refuse, v.t. & i. (rifūz'), reject; deny what is solicited or required; not accept. n. (ref'ūs), what is left as worthless or not wanted.

refūte', v.t. prove falsity or error of; rebut by argument. refū'table, a.; refūtā'tion, n.

regain', v.t. recover possession of; reach (place) again.

rē'gal, a. of or by kings; magnificent. rēgal'ity, n.

regāle', v.t. & i. choice repast. v.t. & i. entertain choicely with; give delight to; feed oneself choicely.

rēgā'lia (-lya), n.pl. insignia of royalty used at coronation, &c.; insignia of an order.

regārd', v.t. & i. gaze upon; give heed to, take into account; have respect or reverence for. n. gaze; attention, heed, care; relation; kindly or respectful feeling; (pl.)

good wishes. ~ant, a. (Herald.) looking backwards. ~ful, a. not neglectful (of). ~less, a. & adv. taking no account of.

regāt'ta, n. meeting for boat or yacht races.

rēgelāte', v.i. (of fragments of ice, snow, &c.) be fused into frozen mass. ~tion, n.

rē'gency, n. office of regent; commission acting as regent; regent's period of office.

regěn'erate, v.t. & i. (-āt) (-rable), invest with new and higher spiritual nature; improve moral condition of; breathe more vigorous life into. a. (-it), spiritually born again; reformed. ~ā'tion, n.; ~tive, a.

rēgěn'erātor, n. (esp.) fuel-saving fire-brick device in furnaces.

rē'gent, n. person administering kingdom during minority, absence, or incapacity of monarch; *member of governing board in some universities.

rē'gicide, n. killer or participator in killing of a king; king-killing. rēgicī'dal, a.

regime, rē- (rězhēm'), n. method of government; prevailing system of things.

rē'gimen, n. prescribed diet and habits; (Gram.) syntactic dependence between words.

rē'giment (-jm-), n. permanent unit of army consisting of several battalions or troops or companies. v.t. form into regiment(s), organize in groups. rēgimen'tal, a. of a regiment. rēgimen'tals (-z), n.pl. regimental uniform. ~ation, n.

rē'gion (-jn), n. tract of country; separate part of the world, &c.; sphere or realm; part round some bodily organ. ~al, a.

rē'gister, n. book in which items are recorded for reference; official list; compass of voice or instrument; recording indicator of speed, &c. v.t. (-trable), set down formally; record in writing; enter or cause to be entered in some register; *express (surprise,

zh, as (rou)ge; ð=1; ß, ū, =ɑ̄; y̆, ў,=I, I; and see p. 4. *=U.S.

3495 O

grief, &c.) by bodily movement, &c. **rĕ'gīstrar**, n. official charged with keeping register. **rĕgīstrā'-tion**, n. **rĕ'gīstry**, n. place where registers are kept.

rēg'nal, a. of the reign.

rēg'nant, a. reigning.

rēgōrge', v.t. & i. cast up after swallowing; flow back from pit, channel, &c.; swallow again.

regress, n. (rē'grĕs), going back; backward tendency. v.i. (rĭgrĕs'), move backward. **rēgrĕs'sion** (-shn), n. backward movement; reversion. **rēgrĕs'sīve**, a.

rēgrēt', v.t. be sorry for loss of; be sorry for something past; grieve at; repent. n. sorrow for loss; repentance or vexation caused by something done or left undone. **~ful**, a. full of regret. **~table**, a. undesirable, unwelcome; deserving censure.

rēg'ūlar, a. following or exhibiting a principle; consistent; systematic; habitual; not capricious or casual; not defective or amateur; acting or done uniformly; correct; (Eccl.) bound by religious rule, belonging to monastic order. n. one of the regular clergy; soldier of the regular or standing army (usu. in pl.). **~ army**, of regular soldiers. ***~ fellow, *~ guy**, (sl.) all round good fellow. **rēgūlā'rĭty**, n.; **~īze**, v.t.; **~īzā'tion**, n.

rēg'ūlāte, v.t. (-lable), control by rule; subject to restrictions; adapt to requirements; adjust (watch, &c.). **~tīve**, a. **~tŏr**, n. (esp.) part of watch or other machine that regulates pace, &c.

rēgūlā'tion, n. regulating or being regulated; prescribed rule; (attrib.) ordinary, usual, formal.

rēgur'gĭtāte, v.i. & t. gush back; cast up again. **~ā'tion**, n.

rēhabil'ĭtāte, v.t. (-itable), restore to rights, privileges, reputation, &c. **~tion**, **~tŏr**, nn.

rēhear', v.t. hear (lawsuit) over again. **~ing**, n.

rēhearse' (-hĕrs), v.t. & i. (-sable), recite, say over; give list of;

enumerate; practise (play, &c.). **rēhears'al** (-hĕr-), n.

Reichstag (rīks'tahg), n. Parliament of the German federation.

reign (rān), n. sovereignty, rule; sovereign's period of rule. v.i. be a sovereign; prevail.

rēimburse', v.t. (-sable), repay (person); refund. **~ment**, n.

rein (rān), n. long narrow strap used to guide horse; (fig.) means of control. v.t. check with reins; (fig.) govern, control.

rein'deer (rān-), n. deer of cold climates used for drawing sledges.

rēinfôrce', v.t. (-ceable), support or strengthen by additional men or material. **~ment**, n. (often pl.) additional troops or ships. reinforced concrete, with metal bars, gratings, or wire, embedded in it.

reins (rānz), n.pl. (arch.) the kidneys; the loins.

rēinstāte', v.t. (-atable), re-establish in former position; restore to privileges, &c.; restore to health or proper order. **~ment**, n.

rēinsure' (-shoor), v.t. & i. (-rable), insure against (loss that one has underwritten). **~rance**, n.

rēit'erāte, v.t. (-rable), repeat over again or several times. **~tion**, **~tor**, nn.; **~tive**, a.

reive, reiver. See reave.

rējēct', v.t. put aside as not to be accepted, believed, used, &c.; vomit. **~ion**, **~or**, nn.

rējoice', v.t. & i. cause joy to, make glad; feel joy, be glad; celebrate an event. rejoicings (-z), n.pl. merrymaking.

rējoin', v.i. & t. say in answer; retort; join (one's companion, &c.) again. **rējoin'der**, n. retort; (Law) reply to replication.

rējū'vĕnāte (-ōō-), v.t. & i. (-nable), make or grow young again. **~tion**, **~tor**, nn.

rējūvĕnĕs'cence (-ōō-), n. a growing young again. **~nt**, a.

rēlapse', v.i. fall back into worse state after improvement. n. a falling back.

rēlāte', v.t. & i. (-table), narrate,

recount; bring into relation; (*p.p.*) connected, allied.

relā′tion, *n.* narration, a narrative; connexion between persons or things; kinsman, kinswoman, relative. **~ship,** *n.* tie of kindred; affinity.

rel′ative, *a.* corresponding in some way; related to each other; having reference to; (Gram.) referring to an expressed or implied antecedent. *n.* (Gram.) relative word; kinsman or kinswoman.

relativ′ity, *n.* (esp.) Einstein's theory of the universe, based on the principle that all motion is relative, and regarding space-time as a fourth dimension.

relax′, *v.t.* & *i.* cause or allow to become loose or slack; enfeeble, enervate; mitigate; grow less strict or energetic. **relăxā′tion,** *n.* recreation, amusements.

relay′, *n.* set of fresh horses to replace tired ones; gang of men or supply of material similarly used; (telegr.) instrument reinforcing long-distance current with local battery. *v.t.* (wireless) broadcast (message, programme, &c., originating at and received from another station). **~ race,** race between teams of which each runner does part of the distance.

release′, *v.t.* (-*sable*), set free, liberate, deliver; unfasten; remit, make over to another; exhibit (cinema film) for first time. *n.* liberation from confinement, fixed position, trouble, &c.; written discharge, receipt; conveyance of right or estate.

rel′égate, *v.t.* (-*gable*), banish, exile; consign to inferior position; transfer to person for decision or execution. **~tion,** *n.*

relĕnt′, *v.i.* relax severity; give way to compassion. **~less,** *a.*

rel′évant, *a.* concerned with the matter in hand; pertinent *to.* **rel′évance,** *n.*; **~cy,** *nn.*

relī′able, *a.* that may be relied upon. **~bility,** *n.*

rell′ance, *n.* trust, confidence; thing depended on.

rĕl′ic, *n.* part of holy person's body or belongings kept after his death; memento, souvenir; (*pl.*) dead body, remains, of person; what has survived destruction or wasting; residue.

rĕl′ict, *n.* man's widow.

relief′, *n.* alleviation or end of pain, distress, or anxiety; money or food given under the Poor-law or to victims of disaster, &c.; delivery of a place from siege; way of carving or moulding in which design stands out from surface; distinctness like this.

relieve′, *v.t.* (-*vable*), bring, give, be a, relief to; bring into relief. **relieving-officer,** *n.* official charged with care of the poor.

relī′gion (-jn), *n.* system of faith and worship; human recognition of a personal God entitled to obedience; monastic state. **relī′gious** (-jus), *a.* imbued with religion; devout; **~** *n.* member of a monastic order.

relinq′uish, *v.t.* give up, cease from; resign, surrender. **~ment,** *n.*

rĕl′iquary, *n.* receptacle for holding relics.

‖ **rĕliq′uiae,** *n.pl.* remains.

rĕl′ish, *n.* distinctive flavour or taste; enjoyment of food or other things; zest; sauce or other appetizer. *v.t.* & *i.* serve as relish to; make piquant, &c.; get pleasure out of, be pleased with; smack *of.*

relŭc′tant, *a.* unwilling, disinclined. **relŭc′tance,** *n.*

relȳ′, *v.i.* put one's trust in; depend with confidence *on.*

remain′, *v.i.* be left over; abide, stay in some place or condition; be left behind. **remain′der,** *n.* residue; remaining persons or things; unsold stock, esp. books.

remains′ (-z), *n.pl.* what remains over; surviving parts or amount; relics of antiquity; dead body.

remand′ (-ah-), *v.t.* send back (prisoner) into custody to allow of further evidence being obtained. *n.* such recommittal.

remark', *v.t. & i.* take notice of, perceive; observe; say by way of comment; make comment on. *n.* noticing; comment; a thing said. ~**able**, *a.* worth notice; exceptional; striking.

rem'edy, *n.* cure for disease or any evil; healing medicine or treatment; redress. *v.t.* rectify; make good. **reme'diable, reme'dial, rem'ediless**, *aa.*

remem'ber, *v.t.* retain in the memory; not forget; make present to, tip; convey greetings from, put in mind of. ~**brance**, *n.* memory, recollection; keepsake; (*pl.*) greetings conveyed through third person. ~**brancer**, *n.* title of certain officials.

remind', *v.t.* put in mind of; cause to remember. **remi'nder**, *n.* speech or thing that reminds.

reminis'cence, *n.* remembering; fact or incident of which one remembers the occurrence. **reminis'cent**, *a.* recalling the past; retrospective; reminding one *of.*

remiss', *a.* careless of duty; negligent; lacking energy. ~**ible**, *a.* that may be remitted. ~**ion**, *n.* release; forgiveness; pardon.

remit', *v.t. & i.* pardon (sins, &c.); refrain from exacting or inflicting (debt, punishment, &c.); abate, slacken; refer (matter) to some authority; transmit. ~**tance**, *n.* money sent to person. ~**tent**, *a. & n.* (fever) that abates at intervals.

rem'nant, *n.* small remaining quantity or piece or number.

remon'strance, *n.* remonstrating.

remon'strant, *a.* of or in remonstrance. *n.* person who remonstrates.

remon'strate, *v.i. & t.* make protest; urge in remonstrance.

remorse', *n.* bitter repentance; compunction. ~**ful**, *a.* filled with repentance. ~**less**, *a.* deaf to compassion.

remote', *a.* far apart; far away in place or time; not closely related; distant from; out-of-the-way, secluded.

remount', *v.t. & i.* go up, get on to (hill, horse, &c.) again; provide with fresh horse(s). *n.* horse to replace one killed or worn out.

remo'vable (-ōo-), *a.* that can be removed. **removabil'ity**, *n.*

remo'val (-ōo-), *n.* dismissal from a post; change to another place.

remove' (-ōov), *v.t. & i.* take off or away from place occupied; convey to another place; dismiss; change one's residence; (*p.p.*) distant from. *n.* stage in gradation; promotion to higher form at school; a form in some schools.

remu'nerate, *v.t.* (-rable), reward; pay for service rendered. ~**tion**, *n.* what is received as pay. ~**tive**, *a.* profitable. ~**tor**, *n.*

renáiss'ance, *n.* revival of arts and letters in 14–16 cc.; style of art and architecture developed by it; any similar revival.

re'nal, *a.* of the kidneys.

renás'cence, *n.* rebirth; renaissance. **renás'cent**, *a.* springing up anew; being reborn.

rencoun'ter, -côn'tre (-ter), *n.* encounter, duel; casual meeting.

rend, *v.t. & i.* (rent), tear or wrench; split or divide.

ren'der, *v.t.* give in return; pay as due; deliver up; present, submit; portray; execute, translate; melt (fat) down. **ren'dering**, *n.* translation or portrayal.

rendezvous (rŏn'divōo), *n.* (*pl.* same, pr. -ōoz), place appointed for assembling or meeting; meeting by appointment. *v.i.* meet at rendezvous.

rendi'tion, *n.* (rare) surrender of place or person; *translation, act of rendering or performing.

ren'egade, *n.* deserter of party or principles; apostate.

renew', *v.t. & i.* make new or as good as new; patch, fill up; replace; begin, make, say, or give anew. **renew'al**, *n.*

renn'et, *n.* curdled milk from

calf's stomach, or artificial preparation, used in curdling milk for cheese, &c.

rĕn′ĕt², n. kinds of dessert apple.

rĕnounce′, v.t. (-ceable), consent formally to abandon; surrender, give up; repudiate; withdraw from, discontinue; forsake.

rĕn′ovāte, v.t. (-able), restore to good condition or vigour; repair. **rĕnovā′tion**, ~tor, nn.

rĕnown′, n. fame, high distinction; being celebrated. **~ed**, a. famous.

rent¹, p.t. & p.p. of rend.

rĕnt², n. tear in garment, &c.; gap, cleft, fissure.

rĕnt³, n. periodical payment for use of land, house, room; hire for machinery, &c. v.t. & i. take, occupy, or use at a rent; let or hire for rent; be let (at). **~charge**, periodical charge on land, &c. reserved to one who is not the owner. **rĕn′tal**, n. sum payable as rent.

rĕnunciā′tion, n. renouncing, document expressing it; self-denial; giving up of things.

rĕp¹, **rĕpp**, **rĕps**, n. corded upholstery fabric.

rĕp², n. (sl.) dissolute person.

repair′¹, v.i. resort; go (to).

repair′², v.t. restore to good condition, renovate, mend; remedy; make amends for. n. restoring to sound condition; condition for working or using. **~able**, a.

rĕp′arable, a. (of loss, &c.) that can be made good.

repara′tion, n. recompense for injury; compensation; amends.

repartee′, n. witty retort.

repast′ (-ah-), n. a meal, esp. one of specified quality.

repa′triāte (or -pā-), v.t. restore to native land. **~tion**, n.

repay′, v.t. & i. (repaid), pay back; return, retaliate; requite, recompense. **~ment**, n.

repeal′, v.t. annul, revoke. n. repealing, revocation.

repeat′, v.t. & i. say or do over again; recite, rehearse; reproduce; recur. n. (Mus.) passage to

be repeated; repeating or thing repeated. **repeat′ĕdly**, adv. several times. **repeat′er**, n. (esp.) repeating watch; (telegr., &c.) a device for automatically retransmitting signals, &c. from one circuit to another. **~ station**, station having a number of repeaters.

repĕl′, v.t. drive back, repulse; ward off; be repulsive or distasteful to. **repĕll′ent**, a. (of manner, &c.) unsociable, uninviting; (of task, &c.) formidable, unattractive.

repĕnt′, v.t. & i. wish one had not done something; feel regret or penitence about something. **~ance**, n.; **~ant**, a.

repercū′ssion (-shn), n. recoil after impact; (fig.) indirect effect of event, &c.; reverberation.

rĕp′ertoire (-twär), n. stock of pieces, &c. that performer or company is prepared to give.

rĕp′ertorў, n. place for finding something; store of information; repertoire.

repetī′tion, n. repeating or being repeated; copy, replica; (also, in schools, rep) saying by heart. piece to be so said.

repīne′, v.i. fret, be discontented.

replāce′, v.t. (-eable), put back in place; take place of; (pass.) be superseded. **~ment**, n.

replĕn′ish, v.t. fill up again; (p.p.) fully stored. **~ment**, n.

replēte′, a. filled, well stocked, stuffed, sated. **replē′tion**, n.

rĕp′lica, n. duplicate of work made by the artist; (loosely) copy, facsimile. **replicā′tion**, n. making of replicas or copies; echo; (Law) plaintiff's reply to defendant's plea.

replў′, v.t. & i. (-iable), make answer, respond. n. replying; what is replied.

repōrt′, v.t. & i. bring back account of; tell as news; make official or formal statement; inform against; take down (speeches, &c.), or write description of, for publication; give account of. *n.* common talk, rumour; repute; account given or opinion formally expressed after investigation; reproduction or epitome of speech or law case, esp. for newspaper publication; sound of explosion. **repôrt′er,** *n.* (esp.) person reporting for newspaper.

repôse′¹ (-z), *v.t.* (-sable), place (trust, &c.) *in.*

repôse′² (-z), *v.i.* & *t.* (-sable), rest, lay to rest, give rest to; be lying or laid; be supported or based on. *n.* rest; sleep; peaceful state, tranquillity; ease of manner. ~ful, *a.*

repôs′itory (-z-), *n.* receptacle; place where things are stored.

repoussé (repoō′sā), *a.* (of metal) hammered into relief from reverse side. *n.* repoussé work; a piece of it.

rep̆rĕhĕnd′, *v.t.* rebuke, censure. ~hĕn′sible, *a.* blameworthy. ~hĕn′sion (-shn), *n.* censure, blame.

rep̆rĕsĕnt′ (-z-), *v.t.* place likeness of before mind or senses; make out to be; allege that; describe or depict as; play (character); stand for, correspond to; be substitute or deputy for. ~ā′tion, *n.* (esp.) a calling of attention to something.

rep̆rĕsĕnt′ative (-z-), *a.* typical of a class; containing typical specimens; of or based on the representation of constituencies. *n.* specimen or typical embodiment; person's agent; person representing a constituency.

rep̆rĕss′, *v.t.* keep under; put down; suppress. ~ible, *a.;* ~ion, *n.,* ~ive, *a.;* ~or, *n.*

rep̆rieve′, *v.t.* (-vable), suspend the execution of. *n.* remission or commutation of capital sentence.

rep̆rimand (-ah-), *n.* official reproof. *v.t.* administer reproof to.

rep̆rint′, *v.t.* print again; print another edition of. *n.* (rē′print), another printing; a new edition.

repri′sal (-zl), *n.* retaliation.

rep̆roach′, *v.t.* upbraid, scold; (of

look, &c.) convey reproach to. *n.* upbraiding, censure; thing that brings discredit. ~ful, *a.* conveying reproach.

rep̆′robate, *v.t.* (-āt; -bable), express or feel disapproval of; (of God) cast off. *a.* (-it), cast off by God; hardened in sin; unprincipled. *n.* (-it), a reprobate person. rep̆roba′tion, *n.* (esp.) rejection by God. ~tor, *n.*

rep̆rodūce′, *v.t.* & *i.* produce again; produce copy or representation of; carry on (species, &c.) by breeding or propagation. ~cible, *a.* rep̆rodūc′tion, *n.* (esp.) breeding or propagation; a copy of something. rep̆rodūc′tive, *a.*

rep̆roof′, *n.* blame or an expression of it. rep̆rove′ (-oōv), *v.t.* (-vable), rebuke, blame.

rep̆′tile, *n.* crawling animal, of the class including snakes; a mean grovelling person (often attrib.).

repŭb′lic, *n.* a State in which the supremacy of the people is formally acknowledged. **repŭb′lican,** *a.* of or characteristic of a republic; *of the Republican party (opp. *Democratic*). *n.* advocate of republican government; *member of the party favouring liberal interpretation of the Constitution, extension of federal power, and protective tariff. ~ism, *n.*

repū′diāte, *v.t.* & *i.* (-iable), disown, disavow, deny; refuse to recognize or obey (authority) or discharge (obligation). ~ā′tion, *n.*

repŭg′nance, *n.* aversion, disinclination; inconsistency or incompatibility of ideas, tempers, &c. repŭg′nant, *a.* distasteful, contradictory, incompatible.

repŭlse′, *v.t.* (-sable), drive back; rebuff, reject. *n.* defeat, rebuff. repŭl′sion (-shn), *n.* tendency of bodies to repel each other; aversion. ~sive, *a.* exciting repulsion; loathsome.

repū′table, *a.* of good repute. repŭtā′tion, *n.* what is generally said or believed about a person's or thing's character.

---

māte, mēte, mīte, mōte, mūte, moōt; răck, rĕck, rĭck, rŏck, rŭck, rook̄ ̆.

repute', *n.* what is generally thought or supposed ; reputation. **repu'ted**, *p.p. & a.* generally considered to be or regarded as.

request', *n.* asking for something, thing asked for ; being sought after, demand. *v.t.* seek permission to do ; ask, entreat.

req'uiem, *n.* mass for the dead ; musical setting for this.

require', *v.t.* (-*rable*), demand, order ; ask as of right ; lay down as imperative ; need. ~**ment**, *n.* thing needed.

req'uisite (-z-), *a.* needed. *n.* thing needed.

requisi'tion (-z-), *n.* formal demand, usu. made in writing ; order to furnish supplies for army, &c. *v.t.* demand supply or use of ; press into service.

requite', *v.t.* (-*table*), make return for ; reward or avenge ; give in return. **requi'tal**, *n.*

rere'dos (rērd-), *n.* ornamental screen covering wall above back of altar.

rescind', *v.t.* abrogate, revoke, cancel. **resci'ssion** (-zhn), *n.*

re'script, *n.* edict or official announcement.

res'cue, *v.t.* (-*uable*), deliver from attack, custody, danger, or harm. *n.* deliverance, succour.

research' (-sér-), *n.* search, inquiry ; endeavour to discover facts by study or investigation. *v.i.* engage in researches.

resem'ble (-z-), *v.t.* be like ; have similarity to. ~**lance**, *n.*

resent' (-z-), *v.t.* show or feel indignation at ; retain bitter feelings about. ~**ful**, *a.* ; ~**ment**, *n.*

reserva'tion (-z-), *n.* reserve ; express or tacit limitation or exception ; **tract reserved for Indian tribe.

reserve' (-z-), *v.t.* (-*vable*), postpone use or enjoyment or treatment of ; hold over ; retain possession or control of by stipulation ; (*p.p.* as *adj.*) reticent, uncommunicative. *n.* something reserved for future use ; tract reserved for native tribe or wild animals ; (sing. or pl.) troops held in reserve ; forces outside regular army and navy liable to be called out in emergencies ; (in games) extra player chosen in case substitute should be needed ; limitation or qualification ; self-restraint in artistic expression ; reticence, lack of cordiality. **reserv'edly** (-z-), *adv.* guardedly ; without openness. **reserv'ist** (-z-), *n.* member of reserve forces.

res'ervoir (-zervwår), *n.* place where anything is kept in store ; receptacle for fluid, esp. one for storing water.

reside' (-z-), *v.i.* have one's home (at, in, &c.) ; be in residence ; (of rights, &c.) be vested in. **res'idence** (-z-), *n.* residing ; place where one resides ; abode. **res'idency** (-z-), *n.* residence of British political agent at Indian native court. **res'ident** (-z-), *a.* residing ; located ; *n.* permanent inhabitant ; British political agent. **residen'tial** (-z-, -shl), *a.* of private houses ; based on residence. **residen'tiary** (-z-, -shǎ-), *a.* bound to or involving or provided for official residence ; *n.* ecclesiastic bound to reside.

res'idue (-z-), *n.* remainder, what is left over ; the rest of an estate when liabilities have been discharged. **resid'ual** (-z-), *a.* left as residuum ; resulting from subtraction. **resid'uary** (-z-), *a.* of the residue of an estate ; residual. **resid'uum** (-z-), *n.* (pl. -*dua*), amount not accounted for in calculations ; substance left after combustion, &c. ; lowest stratum of population.

resign' (-zīn), *v.t. & i.* relinquish, surrender ; reconcile (oneself) to ; give up office, retire. **resigna'tion** (-z-), *n.* resigning of an office ; uncomplaining endurance. **resigned'** (-zīnd), *a.* having resigned oneself ; content to endure ; submissive.

resil'ience (-zīlyens), *n.* power of resuming the original form after

compression, &c.; **elasticity**.
resíl'ient (-zĭlyĕnt), *a*.

rěs'in (-z-), *n*. adhesive substance exuding from certain plants. *v.t.* apply resin to. **~ous**, *a*.

resíst' (-z-), *v.t. & i.* stop course of; successfully oppose; repel; be proof against; abstain from. **~ance**, *n*. resisting; power of resisting; stopping effect. **~ible**, *a*. **~less**, *a*. too strong to be resisted.

rĕs'oluble (-z-), *a*. capable of being resolved into elements.

rĕs'olute (-zŏlŏot), *a*. firm of purpose; determined; constant.

rĕsolu'tion (-zŏlŏo-), *n*. resolute temper or character or conduct; thing resolved on; formal expression of opinion of meeting; separation into components.

resólve' (-z-), *v.t. & i.* (*-vable*), disintegrate, analyse, break up into parts; convert or be converted into; (Mus.) convert (discord) or be converted into concord; solve, settle; decide upon; pass vote by resolution. *n*. a mental resolution; courage.

rĕs'onant (-z-), *a*. echoing, resounding; continuing to sound. **rĕs'onance** (-z-), *n*.

resórt' (-z-), *v.i.* (with *to*) adopt as expedient or method; go to (person) for aid or advice; frequent. *n*. resorting to an expedient; place frequented for some purpose or quality.

resóund' (-z-), *v.i.* ring or echo; produce echoes, go on sounding, fill place with sound; (of fame, &c.) be much talked of.

resóurce' (-sôrs), *n*. (pl.) means of supplying a want, stock that can be drawn on; expedient, device; means of passing the time. **~ful**, *a*. good at devising expedients.

respéct', *n*. deferential esteem; (pl.) message or attention conveying this; heed or regard to; reference or relation to. *v.t.* regard with deference; avoid insulting or injuring or interfering with; treat with consideration.

respéc'table, *a*. deserving respect; of fair social standing, honest

and decent; of some amount or size or merit. **~bility**, *n*.

respéct'ful, *a*. showing deference.

respéc'tive, *a*. each's own; proper to each; individual.

respíre', *v.i. & t.* (*-rable*), breathe; breathe (air, &c.) in and out again; take breath. **respíra'tion**, *n*. breathing; single taking in and expelling of breath. **rĕs'pirator**, *n*. appliance worn over the mouth and breathed through by invalids, &c. **rĕs'pirătorў** (-z-), *a*.

rĕs'pite, *n*. delay merited in the discharge of an obligation or suffering of a penalty; interval of rest or relief. *v.t.* grant or bring respite to.

resplén'dent, *a*. brilliant, glittering. **~nce**, **~ncy**, *nn*.

respónd', *v.i.* make answer; show sensitiveness *to* (action, stimulus) by behaviour or change; *be answerable or liable to make payment. **respón'dent**, *a*. in the position of defendant; *n*. defendant in a divorce suit.

respónse', *n*. answer given in word or act; set answer of congregation; feeling or movement elicited by stimulus, &c.

responsibíl'itў, *n*. being responsible; charge, trust.

respón'sible, *a*. liable to be called to account; of good credit or position; trustworthy.

respón'sions (-shnz), *n.pl.* first of three examinations for the Oxford B.A. degree.

respón'sive, *a*. answering; by way of answer; responding readily to some influence.

‖ **rĕssa'lah** (-sahla), *n*. in India, a squadron of native cavalry.

‖ **rĕssaldár'**, *n*. native captain in Indian cavalry regiment.

rĕst', *v.i. & t.* be still; cease from exertion or action; lie in sleep or death; be tranquil; give relief or repose to; lie or rely on; be fixed on; lean for support on; be propped against; repose trust in. *n*. repose or sleep; resting; a prop or support or steadying-piece; pause in music, elocution.

metre, &c. ~-house, in India, a building in which travellers may obtain rest and shelter; a dawk-bungalow.

rest², v.i. remain in specified state. n. the remainder, what remains; the others.

rés'taurant (-tor-), n. place where refreshments may be had.

rest'ful, a. quiet, soothing.

rest'-harrow (-ō), n. a shrub.

restitu'tion, n. restoring of property, &c. to its owner; reparation.

rés'tive, a. (of horse) jibbing, refractory; (of person) fretful or obstinate under control.

rest'less, a. disinclined to rest; never still; fidgety.

restora'tion, n. act of restoring; recovery.

restor'ative, a. tending to restore health or strength. n. restorative medicine or food or agency.

restore', v.t. (-rable), give back, make restitution of; replace, put back; re-establish.

restrain', v.t. check or hold in; keep under control; repress; confine. ~êdly, adv. with moderation; without exuberance or exaggeration.

restraint', n. restraining or being restrained; check; confinement; self-control; avoidance of exaggeration; reserve.

restrict', v.t. confine, bound, limit. ~ion, n. something that limits action. ~ive, a.

result' (-z-), v.i. follow as a consequence; end in specified way. n. what results; consequence; issue; product of calculation. ~ant, a. resulting as the outcome of conflicting tendencies; n. composite effect given by such conflict.

resume' (-z-), v.t. & i. (-mable), take again or back; reoccupy; begin again; recommence. resump'tion, n.; ~ive, a.

| résumé (rēz'ōōmā), n. summary.

resur'gent, a. rising again after subsidence or defeat or disappearance. ~nce, n.

resurrect' (-z-), v.t. (sl.) exhume; revive practice or memory of.

resurrec'tion (-z-), n. the coming to life at the last day; revival from disuse, &c.

resus'citate, v.t. & i. (-itable), revive; return or restore to life. ~tion, ~tor, nn.; ~tive, a.

retail, n. (rē'tāl), sale of goods in small quantities. adv. (rē'tāl), by retail. v.t. & i. (rītāl'), sell by retail; be retailed; recount.

retain', v.t. keep possession of; keep in mind; secure services of by preliminary fee. ~er, n. retaining fee; (hist.) dependant of nobleman, &c.

retal'iate, v.t. & i. (-iable), repay in kind; retort upon person; tax imports by way of reprisal. ~tion, ~tor, nn.; ~tive, ~tory, aa.

retard', v.t. make slow or late; delay progress or accomplishment of. ~ation, ~ment, nn.

retch, v.i. make motion of vomiting. n. such motion.

reten'tion, n. retaining. ~ive, a. having the power or characteristic of retaining things.

ret'icence, n. reserve in speech; uncommunicativeness. ~nt, a.

retic'ulate¹, ~lated, aa. having the appearance of or markings like network; divided into mesh-like compartments. retic'ulate², v.t. mark with reticulations. ~tion, n. net-like marking or arrangement (usu. in pl.). ret'icule, n. lady's netted or other bag.

ret'ina, n. (pl. -as, -ae), layer at back of eyeball sensitive to light.

ret'inue, n. great person's suite of attendants.

retire', v.i. & t. (-rable), withdraw from place or company or occupation; retreat; recede; go to bed; compel to retire from office. n. order for troops to retire. retired' (-īrd), a. that has retired from office, &c.; secluded. retire'ment (-īrm-), n. seclusion; state of having retired from office, &c. retir'ing, a. shy; fond of seclusion.

retŏrt', *v.t. & i.* requite in kind; make repartee or counter-charge; (*p.p.*) recurved, bent back. *n.* thing done in retaliation or said as repartee, &c.; vessel with bent neck used in distilling; kinds of receptacle used in gas-making, &c.

retouch' (-tŭch), *v.t.* improve by giving new touches.

retrāce', *v.t.* (*-ceable*), trace back to source; go back over again.

retract', *v.t. & i.* withdraw or pull back; be retracted or retractable; withdraw (promise, &c.); recant. ~ātion, *n.* recanting, revoking. ~ile, *a.* that can be drawn back. ~ility, *n.* ~ion, *n.* pulling back. ~ive, *a.* serving to pull back. ~or, *n.*

retrēat', *v.i.* go back, retire; recede, slope away. *n.* act of or military signal for retreating; withdrawing into seclusion; place of seclusion or shelter.

retrĕnch', *v.t. & i.* reduce amount of, cut down; economize. ~ment, *n.* reduction of expenses; cutting off; inner trench and parapet provided against loss of outer defences.

retribū'tion, *n.* recompense, esp. for ill deeds. retrĭb'ūtive, *a.*

retriēve', *v.t. & i.* (*-vable*), regain possession of; rescue from bad state, restore to good state; repair; find and bring in game. retriēv'al, *n.* recovery, restoration. retriev'er, *n.* dog used for retrieving game.

retrocě'ssion (-shn), *n.* ceding back of ceded territory.

rē'trogrāde, *a.* directed backwards; reversing progress. *v.i.* move backwards, recede; revert.

retrogrěss', *v.i.* move backwards; deteriorate. ~ion, *n.* deterioration; backward movement. retrogrěss'ive, *a.*

rět'rospěct, *n.* what one looks back upon. rětrospěc'tion, *n.* meditation on the past. ~ive, *a.* of or in retrospection; lying behind one; applicable to what has already happened.

retûrn', *v.i. & t.* come or go back; revert; give, send, or pay back; say in reply; elect as member for a constituency. *n.* returning or being returned; what is returned; profits of undertaking; official report.

reū'nion (-nyon), *n.* renewal of unity; social gathering.

reūnīte', *v.i. & t.* join again.

reveal', *v.t.* make known by supernatural means; disclose, betray; show, let appear.

reveil'le (-věl, -vǎll), *n.* (Mil.) waking signal.

rěv'el, *v.i.* make merry, be riotously festive; take keen delight in. *n.* a merry-making.

revelā'tion, *n.* revealing or being revealed; what is revealed; striking disclosure.

rěv'elry, *n.* revelling.

revěnge' (-j), *v.t.* (*-geable*), satisfy oneself by retaliation; avenge; take vengeance. *n.* desire for vengeance; act that satisfies this. ~ful, *a.* eager for revenge; vindictive.

rěv'enūe, *n.* annual income, esp. that of a State; department collecting State revenue.

revěrb'erāte, *v.t. & i.* (*-rable*), echo or throw back or reflect (sound, light, heat); echo, resound; rolling sound. ~ā'tion, *n.* echo, rolling sound. ~tor, *n.* reflector, reflecting lamp.

revēre', *v.t.* (*-rable*), regard with deep and affectionate or religious respect.

rěv'erence, *n.* revering or being revered; deep respect; (joc.) title given to a priest. *v.t.* revere.

rěv'erend, *a.* deserving reverence by age, character, or associations; esp. as prefix to clergyman's name.

rěv'erent, *a.* feeling or showing reverence. rěverěn'tial (-shl), *a.* due to or full of reverence.

rěv'erie, *n.* musing; a day-dream; brown study.

revers'al, *n.* reversing or being reversed.

revěrse', *a.* contrary, inverted, upside down. *v.t. & i.* (*-sable*), turn the other way round or up or inside out; invert, transpose; revoke, annul. *n.* the contrary; defeat, check; back of coin, &c. ~sible, *a.*; ~sibility, *n.*

rever'sion (-shn), *n.* reverting, return to former state or habit; passing of an estate or office at appointed time back to grantor or his heirs; right of succession to such estate. ~ary, *a.* ~er, *n.* holder of reversionary right.

revert', *v.i.* return to former state; recur in thought or talk; fall in by reversion. ~ible, *a.* subject to reversion.

revet'ment, *n.* facing of masonry, concrete, faggots, &c. on rampart or embankment.

review' (-vū), *n.* revision; survey, inspection; retrospect; critique of book, &c.; periodical in which events, books, &c. are reviewed. *v.t. & i.* view again; survey, look back on; hold review of (troops, &c.); write review of (book). **review'er** (-vūer), *n.* writer of reviews.

revile', *v.t.* (-lable) call by ill names; abuse, rail at.

revise' (-z), *v.t.* (-sable). examine and amend faults in. *n.* proofsheet embodying corrections made in earlier proof. **revi'ser**, *n.* one who re-examines for correction. **revi'sion** (-zhn), *n.* revising; revised edition or form.

revi'sory (-z-), *a.* of revision.

reviv'al, *n.* reviving or being revived; reawakening of fervour. ~ism, ~ist, *nn.* organization, organizer, of religious revival.

revive', *v.i. & t.* (-vable), come or bring back to consciousness, life, vigour, notice, or vogue. **revi'ver**, *n.* (sl.) stimulating drink.

revivi'fy, *v.t.* (-vable), restore to animation, activity, vigour, or life. ~fication, *n.*

rev'ocable, *a.* that may be revoked. **revoca'tion**, *n.* act of revoking.

revoke', *v.t. & i.* rescind, withdraw, cancel; (Whist, &c.) neglect to follow suit though able to. *n.* (Whist, &c.) revoking.

revolt', *v.i. & t.* rise or fall away or go over in rebellion; feel revulsion; affect with disgust. *n.* insurrection; rebellious mood; sense of loathing. ~ing, *a.* disgusting, horrible.

revolu'tion (-lōō-), *n.* revolving; single completion of orbit or rotation; fundamental change; forcible substitution of new government or ruler for the old. ~ary, *a.* involving great change; of political revolution. *n.* instigator, &c. of political revolution. ~ize, *v.t.* completely reconstruct.

revolve', *v.t. & i.* (-vable), turn round; rotate; go rolling along. **revol'ver**, *n.* (esp.) pistol that will fire several shots without reloading.

revue', *n.* loosely constructed play or series of scenes satirizing current events.

revul'sion (-shn), *n.* sudden violent change of feeling; (Med.) counter-irritation. ~ive, *a.*

reward' (-wôrd), *n.* return or recompense for service or merit; requital for good or evil. *v.t.* give or serve as reward.

Rey'nard (rĕn-), *n.* the fox.

rhab'domancy, *n.* divination by the rod; dowsing.

Rhadaman'thus, *n.* stern judge. ~thine, *a.*

rhap'sody, *n.* an enthusiastic highflown utterance or composition. **rhapsod'ical**, *a.* rhap'sodist, *n.* person who writes rhapsodies.

Rhe'nish, *n.* Rhine wine.

rhet'oric, *n.* art of speaking or writing effectively; inflated or exaggerated language. **rhetó'ical**, *a.* of the nature of rhetoric; oratorical. **rhetori'cian** (-shn), *n.*

rheum (-ōō-), *n.* watery secretion in eyes, nose, or mouth.

rheumat'ic (-ōō-), *a.* of, suffering from, subject to, causing, or caused by rheumatism. *n.* rheumatic patient; (pl.) rheumatism. **rheumat'icky** (-ōō-), *a.* (colloq.) like or having rheumatism. **rheu'matism** (-ōō-), *n.* disease

---

mãre, mãre, mãre, mõre, mūre; pãrt, pĕrt, põrt: *italics*, vague sounds;

marked by inflammation and pain in the joints.

rheu′mỹ (-ōō-), *a.* affected with rheum ; (of air) damp, raw.

rhĭnŏ′ceros, *n.* large animal with horn or two horns on nose.

rho′dĭum (rō-), *n.* a hard white metal extracted from the ore of platinum.

rhŏdodĕn′dron, *n.* evergreen shrub with large flowers.

rhŏmb, rhŏm′bus, *nn.* (pl. -bs, -buses, -bī) equilateral but not right-angled parallelogram ; diamond or lozenge. **rhŏm′bic**, *a.* rhomb-shaped. **rhŏm′boid**, *n.* parallelogram neither equilateral nor right-angled. **rhomboid′al,** *a.*

rhu′bărb (-ōō-), *n.* plant with fleshy leaf-stalks cooked for food ; purgative from root of a Chinese plant.

rhyme, rime, *n.* identity between terminal sounds of words or verse-lines ; a poem with rhymes ; word providing a rhyme. *v.i.* & *t.* (-mable), write rhymes ; exhibit rhyme. **rhỹ′mer, rhỹme′ster** (-ms-), *nn.* writer of rhymes.

rhỹ′thm (-dh-), *n.* measured flow of words in verse or prose ; movement with regular succession. **rhỹth′mic, ~al** (-dh-), *aa.*

rĭb, *n.* one of the curved bones round the upper part of the body ; ridge along surface serving to support or strengthen or adorn, e.g. curved timber to which boat's planks are nailed. **ribbed,** (-bd), *a.* **rĭbb′ing,** *n.*

rĭb′ald, *a.* scurrilous, irreverent, indecent. *n.* a ribald person. **~ry,** *n.* ribald talk.

ribb′on, rĭb′and, *n.* silk or other fine material woven into narrow band ; piece of this used for adornment ; (pl., sl.) reins.

rī′bēs (-z), *n.* kinds of plant including currants, &c.

rice, *n.* pearl-white seeds of an oriental plant used as food ; the plants. **~paper,** used by Chinese artists for painting on.

rĭch, *a.* wealthy, having riches ; fertile ; valuable ; (of dress, &c.)

splendid, costly ; (of food) containing large proportion of fat, butter, eggs, sugar, &c. ; highly amusing ; abundant. **rĭch′es** (-ĭz), *n.* wealth ; valuable possessions. **rĭch′lỹ,** *adv.* fully.

rĭck¹, *n.* stack of hay, corn, peas, &c. *v.t.* form into rick.

rĭck². See wrick.

rĭck′ets, *n.* children's disease with softening of bones, bow-legs, &c. **rĭck′etỹ,** *a.* of, like, or having rickets ; shaky, insecure.

rĭck′shaw, *n.* =jinricksha.

ric′ochet (-shā), *n.* skipping on water or ground of a cannon-ball or bullet ; hit made after it. *v.i.* & *t.* (-cheted, -cheting, pr. -shăd, -shāing), skip once or more ; hit or aim at with ricochet shot.

rĭd, *v.t.* (past ridded, rid ; p.p. rid), disencumber or relieve of ; abolish. **rĭdd′ance,** *n.*

rĭd(d)′el, *n.* (eccl.) altar-curtain.

rĭd′dle¹, *n.* question designed to test one's ingenuity in divining an answer ; puzzling fact, thing, or person.

rĭd′dle², *n.* coarse sieve. *v.t.* sift ; pierce in many places with shot (also fig.).

rīde, *v.i.* & *t.* (rōde, ridden pr. rĭ′dn ; -dable), sit on and be carried by horse, &c. ; go on horseback, bicycle, train, or other conveyance ; manage a horse ; lie at anchor ; float buoyantly ; oppress, tyrannize over. *n.* journey in public conveyance ; spell of riding on horse, bicycle, &c. ; road, esp. through wood, for riding. **rī′der,** *n.* in vbl. senses ; (also) additional clause amending or supplementing document ; expression of opinion, recommendation, &c. added to verdict. **rī′dĭng¹,** *n.* in vbl. senses ; *a.* used for riding on ; intended for a rider. **~breeches,** breeches of shape usual for riding. **~habit,** lady's long skirt for riding. **~master,** one who teaches riding. **~school,** place where riding is taught.

rĭdge, *n.* line of junction in which

two sloping surfaces meet; long narrow hill-top; mountain range. **ridged** (-jd), **ridg'y**, *aa.*

ri'ticule, *v.t.* (-lable). make a laughing-stock of; represent as absurd; deride. *n.* treatment of a person or thing as ridiculous. **ridic'ulous**, *a.* deserving to be laughed at as foolish or absurd.

riding[1]. See ride.

ri'ding[2], *n.* administrative division of Yorkshire or New Zealand.

rife, *pred.a.* of common occurrence; prevailing, current; numerous.

riff'-raff, *n.* the rabble; disreputable people.

ri'fle, *v.t.* search and rob; make spiral grooves in (gun, &c.). *n.* musket with rifled barrel; (pl.) troops armed with these. ~ brigade, certain regiments of British army. ~man, soldier with rifle; member of rifle brigade. **ri'fling**, *n.* arrangement of the grooves in a rifle.

rift, *n.* fissure, chasm, crack.

rig[1], *n.* trick, dodge, swindle. *v.t.* manage by trickery.

rig[2], *v.t.* provide ship with spars, ropes, &c.; furnish with clothes or equipment; set *up* hastily or as makeshift. *n.* way ship's masts, sails, &c. are arranged; person's look as determined by clothes, &c.; *carriage or equip-age, esp. with its horses. **rigg'ing** (-g-), *n.* ship's spars, ropes, &c.

right (rit), *a.* straight; just; proper, correct, true; on or to the right hand; in good or normal condition; not mistaken. *v.t. & i.* restore to or recover proper position; make reparation; avenge, vindicate, rehabilitate; correct, set in order. *n.* what is just; fair treatment; justification; (pl.) right condition, true state; right-hand region or part or direction. *adv.* straight; all the way, completely, exactly; justly, properly, correctly, truly; to right hand. ~ angle, an angle equal to that made by vertical and horizontal straight lines as in letter L.

~-minded, having virtuous inclinations. ~ whale, kind yielding best whalebone.

righteous (ri'chus), *a.* virtuous, upright, just, honest.

right'ful (rit-), *a.* legitimately entitled to; justifiable.

right'ly (rit-), *adv.* justly, correctly, properly, justifiably.

ri'gid, *a.* that cannot be bent; inflexible, harsh. **rigid'ity**, *n.*

rig'marole, *n.* meaningless talk or string of words.

|| **ri'gor** (*or* ri-), *n.* sudden chill with shivering. || ~ **mortis**, stiffening of body after death.

rig'our (-ger), *n.* severity, strictness, harshness; cruel extremity of cold, &c. **rig'orous**, *a.*

rile, *v.t.* (sl.) raise anger in.

rill, *n.* tiny stream.

rim, *n.* outer ring of wheel not including tire; raised edge or border; margin, verge.

rime[1], old form of rhyme.

rime[2], *n.* hoar-frost. *v.t.* cover with rime. **ri'my**, *a.*

rind, *n.* bark; peel; skin of bacon; outer crust of cheese.

rin'derpest, *n.* disease of ruminants; cattle-plague.

ring[1], *n.* circlet of gold, &c. worn esp. on finger; circular thing; enclosure for circus-riding, boxing, betting, &c.; combination of persons acting together for control of market or policy. *v.t.* encompass; fit with ring; put ring in nose of (pig, bull). ~dove, wood-pigeon. ~leader, instigator in mutiny, riot, &c. ~ouzel, bird allied to blackbird. ~tail, kinds of hawk, eagle, and opossum. ~worm, skin-disease in circular patches.

ring[2], *v.i. & t.* (*rang*, rarely *rung*) *p.p. rung*), give forth clear resonant sound; (of place) resound, re-echo; (of ears) be filled with sensation as of bell-ringing; make ring; ring bell; announce or summon by sound of bell. *n.* ringing sound, resonance; act of ringing bell; set of church bells.

ring′let, n. curly lock of hair; hanging curl. ~ed, ~y, aa.

rink, n. stretch of ice used for curling or skating; floor for roller-skating.

rinse, v.t. (-sable), pour water into and out of to remove dirt, &c.; wash lightly; cleanse thus. n. a rinsing.

ri′ot, n. tumult, disorder; disturbance of the peace by a crowd; loud revelry; loose living; unrestrained indulgence or display. v.i. make or engage in a riot; revel. ri′otous, a.

rip[1], v.t. & i. cut or tear or split, esp. with a single quick motion; strip off or away or open up thus; (of material) be ripped; (of ship, &c.) rush along. n. act of ripping; long tear or cut. ripp′er, n. one who rips; (sl.) first-rate person or thing. ripp′ing, a. (sl.) splendid, first-rate; enjoyable.

rip[2], n. worthless horse; dissolute person.

ripar′ian, a. of or on the river-bank. n. a riparian owner.

ripe, a. ready to be reaped, gathered, eaten, used, or dealt with; mature. ri′pen, v.t. & i. mature; make or grow ripe.

riposte′, n. quick return thrust in fencing (also fig.). v.i. deliver riposte.

rip′ple, n. ruffling of water's surface; small wave(s); babble of water. v.i. & i. form or flow in ripples; sound like ripples; make ripples in. ripp′let, n.

rise (-z), v.i. (rose pr. roz; risen pr. ri′zn), get up from lying or sitting or kneeling; get out of bed; cease to sit for business; make revolt; ascend, soar; project or swell upwards; come to surface; have origin, flow from. n. upward incline; social advancement; increase in rank, price, amount, wages, &c.; origin; riser of stair. ri′ser (-z-), n. (esp.) vertical piece connecting two treads of staircase. ri′sing (-z-), n. (esp.) insurrection; boil or pimple.

ris′ible (-z-), a. inclined to laugh; of laughter. ~bility, n. inclination to laugh; risible faculties.

risk, n. chance of bad consequences. v.t. expose to chance of injury or loss; venture. ris′ky, a. || risqué (ris′kā), a. of doubtful propriety; suggestive of indecency.

riss′ole, n. fried ball or cake of meat or fish mixed with breadcrumbs, &c.

rite, n. a religious or solemn ceremony of observance.

rit′ual, a. of or with rites. n. performance of ritual acts; prescribed order for performing religious service. ~ism, n. attaching of great importance to ritual. ~ist, n.; ~istic, a.

ri′val, n. person or thing that competes with another. v.t. vie with, be comparable to. ~ry, n. being rivals; emulation.

rive, v.t. & i. (rived; riven pr. ri′vn), strike or rend asunder; wrench; split; be split.

riv′er, n. large natural stream of water flowing in a channel. ~ horse, hippopotamus.

riv′erain, **riv′erine**, aa. of or characteristic of a river.

riv′et, n. bolt used in fastening together plates of metal, &c. v.t. clinch; fasten with rivets; fix one's eyes, &c. upon; engross.

riv′ulet, n. small stream.

rix′-dollar, n. (hist.) silver coin and money of account in some continental states.

roach, n. a fresh-water fish.

road, n. way prepared to travel on; way one means to take, route; (usu. pl.) piece of water near the shore in which ships can ride at anchor. ~hog, reckless motorist, &c. *~house, inn. ~metal, broken stone for road-making. ~stead, road for ships (see above). ~way, main part of road.

roam, v.i. & t. ramble, wander about. n. a rambling walk.

roan[1], a. (of animal) with coat of which the prevailing colour is thickly interspersed with an-other. *n.* a roan horse, cow, &c.

roan², *n.* soft sheepskin leather used in bookbinding.

roar (rōr), *n.* loud deep hoarse sound as of lion, or the voice in rage or pain or loud laughter. *v.i.* & *t.* emit roar; talk or sing or laugh loud; (of horse) make loud noise in breathing from disease. **roarer** (rōr-), *n.* (esp.) roaring horse. **roar′ing** (rōr-), *a.* noisy; boisterous; brisk.

roast, *v.t.* & *i.* cook or heat by exposure to open fire or sun; undergo roasting; (sl.) banter. *a.* roasted. *n.* roast meat.

rob, *v.t.* & *i.* violently or feloniously despoil; deprive of; commit robbery. ~ber, ~bery, *nn.*

robe, *n.* long loose garment; (often pl.) such garment as sign of rank or office or profession; *dressed skin of buffalo, &c. used as rug or garment. *v.t.* & *i.* invest (person) in robe; assume one's robes.

rob′in (also ~ redbreast), *n.* a small red-breasted bird; *the migratory thrush.

ro′bot, *n.* an apparently human automaton; an intelligent and obedient but impersonal machine; machine-like person.

robust′, *a.* of strong health and physique; not weakly; vigorous; sensible, straightforward. **ro-bust′ious**, *a.* boisterous.

roc, *n.* gigantic bird of Eastern tales.

roch′et, *n.* surplice-like vestment of bishop or abbot.

rock¹, *n.* solid part of earth's crust; a mass of this; large detached stone or boulder. ~ crystal, silica or quartz in hexagonal prisms. ~ dove or ~ pigeon, kind haunting rocks. ~ salt, salt found stratified in free state. ~ work, rockery.

rock², *n.* (hist.) distaff.

rock³, *v.t.* & *i.* make oscillate; oscillate; move to and fro in cradle or in the arms; sway from side to side. **rock′er**, *n.* one of

the curved bars on which a cradle, &c. rocks; *rocking-chair.

rock′ery, *n.* rough stones piled for growing plants on.

rock′et¹, *n.* kinds of flowering plant.

rock′et², *n.* cylindrical case that can be projected by ignition of contents, used in fireworks, signalling, &c. *v.i.* (of pheasant, &c.) fly straight upwards; fly fast and high.

rock′y, *a.* of rock; full of rocks; rugged, hard, as rock.

roco′co, *a.* with much conventional decoration; (obs.) antiquated. *n.* the rococo style.

rod, *n.* slender straight round stick or metal bar; wand, switch; cane or birch for flogging; measure of 5½ yards.

rode, *p.t.* of ride.

ro′dent, *n.* animal of the order *Rodentia* or gnawers, including rats, moles, beavers, &c.

*rode′o (-dā-), *n.* round-up of cattle for branding; exhibition of cowboys' skill at riding, &c.

rodomontade′, *n.* boastful talk, brag. *v.i.* talk boastfully.

roe¹, *n.* (collect. sing.) small kind of deer. ~ buck, male roe.

roe², *n.* mass of eggs in female fish. soft ~, male fish's milt.

roga′tion, *n.* (usu. pl.) special supplications chanted on the rogation-days or three days before Ascension Day.

rogue (-g), *n.* rascal, swindler, knave; mischief-loving child; arch or sly person; elephant living apart from the herd and of savage temper; any large wild animal of similar character; horse inclined to shirk work on racecourse or in hunting-field. **ro′guery** (-ge), *n.*; **ro′guish** (-gi-), *a.*

*roil (rĭl), *v.t.* render (water, &c.) turbid; annoy. ***roil′y** (rĭl-), *a.* turbid.

roi′nek, rooi-, *n.* new-comer, esp. British or European immigrant, in S. Africa; (in Boer war) British soldier.

rois'terer, *n.* noisy reveller; jovial swaggerer. ~**ing**, *a. & n.* of, or conduct of, a roisterer.

rôle (rōl), *n.* actor's part; one's task or function.

rŏll, *n.* cylinder formed by turning paper, cloth, &c. over and over on itself without folding; document in this form, register, list; more or less cylindrical mass of something; rolling motion or gait; continuous sound of thunder or drum or shouting. *v.i. & t.* move or send or go in some direction by turning on axis; sway or rock; undulate, show undulating motion or surface; sound with vibration; flatten with roller; make into or form a roll; make by rolling. ~**call**, calling over of list of persons. rŏ'**ller**, *n.* (esp.) cylinder used alone or as part of machine for smoothing, pressing, crushing, spreading printer's ink, rolling cloth on, &c.; long swelling wave. rŏ'**ling**, *a.* turning on an axis; moving from side to side. ~**pin**, roller for pastry-making. ~**stock**, railway company's wagons and trucks.

rŏll'ick, *v.i.* be jovial and boisterous (esp. in part. as adj.).

rŏ'ly-pŏ'ly, *n.* pudding of paste covered with jam and rolled up; (attrib.) podgy.

Romā'ic, *n.* language of modern Greece. *a.* of or in Romaic.

‖ **romal'**, **rŏomaul'** (-ahl), *n.* (E.-Ind.) silk or cotton handkerchief; thin silk or cotton fabric with handkerchief pattern.

Rō'man, *a.* of the ancient or modern city of Rome; of the people or the State or the Christian Church of Rome. *n.* member of ancient Roman State; inhabitant of Rome; Roman Catholic; (Print.) roman type. ~**candle**, tube discharging coloured balls in fireworks. ~ **Catholic**, member of the Church of Rome. ~ **numerals**, letters denoting numbers used by ancient Rome and still used for

certain purposes. ~ **type**, plain upright type, opp. *italic*.

románce', **R**~, *n.* vernacular language of old France developed from Latin; (collect.) the languages so developed (*R*-); medieval tale of chivalry; tale with scenes and incidents remote from ordinary life; episode or love affair suggesting romance. *a.* (of languages) developed from Latin (*R*-). *v.i.* exaggerate or distort the truth. **román'cer**, *n.* writer of romances; a fantastic liar.

Rōmanĕsque' (-k), *a.* (Archit.) in the style prevalent between the classical and Gothic periods. *n.* this style.

Román'ic, *a.* (of languages) Romance; Romance-speaking. *n.* Romance languages.

Rō'manize, *v.t. & i.* (-zable), make Roman or Roman-Catholic; adopt or cause to adopt Roman-Catholic beliefs or practices. ~**zation**, ~**ism**, ~**ist**, *nn.*

román'tic, *a.* marked by or suggestive of or given to romance; fantastic, visionary; (of literary or artistic method, &c.) preferring grandeur or passion or irregular beauty to finish and proportion. *n.* romanticist. ~**ticism**, *n.* adherence to romantic methods. ~**ticist**, *n.* writer of the romantic school.

Rŏm'any, *n.* a gipsy; the gipsy language. *a.* gipsy.

Rōme, *n.* city, ancient State, Empire, or Church of Rome. ~**ward**, *a. & adv.*, ~**wards**, *adv.* in the direction of Roman-Catholicism. **Rō'mish**, *a.* papistical.

rŏmp, *v.i.* play together with chasing, wrestling, &c. *n.* child given to romping; (of girl or woman) tom-boy. **rŏmp'er**, *n.* (sing. or pl.) child's overall.

rŏn'deau (-dō), **rŏn'del**, *nn.* artificial forms of short poem with refrain.

Röntgen (rŭnt'yen) (or **X**-)**rays**, *n.pl.* form of radiation penetrating many substances impervious

---

to ordinary light. **rönt′genogram** (rŭntgen-). n. photograph taken by Röntgen rays.

rood, n. crucifix, esp. on rood-screen; quarter of an acre. **~-loft**, gallery on rood-screen. **~-screen**, wooden or stone carved screen separating nave and choir.

roof, n. upper covering of house or building; top of covered vehicle. v.t. cover with roof; be roof of. **~-tree**, ridge-pole of roof. **roof′er**, n. (colloq.) letter of thanks sent by departed visitor. **roof′ing**, n. material used for roof.

rook[1], n. (Chess) the castle.

rook[2], n. black hoarse-voiced bird of crow tribe; sharper, esp. at dice and cards. v.t. win money from at cards, &c., esp. by swindling; charge extortionately. **~ery**, n. colony of rooks; crowded cluster of mean houses.

room, n. space occupied or that might be occupied by something; capaciousness or ability to accommodate contents; opportunity, scope; apartment in a house, (pl.) apartments or lodgings. v.i. *occupy room(s) or share room(s) with. *room′er, n. occupier of room(s) only, eating out. room′ful (-ŏol), n. (pl. -ls), room′y, a. spacious, not confined.

roost, n. bird's resting-place. v.i. settle for sleep; be perched or lodged for the night. **~er**, n. (esp.) the domestic cock.

root[1], n. part of plant that fixes it to the earth and conveys nourishment from the soil to it; (pl.) fibres or branches of this; (usu. pl.) plant(s) with edible roots; part of organ, &c. serving as a root; source, means of growth, basis; (Math.) the factor of a quantity which multiplied by itself gives that quantity; original element from which words are formed. v.t. & i. take or cause to take root; establish firmly; pull up by the root;

turn up ground in search of food; (often **rout**, pr. rowt) find or bring out after search, &c.; rummage. **root′let**, n. small root. **root′y**, n. (Mil. sl.) bread.

root[2], v.i. (sl.) be active for another by giving encouraging applause or support. **~er**, n.

rope, n. stout line made by twisting together strands of hemp, flax, hide, or wire. v.t. (rope), fasten with rope, put rope on; enclose or mark off with rope; *(western U.S.) catch with lariat. **~dancer**, performer on tightrope. **~-walk**, long piece of ground in which rope is twisted. **ro′py**, a. (of liquid) developing gelatinous stringy formation.

ro′quet (-kī), n. striking of a croquet-ball against another. v.t. & i. make roquet; hit (ball) thus.

ror′qual, n. whale with dorsal fin.

rosa′ceous (-zāshus), a. of the Rosaceae or family of plants including the rose.

ro′sary (-z-), n. rose garden, bed, arbour, or pergola; prayer made up of aves, glorias, and paternosters; string of beads for keeping count of these.

rose[1] (-z), n. (prickly shrub bearing) a beautiful and fragrant red, yellow, or white flower; nozzle of watering-pot; light crimson, pink. **~bud**, bud of the rose; a young girl. **~-colour**, rosy red, pink; (fig.) pleasant state or outlook. **~-water**, scent made from roses. **~-window**, circular window, usu. with spoke-like mullions. **~-wood**, kinds used in cabinet-making and named from their smell.

rose[2], p.t. of rise.

ro′seate (-z-), a. rose-coloured.

rose′mary (-zm-), n. evergreen fragrant shrub.

rosette′ (-z-), n. rose-shaped ornament made of ribbons, &c., or carved in stone, &c.

Rosicru′cian (-zĭkrŏōshn), a. of a society devoted to occult lore. n. member of this.

rŏs'in (-z-), *n.* resin, esp. in solid form. *v.t.* rub with rosin.

rō'ster (*or* rŏ-), *n.* list or plan showing turns of duty.

rŏs'tral, *a.* (of column, &c.) adorned with actual or sculptured beaks of captured ships; (Nat. Hist.) of or on the rostrum.

rŏs'trate, *a.* (Nat. Hist.) having a rostrum. rŏstra'tĕd, *a.* rostrate; (of column, &c.) rostral.

rŏs'trĭfōrm, *a.* beak-like.

rŏs'trum, *n.* (pl. *-ra*, *-s*), platform for public speaking: pulpit, office, &c. that enables one to gain the public ear; (Rom. Ant.) beak of war-galley; (Nat. Hist.) beak, stiff snout, beak-like part.

rō'sÿ (-z-), *a.* coloured like a red rose.

rŏt, *v.i.* & *t.* undergo decay by putrefaction or from want of use; cause to rot, make rotten. *n.* decay, rottenness; a sheep-disease; (sl.) nonsense, undesirable state of things; (Crick., &c.) sudden series of failures.

rō'ta, *n.* list of persons acting, or duties to be done, in rotation.

rō'tarÿ, *a.* acting by rotation. R~ Club, U.S. and British society for international service to humanity. Rotā'rian, *n.* member of Rotary Club.

rotāte', *v.i.* & *t.* (*-atable*), move round axis or centre; revolve; arrange or take in rotation. ~tion, *n.* rotating: recurrent series or period; regular succession. ~tional, rō'tative, *aa.* ~tor, *n.* revolving apparatus or part. rō'tatorÿ, *a.*

rōte, *n.* mere habituation: unintelligent memory.

rō'tograph (-ahf), *n.* photographic print, esp. of MS. or book.

rō'tor, *n.* rotary part of machine: upright revolving cylinder on ship taking the place of masts and sails.

rŏtt'en, *a.* affected with rot; perishing of decay; inefficient, worthless; (sl.) beastly.

rŏtt'er, *n.* (sl.) person or thing of little worth.

rŏtŭnd', *a.* rounded, plump; sonorous, grandiloquent. rŏtŭn'da, *n.* circular building, esp. with dome. rŏtŭn'dĭtÿ, *n.*

rou'ble (rōō-), *n.* Russian silver coin (formerly 2*s.* 1½*d.*).

|| roué (rōō'ā), *n.* debauchee.

rouge (rōōzh), *n.* red powder used to colour cheeks and lips. *v.t.* colour, adorn oneself, with rouge. ~-et-noire (-ā-nwahr'), card-game on table with red and black marks on which stake is laid.

rough (rŭf), *a.* of uneven or irregular surface; not smooth or level; hairy, shaggy; coarse in texture; violent; stormy, boisterous; riotous; harsh, unfeeling; deficient in finish; incomplete; approximate. *adv.* in rough manner. *n.* turbulent fellow of the lower-class. *v.t.* secure (horse) against slipping by insertion of projecting nails or spikes in shoes. ~cast, *a.* coated with mixed lime and gravel; (of plan, &c.) imperfectly elaborated; *n.* plaster of lime and gravel; *v.t.* coat with roughcast; prepare (plan, &c.) in outline. ~hew, shape out roughly. *~*-house, (sl.) horse-play; indulge in horse-play. ~ luck, (colloq.) worse fortune than one deserves. *~*-neck, (sl.) coarse vulgar person. ~shod, (of horse) having shoes with projecting nail-heads.

roughen (rŭ'fn), *v.t.* & *i.* make or grow rough.

roulade (rōōlahd'), *n.* quick succession of notes.

rouleau (rōōlō'), *n.* (pl. *-s* or *-x*, pr. -z), cylindrical packet of coins; coil or roll.

roulette (rōō-), *n.* gambling game on table with revolving centre.

round, *a.* spherical or circular or cylindrical; entire, continuous, all together; candid. *n.* round object; revolving motion, circuit, cycle, series; (Mil.) officer's inspection of guards and sentries; (Golf) playing of all holes in

---

māte, mēte, mīte, mōte, mūte, mōōt; răck, rĕck, rick, rŏck, rŭck, rōōk;

course once; (Mus.) kind of canon for three or more equal voices; one bout or spell; one stage in competition. *adv.* circularly; with rotation; with return to starting-point; by circuitous way. *prep.* so as to encircle or enclose; about. *v.t.* & *i.* invest with or assume round shape; pass round or double; make a turn. ~about, *a.* circuitous, circumlocutory; *n.* circuitous way, piece of circumlocution; merry-go-round. ~arm, (of bowling) delivered with arm horizontal. ~head, member of the Parliament party in 17th-c. civil war. ~ numbers, numbers stated without odd units, &c. ~ robin, written petition with signatures in circle to conceal order in which they were written. ~'s'man, tradesman's employee going round for orders, &c.; *police officer below sergeant with duties of inspection.

roun'del, *n.* small disk; rondeau.

roun'delay, *n.* short simple lay with refrain; bird's song.

roun'der, *n.* (pl.) a ball game; (sing.) player's complete circular run as unit of scoring in it; *(sl.) habitual loafer or drunkard.

round'ly, *adv.* bluntly, plainly; in thoroughgoing way.

roup¹ (roop), *n.* & *v.t.* (Sc.) sale, sell, by auction.

roup² (roop), *n.* kinds of poultry-disease. rou'py (roō-), *a.*

rouse (-z), *v.t.* & *i.* (-*sable*), stir up from sleep or quiescence; cease to sleep; become active.

rout¹, *n.* disorderly retreat of defeated troops; party of revellers or rioters; (arch.) large evening party. *v.t.* put to rout.

rout². See root.

route (root, Mil. rowt), *n.* way taken in getting from starting-point to destination; (Mil.) formal written marching orders. ~march, march of battalion, &c. for training purposes.

routine (rootēn'), *n.* fixed order of doing things.

rōve, *v.i.* wander without settled destination; move from place to place; (of eyes) look in changing directions. rō'ver¹, *n.* wanderer; senior boy scout; (Croquet) player or ball that has passed all hoops but not pegged out.

rō'ver², *n.* pirate.

row¹ (rō), *n.* more or less straight line of objects; a rank or file; line of seats.

row² (rō), *v.i.* & *t.* propel boat with oars; convey in boat; row race with; be member of boat's crew. *n.* spell of rowing.

row³, *n.* (colloq.) disturbance, noise, dispute; free fight; being reprimanded. *v.t.* reprimand, rate. row'ing, *n.* scolding.

rowan (rō'an, row'an), *n.* (Sc.) the mountain ash; its berry.

rowd'y, *a.* noisy and disorderly. *n.* a rowdy person. ~ism, *n.*

rowel, *n.* spiked revolving disk at end of spur.

row'lock (rŭl-), *n.* appliance serving as fulcrum for oar.

roy'al, *a.* of, from, suited to, worthy of, a king; belonging to family of, in service or under patronage of, a king or queen; splendid, first-rate. *n.* a royal stag, mast, or sail (see below); a size of paper. ~ mast, ~ sail, above topgallant mast and sail. ~ stag, stag with head of 12 or more points. ~ standard, square banner with royal arms. roy'alist, *n.* supporter of monarchy. roy'alty, *n.* being royal; royal persons; royal licence to work minerals; payment by lessee of mine to landowner; payment to patentee for use of patent or to author, &c. for each copy sold.

rŭb, *v.t.* & *i.* subject to friction; polish, clean, abrade, chafe, make dry, make sore, by rubbing; take (stain, &c.) *out*; freshen or brush *up*; come into contact with; get frayed or worn by friction. *n.* spell of rubbing. rŭbb'ing, *n.* (esp.) reproduction on paper of sepulchral brass or stone by rubbing.

---

māre, mēre, mīre, mŏre, mūre; pārt, pĕrt, pōrt; *italics*, vague sounds;

rŭbb'er[1], *n.* tough elastic substance made from coagulated juice of certain plants; india-rubber; person or appliance employed to rub; *(colloq.)* rubber overshoe. *v.i.* stare impertinently. *~neck*, (sl.) inquisitive person; excursion motor-car.

rŭbb'er[2], *n.* three successive games between same sides or persons at whist, cribbage, backgammon, &c.; winning of two games in rubber; third game, when each side has won one.

rŭbb'ish, *n.* waste or worthless matter; litter, trash; nonsense. **rŭbb'ishў**, *a.* of no value.

rŭb'ble, *n.* fragments of stone.

***rube** (rŏŏb), *n.* farmer.

ru'bĭcŭnd (rŏŏ-), *a.* ruddy, red-faced.

ru'brĭc (rŏŏ-), *n.* heading or passage in red or otherwise distinguished lettering; direction for conduct of divine service inserted in liturgical book.

ru'bў (rŏŏ-), *n.* crimson or rose-coloured precious stone; glowing red colour; a size of type (5½ point, as this). *a.* ruby-coloured.

ruche (rŏŏsh), *n.* frill or quilling of gauze, lace, &c.

rŭck[1], *n.* main body of competitors left out of the running.

rŭck[2], **rŭc'kle**, *v.i. & t.* crease, wrinkle (usu. *up*).

ru'cksăck (rŏŏ-), *n.* kind of knapsack slung from shoulders.

rŭc'tion, *n.* (sl.) dispute, row.

rŭdd, *n.* a fresh-water fish.

rŭdd'er, *n.* flat piece hinged to stern of ship or boat for steering with. *~less*, *a.*

rŭd'dle, *n.* red ochre. *v.t.* mark or colour with ruddle.

rŭdd'ў, *a.* freshly or healthily red; of red or reddish-brown.

rude (rŏŏd), *a.* primitive, simple, in natural state; uncivilized, uneducated; roughly made; coarse; violent; vigorous, hearty; insolent, offensive.

ru'dĭment (rŏŏ-), *n.* (pl.) elements or first principles of a subject;

germ of something undeveloped; (sing.) part or organ imperfectly developed as having no function. **rudimĕn'tarў** (rŏŏ-), *a.* not going beyond the rudiments; undeveloped.

rue[1] (rŏŏ), *n.* a bitter-leaved evergreen shrub.

rue[2] (rŏŏ), *v.t.* repent of; wish undone or unbefallen. *~ful*, *a.* dejected, downcast.

rŭff[1], *n.* projecting starched and goffered neck-frill; band of feathers, hair, or colour round bird's or beast's neck; kind of pigeon.

rŭff[2], *n.* bird of sandpiper kind.

rŭff[3], *n.* trumping at whist. *v.t. & i.* trump.

rŭff'ian, *n.* rough lawless person; a bully. *~ism*, *n.*; *~ly*, *a.*

rŭf'fle, *v.t. & i.* disturb smoothness or tranquility of; swagger about. *n.* frill of lace, &c.; ripple.

ru'fous (rŏŏ-), *a.* reddish-brown.

rŭg, *n.* thick woollen wrap or coverlet; floor-mat.

Rŭg'bў or *~* **football**, or (sl.) **rŭgg'er** (-g-), *n.* form of football in which ball may be carried.

rŭgg'ed (-g-), *a.* of rough uneven surface; harsh, austere; *(colloq.)* vigorous, robust.

rugose' (rŏŏ-), *a.* wrinkled, corrugated. **rugŏs'ĭtў** (rŏŏ-), *n.*

ru'in (rŏŏ-), *n.* downfall; fallen or impaired state; (often pl.) remains of building, &c. that has suffered ruin. *v.t.* reduce (place) to ruins; bring to ruin; be the ruin of. **ruĭnā'tion** (rŏŏ-), *n.* perdition. **ru'inous** (rŏŏ-), *a.* in ruins; bringing ruin.

rule (rŏŏl), *n.* principle to which action conforms or should conform; canon, test, standard; normal state of things; sway, government, dominion; a law or code of laws to be observed by a society and its members; order made by judge; carpenter's measure; (Print.) thin slip of metal for separating headings, columns, &c. *v.t. & i.* (*-lable*).

exercise sway or decisive influence over; keep under control; be guided by; pronounce authoritatively that; make line(s) with ruler (of prices, &c.) have a specified general level. **ru'ler** (rōō-), n. person, &c. bearing rule; strip or cylinder of wood, &c. for ruling lines. **ru'ling** (rōō-), n. (esp.) authoritative pronouncement.

rull'ey, n. (pl. -eys), flat four-wheeled dray; lorry.

rum[1], n. spirit made from sugar-cane; *(colloq.) any intoxicating liquor. *~runner, (sl.) smuggler of intoxicants.

rum[2], a. (sl.) queer, strange.

rum'ble, v.i. make sound as of distant thunder, heavy cart, &c. n. rumbling sound; hind part of carriage arranged as extra seat or for luggage.

ru'minant (rōō-), n. animal that chews cud. a. of the ruminants.

ru'minate (rōō-), v.i. chew the cud; (fig.) meditate upon, ponder over. ~tion, n.; ~tive, a.

rumm'age, v.t. & i. (-geable), ransack; make search in; fish out. n. search, esp. of ship by Customs officers. ~sale, sale of unclaimed articles at docks, &c., or of odds and ends at bazaar, &c.

rumm'er, n. large drinking-glass.

rumm'y, a. (sl.) queer, strange. n. a card game, usu. with four to six players and two packs of cards.

rumour (rōōm'er), n. general talk or current statement of doubtful accuracy. v.t. give currency to as a rumour.

rump, n. tail-end of beast or bird; person's posterior.

rum'ple, v.t. crease, touzle.

run, v.i. & t. (-ning; ran; run), go with speed, smooth motion, or regularity; compete in race, &c.; spread rapidly; flow or emit contents; work or be in action (of bus, &c.) ply; be current, operative, or valid; be worded; enter (horse, candidate) for race or contest; set or keep going, control operations of; get (contraband) past coastguard, smuggle in. n. act or spell of running; unit scored at cricket; way things tend to move; rapid fall; *small stream, watercourse; continuous stretch or spell or course; long series or succession; general demand; enclosure for fowls; range of pasture; licence to make free use of.

run'agate, n. (arch.) vagabond.

run'away, n. a fugitive; horse bolting (also attrib.).

rune (rōōn), n. (usu. in pl.) letter(s) of early Teutonic alphabet; mark(s) of mysterious significance resembling them. **ru'nic** (rōō-), a.

rung[1], n. short stick fixed as crossbar, esp. in ladder.

rung[2], p.t. & p.p. of ring[2].

run'let[1], n. cask for wine, &c.

run'let[2], n. small brook.

runn'el, n. brook; gutter.

runn'er, n. a racer; messenger; kinds of twining bean; creeping stem issuing from plant's stem and capable of rooting itself; sliding ring on rod, &c. ~up, competitor beaten only in final round of contest.

runn'ing, a. consecutive; successive; flowing; cursive; discharging (matter). n. act of moving quickly; way race proceeds; discharging matter.

runt, n. ox or cow of small breed.

rupee' (rōō-), n. Indian monetary unit and silver coin, 1s. &c.

rup'ture, n. breaking, breach; breach of harmonious relations; tumour resulting from protrusion of some internal part through an aperture in the membrane, &c. enclosing it; hernia. v.t. & i. (-rable), burst (cell, membrane, &c.); sever (connexion); affect with or suffer hernia.

rur'al (roor-), a. in or of or suggesting the country. **rural'ity,** n.; ~ize, v.t.; ~ization, n.

ruridecā'nal (roor-), a. of rural dean or deanery.

ru'sa (rōō-), n. large E.-Ind. deer.

ruse (rōōz), *n.* **indirect device; stratagem.**

rush[1], *n.* marsh plant with slender pithy stem; its stem; (attrib.) made of rush; (fig.) thing of no value. ~ **candle**, candle with rush pith as wick. ~**light**, rush candle. **rush´ÿ**, *a.* abounding in rushes.

rush[2], *v.t. & i.* impel or carry along violently and rapidly; take by sudden assault; run precipitately or with great speed; go or do without proper consideration; *(sl.)* entertain candidate for election to college fraternity, &c. *n.* act of rushing; violent or tumultuous advance; spurt, charge, onslaught; *contest between two (university) classes for temporary possession of a flag, &c.

rusk, *n.* piece of bread pulled or cut off and rebaked; kinds of light biscuit.

rus´set, *a.* of soft reddish-brown. *n.* russet colour; rough-skinned russet-coloured apple.

Rū´ssia (-sha). ~ **leather**, *n.* a leather prepared with birch-bark oil.

Rū´ssian (-shn) **Russ** (arch.), *n.* native, language, of Russia. *a.* of or from Russia. ~ **boots**, high unlaced and unbuttoned boots with leather uppers round the calves. ~**ize**, *v.t.* ; ~**ization**, *n.* **Russ´ophil**, *n. & a.* friend of or friendly to Russia. **Russ´ophobe**, *n. & a.* opponent of or opposing the Russians. ~**phō´bia**, *n.*

rust, *n.* yellowish-brown coating formed on iron by oxidation and corroding it; plant-disease with rust-coloured spots. *v.i. & t.* contract or affect with rust; lose quality or efficiency by disuse.

rus´tic, *a.* of or like country people or peasants; uncouth; of rude workmanship. *n.* countryman. **rus´ticate**, *v.i. & t.* (-cable), retire to or live in the country; send down (undergraduate) from university for a time as punishment. **rusticā´tion**, *n.* **rusti´cïtÿ**, *n.*

ru´stle (-sl), *n.* sound as of blown leaves or pattering rain. *v.i. & t.* make or cause to make rustle; go with rustle.

rus´tÿ[1], *a.* rusted, affected with rust; rust-coloured; discoloured by age; impaired by disuse.

rus´tÿ[2], *a.* rancid.

rut[1], *n.* track sunk by passage of wheels; beaten track, groove. **rut´ted**, **rut´tÿ**, *aa.*

rut[2], *n.* periodic sexual excitement of male deer, &c.

||**rut**[3], **ruth**[3] (rŭt), *n.* (Anglo-Ind.) native vehicle or carriage.

ruth[2] (rōōth), *n.* pity, compassion, tenderness. ~**less**, *a.*

ruthe´nium (rōō-), *n.* a hard brittle metal found in the ore of platinum.

rÿe, *n.* a grain used for fodder, &c. ; *(colloq.)* rye whisky.

rÿe-grass (rī´grahs), *n.* kinds of fodder-grass.

rÿ´ot, *n.* Indian peasant, husbandman, or cultivating tenant. **rÿ´otwâr**, **-wârÿ**, *a.* (of land tenure in India) characterized by direct settlement between Government and cultivators, without the intervention of zemindar or landlord; *n.* the ryotwary system.

S

sabbatā´rian, *a.* opposed to sabbath-breaking. *n.* person of such views. ~**ism**, *n.*

sabb´ath, *n.* the rest-day appointed for Jews on the last and for Christians on the first day of the week. ~**breaker**, *n.*

sabbat´ic, **-al**, *aa.* of or appropriate to the sabbath. ~ **year**, the seventh year in which Israelites were to cease tilling; *period of freedom from lectures, &c. allowed professor for purposes of travel, research, &c.

sā´ble, *n.* small dark-furred beast; its skin or fur; the tincture or colour black; (pl.) mourning garments. *a.* black, gloomy.

sab´ot (-ō), *n.* shoe hollowed out

from one piece of wood. **săb′otage**, *n.* intentional damage done by workmen to plant, &c.

sā′bre (-*er*), *n.* cavalry sword with curved blade. *v.t.* cut down or wound with sabre. **sā′bretache** (-*ertāsh*), *n.* cavalry officer's satchel hanging from belt by long straps.

săc, *n.* bag of membrane forming a cavity or enclosing a cyst, &c.

săc′charin (-*ka*-), *n.* intensely sweet substance got from coaltar. **săc′charine** (-*ka*-), *a.* of or containing or like sugar.

săcerdō′tal, *a.* priestly; ascribing mysterious powers to, or claiming excessive authority for, the priesthood. ~**ism**, ~**ist**, *nn.*

săch′em, *n.* Amer.-Ind. chief; eminent person.

sā′chet (-*shā*), *n.* small bag of perfume.

săck[1], *n.* large bag of coarse textile stuff; amount which a sack holds; *(Bascb.)* bag serving as base; kinds of loose gown or coat; sacking of town. *v.t.* put in sacks; subject (town, &c.) to unrestrained pillage and licence; *(colloq.)* dismiss from employment. ~**cloth**, coarse stuff such as sacks are made of. **săck′ful** (-*ōōl*), *n.* ~**ing**, *n.* material used for sacks.

săck[2], *n.* (hist.) kinds of white wine from Spain, &c.

săck′but, *n.* obsolete kind of trumpet.

sā′cral, *a.* of the sacrum.

săc′rament, *n.* a symbolic religious ceremony, esp. baptism and the eucharist (*the* ~, the eucharist). ~**al**, *a.* **săcramen′talism**, ~**ist**, *nn.* ascription, ascriber, of great importance or efficacy to the sacraments. **săcramenta′lian**, *n.* sacramentalist; *a.* holding or dictated by sacramentalist views.

sā′crĕd, *a.* consecrated or held dear to a deity; dedicated or appropriated to some person or purpose; hallowed by religious association; inviolable.

săc′rifice, *n.* the slaughter of a victim, or presenting of a gift, or doing of an act, to propitiate a god; such victim or gift or act; the giving up of something. *v.t.* & *i.* offer as sacrifice; offer sacrifice to; give up (one's life, interests, &c.) as of inferior importance to something else. **săcrifi′cial** (-*shl*), *a.*

săc′rilege, *n.* violation of what is sacred. **săcrilē′gious** (-*jus*), *a.*

sā′cring, *n.* (arch.) consecration of elements in the mass; ordination of bishop, sovereign, &c. ~**bell**, bell rung at elevation of the Host.

sā′crist, **săc′ristan**, *nn.* official in charge of the sacred vessels, vestments, relics, &c. of a church; a sexton. **săc′risty**, *n.* sacristan's repository.

sā′crosanct (*or* săc-), *a.* secured against outrage or violation by religious awe. ~**sănc′tity**, *n.*

sā′crum, *n.* the compound bone forming the back of the pelvis.

săd, *a.* sorrowful; showing or causing sorrow; incorrigible (of colour) dull. **sădd′en**, *v.t.* & *i.*

săd′dle, *n.* rider's seat on back of horse or on bicycle; joint of mutton or venison comprising the two loins. *v.t.* & *i.* put saddle on; saddle one's horse; burden (person) with task, &c.; put blame upon. ~**bag**, one of a pair of bags laid across horse behind saddle. **sădd′ler**, *n.* maker of saddles and harness. **sădd′lery**, *n.* saddler's trade or wares.

săd′ism, *n.* sexual delight in cruelty. ~**ist**, *n.* ~**ist′ic**, *a.*

‖ **safā′ri**, *n.* (E.-Afr.) hunting or other expedition.

safe, *a.* uninjured, out of danger; affording security or not involving danger; cautious; reliable; sure. *n.* cupboard for meat, &c.; strong-box for valuables. ~**conduct**, immunity from arrest or harm granted to a person.

safe′guard (-*gärd*), *n.* proviso or other device against foreseen risks. *v.t.* protect by precaution or stipulation. ~**ing**, *n.* (Econ.)

protection of certain industries by levying duties on imports of the same character as the home product.

safe′ty (-ft-), n. being safe; freedom from danger or risks. ~lamp, miner's lamp so protected as not to ignite fire-damp. ~razor, razor with guard protecting skin from cuts. ~valve, automatic vent relieving excessive pressure of steam; (fig.) outlet for excitement.

saf′flower, n. a thistle-like plant, cultivated for the dye obtained from its flowers; the red dye produced from this.

saf′fron, n. orange-coloured stigmas of the Autumnal Crocus; the colour of these. a. saffroncoloured.

sag, v.i. sink unevenly under pressure; hang sideways or show downward curve in middle. n. state of sagging.

sa′ga (sah-), n. medieval tale of Scandinavian heroes.

saga′cious (-shus), a. having or showing insight and practical wisdom. **saga′city**, n.

sage¹, n. kitchen herb with dull greyish-green leaves.

sage², a. wise, judicious, experienced. n. person credited with profound wisdom.

sa′go, n. (pl. -os), starch prepared from palm-pith and used in puddings, &c.

sah′ib (sah-), n. (fem. *mĕm′sahib*), Englishman or European in India as spoken of or to by natives; also used as a title affixed to the name or office of a European; occasionally used as a specific title among Hindus and Mussulmans (*Khan Sahib, Tipu Sahib*).

said, p.t. & p.p. of say.

sail, n. piece of canvas extended on rigging to catch wind and propel vessel; (collect., with number) ships; wind-catching apparatus attached to arm of a windmill; spell of sailing. v.i. & t. progress by use of sail;

start on voyage; navigate ship; traverse sea; go with flight or gait comparable to motion of sailing-ship. **sail′er**, n. ship of specified sailing-power.

sail′or, n. seaman or mariner. ~ing, n. sailor's life.

sain′foin, n. a fodder-plant.

saint, n. canonized person (for use as pref., abbr. *St.*, see **St.**); one of the blessed dead or other of the company of heaven; saintlike person. **sain′ted**, a. canonized or deserving to be so; hallowed. **saint′hood** (-t-h-), n. **saint′like**, ~ly, aa. very free from human weaknesses.

sake, n. used chiefly in phr. *for the ~ of, for ~'s or my* &c. ~, out of consideration for; in the interest of; because of; owing to.

sa′kia (sah-), n. Eastern waterwheel for irrigation.

sal (sahl), **saul**, n. valuable Indian timber (tree).

salaam′ (-lahm), n. Oriental salutation 'Peace'; Indian obeisance. v.i. make salaam.

sa′lable, a. fit for sale; finding purchasers. ~bility, n.

sala′cious (-shus), a. lustful, lecherous. **sala′city**, n.

sal′ad, n. vegetables prepared as food without cooking. ~oil, refined olive-oil.

sal′amander, n. lizard-like animal supposed to live in fire; elemental spirit of fire; cook's implement for scorching things brown.

sala′mé (-lah-), n. Italian sausage highly salted.

sal′ary, n. fixed periodical payment made to person for his services. **sal′aried** (-rid), a.

sale, n. buying-and-selling transaction; public auction; disposal of stock at low prices. ~s′man, ~s′woman, shop assistant; middleman between producer and retailer. ~s′manship, skill in finding customers.

*salerā′tus, n. impure potassium or sodium bicarbonate as ingredient in baking-powder.

săl'ic, Salique' (-ēk), a. ~ law, law excluding females from dynastic succession.

sălicyl'ic, a. made from or involving the use of salicylic acid. ~ acid, an antiseptic and antirheumatic substance.

sā'lient, a. prominent, conspicuous; standing out; (of angles) pointing outwards. n. a salient angle; a bulge in a line of trenches. **sā'lience,** n.

sā'line, a. impregnated with salt(s); like salt. n. solution of salt and water. **salin'ity,** n.

sali'va, n. the liquid of the mouth. **săl'ivary,** a. of or producing saliva.

săll'ow¹ (-ō), n. low-growing kinds of willow.

săll'ow² (-ō), a. of sickly yellow or pale brown. v.i. & t. grow or make sallow.

săll'y, n. rush of besieged upon besiegers, sortie; a piece of banter. v.i. make military sally; go for a walk or expedition. ~port, opening in fortifications provided for making of sallies.

Săll'y Lŭnn, n. kind of tea-cake.

sălmagŭn'di, n. highly seasoned dish of chopped meat, anchovies, eggs, &c.; a medley.

săl'mi (-ē), n. ragout, esp. of game-birds.

salmon (săm'on), n. silver-scaled fish with orange-pink flesh. a. salmon-coloured. ~colour, orange pink. ~ trout, fish resembling salmon.

‖ salon (săl'awn), n. reception-room or reception of great lady.

saloon', n. large room fit for assemblies, &c.; large cabin for ship's passengers; railway carriage without compartments; public room or gallery for specified use: *drinking-bar.

sălpiglŏss'is, n. a garden flower allied to petunia.

săl'sify, n. plant with fleshy root cooked as vegetable.

salt (sawlt), n. substance obtained from sea-water by evaporation or from the earth by mining or pumping, and used as seasoning or preservative of food; sodium chloride; (fig.) the élite of; wit; experienced sailor; (Chem.) compound of basic and acid radicals. a. containing, tasting of, or treated with salt; bitter, pungent. v.t. preserve or season or treat with salt. ~cellar, vessel holding salt for table use. ~pan, hollow near sea, or vessel, used in getting salt by evaporation.

sălta'tion, n. leaping, dancing; sudden transition. **săltă'tory,** a.

săl'tīre, n. a St. Andrew's cross (X) dividing a shield, &c. into four compartments.

saltpetre (sawltpē'ter), n. substance used in making gunpowder, &c.; potassium nitrate.

salu'brious (-lōō-), a. healthgiving. **salu'brity** (-lōō-), n.

Salu'ki (-ōōġi), n. breed of dog, Arabian gazelle-hound.

săl'utary, a. wholesome in operation; resulting in good.

salute' (-ōōt), n. gesture of respect, esp. at meeting or parting; (Mil. Naut.) prescribed movement or use of flags or discharge of guns in sign of respect; (joc.) a kiss. v.t. make salute or salutation to; greet; kiss. **sălūtā'tion,** n. act of, words used in, saluting.

săl'vage, n. rescue of property from loss at sea or by fire; payment made for its rescue. v.t. rescue thus; *(army sl.) appropriate for one's own use.

săl'varsăn, n. drug used esp. in syphilis. **P.**

sălvā'tion, n. fact or state of being saved from sin and its consequences. **S~ Army,** religious organization based on a military model. ~ist, member of Salvation Army; revivalist.

salve (sălv), n. healing ointment; something that soothes. v.t. (-vable), anoint; smooth over or palliate; soothe; harmonize.

săl'ver, n. tray for handing refreshments, &c.

săl'vō¹, n. (pl. -os), a reservation or proviso.

săl'vō², n. (pl. -oes), simultaneous

discharge of guns as salute, or in battle ; round of applause.

săl volăt'ĭlē, *n.* solution of ammonium carbonate, used as restorative in fainting, &c.

săl'vor, *n.* person or ship effecting salvage.

Săm, *n.* In phr. *stand* ~, bear the expense. ~ Browne, army officer's belt and straps.

săm'bō, *n.* half-breed, esp. of negro and Indian parents ; *(S-),* name used in speaking of or to any male negro.

săm'būr, *n.* Indian elk ; often applied to soft leather produced from its hide.

săme, *a.* uniform ; unvarying ; unchanged ; identical ; aforesaid ; previously referred to.

Sā'mian, *a.* & *n.* (native) of Samos. ~ ware, fine pottery found on Roman sites.

săm'ĭte, *n.* rich medieval dress-fabric of silk.

săm'lĕt, *n.* young salmon.

Sămm'ў¹, *n.* (S.-Afr.) Indian who washes clothes.

Sămm'ў², *n.* (Anglo-Ind. army sl.) a Hindu idol (corruption of *swamy).* ~house, idol-temple.

sámová̇r', *n.* Russian tea-urn.

Săm'oyĕd (-oy-), *n.* light-coloured Arctic sledge-dog.

*sămp, *n.* (porridge of) coarsely-ground Indian meal.

săm'păn, *n.* any small boat of Chinese pattern ; *an eight-foot punt.

săm'phĭre, *n.* cliff plant used in pickles.

sa'mple (sah-), *n.* small part taken from a quantity to give an idea of the whole ; specimen or pattern. *v.t.* take samples of ; try the qualities of.

sa'mpler (sah-), *n.* girl's piece of embroidery.

săm'sonite, *n.* an explosive.

săm'urai (-ōōrī), *n.* member of military caste in old Japan ; army officer in modern Japan.

sănăto'rium, *n.* (pl. *-ia),* establishment for treatment of invalids ; place resorted to for its climate.

săn'ative, ~tory, *aa.* tending to health, curative.

sănc'tĭfў, *v.t.* (*-iable).* consecrate, make holy ; purify from sin. ~fication, *n.* sănctĭmō'nious, *a.* making a show of piety. sănc'timony, *n.* sanctimoniousness.

sănc'tion, *n.* penalty or reward attached to a law ; influence that causes a rule to be observed ; authoritative permission. *v.t.* attach or give sanction to ; authorize or countenance (action).

sănc'tity, *n.* saintliness : sacredness or inviolability.

sănc'tŭarў, *n.* place recognized as holy or inviolable ; church or holiest part of it ; private retreat ; place of protection.

sănc'tum, *n.* holy place ; person's private room.

sănc'tus, *n.* the hymn 'Holy, holy, holy' in the Communion.

sănd, *n.* powder produced by the wearing down of flint, &c. ; (pl.) expanse of it. *v.t.* sprinkle or mix with sand. ~bag, *n.* bag filled with sand for use in fortification or as weapon ; *v.t.* & *i.* fortify with, fill and place, sandbags ; hit (person) with sandbag. ~glass, reversible glass with sand, used in measuring time. ~martin, kind nesting in sandy banks. ~paper, *n.* roughened paper for smoothing wood, &c. ; *v.t.* rub with this. ~piper, kinds of bird. ~stone, rock of compressed sand.

săn'dal, *n.* sole without uppers attached to the foot by thongs.

săn'dalled (-ld), *a.*

săn'dalwŏŏd, *n.* kinds of scented wood.

sănd'-blind, *a.* dim-sighted.

sănd'wĭch, *n.* two slices of bread with meat or other relish between. *v.t.* insert (thing, statement, &c.) between others of a different kind. ~board, pair of boards with advertisements carried by ~man.

sănd'ў, *a.* abounding in sand ; yellowish-red (of hair).

---

sāne, *a.* of sound mind; not mad; (of views) moderate, sensible.

sang, *p.t.* of sing.

săng'a, -ar (-ngg-), *n.* breastwork of stones in Indian hill-fighting.

sang-froid (sahnfrwah'), *n.* coolness in danger or difficulty.

săng'uinary (-nggwi-), *a.* attended by or delighting in bloodshed.

săng'uine (-nggwin), *a.* habitually hopeful; optimistic; bright and florid; blood-red.

sanguin'eous (-nggwi-), *a.* of blood; of full-blooded temperament; blood-coloured.

săn'hedrim (-ni-), *n.* supreme council and court of justice in ancient Jerusalem.

săn'itary, *a.* of the conditions that affect health, esp. with regard to dirt and infection. **sănitā'tion**, *n.* improving of sanitary conditions.

săn'ity, *n.* saneness.

sank, *p.t.* of sink.

sāns (-z), *prep.* (arch.) without. **~culótte'**, *n.* republican of lower classes in French Revolution. **~sê'rif**, *a.* without serifs.

Săn'skrit, -crit, *n.* the ancient and sacred language of India.

Saorstat Eireann (sayors'tath âr'an), *n.* the Irish Free State.

săp[1], *n.* the vital juice of plants; (fig.) vitality. *v.t.* drain of sap; exhaust the vigour of. ***~head**, foolish person. **~less**, *a.* (esp.) effete. **~ling**, *n.* young tree. **săpp'y**, *a.* full of sap.

săp[2], *n.* digging of siege-trenches; covered siege-trench; (sl.) studious or hardworking person. *v.t. & i.* approach (place) by sap; dig siege-trenches; undermine (wall, &c.); destroy (faith, &c.) insidiously; (sl.) work hard at books, &c. **săpp'er**, *n.* (esp.) private of the Royal Engineers.

săp'an-wood, -pp-, *n.* wood yielding red or yellow dye from tropical Asia.

săp'id, *a.* savoury; not tasteless; not insipid. **sapid'ity**, *n.*

sā'pience (*or* săp-), *n.* wisdom; knowledge. **sā'pient** (*or* săp-), *a.* aping wisdom; would-be wise.

săponā'ceous (-shus), *a.* soapy.

Sapphic (săf'ik), *a. & n.* of Sappho (Lesbian poetess). **~ stanza, ~ verse**, in Greek metres used by Sappho.

sapphire (săf'īr), *n.* a transparent blue precious stone; its colour, azure. *a.* of sapphire blue.

săp'rophyte, *n.* plant living on decayed vegetable matter.

să'raband, *n.* a slow Spanish dance.

Să'racen, *n.* Arab or Moslem of time of crusades. **Săracĕn'ic**, *a.* (esp.) of Moslem architecture.

Sărato'ga, *n.* lady's large travelling trunk.

săr'casm, *n.* a taunt; bitter or wounding remark. **sarcăs'tic**, *a.*

sărcoph'agus, *n.* (pl. *-gī*), stone coffin.

sărd, *n.* a variety of cornelian.

săr'dine[1], *n.* (Bibl.) sard.

sărdine'[2] (-ēn), *n.* small fish of herring kind usu. tinned in oil.

sardŏn'ic, *a.* grimly jocular; full of bitter mockery.

sard'onyx, *n.* onyx in which layers alternate with sard.

săr'ee, sar'ī (-ah-), *n.* Indian lady's mantle or robe, drawn about the head and body; the material of which this is composed.

sargăss'ō, *n.* (pl. *-os*), kinds of floating sea-weed.

sărong', *n.* kind of tartan skirt worn by Malays and Javanese.

sărsaparill'a, *n.* kinds of smilax; drug made from their roots.

săs'enét, săr'c- (-sn-), *n.* soft silk fabric used in lining.

sartôr'ial, *a.* of tailors or clothes.

săsh[1], *n.* scarf worn baldric-wise as part of uniform or round waist as ornament.

săsh[2], *n.* frame holding windowglass, usu. made to slide up and down in grooves.

săss'afras, *n.* N.-Amer. tree with medicinal bark.

Săssenach (-*ch* soft guttural), *n. & a.* (Sc.) English(man).

sat, *p.t.* of sit.

Sā'tan, personal name for the Devil. **satăn'ic**, *a.* diabolical.

sătch'el, *n.* small bag of leather, &c. ; a school-bag.

sāte, *v.t.* (*-table*), gratify to the full ; cloy, surfeit.

sateen', *n.* glossy cotton or woollen fabric.

săt'ellite, *n.* hanger-on, dependant ; (Astron.) heavenly body revolving round another.

satiate (sāsh'iāt), *v.t.* sate.

sati'ety, *n.* glutted state ; feeling of having had too much.

săt'in, *n.* silk fabric with glossy surface on one side. ~ět, ~ětte', *nn.* satin-like fabric partly or wholly of cotton or wool. săt'iny, *a.*

săt'inwood, *n.* choice wood of tropical tree.

săt'ire, *n.* composition in which vice or folly is held up to ridicule ; use of ridicule, sarcasm, or irony to expose folly. sati'ric, *a.* of or containing satire. ~al, *a.* satiric ; given to the use of satire. săt'irist, *n.* writer of satires ; satirical person. săt'irize, *v.t.* (*-zable*), assail with satire.

sătisfăc'tion, *n.* satisfying or being satisfied ; thing that satisfies desire or gratifies feeling ; payment of debt ; atonement ; amends for injury. ~tory, *a.* causing satisfaction ; adequate.

săt'isfy, *v.t.* (*-iable*), meet the wishes of ; content ; be accepted as adequate ; pay, fulfil, comply with ; still the cravings of ; convince ; be sufficient.

săt'răp, *n.* ancient-Persian provincial governor ; modern subordinate ruler (with implication of tyranny or luxury).

săt'ūrāte, *v.t.* (*-rable*), fill with moisture, soak, steep ; imbue with or steep in learning, traditions, &c. sătūrā'tion, *n.*

Săt'urday (*-erdi*), *n.* seventh day of the week.

Săt'urn, *n.* Roman god of agriculture ; a planet.

săturnā'lia (*-ter-*), *n.pl.* Roman festival of Saturn (*S-*) ; scene or time of wild revelry. ~n, *a.*

Satūr'nian, *a.* of Saturn. ~ verse, a native Roman metre.

săt'urnine (*-ter-*), *a.* of or indicating a sluggish gloomy temperament.

săt'yr (*-er*), *n.* one of the half-human half-bestial woodland beings in the train of Bacchus ; beastly-minded man.

sauce, *n.* liquid added to food to give relish ; *compote of fruit ; (colloq.) sauciness. *v.t.* add sauce to ; (fig.) make piquant ; (colloq.) speak saucily to. ~pan (*-an*), cooking-pot with lid and handle.

sau'cer, *n.* curved plate placed under cup, flower-pot, &c., to intercept spillings, &c.

sau'cy, *a.* impudent, cheeky ; (sl.) smart-looking.

saun'ter, *v.i.* walk in leisurely way. *n.* leisurely gait.

saur'ian, *n.* member of the order including lizards, crocodiles, &c.

sau'sage (sŏs-), *n.* minced meat enclosed in case of thin membrane ; (army sl.) kite-balloon.

Sauterne (sōtẽrn'), *n.* a white wine.

săv'age, *a.* uncivilized ; in primitive state ; fierce, cruel ; (colloq.) angry. *n.* member of savage tribe ; brutal or barbarous person. *v.t.* (of horse, &c.) attack and bite or trample (person). **săv'agery** (*-ij-*), *n.* savage conduct or state.

savănn'ah, *n.* grassy plain in (sub)tropical regions of America.

savant (săv'ahn), *n.* man of learning, esp. distinguished scientist.

sāve, *v.t. & i.* (*-vable*), rescue or preserve from danger or harm ; effect the spiritual salvation of ; keep for future use ; lay (money) by ; reduce requisite amount of ; (Football, &c.) avert a threatened score. *n.* act of saving in football, &c. *prep.* except, but. *conj.* but. sā'ving, *a.* (esp.) making a reservation or exception ; redeeming ; *n.* (esp.) something saved ; (pl.) amount of money put by. sā'vings-bank, institution receiving small deposits.

săv'eloy, *n.* highly seasoned dried sausage.

---

ah, awl, **oil,** boor, **cow,** dowry ; **chin,** go, **bang,** so, **ship,** thin ; **dh,** as *th*(e) ;

să'viour (-vyer), *n.* deliverer, redeemer; saver from ruin, &c.

savoir faire (săv'wär făr), *n.* quickness to see and do the right thing; address, tact.

să'vory, *n.* aromatic kitchen herb.

să'vour (-vor), *n.* characteristic taste or smell; admixture or suggestion of some quality. *v.i. & t.* smack or suggest the presence of. **să'voury** (-vorı), *a.* with appetizing taste or smell; *n.* dish of the savoury kind at beginning or end of dinner.

savoy', *n.* kind of cabbage.

Savoy'ard (-oi-), *n.* native of Savoy.

saw¹, *p.t.* of **see**.²

saw², *n.* old saying, maxim.

saw³, *n.* implement with toothed edge for cutting wood, &c. *v.t. & i.* (*p.p.* **sawn**, **sawed**), cut or make with saw; make to and-fro motion like hand-saw. **~bones**, (sl.) surgeon. ***~buck**, saw-horse. **~dust**, fine wood-fragments produced in sawing. **~fish**, kind armed with toothed snout. **~horse**, rack supporting wood for sawing. **~mill**, mill driven by steam, &c. for mechanical sawing. **~pit**, pit in which lower of two men working two-handed saw stands. **saw'yer**, *n.* workman who saws timber; *uprooted tree floating or stranded in river; name of a New Zealand beetle.

săxe, *n.* a shade of dull blue.

săx'horn, *n.* instrument of trumpet class.

săx'ifrage, *n.* kinds of Alpine or rock plant.

Săx'on, *n.* member, language, of a Teutonic people by whom parts of England were occupied in 5th-6th cc.; native of Saxony; Anglo-Saxon. *a.* of the Saxons; in Saxon.

săx'ony, *n.* a fine wool or cloth made of it.

săx'ophone, *n.* powerful keyed brass reed instrument with large inverted bell.

say, *v.t. & i.* (**said** pr. sĕd), utter or recite in speaking voice; state;

speak, tell, express; adduce or plead; repeat, rehearse. *n.* what one has to say; share in decision. **say'ing**, *n.* (esp.) common remark, maxim.

‖ **sa'yer** (-ah-), *n.* in India, a general name for imposts of the nature of transit and excise duties.

scăb, *n.* crust formed over sore in healing; kinds of skin-disease and plant-disease; blackleg. **scăbb'y**, *a.*

scăbb'ard, *n.* sheath of sword, bayonet, dagger, &c.

scă'bies (-z), *n.* the itch.

scă'bious, *n.* kinds of wild and garden flower.

scă'brous, *a.* rough-surfaced; (of subject, situation, &c.) hard to handle with decency.

scăff'old, *n.* temporary platform supported on poles for use of builders; platform on which criminal is executed. **~ing**, *n.* structure of poles and planks providing builders with platforms; timber for it.

scagliola (skălyō'la), *n.* Italian plasterwork imitating stone.

scald (-aw-), *v.t.* injure or pain (skin, person, &c.) with hot liquid; rinse with boiling water; heat (milk) to near boiling-point. *n.* injury to skin by scalding.

scale¹, *n.* one of the thin horny overlapping plates protecting the skin of fishes, reptiles, &c.; thin plate or flake; scab; (without *a* or pl.) tartar on teeth. *v.t. & i.* (-lable), remove scales or scale from; (of skin, &c.) form or come off in scales. **scă'ly**, *a.*

scale², *n.* pan of weighing-balance; (pl.) a balance or weighing instrument. *v.t.* (of thing weighed) show specified weight.

scale³, *n.* series of degrees; graded system; set of sounds belonging to a musical key arranged in order of pitch; relative dimensions (of plan, map, &c.); an instrument for use in measuring, &c. *v.t.* (-lable), climb with ladder or otherwise.

---

scalēne′, *a.* unequal-sided.

scăll′ion (-lyon), *n.* Welsh onion.

scăll′op, scŏ–, *n.* bivalve shell-fish with shallow shells edged with small semicircular lobes; (pl.) edging imitating scallop-edge. *v.t.* cut in scallops. **~ing,** *n.* scallop-edging.

scăll′ywăg, *n.* (sl.) scamp; scapegrace; *native white in southern States accepting reconstruction measures after the Civil War.

scălp, *n.* skin and hair of the upper part of the head; this torn off as trophy by Red-Ind. victor. *v.t.* take scalp of; criticize savagely; *(sl.) make small quick profit by speculating in tickets, &c.

scăl′pel, *n.* light surgical knife.

scăl′per, scau′per (-aw-), *n.* gouge used by engravers.

scămm′ony, *n.* a purgative resin.

scămp, *n.* rascal, good-for-nothing. *v.t.* do (work) negligently.

scăm′per, *v.i.* run like frightened animal or playing child; take a scamper through. *n.* scampering run; gallop on horseback; rapid tour or course of reading.

scăn, *v.t. & i.* test metre (of line, &c.) by examining feet, &c.; (of line, &c.) be metrically correct; scrutinize closely (horizon, face, &c.).

scăn′dal, *n.* general feeling that something is an outrage; what causes such feeling; malicious gossip. **~ize,** *v.t.* shock. **~ous,** *a.* outrageous; causing or given to scandal; shameful.

Scăndinā′vian, *a.* of the region including Denmark, Sweden, Norway, and Iceland. *n.* the S. family of languages; a S. native.

scăn′dium, *n.* an element found in the Scandinavian yttrium metals.

scăn′sion (-shn), *n.* metrical scanning.

scăn′sŏr′ial, *a.* (of birds, &c.) climbing; adapted for climbing.

scănt, *a.* barely or not sufficient. *v.t.* stint (food, &c.).

scănt′ling, *n.* small beam, esp. one under 5 in. square; size to

which stone or timber is to be cut; modicum, small amount.

scăn′ty, *a.* barely sufficient; of small amount or extent.

scāpe, *n.* shaft of column; long leafless flower-stalk springing from root.

scāpe′goat, *n.* person bearing blame due to others.

scāpe′grāce, *n.* rascal; ne'er-do-well (often playfully of child).

scăp′ūla, *n.* (pl. *-lae*), the shoulder-blade. **scăp′ūlar,** *a.* of the scapula; *n.* kinds of monastic vestment; bandage for shoulder-blade.

scär¹, *n.* mark left on the skin, &c. by a wound, &c. *v.t. & i.* mark with scar; form into a scar.

scär², scaur (-ōr), *n.* precipitous craggy part of mountain side.

scă′rab, *n.* ancient gem cut in the form of a beetle.

scă′ramouch, *n.* buffoon, boastful coward; idler, scamp.

scārce, *a.* not plentiful; rare; hard to find. *adv.* scarcely. **~ness,** *n.* (esp.) rarity.

scārce′ly, *adv.* hardly, only just; surely not.

scār′city, *n.* insufficiency; prevailing want of food; dearth.

scāre, *v.t.* (*-rable*), strike with sudden terror; startle and frighten. *n.* unreasoning terror; commercial panic. **~crow,** figure set in field, &c. to scare birds; badly dressed or grotesque-looking person.

scärf¹, *n.* a joint uniting two pieces of timber endwise. *v.t.* join with scarf.

scärf², *n.* (pl. *-ves, -fs*), long strip of material worn round neck, over shoulders, or from shoulder to opposite hip; necktie. **~pin,** **~ring,** ornamental fastenings for necktie. **~skin,** outer layer of the skin, epidermis.

scā′rify (*-sli*), (Surg.) make slight incisions in; scratch skin or surface of all over; (fig.) criticize mercilessly; loosen surface of soil. **~fication,** *n.*

scärlati′na (-tē-), *n.* scarlet fever.

scar'let, n. brilliant red colour; scarlet cloth or clothes. a. of this colour. ~ fever, infectious fever with scarlet rash. ~runner, scarlet-flowered climbing bean.

scarp, n. steep slope, esp. the inner side of the ditch in fortification. v.t. make steep or perpendicular.

scathe (-dh), n. harm suffered. v.t. injure by blasting or withering up. ~less, a. unharmed.

scat'ter, v.t. & i. throw or put here and there; sprinkle; disseminate; disperse; flee or make flee in all directions.

scav'enger (-j-), n. person employed to remove refuse from the streets; animal feeding on carrion. ~ging, scavenger's work.

|| **scenā'riō** (shä-), n. (pl. -os), table of scenes, &c. in play or opera or cinema play.

scēne, n. theatre-stage, arena for display (now only fig.); place of actual or fictitious occurrence; piece of continuous action that forms part of a play; agitated colloquy, esp. with display of temper; hangings and woodwork used in dressing up a stage; landscape or view. scē'nery, n. stage scenes; the natural features of a district. scē'nic, a. of or on the stage; picturesque.

scent, v.t. discern by smell; make fragrant or rank; apply perfume to; sniff to detect the odour of. n. characteristic odour of something; fragrance; smell left by an animal enabling hounds to track it; (Hare and Hounds) paper laid to guide runners; sense of smell.

scep'tic (sk-), n. person who questions the truth of religious doctrines; person indisposed to accept as true the received opinion on any particular subject. ~al, a.; scep'ticism (sk-), n.

scep'tre (-ter), n. rod symbolizing sovereignty. scep'tred (-terd), a.

sched'ule (sh-, *skē-), n. table of details or items. v.t. (-lable), make schedule of; include in schedule.

schēme (sk-), n. systematic arrangement proposed or in operation; outline, syllabus; plan of action; artful design. v.i. & t. make plans; intrigue. schē'mer (sk-), n. contriver; plotter.

schipp'erkē (sk-, sh-), n. kind of lapdog.

schi'sm (si-), n. a separation or division in a Church; offence of causing such separation. schismăt'ic (siz-), a. tending to or guilty of schism; n. schismatic person. ~al, a.

schist (sh-), n. crystalline rock whose components are arranged in layers. schis'tōse (sh-), a. schist-like, laminated.

schnapp(s (shn-), n. a spirit resembling Holland gin.

schŏl'ar (sk-), n. child at elementary school; learned person; student receiving assistance from university or other funds after a competitive examination. ~ly, a. erudite; of, or as of, a learned man. ~ship, erudition; position of a scholar (last sense).

scholăs'tic (sk-), a. of schools or education; academic or pedantic; dealing in logical subtleties. scholăs'ticism (sk-), n.

schō'liăst (sk-), n. writer of scholia. **schō'lium** (sk-), n. (pl. -ia), ancient grammarian's marginal note on passage or word in classical author.

school[1] (sk-), n. shoal of fish.

school[2] (sk-), n. institution for giving instruction to the young; its buildings; its pupils; lesson-time; group of thinkers or artists with common inspiration or characteristics. v.t. discipline, bring under control; train or accustom to; tutor. ~boy, ~girl, boy or girl still at school. ~fellow, member, past or present, of same school. ~house, head master's boarding-house as opposed to others. ~ma'am, schoolmistress. ~man (-an), theologian dealing with doctrine by the rules of Aristotelian logic. ~master, ~mistress, head or assistant master or mistress in school.

schōon´er (sk-), *n.* fore-and-aft rigged ship.

schottische (shŏtēsh´), *n.* kind of polka.

sciág´raphy (sī-), skī-, *n.* art of shading in drawing, &c.; photography by Röntgen rays (usu. sk-). **sci´agram**, *n.* Röntgen-ray picture.

sciăt´ic, *a.* of the hip; of having sciatica. **sciăt´ica**, *n.* neuralgia of hip and thigh.

sci´ence, *n.* systematic and formulated knowledge; any branch of such knowledge; the physical or natural sciences as a whole; trained skill in boxing, games, &c. **scientif´ic**, *a.* according to the principles of science; of or concerned with science or the sciences; having or requiring trained skill. **sci´entist**, *n.* person learned in one or more of the natural sciences.

|| **sci´licet**, *adv.* (abbrev. *sc.*, *scil.*) that is to say.

scim´etar, -**itar**, *n.* short curved Oriental sword.

scintill´a, *n.* shred or atom.

scin´tillate, *v.i.* sparkle, twinkle; emit sparks. **scintilla´tion**, *n.*

sci´olism, *n.* assumption of knowledge; conceit based on fancied wisdom. **sci´olist**, *n.*

sci´on, *n.* shoot cut for grafting; young member of family.

sciss´ors (-zorz), *n.pl.* cutting implement of pair of blades.

sclerŏt´ic, *a.* hard, firm. *n.* hard opaque coating of eye outside iris forming the white of the eye.

scŏff¹, *v.i.* speak derisively of; mock or jeer *at*. *n.* mocking words; taunt. **scŏff´er**, *n.* (esp.) person who jibes at religion.

scōld, *v.i. & t.* find fault noisily; rail; rate or rebuke. *n.* railing or nagging woman. **~ing**, *n.* a rebuke or rating.

sconce¹, *n.* bracket-candlestick.

sconce², *n.* (colloq.) the head.

sconce³, *n.* fort or earthwork.

sconce⁴, *v.t.* (-ceable). inflict forfeit

for offence against table etiquette. *n.* such forfeit.

scōn(e) (or -ŏn), *n.* soft cake of barley-meal or wheat-flour.

scoop, *n.* short-handled deep shovel for grain, flour, specie, &c.; gouge-like instrument; coal-scuttle; (sl.) exclusive piece of news. *v.t.* lift, hollow, make, with a scoop.

scoot, *v.i.* (sl.) dart, shoot along; make off. **scoot´er**, *n.* child's scooting toy; machine worked by motor as substitute for bicycle.

scope, *n.* outlook; sphere of observation or action; extent to which person or thing may or can range; outlet, vent.

scorbū´tic, *a.* of or affected with scurvy. *n.* scorbutic person.

scorch, *v.t. & i.* burn surface of so as to discolour or injure or pain; become so discoloured; (of motorist or cyclist) go at unreasonably high speed. **~er**, *n.* (sl.) fine specimen of its kind.

score, *n.* notch cut; line cut or scratched or drawn; reckoning; number of points made by player or side in game; detailed table of these; (Mus.) copy of concerted piece. *v.t. & i.* (-*rable*). mark with incisions or lines; slash, furrow; enter item to customer; record (runs, &c.) in game score; make or be credited with so many at cricket, &c.; (Mus.) write out score; secure an advantage. **scōr´er**, *n.* (esp.) keeper of score at cricket, &c.

scōr´ia, *n.* (pl. -*iae*). slag; (pl.) clinker-like masses of lava.

scorn, *n.* disdain, contempt, derision; object of contempt. *v.t.* hold in contempt; abstain from, refuse to do, as unworthy. **~ful**, *a.* contemptuous.

scōrp´ion, *n.* lobster-like arachnid with jointed stinging tail.

scŏt¹, *n.* (hist.) tax or rate. **~free**, *a.* exempt from payment; unharmed or unpunished.

Scŏt², *n.* native of Scotland.

scŏtch¹, *v.t.* (arch.) disable or wound; prevent (wheel, barrel) from moving downhill by means of wedge, &c. *n.* line marked on ground in hop-scotch; wedge used to scotch wheel, &c.

Scotch², *a.* of Scotland or its inhabitants. *n.* the form of English spoken in the Scottish Lowlands. Scots, Scottish, *a. & n.* Scotch. (The Scotch usually prefer *Scottish* or *Scots* (*Scotsman*, *~woman*), but the English rarely use these forms except in official contexts). **Scott'icism**, *n.* Scotch phrase, &c.

scoun'drel, *n.* wicked unscrupulous person; villain. **~ism**, *n.*

scour¹ (-owr), *v.t.* rub bright or clean; rub out; clear out. *n.* act or process of scouring.

scour² (-owr), *v.i. & t.* rove, range; go along hastily, esp. in search or pursuit.

scourge (skĕrj), *n.* (arch.) whip for chastising persons; person or thing regarded as instrument or manifestation of divine wrath. *v.t.* chastise; afflict.

scout¹, *n.* man sent out to reconnoitre; boy scout (see boy); ship designed for reconnoitring; small fast single-seat aeroplane. *v.i.* go out or act as scout. **~master**, officer directing scouts or boy scouts.

scout², *v.t.* reject with scorn.

scout³, *n.* a college-servant at Oxford.

scow, *n.* flat-bottomed boat.

scowl, *v.i.* wear sullen look; frown. *n.* scowling aspect.

scrab'ble, *v.i.* scrawl; scratch or grope or scramble about.

scrag, *n.* skinny person or animal; inferior part of neck of mutton; (sl.) neck. *v.t.* garotte; throttle. **scrāg'g'y**, *a.* thin and bony.

scram'ble, *v.i. & t.* make way by clambering, &c.; struggle with competitors to secure a share of something. *n.* climb or rough walk; eager struggle for share of something.

scran, *n.* (sl.) food, victuals.

scrap, *n.* small detached piece; shred or fragment; (pl.) odds and

ends, leavings; picture or passage cut from newspaper; (sl.) quarrel, fight. *v.t. & i.* discard as past use; break up; (sl.) quarrel or fight. **~book**, book in which cuttings, &c. are kept.

scrape, *v.t. & i.* (-*pable*), level, polish, clean, graze, or abrade with scraping implement; erase; draw along with grating or vibration, play fiddle, &c. thus; move one's feet noisily on the floor; make a clumsy bow; be parsimonious; get or amass by economy or with difficulty. *n.* act or sound of scraping; awkward predicament. **scra'per**, *n.* (esp.) metal edge outside door for scraping boots on.

scrapp'y, *a.* fragmentary; disconnected; full of fight, pugnacious.

scratch, *v.t. & i.* score or wound slightly with claws or nails or something pointed; rub with the nails to relieve itching; make hole, strike out, mark through, by scratching; erase name of, withdraw, from list of competitors, &c. *n.* wound or mark or sound made by scratching; slight wound or cut; act of scratching oneself; starting-line for race; competitor in handicap receiving no start. *a.* scratched together; impromptu; done at short notice. **scratch'y**, *a.*

scrawl, *v.i. & t.* write in hurried untidy way. *n.* hurried writing.

scrawn'y, *a.* lean, scraggy.

scream, *v.i. & t.* utter piercing cry; laugh uncontrollably; speak or sing with excessive loudness. *n.* piercing cry; paroxysm of laughter; (sl.) ludicrous occurrence. **~** of a bunch, lot of good fellows, (contempt.) good-for-nothings.

scree, *n.* slope covered with loose stones (often in pl.).

screech, *n.* scream of fright or pain or anger. *v.t. & i.* utter screech; say in screeching tone. **~owl**, the barn owl.

screed, *n.* long tiresome letter or passage or harangue.

screen, n. piece of furniture designed to shelter from observation, draughts, or excess of heat or light; partition between nave and choir; sheet for display of lantern pictures; riddle for sorting coal, &c. into sizes. v.t. shelter; hide; protect from detection or penalties; show on cinema screen; sort (coal, &c.) with screens.

screw (-ōō), n. cylinder with spiral ridge called the thread running round it outside (male ~) or inside (female ~); metal male screw with slotted head for holding pieces of wood, &c. together; wooden or other screw as part of appliance for exerting pressure; oblique curling motion; miser or extortioner; (sl.) salary; unsound horse. v.t. & i. fasten or tighten with screw; press hard on, oppress; be miserly; extort out of. ~driver, tool for turning screws by the slot. ~ propeller, shaft with spiral blades projecting from ship's stern and propelling it by revolving. ~ steamer, propelled by screw propellers. **screwed** (-ōōd), a. (sl.) drunk.

scrib'ble, v.i. & t. write hurriedly or carelessly; be an author or writer. n. scrawl, hasty note.

scribe, n. person who can write; (hist.) clerk or secretary; (Bibl.) interpreter of Jewish law.

scrimm'age, scru-, n. tussle, confused struggle, brawl (usu. scri-); (Rugby footb.; usu. scru-; abbr. scrum) mass of all the forwards with ball on ground in the middle. v.i. & t. be engaged in scrimmage.

scrimp, v.t. & i. skimp. ~y, a. scanty, stinted.

scrim'shank, v.i. (Mil. sl.) shirk duty. scrim'shanker, n.

scrip[1], n. (arch.) wallet.

scrip[2], n. provisional certificate of money subscribed to company, &c.; (collect.) such certificates.

script, n. handwriting; type imitating handwriting. scriptō'rium, n. (pl. -ia), writing-room.

scrip'ture, n. the Bible; (attrib.) taken from or relating to Bible; sacred book. scrip'tural (-choo-), a. based on the Bible.

scriv'ener, n. (hist.) drafter of documents; a notary.

scrof'ula, n. constitutional disease with glandular swellings. ~lous, a. affected with scrofula.

scroll, n. roll of parchment or paper; book of the ancient roll form; sculptured ornament imitating roll of parchment.

scro'tum, n. (pl. -ta), the pouch containing the testicles.

scrounge (-j), v.t. (colloq.) appropriate without leave.

scrub[1], v.t. & i. rub hard with something coarse or bristly. n. scrubbing.

scrub[2], n. brushwood, stunted trees; insignificant person; stunted animal or plant. ~by, a.

scruff, n. back of the neck.

scrum. See scrimmage.

scrump'tious (-shŭs), a. first-rate.

scrunch, n. & v.t. & i. crunch.

scru'ple (-ōō-), n. weight-unit of 20 grains; very small quantity; feeling of doubt or hesitation about something. v.t. hesitate owing to scruples. scru'pulous (-ōōp-), a. careful not to offend; conscientious; marked by extreme care. scrupulŏs'ĭty, n.

scru'tātor (-ōō-), n. investigator.

scru'tineer' (-ōō-), n. official conducting scrutiny of votes.

scru'tinize (-ōō-), v.t. (-zable), look closely at; examine critically.

scru'tiny (-ōō-), n. critical gaze; detailed examination; official examination of votes cast in election to test their validity.

scud, v.i. run or fly straight and fast; skim along; (Naut.) run before the wind. n. scudding motion; vapoury driving clouds.

scuf'fle, v.i. struggle confusedly with pushing about, &c. n. piece of scuffling; disorderly fight.

scull, n. one of the small oars of which a pair is worked by rower. v.i. & t. use sculls; propel boat with sculls. scull'er, n. sculling boat; one who sculls.

scŭll'er'y, n. back kitchen in which dishes are washed, &c.

scŭll'ion (-yon), n. dish-washer.

scŭlp'tor ~**'tress,** nn. person, woman, who sculptures.

scŭlp'ture, n. art of forming representations by chiselling, carving, casting, or modelling; a work or works of sculpture. v.t. & i. (-rable), represent in or adorn with or do sculpture. ~ral, a. sculpturesque' (-cherĕsk), a. fit for or suggesting a sculpture.

scŭm, n. impurities that rise to surface of liquid; (fig.) the worst part or offscourings of.

scŭpp'er¹, n. hole in ship's side letting off water from deck.

scŭpp'er², v.t. (sl.) surprise and massacre; sink (ship, crew); do for.

scŭrf, n. flakes on surface of skin; scaly incrustations on metal, &c. **scŭrf'y,** a.

scŭr'rilous, a. grossly or obscenely abusive. **scŭr'ril(e),** a. (arch.) scurrilous. **scŭrril'ity,** n. scurrilous quality; scurrilous talk.

scŭr'ry, v.i. run hurriedly, esp. with short quick steps. n. act or sound of scurrying; bustle.

scŭrv'y, a. paltry, dishonourable, contemptible. n. a disease due to lack of fresh food.

scŭt, n. short tail, esp. of rabbit, hare, or deer.

scŭtch'eon (-chon), n. escutcheon.

scŭtt'er, v.i. run in fussy or startled way.

scŭt'tle¹, n. coal-scuttle; amount of coal that fills a coal-scuttle.

scŭt'tle², n. hole with lid in ship's deck or side or in roof or wall. v.t. make hole in ship, esp. for purpose of sinking.

scŭt'tle³, v.i. scurry; make off; retreat in undignified way. n. hurried gait; act of scuttling.

scythe (-dh), n. mowing and reaping implement swung with both hands. v.t. cut with scythe.

sea, n. expanse of salt water; the ocean; swell of the sea, great billow; vast quantity or expanse of something. ~**board,** coast region. ~**breeze,** breeze at sea; breeze on land from direction of sea. ~**conny,** steersman or quartermaster in a ship manned by lascars. ~**cow,** manatee or other sirenian. ~**dog,** kinds of seal; dogfish; old sailor. ~**faring,** a. occupied in sea voyages; n. such occupation. ~**front,** part of town facing the sea. ~**god,** ~**goddess,** god or goddess supposed to reign over the sea. ~**gull,** a sea bird. ~**horse,** steed of a sea-god's chariot; walrus, hippocampus. ~**kale,** a table vegetable. ~**level,** mean level of sea's surface as used in reckoning heights of hills, &c. and as barometric standard. ~**lion,** kinds of large eared seal. ~**man** (-an), sailor; person expert in navigating ship. ~**mew,** gull. ~**piece,** picture of a scene at sea. ~**plane,** aeroplane constructed for rising from and alighting on water. ~**port,** town with harbour. ~**rover,** pirate. ~**scape,** sea-piece. ~**serpent,** kinds of snake living in sea; an imaginary sea monster. ~**sick,** suffering sickness caused by motion of ship, &c. ~**side,** places or an unspecified place close to sea as residence or resort. ~**urchin,** echinus. ~**weed,** plant growing in sea.

seal¹, n. piece of wax, &c. impressed with device and attached to document, or to envelope or receptacle or door; gem or metal stamp used in making seal; act or gift regarded as ratification of. v.t. affix seal to; stamp or fasten or certify as correct with seal; ratify; close securely or hermetically; stop up; set significant mark on. **sealing-wax,** composition for sealing letters, &c.

seal², n. kinds of amphibious marine animal of which some have valuable fur. v.i. hunt seals. ~**skin,** skin of fur-seals as material for garments, &c.

seam, n. line of junction between two edges, esp. those of two pieces of cloth, &c. turned back and sewn together; line of separation between strata; thin stratum separating thicker ones. *v.t.* join by sewing; mark or score with seams, fissures, wrinkles, &c. ~less, *a.* (esp. of garment) made in one piece.

seam'stress, semp'- (sĕms-), *n.* sewing-woman. seam'y, *a.* marked with or showing seams.

|| séance (sā'ăhns), *n.* a sitting of a society, &c.; a meeting for exhibition or investigation of spiritualistic phenomena.

Seanad Eireann (shăn'adh āir'an), *n.* Upper Chamber of the Irish Free State Legislature.

sear, *v.t.* wither or blast; scorch with hot iron; make callous.

search (sĕr-), *v.t. & i.* look to find something; probe or penetrate into; (*part.*, of scrutiny, &c.) thorough or critical. *n.* act of searching; investigation; quest. ~light, electric arc-light arranged to send concentrated beam in desired direction.

seas'on (-zn), *n.* one of the divisions of the year; proper or fit time; time when something is plentiful or in vogue or active. *v.t. & i.* bring or come into efficient or sound condition by exposure, use, lapse of time, &c.; flavour or make piquant. ~able, *a.* suitable to the season; opportune. ~al, *a.* depending on or varying with the seasons. ~ing, *n.* (esp.) flavouring materials.

seat, *n.* thing made or used for sitting on; chair, &c. on which sitter rests, occupation of this as member of council, committee, &c.; country-house; manner of sitting a horse. *v.t.* make sit; provide sitting accommodation for; place (oneself) in sitting posture; put new seat to; establish in a position. ~sea'ter, *n.* motor-car, aeroplane, &c., with seats for specified number.

sébā'ceous (-shus), *a.* fatty; secreting oily matter.

séc, *a.* (of wine) dry.

sé'cant (*or* sē-), *a.* cutting. *n.* secant line, esp. radius of circle produced through end of arc to meet tangent to other end.

sécateurs (sĕk'ateřz), *n.* pruning-shears.

séco'otine (-ēn), *n.* kind of glue.

sécède', *v.i.* withdraw formally from a Church or other body.

séce'ssion (-shn), *n.* act of seceding. ~ist, *n.* *(esp., hist.)* believer in State's right of secession.

*séck'el, *n.* kind of small juicy pear.

séclude' (-ōod), *v.t.* keep retired or away from company or resort. séclu'sion (-ōozhn), *n.* secluding; secluded place or state.

séc'ond, *a.* next after the first; of subordinate importance or value; inferior. *n.* person who wins second place; second-class honours; supporter chosen by duellist or pugilist to see fair play; the sixtieth part of a minute or of an angular degree; (pl.) goods of second quality, esp. coarse flour. *v.t.* back up, give one's support to; (Mil.; pr. sĭkŏnd') remove (officer) temporarily from his regiment or corps with a view to staff or other extra-regimental employment. ~ division, prison treatment less rigorous than that of ordinary offenders. ~hand, (of clothes, books, furniture, &c.) bought after use by another. ~rate, of inferior quality. ~ sight, faculty enabling the owner to see future or distant occurrences as if present. ~string, person or thing kept in hand as a resource if the one preferred should fail. ~ wind, recovery of one's wind in course of exercise after being out of breath. ~ly, *adv.* in the second place.

séc'ondary, *a.* not primary; of the second rank or kind; supplementary. ~ education, ~ school, for those who have had primary instruction.

sĕc'onder, *n.* person who formally seconds a motion in order that discussion may proceed.

se'crĕcȳ, *n.* keeping of secrets; privacy; concealment.

se'crĕt, *a.* kept from general knowledge or view; unrevealed; confidential; (of place) secluded; (of person) keeping a matter to himself. *n.* a secret matter; privacy.

sĕc'rĕtaire, *n.* escritoire.

secrĕtâr'ial, *a.* pertaining to a secretary. **secrĕtâr'iate**, *n.* secretaryship; body of secretaries.

sĕc'rĕtarȳ, *n.* person employed to deal with correspondence, collect information, and prepare business; minister in charge of a specified State department. **~ bird**, African bird with crest likened to pen stuck behind the ear. **~ship**, *n.*

secrēte', *v.t.* (*-table*), put into place of concealment; (Physiol.) produce by secretion. **~tion**, *n.* act of secreting; (Physiol.) the sorting out by a gland or other organ of some special substance from blood or sap; substance so sorted out. **secrē'torȳ**, *a.* of physiological secretion.

secretive (sē'kri-, sĭkrē'-), *a.* given to making secrets; intentionally uncommunicative.

sĕct, *n.* a party in a Church; any religious denomination; adherents of a school of thought.

sĕctâr'ian, *a.* of or confined to a religious denomination. *n.* bigoted adherent of a sect. **~ism**, *n.* **sĕc'tarȳ**, *n.* sectarian.

sĕc'tion, *n.* severance with the knife; part cut off; one of the parts into which something is divided; (in the colonies and U.S.) one of the areas into which undeveloped land is divided; part of community, &c., having separate interests or characteristics; the cutting of a solid by a plane, the plane figure given by this. **~al**, *a.*

sĕc'tor, *n.* the part of a circle, ellipse, &c. enclosed by two of

its radii and the arc cut off by them; plane figure of this shape; (Mil.) any of the parts into which the space occupied by opposing armies is distributed.

sĕc'ular, *a.* concerned with the affairs of this world; temporal; lasting for ages; occurring once in an age or century. *n.* a layman; one of the secular clergy (parish priests, &c.). **~ism**, *n.* doctrine that the basis of morality should be non-religious. **~ist**, *n.*; **~istic**, *a.*; **sĕculâr'itȳ**, *n.* **~ize**, *v.t.* make secular; make worldly. **~ization**, *n.*

secūre', *a.* untroubled by danger or fear; impregnable; safe. *v.t.* (*-rable*), fortify; confine, fasten, or close securely; obtain; guarantee; make safe.

secūr'itȳ, *n.* secure state of feeling; thing that serves as a guard or guarantee or pledge; certificate of stock, &c.

sēdän', **~ chair**, 17th–18th c. vehicle seated for one and carried by two chairmen on poles; *(sedan)* enclosed automobile seating four or more persons including driver.

sēdäte', *a.* collected, composed; free from agitation; serious.

sĕd'ative, *a.* tending to soothe. *n.* sedative drug.

sĕd'entarȳ, *a.* sitting much; done in a chair. **sēdēr'ûnt**, *n.* sitting of ecclesiastical or other court, or of a company in conversation.

sĕdge, *n.* waterside plants resembling coarse grass, growing in a mass. **sĕdg'ȳ**, *a.*

sēdī'lia (or *-li-*), *n.pl.* stone seats for priests in south wall of chancel, usu. canopied.

sĕd'iment, *n.* matter that settles to bottom of liquid; dregs.

sēdī'tion, *n.* conduct or speech inciting to rebellion. **~ious**, *a.*

sēdūce', *v.t.* (*-cible*), lead astray; induce to commit sin or crime; deprive of chastity. **sēdūc'tion**, *n.* seducing; thing that tends to seduce; attractive quality. **~ive**, *a.* alluring.

sĕd'ŭlous, *a.* persevering, diligent, assiduous; painstaking.

see¹, *n.* diocese of a bishop.

see², *v.i. & t.* (*saw*, *seen*), have or use the power of perceiving with the eye; descry, observe, look at; discern mentally; be a passive spectator of; grant interview to; accompany as escort.

seed, *n.* the germs of flowering plants that are sown for reproduction; a single grain of this; offspring; the germ of some movement or development. *v.i. & t.* go to seed; produce or let fall seed; arrange (draw) so that strongest players do not meet in earlier rounds of tournament. ~**ling**, young plant raised from seed. ~**s'man** (-*an*), dealer in seeds. **seed'y**, *a.* shabby-looking; out of sorts, feeling ill.

see'ing, or ~ **that**, *prep. & conj.* since; inasmuch as.

seek, *v.t. & i.* (*sought* pr. sawt), make search or inquiry for; try to get, ask; resort to for advice or health.

seem, *v.i.* have the air or appearance of being; have the sensation of; be apparently perceived to do or have done. ~**ing**, *a.* ostensible; apparent but perhaps not real. ~**ingly**, *adv.* in appearance at least. ~**ly**, *a.* decorous, becoming.

seen, *p.p.* of **see²**.

seep, *v.i.* ooze out, trickle, percolate. ~**age**, *n.*

seer¹, *n.* one who sees visions; inspired person; prophet.

‖ **seer²**, *n.* an E.-Indian weight, varying in different parts of India from over 3 lb. to 8 oz.; also, a measure of capacity (1 litre, or 1·76 pint).

seer'fish, *n.* an E.-Indian fish of mackerel kind.

seer'hand, *n.* kind of Indian muslin.

seer'sucker, *n.* thin cotton fabric with crapy or slightly puckered surface.

see'saw, *n.* backward-and-forward or up-and-down motion as of a saw; game in which two children sit one at each end of a plank and move each other up and down; vacillation. *v.i.* play at seesaw; move with seesaw motion; vacillate.

seethe (-dh), *v.i. & t.* be agitated or in ebullition; boil.

seg'ment, *n.* part cut off or separable from the other parts of something; part of circle or sphere cut off by straight line or plane intersecting it. ~**al**, *a.*

seg'regate, *v.t.* (-*pable*), take from the rest and set apart for some purpose. **segrega'tion**, *n.*

Seid'litz pow'der (sĕd-), *n.* an aperient.

seigneur (sānyĕr'), **seignior** (sā'nyor), *n.* feudal lord; lord of manor. **seign(i)orage** (sā'nyorij), *n.* duty levied on bullion coined; mining royalty, &c. **seigniory** (sā'nyori), *n.* feudal lordship; a feudal domain. **seignor'ial** (sānyôr-), *a.* of a seigneur.

seine (sān), *n.* large fishing-net.

seise. See **seize**.

seis'in (sēz-), *n.* possession of land by freehold.

seis'mic (sīz-), *a.* of earthquake(s). **seismograph** (sīz'mograff), **seismōm'eter**, ~'**moscope**, *nn.* instruments showing occurrence, force, place, &c., of earthquakes. ~**mŏg'raphy**, ~**mŏl'ogy**, *nn.* recording, study, of seismic phenomena.

seize (sēz), *v.t. & i.* (-*zable*) (Law: usu. spelt *seise*) put in possession of; take possession of by warrant or legal right; confiscate; take or lay hold of forcibly or suddenly; snatch; comprehend quickly or clearly. **seizure** (sē'zher), *n.* seizing or being seized; a stroke of apoplexy, &c.

sĕl'dom, *adv.* rarely; not often.

sēlĕct', *a.* chosen for excellence; picked, choice; exclusive. *v.t.* pick out as best or most suitable. **sēlĕc'tion**, *n.* selecting; what is selected. ~**ive**, *a.*; ~**or**, *n.*

sēlē'nium, *n.* a non-metallic element.

selenog'raphy, *n.* study or mapping of the moon.

self, *n.* (pl. *selves*), person's or thing's own individuality or essence ; one's own nature or state or interests or pleasure ; (Commerc., joc.) myself, yourself, himself, &c.

self- is prefixed to a large number of words which explain themselves ; e.g. *self-taught*, taught by oneself. In the list which follows only such words are given as seem to require further explanation. **self-act'ing**, *a.* automatic. **~asser'tion**, *n.* insistence on one's claims. **~bind'er**, *n.* reaping-machine that binds sheaves as it goes. **~cen'tred**, *a.* preoccupied with one's own personality or affairs. **~col'oured**, *a.* of one colour all over. **~command'**, *n.* power of controlling one's emotions. **~con'scious**, *a.* (esp.) embarrassed or unnatural in behaviour from inability to forget oneself. **~contained'**, *a.* compact or complete in itself ; uncommunicative. **~defence'**, *n.* (esp.) in phr. *in ~defence*, not by way of aggression ; *art of ~defence*, boxing. **~deni'al**, *n.* voluntary abstention from pleasurable things. **~destruc'tion**, *n.* suicide. **~determina'tion**, *n.* free will ; (Pol.) choice of polity or allegiance exercised by a nation. **~deter'mined**, *a.* exercising or effected by free will. **~devo'tion**, *n.* giving up of oneself to a cause, &c. **~esteem'**, *n.* favourable opinion of one's character and abilities. **~ev'ident**, *a.* needing no demonstration. **~examina'tion**, *n.* analysing of one's motives, &c. **~exis'tent**, *a.* not derivative. **~forget'ful**, *a.* unselfish. **~help'**, *n.* practice of fending for oneself. **~import'ant**, *a.* (esp.) pompous. **~indul'gence**, *n.*, **~indul'gent**, *a.* yielding to temptations of pleasure or ease. **~in'terest**, *n.* exclusive regard to one's own advantage. **~love'**, *n.* self-

esteem, self-interest ; selfishness. **~mortifica'tion**, *n.* asceticism. **~possessed'**, *a.* unperturbed, cool. **~preserva'tion**, *n.* instinct impelling living things to go on living and avoid injury. **~reli'ant**, *a.* relying on one's own energies ; ready to take responsibility. **~respect'**, *n.* consciousness of conforming to a worthy standard of conduct and thought. **~restraint'**, *n.* avoidance of excess of any kind. **~right'eous**, *a.* laying stress on one's own virtue. **~sac'rifice**, *n.* postponing of one's interest and desires to others'. **~'same**, *a.* the very same. **~sat'isfied**, *a.* conceited. **~seek'ing**, *a.* & *n.* seeking one's own advantage only. **~sown**, *a.* sprung from chance-dropped seed. **~start'er**, *n.* electric appliance for starting motor without turning crank-handle. **~styled'**, *a.* having taken the name without right. **~suffi'cient**, *a.* presumptuous, forward, bumptious. **~suffi'cing**, *a.* independent. **~will'**, *n.* wilfulness, obstinacy.

sel'fish, *a.* deficient in consideration for others ; actuated by self-interest. **self'less**, *a.* oblivious of self ; incapable of selfishness.

sell, *v.t.* & *i.* (*sōld*), make over or dispose of in exchange for money ; keep stock of for sale ; betray for money or other reward ; (sl.) disappoint, trick, take in.

selt'zer, **~wa'ter** (waw-), *nn.* a mineral water. **~zogène**, *n.* apparatus making aerated waters.

sel'vage, **-vèdge**, *n.* edge of cloth so woven that it cannot unravel. **sel'vaged**, **-vedged**, *a.*

seman'tics, *n.pl.* semasiology.

sem'aphore, *n.* signalling apparatus of post with arms used on railways, &c. ; military signalling by operator's two arms or two flags. *v.i.* & *t.* signal, send, by semaphore.

semasiol'ogy (or -ă-), *n.* branch of philology concerned with meanings.

sĕm'blance, n. outward aspect; superficial appearance.

sē'men, n. generative fluid.

sēmĕs'ter, n. college or university half-year in U.S., Germany, &c.

sĕmi-, *pref.* the half of, partly, little more than, occurring in each half. ~brēve, *n.* whole note or time occupied by it. ~chōrus (-k-), *n.* half or part of a choir; passage performed by it. ~cīrcle, *n.* half of a circle or its circumference. ~cō'lon, the stop (;). ~dĕtăched' (-cht), *a.* (of house) joined to another on one side only. ~fī'nal, *n.* the match or round preceding the final. ~offi'cial (-shl), *a.* coming, but not formally owned as coming, from an official source. ~quā'ver, *n.* half a quaver; note with double-hooked shaft. ~tōne, *n.* interval approximately equal to half a tone on the scale. ~vowĕl, *n.* sound, or letter representing it, that is partly vowel and partly consonant.

sē'minal (*or* sĕ-), *a.* of seed or semen; germinal, reproductive; pregnant with consequences.

sĕm'inary, *n.* place or society or state of things favourable to the production of some quality or class; R.-C. training-school for the priesthood; (now rare) school; *private or endowed school or theological school.

Sĕmĭt'ic, *a.* descended from Shem; Jewish; of the same family of languages as Hebrew. **n.** Semitic languages.

sēmoli'na (-lē-), *n.* hard grains left after bolting of flour.

sĕmpitĕr'nal, *a.* eternal.

sĕmpstress. See seamstress.

sē'nary, *a.* on basis of six.

sĕn'ate, *n.* State council of ancient Rome; modern legislature; upper chamber in some parliaments; governing body of some universities. **sĕn'ator**, *n.* member of senate. **sĕnatō'rial**, *a.*

sĕnd, *v.t.* & *i.* (*sĕnt*), have conveyed, or bid go, to a destination; dispatch messenger or message; propel or cause to move or issue; grant or inflict. ~off, *n.* friendly demonstration at or before person's departure.

sēnĕs'cent, *a.* growing old.

sĕn'ĕschal (-shl), *n.* steward of medieval great house.

sē'nīle, *a.* incident to, or characteristic of, old age. **sĕnil'itȳ**, *n.*

sē'nior, *a.* older in age or standing; of higher degree. **n.** person of advanced age or long service; one's elder or superior in standing. **sēniŏr'itȳ**, *n.*

sĕnn'a, *n.* aperient prepared from cassia.

sĕnn'ĕt, *n.* (hist.) signal on trumpet, &c.

sĕnn'ight (-It), *n.* (arch.) week.

sĕnsā'tion, *n.* perception by means of the senses; stirring of strong common emotion amongst an audience or community; situation, &c. that effects this. ~al, *a.* ~alism, *n.* doctrine that sensation is the only source of knowledge; addiction in writers, &c. to the use of sensation. ~alist, *n.*

sense, *n.* any of the special bodily faculties by which sensation is roused; ability to perceive; (pl.) person's sanity or presence of mind regarded as based on the normal action of the senses (sight, hearing, smell, taste, and touch); practical wisdom; meaning. *v.t.* perceive by sense; *(colloq.)* understand. ~less, *a.* wildly foolish; in a state of unconsciousness.

sĕn'sible, *a.* having or showing good sense; judicious; not unaware or unmindful *of*; perceptible by the senses. ~bility, *n.* capacity to feel; susceptibility to.

sĕn'sitive, *a.* very open to or acutely affected by external impressions; touchy or quick to take offence; responsive to or recording slight changes. ~plant, kind of mimosa drooping at a touch. **sĕnsitiv'itȳ**, *n.* degree of sensitiveness.

sĕn'sitize, *v.t.* (-zable), render sensitive; prepare paper to receive photographic impressions. ~za-tion, n.

sen'sory, sensor'ial, aa. of the senses or sensation or the sensorium. sensor'ium, n. the seat of sensation in the brain.

sen'sual (-sū-, -shōō-), a. depending on the senses only and not the intellect or spirit; self-indulgent, carnal, licentious. ~ist, ~āl'ity, nn. pursuer, pursuit, of fleshly gratification. sen'suous, a. stimulating or operating through the senses; aesthetic.

sent, p.t. & p.p. of send.

sen'tence, n. word or set of words complete in itself; declaration of punishment to be inflicted; such punishment. v.t. state sentence of; declare condemned to.

senten'tious (-shus), a. aphoristic, pithy; affectedly or pompously formal. ~ly, adv.

sen'tient (-shi-), a. that feels or is capable of feeling.

sen'timent, n. a mental feeling; motto, thought expressed in words; tendency to be swayed by feeling; mawkish tenderness. sentimen'tal, a. swayed or dictated by shallow emotion; designed to excite or gratify the softer emotions. ~ist, ~ity, nn.

sen'tinel, sen'try, nn. soldier posted to keep guard; (-try) soldier's watch or duty. sentry-box, cabin for sentry.

sep'al, n. calyx-leaf.

sep'arable, a. capable of being disjoined. ~bility, n.

sep'arate, a. physically disconnected; distinct, individual; of individuals. v.t. & i. (-āt) make separate, sever; come asunder; secede from; go different ways; part company; cease from cohabitation. separā'tion, n. separating; disunion. sep'aratism, sep'aratist, nn. withdrawn, one who withdraws or advocates withdrawal, from political union, religious body, &c. ~ive, a.

se'pia, n. brown pigment made from fluid secreted by cuttle-fish.

se'poy, n. Indian soldier in British-Indian army.

sep'sis, n. septic state.

sept, n. clan, esp. in Ireland.

Septem'ber, n. ninth month.

septe'nary, a. & n. of or involving the number seven; set of seven. septenn'ate, n. seven-year period of office. septenn'ial, a. of or for every seven years.

sep'tic, a. causing or caused by putrefaction.

septicae'mia (-sē-), n. blood-poisoning. ~ic, a.

septuagenā'rian, n. person between 69 and 80.

Septuages'ima, or ~ Sunday, n. the third Sunday before Lent.

Sep'tuagint, n. the Greek version of the Old Testament.

sep'ulchre (-ker), n. tomb. v.t. lay in sepulchre. sepul'chral (-kral), a. of sepulchres or sepulture; (of voice, &c.) funereal, gloomy. sep'ulture, n. burying, laying in sepulchre.

se'quel, n. what follows after; after effects; upshot. seque'la, n. (pl. -lae), disease, &c. consequential on another.

se'quence, n. succession; coming after or next; unbroken series; set of things belonging next each other. se'quent, a. coming after; following as a result or logical conclusion.

seques'ter, v.t. seclude, isolate, set apart. se'questrable, a. liable to sequestration. se'questrate, v.t. confiscate; (Law) divert or appropriate income of (property) to satisfaction of claims against its owner. ~tion, n. ~tor, n. person administering sequestered estate.

se'quin, n. former Venetian gold coin about 9s.; coin-like ornament sewn on dresses, &c.

serac', n. one of the castellated masses formed in glacier ice by intersection of crevasses.

sera'glio (-ahlyō), n. (pl. -os), harem; Turkish palace.

serai'[1] (-rī, -rah'ī), n. in various Eastern countries, a building for the accommodation of travellers with their pack-animals.

serai'² (-rī, -rah'ī), n. (Anglo-Ind.) a long-necked earthenware (or metal) flagon for water.

serang', n. (Anglo-Ind.) native head of a Lascar crew.

|| **sera'pé** (-ah-), n. shawl or plaid worn by Spanish-Americans.

sě'raph, n. (pl. -*im*, -*phs*), one of the highest of the nine orders of angels. **seraph'ic**, a. fervent or beautiful as a seraph.

Sěrb, ~**ian**, aa. & nn. (native, language) of Serbia.

sěre, a. withered, dried up.

sěrenáde', n. music sung or played at night below person's window. v.t. give serenade to.

sěrēne', a. clear and calm; placid, unperturbed. **sěrēn'itý**, n. sereneness.

sěrf, n. (hist.) one of the class of labourers bound to and transferred with the soil. ~**age**, ~**hood**, ~**dom**, nn. serf's condition.

sěrge, n. a durable twilled worsted fabric.

sergeant (sär̄j'ant), n. army warrant officer (*regimental* ~-*major*, *company* ~-*major*) or non-commissioned officer (*colour*-~, *sergeant, lance*-~); police officer between inspector and constable.

sěr'ial, a. of or in a series; (of story, &c.) issued in instalments. n. serial story.

|| **sěriā'tim**, adv. point by point in order.

sěr'iēs (-z), n. number of things of which each is similar to the preceding; sequence, succession.

sěr'if, n. fine cross-line finishing off stroke of a letter.

sěr'io-cǒm'ic, a. combining the serious and the comic; jocular.

sěr'ious, a. thoughtful, earnest; important; demanding thought; sincere; not negligible.

serjeant (sär̄j'ant), n. member of highest class (abolished 1880) of barristers.

sěrm'on, n. piece of religious exhortation delivered from the pulpit; an admonition. ~**ětte'**, n. short sermon. ~**ize**, v.i. talk like a preacher.

sěr'ous, a. of or like serum.

sěrp'ent, n. snake, esp. of large kinds; treacherous or cunning person; obsolete wind-instrument; kind of firework. **sěrp'entine**, a. like or as of a serpent; writhing, tortuous, meandering; cunning, treacherous; n. kinds of dull-green mottled stone; a skating-figure.

sě'rrate, **sěrrā'tĕd**, aa. notched like a saw. **sěrrā'tion**, n.

sěr'rāfile (-refīl), n. (Mil.) (pl.) the line of supernumerary and non-commissioned officers placed in the rear of a squadron or troop; one of these.

sě'rried (-rid), a. shoulder to shoulder; in close order.

sěr'um, n. watery animal fluid, esp. the thin part of blood as used for inoculation.

sěrv'ant, n. person who has undertaken to carry out the orders of an employer, esp. one engaged in household work; word of civility used in signatures to letters.

sěrve, v.t. & i. (-*able*), be servant to; do service or be useful to; suffice, satisfy; set food on table; distribute, hand food or goods; make legal delivery of (writ, &c.); set ball in play at tennis; treat; (colloq.) retaliate on. n. (Tennis, &c.) service or turn to serve.

sěrv'ice, n. being servant; servant's status; master's or mistress's employ; department of royal or public employ, persons engaged in it, (pl.) esp. the armed forces; set of vehicles, &c. plying at stated times; work done for another; benefit conferred on, exertion made for, another; use, assistance; liturgical form for use on some occasion; meeting of congregation for worship; legal serving of writ, &c.; set of dishes, &c. for serving meal; (Tennis, &c.) act or manner or turn of serving. **sěrv'iceable** (-səbl), a. useful, durable.

---

mäte, mēte, mīte, mōte, mūte, mōōt; răck, rĕck, rick, rŏck, rŭck, rōōk;

serviette′, *n.* table-napkin.

serv′ile, *a.* of slaves; like or as of a slave; cringing, mean-spirited; without independence. **servil′-ity**, *n.* **serv′itor**, *n.* henchman or servant (arch.); (Oxf. Univ.; hist.) student assisted out of college funds in return for menial services. **serv′itude**, *n.* slavery or bondage.

ses′ame, *n.* E.-Ind. plant or its oil-yielding seeds.

sesquipedā′lian, *a.* a foot and a half long.

sess′ile (or -īl), *a.* (of flower, leaf) attached directly by the base without stalk.

se′ssion (-shn), *n.* being assembled for deliberative or judicial business; period during which such meetings are held; (Sc. & U.S.) school or university term. **Court of Session**, supreme civil court of Scotland. **se′ssion′al** (-shon-), *a.*

ses′terce, *n.* the ancient-Roman coin (about 2*d.*) used in stating sums of money.

set², *v.t. & i.* (*set*), put, lay; cause to stand; station; place ready; dispose suitably; fix in position; cause to work; apply oneself *to* work; impose or propound for solution or answer; give an edge to (razor, saw); unite and secure in place after fracture; sow or plant or imbed; arrange (type) ready for printing; provide (song, words) with music; make insertions in surface with (gold, gems, &c.); curdle, solidify, harden; take shape; develop into maturity; (of sun, moon) sink below the horizon; (of tide, current of feeling, &c.) have motion, gather force, show or feel tendency; (*p.p.*, of batsman) playing with confidence; (of dog) take rigid attitude showing presence of game; (of garment) adapt itself to figure; affix (one's seal, signature, name, &c.) *to*; adjust hands or mechanism of (clock, trap); fix the eyes on; direct and keep (one's hopes) *on*; clench (one's teeth). *n.* setting of sun;

direction of current or wind; attack directed *at*; configuration; hang or fit; slip or shoot for planting. **~back′**, a check or relapse. **~down′**, a rebuff or snub. **~off′**, thing set off against another; counterpoise, compensation. **~out′**, things set out, a display. **~square**, draughtsman's appliance for drawing lines at certain angles. **~to′**, bout of fighting or argument.

set², *n.* number of things or persons that belong or consort together; series, collection, group, clique; group of games in tennis, &c. counting as unit to side winning more than half of them.

se′ton, *n.* thread or tape passed below skin and left with ends protruding to draw off a discharge.

settee′, *n.* seat accommodating two or more.

sett′er, *n.* dog trained to set.

sett′ing, *n.* music of a song, &c.; environment or accessories setting a thing off.

set′tle¹, *n.* bench with high back and box below seat.

set′tle², *v.t. & i.* establish or become established in an abode or place or way of life; sit or make sit down for a stay; cease from wandering; determine, agree upon, decide, appoint; (of bird, fly, &c.) alight; colonize (country); subside, sink; descend as sediment; deal effectually with; dispose of; pay (bill). **~ment**, *n.* terms on which property is settled on person or deed stating these; in India, the process of assessing the Government land-tax over a specific area; a colony; place of abode; company of persons established in a poor district as a centre of social life; (U.S. & colonies) a small village. **sett′ler**, *n.* early colonist.

sev′en, *a. & n.* one more than six, 7, VII. **~fold**, *a. & adv.* **sev′enth**, *a. & n.* ~ly, *adv.* in the seventh place.

seventeen′, *a. & n.* seven and ten, 17, XVII. ~th, *a. & n.*

sev′entÿ, *a. & n.* seven times ten, 70, LXX. ~fold, *a. & adv.*

sev′entieth, *a. & n.*

sev′er, *v.t. & i.* disjoin, separate, divide in two; cut or break off; take away. ~ance, *n.* severing; severed state.

sev′eral, *a.* a good many, three or more; separate, diverse, distinct, individual, respective. *pron.* three or more of the previously mentioned persons or things. **sev′erallÿ**, *adv.* separately, respectively.

sévére′, *a.* austere, strict; unsparing; vehement; arduous, exacting; unadorned, concise, not luxuriant; censorious. **sóvé′ritÿ**, *n.* severe quality; harsh treatment or manifestation.

Sèvres (sä′vr), *n.* kind of porcelain.

sev′erÿ, *n.* (Archit.) compartment of vaulted ceiling.

sew (sō), *v.t. & i.* (p.p. *sewn, sewed,* pr. sōn, sōd), use needle and thread or sewing-machine; fasten or join or enclose by sewing. **sewing-machine**, apparatus in which needle is worked mechanically.

sew′age, *n.* matter conveyed in sewers. **sew′er**, *n.* covered underground drain carrying off refuse of houses and towns. **sew′erage**, *n.* drainage by a system of sewers.

sewn, *p.p.* of sew.

sex, *n.* being male or female; males or females collectively; ~ appeal, attractiveness to opposite sex.

sexagenār′ian, *a. & n.* (person) between 59 and 70.

Sexages′ima, or ~ Sunday, *n.* the second Sunday before Lent.

sexages′imal, *a.* proceeding by sixties; of sixty; sixtieth.

sexcenté′narÿ, *n.* 600th anniversary.

sexénn′ial, *a.* lasting six years; occurring once in six years.

sex′tan, *a.* (of fever, &c.) recurring every fifth day.

sex′tant, *n.* instrument including a graduated arc equal to a sixth of a circle for taking angular measurements.

sextét′, *n.* (musical work for) six voices, singers, instruments, or players, in combination.

sex′tō, *n.* (pl. -os), book formed by folding sheets into six leaves.

sextodé′cimō, *n.* (abbr. 16mo), sheet of paper folded in 16 leaves; book made by folding thus.

sex′ton, *n.* officer charged with care of a church and its belongings and with bell-ringing and grave-digging.

sex′tuple, *a.* a sixfold. *v.t. & i.* multiply, exceed by, six times.

sex′ual, *a.* of sex, a sex, or the sexes.

shabb′ÿ, *a.* worn or threadbare; dressed in shabby clothes; close-fisted, mean; paltry, scurvy.

shab′rack, *n.* cavalry saddle-cloth.

‖ **shabun′der** (-ah-), *n.* an officer at native ports in the Indian seas.

shack¹, *n.* (U.S., Can.) rough cabin or shanty of logs, mud, &c.

shack², n. bait picked up at sea, refuse fish; usu. ~bait.

shack³, v.t. chase after (a ball, &c.), retrieve.

shac′kle, *n.* fetter enclosing ankle or wrist; (pl.) handcuffs; kinds of coupling-appliance. *v.t.* fetter, hamper.

shad, *n.* kinds of fish.

shadd′ock, *n.* fruit like large orange; tree bearing it.

shade, *n.* comparative darkness or obscurity; the darker parts of a picture; (usu. pl.) cool retreat; slight difference, small amount; unreal thing; screen excluding or moderating light or heat; glass cover. *v.t. & i.* (-able), screen from light; make dark; pass by degrees into another shade of colour, opinion, &c. **sha′dÿ**, *a.* giving or situated in shade; of doubtful honesty, disreputable; inferior.

shăd'ow (-dō), n. patch of shade; dark figure projected by body that intercepts rays of light; person, &c. attending another like such shadow; unsubstantial or unreal thing; phantom or ghost; shade; dark part of room, &c.; obscurity; shelter or protection. v.t. set forth vaguely or prophetically; dog, watch secretly. **shăd'owy** (-ōī), a. not luminous; gloomy; unsubstantial, unreal.

shaft (-ah-), n. rod of spear, lance, or arrow; slender cylinder connecting the parts of a machine; stem, stalk; column between base and capital; arrow; ray of light; one of the bars between which horse, &c., is harnessed to vehicle; hole serving as access to mine, &c.

shăg, n. a rough mass of hair; coarse kinds of fine-cut tobacco. **shăgg'y** (-g-), a. hairy, roughhaired; rough, rugged.

shagreen', n. kinds of untanned leather with roughened surface; shark-skin.

shah, n. king of Persia.

shăke, v.t. & i. (shŏŏk, shāken; -kable), move violently or quickly up and down or to and fro; tremble or rock or vibrate, or cause to do so; jolt or jar; brandish; weaken or make less stable. n. shaking, jolt, jerk, shock; (Mus.) rapid alternation of two notes. ~down, bed improvised of straw or bedding laid on floor. **Shā'ker**, n. member of American religious celibate sect.

Shākespear'ian (-pēr-), a. of, as of, Shakespeare.

shăk'ō, n. (pl. -os), form of peaked military cap.

shā'kў, a. unsteady, trembling, infirm, tottering, wavering.

shāle, n. kinds of clay rock like slate but softer. **shā'lў**, a.

shall (-ăl, -ál), v.aux. (pres. I &c. shall, thou shalt; past & condit. I &c. should, thou shouldest; neg. forms shall not or shan't, should not or shouldn't) forming compound tenses or moods express-

ing command, obligation, condition, intention, prophecy, and other senses.

shalloon', n. light cloth for linings and dresses.

shăll'op, n. light boat.

shăl(l)ŏt', n. kind of onion.

shăll'ow (-ō), a. of little depth; superficial. n. shallow place; shoal. v.i. & t. decrease in depth.

shalt. See shall.

shăm, v.t. & i. feign, pretend to be. n. piece of pretence; person pretending to be what he is not; counterfeit thing. a. pretended, counterfeit.

‖ **sha'ma¹** (-ah-), n. cereal cultivated in India, yielding a milletlike grain used as food.

‖ **sha'ma²** (-ah-), n. an Indian song-bird.

‖ **shăm'ba**, n. (E.-Afr.) cultivated plot of ground.

shăm'ble, v.i. go with shuffling ungainly gait. n. such gait.

shăm'bles (-lz), n.pl. butchers' slaughter-house; scene of carnage.

shāme, n. feeling of humiliation excited by consciousness of guilt or from some other cause; state of disgrace or ignominy or discredit. v.t. make ashamed, bring disgrace on; force by shame into or out of something. ~faced, a. bashful, shy. ~less, a. lacking shame; impudent, cynical.

shămm'ў, n. chamois-leather.

shampoo', v.t. treat head of person with lather and rubbing. n. a shampooing.

shăm'rock, n. kinds of trefoil or clover serving as national emblem of Ireland.

shăn'drўdăn, n. light two-wheeled Irish cart; rickety old-fashioned vehicle.

shăn'dўgăff, n. beer and gingerbeer mixed.

shanghai' (-hī), v.t. (Naut. sl.) drug and ship as sailor. n. (Austral.) a catapult.

shănk, n. leg or part of it between knee and ankle; stem or shaft of something.

shan't. See shall.

shăntŭng', n. soft undressed Chinese silk, usu. undyed.

shăn'tŷ, n. hut, hovel.

shape, n. configuration, form; external appearance, guise; orderly arrangement, proper condition; pattern or mould. v.t. & i. (-pable), fashion into desired or definite shape; form, devise, plan; direct one's course; call up image of; assume form. ~less, a. lacking definite form; irregularly made. ~ly, a. well formed or proportioned.

shărd, shĕrd, n. (arch.) fragment of broken pottery.

share, n. the part that falls to an individual out of a common stock or burden or achievement; one of the equal parts of a company's capital entitling holder to profits; the cutting part of a plough. v.t. & i. (-rable), apportion among others; possess or use or endure jointly with; have share or be sharer (with person in thing). ~holder, owner of shares in a company.

shărk, n. large voracious sea-fish; extortioner or swindler.

shărp, a. with fine edge or point, not blunt; peaked or pointed; abrupt or angular or steep; keen, pungent; shrill, piercing; biting, harsh; severe, painful; acute, sensitive; vigilant, clever; unscrupulous; speedy; (Mus.) above normal pitch, (of note) a semitone higher than the named note, (of key) having sharp or sharps in signature. n. (Mus.) a sharp note. ~-set', hungry. ~shooter, skilled shot posted where marksmanship is required. sharp'en, v.t. & i. make or grow sharp; give an edge to; make quick; make hungry; make painful or severe. shărp'er, n. person who lives by fraud.

∥ shăs'ter, ∥ shas'tra (-ah-), n. one of the sacred Hindu writings. ∥ shastri, n. one learned in these.

shătt'er, v.t. & i. break suddenly in pieces; wreck, utterly destroy.

shāve, v.t. & i. (-vable), clear off hair, beard, &c. by passing along the skin a sharp-edged blade; pare (wood, &c.); pass close to without touching. n. being shaved by oneself or another; narrow margin by which contact or failure or success is missed. *~tail, (army sl.) second lieutenant. shā'ver, n. (esp., sl.) youngster. shā'vings (-z), n.pl. planing-refuse.

Shā'vian, a. of, in the manner of, G. B. Shaw, a dramatist.

shaw, n. thicket or copse.

shawl, n. rectangular piece of woven or netted fabric worn over shoulders or head or round neck.

shawm, n. medieval form of oboe.

shay, n. (arch., joc.) chaise.

shē, pron. (obj. her, poss. her and hers, pl. they, &c.), the female in question (also of a ship, train, country, or other thing personified as female).

shē'a, n. W.-Afr. tree yielding a vegetable butter (~-butter).

shead'ing (-ee-), n. administrative tithing or division, of which there are six, in the Isle of Man.

sheaf, n. (pl. -ves), bundle of corn-stalks tied together after reaping; bundle of arrows, papers, or other long objects. v.t. (also sheave) make into sheaves.

shear, v.t. & i. (sheared) p.p. shŏrn, rarely sheared), cut with sword, &c.; clip, take off, with shears; (fig.) fleece or strip bare; (Mech.) distort or rupture by the strain called shear. n. (Mech.) the kind of strain to which the rivet of pivoted shears is subjected; (pl.) clipping-instrument of two blades moving on a rivet; (pl.) hoisting apparatus of two or more poles. ~ling, sheep once shorn.

sheath, n. (pl. pr. -dhz), close-fitting cover, esp. for blade or tool; investing membrane, &c. sheathe (-dh), v.t. (-ɦable), put into sheath; protect with a casing.

sheave, n. wheel with grooved edge as in a pulley.

*shĕbăng´, n. (sl.) hut, dwelling; institution, business.

shĕd¹, v.t. (shed), let or have fall off (hair, clothes, feathers, horns, leaves); let or make flow (tears, blood); diffuse or radiate.

shĕd², n. a roofed shelter for storing things, keeping cattle in, &c.

sheen, a. bright, gleaming. n. radiance, brightness. sheen´ÿ, a.

sheep, n. (pl. same) timid beast kept in flocks for the mutton and wool and leather it yields; (pl.) pastor's flock; sheepish person. ~côte or ~côt, a shelter for sheep. ~fold, enclosure for penning sheep in. ~run, large sheep-walk, esp. in Australia. ~shank, a pair of hitches shortening a rope without cutting it. ~walk, tract of land as sheep-pasture. sheep´ish, a. (esp.) bashful or embarrassed in manner.

sheer¹, a. mere, unqualified, absolute; perpendicular. adv. perpendicularly; directly; clean.

sheer², v.i. swerve or change course (esp. of ship).

sheet, n. rectangular piece of linen, &c. as part of bedclothes; broad thin flat piece of iron or glass or other material; complete piece of paper as made; wide expanse of water, flame, &c.; rope or chain at lower corner of sail for changing its tension or position. v.t. cover with sheet; secure (sail) with sheet. ~anchor, large anchor used only in emergencies; (fig.) last dependence.

sheik(h) (-āk, -ēk), n. Arab chief; head of Arabian or Mohammedan tribe, family, or village.

shĕk´el, n. a Jewish weight and coin; (pl., sl.) money, riches.

shĕl´drāke, n. a bright-plumaged wild duck; *merganser. shĕl´dŭck, n. female sheldrake.

shĕlf, n. (pl. -ves), horizontal slab or board projecting from wall or forming one tier of bookcase or cupboard; ledge on cliff-face, &c.; reef or sand-bank.

shĕll, n. hard outer case enclosing birds' eggs, nuts, some seeds and fruits, some molluscs and crustaceans, &c.; the mere walls of a house; explosive artillery projectile; light coffin. v.t. & i. take out of shell; remove shell or pod from; bombard or fire shells at. ~back, (sl.) old sailor. ~fish, aquatic shelled mollusc (e.g. oyster) or crustacean (crab, &c.). shĕll´ÿ, a.

shĕllăc´, n. lac melted into thin plates for making varnish. v.t. varnish with this.

shĕl´ter, n. protection against exposure to harm; screen or cabin affording shelter. v.t. & i. serve as shelter to; shield; take shelter.

shĕlve¹, v.t. & i. (-vable), put (books, &c.) on shelf; lay aside or defer consideration of.

shĕlve², v.i. slope gently.

shĕp´herd (-perd), n. man who tends flock, (fig.) a pastor. v.t. tend or drive sheep; (fig.) marshal like sheep. ~ess, n.

Shĕ´raton, n. severe 18th-c. style of furniture.

shĕrb´et, n. Eastern cooling drink of fruit-juice, &c.; effervescing drink made by mixing a chemical powder with water.

shereef´, n. a descendant of Mahommed, used as title of certain Arab princes.

shĕ´riff, n. a county or other official entrusted with certain administrative functions.

shĕr´rÿ, n. a white Spanish wine.

shew, shewbread. See show.

shibb´olĕth, n. a word or custom or principle regarded as a test; a party catchword.

shield, n. piece of defensive armour usu. carried on the left arm to ward off cuts and thrusts; (fig.) person or thing that protects one; (Herald.) representation of shield with coat of arms on it. v.t. protect or screen.

shift, v.t. & i. change or move from one position to another; change form or character; use expedients. n. an expedient or resource; a contrivance or piece

māte, mēte, mīte, mōte, mūte; pärt, pĕrt, pört; italics, vague sounds;

of evasion; rotation; a relay of workmen, time for which relay works; (arch.) chemise. ~less, *a.* bad at finding expedients; incapable. shift'y, *a.* (of wind) variable; addicted to indirect courses or deceit.

shig'ram, *n.* Bombay name for a kind of hack gharry, or palanquin-carriage.

shikar´, *n.* (Anglo-Ind.) hunting; sport (shooting and hunting); game. *v.i. & t.* hunt animals for sport; hunt (animal).

shikar´ee (-rî), -rî, shéká´rry, *n.* (Anglo-Ind.) hunter; sportsman's native attendant.

‖ shik'ra, *n.* small Indian hawk, sometimes used in falconry.

shille'lagh (-âla), *n.* cudgel.

shill'ing, *n.* silver coin, 20 to the £, or 12*d.* (abbr. *s.*)

shill'y-shall'y, *n.* vacillation. *a.* vacillating. *v.i.* vacillate.

shimm'er, *n.* tremulous or faint light. *v.i.* shine with this.

shin, *n.* the bony front of the lower leg. *v.t.* kick the shins of.

*shin'dig, *n.* (sl.) social function.

shin'dy, *n.* free fight; commotion.

shine, *v.i. & t. (shône)*, emit or reflect light; be bright, glow; be brilliant or admirable in some respect or sphere; (colloq., with past and p.p. *shined*) put a shine on (boots, grate, &c.). *n.* sunshine; lustre on a surface, a polishing; (sl.) shindy, fuss; *(pl., sl.) capers, tricks. shi'ner, *n.* (sl.) sovereign or other coin; (pl.) money; *kinds of small fresh-water fish.

shingle¹ (shing'gl), *n.* slip of wood used as roof-tile; *a small signboard. *v.t.* cover (roof of house) with shingles; crop the hair so as to give the effect of overlapping shingles; *chastise with a shingle.

shingle² (shing'gl), *n.* pebbles in a mass as on sea-shore. shing'ly (-ngg-), *a.*

shingles (shing'glz), *n.pl.* acute skin inflammation along nerve tracks.

Shin´tô, *n.* the native religious system of Japan, partly ousted by Buddhism; adherent of this. ~ism, ~ist, *nn.*

shint'y, *n.* game resembling hockey; stick used in it.

shi'ny, *a.* with bright surface; (of cloth, &c.) worn smooth.

ship, *n.* large sea-going vessel, esp. one with bowsprit and three or more masts; (boating sl.) boat. *v.t. & i.* put or receive (goods, &c.) on board ship; go or take service on board ship as passenger or sailor; fix (mast, rudder, &c.) in its working place; lay (sculls, oars) inside boat. ~money, (hist.) tax for providing navy. ~shape, in good order, well arranged. ~wreck, *n.* ship's undesigned sinking or destruction; (fig.) utter ruin; *v.t. & i.* bring to or suffer ruin or failure. ~wright, shipbuilder. ship'ment, *n.* putting of goods, &c. on board; goods shipped. shipp'er, *n.* (esp.) importer or exporter. shipp'ing, *n.* (esp.) ships, the ships of a country, &c.

shire, *n.* county; chiefly used as suffix (pron. -sher) in names of many counties.

shirk, *v.t. & i.* avoid or get out of (duty, &c.). *n.* a shirker.

*shir(r), *n.* elastic webbing; elastic thread woven into fabric; gathered trimming, gathering in costumery. *v.t.* gather (material) with parallel threads run through.

shirt, *n.* man's sleeved undergarment; woman's blouse with collar and cuffs. ~ing, *n.* shirt material. shirt'y, *a.* (sl.) in a bad temper; angry.

shiv'er¹, *n.* small fragment, splinter. *v.t. & i.* break to shivers.

shiv'er², *v.i.* tremble with cold or fear; show or feel a vibratory movement or thrill. *n.* momentary shivering. shiv'ery, *a.*

shoal¹, *n.* great number of fish swimming together; multitude of persons or things. *v.i.* (of fish) form shoals.

shoal², a. (of water) shallow. n. shallow place in sea, &c.; submerged sandbank. v.i. get shallower. **shoal'y**, a.

shock¹, n. group of corn-sheaves stood together in field.

shock², n. unkempt mass or head of hair.

shock³, n. violent concussion or impact; sudden and disturbing physical or mental impression; state produced by this. v.t. affect with horror or disgust; appear scandalous or improper or outrageous to. ~er, n. sensational novel, &c. ~ing, a. scandalous, improper; very bad.

shod, p.t. & p.p. of shoe.

shod'dy, n. fibre got by shredding old cloth; cloth partly made of this. a. counterfeit and trashy.

shoe (-ōō), n. outer covering of leather or other material for the foot; thing like a shoe in use or shape. v.t. (shŏd; part. shoeing), fit with shoes or shoe. ~black, boy, &c., who cleans shoes of passers-by. ~flower, (Anglo-Ind.) the flower of the Hibiscus Rosasinensis. ~horn, horn or metal scoop for helping shoe over the heel. ~maker, maker of boots and shoes.

shone, p.t. & p.p. of shine.

shook, p.t. of shake.

|| **shool'dar'y**, n. (Anglo-Ind.), a small tent with steep sloping roof.

shoot, v.i. & t. (shŏt), come or go swiftly or suddenly; discharge or propel quickly (gun, bullet, &c.); wound or kill with gun; shoot game or fire at target; (of bud, &c.) issue; (of plants) put forth buds; jut out or rise sharply up; (Assoc. football) take a shot at goal; (Joinery) plane edges of board accurately; (Cinemat.) photograph with cine-camera. n. bud or young branch; inclined plane down which water may flow or objects slide; shooting-party. *int. say what you have on your mind. shoot'er, n. (esp.) ball that shoots at cricket.

shoot'ing, n. (esp.) right of shooting over estate, &c.; an estate rented to shoot over. ~box, sportsman's lodge for use in shooting season. ~star, point of light seen to glide across sky.

shop, n. building or room for retail sale of goods; workshop or place of manufacture; one's place of business; talk about one's work. v.i. visit shops to buy things. ~keeper, owner of retail shop. ~lifter, pretended customer who steals goods. ~steward, person elected by his fellow workmen as their spokesman on conditions of work, &c. ~walker, person directing customers in large shop.

shore¹, n. beam set obliquely against wall, &c. to prop it up. v.t. (~rable), prop with shore.

shore², n. land that skirts sea or lake or river. ~ward, adv. & a.

shorn, p.p. of shear.

short, a. not long in space or time; not tall; soon traversed or finished; of less than the named amount, &c.; failing to reach the measure or quality of; soon over; concise; angrily curt; (of pastry, clay, metal) crumbling or breaking easily. adv. abruptly; before or without reaching the end; without going to the length of. n. a short vowel or syllable or the short mark (˘); (pl.) garment like trousers cut off above the knee. ~bread, cake, of flour, butter, and sugar; *rich teacake often served with fruit. ~ circuit, electric circuit made through a small resistance. ~coming, failure to reach a standard or perform a duty; defect. ~ commons, scanty allowance of food. ~hand, kinds of writing enabling reporter to keep pace with speaker. ~handed, not having the full number of men required. ~horn, a breed of cattle. ~sighted, having short sight; deficient in foresight. ~tempered, easily angered.

short'age, n. a deficiency in number or amount. **short'en**, v.i. & t. become or make shorter or short; curtail. **short'ly**, adv. before long, soon; in a few words, briefly.

shot¹, p.t. & p.p. of shoot. a. woven of different-coloured warp and woof so that the colour changes with the point of view.

shot², n. attempt to hit something by shooting, throwing, or striking, or to attain an end or solve a question; discharging of a gun, &c.; person of specified skill in shooting; cannon-ball; (collect.) leaden pellets used at each discharge of gun. v.t. load (gun), weight, with shot.

should (-ŏŏd), p.t. of shall.

shoul'der (shōl-), n. point of body at which arm or foreleg or wing is attached; projection or expansion comparable to human shoulder; (pl.) the back from shoulder to shoulder; (sing.) beast's foreleg as joint of meat. v.t. & i. push with the shoulder, jostle; hoist on to or lay across one's shoulders; assume responsibility. ~blade, either flat bone of back jointed with the armbone.

shout, n. loud cry from person or company calling attention or expressing joy, defiance, approval, &c. v.i. & t. emit shout or shouts; speak loudly.

shove (-ŭv), v.t. & i., & n. push (colloq.). ~halfpenny, modern form of shovelboard.

sho'vel (-ŭv-), n. spade-like scoop for shifting earth, &c. v.t. shift with shovel or spade. ~board, game of propelling disks or coins over partitioned surface.

sho'veller (-ŭv-), n. (esp.) the spoonbill duck.

show (-ō), v.t. & i. (p.p. shown, rarely showed; also spelt shew, shewn, shewed), let be seen; disclose, manifest; offer for inspection; exhibit; demonstrate, make understand. n. showing; outward appearance; ostenta-

tion, pomp; pageant or display; (sl.) concern or undertaking. **shew'bread**, twelve loaves displayed in Jewish temple and renewed each Sabbath. **show'man** (-an), manager of menagerie or travelling show. ~room, room in which goods are kept for inspection.

show'er, n. brief fall of rain or of hail or sleet; great number of descending missiles, letters, presents, kisses, &c.; *social gathering in honour of a bride at which each guest brings a present. v.i. & t. descend or send or give in a shower. **show'ery**, a. rainy.

show'y (-ōi), a. of attractively brilliant appearance; making a good show.

shrank, p.t. of shrink.

shräp'nel, n. shells packed with bullets and timed to burst short of the objective; part of bomb, &c. so scored as to break and scatter.

shred, n. scrap, rag, paring, worn-out fibre. v.t. & i. cut or tear to shreds; fray.

shrew (-ŏŏ), n. small beast like long-snouted mouse feeding on insects; scolding woman. ~ish, a. given to scolding.

shrewd (-ŏŏd), a. sagacious, penetrating; (of guess, &c.) near the truth; (of cold, &c.) sharp, severe.

shriek, v.i. & t., & n. scream.

shriev'alty, n. sheriffship.

shrift, n. shriving.

shrike, n. kinds of bird with hooked toothed beak.

shrill, a. piercing and high-pitched in sound. v.i. & t. sound shrilly; utter or send out (song, &c.) thus.

shrimp, n. sea crustacean an inch or two long; diminutive person.

shrine, n. casket or tomb holding relics; sacred or revered place.

shrink, v.i. & t. (shrănk; shrŭnk), grow smaller; make (flannel, &c.) smaller by soaking or other treatment; recoil or retire or flinch. ~age, n. tendency to diminish in size or number; amount of diminution.

shrive, v.t. (arch.; shrōve, shriven), give absolution to; confess.

shriv'el, v.i. & t. contract into wrinkled or withered up state.

shröff, n. banker or money-changer in the East; in the Far East a native expert employed to detect bad coin. v.t. examine, sift (coin, &c.).

shroud, n. winding-sheet; (fig.) concealing agency; (usu. in pl.) set of ropes forming part of standing rigging. v.t. clothe for burial; cover or disguise.

Shrōve'-tíde, Shrove Tuesday, nn. the three days, the day, before Ash-Wednesday.

shrub¹, n. (arch.) drink of rum and lemon-juice, &c.

shrub², n. woody plant of less size than tree. shrub'bery, n. plantation of shrubs.

shrug, v.t. & i. raise the shoulders momentarily as gesture of indifference, &c. n. such motion.

shrunk, p.t. & p.p. of shrink.

shudd'er, n. spasm of shivering. v.i. experience a shudder.

shuf'fle, v.i. & t. drag one's feet, walk thus; change position of playing-cards, papers, &c. by mixing; shift (persons) into each other's place; juggle with words, equivocate; make or let slip off. n. act of shuffling; shuffling gait or step; interchange of positions; piece of equivocation. shuf'ler, n. (esp.) prevaricator.

shun, v.t. keep clear of; eschew.

'shun, abbr. of attention! as word of command.

shunt, v.t. & i. divert (train, &c.) or diverge on to a side track. n. a shunting; (Electr.) a conductor joining two points of a circuit and enabling part of current to be diverted.

shut, v.t. & i. (shut), move (door, lid, lips, &c.) into position to stop an aperture; close door, &c. of (room, box, eye, &c.); bring (knife, book, &c.) into folded-up

or contracted state; become shut. shut'ter, n. (esp.) appliance for blocking up window or excluding light from camera lens; one of the separate parts of a compound shutter.

shut'tle, n. boat-shaped weaving-implement on which weft-thread is shot across between warp-threads. shut'tlecock, n. cork fitted with crown of feathers so as to fly when struck with battledore.

shý¹, v.t. & i., & n. (colloq.) throw, esp. at a mark.

shy², a. avoiding observation; bashful; elusive; *(sl.) short (of). v.i. start aside in alarm. shý'er, n. shying horse.

*shý'ster, n. tricky unreliable person; person without professional honour, esp. tricky lawyer.

Sïamēse' (-z), a. of Siam. n. Siamese native or language.

sib'ilant, a. hissing. n. a sibilant letter or set of letters. sib'ilance, n. sib'ilāte, v.t. & i. pronounce with sibilance.

sib'yl, n. pagan prophetess; fortune-teller; old hag. sibyll'ine, a. oracular.

sice¹, n. the six on dice.

sice², sȳce, n. (Anglo-Ind.) groom; also, an attendant who follows on foot a mounted horseman or a carriage.

sick, a. vomiting or disposed to vomit; surfeited or tired of; ill, despondent; (sl.) mortified. sick'en, v.i. & t. grow ill or show signs of illness; feel nausea or loathing. sick'ener, n. (esp.) event, &c. that makes one weary of something.

sic'kle, n. reaping-hook with semicircular blade.

sick'ly, a. apt to be ill or cause illness; languid, pale; inducing nausea; mawkish.

sick'ness, n. being ill, disease. sleeping-~, fatal African disease marked by somnolence and nerve-paralysis. sleepy ~, a world-wide recently identified disease, distinct from sleeping sickness, though lethargy is a mark of both.

side, n. one of the surfaces bounding an object; either surface of thing regarded as having only two; one of the lines bounding a superficial figure; the part of the body that is to the right or left; one aspect of a thing; one of two contrasted parties or sets of opponents; slope of a hill; (sl.) swaggering gait or assumption of superiority. v.i. in phr. side with, espouse the cause of. ~arms, swords or bayonets. ~board, table or chest against dining-room wall. '~burn, short side whisker. ~car, jaunting-car; car for passenger(s) attachable to side of motor-cycle. ~light, (fig.) incidental illustration of or information on a subject. ~long, oblique; not direct. ~saddle, saddle for rider with both feet on same side of horse. ~show, minor attraction at an exhibition, &c. ~slip, v.i. skid; (Aeronaut.) move sideways instead of forwards; n. skid; side movement, ~s'man (-an), assistant to churchwarden. ~stroke, kinds of swimming. ~track, n. siding or by-path; v.t. shunt; postpone consideration of or dealing with. ~walk, (esp.) '*foot-way at side of road. ~ways, adv.

sidēr'eal, a. of, determined by means of, the stars.

|| **sidi** (seed'ī), n. an African, negro; now chiefly used in comb. ~boy.

si'ding, n. short track by side of railway for shunting; '*boards forming sides of timber building.

si'dle, v.i. walk sidelong, esp. in deferential approach.

siege, n. operations of encamped force for gaining possession of fortified place; besieging or being besieged (often fig.).

siĕnn'a, n. a rich reddish-brown pigment or its colour.

siĕ'rra, n. chain of jagged mountains, esp. in Spain or America.

siĕs'ta, n. midday rest usual in hot countries.

sieve (sĭv), n. utensil with network or perforated bottom through which liquids or fine particles can pass. **sift,** v.t. separate with or pass through a sieve; subject (facts, &c.) to close scrutiny.

sigh (sī), v.i. draw deep breath as in weariness, &c.; mourn or yearn for; express with sighs. n. act or sound of sighing.

sight (sīt), n. faculty of vision; seeing or being seen; range of or region open to vision; scene or spectacle; precise aim with gun or observing instrument, appliance attached to gun, &c. for assisting this; (colloq.) large quantity. v.t. catch sight of, esp. by coming near; adjust sights of (gun, &c.). ~seer, person going round to see the sights. **sight'ly** (sīt-), a. not unsightly.

sign (sīn), n. mark traced on surface, &c.; thing used as symbol of something; indication; symptom or presage or token of; miracle as evidence of supernatural power; password; '*trace or spoor of animal; signboard; gesture used instead of words. v.t. & i. mark with a sign; affix one's name or initials to; make a sign to. ~board, board with inscription, &c. on or in front of inn, shop, &c. ~post, post supporting signboard or set up at cross-roads, &c. to guide travellers.

sig'nal, a. of marked quality or importance; notable. n. sight or sound meant to convey orders or information; message made up of such signals. v.t. & i. make signals; direct, transmit, or announce by signal. **sig'nalize,** v.t. (-zable), make notable; lend distinction to.

sig'natory, n. party to a treaty or other signed agreement.

sig'nature, n. signed name or initials; (Mus.) indication of key or time following clef; (Print.) indication letter or figure at foot of first page of book-sheet.

sig'nĕt, n. small seal, esp. one set in finger-ring.

---

signif'icance, *n.* expressiveness; meaning; importance; reason why thing is significant.

signif'icant, *a.* full of meaning; highly expressive; important.

significa'tion, *n.* (esp.) sense or acceptation of a term, &c.

sig'nify, *v.t.* & *i.* (-*iable*), be a sign or presage of; have as meaning; intimate or announce.

Signor (sē'nyor), Signora (sēn-yōr'a), Signorina (sēnyorē'na), *nn.* (pl. -*ri*, -*re*, -*ne*). Italian gentleman, married lady, unmarried lady (as titles = *Sir* and *Mr.*, *Madam* and *Mrs.*, *Miss*).

Sikh (sik, sēk), *n.* member of a military sect in the Punjab.

si'lence, *n.* abstinence from speech or noise; secrecy; taciturnity; absence of sound. *v.t.* (-*ceable*), reduce to silence by stifling, overpowering, confuting, &c. si'lencer, *n.* (esp.) apparatus deadening sound of gas escaping from oil-engine, &c. si'lent, *a.* keeping or marked by or done in silence; soundless, mute; tacit, taciturn.

silhouëtte' (-lŏŏ-), *n.* portrait of head or figure cut from black paper or done in solid black on white; outline of object seen against the light. *v.t.* represent by, or exhibit in, silhouette.

sil'ica, *n.* a mineral forming quartz and the chief part of flint, sand, &c. sili'ceous (-ishus), *a.*

silk, *n.* fibre composing silkworms' cocoons; thread prepared from it; cloth woven of this; (pl.) silk garments; (attrib.) made of silk; *silk-like filiform styles of female flower of maize; artificial ~, imitation of silk by fibre mechanically produced. ~worm, caterpillar of mulberry-feeding moth. sil'ken, *a.* made of silk. sil'ky, *a.* like silk in softness or lustre.

sill, *n.* slab of wood or stone at foot of window or doorway.

sill'abub, *n.* dish of cream or milk curdled with wine, &c.

sill'adar, *n.* (Anglo-Ind.) irregular cavalryman who provides his own horse and arms.

sill'y, *a.* foolish, imprudent, thoughtless; weak of intellect; (arch.) harmless, innocent. *n.* a silly person. ~ point, ~ short-leg, placed close up to batsman.

si'lo, *n.* (pl. -*os*), pit or airtight chamber for storing green crops for fodder.

silt, *n.* sediment deposited by moving water. *v.i.* & *t.* block or be blocked up with silt.

Silū'rian, *a.* & *n.* (of) a series of rocks forming the lowest subdivision of the Palaeozoic.

sil'van, syl'-, *a.* of the, having, woods; rural.

sil'ver, *n.* a white lustrous precious metal; coins made of it; vessels or implements made of it. *a.* made of silver. *v.t.* & *i.* coat or plate with silver; make or become silvery. ~ fox, fox with valued black fur and white tail-tip. ~gilt', of silver gilded over. ~ paper, tinfoil. ~ point, art of drawing, drawing done, with silver pencil on prepared paper. ~ side, best side of round of beef. ~smith, a worker in silver. ~-tongued, eloquent. ~weed, silvery-leaved wayside plant. sil'very, *a.* like silver in whiteness and lustre; having the clear soft resonance of a silver bell.

sim'ian, *a.* monkey-like. *n.* an ape or monkey.

sim'ilar, *a.* having resemblance to; of the same kind; (Geom.) identical in shape. similä'rity, *n.*

sim'ile, *n.* a comparison of two things for the purpose of illustration or ornament.

simil'itude, *n.* guise or outward appearance; simile; copy.

simm'er, *v.i.* & *t.* be or keep just bubbling or singing below boiling-point; be in a state of suppressed anger or laughter. ~ simmering state.

simo'niac, *n.* person guilty of simoni'acal, *a.*

si'mony, *n.* trafficking in church preferment.

simoōm', n. hot desert sand-wind.

*simp, (sl.) n. fool, simpleton.

sim'per, v.i. & t. smile in silly or affected way. n. such smile.

sim'ple, a. of one element or kind; not complicated or elaborate or adorned; unsophisticated, artless, natural; inexperienced; humble; easily solved or understood or done. n. (arch.) herb used in medicine. ~hearted, ~minded, aa. ingenuous.

sim'pleton (-plt-), n. foolish or half-witted person.

simpli'city, n. artlessness; weakness.

sim'plify, v.t. make simple or easy to understand. ~fication, n.

simulā'crum, n. (pl. -ra), shadowy likeness or mere pretence of.

sim'ūlate, v.t. (-lable), feign; pretend to have or feel; counterfeit. sim'ūlant, a. having the appearance of. simulā'tion, ~tor, nn.

simultā'neous, a. occurring at the same time. simultāne'ity, n.

sin, n. transgression against divine law; an offence against any code. v.i. commit sin; offend against.

since, prep. in the period between some specified time and the present. conj. since the time when; seeing that; inasmuch as. adv. since then or that.

sincē're, a. not given to simulation; not simulated or assumed. sincē'rity, n.

sin'ciput, n. head from forehead to crown.

‖ sī'nè, L. prep.=without. ‖ ~ die (dī'ē), indefinitely (of adjourning). ‖ ~ quā nōn, indispensable condition or qualification.

sī'necure (or sǐ-), n. office of honour or profit with no duties attached to it. ~cūrist, n. holder of sinecure.

sin'ew, n. tough fibrous animal tissue; a tendon; (pl.) muscles, bodily strength; (usu. pl.) motive power of. sin'ewy, a.

sin'ful, a. of the nature of sin; guilty of sin.

sing, v.i. & t. (sáng or arch. sŭng; sŭng), utter words with musical modulations; make humming or whistling sound; celebrate in verse. *n. (colloq.) large social gathering for singing. ~song, monotonous rhythm or cadence in reading, &c.; (colloq.) impromptu vocal concert. ~er, n.

singe (-j), v.t. & i. (geing) apply fire to the surface or edge of; rid thus of hair or feathers or nap; suffer singeing.

single (sing'gl), a. one only, not double or multiple; individual; of, for, or with one person or thing; unmarried. n. a single game; hit, &c. that counts one. v.t. choose out for attention or treatment of some kind. ~ file, advance in which every member of the party is straight behind its leader. *~ foot, horse's racking gait. ~handed, without assistance from others. ~hearted, free from duplicity or mixed motives. ~minded, true to one object. ~stick, (fencing with) basket-hilted stick.

sing'let (-ngg-), n. man's close-fitting undershirt or vest of cotton or wool.

sing'leton (-gglt-), n. player's only card of a suit; lone person.

sing'ūlar (-ngg-), a. extraordinary, uncommon, surprising; eccentric; (Gram.) of the form used in speaking of a single thing or person. n. (Gram.) the singular number, a singular word. singūlā'rity (-ngg-), n.

Sinhalese' (-nalēz), a. of Ceylon. n. Sinhalese native or language.

sin'ister, a. of evil omen; ill-looking; wicked, flagitious; (Herald.) on left side of shield (i.e. right as seen by observer).

sink, v.i. & t. (sánk or arch. sŭnk; sŭnk or in adj. use usu. sŭnken), fall slowly downwards; decline; disappear below horizon or surface of liquid; droop; subside; gradually expire; lower or let droop; send (ship, &c.) to the bottom; bore or construct below ground; engrave; invest (money); decrease the value of. *n.* receptacle with outflow pipe into which dirty water, &c. is thrown. sinking-fund, moneys set aside for the gradual extinction of a debt.

sink'ing, *n.* (esp.) internal sensation of collapse caused by hunger or apprehension.

Sinn Fein (shin fān), *n.* Irish movement aiming at national revival in language, &c., as well as independence.

sinn'er, *n.* a sinful person.

sin'ter, *n.* a mineral incrustation.

sin'uous, *a.* with many curves; meandering. sinūos'itý, *n.* (esp.) a bend in a stream, &c.

sip, *v.t. & i.* drink by successive spoonfuls or small mouthfuls. *n.* one such mouthful.

si'phon, *n.* a curved tube for conveying liquids over edge of vessel; bottle with tap from which aerated water is forced out by pressure of gas.

sipp'et, *n.* one of the pieces of toast or fried bread served with soup, mince, &c.

sir, *n.* used as vocative to master or superior or male stranger, or to boy or inferior who is being rebuked; title preceding Christian name of knight or baronet.

sīr'ar, *n.* (Anglo-Ind.) the Government of India; head of government or household; house-steward; native accountant.

sīrd'ar, *n.* Oriental military chief or general; (since 1882) British commander-in-chief of Egyptian army.

sīre, *n.* father or male ancestor; horse's or other beast's male parent; (voc.) Your Majesty.

sīr'en, *n.* (Gk. Myth.; pl.) winged women living on a rock and with sweet songs luring mariners to destruction; sweet singer; dangerously fascinating woman or pursuit; hooting-instrument used for sound-signals.

Si'rius, *n.* the dogstar.

sirkar. See sircar.

‖ sīrk'ī, *n.* (Anglo-Ind.) upper part of the culm of a species of tall reed-grass, native to India; matting made of this.

sīr'oin, *n.* best part of loin of beef.

sirōc'ō, *n.* (pl. -os), hot moist oppressive wind reaching Italy from Africa.

si'rrah, arch. voc. of *sir*, used in anger, &c. *sirree', (colloq.) vocative of *sir*.

sis'al, *n.*, ~ grass, ~ hemp, fibre from leaves of agave.

sis'kin, *n.* a small songbird.

siss'ōō, *n.* valuable Indian timber-tree; timber obtained from it.

*siss'ý, *n.* effeminate boy or man; (voc.) sister, young girl.

sis'ter, *n.* daughter of same parents as another person; female fellow-member of class or sect or human race; nun or member of sisterhood; hospital nurse in authority over others; institution, &c. on same lines or of same origin (usu. attrib., as *the ~ university*). ~-in-law, one's husband's or wife's sister or brother's wife. ~hood, *n.* (esp.) society of women bound by monastic vows or devoting themselves to religious or charitable work. sis'terlý, *a.*

Sisýphē'an, *a.* (of toil) endless and fruitless; vainly toilsome.

sit, *v.i. & t.* (săt), rest upon the buttocks; keep one's seat on (horse, &c.); (of Parliament, &c.) be in session; (of bird) rest on perch, hatch eggs by sitting on them in nest; (of things) lie or rest or be situated; (with *for*) represent constituency in Parliament; let artist take one's portrait. sitt'er, *n.* (esp.) person sitting for portrait; (sl., with reference to shooting bird sitting) easy job, easy shot at goal, &c. sitt'ing, *n.* (esp.) time for which person or assembly sits continuously; seat in church appropriated to a person. ~-room, parlour.

sit'ār, *n.* a form of guitar, properly having three strings, used in India.

site, *n.* ground on which town or building stands, stood, or is to stand.

‖ **sitrin'gee** (-j-) *n.* (Anglo-Ind.) coloured cotton carpet or rug.

sit'ūate, (arch.), **sit'ūāted**, *aa.* in specified situation.

situā'tion, *n.* site and surroundings of a place, &c.; posture of affairs; the way one is placed; post as servant or wage-earner.

six, *a. & n.* one more than five, 6, VI. ~**fold**, *a. & adv.* ~**penny bit**, piece, silver 6*d.* **sixth**, *a. & n.* next after fifth. ~ **form**, highest form in public school. **sixth'ly**, *adv.* in the sixth place.

sixte, *n.* one of the positions in fencing.

sixteen', *a. & n.* one more than fifteen, 16, XVI. ~**th**, *a.* next after fifteenth. **six'teenmō'** or 16mo, 16 leaves or 32 pages to sheet of printed book.

six'ty, *a. & n.* six times ten, 60, LX. ~**fold**, *a. & adv.* **six'tieth**, *a. & n.*

si'zar, *n.* undergraduate at Cambridge, &c., receiving college assistance on the ground of poverty.

size, *n.* relative bigness or dimensions; glutinous substance used to give surface to paper, stiffen calico, &c. *v.t.* sort in sizes or make conform to a size; glaze or stiffen with size; (with *up*) estimate size of, (colloq.) form judgement of (person).

sizz'le, *n. & v.i.* (make) sound as of frying.

sjäm'bök (sh-), *n.* heavy hide whip used in S. Africa.

skald (-awld), *n.* ancient-Scandinavian poet. **ska'ldic** (-awl-), *a.*

skāte[1], *n.* kinds of ray-fish.

skāte[2], *n.* one of a pair of implements attachable to the boots and enabling wearer to glide over ice. *v.i. & t.* go, perform, on skates.

skėdåd'dle, *v.i.* (sl.) make off.

skein (-ān), *n.* bundle of yarn or thread or silk.

skėl'éton, *n.* the hard framework of an animal or plant; the dried

bones of a person, &c., as in life; an epitome or abstract; nucleus. **skėl'étal**, *a.*

sketch, *n.* a rough, merely outlined, or unfinished drawing or painting; a rough draft or general account of something; a short light entertainment. *v.i. & t.* make sketches; draw or design or describe (object, plan, events) in sketchy way. **sketch'y**, *a.* lacking detail or finish.

skew, *a.* set askew; not in straight line or at right angles, oblique.

skewb'ald (-awld), *a.* with patches of white and some colour other than black.

skew'er, *n.* wooden or metal pin with which meat is held together. *v.t.* run skewer through.

ski (shē, skē), *n.* Norwegian snow-shoe of wood about 8 ft. by 4 in. *v.i.* (ski'd) go on ski.

skid, *n.* piece of wood, &c. serving as support or roller or check; iron shoe or other device to check vehicle's pace; slide of wheel on muddy ground; *timber track on which logs are drawn or slid. *v.t. & i.* support or move or check with skid; (of wheel, &c.) slide instead of keeping true motion.

skier (shē'er), *n.* person using ski.

skiff, *n.* kinds of small light boat.

skil'ful, *a.* expert; adroit.

skill, *n.* practised ability; expertness. **skilled** (-ld), *a.* (esp.) not untrained or amateur.

skill'y, *n.* thin gruel or soup.

skim, *v.t. & i.* take the scum or cream off; read superficially; glide over (surface) with light or occasional contact or parallel flight, &c. ~ **milk**, milk from which cream has been skimmed.

skimm'er, *n.* skimming utensil.

skimp, *v.t. & i.* supply scantily with necessaries; be parsimonious with; live parsimoniously. **skimp'y**, *a.* insufficient; lean.

skin, *n.* natural covering of the body or one layer of this; peel or rind; complexion; hide of flayed animal. *v.t.* strip the skin from ; flay, peel ; heal over with new skin. ~**deep**, merely superficial. ~**flint**, miser. *~**game**, (sl.) swindle. skin′**ny**, a. lacking flesh ; rather thin.

skip², v.i. & t. caper, frisk ; jump lightly from ground ; use skipping-rope ; omit parts in reading. n. skipping motion, esp. slight jump ; spell of skipping with the rope. ~**jack**, jumping toy made from merrythought ; kinds of jumping insect, &c. skipping-**rope**, length of rope used in girls' game of skipping.

skip², n. captain of side at bowls or curling.

skip², n. cage, bucket, &c., in which men or materials are lowered or raised in mines or quarries.

skipp′er, n. captain of ship, esp. of small trading ship ; *(army sl.) first sergeant of a company.

skirl, n. sound of bagpipes. v.i. make skirl.

skirm′ish, n. irregular or unpremeditated fight. v.i. engage in desultory fighting.

skirt, n. woman's outer garment hanging from the waist, or this part of a complete dress ; part of coat, &c. that hangs below the waist ; border or outlying part ; *(sl.) girl. v.t. & i. go or be situated along the edge of ; coast along side of.

skit, n. light piece of satire or burlesque.

skitt′ish, a. (of horse, &c.) playful, fidgety, excitable ; (of persons) sportive, given to indiscretions.

skit′tle, n. one of the nine wooden pins set up to be bowled at in the game of skittles.

skôff, scôff, n. food.

skŭ′a, n. a large gull.

skŭlk, v.i. move stealthily or lurk ; shirk danger or duty.

skŭll, n. bony case of the brain ; the bones of the head.

skŭnk, n. N.-Amer. animal of weasel kind ; its fur ; (sl.) mean rascal. *v.t. (sl.) defeat (opponent) without his scoring.

skÿ, n. the vault of heaven, the firmament ; heaven ; a region. v.t. (-ied), hit (ball) high into the air ; hang (picture) high on wall. ~**blue**, azure. ~**lark**, n. the common lark ; v.i. play about ; play tricks. ~**light**, glazed opening in roof or ceiling or sloping wall. ~**scraper**, very tall building. skÿ′er, n. high hit at cricket.

Skye or ~ **terrier**, n. a breed of dog.

slāb, n. flat thin piece of some rigid material.

slăck, a. sluggish ; not busy ; remiss ; relaxed ; loose. n. slack part of a rope ; small coal ; (pl.) trousers. v.t. & i. idle or be remiss ; slake (lime, thirst) ; fall off in vigour, speed, &c. ~**lime**, slaked lime. slăck′en, v.t. & i. loosen, relax ; be remiss. slăck′er, n. (esp., sl.) idler ; person who scamps his work.

slăg, n. vitreous smelting-refuse ; clinkers.

slain, p.p. of slay.

slāke, v.t. assuage or satisfy (thirst, &c.) ; disintegrate (lime) by combination with water.

slăm, v.t. & i. shut with a bang ; throw or put down with a bang. n. sound made thus.

slạn′der (-ah-), n. false report maliciously uttered to person's injury. v.t. utter slander about. ~**ous**, a.

slăng, n. expressions in common colloquial use but not regarded as standard English ; words or uses of them peculiar to a class. v.t. (sl.) use abusive language to. slăng′y, a. of the nature of slang.

slănt (-ah-), v.i. & t. be or put in an oblique position ; slope. n. position between horizontal and vertical.

slăp, v.t. strike with palm of hand ; smack. n. such stroke. ~**dash**, a. impetuous ; happy-go-lucky ; adv. at random.

slăsh, v.i. & t. make sweeping cut with sword, knife, whip, &c. ; make long gashes in. n. slashing stroke or gash. ~**slăsh′ing**, n. place in forest where trees have been felled or blown down.

zh, as (rou)ge ; ė =ı̆ ; n̄, ŭr, =ẽr ; ŷ, ȳ, =ı̆, ī ; and see p. 4. * =U.S.

slăt, *n.* strip of wood or metal.

slāte, *n.* kinds of rock easily split into thin smooth plates ; trimmed plate of this used esp. in roofing or for writing on. *v.t.* (*-table*), roof with slates ; reprimand or criticize severely ; *(pol.)* suggest as candidate. **slā'tў**, *a.*

slătt'ern, *n.* untidy or slovenly woman. **~ly**, *a.* untidy.

slaught'er (*-awt-*), *n.* killing of animal(s) for food ; slaying, esp. of many persons or animals at once. *v.t.* kill thus. **~house**, shambles. **~ous**, *a.* murderous.

Slav (*-ahv*), *a.* & *n.* (member) of any of the E.-Eur. peoples allied in race to the Russians.

slāve, *n.* one who is another's property ; helpless victim of some dominating influence ; a drudge. *v.i.* work like a slave ; drudge. **~-driver**, overseer of slaves at work ; (fig.) exacting employer. **slā'very**, *n.* (sl. ; pl. *-eys*), maid-of-all-work.

slā'ver¹, *n.* ship or person engaged in the slave-trade.

slāv'er², *n.* saliva running from the mouth ; (fig.) gross flattery. *v.i.* & *t.* let slaver flow ; beslaver in kissing, &c. ; (fig.) fawn upon or flatter.

slā'very, *n.* slave's condition ; slave-holding as an institution.

slā'vish, *a.* abject, servile.

Slavō'nian, Slavŏn'ic, *aa.* of the Slavs. *nn.* Slavonic language or person.

*slaw, *n.* salad of sliced cabbage.

slay, *v.t.* (*slew* pr.*-ōō* ; *slain*), kill.

slĕdge¹, **slĕd, sleigh** (*slā*), *nn.* vehicle on runners instead of wheels, for use esp. on snow. *vv.i.* & *t.* go, convey, in sleigh, &c.

slĕdge², **~-hammer**, *nn.* blacksmith's heavy hammer.

sleek, *a.* soft and smooth ; sleek haired or skinned ; of well-fed comfortable appearance. *v.t.* make sleek by stroking.

sleep, *n.* condition in which the eyes are closed and the nervous system inactive ; a spell of this. *v.i.* & *t.* (*slĕpt*), be or fall asleep ;

be dormant or inactive ; lie in the grave. **~-walker**, somnambulist. **sleep'er**, *n.* sleeping person ; one of the logs on which rails rest. **sleeping-sickness**, see sickness. **sleep'less**, *a.* failing to get sleep. **sleep'y̆**, *a.* feeling the need of sleep ; habitually indolent ; lacking life ; (of pears) over-ripe. **sleepy sickness**, see sickness.

sleet, *n.* snow or hail falling mixed with rain. **sleet'y̆**, *a.*

sleeve, *n.* part of garment that encloses the arm.

sleigh. See sledge¹.

sleight (*slīt*), *n.* dexterity ; artifice. **~ of hand**, juggling.

slĕn'der, *a.* of small girth or breadth ; slim ; scanty.

slept, *p.t.* & *p.p.* of sleep.

sleuth'-hound (*slōō-*), *n.* bloodhound (fig. of detective, &c.).

slew¹, slue (*slōō*), *v.t.* & *i.*, & *n.* turn or swing from one direction to another (often *round*).

slew², *p.t.* of slay.

slice, *n.* thin broad piece cut off or out as with a carving-knife ; a share of ; slicing motion ; cook's flat scoop. *v.t.* & *i.* (*-ceable*), cut into slices ; take (piece) off with carving motion ; strike (water, ball) incorrectly in rowing and golf.

slick, *adv.* (colloq.) without friction ; completely ; clean, right. ***slick'er**, *n.* waterproof coat.

slide, *v.i.* & *t.* (*slĭd* ; *-dable*), progress smoothly over a surface ; slide on the feet on ice ; glide or cause to glide or go smoothly or imperceptibly. *n.* act of sliding ; track for people or toboggans or goods or part of machine to slide on ; slip of glass with object or picture sliding into microscope or magic lantern. **sli'ding scale**, schedule for automatically varying a thing.

slight (*-īt*), *a.* slender, frail-looking ; inconsiderable ; scanty ; inadequate. *v.t.* treat or speak of as not worth attention ; fail in courtesy or respect to. *n.* marked failure of respect.

---

mãte, mēte, mīte, mōte, mūte, mōōt ; răck, rĕck, rick, rŏck, rŭck, rŏŏk ;

slim, a. of slender make; not stout or thick-set; (sl.) crafty.

slime, n. fine oozy mud or glutinous substance. **slī′my**, a. of or like or covered with slime; slippery; servile.

sling[1], n. strap used in hurling stones; kinds of appliance for supporting a hanging weight. v.t. & i. (*slung*), hurl with sling; throw; suspend.

sling[2], n. kind of toddy.

slink, v.i. (*slunk*), go stealthily or with sneaking air. n. (sl.) a slinking fellow.

slip[1], n. cutting from a plant; slim girl or boy; narrow piece of material or paper.

slip[2], v.t. & i. slide momentarily by accident; lose footing or balance thus; make casual mistake; make way unobserved or quietly; let go or cease to check or hold; escape from, give the slip to. n. act of slipping; casual mistake; leash for slipping greyhounds; artificial slope; inclined plane on which ships are built or repaired; *place for vessel to lie between wharves; one of the fielders behind wicket on off side, (sing. or pl.) this part of the field; under-bodice; pillow-case. ~shod, slovenly about the feet; (fig.) careless or inaccurate. **slipp′er**, n. loose indoor shoe. **slipp′ery**, a. hard to move on or treat without slipping; hard to hold on to; shifty, unreliable. **slipp′y**, a. slippery.

slit, v.t. & i. make long cut in; tear lengthwise; cut in strips. n. long cut; long narrow aperture.

slith′er (-dh-), v.i. (colloq.) go sliding and bumping.

slobb′er, v.i. & t. beslaver; display maudlin emotion. n. slaver; maudlin talk. **slobb′ery**, a.

sloe, n. the blackthorn or its bluish-black fruit.

slog, v.i. & t. hit hard, esp. with bat or fist; work or walk doggedly. n. hard random hit.

slō′gan, n. Highland war-cry; party catchword; motto.

sloid, sloyd, n. a system of manual training used in schools.

sloop, n. kind of one-masted fore-and-aft rigged ship.

slop[1], n.v.i. & t. spill; flow or let flow over edge of vessel; wet thus. ~shop, shop selling ready-made clothes. **slopp′y**, a. wet with rain-pools or slops; slipshod; maudlin. **slops**, n.pl. dirty or waste water of kitchen, &c.; liquid food; ready-made clothes.

slop[2], n. (sl.) policeman.

slope, n. position or direction downwards; piece of rising or falling ground. v.i. & t. (-pable), have or show slope; slant; (sl.) make off, saunter *about*.

slot[1], n. slit provided in machine for something to be inserted or work in. ~ machine, one operated by coin placed in slot.

slot[2], n. track of deer, &c.

slōth, n. laziness, indolence; kinds of S.-Amer. mammal of sluggish habits. ~bear, large-lipped black shaggy honey-eating bear of India and Ceylon. **slōth′ful**, a. indolent.

slouch, n. ungainly carriage of body; downward droop of hat-brim. v.i. & t. stand or go with slouch; droop; give slouch to.

slough[1] (-ow), n. miry place hard to pass through or get out of (often fig.). **slough′y** (-owl-), a.

slough[2] (slŭf), n. snake's cast skin; dead tissue dropping off from living flesh. v.t. & i. cast off (skin); drop off as slough.

slo′ven (-ŭv-), n. person of careless untidy habits. ~ly, a. careless in person or methods of work.

slow (-ō), a. taking a relatively long time; dull-witted, stupid; reluctant *to* do; (of clock, &c.) behind true time. adv. slowly. v.i. & t. reduce one's speed; reduce the speed of (train, &c.). ~coach, person slow in action.

slow-worm (slō′-wērm), n. reptile between snake and lizard.

sloyd. See sloid.

slūdge, n. thick mud.

---

māre, mēre, mīre, mōre, mūre; pärt, pĕrt, pört; *italics*, vague sounds;

slue. See slew¹.

slug¹, n. kinds of shell-less snail; roughly formed bullet. slŭg′ard, n. lazy person. slŭg′ish (-gi-), a. slowly-moving, inert, indolent.

*slŭg², v.i. & t. hit hard, slog; work doggedly.

sluice (-ōōs), n. sliding gate for adjusting outflow or inflow of water; channel carrying off surplus water. v.t. & i. (-ceable), let water off with sluice; flood or scour with flow of water.

slŭm¹, n. dirty crowded district in a town. slŭmm′y, a.

*slŭm², n. (Army sl.) soup, stew.

slŭm′ber, n. & v.i. sleep. ~ous, a. (esp.) soporific; peaceful.

slŭmp, n. sudden fall in prices or demand. v.i. fall thus.

slung, p.t. & p.p. of sling.

slunk, p.t. & p.p. of slink.

slŭr, v.t. make continuous or run into one; mark (notes) with a slur; obscure, minimize. n. stigma; piece of slurring; (Mus.) curved line over notes that are to be slurred.

slŭsh, n. thawing snow; mud; (fig.) silly sentiment. slŭsh′y, a.

slŭt, n. slovenly woman; (joc.) girl. slŭtt′ish, a.

slȳ, a. crafty, wily; secretive; underhand. ~boots, sly person.

smăck¹, n. flavour; a tincture or dash of. v.i. taste of; be suggestive or show a tinge of.

smăck², n. sloop, esp. for fishing. ~s′man (-an), man on smack.

smăck³, n. slap, sounding blow, loud kiss. v.t. & i. strike with palm or something flat; part lips audibly; crack (whip).

small (-awl), a. not large or big; little in size, power, importance, number, or amount; mean, paltry. ~arms, hand fire-arms. ~fry, young fish in a shoal; (fig.) the youngsters of a family or school, &c. ~hours, night-time after midnight. ~pox, a contagious disease, often fatal or disfiguring. ~talk, ordinary talk on social occasions.

smalt (-awlt), n. glass colour deep blue with cobalt; pigment made by pounding it.

smart, a. of some severity, sharp; brisk; quick-witted; quick in movement; of fresh or well-dressed or fashionable appearance. v.i. feel acute pain; be painful; rankle. n. stinging pain. smart′en, v.t. & i. break to pieces; bring or come to disaster; utterly defeat; bring or drive (fist, vehicle, &c.) violently down, into, &c.; hit (ball) violently downwards over net. n. breaking to pieces or the sound of it; violent fall or collision; sudden disaster or bankruptcy; smashing stroke in lawn-tennis. adv. with a smash.

smattering, n. a slight knowledge of something. smatt′erer, n. person with a smattering.

smear, v.t. & i. daub grease, ink, &c. on surface; stain or obscure thus; be blurred. n. mark left by smearing. smear′y, a.

smell, n. the sense peculiar to the nose; the quality perceived by this; act of inhaling to test smell. v.i. & t. (smelt), possess or exercise sense of smell; perceive or detect by smell; have or emit a smell; be redolent of. ~er, n. (esp., sl.) nose, a blow on it. ~y, a. evil-smelling.

smelt¹, p.t. & p.p. of smell.

smelt², v.t. melt (ore); extract (metal) thus.

smelt³, n. a small edible fish.

smew, n. kind of duck.

smi′lăx, n. kinds of climbing plant.

smile, n. a relaxation of the features expressive of pleasure, amusement, contempt, &c.; bright aspect of nature, &c. v.i. & t. give or wear a smile; express (assent, &c.) with smile.

smirch, v.t. & n. stain, soil.

smirk, n. conceited or inane smile. v.i. & t. smile thus.

smite, v.t. & i. (smōte; smitten rarely smit; -table), strike, hit, chastise; defeat; kill, injure; *p.p.* captivated by. *n.* (sl.) hard hit at cricket.

smith, *n.* worker in iron or other metal. smith'ery, *n.* smith's work. smith'y (-dh-), *n.* blacksmith's workshop; forge.

smitten, *p.p.* of smite.

smock, *n.* chemise (arch.); smockfrock. *v.t.* adorn with close gathers like those of a smockfrock. ~-frock, linen gown with body adorned with gathers or *smocking* as old-fashioned costume of agricultural labourers.

smoke, *n.* visible vapour emitted by burning substance; spell of tobacco-smoking. (sl.) cigar; *Cape* ~, a cheap kind of brandy drunk in South Africa. *v.i. & t.* (-kable), emit smoke or steam; (of chimney or room-fire) discharge smoke into room; stain, dim, fumigate, preserve, drive out, with smoke; inhale or exhale smoke of (cigar, tobacco, pipe, &c.); (school sl.) blush; (Austral. sl.) get away as quickly as possible, 'slope'. ~-stack, funnel of steamer or locomotive. smo'ker, *n.* (esp.) person who smokes tobacco; (colloq.) carriage for smokers in train, concert at which smoking is allowed; *men's informal gathering. smo'ky, *a.* suggestive of or pervaded by smoke.

smooth (-dh), *a.* of even surface; free from projections and roughness; (of passage, progress, &c.) untroubled by storm or obstacles; not hairy; conciliatory or plausible or flattering. *v.t.* make smooth, get rid of. ~-bore, unrifled gun. ~-spoken, ~-tongued, plausible, flattering.

smote, *p.t. & p.p.* of smite.

smo'ther (-ŭdh-), *v.t.* kill by stopping breath of or excluding air from; suppress; hush up; overwhelm with caresses. *n.* dense smoke, steam, or dust.

smou'lder (smōl-), *v.i.* burn without flame or in suppressed way (often fig.). *n.* such burning.

smudge, *n.* blurred dirt-mark, esp. on paper or the face. *v.i. & t.* (-geable), produce smudge; become blurred; blur. smudg'y, *a.*

smug, *a.* self-complacent; prim; unenterprising. *n.* (university sl.) man lacking social qualities and athletic interests.

smu'ggle, *v.t. & i.* convey by stealth, esp. to evade payment of custom-duty; be a smuggler.

smut, *n.* flake of soot, smudge made by it; obscene talk; plantdisease with blackening of grain, &c. *v.t.* mark or infect with smut(s). smutt'y, *a.*

snack, *n.* a slight hasty meal; a share, portion.

snaf'fle, *n.* simple bridle-bit without curb.

snag, *n.* jagged projecting stump or point. snagged (-gd), snag'gy (-gi), *aa.* beset with snags.

snail, *n.* kinds of mollusc, esp. the common creeping snail.

snake, *n.* kinds of scaly limbless reptile, some poisonous, others harmless to man. *v.t.* draw (log, &c.) along, out, or up. ~-stone, porous or absorbent substance regarded as efficacious in curing snake-bite or as a remedy against poison. sna'ky, *a.* snake-like; treacherous-looking.

snap, *v.i. & t.* make sudden audible bite (esp. of dogs); speak with sudden irritation; break in two with sharp noise; close or work with a click; photograph or shoot by snap-shot; seize or jump at eagerly. *n.* act or fact or sound of snapping; spring fastening; sudden brief spell of specified weather; (attrib.) brought about by surprise; (sl.) photograph taken by snapshot; a round game of cards; (sl.) easy task. *adv.* with a snap. ~-dragon, plant with flowers that can be made to gape and shut like mouth; Christmas game of snatching raisins from dish of lighted brandy. ~-shot, *n.* shot fired without time for deliberate aim; taking of photograph with hand camera working instantaneously or picture so got; *v.t. & i.* take such photograph; get such photograph of. **snapp'ish, snapp'y,** *aa.* given to snapping; petulant.

snare, *n.* trap, esp. of the running-noose kind, for small animals (also fig.). *v.t.* (*-rable*), take in snare (lit. & fig.).

snarl, *v.i. & t.* show teeth and growl, as a dog; speak ill-temperedly. *n.* act or sound of snarling; snarled remark, &c.

snatch, *v.t. & i.* seize quickly, eagerly, or unexpectedly; take thus (*up, down, away, off, from*). *n.* sudden outstretching of hand to get something; sudden endeavour; short burst or spell. **snatch'y,** *a.* in short spells; variable.

sneak, *v.i. & t.* go furtively; (school sl.) peach; (sl.) carry off unobserved; filch. *n.* cowardly underhand person; telltale; ball bowled to run along ground at cricket. *sneak'ers,* n.pl. soft-soled noiseless shoes. **sneak'ing,** *a.* (esp., of feelings) persisting in spite of reason.

sneer, *n.* derisive smile or remark. *v.i. & t.* put on or utter sneer; affect by sneering.

sneeze, *n.* explosive sound made through the nostrils. *v.i.* make sneeze. **~weed,** *the plant Helenium autumnale* or other species of the same genus; (Austral.) an odorous herb convertible into snuff. **~wood,** a South-African timber tree; its timber.

snell, *n.* short line of gut, &c. fastening fish-hook to line; snood.

snick, *v.t.* make slight cut in; (Crick.) deflect ball with slight touch. *n.* such cut or touch.

snick'er, *v.i.* neigh or whinny gently. *n.* such sound.

snide, *a.* (sl.) counterfeit, bogus, *n.* snide jewellery, &c.

sniff, *v.i. & t.* draw in air audibly with the nose; smell (flower, &c.) by sniffing. *n.* act or sound of

sniffing; a breath of air, &c. **sniff'y,** *a.* (colloq.) disdainful, not devoid of bad smell.

snigg'er (-g-), *n.* half-suppressed laugh. *v.i.* laugh thus.

snip, *v.t. & i.* cut with scissors. *n.* such cut; piece cut off.

snipe, *n.* marsh game-bird with long straight bill. *v.i. & t.* go snipe-shooting; (Mil.) fire shots from cover; shoot at thus, esp. *n.* one who fires from cover.

snipp'et, *n.* small piece cut off; (pl.) odds and ends of news.

sniv'el, *v.i.* run at the nose; be lachrymose. *n.* running mucus; lachrymose state or talk.

snob, *n.* person whose conduct or opinions are influenced by considerations of social position or wealth. **snobb'ery,** *n.;* **~bish,** *a.*

snood, *n.* (Sc.) fillet for the hair; any of the short lines attaching hooks to sea-fishing line.

snook'er, *n.* game on billiard-table combining pool and pyramids.

*snoop, *v.i.* (colloq.) pry or sneak about.

snooze, *v.i. & n.* nap, doze.

snore, *n.* rattling or grunting noise often made by sleepers in breathing. *v.i.* make this.

snort, *n.* explosive sound made in driving breath out through the nose, esp. by horses or by indignant person. *v.i. & t.* make this sound; express (defiance, &c.) or say with it. **snort'er,** n. (esp., sl.) violent gale; performance, &c. remarkable for force.

snout, *n.* beast's nose and mouth; (contempt.) person's nose; a nozzle.

snow (-ō), *n.* the light white flakes in which frozen vapour falls to earth; white substance or colour. *v.i. & t.* fall in snow; fall or sprinkle like snow; turn (hair) white. **~ball,** *n.* snow pressed or rolled into hard ball, esp. as missile; the guelder-rose; *v.i. & t.* throw snowballs at; have game of this. **~drift,** bank of snow heaped by wind. **~drop,** early white-flowered plant. **~-line**, level above which snow lies permanently in a region. **~-plough**, machine pushing snow aside to clear track. **~-shoes**, boards or strung frames attachable to feet for walking on snow without sinking in. **~ under**, cover (as) with snow, overwhelm with numbers, &c. **snow'y** (-ŏĭ), a. tending to snow; snow-white.

snŭb, v.t. rebuff with words or coldness. n. a snubbing. a. (of nose) stumpy or turned up. ***snŭbb'er**, n. device for checking recoil of motor-car springs.

snŭff¹, n. black excrescence on wick of lighted candle. v.t. & i. rid (candle) of snuff; put out or trim with snuffers or fingers. **snŭff'ers** (-z), n.pl. wick-trimming scissors.

snŭff², v.i. & t. sniff (now rare); take snuff. n. powdered tobacco for sniffing up as stimulant or sedative; medicinal powder similarly used. **snŭff'y**, a. discoloured with snuff-taking.

snŭf'fle, v.i. & t. make sniffing sounds; speak like one with a cold. n. snuffling utterance.

snŭg, a. sheltered, well-enclosed; comfortable; (of income, &c.) sufficing for comfort. **snŭg'ery** (-g-), n. person's private room arranged for comfort; bar-parlour of inn. **snŭg'gle**, v.i. & t. lie or draw close for warmth or in affection.

sō, adv. in that way; in the same way; to the same extent as; to a surpassing degree; accordingly, as it seems; also. conj. (arch.) provided that. int. of approval, &c. pron. (after say, &c.) that, it, those things; (after or) that sort of number or amount. **~and-so**, substitute for name of person or thing. **~called**, called by but doubtfully deserving that name. **~ far as**, to the extent to which. **~ long**, farewell till our next meeting. **~ long as**, provided that. **~ so**, (colloq.) not very well or good; fair.

soak, v.t. & i. place or leave or lie in liquid for saturation; drench; make wet by percolation; take up (liquid) by absorption; booze, be a soaker. n. a soaking. **soak'er**, n. (esp.) soaking shower; hard drinker.

soap, n. substance used in washing, consisting of fat or oil combined with alkali. v.t. & i. apply soap to; wash with soap. **~-bubble**, iridescent globe made by blowing through pipe after dipping it in soap-suds. **~-stone**, kind of massive talc with greasy feel. **~-suds**, froth of soapy water. **soap'y**, a. like or impregnated with soap; (fig.) unctuous or flattering.

soar (sōr), v.i. fly high; mount to a great height (also fig.).

sŏb, n. convulsive drawing of breath, esp. in weeping. v.i. & t. weep or breathe or speak with sobs. ***~-stuff**, pathos, sentimental writing.

sō'ber, a. not drunk; not given to drink; moderate, sane, tranquil; (of colours) quiet. v.t. & i. make or become sober. **sobri'ety**, n. soberness.

sō'briquet (-kā), **sou-** (sōō-), n. nickname.

sŏcc'er, n. (sl.) Association football.

sō'ciable (-sha-), a. fitted for or disposed to companionship or conversation. n. carriage, double tricycle, or settee, with special arrangement of seats; *informal reception. **~bility**, n.

sō'cial (-shl), a. living in communities; unfitted for solitary life; concerned with the mutual relations of men or classes; relating to society. n. social gathering. **sō'cialism** (-sha-), n. principle that individual liberty should be completely subordinated to the interests of the community; social equality; collectivism. **~ist**, n.; **~istic**, a.; **~ize**, v.t. make social or socialistic. **~ization**, n. **sŏcĭ'al'ĭty** (-shl-), n. **soci'ety**, n. social mode of life;

any social community; the upper classes, people of fashion; company or companionship; an association of persons; *voting members of church congregation.

sŏciŏl'ogy, n. study of the history and nature of human society. sŏciŏlŏg'ical, a.; ~gist, n.

sŏck¹, n. short stocking not reaching knee; inside sole for use in shoe; light shoe of ancient comic actors.

sŏck², v.t. hit. n. blow of fist or missile. adv. squarely.

sŏck'ĕt, n. natural or artificial hollow for something to fit into or revolve in. ~ed, a.

sŏ'cle, n. plinth, esp. as pedestal of statue or column.

Sŏcrăt'ic, a. of, like, following, worthy of, Socrates.

sŏd, n. piece of turf pared off; (poet.) surface of the ground.

sŏ'da, n. one of the compounds of sodium in common use, esp. sodium carbonate or bicarbonate; soda-water. ~water, water made effervescent for use as a drink.

sŏdd'en, a. saturated with liquid; heavy and doughy; stupid with drink. v.t. make sodden.

sŏ'dĭum, n. an alkaline metal.

sŏd'omy, n. unnatural sexual intercourse, esp. between males.

sŏ'fa, n. long stuffed seat with raised end(s) and back.

soft (-aw-), a. not hard; yielding to pressure; malleable or plastic or easily cut; smooth or fine textured; moist or rainy; not loud or strident, low-toned; (of air, &c.) balmy; gentle, quiet, conciliatory; easily touched, compassionate; flabby, feeble, luxurious, half-witted. n. silly weak person. adv. softly. int. (arch.) hold, stop, not so fast. *~ drink, (sl.) non-alcoholic liquor. ~ job, work light in proportion to the pay. ~ sawder, flattery, blarney. ~ soap, liquid soap, (fig.) flattery. sŏften (saw'fn), v.i. & t. make or grow soft. sŏ'fty (saw-), n. half-witted person.

sŏgg'y (-g-), a. waterlogged.

‖ soi-disant (swah dē'zahñ), a. self-styled, pretended.

soil¹, v.t. & i. smear or stain with dirt, &c.; tarnish, defile; show stains, &c. n. dirty mark. ~pipe, sewage or waste-water pipe. soil'less (-l-l-), a.

soil², n. the ground; upper layer of earth; mould.

soirée (swăr'ā), n. evening party, esp. for talk or discussion.

sojourn (sŭj'ern), n. temporary stay at a place. v.i. make sojourn.

sŏ'la, n. tall pithy-stemmed swamp-plant of India; the pith of this employed in making light hats. ~ tŏpi, Indian sun-helmet of the pith.

sŏl'ace, n. & v.t. (-ceable), comfort in distress or disappointment.

sŏ'lan, ~ goose, n. gannet.

sŏ'lar, a. of or reckoned by the sun.

sŏlā'tĭum (-shĭ-), n. (pl. -ia), sum, &c. received as compensation.

sold, p.t. & p.p. of sell.

sŏl'der (sŏd-), n. fusible alloy used in joining the edges of less fusible metal. v.t. join with solder.

sŏl'dier (-jer), n. member of army; private or N.C.O. in army; military commander of specified ability; (sl.) red herring. v.i. serve as soldier. ~like, ~ly, aa. ~ship, n. military skill. sŏl'diery (-jeri), n. soldiers as a class.

sole¹, n. kinds of flat-fish; undersurface of foot, part of shoe or stocking below this; lower surface or base of certain things (e.g. plough, golf-club). v.t. (-lable), provide (boot) with sole.

sole², a. one and only; exclusive or restricted to a single person, &c.; (arch.) alone, unique.

sŏl'ecism, n. flagrant offence against grammar, idiom, or etiquette. sŏlĕcis'tic, a.

sŏl'emn (-m), a. accompanied with ceremony; impressive; grave or deliberate; pompous. solĕm'nity, n. solemn rite; solemnness. sŏl'emnize, v.t. (-zable), celebrate (festival); duly perform (rite, esp. wedding). ~zation, n.

sol-fa (-ah). *n.* use of the note-names in singing. *v.i.* & *t.* sing thus and not with words.

soli'cit, *v.t.* ask repeatedly or urgently; importune; request or invite. solicita'tion, *n.*

soli'citor, *n.* (esp.) member of branch of legal profession chiefly concerned with advising clients and preparing their cases.

soli'citous, *a.* anxious, concerned; eager to do; desirous of. soli'citude, *n.* being solicitous.

sol'id, *a.* of stable shape; of the same material throughout; sound or reliable; of three dimensions. *n.* a body or substance of stable shape; (Geom.) a body or magnitude of three dimensions. solidá'rity, *n.* community of interests, feelings, and action. solid'ify, *v.t.* & *i.* (*-fiable*), make or become solid. ~fication, *n.*; solid'ity, *n.*

soli'loquy, *n.* talking to oneself; piece of such talk. ~quize, *v.i.* indulge in soliloquy.

sol'itaire, *n.* a gem set by itself or the stud, &c. adorned with it; kinds of game for single player.

sol'itary, *a.* living alone; without companions; unfrequented; single; lonely; sole. *n.* a recluse. sol'itude, *n.* being solitary; a solitary place.

so'lo, *n.* (pl. -os), song or instrumental piece for single performer; (Cards) kind of whist in which one player opposes three or undertakes certain other tasks. ~ist, *n.* performer of solo.

sol'stice, *n.* time at which the sun is farthest from the equator and appears to pause before returning. solsti'tial, *a.*

sol'uble, *a.* dissolvable in liquor; (of problem) solvable. ~bility, *n.*

so'lus, *pred. a.* alone, unaccompanied (esp. in stage directions).

solu'tion (-lōō-), *n.* dissolving or being dissolved; conversion of solid or gas into liquid state by mixture with a liquid called the solvent; solving of a problem.

solve, *v.t.* (*-vable*), find or supply the answer to or way out of (difficulty, &c.). solvabil'ity, *n.*

sol'vency, *n.* being pecuniarily solvent. sol'vent. *a.* capable of acting as dissolver; having money enough to meet one's liabilities; *n.* solvent liquid or substance; an agency that saps belief, &c.

som'bre (-ber), *a.* gloomy, dismal; dark-coloured.

sombre'ro (-ārō), *n.* (pl. -os), broad-brimmed felt hat.

some (sŭm, sum, acc. to emphasis), *a.* an unspecified amount or number of; an appreciable or considerable amount of; conjecturally the specified number or amount; (sl. & U.S.) of surpassing magnitude or quality; worthy of the name. *pron.* some people; some specimens of the class in question; some number or amount of. *adv.* (sl. & U.S.) somewhat; rather; a good deal. ~body, some person; a person of importance. ~how, in some way or for some reason or other. ~one, somebody. ~thing, *n.* some thing, esp. as substitute for more precise term. ~time, (arch.) formerly, quondam. ~times, now and then; at one time or other. ~what, in some degree; a certain amount. ~where, in or at some place.

Som'erset House (sŭ-), *n.* London building used for keeping of proved wills and Inland revenue offices.

so'mersault, -set (sŭ-), *n.* acrobatic feat of turning heels over head and alighting on feet.

somnam'bulism, *n.* walking about during sleep. ~ist, *n.*; ~istic, *a.*

somnif'erous, *a.* inducing sleep, narcotic.

som'nolent, *a.* half asleep; inducing sleep. som'nolence, *n.*

son (sŭn), *n.* one's male child; descendant; native of a country; devotee or slave of. ~in-law, daughter's husband. ~ship, *n.*

so'nant, *a.* (Phonet.) involving voice. *n.* a sonant letter.

ɛh, as (rou)ge; ð =1; ᵫ, ŭr, =ēr; ȝ, s̝, =1, l; and see p. 4. ° = U.S.

3495 Q

sona′ta (-nah-), *n.* instrumental piece in several movements.

sŏng, *n.* singing; vocal music; set of words for singing; poetry; a poem. ~**bird,** bird of the singing kinds. ~**ster,** *n.* singer; song-bird; poet. ~**stress,** *n.*

sŏnn′ĕt, *n.* piece of rhymed verse containing fourteen ten-syllable lines; (loosely) any short poem. **sonnéteer′,** *n.* composer of sonnets.

so′nny (sŭ-), *n.* small boy.

sonŏr′ous, *a.* having a resonant or rich or powerful sound.

‖ **soo′jee,** *n.* (food prepared from) flour of Indian wheat.

sōōn, *adv.* after no long interval; relatively early; readily, willingly.

soot, *n.* black powdery substance rising in the smoke of coal, wood, &c., and adhering to the sides of chimneys, &c. *v.t.* mark with soot; apply soot as fertilizer.

sooth, *n.* (arch.) verity, the truth. ~**sayer,** diviner, prognosticator.

soothe (-dh), *v.t.* (-*thable*), calm (person, nerves, &c.); alleviate (pain); humour (person, vanity).

soot′y, *a.* of soot; black as or with soot.

sŏp, *n.* piece of bread, &c. soaked in gravy, milk, &c.; bribe offered to pacify. *v.t. & i.* soak; take up by absorption; drench; be wet through.

sŏph′ism, *n.* a false argument meant to deceive. **sŏph′ist,** *n.* reasoner willing to avail himself of fallacies that will help his case. **sophis′tic,** ~**al,** *aa.* sophis′ticāte, *v.t. & i.* spoil the simplicity or naturalness of; corrupt or tamper with. ~**tion,** ~**tor,** *nn.* **sŏph′istry,** *n.* use of sophisms; a sophism.

soph′omŏre, *n.* second-year student at college or university. **sŏphomŏr′ic,** *a.* immature, bombastic.

sŏporif′ic, *a.* sleep-producing. *n.* a soporific drug or agency.

sŏpp′y, *a.* soaked; swampy; full of mawkish sentiment.

soprā′nō (-ah-), *n.* (pl. -os), highest female or boy's voice, treble; soprano singer.

sŏr′cery, *n.* witchcraft. **sŏr′cerer,** ~**ess,** *nn.* man, woman, practising sorcery.

sŏrd′id, *a.* squalid, mean; humiliating; inspired by low or mercenary or selfish ends.

sōre, *a.* (arch.) grievous; suffering bodily or mental pain; with the skin broken or inflamed or ulcerated. *n.* a sore place, esp. with suppuration; a sore subject. *adv.* grievously.

sŏr′ghum (-gum), *n.* kinds of grass including millet and Chinese sugar-cane.

sŏr′rel, *n.* kinds of sour-leaved herb.

sŏr′row (-ō), *n.* mental pain or what causes it. *v.i.* feel sorrow; mourn. ~**ful,** feeling or causing sorrow.

sŏr′ry, *a.* pained at or regretful over something; feeling pity for some one; ridiculously bad. **sŏr′rily,** *adv.*; **sŏr′riness,** *n.*

sŏrt, *n.* a kind or variety. *v.t.* arrange in sets according to size or quality or other standard; pick out as of one sort.

sŏr′tie (-ē), *n.* sally of besieged party.

sŏrti′tion, *n.* lot-casting; distribution by lot.

S.O.S. (ĕsōs), wireless code-signal of extreme distress.

sŏt, *n.* man constantly stupid with drink. **sŏtt′ish,** *a.*

‖ **sŏttō vō′ce** (-chē), *adv.* in an undertone.

sou (sōō), *n.* the French ½d.

‖ **souc′ăr** (-ow-), *n.* Hindu banker or money-lender.

sou′chŏng (sōōsh-), *n.* a choice black tea.

Soudanese (sōōdănĕz′), *a.* of the Soudan. *n.* Soudanese native.

soufflé (sōōf′lā), *n.* dish made of beaten white of egg.

sough (sŏŏh, sow, sŭf), *n.* sighing or moaning of wind. *v.i.* make a sough.

sought, *p.t. & p.p.* of seek.

soul (sōl), *n.* the immaterial part of man regarded as immortal; the organ of emotion, thought, and will; human being; spirit, essence. ~less, *a.* (esp.) destitute of the humane emotions.

sound[1], *n.* audible air-vibration; what is or may be heard; mere noise as opposed to meaning. *v.i. & t.* emit sound; convey specified impression; (part.) of imposing sound or import; produce sound from (bugle, &c.); give signal thus; celebrate; pronounce; test condition of (heart, &c.) with stethoscope, &c.

sound[2], *a.* free from disease or defects or corruption or heresy; of good quality throughout; reliable; not fallacious; (of sleep) unbroken. *adv.* soundly.

sound[3], *n.* a strait; swimming-bladder of cod and some other fishes; kind of surgical probe. *v.t. & i.* measure depth of sea, &c. with the lead; examine surgically; try to elicit the views of. **sound'ings** (-z), *n.pl.* depth of sea, &c. as taken with the lead.

soup (sōōp), *n.* liquid food made by stewing bones, meat, vegetables, &c. ~and fish, (sl.) evening dress.

‖ **soupçon** (sōō'psawn), *n.* a dash or trace or tinge of.

sour (-owr), *a.* tasting like unripe fruit or vinegar; (of bread, &c.) spoilt by fermentation, &c.; (of soil) dank; peevish or morose. *v.t. & i.* turn sour. ~sop, a W.-Ind. fruit and tree.

source (sōrs), *n.* place from which stream issues; fountain-head; origin; place of origin.

souse, *v.t. & i.* put in pickle; send or go with a plunge into liquid. *n.* plunge into liquid; sound of this. *adv.* with a souse.

soutane (sōōtahn'), *n.* long buttoned gown worn by R.-C. priests as outer garment.

south, *n.* point of horizon directly opposite north. *adv.* towards or in the south. *a.* situated in or towards the south; facing south;

coming from south. ~east, region half-way between south and east (*adv. & a.* like *south*). ~easter, wind from south-east. ~easterly, towards or coming from the south-east. ~eastern, belonging to the south-east, or in that direction. ~eastward, towards the south-east. ~eastwardly, in a south-eastern direction. ~eastwards, towards or in the south-east. ~ pole, see pole[2]. ~west, &c., like *south-east*, &c. **sou'therly** (sŭdh-), *a. & adv.* (of direction) towards, (of wind) from, south, or thereabouts. **sou'thern** (sŭdh-), *a.* situated in or belonging to or characteristic of the south. ~ Cross, a constellation. **sou'therner** (sŭdh-), *n.* native of the south. **south'ward**, *a., adv., & n.; ~wards, adv.* **sou'thernwood**, a scented wormwood. **southron** (Sc.; sŭdh'ron), *n.* southerner or Englishman.

souvenir (sōō'vener), *n.* thing given or kept in memory of a person or place or event.

sou''-wes'ter, *n.* south-west wind; waterproof hat with neck-flap.

sov'ereign (-vrĭn), *a.* supreme and exempt from external control; having supreme power. *n.* a sovereign ruler; British gold coin of £1. **sov'ereignty** (-vrĭn-), *n.* supreme power.

Sŏv'iĕt, *n.* any of the councils elected by the workers and soldiers of a district in revolutionary Russia, or of a smaller number elected by these, or the all-Russian congress of delegates from these latter.

sow[1] (sō), *v.t. & i.* (p.p. *sowed* or *sown*), scatter or plant seed for reproduction; propagate.

sow[2], *n.* female pig. ~bread, kinds of cyclamen.

‖ **sowar'**, *n.* (Anglo-Ind.) native horseman or mounted orderly, policeman, &c.; native trooper, esp. one belonging to the irregular cavalry.

sowar'ry (-ah-), *n.* (Anglo-Ind.) mounted attendant of a person of high rank, State official, &c.

soy, n. (sauce prepared from) soya-(bean).

soy'a-bean, n. Asiatic plant rich in oil, used as food, &c.

spa ((-ah), n. place resorted to for medicinal water.

space, n. an interval between things; regions beyond ken; room available or required; a period or interval of time. v.t. (-ceable), set at intervals. spā'-cious (-shus), a. having ample space; roomy.

spade¹, n. broad-bladed digging-tool with long handle. ~~work, preparatory work of an arduous kind. spāde'ful (-dfool), n.

spade², n. one of the four patterns of playing-card pip.

spādg'er, g'ick, nn. (sl.) sparrow.

spake, p.t. of speak.

spal'peen', n. (Ir.) mean fellow; youngster.

span¹, n. utmost distance between tips of thumb and little finger; nine inches; short distance or time; distance from support to support of an arch or roof; an arch of a bridge; pair of draught animals. v.t. measure by hand-spans; (of bridge, roof, &c.) cross or cover, esp. with single span.

span², p.t. of spin.

spān'drel, n. space between either shoulder of arch and surrounding rectangular framework.

spangle (spăng'gl), n. (usu. in pl.), small piece(s) of glittering metal sewn on garments, &c. (fig. of stars, &c.). spangled (g'gld), a.

Spăn'iard (-yard), n. native of Spain. Spăn'ish, a. of Spain or the Spaniards or their language.

span'iel (-yel), n. kinds of large-eared long-haired dog.

spănk, v.t. & i. slap with the hand; go at a great pace. n. a slap. spănk'er, n. (esp.) fast horse or fine specimen of something (sl.); fore-and-aft sail on mizen-mast. spănk'ing, a. (sl.) excellent.

spăn'ner, n. gripping-tool for working nuts, &c.; wrench.

spăr¹, n. stout pole of the kind used for ship's yards, &c.

spăr², n. kinds of crystalline mineral.

spăr³, v.i. (of game-cock, &c.) strike out with the spurs; box; (fig.) engage in banter or repartee.

spāre, v.t. & i. (-rable), abstain from hurting or destroying; let off, dispense with; find (time, &c. for something); let person have (thing, &c.) out of one's superfluity. a. that is to spare; superfluous; kept in reserve; frugal; lean. n. spare part for substitution in machine; *(bowling or ninepins) knocking down all the pins with two bowls. ~ rib, joint of pork consisting of ribs closely trimmed. ~ room, guest-chamber.

spárk, n. fiery particle of burning substance; flash of light between two neighbouring electric conductors; a gay young fellow. v.i. & t. emit sparks; apply electric spark to, ignite or affect thus. sparking-plug, device for firing explosive mixture in motor-engine.

spár'kle, v.i. seem to emit sparks; radiate or emit or reflect successive small flashes; be bright with shifting points of light. n. sparkling effect; glitter. spárk'-let, n. small spark; least possible amount of a quality.

spā'rrow (-ō), n. small bird haunting houses, &c. ~~hawk, small kind of hawk.

sparse, a. thinly scattered.

Spárt'an, n. native of ancient Sparta. a. as of the Spartans.

spā'sm, n. convulsive muscular contraction; violent access of emotion. spasmōd'ic (-âz-), a. sudden and violent; intermittent.

spăt¹, n. spawn of shellfish.

spăt², p.t. of spit.

spăt³, abbr. of spatterdash.

spătch'cŏck, n. a fowl split open and grilled immediately after being killed. *v.t.* cook thus; insert (item of news, &c.) sandwich-fashion in middle of something.

spate, *n.* sudden river-flood.

spā'tial (-shl), *a.* of or in or relating to space.

spätt'er, *v.t. & i.* fly or send (mud, &c.) flying in drops or splashes; besprinkle. *n.* a spattering fall. **~dash** (now usu. *spat*), gaiter of cloth, &c. covering instep and ankle. *~dock,* the yellow waterlily.

spăt'ŭla, *n.* instrument with edgeless blade for spreading ointment, mixing pigments, &c.

spăv'in, *n.* kind of tumour on horse's leg. **spăv'ined** (-nd), *a.*

spawn, *n.* eggs of fish, frogs, molluscs, &c.; (contempt.) progeny. *v.i. & t.* produce or deposit spawn; produce by spawning; (contempt.) generate.

speak, *v.i. & t.* (*spŏke* & arch. *spāke; spŏken*), utter words in the ordinary way; say something; hold conversation; make a speech; utter or pronounce. **speak'easy,* n. an illicit bar.

speak'er, *n.* (esp.) person of specified skill in speech-making; official president of House of Commons. **speaking-trumpet,** instrument magnifying sound of voice. **~tube,** tube conveying voice from one room, &c. to another.

spear, *n.* hunter's or foot-soldier's thrusting or hurling weapon. *v.t.* pierce or wound with spear. **~mint,** common garden mint.

spĕc, *n.* (sl.) speculation.

spĕ'cial (-shl), *a.* of a peculiar or restricted kind; of or for a particular person, occasion, or thing. *n.* a special constable, edition, train, &c. **~ constable,** private person sworn in for special occasion. **~ edition,** newspaper containing later intelligence than earlier editions. **~ train,** extra train for special purpose. **spĕ'cialist** (-sha-), *n.* person devoting himself to a

single branch of his profession or subject. **spĕcial'ity** (-shi-), *n.* specialness; particular item; distinctive quality. **spĕ'cialize** (-sha-), *v.t. & i* (*-zable*), make special; adapt for a particular purpose; be a specialist. **~zation,** *n.* **spĕ'cialty** (-shl-), *n.* a speciality.

spĕ'cie (-shĭē), *n.* money in the shape of coin.

spĕ'cies (-shĭēz), *n.* a class of things having some common characteristics; a subdivision of a genus; a sort, kind.

specĭf'ic, *a.* definite, distinctly formulated; possessing the properties that characterize a species. *n.* a specific remedy. **spĕ'cĭfy,** *v.t.* (*-fiable*), make specific or definite; mention expressly; give the name of. **specĭfica'tion,** *n.* (esp.) any or all of the details specified in a contract or patent.

spĕ'cimen, *n.* part or piece to show nature of the whole; a sample.

spĕ'cious (-shus), *a.* fair-seeming; plausible.

spĕck[1], *n.* small spot or stain or particle. *v.t.* mark with specks. **spĕck[2],** *n.* (U.S. & S.Afr.) fat meat, bacon, pork; fat of seals, whales, &c.; blubber.

spĕc'kle, *n.* small spot, esp. as natural marking on skin, &c. *v.t.* mark thus (usu. in *p.p.*).

spĕc'tacle, *n.* a public show or noteworthy scene; (pl.) pair of lenses to correct or assist defective eyesight, set in a frame. **spĕc'tacled** (-ld), *a.* wearing spectacles. **spĕctăc'ŭlar,** *a.* of the nature of a show.

spĕctā'tor, *n.* looker-on; person present at a performance.

spĕc'tral, *a.* ghost-like, unreal; of the spectrum.

spĕc'tre (-ter), *n.* a ghost; fear of an expected calamity.

spĕc'troscōpe, *n.* instrument for producing and examining spectra.

spĕc'trum, *n.* (pl. *-ra*), the

---

gh, as (*rou*)ge; ŏ=I; ñ, ŭr, =ẽr; y̆, y̆, =I, ī; and see p. 4. *=U.S.

coloured band into which a beam of light is decomposed.

spec'ulate, v.i. & t. indulge in thought of a conjectural theoretical kind; wonder or guess how, &c., buy and sell stocks or goods in the hope of profiting by changes in market value; deal in transactions of a risky kind. ~tion, ~tor, nn.; ~tive, a.

spec'ulum, n. (pl. -la), surgical instrument for dilating orifices to facilitate examination; mirror used for some scientific purpose.

sped, p.t. & p.p. of speed.

speech, n. speaking; a spoken remark or what is said continuously by one speaker; language. speech'ify, v.i. make speeches; hold forth oratorically in conversation. speech'less, a. unable to speak for overpowering emotion.

speed, n. dispatch, rapidity; relative pace of motion or action. v.i. & t. (sped), go fast; smooth the way of; give prosperity to. ~om'eter, speed-indicator in motor-car, &c. ~trap, trap to catch speeding motorists. *~way, course for fast driving of horses or motors. speed'y, a. prompt, expeditious; going at great pace.

speed'well (-el), n. a blue-flowered plant.

spell[1], n. words used as charm; fascination exercised by person or thing. v.t. & i. (spelt or spelled), write or name the letters of (word); spell words correctly. ~binder, speaker who can hold audience spellbound. ~bound, held with attention as by a spell.

spell[2], n. time devoted to or taken by something; (Austral.) a period of rest from work, &c.

spelt[1], p.t. & p.p. of spell[1].

spelt[2], n. German wheat.

spel'ter, n. zinc.

spen'cer, n, kinds of short over-jacket.

spend, v.t. & i. (spent), pay out (money); expend or use up; pass in some place or occupa-tion; (p.p.) exhausted. ~thrift, person who wastes his money.

Spenser'ians (-z), n.pl. stanzas of the kind used in Spenser's Faerie Queene.

spent, p.t. & p.p. of spend.

sperm, n. semen. ~whale, whale yielding spermaceti.

spermace'ti, n. substance got from head of sperm-whale.

spermat'ic, a. of sperm.

spermatorrhoe'a (-rēa), n. involuntary spermatic emission.

spermatozo'ön, n. (pl. -zoa), fertilizing filament in semen.

spew, v.t. & i. (vulg.) vomit.

sphag'num, n. (pl. -na), kinds of moss growing in bogs and peat, and used as packing, &c.

sphere, n. solid figure having all points of its surface equidistant from a point within it; a ball or globe so shaped; field of action or province or scope. spher'ical, a. sphere-shaped; concerned with spheres. spher'oid, n. body of approximately spherical shape. spheroid'al, a.

sphinc'ter, n. ring-muscle closing and opening orifice.

sphinx, n. figure of couching lion with woman's head.

spice, n. aromatic or pungent vegetable substance used as flavouring. v.t. flavour with spice or with wit, &c. spi'cery, n. spices; aromatic scents.

spick and span, a. trim, smart.

spi'cy, a. having much spice, aromatic; piquant, racy.

*spiel, n. talk, speech. v.i. make speeches.

spi'der, n. kinds of eight-legged web-spinning animal.

spif'licate, v.t. (joc.) castigate.

spig'ot, n. vent-peg or part of tap by which flow is controlled.

spike, n. sharp projecting point; long nail; an inflorescence of many sessile flowers set closely on long common axis. v.t. furnish with spikes; transfix; plug vent of gun with spike.

spike'nard (-kn-), n. aromatic substance got from an Eastern plant.

māte, mēte, mīte, mōte, mūte, mōōt; răck, rĕck, rĭck, rŏck, rŭck, rōōk;

spill[1], *v.t. & i.* (**spilt** or **spilled**), let (liquid, powder) run out from receptacle; (of liquid, &c.) run out thus; shed; (of horse, vehicle, &c.) throw or upset or let fall. *n.* (colloq.) fall from horse or vehicle.

spill[2], *n.* strip of wood or folded piece of paper for lighting candles, &c.

spill′ikin, **spĕl′ican**, *n.* one of the wooden or ivory slips thrown in a heap in the game of *spillikins*, to be removed each without disturbing the rest.

spilt, *p.t. & p.p.* of spill[1].

spin, *v.i. & t.* (**spăn** or **spŭn**, **spŭn**), make thread by drawing out and twisting together the fibres of wool, &c.; make (web, &c.) by extrusion of fine viscous thread; compose (story, &c.); turn or cause to turn like a top or wheel. *n.* revolving motion. **spinning-jenny**, early form of spinning-machine. **~wheel** (hist.), household spinning-apparatus with flywheel and treadle.

spin′ach (-nĭj), *n.* a vegetable eaten boiled.

spi′nal, *a.* of the spine.

spin′dle, *n.* slender rod serving to twist and wind thread in spinning; a varying quantity of yarn or thread.

spin′drift, *n.* scudding spray at sea.

spine, *n.* the backbone or vertebral column; the central line of a roof or the like; thorn or prickle. **~less**, *a.* (esp.) lacking backbone or character.

spin′el, *n.* scarlet ruby-like precious stone.

spin′ĕt, *n.* (hist.) musical instrument of harpsichord kind.

spinn′aker, *n.* large extra sail of racing yacht.

spinn′erĕt, *n.* spinning-organ in spider, silk-worm, &c.

spinn′ey, *n.* (pl. *-eys*), copse.

spin′ster, *n.* unmarried woman.

spĭr′acle, *n.* air-hole, blow-hole.

spirae′a, *n.* kinds of garden plant allied to meadowsweet.

spīr′al, *a.* coiled in a plane, or as round a cylinder or cone. *n.* spiral curve or course.

spīr′ant, *a. & n.* **~** *letter* or *sound*, consonant during the pronunciation of which the passage of breath does not wholly cease.

spire, *n.* tapering structure in form of tall cone or pyramid rising from tower-top.

spi′rit, *n.* the element in man regarded as separable from and animating the body; a person from the mental or moral point of view; an apparition; a person's disposition or mental attitude; exhibition of courage or energy or vivacity; (pl.) state of cheerfulness or despondency; (sing. or pl.) distilled alcoholic liquor. *v.t.* convey mysteriously *away.* **spi′rited**, *a.* showing courage or enterprise. **spi′ritless**, *a.* despondent; lacking energy; abject.

spi′ritual, *a.* concerned with the spirit or soul or with religion; unworldly; mental, intellectual. **spiritūal′ity**, *n.*; **spi′ritūalize**, *v.t.*; **~zā′tion**, *n.*

spi′ritūalism, *n.* belief in the possibility of communication with the dead or other spirits. **~ist**, *n. & a.*

spi′rituous, *a.* of the nature of or containing distilled spirit.

spirt. See spurt.

spit[1], *n.* pointed rod on which a joint of meat, &c. is stuck for roasting; point of land running out into the sea, &c. *v.t.* stick (meat, &c.) on spit; run (person, &c.) through with sword, &c.

spit[2], *v.i. & t.* (**spăt** & arch. **spĭt**), eject saliva from the mouth; (fig.) utter curses, &c.; (of cat) show anger by spitting sound. *n.* spittle. **~fire**, angry cat; hot-tempered person; snappish dog.

spit[3], *n.* spade-depth.

spite, *n.* ill will; malice. *v.t.* mortify intentionally; show malice towards. **~ful**, *a.* animated or dictated by spite.

spit′tle, *n.* saliva. **spittoon′**, *n.* pan to spit into.

splash, *v.t. & i.* agitate liquid so that drops of it fly about; be thus agitated or flung about; wet or stain or spatter by splashing; fall into or go through water or mud with splashing. *n.* splashing or the sound or mark made by it; a daub or patch of colour. ~-**board,** mudguard in front of driver.

splay, *v.t. & i.* construct (aperture) with divergent sides; be so shaped or set; carry one's feet with toes turned abnormally out. *n.* extent to which aperture is splayed. *a.* splayed.

spleen, *n.* abdominal organ acting on the blood; moroseness, irritability. ~-**wort,** kinds of fern.

splěn′did, *a.* magnificent, admirable, glorious. **splěn′dĭd′erous,** *a.* (sl.) extremely good. **splěn′dour** (-der), *n.* splendidness.

splěnět′ic, *a.* morose; liable to fits of ill-temper. **splěn′ic,** *a.* (Anat., Med.) of the spleen.

splice, *v.t.* (-*ceable*) unite (pieces of rope or wood) into one length by interweaving strands or by scarfing; (sl.) join in matrimony. *n.* junction by splicing.

splint, *n.* slip of wood, &c. bound on to keep broken bone in position while it sets.

splin′ter, *n.* pointed, sharp-edged, or narrow fragment broken off from some hard material. *v.i. & t.* break into splinters; come off as a splinter.

split, *v.i. & t.* (*split*) divide into parts; burst by explosion or pressure from within; deprive of or lose unity. *n.* splitting; fissure, rent; schism.

splŏtch, *n.* daub, smear.

*splurge, *n.* ostentatious display of wealth, &c. *v.i.* make splurge.

splŭtt′er, *v. & n.* sputter.

spoil, *n.* (in collect. sing. or pl.), plunder taken from enemy; emoluments of office, &c.; things found or acquired. *v.t. & i.* (*spoilt* or *spoiled*), plunder, deprive of; impair; make useless or inefficient; injure by indulgence; (of

food, &c.) decay or go bad. ~-**sport,** meddler.

spoke², *n.* any of the radiating bars connecting wheel's hub and felloe, or of the projecting handles of a steering-wheel; rung of ladder. ~-**shave,** tool for planing spokes, &c.

spoke², *p.t.* of speak.

spokes′man (-ks-), *n.* (pl. -*men*), person deputed to voice the opinions of others.

spŏliā′tion, *n.* pillaging; depredation; despoiling.

spŏn′dee (-dĭ), *n.* metrical foot of two long syllables. —**dā′ic,** *a.*

sponge (-ŭnj), *n.* kinds of aquatic animal or animal-colony; skeleton of a sponge used as absorbent in bathing, cleansing surfaces, &c.; mop for cleaning cannon-bore; hard drinker; sponger. *v.t. & i.* (-*geable*), wet or cleanse with sponge; soak up with sponge; live as a parasite *on.* **spo′nger** (-ŭnj-), *n.* (esp.) person who habitually sponges on others. **spo′ngy** (-ŭnj), *a.* of porous elastic absorbent texture.

spŏn′son, *n.* platform projecting from ship's side.

spŏn′sor, *n.* godfather or godmother; person who answers or gives security for another. ~-**ship,** *n.*

spŏntā′neous, *a.* resulting from natural impulse; not forced or suggested or caused from outside; not deliberate or laboured. **spŏntānē′ĭty,** *n.*

spoof (sl.), *n.* hoaxing; jocular deception. *v.t.* subject to spoof.

spook, *n.* a ghost.

spool, *n.* bobbin or reel.

spoon, *n.* shallow oval bowl with long handle; kinds of hollow-faced golf-club; (sl.) person in love. *v.t. & i.* lift with spoon; (Crick., &c.) strike feebly upwards; (sl.) make love. ~-**bill,** kinds of bird. **spoon′y** (sl.), *a.* in love; amorous; *n.* mild simpleton.

spoon′erism, *n.* accidental transposition of sounds in successive words.

spoon'ful (-ŏŏl), n. (pl. -ls), amount that fills a spoon.

spoor, n. animal's trail.

sporad'ic, a. occurring only here and there. ~al, a.

spore, n. one of the germs by which flowerless plants are reproduced.

spo'rran, n. pouch hung in front of kilt.

sport, n. fun or frolic; a pastime of an outdoor or athletic kind; such pastimes collectively; (pl.) meeting for athletic competitions; an animal or plant that deviates from type; (sl.) sportsman, good fellow. v.i. & t. gambol, play; toy or play or trifle with; (colloq.) exhibit on one's person or premises. ~ing, a. sportsmanlike; devoted to sport. ~ive, a. playful. sports'man (-an), person fond of hunting and such sports; person ready to risk failure or to act fairly towards opponents. ~like, a.; ~ship, n.

spot, n. small mark or stain; pimple on skin; blemish in character; a particular area or place or locality. v.t. & i. mark with spot(s); (of material) show spots readily; (colloq.) pick out or detect or identify. spotted fever, cerebro-spinal meningitis. spot'less, a. absolutely clean; (fig.) without blemish. spott'y, a.

spouse (-z), n. husband or wife; (pl.) married pair.

spout, n. projecting tube or lip for liquid to issue from; jet of liquid. v.t. & i. discharge or issue in a jet; discharge liquid; (colloq.) declaim or recite.

sprain, v.t. wrench (joint) so as to cause pain and swelling. n. such injury.

sprang, p.t. of spring.

sprat, n. a small sea-fish; small child, thin person.

sprawl, v.i. & t. fall or lie with limbs flung out; throw limbs about; be of irregular form.

spray, n. branched shoot or twig with its flowers or leaves; piece of jewellery of similar form;

liquid flying in fine drops. v.t. sprinkle with spray. spray'er, n. apparatus for sprinkling with insecticide or other spray.

spread (-ĕd), v.t. & i. extend the surface of, cause to cover larger surface, by unrolling, unfolding, smearing, flattening, &c.; diffuse or be diffused; lay out on a surface. n. extent or compass of a thing; expanse; diffusion; (sl.) meal provided; *(Commerc.) difference between cost of manufacture and selling price. ~ eagle, figure of eagle with wings and legs spread in heraldry, &c. ~ eagleism, noisy nationalism, with reference to the spread eagle as U.S. emblem.

spree, n. bit of fun; carouse, drunken frolic.

sprew (-rōō), (S.-Afr.) a bird of the genus Spreo, characterized by its iridescent plumage; a glossy starling.

sprig, n. small wedge-shaped headless nail; twig or shoot of some plant; (fig.) scion.

spright'ly (-īt-), a. vivacious, lively, brisk.

spring, v.i. & t. (sprăng, sprŭng), well up from below ground; burst forth from soil or root or stem; rise from a base; be descended from; jump from the ground; bring suddenly into action or view. n. springing motion; place where water or oil wells up; motive or source of action; the season of early vegetation; piece of metal, &c. used to exert elastic force. ~bok, S.-Afr. gazelle. ~halt, horse-disease with convulsive movement in lifting hind leg. ~ tide, high tide occurring after full and new moon. ~tide, season of spring. springe (-j), n. noose or snare. spring'er, (esp.) support from which arch springs; breed of spaniel. spring'y, a. having elasticity.

sprinkle (spring'kl), v.t. scatter in small drops or particles. sprink'ling, n. (esp.) a few here and there.

sprint, n. & v.i. run for short distance at utmost speed.

sprit, n. small spar extending fore-and-aft sail diagonally.

sprite, n. elf or fairy.

sprout, v.i. & t. put forth shoots, hair, &c.; have sprout. n. shoot of plant; (pl.) Brussels sprouts.

spruce¹ (-ōōs), a. of trim smart appearance.

spruce² (-ōōs), n. (also ~ fir), kind of fir. ~ beer, medicinal infusion from spruce.

sprue (-ōō), n. tropical disease with ulcerated mouth, &c.

spru'it (-rōo-), n. (S.-Afr.) small stream or watercourse, usually almost or altogether dry except in the wet season.

sprung, p.t. & p.p. of spring.

spud, n. kind of weeding implement; (sl.) potato.

spume, n. & v.i. froth, foam. **spū'mў**, a.

spun, p.t. & p.p. of spin.

spunk, n. mettle, grit.

spur, n. pricking instrument worn on horseman's heel; thing that acts as an incitement; projection on back of cock's leg or at base of flower; ridge running out from mountain mass. v.t. & t. put spurs to; incite to action.

spurge, n. plant with juice used to destroy weeds.

spur'ious, a. not genuine; counterfeit; pretended.

spurn, v.t. push away with the foot in contempt; reject (offer, &c.) contemptuously.

spu'rrier, n. spur-maker.

spurt, **spirt**, v.i. & t. burst forth in a jet; eject thus (usu. -irt); increase the pace; go at high speed for short time (usu. -urt). n. a jet or burst; a sprint.

sput'ter, v.i. & t. move the lips with repeated spitting action; speak with incoherent haste.

spū'tum, n. ejected saliva.

spy, n. person secretly collecting and reporting information. v.i. & t. act as spy (upon); discern by scrutiny. ~glass, telescope.

squab (-ŏb), n. unfledged bird;

short fat person; cushion, couch. a. short and plump.

squa'bble (-ŏ-), n. & v.i. quarrel about trifles.

squad (-ŏd), n. party of men being drilled or employed together.

squa'dron (-ŏd-), n. division of cavalry regiment consisting of two troops; number of warships grouped into a temporary unit; division of R.A.F. consisting of three flights. ~leader, officer of R.A.F. in command of a squadron.

squail, n. (pl.) table-game like bowls and curling; disk used.

squa'lid (-ŏl-), a. dirty or wretched with neglect or want.

squall (-awl), v.i. scream (usu. of babies). n. scream; sudden violent storm of wind, esp. at sea and with rain. **squa'lly** (-aw-), a. (of weather) boisterous.

squa'lor (-ŏl-), n. squalidness.

squa'nder (-ŏ-), v.t. spend wastefully; scatter lavishly.

square, a. of the shape of an equilateral rectangle; of equal breadth and length; (of number) that is a square; tallying or even (with); in proper position or relation (with); (of dealings, &c.) honest or fair. adv. squarely. n. an equilateral rectangle; an area or flat object or piece of material of approximately this shape; a space in town enclosed by houses; body of troops presenting four fronts; L-shaped or T-shaped gauge; product of a number multiplied by itself; *(sl.) a square meal. v.t. & t. (-rable), make square; be square or tally with; (sl.) secure silence or acquiescence of by persuasion or bribery. ~ leg, fielder on batsman's left nearly level with wicket. ~root, factor that multiplied by itself gives so and so.

squash (-ŏ-), v.t. & t. squeeze flat or into pulp; force into small space; snub or suppress; pack tight. n. crowded state; a crowd; game played with soft ball and rackets.

---

māte, mēte, mīte, mōte, mūte, mōōt; răck, rĕck, rick, rŏck, rŭck, rōōk;

squat (-ŏt), *v.i.* sit on one's heels or on ground with knees drawn up. *a.* short and thick; dumpy.

squa'tter (-ŏt-), *n.* (esp.) Australian sheep-farmer; *person settling on land without title.

squaw, *n.* Amer.-Ind. woman.

squawk, *n.* gull's or similar cry. *v.i.* utter squawk.

squeak, *n.* short shrill cry or sound; (sl.) close affair. *v.i.* utter or emit squeak; (sl.) peach.

squeal, *n.* shrill sustained cry as of child or animal in pain or terror. *v.i.* utter squeal; *(sl.)* confess, betray by confession.

squeam'ish, *a.* fastidious; of delicate stomach or conscience.

squeegee', *n.* implement with rubber edge, used to push moisture off a smooth surface.

squeeze, *v.t. & i.* (-zable), exert pressure on from opposite or all sides; oppress, crush; extract information by pressure; wring (water, juice, &c.) from something; force (object) or force oneself into or through a tight place. *n.* act of squeezing; crowded state; a forced exaction or impost made by Asiatic officials or servants; a forced charge or levy. **squeezabil'ity**, *n.* (esp.) lack of moral firmness.

squelch, *v.i. & t.* (colloq.) make sucking sound as of hoof drawn out of stiff mud; suppress.

squib, *n.* small firework thrown by hand; lampoon.

squid, *n.* kinds of cuttle-fish.

squiff'y, *a.* (sl.) slightly drunk.

squill, *n.* plant of lily kind used in medicine.

squint, *v.i.* have the eyes turned in different directions; (colloq.) look sidelong or through small aperture. *n.* squinting set of the eyeballs; (colloq.) a glance.

squire, *n.* landed gentleman; (hist.) knight's attendant; *justice of the peace, local judge. *v.t.* escort (lady). **squir'archy** (-ki), *n.* the landed class. **squireen'**, *n.* small landowner, esp. in Ireland.

squirm, *v.i.* (colloq.) writhe like a worm; wriggle.

squi'rrel, *n.* bushy-tailed arboreal rodent.

squirt, *v.t. & i.* shoot out in a jet, esp. from a syringe; direct such jet upon. *n.* syringe; jet of water, &c. from it.

St, abbrev. of *Saint* prefixed to names.

stab, *n.* a thrust or wound with a sharp pointed implement or weapon; sudden acute pain or attack. *v.t. & i.* pierce or wound with something pointed; aim stab *at*.

sta'ble¹, *a.* abiding; likely to endure; firm, steady, constant. ~**bility**, *n.* **stab'ilize**, *v.t.* make stable. **stab'ilizer**, *n.* (esp.) aircraft's fixed horizontal tail-plane.

sta'ble², *n.* building in which horses are kept; racehorses of a particular stable. *v.t.* put or keep or accommodate in a stable. ~**companion**, horse of same stable; (colloq.) member of same school, club, &c. **sta'bling**, *n.* stable-accommodation.

stab'lish, *v.t.* make stable.

stacca'to (-aht-), *a.* (Mus.) with sharp separation of notes.

stack, *n.* pile of hay or sheaves or the like; number of things laid on one another; number of chimneys side by side. *v.t.* form into stacks.

sta'dium, *n.* (pl. *-ia*), foot-race course in anc.-Gk. athletic contests; modern athletic ground.

staff (-ahf), *n.* (pl. *-s*, and arch. and mus. *staves*), stick or pole as weapon or support or as symbol of office; (Mus.) the set of parallel lines on which notes are written; body of officers attached to a commander; body of assistants by whom an institution or business is carried on. *v.t.* provide (institution, &c.) with staff.

stag, *n.* male of red or other large deer; (Stock Exch.) person who applies for allotments in new concerns with a view to selling at once at a profit. **~beetle**, kind of beetle with antler-like mandibles.

stage, n. a platform of boards; the part of a theatre on which the actors perform; the acting profession; the theatres of a country; scene of action; one phase or period of a development; stopping-place; interval between stopping-places. v.t. (-geable), put (play) on the stage; (fig.) arrange with a view to effect. **~coach**, running by stages between two places. **stā'ger**, esp. old **~**, person of experience.

stagg'er (-g-), v.i. & t. go unsteadily as if about to fall; make stagger; shake conviction, &c. of. n. act of staggering; (pl.) giddiness as horse and cattle disease. **stagg'erer** (-g-), n. (esp.) event, &c. that staggers one.

stag'nant, a. without current or tide; motionless; inert, sluggish; unchanging. **stagnāte'**, v.i. be stagnant. **stagnā'tion**, n.

stā'gy̆, a. theatrical.

staid, a. of sober demeanour.

stain, v.t. & i. discolour, soil; make coloured mark on; (fig.) sully, blemish; be stainable. n. colouring liquid for staining; stained spot; fact that sullies a person's reputation. **stain'less**, a.

stair, n. (pl.) set of fixed steps connecting different floors; one such step. **~case**, flight or flights of stairs.

stāke, n. stout stick or post pointed for driving into ground; post to which a person was tied who suffered death by burning; amount risked in a wager or match; (pl.) amount contended for in a match; horse-race, &c., for stakes. v.t. (-kable), fix, or mark out or off, or hedge in, with stakes; risk (money, credit, &c.) on an issue.

stăl'actite, n. deposit of carbonate of lime hanging like icicle from roof of cave. **stăl'agmite**, n. similar deposit rising like spike from floor of cave.

stāle, a. lacking freshness; out of condition from lapse of time or over-use. v.t. & i. (-lable), make stale by over-use.

stā'lemāte' (-lm-), n. state of chess-game counting as draw; (fig.) deadlock in proceedings. v.t. reduce (opponent) to standstill without defeating him.

stalk[1] (-awk), n. slender stem of plant or flower, &c.

stalk[2] (-awk), v.t. & i. make furtive approach to with a view to killing or catching; walk with slow strides or in haughty manner. n. stalking gait; attempt to stalk game, &c.

stall (-awl), n. compartment for one animal in stable or cowhouse; space appropriated to one dealer in market or bazaar; a numbered seat in theatre; (pl.) row of seats lining wall of choir or chancel; (sing.) one such seat, or canonry, &c. entitling holder to it. v.t. & i. put or keep (beast) in stall; (of motor engine) stop working; (of aeroplane or airman) become unstable by loss of speed.

stǎll'ion (-yon), n. male horse.

stǎl'wart (-awl-), a. tall and strong; courageous. n. resolute member of party in politics, &c.

stā'men, n. male or pollen-bearing organ in flower.

stăm'ina, n. staying power.

stămm'er, v.i. & t. speak haltingly; utter (excuse, &c.) stammeringly. n. such speech.

stămp, v.t. & i. bring foot down with force on the ground or on an object; crush (ore, &c.) with downward blows; mark (paper, &c.) with stamped impress; affix postage stamp to; (of action, &c.) serve to distinguish. n. stamping of foot; stamped impress; piece of printed paper affixed as indication of amount of postage paid on a letter or to ensure validity of a document.

stampēde', n. rush of horses or cattle or people under sudden common impulse, esp. panic.

ah, awl, oil, boor, cow, dowry; chin, go, bang, 'so, ship, thin; dh, as th(e);

v.i. & t. (-dable), make, or cause to make, such rush.

stance, *n.* position taken for stroke in golf or cricket.

stanch. See staunch.

sta'nchion (-ahnshn), *n.* firm metal or timber post, esp. as upright giving lateral support.

stand, *v.i. & t. (stood)*, be in stationary upright position; rise up; assume stationary position; maintain position; (of ship) sail in specified direction; place (thing) on its base or end; successfully endure, put up with; (colloq.) pay for on another's behalf or give (drink, &c.). *n.* stationary position; resistance to attack; pedestal or rack, &c. on or in which things may be placed; structure with tiers of seats for spectators at races, &c. ~by, basis of reliance. ~offish, cold or distant in manner. ~point, point of view. ~still, arrest of progress. ~ treat, pay cost of entertainment.

stan'dard, *n.* distinctive flag; specimen or specification by which something may be tested; required degree of some quality; (attrib.) corresponding to the standard, of recognized authority or prevalence; upright stock on which rose, &c. is grafted; an upright support for a lamp, &c. **stan'dardize**, *v.t. (-zable)*, make conform to a standard.

stan'ding, *a.* of a permanent kind; constantly ready for use; on one's feet; (of jump) done from both feet without run. *n.* established repute or position.

stand'ish, *n.* (arch.) inkstand.

*stand'patter, *n.* politician who is for strict adherence to party platform, esp. on tariff.

stan'hope (-nop), *n.* kind of light open carriage.

stank, *p.t.* of stink.

stann'ary, *n.* tin-mine; tin-mining district. **stann'ic**, *a.* of tin.

stan'za, *n.* one of the metrically equal groups of lines into which some poems are divided.

sta'ple, *n.* piece of wire or metal bent into U-shape for driving into wood, &c.; important or principal article of commerce in a district or country; chief element in something; quality of fibre in wool or flax or cotton.

star, *n.* any celestial body normally seen as a point of light; rayed figure or object representing a star as ornament, &c.; asterisk; brilliant or prominent person; chief actor or actress; person's destiny or luck, (pl.) influences deciding one's lot. *v.t. & i.* mark or adorn with star(s); perform as star actor. ~fish, sea animal with five or more radial arms. ~light, light of the stars.

star'board (-berd), *n.* right side of ship, &c., from point of view of person facing forward. *v.t.* turn (helm) to starboard.

starch, *n.* principle present in potatoes, corn, and other plants, having digestive value and used also as stiffening for linen, &c. *v.t.* stiffen with starch. **starch'y**, *a.* like starch; stiff of manner.

stare, *v.i. & t. (-rable)*, (of eyes) be wide open; look with staring eyes and fixed gaze at. *n.* staring gaze. **star'ing**, *a.* (esp.) too conspicuous to escape attention (of colour, pattern, &c.).

stark, *a.* rigid, esp. in death; (of folly, &c.) sheer or unmitigated; (arch.) resolute, strong. *adv.* completely (~ *mad,* naked).

star'ling, *n.* small bird noted for chatter, thievery, &c.

starr'y, *a.* set with stars; bright as a star; star-like.

start, *v.i. & t.* make sudden involuntary movement due to surprise, &c.; begin journey or operations; set up or set going; send off (runners in race, &c.) by word or signal; (of ship's timbers) burst away at joint. *n.* sudden involuntary movement; departure from starting-place; sending or going off of competitors in race; commencement of operations; amount of distance or time allowed to competitor in race, &c. **stárt'er**, n. (esp.) person giving signal for start of race; competitor actually starting in race. **stárt'ing**, n. In comb. **~gate**, removable barrier for securing fair start in horse-races. **~post**, place from which competitors start in race **~price**, the odds on or against a horse at the start of a race.

stár'tle, v.t. give shock of surprise to. **stárt'ler**, n. startling fact or statement.

stárve, v.i. & t. (-vable), die or suffer acutely from lack of food or (arch. or dial.) cold; (part., colloq.) hungry; keep without or short of food. **stárvá'tion**, n. **stárve'ling** (-vl-), n. person who is or looks ill-fed.

stá'sis, n. stoppage of circulation of any of the fluids of the body.

státe, n. existing position or condition of something; rank; ceremonial pomp; a civil community having its own government and law. v.t. (-table), put into form of a statement; say as of knowledge that. **~-house**, capitol; meeting-place of a State legislature. **~-rights**, rights and powers not delegated to United States but reserved to individual States. **~-room**, room reserved for ceremonial occasions; passenger's private cabin on ship. **státe'ly** (-tll), a. marked by great dignity; imposing; elevated. **státe'ment** (-tm-), n. presentation of a fact or problem. **státes'man** (-an), n. sagacious far-sighted practical politician; influential public man.

stát'ic, -al, aa. of statics; at rest, in equilibrium. **stát'ics**, n.pl. branch of physics concerned with bodies at rest and forces in equilibrium.

stá'tion, n. place held by some person or used for some purpose; in India, a place where the English officials of a district, or the officers of a garrison (not in a fortress) reside; the aggregate society of such a place; rank of life; post of observation or defence; stopping-place for railway trains. v.t. assign (person) his station. **~-master**, official controlling railway station. **stá'tionary** (-sho-), a. still, not in motion; not progressive. **stá'tioner** (-sho-), n. dealer in stationery. **stá'tionery** (-sho-), n. writing-materials and connected goods.

stá'tist, státistí'cian (-shn), nn. expert in statistics. **statís'tical**, a. **statís'tics**, n.pl. numerical facts systematically collected on a subject; science of statistics.

stát'uary, a. of or for statuemaking. n. the statuary art; a sculptor.

stát'ue, n. sculptured figure of person or animal. **státuésque'** (-k), a. statue-like in pose or immobility. **státuétte'**, n. statue of much reduced scale.

stát'ure (-yer), n. bodily height.

stá'tus, n. position held by a person or community; one's standing or rank; the status quo, or ~ quo ante, the posture of affairs as it was up to some date or event.

stát'utable, a. according or not contrary to statute law.

stát'ute, n. a legislative enactment; an ordinance made by a corporation. **stát'utory**, a. of the nature of, or enacted by, a statute.

staunch, stanch (-ahn-), v.t. (usu. -an-), check flow of (esp. blood, wound). a. (usu. -aun-), constant to obligations or purpose; untiring in service or loyalty.

stáve, n. one of the wooden strips of which a cask's sides consist; a fragment of song. v.t. (stóve or staved), (with in) break hole in (cask, boat); (with off) ward off with difficulty or for a time.

stay, n. rope connecting a mast or spar with other part of ship as support; a prop or support; a check or delay; a sojourn or its duration; stamina or staying-power; (pl.) corset. *v.t. & i.* check or cause to stop; abstain from departing; occupy temporary quarters at; maintain position; show capacity for prolonged effort. stay′er, *n.* (esp.) person or animal of great staying-power.

stead (stĕd), *n.* place; room. In phr. *in one's ~*, in lieu or instead of him; *stand one in good ~*, serve his need well. stead′fast (-ast), *a.* showing constancy; immovable. stea′ding (stĕd-), *n.* farmstead.

stead′y (stĕd-), *a.* firm in position; constant in motion or direction or action; not hurried or perturbed; free from wildness or intemperance. *v.t. & i.* (-iable), make or become steady.

steak (stāk), *n.* slab of meat or fish suitable for grilling.

steal, *v.t. & i.* (stōle, stōlen), secretly carry off or appropriate; come or go noiselessly or unnoticed. stealth (stĕl-), *n.* evasion of notice. stea′lthy (stĕl-), *a.* practising or done by stealth; carefully noiseless.

steam, *n.* the gas into which boiling water turns, fitted for use as motive power; any vapour or exhalation; (attrib.) worked by steam. *v.t. & i.* subject to action of steam as method of cooking, softening, &c.; send off steam; (of steam-ship or those on board) go, be driven, by steam. ~boat, steam-ship. ~engine, locomotive or stationary engine worked by steam. ~roller, (esp.) force for crushing opposition. ~ship (abbr. *s.s.*), ship propelled by steam. steam′er, *n.* (esp.) steam-ship or steam-driven boat; utensil for steaming vegetables, &c.

stē′arin, *n.* fatty substance in suet and tallow. stē′atite, *n.* kind of talc, soapstone.

steed, *n.* a horse.

steel, *n.* kinds of alloy of iron with carbon or other elements; steel rod for whetting knives on; (attrib.) made of, or hard as, steel. *v.t.* harden (oneself) against

a thing or to do some action. ~yard, weighing-apparatus with graduated arm along which a weight slides. steel′y, *a.* suggestive of steel.

steep¹, *v.t.* keep in liquid or some medium till saturated or impregnated.

steep², *a.* (of slope) descending or rising rapidly; hard to climb up; (sl., of story, &c.) taxing patience or credulity. *n.* (poet.) steep hill. steep′en, *v.i. & t.* steep′le, *n.* high church tower running into spire. ~chase, cross-country horse-race or foot-race. ~jack, workman who repairs steeples, tall chimneys, &c.

steer¹, *n.* a young male ox.

steer², *v.t. & i.* manage rudder or guiding-apparatus; direct (ship, motor-car, &c.) thus. ~age, *n.* steering; direction; the accommodation to which lower-class passengers are restricted in ship. ~s′man, person steering.

stein′bock (stīn-), *n.* kinds of small South African antelope; the Alpine ibex.

stěll′ar, *a.* of stars.

stĕm¹, *n.* the main body of a tree or plant springing from the root; (fig.) family stock; slender shaft; (Philol.) the common base from which a set of inflected or derivative forms is made; the upright or forward-slanting piece at ship's bow by which the converging sides are connected.

stĕm², *v.t.* make headway against; resist the force of; not be carried away by (current, &c.).

stĕnch, *n.* overpowering or noxious or persistent stink.

stĕn′cil, *n.* thin plate of metal, &c., punched with pattern, which is reproduced on other surfaces by washing it with colour, &c. *v.t.* reproduce (pattern) or mark (surface) by use of stencil.

stĕnŏg′raphy, *n.* shorthand. ~pher, *n.*; stěnŏgráph′ic, *a.*

stěntō′rian, *a.* (of voice) loud; (of person) with stentorian voice.

stĕp, *v.i. & t.* go or come in specified direction by alternate change of the feet; perform (dance) (Naut.) set up (mast) in ship. *n.* complete movement of one leg in walking or running or dancing; distance gained by it; footstep or footfall; surface trodden on in ascending or descending; a degree in a scale of promotion, &c.; (pl.) short ladder with flat steps. **stepping-stone,** *n.* stone placed in stream, &c. to provide dryshod crossing; (fig.) a means to an end.

step-, *pref.* made nominally so by death of one and remarriage of the other of a wedded pair, e. g. ~*child*, *-son*, *-daughter*, &c.

stěp'ney, *n.* (pl. *-eys*), extra rim and tire formerly carried on motor-car to be attached to wheel whose tire has collapsed.

stěppe, *n.* level treeless plain.

stereo-, *pref.* solid. **stěrěŏg'raphy,** *n.* the delineation of solid form on plane surface. **stě'rěoscōpe,** *n.* optical apparatus by which two views of something taken at slightly different angles are combined into one picture. **stěrěoscŏp'ic,** *a.* **stě'rěotype,** *n.* printing-plate cast from a mould of set-up type; *v.t.* make stereotypes; print from stereotypes; (fig.) fix the form permanently; (*p.p.*) conventional, unvarying.

stě'rile (or *-īl*), *a.* barren, unproductive; not bearing seed; (Med.) sterilized. **steril'ity,** *n.* **stě'rilize,** *v.t.* (*-zable*), rid of microbes, &c. by boiling or other means.

stěr'ling, *a.* (of money and gold and silver) of the standard British value; (of character, &c.) sound, genuine; of solid worth.

stěrn¹, *a.* enforcing obedience; testing endurance; severe.

stěrn², *n.* ship's or boat's hinder end; rump; tail. ~*most,* *a.* nearest to stern. ~ *sheets,* space in boat between stern and rowers' thwarts.

stěr'num, *n.* (pl. *-na*), the breastbone.

stěrt'orous, *a.* (of breathing) laboured and noisy.

stět, direction on proof-sheet to printer to disregard a correction.

stěth'oscōpe, *n.* instrument making patient's heart-action and other internal sounds audible to user. **stěthoscŏp'ic,** *a.*

stět'son, *n.* slouch hat worn by Anzac soldiers.

stē'vedōre, *n.* man employed in ship-loading.

stew¹, *v.t. & i.* cook by long simmering in vessel with little liquid; sweat or welter in hot close atmosphere; (sl.) swot. *n.* dish of stewed meat; (sl.) acute apprehension. ~*stewed,* *a.* (sl.) drunk.

stew², *n.* tank or pond for storing live fish.

stew'ard, *n.* person paid to manage another's estate or house, or to cater for some society or ship; official managing an entertainment, meeting, or show. ~*ess,* *n.* (esp.) female attendant in passenger ship. ~*ship,* *n.* (esp.) charge committed to one.

stick¹, *v.t. & i.* (*stuck*), stab or transfix; impale on spike, &c.; *cheat; thrust point of (needle, &c.) into; remain stuck in; keep position as if rooted or embedded; adhere to something; attach or fasten with glue, &c.; remain constant to a person, purpose, &c.; (colloq.) put up with.

stick², *n.* thin wooden rod serving various purposes; rod-shaped piece of chocolate, sealing-wax, or the like; (colloq.) stiff or shy or dull person. ~*insect,* any insect of the family *Phasmidae*, from its resemblance to branches or twigs of trees.

stick'lac, *n.* lac in its natural state of incrustation on twigs.

stic'klebäck (*-klb-*), *n.* small spiny-backed fish.

stick'ler, *n.* person who pertinaciously insists on the importance of accuracy, discipline, &c.

stick'y, *a.* tending to stick or adhere to things.

---

stiff, *a.* hard to bend or mould; not soft; difficult to achieve or perform; (of limb, &c.) aching owing to previous exertions; cold or formal in manner. stiff-necked, stubborn, mulish. stiff'en, *v.t. & i.*

sti'fle, *v.t. & i.* smother; cause difficulty of breathing or feeling of oppression or constraint to; feel such oppression.

sti'fle, *n.* horse's joint between hip and hock.

stig'ma, *n.* moral spot or stain or brand; (pl. *-ata*) marks corresponding to Christ's wounds; (Anat. &c.; pl. *-s, -ata*) kinds of small spot or orifice on or in surface. stig'matize, *v.t.* (*-zable*), cast imputation at; describe opprobriously *as.*

stile, *n.* set of steps or posts to enable persons to pass over a fence, wall, &c.; upright timber of door or window.

stilett'ō, *n.* (pl. *-os*), small dagger; seamstress's eyelet-pricker.

still[1], *n.* apparatus for distilling spirits, &c. ~room, housekeeper's room in large house.

still[2], *a.* motionless; hushed; undisturbed by movement or noise. *n.* hushed state; interval of quiet. *v.t.* quiet; calm; lull to rest. *adv.* nevertheless; for all that. ~born, born dead. ~ life, fruit or furniture or the like as painting subjects. still'ȳ, *a.* without sound.

stilt, *n.* one of a pair of poles with brackets raising walker's feet several inches above the ground. stil'tĕd, *a.* high-flown or bombastic (of style).

Stil'ton, *n.* kind of cheese.

stim'ūlant, *a.* producing transient increase of vital energy. *n.* a stimulant drug or food.

stim'ūlate, *v.t.* (*-lable*), apply stimulus to; spur to action or increased vigour. ~tion, *tor*, *nn.*; ~tive, *a.*

stim'ūlus, *n.* (pl. *-lī*), rousing influence; thing that evokes activity in tissues, &c.

sti'mȳ, *n.* (Golf) player's position with opponent's ball obstructing his put. stim'ied (*-mid*), *a.*

sting, *n.* tubular point with which poison is injected by bee or nettle or the like; wound, puncture, or pain produced by it; any acute bodily or mental pain; pungency. *v.t. & i.* (*stŭng*), puncture with sting; cause sharp pain to; wound the feelings of; be pungent; (of bodily part) feel acute pain: *(sl.) cheat.

sting'er, *n.* (esp., colloq.) smart blow; sharp frost. sting'gy (*-ji*), meanly averse to spending; niggardly.

stink, *v.i.* (*stănk* or *stŭnk*; *stŭnk*), have foul or nasty smell. *n.* foul or nasty smell; (pl., sl.) chemistry or natural science as subject of study. ~wood, (S.-Afr. & Austral.) name given to various trees the wood of which has an unpleasant odour; the wood of any of these trees.

stint, *v.t.* supply on a niggardly scale; keep so supplied. *n.* limitation of supply or effort; allotted amount of work, &c.

sti'pend, *n.* a salary. stipen'diarȳ (or *sti-*), *a.* receiving fixed pay; *n.* paid police magistrate.

stip'ple, *v.i. & t.* use dots instead of lines in engraving or painting or drawing. *n.* dotted work.

stip'ūlate, *v.t. & i.* state to be part of one's terms. ~ā'tion, *n.* a demand stated as condition of consent to an agreement.

stir, *v.t. & i.* cause motion in; set or keep moving; excite, rouse; touch the feelings of. *n.* slight motion seen or heard after stillness; act of stirring; liveliness or display of interest on the part of many people.

sti'rrup, *n.* rider's foot-rest.

stitch, *n.* acute pain in side induced by running, &c.; single pass of needle, or the work effected by it, in sewing or crochet or the like. *v.t. & i.* sew. ~wort, a plant.

stith'y (*-dhi*), *n.* anvil, forge.

sti´ver, *n*. the most trifling coin.

stoat¹, *n*. any beast of weasel or ferret kind, esp. the ermine.

stoat², *v.t.* sew up (tear, cloth edges) with invisible stitches.

stock, *n*. stump or butt or trunk (now rare) or branch; (pl.) timbers on which a ship rests while building; (pl., hist.) timber frame in which offender's ankles were held as he sat exposed to ridicule, &c.; the goods or equipment for carrying on a business; the animals belonging to a farm; money contributed by way of loan to form a State fund or the capital of a company; kinds of fragrant garden plant; stiff neck-band of leather, &c.; hard solid brick of best quality; *fat~*, animals fit for slaughter as food. *v.t.* equip with what is needful; keep (goods) in stock. **~broker**, person who buys and sells stocks on commission. **~ company**, semi-permanent company in theatre. **~dove**, small wild pigeon. **~ exchange**, place where stocks are publicly bought and sold. **~fish**, cod, &c. dried in sun without salt. **~jobber**, person who buys and sells stocks with a view to profiting by fluctuations in price; *(contempt.)* stockbroker. **~man**, man employed to look after cattle or other live stock, (Austral.) one who tends and drives horned cattle and horses. **~still**, as still as a post. **~whip**, thick tapering thong of 12–14 ft., affixed to a handle of 1½ ft.

stockāde´, *n*. line of upright stakes as defence, &c.

stock´inĕt, -ette, *n*. elastic material for underclothing, &c.

stock´ing, *n*. knitted or woven covering for foot and leg.

stock´ȳ, *a*. thickset.

stodge (sl.), *n*. stodgy food; full meal. *v.i. & t.* eat greedily.

stod´gȳ, *a*. (of food) heavy, indigestible; (of book, style, &c.) overfull of facts or details.

stoep (-ōōp). *n*. (S.-Afr.) terraced verandah in front of house.

stō´gie (-g-). n. kind of heavy boot; long slender cigar.

stō´ic, *n*. person of great fortitude or austerity. **stō´ical**, *a*. showing great power of resisting pain and hardship or temptation. **stō´icism**, *n*.

stōke, *v.t. & i*. (*-kable*), keep (fire, furnace) going; stoke fire of (engine). **stō´ker**, *n*. man who feeds and tends furnace.

stōle¹, *n*. vestment consisting of a long narrow band hanging down in front from back of neck; woman's wrap similarly worn.

stōle², stolen, *p.t.* of steal.

stŏl´id, *a*. slow to feel or betray feeling; not easily moved; stubborn. **stolid´itȳ**, *n*.

stŏm´ach (-ŭmak), *n*. the cavity into which food passes for digestion; (loosely) the belly; appetite or inclination or courage *for*. *v.t.* find sufficiently palatable to swallow or keep down; (fig.) put up with. **stŏ´macher** (-ŭmach-), *n*. (hist.) breast-piece of woman's dress. **stomăc´hic** (-k-), *a*. of the stomach; promoting digestion or appetite; *n*. a stomachic draught or drug.

stōne, *n*. piece of rock of any shape and of no great size; stones or rock as a substance or material; thing resembling stone in hardness or pebble in shape; weight of 14 lb. *v.t.* (*-nable*), pelt with stones; rid (fruit) of stones. **~ age**, period in which weapons and tools were made of stone. **~blind**, quite blind. *~~boat*, runnerless sled for carrying stones. **~chat**, kind of small bird. **~crop**, kinds of creeping plant. **~fruit**, fruit with seed enclosed in hard shell surrounded by pulp. **~pine**, S.-Ital. kind with spreading top. **~wall**, *v.i. & t.* (Pol.) obstruct by stonewalling. **~walling**, (Pol.) esp. Austral.) parliamentary obstruction; (Crick.) excessively cautious batting. **~ware**, pottery of flinty clay.

stō'ný, a. abounding in stones; hard or unfeeling. ~**broke**, (sl.) with no money left.

stood, p.t. of **stand**.

stook (Sc. & north.) group of cornsheaves. v.t. arrange in stooks.

stool, n. movable seat without a back; evacuation of bowels or accommodation provided for it. ~**ball**, old game of cricket or rounders.

stoop¹, v.i. & t. bend down; carry one's head and shoulders bowed forward; abase oneself or condescend to do; (arch., of hawk, &c.) swoop down. n. stooping carriage of body.

stoop², n. (U.S., Can.) unroofed platform or (colloq.) porch or verandah at house door, approached by means of steps.

stop, v.t. & i. stuff up; prevent passage of; prevent motion or action of; cease to permit or supply; withhold or keep back out of a sum; cease from action or speech; halt or pause; (colloq.) sojourn or remain somewhere. n. a pause or cessation; mark indicating a pause in printed or written matter; (Mus.) device in instrument to assist change of pitch; set of pipes having special tone in organ. ~**cock**, tap. ~**gap**, temporary substitute. ~~**press**, late news inserted in paper after printing has begun. ~**watch**, timepiece with mechanism for starting and stopping it at will for exact timing of races, &c. **stopp'age**, n. blocked state; a cessation. **stopp'er**, n. (esp.) plug for closing bottle, &c.; v.t. close or provide with stopper.

store, n. abundance; (sing. or pl.) a fund or good supply of; (pl.) shop dealing in many different kinds of commodity on a large scale; (sing. or pl.) warehouse or storing-place; *building or room for retail of goods; an animal kept for fattening. a. (of cattle, &c.) kept for fattening. v.t. (-rable), equip or furnish plentifully with;

lay up for future use; deposit or keep in warehouse. ~**house**, granary or other storing-house; abundant source of information, &c. **stor'age**, n. storing of goods; space available for this; cost of warehousing.

storey. See **story¹**.

stork, n. tall stately, usu. white, wading bird.

storm, n. violent disturbance of the atmosphere, with thunder or strong wind or heavy fall of rain, &c.; commotion in human relations or in the mind comparable to it; assault by troops on fortified place. v.t. & i. take (fortress, &c.) by storm; (of crowd) make way by force into; talk violently; rage. ~**cock**, kinds of bird. **storm'ý**, a. boisterous; subject to storms; violent or quarrelsome. ~ **petrel**, sea-bird associated with storms.

‖ **stor'thing** (-ti-), n. Norwegian parliament.

stor'ey¹ (pl. -ies), **stor'ey** (pl. -eys), n. any of the parts one above the other into which a house is divided. **stor'ied** (-rid), a.

stor'y², n. legends or tradition; account given of an incident; piece of narrative or tale; (Nursery) a lie. ~**teller**, writer of stories; anecdote monger; (Nursery) liar. **stor'ied²** (-rid), a. famed in story; legendary.

stoup (-ōōp), n. flagon or beaker.

stout, a. undaunted, resolute; of considerable thickness or strength; corpulent. n. strong variety of porter.

stove¹, p.t. & p.p. of **stave**.

stove², n. kinds of closed apparatus in which heat is produced by coal, coke, wood, gas, or oil.

***stō'ver** (-er), n. (dial. & U.S.) fodder of corn-straw, &c.

stow (-ō), v.t. pack closely or compactly; (sl.) cease to indulge in (chaff, noise, &c.). ~**age**, accommodation for stowing things; money paid for stowing. ~**away**, person going on board ship and hiding till at sea.

---

strâd′dle, *v.t.* & *i.* separate (one's feet or legs) laterally; stand or sit across with straddled legs. *n.* act or attitude of straddling.

strafe (-ahf), *v.t.* (Mil. sl.) worry with shells, bombs, sniping, &c.; reprimand or thrash.

strâg′gle, *v.i.* lack compactness; be or move in loose irregular order; stray or lag behind.

straight (-āt), *a.* without curves or angles; not curved or crooked; (of object) in a straight line with or parallel or perpendicular to; correctly placed or in proper order; going direct to the mark; honest or candid. *adv.* in a straight line; direct; with good aim. ~ **arm**, straightforward thrust. ~**forward**, *a.* devoid of guile or complexity. *~ ticket*, party programme without modification. ~**way**, immediately. **straight′en** (-āt-), *v.t.* & *i.*

strain[1], *n.* a breed or stock.

strain[2], *v.t.* & *i.* stretch tightly; make taut or tense; injure by over-exertion or exacting too much; wrest from true meaning; hold in tight embrace; *(p.p.)* forced or factitious; strain one's muscles or faculties; tug *at*; come near breaking under pressure; pass (liquid) through **strainer**. *n.* condition of a body subject to stress; severe demand upon person or thing; injury due to such demand; (pl.) music or verse of specified tendency; (sing.) tone or tendency in speech or writing. **strain′er**, *n.* (esp.) appliance through which liquid is poured to be cleared of matter suspended in it.

strait, *a.* narrow; strict. *n.* narrow water-passage connecting two seas or large bodies of water; (pl.) ill-supplied state, need, difficulty. ~**laced**, *a.* over-scrupulous; puritanical. **strait′en**, *v.t.* restrict, confine (arch.); reduce to straits.

strand[1], *n.* land along sea or other water. *v.t.* & *i.* run aground; *(p.p., fig.)* in difficulties.

strand[2], *n.* one of the strings or wires twisted round each other to make a rope.

strange (-j), *a.* foreign, alien; unfamiliar or not known (*to*); surprising; eccentric.

strā′nger (-j-), *n.* person in a place or company that he does not belong to; person strange to some one or to something; *used as voc. for sir, &c.*

strangle (străng′gl), *v.t.* kill by squeezing the windpipe.

străng′ŭlāte (-ngg-), *v.t.* (-lable) prevent circulation through (vein, intestine) by compression. ~**tion**, *n.* strangling.

străp, *n.* strip of leather or other material, esp. one fitted with a buckle to serve as a band. *v.t.* secure with strap; apply strapping to; thrash with strap. **străpp′ing**, *a.* stalwart; tall and strong; *n.* (esp.) adhesive plaster in strips for surgical use; a flogging.

strappā′dō, *n.* (pl. *-os*) torture in which victim was let fall from a beam to the distance allowed by the rope attaching him to it. *v.t.* subject to this.

strata. See **stratum**.

străt′agĕm, *n.* a device for deceiving the enemy; a clever plan.

străt′egy, *n.* the art of war, esp. the part of it concerned with the conduct of campaigns. **stratē′gic**, *-al* (or *-ē-*) *aa.* of, dictated by, serving the ends of, strategy. **străt′egist**, *n.* expert in strategy.

strāth, *n.* Scotch river-valley. ~**spey** (-ā), *n.* a Scotch dance.

străt′ify, *v.t.* & *i.* (-fiable) form into strata. ~**fication**, *n.*

strā′tum, *n.* (Geol.: pl. *-ta*) layer of deposited matter forming part of earth's crust (also *fig.*).

strā′tus, *n.* (pl. *-tī*), low horizontal sheet of cloud.

straw, *n.* dry cut stalks of grain as material; single stalk of this; straw hat. ~**berry**, wild and garden fruit or the plant bearing it. *~boss*, assistant foreman.

---

straw'ÿ, a. of flavour of inferior eggs and tea.

stray, v.i. go astray *from* (the track, flock, virtue, &c.); wander aimlessly. n. strayed beast or child; (Wireless, usu. in pl.) atmospherics. a. strayed; sporadic or isolated.

streak, n. irregular line or band, esp. one distinguishable by colour; (fig.) strain or element in character. v.t. mark with streaks. streak'ÿ, a.

stream, n. body of running water; moving mass or crowd; large quantity of something that moves along. v.i. flow out or along; run with liquid; (of banner, &c.) be blown out horizontally. stream'er, n. pennon; ribbon attached at one end to float in wind. stream'lêt, n.

street, n. town or village road lined with houses.

strength, n. being strong; degree of strongness; number of persons present or available. strëng'then, v.t. & i. add to the strength or number of; grow stronger.

strën'ious, a. making or requiring great exertions.

strëptocôcc'us, n. (pl. -ci pr. -kī), chaplet-shaped bacterial organism.

stress, n. pressure or tension or compulsion; emphasis, accent. v.t. lay stress on; emphasize.

stretch, v.t. & i. make taut; increase the length or size of by tension; undergo such increase; exert to the utmost; misrepresent by exaggeration; reach out (one's hand, legs, &c.); be of specified extent, run or be spread out in specified direction. n. act of stretching; expanse or tract; spell. stretch'er, n. (esp.) handbarrow on which disabled person can be laid and carried; board in boat for rower to steady his feet against.

strew (-ōō), v.t. (p.p. strewn, strewed), scatter (sand, &c.) over a surface; spread (surface) with sand, &c.

stri'a, n. (pl. -ae), slight score or ridge on a surface. strī'tëd, a. marked with striae. strī'tion, n. making or possession or arrangement of strias.

stricken. See strike.

stric'kle, n. rod used in strike-measure.

strict, a. precisely defined or limited; requiring implicit obedience; without deviation.

stric'ture, n. (usu. in pl.), comment(s) of a critical or censorious kind; (Med.) constricted state of a duct.

stride, v.i. & t. (strōde; -dable), walk with long steps; traverse in one step; bestride or stand astride of. n. single walking or running step; gait in regard to length of stride.

stri'dent, a. of loud harsh sound.

strife, n. quarrels, hostilities.

strike, v.t. & i. (past struck; p.p. struck and arch. stricken; -kable), hit; deliver blows (lit. or fig.); propel with blow; come sharply into contact with; dash against or on something; make (coin, medal) by stamping; agree on (bargain); enter the mind or rouse the attention of; extract (fire, spark) by percussion; ignite (match) by rubbing; take down or remove (flag, sail, tent); put oneself into (an attitude); (of clock) sound the time, (of hour, &c.) be sounded; (of workmen) go on strike; lower flag in sign of surrender; take root. n. concerted refusal of workmen to work till higher wages are paid or some grievance is remedied (*general* ~, strike by workmen of all or most trades with a view of securing some common object; *sympathetic* ~, strike by unaggrieved trade to give moral support to aggrieved one on strike); *(bowling or ninepins) levelling all the pins with one bowl; *(Baseball) batsman's actual hitting of, or attempt to hit, pitched ball; *(sl.) sudden success at finding petroleum.

&c. or in financial operation. ~-breakers, outsiders got in to replace strikers. ~-measure, measuring of grain, &c. by passing rod across top of heaped vessel to ensure its being full and no more. ~pay, subsistence money paid to strikers by trade-union. strik'en, *p.p.* & *adj.* smitten with disease or famine or grief; far gone in years. stri'ker, *n.* (esp.) workman on strike.

string, *n.* twine or fine cord; a length of this or some other material serving to tie or attach or work something; one of the stretched pieces of cord or catgut or wire producing the notes of musical instruments; set of things threaded on a string; set of things, &c. coming successively (*first, second, ~*, competitor, &c. relied on in this order). *v.t.* & *i.* (*strung*) thread on a string; put (facts, &c.) together; bring (person, &c.) to state of tension; put a stringed instrument in tune; provide with strings. stringed (-ngd), *a.* (of musical instrument) provided with strings.

strin'gent (-j-), *a.* strict, binding, precise; leaving no discretion. strin'gency (-j-), *n.*

string'y (-ngi), *a.* fibrous; like string.

strip, *v.t.* & *i.* remove clothes or covering from; dismantle; deprive of covering or belongings; put off one's clothes. *n.* long narrow piece of something.

stripe, *n.* long narrow band differing in colour or texture from the surface on either side; (Mil.) N.C.O.'s chevron (pl., exc. of lowest grade); (usu. pl.) a blow with scourge; flogging. striped (-pt), *a.*

strip'ling, *n.* youth whose figure has not yet filled out.

strive, *v.i.* (*strŏve, striven*), try hard, struggle; engage in strife *with*; contend *against.*

strode, *p.t.* of stride.

strōke, *n.* blow; shock given by blow; sudden favourable turn of luck; movement of a recurrent or regulated kind; the oarsman nearest the stern who sets the stroke; the sound of a clock's bell; sweep of the pen or pencil or brush, mark left by it. *v.t.* (*-kable*), pass the hand gently along (hair, head, &c.); act as stroke to crew.

strŏll, *v.i.* walk leisurely along; rove from place to place. *n.* short leisurely walk. strŏll'er, *n.* (esp.) strolling actor.

strŏng (in *stronger, -est,* pr. -ngg-), *a.* having power of resistance; tough, firm, healthy; muscular; powerful in numbers or resources; having any quality in a great degree; energetic, decided, vigorous. ~-box, -room, box or room of especial strength for keeping valuables. ~-hold, fortress or citadel.

strŏp, *n.* appliance for sharpening razors; (Naut.) band of rope or iron round pulley. *v.t.* sharpen on strop.

strō'phē (or -ŏ-), *n.* ~ *and antistrophe,* two sections of an anc.-Gk. choric ode answering metrically to each other.

strove, *p.t.* of strive.

struck, *p.t.* & *p.p.* of strike.

strŭc'ture, *n.* way in which things hold together; the supporting framework or essential parts; a building or any complex whole. strŭc'tural (-cher-), *a.* (esp.) of the essential framework.

strŭg'gle, *v.i.* throw the limbs about in violent effort to get free; make one's way with difficulty; make great efforts under difficulties. *n.* spell of struggling; effort under difficulties; hard contest.

strŭm, *v.i.* & *t.* play tune, &c. monotonously on piano, &c. *n.* strumming sound.

strŭm'pĕt, *n.* prostitute.

strung, *p.t.* & *p.p.* of string.

strŭt, *n.* bar forming part of a framework or strutting gait. *v.i.* & *t.* walk in stiff pompous way;

strengthen or support (framework) with strut.

strÿc'hnīne (-k- ; *or* -ēn), *n.* poisonous alkaloid used in small doses as nerve-stimulant.

stūb, *n.* stump of tree, tooth, &c., remaining rooted; fag-end of cigar, pencil, &c. *v.t.* rid (ground) of stubs; dig (root, &c.) up.

stŭb'ble, *n.* stumps of grain left sticking in ground.

stŭbb'ly, *a.* short and stiff.

stŭbb'orn, *a.* unyielding; not docile or amenable to control.

stŭcc'ō, *n.* (pl. -oes). kinds of plaster for facing walls. *v.t.* face with stucco.

stuck, *p.t. & p.p.* of stick.

stŭd¹, *n.* projecting nail-head or similar knob on a surface; post to which laths are nailed; removable double-headed button for two or more button-holes. *v.t.* set with or as with studs.

stŭd², *n.* number of horses kept for breeding, racing, &c.

stŭdd'ing, *n.* wood, lath and plaster, &c., of partitions.

stū'dent, *n.* person undergoing instruction in some branch of learning; person of studious habits; a bookish person.

stū'dīō, *n.* (pl. -os). artist's workroom; room in which cinema or broadcast items are performed.

stū'dious, *a.* given to study or reading; attentive to; careful.

stŭd'ÿ, *n.* acquiring of information, esp. from books; pursuit of some branch of knowledge; meditation; piece of work, esp. in painting, done as practice or experiment; room used for literary work or owner's private business. *v.t. & i.* (-diable). make an object of study; devote time and thought to understanding (subject, &c.); scrutinize; (*p.p.*) deliberate or intentional.

stŭff, *n.* material; substance or things of uncertain kind or inferior quality; woollen fabric. *v.t. & i.* pack tightly or cram into; block up; eat greedily, overeat oneself; (colloq.) gull or

hoax, stŭff'ing, *n.* (esp.) seasoning used in stuffing meat, &c. ; padding of furniture, &c. stŭff'ÿ, *a.* lacking ventilation; close or oppressive or fusty; (sl.) angry.

stŭl'tifÿ, *v.t.* (-fiable). exhibit in ridiculous light; undo the work or effect of. ~fication, *n.*

stŭm'ble, *v.i.* lurch forward, have partial fall; be checked in speech; (with *at*) feel scruples or doubts about; (with *upon*) come across unexpectedly. *n.* act of stumbling. stumbling - block, circumstance causing difficulty or hesitation.

stū'mer, *n.* (sl.) worthless cheque; counterfeit coin or note.

stŭmp, *n.* part of a felled or fallen tree that remains projecting from the ground; remnant of something; any of the three uprights of a cricket wicket; wooden leg; (pl., colloq.) legs. *v.i. & t.* walk on, or as on, wooden legs; (of wicket-keeper) put out batsman while he is out of his ground; (of question, &c.) be too hard for; embarrass, stŭm'per, (sl.) wicket-keeper. stŭmp'ÿ, *a.* thickset.

stŭn, *v.t.* knock senseless; overwhelm or stupefy by shock. stŭnn'ing, *a.*, stŭnn'er, *n.* (sl.) amazingly good, first-class, (specimen).

stung, *p.t. & p.p.* of sting.

stunk, *p.t. & p.p.* of stink.

stŭnt¹, *v.t.* check growth of; (*p.p.*) undersized or ill-developed.

stŭnt², *n.* (sl.) special effort or display; esp. aerobatics.

stīpe, *n.* (Surg.) pledget or fomentation-flannel.

stū'pefÿ, *v.t.* (-fiable). dull the wits or senses of. stŭpēfăc'tion, *n.*

stŭpen'dous, *a.* amazing; of vast size or importance.

stū'pid, *a.* unintelligent; uninteresting. stŭpid'itÿ, *n.*

stū'por, *n.* dazed or torpid state; utter amazement.

stŭrd'ÿ, *a.* not easily knocked down or pushed aside; strong; of independent character.

stūr'geon (-jn), *n.* kinds of large edible fish.

---

stŭtt'er, v.i. & t. speak with checks at and repetitions of certain sounds; utter thus.

stȳ¹, n. (pl. -ies), enclosure in which pigs are kept; filthy room or dwelling.

stȳ², n. (pl. -ies), inflamed swelling on edge of eyelid.

Stȳ'gian, a. of or as of Styx or Hades; murky.

stȳle¹, n. (Bot.) narrowed extension of ovary bearing stigma.

stȳle², n. pointed rod with which the ancients wrote on wax-coated tablet; pen or pencil; style-shaped implement; manner of writing, speaking, &c.; mode of address; shape or make or appearance of a garment or vehicle or the like. v.t. describe by specified term or designation.

stȳ'lish, a. in the prevailing fashion; well-appointed. **stȳ'list**, n. writer or other artist intent rather on style than matter. **stylis'tic**, a. **stȳ'lograph** (-ahf), colloq. **stȳ'lo** (pl. -os), reservoir pen. **stylograph'ic**, a.

stȳp'tic, a. that checks bleeding. n. a styptic substance.

suasion (swā'zhn), n. reasoning or advice as incentive.

suave (sw-), a. bland, polite; of soft flavour. **suav'ity** (sw-), n.

sub¹, n. (colloq.) subaltern; subscription; substitute.

‖ **sub²**, L. prep. = under, used esp. in: ‖ **sŭb ju'dĭcĕ** (jōō-), under judicial consideration, still to be decided. ‖ **— rō'sa** (-z-), in confidence, under pledge of secrecy. ‖ **— sĭlĕn'tĭo** (-shĭō), tacitly, in secret fashion. ‖ **— vō'cĕ** (abbr. s.v.), in the article on that or a specified word.

sub-, pref. denoting inferiority of rank or defect of quality; below, under; deputy.

subahdār' (sōoba-), (Anglo-Ind.) n. chief native officer of company of Sepoys.

subā'cid, a. slightly acid.

sub'altern, n. commissioned officer of lower rank than captain.

subāq'ueous, a. below water.

subaudi'tion, n. mental supplying of what in sense is taken to be implied, though not expressed.

subclass', n. subdivision of a class.

subcon'scious (-shŭs), a. partially or imperfectly conscious.

subcon'tract, n. contract under a previous contractor.

subcutā'neous, a. below the skin.

subdivīde', v.t. & i. divide further. **—divi'sion** (-zhn), n. subdividing; one of the parts resulting.

subdūe', v.t. (-uable), get the upper hand of; tame; soften, tone down. **subdū'al**, n.

subĕd'itor, n. assistant editor of a newspaper or other literary undertaking. **—ship**, n. **subĕd'it**, v.t. act as sub-editor of.

subjā'cent, a. situated below.

sub'ject¹, a. under government; politically dependent; owing obedience to; liable or exposed or prone to. adv. (with to) conditionally upon; on the assumption of. n. person subject to political rule; member of a State or of a subject State; (Gram.) thing about which something is predicated; theme of discussion, description, &c.; person of such-and-such proclivities.

subject'², v.t. subdue; expose; render liable; submit to. **subjĕc'tion**, n.

subjĕc'tive, a. relating to the subject as opposed to the object; (pop.) imaginary; (of art and artists) expressing the artist's point of view rather than transcribing external realities. **subjĕc'tivism**, n. doctrine that all knowledge is subjective only and incapable of objective proof. **subjĕctiv'ity**, n.

subjoin', v.t. add at the end.

sub'jugāte (-jŏŏ-), v.t. (-gable), bring into subjection. **—tion**, n.

subjunc'tive, a. — mood, a. & n. a mood named as being common in subjoined or dependent clauses.

sublease', n. letting to another party of what the lessor himself holds on lease. **sublĕt'**, v.t. let to another person.

sŭb′limate[1], *n.* product of sublimation. **sŭb′limāte**[1], *v.t.* (*-mable*), subject to or produce by sublimation (rare exc. in *p.p.*).

sŭblimā′tion, *n.* process of converting a substance by heat into vapour and allowing this to solidify; also used fig. of emotions, &c.

sublime′, *a.* exalted; surpassing; so impressive as to inspire awe or wonder. *v.t.* (*-mable*), make sublime; subject to or extract by sublimation.

sŭblim′inal, *a.* (Psychol.: of sensations) present without being consciously apprehended.

sublim′ity, *n.* being sublime.

sŭblu′nary (-lōō-), *a.* merely terrestrial; of this world.

sŭb′marine (-ēn), *a.* below sea. *n.* submersible boat, esp. for torpedo work.

submĕrge′, *v.t. & i.* (of water, &c.) cover the whole of; contain below the surface; (of submarine, &c.) sink; (*p.p.*, fig.) plunged in debt or want. **submĕrg′ence**, *n.*

submĕrsed′ (-st), *a.* put or growing under water. **~sible**, *a.*; **~sibility**, *n.*; **~sion**, *n.*

submĭs′sion (-shn), *n.* submitting; theory, &c. submitted. **~ive**, *a.* unresisting; meek, tractable.

submit′, *v.t. & i.* accept without resistance; give way; yield; present for consideration; represent.

subnŏrm′al, *a.* below normal.

subŏr′dĭnate, *a.* of inferior importance or rank. *n.* person working under another. **subŏr′dĭnate**, *v.t.* (*-nable*), treat or regard as subordinate. **~tion**, *n.* subordinate state. **~tive**, *a.*

suborn′, *v.t.* induce to commit perjury or other crime. **~ā′tion**, *n.*

subpœ′na (-pēn-), *n.* writ commanding person's attendance in court of justice.

subscribe′, *v.t. & i.* (*-bable*), sign (one's name to a document); express adhesion *to*; contribute to fund or object. **subscri′ber**, *n.*

sŭb′script, *a.* written below.

subscrip′tion, *n.* subscribing; share or sum subscribed.

sŭb′sequent, *a.* coming after; posterior *to*. **sŭb′sequence**, *n.*

subsĕrve′, *v.t.* (*-vable*), serve as means towards. **~vience**, *n.* **~vient**, *a.* conducive as means *to*; obsequious.

subside′, *v.i.* fall to the bottom; sink to normal level; cave in; settle down lower in ground or water; abate, die away; fall silent, subside. **~dence**, *n.*

subsid′iary, *a.* serving to help or supplement; not of primary importance; supplementary *to*.

sŭb′sidīze, *v.t.* (*-zable*), pay subsidy to; support by subsidies.

sŭb′sidy, *n.* money grant to sovereign, or to another State in return for support; money grant from State to private concerns held to be of public utility or to meet urgent necessities.

subsist′, *v.i. & t.* exist; support life; find sustenance for. **~ence**, *n.* subsisting; what one lives on or by.

sŭb′soil, *n.* stratum of earth just below surface.

sŭb′stance, *n.* the essence or most important part of anything; gist, purport; matter; reality; solidity; actual possessions.

substăn′tial (-shl), *a.* having substance; not illusory; not inconsiderable; not of doubtful credit.

substăn′tiāte (-shĭ-), *v.t.* (*-tiable*), give good grounds for (charge, statement). **~tion**, *n.* **~tor**, *nn.*

sŭb′stantive, *a.* expressing existence; having separate existence; not subsidiary. *n.* noun. **substan′tival**, *a.*

sŭb′stitūte, *n.* person or thing performing some function instead of another. *v.t.* (*-tutable*), put in exchange (*for*). **~tion**, *n.* **~tor**, *nn.*

substrā′tum, *n.* lower layer; basis.

substruc′tion, *n.* vaults or other masonry, &c. serving as foundation. **sŭb′structure**, *n.* an underbuilding; a foundation; basement.

sŭbtĕn'ant, n. tenant holding of a tenant. ~ncy, n.

sŭbtĕnd', v.t. (of line) be opposite (angle, arc).

sŭb'terfūge, n. evasion, esp. in argument or excuse.

sŭbterrā'nean, a. underground.

sŭbtī'tle, n. secondary title of a book, &c.

subtile, subtil (sŭ'tl), a. pervasive by tenuity; insidious; hard to analyse or apprehend; ingeniously minute. **subt'īlize** (sŭt-), v.t. subtlety, subtilty (sŭt'ltī), n. subtileness; a fine distinction.

subtract', v.t. deduct (part, quantity, number) from, esp. with a view to ascertaining the remainder. ~ion, n. (esp.) subtracting process. ~or, n. **sŭb'trahĕnd**, n. what is to be subtracted in a subtraction sum.

sŭb'ûrb, n. outlying district of city. **suburb'an**, a.

subvĕn'tion, n. grant of money in aid of an institution, &c.

subvĕr'sion (-shn), n. subverting. ~ive, a. tending to subversion.

subvĕrt', v.t. effect destruction or overthrow of (religion, &c.).

sŭb'way, n. underground passage, esp. for foot-passengers; *underground railway.

succeed' (-ks-), v.t. & i. come next after and take the place of; be successor to; inherit; attain one's purpose.

success' (-ks-), n. favourable issue; attainment of one's object; prosperity; person or thing that turns out well. ~ful, a.

succes'sion (suksĕshn), n. a following in order; series of things in succession; right of succeeding to, esp. a throne. ~ive, a. following in succession; running. ~or, n. person or thing succeeding to another.

succinct' (-ks-), a. (arch., of clothes or wearer) girded up; (of style, &c.) terse, brief.

*succ'otăsh, n. beans and Indian corn boiled together.

succ'our (-ker), v.t. come to the assistance of. n. aid given at time of need.

succ'ûlent, a. juicy; thick and fleshy. **succ'ûlence**, n.

succumb' (-m), v.i. be vanquished; give way to; die.

such, a. of the kind or degree indicated by the context or circumstances. pron. that; the action, &c. referred to; other such things. ~and-such, (a) certain. ~ as (arch.), all who. ~like (vulg.), a. of such kind; pron. other such things.

suck, v.t. & i. draw (milk, liquid) into the mouth; imbibe or gain (knowledge); roll the tongue about, squeeze in the mouth (sweets, &c.); use sucking action. n. act or spell or process of sucking; (school sl.) (pl.) sweets, (sing., or in pl. as excl.) a sell. ~in, (sl.) a sell. **sucking-pig**, unweaned pig.

suck'er, n. (esp.) shoot springing from plant's root beside and not from the stem; organ in animals or part of apparatus adapted for adhering by suction to surfaces; pump-piston; *(sl.) simpleton, greenhorn.

suck'le, v.t. feed (young) from breast or udder.

suck'ling, n. unweaned child or other mammal.

suc'tion, n. sucking; removal of atmospheric pressure from any interior space so as to allow the pressure to act externally.

sŭdd, n. vegetable matter obstructing the White Nile.

sŭdd'en, n. occurring unexpectedly or without warning; abrupt; hurried.

sūdorif'ic, a. promoting or secreting sweat. n. a sudorific drug.

Sud'ra (sōō-), n. lowest of four great Hindu castes.

sŭds (-z), n.pl. soap-froth.

sūe, v.t. & i. (-uable), prosecute in court; make petition to.

suède (swād), n. undressed kid-skin.

sū'ĕt, n. fat enclosing kidneys of ox, &c.

---

māte, mēte, mĭte, mōte, mūte, mōōt; rǎck, rĕck, rĭck, rŏck, rŭck, rŏŏḳ;

sŭff'er, *v.t.* & *i.* undergo, be subjected to, pain or damage or punishment; allow to go on. ~ance, *n.* tacit consent; abstention from objection. ~ing, *n.* what one has to endure.

suffice', *v.i.* & *t.* (-ceable), be enough; meet the needs of. **suffi'ciency** (-shn-), *n.* enough of something; a competence. **suffi'cient** (-shnt), *a.* sufficing; enough of.

sŭff'ix[1], *n.* letter or syllable(s) appended in word-formation. **suffix'**[2], *v.t.* append thus.

sŭff'ocāte, *v.t.* & *i.* (-cable), kill by stopping respiration; impede breath or utterance of; gasp for breath. **suffocā'tion**, *n.*

sŭff'ragan, *n.* assistant bishop in charge of part of diocese. *a.* (of see or bishop) subordinate.

sŭff'rage, *n.* (usu. pl.) intercessory petition(s) in liturgy; vote; right of voting at elections. **sŭffragette'**, *n.* woman who agitated for woman suffrage. **sŭff'ragist**, *n.* advocate of extending the franchise, esp. to women.

suffūse' (-z), *v.t.* (of liquid, hue, blush, tears, &c.) spread as from within over the surface of. **suffū'sion** (-zhn), *n.*

su'fi (sōō-), *n.* Mohammedan pantheist.

su'gar (shŏŏ-), *n.* kinds of sweet crystalline substance for use in cookery, &c.; flattery; (Chem.) kinds of soluble sweet fermentable carbohydrate. *v.t.* & *i.* sweeten or coat with sugar; (U.S. & Canada) make maple-sugar. ~cane, grass yielding sugar. ~loaf, conical mass of refined sugar. ~plum, sweetmeat. **su'gary** (shŏŏ-), *a.*

suggest' (suj-), *v.t.* cause (idea) to present itself; give a hint or inkling of; propose for acceptance. ~ible, *a.* (esp.) open to hypnotic suggestion. ~ibility, *n.* suggesting; theory or plan suggested; suggesting of prurient ideas. **sugges'tive** (suj-), *a.* full of suggestion; suggesting the idea of; suggesting prurient ideas.

su'icide, *n.* self-murderer; self-murder. **suici'dal**, *n.*

suit (sūt), *n.* suing, petition; prosecution of woman's hand; prosecution of claim in law-court; any of the four sets into which pack of cards is divided; set of clothes; set of pyjamas or armour or sails. *v.t.* & *i.* adapt or make appropriate *to*; (*p.p.*) well fitted to; meet the requirements of; agree with; comport with; be convenient. ~case, travelling bag.

suit'able (sūt-), *a.* suited *to* or *for*; fitted for the purpose. ~bility, *n.*

suite (swēt), *n.* retinue; set of rooms, furniture, &c.; set of dance-tunes.

suit'or (sūt-), *n.* wooer; plaintiff or petitioner in suit.

sŭlk, *v.i.* be sulky. *n.pl.* sulky fit or state. **sŭl'ky**, *a.* silent or inactive or unsociable from resentment or ill temper.

sŭll'age, *n.* filth, refuse.

sŭll'en, *a.* passively resentful; unforgiving; ill-humoured.

sŭll'y, *v.t.* (-iable), soil, tarnish; be a stain on; discredit.

sŭl'phate, *n.* a salt of sulphuric acid. **sŭl'phide**, *n.* compound of sulphur with element or radical. **sŭl'phite**, *n.* salt of sulphurous acid.

sŭl'phonal, *n.* a hypnotic drug.

sŭl'phur (-er), *n.* pale-yellow nonmetallic element burning with blue flame and stifling smell; kinds of sulphur-coloured butterfly. *v.t.* treat with sulphur. **sŭl'phurāte**, *v.t.* impregnate with sulphur. **sŭlphūr'eous**, *a.* of or like sulphur. **sŭlphūrĕt'ĕd**, *a.* having sulphur in combination. **sŭlphūr'ic**, *a.* combining sulphur in its higher combining proportion. **sŭl'phūrous**, *a.* containing sulphur in its lower combining proportion.

sŭl'tan, *n.* Mohammedan sovereign. **sŭlta'na** (-tah-), *n.* sultan's wife; kind of seedless raisin. **sŭl'tanate**, *n.* sultanship.

sŭl'try, a. hot and close.

sŭm, n. total resulting from addition of items; summary; particular amount of money; an arithmetical problem. v.t. & i. collect into or express as one total; (with *up*) set out arguments on both sides, gather up in review.

sŭm'marize, v.t. (-zable), make or be a summary of.

sŭmm'ary, a. dispensing with details or formalities; done with dispatch. n. brief account; résumé, epitome.

summā'tion, n. finding of total.

sŭmm'er¹, n. second or hot season. v.i. & t. pass the summer; pasture (cattle) for the summer. ~ time, that indicated by clocks advanced in summer by one hour to prolong use of daylight.

sŭmm'er², n. large beam or stone serving as lintel or base of arch or the like.

summersault. See somersault.

sŭmm'it, n. highest point, top (esp. of mountain, or fig. of ambition, fortune, &c.).

sŭmm'on, v.t. send for; demand the presence of; bid (esp. witness or defendant) appear; convoke; demand surrender of; muster *up* courage, &c., to do.

sŭmm'ons (-z), n. (pl. *-ses*), authoritative call to attend or do something; citation to appear in court; v.t. serve with summons.

|| **sŭ'mmum bō'num**, n. the chief good.

sŭmp, n. pit or well for reception of superfluous water, &c.

sŭm'pitan (-an), n. blow-gun made by Malays from a hollowed cane, from which poisoned arrows are shot.

sŭmp'ter, n. pack (~-*horse*, ~-*mule*, &c.).

sŭmp'tuary, a. regulating expenditure (of laws against luxury).

sŭmp'tuous, a. of costly richness.

sŭn, n. the heavenly body that the earth travels round and receives light and warmth from; such

light or warmth; any fixed star with satellite(s). v.t. & i. expose to sun; sun oneself. ~-bath, exposure of naked body to sun. ~bathe, take sun-bath. ~beam, ray of sun. ~blind, external window-shade. ~dew, small bog-plant. ~dog, parhelion. ~down, sunset. ~downer, (Austral.) tramp who times his arrival for the evening; (S.-Afr.) drink at sundown. ~fish, a fish of large globular kind. ~flower, plant with large golden-rayed flowers. ~-parlour, a room with windows on three sides, so arranged as to get sun at all hours. ~rise, (moment of) sun's rising. ~set, (moment of) sun's setting. ~shade, parasol. ~shine, sunlight, area illuminated by it; cheerfulness or bright influence. ~spot, one of the dark patches sometimes observed on sun's surface. ~stroke, acute prostration from excessive heat of weather.

*sŭn'dae** (-dì), n. ice cream served with crushed fruit or syrup.

Sŭn'day (-dì), n. first day of the week. ~school, held on Sunday for religious teaching.

sŭn'der, v.t. sever.

sŭn'dry, a. divers, several. n. (in pl. only) oddments; items that need not be specified.

sung, p.t. & p.p. of sing.

sunk, p.t. & p.p. of sink.

sŭnn, ~-hemp, nn. E.-Ind. hemplike fibre.

sŭnn'y, a. bright with or as sunlight; diffusing cheerfulness.

|| **sŭnnyas'ee**, -yas'ī (-ah-), n. Brahmin in the fourth stage of his life; wandering fakir or religious mendicant.

sŭp¹, v.t. & i. drink by sips. n. mouthful of liquid.

sŭp², v.t. take supper; make one's supper *off* or *on* specified food.

su'per, n. (sl.) supernumerary actor. a. (of feet, yards, &c.) superficial in square measure; (shop) superfine.

sŭperănn'ūāte, v.t. (-uable), dismiss or discard as too old; send into retirement with a pension. **superánnuā'tion**, n.

superb' (sŏŏ-, sŭ-), a. of the most impressive or exalted kind.

sū'percárgō, n. (pl. -oes), person in merchant ship managing sales, &c. of cargo.

supercil'iary, a. of the brows, over the eye. **supercil'ious** (-yus), a. exhibiting contemptuous indifference; insolently nonchalant.

supererogā'tion, n. doing of more than duty requires. **supererog'atory**, a.

superfi'cial (-shl), a. of or on the surface only; without depth. **superficiál'ity** (-shi-), n.

superfi'cies (-shiez), n. a surface, esp. with reference to its area.

sū'perfine, a. affecting great refinement; of extra quality.

superflu'ity (-lōō-), n. superfluous amount; what is over.

super'fluous (sŏŏpér'flŏŏ-), a. not needed; more than enough.

superhū'man, a. more than human.

superincum'bent, a. lying on the top of something.

superindūce', v.t. (-cible), bring on (sleep, &c.) by external influence.

superintend', v.t. & i. arrange and oversee the working of. **~ence**, n. **~ent**, n. official manager.

super'ior (sŏŏ-), a. higher in place, upper; better in some respect; superior to the average; inaccessible to temptation, adversity, &c. n. person superior to one in rank or in some quality; head of monastery, &c. **superiŏr'ity** (sŏŏ-), n.

super'lative (sŏŏ-), a. of the highest degree; (Gram.) ~degree, the adj. and adv. forms expressing the highest or a very high degree. n. the superlative degree or form; a word in the superlative.

sū'permän, n. (pl. -en), the ideal man, superior to moral restrictions, of Nietzsche. **~mün'däne**, a. superior to earthly things.

supérn'al, a. heavenly; divine.

supernā'tural (-chŏŏ-), a. due to or manifesting some agency above the forces of nature. **~ism**, **~ist**, nn. belief, believer, in the existence of the supernatural.

supernū'merary, a. in excess of the normal or necessary number. n. extra person.

superpōse' (-z), v.t. lay (thing) on or upon another. **superposi'tion**, n. such laying.

superscrip'tion, n. inscription over something.

supersēde', v.t. (-dable), appoint or adopt another person or thing in the place of; oust or take the place of. **~sē'ssion** (-shn), n. superseding.

supersti'tion, n. credulity regarding the supernatural; misdirected reverence. **supersti'tious** (-shus), a. marked by superstition.

sū'perstructure, n. what rests on a foundation; a building in relation to its foundation.

sū'pertäx, n. tax on incomes above a certain amount levied in addition to ordinary income-tax.

supervēne', v.i. occur as an interruption in or change from some state. **~vēn'tion**, n.

supervise' (-z), v.t. (-sable), oversee; watch or direct the carrying on or work of. **~vi'sion** (-zhn), n. **sū'pervisor** (-z-), n. *(esp.) officer of elected board administering a township.

supine'¹, a. lying facing upwards; quiescent, indolent.

sū'pine'², n. Latin verbal noun used in special constructions.

supp'er, n. a meal taken late in the day.

supplant' (-ah-), v.t. oust, esp. by craft.

sup'ple, a. easily bent; flexible; artfully compliant; adroit.

sup'plement¹, n. thing added to supply deficiencies, amplify previous account, &c.; an addition to the regular number of a periodical. **supplement²**, v.t. make additions to (information, &c.). **supplemén'tal, ~ary**, aa.

sŭpp'liant, _a._ supplicating; expressive of supplication.

sŭpp'lĭcāte, _v.i._ & _t._ (-_cable_). make humble petition to or for. supplǐcā′tion, _n._; ~tory, _a._

supply′, _v.t._ furnish, provide; fill (place) as substitute. _n._ providing of what is needed; stock, store; (pl.) necessaries.

support′, _v.t._ carry weight of; prop up; give strength to, encourage; endure, tolerate; supply with necessaries; lend assistance to. _n._ supporting or being supported; person or thing that supports. support′er, _n._

suppōse′ (-z), _v.t._ (-_sable_). assume in default of knowledge; be inclined to think; (_p.p._) reputed. supposĭ′tion (-zĭ-), _n._ thing supposed; supposing. suppŏsĭti′tious (-ztĭshus), _a._ spurious.

suppŏs′ĭtŏry (-z-), _n._ medicinal cone or cylinder placed in orifice to dissolve.

supprĕss′, _v.t._ (-_ible_). put an end to the existence or activity of; avoid giving vent to; withhold from publication; keep secret. ~ion, -or, _nn._

‖ **supprĕs′sĭō vē′rī,** _n._ hiding of truth; tacit misrepresentation.

sŭpp′ūrāte, _v.i._ form pus; fester. suppūrā′tion, _n._

suprĕm′acý (sōō-), _n._ being supreme; highest authority.

suprēme′ (sōō-), _a._ highest in authority or rank; of the uttermost importance or merit.

sur′a¹ (-ōō-), _n._ the fermented sap of various species of palm.

sur′a² (-ōō-), _n._ in Hindu demonology, a good angel or genie.

sur′ah, _n._ kind of soft twilled, usu. one-coloured, silk.

surăt′ (sōō-), _n._ kind of cotton grown in the Bombay Presidency; also coarse cotton goods usu. uncoloured.

surcease′ (ser-), _v.i._ & _n._ (arch.) cease; cessation.

sur′chärge¹, _n._ extra load or charge; fine for under-stamping, &c.; expenditure marked as unauthorized and to be refunded.

surchärge′² (ser-), _v.t._ (-_geable_). overload; exact surcharge from; fine (person) as surcharge.

sur′cingle, _n._ band round a horse's body.

sur′coat, _n._ (hist.) mantle worn over armour.

sŭrd, _a._ & _n._, (Math.: also ~ _number_, _root_), irrational; (Phonet.: also ~ _letter_, _sound_), unvoiced letter or sound.

sure (shoor), _a._ having adequate reason for belief; convinced of; reliable, unfailing; faithful. _adv._ certainly (arch.). ~ly, _adv._ with certainty. surety (shoor′tĭ), _n._ certainty (arch.); security; person who goes bail for another's appearance in court or payment of sum.

sŭrf, _n._ foam of sea breaking on shore or reefs.

sŭr′face (-ĭs), _n._ the outside of a body; outward aspect of material or immaterial thing. ~~car, electric street-car. ~~man, workman keeping permanent way of railway in order.

sur′feit (-fĭt), _n._ excess, esp. in food; satiety. _v.t._ & _i._ overfeed; satiate with, be satiated.

sŭrge, _v.i._ move in or as in waves. _n._ surging motion; waves.

sur′geon (-jn), _n._ person skilled in surgery; medical practitioner having a diploma qualifying him to practise surgery. sur′gery, _n._ manual treatment of injuries or disorders of the body; surgeon's consulting room; medical practitioner's dispensary. sur′gical, _a._ of or by surgery; of surgeons.

sur′icate (-at), _n._ S.-Afr. animal resembling polecat and ferret.

sur′ly, _a._ sour in manner; rudely unsociable; churlish.

‖ **sur′ma** (soor-), **soor′ma,** _n._ (E.-Ind.) black powder consisting of sulphide of antimony or lead, used by Indian women for staining the eyebrows and eyelids.

surmise′ (sermīz), _n._ suspicion of the existence or nature of something. _v.t._ & _i._ (-_sable_). suspect the existence of; form a surmise.

surmount' (-er), *v.t.* overcome; get the better of; be on top of.

surmul'let (-er), *n.* red mullet.

surn'ame, *n.* the name common to all members of a family. *v.t.* (-mable), give (person) surname.

surpass' (-pahs), *v.t.* outdo, excel; (part.) supereminent.

surp'lice, *n.* loose white vestment worn by officiating clergy and choristers. **surp'liced** (-st), *a.*

surp'lus, *n.* amount left over when requirements have been met. **surp'lusage**, *n.* wasteful excess.

surprise (serpriz'), *n.* catching of person(s) unprepared; emotion excited by the unexpected; event, &c. exciting this. *v.t.* (-sable), capture by surprise; attack or come upon at unawares; astonish. **surpris'ing** (serpriz'-), *a.* unlooked-for.

‖ **surra** (soo'ra, su'ra), *n.* disease of horses and other domestic animals in India, China, and other countries.

surren'der, *v.t. & i.* relinquish possession of, esp. to another upon his demand; give oneself up, cease from resistance. *n.* surrendering.

surrepti'tious (-shus), *a.* done by stealth; underhand.

*****surrey**, *n.* kind of four-wheeled two-seated pleasure carriage or automobile.

surrogate, *n.* deputy of bishop or his chancellor; *"judge with jurisdiction over probate of wills, &c.

surround', *v.t.* come or be all round; encompass, environ. **-ings**, *n.pl.* all that environs one.

surt'ax, *n.* additional tax.

surt'out (-oo), *n.* overcoat.

surveill'ance (serval'-), *n.* watch kept on suspected person, &c.

survey[1] (serva'), *v.t.* take general view of; scan; determine the boundaries, size, position, &c. of country, estate, &c. **surv'ey**[2] (-va), *n.* casting of eyes or mind over something; piece of landsurveying. **surveyor** (serva'er), *n.* official inspector of; person who surveys land professionally.

survi'val (ser-), *n.* surviving; relic of the past.

survive' (ser-), *v.t. & i.* (-vable), outlive; be still alive or existent. **surviv'or**, *n.*

sur'wan, *n.* (Anglo-Ind.) cameldriver.

suscep'tible, *a.* impressionable; touchy; admitting of; accessible or sensitive to. **-bility**, *n.* **suscep'tive**, *a.* concerned with the receiving of emotional impressions.

su'si (soo-), *n.* E.-Ind. cotton fabric with stripes of different coloured silk.

suspect', *v.t.* have an impression of the existence or presence of; be inclined to think that; doubt the innocence or genuineness or truth of. *pred.a.* open to suspicion. *n.* suspected person.

suspend', *v.t.* hang up; delay, put off; deprive of office for a time. **suspen'der**, *n.* (esp., pl.) *"trouserbraces; attachments holding up socks, &c.

suspense', *n.* anxious uncertainty about some issue; undetermined state. **-sion**, *n.* suspending. **-sive**, **-sory**, *aa.*

suspi'cion (-shn), *n.* feeling of one who suspects; partial or unconfirmed belief, esp. that something is wrong. **suspi'cious** (-shus), *a.* feeling or justifying suspicion; distrustful.

sustain', *v.t.* bear weight of; keep from falling; enable to last out; undergo, suffer (loss, &c.); uphold, decide in favour of; keep up. **sus'tenance**, *n.* nourishing quality, food (lit. or fig.). **sustenta'tion**, *n.* (rare), supporting of life.

sut'ler, *n.* camp-follower selling food, &c.

Su'tra (soo-), *n.* set of aphorisms in Sanskrit literature.

suttee', *n.* Hindu widow who immolates herself on her husband's pyre; this custom. **-ism**, *n.*

su'ture, *n.* seam-like articulation of two bones or parts at their edges; (Surg.) stitching of wound, thread or wire used.

su'zerain, *n.* feudal lord; sovereign or State having general or nominal control over semi-independent State. **su'zerainty**, *n.*

swab (-ŏb), *n.* mop or absorbent pad or cloth for cleaning; (Naut. sl.) epaulet, clumsy fellow. *v.t.* clean with swab.

swa'ddle (-ŏ-), *v.t.* wrap (esp. infant) up tight and warm. **swaddling clothes**, baby-wraps.

Swade'shi (-dā-), *n.* movement in India for boycotting British goods as means of bringing political pressure to bear.

swăg, *n.* (sl.) burglar's booty; gain made by jobbery, &c.; (Austral.) tramp's or bush-traveller's bundle.

swăg'ger¹ (-ger), *v.i.* behave arrogantly; talk boastfully. *n.* swaggering gait or manner or talk; dashing behaviour. *a.* smart or fashionable.

swă'gger² (-ger), *n.* (Austral. sl.) tramp or bush-traveller.

swain, *n.* young rustic; bucolic lover; (joc.) suitor.

swāle, *v.t. & i.* burn, set fire to (gorse, brushwood, &c.).

swa'llow¹ (-ŏlō), *v.t. & i.* make or let pass down one's throat; engulf; accept credulously; recant (one's words). *n.* gullet; act of swallowing.

swa'llow² (-ŏlō), *n.* kinds of fork-tailed swift insectivorous bird. **~tail**, forked tail; kinds of butterfly and humming-bird; swallow-tailed coat.

swam, *p.t.* of swim.

Swam'i (-ah-), *n.* a Hindu idol; title for a Hindu religious teacher; also (attrib.) applied to jewellery ornamented with figures of Hindu deities. **~house**, idol-temple or shrine.

swamp (-ŏ-), *n.* piece of wet spongy ground; marsh. *v.t.* overwhelm, flood, soak (with water, &c.); overwhelm by superior numbers or quantity. **swa'mpy** (-ŏ-), *a.*

swan (-ŏn), *n.* large long-necked usu. white water-bird. **~song**,

person's last production or achievement. **swa'nnery** (-ŏ-), *n.*

swănk (sl.), *n.* showing off; swagger. *v.i.* behave with swank.

swarāj' (-ahj), *n.* Home-rule or self-government as the watch-word of Indian Nationalists. **~ist**, *n. & a.*

swărd (-ŏrd), *n.* expanse of short grass.

sware, *p.t.* of swear.

swarm¹ (-ŏrm), *n.* large number of insects, birds, horsemen, &c. moving about; cluster of bees. *v.i.* move in or (of bees) form a swarm; congregate in numbers.

swarm² (-ŏrm), *v.i. & t.* climb (rope, pole, &c.) by clipping with knees and hands.

swar'thy (-ŏrdhi), **swart** (-ŏrt arch.), *aa.* dark-hued; sunburnt.

swash (-ŏ-), *v.i. & t.* make the sound of water washing about. *n.* sound of swashing water. **~buckler**, bully, bravo.

swăs'tika, *n.* cross of equal arms with rectangular continuations.

swăth (-aw-; pl. pr. -dhz), **swāthe¹** (-dh), *nn.* band of cut grass, or of cleared ground, left after one passage of mower; (-e only) wrapping, bandage. **swāthe²** (-dh), *v.t.* (-thable), enclose (limb, person) in bandages or wraps.

sway, *v.i. & t.* have unsteady swinging motion; waver; give swaying motion to; have influence over; rule over. *n.* swaying motion; rule, government.

swear (swâr), *v.t. & i.* (*swŏre* & arch. *swāre; swŏrn*), take oath; promise on oath; use profane oaths; cause to take oath; administer oath to. *n.* spell of profane swearing.

sweat (-ĕt), *n.* moisture exuded from the skin; perspiration; sweating state; (colloq.) drudgery or toil. *v.i. & t.* exude sweat; emit like sweat; toil, drudge; get maximum of work for minimum of pay out of. **swea'ter** (-ĕt-), *n.* (esp.) thick woollen jersey; sweating employer. **swea'ty** (-ĕt-), *a.*

Swëde, *n.* native of Sweden; (s-) Swedish turnip. **Swë′dish,** *a.* & *n.* (language) of Sweden.

sween′ỹ, *n.* atrophy of muscle, esp. of shoulder, in horse.

sweep, *v.i.* & *t.* (swěpt), glide swiftly; go majestically; extend in continuous curve or line or slope; impart sweeping motion to; clear everything from; clear of dust or soot or litter with broom. *n.* sweeping motion or extension; curve in road, &c.; long oar worked by standing rower(s) on barge, &c.; chimney-sweep. **~stake(s),** gamble on horse-race, &c., in which entrance money goes to drawer(s) of winner.

sweet, *a.* tasting like sugar or honey; smelling like perfumes; melodious; fresh; not sour or bitter; gratifying; dear, beloved; amiable, gentle; (colloq.) very pretty. *n.* sweetmeat; (usu. pl.) sweet dish(es) such as puddings, tarts, jellies; (pl.) delights; darling. **~bread,** pancreas or thymus-gland, esp. of calf as food. **~ brier,** wild fragrant-leaved rose-tree. **~heart,** either of pair of lovers. **~meat,** sugar-plum or bonbon. **~ pea,** garden annual with showy scented flowers. **~potato,** tropical plant with tuberous roots used for food. **~ william,** garden flower of many coloured varieties. **sweet′en,** *v.t.* & *i.* **sweet′ing,** *n.* kind of apple.

swell, *v.i.* & *t.* (p.p. swŏllen, arch. swŏln, rarely swelled), (cause to) grow bigger or louder; dilate, expand; rise or raise *up*; bulge *out*; increase in volume or force or intensity. *n.* act or state of swelling; heaving of sea after a storm; (colloq.) person of distinction or of good society, or of fashionable appearance. *a.* (colloq.) of distinction; smart, finely dressed. **~ mob,** class of well-dressed pickpockets. **swell′ing,** *n.* (esp.) temporary protuberance due to bruise, &c.

swěl′ter, *v.i.* be oppressive or oppressed with heat.

swept, *p.t.* & *p.p.* of sweep.

swerve, *v.i.* & *t.* (-vable), diverge from regular line of motion (lit. & fig.); cause (ball) to swerve in air. *n.* swerving motion.

swift, *a.* speedy, quick, prompt. *adv.* swiftly. *n.* long-winged insectivorous bird.

swig (sl.), *v.t.* & *i.* take draughts of. *n.* draught of liquor.

swill, *v.t.* & *i.* rinse (often *out*); drink greedily. *n.* rinsing; inferior liquor; hogwash or slops.

swim, *v.i.* & *t.* (swăm; swŭm), float on or at surface of liquid; progress in water by working limbs or body; make swim; be flooded with moisture; walk, &c. with gliding motion; have dizzy effect or sensation. *n.* spell of swimming. **swimm′ingly,** *adv.* with easy unobstructed progress.

swin′dle, *v.t.* & *i.* cheat; defraud. *n.* imposition; fraud.

swine, *n.* (sing. & pl.) kinds of nonruminant carnivorous animal, (pop.) pig, hog; bestial or degraded person, lover of filth. **swi′nish,** *a.* bestial, filthy.

swing, *v.i.* & *t.* (swŭng), move with to-and-fro motion; sway like a pendulum, door, &c.; oscillate; go with swinging gait. *n.* act of swinging; oscillation; swinging gait or rhythm; seat slung by ropes or chains for swinging.

swinge (-j), *v.t.* (part. -geing), strike hard; (part.) huge.

swingle (swing′gl), *n.* swinging bar of flail; flax-beating implement. *v.t.* beat (flax). **~tree,** pivoted bar to which traces are attached in cart, plough, &c.

swipe, *v.i.* & *t.* (Crick.) hit hard and recklessly; *(sl.)* steal. *n.* reckless hard hit; (pl.) inferior beer.

swirl, *n.* whirling motion of water as drawn by suction; eddy. *v.i.* flow with or show swirl.

swish, *v.t.* & *i.* flog with birch; swing (cane, &c.) audibly through air; make a move with such sound. *n.* swishing sound or motion.

---

zh, as (rou)ge; ё = I; ịr, ûr, =ĕr; ỹ, ў, = I, I; and see p. 4.   * = U.S.

3495 E

Swiss, *a.* of Switzerland. *n.* Swiss native. ~ roll, kind of jam-sandwich rolled up.

switch, *n.* flexible shoot cut from tree; kinds of mechanism for making and breaking connexion of railway points, electric circuit, &c. *v.t. & i.* whip with switch; transfer with switch; turn *off* or *on*. ~back, zigzag railway for steep slopes.

swiv'el, *n.* ring and pivot connecting two parts so that one can revolve without the other. **swiv'elled** (-ld), *a.*

swollen, swoln, *p.p.* of swell.

swoon, *v.i., & n.* (have) fainting fit.

swoop, *v.i.* come down with the rush of a bird of prey; make sudden attack. *n.* plunge of bird of prey; sudden raid.

swŏp, swap (-ŏ-), *v.t. & i.* (sl.) exchange, barter.

sword (sŏrd), *n.* weapon with long blade for cutting or thrusting; (Mil. sl.) bayonet. ~bill, long-billed humming-bird. ~fish, fish with upper jaw elongated to sharp weapon. ~grass, gladiolus; kinds of sedge. ~man (-an), person of some skill in use of sword. ~s'manship, *n.*

swore, *p.t.*, **sworn**, *p.p.*, of swear.

swŏt (school sl.), *v.i. & t.* work hard, esp. at books; *hit hard. n.* hard study; task requiring it; one who swots; *hard blow.

swum, *p.p.* of swim.

swung, *p.t. & p.p.* of swing.

syb'arite, *n.* luxurious effeminate person. **sybarit'ic**, *a.*

sy̆c'amine, *n.* (Bibl.) black-mulberry tree.

sy̆c'amŏre, *n.* large timber-tree allied to maple.

syce. See sice².

sy̆c'omŏre, *n.* kind of fig-tree.

sy̆c'ophant, *n.* flatterer, toady. **sy̆c'ophancy̆**, *n.*; **sy̆cophăn'tic**, *a.*

sy̆'ēnīte, *n.* kind of grey crystalline rock. **sy̆enĭt'ic**, *a.*

sy̆ll'abary, *n.* set of characters representing syllables. **sy̆llăb'ic**, *a.* representing a syllable; of or in syllables. **sy̆ll'able**, *n.* word

or part of word containing one vowel-sound; *v.t.* (poet.) utter (name, word).

sy̆ll'abus, *n.* (pl. *-bī, -buses*). abstract of subjects of a lecture or course; programme of hours.

sy̆ll'ogism, *n.* form of reasoning consisting of two propositions, called major and minor premise, from which a third called the conclusion is deduced. **sy̆llogis'tic**, *a.* **sy̆ll'ogīze**, *v.i. & t.* use syllogisms; put into syllogistic form.

sy̆lph, *n.* elemental spirit of the air; slender sprite.

sy̆m'bol, *n.* an emblem or representation of something; mark or character. ~ŏl'ic, ~ical, *aa.*; ~ism, *n.* ~īze, *v.t.* (*-zable*), be a symbol of; represent or refer to by a symbol; treat as symbolic.

sy̆mm'etry̆, *n.* right proportion of parts; harmony. ~sy̆mmĕt'rical, *a.*

sy̆mpathĕt'ic, *a.* expressing or feeling sympathy; (of pain, &c.) caused by pain to some one else or in another part.

sy̆m'pathīze, *v.i.* feel or express sympathy (*with*).

sy̆m'pathy̆, *n.* participation in feeling; being affected similarly to another by his sensations, &c.; compassion *for*.

sy̆m'phony̆, *n.* harmonious sounds; elaborate orchestral composition of several contrasted but related movements; instrumental prelude, interlude, or close, to a song accompaniment.

sy̆mpōs'ium (-z-), *n.* (pl. *-ia*). philosophical or other friendly discussion; set of articles on one subject from various writers.

sy̆mp'tom, *n.* manifestation in the body that indicates disease; sign of the existence of something. **sy̆mptomăt'ic**, *a.*

sy̆n'agogue (-ŏg), *n.* Jewish congregation or its place of meeting.

sy̆n'chronous (-ngk-), *a.* of the same date or moment; simultaneous. **sy̆n'chronīze** (-ngk-), *v.i. & t.* (*-zable*), occur at the same time; ascertain or set

---

māte, mēte, mīte, mōte, mūte, mōŏt ; răck, rĕck, rick, rŏck, rŭck, rōŏk ;

forth the time-correspondence of. ~zā'tion, n.

sÿnc'opāte, v.t. (-pable), shorten by omission of interior letter(s) ; (Mus.) invert rhythm of (note, tone) by beginning it on unaccented beat. ~ā'tion, n. sÿnc'opē, n. syncopation ; (Med.) fainting.

sÿn'dic, n. member of syndicate or committee ; foreign magistrate.

sÿn'dicalism, n. a movement among industrial workers having as its object the transfer of the means of production and distribution from their present owners to unions of workers.

sÿn'dicate, n. committee of delegates or syndics ; association of persons or bodies formed to advance common interests.

sÿne, Sc. for since.

sÿnec'doche (-kĭ), n. (Gram.) extended acceptation by which a part may be named for the whole (e. g. 50 sail, i.e. ships).

sÿn'od, n. assembly of a Church for deliberation ; a council or convention. sÿnŏd'ic, ~al, aa.

sÿn'onÿm, n. word identical in sense and usage with another of the same language. sÿnŏn'ÿmous, a. sÿnŏn'ÿmÿ, n. redundant collocation of synonyms for emphasis.

sÿnŏp'sis, n. (pl. -psēs), summary ; conspectus. sÿnŏp'tic, a. affording a synopsis. ~al, a.

sÿnovī'tis, n. inflammation of membrane secreting the lubricating fluid in a joint.

sÿn'tâx, n. sentence-construction or its rules. sÿntăc'tic, a.

sÿn'thesis, n. (pl. -esēs), combining of elements or parts or ingredients into a system or whole. sÿnthĕt'ic, a. proceeding by or resulting from synthesis ; (of rubber, indigo, &c.) artificial.

sÿph'ĭlis, n. venereal disease.

syphon, syren. See si-.

Sÿr'iăc, n. & a. (in) the language of ancient Syria.

sÿrĭn'ga (-ngg-), n. shrub with white scented flowers.

sÿr'inge (-j), n. tube with nozzle and piston into which liquid is drawn to be ejected in stream. v.t. sluice or spray with syringe.

sÿr'up, n. water thickened with sugar ; condensed sugarcane juice ; refined molasses, treacle. sÿr'upÿ, a.

sÿstăl'tic, a. having systole and diastole ; pulsatory.

sÿs'tĕm, n. complex whole ; set of connected things or parts ; organization ; method ; (principle of) classification. sÿstĕmăt'ic, a. methodical ; according to a plan ; not casual. sÿs'tĕmatize, v.t. (-zable) ; ~zā'tion, n.

sÿs'tolē, n. contraction of heart or other organ alternating with diastole.

T

ta (tah), int. (nursery, joc.), ~ thank you.

Taal (tahl), n. The ~, Cape Dutch language.

tăb, n. small flap of some material attached to a thing as handle or ornament ; keep ~s on, keep under observation.

tăb'ard, n. (hist.) knight's garment worn over armour ; herald's official dress.

tăb'arĕt, n. fabric of alternate satin and watered-silk stripes.

tăbb'ÿ, n. kind of watered silk ; female cat ; old maid or female gossip. ~cat, cat of grey with dark stripes.

tăb'ernacle, n. the tent used as a sanctuary by the Israelites ; a temporary habitation ; nonconformist meeting-house ; canopied niche or receptacle ; *large church.

tăb'inĕt, n. watered fabric of silk and wool.

tă'blature (-cher), n. mental picture ; graphic description.

tā'ble, n. piece of furniture with flat top on which things may be placed ; slab of wood or stone ; set of facts or figures arranged in columns ; level area, flat surface.

TABLE [514] TAILOR

v.t. lay on the table; tabulate. **~d'hôte** (tabl-dōt'), hotel dinner provided for all comers at fixed hour and price. **~land,** level tract at higher level than surrounding country.

tāb'leau (-lō), *n.* (pl. *-eaux* pr. -ōz), dramatic or effective situation suddenly brought about. **~ vivant** (tăb'lō vē'vahň; pl. *-eaux -ts*), group of silent motionless persons arranged to represent a scene.

tāb'let, *n.* small slab, esp. for the display of an inscription; (usu. pl.) set of thin slips for entering memoranda on; dose of some drug in form of small slab.

tāb'loid, *n.* compressed dose of some drug. **P.**

taboo', *n.* (among Polynesians, &c.) setting apart of a person or thing as sacred or accursed; a ban or prohibition by general consent. *a.* inviolable or prohibited. *v.t.* put under taboo.

tā'bor, *n.* (arch.) small drum.

tāb'ouret (-bŏrit), *n.* low stool.

tāb'ūlar, *a.* shaped like a table-top or board; splitting into slabs; displayed systematically in columns. **tāb'ūlāte,** *v.t.* (*-lable*), arrange (figures, &c.) in tabular form. **tābūlā'tion,** *n.*

tāch, *n.* (Bibl.) clasp, link.

tā'cit, *a.* unspoken, not worded; implied but not expressed. **tā'citurn,** *a.* given to silence, talking little. **tăcitūr'nity,** *n.*

tāck, *n.* small sharp broad-headed nail; long stitch used in fastening materials lightly together; rope, &c. for securing sail-corner in certain position; ship's obliquely windward course as determined by position of sails; (fig.) line of action; (Naut.) food. *v.t. & i.* nail with tacks; stitch slightly together; annex or append to; (Naut.) make tack or series of tacks; (fig.) change one's policy.

tā'ckle, *n.* gear or appliances for something; ropes and pulleys used in working sails, hoist-

ing weights, &c.; (Footb.) act of tackling. *v.t.* grapple with; try to defeat or solve or accomplish; (Footb.) seize and stop (player carrying ball).

tact, *n.* delicate perception of the right thing to do or say; adroitness in dealing with others. **~ful, ~less,** *aa.*

tac'tics, *n.pl.* (often as sing.), art of disposing troops or warships; procedure adopted for carrying out a policy. **tac'tical,** *a.*; **tacti'cian** (-shn), *n.*

tac'tile (*or* -ll), **tac'tūal,** *aa.* of or having the sense of touch.

tăd'pōle, *n.* larva of frog, toad, &c., esp. while it presents only a round head and a tail.

tael (tāl), *n.* Chinese weight (1½ oz.) and money of account (about 3s.).

tăffē'eta, *n.* light thin lustrous silk fabric.

tăffē'rail, tăff'erel (-fril), *n.* rail round ship's stern.

Tăff'y, *n.* (colloq.) Welshman.

tāg, *n.* metal point of shoelace, &c.; loose or ragged end; stock phrase. *v.t.* furnish with tag(s); tack or fasten on. **~-day,** day for public solicitation of funds.

tahsil'dār (-seel-), *n.* (Anglo-Ind.) chief revenue officer of a subdivision of a district.

tail¹, *n.* member prolonging animal's body backwards; slender prolongation or appendage; lower or inferior or later part of something. *v.i.* dwindle away, fall off in size or number. **~board,** hinged or removable back of cart. **~coat,** man's coat divided behind into tails. **~light,** light carried at back of train, car, cycle, &c. **~race,** part of mill-race below the wheel.

tail², *n.* provision limiting possession of an estate to a person and his heirs or to a special class of these. *a.* limited by a tail.

tail'or, *n.* maker of outer garments, esp. for men. *v.i. & t.* be or work as tailor; make clothes for. **~ess,** *n.* **~bird,** kinds of

Asiatic passerine birds with nests of joined leaves.

taint, *n.* sullying spot, blemish; latent disease. *v.t.* & *i.* introduce corruption or disease into; infect, be infected.

take, *v.i.* & *i.* (*took, tāken; -kable*), seize, grasp, capture; appropriate, steal; receive into the mind; receive as medicine; convey or conduct; catch or come upon; captivate; win; secure photograph of; prove attractive, be in demand. *n.* amount of fish caught, money received, &c. ~**in,** a deception or trick. ~**off,** piece of mimicry; place jumper springs from. tā′king, *n.* state of agitation; (*pl.*) amount of money received; *a.* attractive or captivating; catching or infectious.

tăl′apoin, *n.* Buddhist monk; kind of W.-Afr. monkey.

tălc, *n.* kinds of mineral, often in thin glass-like plates.

tāle, *n.* narrative or story; report of alleged facts; full number.

tăl′ent, *n.* weight and money of account of some ancient nations, varying from 56 lb. and £200 upwards; faculty or aptitude for something; high mental ability. ~**money,** bonus to professional cricketer, &c. for especially good performance. tăl′ented, *a.* having high ability.

tāl′ĭpŏt, *n.* a palm of South India, noted for its great height and enormous fan-shaped leaves.

tăl′isman (-z-), *n.* object endowed with magical powers.

talk (tawk), *v.i.* & *t.* say words; hold conversation; gossip or spread reports; discuss; give utterance to; use as a medium of communication. *n.* conversation or a spell of it; rumour; mere words. ta′lkative (tawk-). *a.* fond of talking.

ta′lkies, *n.pl.* (colloq.) cinematographic film in which the characters speak.

tall (tawl), *a.* of more than average stature or height; higher than

surroundings; (sl.) boastful, hard to believe, excessive. ~**boy,** high chest of drawers or one mounted on high legs or a table.

tăll′ow, *n.* harder kinds of fat melted down for use in making candles, soap, &c.

tăll′ẏ, *n.* piece of wood scored with notches for the items of an account and split into halves of which each party kept one; such half; account or score so kept; counterpart or duplicate of a thing. *v.i.* correspond (*with*).

tăll′y-hō′, *int.* & *n.* huntsman's view-halloo; *a*large four-in-hand coach or drag. *v.i.* & *t.* cry tally-ho; urge on (hounds) thus.

Tăl′mud, *n.* body of Jewish law and legend as expounded in the Academies of Palestine (200-375) and Babylon (200-500).

tăl′on, *n.* claw, esp. of bird of prey (usu. in *pl.*).

talūk′ (-ook), **-ook,** *n.* district in India subject to revenue collection by native officer; tract of proprietary land in India. talŭk′dār (-oo), *n.* such officer; proprietor of a taluk.

tăm′arind, *n.* tropical tree or its fruit, used in medicine, &c.

tăm′arĭsk, *n.* feathery-leaved evergreen common at seaside.

tama′sha (-mah-), *n.* (Ang.-Ind.) a show or function or occasion.

‖ tămbouk′′ĭ (-oo-), *n.* of or belonging to Tembuland. ~**grass,** ~**wood,** a wild grass and timber of S. Africa.

tăm′bour (-oor), *n.* drum (arch.); circular frame for stretching embroidery - work on. **tambourine′** (-borēn), *n.* musical instrument made of a hoop with parchment stretched on one side and small cymbals set in slots.

‖ tămbreet′, *n.* (Austral.) a native name of the ornithorhyncus or duckbilled platypus.

tāme, *a.* (of animals) domesticated, tractable; lacking spirit; uninteresting, insipid. *v.t.* (*-mable*), make tame, domesticate ; break in ; humble. **~less**, *a.* untamable. **tămabĭl'ĭty̆**, *n.*

Tăm'ĭl, *n.* member, language, of non-Aryan race of S.-E. India.

Tămm'any̆, *n.* organization of the Democrats in New York, sometimes used as a byword for political and municipal corruption.

tăm-o'-shăn'tĕr, tămm'y̆, *n.* round Scotch cap.

tămp, *v.t.* plug (blasting-hole) with clay, &c. to intensify force of explosion. **tămp'ing**, *n.* substance used for this.

tăm'pan (-*an*), *n.* a S.-African species of insect remarkable for the venom of its bite.

tăm'per, *v.i.* meddle ; make unauthorized changes ; exercise underhand influence.

tăn, *n.* bark of oak, &c. crushed in use for tanning hide ; the yellowish brown of tanned leather ; the bronze of sunburnt skin. *a.* yellowish-brown. *v.t.* & *i.* convert (hide) into leather by steeping in infusion of tan ; (of sun, &c.) bronze skin ; (of skin, &c.) become bronzed ; (sl.) thrash.

tan'a (tah-), **tănn'a**, *n.* in India, a police station, formerly a military station or fortified post.

tanadăr' (tah-), **tăunadăr'**, *n.* head officer of police station, formerly commander of a military post.

tăn'dem, *adv.* with two or more horses, &c. harnessed one behind another. *n.* vehicle driven tandem ; bicycle, &c. with two or more seats behind each other.

tăng, *n.* part of tool that fits into handle ; pungent taste ; resonant sound of bell. *v.t.* & *i.* make a resonant sound.

tăng'a (-ngg-), *n.* a name (originally of a weight) given in India, Persia, and Turkestan to various coins (or moneys of account).

tăn'gent (-j-), *n.* straight line that meets a curve at a point but if produced does not intersect it at that point. **~gĕn'tial** (-jĕnshl), *a.*

Tăngerine' (-jĕrēn), *a.* of Tangiers.

n. a native of Tangiers ; kind of small orange.

tăn'gible (-j-), *a.* perceptible by touch ; real, palpable. **~bility**, *n.*

tangle (tăng'gl), *n.* confused mass of intertwined string, &c. ; confused state. *v.t.* & *i.* bring or come into a tangle ; ensnare.

tăng'ō (-nggō), *n.* (pl. *-os*), S.-Amer. dance.

tănk, *n.* Indian reservoir for irrigation, &c. ; large receptacle for storing liquid ; *natural pool or pond ; (Mil.) steel box travelling by motor power, containing crew and guns, and serving as peripatetic fort in battle.

tănk'ard, *n.* tall mug of pewter, &c. for beer.

tănk'er, *n.* ship with tank for carrying mineral oil in bulk.

tăn'ner¹, *n.* one who tans.

tăn'ner², *n.* (sl.) sixpence.

tănn'ĭc ā'cĭd, tănn'ĭn, *nn.* kinds of astringent vegetable substance.

tăn'sy̆ (-zĭ), *n.* an aromatic herb.

tăn'talize, *v.t.* (-*zable*) torment with disappointment ; raise and then dash the hopes of. **~zation**, *n.* **tăn'talum**, *n.* a metal used for electric-lamp filaments. **tăn'talus**, *n.* stand containing visible but inaccessible spirit-decanters.

tăn'tamount, *pred.a.* coming to the same thing as ; equivalent.

tăn'tra, *n.* each of a class of recent Sanskrit religious works dealing chiefly with magic.

tăn'trum, *n.* burst of petulance.

Tao'ism (tah-ō-, tow-), *n.* religious doctrine of Lao-tsze, Chinese philosopher.

tăp¹, *n.* cock through which liquid is drawn from cask or through pipes ; wine or beer from a particular tap. *v.t.* prepare (cask, liquor) for draught by inserting tap ; draw off fluid by incision ; draw supplies or information from. **~room**, inn-room in which liquor is drawn or served. **~root**, long tapering root from which rootlets spring.

tăp², *v.i.* & *t.* strike a light blow ; knock gently. *n.* light blow or

---

sound; (pl.) men's dinner-call in barracks; *(Mil. & Nav., pl.) signal on trumpet, &c. for extinguishing lights in quarters. ~-dancing, dancing with rhythmical tapping of feet.

tāpe, n. narrow strip of linen, &c. serving as flat string; strip of paper paid out with successive messages from recording telegraph instrument; piece of tape or thin strip of metal marked for measuring (also ~-*measure*).

tā′per, n. wick with coat of wax, &c. for conveying light; (arch.) candle. a. diminishing in thickness towards one end. v.t. & i. be or make taper.

tăp′estry, n. fabric in which a weft of coloured wools or silks forming pictures or designs is worked into a warp of hemp or flax; woven fabrics imitating this. **tăp′estried** (-rĭd), a.

tăpi̇o′ca, n. grains prepared from cassava for use as food.

tā′pir (-er), n. American mammal with flexible proboscis.

tā′pis (-ē, -ĭs), n. On the ~, under discussion.

tăpp′et, n. arm, cam, &c., used in machinery to impart intermittent motion.

tăp′ster, n. attendant serving liquor at an inn, &c.

tăr, n. dark thick liquid distilled from wood or coal; (colloq.) sailor. v.t. coat with tar.

tă′ra ~-fern, n. edible fern of New Zealand, &c., a variety of the common brake.

tărăntĕll′a, n. rapid whirling S.-Ital. dance; music for it. **tarăn′tism**, n. hysterical impulse to dance. **tarăn′tŭla**, poisonous S.-European spider.

tarăx′acum, n. drug made from dandelion.

tăr′bōosh, n. tasselled skull-cap worn by Mohammedans.

tărd′ȳ, a. slow to act, come, or happen; behind time.

tāre², n. (usu. in pl.) vetch, esp. the kind grown as fodder; (pl.) noxious weeds among corn.

tāre², n. amount deducted for wrapping, &c. in ascertaining net weight; weight of motor vehicle without fuel or load.

tărg′et (-g-), n. shooting-mark, esp. a round butt divided by concentric circles; butt for scorn, &c.; objective. targe, n. (arch.) buckler or shield.

tă′riff, n. schedule of customs duties; duty on goods; table of fixed charges at hotel, &c.

tăr′atan, n. thin open muslin.

tārn, n. small mountain lake.

tărn′ish, v.t. & i. dull lustre of or discolour (metal) by oxidation; lose lustre or colour; sully or dim (reputation, &c.). n. tarnished state or look.

tărpaul′in, n. canvas coated with tar; sheet or covering of this.

tăr′pon, n. a large sea-fish common on south coast of U.S.

tă′rragon, n. kind of wormwood.

tărrago′na, n. Spanish wine like port.

tă′rry¹, a. smeared with tar.

tă′rry², v.i. defer going or coming; linger; stay; wait.

tărs′ia, n. wood mosaic.

tărs′us, n. (pl. -rsī), the seven small bones of the ankle; bird's shank. **tărs′al**, a.

tărt¹, a. of acid taste; bitter or acrimonious.

tărt², n. fruit pie; piece of pastry with jam, &c. in it.

tărt′an, n. cloth woven in coloured stripes crossing at right angles.

tărt′ar¹, n. substance deposited in cask by fermentation of wine; incrustation that forms on the teeth. **tărtâ′ric**, a.

Tărt′ar², n. native of Tartary; intractable person or child.

Tărt′arus, n. place of torture in Hades; hell. **Tărtâ′rean**, a.

tărt′lĕt, n. tart of size for single portion.

task (tah-), n. piece of work to be done. v.t. impose task on; (of task) prove trying to.

tăss′el, n. tuft of cords, &c. attached to curtain, garment.

---

māre, mēre, mīre, mōre, mūre; părt, pĕrt, pŏrt: *italics*, vague sounds;

umbrella, &c.; **tassel-like** cat-kin, &c. **täss'elled** (-ld), a.

täste, n. the sense peculiar to the tongue or mouth; the quality in substances discerned by it; liking for certain food, &c.; personal preference; aesthetic discernment. v.t. & i. (-table), perceive or try the taste of; eat small portion of; have specified taste; smack of. ~**ful**, a. done in, having, good taste. ~**less**, a. insipid; without taste. **tā'ster**, n. (esp.) person who selects teas, wines, &c. by tasting. **tā'sty**, a. savoury, not insipid.

tat¹. See tatting.

tat² (taht), taut, n. (E.-Ind.) coarse canvas made from various fibres, esp. jute, and used as sacking.

tat³, tatt. See tattoo³.

tat⁴, tatt. See tatting.

tätt'er, v.t. & i. tear or fall into pieces. n.pl. torn state. ~**dema'l-lion** (or -mä-), n. ragged fellow.

tätt'ing, n. edgings, &c. made by netting thread; process of making them. **tät**, v.t. & i. do this.

tät'tle, v.i. gossip idly; repeat or discuss scandal. n. gossip, idle talk.

tattoo¹ (tatōō'), n. beat of drum, esp. in camp, &c. (also of bugle-call) at night; elaboration of this with music and marching as spectacle.

tattoo² (tatōō'), v.t. mark (skin, &c.) by puncturing and rubbing in pigment. n. practice of tattooing; tattooed pattern.

tätt'oo³, n. a native-bred Indian pony; abbrev. tat(t).

tätt'y, n. (Anglo-Ind.) matting of cuscus-grass hung and kept wet to cool and perfume the air; abbrev. tat(t).

taube (towb'e), n. (obs.) type of German aeroplane.

taught, p.t. of teach.

taunt, n. thing said to anger or wound a person. v.t. assail with taunt; reproach with.

taut, a. drawn tight; fit for use. **taut'en**, v.t. & i.

tautŏl'ogy, n. repetition, esp. the

addition of words that add nothing to the sense. **tautŏlŏ'gi-cal**, a.; ~**gize**, v.i.

täv'ern, n. inn or restaurant.

taw, n. large playing-marble.

tawd'ry, a. pretentious but common; like cheap finery.

tawn'y, a. of orange-brown colour.

taws(e) (-z), n. (Sc.) slit thong for chastising children.

täx, n. legally levied contribution to State revenue. v.t. impose tax on; be a severe test of; (Law) fix proper amount of (costs); charge (person) openly with. ~**able**, a.; ~**ability**, n. **täxā'tion**, n. taxes or their imposition.

täx'i, ~**cab**, nn. motor cab (orig. with taximeter). v.i. & t. (-i'd), go, convey, in taxi; (Aeronaut., of machine and pilot) go along ground or water. **täxim'-èter**, n. automatic fare-indicator.

täx'idĕrmy, n. art of preparing, stuffing, and mounting the skins of animals with lifelike effect. ~**mist**, n.

tazza (taht'tsa), n. saucer-shaped cup, esp. one mounted on a foot.

tea, n. dried leaves of the tea-plant; infusion of it as a drink; afternoon meal. ~**cloth**, small ornamental linen table-cloth; also drying-cloth. ~**cup**, (esp.) china cup holding about quarter-pint. ~**fight**, (sl.) tea-party. ~**garden**, place where tea is served out-of-doors to customers. ~**gown**, lady's loose ornamental gown. ~**plant**, kinds of Chinese and Indian shrub yielding tea. ~**rose**, pale yellow tea-scented variety of rose.

teach, v.t. & i. (taught pr. tawt). impart knowledge or skill; give instruction or lessons; instil, inspire with. ~**able**, a. (esp.) apt at learning. ~**ability**, n.

teak, n. durable E.-Ind. timber used in ship-building, &c.

teal, n. (collect. sing. for pl.) small fresh-water duck.

team, n. set of draught animals; a side of players at football, &c. *~**ster**, n. team-driver.

tea'poy, n. small three- or four-legged table, esp. for tea.

tear¹ (tār), v.t. & i. (tōre, tōrn), break coherence of by pulling apart; make rent in (clothes, &c.) by tearing; disunite; pull *away, down, from, off, up, out,* by tearing or snatching; go vehemently; suffer tearing. n. torn hole or slit.

tear², n. drop let fall from the eye. ~**ful,** a. in or given to tears.

tear'ing (tār-), a. vehement.

tease (-z), v.t. (-*sable*), importune or banter; pick (wool, &c.) into separate fibres, comb or card; dress (cloth) with teasels. **teas'el, -zle** (-z-), n. dried prickly flowerhead used for raising nap on cloth; plant producing these. **teas'er** (-z-), n. (esp., sl.) hard question or task.

teat, n. nipple of breast or udder.

tec′hnical (těk-), a. of, in, or peculiar to a particular art or science or craft; pertaining to the mechanical arts. ~**ǎl′ity,** n. being technical; a technical term. **tec′hnics** (těk-), n.pl. doctrine of the arts; technique. **technique** (těknēk′), n. manner of artistic execution; mechanical skill in art. **technŏl′ogў,** n. a treatise on the arts; explanation of terms of art. ~**ŏ′gical,** a.

Tědd′ў bear (bār), n. child's toy bear.

Tē Dē′um, n. a canticle.

tē′dious, a. tiresomely long; prolix. **tē′dium,** n. weariness produced by tediousness.

tee¹, n. small mound on which golfer places ball before making first stroke; mark aimed at in curling, quoits, &c. v.t. & i. place ball on tee.

tee², n. umbrella-shaped, usu. gilded, ornament crowning tope or pagoda.

teem, v.i. swarm *with*; be prolific.

teen, n. woe, misfortune.

teens, n.pl. the ages 13 to 19, esp. in the phrase *in one's* ~.

teeth. See tooth.

teethe (-dh), v.i. cut one's teeth, esp. the milk-teeth.

teetō′tal, a. of or advocating total abstinence. ~**ism,** n. ~**ler,** n. total abstainer.

teetō′tum, n. top with four sides lettered to decide spinner's luck; any top spun with the fingers.

těg′ūment, n. a covering; the skin as the covering of the body.

‖ **tehr, tahr** (tār), n. Himalayan wild goat.

tělaesthē′sia (-zha), n. (Psych.) direct perception of distant occurrences or objects not effected by the recognized senses.

těl′amon, n. (Archit.) male figure as bearing pillar.

těl′ĕgrăm, n. message by telegraph.

těl′ĕgraph (-ahf), n. instantaneous conveyance of messages by means of electricity or by signals; semaphore; apparatus for this; scoring-board with large figures. v.i. & t. send message by telegraph; make signals; convey, &c. by signals. **telĕgrǎph′ic,** a. **tělěg′raphist,** n. operator of telegraph. **tělěg′raphў,** n. use of the telegraph; making, &c. of telegraphic apparatus.

tělěkinē′sis, n. (Psychol.) movement at a distance from the motive cause or agent without material connexion.

těl′ĕmǎrk, n. expert swing turn in skiing used to change direction or to stop short.

tělĕmĕchǎn′ics, n.pl. art of transmitting power by wireless, and so controlling machinery from a distance.

tělĕŏl′ogў, n. doctrine of final causes. ~**ŏ′gical,** a.; ~**gist,** n.

tělĕp′athў, n. communication of impressions from mind to mind without the aid of the senses. **tělĕpǎth′ic,** a. **tělĕp′athist,** n. believer or expert in telepathy.

těl′ĕphone, n. apparatus for transmitting speech or sounds to distant hearer. v.i. & t. send message by telephone. **tělĕphŏ′nic,** a. **tělĕph′onist,** n. telephone operator. **tělĕph′onў,** n.

télé·photŏg'raphy, n. photographing of distant objects by means of a combination of telescope and ordinary photographic lens.

těl'ergy, n. force effecting telepathy.

těl'éscōpe, n. tube, or set of tubes sliding into each other, with lenses or mirrors for magnifying the image of a distant object. v.t. & i. be capable of increase or decrease of length by sliding like telescope tubes; cause to do this; (of railway carriages, &c.) be driven into each other. **tělėscŏp'ic,** a. **tėlės'cŏpy,** n. use and making of telescopes.

tělévi'sion (-zhn), n. electrical transmission of images.

těll, v.t. & i. (tōld), relate or narrate; utter or express in words; betray secret or inform against person; produce marked effect. **~tale,** person who peaches. **těll'er,** (esp.) one of four M.P.'s selected to count votes in House of Commons divisions.

těl'pher, n. travelling unit in telpherage. **~age,** n. automatic electric transport of goods, &c.

těmě'rity, n. rashness.

těm'per, v.t. bring to proper consistence or hardness; mitigate severity of. n. degree of hardness and elasticity in steel, &c.; composure under provocation, &c.; disposition or mood; anger.

těm'pera, n. distemper-painting.

těm'perament, n. the whole of a person's natural tendencies as determined by his physical constitution; idiosyncrasy. **~al,** a.

těm'perance, n. avoidance of excessive indulgence, esp. in alcohol; (attrib.) non-alcoholic.

těm'perate, a. avoiding excess; remote from extremes.

těm'perature, n. thing's degree of heat.

těm'pěst, n. violent storm. **těmpěs'tŭous,** a. stormy; turbulent.

Těm'plar, n. member of the medieval military religious order of the Temple; occupant of chambers in Inner or Middle Temple.

těm'ple¹, n. building treated as the dwelling-place or devoted to the worship of a god.

těm'ple², n. flat part of head between forehead and either ear.

těm'poral, a. of in or denoting time; earthly; secular; lay. **temporăl'ity,** n. (esp., pl.) religious body's temporal possessions.

těm'porary, a. lasting or meant to last only a short time.

těm'porīze, v.i. so act as to gain time by concealing one's intentions; avoid committing oneself.

těmpt, v.t. risk angering; rouse or try to rouse appetite or impulse in; draw or allure into. **~ā'tion,** n. tempting or being tempted; thing that attracts; impulse. **~er, ~ress,** nn.

těn, a. & n. one more than nine, 10, X. **~fold,** a. & adv. **~těnth,** a. & n.; **~ly,** adv.

těn'able, a. that can be maintained against attack or objection; that can be held for period or by class of persons. **~bility,** n.

těn'ace, n. (Whist). Major, minor, **~,** best and third best, second and fourth best, cards in play of a suit.

těnā'cious (-shŭs), a. clinging tightly; slow to relinquish anything; retentive. **těnā'city,** n.

těn'ancy, n. tenant's position.

těn'ant, n. person who rents land or house from a landlord; occupant of a place. v.t. hold or live in as tenant. **~ry,** n. the tenants of an estate, &c.

těnch, n. a fresh-water fish.

těnd¹, v.i. have a certain tendency.

těnd², v.t. take care or be in charge of; look after.

těn'dance, n. tending.

těn'dency, n. aptness to move or act in a particular direction or way; bent or drift.

těndĕn'tious (-shŭs), a. designed to advance a cause.

těn'der¹, v.t. & i. make offer of or present for acceptance; send in a tender. n. an offer; statement of sum for which one will contract to do something.

---

tĕn'dĕr³, n. (esp.) vessel attending larger one with stores, &c.; car attached to locomotive with coal. &c.

tĕn'dĕr³, a. not tough; needing careful treatment; delicate; susceptible; loving, affectionate. **~foot**, (sl.) person new to his surroundings; greenhorn. ***~loin**, undercut of sirloin; (sl.) (T-) amusement district of New York and other cities.

tĕn'don, n. cord of dense tissue attaching muscle to bone, &c.; sinew. **tĕn'dinous**, a.

tĕn'drĭl, n. one of the thread-like shoots by which some climbing plants cling.

tĕn'ĕment, n. an abode or dwelling-place, esp. a flat or suite of rooms or room rented in a house.

tĕn'ĕt, n. doctrine held by a party, sect, &c.

tĕnn'er, n. (colloq.) £10 note.

tĕnn'is, n. ball-game played with rackets in walled court with net; lawn-tennis.

tĕn'on, n. projection that fits into mortise.

tĕn'or, n. prevailing course or routine of one's life or habits; general purport; (Mus.) music for, singer with, highest adult male voice.

tĕnse¹, n. form taken by verb to indicate time of action, &c.

tĕnse², a. stretched to tightness; strained or highly strung.

tĕn'sĭle (or -ĭl), a. of tension; capable of being stretched.

tĕn'sion (-shn), n. effect produced by forces pulling against each other; tense or highly strung state; suppressed excitement.

tĕnt¹, n. portable shelter or dwelling of canvas for encamped soldiers, &c. **tĕn'tĕd**, a.

tĕnt², n. (arch.) roll of linen, &c. used to probe or cleanse or plug a wound, &c. v.t. apply tent to.

tĕnt³, n. deep-red wine much used in the Eucharist.

tĕn'tacle, n. slender flexible appendage serving as organ of touch in some animals. **tĕn'tacled** (-ld), **tĕntăc'ŭlar**, aa.

tĕn'tative, a. done as an experiment or to feel the way. **~hooks**, hooks to which the cloth is fastened.

tĕn'ter, n. cloth-stretching frame. **~hooks**, hooks to which the cloth is fastened.

tĕn'ūous, a. of thin or rarefied or fine-drawn quality or meagre amount. **tĕnū'ity**, n.

tĕn'ure (-yer), n. the holding of property or office; the conditions or period of such holding.

tĕp'id, a. between cool and warm. **tĕpid'ity**, n.

tĕr'aph(im), n. (pl. -phs, -phim, -phims), small image as domestic oracle among ancient Hebrews.

tĕrătŏl'ogy, n. the narration or study or doctrine of miracles; the study of animal and vegetable monstrosities. **~o'gical**, a.

tĕr'cel, tier'cel, n. male hawk.

tĕrcĕntě'nary, a. of 300 years. n. 300th anniversary.

tĕ'rĕbinth, n. a turpentine-yielding tree. **tĕrĕbin'thine**, a. of the terebinth; of turpentine.

tĕrĕ'dō, n. (pl. -os). mollusc boring into submerged timber.

tĕrgivĕrsā'tion, n. act of apostasy; change of principles; making of conflicting statements.

tĕrm, n. limited period; period during which university or school or judicature is at work; (pl.) stipulations made, conditions offered or accepted, payment offered or asked, footing or relation between parties; word or phrase considered as the name or symbol of something; (pl.) phraseology or language. v.t. name, call so-and-so.

tĕr'magant, n. virago, scold.

tĕrm'inable, a. that can be terminated; (of annuity) payable for a term of years only.

tĕrm'inal, a. of or forming the last point or terminus; of a, occurring in each, term. n. the terminal part of something; *railway terminus.

tĕrm'ināte, v.t. & i. bring or come to an end; end in. **~tion**, n. ending; way something ends; last syllable of word. **~tor**, n.

---

māre, mēre, mīre, mōre, mūre; părt, pĕrt, pŏrt; italics, vague sounds;

tĕrmĭnŏl'ogy, *n.* the terms used in a science, &c. **~ŏgical**, *a.*

tĕr'mĭnus, *n.* (pl. usu. -ī), station at end of railway line, &c.

tĕr'mĭte, *n.* an insect destructive to timber; the white ant.

tĕrn, *n.* a sea-bird; sea-swallow.

tĕrn'arў, *a.* composed of three.

Tĕrpsĭchŏre'an (-ko-), *a.* of dancing or the muse Terpsichore.

tĕr'ra, L. & It. for earth. **~ cotta** (kŏt'a), fine hard brownish-red pottery; a work of art made in it; its colour. **~ fĭrma** (fĕrm'a), dry land.

tĕr'race, *n.* raised level table; natural shelf or one made for vine-growing, &c. in hillside; row of houses.

tĕrrain', *n.* a tract of country.

tĕr'rapĭn, *n.* kinds of turtle and tortoise.

tĕrrā'quĕous (or -ă-), *a.* of land and water.

tĕrrēne', *a.* terrestrial; consisting of earth.

tĕrres'trial, *a.* of or on the earth; of or on dry land. *n.* inhabitant of the earth.

tĕr'rible, *a.* exciting or fit to excite terror; grievous.

tĕr'rier, *n.* kinds of small active dog fond of burrowing; (colloq.) member of Territorial Force.

tĕrrĭf'ic, *a.* causing great terror; of tremendous intensity; violently impressive. **tĕr'rĭfў**, *v.t.* (-able), frighten severely.

tĕrrĭne' (-ēn), *n.* pot such as pâté de foie gras is sold in.

tĕrrĭtōr'ial, *a.* of territory or land; landed; of districts. *n.* member of Territorial Army. **T~ Army** or **Force**, home-defence army raised on local basis.

tĕr'rĭtorў, *n.* land, or region, under the dominion of a ruler or State; "(T-) part of the national territory separately organized but not yet given State rights.

tĕr'ror, *n.* extreme fear; terrifying person or thing. **~ism**, *n.* systematic intimidation. **~ist**, *n.* **tĕr'rorĭze**, *v.t.* (-zable), practise terrorism upon. **~zā'tion**, *n.*

tĕr'rў, *a.* (of pile-fabrics) with loops uncut. *n.* terry velvet, &c.

tĕrse, *a.* concise; brief and forcible in style.

tĕr'tian (-shn), *a.* & *n.* (fever, disease) whose paroxysms occur every other day.

tĕr'tiarў (-sha-), *a.* of the third degree.

tĕr'tius (-shŭs), *a.* (in schools) third of the name.

tĕss'ĕllātĕd, *a.* of or resembling mosaic; having finely chequered surface. **~ā'tion**, *n.* tessellated chequering. **tĕss'ĕra**, *n.* (pl. -ae), one of the small cubes or blocks of which mosaic consists.

tĕst[1], *n.* trial determining a thing's quality or genuineness or fitness for a purpose; standard serving this end. *v.t.* put to the test; tax or severely try. **~match**, one of the matches (out of those in a cricket tour, &c.) that are to count towards the total result.

tĕst[2], *n.* the hard unarticulated shell of some invertebrates. **tĕstā'ceous** (-shŭs), *a.* with such shell. **tĕstā'cean** (-shn), *n.* shell-fish or other testaceous mollusc.

tĕs'tament, *n.* a will; *Old, New, T~*, divisions of the Bible; (colloq.) copy of the New Testament. **tĕstamĕn'tarў**, *a.* of or by or in a will.

tĕstā'mur (-er), *n.* certificate of having passed university examination.

tĕs'tāte, *a.* leaving a will. *n.* person who dies testate. **tĕstā'tor**, **tĕs'ter**, *n.* canopy over a bed; (arch.) sixpenny piece.

tĕs'ticle, *n.* either of the semen-secreting glands.

tĕs'tĭfў, *v.i.* & *t.* (-fiable), bear witness *to*; give evidence; solemnly declare (one's faith, &c.).

tĕstĭmō'nial, *n.* certificate of character or qualifications; gift testifying to the esteem felt for the recipient.

tĕs'tĭmonў, *n.* witness borne; thing that testifies *to* something; (Bibl.) the tables of the

---

Mosaic law; (pl.) the teachings of God.

tes′ty, *a.* irascible; short-tempered.

tet′anus, *n.* disease with continuous painful contraction of voluntary muscles.

tetch′y, *a.* easily put out; touchy; ticklish to deal with.

tête-à-tête (tāt′ahtāt′), *n.* the being together of two persons without listeners; their talk.

teth′er (-dh-), *n.* rope, &c. by which grazing animal is restricted to a radius; scope of one's knowledge, &c. *v.t.* fasten with tether.

tet′rachord (-k-), *n.* scale series of four notes. ~al, *a.*

tet′rad, *n.* the number four; set of four.

tet′ragon, *n.* plane rectilineal figure of four angles and four sides. tetrăg′onal, *a.*

tetrahē′dron (-a-h-; *or* -hē-), *n.* (pl. -*ra*, -*rons*), solid figure contained by four plane sides or faces. ~ral, *a.*

tetrăl′ogy, *n.* group of four dramatic or operatic works.

tetrăm′eter, *n.* verse of four measures.

te′trarch (*or* -ē-; -k), *n.* ruler of a quarter or other division of a Roman province. ~y, *n.* tetrarch's office or district.

tett′er, *n.* kinds of skin-disease.

Teuton′ic, *a.* of the Germans; of the races or languages closely allied to the German. *n.* the Teutonic language before its division into German, &c.

text, *n.* the wording of a composition; authentic form of a document or passage or book; passage serving as a theme to comment upon; any sentence selected from Scripture. ~book, manual; book set for study. těx′tŭal, *a.* of or in the text.

tex′tile (*or* -il), *a.* of weaving; woven. *n.* (usu. in pl.) textile fabric(s). těx′ture, *n.* arrangement of threads in textile fabric; arrangement of constituent parts, structure, (of skin, rock, &c.).

|| **thakur, thakoor** (thah′koor), *n.* (E.-Ind.) used as a title and term of respect, = Lord, Master, &c.; also applied to a chief or noble, esp. of the Rajpoot race.

tha′ler (tah-), *n.* German silver coin (3*s.*).

thăl′lium, *n.* rare soft white metallic element used in alloys and glass-making.

than (dhan), *conj.* & *prep.* introducing second member of comparison.

thane, *n.* gentleman below rank of earl and above that of ordinary freeman in Anglo-Saxon times.

thank, *v.t.* express gratitude to. *n.* (always pl. exc. in comb.) expressions of gratitude. ~offering, gift made in gratitude. ~sgiving, (esp.) rendering of thanks to God ("*T*~ *Day*, day set apart annually for this). **thănk′ful**, *a.* grateful (*for*); greatly pleased *that*. ~less, *a.* ungrateful; earning no thanks.

thar (tär), *n.* goat-antelope of Nepal.

that, *a.* (dhăt; pl. *those* pr. dhŏz), serving to identify with a gesture or to particularize without needless description, often in contrast with *this*. *demonst. pron.* (dhăt; pl. *thōse*), representing in the sing. a noun denoting a thing with the adj. *that* or the, and in the pl. a noun denoting persons or things with the adj. *those* or *the*. *adv.* (dhăt), ~ *far*, ~ *much*, as far, as much, as that. *rel. pron.* (dhat), introducing a clause that identifies by defining or restricting. *conj.* (dhat), introducing substantival clauses and adverbial clauses of purpose or consequence.

thătch, *n.* roofing of straw or rushes. *v.t.* roof with thatch.

thaumatŭrgy, *n.* working of wonders, the miraculous. ~gic, *a.*

thaw, *v.i.* & *t.* release or escape from frozen state; warm into liquid state or animation. *n.* cessation of frost.

the (dhĭ *before vowel*, dhe *before consonant*), *a.* serving to describe as unique, or particularize as needing no identification, or to denote a particular person or thing. *adv.* preceding comparatives (e. g. *the more the merrier*).

theatre (thi'ăter), *n.* building for dramatic performances; room or building of similar form for lectures, surgery, &c.; scene or locale *of.* theăt'rical, *a.* of or for the theatre or acting; sensational or showy or flashy; (*n.pl.*) dramatic performance(s).

thee. See thou.

theft, *n.* stealing; larceny.

their (dhâr), *a.* of or belonging to them. **theirs** (dhârz), *pron. & pred.a.* corresponding to *their*.

thē'ism, *n.* belief in a divine creation and conduct of the universe. **thē'ist**, *n.*; **theīs'tic**, *a.*

them. See they.

theme, *n.* a subject or topic; school exercise on set theme; (Mus.) the or a leading melody in a piece. **themăt'ic**, *a.* (Mus.).

themselves (dhemsĕlvz'), *pron.* serving as emphatic and reflexive form to *they*.

then (dh-), *adv.* at that time, after that, next; under those circumstances; accordingly. *n.* that time. *a.* then-existing.

thence (dh-), *adv.* from there; from that. **~forth, ~forward**, *adv.* from that time forward.

theŏc'racy, *n.* government or a State in which God is the sovereign and religion the law. **theŏcrăt'ic**, *a.*

theŏd'olite, *n.* instrument for measuring angles in surveying.

theŏg'ony, *n.* an account or theory of the genesis of gods.

theŏlō'gian, *n.* person learned in theology. **theŏlō'gical**, *a.* of, in, or for the study of theology.

theŏl'ogy, *n.* the science treating of God and His relations to man.

theŏph'any, *n.* a visible manifestation of a god.

theŏrb'ō, *n.* (pl. -ŏs), double-necked lute of 17th century.

thē'orem, *n.* (Geom.) proposition to be proved.

theŏrĕt'ic, -al, *aa.* of, in, or of the nature of theory; unpractical. **theŏrĕt'ics**, *n.pl.* theory as opposed to practice.

thē'orist, *n.* person given to theoretics; holder of a theory.

thē'orize, *v.i.* evolve theories; indulge in theoretics.

thē'ory (thi-), *n.* a view held; supposition explaining something; the sphere of speculation as distinguished from that of practice.

theŏs'ophy, *n.* any speculative system basing knowledge of nature on intuitional or traditional knowledge of God. **theŏsŏph'ic, ~al**, *aa.*; **theŏs'ophist**, *n.*

thērapeut'ic, *a.* of, for, or tending to the cure of disease. **thērapeut'ics**, *n.pl.* curative branch of medicine. **thē'rapy**, *n.*

there (dhâr), *adv.* in or at that place; yonder; at that point; to that place or point. *n.* (after *prep.* only) that place or point. *int.* drawing attention to something. **~about(s)**, near the place or amount or time. **~after**, thenceforward. **~at**, at that; at that place; on that account. **~by**, by that means or agency. **~fore**, for that reason; accordingly. **~in**, in it or them; in that respect. **~of**, of that; of this. **~to**, to that place, &c. **~upon**, as an immediate consequence of; directly after that. **~with**, with it; thereupon. **~withal**, besides.

therm, *n.* unit of heat used in measuring gas.

thĕrm'al, *a.* of heat; of hot springs. **thĕrm'ic**, *a.* of heat.

thĕrman'tidŏte, *n.* apparatus for cooling the air, used in India.

thĕrmi'on, *n.* an ion emitted by an incandescent substance. **thĕrmiŏn'ic vălve**, *n.* appliance converting wireless waves to vibrations audible in telephone for broadcasting.

thĕrmodynăm'ics, *n.* science of the relation between heat and mechanical energy.

---

thermŏm'ĕter, *n.* instrument for measuring temperature, usu. by the expansion of mercury or alcohol in a sealed and graduated glass tube. **thermŏm'ric, ~al,** *aa.* ; **thermŏm'ĕtry,** *n.*

ther'mŏs, *n.* vacuum flask. **P.**

thēsaur'us, *n.* (pl. -rī), storehouse of information, &c. ; dictionary or encyclopaedia.

these. See this.

thē'sis (or -ĕ-), *n.* (pl. *theses* pr. -ēz), proposition that one essays to prove ; composition supporting thesis.

Thĕs'pian, *a.* of tragedy or the drama. *n.* actor or actress.

thews (-z), *n.pl.* person's muscular strength.

they (dhā), *pron.* (obj. **them,** poss. *their*), serving as pl. of *he, she, it.*

thick, *a.* of considerable or specified thickness ; made of thick material ; closely set ; dense ; hard to penetrate ; of stiff consistence ; (sl.) intimate or inseparable ; (of line, &c.) broad, not fine. *n.* thick part of any tapering object ; crowded or important point of. *adv.* with thick voice. **~set,** set closely together ; having stout limbs and sturdy frame. **~skinned,** not sensitive to criticism or rebuff. **thick'en,** *v.t. & i.* make or become thicker. **thick'ĕt,** *n.* a tangle of shrubs or trees. **thick'ness,** *n.* dimension other than length and breadth ; being thick in any sense ; a layer of material.

thief, *n.* (pl. -*ves*), one who takes away by stealth what belongs to another. **thieve,** *v.i.* steal things. **thiev'ery,** *n.* stealing. **thiev'ish,** *a.* given to thievery.

thigh (-ī), *n.* the leg above the knee.

thim'ble, *n.* metal finger-cap used to push needle with. **~rig,** sharpers' game at fairs, &c. with three thimbles and a pea. **~ful** (-bl-fŏŏl), *n.* (pl. -*ls*), small dram, drop of spirits, &c.

thin, *a.* of little thickness ; having little flesh, skinny, meagre ; of

watery consistence ; of feeble sound ; (of infusions, &c.) weak ; not crowded or numerous ; (of excuse, &c.) easily seen through. *v.t. & i.* make or grow thin. **~-skinned,** abnormally sensitive.

thine. See thy.

thing, *n.* any possible object of thought ; a material object ; a person or animal regarded in pity or contempt or affection ; (pl.) the course of events, one's belongings or clothes or implements. **~amy, ~umajig, ~umbob,** *nn.* person or thing whose name one forgets.

think, *v.i. & t.* (*thought* pr. -awt), have one's mind at work ; hold the opinion ; have the half-formed intention of. **think'er,** *n.* (esp.) person of philosophic mind. **think'ing,** *a.* (esp.) reflective ; given to independent thought.

third, *a.* next after second. *n.* one of three equal parts. **~ degree,** a close interrogation or severe treatment of a prisoner by the police to extort an admission or confession. **~ man,** (Crick.) fielder between point and short slip. **third'ly,** *adv.* in the third place.

thirst, *n.* sensation or state of requiring drink ; vehement desire *for* or of glory, &c. *v.i.* crave *for* or *after* ; be physically thirsty. **thirs'ty,** *a.* feeling thirst ; craving for some satisfaction ; (of soil) parched ; (of work) causing thirst.

thirteen', *a. & n.* one more than twelve, 13, XIII. **~th,** *a. & n.*

thirt'y, *a. & n.* three times ten, 30, XXX. **~two-mo,** 32mo, book with 32 leaves to the sheet.

this (dh-), *a. & pron.* (pl. *thēse* pr. -z), the person or thing close at hand or drawn attention to.

this'tle (-sl), *n.* kinds of prickly plant common as weeds ; Scottish national emblem and order of knighthood. **~down,** thistle-seeds. **this'tly** (-sll), *a.* overgrown with thistles.

thith′er (dhidh-), *adv.* to that place. ~**wards,** *adv.*

thôle, n. peg in gunwale of rowing-boat serving as fulcrum for oar; one of two such pegs making a rowlock.

thong, n. strip of hide or leather.

thŏr′ax, n. the part of the trunk between the neck and the abdomen. **thŏrā′cic,** a.

thŏr′ium, n. a rare white metallic element, burning brightly when heated in oxygen.

thôrn, n. a prickle on a plant; kinds of thorny plant, esp. the hawthorn. **thôrn′y,** a, abounding in thorns; difficult to tackle.

thorough (thŭ′rō), *adv.* & *prep.* (arch., poet.) through. *a.* complete; radical; in all respects; out-and-out. ~**bâss,** bass part with harmonies; the science of harmony. ~**bred,** a. of pure breed; (of horse) of pedigree recorded in the stud book; n. thoroughbred horse or person. ~**fare,** right of way; road, &c. not closed at either end. ~**going,** uncompromising; out-and-out. ~**paced,** practised.

thŏrp, n. (arch.) village.

those. See this.

thou (dh-; obj. *thee*), *pron.* of 2nd pers..now replaced by *you*, except in addresses to God or in Quaker or dialect speech.

though (dhō), *adv.* (colloq.) all the same, none the less, however. *conj.* and yet.

thought (-awt), n. thinking as a process or a faculty; a conception or mental image formed in the process. *p.t. & p.p.* of *think.* **thought′ful** (-awt-), a. engaged in meditation; giving signs of original thought; considerate. ~**less,** a. careless of consequences; due to want of thought.

thou′sand (-z-), a, & n. ten hundred, 1000, M. ~**fold,** a. & adv.; ~**th,** a. & n.

thrall (-awl), n. (rhet., poet.) bondsman; bondage. **thra′ldom** (-awl-), n. bondage.

thrāsh, thresh, *v.t. & i.* (usu. -*esh*)

separate the grain from corn by beating with flails or trampling or with machinery; (-*ash*) beat with stick or whip; (colloq.) defeat in fight or contest. **thrāsh′er, thresh′er,** n. kind of shark; *thrush; person or machine that threshes.* **thrāsh′-ing,** n. a whipping; a defeat. **thrēsh′ing,** n. process of threshing corn. ~**floor,** ~**machine,** on, with, which corn is threshed. **thrāson′ical,** a. bragging.

thread (-rĕd), n. a length of spun flax, cotton, silk, or other such fibre; thin cord of twisted yarns; theme of argument, &c.; the ridge or groove running spirally round a screw. *v.t.* pass thread through (needle, beads); make way through. ~**bare,** with nap worn off and threads showing; hackneyed.

threat (-rĕt), n. declaration of intention to punish or hurt; indication of coming evil. **threa′-ten** (-rĕtn), *v.t. & i.* use threat to; intimidate with; portend; (of evil) seem to impend.

three, a, & n. one more than two, 3, III. ~**fold,** a. & adv, thrice repeated; consisting of three. ~**pence** (thrĕp-), 3d. ~**penny bit, piece** (thrĕp-), silver 3d. ~**ply,** (esp., as n.) wood made by gluing together three layers. ~**quarter,** a. (of portrait) including body to below hips or presenting face between full and profile; n. (Rugby footb.) player stationed between halves and full-back. ~**score,** sixty.

thrē′nody, n. song of lamentation.

thresh. See thrash.

thresh′öld, n. plank or stone forming bottom of doorway; entrance.

threw, *p.t.* of throw.

thrice, *adv.* three times.

thrift, n. saving ways; sparing expenditure; the sea-pink. ~**less,** a. wasteful. **thrif′ty,** a. economical.

thrill, n. a nervous tremor due to intense emotion; a wave of sensation; a tremulous sound. *v.i.* & *t.* feel thrills or vibrate (*with*); stir thrills in. thrill′er, *n.* (esp.) sensational play or tale.

thrive, *v.i.* (thrŏve, thriven), prosper; grow vigorously.

throat, *n.* front part of the neck, or either or both of the passages through it to the stomach and lungs; narrow passage or entrance. throat′y̆, *a.* (of voice) hoarsely resonant.

thrŏb, *v.i.* (of heart, arteries, blood) pulsate with abnormal force; (of persons, pain, &c.) have or give the feeling of pulsation. *n.* palpitation; single beat of pulsation.

thrōe, *n.* (usu. in pl.) a violent spasm, esp. (pl.) those of childbirth.

throne, *n.* chair of state for sovereign, bishop, &c. *v.t.* enthrone.

throng, *n.* press of people; crowding; a crowd. *v.i.* & *t.* come in great numbers; flock into; crowd.

thrŏ′stle (-sl), *n.* song-thrush.

thrŏt′tle, *v.t.* compress the throat of; strangle, choke; check with throttle-valve. *n.* throttle-valve. ~valve, valve regulating supply of steam, &c. in engine, &c.

through (-rōō), *prep.* from end to end or side to side of; between the sides of; by agency, means, or fault of; by reason of. *adv.* through something; from end to end; *finished (speaking). *a.* going, concerned with going, through; (of travelling) going all the way without change of line, &c. ~out, *adv.* in every part or respect; *prep.* from end to end of; in every part of.

throw (-ō), *v.t.* & *i.* (threw pr. -rōō; thrown pr. -ōn), launch (object) into the air with some force; fling off (rider) thus; use as missile; throw ball, &c. with jerking motion of arm; worst decisively in wrestle, &c.; throw dice; put (garment, &c.) carelessly over something; twist (silk, &c.) into thread. *n.* act

of throwing or being thrown. ~off′, the start in hunt or in any quest or joint operation. ~ out, reject (bill, &c.) by votes; put (batsman) out by throwing at wicket; embarrass (speaker) by interruption.

thrŭm[1], *n.* unwoven end of a warp-thread left when the finished web is cut away; any short loose thread.

thrŭm[2], *v.t.* & *i.* pluck at (strings); thrum harp, &c.; strum; drum with the fingers, &c.; make drumming sound. *n.* sound of thrumming.

thrŭsh[1], *n.* kinds of song-bird.

thrŭsh[2], *n.* throat-disease in children; foot-disease in horses.

thrŭst, *v.t.* & *i.* push; make a lunge or stab with weapon; intrude oneself, force (person) *upon. *n.* a stab or lunge; pushing force exerted by one part of a structure on another.

thŭd, *n.* sound made by impact of non-resonant things.

thŭg, *n.* member of an extinct association of robbers and stranglers in India; cut-throat, ruffian. ~gee′, ~gery, ~gism, *nn.* thugs′ practices.

thŭmb (-um), *n.* the one of the five fingers opposable to the other four. *v.t.* soil or wear (book, document). ~print, impression of thumb taken as means of identifying person. ~screw, instrument of torture squeezing the thumb.

thŭmp, *v.t.* & *i.* hit so as to produce a thud; hit with fist; pummel. *n.* sound of thumping; a blow with fist. thŭm′per, *n.* (esp., sl.) big specimen; outrageous lie. thŭm′ping, *a.* (sl.) big.

thŭn′der, *n.* the sound made by lightning; any loud rumbling; (usu. pl.) authoritative censure or threats. *v.i.* & *t.* emit thunder or thunders; utter or say out loudly. ~bolt, lightning-flash regarded as missile or destroying agency; punitive decree, &c. ~struck, utterly taken aback by an event or discovery. **thŭn′-dering**, *a.* & *adv.* (sl.) very big; very. **thŭn′derous**, *a.* as loud as thunder. **thŭn′der̆y**, *a.* oppressive.

thŭr′ible, *n.* censer.

Thŭrs′day (-zdi), *n.* the fifth day of the week.

thŭs (dh-), *adv.* in this way; in the manner indicated; accordingly; so far; to this extent.

thwăck. See whack.

thwart (-ôrt), *v.t.* frustrate or foil. *n.* rower's seat.

thȳ (dh-), *attrib.a.* of or belonging to thee. **thine** (dh-), *pron.* & *a.* related to thy as mine to my.

thȳl′acine, *n.* zebra-wolf, a Tasmanian carnivorous marsupial.

thyme (tīm), *n.* kinds of herb with fragrant aromatic leaves.

thȳ′mol, *n.* a strong disinfectant.

thyr′oid (-īr-), *a.* (Anat.) ~ cartilage, in larynx enclosing vocal chords. ~ **gland** or **body**, vascular body adjacent to larynx.

thyrs′us (-êr-), *n.* (pl. -si) staff tipped with pine-cone ornament as attribute of Bacchus.

thȳsělf′ (dh-), *pron.* serving as refl. and emphat. form of *thee*, *thou*.

tiâr′a, *n.* conical cap of ancient Persians, &c.; Pope's diadem; jewelled band worn in the front of the hair by ladies.

tĭb′ĭa, *n.* the shin-bone.

tic, *n.* ~ **douloureux** (dŏlŏrōō′). *n.* neuralgia with twitching of face muscles.

‖ **tĭcc′a** (or tĕ′kah), *a.* (E.-Ind.) engaged on contract, hired. ~ **garry**, hired carriage.

tick¹, *n.* the beat or sound of a watch or clock; a slight sound; a small mark, *v.i.* & *t.* (of clock). make tick; set tick against. ~ **off**, (sl.) reprimand. ~ **over**, (of motor) run slowly with gears disconnected. ~ **er**, *n.* (sl.) watch. ~-**tack**, *n.* manual signalling on race-course.

tick², *n.* kinds of insect parasite.

tick³, *n.* case of mattress or bolster; ticking.

tick⁴ (sl.), *n.* credit, booking of debts; **go tick**, defer payment. *v.i.* & *t.* go tick, give tick; buy or sell (thing) on tick.

tick′ĕt, *n.* card or paper securing admission, &c. to its holder, or serving as label or notice; *(pol.)* list of party candidates. *v.t.* attach label to.

tick′ing, *n.* strong material for bed-ticks.

tic′kle, *v.i.* & *t.* itch, make itch, with light touches; stir sense of humour in; poke or knead in the ribs, &c. to produce convulsive laughter. **tick′lish**, *a.* sensitive to tickling; (of affairs) difficult to handle.

tick′y, **tikk′ie**, *n.* (S.-Afr., colloq.) threepenny-piece.

tĭcpolŏng′a (-ngga), *n.* venomous serpent of India and Ceylon.

tīde, *n.* the rise and fall of the sea occurring twice in a lunar day; a trend of opinion or feeling. *v.i.* be carried by the tide. **ti′dal**, *a.* of, due to, or affected by the tide.

ti′dings (-z), *n.pl.* news received.

ti′dy, *a.* neat, orderly; methodically arranged; (colloq.) considerable. *n.* antimacassar; bag or receptacle for odds and ends. *v.t.* make tidy; put in order.

tie, *v.t.* & *i.* (part. *tying*), fasten with cord; form into knot or bow; tie lace, &c. of shoe, &c.; hamper; make equal score or run dead heat or draw game. *n.* necktie; uniting or connecting element; thing that hampers; draw or dead heat or equal score; match between winners of previous contests. *~-up, strike or lock-out.

tier, *n.* (pl.) two or more rows of things, or platforms, &c., parallel but at different levels; (sing.) one of such rows, &c.

tierce, *n.* (Fencing) position for guard, parry, or thrust; sequence of three cards; medium-sized cask for wine or provisions.

tiff, *n.* quarrel between lovers or friends. *v.i.* have a tiff.

tiff², *n.* draught of liquor. *v.t. & i.* sip, drink ; (Anglo-Ind.) lunch.

tiff'anȳ, *n.* gauzy silk or muslin.

tiff'in, *n.* (Anglo-Ind.) light meal, esp. of curried dishes and fruit ; lunch. *v.i. & t.* take tiffin, lunch ; provide with tiffin.

ti'ger (-g-), *n.* large striped feline beast of prey ; smart-liveried small boy as groom ; *(sl.) supplementary cheer, prolongation, final burst (*three cheers and a tiger*). ~-cat, kinds of smaller animal resembling tiger. ~-lily, with dark-spotted orange flower.

ti'gerish (-g-), *a.* (esp.) as cruel or relentless as a tiger.

tight (tit), *a.* pulled from both ends or every direction ; close packed or firmly fixed ; compact ; gripping or clasping close ; (sl.) drunk. *n.pl.* tight costume of acrobats, &c. *adv.* tightly. ~-rope, rope stretched tight for performer to walk, &c. on. *~-wad, (sl.) stingy person. tight'en (tit-), *v.t. & i.* make or become tight.

ti'gress, *n.* female tiger.

til, *n.* (E.-Ind.) the plant *Sesamum indicum*, chiefly used in comb. ~-oil, ~-seed oil, oil obtained by burning til seeds.

til'burȳ, *n.* light two-wheeled carriage.

til'de (-dā), *n.* the mark placed in Spanish over n (ñ) to indicate a following y-sound.

tile, *n.* thin piece of burnt clay for roofing, &c. ; (sl.) hat. *v.t.* cover, &c. with tiles.

|| tilk'a, *n.* Hindu caste-mark on forehead.

till¹, *prep.* up to, as late as. *conj.* up to the time when ; to the degree that.

till², *n.* money-drawer in shop-counter.

till³, *v.t.* cultivate (land). till'age, *n.* preparation of land for crop-bearing ; tilled land.

till'er, *n.* lever by which rudder is turned.

tilt¹, *n.* unlevel position ; movement in which one end or side becomes higher than the other ;

act of tilting with lance. *v.i. & t.* be or become or put on the tilt ; (of medieval knights, &c.) charge with lance at each other or *at* a mark ; (fig.) direct argument or satire *at* or *against*.

tilt², *n.* awning of cart.

tilth, *n.* tillage.

tim'ber, *n.* wood as material for building or carpentry ; a beam ; large standing trees. ~-toes, (sl.) wooden-legged or heavy-treading person. tim'bered (-erd), *a.* made of, or partly of, timber ; (of country) wooded.

timbre (tăm'ber), *n.* characteristic quality of a musical sound or a voice apart from its pitch.

tim'brel, *n.* (Bibl.) tambourine.

time, *n.* the successive states of the universe regarded as a whole ; any definite or indefinite portion of time ; a period with its events or characteristics ; a season or distinguishable part of the year or day ; amount of time allowed, taken, or available ; an appointed interval ; a breathing-space ; so many reckonings of a multiplicand (pl.) ; pace at which musical notes or steps succeed one another ; time of day as shown by clock, &c. *v.t.* (-mable), choose right time for ; appoint time for ; take the time of (race, &c.). ~-honoured, venerable by antiquity. ~-keeper, one who records time ; clock or watch. ~-piece, clock or watch. ~-server, supple person ; selfish opportunist. ~-table, synopsis of hours of work, starting and arrival times of trains, &c. time'lȳ (-ml-), *a.* opportune, occurring at right time.

tim'id, *a.* easily frightened ; apprehensive. timid'itȳ, *n.*

tim'orous, *a.* timid ; shrinking or shy with timidity.

tin, *n.* a white metal much used for coating iron to preserve it from rust ; a vessel or box of tin or tin-plate ; (sl.) money. *v.t.* coat with tin ; seal up (fruit, meat,&c.) in tins for preservation.

~foil, foil of tin or some white alloy for preservative wrappings. ~hat, (sl.) helmet. ~Lizzie, nickname for Ford motor-car. ~plate, sheet-iron coated with tin. ~tack, tin-coated tack.

tinc′ture, n. colour or other surface marking in heraldry; a tinge of colour; a smack of some quality or accomplishment; medicinal solution of a drug. v.t. (-rable), colour slightly; tinge; imbue or slightly modify the appearance or character of. tinctor′ial, a. of or for dyeing.

‖ tin′dal, n. (E.-Ind.) native petty officer or lascars; foreman of a gang of labourers.

tin′der, n. inflammable material in which the spark from flint and steel used to be caught; dry rotten wood.

tine, n. one of the prongs or teeth or points of a fork, comb, deer's horn, &c.

tinge (-j), v.t. (-geable), colour slightly (with). n. tendency to or trace of some colour; slight admixture of a feeling or quality.

tingle (ting′gl), v.i. feel pricking or thrilling sensation.

tink′er, n. itinerant mender of kettles, &c. v.i. work indifferently.

tinkle (ting′kl), n. sound of or as of small bell. v.i. & t. make or cause (bell) to make tinkle. tink′ler, n. (sl.) small bell.

tin′sel, n. decorations of bright metal foil or threads; tawdry brilliance; flashiness; (attrib.) flashy. tin′selled (-ld), a.

tint, n. one of the varieties of a colour; a faint colour spread over a surface. v.t. colour slightly or conventionally; wash or suffuse with colour.

tintinnābulā′tion, n. tinkling.

ti′ny, a. very small.

tip, n. the finer end of a thing; the extremity remote from base or butt or root; piece added to give durability to a tip, &c.; slight glancing stroke with cricket-bat, &c.; slight tilting push; gift

given to schoolboy, waiter, driver, &c.; piece of information as to probable winner of race; a good dodge or recipe. v.t. & i. put tip on; give tip to; strike (ball, &c.) with tip or side of bat, &c.; tilt, incline; upset. ~-and-run, cricket in which batsman must run if bat touches ball. ~cat, game with a stick and short tapering piece of wood. ~staff, sheriff's officer. ~toe, the point of the toe. ~top, exceedingly good.

tipp′et, n. covering of fur, &c. for the shoulders.

tip′ple, v.i. & t. be given to drink; habitually drink a good deal of. n. alcoholic drink.

tip′ster, n. purveyor of sporting tips.

tip′sy, a. unsteady in gait or speech with drink; drunk.

tirade′, n. piece of vehement denunciation or rant.

tire[1], n. metal rim enclosing felloe; rim-cover of rubber, &c. attached to wheel; (arch.) headdress, attire. v.t. put tire or tires on; (arch.) dress (hair), attire.

tire[2], v.t. & i. become unequal to or indisposed for further exertion, grow sick of; reduce to these states. ~less, a. of inexhaustible energy. ~some, a. trying to the temper; annoying; tedious.

ti′rō, n. a beginner.

tiss′ue (-sū, -shōō), n. a woven fabric, esp. of gauzy texture; (fig.) a network of lies, &c.; any of the coherent substances of which organic bodies are composed. ~paper, thin soft unsized paper for wrappings, &c.

tit, n. titmouse; (arch.) horse, girl. ~lark, small lark-like bird.

Ti′tan, n. the sun (poet.); person far beyond others in genius or power; huge person or animal, &c. ~ess, n.; titān′ic, a.

titā′nium, n. a dark-grey metallic element.

tit′bit, n. dainty morsel; piquant item of news, &c.

tithe (-dh), n. a tenth; originally a tenth of the annual produce of land devoted to the support of the clergy, now converted into rent charge. *v.t.* (-*thable*), subject (property, owner) to tithe.

tit'lllāte, *v.t.* (-*lable*) stimulate as by tickling. ~**tion**, ~**tor**, *nn.*

tit'ivāte, *v.t. & i.* (colloq.) make smart; smarten oneself.

ti'tle, *n.* name of a book or other work of art; heading of a chapter, &c.; word or phrase indicative of a person's status; right to ownership of property; just or recognized claim to thing or *to* do something. ~**deed**, legal document establishing right to property. ~**page**, page of book exhibiting its name, authorship, &c. **ti'tled** (-ld), having title of nobility.

tit'mouse, *n.* (pl. -*mice*), kinds of small active bird.

titt'er, *v.i.* laugh covertly. *n.* such laugh.

tit'tle, *n.* small mark, an iota; least quantity or trifling point.

tit'tle-tattle, *n. & v.i.* gossip.

tit'up, *v.i.* go mincingly or jerkily; bob up and down. *n.* such gait or movement.

tit'ular, *a.* such in name irrespective of the reality; giving or serving as a title. *n.* nominal holder of a benefice, &c.

tmē'sis, *n.* (Gram.) intrusion of a word or words between the parts of a compound word.

to, *prep.* (tōō *emphat.* or at end of clause, tŏŏ *before vowel*, tŏ *before consonant*), in the direction of; as far as; not short of; also, introducing indirect obj. of vb. &c., or as mark of inf. *adv.* to or in the required position; to a standstill; in closed state. ~ and fro, backwards and forwards; from place to place. ~**day'**, this day; on or during this day. ~**mo'rrow**, the day after to-day. ~**night'**, the coming or present night.

toad, *n.* frog-like amphibian breeding in water but living chiefly on land; repulsive person. ~**eater**, toady. ~**flax**, a yellow-flowered plant. ~**stool**, kinds of umbrella-

shaped fungus. **toad'ȳ**, *n.* sycophant; obsequious parasite; *v.t.* play the toady to. ~**ism**, *n.*

toast, *n.* bread sliced and browned, esp. before the fire; the drinking of a health or the sentiment, &c. so honoured. *v.t. & i.* brown (bread) or cook (bacon, &c.) or warm (oneself, &c.) before the fire; drink to the health of.

tobăcc'ō, *n.* (pl. -os), narcotic leaves from which cigars and snuff are made, esp. the preparations for use in pipes or cigarettes. ~**nist**, *n.* dealer in tobacco.

tobŏgg'an, *n.* hand-sledge, used esp. in the sport of coasting down snow or ice slopes.

tō'bȳ, *n.* mug in the shape of a man in a three-cornered hat.

Tŏc H, *n.* society with many branches carrying on comradeship from the great war.

tō'cō, *n.* (sl.) blows or reprimands.

tŏc'sin, *n.* alarm-signal on bell.

tŏd, *n.* (dial.) fox.

tŏd'dle, *v.i.* go with small child's short unsteady steps; (joc.) saunter, walk. *n.* toddling child; (joc.) a stroll.

tŏdd'ȳ, *n.* drink of whisky or other spirit with hot water and sugar; palm-tree sap, or fermented liquor made from it.

tō'dȳ, *n.* W.-Ind. bird related to kingfisher.

tōe, *n.* any of the five members in which front of human foot ends; corresponding part in bird or beast; part of shoe or stocking covering toes. *v.t.* kick (sl.); touch with the toes; (Golf) strike faultily with tip of club.

tŏff, *n.* (sl.) gentleman or one who passes or dresses as such.

tŏff'ee (-fĭ), *n.* sweet-stuff of boiled butter and sugar.

tŏg, *v.t.* (sl.), fit with or dress in togs (usu. ~ *out*).

tō'ga, *n.* civil attire of citizen of ancient Rome; a plain piece of woollen stuff so disposed as to drape the whole person except the head and right arm.

---

ah, as (rou)ge: ŏ = ĭ; ff, ûr, = ĕr; y, y̆, = ĭ, ĭ; and see p. ŏ. ° = U.S.

togeth'er (-dh-), *adv.* in or into company or combination or juxtaposition; simultaneously.

togs (-z), *n.pl.* (sl.) clothes. **tog'ger'y** (-g-), *n.* (sl.) togs.

toil, *v.i.* work laboriously or incessantly at; make slow painful progress. *n.* severe labour; drudgery. ~**some**, involving toil. ~**worn**, said of persons, faces, limbs, &c.

toil'et, *n.* process of dressing; style of dress; a costume; (attrib.) used in the toilet.

toils (-z), *n.pl.* net, snare.

tō'ken, *n.* indication; something that serves as a symbol, keepsake, distinctive mark, or guarantee. ~ **money**, coins of higher nominal than intrinsic value.

tō'la, *n.* unit of weight in Indian empire, =180 grains troy.

tŏl'erable, *a.* not beyond endurance; fairly good.

tŏl'erance, *n.* tolerant temper or ways. **tŏl'erant**, *a.* disposed or accustomed to tolerate others or their opinions; broad-minded. **tŏl'erāte**, *v.t.* allow the existence or occurrence of without authoritative interference; put up with. ~**ā'tion**, *n.* tolerating, esp. the recognition of free thought and practice in religious matters.

tōll¹, *n.* charge payable for permission to pass a barrier, use a market or harbour, &c.; (hist.) proportion of corn kept by miller as payment for grinding. ~**bar**, ~**gate**, barriers preventing passage without payment of toll.

tōll², *v.t. & i.* sound (bell) with slow succession of strokes; strike (hour) or announce or mark (death) thus. *n.* tolling sound.

tolū' (or **tō'lū**), *n.* a S.-Amer. tree and balsam. **tŏ'lūēne**, **tō'lŭŏl** (or **tō-**), *n.* liquid with smell like benzene and burning taste, yielding many compounds.

tŏm, *n.* a male, esp. a male domestic bird or cat. ~**boy**, romping girl. ~ **cat**, male cat. ~**fool'**, *n.* buffoon; *v.i.* show misplaced

levity or ineptitude. ~**fool'ery**, mummery; trifling. ~**nŏdd'y**, simpleton. ~**tit'**, titmouse, esp. the blue tit.

tŏm'ahawk (-a-h-), *n.* war-axe of N.-Amer. Indians. *v.t.* kill or wound with tomahawk.

toma'tō (-ah-), *n.* (pl. -oes) pulpy red or yellow fruit; the plant bearing it.

tomb (tōōm), *n.* a grave; burial-vault; sepulchral monument. ~'**stone**, memorial stone standing or laid over grave.

tŏm'băc, **-k**, *n.* kinds of copper-and-zinc alloy.

tŏm'bola, *n.* kind of lottery with fancy articles for prizes.

tōme, *n.* large book or volume.

tŏmm'y, *n.* (sl.) food; Tommy Atkins. **T~ Atkins**, British private soldier. ~ **rot**, (sl.) nonsense; folly.

tŏm'tŏm, *n.* native Indian drum; gong. *v.i.* beat tomtom.

ton (tŭn), *n.* measure of weight, 20 cwt.; unit of measurement for ship's tonnage, 100 cub. ft. **to'nnage** (tŭ-), *n.* ship's cubic content or carrying-capacity; sum of the tonnage of shipping; charge per ton on freight.

tonăl'ity, *n.* (esp.) relation between the tones of a musical scale; colour-scheme of picture.

tōne, *n.* sound, esp. with reference to pitch, quality, and strength; musical sound; modulation of voice to express emotion, &c.; proper condition of the bodily organs; tint or shade of colour; prevailing character of morals, sentiments, &c. *v.t. & i.* give desired tone to; modify tone of; be in harmony *with*.

tŏng'a (-ngga), *n.* light and small two-wheeled carriage or cart used in India.

tŏngs (-z), *n.pl.* (also *pair of* ~), kinds of two-limbed gripping implement for lifting what is not to be handled.

tongue (tŭng), *n.* muscular organ in the mouth used in tasting, speaking, masticating, &c.;

faculty or manner of speaking; a language; tongue-like piece or part. ~-tied, incapable of or slow of speech.

ton'ic, a. tending to restore bodily tone; bracing. n. a tonic medicine or agency; (Mus.) keynote. ~ sŏl-fa' (-ah), a musical notation used esp. in teaching singing.

ton'jon, tom-, n. (E.-Ind.) kind of sedan-chair slung on a pole and carried by four bearers.

tonk, v.t. (sl.) hit (bowling, person) hard; defeat easily in contest.

tonnage. See ton.

tonn'eau (-nō), n. rounded rear body of some motor-cars.

ton'sil, n. gland at either side of back of mouth. tonsilli'tis, n. inflammation of tonsil.

ton'sure (-sher), n. shaving of the head or of a patch on the crown as clerical symbol; bare patch so made. v.t. subject to tonsure.

tontine' (-ēn), n. loan or fund the surviving subscribers of which receive annuities increasing as they become fewer.

too, adv. in addition; as well; moreover; in an excessive degree.

took, p.t. of take.

tool, n. instrument designed to help or enable the hand(s) to apply force; person used to forward another's purposes. v.t. & i. dress (stone) with chisel; impress design on (leather bookcover); (sl.) drive (team, coach, &c.); convey or go in carriage, &c.

toon, n. E.-Ind. tree with close-grained red wood, much used for furniture, &c.

toot, n. sound of horn, &c. v.i. & t. emit toot; sound (horn, &c.).

tooth, n. (pl. teeth), any of the set of bone-like bodies rooted in the jaws and used esp. in biting; projection comparable to a tooth. ~ache, ache in tooth. ~brush, brush for cleaning the teeth. tooth'ful (-ool), n. (sl.) drop of brandy, &c. ~some, a. (of food) delicious.

too'tle, v.i. & t., & n. toot (esp. with repetition); twaddle.

top¹, n. the summit or the upper part or the surface of something; the highest place or rank; the highest degree; (attrib.) of or at or on the top; platform round top of lower mast; (pl.) parts of hunting-boots representing flaps turned down round calves. v.t. & i. cover top of or crown with; cut off top of (tree); be at the top of; surpass. ~-boots, boots with tops. ~coat, overcoat. ~gäll'ant (tŏp-, tŏg-), mast, sail, yard, rigging, immediately above topmast and topsail. ~hat, high silk hat. ~heavy, apt to topple from being over-weighted above. ~knot, bow of ribbon or bunch of hair or tuft of feathers worn or growing on top of head. ~mast, mast next above the lower mast. ~sail (-sl), square sail next above lowest. topp'er, n. (esp.) top-hat. topp'ing, a. (sl.) excellent.

top², n. toy to which spinning motion is given by means of whip or piece of cord.

to'paz, n. a precious stone of various colours, esp. yellow.

tope¹, n. kind of small shark.

tope², v.i. drink to excess. to'per, n. person given to drink.

tope³, n. (Anglo-Ind.) a clump, grove, or plantation of trees; in Upper India, chiefly of fruit-trees.

tope⁴, n. Buddhist monument, usu. dome or tower.

to'pi, to'pee, n. originally applied by Indian natives to the European hat, now specialized in Anglo-Ind. as a name for the sola topi, sun-hat or helmet. ~wal-lah, ~wala, Indian name for a European because he wears a hat.

to'piary, a. of the clipping of trees, &c. into fantastic shapes.

top'ic, a. subject of conversation or theme of discourse; thing talked of. top'ical, a. having reference to current events.

tŏp'most, *a.* uppermost.

topŏg'raphy, *n.* local geography; features of a district or description of them. **topŏg'rapher**, *n.* expert in topography. **tŏpo-grăph'ic**, **~al**, *aa.*

tŏp'ple, *v.i. & t.* be unsteady or hang as if about to fall; fall or cause to fall.

tŏpsytŭrv'y̆, *adv. & a.* upside down; in inverted position or way; in confusion. **~dom**, *n.*

tŏque (-k), *n.* woman's brimless hat.

tŏr, *n.* rocky hill-top.

tŏrch, *n.* inflammable stick or rope that can be carried as a light.

torchon (tôr'shŏn), *n.* coarse loose kind of lace.

tore, *p.t.* of tear.

to'rēador, *n.* Spanish, usu. mounted, bull-fighter.

torment, *n.* (tôrm'ent), severe bodily or mental suffering or the cause of it. *v.t.* (tôrmĕnt'), subject to torment; importune; tease. **~or**, **~ress**, *nn.*

tŏrm'entil, *n.* a trailing yellow-flowered herb.

torn, *p.p.* of tear.

tōrnā'dō, *n.* (pl. *-oes*), very violent storm over a limited area.

torpē'dō, *n.* (pl. *-oes*), a fish inflicting electric shocks when touched; kinds of explosive mine or petard; cigar-shaped self-propelled submarine missile that can be aimed at a ship, &c. and explodes on touching it. *v.t. & i.* hit or damage with, discharge, torpedoes; (fig.) make ineffective. **~boat**, small fast war-ship discharging torpedoes.

tŏrp'id, *a.* benumbed, stupefied; sluggish; dull. **torpĭd'ity**, *n.*

tŏrp'or, *n.* suspended animation; apathy.

Tŏrps, *n.* (Nav. sl.) ship's torpedo officer.

tŏrque (-k), *n.* metal necklet worn by ancient Britons, Gauls, &c.

tŏ'rrent, *n.* rush of water; downpour of rain; volley of abuse. **torrĕn'tial** (-shl), *a.*

tŏ'rrid, *a.* intensely hot.

tŏr'sion (-shn), *n.* (scient.) twisting. **tŏr'sional** (-sho-), *a.*

tŏrs'ō, *n.* (pl. *-os*), trunk of a statue apart from head and limbs; unfinished work.

tŏrt, *n.* breach of a duty imposed by law whereby some person acquires a right of action for damages.

tŏrt'oise (-tus), *n.* four-legged reptile enclosed in a horny shell. **~shell** (-tashĕl), esp. as material with patches of brown and transparent yellow used for combs, spectacles, &c.; (attrib.) of or like tortoiseshell.

tŏrt'ŭous, *a.* winding, indirect; involved. **tŏrtŭŏs'ity**, *n.*

tŏr'ture, *n.* infliction of pain, esp. to extort something from victim; agony. *v.t.* (-rable), subject to torture; distort.

Tŏr'y̆, *n.* member of the political party opposed to change and supporting existing institutions; a Conservative. **~ism**, *n.*

tŏsh, *n.* (sl.) twaddle, nonsense, easy bowling, &c.

tŏss, *v.t. & i.* move with fitful to-and-fro motion; fling or roll about; drain (liquor) *off* at a draught; throw upwards; throw up coin to decide question by which face falls uppermost. *n.* tossing motion; upward throw or lob of ball, &c.; tossing of coin or decision so given.

tŏt¹, *n.* (colloq.) small child; small mug; dram of liquor.

tŏt², *n.* (colloq.) addition sum or its result. *v.t. & i.* add together; (of expenses, &c.) mount *up*.

tō'tal, *a.* complete; comprising the whole. *n.* sum of all items; total amount. *v.t. & i.* amount to; reckon total of. **totăl'ity**, *n.* being total; an aggregate.

tō'talizātor, **-izer**, **tōte¹** (sl.), *nn.* device registering number and amount of bets staked on race with a view to dividing the total among betters on winner.

tō'talize, *v.t.* combine into a total.

*****tōte²**, *v.t.* carry, bear (burden, load).

tō'tĕm, *n.* hereditary emblem of a tribe or clan or group of primitive people giving its name to the tribe, &c. **~ism**, *n.* stage of development of which totems are characteristic.

tŏtt'er, *v.i.* be insecure on base, &c.; oscillate as if about to fall; go with feeble steps.

tō'ty, *n.* (Anglo-Ind.) man of low caste employed as messenger and odd man.

tou'can (tōō-), *n.* large-billed S.-Amer. bird.

touch (tŭch), *v.i. & t.* come into or be in contact with; strike lightly; deal with (subject) momentarily; tint in parts or slightly *with*; concern; stir sympathy or other emotion in. *n.* act or fact of touching; the sense of feeling; style of execution or treatment; (Footb.) sides of field outside touch-lines. *~-back*, (Amer. footb.) touching ball to ground behind one's own goal-line to anticipate opponent. *~-down*, (Rugby footb.) touch ball on ground behind one's own goal-line to anticipate opponent; *(Amer. footb.) score six points by touching the ball to ground behind opponents' goal-line. *~-down*, (Rugby footb.) act of touching down. *~-hole*, hole through which fire was set to the charge in guns. *~-line*, (Footb.) either side-boundary of ground. *~-paper*, paper steeped in nitre so as to burn slowly for igniting fireworks, &c. *~-stone*, black jasper, &c. used for testing alloys of gold, &c.; (fig.) standard, criterion. *~-wood*, wood in soft rotten state usable as tinder.

tou'ching (tŭ-), *a.* pathetic or moving; *prep.* about; as regards.

tou'chy (tŭ-), *a.* apt to take offence; over-sensitive.

tough (tŭf), *a.* of strongly cohesive substance or great endurance; hard to masticate; not easily injured or broken; hard to tackle or overcome; *(sl.)* depraved, criminal, vicious. *~n.*

street ruffian. **tough'en** (tŭf-), *v.t. & i.*

toupee (tōō-), **toupet** (tōō'pā), *n.* front of false hair.

tour (toor), *n.* roving journey, including stops at various places; short journey for pleasure; rambling excursion. *v.i. & t.* go on a tour; go through (country, &c.) so. **tour'ist** (toor-). *n.* holiday traveller.

tour'maline (toor-), *n.* a mineral with electric properties and used as gem.

tour'nament (toor-), *n.* medieval tilting-match between two sides, or meeting for tilting and similar contests (arch. *tourney*); contest in any game of skill between a number of competitors.

tourniquet (toorn'ĭkĕt), *n.* appliance for stopping blood-flow in artery.

tou'sle (-zl), *v.t.* pull about; make (hair, person) untidy.

tout, *n.* spy on horses in training supplying information to tipsters, &c.; person soliciting custom. *v.i.* act as tout; employ touts; canvass, solicit custom.

‖ **tout ensemble** (tōōt ahǹsahn'bl), general effect of a thing as viewed in a glance.

tow[1] (tō), *n.* fibres of flax, &c. prepared for spinning.

tow[2] (tō), *v.t.* draw along through water by rope or chain; drag along behind one. *n.* towing, being towed. *~-line*, *~-rope*, rope for towing (also *towing-line, rope*). *~-path*, path along canal, &c. to tow barges from (also *towing-path*). **tow'age** (tō'ĭj), *n.* towing or its cost.

toward[1] (tō'ard), *a.* (arch.) towardly; (pred. only) about to occur; in train.

to'wardly (tōar-), *a.* (arch.) promising; propitious.

towards(s) (tōrdz, towŏrdz'), *prep.* in the direction of; not much short of or less than; in relation to; as contribution to.

tow'el, *n.* cloth for drying with after washing. **towe'lling**, *n.*

material for towels; (sl.) thrashing or severe defeat.

tow´er, n. tall strong structure, often forming part of church or other large building; fortress, &c. having a tower; (fig.) source *of* strength, protector. *v.i.* be of outstanding height or greatness; soar aloft; (part.) high, lofty, (of rage, &c.) violent. **tow´ered** (-erd), a. having towers.

town, n. any collection of houses larger than a village and having a more independent local government; the inhabitants of a town. ~ **clerk**, secretary to the corporation of a town. ~ **council**, elective body administering town. ~ **hall**, the municipal building of a town. **~ship**, one of the parishes into which a large original parish has been divided; *(U.S. & Can.)* administrative subdivision of a county, tract of land six miles square; (Austral.) site laid out for town. **~s´man**, **~s´people**, inhabitant, people, of a town.

tŏx´ic, a. of, or caused by, or acting as poison. **tŏxĭcŏl´ogў**, **~gist**, *nn.* **tŏx´in**, n. a poison, esp. one secreted by a microbe and causing some particular disease.

toy, n. a plaything; a trinket or curiosity; (attrib.) mimic, not meant for real use. *v.i.* exchange caresses; play or dally *with*.

trāce, n. mark left behind; indication of the existence or occurrence of something; slight amount or trace; strap or chain or rope by two of which a poled vehicle is drawn. *v.t.* (-ceable), follow or make out the course of by means of traces; detect or make out by scrutiny, &c.; make tracing of, delineate. **~ability**, n. **trā´cerý**, n. stone open-work as in head of a Gothic window; laced ornamentation. **trā´cing**, n. a reproduction of the lines of a drawing, &c. made with the aid of transparent paper, &c.

trache´a (-kēa), n. the windpipe.

trācheŏt´omý (*or* ă; -kĭ-), n. surgical incision in trachea.

trăck, n. continuous line showing where something has passed; a path, esp. one beaten by use; prepared racing-path; a two-rail railway line; (pl.) footsteps. *v.t.* follow or hunt down or find out by means of traces. *~=athletics, running, jumping, putting the weight, &c.* **~less**, a.

trăct, n. a region or expanse of indefinite extent and shape; (Anat.) area of organ or system; a short treatise. **Trăctār´ian**, a. & n. (adherent of) Tractarianism. **~ism**, n. the Oxford High-Church movement, whose leaders issued *Tracts for the Times.*

trăc´table, a. easily managed; docile. **~bility**, n.

trăc´tāte, n. (arch.) treatise.

trăc´tion, n. hauling; drawing force. ~ **engine**, steam engine for drawing load on roads, ploughs, &c. **trăc´tor**, n. traction engine; aeroplane with engine in front.

trāde, n. dealing in commodities for profit; a particular branch of this or persons engaged in it; person's commercial or industrial calling. *v.i. & t.* (-dable), deal in the way of trade; have commerce with. ~ **mark**, manufacturer's registered device or name to distinguish his goods. **~s´man** (-an), shopkeeper. **~s´people**, tradesmen and their families. ~ **union**, association of workmen for the protection and promotion of common interests. ~ **wind**, constant wind blowing towards the equator from NE. and SE.

trādi´tion, n. oral transmission of knowledge or belief from one generation to another; tale or belief or custom so transmitted. **~al, ~arý**, aa.

traduce´, *v.t.* (-cible), slander. **~ment**, n. censure, obloquy.

trăf´fic, *n. & t.* trade (*in* goods, &c.); sacrifice (honour, &c.) for gain. *n.* trading; dealings with

---

măte, mēte, mĭte, mōte, mūte, mŏŏt; răck, rĕck, rĭck, rŏck, rŭck, rŏŏk;

coming and going of persons and vehicles, or conveyance of goods by road, rail, or water.

trăg'acănth, *n.* a gum used esp. as a vehicle for drugs.

tragĕ'dian, *n.* author of or actor in tragedies. **tragĕdĭĕnne'**, *n.* tragic actress.

tră'gĕdў, *n.* a drama of elevated theme and diction and with unhappy ending; a tragical occurrence. **tră'gic**, *a.* of or in the style of tragedy; tragical. **tră'gical**, *a.* calamitous; of a terrible nature. **trăgĭcŏm'ĕdў**, *n.* a play, or an event, in which tragic and comic elements are combined.

trail, *v.t. & i.* draw along as an appendage; be so drawn; walk wearily along; (of plant) hang or spread downwards; (Mil.) carry (rifle) hanging level in one hand muzzle forward. *n.* a trailing growth; soldier's position with rifle trailed; track or scent or other sign of passage left behind by moving object; beaten track through wild region. **trail'er**, *n.* (esp.) trailing plant; wheeled vehicle drawn by another.

train, *v.t. & i.* put in the way to efficiency by instruction and practice; make physically fit for contest; guide growth of (plant); direct (cannon) on mark; (colloq.) travel by train. *n.* trailing prolongation of robe or gown; string of persons or animals; person's retinue; succession of events; a locomotive with the wagons it draws; railway travel; a line of gunpowder laid as an explosive charge. **~bands**, (hist.) citizen soldiery of 16th–18th centuries. **~bearer**, person holding up train of another's robe. ***~man**, brakeman or porter on railway train. **train'er**, *n.* (esp.) person who trains racehorses or athletes.

train'-oil, *n.* whale-blubber oil.

trait (trā), *n.* item in a portrait, description, or character.

trait'or, *n.* person guilty of a be-

trayal; one who acts disloyally. **~ous**, *a.*; **~tress**, *n.*

trajec'torў, *n.* path of a body moving under given forces.

trăm, *n.*, (also **~car**) car for passengers, &c. moved by horse or cable or electric traction along tramway; (also **~way**) line of rails laid in road for tram-cars. *v.i.* travel by tram.

trămm'el, *n.* kind of fishing-net; (usu. pl.) hampering influence, restraint. *v.t.* hamper.

trămp, *v.i. & t.* walk with firm heavy tread; traverse (road, &c.) on foot. *n.* sound (as) of troops marching; person who tramps the roads esp. as a vagrant; freight-ship running on no regular line. **trăm'ple**, *v.t. & i.* tread heavily on.

trance (-ah-), *n.* abnormal state of suspended consciousness.

trănq'uil, *a.* serene, undisturbed. **trănquill'itў**, *n.*; **~lize**, *v.t.*

trănsăct' (-z-), *v.t.* do or carry on (business). **~ion**, *n.* any piece of commercial or other dealing; (pl.) proceedings of a society. **~or**, *n.*

trănsăl'pīne (-z-), *a.* beyond the Alps from the Italian point of view; extra-Italian.

trănsatlăn'tic (-z-), *a.* on the American side of the Atlantic; (of ship, &c.) crossing the Atlantic.

trănscĕnd', *v.t.* be or pass beyond the range of; be too high for; surpass; soar above. **trănscĕn'dence**, **~dencў**, *nn.* **~dent**, *a.* of supreme merit or quality. **trănscĕndĕn'tal**, *a.* not based on experience; supernatural. **~ism**, **~ist**, *nn.* belief, believer, in some form of transcendental philosophy.

trănscŏntinĕn'tal (-z-), *a.* traversing a continent.

trănscrībe', *v.t.* copy out; reproduce in ordinary writing. **trăn'script**, *n.* product of transcription. **trănscrĭp'tion**, *n.* act of transcribing.

trăn'sĕpt, *n.* transverse part of cruciform church; arm of this.

transfer, v.t. (tränsfér'), shift from one position or receptacle to another. n. (träns'fer), transference; conveyance of property to new owner, document effecting this; design, &c. that can be transferred from one surface to another. ~able, a.; ~ability, n. ~ence, n. transferring.

transfig'ure (-ger), v.t. change the aspect of; invest with a more spiritual or elevated character. **transfigura'tion**, n.

transfix', v.t. pierce with lance, &c.; (of horror, &c.) root (person) to the spot; paralyse the faculties of.

transform', v.t. change the form or character of. ~a'tion, n. transforming or being transformed. **transfor'mer**, n. apparatus for changing the voltage of an alternating current supply.

transfuse' (-z), v.t. cause (fluid, &c.) to pass from one vessel, &c. to another; inject (extraneous blood or other liquid) into the veins or blood of. ~sion, n.

transgress' (-z-), v.t. & i. infringe (law, &c.); outstep (limit laid down); sin. ~ion, n. (esp.) a sin. ~or, n.

trans'ient (-z-), a. quickly passing away; fleeting. **trans'ience**, n.

trans'it (-z-), n. passing across, over, through, or from place to place; passage of heavenly body across the sun's disk, &c.

transi'tion, n. passage from one state, subject, or set of circumstances to another. ~al, a.

trans'itive, a. (of verb) requiring a direct object expressed or understood.

trans'itory (-z-), a. of a passing nature; merely temporary.

translate', v.t. (-table), give the sense of in another language; interpret (obscure statement, conduct, &c.); remove (bishop) to another see. **transla'tion**, n. art or act or product of translating. ~tor, n.

translit'erate (-z-), v.t. (-rable), write word in the more or less corresponding letters of another language. ~tion, ~tor, nn.

translu'cent (-zloo-), a. allowing light to pass through. ~nce, n. ~ncy, n.

transmarine' (-z-, -ēn), a. beyond sea.

trans'migrate (-z-; or -mi-), v.i. migrate. ~tion, n. migration.

transmiss'ible (-z-), a. that may be transmitted. ~bility, n.

transmi'ssion (-zmishn), n. sending from one place to another.

transmit' (-z-), v.t. effect conveyance of; pass on; communicate. **transmi'tter**, n. apparatus for transmitting wireless signals. ~ting station, n. station sending out telegraphic messages or telephony by wireless.

transmute' (-z-), v.t. (-table), change the form, nature, or substance of. ~tabil'ity, ~ta'tion, nn.; ~tative, a.

transocean'ic (-zōsh-), a. beyond, crossing, the ocean.

tran'som, n. a cross-beam, esp. a lintel or a horizontal bar in a mullioned window.

trans'par'ent, a. that can be clearly seen through; plainly apparent. **transpar'ence**, n. being transparent. ~cy, n. transparency; kinds of picture, &c. visible by the passing of light through them.

transpire', v.t. & i. (-rable), emit (vapour) or pass off through pores of skin, &c.; emerge into knowledge; (vulg.) happen. ~ration, n.

transplant' (-lah-), v.t. uproot and replant elsewhere. ~ation, n.

transport, v.t. (tränspôrt'), convey by land or sea; (hist.) deport (convict) beyond sea; fill with ecstasy, rage, &c. n. (träns'pôrt), transporting; ship conveying troops, military stores, &c. **transporta'tion**, n.

transpose' (-z), v.t. (-sable), change the order or serial place of; (Mus.) put into another key. **transposi'tion** (-zish-), n.

trans-ship' (-nsh-), v.t. shift to or from another ship or conveyance. ~ment, n.

trănsubstăn'tiāte (-sht-), v.t. change into a different substance. ~tion, n. (esp.) conversion of the eucharistic elements into the body and blood of Christ.

trănsverse' (-z-), a. set or acting crosswise.

trăn'ter, n. (dial.) carrier, hawker.

trăp¹, n. animal-catching apparatus or device; scheme for enticing or detecting; contrivance for throwing something into the air to be shot or struck at; curve in drain-pipe, &c.; two-wheeled spring carriage; trap-door. v.t. catch in trap; ensnare or beguile. ~door, horizontal door in floor or roof or ceiling.

trăp², n. kind of dark volcanic rock.

trăp³, v.t. furnish with trappings. n. (pl.) baggage or belongings.

trāpes (-ps), v.i. (colloq.) trudge wearily or like a slattern.

trapēze', n. gymnastic apparatus of cross-bar and two ropes hung as a swing. trapē'zium, n. any irregular quadrilateral. trăp'ēzoid, n. quadrilateral with no two sides parallel.

trăpp'ings (-z), n.pl. ornamental cloth spread over horse in processions, &c.; embellishments.

trăsh, n. worthless stuff; rubbish; nonsense. trăsh'y, a.

trăv'ail (-vīl), n. pangs of childbirth; laborious effort. v.i. toil; be in labour.

trăv'el, v.i. & t. make journey(s); go in specified manner, &c.; (of eye, memory, &c.) pass from point to point. n. travelling; spell of it. trăv'eller, n. person who travels or is travelling; commercial traveller. traveller's joy, a wild clematis. trăv'elogue (or -ōg), n. illustrated lecture-narrative of expedition, &c.

trăv'erse, v.t. (-sable), go or be right through or across; oppose (allegation, &c.) with denial or objections; shift direction of (gun) laterally. n. contradiction of opponent's allegation; thing, esp. part of structure, that crosses another.

trăv'estȳ, n. an imitation or description that misrepresents the original. v.t. make or be a travesty of.

trawl, n. large wide-mouthed net dragged by boat along bottom of fishing-bank; *long sea-fishing line buoyed and supporting short lines with baited hooks. v.i. use trawl. traw'ler, n. trawling boat; man engaged in trawling.

tray, n. flat shallow vessel used for carrying small articles.

trea'cherȳ (-ĕch-), n. violation of faith; perfidy. trea'cherous (-ĕch-), a. guilty of or involving treachery; (of memory, &c.) apt to fail at need.

trea'cle, n. uncrystallized syrup got in refining sugar.

tread (-ĕd), v.i. & t. (trŏd, trŏdden), set one's foot or feet down; (of foot) be set down; traverse (road, &c.) on foot; press in or down by treading; perform (dance). n. manner or sound of walking; top surface of stair. ~mill, cylinder turned by treading on steps projecting from it. trea'dle (-ĕdl), n. lever worked by foot and working bicycle or lathe or other machine; v.i. work treadle.

trea'son (-z-), n. violation by a subject of his allegiance to sovereign or State; betrayal; treachery. ~able, ~ous, aa. involving or (-ous) guilty of treason.

trea'sure (-ĕzher), n. accumulated wealth; precious metals or gems or a hoard of them; valued thing or person. v.t. (-rable), set store on as dear or valuable; hoard, store up. trea'surer (-ĕzhe-), n. person responsible for the funds of an institution or society; *officer below Secretary of the Treasury.

trea'surȳ (-ĕzhe-), n. place where treasure is kept; funds or revenue of a State or institution or society; the State department controlling the revenue.

treat, v.t. & i. act or behave towards in a specified way; deal with or apply process to; provide with gratuitous entertainment; negotiate. *n.* thing that gives rare pleasure; feast given to school-children, &c.

treat′ise, *n.* written or printed exposition of a subject.

treat′ment, *n.* mode of dealing with a person or thing.

treat′y̆, *n.* formally signed contract between States; negotiations or bargaining between persons.

tre′ble, *a.* three times as great as; pertaining to the highest vocal or instrumental part. *n.* (Mus.) soprano voice or singer. *v.t. & i.* multiply, be multiplied, by three.

tree, *n.* perennial plant with single woody self-supporting main stem called the *trunk*; piece or framework of wood. **~creeper**, kinds of small bird.

tre′foil (*or* -ĕ-), *n.* kinds of plant with three-lobed leaves, clover, shamrock, &c.; ornament in architecture, &c.

trek (S.-Afr.), *v.i. & t.* (of ox) draw vehicle, pull load; migrate or journey with one's belongings in ox-wagons. *n.* act of trekking; migration of body of persons in this way. **trek′ker**, *n.*

trell′is, *n.* grating of light wooden or metal bars, used as support for creepers, fruit-trees, &c. **trell′ised** (-st), *a.*

trem′ble, *v.i.* shake with fear, excitement, or weakness; quiver. *n.* trembling, shiver.

tremén′dous, *a.* terrific, momentous; (colloq.) great.

trem′or, *n.* thrill of fear or other emotion; emotional vibration of voice; trembling; quiver.

trem′ulous, *a.* trembling, vibrating, quivering; agitated.

trench, *v.t. & i.* cut or dig into pits or ditches; dig so as to bring subsoil to top; encroach (*up*)*on*; verge or border closely (*up*)*on*. *n.* deep ditch, esp. one dug by troops as shelter from enemy's fire; groove, wrinkle.

trench′ant, *a.* sharp, keen; incisive, decisive. **trench′ancy̆**, *n.*

trench′er, *n.* (esp.) wooden platter for cutting bread on.

trend, *v.i.* bend or turn away in specified direction; show a certain tendency. *n.* general direction or tendency or drift.

trepán′¹, *n.* surgeon's cylindrical saw for making opening in the skull. *v.t.* use trepan on.

trepán′², *v.t.* decoy, ensnare.

tréphine′ (-ēn-, -īn-), improved form of trepan with centre-pin, &c. *v.t.* use trephine on.

trepidá′tion, *n.* tremulous agitation; perturbation of mind.

trés′pass, *v.i.* enter unlawfully upon another's ground; (arch.) transgress, sin; encroach (*up*)*on* person's time, &c. *n.* act of trespassing; (arch.) a sin or offence.

tress, *n.* (pl.) a woman's or child's flowing hair; (sing.) a lock or curl or braid of hair.

tré′stle (-sl), *n.* kind of timber support used in making a temporary table, platform, &c.

trét, *n.* (hist.) allowance of 4 lb. in 104 lb. formerly made to purchasers of some goods.

trews (-ōoz), *n.pl.* tartan trousers worn by some Scots regiments.

tri′ad, *n.* group of three.

tri′al, *n.* putting to the test; probation; thing that tries one's endurance, &c.; law-court's investigation of a cause.

tri′angle (-nggl), *n.* figure bounded by three straight lines; musical instrument consisting of steel rod bent into triangle; tripod of three poles joined at top for hoisting, &c.; triangle-shaped frame. **triăng′ūlar** (-ng-), *a.* triangle-shaped, three-cornered. **triăng′ūlāte** (-ng-), *v.t.* divide (area) into triangles for surveying purposes. **~tion**, *n.*

tri′as, *n.* division of rock underlying the jurassic. **triăss′ic**, *a.*

tribe, *n.* group of people under recognized chiefs; set of people lumped together (usu. contempt.) ; (Zool., &c.) subdivision of order or family. **tri′bal**, a.

tri′brach (-k), n. metrical foot of three short syllables.

tribulā′tion, n. affliction.

tribū′nal (or -i-), n. court of justice.

trib′une¹, n. apse of basilica ; bishop's throne ; dais, rostrum.

trib′une², n. an officer of anc. Rome chosen by the people ; popular leader or demagogue.

trib′ūte, n. periodical payment exacted by one prince or State from another ; thing done or said or given as a mark of respect, &c. **trib′ūtary**, a. of the nature of or paying tribute ; (of stream, &c.) running into or auxiliary to a greater one ; n. tributary State or person or stream.

trice, v.t. (Naut. ; with up) haul up and lash in place. n. short time ; an instant.

tri′ceps, n. a muscle with three points of attachment.

trichino′pŏli, n. (abbr. **trich′i**), kind of Indian cheroot.

trichinō′sis (-k-), n. disease due to presence of hair-like worms in the muscular tissue.

trichŏt′omy (-k-), n. classification into three parts.

trichromăt′ic (-kr-), a. of or in three colours.

trick, n. stratagem, piece of guile, dodge ; a practice, habit ; practical joke ; piece of juggling or out-of-the-way feat ; the cards played in, or the winning of, one round. v.t. cheat or beguile. **trick′ery**, n. deceitful conduct.

tric′kle, v.i. flow drop by drop. n. trickling flow.

trick′ster, n. deceiver, knave.

trick′sy, a. given to pranks.

trick′y, a. crafty ; prone to deceit ; full of pitfalls ; ticklish.

tri′colour (-ŭler), n. French national flag of three vertical stripes of blue, white, and red.

tri′cycle, n. three-wheeled velocipede. v.i. go on tricycle.

tri′dent, n. three-pronged fish-spear borne as sceptre by Neptune and Britannia.

trienn′ial, a. lasting three years ; happening or done every three years. n. triennial plant ; every third anniversary of event.

tri′fle, n. thing of slight value or importance ; small amount ; cold sweet of whipped cream, sponge-cake, &c. v.i. be frivolous ; indulge in levity ; amuse oneself. **tri′fling**, a. of no importance.

trifō′liate, a. three-leaved ; (of leaf) having three leaflets.

trifō′rium, n. (pl. -ia), arcade or gallery above nave and choir arches.

tri′fŏrm, a. having or appearing in three forms.

trig, a. trim, spruce, smart. v.t. smarten, deck ; wedge or prop up ; check motion of (wheel, &c.) with wedge, &c. n. wedge, &c. used to trig wheel.

trigg′er (-g-), n. lever by pressing which a catch is released and some mechanism set in motion, esp. that of a gunlock.

trig′lyph, n. tablet with three vertical grooves occurring at regular intervals in a Doric frieze.

trigonŏm′etry (-k-), n. science of the relations between the sides and the angles of triangles.

trilăt′eral, a. three-sided. n. triangle ; trilateral district, &c.

tril′by, n. soft felt hat of Tyrolean shape ; (pl., sl.) feet.

trilĭng′ual (-nggw-), a. of, in, speaking, three languages.

trill, n. quavering or vibrating sound. v.i. & t. produce trill ; warble ; pronounce with trill.

trill′ion (-lyon), a. & n. a million million million ; *a million million.

tri′lobite, n. kind of fossil crustacean.

tril′ogy, n. set of three connected plays or other literary works.

trim, a. in good order, neat ; not loose or ungainly. v.t. & i. clip or garnish the edges, &c. of (shrub, turf, beard, garment, dish of food, &c.) ; clip (twigs, &c.) off or away ; adjust balance or inclination of (ship, sails) ; (colloq.) rebuke, thrash. n. state of readiness or fitness. **trimm′ing**, n. (esp.) anything used to adorn a garment; (pl.) accessories.

trim′eter, n. verse consisting of three measures.

trinitrotol′uol, **-uene**, nn. a high explosive (abbr. T.N.T.).

trin′ity, n. a union of three parts; *the T~*, the three persons of the Godhead. **Trinitā′rian**, n. believer in the Trinity.

trink′et, n. trifling ornament, esp. one worn on the person.

trinō′mial, **trinom′inal**, aa. employing three names.

tri′ō, n. (pl. *-os*), composition for three parts; set of three performers; three persons, &c.

tri′olet, n. eight-line poem with strict rhyme-scheme.

tri′onal, n. a hypnotic and anaesthetic drug.

trip, v.i. & t. go lightly and quickly along; catch one's foot and stumble; commit a blunder or moral lapse; cause (person) to fall by entangling his feet. ~, n. travelling-excursion, esp. for pleasure; ship's voyage; stumble, tripping-up.

tripart′ite, a. divided into three parts. **tripartī′tion**, n.

tripe, n. part of stomach of ox, &c. as food; (sl.) inferior stuff, nonsense, easy bowling, &c.

tri′plāne, n. aeroplane with three planes.

tri′ple, a. threefold; consisting of three parts. v.t. treble (rare). **trip′let**, n. set of three things, esp. three successive lines of rhyming; (pl.) three children at a birth. **trip′licāte**, v.t.; **trip′licate**, a.; ~ā′tion, n.

tri′pod (*or -I-*), n. three-legged or three-footed stand. **tri′pŏs**, n. honour examination at Cambridge or list of the successful candidates in three classes.

tripp′er, n. person who goes on a pleasure trip, esp. for a day.

trip′tych (*-k*), n. altar-piece, &c. of three folding panels.

trī′rēme, n. ancient warship with three banks of oars.

trisect′, v.t. divide into three equal parts. ~**ion**, n.

trisyll′able, n. word of three syllables. **trisyllăb′ic**, a.

trite, a. well-worn; hackneyed.

tri′ton, n. attendant of the sea-god Poseidon with fish-tail.

trit′ūrate, v.t. (*-rable*), grind to powder or paste. ~**tor**, n.

tri′umph, n. processional entry into anc. Rome of victorious general; being victorious; signal success. v.i. attain victory or success; exult *over*. **triŭm′phal**, a. of or used in or celebrating a triumph. **triŭm′phant**, a. victorious; successful; exultant.

triŭm′vir, n. (pl. *-rs*, *-rī*), member of a board of three. **triŭm′virate**, n. any party or set of three persons.

tri′ūne, n. three in one.

triv′et, n. iron tripod or bracket for kettles, &c. to stand on.

triv′ial, a. ordinary; insignificant; trifling. **triviăl′ity**, n. (esp.) commonplace remark.

trō′chee (*-kī*), n. metrical foot consisting of a long and a short syllable. **trochā′ic** (*-k-*), a. of or in trochees; n.pl. trochaic verse.

trod, trodden, p.t. & p.p. of tread.

trog′lodyte, n. cave-dweller.

Trō′jan, a. of Troy. n. native of Troy; (colloq.) first-class worker or fighter.

troll¹, v.t. & i. sing in snatches; fish by drawing bait along in the water.

troll², n. kinds of supernatural being in Scandinavian mythology.

troll′ey, n. (pl. *-eys*), kinds of low truck; contact-wheel of electric tram-car worked by overhead wire; *electric street-car (also ~car)*.

troll′op, n. disreputable or slatternly girl or woman.

trŏmbōne′, n. powerful instrument of trumpet-kind with sliding tube.

trōop, n. set of congregated persons or animals; captain's cavalry unit; (pl.) embodied soldiers. *v.i.* come together or go along in numbers. **troop'er,** *n.* cavalry private; *member of State police-force.

tro'pæ'olum, *n.* Indian cress, kinds of trailing plant with spurred yellow or scarlet flowers.

trope, *n.* figure of speech.

tro'phy (*or* -ŏ-), *n.* pile of the enemy's spoil set up by ancient army after victory; thing kept as prize or memento.

trop'ic, *n.* parallel of latitude 23° 27′ N. or S. of equator; circle of celestial sphere limiting sun's N. or S. declination; (pl.) the regions of the torrid zone. **trop'ical,** *a.* of or as of the tropics.

trot, *n.* quadruped's medium pace, lifting one fore-foot and hind-foot simultaneously; human being's gentle run; a spell of trotting. *v.i. & t.* go at the trot; (joc.) go on foot; make (horse, &c.) trot. **trot'ters,** *n.pl.* animal's feet as food; (sl.) person's feet.

troth, *n.* faith; fidelity.

tro'tyl, *n.* trinitrotoluol.

trou'badour (-ōō-, -oor), *n.* medieval romantic or amatory poet.

trou'ble (trŭb-), *n.* disquiet; disturbed, harassed, grieved, or incommoded state or its cause; pains bestowed. *v.t. & i.* ruffle (water, peace, &c.); inflict trouble on or be a trouble to; trouble oneself. ~**some,** *a.* causing difficulty or annoyance or discomfort. ~**lous,** *a.*

trough (-awf), *n.* long narrow shallow receptacle for liquid, &c. to stand in; channel or hollow comparable to this.

trounce, *v.t.* (-ceable). inflict severe punishment or defeat on by word or deed.

troupe (-ōō-), *n.* set of acrobats, performing animals, or the like.

trous'ers (-zerz), *n.pl.* loose two-legged outer garment from waist to ankles.

trouss'eau (-ōōsŏ), *n.* (pl. -s *or* -x pr. -z), bride's outfit.

trout, *n.* fresh-water fish yielding sport to fly-fishers. ~**let,** *n.*

tro'ver, *n.* action to recover value of goods wrongfully taken or detained.

trow (-ō), *v.t.* (arch.) think or be of the opinion that.

trow'el, *n.* flat-bladed tool for spreading mortar, &c.; scoop for lifting small plants, &c.

troy, *or* ~**weight,** *nn.* the weight used for gold, silver, and gems.

tru'ant (-ōō-), *n.* child who absents himself from school without leave; person neglecting a duty, &c. **tru'ancy,** *n.*

truce (-ōō-), *n.* cessation of hostilities by agreement for a time.

truck[1], *v.t. & i. & n.* barter, exchange; *small commodities, esp. vegetables raised for market. ~ **system,** paying in goods instead of money.

truck[2], *n.* kinds of vehicle for moving goods or cattle.

truc'kle, *n.* a small wheel or castor; truckle-bed. *v.i.* cringe *to*; act in a servile manner. ~**bed,** a low wheeled bed that can be pushed in below a higher one.

truc'ulent, *a.* of or showing bellicose merciless temper.

trudge, *v.i.* go on foot; toil along. *n.* a walk.

trud'gen, *n.* (also ~ stroke), swimming with alternate right and left over-arm strokes.

true (-ōō), *a.* in accordance with fact or reality; genuine; loyal or faithful or constant (*to*). ~ **bill,** grand jury's verdict sending case for trial.

truf'fle, *n.* subterranean fungus used for seasoning dishes.

tru'ism (-ōō-), *n.* statement too obviously true or too hackneyed to be worth making.

trull, *n.* harlot.

tru'ly (-ōō-), *adv.* with truth; sincerely; loyally; accurately.

trump[1], *n.* (whist, &c.) card of the suit that ranks above other suits for one game; (colloq.) a good fellow. *v.t. & i.* defeat with trump; play a trump. ~ **card,**

zh, as (rou)ge; ė = ɪ; ñ, ûr, = ŏr̄; ȳ, y̆, = ɪ, ɪ; and see p. 4.   * = U.S.

3495   s

card dealt last and deciding which suit is trumps.

trump², *n.* (arch.) trumpet-blast.

trump´ery, *n.* worthless finery; things of no real value; unsound reasoning. *a.* tawdry and worthless; fallacious.

trump´ét, *n.* wind-instrument of loud clear tone; trumpet-toned organ-stop; ear-trumpet. *v.i.* & *t.* blow the trumpet; proclaim loudly, advertise. ~ major, chief trumpeter of cavalry regiment. **trump´éter**, *n.* (esp.) cavalryman giving signals on trumpet.

trun´cate, *v.t.* (-table), cut off the tip of. ~tion, *n.*

trun´cheon (-chn), *n.* short staff or baton as symbol of authority; policeman's short club.

trun´dle, *v.t.* & *i.* roll or bowl along; push or draw (wheel-barrow); bowl at cricket (colloq.).

trunk, *n.* woody stem of tree; person's or animal's body; the main body of anything; elephant's prehensile nose; travelling-box or portmanteau. ~ call, call on telephone trunk-line. ~line, main line of railway, &c.; telephone line from town to town. ~road, main highway.

trunn´ion (-yon), *n.* projection on either side of cannon enabling it to rest on the carriage.

truss, *n.* bundle of hay or straw; timber helping to support roof or bridge; surgical appliance worn on the body in rupture. *v.t.* make into trusses; support with truss(es); tie up (fowl) compactly for cooking.

trust, *n.* firm belief that a person or thing may be relied upon; charge, &c. committed to one; trusteeship; property committed to trustee(s); combination of producing firms designed to prevent outside competition. *v.t.* & *i.* put trust in; treat as reliable; commit to care of; hope earnestly; allow credit to. ~deed, document creating a legal trust. ~worthy, deserving of trust. **trustee´**, *n.* person or

member of board entrusted with the administration of trust property. **trust´ful**, ~ing, *aa.* believing; not given to suspicion. **trus´ty**, *a.* loyal, faithful.

truth (-ōō-), *n.* (*pl. pron.* -dhz) being true or truthful; what is true; a true statement. ~ful, *a.* wont to tell the truth; true.

try, *v.t.* & *i.* (-ier, -iable), test; make severe demands on; make an attempt at; apply or become candidate *for*; (of judge, &c.) examine and pronounce upon (case). *n.* attempt; (Rugby footb.) touching-down of ball by player behind adversaries' goal-line, giving the right to player to carry ball in front of goal and try to score a goal from a place-kick. "~ out, (colloq.) enter as competitor for (prize, &c.). ~sail (-sl), small fore-and-aft sail set with gaff. **try´ing**, *a.* (esp.) exhausting; exasperating; difficult to bear.

try´ansöme, *n.* kinds of blood-parasite.

tryst, *n.* (arch.) time and place for meeting; assignation.

Tsar, &c. See Czar, &c.

tsèt´se, *n.* S.-Afr. fly fatal to horses, cattle, dogs, &c.

tub, *n.* open wooden vessel used for washing and other purposes; (colloq.) sponge-bath or use of it; (colloq.) broad short ship or boat; boat used for rowing practice, as ~pair, -four, &c. (for so many oarsmen). *v.t.* & *i.* bathe in tub; take out (racing crew) in tub-pair, &c., for practice; plant or pack in tub.

tu´ba, *n.* large low-toned trumpet; kind of organ-stop.

tübb´y, *a.* tub-shaped; (of persons) short and fat.

tübe, *n.* long hollow cylinder; structure serving for passage of fluid, &c., or as receptacle; a tubular electric railway.

tü´ber, *n.* one of the swellings formed at the root of some plants and putting forth buds.

tü´bercle, *n.* one of the small

mäte, mēte, mīte, mōte, mūte, mōōt; răck, rĕck, rick, rŏck, rŭck, rŏŏk;

granular tumours formed in the lungs or other organs in consumption. tuberc′ular, *a.* (esp.) of the nature of tuberculosis. tuberculo′sis, disease marked by tubercles and a characteristic bacillus, esp. consumption of the lungs. tuber′ulous, *a.*

tu′berose, -ous, *aa.* having tubers. *n.* (-ose) plant with creamy-white fragrant flowers.

tu′bing, *n.* indefinite length of tube or quantity of tubes.

tu′bular, *a.* tube-shaped; having or consisting of tubes.

tuck, *n.* fold sewn in a garment; (sl.) eatables, esp. sweets, &c. *v.t.* make tuck(s) in (garment); roll or gather *up* (sleeve, skirt, &c.); dispose or stow compactly. ~in, (sl.) eat heartily. ~in, ~out, (sl.) feast. ~shop, pastrycook's, esp. one frequented by schoolboys. tuck′er¹, *n.* (-se) kind of lace or linen falling collar worn by women and children; (sl.) food.

*tuck′er, *v.t.* tire, weary.

Tuesday (tū′zdi), *n.* third day of the week.

tu′fa, tuff, *nn.* kinds of coarse rock.

tuft, *n.* number of feathers, threads, hairs, or grass-blades growing or joined together in a cluster or knot; small chin-beard. ~hunter, one who seeks the society of titled persons. tuf′ty, *a.*

tug, *v.t.* & *i.* pull hard, pull violently at; tow. *n.* hard pull; small powerful steamboat for towing ships. ~of-war, trial of strength between two sides pulling opposite ways on a rope.

tui (tōō′i), *n.* species of New Zealand bird, a mocking-bird, or parson-bird.

tui′tion, *n.* giving of lessons; instruction.

tu′lip, *n.* plant with single bright bell-shaped flower.

tulle (tūl), *n.* soft fine material for veils and dresses.

tul′si (tōōl-), *n.* (E.-Ind.) species of basil, sacred to Vishnu, culti-

vated by the Hindus as a sacred plant.

tul′war, *n.* Indian sabre.

tumasha. See tamasha.

tum′ble, *v.i.* & *t.* have a fall; suffer downfall; turn somersaults and do acrobatic feats; toss to and fro; disarrange, rumple. *n.* a bodily fall; untidy state. ~down, in ruinous state; in bad repair. tumb′ler, *n.* (esp.) acrobat; kinds of pigeon with peculiar flight; stemless drinking-glass. ~ful, *a.*

tum′brel, -il, *n.* tip-cart, esp. for dung; ammunition cart.

tu′mid, *a.* swollen, swelling, inflated, pompous. tumid′ity, *n.*

tu′mour (-mer), *n.* a local swelling, esp. from morbid growth.

tum′-tum, *n.* W.-Ind. dish of boiled plantains beaten soft in a mortar. tum′-tum², *n.* (Anglo-Ind.) light vehicle, dog-cart.

tu′mult, *n.* riot, angry demonstration of a mob; uproar or din; confused state of mind. ~uous, *a.* vehement, uproarious.

tu′mulus, *n.* (pl. -lī) sepulchral mound.

tun, *n.* large cask for wine; brewer's fermenting-vat.

*tu′na, *n.* Californian tunny.

tune, *n.* the succession of notes or chords forming the music of a song or other piece; melody or air; correct intonation in singing or playing. *v.t.* & *i.* (-nable) adjust the notes of (piano, &c.) or the instruments of (band) to be in tune with each other; (fig.) be in harmony *with.* tuning-fork, implement giving a particular note when struck. tune′ful (-fl), *a.* melodious.

tung′sten, *n.* a metallic element.

tu′nic, *n.* kinds of sleeved garment extending below waist; (colloq.) undress military coat, esp. of private; (Zool.) leathery envelope of ascidia, &c.; (Anat.) membrane enclosing an organ.

tunn′el, *n.* artificial subterranean passage. *v.i.* & *t.* make tunnel; make one's way by tunnelling.

tunn′y, *n.* large edible sea-fish.

tŭp, n. (dial.) a ram.

tū·pélo, n. kinds of large tree growing in swamps in southern U.S.

tuque (tūk), n. kind of Canadian knitted cap.

‖ tū quŏ´que, n. answer made to a charge by accusing the accuser of the same thing.

tŭrb´an, n. man's oriental headdress of coiled linen or silk; kinds of woman's brimless hat.

tŭrb´ĭd, a. muddy, thick; not clear or lucid. turbĭd´itў, n.

tŭrb´ine, n. kinds of rotary motor driven by water or air or steam.

tŭrb´ot, n. large flat-fish.

tŭrb´ūlent, a. given to making disturbances; riotous, insubordinate. tŭrb´ūlence, n.

Tūrc´ō, n. (pl. -os), member of French Algerian troops. ~phil, ~phobe, see Turk.

tūreen´, n. deep covered dish for soup.

tŭrf, n. short grass with the surface earth bound together by its roots; the ~, horse-racing; (Ir.) peat or a slice of it cut as fuel. v.t. lay (ground) with turf. tŭrf´ў, a.

tŭr´gĭd, a. (of language, &c.) bombastic, rhetorical. turgĭd´itў, n.

Tŭrk, n. member of the Ottoman race; an unmanageable child. Tūrc´ophil, a. & n. friendly to, friend of, the Turks. ~phobe, a. & n. opposing, or opponent of, the Turks.

Tŭrk´ey, t~, n. (pl. -eys), the country ruled by the Turks; large bird bred as food. ~buzzard, kind of vulture. T~ carpet, of a kind made in Turkey. ~cock, male turkey noted for its strut and gobble; (fig.) pompous person. T~stone, kind used for hones.

Tŭrk´ish, a. of Turkey or the Turks. n. the Turkish language. ~ bath, hot-air bath followed by massage and other treatment. ~ delight, kind of sweetmeat.

Tŭrk´oman, n. (pl. -ns), member of certain Central-Asian Tartar tribes.

tŭrm´eric, n. powdered root used as dye-stuff, stimulant, and condiment.

tŭrm´oil, n. din; commotion.

tŭrn, v.t. & i. move partly or completely round; face or make face in another direction; place with another side up; diverge; have recourse to; subject to or undergo a change of substance, form, or quality; shape in lathe; turn sour. n. act or fact or process of turning; changed direction; road, &c. diverging from another; alternation, rotation, or regular succession; single part of such alternation; act of kindness or malice. ~buckle, device for connecting parts of metal rod. ~coat, person who changes sides. ~cock, man regulating water from the main. ~down, (colloq.) reject (proposal, its maker, &c.). ~in, go into a house, &c. in passing; go to bed. ~out, (esp.) equipage. ~over, semicircular tart made by folding pastry on itself; amount turned over in trade. ~pike, bar or gate across road for toll-collecting. ~screw, screwdriver. ~spit, (hist.) one who turned a spit, (contempt.) one engaged in a menial occupation. ~stile, revolving barrier on a footpath; admission-gate with four revolving arms. ~ turtle, capsize. tŭrn´er, n. (esp.) lathe-worker. tŭrn´erў, n. (esp.) wooden articles made on lathe. tŭrn´ing, n. (esp.) road diverging from larger one.

tŭrn´ip, n. plant with root used as vegetable and fodder.

tŭrp´entine, n. kinds of resin got from terebinth and other trees; oil made from turpentine.

tŭrp´eth, n. cathartic root of an E.-Ind. plant.

tŭrp´ĭtūde, n. baseness.

tŭrq´uoise (-koiz), n. opaque azure gem.

tū´rret, n. small tower forming part of a building; circular iron tower for gun and gunners in ship or fort. ~ed, a.

tŭr'tle¹, *n.* kinds of dove noted for cooing and amativeness.

tŭr'tle², *n.* marine reptile encased in horny shell; turtle soup. ~ soup, made from the green turtle.

tŭsh, *int.* of contempt or annoyance (arch.). **tŭsh'erў**, *n.* literary use of archaisms such as *tush*.

tŭsk, *n.* long pointed tooth, esp. one projecting from mouth as in elephant or boar.

tusser. See tussore.

tŭs'sive, *a.* of a cough.

tŭs'sle, *n.* & *v.i.* struggle, wrestle.

tŭss'ock, *n.* clump of grass, &c.

tŭss'ŏre, tŭss'er, *n.* kinds of Indian silk-worm; their silk; fabric made from it.

tŭt, *int.* of impatience.

tū'telage, *n.* guardianship; restraint exercised over another's conduct. **tū'telarў**, *a.* giving protection.

tū'tĕnäg, *n.* white alloy like German silver; imported from China and E. Indies.

tū'tor, *n.* private teacher; college official directing studies of undergraduates; (Law) guardian of a minor. *v.t.* & *i.* make one's living as tutor; exercise restraint over. ~ess, *n.*; ~ŏr'ial, *a.*; ~ship, *n.*

***tŭxĕ'dō**, *n.* dinner-jacket.

twa'ddle (-ŏ-), *n.* talk not worth hearing. *v.i.* utter twaddle.

twain, arch. form of two.

twăng, *n.* sound made by plucking string of banjo, harp, bow, &c.; quality of voice compared to this. *v.i.* & *t.* emit or make twang.

tweak, *v.t.* grip with fingers or beak and twist or jerk. *n.* such grip and jerk; (sl.) dodge. **tweak'er**, *n.* (sl.) catapult.

tweed, *n.* rough-surfaced cloth used for clothes.

tween'ў, *n.* between-maid, servant assisting two others; (also) small cheap cigar.

tweez'ers (-z), *n.pl.* minute pincers for pulling out hairs or picking up small objects.

twĕlfth, *a.* next in order after eleventh. *n.* each of twelve equal parts; *the* ~, 12 Aug. as opening day of grouse-shooting. Twelfthday, the Epiphany, 6 Jan. ~-night, the night of Twelfthday, formerly celebrated with games and feasting.

twelve, *a.* & *n.* one more than eleven, 12, XII. ~fold, *a.* & *adv.* ~month, period equal in length to a year. ~mo, or 12mo, sheet folded into 12 leaves; book of such size.

twĕn'tў, *a.* & *n.* twice ten, 20, XX. ~fold, *a.* & *adv.* **twĕn'tiĕth**, *a.* & *n.* ~four-mo or 24mo, sheet folded into 24 leaves; book of such size.

twice, *adv.* two times, on two occasions; doubly.

twid'dle, *v.t.* twist idly about. *n.* act of twiddling.

twig¹, *n.* any of the minor shoots of a tree or shrub.

twig², *v.t.* & *i.* (colloq.) observe, notice; catch the meaning of.

twi'light (-īt), *n.* the half light following sunset and preceding sunrise.

twill, *n.* fabric so woven as to have a surface of parallel ridges. *v.t.* weave thus (usu. *p.p.*).

twin, *n.* (pl.) two persons born at a birth; (sing.) one of twins; person or thing that is the counterpart of another. *a.* born as (one of) twins; consisting of two similar parts.

twine, *n.* cord twisted to the thickness used for tying small parcels. *v.t.* & *i.* (-nable), make (string, &c.) by twisting strands; coil or wind round or about something.

twinge (-j), *n.* a transitory sharp pain.

twinkle (twing'kl), *v.i.* shine with rapidly pulsating or dancing light; sparkle; (of eyelids and eyes) close and open. *n.* twinkling; slight flash of light; gleam of amusement in eyes or face.

twĭrl, *v.t.* spin or swing or twist quickly and lightly round. *n.* twirling motion; pen-flourish.

twist, *v.t.* & *i.* wind (strands) about

each other; distort; wrench out of shape; (of ball, river, &c.) take curved course. *n.* twisting; twisted state; a moral obliquity or mental peculiarity; kinds of mixed drink; (sl.) hunger.

twit, *v.t.* taunt (*with*).

twitch, *v.t.* & *i.* give a momentary sharp pull at; quiver or jerk spontaneously. *n.* sharp light pull; slight muscular strain.

twitt'er, *v.i.* (of birds) utter a succession of tremulous sounds. *n.* twittering; state of tremor.

two (tōō), *a.* & *n.* one more than one, 2, II. ~edged, having an edge on both sides; (fig.) cutting both ways, ambiguous. ~fold, *a.* & *adv.* ~handed, to be wielded with both hands; (of game, &c.) for two players. ~pence (tŭp'ns), 2*d.* ~penny (tŭp'eni), *a.* costing 2*d.*; (colloq.) insignificant; *n.* kind of beer; (sl.) one's head. ~ply, of two strands or layers. ~some, *n.* two-handed game.

tyke, *n.* (colloq.) a cur.

tym'panum, *n.* (pl. -na), drum of the ear; (Archit.) space enclosed in a pediment or between a lintel and an arch above.

Tŷ'nwald (-wŏld), *n.* Isle of Man legislature.

type, *n.* person, thing, or event serving as illustration, symbol, or specimen; a letter or other character used in printing; collection or fount of this. *v.t.* & *i.* (-pable) execute on or use typewriter. ~setter, compositor. ~writer, keyed machine enabling user to produce printed characters instead of writing.

tŷ'phoid, *a.* & *n.* (also ~ *fever*), a fever attacking the intestines.

typhoon', *n.* violent hurricane of the China seas. typhon'ic, *a.*

tŷ'phus, *n.* a contagious fever.

typ'ical, *a.* true to type; fit to serve as a type; characteristic.

typ'ify, *v.t.* (-fiable) represent by a type; foreshadow; be a type of. ~fica'tion, *n.*

tŷ'pist, *n.* user of typewriter.

tȳpŏg'raphy, *n.* printing as an art. typograph'ic, ~al, *aa.*

tȳrann'ical (*or tȳ-*), *a.* given to or characteristic of tyranny.

tȳrann'icide (*or tȳ-*), *n.* killer or killing of a tyrant.

tȳ'rannize, *v.i.* exercise tyranny (usu. *over*).

tȳ'ranny, *n.* cruel and arbitrary use of authority.

tȳr'ant, *n.* oppressive or cruel sovereign or commander or master.

tȳre[1], *n.* (Anglo-Ind.) curdled milk and cream.

tȳre[2], tyro. See tire, tiro.

Tzar. See Czar.

U

U, u (ū), *letter,* and *n.* U-boat, German submarine. U-bolt, U-tube, &c., shaped like U.

ūbiq'uity, *n.* being everywhere or in an indefinite number of places at once. ~tous, *a.*

ŭdd'er, *n.* mammary glands of cattle, &c. ~less, *a.*

ŭg'lȳ, *a.* unpleasing or repulsive to sight; vile; threatening; *ill-natured, quarrelsome. ŭg'liĭy, *v.t.* (colloq.) ~ness, *n.*

Uh'lan (ōōl-, ŭl-), *n.* lancer, esp. of German army.

ūkāse', *n.* Russian edict.

ŭl'cer, *n.* open sore on external or internal surface of body; (fig.) corrupting influence. ~ed (-erd), ~ous, *aa.* ŭl'cerate, *v.i.* & *t.*

ŭl'na, *n.* (pl. -ae), inner of two bones of fore-arm. ŭl'nar, *a.*

ŭl'ster, *n.* long loose overcoat.

ŭlter'ior, *a.* situated beyond; not immediate; beyond what is seen or avowed.

ŭl'timate, *a.* last, final; fundamental or primary. ŭltima'tum, *n.* final statement of terms.

ŭl'timō, *adv.* (abbr. *ult.*), in last month.

ŭl'tra, *n.* advocate of extreme views or measures.

ultra-, prefixed to adjj. and their derivatives with the sense 'beyond what is usual or reasonable'.

---

māte, mēte, mīte, mōte, mūte, mōōt; răck, rĕck, rĭck, rŏck, rŭck, rōōk

ŭltramarine′ (-ēn), a. situated beyond sea. n. a blue pigment.

ŭltramŏn′tāne, a. situated south of the Alps; favourable to the absolute authority of the Pope. n. ultramontane person.

ŭltra-vī′olĕt, a. (of invisible rays of the spectrum) beyond the violet rays.

‖ ŭl′tra vīr′ēs (-z), beyond one's power or authority.

ŭ′lūlāte, v.i. howl, hoot. ~tion, n.

ŭm′bel, n. an inflorescence in which flower-stalks spring from one point and form a corymblike flower-head. ŭmbellate, ŭmbellif′erous, aa.

ŭm′ber, n. natural pigment like ochre but darker and browner. a. umber-coloured.

ŭmbilical (-bĭlĭ′- or -bĭl′ĭ-), a. of or connected with the navel; central. ŭmbĭl′icate, a. navel-shaped. ŭmbĭl′icus, n. navel (Bot., &c.) navel-like formation.

ŭm′brage, n. sense of slight or injury; offence; shade, what gives shade. ŭmbrāge′ous (-jŭs), a. abounding in shade.

ŭmbrĕll′a, n. light circular canopy of silk, &c. on stick carried in hand as protection against rain, folded up when not in use.

umlaut (ōōm′lowt), n. vowel-change due to partial assimilation to a following sound.

ŭm′pīre, n. person chosen to decide question; person chosen to pronounce decisions in cricket, &c. v.i. act as umpire.

ŭm′pteen, a. (sl.) a good many.

ŭn-, pref. (1) before adj. = 'not', 'the reverse of'; (2) before nouns = 'lack of', 'freedom from'; (3) before verbs = 'undo', 'remove'. Words with this prefix being practically unlimited, many of those with an obvious meaning are not given here.

ŭnabashed′, a. not ashamed.

ŭnabā′tĕd, a. in full strength.

ŭnaccom′panied (-ŭm-), a. not attended; without accompaniment.

ŭnaccom′plished, a. unfinished; lacking accomplishments.

ŭnaccoun′table, a. not to be explained; (of persons) not responsible.

ŭnaccŭs′tomed, a. not usual.

ŭnadvī′sĕdlў (-z-), adv. indiscreetly, imprudently.

ŭnaffec′tĕd, a. free from affectation; sincere; not affected by.

ŭnalloyed′, a. unmixed; pure.

ŭnanim′ity, n. agreement.

ŭnăn′imous, a. all of one mind; held or given with one accord.

ŭnan′swerable (-ahnser-), a. that cannot be refuted.

ŭnas′ked, a. (esp.) spontaneous.

ŭnassū′ming, a. making little of one's own merits or status.

ŭnattăch′ed, a. not belonging to particular regiment or college, &c.

ŭnawāre′, a. not aware (of).

unawares (ŭnawārz′), adv. unexpectedly; by surprise.

ŭnbăc′ked, a. unsupported; having no backers (esp. in betting); (of horse) unbroken.

ŭnbăl′anced, a. (esp., of the mind) disordered, violently impulsive.

ŭnbănk′, v.t. cause (fire) to burn by removing ashes from top.

ŭnbăr′, v.t. remove bar from (gate, &c.); unlock, open (often fig.).

ŭnbea′ten, a. not beaten; not surpassed.

ŭnbecom′ing (-ŭm-), a. indecorous, not befitting; not suited to.

unbeknown, -st (ŭnbĭnōn′; colloq.), adv. not known.

ŭnbelief′, n. incredulity; disbelief. ŭnbeliev′er, n. atheist, agnostic. ~ing, a. atheistic or agnostic; unduly incredulous.

ŭnbend′, v.t. & i. change from bent position; straighten; relax from strain; be affable. ~ing, a. inflexible; austere.

ŭnbĭd′den, a. not commanded; not invited.

ŭnblŭsh′ing, a. shameless.

ŭnbos′om (-bŏŏz-), v.t. pour out (secrets, &c.); relieve (oneself) of.

ŭnboun′dĕd, a. (esp.) infinite.

ŭnbrī′dlĕd, a. unrestrained.

ŭnbrō′ken, a. not broken; not subdued; not interrupted.

---

unbŭrd´en, v.t. (esp.) relieve (one-self) by confession, &c.

uncall´ed-for (-kawl-), a. impertinently intruded.

uncănn´y̆, a. weird, mysterious.

uncerémo´nious, a. informal; abrupt; wanting in courtesy.

uncert´ain (-tin), a. not certainly knowing or known; not to be depended on; changeable.

unchan´cy̆ (-ahn-),a. (Sc.) unlucky; unseasonable; uncanny.

unchă´ritable, a. (esp.) censorious; severe in judgement.

unchristian (-kris´tyan), a. contrary to the Christian character.

unchurch´, v.t. deprive of status as a church; excommunicate.

un´cial (-shl), a. of, written in, a kind of writing resembling capitals found in 4th-8th cent. MSS. n, uncial letter or MS.

uncîrc´umcised (-zd), a. (fig.) heathen; unregenerate.

unciv´il, a. ill-mannered; rude.

uncle (ŭng´kl), n. father's or mother's brother, aunt's husband; (sl.) pawnbroker.

unclean´, a. not clean, foul; unchaste; ceremonially impure.

unco´ŏ, adv. (Sc.) very; exceptionally.

uncock´, v.t. let down hammer of (gun) gently.

uncoil´, v.t. unwind.

uncome-ăt´-able (-um-),a. (colloq.) not accessible or attainable.

uncomely (-kŭm´li), a. wanting grace or beauty.

uncŏmm´on, a. unusual, remarkable. adv. (colloq.) remarkably.

uncommū´nicative, a. reserved.

uncŏm´promising (-z-), a. refusing compromise; unyielding.

unconcern´, n. freedom from anxiety; indifference. ~ed, a. free from anxiety. ~edly, adv.

uncondi´tional, a. not subject to conditions; absolute.

uncŏn´scionable (-sho-), a. inconsiderate; making excessive or shameless demands.

uncon´scious (-shus), a. not aware of; devoid of consciousness.

unconsid´ered (-erd),a.disregarded.

unconstitu´tional, a. opposed to a country's constitution.

unconstraint´, n. freedom from constraint. ~ned, a.

unconvĕn´tional (-sho-), a. not bound by convention or custom; free in character or treatment.

uncork´, v.t. draw cork from (bottle); give vent to (feelings).

uncou´ple (-kŭ-), v.t. release (dogs, &c.) from couples or coupling.

uncouth´ (-ōō-), a. strikingly lacking in ease or polish.

unco´venanted (-kŭ-), a. not based on or subject to a covenant.

unco´ver (-kŭ-), v.t. & i. remove covering from; disclose.

uncrit´ical, a. disinclined or incompetent to criticize; not according to the principles of criticism.

uncrow´ned, a. (esp.) of person having power but not office of a king.

unc´tion, n. anointing for medical purposes or as rite; thing used in anointing; affected enthusiasm; gush; gusto. unc´tuous, a. full of unction; greasy.

uncŭt´, a. (esp. of book) with full untrimmed margins.

undaun´tĕd, a. fearless.

undĕceive´,v.t. free from deception. ~d, a. not deceived.

undĕci´dĕd, a. not settled; irresolute.

undĕfĕn´dĕd, a. (esp. of suit) in which no defence is put in.

undĕmŏn´strative, a. not given to showing strong feelings.

undĕnī´able, a. that cannot be denied or disputed.

undĕnŏminā´tional, a. (esp.) of no particular sect.

un´der, prep. in or to a position lower than; below; inferior to, less than; liable to; bound by; in the time of. adv. in or to a lower place or subordinate position.

underăct´, v.t. act inadequately.

underbid´, v.t. make bid for custom lower than (another).

underbred´, a. vulgar, ill-bred.

undercharge´, v.t. charge too little for (thing) or to (person).

un'derclothes (-ōz, -ōdhz), *n.pl.* clothes worn beneath outside garments.

un'dercroft (-craw-), *n.* crypt.

un'dercurrent, *n.* current flowing beneath surface (often fig.).

undercut', *v.t.* reduce (prices) in competition; (Golf) hit (ball) so that it rises high.

underdo' (-ōō), *v.t.* cook insufficiently (esp. in p.p. *underdone*).

underdress', *v.t.* & *i.* dress too plainly or lightly.

under-ēs'timate, *v.t.* form too low an estimate of.

undergō', *v.t.* be subjected to; suffer.

undergrăd'uate, *n.* student beneath rank of graduate.

un'derground', *adv.* & *a.* beneath the ground.

un'derhănd¹, *adv.* & *a.* clandestine(ly); not above-board.

un'derhănd², *a.* & *n.* (Crick.) (bowling) from level of the knee.

underlay', *v.t.* lay something under (thing), esp. (Print.) lay paper under (types, illustrations) to secure a better impression. *n.* piece of paper for underlaying.

underlĕt', *v.t.* sublet.

underlie', *v.t.* lie or be situated under (stratum, &c.); be the basis of (conduct, &c.).

underline', *v.t.* draw line under (word, &c.) to secure emphasis or represent italics. *n.* (ŭn'der-), (Print.) descriptive line(s) below an illustration.

un'derlinen, *n.* linen or other underclothing.

un'derling, *n.* a subordinate.

underman', *v.t.* furnish (ship, &c.) with too few men.

undermine', *v.t.* make mine or excavation under (injure (reputation, &c.) by secret means; injure (health, &c.) insidiously.

un'dermōst, *a.* in lowest place.

underneath', *adv.* & *prep.* at or to a lower place (than); below.

underpay', *v.t.* pay (workmen) inadequately.

underpin', *v.t.* place support of masonry under (wall, bank).

un'derplŏt, *n.* subordinate plot of play or novel.

underprŏp', *v.t.* put prop under.

underquōte', *v.t.* announce lower price than (other dealer).

underrāte', *v.t.* under-estimate.

undersĕll', *v.t.* sell cheaper than (person).

undersigned' (-sīn-), *a.* whose signature(s) appear(s) below.

undersized', *a.* of less than the usual size.

understănd', *v.t.* & *i.* (-stŏŏd), comprehend, perceive the meaning of; infer; take for granted; supply (word) mentally.

understand'ing, *n.* intelligence, intellect, insight; thing agreed upon; stipulation; (pl., sl.) feet, legs, shoes, &c.

understāte', *v.t.* put (numbers, &c.) too low. **—ment**, *n.*

understŏck', *v.t.* supply (farm, &c.) with insufficient stock.

un'derstrăpper, *n.* a subordinate.

un'derstŭdy, *n.* one who studies theatrical part in order to replace usual actor at short notice. *v.t.* be understudy of.

undertāke', *v.t.* & *i.* (-tŏŏk, -tāken; -takable), bind oneself to perform; make oneself responsible for. **un'dertāker**, *n.* (esp.) one who manages funerals. **undertā'king**, *n.* (esp.) task, enterprise, **un'dertāking**, *n.* management of funerals as a trade.

undertĕn'ant, *n.* tenant's tenant.

un'dertōne, *n.* subdued tone, esp. in speaking; subdued colour.

un'derwear (-wār), *n.* underclothing.

un'derwood, *n.* brushwood.

un'derworld (-wĕr-), *n.* antipodes; infernal regions; lowest social stratum.

underwrite', *v.t.* & *i.* (esp.) sign and deliver (policy of insurance); practise marine insurance. **un'derwriter**, *n.* marine insurer.

undėsīgn'ėdly (-zīn-), *adv.* without intention.

un'dies, *n.pl.* (sl.) underclothing.

undigĕs'tėd, *a.* (esp. fig., of facts, &c.) ill-arranged.

ŭndĭg'nĭfĭed, *a.* lacking or inconsistent with dignity.

ŭndĭsguis'édlỹ (-ĭz-), *adv.* openly, without disguise.

ŭndo' (-ōō), *v.t.* annul; unfasten (parcel, coat, &c.); ruin the prospects or reputation of. **ŭndone'** (-dŭn), not done; ruined.

ŭndoub'tédlỹ (-owt-), *adv.* without doubt.

ŭndress'¹, *v.t. & i.* take off the clothes of; take off one's clothes.

ŭn'dress², *n.* ordinary dress, opp. to full dress or uniform (often fig. and attrib.).

ŭndue', *a.* excessive; disproportionate; improper.

ŭn'dūlāte, *v.i.* have wavy motion or look. **~ā'tion**, *n.* wavy motion or form; gentle rise and fall. **~tory**, *a.* rising and falling.

ŭndū'lỹ, *adv.* wrongly, improperly; excessively.

ŭndy'ĭng, *a.* immortal.

ŭnearth' (-ẽr-), *v.t.* draw out from concealment; discover. **~lỹ**, *a.* supernatural, not of this world; weird.

ŭnĕcŏnŏm'ĭc, *a.* (esp. of rent) too low to repay owner and builder.

ŭnea'sỹ (-z-), *a.* disturbed or uncomfortable in body or mind.

ŭnĕmploy'able, *a. & n.* (person) unfitted or unsuitable for paid employment. **ŭnĕmploy'ed**, *a.* not used; lacking employment. **ŭnĕmploy'ment**, *n.* lack of employment; state of things in which many workers cannot find work.

ŭnĕnd'ĭng, *a.* having no end.

ŭnē'qual, *a.* not equal *to*; of varying quality.

ŭnĕquĭv'ocal, *a.* not ambiguous; plain; unmistakable.

ŭnĕrr'ĭng, *a.* not erring or failing or missing the mark.

ŭnĕssĕn'tial (-shl), *a.* not essential; not of the first importance.

ŭnē'ven, *a.* not level or smooth; not uniform or equable.

ŭnexam'pled (-ĭgzah-), *a.* without precedent.

ŭnĕxcĕp'tionable (-shon-), *a.* with which no fault can be found.

ŭnĕxpīred', *a.* still running.

ŭnfail'ĭng, *a.* not failing; not running short.

ŭnfair', *a.* not equitable or honest or impartial.

ŭnfă'shioned (-shn-), *a.* not brought into shape.

ŭnfa'sten (-ahsn-), *v.t.* unloose; unfix. **~ed**, *a.* not secured.

ŭnfeel'ĭng, *a.* lacking sensibility; harsh; cruel.

ŭnfeign'édlỹ (-ān-), *adv.* sincerely.

ŭnfĕm'ĭnine, *a.* (esp.) not beseeming a woman.

ŭnfĭt', *a.* not fit, unsuitable. *v.t.* make unsuitable *for*. **~ted**, *a.* not fit, not fitted. **~tĭng**, *a.* unsuitable.

ŭnfĭx', *v.t.* loosen, detach.

ŭnflédged', *a.* (fig.) undeveloped.

ŭnfōld', *v.t. & i.* spread out; reveal; become opened out; develop.

ŭnformed', *a.* shapeless.

ŭnfōr'tūnate, *a.* unlucky; unhappy; ill-advised. *n.* unfortunate person.

ŭnfoun'déd, *a.* without foundation; not yet founded.

ŭnfūn'déd, *a.* (of debt) floating; not funded.

ŭnfurl', *v.t. & i.* spread out (sail, &c.); become spread out.

ŭnfūr'nished, *a.* not supplied *with*; without furniture.

ŭngain'lỹ, *a.* ill-made; awkward-looking; clumsy.

ŭngăllant' (-găl'ant), *a.* not attentive to women; not brave.

ŭngĕn'tle, *a.* harsh; rude; ill-bred. **~manly**, *a.* violating the code observed by gentlemen.

ŭngo'vernable (-gŭ-), *a.* unruly; licentious; wild; violent.

ŭngrā'cious (-shus), *a.* not kindly or courteous.

ŭngrammăt'ĭcal, *a.* contrary to rules of grammar.

ŭngroun'déd, *a.* unfounded.

ŭngrŭdg'ĭng, *a.* done or given with good will.

ŭnguar'ded (-găr-), *a.* not guarded; incautious; thoughtless.

ŭng'uent (-nggw-), *n.* any soft substance used as ointment or for lubrication.

ŭng′ŭlate (-ngg-), *a.* hoofed. *n.* hoofed mammal.

ŭnhăll′owed (-ō-), *a.* having evil associations; unholy.

ŭnhănd′, *v.t.* take one's hands off (person).

ŭnhăn′dў, *a.* not dexterous; clumsy.

ŭnhăpp′ў, *a.* unlucky; wretched.

ŭnhealth′ў (-hĕl-), *a.* sickly; not conducive to health.

ŭnhinge′ (-j), *v.t.* remove from the hinges; (fig.) make crazy.

ŭnho′lў, *a.* impious, wicked.

ŭnhōōk′, *v.t.* open (dress, &c.) by detaching its hooks.

ŭnhôrse′, *v.t.* throw (rider) from the saddle, cause to dismount.

ŭnhouse′, *v.t.* deprive of shelter; drive from house.

ŭnĭcăm′eral, *a.* one-chambered.

ū′nĭcôrn, *n.* fabulous animal with horse's body and single straight horn; narwhal; kinds of horned beetle, &c.

ū′nĭform, *a.* unvarying; conforming to same rule. *n.* uniform dress worn by members of same body. **ū′niform′itў**, *n.* being uniform; sameness; consistency.

ū′nĭfў, *v.t.* (-fiable), make one or uniform. ~fication, *n.*

ŭnĭlăt′eral, *a.* (of contracts, &c.) binding one side only.

ŭnĭlĭt′eral, *a.* (of word-roots, &c.) consisting of one letter.

ŭnĭmpeach′able, *a.* giving no opening to censure.

ŭnĭnform′ed′ (-md), *a.* ignorant; uninstructed.

ŭnĭnspired′, *a.* commonplace.

ŭnĭntĕll′ĭgĭble, *a.* not such as can be understood.

ŭnĭnvi′ting, *a.* unattractive.

ū′nĭon (-yon), *n.* uniting together; coalition; marriage; concord, agreement; parishes consolidated for administration of poor-laws; workhouse of such union; fabric of mixed materials. **U~ Jack**, national ensign of United Kingdom. *~ suit, combinations* **ū′nĭonĭsm** [(garment). **ū′nĭonĭst** (-nyo-), *n.* member of a trade-union; upholder of legislative

union between Great Britain and Ireland. ~ism, *n.*

ūnique′ (-ēk), *a.* being the only one of its kind; having no like or equal or parallel.

ūnĭsĕx′ŭal, *a.* having pistil or stamens but not both.

ū′nĭson, *n.* unity of pitch; concord; agreement.

ū′nĭt, *n.* the number one; individual thing, person, or group; quantity chosen as standard by which other things may be expressed.

ūnĭtā′rĭan, *n.* one who denies doctrine of the Trinity. ~ism, *n.*

ū′nĭtarў, *a.* of unit or units.

ūnite′, *v.t. & i.* (-table), join together; make or become one; combine; consolidate; agree.

ū′nĭtў, *a.* oneness; being one or single or individual; concord.

ū′nĭvălve, *n.* mollusc of one valve.

ū′nĭvers′al, *a.* general; belonging to or done by all persons or things; applicable to all cases. **ū′niversăl′itў**, *n.* **ūnivers′alĭze**, *v.t.* (-zable), treat as or make universal.

ū′nĭverse, *n.* all existing things; all creation; all mankind. **ū′nĭvers′itў**, *n.* educational institution for instruction or examination of students, with the power of conferring degrees.

ŭnkĕmpt′ (ŭn-k-), *a.* of rough or uncared-for appearance.

ŭnknown′ (un-nōn), *a.* not known; unidentified. *n.* unknown person or quantity.

ŭnlā′boured (-berd), *a.* (of style) easy, spontaneous.

ŭnlearn′ (-lêrn), *v.t.* expel from one's memory; rid oneself of (false information, habit, &c.). ~ed (-ĭd), *a.* not well educated. **ŭnlearnt** (-lêrnt), or ~ned (-nd), *a.* (of lesson, &c.) not learnt.

ŭnleash′, *v.t.* remove leash of (dog); also used fig.

ŭnlea′vened (-lĕ-), *a.* not mixed with fermenting matter.

ŭnlĕss′, *conj.* if not; except when.

ŭnlĕtt′ered (-erd), *a.* illiterate.

ŭnlicked′, *a.* not licked into shape; (sl.) undefeated.

unlike', *a. & prep.* not like.

unlike'ly, *a.* improbable; unpromising.

unlim'ber, *v.t.* detach (gun, guncarriage) from limber.

unlim'ited, *a.* boundless; unrestricted; very numerous.

unload', *v.t.* remove load from (ship, cart, &c.); withdraw charge from (gun, &c.).

unlock', *v.t.* release lock of (door, &c.); (fig.) open the mind.

unlooked'-for, *a.* not expected.

unloose', *v.t.* loose; untie.

unlove'ly (-lŭv'-), *a.* not amiable or attractive.

unluck'y, *a.* unfortunate; unsuccessful; hapless; ill-contrived.

unmake', *v.t.* destroy; annul.

unman', *v.t.* deprive of manly qualities; cause to weep, &c.

unman'ageable, *a.* not manageable; uncontrollable.

unman'nerly, *a.* rude; ill-bred.

unmarked', *a.* not marked; unobserved.

unmask' (-mah-), *v.t. & i.* remove mask from; take off one's mask; show up (villainy).

unmatched', *a.* unrivalled.

unmean'ing, *a.* without meaning.

unmeant' (-měnt), *a.* not intended.

unmeasured (-mězh'erd), *a.* not measured; unbounded.

unmen'tionable, *a.* too bad to be mentioned.

unmer'ciful, *a.* cruel; severe.

unmer'ited, *a.* not deserved.

unmista'kable, *a.* that cannot be mistaken or doubted.

unmit'igated, *a.* unqualified; absolute.

unmoor', *v.t.* loose the moorings of (vessel, &c.).

unmoved' (-ōōvd), *a.* not moved; not changed in purpose.

unmu'sical, *a.* unskilled in or indifferent to music.

unmuz'zle, *v.t.* (esp. fig.) relieve of obligation to remain silent.

unna'mable, *a.* too bad to be named.

unna'tural, *a.* contrary to or doing violence to nature; lacking natural feelings; artificial.

unne'cessary, *a.* not necessary; more than is necessary.

unnerve', *v.t.* deprive of nerve or strength or resolution.

unnum'bered (-erd), *a.* countless.

unoffend'ing, *a.* harmless.

unoffi'cial (-shl), *a.* (esp. of news) not officially confirmed.

unpack', *v.t.* open and remove contents of (box, package, &c.).

unpaid', *a.* remaining due.

unpaired', *a.* (esp. of M.P.) absent from division without pairing.

unpa'ralleled, *a.* having no parallel or equal.

unparliamen'tary (-la-), *a.* contrary to parliamentary usage.

unpeople (-pē'pl), *v.t.* depopulate.

unpick', *v.t.* undo sewing of garment, &c.; take out (stitches).

unplaced', *a.* not placed, esp. in race or list.

unplay'able, *a.* not playable, esp. of ball or serve in games.

unplea'sant (-lěz-), *a.* disagreeable. **~ness**, *n.* (esp.) misunderstanding; quarrel.

unpolled', *a.* (of electors, votes) not polled or recorded.

unpop'ular, *a.* disliked.

unprac'tised, *a.* not experienced; not put into practice.

unprec'edented, *a.* for which there is no previous example.

unprej'udiced (-jŏŏ-), *a.* impartial.

unpremed'itated, *a.* not deliberately planned.

unpresen'table (-z-), *a.* not fit to be presented to company; not fit to be seen.

unpretend'ing, *a.* not given to display; making little show.

unprin'cipled (-ld), *a.* lacking good moral principles; without principle.

unprofes'sional (-sho-), *a.* not belonging to a profession; contrary to professional etiquette.

unprof'itable, *a.* without profit; serving no purpose.

unprovi'ded, *a.* not supplied (with money, &c.); not prepared.

unprovoked', *a.* without provocation.

---

unpŭb'lished, *a.* not made public; (of MS., &c.) not published.

unqual'ified (-ŏlĭfīd), *a.* not competent; not legally or officially qualified; not modified.

unques'tionable (-cho-), *a.* that cannot be questioned or doubted.

unques'tioned (-cho-), *a.* not disputed; not interrogated.

unqui'et, *a.* restless; agitated.

unrav'el, *v.t.* separate the threads of; disentangle (lit. & fig.).

unread' (-rĕd), *a.* (of book, &c.) not read; (of person) not well-read. unread'able, *a.* (esp.) too dull to be worth reading.

unrea'dy (-rĕd-), *a.* (esp.) not prompt in action.

unreal (-rī'al), *a.* illusive; sham; visionary.

unrea'son (-z-), *n.* lack of reason; nonsense, folly. ~able, *a.* exceeding the bounds of reason.

unrecip'rocated, *a.* (esp. of the affections) not requited.

unreclaimed', *a.* not reformed; (of land) in uncultivated state.

unredeemed', *a.* not redeemed; (of promise) not fulfilled; (of bills, &c.) not recalled by payment; not taken out of pawn; (of faults, &c.) not mitigated or relieved (*by* merits, &c.).

unreel', *v.i. & t.* unwind, become unwound, from reel.

unreflect'ing, *a.* thoughtless.

unreformed', *a.* not amended.

unregen'erate (-at), *a.* having had no moral awakening.

unrehearsed' (-hĕr-), *a.* without rehearsal; not prepared beforehand.

unrelieved', *a.* not succoured; lacking the relief given by contrast or variation.

unremitt'ing, *a.* incessant.

unrequi'ted, *a.* (of affection, &c.) not returned.

unreserve' (-z-), *n.* frankness.

unreserv'edly, *adv.* without reservation.

unrest', *n.* disturbed or agitated condition.

unrid'dle, *v.t.* solve (mystery, &c.).

unrighteous (-rī'chus), *a.* unjust; wicked; sinful.

unrip', *v.t.* rip open or apart.

unri'valled, *a.* having no equal; peerless.

unroll', *v.t. & i.* open (roll of cloth, &c.); (of roll) be opened; display, be displayed.

unru'ly, *a.* lawless; refractory.

unsan'itary, *a.* lacking sanitation.

unsa'voury, *a.* uninviting; disgusting.

unsay', *v.t.* retract (statement).

unscal'able, *a.* that cannot be climbed.

unscathed' (-dh-), *a.* without suffering injury.

unscrew' (-ōō), *v.t.* unfasten by removing screws; loosen (screw).

unscrip'tural, *a.* not in accordance with Scripture.

unscru'pulous (-ōōp-), *a.* having no scruples; unprincipled.

unseal', *v.t.* open (letter, sealed receptacle).

unseas'onable, *a.* not suitable to time or occasion; ill-timed.

unseat', *v.t.* remove from seat; throw from horseback.

unsectar'ian, *a.* free from sectarian limitations.

unseem'ly, *a.* improper; unbecoming. *adv.* unbecomingly.

unseen', *a.* not seen; invisible. *n.* unprepared passage for translation (also ~ *translation*).

unsel'fish, *a.* regardful of others rather than of oneself.

unset'tle, *v.t.* disturb; discompose; disincline to routine, &c. unset'tled (-ld), *a.* not settled; liable to change; not paid.

unsex', *v.t.* make unfeminine.

unsha'ken, *a.* not shaken, esp. in resolution.

unship', *v.t.* remove (oar, tiller, part of apparatus) from place where it is fixed or fitted.

unshrink'ing, *a.* unhesitating; fearless; firm.

unsight'ed (-it-), *a.* not yet in sight; (of gun) not furnished with sights.

unsight'ly (-it-), *a.* repulsive to look at.

unskilled' (-ld), *a.* without special skill or training.

ŭnsŏphĭs'tĭcātĕd, *a.* artless; innocent; not adulterated.

ŭnsound', *a.* not sound; diseased; rotten; erroneous; unreliable.

ŭnspeak'ăble, *a.* good or bad beyond description; unexpressible.

ŭnspŏtt'ĕd, *a.* not marked with any stain; not contaminated.

ŭnstā'ble, *a.* not fixed; inconstant; irresolute.

ŭnstĕa'dÿ (-stĕd-), *a.* not firm or steady; shaking; reeling.

ŭnstĭtch', *v.t.* undo stitches of.

ŭnstŏp', *v.t.* free from obstruction; remove stopper from.

ŭnstrained', *a.* not forced; not put through a strainer.

ŭnstring', *v.t.* remove the strings of; weaken nerves of (usu. in P.P. *unstrung*); remove (beads, &c.) from string.

ŭnstrĕssed', *a.* not pronounced with stress.

ŭnstŭd'iĕd, *a.* not premeditated; easy; natural; spontaneous.

ŭnsŭbstăn'tial (-shl), *a.* having little or no solidity or reality.

ŭnsuit'ĕd (-ŏot-), *a.* not fit *for*; not adapted *to*.

ŭnswōrn', *a.* not bound by oath.

ŭnsŷmmĕt'rĭcal, *a.* not characterized by symmetry.

ŭntăck', *v.t.* disjoin, separate; remove tacks from.

ŭntĕn'dĕd, *a.* not watched or looked after.

ŭnthink'ăble, *a.* such as it is impossible even to form a notion of; (colloq.) unlikely.

ŭnthink'ing, *a.* thoughtless.

ŭnthread' (-rĕd), *v.t.* take thread out of (needle).

ŭntie', *v.t.* undo knot or cords of; liberate from bonds.

ŭntĭl', *prep.* till, to; till the time, point, or degree that.

ŭntī'melÿ (-ml-), *a. & adv.* inopportune(ly); premature(ly).

ŭn'tō (-ŏo), *prep.* (arch.) to.

ŭntōld', *a.* not told; uncounted; beyond count.

ŭntō'ward (-tō'ard), *a.* (arch.) perverse; awkward; unlucky.

ŭntrained', *a.* not instructed; not prepared for race, &c.

ŭntrue' (-ŏo), *a.* not true; false; not faithful or loyal *to*; deviating from correct standard.

ŭn'truth' (-rŏo-), *n.* being untrue; falsehood; lie.

ŭntū'tored (-rd), *a.* uninstructed; not taught or schooled.

ŭnū'sual (-zhŏo-), *a.* not usual; remarkable.

ŭnŭtt'erable, *a.* above or beyond description.

ŭnvăl'ūed, *a.* not esteemed or prized; not priced.

ŭnvâr'nished, *a.* not varnished or embellished.

ŭnveil' (-văl), *v.t.* disclose; uncover; reveal (secrets, &c.).

ŭnvĕrsed', *a.* not experienced or skilled *in*.

ŭnwa'rrantable (-wŏ-), *a.* unauthorized; not guaranteed.

ŭnwear'ÿing, *a.* indefatigable; persistent; continual.

ŭnwĕll', *a.* not in good health; indisposed.

ŭnwĕpt', *a.* not wept for.

ŭnwiel'dÿ, *a.* cumbersome or clumsy or hard to manage.

ŭnwill'ing, *a.* reluctant; not willing or inclined.

ŭnwind', *v.t. & i.* draw out at length; become drawn out.

ŭnwise' (-z), *a.* foolish; imprudent; injudicious.

ŭnwished', *a.* not desired.

ŭnwitt'ing, *a.* unaware of the state of the case.

ŭnwor'ldlÿ (-wêr-), *a.* not worldly; spiritual.

ŭnworthy (-wêrdh'ĭ), *a.* not worthy or befitting the character *of*; discreditable.

ŭnwritt'en (-tn), *a.* not written; oral; traditional.

ŭnyield'ing, *a.* firm; obstinate.

ŭnyōke', *v.t. & i.* release from yoke; (fig.) cease work.

ŭp, *adv.* to or in a higher place, amount, value, &c.; to the place in question; completely or effectually. *prep.* to a higher part of; at a higher part of. ~ **against,** confronted with (task). ~ **to** (a person), confronting him as his part.

ū′pas, n. (usu. ~-*tree*), Javanese tree yielding arrow-poison.

upbraid′, v.t. chide, reproach.

up′bringing, n. education.

up′cast (-ah-), n. upward throw; shaft through which air passes out of mine.

up-coun′try (-kŭ-), adv., up′country (-kŭ-), a. towards the interior; inland.

upheav′al (-p-h-), n. heaving up, esp. of part of earth's crust; (fig.) vast social or other change.

up′hill (-p-h-), adv., up′hill (-p-h-), a. (sloping) upwards; (fig.) arduous, difficult, laborious.

uphold′ (-p-h-), v.t. give support or countenance to; maintain, confirm (decision, verdict).

upho′lster (-p-h-), v.t. furnish (room, &c.) with hangings, furniture, &c.; provide (chair, &c.) with covering, &c. ~er, ~ery, *nn.*

up′keep, n. cost or means of maintenance.

uplift′, v.t. raise up. *up′lift, n. intellectual or moral improvement of community.

up′land, n. (usu. in pl.), the higher parts of a country. a. higher in situation.

upon′ prep. on; *take* ~, assume.

up′per, a. higher in place; situated above; higher in rank or dignity. n. upper part of shoe. ~most, a. highest in rank or place; on or to the top. up′pish, a. self-assertive; pert.

upraise′ (-z), v.t. raise up; exalt.

upright, attrib.a. (up′rīt), erect, vertical; strictly honourable or honest. pred.a. (ŭprīt′), in upright position. n. (ŭp′rīt), post or rod fixed upright.

uprise′ (-z), v.i. rise up. upri′sing (-z-), n. rising from bed; rebellion, riot.

up′roar (-ōr), n. tumult; noisy clamour. uproar′ious, a. noisy.

uproot′ (-ōō-), v.t. tear up by the roots.

upset′[1], v.t. & i. overturn; be overturned; disturb the temper or digestion of. n. upsetting.

up′set[2], a. In phr. ~ *price*, lowest selling price of property in auction, &c.; reserve price.

up′shot, n. final issue; conclusion; general effect.

up′side-down′, adv. & a. with the upper part under; inverted; in total disorder.

up′sides (-dz), adv. In phr. *get* ~ *with*, turn the tables on.

upstairs′ (-z), adv., up′stair(s), a. on, to, of, an upper story.

upstand′ing, a. well set up, erect; (of wages) fixed, not variable.

up′start, n. person who has risen suddenly from humble position (often attrib.).

up′stroke, n. upward line in writing.

up′take, n. (Sc.) apprehension.

up′throw (-ō), n. (esp.) upward displacement of rock on one side of fault.

up′ward, -s (-z), adv. towards a higher place.

urā′nium, n. heavy white metallic element found in pitch-blende, &c.

urb′an, a. of, or living or situated in, a city or town.

urbāne′, a. courteous, suave; refined. urban′ity, n.

urch′in, n. boy; youngster.

Urdu (oordōō′), n. Hindustani.

ur′ea, n. (Chem.) soluble colourless crystalline compound.

urē′ter, urē′thra, nn. ducts by which urine passes into and from the bladder.

urge, v.t. (-*geable*), drive forcibly, impel; entreat earnestly; advocate pressingly. n. impulsion, yearning. ur′gent, a. pressing; requiring immediate attention; importunate. ur′gency, n.

ur′ic, a. of urine.

ur′im, n. ~ *and thummim*, objects connected with breastplate of the Jewish high priest.

ur′ine, n. fluid discharged from the bladder. ur′inal, a. place provided, invalid's bed convenience, for passing urine.

urn, n. vase anciently used for storing ashes of the dead; vase-shaped vessel with tap for tea, coffee, &c.

māre, mēre, mīre, mōre, mūre; pärt, pĕt, pürt; *italics*, vague sounds;

ū̓r'sine (*or* -ĭn), *a.* of or like a bear.

us (ŭs, ŭs), pl. obj. of I.

ū̓'sage (-zĭj), *n.* manner of using; treatment; customary practice.

ūse¹, *n.* using; employment; right of using; custom, wont.

ūse² (-z), *v.t. & i.* (-sable), employ for a purpose; consume as material; avail oneself of; (*p.t.*, *pr.* ŭst) be accustomed; (*p.p.*, *pr.* ŭst) accustomed.

ūse'ful (-sf-), *a.* of use, serviceable; efficient. ūse'less, *a.* unavailing; serving no useful purpose; (sl.) fit for nothing.

ū̓'ser¹ (-z-), *n.* one who uses anything. ū̓'ser² (-z-), *n.* (legal) continued use or enjoyment of a right.

ŭsh'er, *n.* officer or servant acting as doorkeeper of court, &c., showing persons to seats, or walking before persons of rank; under-teacher. *v.t.* act as usher to; precede (person) as usher; show in. ~ship, *n.*

ū̓s'quebaugh (-aw), *n.* whisky; cordial made of brandy, &c.

ū̓'sual (-zhōō-), *a.* such as commonly occurs; habitual.

ū̓'sufruct (-z-), *n.* right of enjoying the use of another's property without power to alienate.

ū̓'surer (-zhu-), *n.* one who practises usury.

ūsū́rp' (-z-), *v.t. & i.* seize by force; assume wrongfully. ūsurpā'tion, ~er, *nn.*

ū̓'sury (-zhu-), *n.* lending of money at exorbitant interest; usury interest. ūsū́r'ious (-z-), *a.*

‖ ŭt, *conj.* as. ‖ ~ sū'pra, ‖ ~ ĭn'fra, as shown above, below.

ūtĕn'sĭl, *n.* vessel or appliance in common and domestic use.

ū̓'tĕrus, *n.* the womb. ū̓'terine (*or* -ĭn), *a.* of the uterus.

ūtĭlĭtā'rĭan, *n.* holder of utilitarianism. *a.* based on or inspired by utility or utilitarianism. ~ism, doctrine that the morality of actions is to be tested by their utility.

ūtĭl'ĭty, *n.* usefulness; profitableness. ~ man, actor of small parts.

ū̓'tĭlĭze, *v.t.* (-zable), make use of; turn to account. ~zā'tion, *n.*

ŭt'most, *a.* furthest; extreme.

Utō'pia (ū-), *n.* imaginary island with perfect social and political system. Utō'pian (ū-), *a. & n.* visionary.

ū̓'tricle, *n.* cell or small cavity.

ŭtt'er¹, *a.* (sup. -most), complete; extreme; total; unqualified.

ŭtt'er², *v.t.* emit audibly; express in words; put (notes, base coin, &c.) in circulation.

ŭtt'erance, *n.* uttering; spoken words; articulation.

ū̓'vula, *n.* (pl. -ae), pendent fleshy part of soft palate.

ūxō̓r'ious, *a.* excessively fond of one's wife.

V

vā'cancy, *n.* empty space; unoccupied post, available place.

vā'cant, *a.* empty; without occupant or contents; stupid.

vacāte', *v.t.* (-table), leave vacant; cease from occupying. ~tion, *n.* fixed period of cessation from work.

văc'cināte (-ks-), *v.t.* inoculate with vaccine to give immunity against smallpox; treat similarly against other diseases. ~tion, ~tor, *nn.*

văc'cine (-ks-), *n.* virus of cow-pox as used in vaccination; virus of other diseases similarly used.

vă'cillate, *v.i.* waver; show indecision. ~tion, ~tor, *nn.*

vacū'ity, *n.* state of emptiness.

văc'uous, *a.* (of look, &c.) vacant.

văc'uum, *n.* (pl. -ums, -a), space entirely devoid of matter; space exhausted of air. ~ cleaner, apparatus for removing dust, &c. by suction. ~ flask, vessel with two walls separated by vacuum jacket so that liquid in inner receptacle retains its temperature.

vāde-mē'cum, *n.* handbook, &c. carried about the person.

văg'abònd, *a.* having no fixed dwelling. *n.* wanderer; idle scamp. ~age, ~ism, *nn.*

---

vagār′y, *n.* unaccountable proceeding; freak.

vagī′na, *n.* sheath-like part; passage to womb.

vā′grant, *a.* wandering; unsettled. *n.* vagabond; idle and disorderly person. vā′grancy, *n.*

vāgue (-g), *a.* indistinct; ill-defined; uncertain.

vail, *n.* (arch.) gratuity.

vain, *a.* of an empty nature; showy and valueless; conceited, proud. ~glōr′y, *n.* boastfulness. ~glōr′ious, *a.* boastful.

văl′ance, *n.* short curtain round frame or canopy of bedstead. văl′anced (-st), *a.*

vāle[1], *n.* valley.

|| vā′lē[2], *int.* & *n.* farewell.

vălēdic′tion, *n.* saying of farewell. ~tory, *a.*

văl′entine, *n.* sweetheart chosen on St. Valentine's day; verses or picture sent to one's valentine on same date.

valēr′ian, *n.* kinds of flowering herb.

văl′et, *n.* gentleman's servant.

vălētūdinār′ian, *n.* person compelled or (usu.) disposed to live the life of an invalid.

Vălhăll′a, *n.* (Norse myth.) banquet-hall of slain heroes; roll or burial-place or collected monuments of a nation's illustrious dead.

văl′iant (-ya-), *a.* brave.

văl′id, *a.* sound, well-grounded; having binding force. ~ity, *n.*

văl′idāte, *v.t.* make valid; ratify. vălidā′tion, *n.*

valise′ (-ēs), *n.* small portmanteau; soldier's knapsack.

văll′ey, *n.* (pl. -*eys*), low area more or less enclosed by hills.

văl′our (-ier), *n.* courage, esp. in battle. văl′orous, *a.*

valse (vahls), *n.* waltz.

văl′uable, *a.* of great value or use. *n.* (pl.) precious things.

vălūā′tion, *n.* value set upon anything; professional valuer's fixing of the value of property.

văl′ūe, *n.* worth or utility; price equal to the worth of the thing

bought; equivalent. *v.t.* estimate value of; esteem, have high opinion of.

vălve, *n.* kinds of device for controlling the passage of liquid or gas or the like through pipes, &c.; (Anat.) membranous part of organ allowing flow of blood, &c. in one direction only; one shell of oyster, &c. văl′vūlar, *a.* of an anatomical valve.

vămp[1], *n.* upper leather of front of shoe. *v.t.* & *i.* repair by patching; improvise.

*vamp[2], *n.* (sl.) adventuress; flirting woman or girl. *v.t.* & *i.* (of woman) allure; flirt.

văm′pīre, *n.* ghost that sucks blood of sleeping persons; blood-sucking bat; person who preys on others; *adventuress, woman who exploits men.

văn[1], *n.* winnowing-machine; wing of large bird.

văn[2], *n.* front of an army or fleet when advancing or in battle array. ~guard, advance guard.

văn[3], *n.* large covered vehicle for conveyance of goods.

vanā′dium, *n.* rare white metallic element.

văn′dal, *n.* wilful or ignorant destroyer of works of art, &c. ~ism, *n.*

vāne, *n.* weather-cock; blade of windmill, screw-propeller, &c.

vanill′a, *n.* plant of orchid kind; its fruit; extract of this.

văn′ish, *v.i.* disappear; fade away; dwindle to nothing.

văn′itȳ, *n.* unsubstantial or unreal thing; empty display; vain pride in oneself. ~bag, ~case, carried on the person and containing small mirror, &c.

vănq′uish, *v.t.* conquer, overcome.

va′ntage (vah-), *n.* advantage.

văp′id, *a.* insipid; lacking interest; dull. vapid′itȳ, *n.*

vā′porīze, *v.t.* & *i.* (-*zable*), convert or be converted into vapour. ~zā′tion, ~zer, *n.* vaporizing apparatus. vā′porous, *a.* in the form of or consisting of vapour.

vā′pour (-per), *n.* moisture in the air; steam or mist or smoke; (pl.) nervous irritability or depression. *v.i.* indulge in extravagant talk. **vā′poury**, *a.* resembling vapour.

vār′iable, *a.* apt to vary; not constant. *n.* a variable quantity or thing. **~bility**, *n.*

vār′iance, *n.* state of discord or discrepancy.

vār′iant, *a.* different; variable. *n.* a different form, spelling, type, reading, &c.

vāriā′tion, *n.* deviation from a standard or type; difference.

vā′ricose, *a.* (of vein, &c.) permanently and abnormally dilated.

vār′iegāted, *a.* showing patches of different colours.

vari′ety, *n.* diversity; absence of uniformity; collection of different things; sub-species of a class. **~ entertainment**, show, of mixed kind, e.g. of dramatic trifles, songs, juggling, and acrobats; so **~ theatre.**

vāriō′rum, *a.* with the notes of various commentators.

vār′ious, *a.* of several kinds; diverse; divers.

vār′let, *n.* menial; rascal.

vār′nish, *n.* resinous solution applied to a surface to make it shine. *v.t.* apply varnish to.

vār′ÿ, *v.t.* & *i.* make or become different; modify; fluctuate.

văs′cular, *a.* having vessels for conveying blood, sap, &c.

vase (vahz), *n.* vessel of the water-jar kind, used mainly as ornament or to hold cut flowers.

văs′eline (-ēn), *n.* ointment and lubricant got from petroleum. P.

văss′al, (hist.) holder of land by feudal tenure; (joc.) dependant. **~age**, *n.* vassal's condition.

vast (vah-), *a.* of huge extent, amount, or size; (colloq.) great.

văt, *n.* large tub, cistern, or other vessel. **~ful**, *n.* (pl. *-ls*)

Văt′ican, *n.* the Pope's residence; papal government.

vati′cinate, *v.i.* & *t.* prophesy, foretell. **~ation**, *n.* prophecy.

vaude′ville (vōdv-), *n.* dramatic trifle interspersed with songs and dances; * variety entertainment.

vault, *n.* arched roof or ceiling; room, cellar, tomb, or other space covered in with vault; the sky; any subterranean cellar; grave lined with brick, &c.; act of vaulting. *v.i.* & *t.* make (roof, ceiling) in arched form; spring over something with the hand(s) resting on it. **vault′ing**, *n.* the arched work composing a vaulted roof or ceiling.

vaunt, *v.i.* & *t.* & *n.* boast.]

veal, *n.* calf-flesh.

Ve′da (vā-), *n.* (also in pl.) Hindu scriptures written in old Sanskrit. **Ve′dic** (vā-), *a.*

Vedān′ta, *n.* system of Hindu philosophy founded on the Veda. **~tic**, *a.*

vēdětte′, *n.* mounted sentinel placed in advance of outpost.

veer, *v.i.* (of wind) change direction; (fig.) change one's opinion.

vĕ′gětable, *a.* of the plant kind; derived from or concerned with plants. *n.* a plant, esp. one of the kind grown for food.

vēgětā′rian, *n.* believer in vegetable diet and in abstinence from meat. **~ism**, *n.*

vĕ′gětāte, *v.i.* live a plant's life; be stationary. **~tive**, *a.* **~ation**, *n.* plants collectively; plants growing in a place.

ve′hement (vēïm-), *a.* violent; fervent. **ve′hemence** (vēïm-), *n.*

ve′hicle (vēï-), *n.* carriage or cart or other land conveyance; means of expressing or diffusing opinions, &c. **vehic′ular**, *a.*

veil (vāl), *n.* piece of transparent material to hide or protect the face; curtain; pretext. *v.t.* & *i.* cover with veil; hide, conceal.

vein (vān), *n.* membranous tube through which blood flows; rib of leaf; fissure in rock filled with deposited matter; streak; temporary mood.

vĕld(t) (-lt), *n.* S.-Afr. tract of land with little or no forest; wild grassland.

---

vélle´ity, *n.* wishful state not prompting to action.

vell´um, *n.* fine parchment.

velo´cipède, *n.* (arch.) bicycle or tricycle.

velo´city, *n.* rate of motion, esp. of inanimate things.

velours´ (-oor), *n.* kinds of plush used for hats, &c.

vel´vet, *n.* silk fabric with thick short pile ; (attrib.) made of, or soft as, velvet. **velveteen´**, *n.* cotton fabric with velvet-like pile. **vel´vety**, *a.*

ve´nal, *a.* mercenary ; guilty of taking bribes. **venal´ity**, *n.*

vend, *v.t.* (-*dible*), carry on the sale of (goods). **ven´dible**, *a.* saleable. **vendee´**, *n.* one to whom thing is sold. **ven´dor**, *n.* seller.

vendett´a, *n.* blood-feud.

veneer´, *v.t.* cover (wood, table, &c.) with thin coating of finer wood. ~ *n.* thin coat of wood ; superficial disguise.

ven´erable, *a.* entitled to veneration ; title of an archdeacon.

ven´erate, *v.t.* regard with deep respect ; feel veneration for. **venera´tion**, *n.* profound respect ; reverent regard. ~**tor**, *n.*

venér´eal, *a.* of sexual intercourse.

ven´ery, *n.* (arch.) hunting.

Vene´tian (-shn), *a.* of Venice. *n.* a Venetian person. ~ **blind**, window-blind of slats hung on cords. ~ **mast**, tall particoloured pole used in decorations.

ven´geance (-jans), *n.* retribution ; punishment inflicted on a wrong-doer. **venge´ful** (-jf-), *a.* bent on vengeance.

ve´nial, *a.* trivial ; far from unpardonable. **venial´ity**, *n.*

ven´ison (-nzon), *n.* deer-flesh.

ven´om, *n.* the poison of snakes, &c. ; (fig.) rancour, spite, esp. as expressed in words. ~**ous**, *a.*

ve´nous, *a.* of the veins.

vent, *n.* small outlet or inlet for air, smoke, &c. ; anus of fish, &c. *v.t.* utter ; pour forth.

ven´tilate, *v.t.* (-*lable*), cause air to circulate in (room, &c.) ; purify by air ; submit to discussion.

~**tion**, *n.* ~**tor**, *n.* appliance for ventilating room, &c.

ven´tral, *a.* of or on the belly.

ven´tricle, *n.* cavity or chamber in the body, esp. one of those in the heart or brain.

ventril´oquism, *n.* act or art of producing vocal sounds in such a manner that they appear to come from another place. ~**ist**, *n.*

ven´ture, *n.* risky undertaking ; hazard ; speculative action. *v.t.* & *i.* summon up courage to do ; dare to utter ; hazard. ~**some**, *a.* disposed to take risks ; hazardous.

ven´ue, *n.* district in which a case must be tried ; (pop.) meeting-place, rendezvous.

Ve´nus, *n.* Roman goddess of love ; the planet second in order from the sun ; a beautiful woman.

vera´cious (-shus), *a.* truthful ; not false. **verac´ity**, *n.* truthfulness.

veran´dah (-*da*), *n.* open portico along side of house.

verb, *n.* the part of speech which serves to express action, passion, or existence. **verb´al**, *a.* of or concerned with words ; oral ; word for word. **verba´tim**, *adv.* & *a.* word for word.

verbe´na, *n.* kinds of fragrant-leaved flowering plant.

verb´iage, *n.* needless array of words. **verbose´**, *a.* prolix ; exuberant in use of words. **verbos´ity**, *n.* verbiage. ‖ **verb´um sat. sapien´ti** (abbr. *verb. sap.*), a word is enough to the wise.

verd´ant, *a.* abounding in green foliage ; green and fresh ; (sl.) inexperienced. ~**ncy**, *n.*

verd-antique´ (-ēk), *n.* an ornamental building-stone.

verd´ict, *n.* decision of jury ; opinion arrived at.

verd´igris, *n.* green rust of copper.

verd´ure (-dyer), *n.* mass of green vegetation.

verge, *n.* border-line or brink. *v.i.* incline downwards or in specified direction.

ver´ger, *n.* staff-bearer of bishop, &c. ; official who has care of the interior of a church, &c.

---

mãre, mẽre, mĩre, mõre, mũre ; pãrt, pẽrt, põrt ; *italics*, vague sounds ;

vĕ'rĭfў, *v.t.* (-*fiable*), ascertain the truth or correctness of; bear out or fulfil (prediction, &c.). **vĕrĭfĭcā'tion**, *n.* confirmation.

vĕ'rĭlў, *adv.* in truth.

vĕrĭsĭmĭl'ĭtŭde, *n.* air of being true; likelihood.

vĕ'rĭtable, *a.* real, actual; agreeable to fact.

vĕ'rĭtў, *n.* truth; a true statement or fact.

vĕr'juice (-ōos), *n.* sour juice of unripe fruit.

vĕrmĭcĕll'ĭ, *n.* wheaten paste in threads for cooking.

vĕrm'ĭcĭde, *n.* drug for killing worms.

vĕrm'ĭfŏrm, *a.* worm-shaped.

vĕrmĭl'ĭon (-yon), *n.* bright red colour. *a.* vermilion coloured.

vĕrm'ĭn, *n. collect.* (usu. with pl. verb), creatures injurious to crops, &c.; parasites; vile persons. **~ous**, *a.*

vernăc'ular, *a.* (of language) of one's own country. *n.* the native tongue; homely speech.

vĕrn'al, *a.* of or in the spring.

vĕrn'ier, *n.* small movable scale for obtaining fractional parts of the subdivisions of a fixed scale.

vĕ'ronal, *n.* an opiate.

verŏn'ĭca, *n.* a flowering shrub.

vĕrs'atĭle, *a.* turning readily from one occupation to another; capable of dealing with many subjects. **versatĭl'ĭtў**, *n.*

verse, *n.* metrical composition; a verse line; a stanza; numbered subdivision of a Bible chapter.

versed (-st), *a.* experienced *in.*

vĕrs'ĭcle, *n.* liturgical sentence to be said or sung by minister and congregation alternately.

vĕrs'ĭfў, *v.t. & i.* (-*fiable*), turn into or relate in verse; make verses. **versĭfĭcā'tion**, *n.* **vĕrs'ĭfĭer**, *n.* maker of verses.

vĕr'sion (-shn), *n.* a particular translation of a book, &c., or account of an incident, &c.

vĕrs'ō, *n.* left-hand page of open book, or back of recto.

verst, *n.* Russian measure of length, about two-thirds of a mile.

|| **vĕrs'ŭs**, *prep.* (abbrev. *v.*), against (as *Notts* v. *Surrey*).

vert, *n. & a.* (Herald.) green.

vert'ĕbra, *n.* (pl. -*ae*), single segment of the backbone. **vert'ĕbral**, *a.* **vert'ĕbrate**, *a.* having a backbone; *n.* back-boned animal.

vert'ĕx, *n.* (pl. -*ĭcēs*), thing's topmost point. **vert'ĭcal**, *a.* perpendicular; straight up and down; upright.

vertĭ'gō, *n.* (pl. -*os*), dizziness.

vĕrv'ain, *n.* plant formerly credited with sacred properties.

verve (vĕrv), *n.* enthusiasm; energy; vigour.

vĕrv'et, *n.* small S.-Afr. monkey often employed by organ-grinders.

vĕ'rў, *a.* real; true; truly such. *adv.* in the fullest sense; in a high degree.

Vĕr'(e)ў, *n.* — *light*, projected from ~ *pistol*, for temporarily illuminating part of battlefield, &c. P.

vĕs'ĭcle, *n.* small bladder or blister or bubble.

vĕs'per, *n.* (pl.) evening-service. **~ine**, *a.* of, done or appearing in, the evening.

vĕss'el, *n.* receptacle for holding liquid, &c.; ship or boat; (Anat.) duct, canal, holding or containing blood or other fluid.

vĕst, *n.* body-garment worn next the skin; (shop) waistcoat. *v.t. & i.* place the right to (property, power) *in* a person; (of property, &c.); be so vested *in.*

vĕs'ta, *n.* a wax match.

vĕs'tal, *a.* vowed to chastity; virgin. *n.* vestal virgin; nun.

vĕs'tĭbule, *n.* ante-chamber; entrance-hall; *enclosed platform at end of railway train.

vĕs'tĭge, *n.* trace, evidence; (loosely) particle.

vĕst'ment, *n.* garment, esp. one worn officially.

vĕs'trў, *n.* part of church in which vestments are kept; in nonconformist churches, a room used esp. by minister and deacons; a parochial assembly. **~man**, *n.*

---

ves'ture, *n.* (poet.) clothing.

vesu'vian, *n.* fusee.

vet, (colloq.) *n.* veterinary surgeon. *v.t.* examine or treat.

vetch, *n.* kinds of plant of bean family used for fodder.

vet'eran, *n.* person with long experience of service.

vet'erinary, *a.* of or for the diseases of domestic animals. *n.* a veterinary surgeon.

ve'to, *n.* (pl. *-oes*), constitutional right to reject a legislative enactment; any prohibition. *v.t.* exercise veto against; forbid.

vex, *v.t.* cause distress or annoyance to; disturb. **vexa'tion**, *n.* being vexed; annoying circumstance. **vexa'tious** (*-shus*), *a.* vexing; designed merely to annoy. **vexed** (*-kst*), *a.* much debated.

‖ **via** (vi'a), *prep.* passing through; going by way of.

vi'aduct, *n.* arches or other structure carrying railway or road across valley or dip.

vi'al, *n.* small vessel for holding liquid medicine.

‖ **vi'a me'dia**, *n.* middle course between extremes.

vi'ands (*-z*), *n.pl.* articles of food; victuals.

vi'at'icum, *n.* the eucharist as administered to the dying.

vibrate', *v.i. & t.* move rapidly to and fro; thrill; quiver; oscillate. **~tion**, *n.* vibrating; oscillating. **~tor**, *n.* vibrating part in electric instruments. **~tory**, *a.*

vic'ar, *n.* parson of parish of which the tithes have been impropriated. **~age**, *n.* vicar's house or office. **vicar'ial**, *a.* of a vicar. **~ious**, *a.* acting as substitute; done or suffered by one person on behalf of another.

vice¹, *n.* habitual indulgence in evil; any particular form of depravity; serious fault; defect or blemish; (in horse) ill-temper.

vice², *n.* appliance with two jaws in which things may be gripped and held steady.

‖ **vi'ce³**, *prep.* in place of; in succession to.

vice-, prefix in nouns denoting official who acts for or is second in rank to another.

vicege'rent (*-sj-*), *n.* holder of delegated authority.

vice'roy (*-sr-*), *n.* ruler with royal authority in a dependency. **~alty**, *n.* viceroy's office. **vice-re'gal** (*-sr-*), *a.* belonging to a viceroy. **vice'reine** (*-srān*), *n.* viceroy's wife.

vi'ce ver'sa, *adv.* the other way round.

Vichy (water) (vē'shē), *n.* a mineral water.

vi'cinage, *n.* neighbouring district. **vicin'ity** (*or* vī-), *n.* neighbourhood; nearness.

vi'cious (*-shus*), *a.* of the nature of or addicted to vice; ill-tempered; (of reasoning) faulty, unsound.

viciss'itude (*or* vī-), *n.* a change of fortune; (pl.) ups and downs.

vic'tim, *n.* person or animal slain sacrificially; person sacrificed to attain some object; sufferer from some untoward event. **vic'timize**, *v.t.* (*-zable*), make (person, &c.) the victim of a swindle, one's spite, &c. **~za'tion**, *n.*

vic'tor, *n.* conqueror; winner of a contest.

victo'ria, *n.* light open four-wheeled carriage with seat for two. V~ Cross (abbr. *V.C.*), decoration for conspicuous act of bravery. **Victo'rian**, *a.* of, in, or characteristic of, the reign of Queen Victoria; *n.* person of that period.

vic'tory, *n.* the winning of a battle or contest. **victo'rious**, *a.* conquering; triumphant. **vic'tress**, *n.* female victor.

victual (vi'tl), *n.* (in sing. or usu. pl.), food and drink; provisions. *v.t. & i.* supply with victuals; take in store of victuals. **victualler** (vit'ler), *n.* food-purveyor; licensee of a public-house (usu. *licensed* ~).

vicu'gna, **-u'na** (*-ōōnya*), *n.* S.-Amer. wool-yielding mammal.

‖ **vi'de**, *v. imperat.* (abbr. *v.*), see (specified passage or work). ‖ **~**

supra, infra, see above, below. || vide'licet, *adv.* (abbr. *viz.*, usu. spoken as *namely*), that is to say ; namely.

vie, *v.i.* enter into rivalry *with*.

view (vū), *n.* inspection by eye ; survey, prospect ; range of vision. *v.t.* survey with eyes or mind ; hold specified view of. ~less, *a.* invisible.

vigés'imal, *a.* of or pertaining to twenty ; based on the number twenty.

vi'gil, *n.* eve of a festival ; watching, keeping awake. ~ant, *a.* watchful ; on the watch. ~ance, *n.* *~ance committee, self-organized body for maintenance of order in unquiet time or place, or for keeping watch over the morals of a district. *vigilan'te, *n.* member of vigilance committee.

vignette (věnyět'), *n.* illustration in book not enclosed in definite border ; portrait showing only head and shoulders with shaded background.

vig'our (-ger), *n.* activity and strength of body or mind. vig'orous, *a.* active ; forcible.

vi'king, *n.* northern sea-robber of 8th-10th cc.

|| vila'yet (-ahyět), *n.* Turkish province.

vile, *a.* depraved, base ; worthless ; despicable.

vil'ify, *v.t.* speak ill of ; defame. vilifica'tion, *n.*

vill'a, *n.* country residence ; detached suburban house. ~dom, *n.* suburban society.

vill'age, *n.* assemblage of dwellings in the country ; *minor municipality governed by a president and three or more trustees. vill'ager, *n.* dweller in village ; rustic.

vill'ain (-ǎn), *n.* wicked schemer ; (joc.) sly rogue. ~ous, *a.* worthy of a villain. vill'ainy (-lǎn-), *n.* crafty wickedness.

vill'ein (-lǐn), *n.* (hist.) feudal tenant. ~age, *n.* villein's tenure or relation to superior.

vim, *n.* (sl.) forcibleness, energy.

vinaigrette' (-nǐg-). *n.* smelling-salt bottle.

vin'dicate, *v.t.* (-cable), justify ; establish the truth of ; avenge. ~tion, ~tor, *nn.* ; ~tory, *a.*

vindic'tive, *a.* bent on revenge ; (of act, &c.) inspired by resentment or meant to punish.

vine, *n.* the plant that bears grapes ; *climbing plant.

vin'egar, *n.* acid liquid got from various alcoholic liquors. vin'é-gary, *a.* sour.

vi'nery, *n.* greenhouse for vines. vine'yard (-ny-), *n.* vine-plantation.

vi'nous, *a.* of, like, or due to wine.

vin'tage, *n.* the grape-gathering season or its yield ; wine. vint'ner, *n.* (arch.) wine-seller.

vi'ol, *n.* medieval instrument from which the viola, &c. were developed. vio'la1, *n.* large violin used for alto or tenor.

vi'ola2, *n.* pansy of single-coloured kinds.

vi'olate, *v.t.* (-lable), transgress ; infringe ; break in upon ; ravish. viola'tion, vi'olator, *nn.*

vi'olence, *n.* force ; violent conduct or treatment ; impetuousness.

vi'olent, *a.* of great and impetuous force ; vehement ; intense.

vi'olet, *n.* kinds of wild and garden flower, usu. of bluish-purple ; its colour. *a.* violet-coloured.

violin', *n.* four-stringed musical instrument played with bow. ~ist, *n.* violin-player.

vi'olist, *n.* viol-player.

violoncell'o (-chě-), *n.* (usu. abbr. 'cello ; pl. -os), large bass viol. ~cell'ist (-chě-), *n.*

vi'per, *n.* kinds of venomous snake, esp. the adder ; (fig.) malignant or treacherous person. ~ous, *a.* (fig.).

virā'go, *n.* (pl. -os), fierce or abusive woman.

vi'relay, *n.* form of short-lined poem on two rhymes.

vir'gin, *n.* girl or woman who has not known sexual intercourse. *a.* chaste, unsullied ; never yet used. ~ity, n. virgin's state.

vir′ginal, a. of virgin purity; n. (sing. or pl.) kind of spinet.

Virgin′ia, n. tobacco from Virginia. ~ creeper, vine-like creeper. *~reel, dance like Sir Roger de Coverley.

virile (vi′-, vir′-), a. having masculine vigour or strength; of a mature man. viril′ity, n.

virtu′ (-ōō), n. connoisseurship in art. virtuo′so, n. (pl. -si pr. -sē), art-connoisseur. virtuos′ity, n.

virt′ual, a. such in practice though not in name.

vir′tue, n. moral goodness; any particular form of moral excellence; female chastity. virt′uous, a. practising virtue; morally good; chaste.

vi′rulent (-rōō-), a. powerful; venomous, malignant. ~nce, n.

vir′us, n. the poisonous element by which infection is communicated.

visa. See visé.

vis′age (-z-), n. the face, esp. as revealing temperament, &c.

visard. See visor.

vis-à-vis (vēzahvē′), adv. facing. prep. opposite to; in face of. n. person facing one.

vis′cera, n.pl. the internal organs of the body. vis′ceral, a.

viscid, viscosity. See viscous.

vis′cose, n. cellulose dissolved to the viscous state in which it can be spun into yarn for use as artificial silk.

viscount (vi′k-), n. peer ranking between earl and baron. ~ess, n. viscountcy, ~cy (vi′k-), n. viscount's patent.

vis′cous, vis′cid, aa. of a semifluid clinging consistence like treacle or egg-yolk. viscos′ity n.

visé, visa (vē′zā, -zah), n. indorsement on passport. v.t. mark with visé.

vis′ible (-z-), a. to be seen; conspicuous. visibil′ity (-z-), n. (esp.) atmospheric conditions for discerning distant objects.

vi′sion (-zhn), n. act or faculty of seeing; thing seen in a dream. vi′sionary (-zho-), a. apt to see

or believe in visions; unpractical; n. person of unpractical ideals; mystic.

vis′it (-z-), v.t. & i. go to call on or stay with or to inspect or stay at; punish or afflict; *~with, (colloq.) chat with. n. act or spell of visiting. ~ant, n. visitor. ~a′tion, n. official visit of inspection; affliction as a punishment from God. ~or, n. person who pays or comes on a visit; official with duty of inspecting, &c.

vis′or (-z-), -zor, vis′ard (-z-), -zard, nn. (hist.) movable part of helmet covering face; mask; *(visor) stiff rounded peak in front of man's cap.

vis′ta, n. long narrow view as between rows of trees (also fig.).

vis′ual (-z-), a. of, concerned with, or used in, seeing. ~ize, v.t. (-zable), make visible; shape into a mental image. ~ization, n.

vi′ta-glass (-ah-), n. a kind of glass allowing ultra-violet rays to pass. P.

vi′tal, a. of, concerned with, or essential to, organic life; essential to success, &c.; fatal. n.pl. the vital organs of the body. ~ism, n. doctrine that life originates in a vital principle distinct from physical forces. ~ist, n. ~istic, a. vital′ity (or vit′-), n. vital power; hold on life; persistent energy. vi′talize, v.t. (-zable), endow with life; put vigour into. vitaliza′tion, n.

vi′tamin, n. kinds of factor contained by particular foodstuffs, and regarded as necessary to health.

vit′iculture, n. vine-growing.

vi′tiate (-shi-), v.t. deprive of efficacy; spoil. ~tion, ~tor, nn.

vit′reous, a. of, like, or of the nature of glass. vit′rify, v.t. & i. (-fiable), turn into glass or a vitreous substance. vitrifac′tion, ~fica′tion, nn. such conversion.

vit′riol, n. sulphuric acid or any of its salts; (fig.) caustic speech. vitriol′ic, a. corrosive as vitriol (esp. of abuse, &c.).

māre, mēre, mīre, mōre, mūre; pärt, pĕrt, pŭrt; italics, vague sounds;

vitu'perate, *v.t.* revile, abuse. ~tion, ~tor, *nn.*; ~tive, *a.*

viva'cious (-shus), *a.* sprightly, animated. viva'city, *n.*

viva'rium, *n.* (pl. -ia) place in which live wild creatures are kept.

vi'va vo'ce, *adv.* orally. *a.* oral. *n.* (abbr. *viva*), oral examination.

vi'vers (-z), *n.pl.* (Sc.) food, victuals.

viv'id, *a.* bright; intense; lively; incisive; graphic.

viv'ify, *v.t.* put life into; make lively or animated.

vivip'arous, *a.* bringing forth young alive.

vivisec'tion, *n.* dissection or other experiment performed on a live animal. viv'isect, *v.t.* subject to vivisection. ~or, *n.*

vix'en, *n.* she-fox; spiteful woman. ~ish, *a.*

viz. See videlicet.

vizard, vizor. See visor.

vizier' (-ēr), *n.* Minister of State in Mohammedan countries.

vō'cable, *n.* a word.

vocab'ulary, *n.* list of words in a language, arranged alphabetically with definitions.

vō'cal, *a.* of, with, or for the voice; uttered by the voice. ~ist, *n.* vocal performer. ~ize, *v.t. & i.* (-zable), make sonant; impart vowel sound to; use the singing voice. ~iza'tion, *n.*

voca'tion, *n.* person's sense of being called to a task; occupation or calling. ~al, *a.*

voc'ative, *a.* used in addressing. *n.* vocative case or word.

vocif'erate, *v.t. & i.* shout, clamour; speak loudly and insistently. ~tion, ~tor, *nn.* vocif'erous, *a.* clamorous; loud and insistent in speech.

vod'ka, *n.* Russian spirit distilled from rye, &c.

vogue (-g), *n.* popular favour; the fashion.

voice, *n.* sound uttered by the mouth; a distinguishable quality of voice; the expressed opinion, &c. of; (Gram.) the verbal forms proper to a certain relation of

the subject to the action. *v.t.* (-ceable), give voice to.

void, *a.* empty, vacant; not valid. *n.* empty space; sense of loss. *v.t.* invalidate; emit; evacuate.

vol'atile, *a.* evaporating rapidly; of gay temperament; mercurial. volatil'ity, *n.* vol'atilize, *v.t. & i.* (-zable), turn into vapour. volatiliza'tion, *n.*

volca'no, *n.* (pl. -oes) mountain or hill with opening(s) through which lava, cinders, gases, &c. are expelled. volca'nic, *a.* of, like, or produced by a volcano.

vole, *n.* kinds of rodent.

voli'tion, *n.* act or faculty of willing. ~al, ~ary, *a.*

volksraad (fōlks'raht; or fōl-), *n.* (hist.) legislative assembly of the Orange Free State.

vol'ley, *n.* (pl. -eys), simultaneous discharge of a number of rifles, missiles, &c.; (tennis, &c.) player's return of a ball before it has touched the ground. *v.t. & i.* send, fly, utter, or sound in a volley or volleys; return (ball) before it touches ground.

vol'plane, *v.i.* (of aeroplane or its pilot) descend by gliding without use of engine. *n.* such descent.

volt (or -ō-), *n.* unit of electromotive force. volt'age, *n.* electromotive force measured in volts. volta'ic, *a.* galvanic. volt'meter, an instrument for measuring voltages.

volte-face' (-tfahs), *n.* complete change of front.

vol'uble, *a.* with incessant flow of words. volubil'ity, *n.*

vol'ume, *n.* set of printed sheets bound together and forming a book; moving mass of water or smoke; swell of sound; bulk. volu'minous (-lōō-), *a.* running to many volumes or great length; (of drapery, &c.) loose or ample.

vol'untary, *a.* having free will; not subject to or done by compulsion. *n.* organist's solo in church before, during, or after service. ~ism, *n.* support of voluntary action.

vŏlunteer', *n.* person who comes forward with offer of service at need; member of non-professional military corps. *v.t. & i.* come forward or serve as volunteer; proffer (assistance, &c.).

vŏlŭp'tūarў, *n.* person given up to luxury and sensual gratification. **vŏlŭp'tūous**, *a.*

vŏlūte', *n.* spiral scroll in stonework, esp. on capitals.

vŏm'ĭt, *v.t. & i.* eject food, &c. from stomach through mouth; (fig., of volcano, chimney, &c.) eject violently, belch forth. *n.* matter vomited.

*****vŏō'dŏō**, *n.* use of or belief in witchcraft prevalent among W.-Ind. and U.S. creoles and negroes. *v.t.* bewitch.

voor'looper (vōrlō-), *n.* (S.-Afr.) leader of ox-wagon.

vorā'cious (-shŭs), *a.* greedy, ravenous, **vorā'cĭtў**, *n.*

vort'ĕx, *n.* (pl. *-ĭcēs*), whirlpool; whirlwind; whirling motion or mass. **vort'ical**, *a.* having a whirling motion. **vort'icĭst**, *n.* (esp.) painter of recent school using vortices.

vō'tarў, *n.* person vowed to the service of a god, &c. or devoted to a pursuit. **vō'tarĕss**, *n.*

vōte, *n.* ascertainment or expression of will or opinion by means of ballot, show of hands, roll-call, voice, or otherwise; the right to take part in such vote; number of votes given. *v.i. & t.* (*-table*), give one's vote; decide by majority of votes; (colloq.) pronounce by general consent to be (a success, failure, &c.). **vō'ter**, *n.* (esp.) person with right to vote at election.

vō'tive, *a.* given or consecrated in fulfilment of a vow.

vouch, *v.i.* (with *for*) guarantee, confirm, bear witness to. **vouch'er**, *n.* document establishing the payment of money or the truth of accounts.

vouchsāfe', *v.t.* condescend to grant or *to* do something.

vow, *n.* solemn promise or engagement. *v.t.* promise or threaten by vow; aver.

vow'ĕl, *n.* sound capable of forming a syllable; letter representing this, e.g. a, e, i, o, u.

|| **vŏx hūmā'na** (-mā-, -mah-), *n.* organ-stop with human-voice tones. || **vŏx pŏp'ŭlī**, *n.* public opinion; the general verdict.

voy'age, *n. & v.i.* journey, esp. to some distance, by water.

Vŭl'can, *n.* god of fire and smiths; a smith. **vŭl'canĭte**, *n.* hard vulcanized rubber. **~ize**, *v.t.* (*-zable*), treat rubber with sulphur at high temperature.

vŭl'gar, *a.* coarse; mean; low; common; offending against good taste. **vŭl'garĭsm**, *n.* word or phrase used only by the uneducated. **vŭlgăr'ĭtў**, *n.* **vŭl'garize**, *v.t.* (*-zable*), infect with vulgarity; spoil by making too common or well known. **~izā'tion**, *n.*

Vŭl'gate, *n.* fourth-century Latin version of the Bible.

vŭl'nerable, *a.* not proof against wounds; offering an opening to criticism, &c. **~bility**, *n.*

vŭl'picide, *n.* unsportsmanlike fox-killing or fox-killer.

vŭl'pine, *a.* of or like the fox; of crafty aspect or nature.

vŭl'ture, *n.* kinds of large bird of prey; rapacious person.

W

wad (wŏd), *n.* lump of soft material used to stop hole, &c.; disk of felt, &c. keeping powder or shot compact in gun. *v.t.* secure or stuff up with wad; stuff or protect with wadding. **wa'dding** (wŏd-), *n.* soft material used as stuffing.

waddle (wŏ'dl), *v.i.* walk with slow rocking gait. *n.* such gait. **wădd'ў**, *n.* Australian war-club.

wāde, *v.i. & t.* (*-dable*), walk through water or other impeding medium. *n.* spell of wading. **wā'der**, *n.* kinds of long-legged water-bird; (pl.) high water-proof fishing-boots.

wad′i, -ȳ (wŏ-), n. rocky water-course dry except in rainy season (chiefly of Eastern countries).

wā′fer, n. thin honeycomb-faced biscuit; thin disk of unleavened bread used in the Eucharist; disk of dried paste used to stick papers, &c. together; disk of red paper stuck on law papers instead of seal. v.t. fasten or seal with wafer.

waft (wah-), v.t. & i. convey smoothly through the air or along the water. n. whiff of perfume, &c.

wag, v.t. & i. shake or wave to and fro. n. single wagging motion; facetious person. ~**tail,** kinds of small bird.

wāge, n. workman's or servant's periodical pay (usu. pl.). v.t. engage in or carry on (war, &c.). **wā′ger,** n., & v.t. & i. bet one.

wăgg′ery (-g-), n. facetiousness; a practical joke. **wăgg′ish** (-g-), a. given to waggery; facetious.

wăg′gle, v.i. & i. (colloq.) wag; move unsteadily. **wăgg′ly,** a.

wăg′on, n. four-wheeled vehicle for heavy loads; open railway truck. **wăg′oner,** n. driver of wagon. **wăgonětte′,** n. four-wheeled open carriage with facing side-seats.

waif, n. ownerless object or animal; homeless and helpless person; abandoned child.

wail, n. prolonged plaintive cry; wail-like sound. v.i. & i. utter wail; lament for.

wain, n. (poet., &c.) wagon.

wain′scot, n. boarding or wooden panelling on room-wall. ~**ing,** wainscot or material for it.

waist, n. part of human body below ribs and above hips; part of garment corresponding to waist; *bodice; part of ship between forecastle and quarter-deck. ~**band, ~belt,** worn round waist. ~**coat** (wā′skŏt, wĕs′kŏt), garment worn below coat.

wait, v.i. & i. defer action; await or abide (opportunity, &c.); act as waiter; attend *upon.* n. act or period of waiting; (pl.) Christ-mas carol-singers or musicians

going round at night. **wait′er,** n. an attendant at table; tray, salver. **wait′ress,** n.

waive, v.t. forbear to insist on or exercise; forgo. **waiv′er,** n. explicit waiving of a right, &c.

wāke¹, n. track left by ship on water (also fig.).

wāke², v.i. & i. (past **wŏke, wāked;** p.p. *wāked,* **wōken**), cease or rouse from sleep; be awake; rouse from sloth or inattention; hold wake over (corpse); disturb with noise. n. fair or merrymaking; (Ir.) watching of corpse before burial. ~**ful,** a. unable to sleep; vigilant, sleepless. **wā′ken,** v.t. & i. wake up; make or become awake.

wāle, weal¹, n. ridge raised on flesh by whip, &c. v.t. make wale on.

wā′ler, n. horse for Indian Army from New South Wales.

walk (wawk), n. gait or step; manner of walking; excursion on foot, stroll; track for foot-passengers; round of milkman, &c. v.i. & i. progress by advancing each foot alternately; travel or go on foot; (of farmer, &c.) take charge of (hound puppy); (arch.) conduct oneself in specified way. *~out,* labourers' strike. ~ **over,** go over course as winner owing to absence of competitors. ~**over,** contest won by walking over; easy victory.

wall (wawl), n. upright structure serving as defence of town, side of a building, partition, boundary fence, &c. v.t. provide with wall; block *up* with wall. ~**flower,** a fragrant garden plant; lady who sits out dances for lack of partner. ~**paper,** covering for room-walls.

wa′llabȳ (wŏ-), n. kinds of smaller kangaroo.

wa′lla(h) (wŏ-), n. (Anglo-Ind.) person or thing employed about or concerned with something or some man; *competition* ~, member of I.C.S. appointed by competitive examination; *punkah* ~,

---

māte, mēte, mīte, mōte, mūte, mōōt; răck, rĕck, rick, rŏck, rŭck, rōōk;

servant who works punkah; canal ~, ship built for voyage by Suez Canal.

wallaroo' (wŏ-), n. kinds of larger kangaroo.

wa'llet (wŏ-), n. bag for food, &c. on a journey; leather case for tools, &c. or for papers.

wall-eye (wawl'ī), n. disease of the eye shown by whiteness of the iris; eye affected with this. ~eyed (wawl'īd), a.

wa'llop (wŏ-), v.t. (sl.) thrash; (part.) big, strapping.

wallow (wŏl'ō), v.i. roll about in mud, sand, water, &c.; (fig.) take gross delight in.

wa'lnut (wawl-), n. edible nut in pair of boat-shaped shells; the tree or its timber.

wa'lrus (wŏ-), n. a long-tusked amphibious mammal.

waltz (wawls), n. dance in which partners progress gyrating round each other in embrace; piece of waltz-music. v.i. dance waltz; dance round, &c. in joy.

wampee' (wŏ-), n. grape-like fruit grown in China and E. Indies; tree yielding this.

wa'mpum (wŏ-), n. strings of shell-beads used by N.-Amer. Indians for money or ornament.

wan (wŏn), a. pale, as with illness; languid of look; of cold or dreary aspect.

wand (-ŏ-), n. long slender rod; staff as symbol of authority; conductor's baton.

wa'nder (wŏ-), v.i. go from place to place without settled plan; stray; diverge from the right way; talk irrelevantly; be inattentive or delirious.

wanderoo' (wŏ-), n. kind of monkey with leonine mane and tail.

wāne, v.i. (of moon) decrease in size after the full; decline or fall off. n. process of waning.

wangle (wăng'gl), (sl.), v.t. accomplish or secure (job, result) by artful contrivance; a fake.

want (wŏ-), n. lack or need of, deficiency; poverty, indigence; desire. v.t. & i. be without or in-

sufficiently provided with; wish, long for; fall short of. wa'nting (wŏ-), a. missing or non-existent; lacking; unequal to requirements; half-witted; prep. without; minus.

wa'nton (wŏ-), a. sportive, capricious; luxuriant, wild; unchaste; purposeless. n. unchaste woman; wanton person. v.i. sport, gambol; move capriciously.

wa'piti (wŏ-), n. large N.-Amer. deer.

war (wŏr), n. quarrel usu. between nations conducted by armed force; (fig.) hostile relations between persons. v.i. make war; (part.) rival, competing, antagonistic. ~cry, phrase or name formerly shouted in battle; party catchword. ~paint, put by savages on face and body before battle; (fig.) full dress. ~path, march of Amer. Indians to make war; (fig.) on the ~, engaged in any kind of conflict. ~plane, military aeroplane. war'fare (wŏr-), n. state of war; campaigning. war'like (wŏr-), a. martial, military, bellicose.

war'ble (wŏr-), v.i. & t. sing in gentle continuous trilling manner; *yodel. n. warbling sound. war'bler (wŏr-), n. kinds of small bird.

ward (wŏrd), n. custodianship, custody; minor under care of guardian or Court of Chancery; division of a town; division in prison, hospital, or workhouse; (pl.) the indentations in lock and key. v.t. parry (blow); keep off danger, &c. ~robe, place where clothes are kept; person's stock of clothes. ~room, officers' room on man-of-war. war'den (wŏr-), n. president or governor; (arch.) watchman, sentinel. war'denship (wŏr-), n. war'der (wŏr-), n. jailor. war'dress (wŏr-), n. female jailor. war'd-ship (wŏr-), n. tutelage; guardian's control.

wāre[1], n. pottery, metal, &c., in

the form of manufactured articles; (pl.) what one has for sale. ~house, n. (-s), building in which goods are stored or shown for sale; v.t. (-z), place or keep in warehouse. ~houseman (-an), n. person taking temporary charge of others' furniture; a wholesale dealer in goods.

ware², a. (wār), (poet.) aware. v.t. (wŏr, wār), (colloq.) look out for, be careful of.

warfare, ~like. See war.

war'lock (wŏr-), n. sorcerer.

warm (wŏrm), a. moderately hot; with temperature of skin raised above normal; (of clothing) fit to keep wearer warm; (of feelings, &c.) hearty, excited, affectionate; (in hide-and-seek) near the object sought. v.t. & i. make or become warm; (sl.) thrash. n. act of warming oneself or something. ~-hearted, of affectionate or sympathetic disposition. ~-pan, vessel for warming beds; (fig.) person allowed to hold office as stopgap. warmth (wŏr-), n. warmness.

warn (wŏrn), v.t. make aware of; put on guard against; admonish by way of caution or threat. war'ning (wŏr-), n. what is said or done to warn person; event that serves to warn; notice to terminate employment.

warp (wŏrp), n. threads stretched in loom to be crossed by weft; contorted state of warped wood; mental bias; rope used in warping a ship. v.t. & i. make or become contorted; distort or bias (person's mind); suffer such distortion; haul (ship) along by means of a rope fixed to an external point.

wa'rrant (wŏ-), n. thing that bears one out in doing something; an authorization, esp. in writing. v.t. serve as warrant for; bear out; guarantee (goods). ~officer, of the class holding warrants from Admiralty or War Office. wa'rrantable (wŏ-), a. that can be warranted; legitimate. ~tor,

~tee', nn. person giving, receiving, a guarantee of the quality, &c. of goods. wa'rranty (wŏ-), n. authority or justification; vendor's express or implied undertaking.

wa'rren (wŏ-), n. rabbit colony.

wa'rrior (wŏ-), n. distinguished or veteran soldier; fighting man.

wart (wŏrt), n. small excrescence on the skin; protuberance on tree-trunk. war'ty (wŏr-), a.

war'y (wŏr-), a. cautious, circumspect; on the look-out for danger.

was, p.t. 1st and 3rd pers. sing. of be.

wash (wŏ-), v.t. & i. cleanse with liquid; (fig.) purify; wash oneself, esp. one's face and hands; (of fabric, &c.) bear washing; carry along in specified direction, go sweeping over; ~ up, clean table utensils after use. n. washing; motion of agitated water; lotion or liquid cosmetic; thin coat of liquid colour applied to paper or wall. ~house, laundry. ~-leather, chamois and similar kinds. ~-out, (Army sl.) complete failure to effect something; fiasco; *washing away of a road, dam, &c. ~-tub, utensil in which linen is washed. wa'sher (wŏ-), n. a machine for washing; circlet of metal, leather, &c., used as tightener in taps and at junctions of joints. wash'erwoman, n. laundress. wa'shing (wŏ-), n. linen for, at, or from the wash. wa'shy (wŏ-), a. weak, watery.

wasp (wŏ-), n. winged insect with venomous sting. wa'spish (wŏ-), a. irritable; snappish.

wassail (wŏ'sl, wä'sl), n. festive drinking. v.i. hold wassail.

wast, p.t. 2nd pers. sing. of be.

waste, a. not inhabited or cultivated; superfluous; left over. v.t. & i. (-table), lay waste; squander; use extravagantly; dwindle or pine. n. barren expanse of ground; extravagance; wanton destruction. ~-pipe, pipe carrying off superfluous or used water or steam. wä'stage, *n.* amount lost by waste. **wā'ste-ful** (-tf-), *a.* extravagant; not economical. **wā'ster,** *n.* article spoilt in manufacture; (sl.) ne'er-do-well. **wā'strel,** *n.* thing spoilt in making; street arab; ne'er-do-well.

watch (wŏ-), *n.* state of being on the look-out for something; attention; vigilance; (hist.) watchmen or body of watchmen; one of the divisions of the night; (Naut.) four-hour spell of duty or half of crew taking it; a timepiece for carrying on the person. *v.i. & t.* be vigilant; keep watch; be on the watch for; keep under observation; keep guard over. ~dog, dog kept to give alarm against burglars, &c. ~man, (hist.) man keeping order in the streets; (poet.) sentinel; (mod.) man employed to look after empty building, &c. at night. ~tower, fortified post of observation. ~word, (hist.) military password; (mod.) phrase summarizing some party principle. **wa'tchful** (wŏ-), *a.* vigilant; on the watch.

wa'ter (waw-), *n.* liquid compound of oxygen and hydrogen; kinds of liquid consisting chiefly of this; a sea, river, or lake; the degree of brilliance and transparence in diamonds, &c. *v.t. &* *i.* sprinkle or adulterate or dilute with water; provide or fill (horse, engine, &c.) with water; (of mouth, eyes) secrete or run with water; (*p.p.,* of silk fabric, &c.) having irregular wavy gloss. ~colour, pigment mixed with water and not oil; picture painted with water-colours. ~course, small stream. ~cress, creeping water-plant used as salad. ~fall, stream falling over precipice. ~fowl, bird(s) frequenting the water. ~gauge, appliance showing height of water in reservoir, &c. ~hen, red-billed diving bird. ~ing-place, drinking place for beasts; spa; seaside health-resort. ~lily,

kinds of water-plant with floating leaves and flowers. ~line, line along which surface of water touches ship's side. ~logged, hardly able to float from being filled with water. ~man (-ăn), boatman plying for hire; skilled oarsman. ~manship, skill shown by expert oarsman. ~mark, faint translucent design on sheet of paper, indicating maker, size, &c. ~melon, elliptical smooth kind with watery juice. ~plane, aeroplane that can alight on and rise from the water. ~polo, swimmers' handball game with goals. ~power, mechanical force obtained from weight or motion of water. ~proof, *a.* impervious to water; *n.* such material or garment or sheet. ~rate, charge for use of public water-supply. ~shed, line of separation between river-basins. ~spout, column of water drawn up from sea to meet a whirling cloud. ~tight, so tightly closed as to prevent ingress or egress of water. ~way, navigable channel. ~wheel, kinds of wheel worked by water and working machinery. ~works, establishment for managing public water-supply. **wat'ery** (waw-), *a.* soppy; too thin or weak; rainy-looking.

wa'terbury (waw-), *n.* kinds of cheap American watch.

watt (wŏt), *n.* unit of electric power.

wa'ttle¹ (wŏ-), *n.* interlaced rods and twigs as material of fences, walls, or roofs; kinds of Australian acacia used as national emblem; (dial.) a wicker hurdle. *v.t.* construct of wattle; interlace (twigs, &c.).

wa'ttle² (wŏ-), *n.* fleshy appendage on head or throat of turkey and other birds. wattled (wŏt'ld), *a.* having wattle(s).

waul, *v.i.* squall; cry like a cat.

wāve, *v.i. & t.* (*-vable*), show motions like those of a flag in the wind; hold up and shake with waving motion; wave one's hand as a signal or direction; give a wavy form to (hair, &c.); undulate. *n.* ridge of water raised above the level of the surface; such ridge advancing and breaking on the shore; ridge-and-trough oscillation in a fluid medium conveying heat, light, sound, or electricity; a wavy line or surface; a waving of the hand. **~length**, distance between the crests of two successive waves. **~meter**, (Wireless) instrument used for measuring wavelengths, &c. **wāve'let** (-vl-), *n.*

wā'ver, *v.i.* be undecided; oscillate unsteadily; show signs of giving way; (of flame) flicker.

wā'vy, *a.* showing alternate contrary curves; undulating.

wǎx[1], *v.i.* grow larger; pass into a state or mood (*wax fat*, &c.).

wǎx[2], *n.* (sl.) fit of anger.

wǎx[3], *n.* plastic substance secreted by bees; this used as material for candles and other purposes; kinds of substance resembling wax; (attrib.) made of wax. *v.t.* smear or polish or treat with wax. **~bill**, kinds of small bird. **~cloth**, kinds of cloth coated with wax; floor-cloth. **~wing**, kinds of small bird. **~work**, wax modelling. **wǎx'en**, *a.* smooth and translucent as wax; plastic as wax.

wǎx'y, *a.* resembling wax; (sl.) in a rage; easily enraged.

way, *n.* road or track for passing along; course, route; method or plan for attaining an object; habitual course or manner of action; a concerned frame of mind; a specified state or condition; (pl.) structure of timber, &c. down which new ship slides at launch. **~bill**, list of passengers or parcels on conveyance. **~farer**, traveller, esp. on footway. **~lay'**, lie in wait for, esp. to rob or interview. **~leave**, rented right of way. **°~side**, side of road. **°~station**, stop intermediate between important stations on railroad. **°~train**, one stopping at way-stations.

way'ward, *a.* childishly self-willed; capricious.

wayz'goose, *n.* printing-house's annual feast or holiday.

wē, pl. subj. of I.

weak, *a.* wanting in strength or power or number; fragile; feeble; unsound. **weak'en**, *v.t.* & *i.* make or become weak; enfeeble. **~ling**, *n.* feeble person or animal. **~ly**, *a.* not robust; ailing. **~ness**, *n.* infirmity; weak point; inability to resist temptation; foolish liking *for*.

weal[1]. See wale.

weal[2], *n.* welfare; happiness.

weald, *n.* a district in S. England. **~en**, *a.* of the weald.

wealth (wĕl-), *n.* riches; being rich; abundance. **wea'lthy** (wĕl-), *a.* rich; opulent.

wean, *v.t.* induce (suckling) to feed otherwise than from the breast; cure *of*, rescue *from*, habit, specified company, &c. *n.* (Sc.) a child. **~ling**, *n.* new-weaned child, &c.

wea'pon (wĕp-), *n.* implement for inflicting bodily harm; means employed in any conflict.

wear[1]. See weir.

wear[2] (wār), *v.t.* & *i.* (p.t. & p.p. *wōre*), bring (ship) or come about by putting up of helm.

wear[3] (wār), *v.t.* & *i.* (*wōre, wōrn*), be dressed in or have on; carry or exhibit on one's person; injure appearance or efficiency of by wearing or using; make (hole, &c.) by attrition; sap the energy of; have lasting quality. *n.* use as clothes; things worn; capacity for resisting the effects of wear or use.

wear'y, *a.* tired or tiring. *v.t.* & *i.* tire. **wear'iness**, *n.* **~isome**, *a.* tedious; monotonous.

weas'el (-zl), *n.* small nimble carnivorous beast.

wea'ther (wĕdh-), *n.* state prevailing of such natural conditions as temperature, sunshine, wind, and rain. *v.t.* & *i.* expose to, or affect by, atmospheric changes; suffer discoloration, &c. from

---

māte, mēte, mīte, mōte, mūte, mōōt; rǎck, rěck, rǐck, rǒck, rǔck, rōōk;

such exposure; get to windward of; come safely through (storm). ~beaten, seasoned or injured by exposure to storms. ~board, sloping board attached at bottom of door to keep out rain; (pl.) a series of horizontal boards with overlapping edges, used as outside covering for walls, &c. ~bound, kept from proceeding by bad weather. ~chart, diagram of weather over wide area. ~cock, revolving metal bird or other pointer showing whence wind blows; (fig.) changeable person. ~glass, barometer. ~vane, weathercock.

weave, v.t. & i. (wōve; wōven and wōve), form fabric by interlacing threads, or form fabric out of (threads), esp. in a loom; construct or arrange (story, facts) as by weaving. weav'er, n. loom-worker; kinds of bird making textile nest.

weazen. See wizened.

web, n. woven fabric; amount woven in one piece; cobweb or gossamer or the like; membrane connecting toes, &c., as in bat and duck; connective tissue. webbed (-bd), web-foot'ed, aa. having space between toes, &c., filled with web. webb'ing, n. strong narrow fabric used for girths, &c.; strong edging to finer fabric.

wed, v.t. & i. (wedded; wedded or rarely wed), marry; (fig.) unite (quality to another); (p.p.) firmly attached to a pursuit, &c.

wedd'ing, n. marriage ceremony. ~ring, that used at wedding and worn by married woman.

wedge, n. piece of wood or metal, sharp at one end and gradually growing thicker; anything resembling a wedge. v.t. (-geable), force open or apart, fix firmly, with wedge; thrust or pack tightly between other things or persons.

Wedg'wood, n. kind of pottery. P.

wed'lock, n. the married state.

Wednesday (wĕnz'dĭ), n. fourth day of the week.

wee, a. tiny, very small. W~ Frees, nickname for part of the Free Church of Scotland that refused union with the United Presbyterian Church in 1900.

weed, n. wild herb growing where it is not wanted; lanky and weakly horse or person; (colloq.) cigar. v.t. & i. rid of weeds or of inferior parts or members.

weeds (-z), n.pl. mourning worn by widow.

weed'y, a. full of weeds; lanky and weak.

week, n. any period of seven days; the six days other than Sunday. ~day, day other than Sunday. ~end, Sunday and parts of Saturday and Monday as holiday, &c. week'lÿ, a. once a week; of, for, or lasting a week; adv. once a week; n. weekly newspaper.

ween, v.t. (poet.) think or be of the opinion.

weep, v.i. & t. (wept), shed tears for; lament for; shed moisture; abound with wet. weep'er, n. one who sheds tears; funeral sash or widow's veil; (pl.) white cuffs.

weev'il, n. destructive granary-beetle. weev'illed (-vld), a.

weft, n. cross-threads of web; (formerly) woof; (poet. &c.) web.

weigh (wā), v.t. & i. find the weight of; compare merits of; be of specified weight or importance; have influence. ~anchor, raise it to start voyage. ~bridge, machine for weighing loaded vehicles. weighing-machine, one of more complicated kind than balance-scales.

weight (wāt), n. gravity as a property of bodies; quantity measured by scales; a body of known weight for use in weighing; a heavy body; a load or burden; influence; importance. v.t. attach a weight to; impede or burden with. weighty (wā'tĭ), a. heavy; momentous; deserving consideration or carrying weight.

weir, wear[1] (wēr), n. river-dam raising level of upper stream.

---

weird (wērd), *n.* (rare) one's destiny. *a.* connected with fate; unearthly; (colloq.) queer.

Weis'mannism (vīs-), *n.* a theory of heredity, in which transmission of acquired characters is denied.

Welch, *a.* official spelling, in regimental names, of Welsh[1].

wel'come, *int.* of greeting. *n.* kind or glad reception. *v.t.* (-*mable*) receive (guest, news, &c.) with apparent pleasure. *a.* received with pleasure; free to use or accept.

weld, *v.t. & i.* hammer or press (iron, &c.) into unity; form by welding into some article.

wel'fare, *n.* happiness; prosperous or satisfactory condition.

wel'kin, *n.* (poet.) sky.

well[1], *n.* water-spring; source of knowledge or happiness; shaft sunk in ground to obtain water or oil; shaft in house for stairs, &c. *v.i.* gush out. ~head, ~spring, fountain-head.

well[2], *adv.* in a satisfactory or praiseworthy manner; probably or reasonably. *a.* in good health; in satisfactory state. *n.* what is good or well. *int.* expressing astonishment, qualified admission, &c. ~appointed, having all necessary equipment. ~balanced, sane; equally matched. ~behaved, orderly. ~being, welfare. ~born, of good family. ~bred, of good manners; (of horse, &c.) of pure stock. ~doing, virtuous conduct. ~favoured, comely. ~informed, having well-stored mind or access to best information. ~judged, opportunely or skilfully done. ~knit, compact. ~made, shapely. ~nigh, almost. ~regulated, orderly. ~spoken, refined in speech. ~timed, opportune. ~to-do, prosperous. ~turned, happily expressed. ~wisher, person who wishes one well. ~worn, threadbare; trite.

welladay', *int.* of grief.

Wellingtō'nia, *n.* tree reaching great size. Well'ingtons (-z), *n.pl.* kind of high boots.

Welsh[1], *a.* of Wales; in the Welsh language. *n.* the Welsh language. ~man (-an), ~woman, *nn.* ~mutton, of small mountain sheep. ~rabbit, dish of toasted cheese.

welsh[2], ~ch, *v.t. & i.* (of betting man) decamp without paying winner(s). welsh'er, *n.* one who defrauds winner(s) thus.

welt, *n.* rim sewn to shoe-upper for sole to be attached to; a wale. *v.t.* provide with welt; raise wales on; thrash.

wel'ter, *v.i.* wallow; roll in water or mire; be in confused state. *n.* confused mixture. ~handicap, ~race, ~stakes, &c., horse-races for heavy-weight riders. ~weight, heavy-weight rider, also weight carried apart from weight for age as test; (Boxing) 10 st. 7 lb., U.S. 10 st. 5 lb. and below.

wen, *n.* tumour forming permanent swelling below skin.

wench, *n.* girl or young woman (usu. depreciatory); lass.

wend, *v.t. & i.* direct (one's way); (arch.) go.

went, *p.t.* of go.

wept, *p.t. & p.p.* of weep.

were, *wert.* See be.

werewolf, werw- (wēr'wŏŏlf), *n.* human being turned into wolf.

Wesleyan (wĕz'lēan, wĕs'-), *a.* of the sect founded by John Wesley. *n.* member of this.

west, *n.* part of horizon where the sun goes down. *a. & adv.* from, in, or towards the west. wes'terly, *a.* from or to the west. wes'tern, *a.* of or in the west. west'ward(s), *adv.* towards the west.

wet, *a.* soaked, covered, or supplied with water or other liquid; rainy; (sl.) not prohibiting sale of intoxicants. *v.t.* make wet; moisten. *n.* liquid that wets something; rainy weather; (sl.) a drink. ~nurse, woman who suckles another's child.

wĕth´er (-dh-), *n*. castrated ram.

whăck, thwăck, *vv.t.* hit, esp. with stick ; beat. *nn.* a hit. ~**er,** *n.* (sl.) big specimen ; a lie. ~**ing,** *a.* (sl.) huge ; *n.* (sl.) a beating.

whāle[1], *n*. large fish-like marine mammal. *v.i.* hunt whales. ~**boat,** a ship's boat used in whaling. ~**bone,** elastic horny substance from the jaw of some whales. **whā´ler**[1], *n*. whaling ship or seaman on it.

*whāle[2], *v.t.* thrash, drub. **whā´ler**[2], *n.* (sl.) whopper. **whā´ling,** *n.* a beating ; *a.* (sl.) extra-ordinarily big or unusual.

wharf (wôrf), *n.* (pl. -*ves,* -*fs*), platform to which ships or barges may be moored to load and unload. ~**age,** *n.* wharf accommodation or dues. **whar´finger** (wôrfinj-), *n.* wharf-owner.

what (wŏt), *a.* (interrog.) asking for selection from indefinite number ; (exclam.) how great or strange ? *pron.* (interrog.) what thing ? what kind of person ? &c. (exclam.) what an amount ! how much ! (rel.) the thing or things that ; that or those which. ~**ever,** all or any that ; though any or anything ; (after *no* or *any*) at all, of any kind. ~**not,** piece of furniture with shelves for holding knick-knacks. ~**soever,** emphatic form of *whatever*.

What´man (-ŏt-), *n.* W~ (paper), brand of paper used for drawing, &c. P.

wheat, *n.* the plants or the grain of kinds of corn from which English bread is chiefly made. **wheat´ear,** *n.* a small bird. **wheat´en,** *a.* made of wheat. **whee´dle,** *v.t.* fool by flattery ; get (thing) *out of* by wheedling. **wheel,** *n.* circular spoked frame revolving on an axis ; an instrument of torture ; object resembling a wheel ; a steering-wheel ; motion of a line of men, &c. changing front on one end as pivot. *v.t.* & *i.* push or pull along ; go on bicycle, &c. ; (of bird, &c.) go in curves ; change front by a wheel ;

order (line of men) to wheel. ~**barrow,** box on two legs and a wheel, with handles for pushing. ~**wright,** maker and repairer of wheels. **wheel´er,** *n.* pole or shaft horse.

wheeze, *v.i.* breathe with audible friction. *n.* sound of wheezing ; actor's interpolated joke, &c. **wheez´y,** *a.* wheezing.

whĕlk, *n.* kinds of spiral-shelled marine mollusc.

whĕlm, *v.t.* engulf ; overwhelm.

whĕlp, *n.* pup or cub ; unmannerly child or youth. *v.i.* & *t.* bring forth young.

whĕn, *adv.* (interrog.) at what time ? how soon ? how long ago ? *conj.* at the time that ; at whatever time ; upon which ; although ; considering that. *pron.* (interrog.) what time ? (rel.) which time. *n.* time or date. ~**ever,** at whatever time ; as soon as ; every time that. ~**soever,** emphatic form of *whenever*.

whence, *adv.* (interrog.) from what place or source or cause ? (rel.) with *place*, &c.) from which ; to or from the place, &c. whence. *conj.* and thence ; and hence. *pron.* (interrog.) what starting-place or source or cause ? (rel.) which source, &c. *n.* source. ~**soever,** from whatever place or source.

where (wâr), *adv.* (interrog.) in or to what place, position, or state ? in what direction ? at what part ? (rel., with *place*, &c.) in which ; in or to the place, &c. where. *conj.* and there ; and here. *pron.* (interrog) what place ? &c. *n.* place or scene of something. ~**abouts´,** in or near what place ? ~**´abouts,** rough location. ~**as,** taking into consideration the fact that ; in contrast or comparison with the fact that. ~**by,** by which ; by what ? ~**fore,** for what reason ? on account of which ; and therefore ; the reason. ~**in,** in which ; in what point, &c. ? ~**of,** ~**on,** of, on, which ; of, on, what ? ~**soever,**

gh, as (*rou*)ge ; ö = I ; ĉ, ŏr, = ĝr ; ȳ, ȳ, = I, I ; and see p. 4, * = U.S.

8495 T

emphatic form of *wherever*. ~upon, after which; and thereupon. wherever, in or to what place, &c. ~with. wherewith, with which; with what? ~withal, wherewith; (with *the*) the money or other means needed.

whe′rry, *n*. light boat.

whet, *v.t.* sharpen (scythe, &c., appetite). *n*. a whetting; dram, &c. taken to whet appetite. ~stone, stone for tool-sharpening.

wheth′er (wĕdh-), *pron*. (interrog.) which of the two? *conj*. introducing part of a question expressing alternative(s).

whey (wā), *n*. liquid left when milk forms curds.

which, *a*. (interrog.) asking for selection from limited or known alternatives; (rel.) and or now or but or since or though this or these. *pron*. (interrog.) which thing or things? (rel.) which person(s) or thing(s). ~ever, ~soever, the one or the ones out of a limited or known number.

whiff, *n*. puff of air, smoke, odour, &c.; kind of sculling-boat; small cigar. *v.t. & i.* blow or puff lightly. *whiff′et, n*. insignificant creature.

whif′fle, *v.i. & t.* (of wind) blow lightly, shift about; (of flame, leaves) flicker, flutter; make the sound of a light wind in breathing. *n*. slight movement of air.

Whig, *n*. member of the reforming party that preceded the Liberals. ~gery, ~gism, *nn.*; ~gish, *a*.

while, *n*. space of time; time during which something continues. *v.t.* (with *away*) cause (time, an hour, &c.) to pass. *adv*. during which. *conj*. during the time that; for as long as; although; whereas. whiles (wīlz), *conj*. (arch.) while. whi′lom, *adv*. (arch.) formerly; *a*. quondam. whilst, less usual form for *while* as *conj*.

whim, *n*. a sudden fancy or caprice.

whim′per, *v.i.* cry querulously; whine softly. *n*. such sound.

whim′sical (-z-), *a*. capricious; fantastic. whimsical′ity, *n*.

whim′sy (-zI), *n*. whim, crotchet.

whin, *n*. gorse or gorse-bush. ~chat, a small bird.

whine, *n*. dog's or child's long-drawn wail; querulous tone or talk. *v.i. & t.* emit or utter whine; utter whiningly.

whing′er, *n*. short sword, dirk, or long knife.

whinn′y, *n*. gentle or joyful neigh. *v.i. & t.* emit whinny.

whip, *n*. stick with lash attached as implement for urging on or punishing; person of specified skill in driving; person in charge of hounds; person having or sharing responsibility for a political party's discipline; such whip's written notice requesting member's attendance. *v.t. & i.* apply whip to; urge on thus; beat (eggs or cream) to froth; (sl.) outdo; dart; snatch. ~cord, thin tightly twisted cord. ~ hand, hand that holds the whip. ~top, top kept spinning by blows of lash. whipper-in, whip of pack of hounds or party. whipping-boy, (hist.) boy educated with and chastised instead of young prince.

whipp′er-snapper, *n*. small child; presumptuous insignificant man.

whipp′et, *n*. cross-bred dog of greyhound type used for racing; (Mil.) fast light tank.

whip′poorwill, *n*. an American bird allied to goatsucker.

whirl, *v.t. & i.* swing round and round; revolve rapidly; convey or go rapidly. *n*. whirling movement. ~pool, a circular eddy in sea, river, &c. ~wind, circular eddy of wind. whirl′igig (-g-), *n*. kinds of spinning toy; revolving motion.

whirr, *n*. continuous buzzing or clicking sound. *v.i.* make this.

whisht (hw-), *int*. demanding silence (esp. Ir.).

whisk, *n*. bunch of hair, &c. for

---

flapping dust or flies away; beating-up implement for eggs or cream; whisking motion of tail, &c. *v.t.* & *i.* flap *away* or *off*; beat up with whisk; convey or go with light quick motion. whis'ker, *n.* hair of man's cheek; face-bristles of cat, &c. whis'kered (-erd), *a.*

whis'ky, *n.* spirit distilled from malted barley, &c.

whis'per, *v.i.* & *t.* speak with the breath instead of the voice; talk in secret or confidential way; (of leaves, wind, &c.) rustle or murmur. *n.* whispering speech or sound; thing whispered.

whist, *n.* a card-game, usu. for four persons. ~ drive, whist-party with players moving on from table to table.

whistle (wi'sl), *n.* shrill sound made by forcing the breath between nearly closed lips; similar sound made by bird, wind, or missile, or produced by instrument; instrument made to produce whistle. *v.i.* & *t.* emit whistle; summon or give signal thus; produce (tune) thus.

whit¹, *n.* particle, jot.

Whit², *c.* ~sun'day, 7th after Easter, the Feast of Pentecost. Whit'sun, abbrev. of *Whitsunday.* Whit'suntide, Whitsunday and following days.

white, *n.* of the colour of fresh snow or table salt; pale; transparent and colourless; (fig.) innocent or unstained. *n.* white pigment or whiteness; white material or objects. *v.t.* cover with white. ~bait, fish fried in quantities when about 2 in. long as delicacy. ~heat, state of metal heated beyond red heat; (fig.) intense anger or passion. ~ lead, compound of lead used as pigment. ~livered, cowardly. ~man, member of any of the paler races of the European type; (colloq.) honourable well-bred person. ~ meat, poultry, rabbits, veal, pork. ~smith, tin-man, galvanizer of iron. ~thorn,

hawthorn. ~throat, kinds of songbird. ~wash, *n.* solution of lime or whiting for whitening walls and ceilings; (fig.) means used to whitewash character; *v.t.* apply whitewash to; (fig.) attempt to clear (discredited person) of imputations; *defeat person without his scoring. whi'ten, *v.t.* & *i.* make or become white. whi'tening (-tn-), *n.* whiting. whi'ting, *n.* chalk prepared for use in whitewashing, plate-cleaning, &c.; an edible sea-fish. whi'tish, *a.*

White'hall' (-t-hawl), *n.* departmental government; the Government offices.

whith'er (-dh-), *adv.* (interrog.) to what place, point, position, or state? in what direction? (rel.) to which; to the place, &c. to which. *conj.* and thither, and hither. *n.* destination. ~soever, *adv.* to whatever destination.

whiting, ~ish. See white.

whit'low (-ō), *n.* inflamed tumour on finger.

Whitsun. See Whit².

whit'tle, *n.* (arch.) butcher's knife. *v.t.* & *i.* pare (wood) with repeated slicings of knife; use knife thus (also used fig.).

whiz(z), *n.* sound made by body cutting the air at great speed. *v.i.* fly with, or make, a whiz.

who (hōō), *pron.* (obj. *whom* pr. hōōm, poss. *whose* pr. hōōz), what or which person(s)? of what personal rank or authority? (after *person*, &c.) that. whoever (obj. *whomever*, or usu. *whomsoever*, colloq. *whoever* poss. *whose-ever*, or usu. *whosesoever*, colloq. *whoever's*), any one or every one that; though any one. whoso, (arch.) whoever. whosoever (obj. *whomsoever*, poss. *whosesoever*), emphat. form of *whoever*.

whole (hōl), *a.* in good health (arch.); in uninjured, intact, or undiminished state; all that there is in or on. *n.* thing complete in itself; total amount of something. ~hearted, weakened by no doubt or hesitation; heartily felt or done. ~hog: go the ~hog, do thing thoroughly. ~hogger, a thoroughgoing supporter, esp. of protectionism. ~length, a. (of portrait) including whole figure; n. such portrait. ~sale, n. selling of things in large quantities to be retailed by others; a. & adv. on the wholesale plan; on a large scale. ~some, a. promoting physical or moral health; producing a good effect. wholly (hōl'-li), adv. entirely or without abatement; exclusively.

whom. See who.

whoop (hoōp), ~ing. See hoop².

whop, v.t. & i. (sl.) thrash, defeat. whopp'er, n. (sl.) big specimen; great lie. whopp'ing, a. (sl.) very big; n. thrashing.

whore (hōr), n. prostitute.

whorl, n. ring of leaves round stem; raised ridge round cylinder; one turn of spiral.

whor'tleberry (wertelb-). n. bilberry.

whose (hoōz), possessive case of who, and sometimes of which as rel. pronoun.

why, adv. (interrog.) for what reason or purpose? (rel., after reason, &c.) for which. int. expressing discovery, impatience, reflection, objection, conclusion. n. (pl. -ys), reason.

wick, n. strip or thread feeding the flame of lamp or candle with oil or grease; gauze strip inserted in wound to drain it.

wick'ed, a. sinful, immoral; spiteful; playfully malicious.

wick'er, n. plaited osiers, &c. as a material (usu. attrib.). ~work, wicker or things made of it. wick'ered (-erd), a.

wick'et, n. small door or gate; turnstile entrance; (Crick.) three stumps with bails in position; the ground between the wickets; member of batting side as an item to be got rid of. ~keep(er), fieldsman stationed close behind batsman's wicket.

wide, a. having the sides far apart; broad, not narrow; open to full extent; far from the mark; (appended to measurement) in width. adv. at or to many points; with wide interval or opening; so as to miss the mark. n. (Crick.) a wide ball. ~awake, broad-brimmed soft felt hat. ~ball, ball out of batsman's reach and counting one to his side. ~spread, widely disseminated. wi'den, v.t. & i. make or grow wide. widgeon (wij'en), n. kinds of wild duck.

wid'ow (-ō), n. woman whose husband is dead. v.t. make into a widow or widower. ~bird, black-plumaged African bird. ~hood, n. wid'ower (-ōer), n. man whose wife is dead.

width, n. distance or measurement from side to side; strip of material of a known width; (fig.) wideness of views, &c.

wield, v.t. hold and use (power, sword, pen, &c.).

wife, n. a married woman, esp. in relation to her husband. ~like, ~ly, aa. befitting a wife.

wig¹, n. artificial head of hair.

wig², v.t. rebuke sharply. ~ging, n. severe reproof.

wight (wit), n. (arch.) person.

*wig'wag, v.t. & i., & n. (Army sl.) signal with flags.

wig'wam, n. N.-Amer. Indian's tent or hut.

wild, a. in the original natural state; not domesticated or cultivated; uncivilized; tempestuous; lawless; out of control; intensely excited; rash, ill-aimed, random. adv. with reckless or incapable lack of self-control. n. wild tract, desert. ~cat, (fig., of schemes, &c.) reckless, unsound. ~fire, the combustible liquid anciently used in warfare (now used fig.). ~goose chase, pursuit of something unlikely to be caught. wil'derness, n. a desert; state of being wild or disorderly. wil'ding, n. self-sown plant or its fruit.

wildebeest (wě'ldẽbăst), n. (S.-Afr.) the gnu.

wile, n. stratagem or trick (usu. in pl.); use of tricks. v.t. (-lable). lure away, into, &c.

wil'ful, a. committed intentionally; obstinate, wayward.

will, v.aux. (pres. I, he, we, you, they, will, thou wilt; past & condit. I, he, we, you, they, would, thou wouldst or wouldest), forming compound tenses or moods expressing intention, prophecy, conditional result, insistence, habit, &c. v.t. desire (thing); long or wish to; desire that; intend unconditionally; compel by will. n. faculty by which one decides what one shall do; fixed intention; control exercised over impulse; one's disposition towards others; person's directions written in legal form for disposition of his property after death. will'ing, a. not reluctant; cheerfully ready or given.

will-o'-the-wisp' (-dh-), n. phosphorescent light seen on marshy ground; elusive person or thing.

wil'low (-ō), n. pliant-wooded waterside tree yielding osiers and timber for cricket-bats; (colloq.) cricket-bat. ~herb, kinds of wild plant. **will'owy** (-ōi), a. lithe and slender.

willy-nilly (-ĭ̆-ĭ̆), adv. whether one likes it or not.

wilt¹. See will.

wilt², v.i. & t. wither; droop or make (flower, &c.) droop.

wi'ly, a. crafty, cunning.

wim'ple, n. linen head-dress of the kind worn by nuns.

win, v.t. & i. (won pr. wŭn). gain as result of fight, contest, bet, or effort; be the victor; persuade, induce to do. n. a victory in a game. *~out, (colloq.) be successful. win'ner, n. victor. win'ning, a. attractive; charming; n.pl. sum won in gaming, &c. ~post, post marking the end of a racecourse.

wince, v.i. show pain by starting. n. such movement.

win'cey, n. (pl. -eys), woollen (and cotton) material for dresses, &c.

winch, n. crank of wheel or axle; windlass.

Win'chester, n. repeating rifle.

wind¹, n. (wi- in verse often wī-), air moving along, esp. with considerable speed; wind as conveying scent; wind-instruments or their sound; breath as needed in exertion; flatulence; (Army sl.) in phr. get the ~ up, be frightened. v.t. sound (bugle, horn) by blowing (wī-; winded or wound) (wī-; winded) detect presence of by scent; exhaust the wind of; renew wind of by rest. ~bag, wordy orator. ~bound, unable to sail for contrary wind. ~fall, fruit blown down; piece of unexpected good luck, esp. legacy. ~gall, soft tumour on fetlock. ~gauge, anemometer. ~hover, kestrel. ~instrument, played by blowing or air-current. ~mill, mill with sails worked by wind. ~pipe, air-passage from throat to lungs. ~screen, screen of glass in front of motor-car driver. ~stick, (sl.) propeller of aeroplane.

wind², v.i. & t. (wound). go in spiral or curved course; make one's or its way thus; insinuate oneself; coil, wrap with overlapping; turn, twist. ~up, draw up with windlass; coil the whole of; tighten coiled spring of; bring or come to an end; put in order. **winding-sheet**, linen in which corpse is wrapped.

wind'lass, n. machine on wheel-and-axle principle for hoisting and hauling.

win'dow (-ō), n. opening in wall, &c. for admission of light and air; the glass or sashes of a window, &c. ~dressing, art of showing one's wares.

Wind'sor (-z-). ~ chair, strong plain chair of polished wood with curved back. ~ soap, brown scented kind. House of ~, the present royal family.

wind'ward, a. in the direction

from which the wind is blowing. *n.* the windward region. *adv.* to windward of.

wind′y, *a.* exposed to or stormy with wind; wordy.

wine, *n.* fermented grape-juice as drink; fermented drink resembling it made from other fruits, &c.; solution of drug in wine. ~bibber, tippler. ~cooler, vessel in which wine-bottles are cooled with ice. ~glass, glass for drinking wine. ~press, press in which grapes are squeezed.

wing, *n.* one of the limbs or organs by which flying is effected; side extension of something, esp. of building or army; winged flight. *v.t. & i.* equip with wings; send (arrow, &c.) in flight; travel, traverse, on wings; wound in wing or arm. W~ Commander, officer in R.A.F. ranking next to Group Captain.

wink, *v.t. & i.* close and open (one's eye or eyes); wink one eye at a person to give a hint; (with *at*) affect not to notice, connive at. *n.* act of winking.

winkle (wing′kl), *n.* small edible sea-snail.

wi′nnow (-ō), *v.t.* fan (grain) free of chaff, &c.; fan (chaff, &c.) *away* or *from*; sift, examine.

win′some, *a.* (of person or his manner) winning, engaging.

win′ter, *n.* last and coldest of the four seasons. *v.i.* spend the winter *at, in,* &c. ~garden, glass-covered space with plants as lounge. ~quarters, place to which troops retire for winter.

win′try, *a.* characteristic of winter; (of greeting, &c.) lacking warmth.

wipe, *v.t. & i.* (-*pable*), cleanse or dry surface by rubbing with something soft; get rid of (tears), clean (vessel) *out* or make *clean,* by wiping; (sl.) aim sweeping blow at. *n.* a cleaning rub; blow, stroke; gibe; (sl.) handkerchief.

wire, *n.* metal drawn out into the form of thread, cord, or tape; telegraphy or a telegram. *v.t.*

& *i.* (-*rable*), provide, fasten, &c. with wire; telegraph. ~drawn, (of argument, &c.) of extreme or idle subtlety. ~haired, with stiff loose-lying hair (esp. of dogs). ~puller, politician, &c. who sets puppets moving. ~worm, a plant-pest. wire′less (wīr′l-), *a.* (esp. of telegraphy or telephony) worked or sent without wires; *n.* wireless telegraphy or telephony. wir′y, *a.* (esp.) sinewy or untiring.

wis′dom (-z-), *n.* experience and knowledge with the power of judging rightly; sagacity; prudence. ~tooth, molar usu. cut at age of about 20.

wise[1] (-z), *a.* having, showing, or dictated by wisdom; having knowledge; suggestive of wisdom, oracular.

wise[2] (-z), *n.* (arch.) way or manner or degree.

wi′seacre (-zāker), *n.* sententious dullard.

wish, *v.i. & t.* have or express a desire or aspiration for; want or demand (to do); be inclined well or ill to. *n.* a desire; the thing desired. wish′ful, *a.* desirous.

wish′-wash (-ōsh), *n.* (sl.) washy drink or talk. wish′y-washy (-wō-), *a.* thin, sloppy.

wisp, *n.* small bundle or twist of hay, straw, &c.

wist, *p.t.* of wit.

wistā′ria, *n.* a mauve-flowered tree.

wist′ful, *a.* affected with or betraying vague yearnings or unsatisfied desires.

wit, *n.* (sing. or pl.) intelligence; understanding; imaginative and inventive faculty; amusing ingenuity of speech or ideas; person noted for this. *v.t. & i.* (arch.); pres. *wot, wottest;* past *wist).* know; *to wit,* that is to say, namely.

witch, *n.* woman using magic; old hag; fascinating girl or woman. *v.t.* bewitch. ~craft, use of magic. witch′ery, *n.* witchcraft; power exercised by beauty or eloquence or the like.

witenagemot' (-g-), *n.* (hist.) Anglo-Saxon national council.

with (-dh), *prep.* in antagonism to; in or into company of; among, beside; having, carrying, or possessed of; in agreement or disagreement with; by means of; on the side of; in the care or charge of; despite, notwithstanding.

withal' (-dhawl), *adv.* (arch.) moreover; as well.

withdraw' (-dh-), *v.t. & i.* (-*drew* pr. -ōō; -*drawn*), pull aside or back; take away, remove; discontinue the giving or allowing of; retract, unsay; retire or go apart. **withdraw'al** (-dh-), *n.*

with'e (-dh, *also* with), **with'y** (-dhi), *n.* tough flexible branch, esp. of willow or osier.

with'er (-dh-), *v.t. & i.* make or become dry and shrivelled; deprive of or lose vigour or freshness; blast, blight.

with'ers (-dherz), *n.pl.* ridge between horse's shoulder-blades.

withhōld' (-dh-h-), *v.t.* (-*hēld*), refuse to give or put in operation; restrain from action.

within' (-dh-), *adv.* inside, indoors. *prep.* inside; not out of or beyond; not transgressing or exceeding. *n.* the inside.

without' (-dh-), *adv.* outside; out-of-doors. *prep.* outside; not having or feeling or showing; in want of; with freedom from; in absence of. *conj.* unless. *n.* the outside; external sources.

withstānd', *v.t.* (-*stōōd*), oppose; hold out against.

withy. See withe.

wit'less, *a.* silly; thoughtless.

wit'ling, *n.* facetious person.

wit'ness, *n.* person giving sworn testimony; person attesting another's signature to document; spectator of an event; person or thing whose existence serves as testimony. *v.t. & i.* sign (document) as witness to authenticity; be spectator of; serve as evidence or indication of; bear witness.

witt'icism, *n.* facetious or witty remark.

witt'ingly, *adv.* with knowledge of what one is doing.

witt'y, *a.* showing, or full of, verbal wit.

wi'vern, wy'-, *n.* heraldic winged dragon.

wiz'ard, *n.* person of extraordinary powers; genius; magician; conjurer. **wiz'ardry**, *n.*

wiz'ened (-nd), **wiz'en, weaz'en**, *aa.* shrivelled-looking.

wō, whoa (wō'a), *int.* used to stop horse, &c. **wo-back'**, *int.* used in backing horses.

woad, *n.* a blue dye.

wob'ble, *v.i.* sway from side to side; stand unsteadily; vacillate.

wōe, *n.* affliction, bitter grief; (pl.) calamities. **~begone**, *a.* dismal-looking. **~ful**, *a.* feeling affliction; afflicting.

wōld, *n.* open uncultivated tract.

wolf (wŏŏ-), *n.* (pl. -*ves*), wild beast allied to dog hunting in packs. *v.t.* (sl.) devour greedily. **~cub**, young wolf; junior boy scout. **wo'lfish** (wŏŏ-), *a.*

wo'lfram (wŏŏ-), *n.* tungsten ore; tungsten.

wolverene, -ine (wŏŏlverē'n), *n.* N.-Amer. carnivore allied to glutton.

wo'man (wŏŏ-), *n.* (pl. -*en*, pr. wim'in), adult human female; women or the female sex; a female servant. **~hood**, female maturity; womanly character. **womenfolk, ~kind**, women; the female part of one's family. **wo'manish** (wŏŏ-), *a.* effeminate; lacking manliness. **wo'manize** (wŏŏ-), *v.t. & i.* make womanish; (of men) be licentious. **wo'manly** (wŏŏ-), *a.* having the qualities befitting a woman; not girlish.

womb (wŏŏm), *n.* organ of conception and gestation in female mammals.

wŏm'bat, *n.* Australian marsupial mammal about size of badger.

won, *p.t.* of win.

wo'nder (wŭ-), *n.* strange or remarkable thing or specimen or event; amazement. *v.i. & t.* be greatly surprised or filled with wonder; be curious to know. ~ful, *a.* very remarkable. ~ment, *n.* surprised state of mind. wo'ndrous (wŭ-), *a.* strange; wonderful.

wŏn't, contraction of *will not*.

wŏnt, *a.* accustomed to do. *n.* custom; habit. *v.i.* be accustomed. wŏ'ntĕd, *a.* habitual.

wŏō, *v.t.* court; seek the hand or love of; coax or importune.

wood, *n.* growing trees occupying a tract of land; fibrous substance of tree, whether growing or cut for timber or fuel. ~bine, honey-suckle; *Virginia creeper; kind of cigarette (P.). ~cock, a game-bird. ~craft, knowledge of forest conditions. ~cut, print from engraving made on wood. ~land, wooded country. ~man, forester. ~nymph, dryad. ~pecker, kinds of bird clinging to tree-stems in search of insects. ~pulp, wood-fibre prepared as material for paper. ~ruff, a plant. ~work, things made of wood. wŏŏd'ĕd, *a.* having woods. wŏŏd'en, *a.* made of wood; stiff, clumsy; lacking animation. wŏŏd'y̆, *a.* like or consisting of wood.

wŏŏf. See weft.

wŏŏl, *n.* fine wavy hair such as forms the fleece of sheep and goats; woollen yarn or cloth or garments; (joc.) woolly human hair; cotton-wool or similar substance. ~gathering, absent-mindedness. ~sack, Lord Chancellor's seat in the House of Lords; his office. ~work, embroidery of dyed wools. wŏŏl'en, *a.* made of wool; *n.* woollen fabric. wŏŏl'y̆, *a.* like or suggesting wool; *n.* (often *pl.*) woollen garment, esp. sweater.

wŏŏtz, *n.* special kind of steel made in India and imported into Europe and America for edge-tools.

*Wŏp, *n.* (sl.) Mid- or South-European, esp. Italian, in U.S.

word (wĕrd), *n.* any single symbol used in speech or writing and recognizable as a part of speech; statement or remark or saying; talk (usu. *pl.*); news or message; one's promise or solemn assurance; *Word of God*, the Bible. *v.t.* put into words; select words to express. ~painting, graphic or picturesque writing. ~perfect, having what one has to say by heart. ~picture, piece of word-painting. ~play, verbal fencing; punning or pun. ~splitting, subtle verbal distinctions. wor'dy̆ (wĕr-), *a.* verbose or diffuse.

wore. See wear², wear³.

work (wĕrk), *n.* expenditure of energy; a task; employment; a thing done or made; a book or picture or similar production; (*pl.*) operations in building or engineering; (*pl.*) the operative parts of a machine; (*pl.*) buildings and plant of a manufactory. *v.i. & t.* (*-ed*; also *wrought* pr. rawt), make efforts (*for, against,* &c.); be engaged in work; act in specified way; be in agitated motion or fermentation; exact labour from; effect or bring about; excite artificially into some mood; cipher out (sum). ~aday, concerned with ordinary practical life. ~bag, ~basket, ~box, receptacles esp. for holding sewing-materials. ~house, public institution for reception of paupers (or *petty offenders). ~man, hired labourer; person of specified skill at his job. ~man-like, showing practised skill. ~manship, degree of skill in artificer or of finish in his product. *~out, (colloq.) spell of exercise of athletes, &c. ~people, workmen and workwomen. ~shop, room or building in which manufacture is carried on. ~woman, fem. of *workman*. wor'kable (wĕr-), *a.* that can be worked or will work or is practicable. ~ability, *n.*

world (wĕr-), *n.* the universe or all

that exists; the earth, heavenly body supposed to resemble it; specified part of the earth or of mankind; secular interests and affairs; mankind; the people and things concerned in a specified branch of activity; a vast amount. ~power, powerful State whose policy may affect the world at large. ~wide, spread over or known to all the world, wor'ldling (wĕr-), n. worldly person. wor'ldly (wĕr-), a. temporal or secular; engrossed in or concerned with the pursuit of wealth or pleasure.

worm (wĕrm), n. kinds of invertebrate limbless creeping animal; internal parasite; insignificant or downtrodden person; spiral part of screw, &c. v.t. & i. convey oneself or progress with crawling or wriggling motion; insinuate oneself into favour, &c.; draw (secret, &c.) by craft out of person. ~eaten, riddled with holes by gnawing of worms; (fig.) old, antiquated.

wor'mwood (wĕr-), n. a bitter herb; source of mortification.

wor'my (wĕr-), a. full of worms or worm-eaten.

worn, p.p. of wear.

wo'rry (wŭ-), v.t. & i. shake or pull about with the teeth; harass or importune; be a trouble or anxiety to; fret oneself. n. thing that causes anxiety or disturbs tranquillity; disturbed state of mind; anxiety.

worse (wĕrs), a. more bad, less good; in or into worse health; in worse condition. adv. more badly. n. worse thing(s); something less good. wor'sen (wĕr-), v.i. & t. grow or make worse.

wor'ship (wĕr-), n. homage or service paid to God; adoration felt for a person or principle; title of respect for a magistrate, esp. a mayor. v.t. & i. adore as divine; honour with religious rites; idolize; attend public worship. ~ful, a. honourable or distinguished.

worst (wĕr-), a. most bad, most ill.

adv. most badly. n. the worst part, state, or estimate. v.t. get the better of; defeat.

wor'sted (woŏs-), n. woollen yarn; often used attrib.

wort (wĕrt), n. plant, herb (rare); infusion of malt before it is fermented into beer.

worth¹ (wĕr-), v. (arch.) befall; woe ~ the day, a lamentation.

worth² (wĕr-), a. of value equivalent to; deserving or repaying; possessed of. n. what a person or thing is worth; merit. ~less, a. of no value or merit.

worthy (wĕrdhˈĭ), a. estimable or deserving respect; deserving of; adequate; suitable to the dignity, &c. of. n. a worthy person; a person of distinction.

wot, see wit; would, see will.

would'-be (woŏd-), a. & adv. vainly aspiring to or intending.

wound¹ (woŏ-), n. injury done by cut, stab, blow, or tear to animal or vegetable tissues; injury to reputation or pain inflicted on feelings. v.t. inflict wound on.

wound². See wind¹ (v.), wind².

wove, woven. See weave.

*wow, n. anything extraordinary of its kind.

wrack, n. cast-up sea-weed.

wraith, n. person's double seen shortly before or after his death.

wrangle (răngˈgl), n. a noisy argument or dispute. v.i. engage in wrangle. wrā'ngler (-nggˈ-), n. a disputative person; (hist.) first-classman in mathematical tripos; *(western U.S., colloq.) herdsman, cowboy.

wrap, v.t. & i. envelop in folded or soft encircling material; arrange or draw (pliant covering) round or about person, &c. n. shawl or neckerchief or rug. wrapp'er, n. that in which anything is wrapped; dressing-gown.

wrasse, n. a sea-fish.

wrath (-aw-), n. anger, indignation. ~ful, a. angry.

wreak, v.t. give play to.

wreath, n. (pl. pr. -dhz), flowers or leaves fastened together in a circlet; curl or ring of smoke or cloud. **wreathe** (-dh), *v.t. & i.* encircle with or as with wreath (of smoke, &c.) move in wreaths.

wreck, *n.* destruction or disablement, esp. of ship; ship that has suffered wreck; greatly damaged or disabled building or person. *v.t. & i.* cause wreck of (ship, hopes, &c.); suffer wreck. **~age,** *n.* wrecked material; remnants of wreck. **~er,** *n.* one who wrecks; plunderer of wrecked ships. **~ing,** *n.* wrecker's action.

wren, *n.* kind of small bird.

wrench, *n.* violent twist or pull or tearing off; tool for gripping and turning nuts, &c.; (fig.) painful uprooting or parting. *v.t.* inflict wrench on; pull by violence; distort (facts).

wrest, *v.t.* twist, distort, pervert; force or wrench away or extract *from* opponent, &c.

wre'stle (-sl), *n.* contest in which two opponents grapple and try to throw each other to the ground; a tussle, hard struggle. *v.i. & i.* have wrestling match with; struggle *with* or *against*; *(western U.S., colloq.) throw (steer, &c.) for branding.

wretch, *n.* ill-fated or pitiable person; person without conscience or shame. **wretch'ed,** *a.* unhappy or in misery; of bad quality; contemptible; unsatisfactory.

wrick, rick[2], *v.t.* slightly sprain or strain (neck, back, &c.). *n.* such hurt.

wri'ggle, *v.i. & i.* (of worm) twist about, go along thus; make worm-like motions; (fig.) practise evasion. *n.* act of wriggling.

wright (rīt), *n.* maker or builder, usu. in comb. as *wheel~, ship~, play~,* &c.

wring, *v.t.* (**wrŭng**), squeeze tightly; squeeze and twist; break by twisting; extort by importunity. *n.* act of wringing.

wrinkle (ring'kl), *n.* crease or furrow of the skin or face; similar mark in other flexible sur-

face; piece of useful guidance. *v.t. & i.* make wrinkles in; assume wrinkles. **wrink'ly,** *a.*

wrist, *n.* joint of hand and arm. **~band** (riz'band), band forming or concealing end of shirt-sleeve. **~let,** something worn round wrist, esp. band of leather as protection or support.

writ, *n.* what is written (arch.; usu. in *Holy Writ*); written command from law-court, &c.

write, *v.i. & t.* (**wrote,** arch. *writ; written,* arch. *writ; -table*). mark paper or other material with the symbols by which speech is represented to the eye; set down (letter, word, sentence, &c.) thus; compose for publication; write and send letter to; state in book, letter, &c. **wri'ter,** *n.* one who practises the art of writing; clerk in certain offices; author; *W~ to the Signet* (abbr. W.S.), Scottish solicitor. **wri'ting,** *n.* penmanship; document; piece of literary work. **~-case,** case for holding one's writing-materials. **~-master,** one who teaches to write. **~-materials,** pens, ink, paper, &c. **~-paper,** paper for writing on.

writhe (-dh), *v.i.* twist or roll oneself about as in pain; suffer mental torture.

written, *p.p.* of write.

wrong, *a.* out of order or condition; contrary to morality; mistaken or in error. *adv.* amiss; in the wrong direction; with incorrect result. *n.* what is morally wrong; a wrong action; injustice. *v.t.* treat unjustly; mistakenly attribute bad motives to. **~doer,** offender. **~doing,** transgression. **~headed,** perverse and obstinate. **wrong'ful,** *a.* unwarranted; lacking justification.

wrote, *p.t.* of write.

wroth (or rō-), *a.* angry.

wrought (rawt), *p.t. & p.p.* of work. **~iron,** iron forged or rolled, not cast.

wrung, *p.t. & p.p.* of wring.

wry, a. distorted; turned to one side. ~neck, a small bird.

wych-, pref. in tree-names, as wych-alder, ~elm, ~hazel.

wynd, n. (Sc.) alley in a town.

X

X, x (ĕks), letter and n. (as roman numeral) 10; (Alg.; x) first unknown quantity; incalculable influence or factor.

xě'běc (z-), n. (hist.) ship of kind used by Mediterranean pirates.

xěn'on (z-), n. (Chem.) heavy inert gaseous element.

X-rays. See Röntgen.

xy'lŏgrǎph (z-), n. wood-engraving; also a decorative pattern got by mechanical reproduction of wood-grain. xylŏg'rǎphy (z-), n. art of wood-engraving.

xy'lonite (z-), n. celluloid.

xy'lophŏne (z-), n. musical instrument of wooden bars vibrating when struck.

Y

Y, y (wī), letter and n. (Alg.; y) second unknown quantity.

yacht (yŏt), n. light sailing-vessel for racing or pleasure. v.i. cruise or race in yacht. ~s'man (-an), person who yachts.

yăf'fle, yǎf'fl, n. the green woodpecker.

yahoo' (-a-h-), n. bestial person.

yăk, n. Tibetan ox.

Yāle lŏck, n. cylinder lock for doors, &c. P.

yăm, n. a tropical plant or its edible tuber; sweet potato.

Yama (yah-), n. Hindu god of departed spirits and judge of the dead.

yănk[1], v.t. & i. (sl.) pull (lever, &c.) with a jerk. n. sudden hard pull.

Yănk[2], n. (sl.) Yankee.

Yănk'ee (-kǐ), n. (colloq.) native of New England or of the northern States of America. ~Dōōdle, a U.S. song; a Yankee.

yăp, v.i. & n. bark; *talk.

yăpp, n. book-binding with projecting limp leather cover.

yǎrb'orough (-ru), n. whist or bridge hand with no card above a 9.

yārd[1], n. the unit of long measure (3 ft.); spar slung across mast for sail to hang from. ~arm, either end of sail-yard.

yārd[2], n. space enclosed by walls or railings, open to the sky, usu. attached to a building.

yarn, n. any spun thread, esp. coarse wool for knitting, &c.; (colloq.) story, anecdote.

yǎ'rrow (-ō), n. common kind of milfoil.

yăsh'măk, n. Moslem woman's veil.

yaw, v.i. (Naut., Aeronaut.) fall off from course by fault of steersman or ship or by design.

yawl, n. kinds of ship's boat and sail.

yawn, v.i. open the mouth wide, esp. in sleep or boredom; (of mouth or cavity or chasm) gape or be wide open. n. act of yawning.

yaws, n. a tropical epidemic and contagious disease of the skin with small red spots, sometimes ulcerating.

ye (yē, yǐ), pron. of 2nd pers. pl. nom., now replaced by you except in arch. & poet. & joc. use.

yea (yā), particle (arch.) yes.

yean, v.t. & i. (of ewe, she-goat) bring forth. ~ling, n. young lamb or kid.

year, n. the time occupied by one revolution of the earth round the sun (about 365¼ days); period from 1 Jan. to 31 Dec. inclusive, or any period of twelve calendar months; (pl.) age or old age; (pl.) period of several years. ~book, annual publication bringing information up to date. ~ling, animal between one and two years old. year'ly, adv. every year; once a year; by the year; a. occurring, &c. yearly.

yearn (yẽrn), v.i. be filled with longing or tenderness.

yeast, n. yellow frothy substance, got esp. from fermenting malt liquors and used as fermenting agent, in raising bread, &c. yeast'y, a. frothy; in a ferment; (of talk, &c.) empty and swelling.

yell, n. shrill cry of anger, pain, derision, delight, &c.; *students' concerted cheer. v.i. & t. utter yell; utter in yelling tone.

yell'ow (-ō), a. of the colour of buttercups or gold. n. yellow colour or pigment. v.i. & t. turn yellow. ~ fever, a tropical fever with jaundice. ~-(h)ammer, a small bird. ~ men, Chinese, Japanese, Mongols, &c. ~ peril, the danger that yellow men may overwhelm the white civilization. ~ press, sensational and esp. chauvinistic newspapers. ~-wood, name given to several kinds of trees, including satin-wood, podocarpus, &c.

yelp, n. dog's cry of excitement or pain. v.i. utter yelp; *talk in a loud voice, scream.

yen, n. (pl. the same) Japanese monetary unit.

yeo'man (yō-), n. man owning and farming small estate; middle-class farmer or countryman; *(Navy) petty officer in charge of stores (obs.), of signals. ~ry, n. volunteer cavalry force.

*yep, particle, yes.

yes, particle serving as substitute for affirmative answer, &c. n. the word yes.

yes'terday, n. the day preceding to-day or the day in question. adv. in the course of or during yesterday. (poet.) yes'ter-eve, ~ evening, last evening. ~ morn, ~ morning, yesterday morning. ~ night, last night. ~ year, last year.

yet, adv. still; with continuance to this or that time; by this or that time; so far; again, in addition; nevertheless. conj. but at the same time; and yet.

yew, n. dark-leaved evergreen tree or its wood.

Yidd'ish, n. form of German used by Jews in Europe and America.

yield, v.t. & i. produce or return as fruit or profit or result; surrender or make submission to; give consent; concede, admit. n. amount yielded or produced.

yō'del, n. kind of falsetto warbling practised by Swiss and Tyrolese mountaineers. v.i. & t. utter yodel; utter with yodel.

yō'ga, n. Hindu system of philosophic meditation and asceticism designed to effect the reunion of the devotee's soul with the universal spirit. yō'gi, n. devotee of yoga.

yoicks, int. in foxhunting.

yōke, n. wooden neckpiece by which pair of draught oxen is held together; marriage tie or other bond of union; pair of draught oxen; (fig.) sway, dominion, or servitude; wooden shoulder-piece for carrying pair of pails; shoulder-piece of shirt or coat or blouse. v.t. & i. (-kable), put yoke upon; couple or unite (pair); link; be suited or matched. ~fellow, partner, esp. in marriage.

yō'kel, n. country fellow.

yolk (yōk), n. yellow part of egg.

yon'der, adv. over there; in that direction. a. situated yonder. yon, a. (poet., &c.) yonder.

yōre, n. the past; long ago.

york, v.t. bowl out with yorker. york'er, n. ball that pitches immediately under the bat. York'shire (-er). ~ pudding, baked batter eaten with roast beef. ~ terrier, small shaggy dog.

you (ū, yōō, ye), 2nd pers. pron. sing. and pl., subj. and obj. and voc.: the person(s) addressed; (in general statements) one, a person.

young (yu-), a. not far advanced in life, growth, or development; still vigorous; immature; inexperienced. n. (collect.) offspring of animals, young people. ~ man, ~ woman, (esp. with my, her, his) sweetheart. ~un, (colloq.) youngster. young'ling (yu-), n. (poet.) young animal or child. young'ster (yu-), n. child, esp. active or lively boy.

you′nker (yŭ-), *n.* (arch., colloq.) youngster.

your (yōŏr, yŏŏr, yŏr, yer), *attrib.a.* of or belonging to you; (arch., colloq.) that we all know of. yours (ūrz, yōrz) *pron. & pred.a.* the one(s) belonging to you or of you; *a.* belonging to you; at your service. yourself′ (ūr-, &c. as in *your*), *pron.* (pl. *-ves*) (emphat.) you in person, you in particular.

youth (ūth), *n.* (pl. pr. -dhz), being young; the period between childhood and adult age; a young man; young people. ~ful, *a.* young or having the characteristics of youth.

ytter′bium (ĭ-), *n.* a rare metallic element occurring in gadolinite, &c.

ytt′ria (ĭ-), *n.* an earth obtained as a white powder from gadolinite and other rare minerals. ytt′rium (ĭ-), *n.* a rare metal of the cerium group.

yucc′a, *n.* white-flowered garden plant.

Yugoslav. See Jugoslav.

yule (ūl), *n.* the Christmas festival. ~-log, burnt on Christmas Eve. ~-tide, yule.

Z

Z, z (zĕd), letter and *n.* (Alg.: z) third unknown quantity.

zā′nÿ, *n.* (arch.) merry-andrew; fool, buffoon.

Zănzibär′ï, *n. & a.* (native) of Zanzibar.

zari′ba (-rē-), -rē′ba, *n.* hedge or palisade protecting camp or village in the Soudan.

zeal, *n.* fervour in a cause; hearty service. zea′lot (zĕl-), *n.* extreme partisan; fanatic. zea′lous (zĕl-), *a.* fervent.

zē′bra, *n.* striped horse-like quadruped.

zē′bŭ, *n.* E.-Ind. humped ox.

|| zeitgeist (tsītgī-), *n.* spirit of the times, drift of thought and feeling in a period.

Zēlā′nïan, *a.* (Zoogeography) of New Zealand.

zĕmïn′där, *n.* Bengali landowner paying land-tax.

zĕmst′vŏ, *n.* (pl. -os), elective district council in Russia.

zēná′na (-ah-), *n.* part of house in which women of high-caste families are secluded in India; (also ~ *cloth*) a thin dress-fabric. ~ mission, association of women visiting zenanas to spread medical and other reform among inmates.

Zĕnd, *n.* ancient language allied to Sanskrit.

zēn′ïth, *n.* point of heavens directly above observer; acme or culmination.

zĕph′yr (-er-), *n.* the West wind personified; light balmy breeze; athlete's thin jersey; kinds of gauzy fabric.

Zĕpp′elin, *n.* (colloq. Zepp) German dirigible airship.

zē′rŏ, *n.* (pl. -os), figure 0, nought, nil; the point in the scale of a thermometer or other graduated instrument from which positive and negative quantity is reckoned.

zĕst, *n.* piquancy; keen interest or enjoyment.

zeug′ma, *n.* (Gram.) placing of two words in the same relation to another that is suited to one only of them.

zĭb′et, *n.* the Asiatic or Indian civet.

zig′zăg, *n.* a succession of straight lines with abrupt alternate right and left turns; road, ornament, &c. of this form. *a.* forming a zigzag. *adv.* with zigzag course.

zinc, *n.* a white metal much used in the arts.

Zin′gäro (-ngg-), *n.* (pl. -rī), gipsy.

zinn′ia, *n.* a garden flower.

Zi′on, *n.* holy hill of Jerusalem; Jerusalem; the Hebrew theocracy; the Christian Church; the Kingdom of Heaven. ~ism, *n.* colonizing of Palestine as modern Jewish scheme. ~ist, *n. & a.*

zïrc′on, *n.* Ceylon stone of various colours.

zïrcō′nïum, *n.* metal found chiefly in zircon.

zith'er, -n, *n.* stringed instrument with flat sounding-board played on table, &c.

zlŏ'tў, *n.* Polish coin (10*d.*).

zō'dĭăc, *n.* a belt of the heavens outside which the sun and moon and major planets do not pass.

‖ zollverein (tsŏl'fĕrīn), *n.* union of States having a common customs-tariff against outsiders.

zōne, *n.* girdle or belt; encircling band of colour, &c.; any of the five bands into which the arctic and antarctic circles and the two tropics divide the earth. *v.t.* encircle as a zone. zō'nal, *a.*

Zŏō, *n.* (colloq.) zoological garden, esp. that in London.

zŏŏl'ogў, *n.* natural history of animals. zŏŏlŏ'gĭcal, *a.* ~ garden, enclosure with trees, ponds, cages, &c., in which wild animals are kept for exhibition. zŏŏl'ogist, *n.*

zŏŏm, *v.i.* (Aeronaut.) force aeroplane to mount at high speed and steep angle.

zō'ophўte, *n.* plant-like animal (e.g. sea-anemone, sponge). zŏophў'tic, *a.*

Zŏrŏăs'trianism, *n.* religion taught by Zoroaster and his followers, and held by ancient Magi and modern Parsees.

zouave (zŏō'ahv), *n.* member of French-Algerian infantry corps in uniform of oriental kind; woman's short jacket.

zounds (-z), *int.* (arch.) of indignation.

Zulu (zŏō'lŏō), *n.* member or language of a S.-Afr. tribe.

zuur'vĕld(t) (zoor-), *n.* (S.-Afr.) district covered with sour pasturage.

zymŏt'ic, *a.* of fermentation. ~diseases, those caused by multiplication of germs introduced from without.

ADDENDA

A

Aberdeen' (terrier), (ă-), *n.* rough-haired Scotch terrier.

A-bomb, *n.* atomic bomb.

abrā'sive, *n.* a grinding substance.

account. on ~, in part payment; on credit.

ăcĭdō'sĭs, *n.* undue acidity of blood.

ăck'ăck', *a.* anti-aircraft.

act. Also: one of series of short performances in circus or variety programme.

action. ~ stations, positions taken up by troops &c. before going into action.

ā'gar-(ā'gar), *n.* culture medium for bacteria made from seaweed.

agree. Also: *v.t.* determine, consent to.

ai'lĕrŏn, *n.* lateral-control flap on aeroplane wing.

air. ~borne, (of troops) trained

for transport by air to point of attack; (of aircraft) having taken off. ~conditioning, control of temperature, moisture, &c., of air in room, &c. ~cooled, (of engine) cooled by current of air. ~graph, letter transmitted by air-mail in microfilm. ~ hostess, female attendant for passengers in an air-liner. ~screw, *n.* propeller of aircraft. ~ speed, aircraft's speed relative to air through which it is moving. ~strip, strip of ground for taking off and landing of aircraft.

Aire'dale, *n.* large rough-coated terrier.

alert, *n.* warning of air-raid; period of warning.

all. ~in, everything included, (of wrestling) with no restrictions. ~up, (of weight) inclusive of crew, pay-load, and fuel.

a'llergy, *n.* condition marked by

---

māte, mēte, mīte, mōte, mūte, mōōt; răck, rĕck, rĭck, rŏck, rŭck, rŏŏk;

a different reaction on a reinfection. **aller'gic**, *a*. having an ∼; (colloq.) antipathetic to.

almoner. Also: hospital official.

alpha. Also: ∼ plus, *a*. of the highest excellence.

ambiv'alence, *n*. simultaneous love of and hatred of object or person. ∼nt, *a*.

ameri'cium (-ĭshĭ-), *n*. radio-active metallic element.

amphibian. Also: (vehicle) fitted to travel over both land and water.

An'derson shelter, *n*. arched corrugated-steel air-raid shelter.

ångström'a (-ngg-), *n*. bitter bark used as tonic, &c.

Ang'strom (-êrm) ū'nĭt, *n*. a hundred-millionth of a centimetre (as unit for short wave-lengths).

anhȳ'drous, *a*. (chem.) without water of crystallisation.

an'tè, *n*. stake put up by pokerplayer before drawing new cards. *v.t.* put up (ante); *pay up*.

‖**apart'heid** (-t-hāt), *n*. racial segregation in S. Africa.

aperitif (ahpā'rētēf), *n*. alcoholic appetizer.

aphrodis'iac (-z-), *n*. & *a*. (drug) producing venereal desire.

appease. Also: seek to conciliate (potential aggressor) by making concessions.

approve. ∼d school, State school for young offenders.

apron. Also: hard-surface area on airfield for (un)loading aircraft.

a'qualung, *n*. apparatus carried by diver to supply him with air as required.

arête (ărāt'), *n*. sharp mountain ridge.

armour. Also: steel plates, &c. protecting motor-car, train, &c., from projectiles. ∼ed car, train, one supplied with such armour and (usu.) guns. ∼ed column, &c., one equipped with armoured cars, tanks, &c.

a'rris, *n*. sharp edge where two planes, &c., meet.

ar'sine (-ēn), *n*. kind of poison gas.

ascor'bic acid, *n*. vitamin C.

As'dic, *n*. See abbreviations.

ash. *the Ashes*, symbol of victory in cricket test-matches between England & Australia.

As'ian (āsh-), *a*. & *n*. Asiatic.

assault. Also: (euphem.): *n*. rape (of woman). *v.t.* rape (woman).

assembly. ∼ line, group of machines & workers assembling some product.

atomic. Also: resulting from or utilizing disintegration of nucleus of atom, as ∼ bomb, ∼ energy. ∼ number, number of unit positive charges carried by nucleus of atom of element. ∼ weight, ratio between weight of one atom of the element and $\frac{1}{16}$ of weight of atom of oxygen.

aubrie'tia (-sha), *n*. spring-flowering dwarf perennial plant.

au'tarchy (-k-), *n*. absolute sovereignty.

au'tarky, *n*. (esp. economic) self-sufficiency.

authority. ∼itār'ian, *a*. & *n*. (person) favouring obedience to authority as opp. to individual liberty.

aweigh' (awā), *adv*. (of anchor) just lifted from ground in weighing.

axis. Also: (Rome-Berlin ∼) alliance between Germany and Italy in 1939-45 war.

B

baby. Also: ∼-sitter, person employed to remain with children while their parents are out.

bachelor. ∼ girl, unmarried girl living independently.

back. ∼-chat, (sl.) retort. ∼-cloth, ∼-drop, (Theatr.) painted cloth at back of stage. ∼-fire, premature explosion in cylinder of internal-combustion engine. ∼ log, large log forming back of fire. ∼ room, place where secret research or other work goes on.

---

background. Also: (fig.) person's cultural knowledge, education, experience, &c.

bāffle, n. plate, board, &c., hindering or regulating passage of fluid, sound, &c.

Bail'ey bridge, n. emergency bridge for rapid construction.

bāk'ū, n. fine kind of straw.

bălalai'ka (-li-), n. Russian triangular guitar-like musical instrument.

băl'ata, n. dried milky juice of two S.-Amer. trees, used as substitute for gutta-percha.

bale out, v.i. (of airman) leave aircraft by parachute.

ball. ~-point, (of fountain pen) having a tiny ball as its writing point.

ball'etomānia, n. excessive fondness for ballet.

balloon. ~ barrage, anti-aircraft barrier of steel cables supported by captive balloons; barrage ~, one of these. ~-tire, low-pressure motor tire of large section.

bǎllyhoō', n. noisy or vulgar methods of drawing attention.

barbō'la, n. kind of paste made into ornaments for decorating small articles.

barge-board, n. ornamental screen to gable beams.

barȳ'tēs (-z), n. native sulphate of barium, used as white paint.

base[2]. basic slag, finely-ground slag from Bessemer-steel process, used as fertilizer.

basket. ~-ball, game in which goal is scored when ball is thrown into basket fixed 10 ft. above ground.

basque (bahsk), n. continuation of bodice below waist.

băth'yscaphe (-âf), **băth'ysphēre,** nn. large submersible sphere for deep-sea observation.

bau'xite, n. (min.) earthy mineral, the chief source of aluminium.

beachhead, n. position occupied or held on (hostile) coast.

Bĕd'lington (terrier), n. short-haired narrow-headed sporting terrier.

bĕhā'viourism (-vyer-), n. study and analysis of behaviour as method of psychology.

bĕl'ga, n. Belgian unit of exchange (= 5 francs).

bellows. Also: expansible part of photographic camera.

Bĕnĕdic'tine, n. monk of order founded by St. Benedict; a liqueur.

Bĕn'elux, n. Belgium, Holland, and Luxemburg as an economic and political unit.

bĕn'thos, n. fauna and flora found at sea-bottom.

best. ~ man, bridegroom's supporter.

binge (-j), n. (sl.) drinking-bout, spree.

biochem'istrȳ (-kĕ-), n. the chemistry of living organisms.

biology. biological warfare, involving use of living organisms esp. disease germs.

birth. ~ control, prevention of undesired conception.

black. ~ list, list of persons under suspicion, liable to punishment, &c.; ~-list, v.t. ~ market, n. illicit traffic in scarce or rationed goods. ~ out, obscure (window, street, &c.) so that no light is visible from outside or from air; ~-out, n.

blast. Also: high-pressure wave of air spreading outwards from an explosion.

blatant. Also: flagrant.

blĕb, n. blister, bubble, on skin or glass, &c.

blee'der, n. (esp.) person subject to excessive bleeding from a slight injury.

blind. Also: v.i. (of motorist, &c.) go blindly or heedlessly.

blitz, n. (colloq.) blitz-krieg, esp. intensive aerial attack. v.t. damage, destroy, &c., in blitz.

∥blitz'krieg (-ĕg), n. lightning war, violent campaign intended to bring speedy victory.

blŏc, n. combination of parties, nations, &c., for common purpose; **sterling ~,** of countries with currencies tied to sterling.

---

ah, awl, oil, boor, cow, dowry; chin, go, bang, so, ship, thin; dh, as th(e)

block. ~ letters, separate usu. capital letters resembling those used in printing.

blŏke, n. (sl.) fellow.

blood. ~ sports, those involving bloodshed or killing of animals.

blue. ~pencil, censor. ~print, photographic print with white lines on blue ground, usu. with tracing of plan, &c., as negative.

bŏck, n. strong dark-coloured German beer.

*****bŏ-hŭnk,** n. (sl.) Czech immigrant.

*****bŏlo'ney,** n. (sl.) nonsense, bunkum.

bombard. Also: subject to stream of atomic particles.

border. Also: ~line, limit of an area or class. a. that is on such a limit.

book. ~-ends, pair of props to keep row of books upright.

bottle¹. ~green, dark green. ~neck, place where wide road, railway, &c., narrows; anything obstructing even flow of production, &c. ~ party, party to which guests contribute drinks; kind of night-club where drinks ordered in advance may be consumed outside licensed hours.

bow'er³, n. right, left, ~, knave of trumps, other knave of same colour, at euchre.

box. ~ on the ear(s), slap on side of head.~-pleat, two parallel contrary pleats forming raised band.

bŏx-calf¹ (kahf), n. chrome-tanned calfskin with hatched grain.

brain. ~-storm, sudden cerebral disturbance.

brăss'ière (-yār), n. woman's underbodice supporting breasts.

break, n. Also: spell of (good) luck. bad ~, unfortunate remark or ill-judged action.

breeze³, n. small cinders, coke, &c. used to make concrete blocks for building, &c.

Brĕn gun, n. magazine-fed light machine gun.

brief. Also: n. (sl.) airman's instructions. v.t. (air-force sl.) give (airman) instructions for raid, &c.

broad. ~ bean, common flattened

variety. ~'tail, fur of very young lamb of Asia Minor.

brō'mide¹. Also: (sl.) trite remark, cliché (from use of bromides as soporifics). ~ paper, photographic printing-paper coated with silver bromide emulsion.

bulge. Also: (temporary) increase in numbers or volume.

bulk. ~ buying, purchase by one buyer of all or most of producer's output.

bulldozer, n. powerful caterpillar tractor pushing broad steel blade in front.

bump. Also: variation of air pressure causing irregularity in aircraft's motion. ~ off, (sl.) remove by violence, murder.

bŭr'ble, v.i. bubble or gurgle with mirth.

bŭrl, n. knot in wool or cloth.

bŭr'ton, n. light handy two-block tackle.

bush¹. ~-telegraph, rapid spread of information, rumour, &c.

business. ~-like, systematic, prompt, well-ordered.

butter¹. ~ muslin, thin loosely-woven cloth.

buyer's market, conditions where supply exceeds demand and prices are low.

C

căb'riŏle, n. curved leg characteristic of Queen Anne and Chippendale furniture.

cadĕn'za, n. (mus.) flourish of voice or instrument.

căf'tan, n. Eastern long girdled under-tunic.

*****că'gey** (-ji), a. not easily deceived.

cairn. ~ (terrier), small short-legged shaggy-haired terrier.

căl'ipăsh, căl'ipee, nn. gelatinous green and yellow substances in turtle(-soup).

call. ~ up, v.t. summon into armed forces; n. such a summons.

calyp'so, n. West-Indian song, usu. topical and extempore.

can[1]. **~ned music**, (sl.) music recorded for reproduction.

cănăs′ta, n. card game resembling rummy.

‖**cancan** (kahn′kahn), n. high-kicking dance.

candid. **~ camera**, small camera for taking informal pictures of people often without their knowledge.

cannon[2]. (now esp.) aircraft's shell-firing gun.

cap. Also: payment by non-subscriber for day's hunting.

capital. **~ goods**, goods (to be) used in producing commodities. **capitalize.** Also: use to one's advantage.

car′dan joint, n. one transmitting power by a shaft at any selected angle.

career. **~ist**, n. person intent mainly on personal advancement and success in life.

cărm′inative, a. & n. (drug) curing flatulence.

carriage. **~-way**, (part of) road used by vehicles.

cart. **~-wheel**, n. wheel of **~**, sideways somersault.

căscăr′a sagra′da (-ahd-), n. a laxative.

casement. **~ cloth**, cotton cloth used for curtains, &c.

cash[1]. **~ register**, n. till with mechanism for visibly recording sums received.

castor[2]. **~ sugar**, powdered white sugar.

căt′amite, n. sodomite's minion.

caterpillar. **~ wheel**, wheel with broad tread in separate sections, for use on rough ground.

căth′ōde,n. (Electr.) negative pole.

cave[1]. **~-man**, (also) man of primitive passions and behaviour.

ceiling. Also: maximum altitude of given aircraft; maximum altitude (e.g. weather-conditions); upper limit (prices, wages, &c.).

cĕll′ophane, n. tough transparent cellulose material. P.

cellulose. Also: solution of cellulose acetate or nitrate used in varnishing, &c.

central. **~ heating**, heating by hot water or steam conveyed by pipes from central source.

cĕn′trifuge, n. machine for separating parts of mixture, &c., by rotary motion.

chaise. **~ longue** (lŏngg), sofa with rest for back at one end only.

chamber. **~ music**, for performance in room, not at theatre, church, &c.

change. **~-over**, alteration from one system, &c., to another.

‖ **chassé** (shăs′ā), n. gliding dance-step. v.i. make this.

chăt′terbug, n. (sl.) person given to foolish talk or gossip.

cheese. Also: heavy wooden disk used in skittles.

Chĕl′sea (-sĭ) **bŭn**, n. rolled currant-bun.

chest. **~ of drawers**, frame with drawers for clothes, &c.

chew. **~ing gum**, preparation of gum(s), esp. chicle, for prolonged chewing.

chian′ti (kiah-), n. red Italian wine.

chi′cle (-ē-), n. tough elastic gum obtained from sap of a tropical S. Amer. tree.

chlor′inate (kl-). v.t. impregnate, purify (water, &c.), with chlorine.

chrō′matin (k-), n. (Biol.) tissue that can be stained. **chrō′mosōme**, one of rods or threads into which chromatin of cell-nucleus is turned before cell-division.

chrome. **~ leather**, leather tanned with potassium bichromate.

cĭtronĕll′a, n. fragrant ethereal oil, which keeps off mosquitoes.

cĭt′rus, n. & a. (of) genus including lime, citron, orange, lemon, &c.

city. the City, part of London governed by Lord Mayor and Corporation, business quarter of this, commercial circles. **~ editor**, editor of financial part of newspaper.

clear. **~ing house**, place at which bankers exchange cheques, balances being paid in cash.

click′er, n. foreman of a companionship of compositors.

clinical. **~ thermometer**, one for taking patient's temperature.

---

măte, mēte, mīte, mōte, mūte, mōōt; răck, rĕck, rĭck, rŏck, rŭck, rŏŏk;

clôche, *n.* glass for protecting or forcing plants; a shape of woman's hat.

close¹. ~-up, part of cinema picture taken at short range.

close². *closed shop*, a trade &c. restricted to members of a particular trade union.

coach. Also: long-distance bus.

coa'ming, *n.* raised border round ship's hatches, &c.

*cŏ'ca-cŏ'la, *n.* aerated non-alcoholic drink. P.

cod'ling², *n.* small cod.

coel'acănth (sĕl-), *n.* & *a.* (fish) having hollow spine.

coexist. (peaceful) ~ence, (of peoples with different political systems) living in mutual toleration.

cohere. ~r, *n.* detector of electric waves (through coherence of metal filings in tube).

cold. ~ war, the use in peace time of propaganda, obstructive diplomacy, &c., to attain ends normally sought by war.

comic. Also: comic paper. horror ~, pictorial publication full of horrors.

cŏm'infŏrm, *n.* Communist international Information Bureau.

commando. Also: picked soldier trained for special missions.

cŏm'păct, *n.* small case for compressed face-powder, rouge, &c.

cŏm'père (-âr), *n.* introducer of artists at entertainment. *v.t.* & *i.* act as compère (to).

composite. C~ order, one of the five orders of architecture.

comprehensive. ~ school, large secondary school providing courses of varied kinds and lengths.

com'press¹. Also: wet cloth applied to inflamed part.

condition, *v.* Also: make fit.

consult'ant, *n.* consulting physician, engineer, &c.

consumer. ~(s') goods, things which directly satisfy human needs.

contact. Also: (med.) person likely to be contagious through contact with patient; (sl., usu. *pl.*) person(s) with whom one comes into touch. *v.t.* (sl.) get into touch with (person).

contain. ~ment, *n.* (esp.) policy of building up strength against possible enemy in hope of eventual agreement with him.

contin'uum, *n.* (Philos.) unbroken mass, sequence, tissue.

contract¹. ~ (bridge), form of auction bridge.

cŏp, *n.* (sl.) capture; *policeman.

copy. ~-cat, (colloq.) imitator. ~-writer, one who writes or prepares advertising copy for publication.

cŏr'gi (-gĭ), *n.* small Welsh dog.

coro'na, *n.* kind of Havana cigar. P.

cŏ'ronary, *a.* resembling, encircling like, a crown.

cor'porative, *a.* based on corporate action or movement.

corsair. Also: a pirate.

corvette. Also: small fast naval escort-vessel.

cŏsh, *n.* bludgeon. ~-boy, youth or man armed with cosh. *v.t.* strike with cosh.

costume. ~ jewellery, artificial jewellery for decorative purposes.

côtĕrm'inous, *a.* var. of conterminous.

coun'tershaft, *n.* intermediate shaft driven from main shaft, for supplying power to particular parts of system of machinery.

cover, ~age, *n.* area or amount covered, section of community reached by particular advertising medium. ~ girl, girl or woman whose picture illustrates cover of magazine &c.

crash¹. ~-dive, (of submarine) dive suddenly and steeply. ~ helmet, protective helmet of motor cyclist &c.

crêpe. ~ rubber, (also) crinkly rubber used esp. for soles of shoes &c.

cross-cut, *a.* adapted for cutting across grain.

cross-sec'tion, *n.* (fig.) comprehensive representative sample.

crur'al (-oor-), *a.* (Anat.) of leg.

cuckoo. Also: *a.* (sl.) crazy.

curfew. Also: (mil.) prohibition on going in streets during specified night hours.

cūr′ie, *n.* standard unit of radium emanation.

cut. ~throat, *n.* murderer; *a.* intensive, merciless; (of card-games) three-handed.

cy′clotron, *n.* apparatus for accelerating charged atomic particles by passing them repeatedly through same electro-magnetic field.

D

daily, *n.* Also: non-resident maid-servant.

dark. ~ ages, (also) period between break-up of Roman Empire (A.D. 395) and end of 10th c.

dash. ~board, (also) partition between engine and front seat of motor-car.

dēbŭnk′, *v.t.* (colloq.) remove false sentiment from.

dĕcĕl′erāte, *v.t. & i.* diminish speed of; slow down.

dē-Gauss′, dēgauss′, *v.t.* neutralize magnetization of (ship, &c.) with encircling current-carrying conductor (~ing belt), esp. as protection against magnetic mines.

dēgrained′, *a.* (of leather) with grain removed.

dēhȳd′rāte, *v.t.* (Chem.) deprive of water.

demĕn′tia, *n.* feebleness of mind as form of insanity.

dĕmerâr′a (or -ahra), *n.* yellowish-brown raw cane sugar.

dēnier′ (-nēr), *n.* unit of weight in estimating fineness of silk, rayon, & nylon yarn.

dērā′tion, *v.* remove from the list of rationed goods.

deutĕr′ium, *n.* heavy hydrogen, hydrogen of atomic weight 2.

deu′teron, *n.* nucleus of deuterium atom.

dial, *v.* Also: make telephone-call by moving disk to numbers required.

diamanté (dēamahn′tā), *n.* pow-

dered glass, paste brilliants, &c., as ornament.

Dīăsp′ora, *n.* dispersion, the Jews dispersed among Gentiles.

Diesel (dē′zl), *n.* ~ engine, type of oil-engine. ~ oil, heavy mineral oil used in ~ engine.

dīĕt′ician, *n.* person versed in dietetics.

dipole, *n.* (pop.) television aerial.

direction. ~al, *a.* (wireless) transmitted over narrow angle.

dĭrn′dl, *n.* bodice and full skirt imitating Alpine peasant costume. ~ (skirt), full skirt with tight waistband.

dis′cus, *n.* heavy disk thrown in athletic exercises.

dither. Also: vacillate.

dive. Also: (of aircraft) plunge steeply downwards; (of submarine) submerge. ~bomber, aircraft that drops bombs at end of dive.

do². Also: (colloq.) party, outing.

document. ~ary. Also: *a. & n.* (film) based on real life, not on fictional plot.

dog. ~fight, mêlée between aircraft.

dŏgg′ō, *adv.* (sl.) lie ~, make no sign, lie low.

dollar. Also: ~ area, countries whose currencies are linked to that of the U.S.

dŏŏ′dle, *v.i.* scrawl aimlessly while one's attention is engaged elsewhere. *n.* such scrawl.

double. ~ton, *n.* (cards) two cards only of a suit.

double, *n.* Also: (darts) score in outer ring of board, in which value is doubled; (racing) a cumulative bet made on two horses.

dragée (drah′zhā), *n.* chocolate drop, sugar-coated almond, small silver ball for decorating cake.

drape. Also: piece of drapery, curtain.

‖**drĕss′age** (-ahzh), *n.* training of horse in obedience and deportment.

drŏgue (-g), *n.* sea-anchor; wind-sock.

dry. ~-clean, clean with spirit, &c., without use of water.

dub¹. Also: give (cinema film) another recording of sound esp. in a different language.

dud. Also: *a.* counterfeit; useless, futile.

dumb. ~-iron, one of two curved forward ends of side-members of motor-car chassis.

dummy. Also: imaginary whist-player, his cards exposed and played by his partner; (hand of) declarer's partner at bridge.

*dunk. *v.t. & i.* dip (bread &c.) into soup or a beverage while eating.

dur̆al′ŭmin, *n.* hard tough aluminium alloy used for aircraft, &c. P.

dust. *~-bowl, area reduced to desert by drought and dust storms.

E

earth. Also: (Electr.) ground as medium for completion of circuit; rod, &c., in soil or water to connect conductor to earth. *v.t.* connect (conductor) to earth.

E-boat, *n.* enemy motor torpedo-boat.

écru (ā′krōō), *n.* colour of unbleached linen.

ĕc′toplăsm, *n.* viscous substance exuding from body of spiritualistic medium during trance.

edge. be on ~, be irritable.

electrocute. Also: kill in any way by electricity.

eliminate. ~tor, (esp.) apparatus enabling wireless set to use mains current, so eliminating batteries.

ĕm, ĕn, *nn.* units of measurement in printing.

|| ĕn′osis, *n.* union of Cyprus with Greece.

|| entrepreneur (ahn̆treprenĕr′), *n.* person who assumes risk and control of commercial enterprise.

ĕn′tropy, *n.* (Phys.) measure of unavailability of system's thermal energy for conversion into mechanical work.

ĕn′igŏne, *n.* one of a later (and less distinguished) generation.

equity. Also: E~, actors' trade union; *pl.* stocks and shares not bearing fixed interest.

ĕrg, *n.* unit of work or energy.

Er′ŏs (ēr-), *n.* god of love, Cupid.

|| ersatz′ (ārz-), *n. & a.* substitute.

escape. ~ clause, one specifying conditions under which contracting party is free from obligations. ĕscapee′, *n.* one who has escaped. ~ist, *a. & n.* affording, (person) seeking, escape or relief from realities of life.

ethical. Also: (of drugs) conforming to a recognized standard.

euphor′ia, euph′ory, *nn.* feeling of well-being. euphŏr′ic, *a.*

evacuate. Also: remove (person) esp. from place considered dangerous. ~uee′, *n.*

*ĕv′erglade, *n.* marshy tract, esp. (pl.) S. Florida swamp.

exchange. Also: central telephone office to which subscribers' lines are connected.

ĕxŏphthăl′mic, *a.* (med.) causing protrusion of eyeball.

expend. ~able, *a.* likely to be or meant to be sacrificed or destroyed.

ĕxpertise′ (-ēz), *n.* expert opinion or skill or knowledge.

expose. Also: subject (photographic plate, &c.) to light.

F

façade. Also: (fig.) frontal or outward appearance.

făct′ual, *a.* concerned with, of the nature of, fact.

fault. ~ *v.t.* find fault with, blame.

fellow. ~ traveller. Also: one who sympathizes with Communist aims and policy.

fĕrrō-cŏn′crēte, *n.* reinforced concrete.

fifth. ~ column, organized body sympathizing with and working for enemy within country at war, &c.; (loosely) traitors, spies; ~columnist.

fight. fighter, (esp.) *n.* & *a.* (aircraft) designed for aerial combat rather than bombing, &c.

filibuster. ~er, *n.* a filibuster.

finesse. Also: (cards) attempt to take trick by lower card, with higher in reserve.

fire. ~bomb, incendiary. ~watcher, *n.* person keeping watch for fires caused by fire-bombs, &c.

fish². ~plate, either of two plates holding rails together.

fission. Also: splitting of atomic nuclei. ~ bomb, atom(ic) bomb. ~able (-sho-), *a.*

fix. Also: mend, repair.

flåk, *n.* German anti-aircraft fire.

flån (*or* flähn), *n.* open tart.

flare. Also: *v.* spread diagonally outwards. *n.* bright light used as signal, dropped from aircraft to illuminate target, &c.; gradual widening (esp. of woman's skirt).

flat. flatten. ~ out, bring aircraft parallel with ground.

float-plane, *n.* aeroplane with floats for alighting on water.

flog. Also: (sl.) sell.

flood. ~light, copious artificial light projected on buildings, &c. from many directions.

floor. ~ show, entertainment presented on floor of night-club &c.

flush². straight ~, set of cards in regular sequence. royal ~, (Poker) straight flush headed by ace.

fly². Also: ~past, ceremonial flight of planes past an inspecting officer or other personage.

flying. ~ bomb, jet-propelled, airborne torpedo. ~ saucer, saucerlike object reported as having been seen at times flying at great speed.

fog. ~horn, instrument for warning ships in fog.

foot. Also: ~candle, illumination produced by a standard candle at distance of one foot. ~plate,

platform for driver and fireman in locomotive.

formál'déhýde, *n.* colourless gas used in solution as preservative and disinfectant. fôrm'alin, *n.* aqueous solution of this.

foundation. ~ garment, woman's supporting undergarment.

frame, *n.* Also: single complete image in television.

fránk'fûrter, *n.* highly-seasoned German sausage.

freeze. Also: make (credits, assets, &c.) temporarily or permanently unrealizable.

fret². ~saw, saw for cutting fretwork.

frigate. Also: a large escortvessel.

frog¹. ~man, person wearing special shoes and gloves for under-water operations.

frō'zen, *a.* (of credits, &c.) not realizable.

fůg, *n.* fustiness, stuffiness.

fuse². Also: (Electr.) easily-fusible wire placed in circuit, and melted by excessive current.

fusion. ~ bomb, hydrogen bomb.

fuss. ~pot, (colloq.) person who is always making a fuss.

G

gag. Also: choke, retch.

gåg'a, *a.* (sl.) fatuous, senile.

galė'na, *n.* common lead ore.

*Gåll'up pöll, *n.* test of how representative sample of public will vote.

gamma. ~ rays, X-rays of very short wave-length emitted by radio-active substances.

gåmm'ý, *a.* (sl., of limb) crippled.

gang. Also: *v.i.* join up, act in concert, *with.*

gång'ling (-ngg-), *a.* loosely built, lanky.

gårdė'nia, *n.* (kinds of tree and shrub with) fragrant white or yellow flower.

gas. ~mask, mask for protection against poisonous gas.

gasket. Also: copper and fibre packing esp. for gas-tight joints in internal-combustion engine.

gau′chō (gow-), *n.* herdsman of pampas, of mixed European and Amer. Indian descent.

Geig′er counter (gīg-), instrument for detecting charged (atomic) particles or radio-activity.

gěl *n.* semi-solid colloidal solution.

gēne, *n.* (Biol.) one of physiological units held to cause the development in offspring of parental characteristics.

gĕn′ocide, *n.* extermination of a race.

genteel. ~ism, *n.* word used instead of the ordinary natural word because it is thought to be more genteel.

gĕopŏl′itics, *n. pl.* the politics of a country as determined by its geographical features.

George, *n.* (colloq.) automatic pilot of aircraft.

gĕriăt′rics, *n. pl.,* gěrŏntŏl′ogў (g-, j-), *n.* science of old age and its diseases. gěriăt′ric, *a.;* gĕria-tri′cian (-ĭshn), gĕri′atrist, gĕri′-atrў, *nn.*

|| **gesta′pō** (gestah-), *n.* German secret police.

gig′olō (jĭg-), *n.* male professional dancing partner.

glacé (glahs′ā), *a.* (of cloth, &c.) smooth, polished; iced, sugared.

glass. Also: ~wool, glass in fibre form, used esp. for heat insulation.

glide. ~r, *n.* engineless aeroplane.

*** G-man** (jē), *n.* (sl.) Federal criminal investigation officer.

gŏ′dět (-dā), *n.* = gore².

gold. ~ bloc (of countries with currencies tied to gold). ~ brick, thing with only a surface appearance of value, fraud. ~-dig-ger, (sl.) coquette who wheedles money out of men.

goo′fў, *a.* (sl.) silly, infatuated.

Gŏth, *n.* one of Teutonic tribe who invaded Eastern & Western Empires in 3rd–5th centuries &c.; founded kingdoms in Italy, &c.; uncivilized person, vandal.

Goy, *n.* Yiddish for Gentile.

grand. Also: *n.* (sl.) 1,000 dollars.

grape. ~-vine, (fig.) rumour, false report.

grăt′icŭle, *n.* system of lines or angular gradations incorporated in telescope.

|| **grăt′in** (-ăn), *n.* way of cooking with brown crust, e.g. of bread-crumbs or grated cheese; dish so cooked.

grĕg′ory pow′der, *n.* compound powder of rhubarb, an aperient.

griz′zle, *v.i.* (colloq.) whimper, cry fretfully.

ground. ~ speed, aircraft's speed relative to ground. ~ staff, mechanics and other non-flying members of aerodrome staff.

gudgeon. Also: pin holding two blocks of stone, &c., together. ~ pin, that holding piston and connecting-rod together.

guide, *v.t.* Also: ~d, (of missiles) designed for remote control.

gumboot, *n.* rubber boot.

H

hae′matin, *n.* a constituent of haemoglobin.

haemophil′ia, *n.* hereditary incapacity of blood to clot; bleeding.

hăg², *n.* soft place in moor; firm place in bog.

hair, ~cut, trimming of the hair of the head. ~-do (colloq.), (mode of) hairdressing. ~spring, fine spring in watch. ~ trigger, secondary trigger releasing main one.

halā′tion, *n.* (Photog.) spreading of light beyond its proper boundary in negative.

half. ~ něl′son, a hold in wrestling. ~-tone, illustration printed from photographically-produced block in which light and shades are represented by small or large dots.

hălĭto′sis, *n.* (med.) abnormally foul breath.

halt¹. Also: railway stopping-place without regular station buildings.

ham[1]. Also: (sl.) actor who over-acts (also attrib.). **~fisted**, (sl.) clumsy, heavy-handed.

ham′burger, n. ball or cake of chopped meat fried as a steak; a kind of sausage.

hand, v.t. Also: **~out**, information or news officially released.

hang′over, n. aftermath of alcoholic excess.

hay. *~**wire**, n. anything tangled. a. in disorder, crazy.

H-bomb, n. hydrogen bomb.

head. **~light**, powerful light on front of locomotive or car.

Heav′iside (hē-) **layer**, n. layer of atmosphere reflecting back wireless waves.

heavy. **~water**, deuterium oxide, with same chemical properties as ordinary water, but density about 10 % greater.

high. **~light**, outstanding feature. **~light**, v.t. emphasize, make prominent. **~wing**, (of monoplane) with wings set near top of fuselage.

hind[3]. **~sight**, back sight of gun, (joc.) wisdom after the event.

hitch. *~**hike**, v.i. travel by begging lifts from passing vehicles (also simply hitch).

hive. **~off**, (of firm) assign production of some goods to subsidiary company.

hold. **~ing company**, one formed to hold shares in subsidiary companies.

honour. Also: (Golf) right of driving first; (cards) ace, king, queen, knave (&, in bridge, ten).

hook **~worm**, slender worm infesting men and animals.

hop[2]. Also: n. one stage of long-distance flight.

hot. Also: (of dance music) highly elaborated and florid. *~ **dog**, (colloq.) hot sausage sandwiched in roll of bread.

Hoover. n. make of vacuum cleaner. v.t. to use a H. on.

hotel. **~ier**, n. hotel-keeper.

humbug. Also: kind of sweetmeat, usu. flavoured with peppermint.

hŭm′dĭng′er, n. (sl.) exceptionally fine person or thing.

Hūn, n. one of an Asiatic race ravaging Europe in 4th & 5th centuries; (contempt.) German.

hunger. **~march**, march undertaken by unemployed to call attention to their condition.

hut′ment, n. camp, temporary offices, &c., of huts.

hydrō-ēlĕc′tric, a. (of electricity) produced by using water-power.

hydrogen. Also: **~ bomb**, one designed to release a vast amount of atomic energy by the formation of helium from hydrogen.

hydrŏl′ysis, n. decomposition of compound by reaction with water.

hydropŏn′ics, n.pl. art of growing plants without soil, in water impregnated with chemicals.

hȳ′pō, n. (Photog.) hyposulphite of soda, used in fixing.

hypodermic. **~ needle, syringe,** used in hypodermic injection.

I

ice. Also: **dry ~**, solid carbon dioxide.

idle, v.i. Also: (of engine) run slowly in neutral gear or with no load.

ignition. Also: mechanism for starting combustion in cylinder of motor engine.

imā′gō, n. final and perfect stage of insect.

impact. Also: effect, influence.

immune. **~ize**, v.t. make immune.

in. **~patient**, one remaining in hospital during treatment.

incendiary. (Also: of bomb) made of or filled with inflammatory substance(s) and intended to cause fires, n. incendiary bomb.

incommūnicā′dō (-ah-), a. without means of communication, in solitary confinement.

indŏc′trināte, v.t. teach; imbue with a doctrine, idea, or opinion. **~ā′tion,** n.

Indō-Europe′an, a. of the family of languages spoken over greater part of Europe and Asia as far as N. India.

induct'ance, *n*. (Electr.) (measure of) property of causing induction.

infra. ~-**red**, of invisible rays beyond red end of spectrum.

in'-law, *n*. (colloq.) relative by marriage (usu. pl.).

inop'erable, *a*. that cannot be operated on.

insem'inate, *v.t.* sow, implant, impregnate. ~**ā'tion**, *n*.

intermission. Also: (musical selection during) interval in theatre &c.

interplăn'etarў, *a*. between planets.

interzōn'al, *a*. lying or occurring between two or more zones, esp. of occupied Germany.

invert. Also: (Chem.) convert substance that rotates plane of polarized light to right to one that rotates it to left, or vice versa. *a*. (Chem.) of sugar, &c.) inverted. **inver'tase**, *n*. enzyme that inverts sugar.

Iŏn'ic (ī-), *a*. of Ionia. ~ **order**, one of the five orders of architecture.

iron, ~**curtain**, barrier to passage of information at limit of Soviet sphere of influence. ~ **lung**, iron case over patient's body for administering artificial respiration by mechanical pumps.

irradiate, *v*. Also: treat with ultra-violet light or other radiations.

isolate. ~**tionism**, *n*. policy on part of State of keeping aloof from affairs of other States.

isŏs'celes (-ēz), *a*. (of triangle) having two sides equal.

ĭs'otōpe, *n*. one of two or more forms of an element differing from each other in atomic weight.

Is'raël (ĭz-), *n*. Jewish State established in Palestine in 1948. ~**i** (ĭzrăl'ĭ), *a*. & *n*. (inhabitant) of this State.

it. *a*. (colloq.) *n*. sex appeal.

It², *n*. (colloq.) Italian vermouth (*gin and it*).

ivory. Also: ~ **tower**, shelter or

refuge from life's unpleasantnesses.

J

J (jā) **pen**, *n*. broad-pointed kind.

jay. ~-**walker**, careless pedestrian.

Jeru'salem (-rōō-) **artichoke**, *n*. kind of sunflower with edible tuber.

jet². Also: ~ **propulsion**, propulsion by reaction of jet of gas. **jet**, *n*. aeroplane so propelled.

jig. ~-**saw puzzle**, picture pasted on board and cut in irregular interlocking pieces with jig-saw.

jink, *v.i.* (sl.) manœuvre aircraft, be manœuvred, jerkily up and down.

jitt'ers, *n.pl.* (sl.) nerves, state of extreme nervousness. **jitt'ery**, *a*. jumpy, nervy.

*****jive**, *n*. kind of jazz. *v.i.* play jive, dance to jive.

jockey. ~ **for position**, try to gain a position of (or an unfair) advantage.

jŏdhpurs' (-oorz), *n.pl.* long breeches for riding, &c., tight from knee to ankle.

ju'dō (jōō-), *n*. = ju-jutsu.

*****juke-bŏx** (jōōk), *n*. machine that plays gramophone records when coin is inserted.

Ju'lian (jōō-), *a*. of Julius Caesar. ~ **calendar**, introduced by him.

K

‖ **kĕpi** (kā'pē), *n*. French soldier's straight-peaked cap.

kimō'nō, *n*. long loose Japanese robe with wide sleeves; dressing-gown like this.

kiosk. Also: structure for public telephone.

kitt'ў, *n*. (cards) pool.

klăx'on, *n*. powerful electric motor-horn. P.

knock. Also: (of engine) make thumping noise.

know. ~'-**how**, *n*. practical knowledge.

---

kraft (-ah-), *n.* kind of strong packing-paper.

kremlin. *The K~,* (used for) the Russian Government.

L

lama[1]. **lama'sery** (-mah-), *n.* monastery of lamas.

lamé (lah'mā), *n. & a.* (material) with gold or silver thread inwoven.

land. ~**fall,** ship's approach to land at end of voyage. ~**mine,** explosive mine laid in or on ground; parachute mine.

lāt'ex, *n.* fluid secreted by plants, esp. that from which rubber is obtained.

laun'der, *v.t.* wash (clothes, &c.).

lay[4]. ~**-by,** part of road extended to allow vehicle to stop there without interfering with traffic.

leading. ~ **edge,** forward edge of aircraft's wing.

|| **le'bensraum** (lā-, -owm), *n.* 'living-space', territory which State believes it needs for its natural development.

lēm'on[2] **sole,** *n.* kind of plaice.

lėp'rechaun (-k-), *n.* Irish sprite.

leucŏt'omў, *n.* incision into frontal lobe of brain to relieve some cases of mental disorder.

Lew'isite (lōō-), *n.* a poison gas.

ley (lā), *n.* land temporarily under grass.

lĭbĭd'ō, *n.* emotional craving prompting any human (esp. sexual) activity.

lī'ger (-g-), *n.* offspring of lion and tigress.

line. Also: one of the very narrow vertical sections into which televised scenes are photographed and reproduced.

lĭ'nŏcut, *n.* (print from) design cut on block of linoleum.

liquid. Also: (of assets, &c.) easily convertible into cash.

liquidate. Also: put an end to, get rid of (freq. by violent means).

lisle (līl) thread, *n.* fine hard-twisted kind of thread.

liver[2]. ~**ish,** -ў[2], *aa.* having a disordered liver.

lobŏt'omў, *n.* = leucotomy.

logis'tics, *n.pl.* art of moving, quartering, & supplying troops &c. ~**tic,** *a.*

low[2]. ~**-wing,** (of monoplane) with wings set low in fuselage.

lū'dō, *n.* game played on board with dice and counters.

lŷ'sol, *n.* a disinfectant. P.

M

M. & B. 693. May & Baker sulpho-pyridine. P.

măc, *n.* (colloq.) mackintosh.

mā'cédoine (-dwahn), *n.* mixture of fruits or vegetables.

macra'mé (-ahmi), *n.* trimming of knotted cord.

măd'répŏre, *n.* kinds of coral.

magic. Also: ~ **eye,** popular name for selenium cell.

Maginot (mah'zhēnō) **line,** *n.* French fortified line on Franco-German frontier.

măgnā'lium, *n.* light tough alloy of aluminium and magnesium.

magnet. magnetic; ~ **mine,** submarine mine detonated by approach of large mass of magnetic material, e.g. ship.

măg'nėtron, *n.* (Phys.) thermionic tube for generating very high frequency oscillations.

maison(n)ětte' (-z-), *n.* small house; part of house let separately.

make, *v.* ~**-up.** Also: character of a person.

Mă'rathon, *n.* foot-race of abnormal length; contest requiring great endurance.

măr'khŏr, *n.* large spiral-horned wild goat of N. India.

marsh. ~**mallow,** shrubby herb; sweetmeat from its root.

marshal. ~**ling yard,** railway yard in which goods trains, &c., are assembled.

mărti'ni[2] (-ēni), *n.* kind of cocktail.

mass[2]. ~ **observation,** study and

---

mãte, mēte, mīte, mŏte, mūte, mōŏt; răck, rĕck, rĭck, rŏck, rŭck, rōŏk;

reporting of social customs, &c., of ordinary people taken at random. ~ production, production in large quantities of standardized article(s) by standardized mechanical means.

más'toid, a. shaped like female breast. n. conical prominence on temporal bone: (colloq.) mastoiditis. ~i'tis, n. inflammation of (esp. air-cells in) mastoid.

match[1], ~boarding, boards fitting into each other by means of groove and tongue along edges. ~wood, splinters.

matter. Also: discharge of pus. ~-of-fact', prosaic, ordinary, unimaginative.

may'hem, n. (leg.) maiming of person.

mayonnaise' (-z), n. (dish with) creamy dressing of oil, egg-yolk, vinegar, &c.

meadow. ~sweet, meadow plant with fragrant flowers.

mechanize. Also: equip (troops) with tanks, motor transport, &c.

még'alith, n. large stone esp. as monument.

mén'hir (-ēr), n. prehistoric monumental monolith.

menis'cus, n. lens convex on one side, concave on the other.

mén'opause, n. natural cessation of menstruation.

mér'cerized, a. (of cotton) having silky gloss given by treatment with caustic alkali under tension.

merry. ~-go-round, revolving circle of seats for children to ride in.

més'ón, n. particle of mass intermediate between proton and electron.

mic'rofilm, n. (photographic reproduction on) very small film.

mi'crowave, n. wireless wave of less than 50 cm.

mid. ~-wing, (of monoplane) with wings intermediate in position between those of high-wing and low-wing aircraft.

midget. Also: a. very diminutive.

mi'leage (-lij), n. var. of milage.

mim'éograph, n. apparatus for

making copies of written sheets from stencils.

min'gy (-ji), a. (colloq.) stingy.

Mol'otov, proper name used attrib. ~ breadbasket, (sl.) container scattering incendiary bombs, dropped from aircraft. ~ cocktail, (sl.) inflammatory missile hurled by hand as anti-tank weapon.

monitor. Also: detector for acquired radio-activity.

món'tage (-ahzh), n. selection, cutting, and arrangement of shots in cinema film.

mōr'on, n. adult with intelligence of child of nine or ten.

*mōtél', n. hotel or group of cabins by roadside where motorists may stay for the night.

motor. ~ize, v.t. equip (army, unit, &c.) with motor transport.

Moustēr'ian (-ōō-), a. of the palaeolithic epoch of the remains found in the Moustier cave in France.

mūtilàt'eral, a. done by or affecting several of the parties concerned.

mustard. ~ gas, kind of poison gas, a powerful irritant.

|| mȳstique' (-tēk), n. atmosphere of mystery investing some creeds, arts, &c., or persons; professional skill or technique which impresses the layman.

mȳxōmatōs'is, n. virus disease in rabbits.

N

n (ĕn), n. (math.) indefinite number.

nǎnn'ȳ[2], n. child's nurse.

nǎ'palm (-ahm), n. product of naphthaline and coco-nut oil. ~ bomb, one containing jellied petrol.

narciss'ism, n. morbid self-love or self-admiration.

nǎrk, n. (sl.) police spy.

native, n. Also: superior or British-reared oyster.

nav'icert, *n.* certificate that ship's cargo does not contravene war contraband regulations.

Nazi (nah'tsĭ, -zĭ), *n. & a.* (member) of German National-Socialist party.

ne'on, *n.* inert atmospheric gas giving reddish glow when an electric current is passed through it. **~** light, coloured light used in advertisements, utilizing neon, either alone or with other substances, or gases with similar properties.

net'ball, *n.* game in which ball has to be thrown through elevated horizontal ring from which a net depends.

neutral, *n.* Also: position of parts in gear mechanism in which no power is transmitted.

neu'trŏn, *n.* electrically neutral elementary particle of almost the same mass as a proton.

new. ~ look, late 1947 fashion in women's clothes with ankle-length skirts, &c.

news. ~ letter, periodical sent by post to subscribers.

Nŏ'ĕl', Nowĕl' (nō-), *int.* in Christmas carols.

nŏn-belli'gerent, *a. & n.* (State) not taking active or open part in war. **~ency,** *n.*

nŏn-interven'tion, *n.* policy of not intervening in war, disputes between other States, &c.

nŏn-stŏp', *a.* (of trains, &c.) not stopping at intermediate stations; not stopping. *adv.* without a stop.

nostalgia. Also: sentimental yearning for something past.

nougat (nōō'gah), *n.* an almond sweetmeat.

noyau (nwahyō'), *n.* a liqueur.

nucleus. Also: mass forming centre of atom. **nuclear.** (esp.) of atomic nuclei, atomic. **nuclear fission,** splitting up of heavy atom, e.g. of uranium, into two or more new atoms, with enormous release of energy. **nuclear fuel,** source of atomic energy. **nuclear reactor,** atomic pile.

nū'dist, *n.* adherent of the cult of the nude. **~ism,** *n.*

ny'lon, *n.* synthetic plastic material of great tensile strength and elasticity.

O

occlude' (-ōō-), *v.t.* close, obstruct; absorb (gases). **occlusion,** *n.*

occult. **~ism,** *n.* mysticism.

occupa'tional, *a.* (esp.) incident to, arising from, a person's occupation.

oc'tāne, *n.* hydrocarbon of the paraffin series. **high-~,** (of fuels used in internal-combustion engines) not detonating readily during power stroke.

ŏ'dalisque (-k), *n.* Eastern female slave or concubine, esp. in Sultan's seraglio.

oil. ~-bomb, kind of incendiary containing oil.

operation. ŏpera'tional, *a.* designed for or engaged in warlike operations.

ŏp'sonin, *n.* opsonic substance produced by injecting dead cultures of bacteria of patient's disease.

optic. Also: transparent measuring device attached to mouth of spirit bottle.

ŏp'timum, *n.* (biol.). Most favourable conditions; best amount. *a.* best for biological purposes, most favourable.

orange stick, *n.* stick of orange-wood for manicuring nails.

order, *n.* Also: (Archit.) treatment of column and entablature (the Doric, Ionic, Corinthian, Tuscan, Composite, &c.).

ŏr'gandie, *n.* kind of fine stiffish muslin.

ŏrope'sa (float), *n.* float supporting sweeping-wire in mine-sweeping.

Or'pington, *n.* a breed of poultry.

ŏrthochromăt'ic (-k-), *a.* (Photog.) giving correct relative intensity to colours.

oscillate. Also: (of wireless receivers) radiate electro-magnetic waves owing to faulty operation or construction.

---

out. ~**board,** (of motor-boats) having motor attached outside; (of motor) so attached. ~**moded,** *a.* old-fashioned. ~**size,** (size) larger than stock sizes.

overall. Also: *a.* inclusive of everything, total.

over-proof', *a.* containing more alcohol than proof spirit has.

o'vershŏt, *a.* (of wheel) turned by water flowing above it.

overstrung. Also: (of piano) with strings in sets crossing each other obliquely.

o'vertone, *n.* (mus.) harmonic.

oxidā'tion, *n.* chemical combination with oxygen.

ŏx'ў-acĕt'ŷlēne, *a.* consisting of, involving use of, mixture of oxygen and acetylene (which produces intensely hot flame).

P

paediăt'ric, *a.* of or dealing with children's diseases.

Pakistan' (pah-, -ahn), *n.* The Moslem State of India.

pănchromăt'ic (-k-), *a.* (Photog.) equally sensitive to all spectrum colours.

pănjăn'drum, *n.* (mock title for) great personage.

pănn'ikin, *n.* small metal drinking-vessel.

pan'zer (-tser), *a.* (German) armoured (division, &c.).

par. Also: (Golf) number of strokes a scratch player should require for a hole or course.

păr², *n.* (sl.) newspaper paragraph or notice.

parachute. ~ **flare,** flare dropped by parachute to light target for bombs, &c. ~ **mine,** large case containing explosive dropped by parachute from aircraft. ~ **troops,** invading troops landed by parachute. ~**tist,** *n.* user of parachute; *pl.* parachute troops.

părashōō'ter (or **'rashŏt'**, *nn.* (sl.) member of force acting as guard against parachute troops.

pă'ravane, *n.* kite-shaped mine-sweeping device holding sweeping-wire at angle to ship's side.

păr'sĕc, *n.* distance at which annual parallax of star would be one second of arc, as unit of stellar distance.

part. Also: ~**timer,** part-time worker.

passenger. Also: member of a team who does less than his share.

passe-partout (pahspărtōō'), *n.* kind of adhesive tape or paper used for framing photographs, &c.

păt'ina, *n.* incrustation, usu. green, on surface of old bronze; gloss produced by old age on wood-work.

pearlies (pĕrl'iz), *n. pl.* costermongers' dress decorated with many pearl buttons.

|| **pêche** (pāsh) **Mel'ba,** *n.* confection of ice-cream and peaches.

pĕdŏl'ogў, *n.* science of soils.

pelā'gic, *a.* of, in, on, the open sea.

pel'mĕt, *n.* pendant border concealing curtain-rods, &c.

penicill'in, *n.* drug prepared from the mould penicillium.

pē'nis, *n.* male copulatory organ.

pĕn'tŏde, *a.* & *n.* (wireless valve) with five electrodes.

pĕntstē'mon, *n.* bright-flowered garden plant.

pĕ'on, *n.* (Span. Amer.) day-labourer; (Mex.) enslaved debtor. ~**age,** *n.* employment, service, of peons.

pĕristăl'sis, *n.* wave of contraction passing down tube such as the alimentary canal. ~**tic,** *a.*

pĕrm'alloy, *n.* alloy of nickel and iron very sensitive to magnetic forces, used for cores of telegraph cables. **P.**

permanent. ~ **wave,** (abbrev. *perm.*), artificial wave in hair lasting for some months.

perŏx'ide, *n.* compound of oxygen with another element containing maximum proportion of oxygen; peroxide of hydrogen used as bleach, antiseptic, &c. *v.t.* bleach with this peroxide.

pĕr'spĕx, n. transparent plastic substitute for glass. P.

petrŏl'ŏgў, n. study of the origin, structure, &c., of rocks.

phăg'ocŷte, n. leucocyte specially active in destroying bacteria, waste matter, &c., in blood or body-tissues.

phăll'us, n. image of penis used in religious rites as symbol of generation. phăll'ic, a.

phĕnă'cĕtĭn, n. antipyretic drug.

photo. Also: ~-finish, end of a race in which a camera is used to determine the winner; very close finish.

phōtogĕ'nĭc, a. producing light; photographing well.

piccalill'ĭ, n. pickle of chopped vegetables, mustard, and spices.

pick. ~-up, device replacing sound-box in gramophone (for playing record through wireless loud speaker).

pile. atomic ~, apparatus for the study or utilization of atomic energy.

pilot. Also: a. preliminary and experimental. ~ balloon, small balloon used by meteorologists.

pin. ~point, a. (of target) small and requiring accurate shooting or bombing. ~prick, petty annoyance.

ping, n. sound as of bullet's flight, v.i. emit ping. ~pong, table tennis.

pipe. ~-line, line of pipes for conveying liquid esp. oil to a distance, (fig.) goods in transit from producer to consumer or retailer.

pipĕtte', n. slender tube used for transferring or measuring small quantities of liquid.

plănk'tŏn, n. drifting or floating organisms found at or near surface of oceans and lakes.

plăt'ŷpus, n. ornithorhyncus.

Plĭm'soll. ~ line, mark, statutory load-line on hulls of British ships. ~s, n.pl., shoes of rubber and canvas.

plough. ~-back, (fig.) reinvest (profits) in business &c.

plug, v. Also: (colloq.) repeat (music) over and over again.

Plutō (-ōō-), n. small planet whose orbit is beyond that of Neptune.

plutōn'ĭum (-ōō-), n. radio-active element produced from uranium.

plȳ[1]. ~-wood, strong thin board made of layers glued together with the grains crosswise.

polar. pō'larĭze, v.t. confine vibrations in (light- or heat-waves, &c.) to single direction or plane by passing through prism or other means.

police. ~ state. State controlled by means of political police.

pom'elō (pŭ-), n. small shaddock or grape-fruit.

pŏngee' (-ĭ-), n. soft unbleached Chinese silk.

pŏntĭf'ĭcăte, v.i. play the pontiff, assume airs of infallibility.

pool. football ~, competition in which a proportion of entry money is awarded to those who correctly forecast result of some football matches.

Portland cement, n. cement made from calcined chalk and clay, in colour resembling ~ stone, limestone from Portland.

position. Also: v. place in position; find position of.

pŏs'itron, n. positive electron.

post[2]. Also: Last ~, (mil.) last bugle call of day, apart from *Lights out*.

pŏtt, n. a size of paper.

power. Also: v.t. supply (vehicle) with power or a source of power.

pre'-ĕmpt'ĭve, a. (bridge) ~ bid, high bid intended to prevent further bidding.

prē'făb, n. prefabricated house.

prēfăb'ricăte, v.t. make (houses) in sections in factories for assembly at a different place.

prē'pūce, n. loose skin covering end of penis.

pressure. Also: ~ cooker, vessel for cooking food quickly in high-pressure steam. ~ group, group of persons exerting political pressure.

pretty. Also: n. (Golf) fairway.

prō, n. (sl.) professional.

---

mäte, mēte, mīte, mŏte, mūte, mŏŏt; răck, rĕck, rĭck, rŏck, rŭck, rŏŏk;

produce. ~r′gas, combustible gas for fuel, &c., produced by passing air and steam through red-hot carbon.

prŏs′tāte, n. large gland accessory to male generative organs.

protocol. Also: diplomatic etiquette.

psўchĭ′atrў (sĭk-), n. medical treatment of mental disease.

public. ~ relations, relations of department, organization, &c. with the general public. ~ relations officer, person who gives out information to the public in connexion with some department &c.

pull. ~-over, woollen jersey put on over the head.

pul′mōtor (pŏol-), n. apparatus for applying artificial respiration by pumping air, &c., into lungs. P.

pūr′ée (-ā), n. vegetables, meat, &c. cooked and passed through sieve; soup made of this.

put. Also: ~ across, impose (on persons) with, succeed in deceiving; succeed in explaining.

pylon. Also: lattice-work structure, esp. one carrying overhead electric cables.

Q

quantum. ~ theory, hypothesis that radiant energy is discharged in discrete amounts.

queen. Also: court-card between king and knave; chess-piece of greatest value.

quis′ling, n. (sl.) pro-Nazi traitor or fifth columnist.

R

rāce³, n. root (of ginger).

rāchel′. (-sh-), a. (of face-powder) of yellowish-brown shade.

racial. ~ism, n. tendency to, encouragement of, antagonism between different races of men.

răck′et³. Also: (colloq.) scheme for effecting some object illegally.

răcketeer′ing, n. (esp.) organized blackmail by intimidation. răcketeer′, n.

rā′dăr, n. radiolocation.

radio. Also: ~gram, combined wireless receiver and electric gramophone.

rādiolocā′tion, n. system of detecting approach of aircraft, &c., by reflected radio waves.

rēăc′tor, n. atomic pile.

*rēăl′tor, n. real-estate agent.

recĕp′tionist, n. person employed to receive clients.

recession. Also: *trade slump.

rēdeplŏy′ment, n. improved arrangement of plant and use of personnel in factories.

reflā′tion, n. inflation of currency after a deflation.

Reich, n. the German State.

rē′jĕct, n. rejected thing or person.

‖ rentier (rahn̄tyā′), n. person living on investments, &c.

remand. Also: ~ home, place of detention for juveniles.

remember. Also: Remembrance day, 11th November, the anniversary of the armistice of 1918, or the Sunday before this.

remote. ~ control, control of apparatus from a distance by electrically operated device, radio waves, &c.

rēs′édă (-z-), n. dull greyish-green colour.

respirator. Also: gas-mask.

‖ retrous′sé (-ōōsā), a. turned up (of nose).

rĕv, n. (colloq.) revolution (of internal-combustion engine).

revers′ (-vēr), n. turned-back front edge of garment.

rhine′stŏne (rīns-), n. kind of rock crystal; paste diamond.

ribbon. ~ building, development, building along sides of main road.

road′ster, n. horse, bicycle, &c., for ordinary use on road.

rough. ~age, n. bran, &c., eaten as a bowel stimulant.

rule. work to ~, make efficiency impossible by keeping every rule strictly, as substitute for strike.

rŭm′pus, n. (sl.) row, uproar.

run. ~way, *n.* specially prepared section of airfield for the taking-off and landing of aircraft. ~ning-board, foot-board of motor-car, &c.

S

săl ammŏ'niăc, *n.* ammonium chloride, a white crystalline salt.

salvo. Also: number (*of bombs*) dropped simultaneously from aircraft.

Săn'ta Claus (-z), *n.* mythical personage who fills children's stockings with presents at Christmas.

‖ sauerkraut (sowr'krowt), *n.* German dish of pickled cabbage.

scan. Also: (television) resolve (picture) into elements of light and shade for transmission.

schĭzophrēn'ia (sk-), *n.* mental disease characterized by emotional, but not intellectual, instability.

Schnŏrk'el, *n.* long tube for supplying submerged submarine with air for engines and crew.

scramble. Also: *v.t.* cook (eggs) by breaking into pan with butter, milk, &c., stirring slightly, & heating; alter frequency of speech of (telephone conversation) so as to make it unintelligible to eavesdroppers.

screen, *v.t.* Also: scrutinize (personnel), esp. to prevent espionage or political subversion; provide with oscillation damper.

script. Also: written examination answers.

scŭm'ble, *v.t.* soften (oil-colour) by overlaying with thin coat of opaque colour. *n.* scumbled effect or part.

sea. ~-anchor, kind of drag keeping vessel, &c., from drifting or with head to wind. ~shell, shell of shell-fish.

Sea'lyham (-lĭam), *n.* kind of terrier.

seize. Also: (of machinery) become stuck, jam, from undue heat or pressure.

self-. ~-service, *attrib.* (of restaurant, shop, &c.) in which customers help themselves to food or goods to be paid for afterwards. *n.* this kind of service.

seller's market, conditions where demand exceeds supply and prices are high.

set[1]. Also: fix (hair) when damp so that it dries in waves.

set[2]. Also: (Cinema) built-up scene.

shake, *v.* Also: upset the composure of (a person).

shear. ~ hulk, sheer hulk, dismasted ship fitted with ~legs, hoisting shears.

Sher'pa, *n.* one of a Tibetan people living on Himalayas.

Shĕt'land (pony), *n.* small breed native to Shetland Isles.

shock[3]. ~ tactics, sudden and violent action. ~ troops, picked and highly disciplined body of men.

shoe. ~-string, *(colloq.)* small or inadequate sum of money. *a.* barely adequate.

short, *n.* Also: short circuit.

shot[3], *n.* Also: scene in cinematograph film. ~-gun, smooth-bore gun for firing small shot at short range.

Siamese. ~ cat, short-haired kind with café-au-lait colour and chocolate-brown mask and points.

Siegfried (sē'grēd) line, *n.* German fortified line along Franco-German frontier.

sil'icon, *n.* a non-metallic element.

silver. ~ fish, silvery insect found in damp places.

sit. ~-down strike, one in which strikers refuse to leave factory, mine, &c., in which they work.

skĭrt'ing-board, *n.* board along bottom of room-wall.

slăp'-stick, *n.* harlequin's flexible divided lath; boisterous low comedy of rough kind.

slim. Also: *v.i.* reduce weight by dieting, &c.

slip, *n.* Also: (*pl.*) bathing-drawers.

slow. Also: (of surfaces) tending to cause slowness. ~ motion, (of cinema film) taken at higher

---

speed than normal, so that in projection at normal speed all movements seem slow.

small. Also: ~s, *n.pl.* = articles of laundry.

smärm′y, *a.* (colloq.) unctuously ingratiating, fulsome.

smash, *v.* Also: ~ing, *a.* (sl.) extremely good or good-looking.

smithereens′ (-dh-), *n. pl.* small fragments.

smŏg, *n.* mixture of smoke and fog.

snaffle. Also: *v.t.* (sl.) appropriate, purloin.

snag, *n.* obstacle, drawback.

snake. Also: *v.i.* manœuvre aircraft, be manœuvred, in zigzag course.

snip, *n.* Also: (racing sl.) certainty.

sŏck′eye, *n.* blue-back salmon.

sŏd³ (vulg.), *n.* Also: sŏd′omite, *nn.* person guilty of sodomy.

soda. ~-fountain, (shop, counter, equipped with) vessel in which soda-water is stored under pressure for drawing off.

sŏf′fĭt, *n.* downward surface of top of arch, doorway, &c.

soft. Also: ~ wood, wood of spruce or fir, deal.

sō′lo. Also: unaccompanied flight. *a.* alone, unaccompanied.

sŏn′ic, *a.* of sound (-waves). ~ barrier, resistance offered by air to object moving at speed near that of sound.

sound. ~ box, that part of a mechanical gramophone which contains the needle and the diaphragm.

space. ~-ship, craft for travelling through interplanetary space.

spăs′tic, *a.* caused by or subject to spasm(s). *n.* person suffering from cerebral palsy.

spin, *n.* Also: aircraft's diving descent with continued rotation on its axis.

spind′ly, *a.* slender, attenuated.

spiritual. Also: *n.* religious song peculiar to Amer. negroes.

spiv, *n.* man, usu. young and flashy, exploiting community, esp. in black market.

splinter. ~ party, political party

that has broken away from a larger one.

spot. Also: *v.i.* act as observer (esp. from the air) of enemy's position, effect of gunfire, approach of aircraft, &c. spott′er, *n.* ~-light, beam of light concentrated on actor, &c.

sprŏck′ĕt, *n.* projection on wheel engaging links of chain.

stack, *v.* Also: direct (aircraft) to fly round at different heights until they can land.

stagger, *v.* Also: set (like parts of structure, &c.) in overlapping, slantwise, or zigzag arrangement; arrange (hours of work, holidays, &c.) so that they differ from those of others.

stäle², *v.i.* & *n.* (of horse, &c.) (void) urine.

stand. ~ in, deputize *for.* ~-in, deputy, substitute.

stay. ~-in strike, sit-down strike.

Sten, *n.* small, cheap, mass-produced sub-machine gun, fired from hip.

sterile, sterilize. Also: make incapable of producing offspring.

sterling. Also: ~ area, countries whose currencies are linked to the British pound.

stick¹. Also: ~er, adhesive label.

stick². Also: number (*of bombs*) dropped in quick succession from aircraft.

still², *n.* (Cinema) photograph as distinct from moving picture.

stock. Also: ~piling, accumulation of strategic stocks of materials.

stŏŏge, *n.* *(theatr. sl.) person acting as foil for comedian, &c.; (sl.) one who is learning to fly.

storm. ~ troops, shock troops; esp. Nazi semi-military organization; ~ trŏŏ′per, member of this.

stō′vaine, *n.* local anaesthetic, usu. injected into spine.

straddle. Also: drop bombs across (target) with first and last at opposite sides or ends of it.

strap. ~-hanger, passenger holding on to strap for want of a seat.

zh, as (*rou*)ge; ĕ = ĭ; ĭr, ûr, =[ẽr; ў̆, ў̆, = ĭ, ĭ; and see p. 4. * = U.S.

3495 U

străt′osphēre, *n*. layer of atmospheric air lying above troposphere, in which temperature remains constant.

stream′line, *v.t.* shape so as to reduce resistance to air or water.

street. ∼walker, prostitute.

strike. Also: ∼bound, immobilized by ∼.

string. Also: (*pl.*) conditions attached to offer, &c.

‖ **stu′ka** (-ōō-), *n*. German dive-bomber.

Stŷx, *n*. river encompassing Hades; *cross the* ∼, die.

sŭb-fŭsc, *a*. sober-hued.

sub-machine gun, *n*. machine gun of less than usual size.

subsidiary. ∼ (company), company controlled by another holding more than half its issued share capital.

sŭb′title, *n*. film caption.

sŭlphanil′amide, *n*. drug used to counteract streptococcal infections.

sū′perchārger, *n*. mechanical device for forcing extra quantity of explosive mixture into cylinder of internal-combustion engine.

sūpersŏn′ic, *a*. faster than sound.

sūp′ersound, *n*. sound vibrations too rapid to be audible.

sŭrré′alism, *n*. movement in painting, literature, &c., seeking to express subconscious mind by images, &c., in sequences or associations such as may occur in dreams. ∼ist, *n*. ∼ist′ic, *a*.

‖ **svĕlte**, *a*. lightly built, lissom.

swat (-ŏt), *v.t.* slap, crush (fly).

swing. Also: particular kind of jazz music.

switch. ∼board, apparatus for varying connexion between electric circuits.

swiz′zle, *n*. compounded intoxicating drink.

T

table. ∼ tennis, game played on table-top with rackets, net, and light balls.

tăck′ў, *a*. (of varnish, &c.) in the sticky stage before complete dryness.

take. *∼ care of*, be adequate provision against. ∼ off, (of aircraft) become airborne from rest.

tăradid′dle, *n*. (sl.) fib.

tearᴿ. ∼gas, lachrymatory gas.

technical. techni′cian, *n*. person skilled in technical details of an art or subject.

tech′nicolor (tĕk-), *n*. system of colour photography, esp. in films. P.

teens. teen-āger, person in his or her teens.

tĕl′ĕcast, *v.t.* broadcast in television.

tell. Also: direct (person) *to do*.

territorial. ∼waters, marginal waters under jurisdiction of State, esp. that part of the sea within three miles of shore.

thĕr′mite, *n*. mixture of powdered aluminium and iron oxide producing very high temperature on combustion, used in incendiary bombs, for welding, &c.

thĕrmonū′clear bomb, *n*. hydrogen bomb.

thĕr′mostăt, *n*. automatic device for regulating temperature. thĕrmostăt′ic, *a*.

three. Also: ∼decker, novel in three volumes. ∼lane, marked or designed to accommodate three lines of traffic.

thrombō′sis, *n*. clotting in blood-vessel.

throw. Also: ∼back, reversion to an earlier ancestral type.

tĭdd′ler, *n*. (nursery name for) stickleback.

tīg′on, *n*. hybrid offspring of tiger and lioness.

time. ∼ bomb, one designed to explode after interval from time of being dropped, placed in position, &c. ∼lag, interval between cause, &c., and result or consequence.

tĭn. ∼pan alley, (fig.) the world of composers and publishers of popular music.

Tŏkay′, *n*. a Hungarian wine.

token. ~ payment, proportionately small payment made esp. by debtor State as indication that debt or obligation is not repudiated.

tomm'y-gun, n. (sl.) Thompson sub-machine gun.

To'phet, n. Hell.

total. Also: (of warfare) in which all available weapons and resources are employed.

totälität'ian, a. permitting no rival policies or parties.

touch. (sl.) ~ for, get (money) out of.

trace. trä'cer bullet, shell, &c., one having a burning composition in its base which enables its course to be observed.

track. Also: wheel-band of tank, tractor, &c.

trade. ~ cycle, recurrent alternation of trade conditions between prosperity and depression.

traff'icätor, n. electrically operated turn indicator on motor vehicle.

trail. ~ing edge, rear edge of aircraft's wing.

trailer. Also: extracts from film exhibited in advance as advertisement.

transport, n. Also: means of ~.

trau'ma, n. wound, injury; (Psychology), emotional shock. **traumät'ic,** a.

trickle. ~ charger, slow-working accumulator charger.

tri'ode, n. & n. (wireless valve) with three electrodes.

trip'lex glass, n. kind of unsplinterable glass. **P.**

tröp'osphère, n. layer of atmospheric air extending about 7 miles upwards from earth's surface, in which temperature falls with height.

tubercle. tüber'culin, n. preparation from cultures of tubercle bacillus used esp. as test for tuberculosis.

türb'o-, in comb. turbine. ~jet engine, one having a turbine-driven compressor for supplying compressed air to combustion chamber, ~prop(eller) engine, one having a turbine-driven propeller.

Tüs'can, a. of Tuscany. ~ order, one of the five orders of architecture.

twenty. ~five, (hockey, &c.) line drawn across ground 25 yds. from each goal.

twin. ~ set, woman's matching cardigan and jumper.

type. ~script, typewritten matter.

U

ukulele (öokoölä'le, ü-), n. four-stringed Hawaiian guitar.

üll'age, n. what a cask &c. wants of being full.

ultracen'trifuge, n. very high-speed centrifuge.

ültramicroscöp'ic, a. beyond the range of microscopes.

ünderpriv'iléged (-jd), a. belonging to the lower classes of society.

untouch'able, n. non-caste Hindu (whom caste man may not touch).

up-stage, a. (sl.) supercilious.

utility, a. (of clothes, furniture, &c.), made in austere standardized styles.

V

V, abbr. of 'Vengeance' in names of a series of German 'new' weapons used as means of aerial bombardment; **V 1,** a flying bomb; **V 2,** a long-range rocket-propelled torpedo.

vamöse', -öös(e), v.i. (sl.) decamp, make off.

vändyke', n. triangular point of deeply serrated or indented border or edge.

veil. Also: take the ~, become a nun. ~ing, n. material for veils.

vermouth' (-öoth, or vär'möot), n. kind of apéritif.

vi'able, a. capable of living or surviving.

vic, n. V-shaped formation of aircraft.

view. Also: ~point, way of regarding a matter, position.

voile, *n.* thin semi-transparent dress material.

vŏl'-au-vent' (-ŏ-vahṅ), *n.* kind of raised pie.

V sign, initial letter of 'victory' made with fore and middle finger of (right) hand.

vulgar, vulgār'ian, *n.* vulgar person, esp. one who is rich or conspicuous.

vulnerable. Also: (Contract Bridge) having won one game towards rubber.

W

wage. Also: ~ freeze, pegging of wage levels.

ward, warden. Also: member of civilian organization for assistance of civil population in air-raids.

water. ~-closet, place for evacuation of bowels with water-supply for flushing pan. ~glass, solution of sodium silicate used in preserving eggs, &c.

wedge. Also: ~-shaped golf club.

welfare. Also: ~ state, one in which the health and well-being of the citizens are a chief concern of the government.

well. ~-off, in good circumstances, esp. as regards money.

whip. whipping-boy, (fig.) scapegoat.

white. ~ elephant, rare but burdensome possession.

whodŭn(n)'it (hōō-), *n.* (sl.) mystery or detective story.

*__**whoo'pee**__ (wōō-), *n.* make ~, rejoice noisily, have a roaring time.

winceyĕtte' (-si-), *n.* kind of wincey with less wool.

wind[1]. ~sock, canvas cylinder or cone flown from mast-head to show aircraft direction of wind. ~ tunnel, apparatus for testing models of aircraft under known velocities of ~.

wine. ~sap, large red Amer. winter apple.

wing. Also: one of the broad supporting surfaces of an aeroplane; front mudguard of motor vehicle; (Footb., &c.) forward, &c., whose place is either side of centre.

wise. *~-crack, (colloq.) smart pithy remark; *v.i.* make wise-cracks.

wish. ~ful thinking, confusion of wishes and expectations.

wonk'y, *a.* (sl.) shaky, unreliable.

wood. Also: (Bowls) a bowl.

work. Also: ~ing party, committee, orig. of workers and management, investigating improvements in industrial efficiency, &c.

X

xenophōb'ia, *n.* strong dislike of foreigners.

Y

yaourt (yah'oort), **yog(h)urt** (yŏg'-oort), *n.* sour fermented liquor made from milk in Levant.

yellow. Also: (sl.) cowardly.

yes. ~-man, characterless, weakly acquiescent person.

Z

zip, *n.* light sharp sound. ~-fastener (P.), **zipp'er,** *nn.* fastening device consisting of two flexible stringers engaged and disengaged by means of a sliding cam pulled between them.

ah, awl, oil, boor, cow, dowry; chin, go, bang, so, ship, thin; dh, as th(e);
zh, as (rou)ge; ė = I; îr, ûr, = ẽr; ȳ, y̆, = I, I; and see p. 4. * = U.S.

A. PRONUNCIATION OF PROPER NAMES

THIS list is intended as a guide to the pronunciation of some difficult proper names frequently met with. It makes no claim to completeness, and many geographical names in particular have had to be omitted.

One or two general points may perhaps be noted here: Classical names ending in *-es* are usually pronounced (-ēz). In New Zealand and most newly-colonized countries all native names are pronounced with all vowels sounded (and pronounced as Italian vowels, i.e. *a* = ah, *e* = ā or ĕ, *i* = ē or ĭ, *u* = ōō). The U.S. pronunciation of some American place-names differs frcm the usual English pronunciation; in the following list such specifically U.S. pronunciations are preceded by an asterisk. There are many proper names (e.g. Kerr, Smyth) the pronunciation of which varies according to the family or individual referred to; such names have usually been omitted.

The following symbols have been employed in indicating pronunciation, in addition to those in the body of the work:

χ = *ch* in the Scottish pronunciation of *loch*.

ğ = 'soft' *g* in *ginger*.

ṅ indicates that the preceding vowel is nasalized.

Aar'on (är-)	Æ'schylus (-k-)
Abbeville (ăb'vĕl)	Æ'sŏp
Abĕd'nĕgō	Afghan (ăf'găn)
A'bel (ā-)	Afghăn'istăn (ăfg-; *or* -ahn; *or* ăfgănistan')
Ab'ėlárd (ä-)	
Abernĕ'thẏ (ă-)	A'gag (ä-)
Abī'jah (-a)	Agincourt (ăğ'ĭnkôrt)
Aboukir (ahbōōkēr')	A'gra (ah- *or* ä-)
About (ah'bōō)	Aï'da (ah-ē-)
A'brahăm (ä-)	Aix-la-Chapelle (ā'ks-lah-shăpĕl')
Abruz'zi (-brōōtsĭ)	Aix-les-Bains (ā'ks-lā-băṅ)
Abẏ'dŏs	Ajmēr' (ah-)
Accra (ă'kra *or* akrah')	Alabama (ălabah'ma;* -bă-)
Acĕl'dama (-k- *or* -s-)	Alăd'dĭn
Achates (akā'tēz)	Albani (ălbah'nĭ)
Ach'erŏn (ăk-)	A'lbanẏ (awl-)
Achilles (akĭl'ēz)	Alcan'tara (ălcahn-)
Achĭt'ŏphĕl (ak-)	Alcĕs'tĭs (ă-)
Ad'ėlaide (ä-)	Alcĭbī'adĕs (ă-; -z)
A'den (ä-)	Aldĕb'aran (ä-)
Adīrŏn'dăck (ä-)	Alğĕcī'ras (ä-)
Adonā'ĭs (ă-)	Alğēr'ĭa (ä-)
Adŏ'nĭs	Algiers (ălğēr'z)
Adrĭăt'ĭc (ä-)	Allahabad (ăla-habăd')
Ægĕ'an	Alleghany (ălĕgā'nĭ; *or* -ănĭ)
Ægī'na	Almerī'a (ä-)
Æl'fric (ă-)	Alsace (ăl'săs; *or* -ās)
Ænĕ'as	Amiens [French city] (ăm'ĭăṅ)
Æ'nĕĭd	Amiens [in Shakespeare] (ăm'ĭens)
Æ'olus	A'mŏs (ä-)

Amphit'ryon (ă-)
Anăc'reon
An'ăm (ă-)
Anam'as (ă-)
Anchises (ăngkī'sēz)
Andes (ăn'dēz)
An'drŏclēs (ă-; -z)
Andrŏm'ache (ă-; -ākĭ)
Andrŏm'éda (ă-)
Andrŏn'ĭcus [in Shakespeare] (ă-)
Angĕl'ĭcŏ (ă-)
An'gĕvin (ă-)
Angŏr'a (ăngg-; or ăng'gora)
Antæ'us (ă-)
Anthæa (ăn'thĭa)
Anthony (ăn'tonĭ)
Antig'onê (ă-)
Antigua (ăntē'gwa)
Antin'ŏus (ă-)
Antonī'nus (ă-)
Apĕll'ēs (-z)
Aphrŏdī'tê (ă-)
Apŏllīnăr'ĭs
Apŏll'yon
Appalā'chĭan (ă-; or -ăch-)
Aquī'năs
Arăch'nê (-kn-)
Aravalli (arah'vallĭ)
Archimedes (ārkīmē'dēz)
Arctū'rus (ār-)
Arêŏpagĭt'ĭca (ă-: or -g-)
Arêthū'sa (ă-; -za)
Ar'gentine (ār-)
Argyll (ārgīl')
Arĭăd'nê (ă-)
Ar'ĭel (ār-)
Aries (ār'ĭēz)
Aristī'dēs (ă-; -z)
Arīstŏph'anēs (ă-; -z)
A'rĭstŏtle (ă-)
Arizŏ'na (ă-)
Arkansas (ār'kansaw)
Armē'nĭa (ă-)
Artaxerxes (ārtagzĕr'ksēz)
Ar'tĕmĭs (ār-)
Ar'un (ār-)
A'rundel (ă-)
Asia (ā'sha)
Assĭ'sĭ (ăsē-)
Assouan (ăsŏŏăn')
Astăr'tê (ă-)
Astrakhan (ăstrakăn')
Atalăn'ta (ă-)
A'tê (ā- or ah-)
Athènæ'um (ă-)
Athē'nê
Athens (ă-; -z)

At'ropŏs (ă-)
Auchinlech (ăf'lĕk)
Augē'as
Augŭs'tĭne
Aurē'llus
Autŏl'ўcus
Av'alon (ă-)
Avignon (ă'vēnyawń)
A'von (ă-)
Azores (-ôrz)
Az'răel (ă-)
Bā'al
Bā'bel
Băb'ўlon
Băcchus (-k-)
Bach (bahχ)
Ba'den (bah-)
Bā'den-Pow'ell (-ōel)
Bae'dĕker (bā-)
Bagehot (băg'et)
Bahama (ba-hah'ma)
Baize (bī'ê)
Bălêā'rĭc (or balēr'ĭc)
Bal'kan (bawl)
Bā'lĭŏl
Bălmŏ'ral
Bălthazăr' [in Shakespeare]
Balu'chĭstăn (-lŏŏk-; or balŏŏkĭstăn')
Bantu (bah'ntŏŏ; or băn-)
Barăbb'as
Bārbā'does (-ōz)
Bărcêlō'na
Băr'mécĭde
Barŏ'da
Bārŏt'sêland
Bā'săn
Bā'shăn
Băs'ra (-z-; or bŭs-)
Bassa'nĭŏ (-ahn-)
Băstille' (-tēl)
Basu'tŏlănd (-ŏŏ-)
Bată'vĭa (or bătavī'a)
Băt'on Rouge (rŏŏzh)
Bau'cĭs
Bayeux (bā-yŏŏ')
Bayreuth (bī'roit)
Bea'consfield (bĕ- or bē-)
Beauchamp (bē'cham)
Beaulieu (bū'lĭ)
Beaune (bōn)
Bĕchua'na (-kŭahna; or bĕch-)
Bĕĕl'zébŭb (or bēĕl-)
Beethoven (bā'tŏven)
Beh'rĭng (bĕ-; or bār-)
Beira (bī'ra)
Beirut (bā'rŏŏt)

Bĕl'gium (-jum)
Bē'lial
Bĕllägg'ĭō (-j-)
Bellĕ'rophon
Bĕlli'nl (-lē-)
Belvoir (bē'ver)
Bĕnär'ēs (-z; or bĕ-)
Bengal (bĕnggawl')
Bĕn'tham (-tam)
Berkeley (bärk'll)
Bĕrk'ley [America]
Berkshire (bärk'sher)
Bĕrlin'
Berlioz (bär'lĭōs)
Bĕrmū'das (-z)
Berwick (bĕ'rĭk)
Bethune [English surname] (bē'ten)
Bicester (bĭs'ter)
Bid'éford
Big'élow (-g-; -ō)
Bihär'
Bikanir' (-ēr)
Bilbä'ō
Blanc (-ahn)
Blĕn'heim (-nĭm)
Bleriot (blĕ'rĭō)
Bloe'mfontein (-ōō-; -ān)
Blücher (blōō'ker)
Bōadicē'a
Bōanĕrgĕs (-z)
Bŏcca'cciō (-kahch-)
Bō'diham (-dĭam)
Bō'er (or boor)
Bōē'thius
Bohun (bōōn)
Boleyn (bōōl'ĭn)
Bom'pas (-ŭm-)
Boötes (bō-ō'tēz)
Bordeaux' (-dō)
Bōrdō'nē
Bō'rĕas
Bŏs'ton (*baws-)
Bō'tha (-ta)
Bŏttĭcĕll'ĭ (-chĕl-)
Boulogne (bōōlōn')
Bour'bon (boor-)
Bourchier (bow'cher)
Bow (bō)
Bŏz (or -ō-)
Braemär' (brä-)
Brä'senōse (-zn-; -z)
Brazĭl'
Breadal'bane (-awl-)
Brougham (brōōm or brōō'am)
Bruges (brōōzh)
Buccleuch (buklōō')

Būcĕph'alus
Bū'charĕst (-ker-)
Bū'dapĕst'
Buenos Ayres (bō'nozär'ĭz; or bōō'ĭn-)
Bulawayo (bōōlawī'ō)
Bŭr'leigh (-lĭ)
Bȳr'on
Bysshe (bĭsh)
Bȳzăn'tĭum
Căb'ot
Cā'dĭz
Cadog'an (-ŭg-)
Cæd'mon (kä-)
Caen (kahn)
Cæsar (sē'zer)
Cagliostro (kälĭŏs'trō)
Cairo (kīr'ō)
Caius [Roman name] (kī'us)
Caius [Cambridge college] (kēz)
Căl'ais (-ĭs or -ā or ĭ)
Cālĕdō'nĭa
Cālĭg'ŭla
Callĭ'opē
Cä'mbridge
Cămbȳ'sēs (-z)
Cămpa'gna (-ahnya)
Campbell (kăm'bl)
Cā'naan (-nan)
Căn'berra
Căndä'cē
Canō'pus
Carăc'tacus
Carew' (-ōō)
Carew [Thomas, 1589-1639] (kär'ĭ)
Căr'ey
Cärlisle' (lĭl)
Carmär'then (-dh-)
Carnär'von
Cärnĕg'ie (-gĭ; or -ägĭ)
Căról'na
Căsablăn'ca
Căssĭopei'a (-ĕa)
Căstile' (-ĕl)
Căthay'
Catrī'ona (or kătrĭō'na)
Catŭll'us
Căv'ell
Cavour' (-oor)
Cecil (sĕsl or sĭsl)
Cĕcĭl'ĭa
Cellini (chĕlē'nĭ)
Cenci (chĕn'chĭ)
Cĕr'ēs (-z)
Cĕrvän'tĕs (-z)
Cĕsär'ĕwĭtch (-z-)

Ceylon′ (sĭl)	Crœ′cè
Cézanne′ (sā-)	Crœ′sus (krē-)
Chablis (shăb′lĕ)	Culloď′en
Chăl′dees (k-; -z)	Cȳm′bĕlīne (-lēn)
Chăl′kis (k-)	Cȳn′ĕwulf (k-; ōolf)
Chamonix (shăm′ŏnī)	Cȳp′rian
Chapultèpêc′ (chahpōol-)	Cȳrē′nè
Chā′ring Cross (-aws; or chär-)	Cȳther′a
Charlemagne (shärl′emän)	Czech (chĕk)
Chār′on (k-)	Dæ′dalus
Chär′teris (-terz)	Dahō′mey (da-h-)
Charȳb′dĭs (k-)	Dakō′ta
Chăt′ham (-tam)	Dăm′oclês (-z)
Chautau′qua (sha-; -kwa)	Dā′mon
Cherbourg (shĕr′boorg)	Dăn′āē (-ĭ)
Cher′wĕll chär-)	Dăph′nè
Chicago (shikah′gŏ, *shīkaw′gŏ)	Dăr′ĕs (-z)
Chīlè	Darī′us
Chiswick (chĭz′ĭk)	Daudet (dō′dā)
Chloe (klō′ī)	Dăv′entrȳ (or dă′ntrī)
Cholmondeley (chŭm′lĭ)	Da′vŏs (dah-; or davŏs′)
Chopin (shŏp′ăn or shō-)	Debū′ssy (-ē)
Cicero (sĭs′erŏ)	Dĕcam′eron
Cimabu′e (chē-; -ōō-ĭ)	De Crespigny (dekrĕp′ĭnĭ; or-krĕs-)
Cimarŏ′sa (chē-; -z-)	De′gäs (dā-)
Cincinnāt′ī (or -ah-)	Dehra Dun (dā′ra-dōōn′)
Cīr′cè	Dēlagŏ′a
Cīr′encĕster (or sĭs′ĭster)	De la Mare (dĕl′amār)
Clăv′erhouse (or klăv′erz)	Delhi (dĕl′ī)
Clerk′enwĕll (klär-)	Dē′lius
Clī′ŏ	Dĕl′phī
Clough (klŭf, klōō)	Dēmē′ter
Clovĕll′ȳ	Dēmē′trius (or -mĕt-)
Cŏch′in-Chī′na	Dèmŏc′ritus
Cŏckainge′ (-kän)	Dē′mŏs
Cœur de Lion (kẽrdelē′awń)	Dèmŏs′thenês (-z)
Colbourne (kŏ′ben)	Dĕn′bigh (-bĭ)
Cŏl′chĭs (-k-)	Der′bȳ (där-)
Cologne′ (-ōn)	De Reszke (derĕs′kĭ)
Colom′bŏ (-ŭm-)	Dẽr′went
Colŏn′	Descartes (dā′kärt)
Cŏlora′dŏ (-ah-; *-ă-)	Desdēmŏ′na (dĕz-)
Colquhoun (ko-hōōn′)	Des Moines (dĭmoin′)
Cŏ′mŏ	Détroit′
Comte (kaunt)	Deuterŏn′omȳ
Connect′icut (-nĕt-)	Deutsch′lănd (doich-)
Con′stable (kŭn-)	Dĭăn′a
Cophĕt′ūa	Diderot (dē′derŏ)
Cŏr′diller′a (-lyāra)	Dī′dŏ
Cŏrneille′ (-nā)	Dieppe (dē-ĕp′)
Cŏ′rot (-rŏ)	Dijon (dē′zhawń)
Cŏrrĕgg′iŏ (-j-)	Dīŏclē′tian (-shĭan)
Cŏr′tĕs (-z; or -ĭz)	Dĭŏg′énês (-z)
Cow′per (kōō-)	Dĭomē′dês (-z)
Creusa (krēŏŏ′za)	Dĭonȳ′sius (or -ĭs-)
Crichton (krī′ton)	Dĭonȳ′sus
Crīmē′a	

Disraeli (-zrāl-)
Di'ves (-z)
Domi'tian (-shĭan)
Dŏn Giova'nni (jōvah-)
Dŏn Ju'an (jōōan)
Dŏnne
Donne [John, 1573–1631] (dŭn)
Dŏn Quix'ote (or kwĭk'set)
Do'theboys (dōōdhe-)
Doug'las (dŭg-)
Drey'fus (drā-)
Dŭb'lĭn
Dŭl'wich (-lĭj)
Dū'mas (-mah)
Dū Maurier (mōr'lā)
Dŭmfries' (ēs)
Dŭne'dĭn
Dŭr'ban
Durham (dŭ'ram)
Dvorak (dvŏr'zhák)
Ebbw (ĕb'ŏō)
Ecclēsiás'tēs (ĭk-; -zĭ-; -z)
Ed'ĭnburgh (ĕ-; bure)
Egēr'ia (ĭ-)
Ei'ffel-tower (ĭf-)
Einstein (ī'nstĭn)
Eire (âr'ĕ)
El Dorado (ĕldōrah'dŏ)
E'li (ē-)
E'lia (ē-)
E'lў (ē-)
Empĕd'oclēs (ĕ-; -z)
Endўm'ĭŏn (ĕ-)
Eng'land (ĭngg-)
Entĕbb'ĕ (ĕ-)
Eph'ĕsus (ĕf-)
Epicūr'us (ĕ-)
E'rewhŏn (ē-)
Erie (ēr'ĭ)
Erin (ē'rĭn or ĕr'-)
Er'ŏs (ēr-)
Es'tē (ĕ-)
Esthō'nia (ĕ-)
Etherege (ĕth'erĭj)
E'ton (ē-)
Eubœa (ūbē'a)
Eu'clĭd
Euphrā'tēs (-z)
Eu phūēs (-z)
Eurip'ĭdēs (ūr-; -z)
Europe (ūr'op)
Eurўd'ĭcē (ūr-)
Eutēr'pē
Evéli'na (ē-; -ēna)
Ev'elўn (ē- or ĕ-)
Eyck (īk)
Ezē'kiel (ĭ-)

Fä'gĭn (-g-)
Fáll'odon
Fär'quhar (-kwer)
Fät'ĭma
Fa(u)lk'land (fawk-)
Faust (fowst)
Featherstonehaugh (făn'shaw)
Fīde'liō (-dā-)
Fiennes (fĭnz)
Fie'solē (fē-āz-)
Fĭg'arŏ
Fiji (fē-)
Finisterre' ('-ār)
Flŏr'ēs (-ez)
Flŏ'rida
Foch (fŏsh)
Fo'lkestone (fōks-)
Fŏrtūnā'tus
Fräncĕs'ca (or -chĕs-)
Freud (froid)
Frö'bel frēr-)
Frö'bĭsher
Froude (frōōd)
Frowde (-owd; or -ōōd)
Gael (gāl)
Gala'pagŏs (gahlah-)
Gā'lĕn
Gălĭle'o (-āŏ)
Galle (gawl)
Gallip'oli
Galsworthy (gaw'lzwerdhĭ)
Gamā'lĭel
Găn'gēs (-z)
Gĕdd'ēs (g-)
Gĕm'ĭnī (ğ-)
Gĕn'ĕsĭs (ğ-)
Gĕnĕ'va (ğ-)
Gĕn'ŏa (ğ-)
Geoff'rey (ğĕf-)
Ghats (gawts)
Ghirlāndai'o (gēr-; -dĭ'yŏ)
Giaour (jowr)
Gibral'tar (ğ-; -awl-)
Gĭd'ĕa (g-)
Gĭl'ĕad (g-)
Gillĕtte' (ğ-)
Giŏrğiŏ'nē (ğ-)
Giŏtt'ŏ (g-)
Giovanni (ğŏvah'nĭ)
Glamis (glahmz)
Glás'gow (-zgŏ)
Gloucester (glŏs'ter)
Gluck (-ōōk)
Gŏ'a
Gŏd'almĭng
Gŏda'varī (-dah-)
Godĭ'va

Goethe (gër'te)
Goli'ath
Gotham [Notts.] (gŏtam)
Gŏ'tham [New York]
Gounod (gōō'nō)
Gracchus (grā'kus)
Grātia'nō (-shiah-)
Greenwich (grĭn'ĭj)
Greuse (grērz)
Grieg (grēg)
Grĭn'delwald (-vahld)
Groote Schoor (grō'tskoor)
Gros'venor (grŏv-)
Guadeloupe (gwahdĕlōōp')
Guatemala (gwătĭmah'la)
Gudrun (gŏŏd'rōōn)
Guelph (gwĕlf)
Guernsey (gĕrn'zĭ)
Guiana (gĭ-ah'na)
Guinea (gĭn'ĭ)
Guinness (gĭn'ĭs)
Gŭsta'vus (-tah-)
Haar'lem (här-)
Hä'dēs (-z-)
Hä'gär
Hägg'äl
Hague (hāg)
Haifa (hī'fa)
Hai'nault (-awt)
Hait'ī (or hī-)
Hak'luyt (-ōōt)
Hänsĕăt'ĭc
Hare'wood (här-; locally här-)
Här'lĕch (-k)
Hä'run-äl-Räsch'ĭd (-rōō-; -shĭd)
Harwich (hă'rĭj)
Här'wich [America]
Hausa (hou'za)
Havăn'a
Havre (hah'vr)
Hawai'i (-wi-ĭ)
Haw'arden (erd-; or härd-)
Haw'orth (or how'erth)
Hay'dn (hī-)
Hē'bē
Hĕb'rĭdēs (-z)
Hĕc'atē
He'gel (hāg-)
Hĕg'īra (or hĕjī'a)
Hei'delbĕrg (hī-)
Heine (hī'ne)
Hĕll'ĕspŏnt
Hē'mans
Hĕn'gist (-ngg-)
Hĕr'aclēs (-z)
Heraclī'tus
Hĕr'cūlä'neum

Hĕr'cūlēs (-z)
Hĕ'rĕford
Hĕ'rĕward
Hĕr'mēs (-z)
Hĕrmī'onē
Hērŏ'dĭăs
Hērŏd'otus
Hert'ford [England] (härf-)
Hĕrt'ford [America]
Herts (härts)
Hĕspĕ'rĭdēs (-z)
Hiawath'a (-wŏ-)
Hil'debrănd
Hĭmalay'a (or hĭmah'lĭa)
Hin'du-Kush (-dōō kŏŏsh)
Hippŏc'ratēs (-z)
Hippŏl'ўta
Hŏbb'ĕma
Hŏ'bōken
Hoh'enlĭn'den (hŏen-)
Hōl'bein (-bīn)
Hol'born (hōben)
Hōlŏfĕr'nēs (-z)
Hōl'ўrōōd
Hōl'ўwĕll
Hō'mer
Hŏndūr'ăs
Hŏnolu'lu (-lōōlōō)
Hou'ston (hōōs-)
Houyhnhnm (hōō'ĭnem)
Hŭ'dĭbrăs
Hun'yadĭ (hōōn-yah-)
Hū'ron
Hў'derabăd
Hў'ĝeī'a (-ĭa)
Hў'mĕtt'us
Hўpā'tia (-shĭa)
Hўpĕr'ĭon
Iago (I-ah'gō)
Iăn'thē (I-)
Ibē'rĭa (I-)
I'carus (I-)
Idaho (I'da-hō)
I'dō (I-)
Idūmē'a (I-)
Illinois' (I-; -noi)
Illў'rĭa (I-)
Indĭăn'a (I-)
Indĭanăp'olĭs (I-)
Inge (ĭng or ĭnj)
Ingelow (ĭn'ĝllō)
In'ĭgō (I-)
In'terlaken (I-; -lah-)
Iōlăn'thē (I-)
Iŏl'chus (I-; -k-)
Iō'na (I-)
I'owa (I-)

Iphĭgēnĭ'a (I-)
Iquique (ĭkē'kĭ)
Iraq (ĭrahk')
Irawad'ī (ĭ-; -wŏd-)
I'roquois (ĭ-; -kwoi or -kwah)
Isaac (ī'zac)
Isaiah (īzī'a)
I'sis (ī-)
Islam (ĭz'lahm)
I'sleworth (īzelw-)
Ismailia (ĭzmah-ē'lĭa)
Isŏc'ratēs (ĭ-; -z)
Isolde (ĭzŏl'da)
Ispahan (ĭspa-hahn')
Ith'aca (ĭ-)
Ixī'on (ĭ-)

Jaeger (yā'ger)
Jä'ĕl
Jaipur (jīpoor')
Jăĭr'us (or jĭr'us)
Jamaī'ca
Janeir'ŏ (-ēr-)
Jā'nus
Jā'phĕt
Jā'ques [in Shakespeare] (-kwĭz)
Ja'va (jah-)
Jĕ'kȳll
Je'na (yā-)
Jĕ'rome (or Jĕrŏm')
Jĕr'vaulx (-vō)
Jōb
Jodhpur (jŏ'dpoor)
Jōhänn'esbŭrg
Jō'llĕt
Jōsĕ'phus
Jungfrau (yŏŏng'frou)

Kaap'stadt (kah-; -t)
Kabul' (-ōōl; or kaw'bŏŏl)
Kalahār'ī (kah-; -ee)
Kălamazōō'
Kăndahãr' (-da-h-)
Kănsas [state] (-nz-)
Kăn'sas [city] (-ns-)
Kara'chī (-rah-)
Kăttĕgăt'
Kĕ'ble
Kĕ'dăr
Kĕntŭck'ȳ
Kĕ'nȳa (or kĕn-)
Kĕr'guelĕn (-gĕl-)
Keswick (kĕz'ĭk)
Keynes (kănz)
Khărtum' (k-; ōōm)
Khayyam (kĭ-ahm')
Khȳ'ber (k-)]
Kieff (kēēf')
Kiel (kēl)

Kĭl'imanjăr'ŏ
Kĭrkcud'bright (-kŏŏ'brĭ)
Knollys (nōlz)
Kō'bė
Koh'-ī-noor (kō-)
Kreisler (krī'sler)
Kreutzer (kroit'ser)
Lābouchère' (-bōōshãr)
Lăch'ĕsĭs (-k-)
Laĕr'tēs (-z)
Lafitte (lahfēt')
Lā'gŏs
La Junta (lah hŏŏn'ta)
L'Alle'grō (lālā-)
Lancelot (lahnslĕt)
Lăŏc'ōōn
Lapū'ta
Lascelles (lăs'els)
Las Pal'mas (iahs pahl-)
Laurĕn'çŏ Mãrques' (-sŏ; -ks)
Lausänne' (lōz-)
Lăv'ĕngrō
Lā'verȳ (or lā-)
Lăvoi'sier (-vwahzyā)
Leam'ington (lĕm-)
Lĕăn'der (or lē-)
Lĕ'da
Le Feuve (fē'ver)
Leicester (lĕs'ter)
Leigh (lē)
Lein'ster (lĕn-)
Leip'zig (lĭp-)
Leith (lē-)
Lĕ'land
Lĕ'lȳ
Lĕn'ĭn
Leominster (lĕm'ster)
Leonărd'ŏ (lā-on-)
Le Queux (lekū')
Lĕ'thė (or -ē)
Leveson-Gower (lōō'sen-gŏr')
Lĕvĭt'ĭcus
Ley'den (lā- or lī-)
Lhăs'a (la-)
Lie'bĭg (lē-)
Liége (-āzh)
Li'ma (lē-)
Limoges' (-ōzh)
Lĭn'coln (-ken)
Liszt (-st)
Llan- [as the first element in Welsh
   names] (hlăn-)
Llewĕll'ȳn (lōō-)
Loh'ĕngrĭn (lō-)
Lon'don (lŭn-)
Lŏngī'nus (-nj-)
Lŏr'ėlei (-ī)

Lŏs An'gĕlĕs (-ăngg-; -z)
Louisiān'a (lōō-ēz-)
Lou'ĭsville (lŏō-)
Lourdes (loord)
Lou'vre (loo-)
Luga'nō (lōōgah-)
Lў'cĭdăs
Lўcûr'gus
Lў'lў
Lўm'ington
Lympne (lĭm)
Lўsăn'der
Mă'cédon
Machiavĕll'ĭ (măk-)
Mackay (maki')
Macleod (maklowd')
Madeir'a (-ēr-)
Madrās' (or -ahs)
Madrid'
Mâd'ûra
Maecē'năs
Mae'lström (māl-)
Mae'terlinck (mah- or mā-)
Mâf'èking
Măg'dalĕn [Biblical name]
Magdalen [Oxford college]
   (maw'dlĭn)
Măgdalĕ'nĕ [Biblical name]
Magdalene [Cambridge college]
   (maw'dlĭn)
Magĕll'an (-g-)
Măggiŏr'ĕ (-j-)
Mahŏn' (ma-h-; or -ōōn)
Mahony (mah'nĭ)
Mainwaring (măn'ering)
Măl'achĭ (-k-)
Malay'
Mălaya'lam (-lĭahl-)
Măl'herbe (-lârb)
[The] Măll (or mawl)
Măl'orў
Mal'ta (mawl-)
Mal'vern (mawl-)
Măn'et (-ā)
Măr'ion (or mă-)
Marjoribănks (măr'chb-)
Mârque'săs (-kā-)
Mârseilles' (-āls)
Măr'tineau (-nŏ)
Mârtinique' (-ēk)
Măr'ўlănd (*mē-)
Mă'rylebone (-eleben; or mă'rĭben)
Masai' (-sī; or mah'sў)
Măssachu'sĕtts (-ōō-)
Măss'enet (-enā)
Mătabē'lĕ
Mauri'tius (-shyes)

Mazzini (mădzē'nĭ)
Mĕch'lĭn (-kl-)
Mĕdē'a
Mĕd'ĭcĭ (-chĭ)
Mĕdĭ'na (-ē-)
Mĕdĭ'na [America]
Meis'tersinger (mī-)
Mĕlpŏm'ĕnĕ
Mĕn'ai (-nī)
Mĕn'delssohn (-son; or -sŏn)
Mĕnĕlā'us
Mĕrcā'tor
Mĕrcē'dĕs (-z)
Mĕrcū'tĭō (-shī-)
Mĕ'rĕdith
Mē'ropē
Mĕssĭ'na (-sē-)
Mĕtt'ernĭch (-k)
Mey'nell (mē- or mā-)
Mĭăm'ĭ
Mĭch'ĭgan (-shĭ-)
Mĭ'dăs
Mĭlăn' (or mĭl'an)
Mill'ais (-ā)
Mĭnnéăp'olĭs
Mĭnnēsŏ'ta
Mĭnn'ĕsinger
Mĭrăn'da
Missour'ĭ (-oor-; *mĭz-)
Mĭthrĭdā'tĕs (-z)
Mĭtў'lĕ'nĕ
Mōbile' (-ēl)
Moh'ican (mō-; properly mō-hē'-)
Mohun (mōōn)
Mŏ'lière (-liăr)
Mŏna'cŏ (-ah-)
Mŏntaigne' (-ān)
Mŏnta'na (-ah-; *-ă-)
Mŏntréal' (-awl)
Mŏrŏ'nĕ
Mŏr'pheus (-ūs)
Mŏs'cow (-ō)
Moul'main
Mŏzambique' (-bĕk)
Müller (mü'ler)
Multan (mōō'ltahn)
Mŭ'nĭch (-k)
Mŭnĭll'ō
Mўcē'næ
Mўtĭlē'nĕ (or -ĕ)
Nairŏ'bĭ (nīr-)
Nă'omĭ
Nā'pier (or napēr)
Napŏ'léon
Natăl'
Năv'ajo (-a-hŏ)
Nĕm'ĕsĭs

Nĕpal' (-awl)
Nĕva'da (-vah; *-ă-)
Newfoundlănd' (-fĕnd-)
Nĭăg'ara
Nibelung (nē'bĕlŏong)
Nietzsche (nē'che)
Nī'ger
Nĭgĕr'ĭa
Nil'gĭri (-g-)
Nĭn'ĕveh (-vĭ)
Nī'obē
Norwich (nŏ'rĭj)
Nўăs(s)'a
O'ban (ō-)
Ober-ämm'ergau (ō-; -gow)
O'beron (ō-)
Odўss'eus (-ūs)
Od'yssey (ŏ-)
Œ'dĭpus (ē-)
Œnō'nē (ē-)
Ohī'ō (ō-h-)
Oklahō'ma (ō-)
Omaha (ōma-hah'; *-aw)
Oman (ōmahn')
Onehunga (ōnāhŏongga)
Ontā'rĭo (ō-)
Ophē'lĭa (ō-)
Orĕs'tēs (ō-; -z)
Orī'on (ō-)
Orlé'ans (ōr-; -z)
Orleans [America] (ôrlēnz')
Orpheus (ôr'fŭs)
Orsino (ôrsē'nō)
Osīr'ĭs (ō-)
Os'ler (ō-)
Ota'gō (ōtah-)
Othĕll'ō (ō-)
Ottawa (ŏt'a-wa)
Ottūm'wa (ō-)
Ouida (wē'da)
Ouse (ŏoz)
Ov'ĭd (ō-)
Pach'mann (pahk-)
Păderew'skĭ (-ĕvskī)
Păgani'nĭ (-ēn-)
Pagliacci (pällăch'Ĭ)
Pălamē'dēs (-z)
Păl'amon
Pălĕstri'na (-ēn-)
Păll'ăs
Pall Măll' (or pĕl'mĕl')
Pălmўr'a
Pănama' (-ah)
Pă'phos
Pă'raguay (-gwă or -gwĭ)
Parnăss'us
Parŏll'ĕs

Păs'teur (-ĕr)
Patrŏc'lus
Pau (ō)
Pausa'nĭăs
Pavĭ'a
Pĕg'asus
Pĕkĭn'
Pē'leus (-lŭs)
Pĕloponnē'sus
Pē'lŏps
Pĕnĕl'opē
Pĕnnsўlvā'nĭa
Pĕnthēsĭlē'a
Pepys (pĕps or pĕps or pĕp'ĭs)
Pĕr'dĭta
Pĕrgole'sē (-läz-)
Pĕ'rĭclēs (-z)
Pĕ'rrault (-rō)
Pĕrsĕph'onē
Pĕrsĕp'olĭs
Pĕr'seus (-ŭs)
Peru' (-ōō)
Pĕrugi'nō (-ōōgē-)
Peshawar (peshôr')
Pĕstalŏzz'i (-tsĭ)
Pĕsth (-st)
Pē'tra
Pĕ'trärch (-k)
Pĕtru'chĭo (-ōōk- or -ōōch-)
Phæ'dra
Phā'ĕthŏn
Phăr'aoh (-rō)
Phărsā'lĭa
Phĭlē'mŏn
Phŏ'cĭs
Phœ'bē (fē-)
Phœnĭc'ĭa (fē-)
Phrў'nē
Pie'dmont (pē- or pyĕ- or pyă-)
Pĭē'rĭan (or -ēr-)
Pietermă'ritzbŭrg (pē-; or -rĭtz'-)
Pĭla'tus (-ah-)
Pĭnĕr'ō
Pīræ'us
Pĭsc'ēs (-z)
Plăntăg'ĕnĕt
Plā'tō
Plei'ad (plī-)
Plĭn'ў
Plotĭ'nus
Plu'tärch (-ōō-; -k)
Plўm'outh (-eth)
Pole Carew (pōōl' kär'ĭ)
Pŏlĭx'enēs (-z)
Pŏllaiuo'lō (-ll-ōō-ō-)
Pŏlўb'ĭus
Pŏlўc'ratēs (-z)

Pŏly̆phē′mus
Pom′frĕt (pŭm-)
Pŏmpei′i (-ĕī or -āē)
Pŏrt Said (sah′id or säd)
Pŏsei′don (-sī-)
Potŏ′măc
Poughkeep′sie (pŏkĭp-)
Poussin (pŏō′săṅ)
Pŏ′wy̆s
Prăxit′elĕs (-z)
Prētŏr′ia
Pri′am
Promē′theus (-ūs)
Prŏs′erpīne
Prŏ′teus (-ūs)
Proust (prŏost)
Psy̆chē (s-)
Ptŏl′emy̆ (t-)
Puccini (pŏōchē′nĭ)
Pŭnjab′ (-ahb)
Py̆′ramus
Py̆′tchley
Py̆thăg′orăs
Québĕc′
Quill′er-Couch′ (ŏoch)
Qui′rinal (kw-)
Quix′ōte (or -ĕt)
Răb′elais (-elā)
Răc′ine (-sēn)
Rae′bŭrn (rā-)
Rajputana (rahjpŏōtah′na)
Raleigh (raw′lī or rah- or rä-)
Răm′esĕs (-z)
Răn′elagh (-le)
Răph′ael
Ra′walpindī (rah-w-)
Read′ing (rĕd-)
Reger (rā′ger)
Reik′javĭk (rēkya-)
Reu′ter (roi-)
Rheims (rēms)
Rhŏdē′sia (rō-; -z-. or -s-)
Ri′ca (rē-)
Rĭch′elieu (-shelū)
Rio (rē′ō)
Rivièr′a (-āra)
Robespierre (rō′bzpyăr)
Rŏcke′feller (-kf-, *-kĭf-)
Rōma′nēs (-ah-; -z)
Rŏm′ney (or rŭm-)
Rŏntgen (rĕrn′tyɛn)
Rŏō′sevĕlt (-sv-, *-sĭv-)
Rossĕtt′ī (rōz-)
Rōtorua (-ŏōa)
Rouen (rŏō′ahṅ)
Rŏx′burgh (-bre-)
Ruy Blas (rwē blahs)

Sachĕv′erell (-sh-)
Săg′inaw
Saha′ra (sa-hah-)
Sainte-Beuve (săṅt bĕrv)
Saint-Saens (săṅ sahṅs)
Sā′lĕm
Salis′bury̆ (sawlzb-)
Salŏ′mē
Salŏn′ica (or sălonĕ′-)
Săn′chō (-ṅgk-)
San Diego (dē-ā′gō)
Săn Jacin′tō
San Joaquin (wahkēn′)
San Jose (hōsā′)
Săn Juan′ (hwahn)
Săn Re′mō (rā-)
Săn′ta Fé′ (fā)
Săntia′gō (-ah-)
Sărasa′té (-ah-)
Sărato′ga
Săskătch′ewan
Săskatŏōn′
Sault Sainte Marie (sŏō săṅt mär′ī; or săṅt)
Săvonarŏ′la
Sca′fĕll′ (scaw-)
Scăl′iger
Schēhērēza′dĕ (sh-; ezah-)
Schĕnĕc′tady̆ (sk-)
Schu′bĕrt (shŏō-)
Schuyler (skī-)
Schuy′lkĭll (skŏōl-)
Scĭll′y̆ (s-)
Scĭp′iō (s-)
Scri′abĭn
Scy̆ll′a (s-)
Sédăn′
Sĕd′bĕrgh [school] (-rg)
Sĕd′bĕrgh [town] (-ber-)
Seine (săn)
Sĕm′elē
Sĕmī′ramĭs
Sĕn′eca
Sénégal′ (-awl)
Sĕnnăch′erĭb (-k-)
Séquoi′a (-kwoi-)
Sĕt′ebŏs
Sèvres (sā′vr)
Shănghai′ (-ng-hī)
Shrews′bury̆ (-ŏoz- or -ōz-)
Siăm′
Siegfried (sē′gfrēd)
Sierr′a Léone′ (-ăr-; ŏn-)
Sikh (sēk)
Silē′nus
Sĭm′eon

Sī'mon
Simplon (săṅ'plawṅ)
Sī'naï (-nīī)
Sioux (sōō)
Sīs'yphus
Si'va (shē-)
Skīdd'aw (or skīddaw')
Slough (slow)
Smēth'wick (-dhĭk)
Sŏc'ratēs (-z)
Sofī'a
Sō'lon
Sōma'lĭ (-ah-)
Som'ersĕt (sŭm-)
Sŏph'oclēs (-z)
Soth'eby (sūdhe-)
Soudān' (sōō- or sōō-)
Southey (sow'dhĭ)
Southwark (sŭdh'ark)
Sou'za (-ōō-)
Srīna'gar (-ah-)
St. Al'bans (awl-)
Stendhal (stahṅ'dahl)
St. John (sĭn'jon)
St. Lou'is (sănt lōō-)
St. Ma'lō (-ah-)
Stōke Pō'gĕs
Strachan (strawn)
Streath'am (strĕt-)
Stuy'vèsant (stī-)
Su'ēz (-ōō-)
Suma'tra (sōōmah-)
Sumurun (sōōmōōrōōn')
Surăt' (sōō-)
Sŭsquéhănn'a (-kw-)
Swahi'lĭ (swah-hē-)
Swa'zĭlănd (swah-)
Sўnge (-ng)
Sўr'acūse (-z)
Sў'racūse [America]
Tā'gus
Tahī'tī (tah-hē-)
Taj Mahal (tahj mahahl')
Tăngănyi'ka (-ngg-; -yē-)
Tăngier' (-jēr)
Tănnhäu'ser (-hoiz-)
Tărrago'na
Tauchnitz (towk'nĭts)
Tecŭm'seh (-sĕ)
Teh'erān (tăer-)
Teignmouth (tĭn'meth)
Tĕlĕm'achus (-kus)
Tĕnerif(f)e' (-ĕf)
Tĕrpsich'orĕ (-k-)
Tĕ'rra dĕl Fuego (fōōā'gō)
Tĕrtŭll'ian
Thali'a

Thame (tăm)
Thames (tĕmz)
Thăn'ĕt
Thēbes (-bz)
Thĕmĭst'oclēs (-z)
Thē'obald (-awld; or tĭb'ald)
Thēŏc'rĭtus
Thēŏd'oric
Thĕrmŏp'ylæ
Thĕrsī'tēs (-z)
Thē'seus (-ūs)
Thĕs'pĭs
Thĕssaloni'ca
Thĕss'alў
Thĭs'bē (-z-)
Thŏm'as (t-)
Thomas [Ambroise] (tō'mah)
Thŏr'eau (-ō)
Thŭcўd'ĭdēs (-z)
Thū'lē
Tibēr'ĭus
Tĭbĕt'
Tĭbŭll'us
Tici'nō (-chē-)
Tĭf'lĭs
Tī'gris
Tī'mŏn
Tĭntăg'el
Tĭtă'nĭa
Tĭt'ian (-shĭ-)
Tī'tus
Tiv'olĭ
Tōbī'as
Tō'kyō
Tōlĕ'dō (or -ā'dō)
Tō'phĕt
Tŏ'rrĕs
Tŏt'nĕs
Toulon (tōōlawṅ')
Toulouse (tōōlōōz')
Touraine' (tōō-)
Tours (toor)
Tow'cester (-ster)
Trafăl'gar (or trăfalgăr')
Tră'jan
Trăn'skei (-kī)
Transvaal (trah'nsvahl)
Trĕvi'sa (-vez-)
Trichĭnŏp'olĭ
Trĭĕste'
Trĭnc'ōmalee'
Trī'ton
Trŏll'ope (-ep)
Trŏss'ächs (-ks)
Trou'vĭlle (-ōō-)
Tschaikowski (chĭkŏv'skĭ)
Tucson (tōō'sawṅ; or -ăn)

Tuileries (twē'lerē)
Tŭrīn' (or tūr'ĭn)
Tŭrkĕstän'
Tŭskē'gee
Tussaud's' (-sōz)
Tȳ'chō (-k-)
Tȳn'dale (-dl)
Tȳ'rol (or tĭrōl' or tĭrŏl')
Tȳ'rrwhit (-rĭt)
Ugăn'da (ŏo-)
Uh'land (ŏo-)
U'ĭst (ŏo-; or wĭst)
Ulȳss'ēs (ū-; -z)
Uphär'sĭn (ū-)
Ur'anus (ūr-; or ūrā'nus)
Urdu (ūrdŏo' or oordŏo')
Uriah (ūr-)
Ur'iel (ūr-)
Urquhart (ûrkert)
Uruguay (ŏo'rŏogway'; or -ī)
Ush'ant (ŭ-)
Utah (ū'tah, *ū'taw)
U'ther (ū-)
Utrecht (ūtrĕkt')
Valĕn'cia (-shĭa or -sĭa)
Valenciennes' (-sĭĕn)
Valhäll'a
Văl'kȳrie
Văl'ois (-wah)
Vălparai'sō (-z-)
Văn'burgh (-bre)
Vāsăr'ī
Văs'cō da Ga'ma (gah-)
Văth'ĕk
Vaughan (vawn)
Vauxhall (vŏks'hawl')
Ve'da (vā-)
Vēlās'quez (-kwĭz or -kĭz)
Vĕn'ĕzŭē'la
Verde
Ver'dĭ (vār-)
Vĕr'dun (or vār-)
Vĕr'gil
Verne (vārn)
Vērone'se (-āzĭ)
Vē'rulam (-ŏo-)
Vēsū'vius
Vichy (vē'shē)
Vĭĕnn'a
Vī'gō
Vill'iers (lerz)
Vinci (-chī)
Vī'ola
Vĭr'gil
Vĭr'gō
Vosges (vōzh)
Wa'bash (waw-)

Wadham (wŏd'am)
Wag'ner (vah-)
Waldegräve (wawl'g-)
Walpurgis (vălpoor'gĭs)
Wan'tage (wŏn-)
Wapp'ing (wŏ-)
Wär'ing
Warwick (wŏ'rĭk)
Watteau (wŏt'ō)
Wazir'istan (-ēr-; -ahn)
Wear [river] (wēr)
We'ber (vā-)
Wednes'bury (wĕnzb-)
Wei'mar (vī-)
Weiss'hōrn vīs-h-)
Wĕl'wȳn
Wemyss (wēmz)
We'ser (vāz- or wēz-)
Whewell (hūl)
Wies'baden (vēzbah-)
Wind'sor (-nz-)
Wis'bĕch (-z-)
Wiscŏn'sĭn
Wŏŏl'wich (lĭj)
Wŏŏtt'on
Worcester (wŏŏs'ter)
Worms (v-; -z)
Wrĕ'kĭn (r-)
Wȳch'erley
Wȳc'lif
Wȳc'ombe (-om)
Wȳk'eham (-kam)
Wymondham (wĭnd'am)
Wȳō'mĭng
Xăv'ier (z-)
Xĕn'ophon (z-)
Xĕrxĕs (z-; -z)
Xosa (klau'sa)
Yeats (yāts)
Ye'men (yā-)
Yeo'vil (yō-)
Yŏkōha'ma (-hah-)
Yŏsĕm'ĭtē
Ypres (ēpr, wī'perz)
Ysaye (ĭsī'ī)
Yucatan' (ŭ-; -ahn)
Zăchari'ah (-a)
Zeiss (zīs)
Zĕlō'tēs (-z)
Zĕ'nō
Zeus (zūs)
Zĭmba'bwē (-bah-)
Zō'é
Zō'la
Zŏrōäs'ter
Zürich (zūr'ĭk)
Zuy'der Zee' (zī-)

B. ABBREVIATIONS

A

A., alto; answer; avancer (on watch-regulator = to accelerate).
a.(djective).
A.A., Automobile Assoc.; anti-aircraft.
A.A.A., Amateur Athletic Assoc.; Agricultural Adjustment Administration (U.S.).
A.A.A.S., American Association for the Advancement of Science.
A.A.F., Auxiliary Air Force.
A.A.G., Asst. Adjutant-General.
A.A. of A., Automobile Association of America.
A.A.U., Amateur Athletic Union (of U.S.).
A.B., able-bodied seaman.
A.B.C., the alphabet; alphabetical time-table.
A.B.F.M., American Board of Foreign Missions.
ab init.(io) (= from the beginning).
abl.(ative).
Abp., archbishop.
A.B.S., American Bible Society.
abs.(olute).
A.C., Alpine Club; ante Christum (= before Christ); alternating current.
acc., account; accusative.
A.D., anno Domini (= in the year of our Lord).
A.D.C., aide-de-camp; Amateur Dramatic Club.
ad fin.(em) (= towards the end).
ad init.(ium) (= at the beginning).
adj.(ective).
Adj., adjutant.
ad lib.(itum) (= to the extent desired).
Adm., Admiral; Admiralty.
adv.(erb).
advt. advertisement.
æ, third-class in Lloyd's list.
A.E.C., Army Educational Corps.
Aen.(eid).
Aes.(op).
Aesch.(ylus).
aesth.(etics, &c.).
act., ætat., ætatis (= of his &c. age).

A.E.U., Amalgamated Engineering Union.
A.F., Adm. of the Fleet.
A.F.A., Amateur Football Assoc.
A.F.B.S., American and Foreign Bible Society.
A.F.C., Air Force Cross; Australian Flying Corps.
A.F.L., American Federation of Labour.
A.F.M., Air Force Medal.
A.F.S., Auxiliary, Army, Fire Service.
A.F.V., armoured fighting vehicle.
A.G., Adjutant-Gen.; air gunner.
A.H.M.S., American Home Missionary Society.
A.I., American Institute.
A.Inst.C.E., associate of the Institution of Civil Engineers.
a.l.(s.), autograph letter (signed).
A.L.A., American Library Assoc.
Ala, Alabama.   [tuar.).
Alban., of St. Albans (see Canalg.(ebra &c.).
A.M. = M.A.
a.m., ante meridiem (= before noon); anno mundi (= in the year of the world).
A.M.D.G., ad majorem Dei gloriam (= to the greater glory of God).
A.M.G.O.T., Allied Military Government of Occupied Territory.
A.M.P.C., Auxiliary Military Pioneer Corps.
A.M.S., Army Medical Staff.
Anacr.(eon).
anat.(omy &c.).
anon.(ymous &c.).
ant.(iquities).
anthrop.(ology &c.). [Army Corps.
Anzac, Australia & New Zealand
A.O.C., Army Ordnance Corps.
A.O.D., Advanced Ordnance D
A.P.A., Amer. Philological
A.P.C.K., Association
ing Christian Kn
of Ireland).
A.P.D., Army P
A.P.M., Asst. P
Apocr.(ypha).

app.(endix)

appro.(val).

Apr.(il).

A.Q.M.G., Asst. Q.M. General.

A.R., annual return.

A.R.A., associate of the Royal Academy.

arch. (aic &c., architectural).

archaeol.(ogy &c.).

archit.(ecture &c.).

A.R.C.M., A.R.C.O., associate of the Royal College of Music, of the Royal College of Organists.

Argyl.(lshire).

A.R.I.B.A., associate of the Royal Institute of British Architects.

Arist., Aristot., Aristotle.

Aristoph.(anes).

arith.(metic &c.).

Ariz.(ona).

Ark.(ansas).

A.R.P., Air-raid Precautions.

arr.(ives &c.).

A.R.S.A., associate of the Royal Society of Arts, of the Royal Scottish Academy.

A.R.W.S., associate of the Royal Society of Painters in Water-colours.

A.S., Anglo-Saxon.

Asaph., of St. Asaph's (see Cantuar.).

A.S.C., Army Service Corps.

A.S.C.E., A.S.M.E., American Soc. of Civil Engineers, of Mechanical Engineers.

ASDIC, Allied Submarine Detection Investigation Committee (used for form of hydrophone).

A.S.E., A.S.L.E. & F., A.S.R.S., Amalgamated Soc. of Engineers; Associated Soc. of Locomotive Engineers & Firemen; Amalgamated Soc. of Railway Servants.

ASLIB, Assoc. of Special Libraries and Information Bureaux.

Assoc.(iation).

Asst. assistant.

A.S.S.U., American Sunday School Union.

astrol.(ogy &c.).

astron.(omy &c.).

A T.C., Air Training Corps.

... .S., American Temperance ... ty; American Tract Society; ... y Territorial Service.

... rom unit.

A.U.C., ab urbe condita (= from the founding of Rome).

Aug.(ust). [marked].

a.u.n., absque ullâ notâ (= unmarked).

A.V., authorized version.

A.V.C., Army Veterinary Corps.

avdp., avoirdupois.

A 1, first-class in Lloyd's list.

B

B.(ass).

b., born; bowled.

B, black (of pencil).

B.A., bachelor of Arts; British Academy; British Association.

Bart, baronet. [pital.

Bart's, St. Bartholomew's Hospital.

Bath & Well., of Bath & Wells (see Cantuar.).

B.B., balloon barrage.

BB, BBB, double-black, treble-black (of pencil).

B.B.C., British Broadcasting Corporation; a poison gas.

B.C., before Christ; British Columbia.

B.C.A., Bureau of Current Affairs.

B.C.L., bachelor of Civil Law.

B.Com., bachelor of Commerce.

B.D., bachelor of Divinity.

Bdr., bombardier.

bds., boards (in book-binding).

B.E., Order of the British Empire.

B.E.A., British Electricity Authority.

B.E.A.C., British European Airways Corporation.

Beds., Bedfordshire.

B.E.F., British Expeditionary Force.

Berks.(hire).

B.F.B.S., British & Foreign Bible Soc.

b.h.p., brake horse-power.

bibl.(ical &c.).

B.I.F., British Industries Fair.

biog.(raphy &c.).

biol.(ogy &c.).

B.I.S., Bank of International Settlements.

B.L., bachelor of Law.

b.l., bill of lading.

Bn, battalion.

B.N.C., Brasenose College.

B.O.A.C., British Overseas Airways Corporation.

B.O.T., Board of Trade.

bot.(any &c.).

B.P., British Public, Pharmacopoeia.

b.p., boiling-point.

Bp, bishop.

B.R., British Railways.

brev.(et). [tains].

Britt.(anniarum) (=of the Britons, brothers.

B.Sc., bachelor of Science.

B.S.T., British summer time.

Bt, baronet.

B.Th.U., British thermal unit.

Bucks., Buckinghamshire.

B.U.F., British Union of Fascists.

B.U.P., British United Press.

B.V.M., the Blessed Virgin Mary.

B.W., Board of Works.

B.W.G., Birmingham wire gauge.

B.W.T.A., British Women's Temperance Assoc.

B. & S., brandy and soda.

C

C., Centigrade; Conservative.

c., caught; cent(s); century; chapter; circa; circiter; colt; cubic.

C.A., chartered accountant (Scot.).

Caes.(ar).

C.A.G., Civil Air Guard.

Cal.(ifornia).

Cambs., Cambridgeshire.

Can.(ada).

Cant.(icles).

Cantab., of Cambridge.

Cant.T., Canterbury Tales.

Cantuar., of Canterbury (the signature of certain bishops consists of their Christian name(s) or initial(s) followed by an abbreviation of the Latin adj. of place).

C.A.P., chlor-aceto-phenone (a poison gas).

cap.(ut) (=chapter).

caps, capital letters.

Capt.(ain).

Card.(inal).

Carliol., of Carlisle (see Cantuar.).

Cat.(ullus).

C.B., Companion of the Bath; confinement to barracks.

C.B.E., Commander of the B.E.

C.C., County Council(lor); cricket club.

cc., chapters; cubic centimetre(s).

C.C.C., Corpus Christi College; Civilian Conservation Corps (U.S.).

C.C.S., casualty clearing station; Ceylon Civil Service.

Cd, Command Paper, series to 1918 inclusive (presented to Parliament by command of His Majesty). See Cmd.

c.d.v., carte-de-visite.

C.E., Church of England; Civil Engineer.

C.E.M.A., Council for the Encouragement of Music and the Arts.

Cent.(igrade).

Cestr., of Chester (see Cantuar.).

C.E.T.S., Church of England Temperance Soc.

C.F., Chaplain to the Forces.

cf., confer (=compare).

C.G., coastguard; Coldstream Guards.

cg., centigram.

C.G.M., Conspicuous Gallantry Medal.

c.g.s., centimetre, gramme, second (as elements in a system of physical measurements).

C.G.T., Confédération Générale du Travail (France = General Confederation of Labour).

C.H., Companion of Honour.

ch., chap., chapter.

Ch. Ch., Christ Church.

chem.(ical &c.).

Ches.(hire).

Chron.(icles).

Cic.(ero).

Cicestr., of Chichester (see Cantuar.).

C.I.D., Criminal Investigation Dept.; Committee of Imperial Defence.

C.I.E., Companion of the I.E.

c.i.f., cost, insurance, and freight.

C.I.G.S., Chief of Imperial General Staff.

C. in C., Commander-in-chief.

C.I.O., Committee for Industrial Organization (U.S.).

circ., circa, circiter.

C.J., Chief Justice.

cl., centilitre; class; clause.

C.M., common metre.

cm., centimetre.

C.M.B., (certificated by) Central Midwives Board.

Cmd, Command Paper, series from 1919 inclusive. See Cd.

C.M.G., Companion of the Order of St. Michael and St. George.

C.M.S., Church Missionary Soc.

C.N.R., Civil Nursing Reserve.

C.O., Colonial Office; commanding officer; conscientious objector.

Co., company; county (in Ireland).

c/o, care of.

C.O.D., cash on delivery.

C of E., Church of England.

cogn.(ate).

Col., colonel; Colorado; Colossians.

col.(umn).

Coll.(ege).

colloq.(uial &c.).

comp.(arative).

compl.(ement).

con.(ics).

conj., conjugation; conjunction.

Conn.(ecticut).

constr.(uction &c.).

Co-op.(erative Soc.).

Cor., Corinthians; Coriolanus.

Corn.(wall).

Corp.(oral).

correl.(ative &c.).

C.O.S., Charity Organization Soc.

c.p., candle-power.

cp., compare.

C.P., Common Pleas; Clerk of the Peace.

Cpl., corporal.

C.P.R., Canadian Pacific Ry.

C.P.R.E., Council for the Preservation of Rural England.

C.R., Caledonian Ry.

Cr., credit(or).

cres.(cendo).

crim. con., criminal conversation.

C.S.A., Confederate States Army; Confederate States of America.

C.S.C., Conspicuous Service Cross.

C.S.I., Companion of the Star of India.

C.S.M., Company sergt-major.

C.S.N., Confederate States Navy.

C.T.C., Cyclists' Touring Club.

C.U., Cambridge University.

C.U.A.C., C.U. Athletic Club.

C.U.A.F.C., C.U. Assoc. F.C.

cub.(ic.).

C.U.B.C., C.U. Boat Club.

cum.(ulative).

Cumb.(erland).

C.U.R.F.C., C.U. Rugby F.C.

C.V.O., Commander of the Victorian Order.

C.W.A., Civil Works Administration (U.S.).

C.W.S., Co-operative Wholesale Society.

cwt, hundredweight.

c & b, caught and bowled by.

D

d., daughter; dele (=expunge) denarius (=penny); density, departs &c.; died.

D.A.A.G., Deputy A.A.G.

D.A.G., Deputy Adj.-General.

dag., decagram.

dal., decalitre.

dam., decametre.

Dan.(iel).

dat.(ive).

D.B.E., Dame C.B.E.

D.C., da capo (=repeat ab init.); direct current; District of Columbia.

D.C.L., doctor of Civil Law.

D.C.L.I., Duke of Cornwall's L.I.

D.C.M., Distinguished Conduct Medal.

D.D., doctor of Divinity; dono dedit (=gave this as a gift).

D.D.D., dat dicat dedicat (=gives, devotes, and dedicates this).

D.D.T., dichloro-diphenyl-trichloro-ethane.

Dec.(ember).

deg.(ree).

Del.(aware).

del.(ineavit) (=drew this).

Demosth.(enes).

dep.(arts &c.).

Dept., department.

deriv.(ation &c.).

Deut.(eronomy).

D.F.C., **D.F.M.**, Distinguished Flying Cross, Medal.

D.G., Dei gratia (=by God's grace); Dragoon Guards.

dg., decigram.

dial., dialect &c.; dialogue.

dim., diminuendo; diminutive &c.

div.(idend).

D.L., Deputy Lieutenant.

dl., decilitre.

D.L.I., Durham L.I.

D.Lit., doctor of Literature.

D.Litt., = (at Aberdeen) Litt.D.

D.L.O., Dead Letter Office.

D.M.I., Director, Military Intelligence.

dm., decimetre.

D.N.B., Dictionary of National Biography.

do, ditto.

dol.(lar(s)).

D.O.M., Deo Optimo Maximo (= to God the best and greatest).

D.O.R.A., Defence of the Realm Act.

D.O.W.B., Dept. of Works and Buildings.

doz.(en).

D.P., double pole.

D.P.I., Director of Public Instruction.

D.Phil., doctor of Philosophy.

Dr, debtor; doctor.

dr.(achm).

Dram. Pers., dramatis personae (= characters of the play).

D.S., dal segno (= repeat from the mark); Distinguished Service.

D.S.C., D.S. Cross.

D.Sc., doctor of Science.

D.S.M., D.S.O., D.S. Medal, Order.

D.T., delirium tremens.

Dunelm., of Durham (see Cantuar.).

D.V., Deo volente (= God willing).

dwt, pennyweight.

dyn.(amics &c.).

E

E.(ast).

E., second-class in Lloyd's list.

Ebor., of York (see Cantuar.).

E.C., E. Central London postal district.

eccl.(esiastical &c.).

Eccles.(iastes).

Ecclus, Ecclesiasticus.

Ecl., Eclogues of Virgil.

E.C.U., English Church Union.

Ed.(itor &c.).

E.D.D., E.D.S., English Dialect Dictionary, Society.

E.E.T.S., Early English Text Soc.

e.g., exempli gratia (= for instance).

E.G.M., B.E. for Gallantry, Military Division.

E.I., East Indies, East Indian.

E.I.S., Educational Institute of Scotland.

electr.(ical &c.).

ellipt.(ical &c.).

E. long.(itude).

ENE., east north-east.

E.N.S.A., Entertainments National Service Association.

entom.(ology &c.).

E.P.T., Excess Profits Tax.

Eph.(esians).

E.R., E. Riding; Elizabeth Regina (= Queen Elizabeth).

E.R.P., European Recovery programme.

eschat.(ology &c.).

ESE., east south-east.

esp.(ecially).

Esq.(uire).

Esth.(er).

etc.(etera).

eth.(ics &c.).

ethn.(ology &c.).

et seq., et seqq., et sq., et sqq., et sequentia (= and what follows).

etym.(ology &c.).

E.T.U., Electrical Trades Union.

euphem.(ism &c.).

Eurip.(ides).

Euseb.(ius).

Ex(x).(ample)(s).

exam.(ination).

exc., except; excudit (= engraved).

excl.(usively &c.).

ex div.(idend).

Exod.(us).

Exon., of Exeter (see Cantuar.).

exor(s), executor(s).

Ezek.(iel).   [excepted.

E. & O.E., errors and omissions

F

F.(ahrenheit).

f., feet; feminine; filly; foot; franc(s); from.

f.(orte) (= loud).

F, fine (of pencil).

F.A., Football Association.

F.A.A., Fleet Air Arm.

Fahr.(enheit).   [manry.'

F.A.N.Y., First Aid Nursing Yeo-

F.A.P., First Aid Post, Party.

f.a.s., free alongside ship.

F.B.A., fellow of the British Academy.

F.B.I., Federal Bureau of Investigation (U.S.); Federation of British Industries.

F.C., football club.

fcap, fcp, foolscap.

F.C.I.S., fellow of the Chartered Institute of Secretaries.   [Soc.

F.C.S., fellow of the Chemical

F.D., fidei defensor (=defender of the faith).

Feb.(ruary).

fec.(it) (=made).

F.E.I.S., fellow of the E.I.S.

F.E.S., fellow of the Entomological Soc., of the Ethnological Soc.

fem.(inine).

ff., *fortissimo* (=very loud).

F.F.A., **F.F.P.S.**, fellow of the Faculty of Actuaries, of Physicians and Surgeons.

F.G., Foot Guards.

F.G.S., fellow of the Geological Society.

F.H., fire hydrant.

F.H.S., **F.I.A.**, **F.I.C.**, fellow of the Historical Soc., of the Institute of Actuaries, of the Institute of Chemistry.

fi. fa., fieri facias (=see it is done).

fig., figure; figuratively &c.

fin. =ad fin.

fl., florin(s); floruit (see flor.).

f.l., falsa lectio (=false reading).

Fla, Florida.

flor.(uit) (=flourished).

F.L.S., fellow of the Linnean Society.

F.M., Field Marshal.

F.M.S., Federated Malay States.

F.O., Foreign Office; flying officer.

fo, folio.

f.o.b., free on board.

fol.(io).

foll.(owing words &c.).

f.o.r., free on rail.

F.P., field punishment; fire-plug.

fp., *forte-piano* (=loud, then soft).

F.P.S., fellow of the Philological Society.

Fr, Father.

Fr.(ench).

fr.(anc(s)).

F.R.A.S., fellow of the Royal Astronomical Society.

F.R.C.O., fellow of the R.C.O.

F.R.C.P., fellow of the R.C.P.; **F.R.C.P.E.**, ditto of Edinburgh.

F.R.C.S., fellow of the R.C.S.; **F.R.C.S.E.**, ditto of Edinburgh; **F.R.C.S.I.**, ditto of Ireland.

F.R.G.S., fellow of the R.G.S.

F.R.I.B.A., fellow of the R.I.B.A.

Frl., fräulein (=Miss).

F.R.S., fellow of the Royal Society; **F.R.S.E.**, ditto of Edinburgh.

F.R.S.G.S., **F.R.S.L.**, fellow of the Royal Scottish Geographical Soc., the Royal Soc. of Literature.

F.S., Fleet Surgeon.

F.S.A., fellow of the Society of Antiquaries.

F.S.S., fellow of Royal Statistical Soc.

ft, feet, foot.

fur.(long).

fut.(ure).

F.Z.S., fellow of the Zoological Society.

G

g., guinea; gramme(s).

Ga, Georgia.

Gal.(atians).

gal.(lon(s)).

G.B.E., Knight (or Dame) Grand Cross of the British Empire.

G.C., George Cross.

G.C.B., Grand Cross of the Bath.

G.C.F., greatest common factor.

G.C.H., Grand Cross of Hanover.

G.C.I.E., Grand Commander of the Indian Empire.

G.C.M., greatest common measure.

G.C.M.G., Grand Cross of St. Michael and St. George.

G.C.S.I., Grand Commander of the Star of India.

G.C.V.O., Grand Cross of Royal Victorian Order.

Gen., General; Genesis.

gen., general; genitive.

geog.(raphy &c.).

geol.(ogy &c.).

geom.(etry &c.).

Georg.(ics of Virgil).

G.G., Grenadier Guards.

G.H.Q., General Headquarters.

G.I., Government issue (U.S.), freq. for=enlisted man.

Gib.(raltar).

Gk, Greek.

Glam.(organshire).

Glos., Gloucestershire.

gm., gram(me)(s).

G.M., George Medal; Grand Master.

G.M.B., Great Master of the Bath.

G.M.T., Greenwich mean time.

G.N.R., Great Northern Ry.

G.O.C., General Officer commanding.

G.O.M., grand old man.

G.P., general practitioner.

G.P.I., general paralysis of the insane.

G.P.O., General Post Office.

G.Q.G., Grand Quartier Général.

G.R., General Reserve; Georgius Rex (= King George).

gr., grain(s); grammar.

gram.(mar).

grm., gram(me)(s).

gs, guineas.

G.W.R., Great Western Ry.

gym.(nasium &c.).

H

h.(our)(s).

H, hard (of pencil).

Hab.(akkuk).

H. & C., hot and cold.

H.A.C., Honourable Artillery Co.

Hag.(gai).

Hants, Hampshire.

HB, hard black (of pencil).

H.B.M., His (or Her) Britannic Majesty.

H.C.F., highest common factor.

H.E., His Excellency; high explosive.

Heb.(rews).

hectog.(ram).

hectol.(itre).

hectom.(etre).

Herod.(otus).

Herts., Hertfordshire.

Hes.(iod).

H.F., high frequency.

hf bd, half-bound.

hf cf, half-calf.

H.G., High German; Holy Ghost; Home Guard; Horse Guards.

hg., hectogram.

H.H., His (or Her) Highness.

HH, double-hard (of pencil).

hhd, hogshead.

HHH, treble-hard (of pencil).

H.I.H., His (or Her) Imperial Highness.

H.I.M., His (or Her) Imperial Majesty.

H.L., House of Lords.

hl., hectolitre.

H.L.I., Highland Light Infantry.

H.M., Her (or His) Majesty.

hm., hectometre.

H.M.I.(S.), Her Majesty's Inspector (of schools).

H.M.S., Her Majesty's ship.

H.M.T., Her Majesty's trawler.

H.O., Home Office.

Hom.(er).

Hon., honorary; honourable.

Hor.(ace).

Hos.(ea).

h.p., horse-power.

H.Q., head-quarters.

hr, hour.

H.R.H., His (or Her) Royal Highness.

H.S.H., His (or Her) Serene Highness.

H.T., high tension.

ht wkt, hit wicket.

Hunts., Huntingdonshire.

I

I., island(s), isle.

i.(ntransitive).

I.A., Indian Army.

Ia, Iowa.

ib., ibid., ibidem (= in the same place).

I.C.S., Indian Civil Service.

I.D., Intelligence Dept.

id.(em) (= the same).

i.e., id est (= that is).

i.h.p., indicated horse-power.

IHS, Jesus.

Il.(iad).

Ill.(inois).

I.L.P., Independent Labour Party.

imperat.(ive).

imperf.(ect).

in., inch(es).

incl.(usive &c.).

incog.(nito).

Ind.(iana).

ind.(icative).

indecl.(inable).

indic.(ative).

inf.(initive); infra (= below).

infin.(itive).

init.(io) (= at the beginning).

I.N.R.I., Jesus Nazarenus Rex Judaeorum (= Jesus of Nazareth King of the Jews).

inst.(ant) (= in the present month).

int.(erjection).

intr.(ansitive).

inv.(enit) (= designed this).

I. of M., Isle of Man.

I. of W., Isle of Wight.

I.O.G.T., I.O.O.F., Independent Order of Good Templars, Odd-fellows.

I O U (see dictionary).

I.Q., Intelligence quotient.

Ir.(ish).

I.R.A., I.R.B., Irish Republican Army, Brotherhood.

I.R.O., International Refugee Organization.

irreg.(ular &c.).

I.S., input secondary.

Is., island(s), isle.

Isa., Isaiah.

I.S.M., Incorporated Soc. of Musicians.

I.S.O., Imperial Service Order.

ital.(ics).

I.W., Isle of Wight.

J

J., Judge; Justice.

Jam., Jamaica; **James** (N.T. book).

Jan.(uary).

Jer.(emiah).

Jn, junction.

joc., jocose; jocular.

Joseph.(us).

Josh.(ua).

J.P., Justice of the peace.

Jr, junior.

Jud.(ith).

Judg.(es).

jun., junr., junior.

Juv.(enal).

K

Kan.(sas).

K.B., King's Bench.

K.B.E., Knight Commander of the British Empire.

K.C., King's Counsel; King's Coll. (London).

K.C.B., K.C.H., K.C.I.E., K.C.M.G., K.C.S.I., K.C.V.O., Knight Commander of the Bath, of Hanover, of the Indian Empire, of St. Michael and St. George, of the Star of India, of the Royal Victorian Order.

K.G., Knight of the Garter.

kg., kilogram.

K.H., Knight of Hanover.

K.K.K., Ku-Klux-Klan.

K.L.I., King's L.I.

km., kilometre.

Knt, knight.

K.O.S.B., K.O.Y.L.I., King's Own Scottish Borderers, Yorkshire L.I.

K.P., Knight of St. Patrick.

K.R.R., King's Royal Rifles.

K.T., Knight of the Thistle.

Kt, knight.

Ky, Kentucky.

L

L., learner; Linnaeus; Liberal.

l., left; libra(e) (=pound(s)); line; lira, lire; litre(s).

La, Louisiana.

L.A.C., leading aircraftman.

Lam.(entations of Jer.).

Lancs., Lancashire.

l.b., leg-bye.

lb., libra(e)(=pound(s)) in weight.)

L.B.S.C.R., London Brighton & South-Coast Ry.

l.b.w., leg before wicket.

l.c., loc. cit., lower case.

L.C., Lord Chancellor.

L.C.C., London County Council.

L.C.J., Lord Chief Justice.

L.C.M., lowest common multiple.

L.C.P., licentiate of the College of Preceptors.

L.-Cpl, lance-corporal. [Surgery.

L.D.S., licentiate in Dental

L.D.V., Local Defence Volunteers.

L.E.A., Local Education authority.

Leics., Leicestershire.

Lev.(iticus).

lexicog.(raphy &c.).

L.F., low frequency.

L.G., Low German; Life Guards.

L.G.B., Local Government Board.

L.I., Light Infantry; Long Island.

Lib.(er) (=book).

Lieut.(enant).

Lieut.-Col., Lt-Colonel.

Lieut.-Gen., Lt-General.

Lieut.-Gov., Lt-Governor.

Lincs., Lincolnshire.

Linn.(aeus).

lit.(eral &c.).

Lit. Hum., Litterae humaniores (=more humane studies).

Litt.D., litterarum doctor (=doctor of Letters).

Liv.(y).

L.J., Lord Justice.

ll., lines.

LL.B., legum baccalaureus (=bachelor of Laws).

LL.D., legum doctor (=doctor of Laws).

LL.JJ., Lords Justices.

L.M., long metre.

L.M.S., London Missionary Soc.

L.M.S.(R.), London Midland & Scottish (Ry).

L.N.E.(R.), L.N.W.(R.), London & N.-Eastern, N.-Western, (Ry).

L.N.U., League of Nations Union.

loc. cit., loco citato (=in the place quoted).

log., logarithm; logic &c.

Londin., London., of London (see Cantuar.).

long.(itude).

loq.(uitur) (=speaks).

l.p., large-paper.

L.P.T.B., London Passenger Transport Board.

L.R.A.M., licentiate of the Royal Academy of Music.

L.R.C., London (or Leander) Rowing Club.

L.R.C.M., licentiate of the R.C.M.

L.R.C.P., L.R.C.S., licentiate of the R.C.P., R.C.S.

L.R.C.V.S., licentiate of the Royal College of Veterinary Surgeons.

L.S., Linnean Society.

L.S.D., =£ s. d.; Lightermen, Stevedores and Dockers.

L.S.E., London Sch. of Economics.

L.S.O., London Symphony Orchestra.

L.T., low tension.   [chestra.

Lt, Lieutenant.

L.T.A., London Teachers' Assoc.

Lt-Col.(onel).

Lt-Com.(mander).

Ltd, limited.

Lt-Gen.(eral).

Lt-Gov.(ernor).

Lucr.(etius).

LXX, Septuagint.

£, libra(e) (=pounds sterling).

£E, pounds Egyptian.

£ s. d., pounds, shillings, pence.

£T, pounds Turkish.

M

M.(onsieur).

m., maiden over; mark(s) (coin); married; masculine; metre(s); mile(s); minute(s).

M.A., master of Arts.

M.A.B., Metropolitan Asylums Board.

Macc.(abees).

magn.(etism &c.).

Maj.(or).

Maj.-Gen.(eral).

Mal.(achi).

Man.(itoba).

Mar.(ch).

Mart.(ial).

masc.(uline).

Mass.(achusetts).

math.(ematics &c.).

matric.(ulation).

Matt.(hew).

M.B., medicinae baccalaureus (=bachelor of Medicine).

M.B.E., Member of the B.E.

M.C., master of ceremonies; member of Congress; Military Cross.

M.C.C., Marylebone Cricket Club.

M.Com., master of Commerce.

M.Comm., master of Commerce and Administration.

M.D., medicinae doctor (=doctor of Medicine); mentally deficient.

Md, Maryland.

Mddx, Middlesex.

M.E., Middle English.

Me, Maine.

mech.(anics &c.).

med.(icine &c.).

mem.(ento) (=remember).

memo.(randum).

Messrs, Messieurs.

metaph.(orical &c.).

metaphys.(ics &c.).

meteor.(ology &c.).

meton.(ymy).   [Warfare.

M.E.W., Ministry of Economic

m.f., mezzo forte (=half loud).

M.F.H., master of fox-hounds.

m.g., machine gun.

mg., milligram.

M.G.C., Machine-gun Corps.

Mgr, Monseigneur; Monsignor.

M.I., mounted infantry; military Intelligence.

Mic.(ah).

M.I.C.E., =M.Inst.C.E.

Mich.(igan).

mil.(itary).

min.(eralogy &c.).

Minn.(esota).

M.Inst.C.E., member of the Institute of Civil Engineers.

M.I.E.E., M.I.Mech.E., member of the Institute of Electrical Engineers, of Mechanical Engineers.

Miss.(issippi). [neers.

Mk, mark(s).

ml., millilitre.

Mlle, Mademoiselle.

Mlles, Mesdemoiselles.

M.M., Military Medal.

MM., Messieurs.

mm., millimetre.

Mme, Madame.

Mmes, Mesdames.

M.O., medical officer.

Mo., Missouri.

mod.(ern).

mods, moderations.

M.O.H., medical officer of health.

M. O. I., Ministry of Information.

Mon.(mouthshire).

Mont.(ana).

morphol.(ogy &c.).

M.P., member of Parliament. Military Police.

m.p., melting-point.

mp., *mezzo piano* (= half soft).

m.p.g., m.p.h., miles per gallon, hour. [ceutical Soc.

M.P.S., member of the Pharmaceutical Soc.

M.R., Master of the Rolls; Midland Ry; municipal reform(er).

Mr (see dictionary).

M.R.A.S., member of the Royal Asiatic Society.

M.R.C.P., member of the R.C.P.

M.R.C.S., member of the R.C.S.; **M.R.C.S.E.,** ditto of Edinburgh.

M.R.C.V.S., member of the Royal College of Veterinary Surgeons.

M.R.I.A., member of the Royal Irish Academy.

Mrs (see dictionary).

M.R.S.T., member of the Royal Society of Teachers.

MS., manuscript.

M.S.L., mean sea level.

MSS., manuscripts.

M.T., Motor Transport.

Mt, Mount.

M.T.B., motor torpedo-boat.

M.T.O., Mechanical Transport Officer.

mus.(ic &c.).

Mus.B., Mus.Bac., Mus.D., Mus. Doc., musicae baccalaureus, doctor (= bachelor, doctor, of Music).

M.V., motor vessel.

M.V.O., member of the Royal Victorian Order.

M.W.B., Metropolitan Water Board.

Mx, Middlesex. [Board.

myth.(ology &c.).

N

N.(orth).

n., neuter; nominative; noon; noun.

N.A.A.F.I., Navy, Army, & Air Force Institutes.

N.A.L.G.O., National Assoc. of Local Government Officers.

N.A.(S) Nursing Auxiliary (Service).

N.A.T.O., North Atlantic Treaty Organization. [Organization.

naut.(ical &c.).

nav.(al &c.).

N.B., North Britain; New Brunswick; nota bene (= note well).

n.b., no ball.

N.C., North Carolina.

N.C.B., National Coal Board.

N.C.O., non-commissioned officer.

n.d., no date. [Women.

N.C.W., National Council of Women.

N.D.C., National Defence Contribution.

NE., north-east.

Neb.(raska). [(= O.E.D.).

N.E.D., New English Dictionary (= O.E.D.).

neg.(ative &c.).

Neh.(em ah).

nem. con., nem. dis., nemine contradicente, dissentiente (= no one objecting, dissenting).

N.E.R.A., National Emergency Relief Administration (U.S.).

neut.(er).

Nev.(ada).

N.F., Newfoundland.

N.F.S., National Fire Service.

N.F.U., National Farmers' Union.

N.H., New Hampshire.

N.H.S., National Health Service.

N.J., New Jersey.

N.lat.(itude).

N.L.C., N.L.F., National Liberal Club, Federation.

N.Mex., New Mexico.

NNE., north north-east.

NNW., north north-west.

N.O., natural order. [ber.

N°, numero (= in number); number.

N.O.D., Naval Ordnance Dept.

nom.(inative).

non-com., =N.C.O.
Northants, Northamptonshire.
Northumb.(erland).
Norvic., of Norwich (see Cantuar.).
Nos, numbers.
Notts, Nottinghamshire.
Nov.(ember).
n.p., new paragraph.
n.p. or d., no place or date.
N.R.(iding).
nr, near.
N.R.A., National Rifle Assoc.; National Recovery Act, Administration (U.S.).
N.S., new style; Nova Scotia.
N.S.A., National Skating Assoc.
N.S.E.C., National Service Entertainments Council.
N.S.P.C.C., Nat. Soc. for the Prevention of Cruelty to Children.
N.S.W., New South Wales.
N.T., New Testament.
Num.(bers).
N.U.R., N.U.S.E.C., N.U.T., N.U.W.S.S., National Union of Railwaymen, Societies for Equal Citizenship, Teachers, Women's Suffrage Societies.
NW., north-west.
N.W. Prov.(inces).
N.W.T., N.-Western Territories.
N.Y., New York.
N.Z., New Zealand.

O

O.(hio).
ob.(iit) (=died).
Obad.(iah).
O.B.E., Officer of the B.E.
obj.(ect).
obs.(olete).
O.C., officer commanding.
Oct.(ober).
oct.(avo).   [unit.
O.C.T.U., Officer cadets training
Od.(yssey).
O.E., Old English.   [ary.
O.E.D., Oxford English Diction-
O.E.E.C., Organization for European Economic Co-operation.
O.F., Old French.
O.F.M., Order of Friars Minor.
O.F.S., Orange Free State.
O.H.M.S., on H.M.'s service.
O.K., all correct (*okay).

Okla.(homa).
Ol.(ymplad).
O.M., Order of Merit.
O.N., Old Norse.
onomat.(opoeic &c.).
Ont.(ario).
O.P., opposite prompt side; =O
   pip; Old Playgoers (Club).
o.p., out of print; over proof.
op.(us).   [cited].
op. cit., opus citatum (=the work
O pip, observation post.
opt., optative; optics &c.
Oreg.(on).
orig.(inal &c.).
ornith.(ology &c.).
O.S., old style; ordinary seaman; outsize.
O.S.A., O.S.B., O.S.D., O.S.F., of the Order of St. Augustine, Benedict, Dominic, Francis.
O.T., Old Testament.
O.T.C., Officers Training Corps.
O.U., Oxford University.
O.U.A.C., O.U. Athletic Club.
O.U.A.F.C., O.U. Assoc. F.C.
O.U.B.C., O.U. Boat Club.
O.U.D.S., O.U. Dramatic Soc.
O.U.R.F.C., O.U. Rugby F.C.
Ov.(id).
Oxon., Oxfordshire; of Oxford (see Cantuar.).
oz, ounce(s).

P

P., (car-)park.
p., page; perch(es)
p.(iano) (=soft).
Pa, Pennsylvania.
palaeog.(raphy &c.).
palaeont.(ology &c.).
par.(agraph).
pass.(ive).
path.(ology &c.).
Paus.(anias).
P.A.Y.E., pay as you earn (=Income Tax Payments).
P.C., police constable; post-card; Privy Council(lor).
p.c., per cent.; post-card.
P.D., potential difference.
pd, paid.
P.E.N. (Club), poets, playwrights, essayists, editors, and novelists.
perf.(ect).
per pro.(curationem) (=by proxy).
Pars.(ius).

Pet.(er) (N.T. book).

Petriburg., of Peterborough (see Cantuar.).

pf., *piano-forte* (= soft, then loud).

P.G., paying guest.

Ph.D., philosophiae doctor (= doctor of Philosophy).

Phil.(ippians).

Philem.(on).

philol.(ogy &c.).

photog.(raphy &c.).

phr.(ase).

phys.(ics &c.).

physiol.(ogy &c.).

Pind.(ar).

pinx., pnxt., pinxit (= painted this).

pl., plate(s); plural.

P.L.A., Port of London Authority.

Plat.(o).

Plaut.(us).

P.L.C., Poor Law Commissioners.

Plin.(y).

Plot.(inus).

plup.(erfect).

Plut.(arch).

P.M., Police Magistrate; Prime Minister; Provost Marshal.

p.m., post meridiem (= after noon); post-mortem.

P.M.G., Paymaster General; Postmaster General.

P.N.E.U., Parents' National Educational Union.

pnxt, pinxit (= painted this).

P.O., postal order; Post Office; Pilot Officer.

poet.(ical &c.).

pol.(itics &c.).

pol. econ.(omy).

Polyb.(ius).

pop., popular &c.; population.

P.O.S.B., Post-Office Savings [Bank.

P.O.W., prisoner of war.

p.p., past (or passive) participle; per pro.

pp., pages.

pp., *pianissimo* (= very soft).

P.P.C., pour prendre congé (= to take leave).

P.P.S., post-postscriptum (= further postscript).

P.P.U., Peace Pledge Union.

P.R., proportional representation.

P.R.A., President of the Royal Academy.

P.R.B., Pre-Raphaelite Brotherhood.

Preb.(endary).

pred.(icate &c.).

Pref.(ace).

pref., preference &c.; prefix.

prelim.(inary exam.).

prep., preparation; preposition.

pres.(ent).

pret.(erite).

prob.(ably).

Prof.(essor).

Prol.(ogue).

pron.(oun).

Prop.(ertius).

prop., properly; proposition.

pros.(ody &c.).

pro tem.(pore) (= for the time).

Prov.(erbs).

prov., proverbial &c.; provincial.

prox.(imo) (= in next month).

prox. acc., proxime accessit (= came next).

P.S., postscript; prompt side.

Ps.(alms).

psychol.(ogy &c.).

Pt, Part; Port.

pt, pint.

Pte, Private.

P.T., physical training.

P.T.O., please turn over.

P.W.A., P.W.D., Public Works Administration (U.S.), Dept.

pxt, = pnxt.

P. & O., Peninsular & Oriental.

Q

q.(uery).

Q.B., Q.C., Queen's Bench, Counsel.

Q.E.D., Q.E.F., Q.E.I., quod erat demonstrandum, faciendum, inveniendum (= which was to be proved, done, found).

Q.M., Quarter-master.

Q.M.G.(eneral).

Q.M.S.(ergeant).

qr, quarter(s).

qt, quart(s).

q.t., quiet.

qu., quasi (= as it were); query.

quant. suf., quantum suff., quantum sufficit (= as much as suffices).

Que.(bec).

quot.(ation &c.).

q.v., quod vide (= which see).

qy, query.

R

R., Réaumur; Regina (=queen); retarder (on watch-regulator; =to retard); **Rex** (=king); River; Railway.

r., right; rupee.

R.A., Royal Academician; Royal Artillery.

R.A.C., Royal Automobile Club.

rad.(ical).

R.A.F., Royal Aircraft Factory; Royal Air Force.

rall.(*entando*) (=with decreasing pace).

R.A.M., Royal Academy of Music.

R.A.M.C., R.A.O.C., R.A.P.C., R.A.S.C., R.A.V.C., Royal Army Medical, Ordnance, Pay, Service, Veterinary Corps.

R.A.S., Royal Agricultural Society, Royal Asiatic Society, Royal Astronomical Society.

R.B., Rifle Brigade.

R.B.A., Royal Society of British Artists.

R.C., Roman Catholic.

R.C.M., R.C.O., Royal College of Music, Organists.

R.C.P., R.C.S., Royal College of Physicians, Surgeons.

R.D., refer to drawer; Royal Naval Reserve Decoration; rural [dean.

Rd, road.

R.D.C., Royal Defence Corps; Rural district council.

R.E., Royal Engineers.

recd, received.

ref.(erence).

regt. regiment.

rel. pron., relative pronoun.

Rep.(ertory Theatre Company).

R. et I., Rex et Imperator (=King & Emperor); Regina et Imperatrix (=Queen & Empress).

Rev., Revelation; reverend.

R.F., Royal Fusiliers.

R.F.A., Royal Field Artillery.

R.F.C., Royal Flying Corps; Reconstruction Finance Corporation (U.S.).

R.G.A., Royal Garrison Artillery.

R.G.S., Royal Geographical Soc.

R.H., Royal Highlanders.

R.H.A., Royal Horse Artillery.

R.H.G., Royal Horse Guards.

R.Hist.S., Royal Historical Soc.

R.H.S., Royal Horticultural Society, Royal Humane Society.

R.I., Rhode Island; Royal Institute of Painters.

R.I.B.A., Royal Institute of British Architects.

R.I.C., Royal Irish Constabulary.

R.I.I.A., Royal Institute of International Affairs.

R.I.P., requiesca(n)t in pace (=may he, she, or they, rest in peace).

R.M., Reichsmark; resident magistrate; royal mail; Royal Marines.

R.M.A., Royal Marine Artillery; Royal Military Academy.

R.M.C., Royal Military College.

R.M.L.I., Royal Marine Light Infantry.

R.M.S., Royal Mail Steamer.

R.M.S.P., Royal Mail Steampacket Co.

R.N., Royal Navy.

R.N.A.S., R.N.C., R.N.D., R.N.R., R.N.V.R., Royal Naval Air Service, College, Division, Reserve, Volunteer Reserve.

R.N.L.I., Royal National Lifeboat Institution.

Roffen., of Rochester (see Canterbury Rom.(ans). [tuar.).

rom., roman type.

R.P.S., Royal Photographic Soc.

R.R.C., Royal Red Cross.

R.S., Royal Society.

Rs, rupees. [cian.

R.S.A., Royal Scottish Academician.

R.S.E., Royal Society of Edinburgh.

R.S.M., Regimental Sergt-Major.

R.S.P.C.A., Royal Soc. for Prevention of Cruelty to Animals.

R.S.V.P., répondez s'il vous plaît (=please answer).

Rt Hon., right honourable.

R/T, radio telegraphy.

R.T.O., Ry transport officer.

Rt Rev., right reverend.

R.T.C., R.T.R., Royal Tank Corps, Regiment.

R.T.S., Religious Tract Soc.

R.U., Rugby Union.

R.V., revised version.

R.W.F., Royal Welch Fusiliers.

R.W.S., Royal Soc. of Painters in Water-colours.

Ry., railway.
R.Y.S., Royal Yacht Squadron.
℞, recipe.
₨, rupee(s).
₨x, tens of rupees.

S

S., (air-raid) shelter; Signor; soprano; South.
s., second; shilling; singular; son.
S.A., Salvation Army; South Africa; Storm-Abteilung (=Nazi storm-troops).
Sall.(ust).
Salop, Shropshire.
Sam.(uel).
Sarum, of Salisbury (see Cantuar.).
Sask.(atchewan).
S.A.T.B., soprano, alto, tenor, bass.
S.C., South Carolina; special constable.
SCAPA, Soc. for Checking the Abuses of Public Advertising.
sc., scil.; sculpsit (=carved).
scil.(icet) (=to wit).
S.C.M., State certified midwife; Student Christian Movement.
sculps.(it) (=carved).
s.d., several dates.
S. Dak., South Dakota. [tion.
S.D.F., Social Democratic Federa-
SE., south-east.
Sec.(retary).
sec.(ond).
sect.(ion).
Sen.(eca).
sen., senr, senior.
Sept., September; Septuagint.
seq., seqq., =et seq. [end].
s.f., sub finem (=towards the
sf.(orzando) (=with sudden emphasis).
S.G., specific gravity.
s.g.d.g., sans garantie du gouvernement (=without Government guarantee).
Sgt, sergeant.
S.H., School House.
S.H.A.E.F., Supreme Headquarters Allied Expeditionary Force.
sh.(illing).
S.I.C., specific inductive capacity.
sing.(ular).

S.J.A.B., St. John Ambulance Brigade.
S.J., Society of Jesus.
Skr., Sanskrit.
S. lat., South latitude.
S.M., Sergeant-Major; short metre.
s.o., sub-office.
Soc.(iety).
sociol.(ogy &c.).
Song of Sol.(omon).
Soph.(ocles).
S.O.S. (see dictionary).
sov., sovs, sovereign(s) (coin).
S.P.C.K., Society for Promoting Christian Knowledge.
S.P.E., Society for Pure English.
S.P.G., Society for the Propagation of the Gospel.
sp. gr., specific gravity.
S.P.Q.R., senatus populusque Romanus (=the Roman senate and people); small profits and quick returns.
S.P.R., Society for Psychical Research. [search.
sq., sqq., et seq.
S.R., Southern Railway.
Sr, senior.
S.R.N., State registered nurse.
S.R. & O., statutory rules & orders.
S.S., screw steamer; Schutz-Staffel (=Nazi special guard).
SS., Saints.
SSE., south south-east.
S.S.U., Sunday School Union.
SSW., south south-west.
St, Saint; street.
st., stone (weight); stumped.
Staffs, Staffordshire.
stat.(ics &c.).
St. Ex., Stock Exchange.
stg, sterling.
S.T.P., sacrosanctae theologiae professor (=professor of Sacred Theology).
str., stroke oar.
S.T.S., Scottish Text Society.
sub., subaltern; submarine boat; substitute.
subj., subject &c.; subjunctive.
subst., substantive; substitute.
Suet.(onius).
suf.(fix).
Suid.(as).
sup.(ra) (=above).
superl.(ative).

suppl.(ement &c.).

Supt, superintendent.

Surg.(eon &c.).

sus. per col., suspensio per collum (= hanging by the neck).

s.v., sub voce, verbo (= under that word).

SW., south-west.

S.W.G., standard wire gauge.

syn.(onym &c.).

S. & M., Sodor & Man.

T

T.(enor).

T.A., Territorial Army.

Tac.(itus).

T.B., torpedo-boat; tuberculosis.

T.B.D., T.B. destroyer.

T.C., Tank Corps; temporary constable.

T.C.D., Trinity College, Dublin.

tech.(nical &c.).

t.e.g., top edge gilt.

temp.(ore) (= in the period of).

Tenn., Tennessee.

Ter.(ence).

Tex.(as).

T.F., Territorial Force.

theat.(rical &c.).

Theoc.(ritus).

theol.(ogy &c.).

theos.(ophy &c.).

Thess.(alonians).

Thuc.(ydides).

Tib.(ullus).

T.I.H., Their Imperial Highnesses.

Tim.(othy).

Tit.(us).

T.N.T., trinitrotoluene.

T.O., turn over.

Too H., Talbot House.

trans.(itive).

transl.(ation &c.).

T.R.C., Thames Rowing Club.

Treas.(urer).

T.R.H., Their Royal Highnesses.

trig.(onometry &c.).

trs., transpose.

Truron., of Truro (see Cantuar.).

T.S.H., Their Serene Highnesses.

T.U.C., Trades Union Congress.

T.V.A., Tennessee Valley Authority (U.S.).

typ.(ography &c.).

t. & o., taken and offered.

U

u.c., upper case.

U.D.C., Urban District Council; Union of Democratic Control.

U.K., United Kingdom.

U.K.A., United Kingdom Alliance.

ult.(imo) (= in last month).

U.N.O., United Nations Organization.

U.N.E.S.C.O., United Nations Educational, Scientific, and Cultural Organization.

U.N.R.R.A., United Nations Relief and Rehabilitation Administration. [Provinces.

U.P., United Presbyterian; United

u.p., under proof.

U.S., United States. [Army.

U.S.A., U.S. of America; U.S.

U.S.M., U.S. Mail; U.S. Marine.

U.S.M.A., U.S. Military Academy.

U.S.N., U.S. Navy.

U.S.N.A., U.S. Naval Academy.

U.S.S., U.S. Senate; U.S. ship or steamer. [Republics.

U.S.S.R., Union of Soviet Socialist

V

v., verb; versus (= against); vide (= see).

Va., Virginia.

v.a., vb active. [ment.

V.A.D., Voluntary Aid Detachment. var.(iant).

v.aux., vb auxiliary.

vb, verb.

V.C., Vice-Chancellor; Victoria Cross.

V.D., venereal disease. [Cross.

v.dep., vb deponent.

Ven.(erable).

verb. sap., verb. sat. sap., verbum (satis) sapienti = a word to the wise).

v.f., very fair.

V.G., Vicar-General.

v.g., very good.

v.i., vb intr.

V.I.P., very important person.

Virg.(il).

viz, videlicet (= namely). [ing.

v.l., varia lectio (= variant reading).

v.n., vb neut.

voc.(ative).

vol.(ume).

V.R., Victoria Regina (= Queen Victoria); Volunteer Reserve.

v.refl., vb reflexive.
V.S., veterinary surgeon.
Vt, Vermont.
v.t., vb trans.
Vulg.(ate).
vulg.(arly &c.).
vv., verses.

W

W.(est).
w., wide; with.
W.A.A.F., Women's A.A.F.
w.a.f., with all faults.
W.A.F.S., Women's A.F.S.
War.(wickshire).
Wash.(ington).
W.A.T.S., Women's A.T.S.
W.C., W. Central.
w.c., water-closet.
W.C.A., Women's Christian Assoc.;
  Women Citizens' Assoc.
W.D., War Department.
W.D.C., War Damage Contribution.
W.E.A., Workers' Educational Association.
w.f., wrong fount.
W.I., W.Indies; Women's Institute.
Wilts.(hire).
Winton, of Winchester (see Cantuar.).
Wis.(consin).
wk, week.
W/L, wave length.
W.L.A., Women's Land Army.
W. long.(itude).
WNW., west north-west.
W.O., War Office; warrant officer.
Worcs, Worcestershire.
W.P., weather permitting.
W.P.A., Works Progress Administration (U.S.).

W.P.B., waste-paper basket.
W.R., War Reserve (police); West Riding.
W.R.A.F., W.R.N.S., Women's Royal Air Force, Naval Service.
W.R.I., War Risks Insurance.
W.S., writer to the signet.
W.S.P.U., Women's Social and Political Union.
WSW, west south-west.
W/T, wireless telegraphy.
wt, weight.
W. Va, W. Virginia.
W.V.S., Women's Voluntary Services.
Wyo.(ming).

X

xd, x-d., x-div., ex dividend.
Xen.(ophon).
x-i., ex interest.
Xmas, Christmas.
Xt, Christ.
Xtian, Christian.

Y

yd, yard.
ye, the.
Y.M.C.A., Young Men's Christian Association.
Yorks(hire).
Y.P.S.C.E., Young People's Society for Christian Endeavour.
yr, year.
Y.W.C.A., Young Women's Christian Association.

Z

Zech.(ariah).
Zeph.(aniah).
zool.(ogy &c.).

PRINTED IN GREAT BRITAIN
AT THE UNIVERSITY PRESS, OXFORD
BY CHARLES BATEY, PRINTER TO THE UNIVERSITY